ACQUISITIONS EDITOR	Ruth Rominger
DEVELOPMENTAL EDITOR	Lisa Toftemark-Rittby
PROJECT EDITOR	Sheila M. Spahn
DESIGNER	Linda Wooton Miller
PRODUCTION MANAGER	Kelly Cordes and Mandy Manzano
PERMISSIONS EDITOR	Shirley Webster and Cindy Robinson
PRODUCT MANAGER	Lisé Johnson
MARKETING ASSISTANT	Sam Stubblefield
COPY EDITOR	Karen Carriere
INDEXER	Leoni McVey
COMPOSITOR	GTS Graphics
TEXT TYPE	10/12 Minion Regular
COVER IMAGE	© 1994 Eric Dinyer

About the Artist

Eric Dinyer was born in St. Louis, Missouri, in 1960. He received a Bachelor of Fine Arts Degree from Washington University School of Fine Arts in St. Louis, Missouri, in 1982, and a Master of Fine Arts Degree from the School of Visual Arts in Manhattan, New York, in 1986. Dinyer currently resides in Kansas City, Missouri, where he pursues his international freelance career.

Dinyer's work has been featured in numerous national and international magazines, publications, book jackets, and CD covers. Dinyer has also received honors from *Communication Arts* Annual, *Print Regional* Annual, The Society of Publication Designers Annual, The New York Society of Illustrators Annuals, and the Japan Creators Association International Annuals.

For inspiration in creating the artwork for *Managing Organizations in an Era of Change,* Dinyer relied on his own experience with computer technology. He crossed over from traditional media, including oil paints and pencils, to Digital Media (photoshop software, and Fractal design painter software) two years ago.

Dinyer wanted to visually interpret the idea of change and speed in the current global technology paradigm shift through the use of abstract motifs. Dinyer's montages illustrate the impending complexity of a global marketplace, depicting tomorrow's knowledge worker enshrouded in and controlling the rapid dance of technology. Dinyer found satisfaction in the challenge of visually executing the idea of technology which has and will continue to change our world in profound ways.

Address for Orders
The Dryden Press
6277 Sea Harbor Drive
Orlando, FL 32887-6777
1-800-782-4479 or 1-800-433-0001 (in Florida)

Address for Editorial Correspondence
The Dryden Press
301 Commerce Street, Suite 3700
Fort Worth, TX 76102

ISBN: 0-03-096612-4

Library of Congress Catalog Card Number: 94-69149

Credits appear on pages 687–688, which constitute a continuation of the copyright page.

Printed in the United States of America

4 5 6 7 8 9 0 1 2 3   048   9 8 7 6 5 4 3 2 1

The Dryden Press
Harcourt Brace College Publishers

MANAGING ORGANIZATIONS

IN AN ERA OF CHANGE

GARY DESSLER

FLORIDA INTERNATIONAL UNIVERSITY

THE DRYDEN PRESS

HARCOURT BRACE COLLEGE PUBLISHERS

FORT WORTH   PHILADELPHIA   SAN DIEGO   NEW YORK   ORLANDO   AUSTIN   SAN ANTONIO
TORONTO   MONTREAL   LONDON   SYDNEY   TOKYO

Dedicated to Claudia

THE DRYDEN PRESS
SERIES IN MANAGEMENT

Kemper
Experiencing Strategic Management

Kindler and Ginsburg
Strategic and Interpersonal Skill Building

Kirkpatrick and Lewis
Effective Supervision: Preparing for the 21st Century

Kuehl and Lambing
Small Business: Planning and Management
Third Edition

Kuratko and Hodgetts
Entrepreneurship: A Contemporary Approach
Third Edition

Kuratko and Welsch
Entrepreneurial Strategy: Text and Cases

Lee
Introduction to Management Science
Second Edition

Lengnick-Hall, Cynthia, and Hartman
Experiencing Quality

Lewis
Io Enterprises Simulation

Long and Arnold
The Power of Environmental Partnerships

McMullen and Long
Developing New Ventures: The Entrepreneurial Option

Matsuura
International Business: A New Era

Montanari, Morgan, and Bracker
Strategic Management: A Choice Approach

Morgan
Managing for Success

Northcraft and Neale
Organizational Behavior: A Management Challenge
Second Edition

Penderghast
Entrepreneurial Simulation Program

Sandburg
Career Design Software

Shipley and Ruthstrom
Cases in Operations Management

Sower, Motwani, and Savoie
Classic Readings in Operations Management

Van Matre
Foundations of TQM: A Readings Book

Vecchio
Organizational Behavior
Third Edition

Walton
Corporate Encounters: Law, Ethics, and the Business Environment

Zikmund
Business Research Methods
Fourth Edition

THE HARCOURT BRACE COLLEGE OUTLINE SERIES

Pentico
Management Science

Pierson
Introduction to Business Information Systems

Sigband
Business Communication

WHY ANOTHER MANAGEMENT TEXTBOOK?

There are many fine management textbooks available, so let me start this introduction by briefly explaining why I wanted to write this book. I had three main reasons:

THE END OF "COMMAND AND CONTROL"   In the past 10 years remarkable changes have taken place in the ways that firms are organized and managed, but many textbooks still seem to be more focused on the past than on the future. A sprinkling of pedagogical boxes illuminating "the challenge of innovation" notwithstanding, most management textbooks today are firmly rooted in what Peter Drucker called the "command and control approach" of years past. This was a management world of departments, centralized staffs, and a reliance on budgets and imposed controls and procedures. In their book, *Re-engineering the Corporation,* Michael Hammer and James Champy make a similar point when they say that "a set of principles laid down more than two centuries ago have shaped the structure, management, and performance of American businesses throughout the nineteenth and twentieth centuries." Indeed, many management textbooks today are largely indistinguishable in organization, methods, and principles from some of the early classics of the 1960s. *Managing Organizations in an Era of Change* was created for the management world of the 1990s and beyond, a world in which the lines between manager and worker are blurring and in which boundaryless organizations, globalization, team-based structures, empowerment, and response to change are essential for success. Today and in the years ahead, the future will belong to the managers and organizations that do the best job of managing change. *Managing Organizations in an Era of Change* was, therefore, written, first, to help give future managers the concepts and skills they'll need to manage organizations under turbulent and rapidly changing conditions.

REVISED AACSB GUIDELINES   I also wanted to write a book that accommodated the new guidelines of the American Assembly of Collegiate Schools of Business (AACSB). Among other things, these new guidelines should encourage a synthesis of principles of management and organizational behavior, as well as focus management educators' attention on preparing students for team-based careers in the twenty-first century. The new guidelines also call for a more cross-functional approach to management education. I have tried to make sure *Managing Organizations* addresses these issues by integrating more behavioral topics into the text, by emphasizing teams, and by introducing topics like quality, technology, ethics, and service in an interactive manner.

THE EXCITEMENT OF MANAGEMENT   Third, I wrote this book because I wanted to communicate the excitement of being a manager and to do so in a lively, understandable, and practical way. You will, therefore, find hundreds of real-life management examples in this book, as well as the commitment to clear, understandable explanations that I hope adopters of my earlier books have come to expect of me.

HOW THIS BOOK DIFFERS FROM OTHER MANAGEMENT TEXTBOOKS

This book's mission is to provide future managers with the skills they will need to manage organizations under conditions of turbulence and change. Three main features distinguish it from its competitors.

NEW TOPICS   First, while *Managing Organizations in an Era of Change* covers all of the "foundation" management topics (like planning, budgeting, and functional departmentation) about 20 percent of the chapters are new, in that they usually don't appear as chapters in management textbooks. These include Chapter 9 (The Responsive Organization), Chapter 12 (Empowering Employees and Building Commitment), Chapter 17 (Managing Teams), and Chapter 21 (Managing Services). This book's relatively detailed coverage of modern management concepts and techniques is not apparent from a brief review of the table of contents. This coverage includes a heavy emphasis on creating shared visions, creating a sense of mission, developing communication-building techniques, building teams, formulating and communicating values, managing information technology, creating boundaryless organizations, changing employees' values, selecting "value-based" employees, downsizing into "mini" organizations, managing knowledge-based organizations, and managing discontinuous change, to name just a few. I believe that I have been able to include all of this new material by compressing certain traditional foundation material rather than leaving out anything essential.

RESPONSIVENESS THEME   Second, befitting its title, *Managing Organizations in an Era of Change* emphasizes managing and responding to change as its theme in each and every chapter. You will, therefore, find examples of planning for responsiveness in Chapter 5; the central role of core competencies and strategic alliances in responsive organizations in Chapter 6; organizing for responsiveness in Chapter 9; selecting employees for working in responsive organizations in Chapter 10; the interplay of control, commitment, and organizational responsiveness in Chapter 11; the role of transformational leadership in responsive organizations in Chapter 12; building communications for responsiveness in Chapter 16; adaptive organizational cultures in Chapter 13; discontinuous change and corporate renewal in Chapter 18; and using information technology to boost responsiveness in Chapter 20, to name a few examples. At the same time, the contingency aspects of management—and in particular, the need to fit the management approach and organization to the rate of change of the environment—is fully covered, for instance, in Chapters 1, 4, and 9.

MERGING MANAGEMENT AND BEHAVIOR   Third, you will also notice that *Managing Organizations in an Era of Change* is divided into four parts that give nearly equal weight to the management process and to behavior in management, rather than into four or five basic management functions (planning, organizing, staffing, leading, and controlling) as is often the case in management textbooks. There are two reasons for this organization. First, writing a textbook that is both new in the concepts it covers while familiar enough to be acceptable to adopters was bound to be tricky. I believe the book's current organization left more room for adding innovative chapters and behavioral material than did the relatively rigid four or five part process format, while still loosely adhering to the functions, behavior, and models format that many adopters are already familiar with.

Second, the book's organization also highlights its relatively heavy behavioral coverage, when compared to traditional process-oriented books.

Why this heavier emphasis on organization behavior? One reason, as mentioned, is the set of new **AACSB** guidelines. The second reason is that I am convinced that in today's management world, artificially distinguishing between management functions and the behavioral side of what managers do is no longer realistic, if it ever was. In today's team-based, boundaryless organizations with their empowered workers and upside down authority pyramids, behavioral concepts and techniques have assumed enormous importance. Therefore, I think it's more important today to teach management while simultaneously covering behavioral topics more fully than we have in the past.

THE ORGANIZATION OF THE BOOK

I would like to briefly summarize what each of the four parts covers.

PART I: THE MANAGERS' CHANGING WORLD   Part I sets the stage for the rest of the book by explaining what managers do and the challenges they face today (Chapter 1); the managerial and organizational challenges of managing in a global economy (Chapter 2); the ethical foundations of management (Chapter 3); and the challenge of managing responsive organizations in a historical context, while describing the evolution of management thought (Chapter 4).

PART II: THE MANAGEMENT PROCESS   Part II provides a complete and comprehensive discussion of the management functions of planning, organizing, staffing, and controlling. It covers the overall planning process (Chapter 5); strategic planning and management and, in particular, the activities involved with determining what business the firm should be in (Chapter 6); and a brief review of important techniques used for improving the planning process and managerial decision making (Chapter 7). The fundamentals of organizing (including departmentation, delegation, and coordination) are discussed in Chapter 8; and Chapter 9, The Responsive Organization, explains modern methods used by managers to organize their enterprises for responsiveness—methods that include boundaryless and horizontal organization structures. The staffing or human resource management function is fully covered in Chapter 10; and Chapter 11, Achieving Control, discusses basic concepts and techniques of managerial control, while explaining that in today's fast-paced organizations, control must increasingly come from within the employees themselves. Chapter 11, therefore, provides a bridge to the next part of this book—behavior.

PART III: BEHAVIOR AND MANAGEMENT   Part III provides a more comprehensive coverage of organization behavior than is typically included under the "leadership" function in most traditional management textbooks. Furthermore, wherever possible, I have integrated functional management and behavioral material. For example, Chapter 12, Empowering Employees and Building Commitment, emphasizes that in a fast-changing world, empowering employees and gaining their commitment to their teams and their companies is crucial and necessarily relies on effectively implementing the management process. By contrasting the supervisory control techniques of Chapter 11 with the motivation and self-control enhancing techniques of Chapters 13 through 18, Chapter 12 also bridges this management function and behavioral material. Chapters 13, Leadership, and 14, Organizational Culture and Shared Values, describe the leaders' roles in creating the sense of mission and the culture and shared values of the organization. Chapter 15, Motivation and Behavior, discusses one of the important emergent consequences of culture and leadership, namely employee motivation. Since factors other than leadership and culture obviously influence employee motivation, Chapter 15 also reviews some fundamentals of individual behavior, including perception, personality, and attributions. Organizational communication and, in particular, techniques for boosting upward, downward, and lateral communication to enhance organizational responsiveness is covered in Chapter 16. Chapter 17, Managing Teams, provides a brief review of group dynamics and a comprehensive treatment of managing teams in organizations including types of teams, building effective teams, and team-based total quality management programs. Chapter 18, Organizational Change and Development, particularly emphasizes strategic, discontinuous change and corporate renewal, as well as planned change, change advocates, organizational development, and conflict and conflict management techniques.

PART IV: MANAGING OPERATIONS AND SERVICES   Part IV focuses on three important topics. Chapter 19, Operations Management, provides a comprehensive discussion of operations and production management (including operations planning and control and inventory management). It especially emphasizes world-class manufacturing and the responsive organization and, in particular, the use of just-in-time flexible manufacturing systems and computer integrated manufacturing for building organizational responsiveness. Chapter 20, Information Technology and Management Systems, reviews the types of management information systems, but particularly focuses on advances in managerial and data communications and on information technology and its effects on organizational responsiveness. Finally, Chapter 21 focuses on managing services. With about three-fourths of the U.S. workforce now employed in service firms, a complete discussion of the unique aspects of managing services is overdue in management textbooks.

TREATMENT OF CROSS-FUNCTIONAL TOPICS

Most textbooks cover topics that by their nature connect with various disciplines. This book is no exception. In particular, this book contains considerable coverage of quality, diversity, small business management, global management, and ethics. The question of how to treat such cross-functional topics is always a judgment call. Having said that, I want to elaborate on how these topics are treated.

QUALITY MANAGEMENT   Managing quality has emerged as a central management concern for the 1990s and is, therefore, fully approached in this book. Because most quality management programs are team-based, a section of Chapter 17 on Managing Teams is devoted to total quality management programs, including steps in total quality management. Quality management is closely identified with the operations management function, so Chapter 19 on Operations Management similarly contains a section devoted to controlling for quality, which focuses on "quality defined," as well as on total quality management, quality control methods, and the related topic of design for manufacturability. In addition, the relationship of quality to various other topics discussed in this book is emphasized; for example, quality's relationship to service management in Chapter 21; the impact of global competition on quality in Chapter 2; and the importance of the staffing function in building commitment to quality in Chapters 10 and 12.

DIVERSITY   As explained early in this book, the U.S. workforce is becoming increasingly diverse. To mention just one statistic from Chapter 1, minorities and women will account for more than 90 percent of the U.S. labor force's growth over the next 10 years and women alone are projected to account for 64 percent of the net increase in the labor force over this period.

The question is how to integrate the required diversity material? As an author, I had several alternatives ranging from a self-contained diversity chapter to vignettes in each chapter. I decided that the most effective way to communicate the concepts of diversity was to rely on special cases in each chapter, as well as on diversity-related text material as appropriate. In Chapter 10, for example, material including equal employment laws, affirmative action programs, and sexual harassment is fully covered.

Building the diversity theme around each chapter's "Case in Diversity" accomplishes two things. First, it allows for an integration between that chapter's material and a diversity issue that requires a solution. Second, it presents a more realistic picture of diversity issues. As a manager and as a consultant, I am increasingly aware that a mere recitation of diversity topics does not convey the often dramatic similarities and differences in points of view and perspectives that usually underlie diversity-based issues. Carefully chosen realistic case situations do. A synopsis of the "Case in Diversity" for each chapter is as follows:

- **Chapter 1: The Management Challenge Today** A Case in Diversity: "The Challenge of Managing a Diverse Workforce" asks students to address questions such as "What opportunities and dilemmas will managers face as the workforce becomes more diverse?"

- **Chapter 2: Managing in a Global Economy** A Case in Diversity: "Dealing with Diversity Abroad" focuses on discriminatory practices overseas. It asks readers to answer questions such as "Do you think U.S. civil rights laws should apply to American companies' foreign operations?"

- **Chapter 3: Management Ethics and Social Responsibility** A Case in Diversity: "Papa's Grocery" describes a grocery situated in a predominantly African-American section of Los Angeles. It raises issues such as "If the grocery continues to lose money, do you think it will be able to sustain its pattern of social responsibility, or will economic realities have to take precedence?"

- **Chapter 4: Foundations of Modern Management** A Case in Diversity: "McDonald's Corporation" describes how McDonald's adapts both its menus and management methods to the extent that its customers and workers bring with them attitudes and values "as numerous and varied as their countries of origin." The case raises issues such as how a global firm can maintain consistency of purpose while adapting local operations to the diverse needs of local customers and workers.

- **Chapter 5: Planning and Setting Goals** A Case in Diversity: "Margaret F. Gonzalez and Achieving Goals" describes the barriers Gonzalez faces in attracting enterprises to the economically disadvantaged area in her city, and raises issues such as what obstacles and opportunities does she face in attempting to achieve her goals?

- **Chapter 6: Strategic Management.** A Case in Diversity: "Strategic Management at Amigos Canning Company" describes how Ralph Velasco, Jr., the CEO of this Mexican food business changed the strategic direction of his firm. It raises issues such as how a small firm like this can compete by remaining sensitive to demographic changes in the marketplace.

- **Chapter 7: Planning and Decision Making Aids** A Case in Diversity: "Women and Decision Making" asks whether the stereotype sometimes ascribed to women executives (that they tend to be consensus builders and that those who are not "may be characterized as strident, while a man with the same management style is considered decisive") is valid, and if not, what accounts for the stereotype?

- **Chapter 8: Fundamentals of Organizing** A Case in Diversity: "Monsanto Chemical Group" explains that Monsanto Chemical discovered several years ago that many talented women and minorities were leaving because they had the sense that management neither appreciated nor understood them. It asks students to discuss this conflict and Monsanto's solution for it.

- **Chapter 9: The Responsive Organization** A Case in Diversity: "Disability Hiring Initiative by CEOs" describes the Disability 2000-CEO Council, and raises such issues as "Is it possible to completely eliminate the us vs. them mentality among diverse workers?"

- **Chapter 10: The Staffing Function and Human Resource Management** A Case in Diversity: "White Males in the Workplace" raises the question of why some white males feel that they are "the most aggrieved victims of job discrimination." It asks students to consider that issue, and the impact that so-called reverse discrimination may have on interpersonal relations in organizations.

- **Chapter 11: Achieving Control** A Case in Diversity: "New York National Bank" presents some of the management problems banker Serafin Mariel had to navigate while setting up his minority-owned bank in South Bronx, New York.

- Chapter 12: Empowering Employees and Building Commitment A Case in Diversity: "The Japanese and Employee Commitment" raises the interesting issue of how American workers react to supervision by Japanese managers and the effects of Japanese management methods on American workers.

- **Chapter 13: Leadership** A Case in Diversity: "J. Bruce Llewellyn" describes the leadership style of J. Bruce Llewellyn, who controls the Philadelphia Coca-Cola Bottling Company and has been described as one of the nation's most powerful African-American businesspeople.

- **Chapter 14: Organizational Culture and Shared Values** A Case in Diversity: "Organization Culture and the 'Baby Busters'" presents several short scenarios depicting "baby buster"-generation employees who set off to find businesses of their own. It raises such issues as how the values of this new generation may change corporate cultures as baby busters build their own businesses or stay at their existing firms and reach top managerial ranks.

- **Chapter 15: Motivation and Behavior** A Case in Diversity: "Motivated Entrepreneurs" describes some of the hurdles Ana Garcia and Rey Salinas faced when starting their new firms and raises the issue of what personal needs motivated them to launch their own businesses.

- **Chapter 16: Organizational Communication** A Case in Diversity: "Asian-Americans and Organizational Communications" explains how J. D. Hokoyama, head of a Los Angeles management training business, conducts training sessions for Asian-American workers and managers. It addresses the issue of whether workers raised in an Asian culture have a sense of deference to superiors and whether an emphasis on maintaining harmony and loyalty and control of emotions may result in misunderstanding and acrimony in the relatively more direct and harsh organizational communication environment of most U.S. firms. Among the specific questions asked are, "Do you agree with the theory that Asian-American workers need to alter their communication skills in order to get ahead in the U.S. business world? Why? Why not?" And, "Which of the communication barriers described in the chapter are Asian-Americans most likely to encounter in the workplace and how can they best be overcome?"

- **Chapter 17: Managing Teams**   A Case in Diversity: "G.E. Silicones" describes the challenge of achieving team cohesiveness when members of the teams are of varying ethnic backgrounds and genders.

- **Chapter 18: Organizational Change and Development**   A Case in Diversity: "Organizational Change at Avon and Prudential" addresses the programs Prudential and Avon began to solve the problem of why African-American workers in these firms were "leaving for other jobs in droves." Among the specific issues raised is "What sources of resistance to change is the company likely to encounter in pursuing their diversity programs?"

- **Chapter 19: Operations Management**   A Case in Diversity: "Older Workers at Chrysler" raises the issue of the older worker, and asks students to address such questions as "How did Chrysler boost productivity despite the aging of its manufacturing workforce?"

- **Chapter 20: Information Technology and Management Systems**   A Case in Diversity: "Minority IS Managers" describes the challenges faced by a minority manager as he moved up the hierarchy in his information systems career. It asks questions such as "Given the right educational background, do you think minorities have the same opportunities to succeed in information-based organizations as their non-minority counterparts?"

- **Chapter 21: Managing Services**   A Case in Diversity: "Juggling Career and Family" describes how an entrepreneurial Margaret Johnsson developed a thriving business by filling the needs of successful women who wanted an alternative way to juggle family and career.

SMALL BUSINESS/ENTREPRENEURSHIP   There is little doubt that more college graduates are going to take jobs with small, entrepreneurial firms rather than with giant employers. Therefore, I wanted to show, in an integrated way, how a chapter's topic applied specifically in a small business–entrepreneurial environment. Each "focus on small business" box refers to the issues raised within the text itself. To underscore the small business issues, several "focus on small business" questions at the end of the chapter are tied to the boxed element to encourage student discussion of the issues raised.

GLOBAL MANAGEMENT   Many of the challenges managers face today are a direct result of the globalization of industrial economies. And, indeed, there is now an enormous body of knowledge relating to international business and global management. This book contains a comprehensive chapter entitled "Managing in a Global Economy," which covers international business and its impact on managers and management.

ETHICS AND SOCIAL RESPONSIBILITY   Ethics and social responsibility underpin much of what is essential for management education including areas like diversity management. Early in this book (in Chapter 3) a comprehensive treatment of management ethics and social responsibility is included to emphasize the importance of these topics as a foundation for all that managers do.

IN-TEXT LEARNING AIDS

In addition to **video cases** with questions for each part of the book, each chapter has a full complement of in-text learning aids. These include **learning objectives** and a **chapter outline** at the beginning of the chapter; an **opening problem** to set the scene for the chapter, along with a **closing solution** at the end of the chapter that describes how the opening problem was solved and separate questions so that the opening problem and closing solution can be used as a case; the **"focus on small business"** boxes along with questions that can be used to turn each chapter's small business box into a second, small business, case; a third, somewhat longer **Case for Analysis** at the end of each chapter; the **Case in Diversity** comprising a fourth case at the end of each chapter; a full set of **end-of-chapter questions** including separate questions for review, for discussion, and for student action; a list of **key terms** at the end of each chapter along with **marginal definitions** within the chapters; and several **illustrative vignettes** each tied to the text to provide a real example of the concepts being discussed.

RELATED SUPPLEMENT PRODUCTS

- **Study Guide** by Becky Porterfield (University of North Carolina—Wilmington)
- **Test Bank** by Sharon Clinebell (University of Northern Colorado) and Joy Peluchette (University of Southern Indiana)
- **Overhead Transparencies, Transparency Masters, and Teaching Notes** by Ralph Braithwaite (University of Hartford)
- **Instructor's Manual** by Bruce Kemelgor (University of Louisville)
- **Laser Disk with Lecture Active Software**
- **Three sets of videos available** (A Case Approach, Chapter Topics, and Business Concerns Quarterly)
- **Media Instructor's Manual**
- **Management Skills Software** (3.5)

ACKNOWLEDGMENTS

Creating a textbook has taken on many of the aspects of producing a modern Broadway show, not least in terms of the number of people contributing to it, reviewing it, producing it, and marketing it. In acknowledging and thanking everyone who has been involved in this project, I am, therefore, somewhat at a loss, but want to start first with Scott Isenberg and Bob Pawlik, both formerly of The Dryden Press, without whose faith in and commitment to this book you would not now be holding it in your hands. Of those at Dryden on the editorial and production staff with whom I have dealt frequently as this book evolved, I want to thank Ruth Rominger, Lisa Toftemark-Rittby, and Sheila M. Spahn, as well as Linda Wooton Miller, Kelly Cordes, Mandy Manzano, Shirley Webster, Lisé Johnson, Sam Stubblefield, Brett Spalding, Dona Hightower, and Tamra Yoder for all of their expertise and assistance. I also want to gratefully acknowledge Carol Cirulli who helped to prepare most of the cases and vignettes and whose insight into what we needed added significantly to the book. While I am, of course, responsible for the content of this book, I want to express my gratitude to the faculty members who reviewed portions of the manuscript: Russell Kent, Georgia Southern University; Margaret Langford, St. Mary's University; Bruce Kemelgor, University of Louisville; Sharon Clinebell, University of Northern Colorado; Tammy Hunt, University of North Carolina—Wilmington; Joy Peluchette, University of Southern Indiana; Ralph Braithwaite, University of Hartford; Terry Gaston, Southern Oregon State

College; and James McElroy, Iowa State University. This book would not be such a source of expert information without the input and suggestions from these expert reviewers.

Last, but certainly not least, I want to thank my son Derek whose knowledge of and insights into business management continue to be an enormous source of pride for me, and my wife Claudia, who tolerated my self-imposed exile to my university office in order to work on this book each weekend while she managed the reconstruction of our Miami home after Hurricane Andrew.

Gary Dessler
Miami, Florida
August 1994

ABOUT THE AUTHOR

Gary Dessler is a Professor of Business and Chairman of the Department of Management and International Business in the College of Business Administration at Florida International University in Miami. He has a Bachelor of Science Degree from New York University, a Master of Science Degree from Rensselaer Polytechnic Institute, and a Ph.D. in Business Administration from the Bernard M. Baruch School of Business of the City University of New York.

In addition to *Managing Organizations in an Era of Change*, Dr. Dessler has authored numerous other books, including, most recently, *Winning Commitment: How to Build and Keep a Competitive Workforce*, and *Human Resource Management*, Sixth Edition. He wrote the syndicated "Job Talk" column for the *Miami Herald* for 10 years and has written numerous articles on organization behavior, leadership, and quality improvement. His recent consulting assignments have involved strategic planning, executive and management recruiting, establishing human resource management systems, and negotiating multinational joint ventures.

CONTENTS

PART I
THE MANAGER'S CHANGING WORLD
1

CHAPTER 3   MANAGEMENT ETHICS AND SOCIAL RESPONSIBILITY   58

CHAPTER 4   FOUNDATIONS OF MODERN MANAGEMENT   86

**PART II
THE MANAGEMENT
PROCESS
117**

**PART III
BEHAVIOR AND
MANAGEMENT
329**

CHAPTER 13   LEADERSHIP   362

**PART IV
MANAGING
OPERATIONS AND
SERVICES
541**

THE MANAGER'S CHANGING WORLD

THE MANAGEMENT CHALLENGE TODAY

LEARNING OBJECTIVES

After studying this chapter, you should be able to:

- Explain how rapid change has led to a transformation in how companies are organized and managed.
- Describe the five basic management functions of planning, organizing, staffing, leading, and controlling.
- Detail the various ways to classify managers.
- Discuss the major sources of change for businesses, including technological innovation, globalization, deregulation, and the shift to a service society.
- Summarize the features that characterize responsive companies.
- Describe the "new management" that has emerged from companies' efforts to recreate themselves and respond to changing conditions.

Dell Computer founder Michael Dell must have felt like he was riding a whirlwind. Dell sales had soared from $6 million in 1985 to $3 billion in 1993. But with those explosive sales came management problems, culminating in a first-ever quarterly loss of $75 million. Michael Dell had been in business since he was 12, and now, at the age of 29, he faced the business crisis of his career. ■ Dell Computer had been battered by many of the forces that have changed the face of business today. Global expansion—to Germany in 1988 and then to London—stretched Dell's management resources thin, while foreign competitors from Italy's Olivetti to Japan's Toshiba squeezed Dell's profits. Technological innovation was so fast that products like Dell's notebook computer were often outdated five or six months after introduction. Political turmoil—from East Germany to Russia to Brazil—created tremendous new market opportunities and equally big risks. As all of this occurred, Dell sales were almost doubling every single year. ■ By 1993, the personal computer industry faced enormous uncertainties as demand tapered off and price cutting from global competitors set in. Falling prices and profits had already sent several computer firms (including CompuAdd Computers) into bankruptcy court, and even major firms like Apple and IBM were announcing plans to lay off workers. Two long-time computer presidents—Apple's John Sculley and IBM's John Akers—both had to step down. ■ Such turbulence and rapid growth strained Dell's management resources beyond the breaking point. First, inventories soared. Dell had always kept costs down by building computers on demand as the orders arrived from the telemarketing department. But with orders flooding in, Dell had to build and stock computers and more and more computer parts—all without, as it turned out, adequate inventory controls. New-product design was also a problem. Trying to rush its new notebook computer into production, Dell stumbled badly in 1993 by shipping thousands of problem-plagued computers. Then Dell's sub-notebook computer was recalled for mis-wired board connections, and its laptop revenues dropped as a result.[1] Dell's strategy of generating sales almost exclusively through telemarketing also required revamping, since more and more customers wanted the personalized advice they could only get from one-on-one sales discussions. Michael Dell knew that something had to be done. As an article in Computer World put it:[2]

> Threatened by the entry into the direct marketing channel of the newly aggressive IBM PC company, and Compaq Computer Corp., and slammed for its inability to track parts and inventory, and strategic blunders in the notebook industry, Dell executives said that the company is ready to correct the mistakes that . . . have cost [it] dearly.[3]

MANAGING IN AN ERA OF CHANGE

The opportunities and problems facing Dell illustrate the rapid change and unpredictability that managers face today. Intensified global competition, deregulation, technological advances, and political upheavals have triggered an avalanche of change, one that many firms have not survived. Consider some facts: bank failures rose from single-digits in the 1970s to ten in 1980, 120 in 1985, and almost 200 annually in the early 1990s.[4] Some estimate that 20 million people were displaced in the 1980s by restructuring in manufacturing, and the percent of those employed in service jobs jumped from 70 percent in 1980 to almost 78 percent in 1991.[5] U.S. firms, once dominant players in the market for phonographs and television sets, have seen their market share drop to 1 percent for phonographs and 10 percent for television sets. In 1990, the United States, once the undisputed leader in telecommunications apparatus, exported more than $9 billion worth of such apparatus and imported over $22 billion worth.[6] In about ten years, three U.S. airlines—Eastern, People's Express, and Braniff—ceased operations, while many others, including Pan Am and USAir, have either been taken over or have had to sell substantial shares.[7] Major currency prices, once stable, now swing as much as 30 percent per year, and the U.S. banking system faces a crushing trillion dollars in developing-country debt.[8]

In the United States, cutthroat competition has been fed by deregulation, an increase in the globalization of competition, and a tapering off of population growth. The U.S. labor force should grow at 1.3 percent per year through 2005, compared with 1.9 percent annual growth for 1975–1990. Japanese firms have surpassed Chrysler as this nation's third-largest automaker, and Intel Corporation president Andrew S. Grove predicted an industrywide shakeout among PC makers, noting that "there are 500 suppliers—and 450 should not exist."[9] The U.S. public debt ballooned from just under $1 trillion in 1980 to $3.2 trillion in 1990,[10] and in country after country, household debt as a percentage of annual disposable income jumped: from 80 percent in 1980 to over 100 percent in 1990 in the United States, from under 80 percent to almost 120 percent

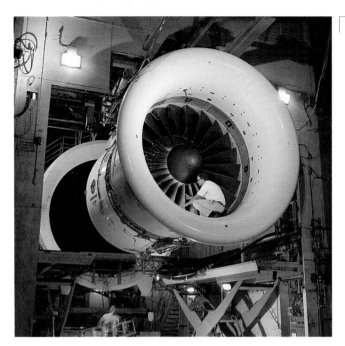

United Technologies, owner of Pratt & Whitney, saw orders for new engines drop drastically as airplane orders dropped at Boeing, Airbus, and McDonnell Douglas. This trend is not expected to reverse itself anytime soon.

in Japan, and from barely 60 percent to 118 percent in Great Britain.[11] The United States' favorable balance of trade evaporated in the 1970s and 1980s: U.S. exports exceeded imports by more than $9 billion in 1975, but imports exceeded exports by $24 billion in 1980, $132 billion in 1985, and $101 billion in 1990.[12] As new competitors spring up overnight, consumers demand ever-better quality, factories demand ever-smarter workers, and computers continue to link buyers and sellers in close-knit chains, executives everywhere understandably ask themselves, what's coming next?[13] The *United Technologies* vignette shows how one firm was buffetted by such issues.

In such an environment, the future belongs to those managers who can best manage change, and a revolution has therefore taken place in the ways that companies are organized and managed. At Harvard, for instance, Professor Rosabeth Moss Kanter points out that rapid change, competition, and the need to get closer to the customer have created changes in how companies must be led. Management expert Peter Drucker says "we are entering a third period of change: the shift from the command and control organization, the organization of departments and divisions, to the information-based organization, the organization of knowledge specialists." The shift from manual to knowledge and service work, shorter product life cycles, information technology, and intense global competition have, in other words, created the need for a new approach to managing, one in which flexibility and the ability to respond to change have taken on enormous importance.

Today's new highly responsive organizations go by many names. But whether we call them "post-entrepreneurial" organizations (as does Kanter) or "information organizations" (as does Drucker), or whether we refer to them by some other name, it is apparent that new management skills are needed to survive and thrive today. *Managing Organizations in an Era of Change* will be our focus in this book, and we will begin with a general view of what managers do.

UNITED TECHNOLOGIES CORPORATION

After taking over as chairman of United Technologies Corporation (UT) in 1986, the difficulties facing Robert F. Daniell must have reminded him of the mythological Hydra: every time he eliminated one problem, two others grew back in its place. Daniell's problems included an overbuilt real estate market that had reduced demand for the air conditioners made by UT's Carrier Corp. and the elevators manufactured by its Otis division. But the chairman's biggest worry concerned the company's jet engine maker Pratt & Whitney. Airline fare wars had led to a series of bankruptcies, and overcapacity had brought on a sea of red ink and the early retirement or mothballing of commercial jets. New engine orders were drastically reduced, and the lucrative spare parts business had fallen sharply. The post-Cold War era also had brought military budget cutbacks and reduced orders from defense contractors. Daniell definitely had a crisis on his hands. The Pratt & Whitney jet engine division typically accounted for as much as two-thirds of UT's profitability.

Daniell decided to tackle the problem by bringing in George David, a conscientious cost cutter who previously had returned Otis and Carrier to profitability. Daniell appointed him president of UT in the hope that David could work the same magic at Pratt. However, David's assessment was not encouraging. "I don't think Pratt has run itself well for decades," David said. "It hasn't paid attention to costs, productivity, or responsiveness. Now it is exposed for the first time to the ravages of cost-based rivals who had to scramble in order to survive."

Daniell and David began making fundamental changes in the way Pratt did business. In the past, the division built an engine entirely on its own, spending as much as $2.5 billion for production, research and development, and other costs. To reduce the considerable risks, Daniell entered an agreement with Daimler Benz wherein R&D costs were shared and potential risks reduced. The company also successfully trimmed costs in areas other than payroll.

It is unclear whether management could have better foreseen the market changes that led to the company's plight. But what is certain is the necessity of implementing a top-to-bottom management restructuring that eliminates waste and produces efficiency and responsiveness, while still meeting customer needs.

SOURCES: James R. Norman, "Welcome to the Real World," *Forbes,* February 15, 1993, 46–47; Stanley Kandebo, "Market Forces Pummel Pratt; Personnel Cuts Expanded," *Aviation Week and Space Technology,* October 26, 1992, 18–19; and Todd Vogel, "United Technology Goes in for a Little Engine Work," *Business Week,* October 21, 1991, 108–10.

WHAT MANAGERS DO

THE BASIC MANAGEMENT FUNCTIONS

A **manager** is someone who gets thing done through others. In other words, managers like Michael Dell do not depend solely on their own efforts for getting the job done. Instead, new skills are required—the skills of a manager. Management writers traditionally classify these skills into the following five basic functions:

PLANNING Planning includes setting goals and deciding on courses of action, developing rules and procedures, developing plans (both for the organization and for those who work for them), and forecasting (that is, predicting or projecting what the future holds for the firm). For example, Michael Dell's plan involved hiring a sales force and improving controls to return his firm to profitability.

ORGANIZING Organizing includes giving each subordinate a task, setting up departments, delegating or pushing down authority to subordinates, establishing a chain of command (in other words, channels of authority and communication), and coordinating the work of the manager's subordinates. Thus, Dell had to organize a telemarketing department and coordinate its work with that of manufacturing.

STAFFING Staffing involves deciding what type of people should be hired, recruiting prospective employees, selecting employees, setting performance standards, and training and developing employees. For example, Dell had to hire senior executives and decide how they would be trained and appraised.

LEADING Leading means getting others to get the job done, maintaining morale, and motivating subordinates. Thus, Dell had to motivate his sales force and maintain morale in the face of the notebook computer's problems.

CONTROLLING Controlling means setting standards (such as sales quotas, or quality standards), comparing actual performance with these standards, and then taking corrective actions as needed. For example, Dell first had to determine why his firm's inventory levels were excessive, and then install new procedures to prevent such a problem from occurring again.

TYPES OF MANAGERS

Managers may be classified in three main ways, specifically by *position,* by *level,* or by *title.* These classifications are illustrated in Figure 1.1. Thus, the managers at the top of an organization like Dell Computer represent the firm's top management. These people are usually referred to as *executives.* Titles including president and vice-president are typically included at this level. On the other hand, on Dell's assembly floor we typically find *first-line managers* such as production supervisors. *Middle managers* such as sales managers and production managers then fit between top managers and first-line managers.

Different levels of managers have much in common. They all get work done through subordinates. They all plan for others, organize the work of others, and are involved in motivating, and controlling. Also they all usually spend a good deal of their time with people—talking, listening, attending meetings and so forth.[14]

But the various levels of management also display many differences. For example, executives and middle managers both have managers for subordinates; they are in charge of other managers. Supervisors (first-line managers) on the other hand, have workers—nonmanagers—as subordinates.

MANAGER

Someone who gets things done through others.

PLANNING

Includes setting goals and courses of action, developing rules and procedures, developing plans (both for the organization and for those who work in it), and forecasting—that is, predicting or projecting what the future holds for the firm.

ORGANIZING

Includes giving each subordinate a task, setting up departments, delegating or pushing down authority to subordinates, establishing a chain of command, and coordinating the work of the manager's subordinates.

STAFFING

Involves deciding what type of people should be hired, recruiting prospective employees, selecting employees, setting performance standards, and training and developing employees.

LEADING

Getting others to get the job done, maintaining morale, and motivating subordinates.

CONTROLLING

Setting standards (such as sales quotas, or quality standards), comparing actual performance with these standards, and then taking corrective actions as needed.

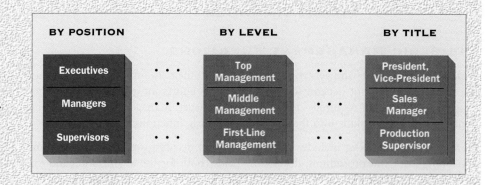

FIGURE 1.1

Three Ways to Classify
Managers

*Managers can be classified
by position, by level, and by
title. Thus, Michael Dell is
president of Dell Computer
and as such is an executive
and a member of the firm's
top management team.*

Managers from different levels also spend their time differently. Top managers typically spend most of their time planning and setting goals and direction. Middle managers then take these goals (like "double sales in the next two years") and translate them into specific projects (like "hire two new salespeople and introduce three new products") for their subordinates to execute. First-line supervisors then concentrate on directing and controlling the employees who work on these projects.

Yet, the manager's job is changing so fast that some—like management expert Peter Drucker—say, "I'm not comfortable with the word manager anymore, because it implies subordinates."[15] Forces such as globalization, computerization, and deregulation have so changed the nature of what managers do that in some respects the job today would be unrecognizable to a time traveler from the 1940s. Let's look more closely at some of the forces prompting change.

THE MANAGER'S ENVIRONMENT

The problems faced by Dell Computer illustrate the tumultuous environment within which firms and their managers now compete. Intensified global competition, deregulation, technological advances, and other sources of change have triggered an avalanche of opportunities and threats to which firms must respond; those that fail to do so do not survive. Several major sources of change and turbulence affect today's business firms.

TECHNOLOGICAL INNOVATION

Technological innovations like information highways, microprocessors, and automated factories are creating a rapidly changing competitive terrain. U.S. patents issued rose from 62,000 annually in the 1960s, to 67,000 in the 1970s, to 77,200 in 1985, and to over 100,000 per year in the 1990s. The number of U.S. trademarks issued has risen from fewer than 20,000 per year in the 1960s to almost 66,000 in the 1980s, and to over 120,000 per year in the 1990s. And this total just reflects U.S. patents and trademarks, not those issued in other countries.

INFORMATION TECHNOLOGY
Merging communications with
computers.

Similarly, **information technology**—merging communications with computers—is changing the face of business. For example, Inter-Design of Ohio sells plastic clocks, refrigerator magnets, soap dishes, and similar products. Its president explains the impact of information technology this way: "In the seventies we went to the Post Office to pick up our orders. In the early 80s, we put in an 800 number. In the late 80s, we got a fax machine. In 1991, pressured by Target [stores], we added electronic data interchange." Now, just two years later, more than half of Inter-Design's orders arrive via modem, straight into company computers. Errors in order entry and shipping have all but disappeared.[16]

Information technology has also hastened what experts call the "fall of hierarchy"; in other words, managers depend less and less on yesterday's stick-to-the-chain-of-command approach to organizing. For example, with **distributed computing** (discussed in Chapter 20), every employee with a PC on his or her desk can tap into the firm's computer network and get the information that he or she needs. Says one manager at Goodyear Tire and Rubber Company: "It used to be, if you wanted information, you had to go up, over, and down through the organization. Now you just tap in. Everybody knows as much about the company as the Chairman of the Board. That's what broke down the hierarchy. It's not why we bought computers, but it's what they did."[17]

In any case, technological innovation pressures firms to move fast. For example, the performance per unit price of computer work stations is rising 70 percent per year. This gives workstation makers like Hewlett-Packard just several months to cover a product's costs and to gain profits.

That's why introducing its notebook computer late can be a disaster for a firm like Dell: by the time the product is introduced it is technologically out of date, and the profits to be gained are virtually nil. So, for the manager, the question is, "How do you organize so as to ensure that your firm can respond at once to such rapid change?"

DISTRIBUTED COMPUTING
The ability for every employee with a PC on his or her desk to tap into the firm's computer network and get the information that he or she needs.

GLOBALIZATION

In 1983, General Electric, long accustomed to being the dominant lighting manufacturer in the United States, had a rude awakening. Its relatively weak competitor, Westinghouse, sold its lamp operations to Dutch electrical powerhouse Philips Electronics; overnight GE's competitive picture had changed. As one GE executive put it, "suddenly we have bigger, stronger competition. They're coming into our market, but we're not in theirs. So we're on the defensive."[18]

The situation did not stay that way for long, though. GE soon bought Hungary's Tungstram electronics and is fast moving into Asia through a partnership with Hitachi.[19] In 1990, GE lighting got less than 20 percent of its sales from abroad; by 1993, the figure was 40 percent, and for 1996 the estimate is more than half.

Globalization refers to the tendency of firms to extend their sales or manufacturing to new markets abroad; and for businesses everywhere, the rate of globalization the past few years has been nothing short of phenomenal.

GLOBALIZATION
The tendency of firms to extend their sales or manufacturing to new markets abroad.

For U.S. firms, this globalization is manifesting itself in many ways. The value of the U.S. import/export trade grew from 9.4 percent of the U.S. economy in 1960 to almost 23 percent in 1991.[20] Also, U.S. exports are reaching new markets with big gains since 1988 to countries ranging from Uruguay and Mexico, to the Netherlands, Hungary, and Kuwait.[21]

Production is becoming globalized, too, as manufacturers around the world put manufacturing facilities where they will be most advantageous. Thus, the Toyota Camry—what many would claim is "obviously" a Japanese car—is produced in Georgetown, Kentucky, and contains almost 80 percent American-made parts. At the same time, the General Motors Pontiac LeMans ("obviously" an American car) actually contains almost two-thirds foreign-made parts.[22]

This globalization of markets and manufacturing has vastly increased international competition. Throughout the world, firms that formerly competed only with local firms—from airlines to carmakers to banks—now find that complacency must give way to facing an onslaught of new foreign competitors.

Many firms have successfully responded to this new international scene, while others have failed. For instance, when Swedish furniture retailer Ikea built its first U.S.

furniture superstore in New Jersey, its superior styles and management systems grabbed market share from numerous domestic competitors, driving several out of business.

Such global competition is, of course, a two-way street. Ford and GM have huge market shares in Europe, for instance, while IBM, Microsoft, Apple, and countless smaller firms have major market shares around the world. As one international business expert puts it, "the bottom line is that the growing integration of the world economy into a single, huge marketplace, is increasing the intensity of competition in a wide range of manufacturing and service industries."[23]

DEREGULATION

DEREGULATION
The act or process of removing restrictions or regulations.

Meanwhile, the comfortable protection provided by **deregulation** to thousands of businesses in dozens of industries around the world has been stripped away in country after country. In the United States, as discussed earlier, a dozen airlines including Eastern, People's Express, Braniff, Pan Am, and Piedmont have either been bought or have gone bust as a result of the pressures for better service and lower costs resulting from U.S. airline deregulation in the 1970s. Similarly (as mentioned), bank failures rose from single-digits in the 1970s to ten in 1980, 120 in 1985, and almost 200 annually in the early 1990s as banking deregulation exposed inefficiencies that less responsive competitors couldn't eliminate in time.[24] Similar changes have swept other countries. The *Morris Air* Small Business box shows how one firm dealt with deregulation.

A NEW WORLD ORDER

As nations ranging from the Philippines to Argentina, Russia, Poland, and Chile join the ranks of democracies, central planning and communism are increasingly replaced by capitalism. This prompted Francis Fukuyama, a state department planner, to declare "the end of history." In an essay in *The National Interest Magazine,* he summarized the conquest of capitalism over communism and the consequences, including the end of the historical conflict between these two great economic ideologies.[25] To Fukuyama the overthrow of Marxist-Leninist ideology means the victory of the principles of liberty and equality, and thus the strengthening of economic liberalism, capitalism, and competition. "Indeed," says Fukuyama, "the meaning of 'great power' will be based increasingly on economic rather than military, territorial, or other traditional measures of might."[26]

One major consequence has been an explosive opening of new markets, new markets with hundreds of millions of potential customers in countries from Russia to Chile. For business firms the opportunities are enormous. (See for instance, the photo of Evan Newmark, head of Investment Banker Goldman Sach's new Moscow office.[27]) Yet with this burgeoning demand comes increased global competition, as seen in the photo of the new Hungarian bus on the streets of Portland, Oregon.[28]

DEMOGRAPHICS AND THE NEW GLOBAL WORK FORCE

In the United States the nature of the work force is changing dramatically, too. Over the next few years, that part of the work force composed of Hispanics, minorities, and women will increase. During the 1990s, the white labor force is forecast to grow less than 15 percent while the black labor force will grow by about 29 percent and the Hispanic labor force will jump by more than 74 percent. During the period 1986–2000, Hispanics will account for nearly 29 percent of the labor force's growth; Asian and other nonwhite races (including Alaskan natives) will account for more than 11

MORRIS AIR

The business philosophy at tiny Morris Air is simple: offer low enough fares and travelers will dream up their own excuses to journey by air. Then all you have to do is operate efficiently, and the increased volume will translate into profits. But that last part is not as easy as it sounds.

The driving force behind Morris Air—some say she is Morris Air—is founder June Morris. With characteristic understatement, Morris says she simply identified a need and filled the niche in starting the company. She believed she had talent, but perhaps more importantly, she found good people and let them use their own abilities in building Morris Air.

The Salt Lake City-based regional carrier now has 2,000 employees, including son Rick Frendt, who is the airline's chairman, and a few others that go as far back as grade school with June Morris. She thinks Utah is a good place to find good employees; work ethics are solid and people well educated and polite. That, too, is important, because despite low fares and cost-conscious operations, Morris insists customer service be the best. Since her management style focuses on the human side, she wants to hear about problems, too. Personally, Morris stays on top of what's happening by monitoring in-flight sur-

veys, reading complaint letters, and occasionally fielding telephone calls.

One way the airline has managed to keep fares low, often below competitors' fare-war prices, is by leasing many of its planes and contracting flight crews. Another tactic is more ingenious, an advertising strategy that encourages flyers to see that their own best interests coincide with those of Morris Air. One of the company's promotional brochures summed it up: "A ticket on Morris Air is a vote for permanent low fares!" When the carrier began Salt Lake

FOCUS ON SMALL BUSINESS

City to Denver service with four flights daily, Delta, American, and United had to slash fares as much as 50 percent.

So far the increased competition has hit Delta the hardest. In mid-1992, 75 percent of passengers boarding flights in Salt Lake were Delta flyers. A little over a year later that number dropped to 67 percent while Morris Air's market share rose from 8 percent to 14 percent. Analysts said the big airline underestimated Morris Air. Whatever the case, it's safe to assume Delta management was less than amused, and

retaliation was swift. Delta notified travel agents in mid-1993 that booking fliers on Morris Air could result in losing lucrative commissions from the big carrier. Delta even gave away free tickets to loyal agents as a further inducement. Morris was forced to hire new reservation agents, but the small carrier quickly won back the 20 percent loss in business.

June Morris patterned much of her airline operations around Texas-based Southwest Airlines. The two carriers have much in common. Both fly 737 jets exclusively and concentrate on short flights of around 500 miles. In the future they will have even more in common. In December 1993, Southwest announced it was buying Morris Air. Deregulation continues to churn airlines and their management.

SOURCES: John Accola, "Tiny Morris Air Is Making the Big Airlines Nervous with Its Cut-Rate Fares," *Rocky Mountain News*, 88A; 90A; Judy B. Rollins, "Morris Air Owner Says Every Cloud Has a Silver Lining," *The Salt Lake Tribune*, January 10, 1993, F8, F9; Julie Schmit and Jefferson Graham, "When Morris Took Flight, Fares Fell," *USA Today*, August 30, 1993, section B, 1; Carlene Canton, "Flying High," *The Costco Connection*, August 1992, vol. 6, no. 8, 1; 15; and Terry Maxon, "Southwest to Buy Carrier," *Dallas Morning News*, December 14, 1993, 1A, 10A.

percent of labor force growth, and (in total) blacks, Hispanics, Asians, and other non-white races should account for 57 percent of labor force growth. If you include non-Hispanic white women, then minorities and women will account for more than 90 percent of the labor force's growth over the next few years. Women alone are projected to account for 64 percent of the net increase in the labor force over this period.[29] Many of these individuals may not have the entry-level skills needed by business and that fact—combined with the work force's rising diversity—will force virtually all U.S. firms to make dramatic changes in their training and other personnel-related programs.[30]

At the same time, more U.S. firms will transfer their operations abroad, not just to seek cheaper labor, but to tap what *Fortune* magazine calls "a vast new supply of skilled labor around the world."[31] Even today, in fact, most multinational firms set up manufacturing plants abroad partly to establish beachheads in promising markets and

East meets West and does business. Evan Newmark, head of Goldman Sachs' new office in Moscow, isn't doing much business yet, but is hopeful it will pick up soon.

Portland, Oregon, opts for new Hungarian buses. While the opening of new world markets has brought additional opportunities for many firms, it has also brought added competition to local markets.

partly to utilize that country's professionals and engineers. For example, ASEA Brown Boveri (a $30 billion-a-year Swiss/Swedish builder of transportation and electric generation systems), already has 25,000 new employees in former Communist countries, and has thus shifted many jobs from Western to Eastern Europe. Exactly how such domestic and international demographic trends will evolve is hard to predict. The only thing for sure is that such labor force changes will create profound uncertainties for countless firms and managers around the world.

A SERVICE SOCIETY

At the same time, an enormous shift from manufacturing jobs to service jobs is taking place in North America and Western Europe. Today over two-thirds of the U.S. work force is employed in producing and delivering services, not things. In fact, the manufacturing work force declined over 12 percent during the 1980s. Of the 21 million or so new jobs added by the U.S. economy throughout the 1990s, virtually all will be in such service industries as fast foods, retailing, consulting, teaching, and legal work. This, in turn, will demand new types of "knowledge" workers and new management methods to manage them.

KNOWLEDGE, WORK, AND HUMAN CAPITAL

Management expert Peter Drucker has said that the typical large business will soon bare little resemblance to the typical manufacturing company of 30 years ago. As Drucker predicts it, "the typical business will be knowledge-based, an organization composed largely of specialists who direct and discipline their own performance through organized feedback from colleagues, customers and headquarters. For this reason, it will be what I call an information-based organization."[32] As a result, the distinguishing characteristic of companies today and tomorrow, say many experts, is the

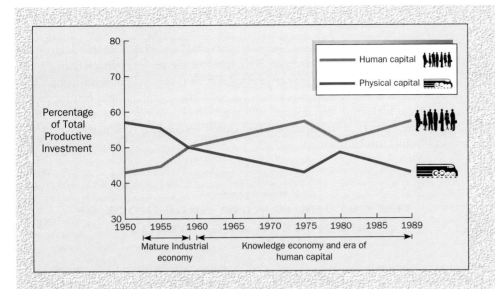

FIGURE 1.2

U.S. Investment in Human
Capital Compared to U.S.
Investment in Physical
Capital, 1950 to 1989

*The human capital
investment in things like
schooling and training has
risen from about 42% of
industry's total productive
investments to about 58%
between 1950 and 1989.*

SOURCE: Richard Crawford, *In
the Era of Human Capital*
(Harper Business, 1991), 31.

growing emphasis on **human capital**[33]—the knowledge, training, skills, and expertise of a firm's workers—at the expense of physical capital like equipment, machinery, and the physical plant.[34]

This is illustrated in Figure 1.2.[35] The human capital investment (including direct outlays for all forms of formal schooling and worker training) rose from about 42 percent of total productive investment to about 58 percent between 1950 and 1990. During the same time, the investment in physical capital as a percentage of total productive investment dropped from about 58 percent to about 45 percent.

This growing emphasis on education and human capital reflects several things. One is the increase in the service-oriented nature of the U.S. economy (service jobs like consulting put a bigger premium on worker education and knowledge than do traditional manufacturing jobs). Another is the fact that manufacturing jobs are changing, too. Particularly in the United States, manufacturing-intensive jobs in the steel, auto, rubber, and textile industries are being replaced by what one expert calls "knowledge-intensive high tech manufacturing in such industries as aerospace, computers, telecommunications, home electronics, pharmaceuticals, and medical instruments."[36] At the same time, even heavy manufacturing jobs are becoming more high-tech: at Alcoa Aluminum's Davenport, Iowa, plant, for instance, a computer stands at each workpost to help each employee control his or her machines or communicate data. As *Fortune* magazine recently put it, "practically every package deliverer, bank teller, retail clerk, telephone operator, and bill collector in America works with a computer [today]."

Jobs today demand a level of expertise far beyond that required of manufacturing workers 20 or 30 years ago. Furthermore, it is not unusual for more than one-fourth of many firms' sales to come from products less than five years old. As a result, "innovating—creating new products, new services, new ways of turning out goods more cheaply—has become the most urgent concern of corporations everywhere."[37] This means that companies are relying more on employees' creativity and skills, thus placing more stress on the employee's brain power. As *Fortune* magazine recently said:

> Brain-Power . . . has never before been so important for business. Every company depends
> increasingly on knowledge—patents, processes, management skills, technologies, informa-

HUMAN CAPITAL
The knowledge, training, skills,
and expertise of a firm's workers.

tion about customers and suppliers, and old-fashioned experience. Added together, this knowledge is intellectual capital.[38]

For managers, the challenge of "intellectual capital" lies in the fact that such workers must be managed differently than were those of the previous generation. As one expert put this, "the center of gravity in employment is moving fast from manual and clerical workers to knowledge workers, who resist the command and control model that business took from the military 100 years ago."[39] Workers like these, in other words, cannot just be ordered around and closely monitored. New management systems and skills will be required.

THE FUTURE IS NOW: SNAPSHOTS OF THE MODERN ORGANIZATION

To fit these new fast-changing, deregulated, globally competitive and increasingly high-tech environments, a new breed of organization is arising. As mentioned earlier, these go by many names: the *post-entrepreneurial organization,*[40] the *information-based organization*[41] and the *post-modern organization.*[42] Whatever they're called, the 1990s have seen the birth of a new business firm, one for which *responsiveness* is now a main concern. Probably no single firm exemplifies all the traits of a post-modern organization. However, examples abound of firms that exemplify specific features. Let's look at a few examples:

ABB ASEA BROWN BOVERI

Zurich-based electrical equipment maker ABB Asea Brown Boveri is one good example of a firm that "dis-organized itself to compete in the fast-moving global market of the next ten years."[43] ABB did four things to make itself super-responsive; it organized around *mini-units, empowered* its workers, *flattened its hierarchy,* and *eliminated central staff.* How did ABB do it?

First, within two years of taking over this $30 billion firm, Chairman Percy Barnevik "de-organized" its 215,000 employees into 5,000 *minicompanies,* each averaging only about 50 workers each.[44] For example, the ABB hydropower unit in Finland is a minicompany that serves just its own Finnish customers. Such direct customer contact transformed the unit into a highly customer-focused little business, one in which employees' efforts are all centered on its local (Finnish) customers. Each of ABB's 50-person units is run by its own manager and three or four lieutenants. Such small units are very manageable: it's a lot easier to monitor what everyone is doing when there are only 50 people to keep track of than when there are 1,000, let alone 5,000 or 10,000.

Next, to speed decision making, the 5,000 minicompanies are autonomous and *empowered.* Their employees have the authority to make most of their own business decisions without checking first with top management.

For example, if a customer has a complaint about a $50,000 machine, a minicompany employee has the authority to approve a replacement on the spot, rather than having to wait for reviews by several levels of management. Giving employees this much authority means, by the way, that ABB's 5,000 businesses must be staffed by, as management expert Tom Peters put it, "high-performance team members," highly skilled employees with the capacity and commitment to make those big decisions.

Next, in a break with most big firms, ABB's 215,000-employee organization has only three management levels (compared to the seven or eight a comparably sized company might have). There is a 13-member top-management executive committee based in Zurich. Below this is a 250-member executive level that includes country managers and executives in charge of groups of businesses. Below this is a third level, consisting of the 5,000 minicompany managers and their management teams. They thus **flattened the hierarchy,** or chain of command. By slicing out layers of management and letting lower-level employees make their own on-the-spot decisions, ABB's employees can respond more quickly to customers' needs and competitors' moves.

FLATTEN THE HIERARCHY
To "slice" out layers of management, letting lower-level employees make their own on-the-spot decisions.

Fourth, since decision making was pushed down to front-line ABB employees, ABB could *eliminate* most headquarters staff advisers. For example, when Barnevik became CEO in 1980, he found 2,000 people working at headquarters, basically reviewing and analyzing (and slowing down) the decisions of the firm's lower-level employees. Within a few months, Barnevik reduced the staff to 200—and he reduced it even further in later years. As ABB acquired other companies, Barnevik took the same approach. For example, when he acquired Finland's Stromberg Company, he reduced its headquarters staff from 880 to 25. Similarly, he reduced German ABB headquarters in Mannheim from 1,600 to 100.

Responsiveness is the net effect of all this reorganization: a lean, flat organization staffed with highly committed employees who are organized into small, empowered teams, each able to respond fast to competitors' moves and customers' needs with no need to wait for approval from headquarters.

SATURN CORPORATION

Perhaps it is a bit ironic: one of the most responsive and progressive companies around is part of the huge General Motors Corporation (which many management experts still use as a prime example of yesterday's unresponsive, bureaucratic organization).

Its *team-based organization* is one thing that sets Saturn Corporation apart. For example, virtually all the work on the shop floor is organized around work teams of 10 to 12 employees. Each team is responsible for a task, such as installing door units, checking electrical systems, or maintaining automated machines. These work teams don't have supervisors in the traditional sense. Instead, they consist of highly trained workers who do their own hiring, control their own budgets, monitor the quality of their own work, and generally manage themselves. Are too many of the parts installed in the door not fitting right? Then the team is in charge of finding the problem and getting the parts supplier to solve the problem. Is there a coworker who is always late or is often out? Then discipline him or her, since the team must manage its own (and its team members') time.

AT&T

AT&T has come a long way since the mid-1980s. On January 1, 1984, the U.S. government split the huge AT&T local phone monopoly into seven regional operating companies (the "Baby Bells"). That left AT&T with the long-distance phone business and with Western Electric, the telephone equipment maker.[45] Decades of operating as a regulated monopoly (with virtually no competition) had made AT&T slow and bureaucratic. Deregulation and divestiture meant that it had to get moving—and fast—if it wanted to compete with the likes of MCI. In the process, AT&T has come far toward remaking itself into a post-modern organization, by **downsizing,** *boosting communications, empowering workers,* and *changing employees' values.*

DOWNSIZING
Eliminating jobs and the employees that went with them.

Here's a synopsis of what they did. Since 1984, the company *downsized* by 140,000 jobs (in other words, AT&T eliminated 140,000 jobs—and the employees that went with them). In addition, chairman Robert Allen reorganized AT&T in order to *promote communication* between the firm's units and to dramatically speed up decision making. AT&T now consists of four major business groups: the telephone network itself, equipment for the telecommunications network, user products (like telephones and answering machines), and computer-maker NCR. The heads of these four groups (along with the company's top financial officer) comprise a five-person presidency known as the "Operations Committee." The Operations Committee meets several days per month and makes major AT&T decisions, reporting to Chairman Allen. Bonuses for the four committee members are tied in part to AT&T's overall performance. That helps to ensure that the four executives don't just think of what is best for their own divisions, but also of what's best for AT&T as a whole. Communication was also encouraged by setting up lots of interdepartmental teams. These teams "mix it up, get people talking, and figure out the businesses and structures that AT&T as a company will need."[46]

EMPOWER
To give authority to employees to make decisions and the training and resources required to make them.

AT&T managers also **empower** their employees. For example, Jerry Stead, president of AT&T's global business communications systems unit, not only never shuts his office door—he had the lock removed.[47] He wants and expects his employees to interact with him often; "I am not a boss" he says and prefers to be called "Coach." His job, as he sees it, is not to "manage" a group of "subordinates." Instead, he wants to get what he calls his "associates" to focus on their customers' needs. Stead's job is to make sure he gets employees the training, authority, and resources they need to satisfy those customer needs.

VALUES
Basic beliefs about what is important and unimportant, and what one should and should not do.

None of this, Allen knew, would be possible without instilling new **values** throughout AT&T. (Values are basic beliefs about what is important and unimportant, and what one should or should not do.) Allen says that one of his highest priorities today is defining and disseminating the new values AT&T will need to compete in the year 2000. These values include respect for individuals, dedication to helping customers, adhering to the highest standards of integrity, innovating, and team work.[48] His senior managers say that they frequently spend as much as 80 percent of their time in high-level meetings discussing their values and how those values apply and can be operationalized. Allen has thus been able to instill the sense of team work, quality, respect for the individual, and responsiveness that he knows his firm will need to compete in the coming decade. At the same time he has helped to banish the back-stabbing and politicking that often strangles an organization's responsiveness.

TOMORROW'S MANAGEMENT TODAY

Let's briefly summarize where we stand. Organizations today need to grapple with a number of revolutionary forces: accelerating product and technological change, globalized competition, deregulation, political instability, demographic changes, and trends toward a service society and the information age. Forces like these have changed the playing field on which firms must compete. In particular, they have dramatically increased the need for firms to be responsive, flexible, and capable of competing in a global marketplace.

Firms like ABB, Saturn, and AT&T are in the vanguard of thousands of other firms that are re-creating themselves to fit these new conditions. From their experiences, and from others, here is a summary of what management experts believe "the new management" will look like:

THE AVERAGE COMPANY WILL BECOME SMALLER, EMPLOYING FEWER PEOPLE This is partly because more people will set up businesses for themselves and partly because many firms like GM and IBM may continue to down-

size or will break themselves up. Even within big firms (like ABB) the operating units will be divided into small, self-contained mini-units.

Cypress Semiconductor is an example. Tom Rogers, president of this California firm, believes that large organizations stifle innovation. So when a new product must be developed he doesn't do it within the existing corporation. Instead, he creates a separate start-up company under the Cypress umbrella. "I would rather see our billion-dollar company of the 1990s be ten $100-million companies, all strong, growing, healthy and aggressive as hell," Rogers says. "The alternative is an aging billion-dollar company that spends more time defending its turf than growing." True to his words, Rogers already has four successful start-ups under development.[49]

THE TRADITIONAL, PYRAMID-SHAPED ORGANIZATION WILL GIVE WAY TO NEW ORGANIZATIONAL FORMS[50]   As at AT&T the new organization will stress cross-functional teams and boosting interdepartmental communications. There will be a corresponding de-emphasis on "sticking to the chain of command" to get decisions made. At General Electric, Chairman Jack Welch talks of the *boundaryless organization,* in which employees do not identify with separate departments, but instead interact with whomever they must to get the job done.

EMPLOYEES WILL BE CALLED UPON TO MAKE MORE AND MORE DECISIONS   Work will be less routine, with less drudgery. Work will require constant learning, "higher order" thinking, and much more worker commitment. The result for employees will be more *empowerment* and less of a 9-to-5 mentality. Experts like Karl Albrecht argue for *turning the typical organization upside down.* They say today's organization should put the customer on top and emphasize that every move the company makes should be toward satisfying the customer's needs. To do so management must *empower* its front-line employees—the front desk clerks at the hotel, the cabin attendants on the Delta plane, and the assemblers at Saturn. In other words, employees need the authority to respond quickly to the customer's needs. The main purpose of managers in this "upside down" organization is to *serve* the front-line employees, to see that they have what they need to do their jobs—and thus serve the customers.

FLATTER ORGANIZATIONS WILL BE THE NORM   Instead of the pyramid-shaped organization with its seven to ten or more layers of management, flat organizations with just three or four levels will prevail. Many companies (including AT&T, ABB, and General Electric) have already cut the management layers from a dozen to six or fewer.[51] As the remaining managers have more people reporting to them, they will be less able to meddle in the work of their subordinates.

WORK ITSELF—ON THE FACTORY FLOOR, IN THE OFFICE, EVEN IN THE HOTEL—WILL BE ORGANIZED AROUND TEAMS AND PROCESSES RATHER THAN SPECIALIZED FUNCTIONS   On the plant floor, a worker will not just have the job of installing the same door handle over and over again. He or she will belong to a multifunction team, one that manages its own budget and controls its own quality.

THE BASES OF POWER WILL CHANGE   In the new organization, says management theorist Rosabeth Moss Kanter, position, title, and authority are no longer adequate tools for managers to rely on to get their jobs done.[52] Instead, "success depends increasingly on tapping into sources of good ideas, on figuring out who's collaboration is needed to act on those ideas, and on working with both to produce results. In short, the new managerial work implies very different ways of obtaining and using power."[53]

Similarly, Peter Drucker has said, "you have to learn to manage in situations where you don't have command authority, where you are neither controlled nor controlling." Thus, managers in the new organization will have to win the respect and commitment of highly trained and empowered employees.

THE NEW ORGANIZATION WILL BE KNOWLEDGE BASED As Peter Drucker says, tomorrow's organization will be "composed largely of specialists who direct and discipline their own performance through organized feedback from colleagues, customers, and headquarters."[54]

Similarly, management specialist Tom Peters says the new organization will be more like consulting firms and hospitals. Teams of highly committed and trained professionals will work in teams, focusing on their customers while largely managing their own activities.[55]

MANAGERS WILL NOT "MANAGE" Yesterday's manager knew that the president and owners of the firm gave him or her the authority to command and control subordinates. Today, most managers realize that reliance on formal authority is a thing of the past. Peter Drucker says that managers have to learn to manage in situations where they do not have command authority, where "you are neither controlled nor controlling." As Rosabeth Moss Kanter put it, managers will have to depend "increasingly on tapping into sources of good ideas, on figuring out whose collaboration is needed to act on those ideas, on working with both to produce results. Thus, the new managerial work implies very different ways of obtaining and using power."[56]

Service management expert Karl Albrecht makes a similar point. He says managers have to turn the organizational pyramid upside down and put the customers and subordinates on top. Doing so emphasizes that managers' real role today is to help their employees get their jobs done by training them, removing roadblocks, and getting employees the resources they need.

This highlights one big difference between the old and new manager. Yesterday's manager thinks of himself or herself as a "manager" or "boss," while the new manager thinks of himself or herself as a "sponsor," "team leader," or "internal consultant." The old manager makes most decisions alone; the new one invites others to join in the decision making. The old manager hoards information in part to build his or her personal power. The new manager shares information to help subordinates get their jobs done.[57]

THE NEW COMPANY WILL STRESS VISION AND VALUES Formulating a clear direction and vision among employees will be more important than ever before. Managers will have to communicate clear values regarding what is important and unimportant, and regarding what employees should do and should not do. As GE CEO Jack Welch has said:

> Every organization needs values, but a lean organization needs them even more. When you strip away the support systems of staffs and layers, people need to relearn their habits and expectations or else the stress will just overwhelm them . . . values [are] what enable people to guide themselves through that kind of change.[58]

Other experts agree. Peter Drucker says today's organizations—comprised as they are of professionals and other employees who largely control their own behavior—require "clear, simple, common objectives that translate into particular actions." In other words, they need a clear vision of where the firm is heading.[59] Similarly, says Rosabeth Kanter, "helping people believe in the importance of their work is essential, especially when other forms of certainty and security have disappeared." Therefore, she says, "good leaders can inspire others with the power and excitement of their vision and give people a sense of purpose and pride in their work."[60]

**MANAGEMENT WILL EMPOWER EMPLOYEES AND BUILD COMMIT-
MENT**   Building adaptive, customer-responsive organizations means that eliciting
employees' self-control will be more important than it has ever been. GE's Jack Welch
put it this way:

> The only way I see to get more productivity is by getting people involved and excited about
> their jobs. You can't afford to have anyone walk through a gate of a factory or into an office,
> who is not giving 120%.[61]

**MANAGEMENT WILL SEEK TO CREATE OPEN, BOUNDARYLESS
ORGANIZATIONS**   Managers will also have to build what Welch calls boundaryless organizations, ones in which the employees don't feel they can interact only with
coworkers at their own level or in their own departments. This will require, says Welch,
an open, trusting sharing of ideas, which in turn means a willingness on the part of
management to listen, debate, and then take the best ideas "and get on with it." Why?
Because creating open, boundaryless organizations means doing more than paying lip
service to the need to "be open." Practicing managers know that it's all too easy to
inadvertently create a politicized, "stab-in-the-back" culture, one that inhibits open
communication. Creating an open, trusting, "I-am-willing-to-listen" culture is therefore a skill today's manager must develop.

MANAGERS MUST BE AGENTS OF CHANGE   As GE's Jack Welch puts it,
"you've got to be on the cutting edge of change. You can't simply maintain the status
quo, because somebody's always coming from another country with another product,
or consumers' taste change, or the cost structure does, or there's a technology breakthrough. If you are not fast and adaptable, you are vulnerable."[62]

SUMMARY

Managers today are facing rapid change and unpredictability. As a result, companies are being organized and managed differently, with a major emphasis on flexibility and the ability to respond to change. These highly responsive organizations go by many names, but they provide evidence that new management skills are needed to survive and thrive in the current environment.

Management is traditionally classified into five basic functions: planning, organizing, staffing, leading, and controlling. Managers can also be classified by their position, level, and title.

Major sources of change and turbulence for businesses include technological innovation, globalization, deregulation, the new world order, the global work force, the shift to a service society, and the emphasis on knowledge work and human capital.

Based on the experience of firms that are re-creating themselves to respond to these new conditions, a profile of the "new management" emerges. In the future, the average company will be smaller and employ fewer people. The traditional, pyramid-shaped organization will give way to new, team-based organizational forms. For employees, work in the "new organization" means that they will be called upon to make more and more decisions. Flatter organizations will be the norm and the bases of power will change. Work itself will be organized around teams and processes rather than specialized functions. The new organization will be knowledge-based, and managers will not "manage" in the traditional sense of exercising formal authority. Instead, they will increasingly depend on tapping into sources of good ideas, and figuring out whose collaboration is needed to act on those ideas and produce results. Formulating a clear unity of direction and beliefs among employees also will be more important than ever. Empowering employees and building commitment will be essential to creating open, boundaryless organizations in which workers do not feel limited to interact only with coworkers at their own level or in their own departments. In summary, managers must learn to be agents of change.

QUESTIONS

■ FOR REVIEW

1. Name some of the forces that have changed the nature of management. Which ones have been most dominant recently?

2. Explain the five basic functions of management.

3. What changes were implemented at ABB Asea Brown Boveri, Saturn, and AT&T, and how did they enhance each firm's ability to compete?

4. Describe the structure of the organizations of tomorrow, and identify the management skills that will be required to manage them.

■ FOR DISCUSSION

5. What will be the most fundamental differences between firms of the future and companies of the recent past? What are the ramifications for the U.S. society as a whole?

6. Discuss the various types of managers and the functions each performs. Is it conceivable that some managerial positions are becoming obsolete?

7. How has information technology changed the face of business? Anticipate changes that could occur in the future.

8. Which types of organizational structures do you think can best replace the traditional pyramid hierarchy? Will the best structure vary depending on the business?

■ **FOR ACTION**

9. Go to the library and research the changes that characterized the Industrial Revolution. How do they compare to the changes experienced in the last 50 years?

10. Find an example of a company that is still operated under the traditional hierarchical structure and formal lines of authority. How could it be restructured to reflect new management techniques?

11. Create your own scenario of what General Motors is likely to look like in the year 2044. How can the company ensure it survives that long?

■ **FOR FOCUS ON SMALL BUSINESS**

12. Explain why flexibility and the ability to respond to change are especially important characteristics for a small company like Morris Air.

13. Why do you think Morris Air has succeeded where many of its counterparts in the airline industry have failed?

14. What changes are companies like Morris Air likely to face in the future?

 CLOSING SOLUTION

DELL COMPUTER

Michael Dell proved meteoric growth is possible from a bare-bones operation. He also discovered the difficulties involved in expanding annual sales much beyond the $2 billion level without making big investments in a formal sales force. Dell has now hired several new top managers and doubled expenditures for internal information systems that will network operations facilities.

Dell hired 1,700 new employees in 1992 and is adding 10 to 15 new-hires per week. The chief responsibility of the new management team will be to revamp Dell's key management processes, from product development to shipping. One primary goal is to upgrade manufacturing productivity by 25 percent.

For example, Dell has long operated a system that saw computer parts flown in from around the globe to the company's Austin headquarters. From the Texas capital, the parts were then redistributed for assembly at yet some other global destination. In the future, regional staging areas will alleviate some of the reshipping and save the company around $10 million annually in the process. Distribution will also be improved by establishing plants in both Mexico and Japan.

Dell Computer's problems will require remedies that are painful in the short term, but, fortunately, they won't be terminal. Almost any company that experiences a 285 percent growth rate over two years is bound to suffer some setbacks and periods of retrenchment. Dell's bare-bones managerial approach worked well up to a point, but it is not sufficient to support the attainment of the company's ultimate goal of $10 billion in annual sales.[63] For that, new management systems will be required.

■ **QUESTIONS FOR CLOSING SOLUTION**

1. Describe some of the changes that have swept the computer industry in general, and Dell in particular, in recent years.

2. What implications have these changes had on the way Dell is organized and managed?

3. How do you envision the computer company of the future being organized? Why?

KEY TERMS

Manager

Planning

Organizing

Staffing

Leading

Controlling

Information Technology

Distributed Computing

Globalization

Deregulation

Human Capital

Flatten the Hierarchy

Downsizing

Empower

Values

CASE FOR ANALYSIS

EASTMAN KODAK COMPANY

When Kay Whitmore took the helm at Eastman Kodak Co. in 1990 he represented a continuum in the line of technically oriented CEOs that have headed up the company. Along with the new post, he also inherited a number of the problems his successors had created. Unfortunately, he persisted with many of the same futile remedies as well.

Understanding Kodak's problems is impossible without reviewing decisions made more than 20 years ago. The early 1970s saw Kodak management wrongly predict the obsolescence of silver halide technology, the same film coating foundation George Eastman relied on when he built the company. Electronic photography, management feared, would quickly replace it. It hasn't yet, except in industrial applications. Kodak developed one of the earliest videocassette recorders, but decided consumers would never be interested. The Japanese gleefully jumped in to fill the vacuum. One market where Kodak did forge ahead was instant photography, and in so doing infringed on Polaroid's proprietaries. Fruits of that effort included big lawsuit losses and a besmirched image. Kodak ultimately had to pay Polaroid almost $1 billion. The company also developed a copier that was superior to Xerox. It failed to aggressively market the product, and Xerox soon passed Kodak by. Kodak sold $4 billion in copiers and information systems in 1991 and 1992. The division lost money.

Whitmore's first stab at restructuring in 1991 could charitably be described as a $1.6 billion debacle. Plans to cut costs through staff reductions backfired. The financial aspects of the early retirement program were so tantalizing that three times the expected number of employees left, forcing the company to find replacements. Worse still, earnings remained virtually flat. The chagrined board managed one cost cut of its own, voting to trim Whitmore's yearly bonus by 70 percent.

Cost-cutting, round 2, saw Christopher J. Steffen (from Honeywell and before that one of the driving forces behind the renaissance at Chrysler) brought in as chief financial officer. Kodak's

market capitalization improved by a couple billion dollars just after the news broke. Steffen's planned changes—which were rumored to include reducing debt by selling Kodak's $5.1 billion acquisition, Sterling Drug—may have peeved Whitmore. Whitmore felt a financial restructuring couldn't be implemented without focusing on what Kodak's new strategy should be. Steffen quit; his tenure at Kodak lasted but 11 weeks.

Kodak will doubtless have to find ways to cut costs. Core businesses like consumer and professional films, X-ray and medical films, as well as movie and graphic arts films continue to grow. The company is gaining back world market share in its core film business, currently at around 55 percent. But in the recent past, the majority of profits from film-related revenues has been squandered on restructuring costs or other ill-conceived ventures such as pharmaceuticals. It seems clear the company will have to break away from the insular management style that has characterized its Rochester, New York, headquarters. Whatever the selected course, Kodak will proceed without Kay Whitmore. He was fired in 1993.

SOURCES: Carol J. Loomis, "The Battle to Shape Up Kodak," *Fortune,* May 31, 1993, 62–63; Mark Maremont and Elizabeth Lesly, "The Revolution That Wasn't at Eastman Kodak," *Business Week,* May 10, 1993, 24–25, and Subrata N. Chakravarty and Amy Feldman, "The Road Not Taken," *Forbes,* August 30, 1993, 40–41.

■ QUESTIONS

1. Describe the changes Kodak has had to deal with in the last two decades.

2. How did top executives fail in their efforts to manage in that era of change?

3. If you were asked to take over from Kay Whitmore, what would be your priorities?

A CASE IN DIVERSITY

THE CHALLENGE OF MANAGING
A DIVERSE WORK FORCE

Without the benefit of a highly accurate crystal ball, future managers will face many unexpected challenges. But one thing that is becoming increasingly clear is that women, racial minorities, and persons with disabilities will make up a far larger percentage of the work force than in the past. The skills required to cope with the cultural, communication, and training hurdles won't be easy to come by. But those that master them will get the most from the workers that are out there, whether they're from Tacoma or Timbuktu.

Take Herb Prokscha, owner of the Winter Park, Florida-based pasta company La Romagnola. Twenty of his 30 production workers were hired through Catholic Refugee Service and come from countries such as Bulgaria, Romania, and Vietnam. Where many might consider language barriers to be the most formidable of obstacles in dealing with such a diverse work force, that hasn't been the case. An interpreter is sometimes required to convey salary and benefit nuances, but job demonstrations have proven a highly effective training tool. Though it may be a throwback to sign-language, employees eager to demonstrate their abilities catch on quickly and are usually able to convey any problems they might be experiencing.

Ethnic concentrations within the company have provided an unexpected advantage instead of a handicap. The natural tendency is for groups to gravitate together. More experienced workers can then assist newer workers with language, work, or general adjustment difficulties. Another benefit is a strong sense of teamwork and self-policing among members of similar ethnic groups. Also, because the majority of workers are immigrants, the veterans are sensitive to the cultural differences of new employees.

For some companies, that's not always true. Often the greatest problems may not come from diverse workers coming in, but from the work force already in place. Helping those workers develop an awareness and sensitivity to cultural, religious, or physical differences is critical. Formal training sessions or even informal get-togethers chaired by knowledgeable moderators can change perspectives. Prejudices often evaporate when coworkers learn of the adversities many workers have suffered and the obstacles they have overcome just to have the opportunity to have a job and provide for a family and future.

Over the past five years, many companies have seen an increase in the number of women, racial minorities, immigrants, and disabled on their payrolls. Managers who do not make the adjustments necessary to cope with such a diverse work force will fail to capitalize on what these disparate groups have to offer their firms. In addition, if that failure to cope leads to an intransigence about hiring minorities, these managers may end up with problems it will take more than a crystal ball to see their way out of.

SOURCES: Ellyn E. Spragins, "Managing Diversity," *Inc.,* January 1993, 33; and Spragins, "The Diverse Work Force," *Inc.,* January 1993, 33.

■ QUESTIONS

1. Describe the opportunities and threats that managers face as their work force becomes more diverse.
2. What steps can managers take to ensure their diverse work force is an integral part of an open, boundaryless organization?
3. Name some ways that managers can be agents of change when dealing with diversity issues.

ENDNOTES

1. Kevin Kelley, "Michael Dell: The Enfant Terrible of Personal Computers," *Business Week,* June 13, 1988, 62; and Patricia Keefe, "Dell Revamps Portable Strategy," *Computer World,* May 24, 1993, 159.
2. Michael Fitzgerald, "Dell Trying to Get Back on Track," *Computer World,* August 23, 1993, 155.
3. Michael Fitzgerald, "Dell to Post First Loss," *Computer World,* July 19, 1993, 109.
4. *The World Almanac and Book of Facts: 1992* (New York: World Almanac, 1991) 157.
5. Dianne Herz, "Worker Displacement in a Period of Rapid Job Expansion: 1983–1987," *Monthly Labor Review,* vol. 113, no. 5, May 1990, 21–41; and *U.S. Department of Labor, Occupational Outlook Quarterly, Outlook: 1990–2005,* Spring 1992.
6. *World Almanac,* 673.
7. Wendy Zellner, Andrea Rothman, and Erik Schine, "The Airline Mess," *Business Week,* July 6, 1992, 51.
8. *World Almanac,* 823; and *The Economist Yearbook: 1992* (London: The Economist Books, 1992), 330–31.
9. Katherine Arnst, "This Is Not a Fun Business to Be in Now," *Business Week,* July 6, 1992, 68.
10. *World Almanac,* 140.

11. *The Economist Yearbook,* 222.

12. *World Almanac,* 73.

13. This is based on Gary Dessler, *Winning Commitment: How Top Companies Get and Keep a Competitive Work Force* (New York: McGraw-Hill, 1993), 3–4.

14. Henry Mintzberg, "The Manager's Job: Folklore and Fact," *Harvard Business Review* (July–August 1975), 489–561.

15. Peter Drucker, "The Coming of the New Organization," *Harvard Business Review,* January–February 1988, 44.

16. Thomas Stewart, "Welcome to the Revolution," *Fortune,* December 13, 1993, 68.

17. Ibid., 72.

18. Ibid., 66.

19. Ibid., 67.

20. "A Portrait of America: How the Country Is Changing," *Business Week,* 1992, 51.

21. "Grabbing New World Orders," *Business Week,* Reinventing America, 1992, 110–11.

22. Charles W. Hill, *International Business* (Burr Ridge, IL: Irwin, 1994), 6.

23. Ibid., 9.

24. *The World Almanac and Book of Facts:* 1992, 157.

25. Francis Fukuyama, "Are We at the End of History?" *Fortune,* January 15, 1990, 75–78.

26. Ibid., 78.

27. Philip Zweig, "Goldman's Spectacular Roadtrip," *Business Week,* November 1, 1993, 110.

28. Thomas Stewart, "How to Manage in the New Era," *Fortune,* January 15, 1990, 68.

29. Ronald Kutcher, "Overview and Implications of the Projections to 2000," *Monthly Labor Review,* September 1987, 3–9.

30. See, for example, Gary Dessler, *Personnel-Human Resource Management* (Englewood Cliffs, NJ: Prentice-Hall, 1991), 494–98.

31. Bryan O'Reilly, "Your New Global Workforce," *Fortune,* December 14, 1992, 52–66.

32. Peter Drucker, "The Coming of the New Organization," *Harvard Business Review,* January–February 1988, 45.

33. Richard Crawford, *In the Era of Human Capital* (New York: Harper, 1991), 10.

34. Ibid.

35. Crawford, *In the Era of Human Capital,* 31.

36. Ibid., 26.

37. Fukuyama, "Are We at the End of History?"

38. Thomas Steward, "Brain Power," *Fortune,* June 3, 1991, 44.

39. Drucker, "The Coming of the New Organization," 45.

40. Rosabeth Moss Kanter, *When Giants Learn to Dance* (New York: Touchstone, 1989).

41. Drucker, "The Coming of the New Organization," 45–54.

42. John Byrne, "Paradigms for Post Modern Managers," *Business Week,* Reinventing America, 1992, 62–63.

43. Tom Peters, *Liberation Management* (New York: Alfred Knopf, 1992), 9.

44. Ibid.

45. David Kirkpatrick, "Could AT&T Rule the World?" *Fortune,* May 17, 1993, 55–66.

46. Ibid., 62.

47. Ibid., 55.

48. Ibid., 64.

49. Bryan Dumaine, "What the Leaders of Tomorrow See," *Fortune,* July 3, 1989, 58.

50. These are based on Walter Kiechel III, "How We Will Work in the Year 2000," *Fortune,* May 17, 1993, 79.

51. Bryan Dumaine, "What the Leaders of Tomorrow See," *Fortune,* July 3, 1989, 51.

52. Rosabeth Moss Kanter, "The New Managerial Work," *Harvard Business Review,* November–December 1989, 88.

53. Ibid., 88.

54. Drucker, "The Coming of the New Organization," 45.

55. Peters, *Liberation Management.*

56. Kanter, *When Giants Learn.*

57. Bryan Dumaine, "The New Non-Manager Managers," *Fortune,* February 22, 1993, 81.

58. Thomas A. Stewart, "How GE Keeps Those Ideas Coming," *Fortune,* August 12, 1991, 42.

59. Drucker, op. cit., 43.

60. Rosabeth Moss Kanter, "The New Managerial Work," 91.

61. Thomas A. Stewart, op. cit., 45.

62. Stratford Sherman, "A Master Class in Radical Change," *Fortune,* December 13, 1993, 82.

63. Sources for this closing solution were Steve Lohr, "Market Place, Is Dell Computer's Long Fall from Wall Street's Good Graces about to Be Reversed?" *The New York Times,* November 29, 1993, C8; and Peter Burrows and Stephanie Anderson Forest, "Dell Computer Goes into the Shop," *Business Week,* July 12, 1993, 138–40.

M A N A G I N G I N A
G L O B A L E C O N O M Y

LEARNING OBJECTIVES

After studying this chapter, you should be able to:

- Define and give examples of an international business.
- List the major reasons why firms are globalizing.
- Describe the globalization of markets, production, and labor.
- Explain why the potential benefits of free trade have prompted many nations to enter into various levels of economic integration.
- Discuss the motivations that drive firms to pursue international business.
- Identify the economic, legal/political, socio-cultural, and technological issues facing the international manager.
- Compare and contrast exporting, licensing, franchising, and foreign direct investment.
- Describe the international planning, organizing, controlling, human resource management, and behavioral issues with which global managers must cope.

OPENING PROBLEM

GENERAL ELECTRIC'S
BRAVE NEW WORLD

Looking down from his hotel window in economically bustling Guangdong, China, GE chairman Jack Welch saw where his company's future lay for the 1990s and beyond. He and his top management team put in place a plan, one that would shift the firm's economic center of gravity from Europe and the United States to Asia and Latin America. By the year 2000, GE's sales to these two booming markets should about double to more than $20 billion and represent more than 25 percent of GE's total sales.[1] Within these markets, GE is placing most of its bets on China, India, Mexico, and Southeast Asia—which together have a population of about 2.5 billion, roughly ten times the U.S. population. ■ Welch knows that it won't be easy. For one thing, political and economic risks loom large: more than 500 million people in India live in poverty, for instance, and in 1993, Indian Prime Minister Rao was under political and (literal) fire from Hindu militants. In China, everyone remembers the Tiananmen Square Massacre. And in Mexico, accusations continue about presidential election irregularities by the country's long-ruling party. Yet Welch and his managers knew that with the relatively slow growth in Europe and the United States, GE's only real alternative was to become a truly global firm. Revenues from outside the United States already represent about 40 percent of GE's total sales and are growing at the rate of 30 percent per year. Soon, the firm whose bulbs light almost every U.S. house will be earning more money outside the United States than within.

THE GLOBAL CORPORATION

SOME DEFINITIONS

INTERNATIONAL BUSINESS

Any firm that engages in international trade or investment, or refers to those business activities that involve the movement of resources, goods, services, and skills across national boundaries.

INTERNATIONAL TRADE

The export or import of goods or services to consumers in another country.

INTERNATIONAL INVESTMENT

The investment of resources in business activities outside a firm's home country.

MULTINATIONAL CORPORATION (MNC)

An internationally integrated production system over which equity-based control is exercised by a parent corporation that is owned and managed essentially by the nationals of the country in which it is domiciled.

GLOBAL CORPORATION

Sells essentially a standardized product throughout the world, components of which may be made in or designed in different countries.

With worldwide sales of products ranging from electric bulbs to power generators, GE is already an international business. An **international business** is any firm that engages in international trade or investment.[2] **International trade** refers to the export or import of goods or services to consumers in another country. Similarly, **international investment** refers to the investment of resources in business activities outside a firm's home country. International business also refers to those activities that involve the movement of resources, goods, services, and skills across national boundaries. These resources may include raw materials, capital, people, and technology. Goods, in this case, may include semifinished and finished assemblies and finished products. Much international business today also involves moving services and skills across national borders. Such services and skills might include investment advice and the transfer of manufacturing know-how from one country to another.[3] More generally, international business refers to all business transactions that involve two or more countries.[4]

The multinational corporation is one type of international business enterprise. The **multinational corporation** (or MNC) may be defined as "an internationally integrated production system over which equity based control is exercised by a parent corporation that is owned and managed essentially by the nationals of the country in which it is domiciled."[5] That is quite a mouthful. What it means, basically, is that the multinational corporation operates manufacturing and marketing facilities in several countries; these operations are coordinated by a parent firm, whose owners are mostly based in the firm's home country. Firms like General Electric, General Motors, and ITT have long been multinational corporations. However, marketing expert Theodore Levitt contends that the multinational corporation's reign as the preeminent vehicle of international trade is nearing its end. It is slowly being displaced, he says, by firms that represent a new type of international enterprise that he calls the global corporation. The multinational corporation, says Levitt, operates in a number of countries and adjusts its products and practices to each. This is a relatively expensive procedure, since products must be "fine-tuned" to the needs of the consumers in each separate country.

The **global corporation,** on the other hand, operates as if the entire world (or major regions of it) were a single entity, says Levitt. Global corporations sell essentially the same things in the same way everywhere. Thus, a global corporation, such as Sony, sells essentially a standardized product, such as "Walkman," throughout the world, components of which may be made in or designed in different countries.[6] As Levitt says:

> The global corporation—or transnational corporation to use the tag some academics prefer—looks at the whole world as one *market*. It manufactures, conducts research, raises capital, and buys supplies wherever it can do the job best, it keeps in touch with technology and market trends all around the world. National boundaries and regulations tend to be irrelevant, or a mere hindrance. Corporate headquarters might be anywhere.[7]

The *Verifone* Small Business box shows that small firms can be global, too.

THE GLOBAL ECONOMY

THE GLOBAL MARKETPLACE

Today, what Levitt predicted is coming true: we are seeing an increase in the globalization of markets and production.[8]

VERIFONE, INC.

Getting a handle on where VeriFone, Inc., chief executive Hatim Tyabji is on any given day isn't easy. Hong Kong is a possibility; Marseilles or Copenhagen would also be good bets; but Bangalore, India, shouldn't be ruled out either. "Being at [San Francisco] headquarters is irrelevant to me," he says, summing up the philosophy of the global manager.

VeriFone manufactures the terminals used for credit card transactions, and Tyabji takes literally the notion that he and his 1,500 employees must stay close to their customers. That's why each new employee is issued a laptop computer. "There is my office," Tyabji says, indicating his own laptop. And

even though it sounds like hyperbole, employees learn to "modem in regularly", as one manager put it. Managers average 60 VAX-mail and Internet messages a day, and for them to receive as many as 200 isn't uncommon.

FOCUS ON SMALL BUSINESS

Requiring employees to hopscotch around the globe might be a disaster for some firms, but not for VeriFone. Despite formidable competitors such as IBM and GTE, the company has a 60 percent market share for card autho-

rization services in the United States. It has also outdistanced rivals in Europe, Asia, and South America, the source of 22 percent of company revenues.

VeriFone employees even use global time differences to their advantage. When VeriFone was in the running to design a payment authorization system for a group of German banks, company employees around the globe joined in a cooperative effort. At day's end, the team concluding its work would forward it on in the direction of the rising sun, where another VeriFone picked up where the first team left off. The effort continued around the clock until completion, at which time the pleasantly surprised bankers awarded the company 80 percent of the business.

SOURCE: David H. Freedman, "Culture of Urgency," *Forbes*, 25–28.

The global acceptance of McDonald's on Paris' Champs Élysées, of the Sony Walkman in Afghanistan, or of a Coke in dusty Porlamar, Venezuela, also symbolize the increasingly global nature of markets and manufacturing today. The *Unilever* Vignette provides another example.

Firms are globalizing for a variety of reasons. Increasingly (as at General Electric, discussed above), firms are doing so because their domestic markets are too limited. As one expert put it, "Even the biggest companies in the biggest countries cannot survive on their domestic markets if they are in global industries. They have to be in all major markets." So markets today include not just North America or Western Europe, but South America, Africa, and Asia and Southeast Asia, too.[9] At the same time, television, telecommunications, and air travel have combined to blur the distinctions that formerly separated one country's market from another. According to this view, says international expert Charles Hill, "the tastes and preferences of consumers in different nations are beginning to converge on some global norm. Thus, in many industries it is no longer meaningful to talk about the 'German market,' 'the American market,' or the 'Japanese market'; there is only the 'global market.'"[10]

The result has been an explosion of exports for U.S. firms. According to the United States Department of Commerce, for instance, the export of U.S.-produced merchandise, agricultural goods, and minerals jumped from $227 billion in 1986 to $394 billion in 1990. Similarly, U.S. exports of private services by private firms jumped from $70 billion in 1986 to $120 billion in 1990. In both cases, this represents four-year increases of almost 75 percent.[11] Booming U.S. export targets are illustrated in Figure 2.1.[12] Between 1988 and 1991, U.S. exports to the Czech Republic and Slovakia jumped by 170 percent, while exports to France jumped by 55 percent, exports to Malaysia increased by 88 percent and those to Kuwait rose by 74 percent, for instance. As one economist sums up, "the global marketplace surely has arrived when villagers in the

UNILEVER

Almost 65 years after its founding in 1930, the Dutch-British company Unilever stands as a classic example of a global or transnational corporation. But even company insiders admit the shape of the organization today is less a result of conscious design than of doing what works. In particular, Unilever managers have been successful adhering to a company philosophy of "thinking globally" while "acting locally."

Unilever's formal organization is what the firm calls a matrix system. It combines giving managers authority for local initiatives with centralized headquarters control, and encourages managers to maintain a transnational perspective. The company has long cultivated local managerial talent for its subsidiaries, whether in Java or the wilds of Colombia. In fact, in all likelihood, managers will see those two locales, and several more as they rotate amongst jobs. Gaining experience in several countries while overseeing multiple product lines is the norm for Unilever managers.

To prepare them for this challenge, as many as 400 Unilever managers a year receive training at the company's international management college outside London. At Unilever, responding to change depends on (1) recruiting and training the best managerial talent available while (2) ensuring that local subsidiaries exercise prudent initiatives while holding fast to the established company policies and culture.

SOURCE: Floris A. Maljers, "Inside Unilever: The Evolving Transnational Company, *Harvard Business Review*, September–October 1992, 46–51.

Middle East follow the Gulf War on CNN, via Soviet government satellite, and through a private subsidiary of a local government enterprise. . . ."[13]

GLOBALIZATION OF PRODUCTION

GLOBALIZING PRODUCTION
Dispersing part of a firm's production process to various locations around the globe.

Globalizing production means dispersing parts of a firm's production process to various locations around the globe. The aim is to take advantage of national differences in the cost and quality of production and then integrate these operations into a unified and efficient system of manufacturing facilities around the world.[14]

The Xerox corporation's worldwide manufacturing system is an example. In the late 1970s and early 1980s, each Xerox company in each country had its own suppliers, assembly plants, and distribution channels. In other words, plants in South America, the United States, Canada, Asia, and Europe each produced according to their own production schedules based on the sales forecasts of the Xerox sales organization in each country. Production managers in each country's plants gave little thought to how their production plans fit into Xerox's global production plans and needs.

This approach became unworkable as international competition in the duplicator market became increasingly intense in the 1980s. Canon, Minolta, and Ricoh penetrated Xerox's U.S. and European markets with low-cost copiers. Between 1983 and 1985, Xerox's market share dropped from 57 percent to 52 percent. In 1985, Canon announced that instead of manufacturing primarily in Japan and selling through a

worldwide distribution network, it would set up manufacturing facilities around the world and coordinate these to gain maximum efficiencies.[15]

This decision prompted Xerox's senior managers to globalize their production process. For example, they created a central purchasing group to consolidate raw material sources and thereby cut worldwide manufacturing costs. They instituted a "leadership through quality" program to improve product quality, streamline and standardize manufacturing processes, and cut costs. Xerox managers eliminated over $1 billion of inventory costs by installing a system that linked customer orders more closely with worldwide production capabilities. And in the early 1990s, Xerox began integrating its product delivery activities; for instance, the company consolidated inventories, which could then be used to supply U.S., Canadian, and Latin American markets. This reduced the need for relatively large inventories in each part of the hemisphere.

For many of us, the clearest evidence of globalized production may be the local content in products like the cars we drive. As mentioned in Chapter 1, for instance, the seemingly "American" Pontiac LeMans actually has little American content. Of the $20,000 GM earns for a LeMans, remember, about $6,000 goes to South Korea where the car is assembled, $3,500 goes to Japan for advanced components, and $1,500 goes to Germany where the LeMans was designed.[16] On the other hand, the seemingly "Japanese" Camry is assembled in Georgetown, Kentucky, and contains about 75 percent American parts and labor.[17] As economist Robert Reich sums up:

> Once upon a time, products had distinct national identities. Regardless of how many international borders they crossed, their country of origin—the name of which was usually imprinted right on them—was never in doubt. . . . But in the emerging high-value economy,

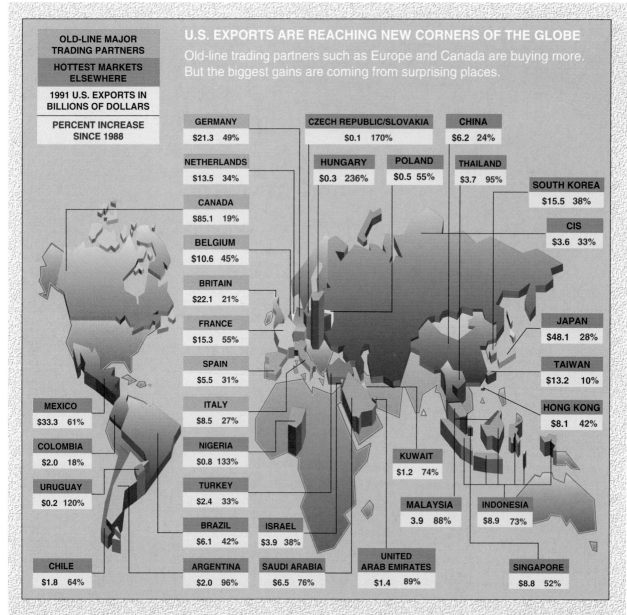

FIGURE 2.1

U.S. Export Targets

SOURCE: "Grabbing New World Orders," *Business Week/Reinventing America*, 1992, 111.

products can be produced efficiently in many different locations and combined in all sorts of ways to serve customer needs in many places. Precision ice hockey equipment is designed in Sweden, financed in Canada, and assembled in Cleveland and Denmark for distribution in North America and Europe, respectively . . . an advertising campaign is conceived in Britain; film footage shot in Canada, dubbed in Britain and edited in New York.[18]

THE GLOBAL WORK FORCE

On the night of November 9, 1993, H. Ross Perot and Vice-President Al Gore debated the pros and cons of NAFTA, the North American Free Trade Agreement. Perot insisted that signing the agreement would create a "great sucking sound" as jobs were pulled from the United States to low-wage Mexican factories. Gore argued that such would not be the case. Whoever was right, companies around the world are undoubtedly tapping a vast new supply of skilled labor from wherever in the world that labor might be.[19] Thus, 3M makes tapes, chemicals, and electrical parts in Bangalore, India, for instance, and Hewlett-Packard assembles computers and designs memory boards in Guadalajara, Mexico. Unlike in earlier days, though, firms like these aren't just chasing after cheap labor. Instead, firms are moving their plants and jobs overseas to tap into the highly educated and skilled employees that are becoming more available in Latin America and Asia.

As a result, the labor force of more and more multinational firms is truly global. In Jamaica, for instance, 3,500 office workers make airline reservations, process tickets, and handle calls to toll-free numbers via satellite dishes for United States companies. Call Quarterdeck Office Systems, a California-based software firm, with a question about how to use one of its programs and your call may be routed to Dublin, Ireland, where the firm has a phone-answering operation. Back in Bangalore, India, an educated work force has drawn Texas Instruments and 30 more firms, including Motorola and IBM, to set up software program offices in the area.[20] In other words, a firm's work force is likely to be globalized, too.[21]

THE GLOBAL MANAGER

Economist and Labor Secretary Robert Reich says that globalization of markets, production, and labor is coinciding with the rise of a new type of manager—a global manager. To global managers (like GE's Jack Welch), the bonds between company and country are thinning. A **global manager** to Reich is a manager who views markets and production globally and who seeks higher profits for his or her firm on a global basis rather than in terms of what is necessarily optimum for his or her firm's home country.[22] As Reich says:

> Gone is the company town, the huge local labor force, the monolithic factory, and the vertically integrated corporation that dominated the entire region. Gone is the tight connection between the company, its community, even its country. Vanishing too are the paternalistic corporate heads who used to feel a sense of responsibility for their local community. Emerging in their place is the new global manager, driven by the irrefutable logic of global capitalism to seek higher profits, enhanced market leadership, and improved stock price. The playing field is the world.[23]

Global managers, then, must be comfortable anywhere in the world.[24] Webster's dictionary defines cosmopolitan as "belonging to the world; not limited to just one part of the political, social, commercial or intellectual spheres; free from local, provincial, or national ideas, prejudices or attachments." The schedule of Patrick Martin, president and general manager of Xerox Americas Corporation (shown in Figure 2.2), helps illustrate this cosmopolitan management style.[25] In Hong Kong, his job is to lead a joint venture with a firm in Chiang Hai, China. In Chiang Hai, he checks out Xerox's manufacturing facility. On the 18th, he is in Beijing for meetings with Chinese political leaders. Then, on the 20th, he's back at U.S. headquarters in Stanford, Connecticut, for meetings with other Xerox managers. In each location, he had to negotiate and make major decisions—opening new plants, hiring top managers, making financial commitments, and so on—with a keen understanding of the cultural differences from country to country.

GLOBAL MANAGER
A manager who views markets and production globally and seeks higher profits for his or her firm on a global basis rather than in terms of what is necessarily optimum for his or her firm's home country.

FIGURE 2.2

Global Management
Schedule for Xerox Americas
Corporation President

*Global managers like
Patrick Martin must be
comfortable circling the
globe doing business with
people of many countries.*

SOURCE: Marlene Piturro,
"Super Manager!" *International Business,* Annual
Editions: *World Trade* 1982,
80.

A MONTH IN THE LIFE OF

Frequent Flier
Patrick Martin

President and General Manager
Xerox Americas Corporation

SEPTEMBER
13 Hong Kong. Xerox regional office
16 Shanghai. Xerox manufacturing complex
18 Beijing. Meetings
20 U.S. headquarters, Stamford, CT
22 Sao Paulo, Brazil
24 Buenos Aires, Argentina
27 Chile
29 Venezuela

OCTOBER
1 U.S. headquarters
6 Brazil

ONCE A MONTH: VISIT BRAZIL, MEXICO, AND CANADA

EVERY 3 OR 4 MONTHS: VISIT FAR EAST

Percy Barnevik, the head of the Swiss firm ABB Asea Brown Boveri, sums up the global manager this way:

> Global managers have exceptionally open minds. They respect how different countries do things, and they have the imagination to appreciate why they do them that way. But they are also incisive, they push the limits of the culture. Global managers don't passively accept it when someone says, "you can't do that in Italy or Spain because of the unions," or "you can't do that in Japan because of the ministry of finance." They sort through the debris of cultural excuses and find opportunities to innovate. . . . Global managers are also generous and patient. They can handle the frustrations of language barriers.[26]

ETHNOCENTRIC
A management philosophy that leads to the creating of ethnocentric or home market-oriented firms.

POLYCENTRIC
A management philosophy oriented toward individual foreign markets.

REGIOCENTRIC
A management philosophy oriented toward larger areas including the global marketplace.

ECONOMIC INTEGRATION AND GLOBAL PHILOSOPHIES

Some experts classify international managers' philosophies in terms of their orientation to the global marketplace. An **ethnocentric** management philosophy leads to the creation of ethnocentric or home-market-oriented firms. A **policentric** management philosophy is oriented toward individual foreign markets. Finally, **regiocentric** or geocentric philosophies (and firms) are those oriented toward larger areas including the global marketplace.[27] These experts argue that a person's international philosophy will influence his or her approach to expanding overseas.

ECONOMIC INTEGRATION AND THE TRIAD

In the early 1930s, the United States was suffering from a severe economic depression. Almost 30 percent of the U.S. labor force was unemployed, plants lay idle, and hungry citizens waited in long lines for handouts of hot meals. Many in Congress believed that raising tariffs—taxes on imported goods—was one solution to America's problems; they promptly voted into effect a wide range of tariffs under the Smoot Halley bill. Congress' move was met by countermoves by other countries. International trade slowed quickly. The nations of the world were pushed into a more severe economic downturn as plants that formerly produced items for export found that the demand had dried up.

The consequence of this Depression-era decision helps to illustrate the basic idea behind free trade. **Free trade** means that all barriers to trade among participating countries are removed.[28] The classic explanation for the advantages of free trade was described by the economist Adam Smith in his book *The Wealth of Nations*. Basically, Smith argued that each country would (if unhindered by subsidies and tariffs) end up specializing in the goods and services they could produce best—for instance, Ireland might produce fine glass, Switzerland might manufacture watches, and Japan might specialize in electronics. Such specialization would lead to higher productivity and efficiency, which would lead to higher income, which in turn could be used to purchase imports from abroad. **Economic integration** refers to attempts by two or more nations to obtain advantages of free trade by minimizing trade restrictions.

Economic integration occurs in several levels. In a **free trade area**, all barriers to trade among member countries are removed, so that goods and services are freely traded among the member countries. At the next higher level of economic integration, members of a **custom union** also dismantle barriers to trade among themselves while establishing a common trade policy with respect to nonmembers. In a **common market**, no barriers to trade exist among members and a common external trade policy is in force; in addition, though, factors of production, such as labor, capital, and technology, are mobile among member countries.

Several important examples of economic integration are at work in the world today. In 1957, the European Economic Community (now called the European Community or EC) was established by the Community's founding members: France, West Germany, Italy, Belgium, the Netherlands, and Luxembourg. They signed the **Treaty of Rome,** founding the EEC in 1957. The main provisions of the Treaty of Rome called for the formation of a free trade area and the gradual elimination of tariffs and other barriers to trade, along with formation of a customs union and eventually a common market. By 1987, the renamed European Community included six other countries (Great Britain, Ireland, Denmark, Greece, Spain, and Portugal) and had signed the Single Europe Act. This act "envisages a true common market where goods, people and money move between the twelve EC countries with the same ease that they move between Wisconsin and Illinois."[29] Some fear that the EC's establishment will lead to a "fortress Europe" in which non-EC firms will find it increasingly difficult to export goods into the EC.[30]

After a series of discussions culminating in a 1991 meeting in Maastricht, Netherlands, the twelve EC countries agreed to submit to their respective legislatures' plans for cementing even closer economic ties between them, including plans for a single European currency by 1999 and free movement of labor. The **Maastricht Accord** was approved by each country by 1993.

Similarly, Canada, the United States, and Mexico have together established a North American Free Trade Agreement (NAFTA). NAFTA will create the world's largest free market, with a total output of about $6 trillion.

FREE TRADE
When all barriers to trade among participating countries are removed.

ECONOMIC INTEGRATION
Refers to attempts by two or more nations to obtain the advantages of free trade by minimizing trade restrictions.

FREE TRADE AREA
A type of economic integration in which all barriers to trade among members are removed.

CUSTOM UNION
Here trade barriers among members are removed and a common trade policy exists with respect to nonmembers.

COMMON MARKET
No barriers to trade exist among members and a common external trade policy is in force; in addition, though, factors of production, such as labor, capital, and technology, are mobile among member countries.

TREATY OF ROME
A treaty signed by France, West Germany, Italy, Belgium, the Netherlands, and Luxembourg, which founded the European Economic Community in 1957.

MAASTRICHT ACCORD
In a series of meetings in 1991 held in Maastricht, the Netherlands, the twelve EC countries agreed to submit to their respective legislatures plans for cementing even closer economic ties between them, including plans for a single European currency by 1999 and free movement of labor. The Maastricht Accord was approved by each country by 1993.

Considerable free trade cooperation has occurred in Asia, too. For example, the Association of Southeast Asian Nations (ASEAN) was organized in 1967. It includes Brunei, Indonesia, Malaysia, the Philippines, Singapore, and Thailand. These countries are cooperating in reducing tariffs and in generally attempting to liberalize trade, although the results at this point have been limited.[31]

Some experts predict a global economy with a triad of three equally important regional economic activity hubs: North America, the EC, and East and Southeast Asia (including Japan, India, and China), as is illustrated in Figure 2.3.[32] Of the three, Asia is widely predicted to have the fastest growth over the next few years—in particular, mainland China, South Korea, Taiwan, Singapore, and Hong Kong. For example, the Chinese economy is growing at an annual rate of about 11.4 percent, compared to about 4 percent for Japan and about 3 percent for the United States.[33]

WHY COMPANIES GO INTERNATIONAL

Firms go international for several reasons. Three primary motivations for firms to pursue international business are to expand sales, to acquire resources, and to diversify

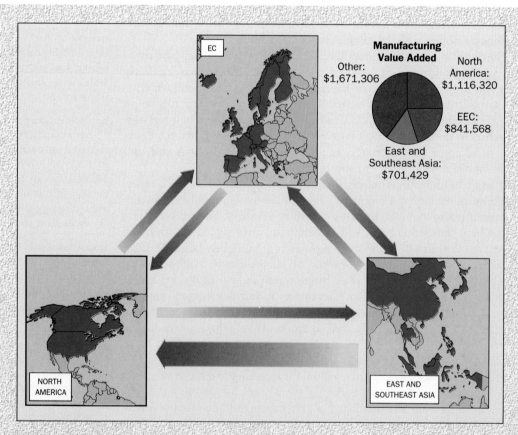

FIGURE 2.3

A Triad of Economic Activity Hubs

SOURCE: Charles Hill, *International Business: Competing in the Global Marketplace* (Burr Ridge: Irwin, 1994), 14.

sources of sales and supplies.[34] "Finding cheap labor" is *not* the primary r
most firms' internationalization efforts (although for some it is certainly a
Instead, *sales expansion* is usually the main motive. Firms like GE are moving r
to Asia because of the relatively fast growth rate of the Asian economies. Tha
lates into more income for Asia's consumers and fast sales increases for firms l

Firms pursue international business for three other reasons. Manufacturers ar
tributors do seek out foreign products and services in part to reduce their cost
example, Florida apparel manufacturers have items assembled in Central Am
where the labor costs are relatively low. In many cases it's high quality that drives f
overseas. For example, Apple Computer enlisted Sony's aid in producing parts fo
new notebook computer. Lastly, companies can smooth out sales and profit swings
seeking markets overseas. For example, a manufacturer of snowblowers might sell
Chile, knowing that as demand for its products in the United States are dropping o
in the spring, it is rising in Chile where the seasons, of course, are reversed.

ASSESSING THE INTERNATIONAL ENVIRONMENT

Going international presents the manager with new and often perplexing problems.
Having been brought up in the United States, for instance, our manager might find
the U.S. legal and political systems both familiar and predictable with, say, none of the
risks of political overthrows that he or she might face by doing business in Peru. Similarly, the U.S. economic environment also has its own familiar set of rules. For example, the president of Ben & Jerry's Homemade, Inc., knows that he can ship his ice
cream from Vermont to New York without paying tariffs when his trucks cross over
the border into Albany. The U.S. manager is familiar with our cultural norms and ways
of behaving. And if our manager decides to build a new plant in another state, transferring the technology—the machinery and know-how—from one state to another
would be a fairly easy matter.

Going abroad, though, creates new complexities and uncertainties for our manager.
He or she must now be adept at assessing a wide array of economic, legal, political,
sociocultural, and technological factors. Let's look at some of these.

THE ECONOMIC ENVIRONMENT

Managers engaged in international business need to be familiar with several features
of the economic environment. These include the economic systems of the countries
in question, the level of each country's economic development, and exchange rates.

THE ECONOMIC SYSTEM   The country's economic system is one important feature of the international marketplace. For example, consider the dilemma facing business managers in Hong Kong today. At the present time, Hong Kong is an example of
a market economy. In a pure **market economy,** the quantities and nature of the goods
and services produced are not planned by anyone. Instead, the interaction of supply
and demand via market forces decides what is produced, in what quantities, and at
what prices.

At the other extreme, the People's Republic of China (PRC), until very recently, has
been entirely an example of a command economy. In a **command economy,** government *central planning agencies* try to determine how much is produced by which sectors of the economy, and by which plants and for whom these goods are produced.
Countries like these (and they included, until recently, the former Soviet Union)

MARKET ECONOMY
The quantities and nature of the goods and services produced are not planned by anyone. Instead, the interaction of supply and demand via market forces decides what is produced, in what quantities, and at what prices.

COMMAND ECONOMY
An economy in which government central planning agencies try to determine how much is produced by which sectors of the economy, and by which plants and for whom these goods are produced.

MIXED ECONOMY
An economy i
tors of the
private
ke

usually base their yearly targets on five-year plans. They then establish specific production goals and prices for each sector of the economy (for each product or group of products) and for each manufacturing plant. It is conceivable that some time in the future, the PRC might move to a mixed economy. In a **mixed economy,** some sectors of the economy are left to private ownership and free market mechanisms, while others are largely owned by and managed by the government. Note that there are few, if any, "pure" market economies or command economies anymore. For example, much of the French banking system is still under government control. And, it was only several years ago that the government of England privatized (sold to private investors) British Airways.

The PRC (which had given Great Britain the right to govern Hong Kong until 1997) will be reassuming Hong Kong's governance in that year. Firms therefore now must decide whether to maintain, increase, or decrease their investments in Hong Kong, given the impending takeover by a traditionally command-economy oriented country.

ECONOMIC DEVELOPMENT   Countries also differ—often dramatically—in their rate of economic development. For example, Figure 2.4 illustrates that growth of gross domestic product—an indicator of economic growth—is estimated to be about 2.8 percent in the United States during 1994.[35] The figure for Hong Kong (5.5 percent) is about twice as large, while the growth rate in other Southeast Asian countries is even higher. This helps to explain why firms like GE are shifting resources to Asia.

In many areas of the world, political and economic liberalization are combining to create booming markets. In the former Soviet bloc, for instance, carmakers are rushing into the market. French automaker Renault sold about 6,000 cars in 1992 in Hungary and the Czech Republic. That may not seem like much, but it's the potential that is whetting carmakers' appetites: there are about 450 cars for 1,000 people in Western Europe, while there are only about 200 cars per 1,000 people in Central European countries.[36] In Pacific countries, the number of households approaching $18 thousand a year in buying power will about quintuple between now and the year 2000, from about 14.5 million to about 73 million households.[37] That means a boom in demand for all those products we associate with middle-class buyers, products like better housing, large appliances, televisions, telephones, and cars.

EXCHANGE RATES   Managers engaged in international business also have to juggle exchange rates. **Foreign exchange** refers to foreign currency. The **exchange rate** (between one country's currency and another) refers to the rate at which one currency can be exchanged for another. As the foreign exchange chart in Figure 2.5 shows, in January 1994 one British pound was worth about $1.49 in U.S. currency. Similarly, a French Franc was worth about 17 cents. Exchange rates can have a big impact on a company's performance. For example, a dramatic drop in the value of the dollar relative to the pound could have a devastating effect on a small U.S. company that suddenly found it needed 30 percent more dollars than it planned to build its factory in Scotland.

THE POLITICAL AND LEGAL ENVIRONMENT

The international manager also must be keenly aware of the legal and political environments of the countries in which he or she is to do business. Consider the uneven playing field between Japan and the United States, for example. A Chrysler Le Baron sells for $18,176 in the United States but $33,077 in Japan. A Buick Park Avenue lists for $27,420 in the United States but $43,617 in Japan. Yet a Honda Accord that retails for $17,645 in the United States sells for only $20,272 in Japan.[38] How could this be?

FOREIGN EXCHANGE
Refers to foreign currency.

EXCHANGE RATE
Refers to the rate at which one currency can be exchanged for another between two countries.

which some sectors of the economy are left to private ownership and free market mechanisms, while others are largely owned by and managed by the government.

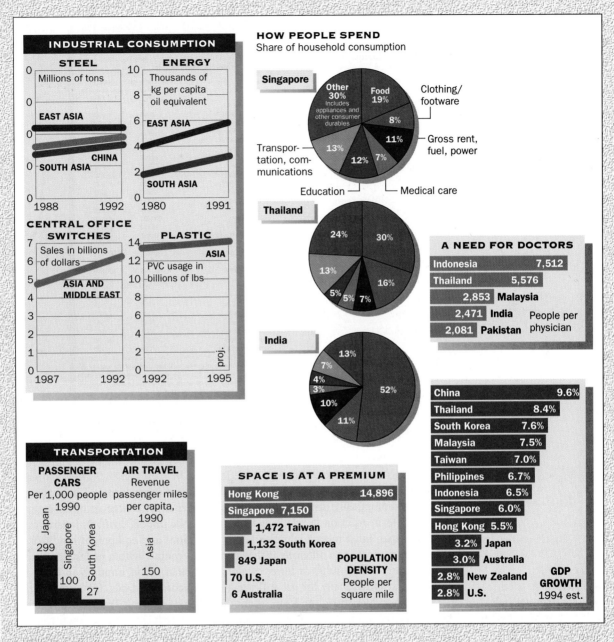

INDUSTRIAL CONSUMPTION

STEEL
Millions of tons

EAST ASIA

CHINA

SOUTH ASIA

1988 — 1992

ENERGY
Thousands of kg per capita oil equivalent

EAST ASIA

SOUTH ASIA

1980 — 1991

CENTRAL OFFICE SWITCHES
Sales in billions of dollars

ASIA AND MIDDLE EAST

1987 — 1992

PLASTIC
ASIA

PVC usage in billions of lbs

proj.

1992 — 1995

HOW PEOPLE SPEND
Share of household consumption

Singapore
Other 30% Includes appliances and other consumer durables
Food 19%
Clothing/footware 8%
Gross rent, fuel, power 11%
7%
Medical care
Education
12%
13%
Transportation, communications

Thailand
30%
16%
7%
5%
5%
13%
24%

India
52%
13%
7%
4%
3%
10%
11%

A NEED FOR DOCTORS
	People per physician
Indonesia	7,512
Thailand	5,576
Malaysia	2,853
India	2,471
Pakistan	2,081

GDP GROWTH 1994 est.
China	9.6%
Thailand	8.4%
South Korea	7.6%
Malaysia	7.5%
Taiwan	7.0%
Philippines	6.7%
Indonesia	6.5%
Singapore	6.0%
Hong Kong	5.5%
Japan	3.2%
Australia	3.0%
New Zealand	2.8%
U.S.	2.8%

TRANSPORTATION

PASSENGER CARS
Per 1,000 people 1990

Japan 299
Singapore 100
South Korea 27

AIR TRAVEL
Revenue passenger miles per capita, 1990

Asia 150

SPACE IS AT A PREMIUM
POPULATION DENSITY
People per square mile

Hong Kong	14,896
Singapore	7,150
Taiwan	1,472
South Korea	1,132
Japan	849
U.S.	70
Australia	6

FIGURE 2.4

Countries differ in their rate of economic development. Note the high (GDP) economic growth rates in China and Thailand for instance. As economies grow, their citizens also spend their incomes differently, with more going to consumer durables, and less to basics like food.

SOURCE: "The New Global Consumer in Charts," *Fortune*, Autumn-Winter, 1993, 77.

FIGURE 2.5

Foreign Exchange

International travelers should be familiar with exchange rates between various countries. For example, on January 14, 1994 one British pound was worth about $1.49

SOURCE: *New York Times*, January 16, 1994, F-28.

FOREIGN EXCHANGE

FRIDAY, JANUARY 14, 1994

NEW YORK (AP) — Foreign Exchange, New York prices.
Rates for trades of $1 million minimum.

	Fgn. currency in dollars Fri	Dollar in fgn. currency Fri
f-Argent (Peso)	1.0100	.9901
Australia (Dollar)	.6935	1.4420
Austria (Schilling)	.0814	12.288
c-Belgium (Franc)	.0274	36.53
Brazil (CruzeiroR)	.0027	370.07
Britain (Pound)	1.4935	.6696
30-day fwd	1.4905	.6709
60-day fwd	1.4880	.6720
90-day fwd	1.4854	.6732
Canada (Dollar)	.7550	1.3245
30-day fwd	.7546	1.3252
60-day fwd	.7543	1.3258
90-day fwd	.7540	1.3262
y-Chile (Peso)	.002403	416.21
China (Yuan)	.1152	8.6783
Colombia (Peso)	.001437	695.72
c-CzechRep (Koruna)	.0339	29.47
Denmark (Krone)	.1473	6.7876
ECU	1.10900	.9017
z-Ecudr (Sucre)	.000499	2004.01
d-Egypt (Pound)	.2994	3.3405
Finland (Mark)	.1761	5.6780
France (Franc)	.1685	5.9340
Germany (Mark)	.5719	1.7485
30-day fwd	.5704	1.7531
60-day fwd	.5692	1.7567
90-day fwd	.5681	1.7602
Greece (Drachma)	.003986	250.90
Hong Kong (Dollar)	.1294	7.2260

ECU: European Currency Unit, a basket of European currencies. The Federal Reserve Board's index of the value of the dollar against 10 other currencies weighted on the basis of trade was 96.73 Friday off 0.09 points or 0.09 percent from Thursday's 96.82. A year ago the index was 92.57

c-commercial rate, d-free market rate, f-financial rate, y-official rate, z-floating rate.

TRADE CONTROL   The answer is that tariffs and other forms of import restrictions can dramatically distort the prices companies must charge in other countries. For example, in addition to relatively high automobile import tariffs in Japan, cars not made in Japan must meet a complex set of regulations and equipment modifications. Side mirrors must snap off easily if they come into contact with a pedestrian; and any manufacturer selling 1,000 or fewer cars of a particular model annually in Japan must test each car individually for gas mileage and emission standards, for instance.

These examples show one form or another of trade control. **Trade control** refers to governmental influences that are usually aimed at reducing the competitiveness of imported products or services. A tariff is the most common type of trade control. **Tariffs** (or duties) are governmental taxes levied on goods shipped internationally.[39] The exporting country collects export tariffs, the importing country collects import tariffs, and the country through which the goods are passed collects transit tariffs.

As the examples above illustrate, a multitude of nontariff barriers exist, too. For example, some countries make direct payments to producers. These are called **subsidies** and can make an otherwise inefficient producer more cost competitive than it would be otherwise. Other countries impose **quotas**—legal restrictions on the import of particular goods—as further barriers to trade.[40]

POLITICAL RISKS   The international manager must be concerned not just with governmental influences on trade but with political risks as well. For example, when the Shah of Iran fell a number of years ago, U.S. firms that had been doing business

TRADE CONTROL
Refers to governmental influences that are usually aimed at reducing the competitiveness of imported products or services.

TARIFFS
Governmental taxes levied on goods shipped internationally.

SUBSIDIES
When a country makes direct payments to help support its producers.

QUOTAS
Legal restrictions on the import of particular goods.

in Iran were surprised to learn that their apparently endless profits were no longer guaranteed.[41] Similarly, companies doing business with South Africa wonder how the new majority rule will affect their businesses. U.S. manufacturers in Peru must be ever vigilant against terrorist attacks. The ethnic violence in the former Yugoslavia brought economic activities for many companies exporting to those countries to a virtual stand-still in 1994.

Political risks can range from major events to relatively invisible ones. As one expert puts it,

> Political problems range from catastrophic events such as revolution or war, through a broad range of destabilizing issues including corruption, labor unrest, crooked elections, religious violence, coupes d'etat and incompetent economic management by government agencies, and then on to narrow but nevertheless dangerous matters such as the political leverage of your competition or ethnic conflict within a specific work-site. All of these phenomena spell trouble if not considered in advance.[42]

LEGAL SYSTEMS   There are also important differences in legal systems and restraints. For example, even some major European companies are sometimes hesitant to enter into business arrangements with U.S. firms because of the fear of litigation in the United States. Legal systems also vary from country to country. Many countries adhere to a system known as common law. **Common law** is law based on tradition and depends more on precedence and customs than on written statutes. England is one example of a country that uses common law. Other countries have a code law system. **Code law** represents a comprehensive set of written statutes. Some countries use a combination of common law and code law. For example, the United States adheres to a system of common law in many areas but adheres to a written Uniform Commercial Code for governing the activities of businesses. **International law** is another consideration. International law is not so much an enforceable body of law as much as agreements embodied in treaties and other types of agreements that countries have agreed to respect. For example, international law governs intellectual property rights (such as whether U2's music can be reproduced in Japan without its permission).

THE SOCIO-CULTURAL ENVIRONMENT

People who travel to other countries quickly learn that they must also adapt to societal differences. In Latin America, for instance, *machismo* ("maleness") is comprised of virility, zest for action, daring, competitiveness, and the will to conquer. This is translated into daily business life by demonstrating forcefulness, self-confidence, courage, and leadership.[43] The differences between the Japanese and American culture manifest themselves in thousands of small ways. In Japan, saving face and achieving harmony are very important. As a result, indirect and vague communication is preferred, with sentences frequently left unfinished so the other person may draw his or her own conclusions. In the Middle East, the people of Arabia, it is said, love the spoken word and tend not to get to the point quickly. This can frustrate Americans (who must be careful not to exhibit impatience or annoyance). And in France, a firm and pumping handshake may be considered uncultured; instead, a quick shake with some pressure on the grip is more appropriate.

VALUES   Research by Geert Hofstede suggests that a society's values are among the most influential of cultural differences. Values are basic beliefs we have about what is good or bad, important or unimportant. Values (such as Westpoint's famous "duty, honor, country") are important because they guide how we behave.

Hofstede argues that cultural differences among countries relate to the following four basic values.

COMMON LAW
Law based on tradition and depending more on precedence and customs than on written statutes.

CODE LAW
Represents a comprehensive set of written statutes.

INTERNATIONAL LAW
Agreements embodied in treaties and other types of agreements that countries have agreed to respect, not so much an enforceable body of law.

POWER DISTANCE
A dimension of cultural differences that refers to the extent to which the less powerful members of institutions accept and expect power to be distributed unequally.

- **Power distance.**[44] According to Hofstede, this dimension refers to the extent to which the less powerful members of institutions accept and expect power to be distributed unequally.[45] He concluded that the institutionalization of such an inequality was higher in some countries (such as Mexico) than it was in others (such as Sweden).

- **Individualism vs. collectivism.** This refers to the degree to which ties between individuals are normally loose rather than close. In more individualist countries, "all members are expected to look after themselves and their immediate families."[46] Individualistic countries include Australia and the United States. In collectivist countries, people are expected to care for each other more. Indonesia and Pakistan are examples of collectivist countries.

- **Masculinity vs. femininity.** According to Hofstede, societies differ also in the extent to which they value assertiveness, which he called "masculinity," or caring ("femininity"). Japan and Austria ranked high in masculinity; Denmark, Costa Rica, and Chile ranked low.

- **Uncertainty avoidance.** This value refers to the extent to which living in the society nurtures a sense of being uncomfortable with unstructured situations in which unknown, surprising, novel incidents occur. In other words, how comfortable are people in this society when it comes to dealing with surprises? The people in some countries (such as Sweden, Israel, and Great Britain) are, according to Hofstede, relatively comfortable dealing with uncertainty and surprises. On the other hand, people in other countries (including Greece and Portugal) tend to be uncertainty avoiders.[47] Those more comfortable with uncertainty "are more tolerant of opinions that are different from what they are used to; they [also] try to have as few rules as possible."[48]

LANGUAGE AND CUSTOMS   Differences in language need to be dealt with by the business manager, too. (Braniff Airlines' "Fly in Leather" slogan was reportedly translated as "fly naked" for the company's Latin American campaign.)[49] The country's traditional manners and customs can also be important. McDonald's found it had to offer mineral water in France, for instance, and Campbell's learned that Japanese drink soup mainly for breakfast. Similarly, a country's predominant religions, cultural orientations (such as music and art), and educational processes can all influence the manner in which business should be conducted in the country. The *Visa* vignette illustrates how socio-cultural factors have influenced one firm's global expansion.

THE TECHNOLOGICAL ENVIRONMENT

A country's technological environment—and in particular the relative ease or difficulty with which technology can be transferred from one country to another—greatly affects international business decisions.

TECHNOLOGY TRANSFER
The transfer of systematic knowledge for the manufacture of a product, for the application of a process, or for the rendering of a service; does not extend to the mere sale or lease of goods.

Technology transfer is the "transfer of systematic knowledge for the manufacture of a product, for the application of a process, or for the rendering of a service and does not extend to the mere sale or lease of goods."[50] Successful technology transfer in turn depends on three things. First, there must be a *suitable technology* to be transferred, for instance, the computer software for designing pollution control filtration devices. Second, *social and economic conditions* must favor the transfer. Pollution-reducing technology that might be highly effective in the U.S. might prove of no significance in a less developed country where political, social, and economic conditions do not encourage pollution reduction. Finally, successful technology transfer depends on the *willingness and ability* of the receiving party to use and adapt the technology.[51]

VISA

James F. Partridge, president of Visa International's Latin American Region, has seen societal differences firsthand. Visa is not a company in the typical sense, but rather an industry group owned by 19,000 financial institutions worldwide. Although it started out as a U.S. company, Visa has become a homegrown entity wherever the member owner happens to be.

"We are not a company based in one country that controls foreign subsidiaries; wherever Visa is distributed it is a local brand, locally managed and locally owned," says Partridge.

Operating across such a range of locales hasn't always been smooth. In opening its first Asian office, an American staff in Singapore set up a traditional hierarchy staffed with their fellow Americans, all of whom went to live in the most expensive housing. They could scarcely have done a better job of stigmatizing relations with their Singapore colleagues. A good deal of time, money, and fence-mending were required to put things right. Jumping to cultural conclusions hasn't paid off either. Partridge says expansion into Japan, known for its protectionist stance in many industries, was smoothly accomplished. Germany, on the other hand, viewed Visa as a threat to its domestic check-guarantee card and attempted to thwart operations. In Brazil, a consortium of banks threatened to shut Visa out of the market unless they were granted exclusivity. Partridge, sensing that global markets were opening and not closing, refused. Ultimately, the would-be bank cartel fell apart, and Brazil became one of Visa's fastest growing markets.

SOURCE: Arthur L. Chait, "In Complexity Lies . . ." *ICC Supplement to Across the Board,* January 1994, 16–21.

Aggressive marketing strategies have enabled Visa to gain ground against American Express, its major rival. Visa now has the majority of the global market in charge volume, largely as a result of the work of Chief Executive Robert Heller (left) and Marketing Vice President Bradford Morgan (right).

If the successful application of the pollution control software required highly trained chemical engineers to whom the receiving country has no access, the technology transfer would not be successful.

TYPES OF INTERNATIONAL VENTURES

Companies have many alternatives when it comes to extending their operations into foreign markets. We look at the main alternatives next.

STARTING INTERNATIONAL OPERATIONS

Most companies do not initially embark on international ventures by making substantial investments in foreign countries. Instead, initial international operations usually focus on either exporting, licensing, or franchising.

EXPORTING Exporting is often the alternative of choice when manufacturers decide to expand their sales overseas. Indeed, exports of merchandise, agricultural goods, minerals, and services have mushroomed over the past few years, increasing at

EXPORTING

Selling abroad, either directly to target customers, or indirectly by retaining foreign sales agents and distributors.

a rate of about 18 percent per year.[52] **Exporting** means selling abroad, either directly to target customers or indirectly by retaining foreign sales agents and distributors.

It is estimated that more than half of all world trade is handled through agents and distributors. This underscores the advantages of using an intermediary familiar with the local market's customs and customers. On the other hand, using intermediaries is tantamount, in some respects, to taking on a partner. Poorly selected intermediaries can prove more trouble than they are worth. Carefully selecting intermediaries, checking business reputations via local agencies of the U.S. State Department, and then carefully drafting agency and distribution agreements is therefore essential if a company chooses to take this route.[53]

Whichever route is taken, exporting has some clear advantages and disadvantages for the internationally aspiring company. It is a relatively quick and inexpensive way of "going international," particularly insofar as it avoids the need to establish manufacturing operations in the host country.[54] Exporting is also a good way of testing the waters in the host country and learning more about its customers' needs. On the other hand, high transportation, tariff, or manufacturing costs can put the exporter at a relative disadvantage. In addition, poorly selected intermediaries (as noted above) can undermine the company's export efforts. One creative way for companies to avoid some of these problems is by selling directly through mail order. For example, L.L. Bean, Lands' End, and the Sharper Image all export globally via their famous catalogs.[55]

The *Small Business Exporters* vignette shows how three firms have had successs with foreign sales agents.

LICENSING Licensing is another way to start international operations. International **licensing** is an arrangement whereby a firm (the licensor) grants a foreign firm the right to use intangible ("intellectual") property such as patents, copyrights, manufacturing processes, or trade names for a specified period of time, usually in return for a royalty.[56]

LICENSING

An arrangement whereby a firm (the licensor) grants a foreign firm the right to use intangible ("intellectual") property such as patents, copyrights, manufacturing processes or trade names for a specified period of time, usually in return for a royalty.

Licensing arrangements have their pros and cons. For example, consider a small, underfunded inventor of a new material and process for reducing and controlling pollution. Entering into a licensing agreement with a well-established European environmental products company could allow our U.S. firm to enter the expanding Eastern European pollution control market without any significant investment. On the downside, the U.S. firm might not be able to control the design, manufacturing, or sales of its products as well as it could if it set up its own facilities in Europe. It is also possible that by licensing its knowledge and know-how to a foreign firm, the small U.S. firm could eventually lose control over its patented property.

FRANCHISING

The granting of a right by a parent company to another firm to do business in a prescribed manner.

FRANCHISING As anyone who has eaten at McDonald's on the Champs Élysées knows, franchising is another way to start operations overseas. **Franchising** is the granting of a right by a parent company to another firm to do business in a prescribed manner.[57]

Franchising is similar to licensing, with several differences. Franchising usually involves a longer time commitment on the part of both parties. Furthermore, franchising usually requires the franchisee to follow much stricter guidelines in running the business than does licensing. In addition, licensing tends to be limited to manufacturers, while franchising is more popular with service firms such as restaurants, hotels, and rental services.

The advantages here are generally the same as those for licensing: this is a quick and relatively low-cost way for a firm to expand its sales in other countries. The significant disadvantage is maintaining quality control. For example, one early French

SMALL BUSINESS EXPORTERS

In 1989, Bird Corporation president Fred Schweser sought out Commerce Department trade specialist Harvey Roffman for help in generating overseas business. Roffman recommended advertising in *Commercial News USA,* a government publication designed to enlighten around 100,000 foreign agents, distributors, buyers, and government officials about American products. Schweser was very soon deluged with responses, and his Elkhorn, Nebraska, company now boasts customers from Japan to the United Kingdom and many points in between. What is Bird Corporation's product? Go-carts.

In another example of exporting success, Arbor Crest Winery was undaunted by the intense competition in the international wine market. "I guess no one told us that we couldn't export so we did," says David Mielke, who owns the Washington company with his brother Harold. In the mid-1980s, once their high-quality wines were selling in almost every state in the nation, the Mielkes decided to look for business opportunities abroad. Overseas distributors now ship 15 percent of the company's product to Canada, Western Europe, and several countries in the Pacific Rim.

And for Russellville, Arkansas-based POM, the overseas market has proven to be even bigger than the one at home. The small manufacturer of parking meters sells a product with an average life span of two decades or more. With the U.S. market nearing saturation, it seemed only natural to look to developing nations, where industrialization was creating newly urbanized streets. The move paid off. Over the last decade, POM, working with distributors, has snagged nearly half of the international parking meter market.

SOURCES: Albert G. Holzinger, "Paving the Way for Small Exporters," *Nation's Business,* June 1992, 42–43; Albert G. Holzinger, "Reach New Markets," *Nation's Business,* December 1990, 18–25; and Christopher Knowlton, "The New Export Entrepreneurs," *Fortune,* June 6, 1988, 89–102.

McDonald's franchisee was forced by McDonald's to close down its Paris restaurants for failing to maintain McDonald's well-known quality standards.

FOREIGN DIRECT INVESTMENT AND THE MULTINATIONAL ENTERPRISE

Many internationally aspiring firms find that exporting, licensing, and franchising can get them only so far. At some point, they find that to take full advantage of foreign opportunities, they have to make a substantial, direct investment of their own funds in another country. In general, **foreign direct investment** refers to operations in one country that are controlled by entities in a foreign country. This might involve a foreign firm building new facilities in another country, as Toyota did when it built its Camry manufacturing plant in Georgetown, Kentucky. Or it might mean that the firm acquires property or operations in a foreign country, as when Matsushita bought control of Rockefeller Center in New York City. Strictly speaking, a foreign direct investment means acquiring control by owning more than 50 percent of the operation. But

FOREIGN DIRECT INVESTMENT
Refers to operations in one country that are controlled by entities in a foreign country.

Fred Schweser, president of Bird Corporation, takes a test drive in one of his company's go-carts. Advertising in the Commerce Department *magazine helped open up foreign markets for Bird.*

in practice, it is possible for any firm (including a foreign firm) to gain effective control by owning less. In any event, a foreign direct investment turns a firm into a multinational enterprise. A **multinational enterprise** is one that controls operations in more than one country. Joint ventures and wholly-owned subsidiaries are two examples of foreign direct investments.

MULTINATIONAL ENTERPRISE
An enterprise that controls operations in more than one country.

JOINT VENTURE
The participation of two or more companies jointly in an enterprise such that each party contributes assets, owns the entity to some degree, and shares risk.

STRATEGIC ALLIANCE
Refers to cooperative agreements between potential and actual competitors.

JOINT VENTURES   The terms **joint venture** and **strategic alliance** are often used interchangeably, although they aren't, strictly speaking, the same thing. Some experts reserve the term *strategic alliances* to refer to "cooperative agreements between potential or actual competitors."[58] For example, several years ago, Boeing combined with a consortium of Japanese companies to produce the 767 commercial jet. However, most experts would probably define strategic alliances as "any agreements between firms that are of strategic importance to one or both firms' competitive viability."[59] Used in that sense, even licensing or franchising agreements may come under the umbrella of strategic alliances.

A joint venture is a specific type of strategic alliance. In fact, it is the classical example of such an alliance.[60] A *joint venture* has been defined as "the participation of two or more companies jointly in an enterprise in which each party contributes assets, owns the entity to some degree, and shares risk."[61]

The joint venture of General Motors and Toyota called New United Motor Manufacturing, Inc. (NUMMI), is an example of a joint venture. At the time, Toyota needed to sharpen its U.S. marketing skills and needed direct access to U.S. customers. General Motors, faced with anemic productivity and morale when compared to Japanese car manufacturers, needed to learn more about Japanese manufacturing systems and technology. The two firms formed NUMMI and had it take over a chronically troubled GM plant in Freemont, California. Within two years the Japanese management methods had made this plant GM's most productive.

As at NUMMI, joint ventures have substantial advantages. Consultant Kenichi Ohmae points out that "in a complex, uncertain world filled with dangerous opponents, it is best not to go it alone."[62] A joint venture arrangement lets a foreign firm (like Toyota) gain useful experience in a foreign country while utilizing the expertise and resources of a locally knowledgeable company. Joint ventures also obviously help both companies share what may be the substantial cost of starting a new operation. But, as with licensing, the joint venture partners also run the risk of giving away proprietary secrets to each other. Furthermore, joint ventures almost always mean sharing control. Each partner runs the risk that the joint venture may not be managed as tightly or in the manner that each would have chosen on its own.

WHOLLY-OWNED SUBSIDIARIES   The year 1991 was a momentous one for Toys-Я-Us, Inc., and for Japan. In that year the company opened its inaugural store in Japan, and thus became the first large U.S.-owned discount store there.[63]

As the name implies, a **wholly owned subsidiary** is owned 100 percent by the foreign firm. Thus, in the U.S. today, Toyota Motor Manufacturing, Inc., and its facility in Georgetown, Kentucky, is a wholly owned subsidiary of Toyota Motor Corporation, which is based in Japan. (NUMMI is a separate and independent operation.)

Wholly owned subsidiaries have advantages and disadvantages. They provide for the tightest controls by the foreign firm. That firm also does not have to fear losing any of its rights to its proprietary knowledge. However, this is a relatively expensive way to expand into foreign markets.

WHOLLY OWNED SUBSIDIARY
A subsidiary that is owned 100 percent by the foreign firm.

MANAGING IN A GLOBAL ECONOMY

Doing business abroad creates new management issues with which the manager must cope. We'll look briefly at some of these issues here and then continue our discussion of international management in each chapter, as appropriate.

MULTINATIONAL PLANNING ISSUES

Planning means setting goals and identifying the courses of action for achieving those goals. Planning therefore always involves identifying opportunities and threats and balancing these with the strengths and weaknesses of the enterprise. Planning in an international arena involves the same basic approach. However, global planning requires that international managers deal with several unique issues as well.

As we have seen, the international planner must address many political, legal, and technological issues. There is the ever-present possibility of political instability, since many countries in which international firms do business have frequent changes of government.[64] Similarly, currency instability, competition from state-owned enterprises (such as Montedison, a chemical firm 50 percent owned by the Italian government), and pressures from national governments (including changing tariff barriers) can all influence a firm's business, often throwing its best laid plans into disarray.

Instabilities like these are not just a characteristic of developing countries. Between 1993 and 1995, Italy embarked on a sweeping privatization of its nationalized businesses. During that time, banks and companies worth about $60 billion were sold, including some of Italy's largest telecommunications, oil and gas, and insurance companies.[65]

At the same time, sweeping criminal investigations created havoc among the country's political and managerial elite. Changes like these created enormous opportunities for foreign firms doing business in Italy. At the same time they increased the risks by boosting both the competitiveness of the newly privatized Italian firms and the uncertainties of dealing with the country's political institutions.

Other complications arise in international planning:[66] A domestic (U.S.) planner faces a relatively homogeneous market, while the international planner faces a relatively fragmented and diverse set of customers and needs. For U.S. planners, data are usually available and are relatively accurate and easy to collect. Internationally, data collection—on demographics, production levels, and so on—can be a formidable task, and the actual data are often of questionable accuracy. Complications in international planning are illustrated in the *Electrolux* vignette.

ORGANIZING THE MULTINATIONAL BUSINESS

As companies evolve from domestic to multinational enterprises, they typically go through several organizational stages.[67] Figure 2.6 illustrates the typical organizational alternatives, which include the domestic organization, the export-oriented organization, the international organization, and the multinational organization.

These alternatives differ in how they maintain authority over the foreign operations. In the **domestic organization,** each division handles its own foreign sales, which may come largely from unsolicited overseas orders. Next, in response to increasing orders from abroad, the firm may move up to an **export-oriented** organization structure. Here, a department (often called an import-export department) is created to coordinate all international activities such as licensing, contracting, and managing

DOMESTIC ORGANIZATION
Division of an organization that focuses on production and sales of domestic markets.

EXPORT-ORIENTED
An import/export department coordinates all international activities, such as managing foreign sales.

Stiff competition from Whirlpool and weak markets forced Electrolux to refocus on its core appliance business. CEO Anders Scharp had to bring together diverse and far-flung companies acquired through several mergers in the 1980s.

ELECTROLUX

When he took over as head of Electrolux's household appliance division in 1983, Leif Johansson faced the challenge of managing 20 different brands sold in 40 countries. Electrolux's product line had been assembled through acquisitions. As a result, Johansson found himself presiding over a hodge-podge of products and brand names, and markets that were highly fragmented. Johansson quickly realized two things. To maximize return on resources, the Swedish firm would have to devise a plan to integrate these far-flung operations and take advantage of similarities in customer needs and product characteristics. But dropping familiar brands would cost Electrolux some consumer loyalty and distribution leverage.

Johansson headed up a task force aimed at reducing product-line proliferation. Together they isolated market similarities that crossed national boundaries. They also determined that consumers' perception of the so-called localness of products was a function of brand name and how the products were promoted and sold, not of where they were manufactured. Working from these findings, the task force devised a plan that offered two regional brands aimed at conservative customers in all European markets and another more innovative brand directed at consumers regarded as more progressive. Local brands were likewise segregated into market groups aimed at young professionals and persons primarily concerned with lower-priced offerings. The plan enabled the company to maintain local brand-name clout, while at the same time standardizing the products and gaining the benefits of mass production in regional plants.

SOURCE: Christopher A. Bartlett and Sumantra Ghoshal, "What Is a Global Manager?" *Harvard Business Review,* September–October 1992, 124–32.

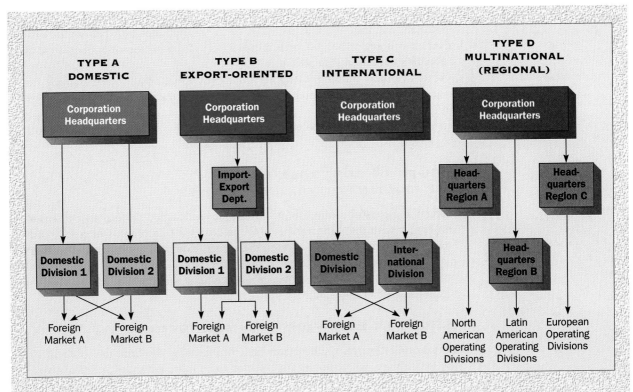

FIGURE 2.6

International Organizations

As firms evolve from domestic to multinational enterprises, their increasing international operations necessitate a more globally oriented organization.

Note: Boxes indicate the sources of authority in respect to foreign operations.

SOURCE: Richard D. Robinson, *Internationalization of Business: An Introduction* (Chicago: Dryden, 1984), 270.

foreign sales. In an **international organization,** the company is divided into separate domestic and international divisions. The international division focuses on production and sales for overseas, while the domestic division focuses on domestic markets.

Finally, the firm may be pushed toward a **multinational form.** Here, each country in which the firm does business may have its own subsidiary. The oil firm Royal Dutch Shell is organized this way. It has separate subsidiaries for Shell Switzerland and Shell U.S.A., for instance.[68]

INTERNATIONAL ISSUES IN HUMAN RESOURCE MANAGEMENT

Globalization also impacts the firm's human resource (personnel) systems. Here issues range from (1) general issues like how to select, train, and compensate managers who are to be sent to foreign posts, to (2) dealing with specific inter-country differences in labor laws. For example, take selecting managers for foreign assignments. Here one vice-president said, "there is too much emphasis on executives' technical abilities and

INTERNATIONAL ORGANIZATION
Usually coupled with a domestic division, this division focuses on production and sales of foreign markets.

MULTINATIONAL FORM
Each country in which the firm does business may have its own subsidiary

too little on their cultural skills and family situations. When international executives' relocations fail, they generally fail either because expatriates can't fathom the customs of a new country or because their families can't deal with the emotional stress that a company's relocation entails."[69]

Cross-cultural training is another important issue. Ideally, such training should focus on the impact of cultural differences, on raising trainees' awareness of the impact on business decisions of these cultural differences, and on other matters like building language and adaptation skills. Yet few firms actually provide such training to their employees.[70]

ISSUES IN CONTROLLING THE MULTINATIONAL ENTERPRISE

Maintaining control means monitoring a manager's actual performance to ensure its consistency with the standards he or she is expected to achieve. Doing so is difficult enough when the manager is around the corner. However, the problems can be enormously complex in the global enterprise. For example, even with computerized technology, geographic distance, language, and cultural barriers can undermine communications and therefore control.

ISSUES IN BEHAVIOR AND MANAGEMENT

Globalizing influences the behavioral side of managing the firm, too. In Latin America, for instance, where bosses are expected to be more autocratic, participative management (in which employees are encouraged to make work-related decisions) can backfire. At the other extreme, Japanese managers value consensus and rarely welcome the kind of take-charge leader who wants to personally make all the decisions.

In their book *Working for the Japanese,* Joseph and Suzy Fucini describe the cultural problems between the Japanese and Americans that eventually caused the Mazda plant in Flatrock, Michigan, to become unionized. Here's how they describe why Denny Pawley, the highest-ranking American at Flatrock, decided to leave the Mazda plant for a new job with United Technologies Corporation:

> Pawley did not quit for the money. He left Mazda because he had become frustrated with the constraints that the company's Japanese management had placed on him. After two years and one month with Mazda, it had become obvious to the burly, high-spirited car man . . . that because he was an American he would never be given real authority at Flatrock. He had, he believed, worked patiently with the Japanese to learn their system, in the belief that one day he would be combining this knowledge with the experience he brought with him from General Motors to create the "third-culture plan" that Mazda's executives had so often talked about. But, as he would later observe, "it started looking more and more to me [like] the real decision-making would always come out of Hiroshima, and [this] just didn't offer me the opportunity to use my broad-based management experience."[71]

Going international thus confronts the manager with new issues and challenges. The effectiveness through which he or she deals with these new issues—whether through planning, organizing, managing human resources, controlling, or managing the behavioral side of his or her firm— will determine whether or not the decision to internationalize was a good one.

SUMMARY

An international business is any firm that engages in international trade or investment. Multinational and global corporations are two types of international business enterprises. Firms are globalizing for a variety of reasons. Some are doing so because their domestic markets are too limited. Others have been spurred by the increasing convergence of tastes and preferences of consumers in different nations brought about by television, telecommunications, and air travel. One result has been an explosion of export trade for U.S. firms.

Globalizing production means dispersing parts of a firm's production process to various locations around the globe. The aim is to take advantage of national differences in the cost and quality of production and then integrate these operations in a unified system of manufacturing facilities around the world. Companies also are tapping a new supply of skilled labor in various countries. The globalization of markets, production, and labor coincides with the rise of a new type of global manager, who can function effectively anywhere in the world.

Free trade means that all barriers to trade among participating countries are removed. Its potential benefits have prompted many nations to enter into various levels of economic integration, ranging from a free trade area to a common market. Firms have three primary motivations to pursue international business: to expand sales, acquire resources, and diversify sources of sales and supplies. Sales expansion is usually the primary motivation. Other reasons for pursuing international business include reducing costs or improving quality by seeking out products and services produced in foreign countries and smoothing out sales and profit swings.

International managers must be adept at assessing a wide array of economic, legal/political, socio-cultural, and technological factors. For example, managers must be familiar with the economic systems, exchange rates, and level of economic development of the countries in which they do business. They also must be aware of import restrictions, political risks, and legal differences and restraints. Important cultural differences will also affect how people in various countries act and expect to be treated. Values, languages, and customs are all examples of elements that distinguish people of one culture from those of another. Finally, the relative ease with which technology can be transferred from one country to another is an important consideration in conducting international business.

Companies have many alternatives when it comes to extending their operations to foreign markets. Exporting is often the route chosen by manufacturers, but licensing and franchising are two other popular alternatives. At some point, a firm may decide to directly invest its own funds in another country. Joint ventures and wholly-owned subsidiaries are two examples of foreign direct investments. Doing business abroad presents the manager with new challenges involving international planning, organizing, controlling, human resource management, and management of the behavioral side of the firm.

QUESTIONS

■ **FOR REVIEW**

1. What are the required characteristics and capabilities of the global manager?

2. Give examples of economic integration of the present or recent past.

3. Name at least five reasons firms elect to pursue international business. What popular reason is actually not a major motivating factor influencing this type of expansion?

4. List the most common problems associated with expanding a company internationally.

5. Explain the difference between foreign direct investment and multinational enterprises, joint ventures, and strategic alliances.

▨ FOR DISCUSSION

6. Do you think there may come a day when all large companies are multinationals? Why or why not?

7. Describe the benefits of free trade and the consequences of trade barriers on the world economy.

8. Discuss the problems firms might encounter managing human resources in foreign countries.

9. A global manager must be adept at assessing a wide array of economic, legal/political, socio-cultural, and technological factors. Which of these do you think would be most difficult to assess, and why?

▨ FOR ACTION

10. Foreign companies can list their stocks in the United States through what are known as American depository receipts. Obtain an annual report for a company that has an ADR. Use it to describe the scope of its international operations.

11. Ask a fellow student from another country about economic, political, and cultural differences in his or her home. Based on that information, develop a list of pros and cons for a U.S. company considering doing business there.

12. The North American Free Trade Agreement will gradually eliminate all tariffs and trade barriers between the United States, Canada, and Mexico, but some types of businesses will be impacted before others. Go to the library and research the specifics of NAFTA. Which U.S. industries will be the first to feel the effects of the agreement?

▨ FOR FOCUS ON SMALL BUSINESS

13. Discuss the advantages and disadvantages of "going global" for a company like VeriFone.

14. Describe the environmental forces that have made it important for even a small company to operate globally.

15. List some reasons why you believe Tyabji has succeeded in his role as a global manager.

CLOSING SOLUTION

GENERAL ELECTRIC

Although GE has had a global presence for decades, it has essentially remained a U.S. company that merely operates abroad. Welch's expansion strategy will change all that. Initial inroads will take the form of small stakes in several foreign locations, with product offerings dictated by the demand in the particular locale. That means the company might directly export jet engines or turbines to China, or establish in-country manufacturing plants for lower technology goods in lesser developed countries such as India. GE managers will also become more internationally oriented. Some of Welch's principle subordinates will assume positions around the world, creating what has been dubbed "global brains" capable of managing operations in any culture or country. GE has already increased personnel in Beijing by 200 percent. The number of management personnel in Asia has doubled. Wherever possible, GE will offer technologies and capital for everything from upgrading their host's manufacturing base to building multi-billion dollar power generating plants.

Jack Welch has correctly concluded that the next big business boom won't happen domestically, it will occur in developing countries with huge populations, problems, and opportunities. GE has the right company infrastructure to capitalize, and in keeping with his fast-moving, flexible corporate philosophy, Welch also will see to it that seasoned decision-makers are on the ground where they need to be around the world. He thinks he has seen the future, and he plans for GE to be a part of it.

SOURCE: Tim Smart et al, "GE's Brave New World," *Business Week,* Nov. 8, 1993, 64–70.

■ **QUESTIONS FOR CLOSING SOLUTION**

1. What changes planned by Jack Welch do you think will transform GE from a multinational corporation to a global corporation?

2. Outline some of the special skills and qualifications GE's international managers will need to master in order to effectively run the company's various overseas operations.

3. How do you think Welch can maintain control of the company as it continues to expand internationally?

KEY TERMS

International Business
International Trade
International Investment
Multinational Corporation (MNC)
Global Corporation
Globalizing Production
Ethnocentric
Policentric
Regiocentric
Free trade
Economic Integration
Free Trade Area
Custom Union
Common Market
Treaty of Rome
Maastricht Accord
Market Economy
Command Economy
Mixed Economy
Foreign Exchange
Exchange Rate

Trade Control
Tariffs
Subsidies
Quotas
Common Law
Code Law
International Law
Power Distance
Technology Transfer
Exporting
Licensing
Franchising
Foreign Direct Investment
Multinational Enterprise
Joint Venture
Strategic Alliance
Wholly-owned Subsidiary
Domestic Organization
Export-oriented
International Organization
Multinational Form

CASE FOR ANALYSIS

NAFTA AND DOING BUSINESS IN MEXICO

Misconceptions about what effect the North American Free Trade Agreement will have on the U.S. worker abound. And predictions by billionaire businessman Ross Perot about "a giant sucking sound" that will take millions of U.S. jobs with it doesn't lessen anxieties.

There also is much skepticism about the obstacles that U.S. companies are likely to encounter when doing business south of the border. Mexico's past is replete with protectionist policies, complex regulations, a nearly nonexistent infrastructure, and ingrained bureaucratic corruption as a way of life. NAFTA calls for the phase-out of most regulatory edicts, but the timetable is ten years. It's doubtful that plant managers will be able to take advantage of bargain-priced labor without providing something in return. The quid pro quo will most likely involve providing housing, education, and medical care, for starters. Down the road, such matters as adequate roads and help with the myriad environmental problems of the region may come into play. The cost of such undertakings is unknown, but it could be very high.

The obstacles may well extend to the plant floor. Turnover tends to be high among workers in Mexico, where the idea of corporate loyalty has not yet taken hold.

"Often, workers will come up from the fields during the off-season to work for just a few months and return. Or a mother will make a few dollars, and then quit to take care of the children again," says one manager at Comair-Rotron, a firm in Tijuana. Absenteeism and tardiness are rife among unskilled workers, who grew up in rural areas and are unaccustomed to the discipline required to comply with strict schedules.

Capable local executives are in short supply. The best Mexican managers tend to opt for more lucrative jobs in the United States. Those that stay behind usually have neither the formal training nor the experience necessary to succeed in U.S. settings. Yet despite the high cost of hiring and training local workers for management jobs, U.S. firms find local know-how is essential for dealing with Mexico's political turmoil and labor conflicts.

SOURCES: Martha H. Peak, "Maquiladoras: Where Quality Is a Way of Life," *Management Review,* March 1993, 19–23; Laurence Hecht and Peter Morici, "Managing Risks in Mexico," *Harvard Business Review,* July–August 1993, 32–34; "Hi, Amigo," *The Economist,* December 12, 1992, 21–23; and Mariah E. deForest, "Are Maquiladoras a Menace to U.S. Workers?" *Business Horizons,* November–December 1991, 82–85.

■ QUESTIONS

1. Do you agree with Ross Perot's prediction that NAFTA will lead to the loss of U.S. jobs? How do your views reflect on the merits of free trade?
2. Describe the economic, legal/political, and socio-cultural factors that U.S. executives must be familiar with in order to do business in Mexico effectively.
3. What are some of the potential benefits for U.S. firms that extend their operations to the Mexican market? Considering the current business climate there, do you think the benefits outweigh the potential costs?

A CASE IN DIVERSITY

DEALING WITH DIVERSITY ABROAD

Solving diversity-based problems for U.S.-based managers is a challenging enough task. Their American counterparts overseas may face infinitely more complex choices, and the options often resemble the frying pan or fire choice. While equal opportunity and individual civil rights are the law of the land here, that frequently isn't the case abroad. So when moral and legal issues run counter to host country customs, business operations or individual employee welfare, or both, are bound to suffer.

Cultural differences are among the most difficult to surmount. AT&T asked New York-based consultants Cornelius Grove and Willa Hallowell to analyze gender and race issues around the world. Among their findings, they wrote that the ethical underpinnings that drive diversity issues at home don't necessarily exist abroad. They additionally reported that many societies consider ethnic differences as an appropriate criterion for employee work placement. For example, European descendants in Mexico are loathe to promote indigenous races to management posts. Japanese managers are only rarely and reluctantly conversant with East Indian employees, even those in positions of responsibility. Despite these findings, the two consultants recommend that U.S.

managers abroad ignore cultural norms and continue placing a premium on equality.

Ali Boureslan has had some practical, hard-knocks experience with discriminatory treatment overseas. When the Arabian American Oil. Co. engineer was transferred to Saudi Arabia, he says he was relentlessly ridiculed by his supervisor because he was of Lebanese extraction and a practicing Moslem. "As an American society, we are not free of this disease," Boureslan says. He was eventually fired. He filed suit against Aramco, and lost. Higher courts sustained the verdict, concurring that Congress never intended to extend anti-bias laws overseas. "It is a chauvinistic and imperialistic view that U.S. law is always better," says Aramco's attorney Paul L. Friedman.

The Equal Employment Opportunity Commission took up Boureslan's cause, as it moved through the slow appellate process. Meanwhile, multinationals pondered the potential Gordian knot of a domestic statute that would run directly contrary to laws of a foreign base of operations. Legal experts generally agree that cases like Boureslan's come down to whether the 1964 Civil Rights Act was intended to extend worldwide. That doesn't mean things are likely to get less complicated anytime soon. Proposals have been made that would extend anti-discrimination laws anywhere U.S. companies do business. For future managers, such fair-minded, well-intentioned legislation will likely not only make running a foreign-based operation infinitely more difficult, but legally perilous as well.

SOURCES: Leon E. Wynter, "Multiculturalism Stalls at the National Divide," *The Wall Street Journal,* Jan. 19, 1994, B1; Susan B. Garland, "Were Civil Rights Laws Meant To Travel?" *Business Week,* Jan. 31, 1991, 36.

■ QUESTIONS

1. Do you think U.S. civil rights laws should apply to American companies' foreign operations? Why or why not?
2. If you were setting policy for an American company operating overseas, what approach would you suggest that managers take in dealing with diversity issues outside the United States?
3. Discuss the contention that it is chauvinistic and imperialistic to believe that U.S. law is always better.

ENDNOTES

1. Tim Smart, Pete Engardio, and Jeri Smith, "GE's Brave New World," *Business Week,* November 8, 1993, 64–65.
2. Charles Hill, *International Business* (Burr Ridge, IL: Irwin, 1994), 4.
3. For a discussion see, for example, Arvind Phatak, *International Dimensions of Management* (Boston: PWS-Kent, 1989), 2.
4. John Daniels and Lee Radebaugh, *International Business* (Reading, MA: Addison-Wesley, 1994), 8.
5. Richard Robinson, *Internationalization of Business: An Introduction* (Hinsdale, IL: Dryden Press, 1984), 271–272.
6. Theodore Levitt, "The Globalization of Markets," *Harvard Business Review,* May–June 1983, 92–102.
7. See, for example, Jeremy Main, "How to Go Global—and Why," *Fortune,* August 28, 1989, 70.
8. Hill, *International Business,* 5; and Paul Dickens, *Global Shift* (New York: Guilford Press, 1992), 32.
9. Main, *How to Go Global,* 70.
10. Hill, *International Business,* 5–6.
11. Ted Rakstis, "Going Global," *Kiwanis Magazine,* October 19, 1991, 39.
12. "Grabbing New World Orders," *Business Week/Reinventing America,* 1992, 110–11.
13. David Francis, "Global Frontiers of Business," *The Christian Science Monitor,* April 11, 1991, 9.
14. Hill, *International Business,* pg. 6; and Michael McGrath and Richard Hoole, "Manufacturing's New Economies of Scale," *Harvard Business Review,* May–June, 1992, 94.
15. Based on ibid., 94–102.
16. Hill, *International Business,* 6.
17. For another perspective on global manufacturing, see Nigel Dunham and Robin Morgan, "The Search for a Truly Pan-European Manufacturing System," *The Journal of European Business,* September–October 1991, 43–47; for an interesting perspective on country content in various items, see Robert Reich, "The Myth of 'Made in the U.S.A.,'" *The Wall Street Journal,* July 5, 1991, A6.
18. Reich, "The Myth of 'Made in the U.S.A.,'" A6.
19. Based on Brian O'Reilly, "Your New Global Workforce," *Fortune,* December 14, 1992, 52–66.
20. Ibid., 64.
21. For example, this may leave many workers in the United States at a disadvantage as jobs go abroad. See Bernstein and Walecia Conrad and Louis Therren, "The Global Economy: Who Gets Hurt?" *Business Week,* August 10, 1992, 43–53.
22. Robert Reich, "Who Is Them?" *Harvard Business Review,* March–April 1991, 77–88.
23. Ibid., 78.
24. Philip Harris and Robert Moran, *Managing Cultural Differences* (Houston: Gulf Publishing Company, 1979), 1.
25. Marlene Piturro, "Super Manager!" *World Trade, International Business,* Annual Editions, 1982, 80–82.
26. William Taylor, "The Logic of Global Business: An Interview with ABB's Percy Barnevik," *Harvard Business Review,* March–April 1991, 94.

27. Howard Perlmutter, "The Torturous Evolution of the Multinational Corporation," *Columbia Journal of World Business,* vol. 4 (January–February 1969), 9–18.

28. For a discussion see, for example, Michael Czinkota, Pietra Rivoli, and Ilka Ronkinen, *International Business* (Ft. Worth: The Dryden Press, 1992), Chapter 2.

29. Czinkota et al., *International Business,* 116.

30. See, for example, Susan Lee, "Are We Building New Berlin Walls?" *Forbes,* January 7, 1991, 86–89.

31. Daniels and Radebaugh, *International Business,* 409.

32. Paul Dickens, *Global Shift* (New York: Guilford Press, 1992), 45; reprinted in Hill, *International Business,* 14.

33. *The Economist Book of Vital World Statistics* (New York: Random House, 1990); and Hill, *International Business,* 13.

34. Daniels and Radebaugh, *International Business,* 9–10.

35. "GDP Growth," *Fortune,* Special Issue, Autumn–Winter 1993, 77.

36. Ibid., 65.

37. Ibid., 64.

38. Bryan Moskal, "The World Trade Topography: How Level Is It?" *Industry Week,* May 18, 1992, 24–36.

39. Daniels and Radebaugh, *International Business,* 178.

40. Czinkota et al., *International Business,* 640.

41. Benjamin Weiner, "What Executives Should Know about Political Risk," *Management Review,* January 1992, 19–22.

42. Ibid., 85.

43. Philip Harris and Robert Moran, *Managing Cultural Differences* (Houston: Gulf Publishing Company, 1979), 227–28.

44. Geert Hofstede, "Cultural Dimensions in People Management," Vladimir Pucik, Noel Tichy, and Carole Barnett, eds. *Globalizing Management* (New York: John Wiley & Sons, Inc., 1992), 139–58.

45. Ibid., 143.

46. Ibid.

47. Ibid., 147.

48. Ibid.

49. Czinkota et al., *International Business,* 205.

50. United Nations, *Draft International Code of Conduct on the Transfer of Technology* (New York: United Nations, 1981), 3; quoted in Czinkota et al., *International Business,* 313.

51. Czinkota, *International Business,* 314.

52. Ted Rakstis, "Going Global," *Kiwanis Magazine,* October 1981, 39–43.

53. Thomas Clasen, "An Exporter's Guide to Selecting Foreign Sales Agents and Distributors," *The Journal of European Business,* vol. 3, no. 2, November–December 1991, 28–32.

54. Hill, *International Business,* 402.

55. Art Garcia, "It's in the Mail," *World Trade,* April 1992, 56–62.

56. See, for example, Daniels and Radebaugh, *International Business,* 544.

57. Czinkota et al., *International Business,* 278.

58. Hill, *International Business,* 411.

59. Daniels and Radebaugh, *International Business,* G-19.

60. Kenichi Ohmae, "The Global Logic of Strategic Alliances," *Harvard Business Review,* March–April 1989, 143–54.

61. Katherine Rudie Harrigan, "Joint Ventures and Global Strategies," *Columbia Journal of World Business,* vol. 19 (Summer 1984), 7–16; Czinkota et al., *International Business,* 320.

62. Ohmae, "The Global Logic," 143.

63. Robert Neff, "Guess Who's Selling Barbies in Japan Now?" *Business Week,* December 9, 1991, 72, 74, 76.

64. Arvind Phatak, *International Dimensions of Management* (Boston: PWS-Kent, 1989), 46–49.

65. John Rossant, "After the Scandals," *Business Week,* November 22, 1993, 56–57.

66. Anant Negandhi, *International Management* (Newton, MA: Allyn & Bacon, Inc., 1987), 231.

67. Richad D. Robinson, *Internationalization of Business: An Introduction* (Hinsdale, IL: The Dryden Press, 1984), 227–28.

68. See also S.M. Davis, "Managing and Organizing Multinational Corporations," C.A. Bartlett and S. Ghoshal, eds., *Transnational Management* (Homewood, IL: Richard D. Irwin, 1992). See also Phatak, *International Dimensions,* 78–104.

69. Paul Blockyn, "Developing the International Executive," *Personnel,* March 1989, 44.

70. Madelyn Callahan, "Preparing the New Global Manager," *Training and Development Journal,* March 1989, 30.

71. Joseph Fucini and Suzy Fucini, *Working for the Japanese* (New York: The Free Press, 1990), 122–23.

CHAPTER 3

MANAGEMENT ETHICS AND SOCIAL RESPONSIBILITY

LEARNING OBJECTIVES

After studying this chapter, you should be able to:

- Explain why ethical decisions can have extended consequences as well as personal implications.

- Differentiate between normative and moral judgments.

- Describe what makes a decision ethical.

- Compare and contrast ways in which moral standards differ from nonmoral ones.

- Discuss the extent to which adhering to the law guarantees the making of ethical decisions.

- List factors that influence ethical behavior at work.

- Name several lessons that can be learned from existing corporate ethics programs.

- Define corporate social responsibility and discuss the differing views on the purpose of the corporation.

- Detail some mechanisms firms use to improve their social responsiveness.

OPENING PROBLEM
GENERAL DYNAMICS

In the 1980s, General Dynamics was faced with allegations of everything from bribing foreign officials to overcharging the government. In one case, senior managers were accused of adding $64 million in improper overhead expenses to defense contract bills. The expenses ranged from country club memberships to dog kennel fees.

■ A company that gets 95 percent of its income from governments should know better, and in 1985 the Defense Department suspended GD from bidding on new Pentagon business. Within a year, the company's share of the Tomahawk cruise missile contract was trimmed by a third, and sales dropped by $24 million. In the management shake-up that ensued, Stanley Pace took over as chairman and chief executive officer. He brought with him some very good ideas about how to restore GD's ethical conduct and in the process reestablish the firm's integrity with the U.S. Defense Department.[1] He would need all the good ideas that he could muster.

THE NATURE OF BUSINESS ETHICS

THE ETHICAL CHALLENGE AT WORK

Ethical choices surround us every day. An engineer discovers a product design flaw that constitutes a safety hazard. Her company, when informed, declines to correct the flaw and she decides to keep quiet, rather than taking the complaint outside the firm.[2] A purchasing agent receives a bottle of whisky from a supplier as a Christmas gift and phones to say thanks.[3] A firm pays a $350,000 "consulting fee" to a government official of a foreign company; in return, he promises to help the firm obtain a contract that should generate $10 million in sales.[4] A sales manager and his wife entertain friends at a top restaurant. He charges the bill to his expense account under the notation "dined with potential customers."[5]

These ethical dilemmas are fictional, but they are representative of real choices that real managers make. For example, senior General Dynamics managers did add $64 million of improper overhead expenses (including the country club memberships and dog kennel fees) to GD's bill for defense contracts in the early 1980s.[6] Sales executives at a firm making artificial eye lenses did provide "free use of a yacht off Florida, travel in Europe, all-expense paid and week-long training seminars in the Bahamas, second homes, and cash rebates for buying their lenses rather than their competitors'."[7] And, on February 10, 1992, Dow Corning did replace its CEO and reveal it had received complaints for decades about medical problems with its silicone breast implants; the complaints ranged from immunological problems to scleroderma—a disease in which the skin thickens and stiffens and there is a buildup of fibrous tissue in the lungs and other organs.[8] Thomas Talcott, a Dow Corning materials engineer for 24 years, had quit in 1976 over the safety of the implants; his warnings went unheeded until 1991, when he testified as an expert witness in one recipient's lawsuit.

SOME CHARACTERISTICS OF ETHICAL PROBLEMS IN MANAGEMENT

Ethical decisions like these have characteristics that make them very serious issues for all managers.[9] First, *most ethical decisions have extended consequences*. For example, the negative consequences of taking a bribe or failing to follow up on product hazards evidence are not limited to the people involved, or to the company itself. Instead, bribes may distort government bidding procedures and lead to the purchase of products, such as defective jet engines, that may be dangerous for the application. Unsafe products like silicone implants can destroy lives and families.

Second, ethical decisions have *unpredictable consequences*. When stockbroker Michael Levine gave inside information to banker Ivan Boesky, he was unaware of the chain of events he was triggering, one of which eventually led to junk bond king Michael Milken going to jail. As one expert put it, "it is not always clear what consequences will follow from most ethical choices."[10]

Ethical decisions also always have *personal implications* (as Levine and Milken learned to their chagrin). In other words, ethical decisions are never entirely divorced from the lives and careers of the managers who make them. For example, questionable ethical decisions, like those regarding breast implants or insider trading, often blow up in the manager's face, taking his or her career and livelihood with them. Even apparently trivial unethical decisions may have a corrosive effect on a manager's reputation, slowly eroding his or her sense of self-worth as "taking the easy way out" becomes habitual.

ETHICS DEFINED

Ethics may be defined as the study of standards of conduct and moral judgment.[11] Ethics, says one expert, "refers to standards of right conduct."[12] Another calls ethics "the principles of conduct governing an individual or a group."[13] Notice that in popular usage *ethics* may primarily refer (as in the first definition) to a theoretical study or (in the latter definition) to the principles of conduct by which people run their lives. In either case, ethical decisions always involve both normative judgments and moral judgments.[14]

NORMATIVE JUDGMENTS   Making ethical decisions first implies a right and wrong way to proceed, and therefore involves a normative judgment. A **normative judgment** states or implies "that something is good or bad, right or wrong, better or worse, or to be or not to be."[15] (Ethics expert Manuel Velasquez points out that normative judgments always express values, since values reflect our beliefs about what is good or bad, important or unimportant.) Thus, a **non-normative judgment** simply names, defines, or reports a certain state of affairs, such as "your office is furnished with a desk and two chairs." The normative version of that non-normative observation might then be "your office is too sparsely furnished." (Similarly, "You are wearing a skirt and a blouse" is a non-normative statement; "That's a great outfit!" is a normative one.)

MORAL JUDGMENTS   However, ethical decisions don't just involve normative, evaluative choices in a general sense. Instead, ethical choices always involve fundamental *moral* principles of right and wrong. (For example, there are grammatical rules regarding what is correct and incorrect regarding word placement. We could make a normative judgment that "that paragraph is ungrammatical." However, that would not be an ethical or moral judgment, just a normative one.)

In ethical judgments, the standards of right and wrong are always moral ones. A decision is therefore ethical (or unethical) to the extent that it does not (or does) violate fundamental moral standards.

Moral standards differ from non-moral ones in five main ways:[16]

1. Moral standards address matters of serious consequence to human well-being. Moral standards against murder, lying, slander, or price-fixing exist because there is a consensus that such actions pose a serious threat to individuals or society's well-being.

2. Moral standards cannot be established or changed by decisions of authoritative bodies like legislatures. Companies, legislatures, even Congress cannot create moral standards by legislating company codes or laws. It is true that a company's code of ethics or a state's body of laws may be written to reflect what is wrong or right in a moral sense. But, the law cannot make something morally right just by saying it is legal. Nor, for that matter, can the law make something that is morally right morally wrong. Instead, the question of what is morally right or wrong transcends the actions of authoritative bodies.[17]

3. Moral standards should also override self-interest. Thus, if you have a moral obligation to do something, you are expected to do it, even if doing so might (for instance) impede your career or cost you money.

4. Moral standards are based on universal, impartial considerations. In other words, moral judgments are never situational. Something that is morally right (or wrong) in one situation is similarly right (or wrong) in another. For example, the fact that your company will benefit if you pay a bribe does not make

ETHICS
The study of standards of conduct and moral judgment; also, standards of right conduct.

NORMATIVE JUDGMENT
States or implies that something is good or bad, right or wrong, better or worse.

NON-NORMATIVE JUDGMENT
Names, defines, or reports a certain state of affairs.

MORAL STANDARDS
A set of beliefs regarding right or wrong that address matters of serious consequences to human well-being. These are also characterized by the fact that they cannot be established or changed by decisions of authoritative bodies like legislatures; should override self-interest; and that they are based on universal, impartial considerations.

the bribe right; the fact that someone is a tyrant doesn't necessarily make it right to kill him.

5. Moral judgments tend to trigger special emotions. For example, violating moral standards may make you feel ashamed or remorseful. Similarly, if you see someone else acting immorally, you may feel indignant or resentful. Immoral decisions thus tend to be associated with strong emotional feelings.[18]

ETHICS AND THE LAW

It is possible to look at a decision that involves ethics (such as firing an employee) and to make the decision strictly based upon what is legal. However, there is no guarantee that the decision will thus be ethical. Nor, for that matter, is there any guarantee that the decision will be unethical just because you failed to follow the law. This is because a decision can be legal but still unethical. While what is legal and what is ethical may overlap, the correlation is far from perfect. As a result, the law, by itself, is an inadequate guide to ethical decision making.

This is certainly the case in aberrant situations such as that which occurred in Nazi Germany, where many transparently unethical laws were passed. However, the same applies in everyday situations, too. For example, firing a 38-year-old employee just before her pension becomes vested may be unethical, but generally it is not illegal. Similarly, charging a naive customer an exorbitant price may be legal but still unethical. A decision can also be ethical but illegal. For example, some municipalities still have so-called blue laws, which prohibit doing business on Sundays. A firm doing business on Sunday would be breaking the law. However, would the firm be acting unethically? Some might say yes, and some no. In any case, it is a mistake to assume that *legal* automatically means *ethical*.[19]

An increasingly prevalent example illustrates this point. Many modern-day retailers pry into their customers' buying habits by using a variety of electronic and infrared surveillance equipment.[20] For example, Videocart, Inc., of Chicago uses infrared sensors in store ceilings to track shopping carts; other firms compile information from credit card purchases to determine individual customers' buying habits. These activities are not illegal at the present time. But many believe that such encroachment into one's privacy is unethical.

FACTORS INFLUENCING
ETHICAL BEHAVIOR AT WORK

What factors influence whether specific individuals in specific organizations make ethical or unethical decisions? There are several.

THE INDIVIDUAL

First, much of the blame for unethical decisions (and the credit for ethical ones) must sit squarely on the shoulders of the one who has the most influence over whether the "right" decision is made or not, namely the individual himself or herself. Managers bring to their jobs their own ideas of what is right or what is wrong. And, as with other facets of one's personality, a person's ethics reflect the sum total of that individual's experiences, education, and upbringing. Every decision you make and every action you take will reflect, for better or worse, the application of your moral standards to the question at hand. As Professor Laroue Tone Hosmer puts it:

Moral standards differ between individuals because the ethical systems of belief—the values or priorities, the convictions that people think are truly important and upon which their moral standards are based—also differ. These beliefs depend upon each person's family background, cultural heritage, church association, educational experience and other factors.[21]

It is difficult to generalize about the characteristics of ethical versus unethical people. In one study, 421 employees were surveyed to measure the degree to which age, gender, marital status, education, dependent children status, region of the country, and years in business influenced ethical decision making.[22] Each respondent was asked to rate the acceptability of ethically loaded situations such as "doing personal business on company time," "not reporting others' violations of company rules and policies," and "calling in sick to take a day off for personal use." With the exception of age, all the other variables—gender, marital status, education, and so on—were poor predictors of whether a person would or would not make the "right" decision. However, older workers in general had stricter interpretations of ethical standards. To that extent, they could reasonably be expected to make more ethical decisions than younger employees, other things equal.

A sort of generation gap in business ethics has been found by other researchers, too.[23] One study by Baylor University researchers surveyed 2,156 individuals who were grouped by age: those aged 21–40 represented the younger group and those aged 51–70 represented the older group. As in the previous study, respondents were asked to rate the acceptability of a number of ethics-related vignettes, such as "an executive earning $50,000 a year padded his expense account about $1,500 a year."[24] The 16 ethical vignettes and related data are presented in Figures 3.1 and 3.2.

In virtually every case, the older group viewed the ethically questionable decision as more unacceptable than did the younger group. This is illustrated in Figure 3.2. A larger percentage of older respondents generally chose "never acceptable" as reflecting their opinions of the managerial choices that had been made. Such findings certainly do not suggest that all older employees are ethical, or that younger ones are unethical. However, they do raise the question of whether the relative lack of experience of younger employees leaves them more open to making the "wrong" decision.

It is also particularly interesting to note that individuals consistently see themselves acting more ethically than others.[25] In other words, most people tend to view themselves as more ethical than "the next guy or gal," and that can give someone a very false sense of ethical security.

THE POWER OF THE SITUATION

To what extent might an otherwise ethical person be coerced by the situation into taking actions that are not just unethical but severely so? That was the question that researcher Stanley Milgram started out to study a number of years ago. His results—repeated many times since then—shed some startling light on the issue.[26] Milgram's experiment, originally conducted at Yale University in the early 1960s, set out to answer this specific question: in a laboratory situation, if an experimenter tells a subject to act with increasing severity against another person, under what conditions will the subject comply, and under what conditions will he or she disobey? In each of these experiments, two people come to a psychology laboratory supposedly to take part in a study of memory and learning. One of them is designated a "teacher" and the other a "learner." They are told that the study is concerned with the effects of punishment on learning. The learner (who is actually one of the researchers) is conducted to a room and seated in a chair with his or her arms strapped and an electrode attached

FIGURE 3.1

Ethical Vignettes

SOURCE: Justin G. Longe-
necker, McKinney and Carlos
Moore, "The Generation Gap
in Business," *Business Horizons*, September–October
1989.

The following are the 16 vignettes used in the study. Those on which the older group's more negative responses were statistically significant are marked with an asterisk.

A.* An executive earning $50,000 a year padded his expense account about $1,500 a year.

B. In order to increase profits, a general manager used a production process which exceeded legal limits for environmental pollution.

C.* Because of pressure from his brokerage firm, a stockbroker recommended a type of bond which he did not consider to be a good investment.

D.* A small business received one-fourth of its gross revenue in the form of cash. The owner reported only one-half of the cash receipts for income tax purposes.

E. A company paid a $350,000 "consulting" fee to an official of a foreign country. In return, the official promised assistance in obtaining a contract which should produce $10 million profit for the contracting company.

F.* A company president found that a competitor had made an important scientific discovery which would sharply reduce the profits of his own company. He then hired a key employee of the competitor in an attempt to learn the details of the discovery.

G.* A highway building contractor deplored the chaotic bidding situation and cutthroat competition. He, therefore, reached an understanding with other major contractors to permit bidding which would provide a reasonable profit.

H.* A company president recognized that sending expensive Christmas gifts to purchasing agents might compromise their positions. However, he continued the policy since it was common practice and changing it would result in loss of business.

I.* A corporate director learned that his company intended to announce a stock split and increase its dividend. On the basis of this information, he bought additional shares and sold them at a gain following the announcement.

J. A corporate executive promoted a loyal friend and competent manager to the position of divisional vice-president in preference to a better-qualified manager with whom he had no close ties.

K. An engineer discovered what he perceived to be a product design flaw which constituted a safety hazard. His company declined to correct the flaw. The engineer decided to keep quiet, rather than taking his complaint outside the company.

L.* A comptroller selected a legal method of financial reporting which concealed some embarrassing financial facts which would otherwise have become public knowledge.

M. An employer received applications for a supervisor's position from two equally qualified applicants but hired the male applicant because he thought that some employees might resent being supervised by a female.

N. As part of the marketing strategy for a product, the producer changed its color and marketed it as "new and improved," even though its other characteristics were unchanged.

O.* A cigarette manufacturer launched a publicity campaign challenging new evidence from the Surgeon General's office that cigarette smoking is harmful to the smoker's health.

P.* An owner of a small firm obtained a free copy of a copyrighted computer software program from a business friend rather than spending $500 to obtain his own program from the software dealer.

to each wrist. The learner is told (in front of the teacher) that he or she is to learn a list of words and will receive an electric shock whenever he or she makes an error.

The experiment's real focus is the teacher. After watching the learner being strapped into place, the teacher is taken to a room and seated before what appears to be a shock generator with a horizontal line of thirty switches ranging from fifteen volts to 450 volts. The teacher is then told to administer the "learning test" to the learner on the other side of the window. Every time the learner gives an incorrect answer, the teacher

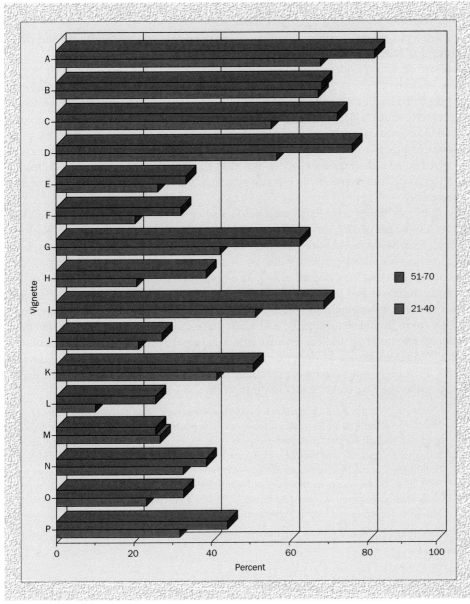

FIGURE 3.2

Ethical Vignettes "Never Acceptable" Responses by Age Group

This figure shows the percent of each age group (young and old) that responded "never acceptable" to each of the 16 (A–P) "ethically questionable" vignettes.

is to give the person an electric shock, starting at 15 volts and increasing in 15 volt increments after that. (Remember that the learner actually receives no shock at all.)

The point of the experiment is to see how far the teacher will go in apparently (and unethically) inflicting increasing pain on a protesting victim. At 75 volts, the learner grunts; at 120 volts he or she complains verbally; at 150 the learner demands to be released from the experiment. The learner's protests become increasingly vehement and emotional, until at 285 volts the learner is screaming hysterically.

According to Milgram, the results of his study "are both surprising and dismaying." Although many of the teachers experienced stress and protested to the experimenter, almost two-thirds turned out to be obedient subjects, continuing to administer shocks until the end of the scale. These subjects, remember, were not from some sadistic fringe of society, but "were ordinary people drawn from working, managerial and professional classes." Milgram concluded that the ordinary person who shocked the victim "did so out of a sense of obligation, a conception of his or her duties as a subject—and not from a peculiarly aggressive tendency."

Interestingly, the "teachers" working under the researchers' authority did not really lose what Milgram called their "moral sense." Instead, they shifted that sense of right and wrong to a consideration of how well they were living up to the expectations that the authority figure had for them. Other explanations have been offered for the worrying behavior of the teachers. However, the fact remains that perfectly normal subjects were much more willing than you might have imagined "just to follow orders" and to substitute the researchers' sense of right and wrong for their own personal value scale. In other words, people in this experiment obeyed simply because they had elected to join the organization (in this case the experiment) and viewed following orders as part of their jobs. It is a scary finding that all employees would do well to remember.

Can such things happen in practice? Psychologist Saul Gellerman concluded that the answer was yes. He describes how more than 40 years ago, information began to reach John Manville Corporation's medical department—and through it the firm's top executives—implicating asbestos inhalation as a cause of asbestosis (a debilitating lung disease) as well as lung cancer among its employees. Subsequent testimony in a California court revealed that Manville had hidden the asbestos danger from its employees rather than looking into safer ways to handle it.[27] A New Jersey court was blunt. That court "found that Manville had made a conscious, cold-blooded business decision to take no protective or remedial action, in flagrant disregard of the rights of others."[28] After reviewing all the evidence, Gellerman concluded that it is inconceivable that 40 years of Manville managers could all have been immoral. Instead, his explanation has the ring of Milgram's findings to it:

> The truth, I think, is less glamorous—and also less satisfying to those who like to explain evil as the actions of a few misbegotten souls. The people involved were probably ordinary men and women for the most part, not very different from you and me. They found themselves in a dilemma, and they solved it in a way that seemed to be the least troublesome, deciding not to disclose information that could hurt their product. The consequences of what they chose to do—both to thousands of innocent people, and, ultimately, to the corporation—probably never occurred to them. . . . The Manville case illustrates the fine line between acceptable and unacceptable managerial behavior.[29]

The *Ethics Survey* vignette further illustrates the often situational nature of ethical decisions.

THE BOSS'S INFLUENCE

Several surveys indicate that the behavior of one's superiors is one of the most important factors influencing ethical decisions.[30] More disturbingly, most managers even seem to feel that unethical actions are acceptable if their superior knows about them and says nothing.

In other words, employees definitely take their ethical cues from what they see their managers doing. One writer gives these examples of how a supervisor can advertently (or inadvertently) lead his or her subordinates ethically astray:

- Tell staffers to "do whatever is necessary" to achieve results.
- Overload top performers to ensure work gets done.
- Look the other way when wrongdoing occurs. Take credit for other's work or shift blame. Play favorites.[31]

The *Intuit* Small Business box shows how one entrepreneur set the ethical tune for his software start-up.

The complexities of Wall Street trading make it difficult to control unethical practices. Mary Jo White, head of the U.S. Attorney's Office for the Southern District of New York, feels that pursuing white-collar criminals is a "special responsibility," no matter how victimless the crime seems. She is investigating phantom trades and misrepresentation of financial information and investment opportunities at several large institutions.

ETHICS SURVEY

An *Industry Week* survey of 1,300 mid-level managers from companies with a minimum of 500 employees suggests that just 2 percent of respondents would go through with a foolproof plan to steal $100,000 from the company; only 1 percent would accept money under the table for the preferential treatment of a supplier or other business associate. But the ethical veneer tarnishes somewhat when ethical questions shift from grand theft and kickbacks to the more usual temptations of daily business life.

When presented with a competitive bidding situation where a rival had several months advantage in development and manufacturing time, respondents varied widely in how they would handle deadline queries from the client. The majority, or 58 percent, would come clean with the facts about the time required to fill the order. Just over a quarter would attempt to deflect the question by highlighting product features deemed superior to the competitor's. However, 13 percent would brazenly inform the client they could match the faster schedule and try and wing it later on.

In the area of discrimination, only one in ten respondents admitted bias against women. The response was about the same for the uneven treatment of minorities. The most aggrieved segment, according to the survey, are gay employees, and the prejudicial severity increased proportionately with the position's visibility and level of responsibility. More than a third would not hire an admitted homosexual for a virtually invisible production line job; just over half would disqualify a management or sales candidate for the same reason.

What the survey proves remains open to question. It was administered on a voluntary and confidential basis. The final query related to the truthfulness of the responses that came before. Sixty-five managers, or 5 percent of the total, admitted they had lied on one or more of the responses.

SOURCE: David R. Altany, "Torn Between Halo & Horns," *Industry Week,* March 15, 1993, 15–20.

ETHICS POLICIES AND CODES

While the boss's actions have been described as possibly "the single most important factor in fostering corporate behavior of a high ethical standard," surveys usually rank ethics policy as very important, too.[32] This is why the report of the U.S. National Commission on Fraudulent Financial Reporting recommended that firms develop and implement codes of conduct.[33]

Many firms do have such codes. One study surveyed corporate management accountants. The researchers found that 56 percent of the respondents' firms had corporate codes of conduct, but the existence of codes ranged widely with firm size. For example (as summarized in Figure 3.3), 77 percent of the firms with net worth more than $100 million had corporate codes of conduct, as compared with about half of mid-size firms, and just less than one fourth of smaller firms. What follows are some other conclusions the researchers arrived at.[34]

INTUIT

Ethical decisions usually come relatively easy when business is good; hard times are often a different matter altogether. Scott Cook faced such a situation in 1984 when he launched Intuit, a software company based in Menlo Park, California. His start-up bankroll of $151,000 was devoured almost instantly as Intuit developed its Quicken check-writing software. Cook's two principal competitors collectively spent $7 million on marketing alone.

Partly because of the hard times, ethical questions seemed to be falling out of the sky. What could he promise customers? What could he promise employees? How could he window-dress the financial condition of his company without flagrantly abusing the truth?

Cook had heard the conventional arguments about the virtual necessity of artful posturing for start-up operations. He disagreed. His view was that any enterprise should be based on being truthful and straightforward with customers. Deception, he believed, only temporarily smoothed the descending pathway to oblivion.

Despite his financial concerns, Cook chose to urge dealers and retailers to buy less of his software than they might

originally request. This piece of advice was unusual in an industry that has long lived by the axiom that oversupplied customers are loyal customers because they will have to work overtime getting rid of surplus product while neglecting competitors. Cook calls that a bad ethical decision, and a bad business one. Keeping customers' inventories at the proper levels has a couple of benefits. Consistent sales levels mean manufacturing schedules can be smoothed out, avoiding frenetic output

**FOCUS ON
SMALL BUSINESS**

followed by virtual shutdowns. Ensuring that customers are properly supplied also reduces customer's inventory costs. Perhaps most important over the long-term, Cook believes Intuit clients develop a trusting relationship with the company that translates into loyalty. Recommendations from salespeople are then taken seriously, and vendors become partners.

Cook thinks it more ethical to maintain uniform pricing as well. Even

though all of Intuit's big accounts get a uniform quote, it does not stop volume dealers from lobbying for an edge. Cook's answer is also always uniform. His price is the best deal possible, and knocking off a percentage for one customer amounts to misleading all the others to whom he made the same pledge.

According to Cook, most start-ups compromise ethical standards because they focus more on the possibility of failure than the potential for success. Businesses that don't shoot straight with customers and do succeed must then operate with a tainted corporate culture, says Cook. The opposite is also true, and employees will look to top managers for ethical guidance. Therefore, although Intuit suffered more than its share of adversity in its first three years of existence, Cook never wavered from one conviction: the ethics established and adhered to from day one would outlast him. Intuit now employs 400 people and annual revenue for 1992 was expected to be around $80 million. "If you've got a choice about the culture you create," asks Cook, "why build it on a foundation of fraud?"

SOURCE: Scott Cook, "The Ethics of Bootstrapping," *Inc.*, September 1992, 87–95.

IMPACT OF CODE   The researchers concluded that "in order for a corporate code of conduct to be effective, the 'tone at the top' must be positive and reflect a proactive management."[35] Among other things, this means that top management must make it clear that it is serious about code enforcement. Top management also must ensure that customers, suppliers, and employees are all aware of the firm's stress on good ethics. The *Levi Strauss* vignette (on page 70) shows how one firm puts its ethics code into practice.

APPROVAL OF CODE   Top management must emphasize its support. The researchers concluded that "it is important for the code to be endorsed by executives at or near the top of the organization chart and by employees throughout the organization."[36] In 95 percent of the firms with codes, the code had been approved by the CEO, board of directors, or both.

COMMUNICATION OF CODE   To influence employee behavior, the ethics code must be communicated. The researchers found that the first step was generally to have

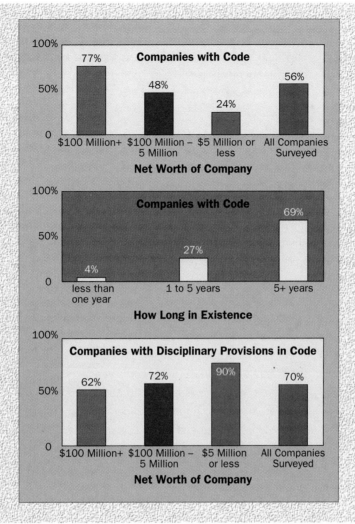

FIGURE 3.3

Survey: Ethics Codes in
Corporate America

*Ethics codes are especially pre-
dominant among larger firms
and most firms with such codes
have had them for 5 or more
years.*

SOURCE: Robert Sweeney and
Howard Siers, "Survey: Ethics
in Corporate America," *Management Accounting*, June
1990.

top management assign responsibility for implementation of the code to a high-rank-
ing manager. He or she in turn communicates the ethics code to employees. Although
this is an important step, only about 57 percent of the firms actually sent a copy of
their conduct codes to all employees.

ETHICS PROGRAMS IN PRACTICE

We can get a better perspective on how to encourage ethical behavior by looking more
closely at how several firms actually manage their corporate ethics programs. We will
look specifically at two firms, Johnson & Johnson and Norton.

THE JOHNSON & JOHNSON PROGRAM

Ethical decision making at Johnson & Johnson has long been symbolized by what the
company calls "our credo." The credo, which is presented in its entirety in Figure 3.4
on page 72, provides the ethical pillars on which the firm is built and on which it

LEVI STRAUSS & CO.

Levi Strauss & Co. has a longer continuous history than many nations, and since its founding in 1853, the company's personal, family, social, and religious values have been maintained. Regarding Levi's long-standing approach to ethical behavior, vice-president of corporate affairs Robert Dunn says, "We have articulated a vision that goes beyond selling our product, and we have committed to it. If there's a conflict, ethical values must prevail."

At Levi Strauss, managers have to do more than talk about ethics. Bonuses and salary increases are partly contingent upon performance evaluations that take ethical behavior into consideration. The policy leads to a mutually desired result: ethical managers are attracted to a company that shares and nurtures their personal values. It has led to something else as well. In 1993 the company's executive management committee renamed itself the Global Leadership Team and announced that in addition to management it would emphasize ethical considerations in all company decisions.

This group also did more than talk. International contractors in China and Burma who were determined to be human rights violators (for instance by using child labor) were terminated. Potentially closing off, even temporarily, the billion-plus Chinese market was widely criticized, but Levi management took the long view and refused to compromise. Ethical actions, the company believed, meant taking into consideration everyone who might be affected by a decision. "The experience of this company is that when we do what we believe is right, the company has benefited from standing by its convictions," says Dunn.

SOURCE: "Lasting Value, Levi Strauss," *Business Ethics,* November–December 1993, 28.

---

continues to produce its pharmaceutical and health products. The credo begins with the statement that "we believe our first responsibility is to the doctors, nurses and patients, to mothers and all others who use our products and services."[37] Other elements include "in meeting their needs, everything we do must be of high quality" and "our suppliers and distributors must have an opportunity to make a fair profit."

Stories abound about how the credo's moral standards channel ethical decision making at the firm. One story concerns how Johnson & Johnson reacted to the discovery of a few poisoned Tylenol capsules several years ago. Given that "our first responsibility is to the doctors, nurses and patients . . ." Johnson & Johnson decided to recall all outstanding capsules, so as to protect all those who might use its product.

Indeed, virtually everything the company does is linked to its credo; in this way, the founders' high ethical standards have taken root throughout the firm. For instance, the company's college recruiting brochure emphasizes that "the Johnson & Johnson credo—a statement of corporate responsibility—spells it out . . ."[38] Many employees keep copies of the credo in their offices, and, reportedly, all employees talk animatedly of the standards and spirit symbolized by the credo.

A worker in Levi's El Paso plant wheels components across the shop floor. Plant closings in the United States and abroad have led management to think long and hard about its treatment of remaining workers. Ethical considerations are a primary part of Levi's management approach.

The short and simple credo has also been described as the glue that holds this complex firm together.[39] Johnson & Johnson is a widely diversified international corporation with over 160 businesses in 50 countries. Its products range from baby powder to toothbrushes and from pain relievers to contact lenses.[40] It is also highly decentralized, with the presidents of its subsidiaries "usually left very much on their own in terms of the way in which they will manage their particular company."[41] By evaluating, promoting, and continually reminding all employees of the credo's importance the firm has, in a sense, created an organization of believers. Whether those believers are working in Asia, South America, France, or the United States, the firm's home office can be assured that the company's ethical values will be adhered to by employees around the world.

THE NORTON COMPANY

Norton is a diversified, multinational manufacturer of industrial products including grinding wheels, abrasives, and advanced ceramics and plastics. Sales today are about $1.5 billion, and the firm has manufacturing plants in 27 countries.

The three main features of the Norton Ethics Program are a code of conduct, an ethics committee of the board of directors, and an annual ethics review.[42] The code itself, called "the Norton Policy of Business Ethics," contains 12 pages. It combines general guidelines with specific rules regarding responsibility to employees, customers,

FIGURE 3.4

Johnson & Johnson's
Corporate Credo

SOURCE: "Corporate Ethics: A
Prime Business Asset," *The
Business Roundtable*,
February 1988.

Our Credo

We believe our first responsibility is to the doctors, nurses and patients,
to mothers and fathers and all others who use our products and services.
In meeting their needs everything we do must be of high quality.
We must constantly strive to reduce our costs
in order to maintain reasonable prices.
Customers' orders must be serviced promptly and accurately.
Our suppliers and distributors must have an opportunity
to make a fair profit.

We are responsible to our employees,
the men and women who work with us throughout the world.
Everyone must be considered as an individual.
We must respect their dignity and recognize their merit.
They must have a sense of security in their jobs.
Compensation must be fair and adequate,
and working conditions clean, orderly and safe.
We must be mindful of ways to help our employees fulfill
their family responsibilities.
Employees must feel free to make suggestions and complaints.
There must be equal opportunity for employment, development
and advancement for those qualified.
We must provide competent management,
and their actions must be just and ethical.

We are responsible to the communities in which we live and work
and to the world community as well.
We must be good citizens — support good works and charities
and bear our fair share of taxes.
We must encourage civic improvements and better health and education.
We must maintain in good order
the property we are privileged to use,
protecting the environment and natural resources.

Our final responsibility is to our stockholders.
Business must make a sound profit.
We must experiment with new ideas.
Research must be carried on, innovative programs developed
and mistakes paid for.
New equipment must be purchased, new facilities provided
and new products launched.
Reserves must be created to provide for adverse times.
When we operate according to these principles,
the stockholders should realize a fair return.

Johnson & Johnson

suppliers, shareholders, local communities, and the general public. The ethics policy is currently printed in eight languages and distributed to every Norton manager. New employees receive a copy of the policy almost immediately. No formal ethics training occurs during the firm's management training program, but frequent ethics seminars emphasize the importance of ethics and the company's ethics code.

Code compliance is monitored in two ways. First, top management annually solicits letters from the top 100 managers worldwide asking them to "specify any significant violations of the ethics policy which have occurred and any important cases which might be regarded as controversial."[43] At this time, managers are also asked to review the performance of their subordinates on ethics. Then, the ethics committee of the firm's board of directors meets to review the annual ethics letters, to discuss and resolve any unresolved ethics issues, and to prepare a final report to the full board of directors.

ETHICS: THE LESSONS LEARNED

After a review of the ethics programs at eleven major firms, one study concluded that several lessons could be learned regarding how to build an effective ethics program:

1. *Emphasize top management's commitment.* "In the experience of these companies with regard to corporate ethics, no point emerges more clearly than the crucial role of top management. To achieve results, the chief executive officer and those around the CEO need to be openly and strongly committed to ethical conduct, and give constant leadership in tending and renewing the values of the organization."[44]

2. *Publish a "code."* Next, firms with effective ethics programs set forth principles of conduct for the whole organization in the form of written documents. These generally cover areas such as fundamental honesty and adherence to laws; product safety and quality; health and safety in the workplace; conflicts of interest; employment practices; fairness in selling/marketing practices; financial reporting; supplier relationships; pricing, billing, and contracting; trading in securities/using inside information; payments to obtain business/Foreign Corrupt Practices Act; acquiring and using information about others; security; political activities; protection of the environment; and intellectual property/proprietary information.[45]

3. *Establish compliance mechanisms.* Establish mechanisms to ensure compliance with company standards. Mechanisms include management attention paid to values and ethics in recruiting and hiring; emphasis on corporate ethics in training; communications programs to inform and motivate employees; periodic certification of adherence to standards; auditing to ensure compliance; and enforcement procedures, including discipline and dismissal.[46]

4. *Involve personnel at all levels.* Developing effective corporate ethics programs requires the involvement by those whose behavior the ethics policies are to influence. Therefore, round-table discussions among small groups of employees regarding corporate ethics and employee surveys of attitudes regarding the state of ethics in their firm are important.

5. *Measure results.* While the end results cannot be precisely measured, all of the firms studied used methods such as surveys and audits to monitor compliance with ethical standards.[47]

CONTRASTING VIEWS
OF SOCIAL RESPONSIBILITY

ETHICS AND SOCIAL RESPONSIBILITY

SOCIAL RESPONSIBILITY
Refers to the extent to which companies should and do channel resources toward improving the quality of life of one or more segments of society other than the firm's own stockholders.

Corporate **social responsibility** refers to the extent to which companies should and do channel resources toward improving the quality of life of one or more segments of society other than the firm's own stockholders. Socially responsible behavior thus might include creating jobs for minorities, controlling pollution, or supporting educational facilities or cultural events. At one level, social responsibility is essentially an ethical issue, since it involves questions of what is morally right or wrong with regard to the firm's responsibilities. As you will see, though, there is less unanimity regarding what is right or wrong in this area than there is with respect to traditional ethical issues such as bribery, stealing, and corporate dishonesty. Many perfectly ethical people strongly believe that a company's only social responsibility is to its shareholders.

The link between ethics and social responsibility is perhaps the clearest when the social responsibility is to the firm's customers or employees. John Manville's alleged asbestos mistreatment of thousands of its employees and Dow Corning's continued merchandising of silicone implants in the face of evidence regarding their safe use are examples.

However, the examples don't end there. In the mid-1980s, Ethel Smith tried to light her Bic Corporation lighter; it exploded in her hands, killing her and severely burning her husband. The firm later admitted that its own tests showed that about 1 percent of its lighters were faulty.[48] And when, on one night in the 1980s, a Union Carbide chemical plant in Bhopal, India, began spewing highly poisonous methyl isocyanate gas into the surrounding town, the firm's managers were chagrined to learn that virtually all the human and mechanical controls aimed at avoiding such disasters had been compromised.[49]

DIFFERING VIEWS ON THE PURPOSE
OF THE CORPORATION

When lighters explode and chemical plants kill thousands the ethics of the situation are fairly clear, and most would probably agree that firms have a social responsibility to serve their various nonowner constituencies in such situations. But when it comes to other aspects of social responsibility, such unanimity does not exist. This is particularly so when the term "social responsibility" is broadened to refer to the role the corporation should play in solving social and community ills. To many social philosophers, a firm's social responsibilities go far beyond clear-cut ethical rights and wrongs. They extend, they say, to whether firms should be responsible for creating jobs for minorities or for supporting educational and cultural events in their communities, for example.

The question can be stated in another way: What is the purpose of a business? Is it simply to maximize profits? Or does business also have a wider social responsibility, one also measured by issues like pollution control and consumer protection?

FRIEDMAN AND MANAGERIAL CAPITALISM   The classical view is that a corporation's primary (and perhaps sole) purpose is to maximize profits for its stockholders. Today, this view is most often associated with economist and Nobel laureate Milton Friedman, who has said:

> The view has been gaining widespread acceptance that corporate officials and labor leaders have a "social responsibility" that goes beyond the interest of their stockholders or their

members. This view shows a fundamental misconception of the character and nature of the free economy. In such an economy, there is one and only one social responsibility of business—to use its resources and engage in activities designed to increase its profits so long as it stays within the rules of the game, which is to say, engages in open and free competition, without deception and fraud. . . . Few trends could so thoroughly undermine the very foundation of our free society as the acceptance by corporate officials of a social responsibility other than to make as much money for their stockholders as possible.[50]

Friedman's position is built on two main arguments.[51] First, stockholders are the owners of the corporation and so the corporate profits belong to them and to them alone. Second, stockholders deserve their profits because these profits derive from a voluntary contract among the various corporate stakeholders. In other words, everyone associated with the productive efforts of the firm benefits—the local community receives tax money, suppliers are paid, employees earn wages, and so on. Everyone gets their due and additional social responsibility is not needed, Friedman argues.

STAKEHOLDER THEORY An alternative view is that business has a social responsibility to consider and serve all the "corporate stakeholders" affected by its business decisions. This view is summarized in Figure 3.5.[52] A **corporate stakeholder** may be defined as "any group which is vital to the survival and success of the corporation."[53] Six stakeholder groups are traditionally identified: stockholders (owners), employees, customers, suppliers, managers, and the local community, although conceivably others could be identified as well.

Friedman's corporation focuses on maximizing its profits. Stakeholder-oriented firms "see their task as harmonizing the legitimate interests of the primary corporate stakeholders."[54] As Evan and Freeman put it:

> The corporation should be managed for the benefit of [all] its stakeholders: its customers, suppliers, owners, employees, and local communities. The rights of these groups must be ensured, and, further, the groups must participate, in some sense, in decisions that substantially affect their welfare.[55]

THE MORAL MINIMUM Between the extremes of Friedman's capitalism and Evan and Freeman's stakeholder firm is an intermediate position known as the moral minimum, which essentially means that at a minimum the firm should do no harm.

CORPORATE STAKEHOLDER
Any group which is vital to the survival and success of the corporation.

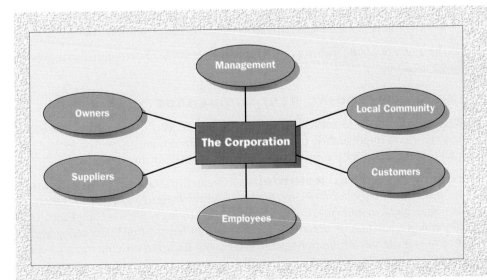

FIGURE 3.5

A Stakeholder Model of the Corporation

One view of social responsibility is that a firm must consider and serve all the stakeholders that may be affected by its business decisions.

SOURCE: Bowie and Beauchamp, *Ethical Theory and Business* (Englewood Cliffs, NJ: Prentice-Hall, 1993), 49–52.

We call it a "moral minimum," implying that however one may choose to limit the concept of social responsibility, one cannot exclude this negative injunction. Although reasons may exist why certain persons or institutions cannot or should not be required to pursue moral or social good in all situations, there are many fewer reasons why one should be excused from the injunction against injuring others.[56]

Moral minimum advocates would agree that the purpose of the corporation is to maximize profits, subject, however, to the requirement that it must do so in conformity with the moral minimum. The **moral minimum** means that corporations should be free to strive for profits *so long as they commit no harm.* By this view, a business would certainly have a social responsibility to not produce exploding lighters or poisonous implants. However, it is unlikely the business's social responsibilities would extend beyond this moral minimum, for instance to donating profits to charity or educating the poor.

MORAL MINIMUM
The standard that corporations should be free to strive for profits so long as they commit no harm.

BEN & JERRY'S AND SOCIAL RESPONSIBILITY   Managers necessarily must make up their own minds regarding where on the social responsibilities scale their firm should lie. For Ben & Jerry's Homemade Ice Cream Company, though, the decision seems never to have been in doubt. Founders Ben Cohen and Jerry Greenfield founded a company that had, as part of its mission:

> To operate the company in a way that actively recognizes the central role that business plays in the structure of a society by initiating innovative ways to improve the quality of life of a broad community: local, national and international.[57]

Ben & Jerry's Homemade operationalizes this social mission in many ways. The firm has "green teams" responsible for assessing the firm's environmental impact in all areas of operation, and for developing and implementing programs to reduce any negative impact. The firm also donates 7.5 percent of its pretax earnings to the Ben & Jerry's Foundation. (This is a nonprofit institution established in 1985 by personal contributions from founders Cohen and Greenfield.) And, in explaining Ben & Jerry's choice of some suppliers, Ben Cohen says:

Some corporation's cultures include community outreach and encouragement of volunteerism by employees.

> Wild Maine Blueberry is another step in how we are defining what caring capitalism is all about. Our goal is to integrate a concern for the community in every business decision we make. We are trying to develop a system that improves the quality of life through socially conscious purchasing of our ingredients. The brownies in Chocolate Fudge Brownie benefit the employment of underskilled persons, the nuts in Rain Forest Crunch benefit the preservation of the rain forest, the peaches in Fresh Georgia Peach support family farms, and the blueberries in Wild Main Blueberry support traditional native American economy.[58]

The Tom's of Maine vignette presents another example of corporate social responsibility in action.

IMPROVING SOCIAL RESPONSIVENESS

While few firms are so socially progressive as Ben & Jerry's, many have established mechanisms to improve their social responsiveness. In this regard, we will look at two final concepts: corporate social monitoring and whistle-blowing.

CORPORATE SOCIAL MONITORING
The process of a firm monitoring how they measure up to the social responsibility aims they have set for themselves.

CORPORATE SOCIAL MONITORING   Some firms monitor how they measure up to the social responsibility aims they have set for themselves, a process known as **corporate social monitoring.** Corporate social monitoring is often accomplished via a corporate social audit. A **corporate social audit** has been defined as a rating system used to evaluate the corporation's performance with regard to meeting its social obligations.

CORPORATE SOCIAL AUDIT
A rating system used to evaluate the corporation's performance with regard to meeting its social obligations.

TOM'S OF MAINE

When considering the magnitude of social ills encountered in just one day's reading of any newspaper, many people inevitably come away thinking, "But what can I do?" Personal care products maker Tom's of Maine doesn't pretend to have the solution. But the firm is at least encouraging employees to make a small contribution to society.

Tom's 65 employees can volunteer two hours a week or a whole day a month assisting in the charity of their choice. If they don't have a cause in mind, the company will help them locate one. One-third of the employees volunteer at schools, churches, various shelters, and other nonprofit institutions. Workers frequently form their own teams in tackling tasks. Participants reportedly enjoy enhanced relationships with one another and come away from the experience with a heightened perspective on serving society.

The company, which has been absorbing the loss of all those days each month for over four years now, thinks it's all worth it. Says company spokesperson Colleen Myers, "It's a morale booster, and better morale translates pretty directly into better productivity."

SOURCE: Ellyn E. Spragins, "Paying Employees to Work Elsewhere," *Inc.*, February 1993, 29.

Tom Chappell, chairman and founder of Tom's of Maine, a manufacturer of natural beauty products, donates 10 percent of pretax profits to charity and encourages employees to volunteer in the community by giving them time off from work with pay to do so.

SULLIVAN PRINCIPLES
A code by Reverend Leon Sullivan that provided for measurable standards by which U. S. companies operating in South Africa could be audited, and contained a number of priciples including nonsegregation of the races in all eating, comfort, and work facilities, and equal pay for all employees doing equal or comparable work for the same period of time.

SINGLE-ISSUE MONITORING SYSTEM
Intended for use by multiple companies to monitor their performance on a single social responsibility issue.

WHISTLE-BLOWING
The activities of employees who try to report organizational wrongdoing.

The so-called Sullivan Principles for Corporate Labor and Community Relations in South Africa[59] was one of the first of such rating systems. The Reverend Leon Sullivan was a black minister and board of directors member for General Motors. For several years he had tried to pressure the firm to withdraw from South Africa. As part of that effort, he formulated the code that became known as the **Sullivan Principles,** whose purpose was "to guide U.S. business in its social and moral agenda in South Africa."[60] The code provided for measurable standards by which U.S. companies operating in South Africa could be audited, and it contained a number of principles including nonsegregation of the races in all eating, comfort, and work facilities, and "equal pay for all employees doing equal or comparable work for the same period of time."[61]

The Sullivan Principles are an example of a **single-issue monitoring system** intended for use by multiple companies. All U.S. firms doing business in South Africa could use these principles to monitor their performance on the single social responsibility issue of equal rights for black African employees.

Other types of rating systems are used as well. For example, some publications monitor the record of consumer products firms over a broad range of social issues, including community affairs, women and minority hiring and treatment, the environment, and military contracting.[62]

WHISTLE-BLOWING   Many firms have a reputation for actively dissuading **whistle-blowing,** the activities of employees who try to report organizational wrongdoing. The *Challenger* space shuttle explosion in the mid-1980s was one of the saddest and most spectacular examples. According to some Morton Thiokol engineers, they had tried repeatedly to "blow the whistle" internally prior to the launch, protesting that with the defects they knew existed in the rocket's O-rings, the launch should not take place with the exceptionally cold weather conditions prevailing at the time.[63] In later congressional testimony, the engineers said that Morton Thiokol managers repeatedly overruled their protests.

Many arguments can be made for firms actually encouraging whistle-blowers. For example, in a firm that adheres to the "moral minimum" view of social responsibility, such whistle-blowers can help the firm avoid doing harm. As one writer has put it, whistle-blowers "represent one of the least expensive and most efficient sources of feedback about mistakes the firm may be making."[64]

Other firms find that the "benefits of muffling whistle-blowers is illusory."[65] Once the damage is done—whether it is a space shuttle explosion, a cigarette lighter exploding, or a breast implant making hundreds of women ill —the cost of making the damage right can be enormous.

Yet, as often as not, firms retaliate against whistle-blowers, either with dismissals or by placing them in marginal jobs.[66] Some do this because of a preoccupation with maximizing profits, while others may not have strong ethics codes. But there is also the lingering belief in many firms that whistle-blowers are either disloyal or "kooks," or both. Such views are probably myopic; many firms can and do benefit from creating an environment that at least permits (and perhaps encourages) employees who observe organizational wrongdoing to report their observations to the highest levels of the firm.[67]

Managers are faced with serious ethical decisions every day. Most decisions of this type have extended and unpredictable consequences, as well as personal implications. *Ethics* can be defined in various ways, but in popular usage the term either refers to the study of standards of conduct and moral judgment or the principles of conduct through which people run their lives. Making ethical decisions implies a right and wrong way to proceed, and therefore calls first for *normative* judgments. In ethical judgments, the standards of right and wrong are always *moral* ones. A decision is therefore ethical to the extent that it does not violate fundamental moral standards.

Moral standards differ from nonmoral ones in that they address matters of serious consequence to human well-being; cannot be established or changed by decisions of authoritative bodies; should override self-interest; are based on universal, impartial considerations; and tend to trigger special emotions.

Making a decision based on what is legal is no guarantee that it will be ethical. Factors that influence whether individuals in organizations make ethical or unethical decisions include individual ideas of right and wrong, situational factors, the boss's influence, and the existence of ethics policies and codes.

A study of ethics programs at eleven major firms concluded that the following factors were important for their effectiveness: the commitment of top management, the establishment of a code of company conduct standards, the involvement and commitment of personnel at all levels, and the use of methods for monitoring compliance with ethical standards.

Corporate social responsibility refers to the extent companies channel resources toward improving the quality of life for segments of society other than the firm's own stockholders. But views differ on the purpose of the corporation. The classical view, most often associated with economist Milton Friedman, is that a corporation's primary purpose is to maximize profits for its stockholders. An alternate view is that business has a social responsibility to consider all the "corporate stakeholders" affected by its business decisions. An intermediate view, known as the moral minimum, holds that the purpose of a corporation is to maximize profits, as long as it commits no harm.

Some firms monitor how they measure up to the social responsibility aims they have set for themselves through a process known as corporate social monitoring. In theory, whistle-blowers, or employees who try to report organizational wrongdoing, can help the firm avoid doing harm. But in practice, many firms retaliate against whistle-blowers by dismissing them or by relegating them to marginal jobs.

SUMMARY

QUESTIONS

■ **FOR REVIEW**

1. List five ways that moral standards differ from nonmoral standards.

2. Give some examples of both positive and negative ethical cues that a boss could give employees. What is the best course of action a worker can take when confronted with negative ethical cues?

3. Summarize Milton Friedman's view on the primary purpose of a corporation and what he regards as the two main underlying arguments supporting his thesis. How do his views differ from the stakeholder theory?

4. What is a corporate social audit, and what was the setting and circumstances that gave rise to the set of principles on which such audits are based?

■ **FOR DISCUSSION**

5. When faced with an ethical dilemma, does a manager's principal area of respon-

sibility lie with the good of the company's shareholders or the persons potentially affected by the operation in question? Can the two be reconciled?

6. Retailers are increasingly offering customers the opportunity to charge their purchases under "same as cash" offers. What some people do not realize is that the arrangement requires them to make minimum monthly payments and pay off the entire balance within the specified period or be liable for all the accrued interest. This practice is legal, but is it ethical? Discuss.

7. How would you interpret the findings of the Baylor business ethics survey described in this chapter (pages 64 and 65)? Do you think older employees tend to be more ethical?

8. Name some practical ways that a company with high ethical standards can ensure employees measure up to expectations. How could actual behavior be monitored?

9. Contrast Ben & Jerry's company mission, its emphasis on improving the community and the environment, and its contributions to charitable causes with the necessity of maintaining profitable operations. Would it be feasible for other companies to emulate Ben & Jerry's?

■ FOR ACTION

10. Recall a situation when you were tempted to do something unethical at work or school simply because everyone else seemed to be doing it. Did you give in to the temptation? (Be honest!) How did you justify your decision?

11. Develop your own version of a code of conduct for students at your university. Then find out whether your school actually has such a code, and compare the two.

12. Just as corporations strive to be socially responsible, so do individuals. Name some ways that you are socially responsible as a student, worker, or volunteer.

■ FOR FOCUS ON SMALL BUSINESS

13. Do you agree that some "artful posturing" is especially important for a start-up operation? Why or why not?

14. If you were running a business like Intuit, would your ethical standards more closely resemble those of Cook or his competitors? Explain.

15. Do you think Cook's business ethics have contributed to Intuit's growth?

CLOSING SOLUTION

GENERAL DYNAMICS

Stanley Pace's approach to restoring the Pentagon's trust was certainly innovative. All company cost claims related to government contracts were reviewed. Any charges that could remotely be regarded as questionable by Defense Department auditors were simply dropped. Pace also created codes of conduct for various positions, and he set down strict rules relating to entertainment, gratuities, and conflicts of interest. As the company's chief ethics officer, Kent Druyvesteyn installed an employee hotline that went directly to his desk. His office also began distributing a book of ethical conduct to all employees. A network of business ethics directors now exists at each of the company's major operating divisions, and incentive compensation for directors and vice-presidents are based in part on ethical behavior. According to Druyvesteyn, GD has transformed itself from an ethical pariah to a model other companies can emulate. He says his office receives from 150 to 200 calls per year from academics, corporations, or professional associations inquiring about GD's ethics program.

■ QUESTIONS FOR CLOSING SOLUTION

1. Would you consider it necessary for every large company to have an ethics officer, along the lines of the one at General Dynamics? Why or why not?

2. How effective do you think company codes of conduct are? Do they serve as a deterrent if an employee is intent on unethical behavior?

3. If you were managing a company, how would you ensure that employees were ethical and socially responsible?

Ethics	Moral Minimum
Normative Judgment	Corporate Social Monitoring
Non-normative Judgment	Corporate Social Audit
Moral Standards	Sullivan Principles
Social Responsibility	Single-issue Monitoring System
Corporate Stakeholder	Whistle-blowing

CASE FOR ANALYSIS

CONSUMERS UNITED INSURANCE

Jim Gibbons had his own ideas about running an ethical business operation. The founder and president of Consumers United Insurance Company believed funding housing, education, and youth groups in inner-city neighborhoods were wise investments. He was ahead of his time in encouraging employee development and self-actualization, a companywide community/family spirit, and the implementation of flexible schedules for workers. His firm, he believed, would stand as a model of how an American business could earn a profit and still make a difference. He was right, and he was wrong.

Gibbons's philosophy was deeply rooted in his past. He embarked on his career in the early 1960s with the view that education was the most critical factor of production. Without it young people would be relegated to lower-rung servitude in perpetuity. With that idea in mind, he and partner Bruce Terris founded Better Homes, Inc., and began buying and upgrading low-end housing in Washington, D.C. That was only the beginning. The company also enlisted tutors for the children of tenants and persuaded physicians to donate health care services. The initial success attracted the attention of then-Attorney General Robert Kennedy, who came to visit. It also attracted federal bureaucrats who urged Better Homes to work in tandem with government programs. By Gibbons's own evaluation, this proved to be a disaster, and he came away convinced such operations could only succeed when run by an innovative entrepreneur. Five years later he got his chance when he began Consumers United Insurance.

Ever progressive, one of his first moves was to make employees owners of the company. As equity holders, they could veto big decisions by Gibbons. The lowest paid worker earned enough to support a family of four. In adverse time, layoffs didn't occur; workers took pay cuts instead, which the company repaid later. Profits were limited to 5 percent, with the rest refunded to policyholders.

Initially, all went well. Through the next decade Consumers grew to 320 employees and was collecting $80 million in premiums a year. By 1986, the company portfolio reached $47 million in invested assets. And the company was as revolutionary as its chief. Consumers offered women the same rates as men, covered domestic partners, and paid for usually excluded services such as chiropractors and homeopathic treatments. It once tried to write special policies for HIV-positive individuals but was thwarted by Delaware's state insurance department.

It was Gibbons's investment policies that really piqued state regulators' interest. In keeping with his sense of responsibility toward inner-city renewal, Gibbons paid $2 million for a 26-acre tract on which the Parkside-Paradise affordable housing project was to be built. The D.C. development included a medical clinic, and besides providing local employment, it would also fund college scholarships through the Young People on the Rise program. Gibbons's mistake this time was again acceding to an alliance with another bureaucracy, this time the D.C. Housing Finance Agency. The agency's foot-dragging placed Consumers' investment in a non-earning limbo for months. Regulators promptly pounced on the firm, declaring the investment a nonperformer.

Consumers might have weathered the Parkside-Paradise write-down had so many other risky investments not also been funded. Though he was loathe to admit it, a host of scam artists had wheedled funds from Gibbons. At one point he invested $6,000 of his own money in a firm doing something called French-intensive gardening. Consumers had already paid, according to regulators, twice what the 200-acre Warrington, Virginia, farm was worth. When he got around to visiting, Gibbons discovered nothing had been planted, and Consumers, which had presold the produce, had to make good by buying and distributing the promised vegetables.

Regulators ultimately placed Consumers into receivership. Most of the remaining 200 employees were let go, along with Gibbons. He claimed the state unreasonably targeted Consumers; the then Delaware commissioner of insurance David Levinson claims he did everything in his power to save the company. Whatever the case, Consumers probably typifies a good corporate citizen gone wrong. Many worthy causes were funded and still operate today. On the other hand, Gibbons's unchecked idealism may have made victims of himself and his employees.

SOURCES: Bill Gifford, "Too Much of a Good Thing," *Business Ethics,* November–December 1993, 21–24; and Dawn Gunsch, "Urban Renewal Is an Investment," *Personnel Journal,* March 1993, 53–55.

■ QUESTIONS

1. Where did Gibbons go wrong in his quest to make Consumers a socially responsible company? Describe his view of social responsibility.
2. Considering the ultimate outcome, would you say that Gibbons's investment decisions represented an ethical use of policy holders' money? Why or why not?
3. What could Gibbons have done to better balance his concern for societal welfare and employees with the financial needs of policy holders?

A CASE IN DIVERSITY

PAPA'S GROCERY

Papa's Grocery is situated in a predominately black section of Los Angeles and features such eclectic delicacies as chitterlings and Creole cuisine. But Papa's has big problems lurking just outside: drugs, crime, and decaying infrastructure. There was no better place for owner Patsy Brown to take a stand and make her original vision a reality back in 1984. "I wanted a place where people know their grocer and butcher," she says, "a place where elderly folks could walk to, where you could send the kids."

Urban development experts almost unanimously agree Brown's modus operandi is right on track. Viable small entrepreneurial businesses founded by locals employ more people and deliver more in the way of civic pride than large corporate entities that have been coaxed to areas that have experienced neglect and civil strife. "Small businesses create a large number of new jobs," says John C. Weicher, Assistant Housing & Urban Development Secretary, "especially in the inner city."

Papa's has done that. In the process of grossing around $1.7 million annually, the grocer has put 24 people to work. But profits have been hard to come by, primarily because the store can't price-compete on many staple items. Big chain stores, taking advantage of their volume purchasing ability, have siphoned off customers. Brown cut prices on staples like rice and bread and beans anyway. So far, the volume hasn't translated into earnings despite top-notch service and a store that's always spic-and-span. She thinks that the store's appearance will ultimately be the attraction that earns long-term patronage. "This is primarily a neighborhood of people with jobs, who, like everybody else, enjoy shopping at nice places," Brown says.

She is irked somewhat by what she perceives as reluctance on the part of bankers to extend credit to black entrepreneurs. She also thinks investors from her own community could do more. "Bankers think of black-owned business as beauty salons and bar-becue stands," she says, "and most wealthy black investors won't put money into black enterprise because they think it's too risky." Papa's was funded entirely by proceeds and savings acquired by Brown's husband, who for years ran a profitable, 200-employee scrap-metal business.

Patsy Brown isn't about to give up. Even though Papa's has failed to generate consistent profits, she has obtained assistance from a city redevelopment agency, and a second, even larger Papa's is slated to open. It will create 30 new jobs and feature a restaurant serving more wholesome fare than most of the fast-food establishments that predominate the area. One city official thinks just these sorts of efforts are critical, even if sustained profitability remains a ways off. "Setting an example to the community as an entrepreneur with dreams is important in and of itself," says Casper Williams, senior manager at L.A.'s Community Development Department.

There will be plenty of rough times ahead, and there aren't any guarantees. But at least Patsy Brown can feel good about her efforts on behalf of her employees and the community.

SOURCE: Jane Birnbaum, "Patsy Brown," *Business Week,* Reinventing America Issue 1992, 190–91.

■ QUESTIONS

1. If Papa's continues to lose money, do you think it will be able to sustain its pattern of social responsibility, or will economic realities have to take precedence?
2. Describe Papa's purpose using one of the three views of social responsibility outlined in the chapter.
3. What else could Papa's do to help meet the needs of the community while also pursuing its financial goals?

1. This problem was researched from Howard Banks, "Corporate Cleaner-upper," *Forbes,* January 11, 1988, 70; James E. Ellis and Dave Griffiths, "General Dynamics: All Cleaned Up with No Place to Grow," *Business Week,* August 22, 1988, 70–71; Barbara Ettorre, "Corporate Accountability '90s Style: The Buck Had Better Stop Here," *Management Review,* April 1992, 18–21; Roger Bennett, "Profile of Harry Crown, Founder of General Dynamics Inc.," *New York Times,* June 16, 1985, 26F; presented in Laroue Tone Hosmer, *The Ethics of Management* (Homewood, IL: Irwin, 1987), 16.

2. Adapted from Justin Longenecker, Joseph McKinney, and Carlos Moore, "The Generation Gap in Business Ethics," *Business Horizons,* September–October, 1989, 10.

3. Deon Nel, Leyland Pitt, and Richard Watson, "Business Ethics: Defining the Twilight Zone," *Journal of Business Ethics,* vol. 8 (1989), 783.

4. Adapted from Longenecker, et al., "The Generation Gap," 10.

5. Adapted from Nel, Pitt, and Watson, "Business Ethics," 783.

6. Roger Bennett, "Profile of Harry Crown, Founder of General Dynamics, Inc.," *The New York Times,* June 16, 1985, 26F; as presented in Laroue Tone Hosmer, *The Ethics of Management* (Homewood, IL: Irwin, 1987), 16.

7. *Ann Arbor News,* July 19, 1985, B-1; presented in Hosmer, *The Ethics of Management,* 16.

8. This is based on Robert Hartley, *Business Ethics: Violations of the Public Trust* (New York: John Wiley & Sons, 1993), 235–38.

9. This is based on Hosmer, *The Ethics of Management,* 13–14.

10. Hosmer, *The Ethics of Management,* 14.

11. *Webster's New World Dictionary of the American Language* (New York: Popular Library, 1972), 200.

12. Hartley, *Business Ethics,* 3.

13. Manuel Velasquez, *Business Ethics: Concepts and Cases* (Englewood Cliffs, NJ: Prentice-Hall, 1992), 9.

14. The following, except as noted, is based on Velasquez, *Business Ethics,* 9–12.

15. Velasquez, *Business Ethics,* 9.

16. This is based on Velasquez, *Business Ethics,* 12–14.

17. Velasquez, *Business Ethics,* 12. For further discussion see Kurt Baier, *Moral Points of View,* abbr. ed. (New York: Random House, 1965), 88.

18. For further discussions of ethics and morality see Tom Beauchamp and Norman Bowe, *Ethical Theory and Business* (Englewood Cliffs, NJ: Prentice-Hall, 1993), 1–19.

19. See, for example, Hartley, *Business Ethics,* 5; and Hosmer, *The Ethics of Management,* 24–25.

20. See Michael McCarthy, "James Bond Hits the Supermarket: Stores Snoop on Shoppers' Habits to Boost Sales," *The Wall Street Journal,* August 25, 1993, B12.

21. Hosmer, *The Ethics of Management,* 15.

22. Paul Serwinek, "Demographic & Related Differences in Ethical Views Amongst Small Businesses," *Journal of Business Ethics,* vol. 11 (1992), 555–66.

23. Longenecker, McKinney, and Moore, "The Generation Gap," 9–14.

24. Longenecker, McKinney, and Moore, 10. For a discussion of the development of a scale for measuring individual beliefs about organizational ethics, see Kristina Froelich and Janet Kottke, "Measuring Individual Beliefs About Organizational Ethics," *Educational and Psychological Measurement,* vol. 51 (1991), 377–83.

25. Thomas Tyson, "Does Believing That Everyone Else Is Less Ethical Have an Impact on Work Behavior?" *Journal of Business Ethics,* vol. 11 (1992), 707–17.

26. Stanley Milgram, *Obedience to Authority: An Experimental View* (New York: Harper & Row, 1974), 1–12. Copyright 1974 by Stanley Milgram. Reprinted by permission of Harper & Row Publishers, Inc. Reprinted in Jerome E. Schnee, Kirby Warren, and Howard Lazarus, *The Progress of Management* (Englewood Cliffs, NJ: Prentice-Hall, 1977), 427–36.

27. This is from Saul Gellerman, "Why Good Managers Make Bad Ethical Choices," *Harvard Business Review,* July–August 1986, 86.

28. Ibid.

29. Ibid.

ENDNOTES

30. For a discussion, see Steven Brenner and Earl Molander, "Is the Ethics of Business Changing?" *Harvard Business Review,* January–February 1977, 57–71; see also Robert Jackyll, "Moral Mazes: Bureaucracy and Managerial Work," *Harvard Business Review,* September–October 1983, 118–30.

31. From Gary Brumback, "Managing Above the Bottom Line of Ethics," *Supervisory Management,* December 1993, 12.

32. Nel, Pitt, and Watson, "Business Ethics," 781; Brenner and Molander, "Is the Ethics Business Changing?"

33. Robert Sweeney and Howard Siers, "Survey: Ethics in Corporate America," *Management Accounting,* June 1990, 34.

34. Ibid., 34–40.

35. Ibid., 34.

36. Ibid., 35.

37. *Corporate Ethics: A Prime Business Asset* (New York: The Business Round Table, February 1988), 81.

38. *Corporate Ethics,* 91.

39. *Corporate Ethics,* 78.

40. Ibid., 79.

41. Ibid.

42. *Corporate Ethics,* 118.

43. Ibid., 122.

44. Ibid., 4.

45. Ibid., 6.

46. Ibid., 7.

47. Ibid., 9.

48. Velasquez, *Business Ethics,* 270–72.

49. Hartley, *Business Ethics,* 147–51. For a discussion of ethics as it relates to various facets of social responsibility, see Velasquez, *Business Ethics,* 211–371.

50. Milton Friedman, *Capitalism and Freedom* (Chicago: University of Chicago Press, 1962), 133.

51. Tom Beauchamp and Norman Bowie, *Ethical Theory and Business* (Englewood Cliffs, NJ: Prentice-Hall, 1993), 49–52.

52. Beauchamp and Bowie, *Ethical Theory and Business,* 80.

53. Ibid., 79.

54. Ibid., 54.

55. William Evan and R. Edward Freeman: "A Stakeholder Theory of the Modern Corporation: Kantian Capitalism," reprinted in Beauchamp and Bowie, *Ethical Theory of Business,* 82. See also Kenneth Goodpaster, "Business Ethics and Stakeholder Analysis," *Business Ethics Quarterly,* vol. 1, January 1991, 53–73.

56. John Simon, Charles Powers, and John Gunnemann, "The Responsibilities of Corporations and Their Owners," in *The Ethical Investor: Universities and Corporate Responsibility* (New Haven, CT: Yale University Press, 1972); reprinted in Beauchamp and Bowie, *Ethical Theory of Business,* 60–65.

57. Ben & Jerry's Homemade, Inc., Employee Handbook.

58. Ben & Jerry's Public Relations Release, October 5, 1990.

59. Karen Paul and Steven Lydenberg, "Applications of Corporate Social Monitoring Systems: Types, Dimensions and Goals," *Journal of Business Ethics,* vol. 11 (1992), 1–10.

60. Karen Paul, "Corporate Social Monitoring in South Africa: A Decade of Achievement, An Uncertain Future," *Journal of Business Ethics,* vol. 8 (1989), 464.

61. Paul, "Corporate Social Monitoring," 464.

62. Paul and Lydenberg, "Applications of Corporate Social Monitoring," 6.

63. Janet Near, "Whistle Blowing: Encourage It!" *Business Horizons,* January–February, 1989, 2.

64. Ibid., 5.

65. Ibid.

66. Ibid., 6.

67. See also S. Gellerman, "Why Good Managers Make Ethical Choices," *Harvard Business Review,* July–August 1986, 85–90.

CHAPTER 4

FOUNDATIONS OF MODERN MANAGEMENT

LEARNING OBJECTIVES

After studying this chapter, you should be able to:

- Trace the roots of modern management.
- Discuss the management techniques that were adopted during the Industrial Revolution.
- List the four principles that serve as the framework for Taylor's scientific management.
- Describe the theories of Fayol, Weber, and the Gilbreths.
- Outline the significance of the Hawthorne studies and their impact on the human relations movement.
- Give examples of the behavioral approach to management.
- Explain how the work of Barnard and Simon led to the development of an integrated theory of management.
- Compare and contrast the management science and systems approaches.
- Discuss the situational or contingency view of management.
- Name the features that will characterize successful firms of the 1990s and beyond.

OPENING PROBLEM
AMERITECH

Ameritech's chief executive officer William Weiss was facing a formidable crisis. The long-time monopoly status of the $11.2 billion Bell operating company had reduced its employees' ability to think competitively. And in 1992, Ameritech posted record earnings, which would make doing so even more difficult. This lack of competitive spirit did not fit with what Weiss saw down the road for Ameritech. Even though one-fifth of the company's present revenues came from competitive operations, Weiss reckoned that in as few as five years, 95 percent would come from competitive markets. In essence, Weiss had to define for his employees a problem that hadn't yet materialized and implement sweeping changes in the attitude of his work force in anticipation of challenges he could only predict. Given this backdrop of record earnings and the natural tendency of employees to resist changes in the status quo, Weiss had to find a way to implement new management methods that would be essential for the firm's survival in a fast-changing business environment.[1]

THE EARLY FOUNDATIONS
OF MANAGEMENT

It would be impossible to imagine a modern society without organized effort or without the managers, like Weiss, who help to synchronize that effort, but the roots of management can actually be traced back to antiquity. Hunters banded into tribes for protection, the Egyptians used organizations to build pyramids and control the rise and fall of the Nile, and the Romans relied on organizing for building their armies and controlling their empire. Management can thus be traced back many, many years, although the formal study of management did not start until much later.

Several issues become apparent when you view management over the ages, as we will see. First, many of the management concepts we take for granted today, such as dividing employees into departments, can be traced to the earliest organizations, including those of the Egyptians and ancient Greeks. Similarly, the close supervision and reliance on coercion and rules that management expert Peter Drucker has called "command and control" managing is also a product of earlier times, in particular of the militaristic organizations of Egypt and ancient Rome.

Second, we will see that the forms that organizations take and the ways that managers manage have always been a product of the environments of the time. As futurist Alvin Toeffler has said (in describing nineteenth-century management):

> Each age produces a form of organization appropriate to its own tempo. During the long epic of agriculture civilization, societies were marked by low transcience. Delays in communication and transportation slowed the rate in which information moved. The pace of individual life was comparatively slow. And organizations were seldom called upon to make what we would regard as high speed decisions.[2]

SCIENTIFIC MANAGEMENT

THE INDUSTRIAL REVOLUTION

INDUSTRIAL REVOLUTION
A period of several decades during which machine power was increasingly substituted for hand labor.

By about 1750, what Toeffler referred to as "the long epic of agriculture civilization" was about to end with the advent of the Industrial Revolution. The **Industrial Revolution** was a period of several decades during which machine power was increasingly substituted for hand labor. During these years (around 1750) several major trends were converging. The scientific and technological discoveries of Galileo, Gilbert, Harvey, and Watt, including the invention of the steam engine and the use of electricity, all contributed to industrialization. England, generally recognized as the epicenter of the Industrial Revolution, had at that time a stable, constitutional government, a sensitivity to laissez-faire (hands-off) economics, and a strong spirit of self-reliance. In his book, *Wealth of Nations,* Adam Smith had described how the division and specialization of work was a pillar of the burgeoning free competitive market system and would lead to enormous increases in productivity and output.[3]

THE INDUSTRIAL ENVIRONMENT

For firms in the 1800s, industrialization meant emphasizing resource accumulation and company growth. Division of work and specialization—two pillars of industrialization—required high volume, and stability. Company growth therefore led to higher profits: as sales, volume, and stability increased, unit costs decreased.

But enlarged operations created new problems for the entrepreneurs of the 1800s. They needed management techniques through which they could run their new, large-scale industrial enterprises. These early entrepreneurs therefore quickly adopted the structures and principles of managers of an earlier day. In so doing, they adopted management practices such as centralized decision making, rigid chain of command, specialized division of work, and autocratic leadership, all of which had been born and nurtured in military and religious organizations like those of ancient Rome and Egypt.

FREDERICK WINSLOW TAYLOR AND SCIENTIFIC MANAGEMENT

The race to accumulate resources and grow was particularly pronounced in the United States. The War of 1812 economically severed the United States from England and spurred the growth of manufacturing operations. Technological advances flourished, and included the steamboat, the cotton gin, the iron plow, the telegraph, the electric motor, and the expansion of a railroad and canal network that opened new markets for producers. In turn, these new markets provided the volume that was a basic requirement for the effective use of division of work.

Historian Alfred Chandler has pointed out that by the late 1800s many new industries were completing the resource-accumulation stage of their existence and beginning to move into what he called a rationalization stage.[4] The management focus shifted from growth to efficiency. As organizations became large and unwieldy, and as competition became more intense, managers needed better ways to utilize the resources they had accumulated. They sought new concepts and techniques that would cut costs and boost efficiency. It was out of this industrial environment that the **classical school of management** emerged.

Frederick W. Taylor was one of the first of what historians today call the classical management writers; he specifically developed a set of principles that became known as **scientific management.** Taylor's basic theme was that managers should study work scientifically to identify the "one best way" to get the job done. The framework for Taylor's scientific management can be summarized as consisting of four principles:

1. *Finding the "one best way."* First management, through observation and "the deliberate gathering . . . of all the great mass of traditional knowledge, which in the past has been in the heads of the workmen . . .", finds the "one best way" for performing each job.

2. *Scientific selection of personnel.* This principle requires "the scientific selection and then the progressive development of the workmen." Management must uncover each worker's limitation, find his or her "possibility for development," and give each worker the required training.

3. *Financial incentives.* Taylor knew that putting the right worker on the right job would not by itself ensure high productivity. Some plan for motivating workers to do their best and to comply with their supervisors' instructions was also required. Taylor proposed a system of financial incentives, in which each worker was paid in direct proportion to how much he or she produced, instead of according to a basic hourly wage.

4. *Functional foremanship.* Finally, Taylor called for a division of work between manager and worker such that managers did all planning, preparing, and inspecting while the workers did the actual work. Taylor proposed using specialized experts, or functional foremen, who would be responsible for specific aspects of the worker's task, such as choosing the best machine speed, determining job priorities, and inspecting the work. The worker was to take orders

CLASSICAL SCHOOL OF MANAGEMENT
An approach to managing emphasizing concepts and techniques that would cut costs and boost efficiency.

SCIENTIFIC MANAGEMENT
Developed by Frederick W. Taylor, a set of principles that encouraged managers to study work scientifically in order to identify the "one best way" to get the job done.

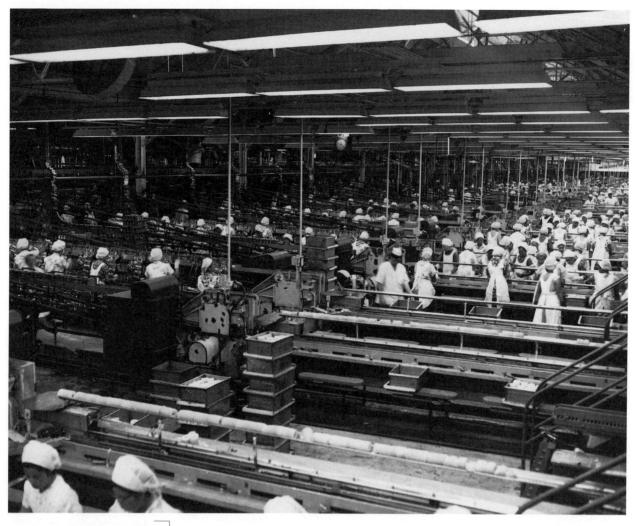

Frederick Taylor was one of the first of many so-called efficiency experts to study workers on production lines with an eye toward developing "one best way" to get the job done.

from each of these foremen, depending upon whether the matter concerned planning, machine speed, or inspecting, for example.[5]

The *General Mills* vignette shows how one modern firm applies a Taylor concept.

FRANK AND LILLIAN GILBRETH

The work of the husband and wife team of Frank and Lillian Gilbreth also exemplifies the techniques and points of view of the scientific management approach. Born in 1868, Frank Gilbreth passed up an opportunity to attend MIT, deciding instead to enter the contracting business. He began as an apprentice bricklayer and became intrigued with the opportunities for improving bricklayers' efficiency. By carefully studying bricklayers' motions, he developed innovations—in the way bricks were stacked, in how bricks were laid, and in the number of motions bricklayers used, for instance—that nearly tripled the average bricklayer's efficiency.[6]

In 1904, he married Lillian Gilbreth, who had a background in psychology, and together they began to develop the principles and practices to more scientifically analyze tasks. In addition to using stopwatches to improve production efficiencies, these

GENERAL MILLS

Taylor's theory of incentives is at work even today. At General Mills, base salaries are less than those at competing manufacturers, even for managers. But if you think top managers at the Minneapolis-based food manufacturer are upset, consider these facts: Compensation for marketing managers in the food industry averages around $90,000; at General Mills the same managers might earn $75,000. If a manager's product and division rings up profit increases and return on capital in line with the rest of the industry, the addition to base pay is only about $10,000, still below the norm. If a manager can push his or her product into the industry's top 10 percent in those same categories, that manager's compensation would total over $115,000, or 28 percent *above* the average.

For example, managers at the company's Yoplait yogurt division established a goal to increase operating earnings by 40 percent for fiscal 1993. The Yoplait managers, many of whom were just past 30 years old, decided to shoot for doubling those profits. They ended up exceeding their own projections, and six of them received bonuses that approached 50 percent of base salary.

The incentives at General Mills have instilled a contagious attitude and culture. Excellence has become commonplace, and performance that is simply average for the industry doesn't make the grade. Although managers at General Mills routinely field calls from recruiters trying to sell them on higher salaries at competing firms, the pitch falls flat. "I spent eight years with a food company that had high base and low variable pay," says marketing head Craig Hettrich. "The effect is stagnation."

SOURCE: Shawn Tully, "Your Paycheck Gets Exciting," *Fortune,* November 1, 1993, 83–98.

experts developed various tools, including **motion-study principles,** to assist them in their quest for efficiency. They concluded, for example, that:

1. the two hands should begin as well as complete their motions at the same time.
2. the two hands should not be idle at the same time except during rest periods.
3. motions of the arms should be made at opposite and symmetrical direction and should be made simultaneously.[7]

Therbligs, another example of the tools used by the Gilbreths, refer to elemental motions like searching, grabbing, holding, and transporting. (The Gilbreths created the term *therblig* by using their last name spelled backwards and transposing the *th.*) *Micromotion study* refers to the Gilbreths' process of taking motion pictures of a worker doing his or her job and then running the film forward and backward at different speeds so that details of the job could be examined and re-examined. Used in

MOTION-STUDY PRINCIPLES
Tools developed by Frank and Lillian Gilbreth to assist them in their quest for efficiency.

conjunction with timing devices, it was (and is) possible to determine precisely how long each component activity of a task takes a worker. The person's performance can then be improved by modifying or eliminating one or more of these activities.

HENRI FAYOL AND THE PRINCIPLES OF MANAGEMENT

The work of Henri Fayol also illustrates the classical approach to management and behavior at work. Fayol had been a manager with a French iron and steel firm for 30 years before writing his book *General and Industrial Management*. In it, Fayol said that managers performed five basic functions: planning, organizing, commanding, coordinating, and controlling.

He also outlined a list of management principles that he found useful during his years as a manager. He argued that other managers should use these principles in planning, organizing, commanding, coordinating, and controlling. Fayol's 14 principles are summarized in Figure 4.1 and include his famous principle of *unity of command:* "for any action whatsoever, an employee should receive orders from one superior only."[8]

FIGURE 4.1

Fayol's 14 Principles of Management

Fayol developed his 14 principles while a manager with a French firm and believed they could help all managers better organize and manage their companies.

SOURCE: Henri Fayol, *General and Industrial Management*, translated by Constance Storrs (London: Sir Isaac Pitman, 1949).

1. *Division of work.* The worker, always on the same part, and the manager, concerned always with the same matters, acquired ability, sureness, and accuracy, which increased their output.

2. Authority and responsibility. Authority is the right to give orders and the power to exact obedience. Distinction must be made between a manager's official authority, deriving from office, and personal authority, compounded of intelligence, experience, moral worth, and ability to lead.

3. *Discipline.* The best means of establishing and maintaining [discipline] are: good superiors at all levels; agreements as clear and fair as possible; sanctions [penalties] judiciously applied.

4. *Unity of command.* For any action whatsoever, an employee should receive orders from one superior only. . . .

5. *Unity of direction.* There should be one head and one plan for a group of activities serving the same objective.

6. *Subordination of individual interests to general interests.* This principle means that in a business, the interests of one employee or group of employees should not prevail over those of the concern. . . . Means of effecting it are: firmness and good example on the part of superiors; agreements as far as is possible.

7. *Remuneration of personnel.* Remuneration should be fair and as far as possible afford satisfaction to both personnel and firm.

8. *Centralization.* The question of centralization or decentralization is a simple question of proportion; it is a matter of finding the optimum degree for the particular concern. What appropriate share of initiative may be left to intermediaries depends on the personal character of the manager, on his moral worth, on the reliability of his subordinates, and also on the condition of the business. The degree of centralization must vary according to different cases.

9. *Scalar chain.* The scalar chain is the chain of superiors ranging from the ultimate authority to the lowest ranks. . . . It is an error to depart needlessly from the line of authority, but it is an even greater one to keep to it when detriment to the business ensues.

10. *Order.* For social order to prevail in a concern, there must be an appointed place for every employee and every employee must be in his appointed place.

11. *Equity.* For the personnel to be encouraged to carry out its duties with all the devotion and loyalty of which it is capable, it must be treated with kindliness, and equity results from the combination of kindness and justice. Equity excludes neither forcefulness nor sternness. . . .

12. *Stability of tenure of personnel.* Time is required for an employee to get used to new work and succeed in doing it well, always assuming that he possesses the requisite abilities. If, when he has gotten used to it, or before then, he is removed, he will not have had time to render worthwhile service.

13. *Initiative.* Thinking out a plan and ensuring its success is one of the keenest satisfactions for an intelligent man to experience. . . . This power of thinking out and executing is what is called initiative. . . . It . . . represents a great source of strength for business.

14. *Esprit de corps.* "Union is strength." Harmony, union among the personnel of a concern, is a great strength in that concern. Effort, then, should be made to establish it.

MAX WEBER AND
BUREAUCRATIC ORGANIZATION THEORY

Max Weber was a contemporary of Taylor, Fayol, and the Gilbreths, and his work, first published in Germany in 1921, provides further insight into the points of view of the classical management writers. However, unlike most of these writers, Weber was not a practicing manager but an intellectual. He was born in 1864 to a well-to-do, cultured family and he studied law, history, economics, and philosophy at Heidelberg University.

During the 1920s, Weber watched the growth of the large-scale organization and correctly predicted that this growth demanded a more formal set of procedures for how to administer organizations. He therefore created the idea of an ideal or "pure form" of organization, which he called *bureaucracy*. This term, as developed by Weber and his followers, did not refer to red tape and inefficiency, as it is often used today. Indeed, **bureaucracy,** for Weber, was the most efficient form of organization, and for him it filled the vacuum caused by the lack of principles regarding how managers should design and manage large organizations. Weber described bureaucracy as having certain characteristics:

1. A well-defined hierarchy of authority.

2. A clear division of work.

3. A system of rules covering the rights and duties of position incumbents.

4. A system of procedures for dealing with the work situation.

5. Impersonality of interpersonal relationships.

6. Selection for employment, and promotion based on technical competence.[9]

The *Autodesk* vignette shows one modern application.

BUREAUCRACY
Weber's "ideal" form of organization that involves the following: a well-defined hierarchy of authority; a clear division of work; a system of rules covering the rights and duties of position incumbents; a system of procedures for dealing with the work situation; impersonality of interpersonal relationships; and selection for employment and promotion based on technical competence.

SUMMARY: THE CLASSICAL APPROACH
TO MANAGEMENT

Generally speaking, the classical approach to management focused on rationalizing resources and on boosting efficiency. To writers like Taylor, Fayol, Weber, and the Gilbreths, an efficiently designed job and organization were of prime importance. They thus focused their efforts on developing analytical tools, techniques, and principles that would enable managers to create such efficient organizations. Human work behavior was not unimportant to the classical writers; instead they simply assumed its complexities away by arguing that financial incentives would suffice to ensure motivation. As a result, intentionally or not, the classicists left the impression that workers could be treated as givens in the system, as little more than appendages to their machines. "Design the most highly specialized and efficient job you can," assumed the classicist, and then "plug in the worker who will then do your bidding if the pay is right."

Yet the classical management approach was effective because it was a product of its time. Technological change was relatively slow and predictable, labor was abundant, markets tended to be highly localized or regionalized, and competitors were known and relatively unchanging. Particularly during the early 1900s, most managers found a strong demand for their products and could focus attention on efficiency rather than on developing new products or adapting to competitors' new initiatives. In such a relatively predictable and stable environment, an emphasis on efficiency and on immutable principles and a rigid organizational chain of command made a good deal of sense. But by the 1920s, things were changing.

AUTODESK, INC.

Some of Weber's theories of the bureaucratic organization are applicable in modern businesses. When Carol Bartz took over Sausalito, California-based Autodesk, Inc., for example, several things were readily apparent. The company makes one of the hottest selling computer-aided design packages, and is the world's sixth largest PC software-producing firm. But its enigmatic founder had relocated to Switzerland, leaving the company virtually adrift in the hands of CEO Al Green. After Green resigned in 1991, Autodesk was in chaos. Programmers squabbled with executives and each other, and very little was accomplished or resolved. Bartz decided that more structure, not less, was what Autodesk needed. With most of the rest of corporate America slashing management layers and downsizing company structures, Bartz's prescription ran against the tide.

Bartz created the company's first human resources department and installed professionals to handle questions from Autodesk's 1,600 employees. To head off maverick programmers intent on charting their own courses, employees were assigned supervisors and instructed to keep their supervisors apprised of work in progress. Bartz also implemented teamwork concepts through the use of *matrix-management,* grouping multiskilled workers on projects that were overseen by team leaders. Surprisingly, many programmers welcomed the heightened focus provided by their leaders. It turned out many were eager for direction.

According to Bartz, a certain number of rules are necessary, even for a group of free-spirited, creatively inclined computer programmers. In Bartz's view, the best organizations have decision makers at every level, and both responsibility and authority are passed down.

The transition to instill healthy bureaucracy wasn't all smooth sailing. Two of the company's divisions that weren't producing were sold off, and a lot of programmers couldn't cope with even the limited structural changes made. However, the overall results proved Bartz right. Net revenues grew 29 percent in her first year on the job. Although management changes, the selling of unprofitable divisions, and heavy investment in new products dampened net income, Bartz has Autodesk on the right track. "She empowers you to be aggressive," says chief financial officer Eric Herr, "and is prepared to help you if you need that help." Bartz proved that she's not one for adopting the latest management fads if "bureaucracy" is what's needed.

SOURCES: Jonathan Littman, "Hard Drive," *Working Woman,* June 1993, 45–83; Laurie Kretchmar, "Rising Star Eclipses Sun," Fortune, June 1, 1992, 148; "Carol Bartz, Star at Sun," *Working Woman,* November 1991, 90; and "What Should Business and Government Do for Women in 1993? And What Can Women Do for Themselves?" *Working Women,* November 1992, 56; Elizabeth Lesly, "Inside the Freshman Class of '92," *Business Week,* October 12, 1992, 118.

Carol Bartz, brought in as CEO of Autodesk in 1992, has gone against most current management theories by adding layers of management and creating more, rather than less structure.

THE BEHAVIORAL SCHOOL
OF MANAGEMENT

THE ENVIRONMENT

Many changes swept across the United States and the world in the 1920s and 1930s. Increasing numbers of people moved from farms to cities and thus became more dependent on each other. Factories became more mechanized and the jobs became more specialized and interdependent. The American frontier was no longer the vast, unexplored area that provided a safety valve for those wishing to start a new life away from the crowded cities.

Slowly, these forces built toward what William Scott has called the **period of collision,** resulting from "environmental conditions which draw people into inescapable proximity and dependency on one another."[10] Thus, an era of rapid growth and optimism gave way to one in which people felt closed in and dependent on one another. Scott believes that if these forces had been left unharnessed, the collision effect might have led to brutal competition, then conflict, and finally a degeneration of society.

This did not happen, since fundamental changes were taking place in society's values. Instead of continuing its hand-off policy, government became more involved in economic matters, and a number of lawsuits were filed to break-up big industrial monopolies. Social movements aimed at giving women the right to vote, electing senators by popular direct vote, establishing a minimum wage, and encouraging trade unions became more popular. Even the literature of the period became more anti-individualistic as people questioned whether a philosophy based on hard work,

PERIOD OF COLLISION
A period resulting from environmental conditions which draw people into inescapable proximity and dependency on one another.

individualism, and maximizing profits—the building blocks of the classical management era—might not actually have some drawbacks.

THE HAWTHORNE STUDIES AND THE HUMAN RELATIONS MOVEMENT

HAWTHORNE STUDIES

A series of studies begun in 1927 at the Chicago Hawthorne Plant of the Western Electric Company, which determined that performance depended on factors other than physical conditions or rate of pay, and that the social situations of the workers (not just working conditions) influenced their behavior and performance at work.

In 1927, the **Hawthorne Studies** began at the Chicago Hawthorne Plant of the Western Electric Company. They eventually added an entirely new perspective to the management of people at work.

Three main sets of studies took place. The first was based on what was then a traditional classical management assumption: that physical conditions influenced worker output and that, in particular, output would rise if the level of illumination at the work place increased. To test this theory, the researchers, led by Elton Mayo and Fritz Roethlisberger of Harvard, isolated a few workers in a separate room of the plant and observed the workers' reactions to changes in the level of lighting. To the researchers' surprise, not only did worker output not fall as illumination was reduced, it actually rose, at least until it was too dark to see.

A second series of studies aimed at explaining this phenomenon was carried out in what became known as the "relay assembly test room studies." A group of workers was again isolated and studied as a series of changes was made, such as modifying the length of the work day and altering the morning and afternoon rest breaks. Again, researchers noted that these factors did not greatly affect worker performance, underscoring a growing belief that performance depended on factors other than physical conditions or rate of pay.

The relay assembly test room studies led the researchers to conclude that the *social situations* of the workers, not just working conditions, influenced their behavior and performance at work. The researchers discovered, for instance, that in countless ways their observations had inadvertently made the workers feel they were each "someone special." The observer had changed the workers' situation by "his personal interest in the girls and their problems. He had always been sympathetically aware of their hopes and fears. He had granted them more and more privileges."[11]

HAWTHORNE EFFECT

The effect which happens when the scientist, in the course of his or her investigation, inadvertently influences the subject's behavior so that it is not the scientist's intended changes that affect the subject's behavior, but how the scientist acts.

These results have been codified as the *Hawthorne effect*. The **Hawthorne effect** is what happens when the scientist, in the course of his or her investigation, inadvertently influences the subjects' behavior so that is not the scientist's intended changes that affect the subject's behavior but how the scientist acts. In the relay assembly test room, for instance, the researchers wanted to place rest periods where they would be most advantageous. They therefore called a meeting during which they showed the workers their output curves, and pointed out the low and high points of the day. "When asked at what times they would like to have their rest, they unanimously voted in favor of 10:00 o'clock in the morning and 2:00 o'clock in the afternoon." Accordingly, the investigators agreed to institute the rest pauses at these times. This involvement in turn boosted employees' morale and performance.

As part of a third series of studies, researchers interviewed thousands of workers and confirmed that workers were driven not so much by pay as by needs, wants, and desires. Workers who felt adrift and degraded by oversimplified jobs sought companionship and security in their work groups. It also became apparent to the researchers that human performance at work depended not just on pay and working conditions, but it depended as much (or more) on the supervisor's leadership style and on the employee's belief that the company was treating him or her as a valued, unique individual. These results confirmed the researchers' initial conclusions from their observations of the Hawthorne studies.

HAWTHORNE'S CONSEQUENCES

The Hawthorne studies were a turning point in the study of management and became the basis for the human relations movement. As the work of the Hawthorne researchers became more widely known, managers and management experts recognized that human behavior at work was a complex and powerful force to be dealt with. This **human relations** movement may be defined as the school of management thought that emphasized that workers were not just givens in the system but instead had needs and desires that the organization and task had to accommodate.

The Hawthorne experiments ended in 1933 as the country fell deeper into the Great Depression. Between 1929 and 1933, U.S. unemployment rose from 3.2 percent to 30 percent. Businesses were failing, unemployment was widespread, incomes were dropping, and national morale was low. Individualism and the hard work ethic seemed to have failed. In their place a new social ethic arose that emphasized the importance of the group, getting along with others, government intervention, and security.

Other changes were occurring as well. The excess production capacity caused by the Depression stimulated corporate research and development activities. These activities, combined with the technological advances that accompanied World War II, resulted in burgeoning product diversification for the period beginning in the late 1930s and early 1940s. Because of this rapid product diversification, workers were called upon to carry out jobs that were very different from those workers faced during the classical management era. With a new emphasis on research, development, and product diversification, fewer jobs were of the assembly line variety as more jobs called for heavy doses of creativity and autonomy on the part of workers. These new demands for creativity and autonomy combined with the new social values and the Hawthorne findings and led to a more behavioral approach to management, one that put more emphasis on boosting employee morale. Such an approach is in use even today, as the *Tennessee Valley Authority* vignette shows.

HUMAN RELATIONS
The school of management thought that emphasizes that workers are not just givens in the system—but instead have needs and desires that the organization and task have to accommodate. Laid the foundation for what became known as organizational behavior.

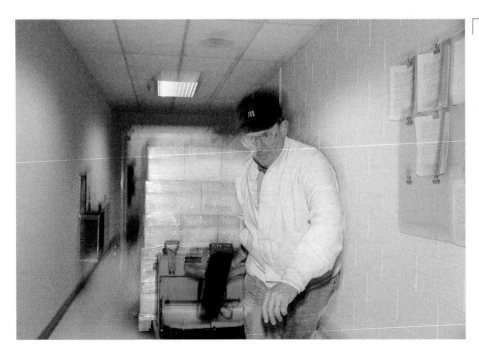

Tennessee Valley Authority CEO William Malec helps out in the company's supply room. Malec, who spends one day a month working among his employees, feels he gains valuable insights by doing so.

TENNESSEE VALLEY AUTHORITY

Tennessee Valley Authority chief financial officer William Malec believes in listening to what his employees have to say. One day a month he works alongside the rank and file. His job might include anything from cleaning bathrooms to delivering mail. In Malec's view, working with someone is the best way to learn what's on the other person's mind, and Malec thinks listening to workers is one of the best long-term methods of improving a firm's efficiency.

His plan is working. After his experience in the purchasing department, Malec got rid of a process limited to specific vendors, and issued plant managers credit cards that could be used at any store, saving $1.3 million annually. During his stint as a janitor, Malec learned how much time was wasted plugging and unplugging vacuum cleaners. He quickly replaced the old appliance with battery-powered models. And he used direct input from employees of the $5-billion federal utility to streamline and expedite everything from car rentals to bookkeeping.

Malec's working-class parents used to complain that their bosses never had time to listen to them because they didn't think workers had anything useful to say. Malec didn't like it then, and he doesn't believe it now. "When you get down into their jobs they will tell you things you don't normally hear," he says. Malec's hands-on approach represents quite a breakthrough in an organization that used to be viewed as just another bureaucratic federal agency. The experience can also be otherwise enlightening. One manager was always extra polite to Malec, but wasn't nearly so nice to mailroom workers. So it was a very sad day for the manager when the letter carrier he didn't recognize but treated badly turned out to be Malec. "This is what we have to change," Malec says.

SOURCE: Toddi Gutner, "Meeting the Boss," *Forbes,* March 1, 1993, 126; and G.E.D. "Cushioning the Blow in Tennessee," *FW,* September 1993, 34.

ENVIRONMENT, INCREASED DIVERSITY, AND CHANGE

Historian Alfred Chandler has suggested that after accumulating and then rationalizing resources, managers traditionally moved to a third stage in which they attempted to better utilize their organizational resources by developing new products and new markets—by diversifying. In the United States, movement into this third stage was hampered by the Depression. However, excess production capacity did ultimately stimulate research and development activities. This, coupled with the technological and managerial advancements that emerged in the years surrounding World War II, finally shifted most American industry into Chandler's third, **diversification** stage.[12]

To understand the evolving management theory, it is important to recognize that this period was characterized by differentiated, complex, and rapidly changing environments. Even before World War II, many firms had embarked upon extensive

DIVERSIFICATION
A style of management whereby managers attempt to better utilize their organizational resources by developing new products and new markets.

research and development activities to utilize their resources by developing new products. For example, at General Electric and Westinghouse, research and development activities resulted in the manufacture of plastics as well as a variety of other products based on electronics. The automobile companies had begun to produce airplane engines, electrical equipment, and household appliances before the war. After the war, companies in the rubber industry—such as United States Rubber and B.F. Goodrich, which had concentrated on tire manufacturing—entered into systematic research and development and began to market such items as latex, plastics, and flooring.

These environmental changes contributed to the development of management theory in several ways. First, the increased rate of change and novelty triggered by diversification meant that managers and management theorists could no longer view organizations as closed systems that were essentially isolated from their environments.[13] Second, efficiency was no longer a manager's main concern. It was eclipsed by the drives to diversify and monitor the activities of previously unrelated companies. Third, this shift toward making organizations more responsive was characterized by a trend toward **decentralization,** which in essence meant letting lower-level employees make more of their own decisions themselves. Decentralization, though, required a new managerial philosophy: allowing subordinates to do more problem solving and decision making meant that managers had to rely on their employees' self-control. This change (coming as it did just after Hawthorne's results became popularized) led to a new emphasis on participative, people-oriented leadership and a more behavioral approach to management.

DECENTRALIZATION
Letting lower level employees make more of their own decisions.

DOUGLAS McGREGOR: THEORY X, THEORY Y

The work of Douglas McGregor is a good example of this more behavioral approach to management. According to McGregor, the classical organization (with its highly specialized jobs, centralized decision making, and top-down communications) was not just a product of the need for more efficiency. Instead, McGregor said it was a reflection of certain basic managerial assumptions about human nature.[14] These assumptions, which McGregor somewhat arbitrarily classified as **Theory X,** held that most people dislike work and responsibility and prefer to be directed; that people are motivated not by the desire to do a good job, but simply by financial incentives; and that, therefore, most people must be closely supervised, controlled, and coerced into achieving organizational objectives.

THEORY X
Assumptions coined by Douglas McGregor; held that most people dislike work and responsibility and prefer to be directed; that people are motivated not by the desire to do a good job, but simply by financial incentives; and that, therefore, most people must be closely supervised, controlled, and coerced into achieving organizational objectives.

McGregor questioned the truth of this view and whether management practices such as specialized division of work are appropriate for the sorts of tasks faced by more modern organizations. He felt that management needed new organizations and practices to deal with diversification and decentralization and participative decision making. These new practices had to be based on a revised set of assumptions about the nature of human beings. What emerged was an alternate set of assumptions, which McGregor called **Theory Y.** Unlike Theory X assumptions, Theory Y assumptions held that people could enjoy work and that an individual would exercise substantial self-control over his or her performance if the conditions were favorable. Implicit in Theory Y is the belief that people are motivated by the desire to do a good job and by the opportunity to affiliate with their peers, rather than just by financial rewards.

THEORY Y
A set of assumptions which holds that people enjoy work and that an individual will exercise substantial self-control over his or her performance if the conditions are favorable.

RENSIS LIKERT AND THE EMPLOYEE-CENTERED ORGANIZATION

Researcher Rensis Likert's work is another example of the trends in management during these post-war years. He concluded that effective organizations differ from ineffective ones in several ways. Less effective **job-centered companies** focus on specialized

JOB-CENTERED COMPANIES
Companies characterized by a focus on specialized jobs, efficiency, and closely supervised workers.

jobs, efficiency, and closely supervising workers, he said. On the other hand, more effective organizations "focus their primary attention on endeavoring to build effective work groups with high performance goals."[15] As Likert noted, in **employee-centered companies:**

> The leadership and other processes of the organization must be such as to insure a maximum probability that in all interactions and all relationships with the organization, each member will, in the light of his background, values and expectations, view the experience as supportive and one which builds and maintains his sense of personal worth and importance.[16]

EMPLOYEE-CENTERED COMPANIES
Companies characterized by participation, supportive leadership, and emphasizing the sense of worth of each member of that organization.

CHRIS ARGYRIS AND THE MATURE INDIVIDUAL

Chris Argyris reached similar conclusions but approached the problem from a different perspective.[17] In his view, the classical *command and control* approach to managing was unhealthy to the workers involved. Argyris argued that healthy people go through a maturation process. As a person approaches adulthood, he or she moves to a state of increased activity, independence, and stronger interests, and passes from the subordinate position of a child to an equal or superordinate position as an adult. Gaining employees' compliance by assigning them to highly specialized jobs with no decision-making power and then closely supervising them inhibits these normal maturation processes by encouraging workers to be dependent, passive and subordinate. Argyris concluded that it would be better to give workers more responsibility and broader jobs.

THE BEHAVIORALIST PRESCRIPTIONS

Behavioral scientists like Argyris, McGregor, and Likert soon translated their ideas into practical methodologies, methodologies that became the heart of the emerging subject of organization behavior. Likert, for example, emphasized leadership style and group processes. "The low-producing managers, in keeping with the traditional practice, feel that the way to motivate and direct behavior is to exercise control through authority."[18] In contrast, "the highest-producing managers feel, generally, that this manner of functioning does not produce the best results, that the resentment created by direct exercise of authority tends to limit its effectiveness."[19] Therefore, said Likert, "widespread use of participation is one of the more important approaches employed by the high-producing managers."[20] He found that this participation applied to all aspects of the job and of work, "as, for example, in setting work goals and budgets, controlling costs, organizing the work, etc."[21]

McGregor had his own prescriptions, too. He said decentralization and pushing decision making down should be the norm in order to free people from the "too-close control of conventional organization." Management should encourage *job enlargement* (in which the variety of tasks an employee performed is increased) so that workers' jobs are made more challenging and interesting. *Participative management* (which he said would give employees some voice in decisions that affect them) would similarly enhance self-control. Finally, he urged using *management-by-objectives* to encourage self-control. When this technique is used, subordinates set goals jointly with their supervisors and are measured on the accomplishments of these goals, thus avoiding the need for day-to-day close supervision.

For Argyris, as for McGregor and Likert, the solution was to decrease what he called the dependency, subordination, and submissiveness of employees. To do this, he recommended taking several steps. For example, Argyris suggested that organizations eliminate submissiveness by instituting communication systems that would provide each employee with "the right to appeal against any executive decision or action of an executive or a superior which affects him and which he considers to be unfair or unjust."[22] He suggested instituting profit-sharing incentive plans in which employees are encouraged to make quality and productivity enhancing suggestions and then share in whatever profits result from their ideas. "The assumption is that the workers at the lowest levels are important human resources who can make important contributions."[23] Firms should also encourage workers to participate in problem solving and institute the sorts of decentralized, team-based structures advocated by Likert.[24] The *Phelps County Bank* small business box shows how one small business is applying this behavioral approach today.

BRIDGING THE ERAS: CHESTER BARNARD AND HERBERT SIMON

The work of Barnard and Simon does not fit neatly into any one school of management theory. Their research actually spanned several schools and contributed to the development of an integrated theory of management.

CHESTER BARNARD   Chester Barnard used his experience as an executive to develop an important new management theory. He was the president of New Jersey Bell Telephone Company and, at various times, president of the United Service Organization (the USO of World War II), president of the Rockefeller Foundation, and chairman of the National Science Foundation.

Barnard was the first major theorist after the Hawthorne studies to emphasize the importance and variability of the individual in the work place. He said, for example, that "an essential element of organizations is the willingness of persons to contribute their individual efforts to the cooperative system." And he added that "the individual is always the basic strategic factor in organization. Regardless of his history or obligations, he must be induced to cooperate, or there can be no cooperation."

Barnard therefore set about developing a theory of how to get workers to cooperate. According to Barnard the question is, how do you get the individual to surrender his or her personal preferences and to go along with the authority exercised by his or her supervisor?[25]

Barnard believed the answer could be found in what he called the person's **zone of indifference,** a range within each individual in which he or she would willingly accept orders without consciously questioning their authority.[26] Barnard saw the willingness to cooperate as the expression of the net satisfactions or dissatisfactions experienced or anticipated by each person. In other words, organizations had to provide sufficient inducements to broaden each employee's zone of indifference and thus increase the likelihood that the boss's orders would be obeyed.

But Barnard, in a clear break with the classicists, said that material incentives by themselves were not enough: "the unaided power of material incentives, when the minimum necessities are satisfied, in my opinion, is exceedingly limited as to most men."[27] Instead, said Barnard, several other classes of incentives, including "the opportunities for distinction, prestige, [and] personal power" are also required.

HERBERT SIMON   Whereas Barnard wrote from the vantage point of an executive, Herbert Simon was a scholar who had mastered organization theory, economics, natural science, and political science, and who went on to win the Nobel Prize in economics. Like Barnard, Simon viewed getting employees to do what the organization needed them to do as a major issue facing managers. He proposed two basic ways to gain such compliance:

ZONE OF INDIFFERENCE
A range within each individual in which he or she would willingly accept orders without consciously questioning the supervisor's authority.

PHELPS COUNTY BANK

By the time Emma Lou Brent took over Phelps County Bank in 1982, she had long heard that small town banks would soon be a thing of the past. She never thought she would one day be CEO of the bank where she began working 20 years earlier as a teller. She also didn't think there was any reason Phelps Bank couldn't compete, as long as she attracted smart people and gave them the right motivation to produce. Brent needed to be right. Her two chief competitors in town were affiliates of big, national bank holding companies, and the region's market consisted of just 35,000 people.

Since she had started at the bottom, Brent had memories of managers who had disregarded her suggestions. Now that she was in charge, she began informally soliciting employee input in decision making. Eventually, she established annual goal-setting meetings for the entire bank staff, managers, and board members. She also initiated a participation-reward program. Anyone could submit an idea they thought might improve service or operations. The best one each month earned the donor $100; the employee with the best idea of the year won a trip for two worth $1,500.

On her way up the corporate ladder, Brent had to learn banking operations slowly, one step at a time. She had a better idea for her 55 employees. She arranged classes taught by the American Institute of Banking, with particular emphasis on problem solving. Once staffers had a handle on regulations and bank services, they were given the latitude to make decisions on their own.

Phelps County Bank personnel, like teller Judy Bieger, are given the latitude to solve customer problems on the spot. CEO Emma Lou Brent has been able to compete with local branches of larger banks by emphasizing personal service.

Brent figured a good way to show employees they were valued was to offer incentives. She decided that an employee stock ownership plan would not only provide for employees' retirement needs, but would also make them owners and give them the incentive to work hard for the customer. Now one of the bank's yearly highlights is the shareholders' dinner when Brent distributes everyone's stock ownership account update, along with objectives for the

FOCUS ON SMALL BUSINESS

coming year. "That's when it really came home to me . . .," says employee Patti Douglas. "Gee whiz, I'm an owner of that bank . . . Anything that I can do for this bank to improve it, I benefit from."

It didn't take long to notice the difference at PCB. Customers who come to the door after closing time are now ushered to a secure room, and customer service reps have the authority to take care of most problems on the spot. Whenever possible, tellers resolve customer complaints and avoid shunting them over to the service representatives. PCB loan officers have been known to close loans after work hours and even at the customer's home if that happens to be most convenient. Douglas even created a product program designed to attract senior citizens. She'd researched it for two years. Peggy Laun, another loan department employee, looked into an electronic tax filing service. She ultimately backed off the idea after discovering the available software wasn't up to speed and the idea would create more problems than it solved.

Brent successfully implemented a can-do culture at PCB. She thought motivated employees would translate into first-rate service providers. The bank's customer service creed sums up the attitude: "Each of us has the authority and the responsibility to do what we feel necessary to solve a customer's problem. We are owners of our bank, and customers expect owners to solve problems." As for those two megabanks that are PCB's competitors—they're currently in second and third place.

SOURCE: John Case, "Total Customer Service," *Inc.*, January 1994, 52–61.

Decisions reached in the highest ranks of the organization hierarchy will have no effect upon the activities of operative employees unless they are communicated downward. Consideration of the process requires an examination of the ways in which the behavior of the operative employee can be influenced. These influences fall roughly into two categories: (1) *establishing in the operative employee himself* attitudes, habits and a state of mind which lead him to reach that decision which is advantageous to the organization, and (2) *imposing on the operative employee decisions reached elsewhere* in the organization. The first type of influence operates by inculcating in the employee organizational loyalties and a concern with efficiency, and more generally by training him. The second type of influence depends primarily upon authority and upon advisory and informational services. It is not insisted that these categories are either exhaustive or mutually exclusive.[28]

Thus, according to Simon, managers can ensure that their employees carry out their tasks in one of two ways. They can *impose control* by closely monitoring their subordinates and insisting that they do their jobs as they have been ordered to do them (thereby using the classicists' command and control approach to managing). Or, managers can foster their employees' *self-control* by better training them, by encouraging participative leadership, or by developing their employees' commitment and loyalty. As rapid change forced employers to depend more and more on their employees' initiative, developing such self-control would soon become a major theme in management writings. First, we should discuss The Quantitative School.

THE QUANTITATIVE SCHOOL

After World War II, a trend developed among management theorists to apply quantitative techniques to a wide range of managerial problems. This movement is usually referred to as **operations research** or **management science** and has been described as "the application of scientific methods, techniques and tools to problems involving the operations of systems so as to provide those in control of the system with optimum solutions to the problems."[29]

OPERATIONS RESEARCH (MANAGEMENT SCIENCE)
The application of scientific methods, techniques, and tools to problems involving the operations of systems so as to provide those in control of the system with optimum solutions to the problems.

THE MANAGEMENT SCIENCE APPROACH

Management science has three distinguishing characteristics. First, management scientists generally deal with well-defined problems that have clear and *undisputable standards of effectiveness*. They want to know, for instance, if inventory costs have been too high and should be reduced by 20 percent, or if a specific number of items should be produced at each of a company's plants to minimize transportation costs to customers.

Second, management scientists generally deal with problems that have *well-defined alternative courses of action*. Thus, a company might have four alternative plants from which to ship products or various levels of product A and product B that can be produced to maximize sales revenues. Finally, management scientists must develop a *theory or model* describing how the relevant factors are related. Like any scientist, management scientists must understand the problem and relationships clearly enough to formulate a mathematical model.

Historian Daniel Wren points out that operations research/management science has "direct lineal roots in scientific management."[30] Like Taylor and the Gilbreths, today's management scientists try to find optimal solutions to management problems. As Taylor and his people used scientific methods to find the one best way to do a job, management scientists use the scientific method to find the best solution to industrial problems. The difference in the two approaches is two-fold. First, modern-day management scientists have at their disposal much more sophisticated mathematical tools and computers. Second, management science's goal is not to try to find a science of management (as did Taylor) as much as to use scientific analysis and tools to solve management problems.

THE SYSTEMS APPROACH

The management science approach is closely associated with what is called the systems approach to management. A **system** is any entity—a hospital, a city, a company, or a person, for instance—that has interdependent parts and a purpose. **Systems approach** advocates argue that viewing an organization as a system helps managers to remember that a firm's different parts, departments, or subsystems are interrelated and must all contribute to the organization's purpose.

According to systems advocates like C. West Churchman, all systems have four basic characteristics.[31] First, all systems operate within an *environment*. An environment may be defined as those things that are outside of and important to the organization, but that are largely beyond its control. For a company this might include clients, competitors, unions, and governments.

Second, all systems are composed of building blocks called elements, components, or *subsystems*. In an organization, these basic building blocks might be departments, like those for production, finance, and sales. The subsystems may also cut across traditional departmental lines. For example, the marketing subsystem might include sales, advertising, and transportation because each of these elements have an impact on the marketing task of getting the product to the customer.

Third, all systems have a central *purpose* against which the organization's efforts and subsystems can be evaluated. For example, the optimal inventory level for a firm that serves top-of-the-line customers would probably be higher than that of a firm whose customers want the best buy in town and are willing to wait for shelves to be restocked.

Fourth, all systems are also characterized by the *interrelatedness* of their elements. Focusing on the interrelatedness among the subsystems (and between the subsystems and the firm's environment) is an essential characteristic of systems thinking. For one thing, interrelatedness emphasizes the fact that a manager can't change one subsystem without affecting the rest. For example, hiring a new production manager might actually have repercussions in the sales and accounting departments. Furthermore, interrelated thinking underscores the need for managers and management theorists to be more sensitive to how the changes taking place in industrial environments affect how companies are organized and managed.

TOWARD A SITUATIONAL MANAGEMENT THEORY

BACKGROUND

This emphasis on the openness of the organization to its environment plus the apparent contradictions between the command and control classical management approach and the employee-centered behavioralist approach led managers and management experts to question which management theory was best. In 1961, Professor Harold Koontz published a paper entitled "The Management Theory Jungle." In it he said that the variety of management schools, terminologies, and assumptions had resulted in confusion and "jungle warfare" among the various schools of thought.[32] As a result of

SYSTEM
Any entity that has interdependent parts and a purpose.

SYSTEMS APPROACH
Viewing an organization as a system means managers remember that a firm's different parts, departments, or subsystems are interrelated and must all contribute to the organization's purpose.

this article, a group of management scholars and practitioners with diverse research and analytical approaches to management met at a symposium in California. Participants left this symposium with a renewed interest in management principles. Management experts began to search in earnest for a way to unify the different management theories.

THE SITUATIONAL THEORISTS

At about the same time (the early 1960s) organizational research studies in England and the United States began to underscore the need for a *situational* or contingency view of management, one in which the appropriateness of the organization and the management principles was contingent on the rate of change in an organization's environment and technology. In one such study, Tom Burns and G.M. Stalker analyzed a number of industrial firms in England. They concluded that whether what they called a "mechanistic" or an "organic" management system was appropriate depended on the nature of the organization's environment.

> We have endeavored to stress the appropriateness of each system to its own specific set of conditions. Equally, we desire to avoid the suggestion that either system is superior under all circumstances to the other. In particular, nothing in our experience justifies the assumption that the mechanistic system should be superseded by the organic in conditions of stability. The beginning of administrative wisdom is the awareness that there is no one optimum type of management system.[33]

They argued that a **mechanistic management system** was appropriate if the company's task was routine and unchanging. Thus, in a textile mill that they studied, it was important to have long, stable production runs that kept surprises to a minimum and thereby prevented the necessity to shut down huge machines. In such unchanging conditions Burns and Stalker found that a mechanistic (or classical) management approach was appropriate, one characterized by an emphasis on efficiency, specialized jobs, elaborate procedures for keeping behavior in line, and an insistence that everyone play by the rules.

On the other hand, Burns and Stalker found that the more behavioral, **organic management system** was appropriate if innovative, entrepreneurial activities were important. In high-tech electronic firms, for instance, companies and their employees are constantly under pressure to come up with new devices so that they can compete effectively with rival firms. Burns and Stalker found that management often ran such firms with an organic approach that emphasized creativity, rather than efficiency. These firms placed less emphasis on specialized jobs and issued fewer rules and procedures. Instead, they delegated decisions to employees who then exercised self-control in getting their jobs done. These findings are summarized in Figure 4.2.

Also in England, Joan Woodward and researchers from the Tavistock Institute analyzed a group of firms to discover the relationship between an organization and its production technology. The organic, flexible system described by Burns and Stalker again appeared to be more appropriate where dealing with unexpected, unpredictable occurrences was of paramount concern. Thus it was used in small, custom-made job shops, and in large factories that were built to run continuously and in which unexpected breakdowns were therefore a main concern. On the other hand, Woodward and her team found that the mechanistic, classical approach was appropriate where predictability and efficiency were paramount, such as where mass production technologies and assembly lines were utilized.[34]

These findings and others like them culminated in what came to be called a situational or contingency approach to management theory. What follows is how Paul Lawrence and Jay Lorsch, two of the original investigators in this area, put it.

MECHANISTIC MANAGEMENT SYSTEM
Management that is appropriate if the company's task was routine and unchanging, and that is characterized by specialized jobs, top-down communications, imposed control, and "sticking to the chain of command" for making decisions.

ORGANIC MANAGEMENT SYSTEM
If innovative, entrepreneurial activities are important, this style of management is more appropriate, and is characterized by enlarged jobs, lateral communications, participative management, and an emphasis on self-control and worker commitment.

FIGURE 4.2

Burns and Stalker's
Mechanistic and Organic
Systems of Management

*Burns and Stalker concluded
that the management system
that was best depended on the
company's environment. The
mechanistic system (roughly
comparable to the classical approach to managing) was
appropriate to routine, unchanging conditions. The
organic system (similar in
many ways to the behavioralist's approach) was best for
fast-changing situations.*

SOURCE: Tom Burns and G.M.
Stalker, *The Management of
Innovation* (London: Tavis-
tack Publications, 1961).

CHARACTERISTICS OF ORGANIC SYSTEMS OF MANAGEMENT

The contributive nature of special knowledge and experience to the common task of the concern

The "realistic" nature of the individual task, which is seen as set by the total situation of the concern

The adjustment and continual redefinition of individual tasks through interaction with others

The shedding of "responsibility" as a limited field of rights, obligations, and methods

The growth of commitment to the concern beyond any technical definition

A network structure of control, authority, and communication

Omniscience no longer imputed to the head of the concern; location of knowledge about the technical or commercial nature of the present task located anywhere in the network

A lateral rather than a vertical direction of communication through the organization; also, a communication between people of different rank, resembling consultation rather than command

Content of communication consisting of information and advice rather than instructions and decisions

Commitment to the concern's task and to the "technological ethos" of material progress and expansion more highly valued than loyalty and obedience

Importance and prestige attached to affiliations and expertise valid in the industrial, technical, and commercial environments outside the firm

CHARACTERISTICS OF MECHANISTIC SYSTEMS OF MANAGEMENT

The specialized differentiation of functions, to which the problems and tasks facing the concern as a whole are broken down

The abstract nature of each task, which is pursued with techniques and purposes more or less distinct from those of the concern as a whole

The use of the formal hierarchy for coordination

The precise definition of rights, obligations, and technical methods attached to each functional role

The translation of rights, obligations, and methods into the responsibilities of a functional position

Hierarchic structure of control, authority, and communication

A reinforcement of the hierarchic structure by the location of knowledge of actualities exclusively at the top of the hierarchy

A tendency for interaction between members of the concern to be vertical; i.e., between superior and subordinate

A tendency for operations and working behavior to be governed by the instructions and decisions issued by superiors

Insistence on loyalty to the concern and obedience to superiors as a condition of membership

A greater importance and prestige attaching to internal (local) than to general (cosmopolitan) knowledge, experience, and skill

During the past few years there has been evident a new trend in the study of organizational phenomena. Underlying this new approach is the idea that the internal functioning of organizations must be consistent with the demands of the organization's task, technology, or external environment, and the needs of its members if the organization is to be effective. Rather than searching for the panacea of the one best way to organize under all conditions, investigators have more and more tended to examine the functioning of organizations in relation to the needs of their particular members and the external pressures facing them. Basically, this approach seems to be leading to the development of a "contingency" theory of organization, with the appropriate internal states and processes of the organization contingent upon external requirements and member needs.[35]

INTO THE FUTURE

Our discussion of the foundations of modern management returns us, in a sense, to some of the ideas we first encountered back in Chapter 1. While no one best way to manage exists, experts have little doubt that the management system that is best for a particular organization depends in part on how fast the firm's environment is changing. And, as we discussed in Chapter 1, today's environments are changing very fast, due to trends like globalization, deregulation, technological innovation, and an increased emphasis on service jobs and information technology. That is why management author Tom Peters—billing the 1980s as "an era of unprecedented uncertainty"—argues that "a clear picture of the successful firm in the 1990s and beyond emerges," and it will be

- Flatter. (They will have fewer layers of managers.)
- Populated by more autonomous units. (They will have more local authority to introduce and price products.)
- Oriented toward differentiation, producing high-value added goods and services and creating niche markets.
- Quality conscious.
- Service-conscious.
- More responsive.
- Much faster at innovation.
- A user of highly-trained, flexible people as the principal means of adding value.[36]

In Figure 4.3 Peters summarizes his vision of where management theory is heading and the forces that are propelling it there. A series of forces (as shown on the left of the chart), including uncertainty, technological revolution, new competitors, and changing tastes, are interacting with one another to create a completely new and rapidly changing context for doing business. This has led to much more uncertainty for managers. As a result, *the company winners today and tomorrow, he says, will have to be designed and managed to be as responsive as possible.* With that in mind, we turn to the next part of our book to see how managers can use the planning, organizing, staffing, and controlling functions to make their firms more responsive.

GENERIC UNCERTAINTY

- Oil @ $5 or $35 a barrel
- 1 trillion Eurodollars
- $80 trillion in annual currency = trading/gyrating exchange rates
- Casino society (junk bonds, availability of venture capital, strong market for initial public offerings, leveraged buyouts)
- $1 trillion in developing-country debt
- Mergers, divestitures, de-integration, joint ventures
- Record business and bank failures (and record start-ups)

TECHNOLOGY REVOLUTION

- Design (fast collection of customer data, reduced design-to-manufacture time)
- Manufacturing (smaller, more flexible factories)
- Distribution (electronic linkages, power to customers)

NEW COMPETITORS

FOREIGN

- Developed (e.g. Japan, Germany)
- Newly industrialized (e.g. Korea)
- Rapidly industrializing (e.g. Brazil)

DOMESTIC

- Smaller firms resulting from the entrepreneurial explosion
- Downsized and de-integrated units within big firms, spun-off elements from big firms

CHANGING TASTES

- More options
- Two-wage-earner families
- More affluence (top third)
- Less affluence (bottom third)
- Saturation of markets for the "commodities" of yesteryear
- Demand for superior quality

OUTCOME

- Uncertainty
- End of isolation
- Demise of mass (markets and production)
- More choices
- Market fragmentation
- Product and service explosion
- Demand for quality and fast response
- More complexity
- Midsize firms
- Cleaned-up portfolios and more competitive big firms' business units

SHAPE OF A WINNER

- Niche-oriented market creators (short production runs)
- Flat (fewer layers)
- Fast (responsive, adaptive)
- Quality-conscious
- Internationalist (even if small)
- Smaller (stand-alone, small within big)
- Gain sharing, participation, adding value through people

FIGURE 4.3

Rapid Change Creates a Need for Responsive Organizations

A series of forces—generic uncertainty, technology revolution, new competitors, and changing tastes—are creating outcomes that include uncertainty, more choices, and more complexity. The result is that the organizational winners of today and tomorrow will have to be responsive, smaller, flatter, and oriented toward adding value through people.

SOURCE: Tom Peters, *Thriving on Chaos*, (New York: Harper & Row, 1987), 37.

SUMMARY

Management techniques have always been a product of the environment of the time. During the Industrial Revolution, the emphasis was on resource accumulation and company growth. These newly emerging large-scale industrial enterprises required new management techniques and organizational structures. Managers responded by adopting concepts such as centralized decision making, a rigid chain of command, specialized division of work, and autocratic leadership.

By the late 1800s, the focus was beginning to shift from growth to efficiency. It was out of this industrial environment that the classical school of management emerged. Writers like Frederick Taylor, Frank and Lillian Gilbreth, Henri Fayol, and Max Weber advocated a scientific management approach. Believing that efficiently designed jobs and organizations were of prime importance, they focused their efforts on developing analytical tools, techniques, and principles that would enable managers to better create such efficient organizations.

The Hawthorne studies, which began in 1927, became the basis for the human relations movement. This new management theory emphasized that workers were not just givens in the system, but had needs and desires that the organization and task had to accommodate. The excess production capacity that resulted from the Great Depression and the technological advances spawned by World War II led to increased product diversification. The new demands for employee creativity and autonomy required to sustain product diversification, combined with evolving social values and the Hawthorne findings, led to a more behavioral approach to management. Douglas McGregor's Theory X and Theory Y, Rensis Likert's theories on employee-centered organizations, and Chris Argyris' views of the mature individual are examples of the behavioral approach of this period.

The work of Chester Barnard and Herbert Simon contributed to the development of an integrated theory of management. Barnard emphasized the importance and variability of the individual in the work setting and developed a theory he called the zone of indifference, which described how to get workers to cooperate in their organizational endeavors. Simon also viewed employee compliance as a major issue facing companies and suggested that managers could either impose control or foster their workers' self-control.

After World War II, a trend developed toward applying quantitative techniques to the solution of a wide range of managerial problems. This movement is usually referred to as operations research or management science. The quantitative school is also closely associated with what is called the systems approach to management, which holds that an organization is a set of subsystems that are interrelated and must all contribute to the organization's purpose.

Situational theorists underscored the idea that the appropriateness of the organization and the management principles were contingent on the rate of change in an organization's environment and technology. The mechanistic and organic management systems outlined by Tom Burns and G.M. Stalker are typical of the situational or contingency approach to management. Although no single best way to manage exists, the rapidly changing environment means that successful organizations of the future must be designed and managed to be responsive and adaptive.

QUESTIONS

■ FOR REVIEW

1. What four principles serve as the framework for Frederick Winslow Taylor's scientific management?

2. Explain the significance of the Hawthorne studies and their impact on the human relations movement.

3. List some of the environmental factors that led to the behavioral approach to management.

4. Describe the three distinguishing characteristics of the management science approach and the four basic characteristics of the systems approach.

5. Contrast the mechanistic and organic management approaches. When is each most effective?

■ FOR DISCUSSION

6. How do the management changes that characterized the Industrial Revolution compare to management trends today? Discuss your answer.

7. Which aspects of Max Weber's bureaucracy are still most effective today? Why are some of his principles no longer so applicable?

8. Do you think most modern organizations implemented the theories advocated in the behavioral approach to management? Why, or why not?

9. Are successful firms of the 1990s going to achieve the characteristics described by management author Tom Peters? Why or why not?

■ FOR ACTION

10. Research the recent changes at IBM. Write a report describing how the company is implementing the modern management techniques described at the end of this chapter.

11. Ask a retired worker to discuss the management changes he or she witnessed after World War II. Compare the practices of the past with your own experience with modern practices.

12. How might the management changes of the last ten years affect your job prospects upon graduation?

■ FOR FOCUS ON SMALL BUSINESS

13. Which of the behavioralist prescriptions discussed in the chapter have been implemented by Emma Lou Brent?

14. How has the management approach at Phelps Bank changed in the 20 years since Brent was first hired as a part-time teller?

15. Consider some forces that will change the bank's way of doing business as it moves into the next century.

CLOSING SOLUTION

AMERITECH

Weiss's first move was to eliminate 7 percent of the company's managers and to revolutionize the way those that remained did things. At first, no one would tackle hard decisions, the company lacked direction and vision, and little was getting accomplished because few would make the necessary commitments required to follow through. That indecisiveness would prove disastrous if it continued because Ameritech's markets were changing fast. Weiss's solution was direct: the most effective way to get people to accept the need for change was not to give them a choice. He created a culture where managers were not only willing to challenge one another, but could even question him. Weiss made it clear that he intended to provide strong leadership from the top, and he expected his managers to do likewise. He reorganized the firm into business units that targeted specific customer segments and needs. Teams were used to design work processes, with each member responsible for results. The firm also began planning an incentive system so workers would have a financial interest in their own productivity.

As in any reorganization, some employees were able to adjust and others weren't. Weiss's response to one and all was that he could offer no guarantees about the future because he simply didn't know how Ameritech would stack up against the competition. One thing he was sure of was that the old monopoly mentality—which held the company was entitled to a profit and workers could count on lifetime employment—was gone for good. Today, Ameritech is not much different from other organizations that have learned the keys to competing successfully in the 1990s and beyond lay in responsiveness and committed employees.

▪ QUESTIONS FOR CLOSING SOLUTION

1. Using the concepts discussed in the chapter, describe Weiss's approach to management.

2. In what ways is Weiss's management style a reflection of the current environment?

3. Does the newly reorganized Ameritech have any of the characteristics of the successful firm described by Tom Peters? If so, which ones?

KEY TERMS

Industrial Revolution

Classical School of Management

Scientific Management

Motion-study Principles

Bureaucracy

Period of Collision

Hawthorne Studies

Hawthorne Effect

Human Relations

Diversification

Decentralization

Theory X

Theory Y

Job-centered Companies

Employee-centered Companies

Zone of Indifference

Operations Research (management science)

System

Systems Approach

Mechanistic Management System

Organic Management System

JAGUAR

Late in the 1980s, Ford outbid rival General Motors for the purchase of Jaguar Cars, Ltd. The price tag was a hefty $2.5 billion, and Ford later had to invest an additional $700 million to keep the defect-prone automaker operating. The timing could scarcely have been worse. The world market for luxury cars was headed into a tailspin, and Jaguar's market share was tiny compared to competitors like Mercedes-Benz and Cadillac. The problems ran deep and wide at Jaguar. Manufacturing experts at Ford had transformed its U.S. plants into the best in the world. But they had their work cut out for them again in trying to recoup Ford's big investment in what clearly was one sick cat.

Ford executives' first inkling of real trouble came soon after acquiring the British automaker. They were aware of the numerous quality problems, but they didn't expect an engineering staff that had grown so accustomed to a dearth of investment funds that they had virtually ceased trying to develop new car models. The only product in the works turned out to be a new sports model that was underpowered and overpriced. The planned car was put on indefinite suspension.

Another problem was readily apparent. Though small compared to other automakers, communication between departments at Jaguar basically didn't exist. Managers were hesitant to offer ideas and marketing people were out of touch with engineers. Such breakdowns didn't bode well for producing significant new offerings at Jaguar.

The culture at Jaguar—the values its workers shared—also stifled worker initiative. Under union rules, workers walked off the job or simply read the paper when daily quotas were reached. Workers were hostile toward management, and the sentiment was reciprocated. Not surprisingly, productivity was so bad that some were comparing it to factory output in the old Soviet Union. German workers were twice as productive; at Toyota's Lexus division, employees produced four times as fast as their counterparts at Jaguar. After completing its acquisition, Ford began emphasizing quality, starting on the factory floor.

The efforts are slowly beginning to bear fruit. Insisting that workers take more responsibility has led to an 80 percent reduction in assembly-line defects. Warranty service work on 1992 models was down 25 percent. At the same time, productivity has increased 35 percent. Though good, the improvements still aren't sufficient to recoup Ford's investment anytime soon. Total worker-hours needed to produce a car has been cut from an average of 418.6 to around 250, but the goal of 126 hours is still far off. Building a Jaguar takes about three times longer than it takes to build one of Ford's top-of-the-line offerings like the Lincoln Town car. Cash incentives from Ford will motivate engineers to iron out quality problems in existing models. It will also breathe new life into the next generation of cars still on the drawing board. But then marketers will have to convince luxury automobile buyers that the quality is really back in Jaguar.

It is encouraging to note that the company's culture and even the attitudes of union members have turned around. "Our members have a new realization that they are the company, that customer satisfaction starts inside the factory," says Chris Liddell, a union leader. The newly motivated work force will be facing a trial by fire for the foreseeable future. Jaguar's return to profitability will hinge on efficiently producing its new offerings. The company spent almost a quarter billion dollars on redesigning the XJ6, which came out in 1994. Robust profitability will only be achieved if Jaguar can successfully create a high-volume car that is less expensive and will be attractive to fleet buyers. Engineers are feverishly trying to put together a competitor for the BMW 540i by 1998. Sales projections for the model (code named X200) are 50,000 by the end of the decade, approximately doubling total sales volume.

Ford executives may ultimately pour as much as $5 billion into Jaguar. Their contention has been that creating a car company with the same mystique and allure of the British automaker would have cost far more. What isn't in dispute is the need for Ford executives to continue implementing management policies that maximize initiative in what had been a stagnated work force. Significant increases in productivity have already been realized. A good deal remains to be done before Jaguar becomes the formidable predator it once was.

SOURCES: Mark Maremont et al., "Would You Pay $2 Billion for a Sick Cat?" *Business Week,* October 23, 1989, 58; Jerry Flint, "Save the Cat," *Forbes,* September 16, 1991, 191; Mark M. Colodny, "Can Mike Dale Fix Jaguar—Again?" *Fortune,* November 5, 1990, 165; Alex Taylor III, "Shaking Up Jaguar," *Fortune,* September 6, 1993, 65–67; Mark Maremont et al., "Can Ford Make a Tiger out of Jaguar?" *Business Week,* October 29, 1990, 73–74; and Mark Maremont et al., "These Repair Jobs Are Taking a Little Longer Than Expected," *Business Week,* April 27, 1992, 117–21.

■ QUESTIONS

1. Which management techniques described in this chapter would have the best chance of reviving Jaguar?
2. Have the problems at Jaguar gone beyond the scope of management theories making them virtually impossible to remedy? Discuss your answer.
3. What characteristics must the Jaguar organization develop to keep up with its global competitors in the future?

A CASE IN DIVERSITY

McDONALD'S

The marketing managers at McDonald's are nothing if not innovative. In the past few years the mega fast-food retailer has established chain outlets on Swiss rail cars, throughout Eastern Europe, and even in India, where cows are regarded as sacred. But, while catering to the widely disparate tastes and preferences of global customers is tough, it's only half of the battle. McDonald's also faces the constant challenge of meeting the needs of its diverse, worldwide work force.

In India, the aversion to eating beef will most likely mean using lamb as a substitute for the main ingredient in the Big Mac. And McDonald's breakfast devotees in Switzerland needn't bother searching the menu for the morning U.S. staple of the Egg McMuffin. The Swiss palate is more attuned to croissant, marmalade, and cheese. Later in the day, customers may select wine or beer with their fast-food feast. In Eastern Europe, patrons may be dazzled by the simple fact that McDonald's outlets have adequate product on-hand. By franchising its stores, the company is able to by-pass most of the regulatory requirements of inert state bureaucracies.

After adapting to the unique tastes of customers from far-flung locales, the company has to get employees up to speed on serving them the McDonald's way. Though challenging, it's not something entirely new. In the United States, McDonald's has long been a pioneer in hiring, training, and maintaining a diverse work force. Besides hiring persons from virtually all ethnic backgrounds, it began employing individuals with mental and physical disabilities almost 30 years ago. The experience is paying off in getting foreign workers into shape, but franchisees and corporate representatives are learning that nothing can be taken for granted.

The attitudes that workers bring with them are as numerous and varied as their countries of origin. The Swiss reputation for orderly efficiency, for example, is often reflected in the workers the company recruits. They sometimes contrast sharply with applicants in countries of the former Soviet bloc, where long lines and delays in shops and markets are an ingrained part of the culture. Employees who have lived a lifetime under an economic system that placed no emphasis on service or customer satisfaction must undergo a rebirth in their thinking. Some of the obstacles in India run even deeper. Western companies are sometimes regarded as imperialistic extensions in a country that threw off the yoke of British colonialism not too long ago. Workers not only must cope with the perception that McDonald's products represent an effrontery to religious beliefs, but may also be a symbol of anti-nationalism.

By franchising, McDonald's can keep better control over the quality and service its foreign workers provide. And since the company now earns most of its profits from restaurants outside the United States, it finds that dealing with a diverse work force is well worth the effort. As the company's founder Ray Kroc was fond of saying: McDonald's "has always been guided by the philosophy that you get back what you put in."

SOURCES: Eben Shapiro, "McDonald's Beef Up Abroad," *Ceres*, July-August 1992, 7; Carla Rapoport, "Bic Mac Attacks Swiss Tracks," *Fortune*, June 1, 1992, 13; "Silver Lining Over Golden Arches," *Economist*, Feb. 13, 1993, 41; "McGoulash to Go," *Economist*, April 6, 1991, 70–71; Jennifer J. Laabs, "The Golden Arches Provide Golden Opportunities," *Personnel Journal*, July 1991, 52–57.

■ QUESTIONS

1. McDonald's has many of the characteristics of the successful firm of the 1990s, as outlined in the chapter. Which do you think play the greatest role in the company's success?
2. McDonald's also hires people with very diverse nationalities, attitudes, and values to work in the United States. What sorts of problems at work do you think McDonald's needs to watch out for? What would you do to make sure problems do not arise?
3. What do you think accounts for McDonald's appeal in such diverse locales as the United States' Main Street and Paris' Champs-Élysées?

ENDNOTES

1. This problem was researched from John Huey, "Managing in the Midst of Chaos," *Fortune*, April 5, 1993, 38–46; Jagannath Dubashl, "Dial 1-800-Get-Moving," *Financial World*, March 31, 1992, 62–63; and "William Weiss, Ameritech," *Fortune*, December 13, 1993, 87–88.
2. Alvin Toeffler, *Future Shock* (New York: Bantam Books, 1971), 43.
3. Adam Smith, *An Inquiry Into the Nature and Causes of Wealth of Nations*, ed., Edward Cannan, 4th ed. (London: Methuen, 1925). Published originally in 1776.
4. Alfred Chandler, *Strategy and Structure* (Cambridge, MA: MIT Press), see also Daniel Wren, *The Evolution of Management Thought* (New York: John Wiley, 1979).
5. D. S. Pugh, *Organization Theory* (Baltimore: Penguin, 1971), 126–27.
6. Claude George, Jr., *The History of Management Thought*, (Englewood Cliffs, NJ: Prentice-Hall, 1972), 99–101.
7. Richard Hopeman, *Production* (Columbus, OH: Charles Merrill, 1965), 478–85.
8. Henri Fayol, *General and Industrial Management*, translated by Constance Storrs (London: Sir Isaac Pitman, 1949), 42–43.

9. Based on Richard Hall, "Intra-Organizational Structural Variation: Application of the Bureaucratic Model," *Administrative Science Quarterly,* vol. 7, no. 3, December 1962, 295–308.

10. William Scott, *Organization Theory* (Homewood, IL: Richard D. Irwin, 1967).

11. F.L. Roethlisberger and William Dickson, *Management and Worker,* (Boston: Graduate School of Business, Harvard University, 1947), 21.

12. Alfred Chandler, *Strategy and Structure* (Cambridge, MA: MIT Press, 1962), 19–51.

13. Warren G. Bennis, "Organizational Development and the Fate of Bureaucracy," address at the Division of Industrial and Business Psychology, American Psychological Association, September 5, 1964, reprinted in L.L. Cummings and W.E. Scott, Jr., *Organizational Behavior and Human Performance* (Homewood, IL: Richard D. Irwin and Dorsey, 1969), 436.

14. Douglas McGregor, "The Human Side of Enterprise," Edward Deci, B. Von Haller Gilmer, and Harry Kairn, *Readings in Industrial and Organizational Psychology* (New York: McGraw-Hill, 1972), 123.

15. R. Likert, *New Patterns of Management* (New York: McGraw-Hill, 1961), 6.

16. Likert, *New Patterns of Management,* 103.

17. Chris Argyris, *Integrating the Individual and the Organization* (New York: John Wiley, 1964).

18. Likert, *New Patterns of Management,* 91.

19. Ibid., 100.

20. Ibid.

21. Ibid.

22. Argyris, *Integrating the Individual,* 211.

23. Ibid., 206.

24. Ibid., 203, 207.

25. Chester Barnard, *The Functions of the Executive* (Cambridge: Harvard University Press, 1968), 84.

26. Ibid., 167.

27. Ibid., 143.

28. Simon, *Administrative Behavior* (New York: Free Press, 1976), 11.

29. See West Churchman, Russell Ackoff, and E. Linard Arnoff, *Introduction to Operations Research* (New York: John Wiley, 1957) 18.

30. Daniel Wren, *The Evolution of Management Thought* (New York: John Wiley, 1979), 512.

31. C. West Churchman, *The Systems Approach* (New York: Delta, 1968).

32. Not everyone agreed with this conclusion. Simon, for example, stated that there was no confusion and that he was "exhilarated by the progress we had made." See Harold Koontz, ed., *Toward a Unified Theory of Management* (New York: McGraw-Hill, 1964), 79.

33. Tom Burns and G.M. Stalker, *The Management of Innovation* (London: Tavistock, 1961), 125.

34. Joan Woodward, *Industrial Organization: Theory and Practice* (London: Oxford University Press, 1965), 64–65.

35. J.W. Lorsch and Paul R. Lawrence, eds., *Studies in Organization Design* (Homewood, IL: Richard D. Irwin and Dorsey, 1970), 1.

36. Tom Peters, *Thriving on Chaos: A Handbook for a Management Revolution* (New York: Harper & Row, 1987), 34.

UNITED PARCEL SERVICE

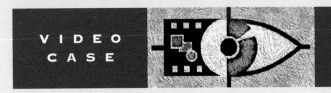

European Community '92 (EC '92), North American Free Trade Agreement (NAFTA), and the General Agreement on Trade & Tariffs (GATT) are all trade pacts that have been completed in this decade. All represent opportunities for expansion by businesses around the world through the dismantling of trade barriers. While the lessening of trade barriers makes it easier to do business, it does present a unique set of challenges. Corporations hoping to be successful must recognize already established local competitors, new efforts by traditional competitors to establish themselves in these same emerging markets, cultural differences, and expanded customer expectations.

Atlanta-based United Parcel Service (UPS) is one company trying to take advantage of new opportunities in the global marketplace. Manager-owned UPS currently provides service to over 185 countries and territories and expects one-third of its revenues to come from international business by the end of the decade. Donald W. Layden, senior vice president of international operations for UPS, recognizes traditional competition from Federal Express, DHL (Worldwide Express), and TNT. Layden also states "Within the countries themselves, several of the European countries have very, very fine, well-organized, well-managed, well-run postal services, and they're also major competitors for the domestic intra-country product."

The international marketplace also presents business challenges due to expanded customer expectations. New York State Transportation Commissioner Thomas M. Downs sees a critical need for companies to focus on the unique needs of the international marketplace. He states, "The international marketplace gives us no slack. It shows no mercy to those who do not compete." Downs said other countries have been quicker than the United States to plan and invest in the kinds of "intermodal" facilities required to improve freight and people-moving systems needed to compete successfully in the world economy. "The Japanese spend more on this in a year than we think of spending in a decade," he said. Downs also stated, "We have to go out and ask our customers what they want, what they think is important, and then judge ourselves by those standards."

UPS recognizes two major needs of the international customer: the ability to use one carrier to fulfill all of its delivery service needs, and the ability to track and follow the movement of all packages throughout the world. Several strategies are being employed to provide the level of service quality international customers expect. Don Layden points out, "Unlike some competitors, we believe the most reliable way to serve the European market is to control the delivery from beginning to end, rather than turn it over to another carrier when it arrives in Europe. Our commitment to international expansion has been neither easy nor inexpensive. However, before we started we knew that we must invest heavily to build the necessary infrastructure in Europe." To create this infrastructure UPS has acquired several foreign express services, gone into joint ventures with others, and used technology to provide the key platforms necessary for expansion.

Two critical acquisitions included the Belgian company Seabourne European Express Parcels and Carryfast Ltd., Britain's largest privately owned express service. Acquiring companies rather than starting UPS operations helps the company eliminate many foreign hurdles. The 1990 acquisition of Seabourne gave UPS a firm that already had a cross-border license. The Carryfast purchase allowed UPS to complete its ground delivery network in Europe, a delivery network that is linked into the UPS global operation. Joint ventures with Unistar Air Cargo and Yamato Transport of Japan have filled in critical pieces of the puzzle in both Asia and Africa.

Technology also plays an important role in linking the various domestic and international operations at UPS. Several systems have been developed and implemented; UPSnet, ISPS, and Totaltrack. Together each system allows UPS and its customers to track packages from pickup to delivery and provide interaction with foreign customs clearance in more than twenty countries. These systems also allow UPS to integrate new acquisitions quickly and still keep local management and employees, allowing them to assimilate into the UPS corporate culture at their own pace.

SOURCES: *PR Newswire*, "UPS Rolls Out New Look; 64,000 Vehicles With New Graphics to Hit the Road Across the Country," *PR Newswire*, October 25, 1993. "UPS Optimistic About Shipping Its Strategy Worldwide," *Los Angeles Times*, July 4, 1992. "Downs Calls For Focus on Needs of Customers," Guy T. Baeher, *The Star-Ledger* (Newark, NJ), July 15, 1993. "UPS Buys Carryfast to Form European Network," *South China Morning Post*, July 20, 1992. "UPS Deploys Mobile Data Service," *Document Delivery World*, April 1, 1994.

■ QUESTIONS

1. Why do you think UPS prefers to expand its global operations through acquisition and joint ventures rather than build new operations from the ground up?
2. What impact do you think local customs and culture play in the development of global operations?
3. What are some of the trends creating turbulence and rapid change for UPS? How is UPS changing its management practices and organizational structure to be more responsive in this fast-changing industry?

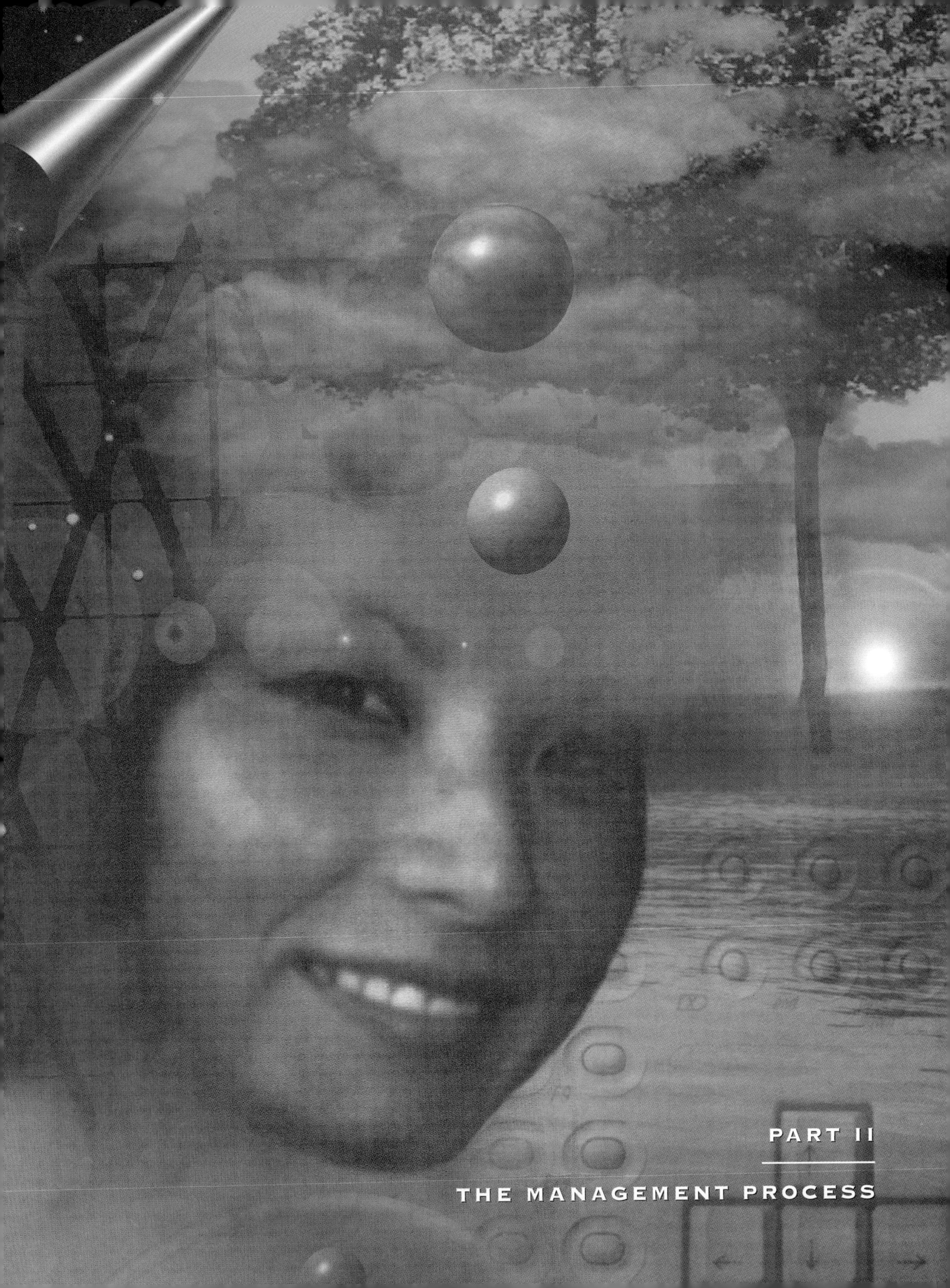

PART II

THE MANAGEMENT PROCESS

CHAPTER 5

PLANNING AND SETTING GOALS

LEARNING OBJECTIVES

After studying this chapter, you should be able to:

- Describe the planning process and the various types of plans.
- Explain the importance of planning.
- Describe each of the steps that comprise the planning cycle.
- Explain the hierarchical aspects of organizational planning processes.
- List the characteristics of effective goals.
- Outline the five-step process that comprises management by objectives and the elements that make it successful.
- Summarize how changes in organizations have led to changes in the planning process.
- List the ten most common planning-related activities.

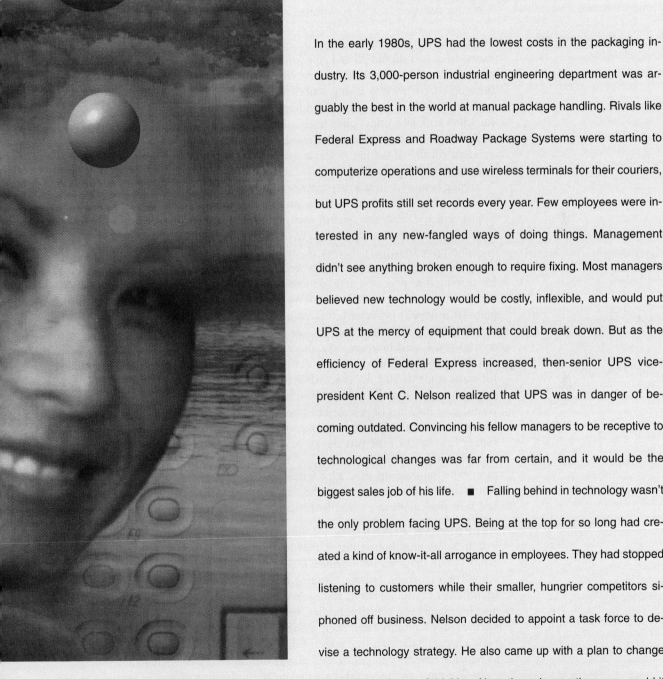

OPENING PROBLEM
UPS

In the early 1980s, UPS had the lowest costs in the packaging industry. Its 3,000-person industrial engineering department was arguably the best in the world at manual package handling. Rivals like Federal Express and Roadway Package Systems were starting to computerize operations and use wireless terminals for their couriers, but UPS profits still set records every year. Few employees were interested in any new-fangled ways of doing things. Management didn't see anything broken enough to require fixing. Most managers believed new technology would be costly, inflexible, and would put UPS at the mercy of equipment that could break down. But as the efficiency of Federal Express increased, then-senior UPS vice-president Kent C. Nelson realized that UPS was in danger of becoming outdated. Convincing his fellow managers to be receptive to technological changes was far from certain, and it would be the biggest sales job of his life. ■ Falling behind in technology wasn't the only problem facing UPS. Being at the top for so long had created a kind of know-it-all arrogance in employees. They had stopped listening to customers while their smaller, hungrier competitors siphoned off business. Nelson decided to appoint a task force to devise a technology strategy. He also came up with a plan to change his managers' way of thinking. Now, the only question was, would it work?[1]

THE NATURE AND PURPOSE OF PLANNING

SOME DEFINITIONS

PLANS

Methods formulated beforehand for doing or making something and consisting of a goal and a course of action.

As at UPS, all companies should have plans. **Plans** are methods, formulated beforehand, for doing or making something. All plans identify *goals* (such as "boost sales by 10 percent") as well as a course of action (such as "by hiring a new salesperson and boosting advertising expenditures by 20 percent"). Plans always identify (at a minimum) *what* you should do and *how* you are going to do it. Planning, therefore, is "the process of establishing objectives and choosing the most suitable means for achieving these objectives prior to taking action."[2]

Planning means, in a sense, "deciding ahead of time," according to planning expert Russell Ackoff, who adds "planning . . . is anticipatory decision making. It is a process of deciding . . . before action is required." Planning is often considered the "first amongst equals" of the five management functions discussed in Chapter 1 (planning, organizing, staffing, leading, and controlling). As Koontz and O'Donnell point out, "planning is unique in that it establishes the goals which are (or should be) the basis of all the other management functions."[3] The people you hire, the motivation techniques you use, and the control systems you implement all relate, in one way or another, to the plans and goals you have for your firm.

Planning is an activity that we all engage in every day, often without giving it very much thought. For example, if you are like most readers of this book, you're probably reading it as part of a management course you are taking. And why are you taking this course? Chances are, the course is part of your program of studies. This program (it is hoped) is *planned*. It identifies your goal (say, getting a degree in business by 1998), and it identifies how you are going to obtain that degree by specifying the courses you'll need in order to graduate.

Of course your plans may well not end with just obtaining the degree (although for many students, just doing so, while working, may be hassle enough for now!). You may also have a broader goal, a *vision* of where you're headed in life. If you do, then your degree may just be one step in a broader- and longer-term plan. For example, let us say you have a dream or a vision of yourself running your own management consulting firm by the time you are 35. Now (you ask yourself), "What do I have to do to achieve this goal?" The answer may be to work for a nationally known consulting firm, thus building up your experience and your reputation in the field. So here is your plan: take this course to get the degree, get the degree to get the consulting job, and then work hard as a consultant to achieve your dream.

RESPONSIVE PLANNING   If there is a problem with this somewhat ideal plan it is, to quote poet Robert Burns, that "the best laid schemes o' mice and men oft go astray."[4] Life plays its little games: a relative's illness makes a student drop out of school; or a recession causes consulting firms to cut back so that no jobs are available. In any case, having a plan in place is not only no guarantee of success—sticking to a plan too rigidly can actually backfire, which is what happens if conditions change and planners don't modify their plans along with them. Particularly under conditions of rapid change, balancing the sense of direction that planning provides with the need to remain responsive in case things change can be a very tricky matter.

In fact, more and more firms are making their planning process as lean and responsive as possible. For example, a few years ago the General Electric Company had a 350-member planning staff that churned out voluminous and detailed planning reports.[5] Today, GE is down to fewer than 20 full-time planners. The *real* planning these days is done by the heads of GE's 13 businesses. Each year each one of these business heads develops five one-page "charts." These charts are actually memos listing possible business opportunities and obstacles over the next two years. So, when Hungary decided to let foreign firms take over state-run companies, GE needed just 60 days to buy 50 percent of Tungsram, Hungary's leading lighting company. This is because Tungsram had been on GE's "charts" for years.[6]

TYPES OF PLANS

Plans may be classified in several ways. Plans differ, first, in *format.* Some plans, for instance, are stated descriptively; they state in words what is to be accomplished and how. Other plans are stated in financial terms and are called budgets, while still others present the plan in charts that show graphically what is to be accomplished and how. We'll look at some examples in the next few chapters.

Plans also differ in terms of the time horizons they cover. Top management usually engages in long-term (five- to ten-year) *strategic* planning, while middle managers focus more on developing intermediate, *tactical* plans (of six months to five years duration). These show how top management's plans are to be implemented by each division's manager. First-line managers then focus on shorter-term *operational* planning. This is the most detailed, day-to day planning of all. It might show, for instance, exactly which workers are to be assigned to which machines or exactly how many units will be produced on a given day.[7]

Plans can also be classified in terms of their purpose or function. For example, firms typically have sales plans, manufacturing plans, staffing plans, capital-investment plans, and performance-improvement plans.

Plans differ in the repetitiveness with which they are intended to be applied. When the J.C. Penney's Company moved its offices from New York City to Dallas several years ago, it needed a *single-use plan* outlining the steps to be taken and the goals to be achieved in this one-time move. A major project like this one involved much planning—for new facilities, for severance pay for employees not making the move, for the replacement of the former employees with new Dallas employees, and for getting trucks to transfer equipment, files, and staff from city to city.

In contrast to single-use plans, **standing plans** are plans established to be used repeatedly, as the need arises.[8] Policies, procedures, and rules are examples of standing plans.

Policies, procedures, and rules differ from each other in degree of specificity. **Policies** usually set broad guidelines for the enterprise. For example, it might be the policy at Saks Department stores that "we sell only high-fashion apparel and top-of-the-line jewelry." **Procedures,** as the name implies, specify how to proceed if some specific situation arises. For example, "Before refunding the customer's purchase price, the salesperson should carefully inspect the garment and then obtain approval from the floor manager for the refund." Finally, a rule is an even more specific guide to action. For example, "Under no condition will the purchase price be refunded after 30 days."

Plans can also be classified according to *scope.* At one extreme, a company's **strategic plan** outlines the course of action the firm plans to pursue in becoming the sort of enterprise that it wants to be, given the firm's external opportunities and threats and its internal strengths and weaknesses. Deciding whether Mom and Pop's Supermarket will compete with Enormous Markets head-to-head by building similar super stores involves strategic planning. Departmental plans are usually narrower in scope. Thus, a firm's manufacturing plan should help to explain how the manufacturing department will contribute to achieving the company's overall strategic plan. Even narrower in scope would be the manufacturing department's single-use plan for opening

STANDING PLANS
Plans established to be used repeatedly, as the need arises.

POLICIES
Set broad guidelines for the enterprise.

PROCEDURES
Specify how to proceed if some specific situation arises.

STRATEGIC PLAN
Outlines the course of action the firm plans to pursue in becoming the sort of enterprise that it wants to be, given the firm's external opportunities and threats and its internal strengths and weaknesses.

a new plant. Perhaps narrowest in scope would be specific procedures and rules that explain what to do, for instance, in case of a plant fire.

WHY PLANNING IS IMPORTANT

PLANNING PROVIDES DIRECTION First, planning is important because it provides direction and a sense of purpose for the enterprise. Several years ago R.R. Donnelley Company was primarily in the business of printing documents and other materials for such clients as investment bankers. Anticipating a change caused by telecommunications and the globalization of its customers, Donnelley decided to reinvent itself. The company invested heavily in advanced technology and expanded overseas. Now, with satellites, Donnelley can print a securities prospectus simultaneously in locations around the globe.[9] Its new vision and strategy provided a new sense of direction for the firm.

PLANNING REDUCES PIECEMEAL DECISION MAKING A plan also provides a unifying framework against which decisions can be assessed. The result, as one expert put it, is that "planning channels efforts toward desired results, and by providing a sequence of efforts, minimizes unproductive behavior."[10] For instance, it would have been wasteful and potentially disastrous for R.R. Donnelley to spend its investment dollars building ever bigger printing factories at its main U.S. location. The globalization of its customers and technological advances demanded that it be capable of transmitting and creating documents via satellite around the globe. Its plan for doing so helped ensure that the firm channeled all its efforts toward those desired results, thus minimizing unproductive behavior (such as building unneeded domestic printing plants).

PLANNING REVEALS FUTURE OPPORTUNITIES AND THREATS Management theorist Peter Drucker says that planning can help identify potential opportunities and threats and at least minimize long-term risks.[11] Thus, Donnelley's plan-

When GE purchased Tungsram Ltd., a Hungarian lightbulb manufacturer, it found itself having to retrain workers not just in manufacturing techniques, but in management techniques and attitudes.

ning process helped identify the opportunity for satellite-transmitted data while GE's planning process helped identify the opportunity for purchasing Hungary's Tungsram.

PLANNING FACILITATES CONTROL Control means ensuring that activities conform to plans; it involves a three-step cycle in which standards are set, performance is measured against these standards, and deviations are identified and corrected.

Planning is the first step in this cycle—specifying what is to be achieved. For example, a company's five-year plan may specify that its profits will double within five years. This goal can then be a standard against which to measure and control the president's performance.

Yet, important though it is, many firms do little or no planning, as the *Proudfoot* vignette illustrates.

THE ORGANIZATIONAL PLANNING PROCESS

THE PLANNING CYCLE

Whether managers are developing broad, top-level strategic plans for the whole company or relatively narrow department plans, planning involves a four-step cycle:

Step 1: *Define your goals.* This step answers the question, "Where do we want to go?"

PROUDFOOT CHANGE MANAGEMENT SURVEY

Many firms do no real planning. Proudfoot Change Management, a consulting firm that helps companies manage change, commissioned a survey of 400 top executives in mid-1993. Proudfoot wanted to know how firms anticipate and plan for change.

Only half of the respondents plan new business moves. The rest simply react, usually by cutting costs, when adversity threatens profits. The CEOs, presidents, and top managers listed customer demands, competition, government regulations, and evolving markets as the primary motivators for change. But surprisingly, 69 percent said they cut expenses even if costs aren't the problem. More often than not, their reaction is simply to cut costs through layoffs. "There is very little anticipation or planning for the future," said Robert Gilbreath, president of Proudfoot.

Only 1 percent had any sort of planning group looking into how the business' direction might be rerouted, an astounding finding considering that 79 percent believed their business would indeed undergo rapid changes in the future. "Basically, it's a self-admission that they don't know what the [heck] they're doing about managing change," said Gilbreath.

SOURCE: Reuters, "Many Firms Flying by Seat of Pants," *The Dallas Morning News,* September 9, 1993.

Step 2: *Conduct a situation analysis.* This step involves forecasting and developing basic planning premises and answers the question, "What are the basic assumptions on which we will base our plans?"

Step 3: *Develop alternative plans.* This answers the question, "How could we get where we want to go?"

Step 4: *Finally, decide on a plan and implement it.* This answers the question, "How will we get where we want to go?"

THE HIERARCHICAL NATURE OF PLANNING

Organizational planning has a hierarchical aspect, which is illustrated in Figure 5.1. Top management's **mission statement** indicates the scope and direction of the organization's activities and answers the question, "What business are we in?"[12] Top-level managers then formulate strategic plans for the enterprise. As we will see later in Chapter 5, the strategic plan identifies the business or businesses in which the firm will compete and lays out a broad framework within which the firm's lower-level managers will carry out their activities. At the next level, middle managers translate these strategic goals into tactical goals for their individual divisions, and plans are formulated for achieving these goals. First-level functional department managers then translate the divisional plans into operational goals, and these departmental goals then become the ends for which operational departmental plans are created. This is illustrated in the *Elyria Foundry* vignette.

MISSION STATEMENT
Broadly outlines the organization's future course and serves to communicate "who we are and where we're heading." Answers the question, "what business are we in?"

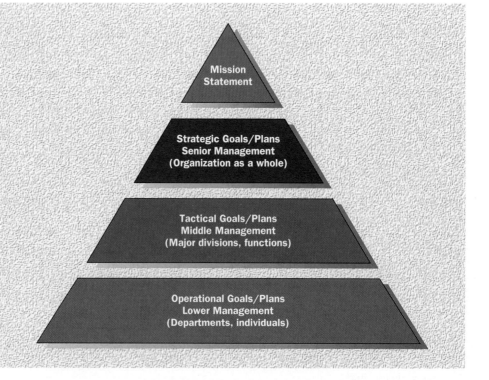

FIGURE 5.1

Levels of Goals/Plans and Their Importance

Organizational planning has a hierarchical aspect. Top management's strategic plans and goals are translated into tactical goals and plans by middle managers.

SOURCE: Richard Daft, *Management,* 3rd ed. (Fort Worth: The Dryden Press, 1994), 185.

ELYRIA FOUNDRY—GOAL SETTING

When Gregg Foster purchased the Elyria Foundry in 1983, the company was heading downhill fast. Turning things around first involved slugging it out with unions and transforming the company culture. But Foster knew the key to long-term prosperity would require establishing a set of strategic goals and then getting employees from the shop floor to the executive suite committed to achieving them. In his view, goals would give everyone something they could sink their teeth into. "They're specific, but they also create a picture of how we want to be."

Foster's plan got off to an uneven start. He didn't come up with many goals but it really didn't matter—the main thing was to provide a broad direction for the firm. He next turned to his department managers, who each submitted 5 to 10 goals that Foster then condensed. The input from lower-level employees then yielded goals ranging from retirement plans participation to qualifying for ISO 9000 (quality management) certification.

From the goals that were proposed, Foster found that literally hundreds of things in both his office and shop could do with fixing. To make Elyria a better company, he decided that the goals that are adopted must have the highest impact on the greatest number of people. To make the final cut, Foster says, the goals must also be measurable, specific, and fit with the firm's overall goals.

SOURCE: Leslie Brokaw, "One-Page Company Game Plan," *Inc.*, June 1993, 111–13.

Workers at Elyria Foundry are unionized, a circumstance which sometimes complicates the process of establishing new goals.

THE HIERARCHY OF GOALS

As illustrated in Figure 5.2, this planning process results in a hierarchy of goals. At the top-management level, the strategic planning process results in the identification of an overall mission for the firm. The president then sets specific goals (such as a 12 percent return on investment), to which each vice president's goal (such as a scrap rate of 3 percent or less) is tied. Below this, the supervisors' goals (such as machine downtime at less than 7 percent) similarly contribute to the higher-level managers' goals. Ideally, the mission statement should thus provide an overall standard for decision making at all levels in the firm.[13]

SETTING GOALS IN ORGANIZATIONS

WHY SETTING GOALS IS IMPORTANT

Setting goals is important for several reasons. First, people usually perform better when they have specific goals to achieve. Second, when an employee's performance is inadequate, it is often because the person either thinks he or she is doing what is expected or does not know what the goals are. Third, goals link planning and control. As products of the planning process, goals specify in concrete terms what each unit and individual in the organization is to achieve. These goals then became the standards against which actual performance can be compared and controlled.

SETTING EFFECTIVE GOALS

As in most human endeavors, there is a right way and a wrong way to set goals. Psychologists, including Edwin Locke and his associates, have conducted hundreds of studies to ascertain the characteristics of effective goals, and the results can be summarized as follows.

CLEAR AND SPECIFIC   Employees who are given specific goals usually perform better than those who are not. One study that illustrates the practical significance of goals was carried out in a logging operation in Oklahoma.[14] The subjects of the study were truck drivers who had to load logs and drive them to the mill. An analysis of each trucker's performance showed that they were often not filling their trucks to the maximum legal net weight. The researchers believed this was largely because the workers were traditionally just urged to "do their best" when it came to loading the truck to its maximum net weight. Therefore, the researchers arranged for a specific goal ("94 percent of a truck's net weight") to be communicated to each driver. The drivers were told that this was an experimental program, that they would not be required to make more truck runs, and that there would be no retaliation if performance suddenly increased and then decreased. No monetary rewards or benefits, other than verbal praise, were given for improving performance. The drivers and their supervisors got no special training of any kind.

The results of the study were impressive. Performance (in terms of weight loaded on each truck) jumped markedly as soon as the truckers were assigned specific hard goals, and it generally remained at this much higher level. This and other evidence clearly indicates that setting specific goals with subordinates, rather than setting no goals or telling them to "do their best" can substantially improve subordinate performance.[15] In fact, goal difficulty and goal clarity have been found to be associated with employee performance in a wide range of settings.[16]

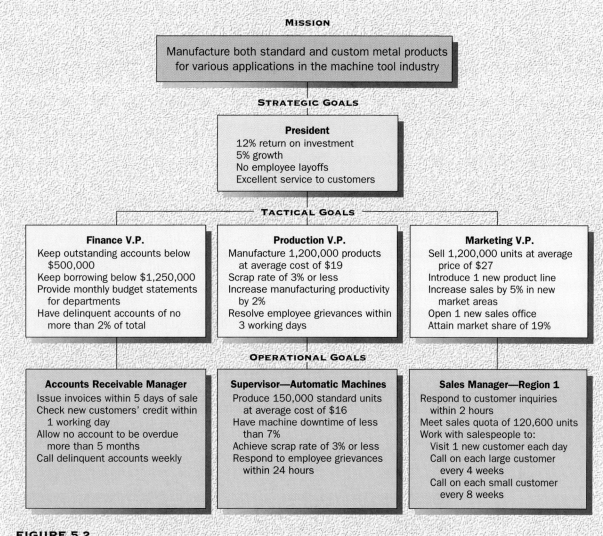

FIGURE 5.2

Hierarchy of Objectives for a Manufacturing Company

The planning process typically results in a hierarchy of goals; for instance, the production vice-president's goals should be formulated to contribute to the president's overall strategic goals.

SOURCE: Richard Daft, *Management*, 3rd ed. (Fort Worth: The Dryden Press, 1994), 192.

MEASURABLE AND VERIFIABLE[17]   Wherever possible, goals should be stated in quantitative terms and should include target dates or deadlines for accomplishment. In that regard, goals set in absolute terms (such as "an average daily output of 300 units") is less confusing than a goal set in relative terms (such as "improve production by 20 percent"). If measurable results will not be available, then "satisfactory completion"—such as "satisfactorily attended workshop" or "satisfactorily completed his or her degree"—is the next best thing. In any case, target dates or deadlines for accomplishment should always be set.

CHALLENGING BUT REALISTIC According to researcher Gary Yukl, goals should be challenging but not so difficult that they appear impossible or unrealistic.[18] In other words, goals should be challenging but realistic. Particularly in areas such as sales management where immediate and concrete performance is both obvious and highly valued, setting goals that are in line with past sales patterns and therefore realistic, yet high enough to be challenging, is widely espoused.[19]

Consider the findings on the effects of goal setting in United Fund Campaigns.[20] In general, researchers have found a direct relationship between the difficulty of the goal (in terms of how far it exceeded the previous year's performance) and subsequent performance. In other words, the more difficult the goal, the more money the campaign raised. This only held true when the goals were viewed as attainable and acceptable, however; for communities with more prior failures than successes, goal difficulty did not lead to better performance. When is a goal too difficult or too hard? Yukl suggests considering prior performance by the same person, performances by people in comparable positions, available resources, likely conditions that will affect performance, and the amount of time until the deadline. As he suggests:

> A goal is probably too easy if it calls for little or no improvement in performance when conditions are becoming more favorable, or if the targeted level of performance is well below that of most other employees in comparable positions. A goal is probably too difficult if it calls for a large improvement in performance when conditions are worsening, or if the targeted level of performances is well above that of people in comparable positions.[21]

ASSIGNED VERSUS PARTICIPATIVELY SET GOALS Should managers assign their subordinates goals, or should they permit their subordinates to participate in developing the goals that are to guide their activities? Considerable research evi-

Wellington Environmental employees meet offsite annually to set goals for the coming year and for the next five years. Getting away from the office has been a major boost for candid discussion.

dence has been collected concerning this question, and we can reach five conclusions concerning the relative superiority of assigned versus participatively set goals.

First, it is apparent that employees who participate in setting their own goals tend to perceive themselves as having had *more impact* on the setting of those goals than do employees who are simply assigned goals.[22] Second, participatively set goals tend to be higher—*more difficult*—than the goals the supervisor would normally assign to their subordinates.[23] Third, even when the participatively set goals are more difficult than the assigned ones, *they are not perceived as such* by the subordinates. In other words, subordinates who participatively set their own goals do not perceive those goals as being more difficult than do those who have goals assigned to them, even though they are, in fact, usually more difficult.[24] Fourth, participatively set goals do not consistently result in higher *performance* than assigned goals (nor, for that matter, do assigned goals consistently result in higher performance than participatively set goals). When, as is usually the case, the participatively set goals are higher and more difficult than the assigned goals, however, then the participatively set goals usually lead to higher performance. Again, though, *it is the fact that the goal is more difficult* that seems to account for the higher performance, not the fact that it was participatively set.[25] Finally, unilateral goals set by managers can encounter employee resistance, regardless of the goal's appropriateness. Insofar as participation creates a sense of ownership in the goals, employees' resistance to the goals can be reduced.[26]

One writer summarizes the characteristics of effective goals by asserting that objectives should be uniformly SMART: specific, measurable, achievable, results oriented, and timely.[27] The *Wellington Environmental* vignette illustrates how one firm sets goals.

WELLINGTON ENVIRONMENTAL

Thom Wellington, president of Wellington Environmental Consulting and Construction, Inc., thinks expanding companies are easy targets if they don't plan carefully. He thinks three things made 1992 a good year for his St. Louis firm: clear one-year goals were established, realistic five-year goals were drawn, and all goal planning and discussion was carried out outside the office.

Wellington also thinks setting goals is what keeps people around. "It gets everybody here going, because we all know what the company goals are."

The company met 80 percent of its one-year goals in 1992. Five-year goals have been established, but they are more general in nature. Categories include the anticipated number of employees, company sales, and physical requirements such as office and warehouse space, trucks, and equipment.

Wellington thinks holding yearly goal-setting meetings away from the home turf may be the most important aspect of the process, even if it's just a few miles away. He says escaping the office makes employees feel more free to speak their minds. The result is a wider range of ideas on how best to cope with the future.

SOURCE: Bradford McKee, "Think Ahead, Set Goals, and Get Out of the Office," *Nation's Business,* May 1993, 10.

MANAGEMENT BY OBJECTIVES

THE MANAGEMENT BY OBJECTIVES PROCESS

MANAGEMENT BY OBJECTIVES
A technique in which supervisor and subordinate jointly set goals for the latter and periodically assess progress toward those goals.

Management by objectives (MBO) is a technique in which supervisor and subordinate jointly set goals for the latter and periodically assess progress toward those goals. A manager could conceivably engage in a modest MBO program by setting goals with his or her subordinates and periodically providing feedback. However, the term *MBO* almost always refers to a comprehensive organization-wide program for setting goals, one usually reserved for managerial and professional employees.

The MBO process generally consists of 5 steps:

1. *Set organization's goals.* Organization-wide strategy and goals are established.
2. *Set departmental goals.* Department heads and their superiors jointly set goals for their departments.
3. *Discuss departmental goals.* Department heads discuss departmental goals with all subordinates and ask them to develop their own individual goals.
4. *Set individual goals.* Goals are set for the subordinate, and a timetable is assigned for accomplishing those goals.
5. *Feedback.* The supervisor and subordinate meet periodically to review the subordinate's performance and to monitor and analyze progress toward his or her goals.[28]

MAKING MBO SUCCESSFUL

Managers can do several things to make their MBO programs more successful. One study analyzed the prescriptions of 42 MBO experts and concluded that, to be successful, goals in MBO should be stated in measurable terms, be specific, and be set so each person's goals are integrated with those of the organization. Most experts also agree that goals should be reviewed and updated periodically, that the time period for goal accomplishment should be specified, and that the goals should be quantifiable and flexible enough to be changed if conditions warrant.[29]

Individuals are strongly motivated to guide their behavior toward the attainment of goals that they have accepted. Therefore, gaining employees' acceptance of the goal should translate into motivation to achieve that goal.[30]

GOAL SPECIFICITY
The degree of precision with which the goal is defined.

GOAL DIFFICULTY
The level of proficiency or performance sought.

Goal specificity—the degree of precision with which the goal is defined—and **goal difficulty**—the level of proficiency or performance sought—are, as we've seen, two determinants of whether or not subordinates will pursue the goals that have been set. This helps to explain, say two experts, why MBO is effective: it is a good method for assuring goal specificity, goal difficulty, and goal acceptance.[31]

Again, however, effective MBO requires more than just setting goals. MBO usually refers to formal, organization-wide programs, and this means that integrating the goals of the individual, of his or her unit, and of the company as a whole is absolutely essential. As Peter Drucker, an early proponent of MBO, said:

This means that the goals of each manager's job must be defined by the contribution he or she has to make to the success of a larger unit of which they are part. The job objectives of district sales managers should be defined by the contribution they and their district sales forces have to make to the sales department. The objectives of the general manager of a decentralized division should be defined by the contribution his or her division has to make to the objectives of the parent company.[32]

Finally, performance appraisals in MBO-based firms should be tied to the employee's goals. In other words, the subordinate and his or her supervisor should meet periodically to assess the former's progress relative to his or her goals; the subordinate then gets feedback and an appraisal concerning how he or she is performing relative to the goals.[33]

PLANNING FOR RESPONSIVENESS

THE EVOLUTION OF PLANNING

As summarized in Figure 5.3, the planning process—particularly strategic, long-term planning—has gone through several significant changes in recent years.[34] These changes reflect broader changes taking place in the management of organizations today and particularly the growing emphasis on flattening hierarchies, pushing down decision making, and positioning the firm to be responsive to increasingly unpredictable environmental changes.

This need to prepare the firm on a continual basis to be responsive to change has had at least three specific effects on corporate planning. First, the role of the planning departments in most firms has changed. During the 1950s, many firms tended to look inward and emphasized improving production processes and organizational efficiencies. Here the planner's role emphasized *analysis*—for instance, analysis of figures concerning material cost and relationships between economic activity and demand for the company's products. Second, with competition increasing in the 1970s, the planner's role shifted to *strategy formulation*. This basically meant assessing competitors' strengths and weaknesses in order to better predict competitive moves and plan for them. During this period, planning staffs tended to

increase dramatically in size and scope as the issues to be addressed became more complex [in terms of] escalating competition in the market place, rapid diversification into new busi-

	1950s	1970s	1990s & Beyond
Role	Analysis	Strategy Formulation	**Facilitation**
Structure	Centralization	Increased Centralization	**Decentralization**
Drivers	Inputs/Outputs	Competition	**Customers**

FIGURE 5.3

The Evolution of Strategic Planning

The role of companies' planning groups has changed over the years. In the 1950s, firms were more inward-looking, and planning focused on sales and cost analysis. Today, responsiveness is paramount, and planners emphasize facilitating the work of the line managers who are closest to the customers on "the firing line." This, in turn, helps make the planning process more responsive.

SOURCE: Arthur Little, *Global Strategic Planning* (New York: Business International Corporation, 1991), 3

ness areas, and expansion into new global markets. Companies forced to form strategies to deal with these forces relied heavily on centralized planning specialists to do so.[35]

Today (and probably in the future) planning is moving to a third stage, to facilitate responsiveness. Planning today is therefore shifting from centralized headquarter planning departments down to the product and divisional managers who are in the best position to sense changes in customer, competitive, and technological trends and react to them. Therefore, firms like General Electric are downsizing their headquarter planning staffs, in GE's case from about 350 employees down to about 20.

In turn, these headquarters planners now perform more of a *facilitation* role. At GE they are called product development managers and their role is to facilitate line managers' planning by training them in planning techniques, for instance, or helping them to acquire the needed data.

PLANNER'S FOCUS   This has coincided with an evolution in the factors, or *drivers,* on which planners focus. In the relatively inward-looking 1950s, planning focused on cost factors and "revolved primarily around the financial and other resource requirements needed to deliver products to the marketplace, i.e. inputs and outputs."[36] With the increased pace of change in the late 1960s and 1970s, companies increasingly needed a systematic way for dealing with competition, which explains why planners and the techniques they used shifted in focus from inputs (raw materials' costs) to the strengths and weaknesses of potential competitors.

Today, the planning focus is shifting again as *the customer* is increasingly driving the planning function. As we'll see in Chapter 6, today it is—as one major strategic consulting firm put it—"the customer, not the competition" that must become the "key parameter against which the success of plans is gauged."[37] Planning's focus is shifting, in other words, to determining who the firm's customers are and should be, and to which of the firm's core competencies—the fundamental things that it is good at—the firm should bring to bear to serve these customers successfully. When R.R. Donnelley (discussed earlier in this chapter) looked at the customers for its technical printing, the company determined that those customers would soon want not just paper and ink printing but all manner of electronic reproduction as well—and globally distributed, at that. Donnelley's long-term plan was thus built on a shrewd understanding of its customers' needs and its own core competencies and strengths (such as its ability to service the needs of financial clients quickly). That proved a lot more useful than any attempt to simply anticipate what its competitors were going to do. Such customer-focused planning works well for small firms too, as the Cin-Made Small Business box illustrates.

WHAT PLANNERS DO

The planning departments of multinational firms like G.E. engage in about ten basic planning-related activities. These can be summarized as follows:

INFORMATION RESOURCE   Planning departments typically obtain, screen, and compile into a useful format each division's planning-related data. Top management can then use this information to assess each division's progress toward its goals. Information compiled by planners includes current financial targets of divisions and progress toward them, divisional strategic plans, competitor intelligence, regional and global economic summaries, and data reporting on the extent to which divisions are adhering to their goals.

COMPETITOR AND MARKET RESEARCH   Planning departments help divisions analyze global competition, for instance, by identifying major global competitors and monitoring their strategies.

CIN-MADE

Bob Frey learned a lot during his career at a big consumer-products company. But the main thing he remembered when he left to buy Cin-Made of Cincinnati, Ohio, in 1984 was that he hated bureaucracy. He decided that at his new paper and cardboard package manufacturing company he would keep track of everything in his head. Bad decision.

For the next three years Cin-Made careened through the market. It had become a rudderless ship in search of a reef. Profit margins all but disappeared. It finally dawned on Frey that he might have thrown the baby out with the bathwater. "I lost sight of some valuable disciplinary techniques," he says. Frey developed a plan.

First, Frey made an analysis of the packaging market and where his company fit into it. He discovered that Cin-Made was one of many companies making a standard commodity that was subject to cutthroat pricing from the lowest-cost producer. But a radical change in one of his primary markets made Frey think he could distinguish Cin-Made.

The change was in motor-oil cans. When motor-oil cans went from paper to plastic containers, Frey made the investment required to convert to the manufacture of chemical canisters. Since users wanted custom features, they didn't quibble about price as long as Frey could deliver the goods. Cin-Made started concentrating on specialty packaging needs that non-custom operations couldn't provide. R&D set sights on keeping the company out in front of the next trend. Frey eventually adopted a policy permitting attrition to occur in his standard packaging operations while concentrating on custom-built machinery. This approach helped keep research fully funded.

FOCUS ON SMALL BUSINESS

"To properly exploit our premium-niche strategy, we have to plow more in R&D," Frey says. "That yields products with higher price tags to reflect that investment. The more things we try out, the better our chances of success."

Company operations are now directed by very specific business planning summaries that Frey creates. These one-page synopses circulate from the shop floor to the boardroom. And even though the scope of the summaries reaches five years, they are updated at least once a month, sometimes more frequently.

The thinking that goes into Frey's summaries is pragmatic, flexible, and far-reaching. For example, Cin-Made is committed to a custom product price strategy and won't be drawn into a pricing war. But since considerable capital was expended on packaging equipment before Frey adopted his specialty-niche strategy, he will compete for high-volume, traditional packaging business to recoup his investment until Cin-Made's newer products carve out their own market segments.

Cin-Made's capital investment strategy represents the same type of trade-off. Frey concedes the half-million dollar investment to meet and compete with custom packagers was too steep. But he thinks he can end-run the competition by investing in newer technology. To do that he encourages R&D personnel to be creative and doesn't insist they justify every penny they spend.

Such strategies have paid off. Pretax profit margins at Cin-Made have increased fivefold. More encouraging, new products may double the company's revenues, and Frey seems to enjoy being the man with the plan.

SOURCE: Teri Lammers, "The One-Page Strategy Guide," *Inc.*, September 1992, 135–38.

FORECASTING   Most corporate planning departments also help divisional planners by developing forecasts. For example, they help provide a consistent framework for the plans of the divisions by developing forecasts of basic economic figures such as gross national product or inflation rates around the world.

CONSULTING SERVICES   Some corporate planners emphasize an assistance and advisory role. For example, they help divisions conduct industry analyses and provide divisional planners with training in the planning techniques they could or should be using.

CREATING A COMMON LANGUAGE   Particularly in large multinational corporations, it is usually important to have a common language that all the divisions can use. Planners often assist in this, for instance, by devising standardized planning reports.

COMMUNICATING CORPORATE CULTURE   Later in this book we'll see that, particularly in multinational firms, it is important to create a common corporate culture, in other words, a consensus about the common values that characterize the firm and provide its identity. Planning departments often help in that regard, for instance, by promulgating codes of ethical standards.

COMMUNICATING CORPORATE OBJECTIVES   In most companies, lower-level divisional plans must be consistent with top management's corporate goals for matters such as market share. These corporate objectives are generally communicated to divisions by the planning departments.

GROUP FACILITATION AND TEAM LEADERSHIP   Corporate planners organize and coordinate meetings and conferences, particularly planning-related meetings of the sort attended by top executives, division heads, and product or industry specialists.

GUARDIAN OF THE PLANNING PROCESS   Whatever planning procedures the firm has decided to use, it is generally the planning department's responsibility to ensure that the process is functioning smoothly.

DEVELOPING PLANNING METHODS   Finally, some planning departments have been and are involved in developing special analytical tools and planning methods. The firm can use these to make its planning process more effective.

PLANNING IN ACTION: AN EXAMPLE

BAT Industries (originally British American Tobacco Company) is the leading international manufacturer of cigarettes. The company has factories in 50 countries, sells over 500 billion cigarettes annually around the world, and is headquartered in London.

The enormity of this enterprise notwithstanding, corporate planning has a staff of only four.[38] The head of group planning reports directly to BAT's chairman. In turn, BAT'S subsidiaries (which are themselves very large) each have their own planning divisions. At BAT, therefore, corporate planning's major role is designing and administering the planning system, for instance, "monitoring the business plans as they come in from the subsidiaries."[39] At the corporate level, the head of planning says that his department's primary roles are (1) formulating policies—in particular, determining what business or businesses BAT Industries wants to be in; (2) formulating objectives, in terms of "where we're trying to get to"; and finally, (3) formulating strategies, which are the methods the firm will use to answer the question, "How will we get there?"

While BAT's divisions formulate their own strategic plans, corporate planning (small though it is) nevertheless plays a crucial role. The business units have to present their plans to the policy committee of the corporate board, for instance, and corporate planning synthesizes and assists the board in assessing those plans. Corporate planning also develops assumptions that the divisions can in turn use. These might include, for instance, assumptions regarding political stability or instability in various sectors of the world, or assumptions about the evolving political legislation regarding smoking.

Corporate planning also assures that BAT's planning cycle is being adhered to. For example, in April, the divisions complete reviews of their businesses regarding matters such as competitive, technological, social, and political trends that may be affecting their businesses. In June, the board adopts a set of planning assumptions based on recommendations prepared by the corporate planning department. (This might include, for instance, political, legislative, and economic projections.) At the same time, the headquarters planning group prepares a financial forecast for the corporation, based on projections from the individual BAT units. In July, the board reviews the financial objectives (as compiled and assessed by the corporate planning department). Modified financial objectives then go out in early August as a set of guidelines to each business unit. They, in turn, rely on these targets in preparing their own plans which are submitted to the board for approval by January. "Once adopted, plans are monitored in quarterly progress reports submitted by the operating units."[40]

Corporate planning also plays a role in maintaining what BAT refers to as "cultural harmony." In such a geographically dispersed company, employees may tend to identify first with their business units, rather than with BAT as a whole. The company uses several techniques to defend itself against such tendencies. Top managers and senior directors travel widely and immerse themselves in the division's businesses so as to, in a sense, "carry the flag" of the firm to all of its far-flung outposts. BAT also has a strong internal accounting/audit group; it carefully monitors each division's compliance with BAT policies regarding matters such as business ethics. Finally, of course, corporate planning plays a role by helping to standardize the assumptions and overall sense of mission that all divisions are to share.

SUMMARY

Plans are methods formulated beforehand for doing or making something. They identify goals as well as action statements—what is to be done and how it will be accomplished. Because of rapid changes, firms are increasingly making their planning processes leaner and more responsive.

Plans may be classified in many ways. They differ in format, time horizons, purpose, function, and degree of repetitiveness. There are single-use plans and standing plans. Plans can also be categorized according to scope.

Planning is important because it provides an enterprise with direction and a sense of purpose. Plans provide a unifying framework that channels efforts toward desired results. Plans also help identify opportunities and threats, and they facilitate control by impacting standard setting, performance evaluation, and problem solving.

The planning cycle involves defining goals, conducting a situation analysis, developing alternative plans, and deciding which plan to implement. The organizational planning process has a hierarchical aspect to it.

Goal setting leads to better employee performance by providing standards against which actual performance can be compared and controlled. To be effective, goals must be clear and specific, measurable and verifiable, and challenging but realistic. Goals can be assigned or participatively set.

Under management by objectives, supervisors and subordinates jointly set departmental and individual goals, and they meet to review and analyze progress. To make MBO programs more successful, managers should define specific goals in terms of measurable results and make sure individual goals are integrated with those of the organization. Goals should also be reviewed and updated periodically.

Because of changes in organizations, planning has shifted from headquarters to product or divisional heads who can more quickly perceive changes in customer preferences. Customers are increasingly the driving force in the planning function.

Company planning departments generally engage in ten planning-related activities, from gathering necessary information to developing analytical tools that can be used to make the planning process more effective.

QUESTIONS

FOR REVIEW

1. List the various ways plans can be classified.
2. Name four reasons why planning is important.
3. Describe the characteristics of effective goals.
4. How has planning evolved over the last 40 years?
5. Summarize the most common planning-related activities.

FOR DISCUSSION

6. Discuss some of the ways a CEO's plans would differ from those of a sales manager.
7. Do you think it is possible to operate a successful business without short-term and long-term plans? Why or why not?
8. What differentiates management by objectives from other types of goal setting?
9. Did the evolution in the planner's role bring about changes in business strategies or vice versa?

FOR ACTION

10. Your instructor will break the class up into small groups. Join with the other members of your group to develop a set of specific plans and goals aimed at rais-

ing enough money for a class trip to Hawaii through the sale of T-shirts with the university logo. Compare your results.

11. Develop a hierarchy of goals for your personal life. Illustrate how the lower-level goals contribute to the achievement of your overall aims.

12. Identify a successful company that is of interest to you. Find out if it has a corporate planning department or whether its planning is informal.

■ FOR FOCUS ON SMALL BUSINESS

13. Why was Frey wrong to believe that his company could succeed without a plan?

14. Outline Frey's vision and strategy for Cin-Made.

15. In what ways do you think planning in small firms differs from that in large firms?

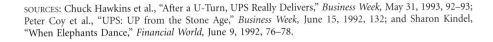

CLOSING SOLUTION

UPS

Kent Nelson, who is now chief executive, felt computer-based systems would eventually outstrip human capability in tracking, routing, and identifying packages. UPS spent around $2 billion on the most technologically advanced equipment to do just that. The company now has a global data network and has equipped drivers with hand-held computers. It also has budgeted another $3.2 billion over the next five years to continue its metamorphosis from a low-tech to a high-tech company. The approach taken to bring employees around didn't require anywhere near that kind of financial outlay, but it did require finesse. The host of dissenters, many of whom were highly-regarded managers, were sent to school. When they returned as committed converts, Nelson put them in charge of departmental steering committees that prioritized the new way of doing things. Nelson called it one of his best decisions. To get back in sync with customers, the marketing staff, which for years had been composed of just seven people, was expanded to 175. Nelson directed that personal interviews with 25,000 customers be conducted to determine service and product preferences and help UPS formulate future plans and achieve its ultimate goal—keeping customers happy.

SOURCES: Chuck Hawkins et al., "After a U-Turn, UPS Really Delivers," *Business Week,* May 31, 1993, 92–93; Peter Coy et al., "UPS: UP from the Stone Age," *Business Week,* June 15, 1992, 132; and Sharon Kindel, "When Elephants Dance," *Financial World,* June 9, 1992, 76–78.

■ QUESTIONS

1. Why was it important for UPS to make planned changes when it was still a leader in its industry?

2. Using the terms defined in the chapter, describe the types of plans Nelson made at UPS.

3. Based on the criteria developed by Edwin Locke and other researchers, would you say Nelson's goals were effective ones? Discuss.

KEY TERMS

Plans
Standing Plans
Policies
Procedures
Strategic Plan

Mission Statement
Management by Objectives
Goal Specificity
Goal Difficulty

CASE FOR ANALYSIS

ITT CORPORATION

Harold Geneen was CEO of the widely diversified ITT (formerly International Telephone and Telegraph). An acknowledged entrepreneurial wiz, he set out to first acquire a disparate collection of European telecommunication companies and then mold them into an efficient, functional whole. He implemented the latest information systems and brought the brightest young managers he could find on board. They began successfully identifying undervalued companies with high profit potential, and once acquired, Geneen molded and shaped them to fit into ITT's overall operations.

Ahead of his time, Geneen implemented a divisional structure that made managers accountable, and rewardable, for their own departments. His systems of control and information flow were soon a part of business lore. He was certain that the frequent appraisal meetings and divisional accountants reporting to headquarters would keep him on top of problems that might arise.

Geneen didn't know that the environment he created would sow the seeds of disaster. The succession of profitable acquisitions, and the autonomy under which managers directed their divisions, effectively loosened a platoon of overconfident managers across Europe. It was a decentralized corporate culture that placed growth above all others. Promotions, prestige, and compensation all came to be tied to it.

Between 1967 and 1970, acquisitions that generated $1.8 billion in revenue occurred. By 1977, 100 companies and 250 separate profit centers became part of ITT. Debt soared. And Geneen's vaunted information systems and whiz-kid managers went into overload trying to stay on top of it all. Financial standards sent down from on high were often misguided or irrelevant to the real needs on the ground. Infighting broke out. Top accountants at headquarters often tried to grab Geneen's attention by pointing out operational flaws within the divisions. Division chiefs retaliated by furnishing distorted numbers to the controllers. Top managers burned up better than 75 percent of their time doing budgets or attending meetings at the corporate headquarters, leaving little time to direct their operations. Product lines were ignored. Divisional plans lacked the necessary substance.

The acquisition momentum at ITT swept aside everything in its path. The early successes, and commensurate financial rewards that went with them, led managers to double and redouble bets. Diversification became the propelling force of the company, whether it made sense or not. Fundamental business practices, goods, services, and markets were obscured by an out-of-control emphasis on acquisitions. ITT lost sight of its primary objective. It was no longer gobbling up other companies to mold and build them into efficient business entities. The acquisition itself had become the central focus.

By the late 1970s, calcified product lines ceased returning adequate rates of profit. Several divisions were experiencing serious operational difficulties. By the late 1980s, new CEO Rand Araskog found himself presiding over a listless giant. He had to sell more than 100 divisions, shrinking the work force more than 60 percent.

SOURCES: "The Icarus Paradox: How Exceptional Companies Bring About Their Own Downfall," *Business Horizons,* January–February 1992, 23–30; and Subrata N. Chakravarty, "When Everything's for Sale, You Lose Something," *Forbes,* December 12, 1988, 34–36.

■ **QUESTIONS**

1. Based on the facts outlined in this case, do you think Geneen's acquisitions were part of an overall plan? Why or why not?
2. Where did Geneen's planning efforts go wrong? What could he have done differently?
3. How would you describe ITT's organizational goals under Geneen's leadership?
4. What do you think Geneen could have done to make ITT more responsive to change?

A CASE IN DIVERSITY

MARGARET F. GONZALES AND ACHIEVING GOALS

All good sales managers devote a big part of their energies prospecting for new business. And when they find them, they work hard to overcome barriers and close the sale. But for Margaret F. Gonzales, director of Los Angeles' East Side enterprise zone, things don't always get easier after the deal is done. Her primary goal is to attract industries and create jobs in an area blighted by a host of urban problems. She must also constantly plot strategies and devise methods to keep them there.

A quarter of the warehouse space in Gonzales' state-mandated territory is empty. Unemployment is a chronic problem, and is probably even higher than official estimates because the actual number of illegal alien residents is unknown. She brings an arsenal of incentives to the table: tax credits for each employee hired, low interest loans, cut-rate utility bills, and a motivated local labor force that comes cheap by surrounding standards. She's up against the predictable obstacles of crime and concerns about maintaining a safe workplace and a decaying infrastructure, among others. Her staff and budget aren't adequate either.

To achieve her goals, Gonzales has enlisted the professional assistance of real estate agents from other areas. She has taken her presentation to some of the tonier addresses to the north as well. Not long ago she pitched the benefits of her Boyle Heights district to several accountants at the Beverly Hills Racquet Club. The tax-shelter highlights of investing in her enterprise zone got a thorough sounding.

Her success stories include a salsa manufacturer's decision to move its factory to the area. An importer also plans an expansion, thanks to Gonzales' efforts to help the company obtain a $1 million Small Business Administration loan. But for every two steps forward, it seems Gonzales has to take a step back. One manufacturer is considering moving out of the area and relocating its operations to Idaho. And United Parcel Service backed out of a plan to construct a distribution center there. The setbacks are not enough to deter Gonzales. "My job is to find out what's making them unhappy and to see if I can fix it," she says.

Gonzales knows hers will always be an on-going effort. She has to stay on top of plans to attract new businesses, as well as methods to keep them there over the long haul. The job is challenging and thought-provoking, but the economic payoff for her constituents makes it worth it.

SOURCE: Ronald Grover, "Local Heroes Making a Difference," Business Week/Reinventing America, 1992, 214–220.

■ QUESTIONS

1. Describe Gonzales' task using the four-step planning cycle outlined in the chapter.
2. Develop a hypothetical set of goals for Gonzales that are clear and specific; measurable and verifiable; and challenging but realistic.
3. How would you tackle the task of getting companies to invest in an economically disadvantaged area? What do you think are some of the unstated objections that the firm's top managers want answered, but may not ask?

ENDNOTES

1. Chuck Hawkins, "After a U-Turn UPS Really Delivers," *Business Week,* May 31, 1993, 92-93, and Sharon Kindel, "When Elephants Dance," *Systems User,* June 9, 1992, 76–78.
2. Leonard Goodstein, Timothy Nolan, and Jay William Pfeiffer, *Applied Strategic Planning* (New York: McGraw Hill, Inc., 1993), 3.
3. Harold Koontz, Cyril O'Donnell, and Heinz Weihrich, *Management* (New York: McGraw Hill Book Company, 1980), 158.
4. Robert Burns, "To a Mouse," 1785.
5. Ronald Henkoff, "How to Plan for 1995," *Fortune,* December 31, 1990, 72.
6. Ibid., 72.
7. See, for example, D. Scott Sink and Thomas Tuttle, *Planning and Measurement in Your Organization of the Future* (Norcross, Georgia: Industrial Engineering and Management Press, 1989), 78–79.
8. Harvey Kahalas, "A Look at Planning and Its Components," *Managerial Planning,* January–February 1982, 13–16; reprinted in Phillip DuBose, *Readings in Management* (Englewood Cliffs, NJ: Prentice-Hall, Inc., 1988), 49–50.
9. Hankoff, "How to Plan," 74.
10. Kahalas, "A Look at Planning," 49.
11. Peter Drucker, "Long Range Planning," *Management Science,* vol. 5 (1959), 238–49.
12. See, for example, Goodstein et al., *Applied Strategic Planning,* 170.
13. Goodstein et al.

14. Gary Latham and J. James Baldes, "The Practical Significance of Locke's Theory of Goal Setting," *Journal of Applied Psychology,* vol. 60, no. 1 (February 1975).

15. See, for example, Gary Latham and Gary Yukl, "A Review of Research on the Application of Goal Setting in Organizations," *Academy of Management Journal,* vol. 18, no. 4 (1964), 824; and Gary Latham and Terrance A. Mitchell, "Importance of Participative Goal Setting and Anticipated Rewards on Goal Difficulty and Job Performance," *Journal of Applied Psychology,* vol. 63 (1978), 163–71.

16. Sondra Hart, William Moncrief, and A. Parasuraman, "An Empirical Investigation of Sales People's Performance, Effort and Selling Method During a Sales Contest," *Journal of the Academy of Marketing Science,* vol. 17, no. 1, Winter 1989, 29–39.

17. The rest of this section, except as noted, is based on Gary Yukl, *Skills for Managers and Leaders* (Englewood Cliffs, NJ: Prentice-Hall, 1991), 132–33.

18. Yukl, *Skills for Managers and Leaders,* 133; and Miriam Erez, Daniel Gopher, and Nira Arzi, "Effects of Goal Difficulty, Self-Set Goals, and Monetary Rewards on Dual Task Performance," *Organizational Behavior & Human Decision Processes,* vol. 47, no. 2, December 1990, 247–69.

19. See, for example, Stephan Schiffman and Michele Reisner, "New Sales Resolutions," *Sales & Marketing Manager,* vol. 33, no. 1, January 1992, 15–16; and Steve Rosenstock, "Your Agent's Success," *Manager's Magazine,* vol. 66, no. 9, September 1991, 21–23.

20. A. Zandernt Newcomb, Jr., "Group Levels of Aspirations in United Fund Campaigns," *Journal of Personality and Social Psychology,* vol. 6 (1967), 157–62; A. Zandernt, J. Forward, and R. Albert, "Adaptation of Board Members to Repeated Failure or Success by the Organization," *Organizational Behavior and Human Performance,* vol. 4 (1969), 56–76; and J.C. Wofford, Vicki Goodwin, and Steven Premack, "Meta-Analysis of the Antecedents of Personal Goal Level and of the Antecedence and Consequences of Goal Commitment," *Journal of Management,* vol. 18, no. 3, September 1992, 595–615.

21. Yukl, "Skills for Managers," 133.

22. Gary Latham and Lise Saari, "The Effects of Holding Goal Difficulty Constant on Assigned and Participatively Set Goals," *Academy of Management Journal,* vol. 22 (1979), 163–68; and Mark Tubbs and Steven Ekeberg, "The Role of Intentions in Work Motivation: Implications for Goal Setting Theory and Research," *Academy of Management Review,* vol. 16, no. 1, January 1991, 180–99.

23. See Latham and Saari, "The Effects of Holding . . ."

24. Gary Latham, Terence Mitchell, and Denise Dossett, "Importance of Participative Goal Setting and Anticipated Rewards on Goal Difficulty and Job Performance," *Journal of Applied Psychology,* vol. 63 (1978), 170.

25. See, for example, Anthony Mento, Norman Cartledge, and Edwin Locke, "Maryland Versus Michigan Versus Minnesota: Another Look at the Relationship of Expectancy and Goal Difficulty to Task Performance," *Organizational Behavior and Human Performance,* vol. 25, no. 3 (June 1980), 419–40.

26. William Werther, "Workshops Aid in Goal Setting," *Personal Journal,* vol. 68, November 1989, 32–38.

27. Howard Klein, "Further Evidence on the Relationship Between Goal Setting and Expectancy Theories," *Organizational Behavior & Human Decision Processes,* vol. 49, no. 2, August 1991, 230–57; and Gerald Bricker, "Performance Agreements: The Key to Increasing Motivation," *Sales & Marketing Management,* vol. 144, February 1992, 69–70.

28. Steven Carroll and Henry Tosi, *Management by Objectives* (New York: Macmillan, 1973).

29. Mark McConkie, "A Clarification of the Goal Setting and Appraisal Processes in MBO," *Academy of Management Review,* vol. 4 (1979), 29–40.

30. Gary Latham and Edwin Locke, "Self-Regulation Through Goal Setting," *Organizational Behavior & Human Decision Processes,* vol. 50, December 1991, 212–47.

31. Maurice Vilere and Sondra Hartman, "Tapping the Benefits of Knowing Where You Are Going: Insights on Goal Setting Theory," *Leadership & Organization Development Journal,* vol. 12, no. 4, 1991.

32. Peter Drucker, *People and Performance: The Best of Peter Drucker* (New York: Harper, 1977), 65.

33. Michael Trapani, "Goals Set/Goals Met," *Life & Health Insurance Sales,* vol. 134, no. 8, August 1991, 14–18.

34. *Global Strategic Planning* (New York: Business International Corporation, 1991), 3.

35. Ibid., 2.

36. Ibid., 3.

37. Ibid., 5.

38. This is based on *Global Strategic Planning,* 60–63.

39. Ibid., 62.

40. Ibid., 63.

CHAPTER 6

STRATEGIC MANAGEMENT

LEARNING OBJECTIVES

After studying this chapter, you should be able to:

- Define strategic management and its functions.
- Outline and describe the five basic steps of the strategic management process.
- Explain how strategic planning fits in with the overall strategic management process.
- Explain stretch and leverage concepts in the application of strategic management plans.
- Differentiate between corporate, competitive, and functional strategies.
- Illustrate the strategic role of core competencies, the necessity of managers viewing their companies as "boundaryless organizations," and the advantages of strategic alliances and virtual corporations.
- Discuss methods of implementing strategy and the difficulties associated with this process.
- Discuss at least five strategic situation analysis tools.

The Nature and Functions of Strategic Management
Why Strategic Management Is Important
The Strategic Management Process
The Strategic Planning Process
Strategy as Stretch and Leverage

Formulating Strategies
Types of Strategies
Corporate Strategies
Competitive Strategies
Functional Strategies

The Responsive Organization: Competing on Capabilities and Core Competencies
The Strategic Role of Core Competencies
Strategic Alliances

Implementing Strategy
The Integrated Nature of Strategy Implementation

Strategic Situation Analysis Tools
The Role of Situation Analysis
Portfolio Analysis Tools for Corporate Strategy
Competitive Analysis: The Five Forces Model
Company Internal Situation Analysis Tools
Organizing the Information: SWOT Analysis

OPENING PROBLEM
KMART CORPORATION

In 1979, Kmart was "king of the discount retailing industry," and Wal-Mart was barely a speck on the retailing scene.[1] With 1,891 stores, Kmart literally dwarfed Wal-Mart's 229 stores, particularly since Wal-Mart's stores were almost all in small to midsized towns in the southern United States. Kmart's enormous size gave it advantages that casual observers at the time assumed made the retailer almost unbeatable: after all, Kmart benefitted from economies of scale in purchasing, distributing, and marketing its merchandise that should have enabled it to beat its competitors hands down in this highly price-sensitive industry. In this setting, Wal-Mart hardly seemed a serious competitor, with average revenues per store barely half of Kmart's $7

changed dr

by the early

world, while

in c
mary t
thinking
business a
strategies and

THE NATURE AND FUNCTIONS OF STRATEGIC MANAGEMENT

WHY STRATEGIC MANAGEMENT IS IMPORTANT

Two experts say the main reason for the reversal of fortunes outlined in the opening Kmart case lies in "a set of strategic business decisions that transformed [Wal-Mart] into a capabilities-based competitor." Wal-Mart had a *vision* of the sort of discount chain it wanted to be and a mission, "to provide customers access to quality goods, to make these goods available when and where customers want them, to develop a cost structure that enables competitive pricing, and to build and maintain a reputation for absolute trustworthiness."[2]

The key to Wal-Mart's strategy—its course of action for achieving this mission—lay in a distribution system that even today is years ahead of its time. Almost from its inception, Wal-Mart had a unique communications and distribution problem. As owner Sam Walton put it, "Our stores were sitting out there in tiny little towns and we had to stay in touch and keep them supplied."[3] By the late 1960s, Walton and his team were investing in sophisticated satellite-based communication equipment and technology, and were developing a distribution system based on huge regional warehouses and the concept of *cross-docking*. At the time, most Wal-Mart competitors—including Kmart—used traditional logistical means to get suppliers' merchandise to their stores: this basically meant that stores would order merchandise through the company's central buying offices when they were running low. The central buying offices then ordered the merchandise from the suppliers, who then produced the merchandise—say, a thousand suits—and sent them directly to the stores. With cross-docking, things are handled differently. Goods are continuously delivered to Wal-Mart's warehouses, where the material is repacked and dispatched to the stores that need it, often without ever sitting in inventory.[4] Among other things, cross-docking dramatically reduced the amount of inventory that had to wait around on Wal-Mart shelves and enabled store managers to know they could get items restocked within a couple of days.

The effects of cross-docking on the company's profits were enormous. The strategy of building distribution around cross-docking drove down Wal-Mart's cost of sales by 2 percent to 3 percent compared with the industry average and in turn kept prices down. This, in turn, reduced sales promotions and built more predictability into Wal-Mart's sales patterns, further reducing the need for high inventories.

Today, Wal-Mart's distribution system remains the most sophisticated in the industry. Nineteen distribution centers and 2,000 company-owned trucks let Wal-Mart replenish store shelves within two days. Sophisticated point-of-sale cash registers monitor the inventory levels of various items in each store and continuously communicate that data to both the distribution center and suppliers. The result, as it turns out, is a uniquely customer-driven merchandising operation. Whereas many other chains have central buying offices that place large orders for merchandise and then try to "push" this merchandise through the stores to customers, Wal-Mart's approach is the opposite. Customer data from point-of-sale machines and local store managers determine what is ordered, and the resulting system is highly responsive to changes in customers' tastes.

The Wal-Mart example underscores the central role played by strategy management in ensuring a firm's success. Management expert Peter Drucker has said that the primary task of top management is:

through the mission of the business, that is, of asking the question "What is our ... and what should it be?" This leads to the setting of objectives, the development of ... plans, and the making of today's decisions for tomorrow's results.[5]

As at Wal-Mart, strategic management, stripped to its essentials, involves determining what business the firm is going to be in, and the course or courses of action (the strategies) the firm will use to get from where it is now to where it wants to go. And, as at Wal-Mart, this often determines success or failure for the firm.

THE STRATEGIC MANAGEMENT PROCESS

Strategic management is the process of identifying and pursuing the organization's mission by aligning the organization's internal capabilities with the external demands of its environment.[6] As shown in Figure 6.1, the strategic management process contains five basic steps: defining the business and developing a vision and mission; translating the mission into specific strategic objectives; crafting a strategy to achieve the objectives; implementing and executing the strategy; and evaluating performance, reviewing the situation, and initiating corrective adjustments.

Let us look at each step in turn.

STEP 1: DEFINE THE BUSINESS AND DEVELOP A MISSION   Peter Drucker said the primary task of top management is thinking through the mission of the business, that is, of asking the question, "What is our business and what should it be?" As authors Thompson and Strickland point out, "Management's answer to 'What is our business and what will it be?' begins the process of carving out a meaningful direction for the organization to take and of establishing a strong organizational identity."[7]

Two companies can compete in the same industry but still define their businesses in different ways. For example, Ferrari and Ford both make cars, but there the similarity ends. Ferrari specializes in high-performance cars, and its competitive advantage is built on handmade craftsmanship and high-speed performance. Ford produces a wide range of automobiles, as well as many of its own supplies and parts; its competitive advantage is built on cost-efficient production and a strong worldwide dealer network. Similarly, Wal-Mart and Kmart are in the same industry. But Wal-Mart

STRATEGIC MANAGEMENT
The process of identifying and pursuing the organization's mission by aligning internal capabilities with the external demands of its environment.

— absolutely

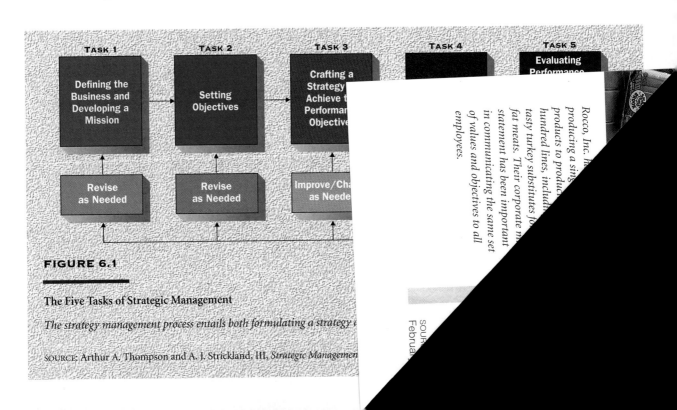

FIGURE 6.1

The Five Tasks of Strategic Management

The strategy management process entails both formulating a strategy

SOURCE: Arthur A. Thompson and A. J. Strickland, III, *Strategic Management*

distinguished itself from Kmart by concentrating its stores in small southern towns, and by building its state-of-the-art cross-docking distribution system. Kmart, on the other hand, opened stores throughout the country (where it necessarily had to compete with a great many other discounters, often for expensive, big-city properties). Also, Kmart based its competitive advantage on its size, which it (erroneously) assumed would provide it with the economies of scale necessary to keep its costs below those of competitors.

As we will see, answering the question, "What business should we be in?" sometimes produces both a vision statement and a mission statement (although the two are often essentially the same). The organization's **vision** is a "general statement of its intended direction that evokes emotional feelings in organization members."[8] As Warren Bennis and Bert Manus say:

> To choose a direction, a leader must first have developed a mental image of a possible and desirable future state for the organization. This image, which we call a vision, may be as vague as a dream or as precise as a goal or mission statement. The critical point is that a vision articulates a view of a realistic, credible, attractive future for the organization, a condition that is better in some important ways than what now exists.[9]

For example, Dr. Edwin Land, who invented the Polaroid camera, had a vision of a company built on providing instant photographs in self-contained cameras.

In turn, the firm's **mission statement** further defines and operationalizes the top manager's vision. A mission statement "broadly outlines the organization's future course and serves to communicate 'who we are, what we do, and where we're headed.'"[10] Mission statements, such as for Otis Elevator, are presented in Figure 6.2. The *Rocco, Inc.* vignette explains a little about why one firm developed its mission statement.

VISION

A general statement of the firm's intended direction that evokes emotional feelings in organization members.

MISSION STATEMENT

Broadly outlines the organization's future course and serves to communicate "who we are and where we're heading." Answers the question, "what business are we in?"

...as expanded from
...le line of poultry
...ng several
...ng these
...higher-
...ission

ROCCO, INC.

When it began as a family-owned manufacturer of animal feed in 1939, Rocco, Inc., sold a single line of products. Today the Harrisonburg, Virginia, company markets several hundred lines of poultry products, employs more than 3,000 people in several states, and earns annual revenues of nearly $400 million. Third-generation family members still sit on the board, but remembering the founder's philosophy more than a half-century later is difficult. The board concluded that it needed a written mission statement to redefine that philosophy and serve as a blueprint for future operation.

Rocco CEO John Darazdi believed the statement had to be clear, concise, and brief. It would not be effective if it was too long or complicated, or filled with unrealistic, high-sounding rhetoric. The document had to be instructive and define what was important to the company. That included customers, products, as well as employee obligations to Rocco. As it turned out, the corporate mission statement was critically important to Rocco. It communicated the expected standards of operation and provided an indispensable guide to every employee in carrying out their duties and responsibilities.

...CE: James J. Darazdi, "Mission Statements Are Essential," *Personnel Journal,*
...y 1993, 24–25.

SEVEN ACTUAL COMPANY MISSION STATEMENTS:

OTIS ELEVATOR

Our mission is to provide any customer a means of moving people and things up, down, and sideways over short distances with higher reliability than any similar enterprise in the world.

DELUXE CHECKS

The mission of Deluxe Checks is to provide all banks, S&Ls, and investment firms with error-free financial instruments delivered in a timely fashion.

McCORMICK & COMPANY

The primary mission of McCormick & Company is to expand our worldwide leadership position in the spice, seasoning, and flavoring markets.

HEWLETT-PACKARD COMPANY

Hewlett-Packard is a major designer and manufacturer of electronic products and systems for measurement and computation. HP's basic business purpose is to provide the capabilities and services needed to help customers worldwide improve their personal and business effectiveness.

THE SATURN DIVISION OF GENERAL MOTORS

To market vehicles developed and manufactured in the United States that are world leaders in quality, cost, and customer satisfaction through the integration of people, technology, and business systems and to transfer knowledge, technology, and experience throughout General Motors.

PUBLIC SERVICE COMPANY OF NEW MEXICO

Our mission is to work for the success of the people we serve by providing our CUSTOMERS reliable electric service, energy information, and energy options that best satisfy their needs.

AMERICAN RED CROSS

The mission of the American Red Cross is to improve the quality of human life; to enhance self-reliance and concern for others; and to help people avoid, prepare for, and cope with emergencies.

FIGURE 6.2

SOURCE: Arthur A. Thompson and A. J. Strickland, III, *Strategic Management: Concepts and Cases,* 6th ed. (Homewood, IL: Irwin, 1992), 4.

STEP 2: TRANSLATE THE MISSION INTO STRATEGIC OBJECTIVES

The next strategic management task is to translate top management's broad vision and mission into operational strategic objectives. For example, strategic objectives for Citicorp include building shareholder value through sustained growth in earnings per share; a continued commitment to building customer-oriented business worldwide; superior rates of return; a strong balance sheet; and a business balanced by customer, product, and geography.[11]

STEP 3: FORMULATE A STRATEGY TO ACHIEVE THE STRATEGIC OBJECTIVES

A **strategy** is a course of action which explains how the enterprise will move from the business it is in now to the business it wants to be in (as stated in its mission), given the opportunities and threats, and its internal strengths and weaknesses. For example, in the 1960s, Wal-Mart planned to move from a relatively small southern-based chain of retail discount stores to the national leader in low costs and prices. One strategy was to reduce distribution costs and minimize inventory and delivery times through the technology-based cross-docking distribution system.

STRATEGY
A course of action which explains how the enterprise will move from the business it is in now to the business it wants to be in.

STEP 4: IMPLEMENT THE STRATEGY

Strategy implementation means translating the strategy into actions and results. Doing so requires drawing upon all of the functions in the management process, namely organizing, staffing, leading, and controlling. For instance, an organization structure capable of implementing the strategy will have to be crafted; employees will have to be hired and motivated; and budgets must be formulated through which progress toward the firm's strategic goals can be measured and controlled. The firm's strategic plan is comprised of its strategies and strategic objectives.

STEP 5: EVALUATE PERFORMANCE AND INITIATE CORRECTIVE ADJUSTMENTS AS REQUIRED

STRATEGIC CONTROL
The process of assessing the firm's progress toward its strategic objectives and taking corrective action as needed.

Finally, **strategic control**—assessing the firm's progress toward its strategic objectives and taking corrective action as needed—operates to keep the company's strategy fresh. It also ensures that all parts and members of the organization are contributing in a useful way toward its implementation. Managing strategy is thus an ongoing, not a stagnant, process: competitors introduce new products, technological innovations make production processes obsolete, and societal trends reduce demands for some products or services while boosting demands for others. As a result, managing strategy is an evolutionary process; managers need to be alert to opportunities and threats that might demand modifying or, in some cases, totally abandoning their strategic plans.

THE STRATEGIC PLANNING PROCESS

STRATEGIC PLANNING
The process of identifying the business a firm is in today and the business it wants to be in in the future, and the course of action or strategy it will pursue, given its opportunities, threats, strengths, and weaknesses.

Strategic planning is part of the overall strategic *management* process. As illustrated in Figure 6.3, it represents the first three of the strategic management steps: defining the business and developing a vision and mission, translating the mission into strategic objectives, and crafting a strategy or course of action to move the organization from where it is today to where it wants to be.

Like any planning, strategic planning follows the planning cycle. This means a company must set objectives, conduct a situation audit, identify its alternatives, and, finally, choose a strategic plan. **Strategic planning** is therefore the process of identifying the business the firm is in today and the businesses it wants to be in in the future, and then identifying the course of action or strategy it will pursue, given its opportunities,

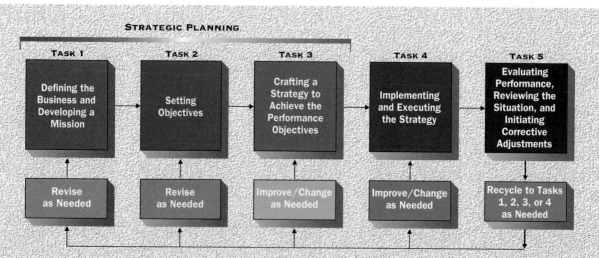

FIGURE 6.3

Strategic Planning's Role in Strategic Management

Strategic planning entails defining the nature of the business, setting strategic objectives, and formulating a strategy or course of action for achieving the objectives.

SOURCE: Arthur A. Thompson and A. J. Strickland, *Strategic Management: Concepts and Cases,* 6th ed. (Homewood, IL: Irwin, 1992), 5.

KING'S MEDICAL COMPANY

Do you think small businesses can't derive much benefit from strategic planning? Think again. King's Medical Company of Hudson, Ohio, is a 13-year-old company currently implementing its third three-year strategic plan. General manager and chief planner William Patton considers the decision-making discipline and the follow-through it promotes to be the focus point to the company's success. "A lot of literature says there are three critical issues to a small company and they're all cash flow. These issues are critical, but the reason a small company survives is planning."

King's Medical is both a proprietor and manager of magnetic-resonance imaging equipment, big-ticket machines that produce X-ray images for the health care industry. Started in 1981, the company grew to more than $13 million in sales by 1992. Company founder Albert Van Kirk, who admits he used to do little planning, wholeheartedly concurs with Patton's views.

According to Van Kirk and Patton, plans are important for several reasons. Plans inspire evaluation and discussion in the formulation stage. Once in place, plans set the company course for the medium term. Managers across the company get involved in the decision-making process and get an idea of how their work integrates in the overall company scheme.

At King's Medical, the planning process begins with the establishment of a leadership group. This is aimed at answering some basic questions like why the firm is in business, where it is currently, and where it hopes to be at the end of the planning period. The answers are correlated and reduced to a mission statement, which is then distributed to all employees.

**FOCUS ON
SMALL BUSINESS**

Next, a business plan is produced through analysis of the industry. Patton considers this to be a standard exercise for a planner. "It's an abbreviated SWOT—evaluating your strengths, weaknesses, opportunities, and threats," he says. The last step of the process is to define specific objectives and action plans to meet each of them.

At the department level, good strategic planning results in each division carrying out a tactical plan that matches the company's objectives. Consistency and a view of the big picture are the keys. "I want to see how these more specific plans fit into our long-range objectives," says Patton. "That helps us create the vertical integration of our planning, to have a set of common ends we're all going after."

At King's, every tactical plan, regardless of where it originates, must address five issues: which objectives it helps to meet; the measurable outcomes, or what it will achieve; the time frame; the cost; and who will be held responsible. Department managers canvas their staffs to formulate plans, and Patton helps fine-tune them. Van Kirk has final veto power and keeps an eye on the outcomes. Through this process, each plan creates its own top-to-bottom communication channel.

Van Kirk says everything at King's Medical comes back to three questions: How does it fit with company goals? Where does this department want to be in the future? And how do you know when it has gotten there. Perhaps ironically, he also feels the emphasis on planning makes the company more flexible. Changes in the marketplace that in the past might have led to a ruinous change of course can be avoided, because the vision spelled out in the plan remains intact. "The key," Van Kirk says, "is keeping on track."

SOURCE: Leslie Brokaw, "The Secrets of Great Planning," *Inc.*, October 1992, 51.

threats, strengths, and weaknesses. Notice that the notion of *strategic fit* therefore plays a big role in strategic planning: top management's job is to develop a strategic plan that positions the company in the right businesses and with the right competitive advantage, given its external opportunities and threats, and the company's resources. Strategic planning is important for small companies too, as the *King's Medical* Small Business box shows.

STRATEGY AS STRETCH AND LEVERAGE

Two strategy management experts, Gary Hamel and C. K. Prahalad, caution against being preoccupied with the concept of strategic fit, however.[12] They agree that every company "must ultimately effect a fit between its resources and the opportunities it pursues."[13] However, they argue that a preoccupation with the concept of fit can unnecessarily limit a company's growth. They say that in practice the concept of "stretch" must supplement the idea of fit. They argue that leveraging resources—supplementing what you have and doing all that's possible, or more, with what you have—can be more important than just fitting your strategic plan to your firm's current limited resources.

For example, "if modest resources were an insurmountable deterrent to future leadership, GM, Phillips, and IBM would not have found themselves on the defensive with Honda, Sony, and Compaq."[14] Similarly, Kmart would not have found itself overtaken by Wal-Mart within barely ten years. Companies, they say, can *leverage* their resources, for instance, by concentrating them more effectively on key strategic goals. Consider how Wal-Mart focused its relatively limited resources on building its cross-docking distribution system and high-tech communications system and thus built a competitive advantage that helped it push Kmart aside.

FORMULATING STRATEGIES

TYPES OF STRATEGIES

CORPORATE-LEVEL STRATEGY
Identifies the portfolio of businesses that, in total, will compose the corporation, and it identifies the ways in which these businesses will relate to each other.

COMPETITIVE STRATEGY
Identifies how to build and strengthen the business's long-term competitive position in the marketplace by analyzing the attractiveness of the business's industry in order to build a relative superiority over competitors.

There are several type of strategies. This is summarized in Figure 6.4. Many companies such as PepsiCo consist of several businesses such as Pepsi, Frito-Lay, and Pizza Hut. These companies therefore need a corporate-level strategy. A company's **corporate-level strategy** identifies the portfolio of businesses that, in total, will compose the corporation, and the ways in which these businesses will relate to each other.

Each of these businesses (such as Pizza Hut) is then guided by a business level/competitive strategy. A **competitive strategy** identifies how to build and strengthen the business's long-term competitive position in the marketplace.[15] It identifies, for instance, how Pizza Hut will compete with Dominos or how Wal-Mart will compete with Kmart.

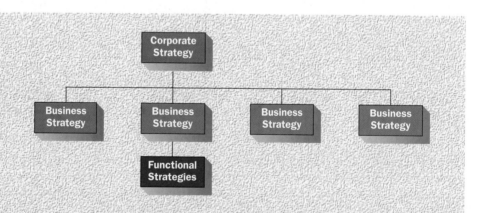

FIGURE 6.4

Relationships among Strategies in Multiple-Business Firms

Companies typically formulate three types of strategies. Corporate strategies identify the mix of businesses the firm will engage in. The business level/competitive strategies identify how each of the firm's businesses will compete; and each business then has several functional strategies identifying how the unit's manufacturing, sales, and other functions will contribute to the business strategy.

SOURCE: James M. Higgins and Julian W. Vincze, *Strategic Management: Text and Cases*, 5th ed. (Fort Worth: The Dryden Press, 1991), 263.

Each business will in turn be comprised of departments, such as manufacturing, marketing, and personnel. **Functional strategies** identify the basic courses of action that each of the business's departments will pursue in order to help the business attain its competitive goals. We'll look at each type of strategy in turn.

CORPORATE STRATEGIES

Every organization has to consider the number of businesses in which it will compete and the relationships that will exist among those businesses. Several standard corporate strategic alternatives are available.

CONCENTRATION   A concentration corporate strategy focuses the organization on one product or product line, usually in one market. Organizations that have successfully pursued a single-business strategy include McDonald's, Kentucky Fried Chicken, Campbell's Soup, and Gerber.

A concentration strategy has advantages and disadvantages. The main advantage is that the organization can focus its strengths on the one business that it knows well, allowing it to do that one thing better than competitors (for instance, Gerber's baby foods stresses that "baby foods are our only business"). It should also boost efficiency through economies of scale—more efficient manufacturing facilities and higher volume supplies buying, for instance.

The big risk in concentration results from a company putting all its eggs in just one basket. Most products go through a product life cycle: demand for the product rises rapidly in the early, introduction stage; slowly levels off as product demand matures and as more competitors enter the market; and finally, demand may decline. As a result, concentrators must always be on the lookout for signs of decline. Thus, McDonald's Corporation, after years of concentrating in the hamburger franchise business, took the first step toward diversifying into building and franchising children's play areas in covered shopping malls.

Concentrating in a single line of business need not mean that the firm isn't going to grow. Indeed, some traditional concentrators such as Coca Cola Corporation have achieved very high growth rates.

Such growth may be achieved in several strategic ways.[16] Companies can grow through **market penetration.** This means taking steps to boost sales of present products by more aggressively permeating the organization's current markets. **Geographic expansion** is another strategic growth alternative. *The Wall Street Journal* has achieved above average growth rates while concentrating on its business publication by aggressively expanding into new geographic markets both domestic and overseas. Growth can also be achieved—even in maturing markets—through **product development,** which means developing improved products for current markets with the goal of maintaining or boosting growth. **Horizontal integration,** acquiring ownership or control of competitors who are competing in the same or similar markets with the same or similar products, is another option. For example, the Humana hospital chain has grown rapidly while remaining a concentrator by acquiring hundreds of hospitals.

VERTICAL INTEGRATION   Vertical integration is another corporate strategy and it means owning or controlling the inputs to the firm's processes or the channels through which the firm's products or services are distributed. (The former is called backward integration, while the latter is called forward integration.) Thus, Ford owns Libby-Owens glass, which supplies it with windshields; major oil companies like Shell not only drill and produce their own oil, but sell it through company-controlled outlets.

DIVERSIFICATION
A strategy of expanding into related or unrelated products or market segments.

RELATED DIVERSIFICATION
Diversifying into other products or markets in such a way that a firm's lines of business still possess some kind of fit.

CONGLOMERATE DIVERSIFICATION
Diversifying into other products or markets that are not related to the firm's present businesses or to one another.

STABILITY OR STATUS QUO STRATEGY
A corporate strategy in which the firm retains its current strategy, focusing on its present products and markets.

INVESTMENT REDUCTION OR DEFENSIVE STRATEGIES
Corrective actions taken to reduce the company's investments in one or more of its lines of business.

RETRENCHMENT
The reduction of activities or operations.

DIVESTMENT
Selling or liquidating individual businesses.

DIVERSIFICATION Diversification means a strategy of expanding into related or unrelated products or market segments.[17]

Diversifying helps to move the organization into other businesses or industries or perhaps just into other product lines. In any case, it helps the firm avoid the problem of having all its eggs in one basket by spreading risk among several products or markets. However, diversification adds a new risk of its own: it forces the organization and its managers to split their attentions and resources among several products or markets instead of one. To that extent diversification may undermine the firm's ability to compete successfully in its chosen markets.

Several forms of diversification are widely used. **Related diversification** means diversifying into other industries in such a way that a firm's lines of business still possess some kind of fit.[18] In general, related diversification means diversifying into a business that has a customer base, product, technical knowledge, or channels of distribution similar or related to the company's present businesses.[19] When women's wear maker Donna Karan expanded into men's clothing, it was an example of related diversification. When Campbell's Soup purchased Pepperidge Farm Cookies, it did so because it felt that Pepperidge Farm's customer base and channels of distribution were very similar to its own. **Conglomerate diversification** means diversifying into products or markets that are *not* related to the firm's present businesses or to one another. For example, Getty Oil diversified into pay television, and several years ago Mobil Oil Company purchased the Montgomery Ward's retail store chain.

STATUS QUO STRATEGIES Unlike the preceding growth-oriented strategies, a **stability** or **status quo strategy** means that the organization is satisfied with its rate of growth and product scope. Operationally, this means that it plans to retain its present strategy and, at the corporate level, will continue focusing on its present products and markets for the foreseeable future. This can be dangerous as a long-term strategy, since competitors' growth (which must come from somewhere) may well come at the status quo firm's expense. It can be effective in the short-term, however, particularly when the firm is successful at doing what it is doing.

INVESTMENT REDUCTION STRATEGIES Sometimes companies must cut back. Delta Airlines, suffering from route over-expansion because of its purchase of Pan Am, recently made the first employee cutbacks in its history, for instance. In any case, whether it is over-expansion, ill-conceived diversification, or some other financial exigency, **investment reduction** or **defensive strategies** are corrective actions taken to reduce the company's investments in one or more of its lines of business.

Several options are available to reduce investment. **Retrenchment** means the reduction of activity or operations. For example, IBM is currently engaged in a massive retrenchment effort, involving dramatically reducing (*downsizing*) its number of employees and closing a multitude of facilities. **Divestment** means selling or liquidating individual businesses. (Divestiture usually denotes the sale of a viable business, while liquidation denotes the sale or abandonment of a nonviable one.) The *U S West* vignette illustrates some of the mechanics of downsizing a company.

STRATEGIC ALLIANCES AND JOINT VENTURES Strategic alliances and joint ventures are a separate corporate strategic option. Either generally refers (as noted in Chapter 2) to a formal agreement between two or more separate companies, the purpose of which is to enable the organizations to benefit from complementary strengths. We'll discuss this increasingly popular option in more detail later in this chapter.

The decision regarding whether to concentrate, diversify, or pursue some other specific corporate strategy, such as status quo, should be based on a thorough analysis of

U S WEST

Staff reductions can boost efficiency, but can also hurt morale among employees that remain.

U S West Communications, Inc., is one of many companies that has felt the double-edge blade of downsizing. Facing competitive pressure that resulted from a changing marketplace and changing technology, U S West began reducing its staff in 1989. In 1993, it announced further cuts that amounted to 14 percent of its 63,000 person work force over three years. Altering operations made streamlining possible, but eliminating so many people made those workers that stayed behind fearful of losing their jobs.

U S West faced the problem squarely. The company clearly spelled out its future direction, and employees were informed about their prospects. Teams were formed to encourage worker involvement. With goals—and the methods of achieving them—clearly defined, workers were instilled with the sense that they once again had control of their own destinies. This established a positive culture. Sound financial planning and an investment in education empowered employees and increased productivity. U S West now relies on a committed work force that understands company goals and will take personal responsibility in achieving them.

SOURCES: Steven Tarr and William Juliano, "Leading a Team Through Downsizing," *HR Magazine,* October 1992, 91; and "U S West to Slash 9,000 Jobs," *Reuters,* September 18, 1993.

When U S West downsized, it used innovative programs to help both those whose jobs were phased out and those who remained. Cliff Walker, a 24-year employee, took a transition leave of absence to pursue other opportunities.

the situation. A number of corporate strategic situation analysis aids are described in the appendix to this chapter.

COMPETITIVE STRATEGIES

Whether an organization decides to concentrate on a single business or diversify into a number of different ones, it should develop competitive strategies for each of these businesses. Strategic planning expert Michael Porter refers to competitive strategy as "the search for a favorable competitive position in an industry." He goes on to say that "competitive strategy aims to establish a profitable and sustainable position against the forces that determine industry competition."[20]

As we'll see in the appendix to this chapter (when we discuss competitive strategy situation analysis aids) formulating competitive strategy requires analyzing the attractiveness of the business's industry. Based on that analysis, the company has to find a sustainable competitive advantage, that is, a basis upon which the business can claim a relative superiority over competitors and thus lay claim to certain customers. Based on the competitive strategic situation analysis, Porter says three basic or generic competive strategic options are possible: cost leadership, differentiation, and focus.

COST LEADERSHIP Just about every company tries to hold down its costs. In this way, a company can price its products and services competitively. **Cost leadership** as a competitive strategy goes beyond this. A business that pursues a cost leadership competitive strategy is aiming to become *the* low-cost leader in an industry. It may do

COST LEADERSHIP
A strategy that means the business aims to be the low-cost leader in the industry.

this by pursuing sheer size and economies of scale (as Kmart attempted), or it may use some combination of other options (as Wal-Mart did when it developed its cross-docking distribution system). In any case, the unique characteristic of the cost leadership strategy is its emphasis on obtaining absolute cost advantages from any and all possible sources. Wal-Mart is a typical industry cost leader. Distribution costs are minimized through the satellite-based cross-docking system, store location costs are minimized by placing the stores on relatively low-cost land outside small- to medium-sized southern towns, and the stores themselves are anything but plush.

Pursuing a cost leadership competitive strategy involves a tricky balance between relentlessly pursuing lower costs while maintaining acceptable quality. Southwest Airlines, for instance, manages to keep its cost per passenger mile below those of most other major airlines while still providing service as good or better than those of its competitors.

DIFFERENTIATION   In a **differentiation strategy,** a firm seeks to be unique in its industry along some dimensions that are widely valued by buyers.[21] In other words, it picks out one or more attributes of the product or service that its buyers perceive as important, and then it uniquely positions itself to meet those needs. In practice, the dimensions along which a firm can differentiate itself range from the relatively ethereal product image boosted by some cosmetics firms, to concrete differences in attributes such as product durability, as emphasized by Caterpillar Tractor. Similarly, Volvo

DIFFERENTIATION STRATEGY
When a firm seeks to be unique in its industry along some dimensions that are widely valued by buyers.

In an increasingly crowded marketplace, businesses may emphasize their unique attributes to capture the consumer's attention. Apple has stressed the user-friendly nature of its line of personal computers from its inception, hoping to differentiate itself from the competition.

stresses the safety of its cars, Apple stresses the usability of its computers, and Mercedes Benz emphasizes reliability and quality. As with Mercedes Benz, firms can usually charge a premium price if they successfully stake out their claim to being substantially different in some coveted way from their competitors.

FOCUS Differentiators like Volvo and low-cost leaders like Wal-Mart generally aim their business at a wide range of potential buyers. The third generic competitive strategy, focus, is different. A business pursuing a **focus strategy** selects a market segment and builds its competitive strategy on serving those in its markets better or more cheaply than its competitors. For example, IBM is a differentiator that (generally speaking) sells to a very wide range of computer buyers. On the other hand, Cray Research builds superfast supercomputers and focuses its effort on market niches that require the special attributes that a Cray computer can provide, such as the U.S. Weather Service.

The basic question in choosing whether to pursue a focus competitive strategy is this: By focusing on a narrow market, can we provide our target customers with a product or service better or more cheaply than can our generalist competitors? In other words, it makes sense to pursue a focus strategy when (as summarized in Figure 6.5) it allows the business to differentiate itself (as far as its customers are concerned) from its generalist competitors or allows it to provide its customers with a product or service more cheaply.

Examples of focusers abound. For example, the Pea in the Pod chain of maternity stores focuses on selling stylish clothes to pregnant working women. By specializing in "working women maternity clothes," the company is able to provide a much wider range of such clothes to its target customers than those customers would find in generalist competitors such as Macy's or J.C. Penney. Focusing thus allows it to differentiate itself. Martin Brower, Inc., focuses on supplying McDonald's franchisees with supplies such as hamburger patties, cups, and napkins. Because they specialize in

FOCUS STRATEGY
When a business selects a market segment and builds its strategy on serving those in its target market better or more cheaply than its generalist competitors.

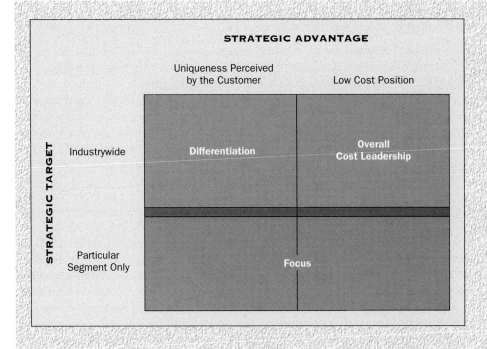

FIGURE 6.5

Three Generic Strategies

The focus strategy is a special example of the differentiation or cost leadership strategies. Focusers succeed by providing their target segments with (1) something they could not get or get as well from industrywide competitors, (differentiator/focusers) or (2) could not get as inexpensively from them (cost leadership/focusers.)

SOURCE: Michael Porter, *Competitive Strategy: Techniques for Analyzing Industries and Competitors* (New York: The Free Press, 1980), 39.

McDonald's franchisees, the company is able to stockpile and purchase in larger quantities items that are unique to the McDonald's stores and can therefore do it more inexpensively than can generalist food suppliers. It is thus a low-cost leader for McDonald's franchisees.

FUNCTIONAL STRATEGIES

At some point each business' choice of competitive strategy (be it low-cost leader, differentiator, or focuser) is translated into functional strategies for each of its departments to pursue. A *functional strategy* is the basic course or courses of action that each department is to follow in enabling the business to accomplish its strategic goals. For example, Wal-Mart, as we've seen, has chosen to compete as the industry's low-cost leader. In order to implement this strategy, the firm had to formulate functional strategies for each of its departments that made sense in terms of moving Wal-Mart toward its desired position as low-cost leader. Thus the distribution department would pursue a strategy (cross-docking) that would ultimately drive distribution costs down to a minimum; the company's land development department would identify locations that both fit the firm's customer profile while keeping construction costs to a minimum; and the merchandise buyers would find sources of supplies that were capable of providing good quality merchandise at the lowest possible prices. Similarly, the basic strategies to be pursued by the company's human resource (personnel) department and its finance departments would have to be consistent with furthering the company's low-cost leader strategic goal. Notice, by the way, that functional strategies cannot be formulated intelligently unless the business has a clear direction in terms of the competitive strategy it wants to pursue.

THE RESPONSIVE ORGANIZATION: COMPETING ON CAPABILITIES AND CORE COMPETENCIES

THE STRATEGIC ROLE OF CORE COMPETENCIES

The ability to respond quickly to technological, product, and competitive changes is increasingly the hallmark of successful management. That is why strategy management experts C. K. Prahalad and Gary Hamel believe that in a world in which the boundaries between markets are increasingly blurred, and in which the life spans of products often end suddenly, a preoccupation with viewing the company as merely a portfolio of businesses can be deadly.[22] Instead, they argue persuasively that the roots of a firm's competitive advantage lie in its *core competencies.* They define these as "the collective learning in the organization, especially how to coordinate diverse production skills and integrate multiple streams of technologies."[23]

As illustrated in Figure 6.6, the corporation, like a tree, grows from its core competency roots. A firm's core competencies—say, Canon's three competencies in precision mechanics, fine optics, and microelectronics—nurture the development of core products—such as miniature electronic controls and fine lenses. In turn, core products like these are combined and engender businesses, such as Canon's camera business, computer business, and fax business. In turn, these businesses create end products such as electronic cameras, video still cameras, laser printers, and the laser fax.

Increasingly, successful companies are those that develop core competencies that can be applied *regardless of how demand for products shifts.* Indeed, such firms can often anticipate such changing tastes. For example, consider how Sony combines its core competencies. To create its tiny consumer electronic products, Sony's managers need

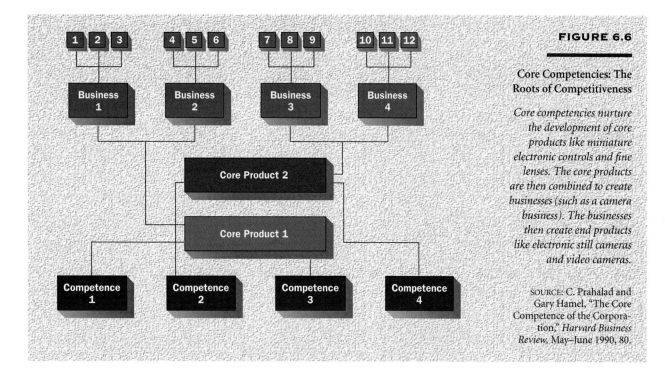

FIGURE 6.6

Core Competencies: The
Roots of Competitiveness

*Core competencies nurture
the development of core
products like miniature
electronic controls and fine
lenses. The core products
are then combined to create
businesses (such as a camera
business). The businesses
then create end products
like electronic still cameras
and video cameras.*

SOURCE: C. Prahalad and
Gary Hamel, "The Core
Competence of the Corpora-
tion," *Harvard Business
Review,* May–June 1990, 80.

to reach across departmental lines and "harmonize know-how in miniaturization, microprocessor design, material science, and ultra thin precision casing—the same skills it applies in its miniature card calculators, pocket TVs, and digital watches."[24] In other words, a major source of competitive advantage lies not just in differentiating a product, becoming the low-cost leader, or even becoming a focuser. Instead, the roots of competitive advantage run deeper, "in management's ability to consolidate corporate-wide technologies and production skills into competencies that empower individual businesses to adapt quickly to changing opportunities."[25] Figure 6.7 shows how Canon's three core competencies—precision mechanics, fine optics, and microelectronics—combine to create the current Canon product line.[26]

CORE COMPETENCIES AND BOUNDARYLESS ORGANIZATIONS As we'll see in Chapter 9 (Organizing for Responsiveness), building a competitive advantage around core competencies forces managers to think of their companies more as "boundaryless organizations." **Boundaryless organizations** "have identifiable [departmental] functions, levels, and outside limits. They simply do not let these distinctions get in the way of transferring knowledge, services, and goods in the most efficient way possible." Boundaryless, then, "refers to the permeability of the functional, hierarchical, customer, and supplier boundaries."[27] In other words, given the need to create core competencies (elements of which may lie in various departments and at various levels in the organization), managers have to take steps to improve the ability of the contributors of core competencies to interact with each other and communicate. Only in that way can a firm such as Canon react quickly to competitors' actions and apply its core competencies to developing and producing the needed new product or service.

STRATEGIC ALLIANCES

A **strategic alliance** is any close association of corporations to achieve common objectives.[28] As mentioned in Chapter 2, a joint venture is the most common form of such an alliance. A joint venture is a partnership between two separate entities. Its general

BOUNDARYLESS ORGANIZATIONS
These businesses have identifiable functions, levels, and outside limits but these are permeable and do not inhibit the exchange of knowledge, services, and goods in the most efficient way possible.

STRATEGIC ALLIANCE
Any close association of corporations to achieve common objectives.

FIGURE 6.7

Core Competencies of Canon

Canon's three core competencies combine to create Canon's product line.

SOURCE: C. Prahalad and Gary Hamel, "The Core Competence of the Corporation," *Harvard Business Review*, May–June 1990, 90.

	Precision Mechanics	Fine Optics	Micro-electronics
Basic camera	■	■	
Compact fashion camera	■	■	
Electronic camera	■	■	
EOS autofocus camera	■	■	■
Video still camera	■	■	■
Laser beam printer	■	■	■
Color video printer	■		■
Bubble jet printer	■		■
Basic fax	■		■
Laser fax	■		■
Calculator			■
Plain paper copier	■	■	■
Battery PPC	■	■	■
Color copier	■	■	■
Laser copier	■	■	■
Color laser copier	■	■	■
NAVI	■	■	■
Still video system	■	■	■
Laser imager	■	■	■
Cell analyzer	■	■	■
Mask aligners	■		■
Stepper aligners	■		■
Excimer laser aligners	■	■	■

purpose is to exploit the strengths or core competencies of the partners and/or to compensate for the weaknesses in one or more of them. For example, a small cash-poor Florida-based company with a patented industrial pollution control filter might form a European joint venture with a subsidiary of a major European oil firm. In this case the joint venture might be a separate corporation based in Europe to which each partner contributes funds and other resources. The oil firm gets access to a product that could revolutionize its distilling facilities; the filter company gets access to the oil firm's vast European marketing network.

THE VIRTUAL CORPORATION   For many firms, the ultimate strategic alliance is the **virtual corporation**, "a temporary network of independent companies—suppliers, customers, even erstwhile rivals—linked by information technology to share skills, costs, and access to one another's markets."[29] Virtual corporations don't have headquarters staffs or organization charts or the organizational trappings (like personnel

VIRTUAL CORPORATION
A temporary network of companies, each of which lends the virtual corporation/network its core competence and is committed to the corporation achieving its objectives.

departments) that we associate with traditional corporations. In fact, virtual corporations are not "corporations" at all, in the traditional sense of common ownership or a chain of command. Instead, virtual corporations are networks of companies, each of which lends the virtual corporation/network its core competence. Information technology-based communication networks (computer information systems, fax machines, electronic mail, and so on) then help the virtual corporations' often far-flung company/constituents stay in touch and quickly carry out their contributions.[30] When managed correctly, the individual contributors to a virtual corporation aren't merely impersonal suppliers or marketers, however. Instead, successful virtual corporation-relationships are built on trust and on a sense of "co-destiny," which means that "the fate of each partner is dependent on the other."[31]

Virtual corporations of some significance exist today. For example, AT&T called on Japan's Marubeni Trading Company to help it link up with Matsushita Electronic Industrial Company when it wanted to speed production of its Safari notebook computer (itself designed by Henry Dreyfuss Associates).[32] Unable to produce its entire line of PowerBook notebooks, Apple turned to Sony Corporation to manufacture one version, thus merging Sony's miniaturization manufacturing skills (core competencies) with Apple's easy-to-use software.[33] Communications company MCI is another virtual corporation proponent: a central part of MCI's strategy is to match its core competencies in network integration and software development with the strengths of other companies making telecommunications equipment.

Hewlett-Packard relies heavily on communication systems such as the in-house video teleconferencing facilities pictured here to meet the challenge of doing business on several continents. This horizontal communication lets employees worldwide reach mutual understanding about issues such as new product designs, research lab activites, engineering modifications, and strategic plans, and helps let Hewlett-Packard participate as a partner in virtual corporations.

Similarly, when start-up company TelePad came up with an idea for a hand-held, pen-based computer, a virtual corporation was their answer for breathing life into the idea: an industrial design firm in Palo Alto, California, designed the product, Intel brought in engineers to help with some engineering details, several firms helped develop software for the product, and a battery maker collaborated with TelePad to produce the power supply.[34]

The *Kingston Technology* vignette provides another example of how one virtual corporation works in practice.

IMPLEMENTING STRATEGY

STRATEGY IMPLEMENTATION
Converting the strategic plan into action and then into results.

Strategy implementation—"converting the strategic plan into action and then into results"[35]—can be a daunting task, drawing as it does on all the management functions: an organization structure is designed to specify the pattern of relationships through which employees will accomplish the activities required to achieve company

KINGSTON TECHNOLOGY

John Tu and David Sun, cofounders of Kingston Technology, do business on a handshake, seldom use contracts, and have never hired a lawyer. And they aren't running a curbside lemonade stand either.

Kingston, located in Fountain Valley, California, is a world leader in upgrading personal computers. Sales in 1992 were $240 million, up from $140 million the year before. Kingston is expected to double that in 1994. Tu and Sun took a look at how the huge, diversified companies of the United States were run and their reaction was, "no thank you." Instead they created a virtual corporation, a network of independent company partners working together in complementary roles. They share capital, know-how, and markets, avoid huge investment requirements of larger enterprises, and still enjoy economies of scale that smaller firms can't match.

Here's an example of how it works. Early one week, a Los Angeles ComputerLand store called Kingston. It had an order from a bank for 100 IBM PCs with extra memory and other upgrades. Within hours, Kingston had the upgrade system designed and passed the specs along to a principal partner, Express Manufacturing. Express filled the order and sent it back before the end of the day. Kingston checked everything out and shipped the order, via Federal Express, to ComputerLand the same day. The bank had its new system in place before the weekend. "You've heard of just-in-time inventory?" asks Sun. "This is just-in-time manufacturing."

Both Kingston and Express work with other companies, but they maintain a primary commitment to one another. "You always have to think of your partners. They are there when we need them, and we are there when they need us." And that's the essence of a virtual corporation.

SOURCE: Michael Meyer, "Here's a Virtual Model for America's Industrial Giants," *Newsweek,* August 23, 1993, 40.

goals; the organization must be staffed with employees who have the skills required to engage successfully in those activities; the organization's leaders must inspire and motivate the firm's employees toward attaining the organization's vision and goals; finally, various procedural and control systems must be implemented in order to track progress toward goals and take corrective action as required.

THE INTEGRATED NATURE OF STRATEGY IMPLEMENTATION

Successful managers know that implementing strategy calls for a coordinated effort, not just from employees but among the management functions as well. For example, McDonald's strategy of expanding overseas required organizing new departments for the overseas operations. Employees with knowledge and skills in the new markets had to be recruited and trained, and new reward systems were needed to inspire and motivate employees (for instance, to move overseas). Control systems had to be modified to facilitate monitoring of what were now far-flung facilities around the globe. At the same time, the company had to be sure that its unique culture—its shared values that emphasized quality, service, cleanliness, and price—remained the glue that bonded McDonald's employees wherever they were. In summary, implementing the organization's strategy entails successfully carrying out all of the five management functions.

SUMMARY

Strategic management is the process of identifying and pursuing an organization's mission by aligning the internal capabilities of the organization with the external demands of its environment.

During this process, decisions are made in the present day that will ultimately lead the firm toward the defined mission of tomorrow. Strategic management involves determining the firm's business or its mission, setting its strategic objectives, formulating a strategy for achieving the strategic objectives, implementing the strategy, and evaluating the performance and initiating corrective adjustments as required.

Strategic planning is an integral part of the overall strategic management process. It involves developing a vision and mission, translating the mission into strategic objectives, and crafting a strategy or course of action to move the organization from where it is to where it wants to be.

Strategies can exceed the bounds of a firm's existing resources. This leveraging of resources can be more important than simply fitting a strategic plan to a firm's current level of resources.

A company's corporate-level strategy identifies the range of businesses that make up the corporation and depicts how these businesses will interrelate. Corporate strategic alternatives include concentration, vertical integration, diversification, investment reduction, strategic alliances, and joint ventures.

Building and strengthening a particular business's long-term competitive position in the marketplace is called competitive strategy. Three of the basic strategic options at this level are cost leadership, differentiation, and focus.

Functional strategies identify the basic courses of action that each of the business's departments will pursue to help attain competitive goals.

How companies coordinate diverse skills and integrate core technologies—in essence, the sum total of learning within the organization—makes up the core competency of the company. The roots of a company's competitive advantage, especially in a world where boundaries between markets are increasingly uncertain, lie in these core competencies.

A strategic alliance is any close association of corporations to achieve common objectives. A joint venture is one example. Another example currently evolving is known as a virtual corporation, which is a temporary network of independent companies lending their particular core competencies to each other.

Strategy implementation can be defined as transforming a strategic plan into action and then into results. The effort calls for a coordinated effort on the part of both employees and management. Success depends on carrying out all five of the management functions.

QUESTIONS

■ FOR REVIEW

1. Name the five basic steps of the strategic management process.

2. Compare and contrast corporate, competitive, and functional strategies and list some of the options available at each level.

3. Describe the characteristics of boundaryless organizations, and explain how they relate to core competency.

■ FOR DISCUSSION

4. Is strategic management only necessary for large publicly held companies, or can small family owned businesses benefit from it as well? Discuss.

5. Can you think of any major corporations that have drastically changed their corporate strategies in recent years? What impact has that had on the competitive and functional strategies?

6. What are the advantages of virtual corporations? Do you believe they represent the wave of the future? Why or why not?

■ FOR ACTION

7. Formulate your own version of a mission statement for the company where you are employed or one with which you are familiar.

8. Make an appointment with your boss or a local executive and ask about his or her company's strategic management process. How does the company carry out the five basic steps outlined in this chapter?

9. Look through some recent business periodicals and find an example of companies that have formed a strategic alliance. How do they complement each other?

■ FOR FOCUS ON SMALL BUSINESS

10. What benefits does King's Medical derive from strategic planning?

11. Do you think all small businesses, no matter what their size, could benefit from a strategic management process? Why or why not?

12. What are some of the drawbacks that can result from a lack of planning?

CLOSING SOLUTION

KMART CORPORATION

After taking over in 1987, CEO Joseph Antonini recognized a primary reason Kmart was taking a whipping from Wal-Mart: the lack of a state-of-the-art control system. Emulating its chief competitor, Kmart installed computerized, point-of-sale cash registers at 20,000 checkout counters. The $1 billion project directly linked the Troy, Michigan corporate headquarters to every store. As a result, checkout times were cut by 25 percent, inventory costs were reduced, and Kmart was able to buy more products centrally, obtaining volume discounts and relieving store managers of the chore. Antonini predicted inventory reductions would save the firm at least $100 million in carrying costs.

Antonini also embarked on a $2.5 billion plan to expand, renovate, relocate, or shut down nearly all of Kmart's 2,300 U.S. stores. "If we don't spend the $2.5 billion by 1995, our stores will be 19 years old, tired, and dated," he said.

Through 1993, results of Antonini's efforts were somewhat disappointing. He also disappointed analysts by scaling back the pace of renovating and enlarging stores. Even though the renewal program was only 50 percent complete, it was curtailed to make way for Super Kmarts—combination discount stores and supermarkets. Antonini may have been reacting to Wal-Mart, which had 30 such superstores. Or, he may have been enamored with the results he had already seen. A Super Kmart prototype in Medina, Ohio, now grosses more than $60 million annually; the store it replaced had yearly sales of $12 million.[36]

■ **QUESTIONS FOR CLOSING SOLUTION**

1. Describe Kmart's strategic objectives. How could the company improve implementation of its strategy?

2. If you were in Antonini's shoes, what competitive strategy would you pursue?

3. What is Kmart's core competency? Do you believe it has lost sight of it? Why or why not?

KEY TERMS

Strategic Management

Vision

Mission Statement

Strategy

Strategic Control

Strategic Planning

Corporate-level Strategy

Competitive Strategy

Functional Strategy

Market Penetration

Geographic Expansion

Product Development

Horizontal Integration

Vertical Integration

Diversification

Related Diversification

Conglomerate Diversification

Stability or
   Status Quo Strategy

Investment Reduction or Defensive
   Strategies

Retrenchment

Divestment

Competitive Strategy

Cost Leadership

Differentiation Strategy

Focus Strategy

Boundaryless Organization

Strategic Alliance

Virtual Corporation

Strategy Implementation

The history of Continental Can Company has been a bit like *The Wizard of Oz,* in which Dorothy went all the way to Oz, only to discover what she was looking for was in her own backyard. Continental was the largest can producer in the United States following World War II. But by 1980, its market share had shrunk to 17 percent. That's when then-chairman S. Bruce Smart, Jr., decided to use the can company as a cash source for acquisitions. The company quickly added energy, forest products, and insurance to its packaging operations. The ensuing battles over strategic direction forced President Donald J. Bainton into early retirement in 1983. "I felt we should have concentrated on the packaging business," he says. "It was the largest—and the best—packaging company in the world."

Before long, Bainton got the chance to prove his point. In 1984, Continental was acquired by Peter Kiewit Sons, Inc., which began selling off most of the company's divisions piece by piece. Although Bainton had gone on to Viatech, Inc. (an international packaging company that he built into a $500 million business), he still had an eye on his old company. In 1992, he was given the opportunity to buy the rights to the Continental Can Company name and corporate logo. Symbolically, the name was important to Bainton, especially considering Viatech purchased Continental's 15-plant plastic container division. But he also had a firm vision of where he would take the company he had served for 29 years. "From the moment Kiewit bought Continental, it was in the back of my mind that when they got to the point of chopping it up and selling off the parts, I wanted at least a part of Continental . . . I wanted to resurrect Continental and literally make it into the company it once was," he says.

Bainton went into the acquisition mode himself. But, unlike the diversifications of the past, he was seeking businesses that fell into Continental's areas of core competency. In the future, for instance, Continental would leave timber and oil to lumberjacks and wildcatters. The company would do what it did best: profitably manufacture metal, flexible-plastic, and rigid-plastic containers.

Management philosophies were also similar to the past, with emphasis on lean structure, a family-like corporate environment, and strict cost control. Bainton got lots of good advice by enlisting ex-employees of Continental as consultants. Also, full-time executives set a new standard for cross-utilization. For example,

executive vice-president Abdo Yazgi served as company counsel, top administrative officer, chief financial officer, and head of human resources. With that kind of structure, Bainton had no trouble running his $500 million operation with a staff of five.

The chairman and CEO also provided managers with incentives and expected them to produce. They knew if they didn't, they would be replaced. A newspaper paraphrased Bainton's motivational approach as "produce—or vamoose." He met monthly with his employees to get strategy, goals, and objectives, and to sign off on budgets. "The rest of the time," he says, "these guys run their businesses by themselves."

Bainton, leery of getting over-staffed, kept a close eye on personnel levels. But surprisingly, he didn't necessarily intervene when his managers proposed additions that he didn't like. He says he didn't mind being disagreed with, and went along nine times out of ten. "But," he adds, "they better get results."

Returning Continental to its former glory won't be easy. Bainton acknowledges the acquisition pickings so far have been pretty slim. "So far, we've looked at more than 1,000 businesses," he says, "and we've bought only four." But he isn't likely to deviate from his strategy either. If the company returns to its $4 billion a year in revenues, it will be strictly in the packaging areas it knows best. After all, Bainton was the one who never wanted to leave his own backyard in the first place.

SOURCES: John H. Sheridan, "On the Resurrection Trail," *Industry Week,* November 16, 1992, 21–24; John R. Dorfman, "Uncanny," *Forbes,* December 20, 1982, 56–58; and Allan Dodds Frank, "More Takeover Carnage?" *Forbes,* August 12, 1985, 40–41.

■ **QUESTIONS**

1. Compare corporate strategies of the failed Continental Can with the new company under Bainton's direction. What are the pros and cons of each?
2. Describe how Bainton has carried out the various tasks in the strategic management process since taking over his old company.
3. Do you think Bainton is taking the right approach in rebuilding the company? What might you do differently?

A CASE IN DIVERSITY

STRATEGIC MANAGEMENT AT AMIGOS CANNING COMPANY

During his more than 40 years in the Mexican food business, Amigos Canning Company CEO Ralph Velasco, Jr., has had to change strategic direction more than once. Soon after joining the San Antonio-based food producer in 1950 he helped engineer the switch from tortilla manufacturing to canning. Lots of diversification followed, and by the mid-1980s the company founded by Velasco's father was producing a number of private label canned food lines for major companies. But in 1989, Amigos lost nearly $500,000, and Velasco began experiencing deja vu all over again. He would have to redirect the company once more, and this time the entire business was at stake.

Before making a move, Velasco consulted with management and marketing experts. Smaller companies like Amigos are attracted to producing under the private labels of the food giants they contract with because no money is required for a sales force. The downside is hard price bargaining and an uncertain future. Big regional food distributors are frequently merged or bought, and past business relationships aren't always continued by new owners or managers. Together with the consultants, Velasco decided to market Amigo products under his own label.

Besides exhibiting an underdog's courage level that is seldom seen, Velasco made two other shrewd moves. He hired a seasoned national sales manager and gave him a substantial stake in the company. He also spent a considerable sum on an aluminized label that differentiated his primary product, bean dip.

Velasco recognized that dips had long been blithely regarded as merely a complimentary item by big chip makers like Frito-Lay and Borden's. Through consumer taste tests and careful quality control he ensured that Amigos produced only the best. Velasco always considered himself a numbers man, so he took the process a step farther. Because he didn't know who actually was buying Amigos products, he invested in finding out exactly which consumers were buying what products. The data helped him fine-tune the company's marketing strategy more effectively.

Perhaps not surprisingly, Velasco's next move is another new strategy direction. It will be a lot like the others, only better. After more market research to define his targets, he plans to launch more new product lines.

SOURCE: Rick Mendosa, "Amigos Canning Company," *Hispanic Business.*

■ QUESTIONS

1. Using the five-step process outlined in the chapter, describe the strategic management approach Velasco took in 1989.
2. How did Amigos' corporate-level strategy change over the years?
3. What kind of competitive strategy did the company pursue by switching to Amigos-brand products?
4. In what ways did Velasco take advantage of the United States' increased diversity in formulating his new strategy?

ENDNOTES

1. This discussion is based on George Stalk, Philip Evans, and Lawrence Shulman, "Competing on Capabilities: The New Rules of Corporate Strategy," *Harvard Business Review,* March–April 1992, 57–58.
2. Stalk et al., "The New Rules," 58.
3. Sam Walton, *Made in America* (New York: Doubleday, 1992), 90.
4. See Stalk, "The New Rules," 58.
5. Peter Drucker, *Management: Tasks, Responsibilities, Practices* (New York: Harper & Row, 1974), 611.
6. See, for example, Allan J. Rowe et al., *Strategic Management* (Reading: Addison-Wesley Publishing Co., 1989), 2; and James Higgins and Julian Vincze, *Strategic Management* (Fort Worth: The Dryden Press, 1993), 5.
7. Arthur Thompson and A. J. Strickland, *Strategic Management* (Homewood, IL: Irwin, 1992), 4.
8. Higgins and Vincze, *Strategic Management,* 5.
9. Warren Bennis and Bert Manus, *Leaders: The Strategies for Taking Charge* (New York: Harper & Row, 1985); quoted in Andrew Campbell and Sally Yeung, "Mission, Vision and Strategic Intent," *Long-Range Planning,* vol. 24, no. 4, 145.
10. Thompson and Strickland, 4.
11. Ibid., 8.
12. Gary Hamel and C. K. Prahalad, "Strategy As Stretch and Leverage," *Harvard Business Review,* March–April 1993, 75–84.
13. Ibid., 77.
14. Ibid., 78.
15. Thompson and Strickland, 38.

16. This is based on Higgins and Vincze, *Strategic Management,* 200–204.

17. Rowe, et al., *Strategic Management,* 246–47.

18. Thompson and Strickland, 169.

19. Rowe, et al., *Strategic Management,* 246.

20. Unless otherwise noted, the following is based on Michael E. Porter, *Competitive Strategy* (New York: The Free Press, 1980); and Michael E. Porter, *Competitive Advantage* (New York: The Free Press, 1985).

21. Porter, *Competitive Advantage,* 14.

22. C. K. Prahalad and Gary Hamel, "The Core Competence of a Corporation," *Harvard Business Review,* May–June 1990, 80.

23. Ibid., 82.

24. Ibid.

25. Ibid., 81.

26. A similar point is made by George Stalk, Philip Evans, and Lawrence Shulman, "Competing on Capabilities: The New Rules of Corporate Strategy," *Harvard Business Review,* March–April 1992, 57–69.

27. Mary Anne Devanna and Noel Tichy, "Creating the Competitive Organization of the 21st Century: The Boundaryless Corporation," *Human Resource Management,* Winter 1990, vol. 29, no. 4, 465.

28. Higgins and Vincze, *Strategic Management,* 304.

29. John Byrne, Richard Brandt, and Otis Port, "The Virtual Corporation," *Business Week,* February 8, 1993, 99.

30. See also J. Carlos Jarillo, "On Strategic Networks," *Strategic Management Journal,* vol. 9, (1988), 31–41; and William Davidow and Michael Malone, "The Virtual Corporation," *California Business Review,* November 1992, 34–42.

31. Byrne et al., "The Virtual Corporation," 99.

32. Ibid., 100.

33. Ibid.

34. Virtual corporations should not be confused with the Japanese Keiretsus strategy. Keiretsus are tightly knit groups of firms governed by a supra board of directors concerned with establishing the long-term survivability of the Keiretsus organization. Interlocking boards of directors and shared ownership help distinguish Keiretsus from other forms of strategic alliances, including virtual corporations. See, for example, Byrne et al., "The Virtual Corporation," 101; Thompson and Strickland, 216; and Kenichi Ohmae, "The Global Logic of Strategic Alliances," *Harvard Business Review,* March–April 1989, 143–54.

35. Higgins and Vincze, *Strategic Management,* 306.

36. David Woodruff, et al., "Attention Kmart Shop . . . Hey, Where Is Everybody?" *Business Week,* January 18, 1993, pg. 38; Laura Zinn, et al., "Attention Shoppers: K-Mart is Fighting Back," *Business Week,* October 7, 1991, 118–20; Chakravarty N. Subrata, "A Tale of Two Companies," *Forbes,* May 27, 1991, 86–96.

A P P E N D I X   F O R   C H A P T E R   6

S T R A T E G I C   S I T U A T I O N   A N A L Y S I S   T O O L S

STRATEGIC SITUATION ANALYSIS TOOLS

THE ROLE OF SITUATION ANALYSIS

Situation analysis plays a central role in strategic planning. A strategic plan's purpose is to balance the internal strengths and weaknesses of a company with its external opportunities and threats. As Thompson and Strickland point out, the purpose of **situation analysis** is to assess the internal and external features of a company that will most directly affect its strategic options and opportunities.[1] Strategy management experts have devised many situation analysis aids. In this appendix we will review some of the most important ones.

PORTFOLIO ANALYSIS TOOLS FOR CORPORATE STRATEGY

Corporate level strategic planning largely involves deciding the mix or *portfolio* of businesses the company will manage. A company might concentrate on one business only; other options are to diversify into related or unrelated products, or perhaps to engage in integrative growth by purchasing suppliers or opening retail outlets.

While most firms want to grow, their ability to grow is obviously limited by the available resources. Particularly in multibusiness companies, reviews are thus periodically made to ascertain the attractiveness of the firm's various business lines to determine whether resources should be shifted from one business to another. This is how Greyhound Corporation moved from a transportation to a consumer products firm; it now derives most of its profits from products like Dial Soap. Three widely used **portfolio management analysis** aids are the growth/share or Boston Consulting Group Matrix, the General Electric Business Screen, and the product/market industry evolution portfolio matrix.

BCG MATRIX The **BCG Matrix,** developed by the Boston Consulting Group (BCG) helps to identify the relative attractiveness of a firm's businesses. As in Figure 6A.1 it compares *business growth rate* and *relative competitive position* (market share) for *each* of the company's businesses. As shown in the figure, each business is represented by a circle, the size of which is proportional to the size of the businesses.

Once all businesses are plotted on the matrix, a decision can be made as to whether the businesses are "stars," "question marks," "cash cows," or "dogs," to use the technique's usual terminology. **Stars** are businesses in high-growth industries in which the company has a high relative market share. For example, Intel's microprocessor business (the heart of computers such as IBM's 486-driven PCs) have a high growth rate and Intel has a relatively high market share. Star businesses usually require large infusions of cash to sustain growth. However, they generally have such a strong market position that much of the needed cash can be generated from sales and profits.

Question marks are businesses in high-growth industries, but with low relative market shares. Such business units (such as the computer business started by Exxon Oil several years ago) have a dilemma: they are in attractive high-growth industries, but have such low market shares that they do not have the clout to fend off larger

---

SITUATION ANALYSIS
An analysis of the features in a company's internal/external environment that will most directly affect its strategic options and opportunities.

PORTFOLIO MANAGEMENT ANALYSIS
An analytical review or aid that determines, particularly in a multibusiness company, the attractiveness of the firm's various business lines to ascertain whether resources should be shifted from one business to another.

BCG MATRIX
A widely used portfolio management analysis aid devised by the Boston Consulting Group that helps to identify the relative attractiveness of a firm's businesses.

STARS
Businesses in high-growth industries in which the company has a high relative market share.

QUESTION MARKS
Businesses in high-growth industries, but with low relative market shares.

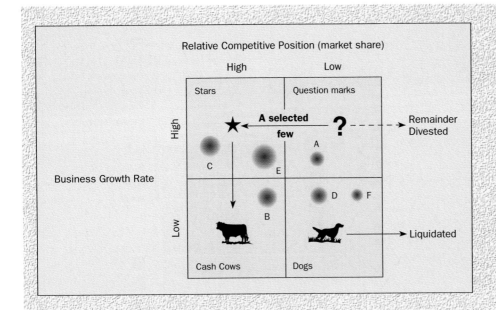

FIGURE 6A.1

BCG Matrix

Once the position of each of the company's businesses is plotted, a decision can be made regarding which businesses will be cash sources, and which cash users.

SOURCE: James Higgins and Julien Vincze, *Strategic Management: Text & Cases* (Fort Worth: The Dryden Press, 1993).

competitors. The company must either divert cash from its other businesses to boost the question mark business's market share, or get out of the business.

Cash Cows are businesses in low-growth industries, but have high relative market shares. Being in a low-growth, unattractive industry argues against making large cash infusions into businesses like these. On the other hand, its high market share generally permits it to continue generating high sales and profits for years. Cash cows can thus be good cash generators for the company's question mark businesses.

Finally, **dogs** are businesses that are in low-growth, unattractive industries and in which the firm has a low relative market share. Having a low market share puts the business in jeopardy relative to its larger competitors. As a result, dogs can quickly become "cash traps," needlessly absorbing cash to support a relatively hopeless and unattractive situation. They are usually sold to raise cash for stars and question marks.

THE GE BUSINESS SCREEN   The **GE Business Screen,** shown in Figure 6A.2, is a nine-cell matrix originally used by GE to analyze its own diversified portfolio. Each company is plotted into the appropriate cell according to its (1) industry attractiveness and (2) business unit position. Industry attractiveness (as illustrated) reflects criteria such as industry size, market growth, and industry profitability. Business unit position reflects criteria such as relative size, market share, and profitability.

Like the BCG matrix, the GE Business Screen focuses on whether the company will boost or reduce its investment in each business. For this reason, it is also called the GE Stop Light Strategy. As in Figure 6A.2, businesses that fall in attractive industries *and which are relatively strong competitors* justify further investment, and the pursuit of the growth strategies discussed in this chapter (market development, product development, diversification, and integration). Businesses in the purple cells in the lower right of the matrix no longer deserve investment: they either become cash cows or are divested. Those falling in the three blue (diagonal) cells need to be monitored for any changes (in industry attractiveness or business strengths) that might signal the need for increased or decreased investment.

CASH COWS
Businesses in low-growth industries, but having high relative market shares.

DOGS
Businesses that are in low-growth unattractive industries and in which the firm has a low relative market share.

GE BUSINESS SCREEN
A nine-cell matrix originally used by GE to analyze its own diversified portfolio and which plots industry attractiveness and competitive position.

FIGURE 6A.2

Company Position/Industry Attractiveness (GE) Screen

SOURCE: Michael Porter, *Competitive Strategy, Techniques for Analyzing Industries & Competitors* (New York: The Free Press, 1980), 365.

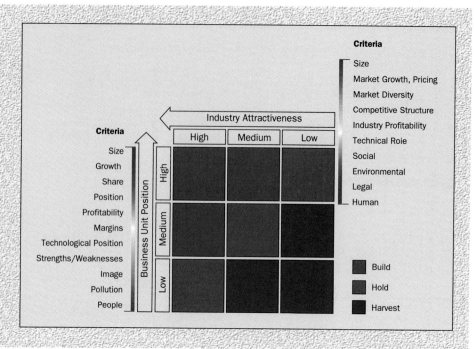

LIFE-CYCLE PORTFOLIO MATRIX
This matrix plots the business unit's competitive position against its industry's life-cycle stage.

DEVELOPMENT STAGE
According to the life-cycle theory, products move first through this stage, during which sales are virtually nil.

RAPID GROWTH STAGE
According to the life-cycle theory, products leave the development stage and enter this stage of introduction as a new and popular product.

MATURITY STAGE
During a product's life-cycle it may reach this stage, during which it experiences a long period of flat or modest sales growth.

DECLINE
That phase in the product's lifecycle when customers' interest in the product diminishes and market saturation occurs.

THE LIFE-CYCLE PORTFOLIO MATRIX As in Figure 6A.3, the **life-cycle portfolio matrix** plots the business unit's competitive position against its industry's life-cycle stage. Basically, life-cycle theory holds that products (such as personal computers) move first through a **development stage,** during which sales are virtually nil. They then move into a **rapid growth stage** upon introduction of the new, popular product. Toward the end of the growth stage is a shakeout period for suppliers, since the industry has attracted many new competitors and since most potential customers already have the product. There then may be a long period of flat or modest sales growth, during the product's **maturity stage.** Finally, there is market saturation, and **decline** as, for various reasons, customers' interest in the product diminishes. In this matrix, the size of the circles usually shows the total size of the industry in which the business is competing; the size of the wedge shows the business's market share.

Life-cycle analysis provides an additional perspective on the strategies to pursue with each of the company's businesses. Thus, in Figure 6A.3, business A is identified as a developing winner, one toward which additional cash investment should be directed. Business F represents a cash cow and potential source of cash for the developing winner. Business C represents a question mark business (although its position late in the growth stage and its weak competitive position could also possibly identify a potential loser to be harvested or divested). Similarly, business G would be a dog to be sold. The *Tandy* vignette (on page 172) illustrates how one firm applied situational analysis.

COMPETITIVE ANALYSIS: THE FIVE FORCES MODEL

Portfolio analysis helps management identify the individual businesses that will form its *portfolio.* A competitive strategy is then formulated for each of those businesses. Competitive strategy has been defined as "that part of a business's strategy dealing with the company's competitive approaches for achieving market success, its offensive

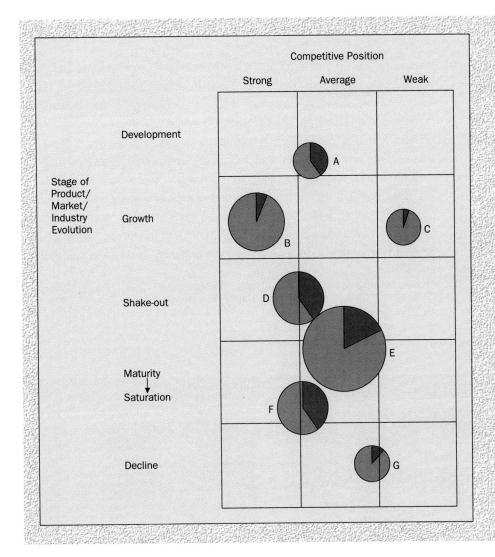

FIGURE 6A.3

**Product/Market/Industry/
Evolution Portfolio Matrix**

SOURCE: James Higgins and
Julian Vincze, *Strategic Management: Text and Cases* (Fort
Worth: The Dryden Press,
1993).

moves to secure a competitive edge over rival firms, and its defensive moves to protect its competitive position."[2]

Recall that businesses can pursue three main competitive strategies: differentiation,
low-cost leader, and focus. Strategy expert Michael Porter argues that the optimal competitive strategy depends on the intensity of competition in an industry. Competitive
intensity in turn depends on five competitive forces, which are shown in Figure 6A.4
(on page 173). The central task in competitive strategy analysis is to analyze the competing forces. The major planning aid for doing so is the Porter Five-Forces Model
shown in Figure 6A.4.[3] Let us look at each of the five forces.

THREAT OF ENTRY Intensity of industry competition depends first on the threat
of new entrants to an industry. The competitive landscape for NBC, CBS, and ABC
changed when Fox introduced its fourth network, for instance. In turn, says Porter,
the threat that there will be new entrants depends on the existing barriers to entry.

There are six major barriers to entry. (1) *Economies of scale* deter entry by forcing
entrants to come in with large-scale investments. The economies of scale barrier may

TANDY CORPORATION

In January 1993, Tandy CEO John Roach announced that Tandy would sell its computer manufacturing operations to AST Research, Inc., of southern California. "Clearly, the best investment, the best opportunity for the company is to focus in the retail area," Roach said at the time.

Tandy came to prominence through its thousands of retail Radio Shack stores. It has now expanded on this original theme with its new Incredible Universe stores. Roach was taking the company portfolio back to its roots. The hope was that the combination of a theme-park atmosphere and very competitive prices would prove to be a "developing winner" and would have customers flocking to the 160,000-square-foot Universe Stores. Tandy would be returning to what it does best and most profitably: retail store operations.

SOURCES: Annetta Miller and Seema Nayar, "Shufflin' at the Shack," *Newsweek,* June 7, 1993, 44; and Tom Steinert-Threlkeld, "Tandy Bids Goodbye to Computers," *Dallas Morning News,* May 27, 1993.

Tandy Corporation's Incredible Universe stores offer shoppers an overwhelming array of consumer electronics goods in a theme-park atmosphere. The 160,000 foot stores are roughly the size of 70 Radio Shacks combined.

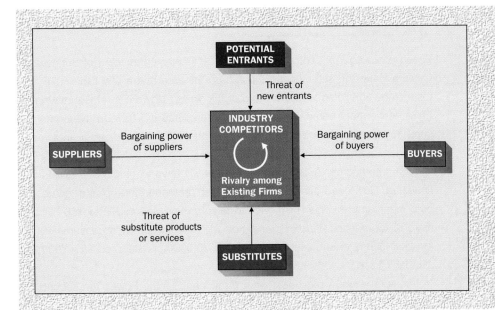

FIGURE 6A.4

Forces Driving Industry Competition

SOURCE: Michael Porter, *Competitive Strategy: Techniques for Analyzing Industries and Competitors* (New York: The Free Press, 1980), 4.

discourage potential candidates from entering the automobile manufacturing business, for instance. *Product differentiation* represents established brand identification and loyalties that stem from the existing competitors' product differences, customer services, or past advertising. (2) The need for *large capital requirements* is another potential barrier. (3) *Switching costs* present a barrier to entry when buyers face substantial one-time costs in switching from current to new suppliers—such as switching from IBM to Apple systems. (4) Access to *distribution channels* can be another barrier, as when the manufacturer of a new food product must persuade the supermarket to give it shelf space. (5) Existing competitors may also have *cost advantages* independent of their size, and such cost advantages can also provide barriers to new entrants. These cost advantages can stem from several origins, such as patents, favorable access to raw materials, favorable locations, and the so-called learning or experience curve. (The latter means that current competitors may simply be better at what they are doing than new entrants would be because they have been doing it for several years.) (6) New entrants will also gauge their plans on the *retaliation* they expect from current competitors. Thus, a history of vigorous retaliation to entrants may deter all but the most courageous to enter the market. The *Intersource* vignette illustrates a new entrant.

INTENSITY OF RIVALRY AMONG EXISTING COMPETITORS Rivalry among existing competitors manifests itself in tactics like price competition, advertising battles, and increased customer service.[4] Furthermore, the rivalry in some industries is more intense and warlike than it is in others. For example, for many years the rivalry among law firms and CPA firms could be characterized as gentlemanly. More recently, it has turned quite cutthroat.

Several aspects of the situation combine to determine just how warlike the competition will be. *Slow industry growth* makes competition more intense, since each firm can gain market share only at the others' expense. *High fixed costs* create strong pressure to cover those costs, which in turn can foster price cutting. Many products (such as the elastic used in apparel) are basically *undifferentiated commodities,* and in such instances pressures for intense price and service competition result. *High strategic*

INTERSOURCE TECHNOLOGIES

Seven years ago, executives at Intersource Technologies, Inc., of Sunnyvale, California, tried to sell General Electric on the idea that a $20 radiowave technology light bulb was the wave of the future. Now GE's refusal may create a new-entrant competitor. However, Intersource will have to overcome some formidable entry barriers before taking on the $60 billion GE in a market it dominates.

First, Intersource CEO Stanley W. Hulett will have to obtain $20 million in financing. He'll need this to underwrite manufacturing start-up and locate a bulb manufacturer. Then he'll have to raise around $40 million to $50 million more for operations. Finally Intersource will have to convince consumers that it makes sense to substitute Intersource's 20,000-hour bulb for GE's 750-hour standard issue.

Intersource got a big boost when American Electric Power, the second largest electric utility in the United States, took a 10 percent stake in the company. The utility is offering technical assistance, and its $6.5 million infusion made it possible for Intersource to complete engineering and design. Making believers out of consumers may prove more difficult. The so-called E-lamps emit less heat and use less energy. Still, many wonder how consumers will take to a $20 light bulb that may save them only a few cents on their monthly utility bill. Without some sort of push from government or other utility companies, Intersource could slowly fade to black.

SOURCE: "The $20 Light Bulb," *Industry Week*, February 15, 1993, 22.

stakes—as when Toyota decided to introduce its Lexus cars in the United States—can drive a competitor to establish its position by dropping prices below what they might otherwise be. When competitors can't "escape"—when there are *high exit barriers* (perhaps due to big investments in highly specialized plants)—rivalry is intensified as well.

PRESSURE FROM SUBSTITUTE PRODUCTS   The attractiveness of an industry and the intensity of its competition also depends upon the availability of substitute products. For example, frozen yogurt is a substitute for ice cream, and rayon is a substitute for cotton. As in these examples, substitute products perform the same or similar function as comparable products in the industry. To the extent that few substitutes are available (as would be the case with certain patented heart medicines), rivalry is reduced and the industry is more attractive to current competitors.

BARGAINING POWER OF BUYERS   The buyers' power is another consideration. For example, a buyer group is powerful if it purchases large volumes relative to the seller's sales: Toyota tends to have a lot of clout with its suppliers, for instance. Similarly, when the products purchased are standard or undifferentiated (such as apparel elastic), and when buyers face few switching costs or earn low profits, then buyers' bargaining power (over suppliers) tends to be enhanced. The buyers' bargaining position is also enhanced if there is a real threat that buyers might integrate backward (and do their own supplying). The apparel industry presents a recent, and classic, example here. As big department stores consolidated in the early 1990s, they tended to centralize their buying and control. The apparel industry suffered as a result as buyers' power increased and apparel profit margins were squeezed.

BARGAINING POWER OF SUPPLIERS Finally, *suppliers* can influence an industry's competitive intensity and attractiveness, for instance, by threatening to raise prices or reduce quality. Several factors contribute to a supplier group's bargaining power. Suppliers tend to have greater bargaining power when they are dominated by a few firms and are more concentrated. Similarly, when few substitute products are available, when the buying industry is not an important customer of the supplier group, and when the supplier's product is an important input to the buyer's business, then the supplier's power rises. Similarly, when the supplier's products are differentiated or have built-in switching costs, or when the supplier group poses a credible threat of forward integration, the supplier will have greater bargaining power.

APPLYING THE FIVE-FORCES MODEL Analyzing an industry with the five-forces model helps a company identify competitive strategic options. For example, where rivalry among existing competitors is intense or there is a real threat of new entrants, a competitive strategy of boosting product differentiation is a sensible option. Boosting switching costs (as American Airlines did when it convinced thousands of travel agents to use its SABER computerized reservation system) can also reduce rivals' (or new entrants') ability to compete, even when the product or service itself is fairly undifferentiated by boosting buyers' switching costs.

COMPANY INTERNAL SITUATION ANALYSIS TOOLS

A strategy balances two sets of forces, *external* and *internal*. Portfolio analysis aids and the five forces model are primarily planning aids for external analyses of factors such as industry growth rates. Now we turn to *internal* analysis of the firm's strengths and weaknesses, and particularly to the company capability profile.

COMPANY CAPABILITY PROFILE The **company capability profile** is a graphical means of assessing a company's managerial, competitive, financial, and technical strengths and weaknesses.[5] As you can see in Figure 6A.5, the capability profile itself lists managerial, competitive, financial, and technical factors that individually represent strengths or weaknesses for any firm. As in the figure, a manager assesses each of the factors and awards it a rating for his or her firm, either above or below neutral. Thus, for the company illustrated in Figure 6A.5, "corporate image/social responsibility" is modestly strong; "use of strategic plans and strategic analysis" and "environmental assessment and forecasting" are weak. Similarly, "product strength" and "customer loyalty" are very strong competitive strengths.

A completed capability profile can help to identify strengths on which the firm can build its strategies, and weaknesses that must be addressed. Remember, though, that the existence of particular weaknesses does not necessarily preclude a strategy that might otherwise be advisable. It may just mean that a gap exists. This must be rectified by eliminating the weakness. One reason why Apple Computer Company has taken steps in the past few years to improve the compatibility between its computers and IBM's is because many commercial buyers found that incompatibility to be a major weakness.

COMPANY CAPABILITY PROFILE
A graphic means of assessing a company's managerial, competitive, financial, and technical strengths and weaknesses.

FIGURE 6A.5

Company Capability Profile

Managers use the capability profile to graphically depict their firm's strengths and weaknesses on these generic attributes.

SOURCE: Alan Rowe et al., *Strategic Management: A Methodological Approach*, 3rd ed. (Reading, MA: Addison-Wesley, 1989).

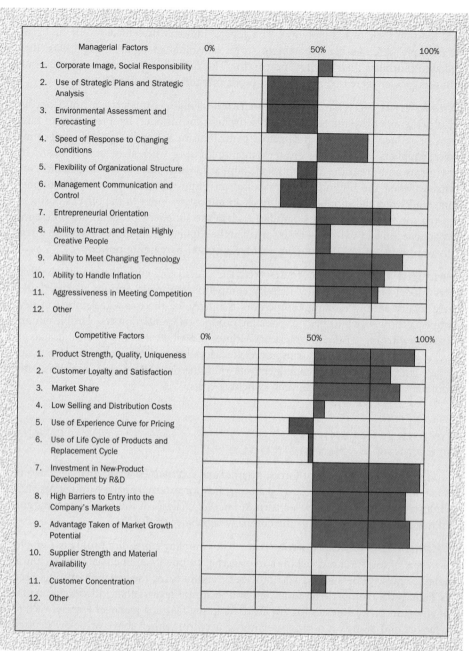

ORGANIZING THE INFORMATION: SWOT ANALYSIS

SWOT

An acronym for the strengths, weaknesses, opportunities, and threats matrix.

SWOT analysis is then used to consolidate the information produced by the external analysis of opportunities and threats, and the internal analysis of strengths and weaknesses. **SWOT** stands for strengths, weaknesses, opportunities, and threats. As illustrated in Figure 6A.6, potential strengths typically include adequate financial resources, economies of scale, and proprietary technology. Potential internal weaknesses include lack of strategic direction, obsolete facilities, and lack of managerial depth and talent. Formulating the strategic plan is then largely a process of balancing these strengths

FIGURE 6A.5

Continued

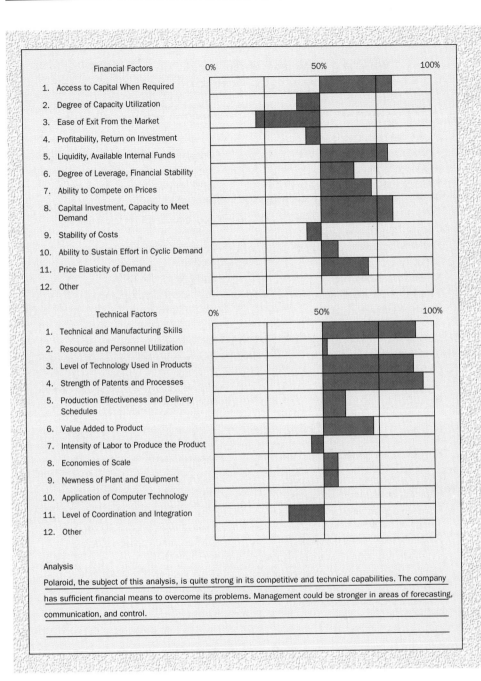

Analysis

Polaroid, the subject of this analysis, is quite strong in its competitive and technical capabilities. The company has sufficient financial means to overcome its problems. Management could be stronger in areas of forecasting, communication, and control.

and weaknesses with the potential external opportunities and threats. Opportunities that your previous analysis might identify include the possibility of serving additional customer groups (market penetration), the chances for entering new markets or segments (market development), or falling trade barriers in attractive foreign markets (a situation that European community–based companies currently face). External threats might include the likely entry of new, lower-cost foreign competitors, rising sales of substitute products, and slowing market growth. The manager considers all such facts, and then develops a corporate, and then a competitive strategy based on his or her analysis.

FIGURE 6A.6

SWOT Analysis

SOURCE: Arthur A. Thompson and A. J. Strickland, *Strategic Management*, 6th ed. (Homewood, IL: Irwin, 1992).

WHAT TO LOOK FOR WHEN SIZING UP A COMPANY'S STRENGTHS, WEAKNESSES, OPPORTUNITIES, AND THREATS

POTENTIAL INTERNAL STRENGTHS

- Core competencies in key areas
- Adequate financial resources
- Well thought of by buyers
- An acknowledged market leader
- Well-conceived functional area strategies
- Access to economies of scale
- Insulated (at least somewhat) from strong competitive pressures
- Proprietary technology
- Cost advantages
- Better advertising campaigns
- Product innovation skills
- Proven management
- Better manufacturing capability
- Ahead on experience curve
- Superior technological skills
- Other?

POTENTIAL INTERNAL WEAKNESSES

- No clear strategic direction
- Obsolete facilities
- Subpar profitability because . . .
- Lack of managerial depth and talent
- Missing some key skills or competencies
- Poor track record in implementing strategy
- Plagued with internal operating problems
- Falling behind in R&D
- Too narrow a product line
- Weak market image
- Weak distribution network
- Below-average marketing skills
- Unable to finance needed changes in stratregy
- Higher overall unit costs relative to key competitors
- Other?

POTENTIAL EXTERNAL OPPORTUNITIES

- Serve additional customer groups
- Enter new markets or segments
- Expand product line to meet broader range of customer needs
- Diversify into related products
- Vertical integration (forward or backward)
- Falling trade barriers in attractive foreign markets
- Complacency among rival firms
- Faster market growth
- Other?

POTENTIAL EXTERNAL THREATS

- Entry of lower-cost foreign competitors
- Rising sales of substitute products
- Slower market growth
- Adverse shifts in foreign exchange rates and trade policies of foreign governments
- Costly regulatory requirements
- Vulnerability to recession and business cycle
- Growing bargaining power of customers or suppliers
- Changing buyer needs and tastes
- Adverse demographic changes
- Other?

Situation analysis plays a central role in strategic planning. Its purpose is to assess internal or external factors that most directly affect a company's options and opportunities. Portfolio analysis is an important situation analysis aid. It involves assessing a company's mix of businesses, using such methods as the Boston Consulting Group Matrix, the GE Business Screen, and the product/market industry evolution portfolio matrix.

A competitive analysis must then be done for each of the businesses in the portfolio. Under the five-forces model, the optimal competitive strategy is determined based on the attractiveness and intensity of competition in the industry. That involves assessing the threat of entry by new competition, the intensity of rivalry among existing competitors, pressure from substitute products, the bargaining power of buyers, and the bargaining power of suppliers.

Formulating a strategy also requires analysis of the company's internal strengths and weaknesses. Using a company capability profile, a business can assess its managerial, competitive, financial, and technical strengths and weaknesses. The SWOT analysis then synthesizes all this information.

■ **FOR REVIEW**

1. What is the purpose of strategic situation analysis? Which variables must be considered when conducting such an analysis for a company?

2. Outline the components of the five-forces model.

■ **FOR ACTION**

3. Conduct a SWOT analysis of your employment prospects in the field of your choice upon graduation. Use market research gathered at the library to back up your analysis. Based on the results, would you still seek a job in that field?

Situation Analysis

Portfolio Management Analysis

BCG Matrix

Stars

Question Marks

Cash Cows

Dogs

GE Business Screen

Life-cycle Portfolio Matrix

Development Stage

Rapid Growth Stage

Maturity Stage

Decline

Company Capability Profile

SWOT

1. Arthur Thompson and A. J. Strickland, *Strategic Management,* 6th ed. (Homewood IL: Irwin, 1992) Chapter 3.

2. Thompson and Strickland, op. cit., 67.

3. Michael Porter, *Competitive Strategy: Techniques For Analyzing Industries and Competitions* (New York: The Free Press, 1980).

4. Porter, Ibid., 17.

5. This is based on Alan Rowe, Karl Dickel, Richard Mason, and Neil Snyder, *Strategic Management: A Methodological Approach* (Reading, MA: Addison-Wesley Publishing Co., 1989), 235–38.

CHAPTER 7

PLANNING AND DECISION-MAKING AIDS

LEARNING OBJECTIVES

After studying this chapter, you should be able to:

■ Describe the importance of forecasting in management.

■ Distinguish between quantitative and qualitative forecasting methods and give examples of each.

■ Explain the four steps in decision making.

■ Compare and contrast programmed and nonprogrammed decisions.

■ List the various aids in making programmed and nonprogrammed decisions.

OPENING PROBLEM
CHRYSLER CORPORATION

Chrysler faced a major decision just after it introduced its new LH cars. Its Dodge Intrepid, Eagle Vision, and Chrysler Concorde had been built with two goals in mind: to reestablish Chrysler's reputation for quality and to boost consumer confidence. More than three years and $1.6 billion had gone into a design that increased interior space, and enhanced stability by shifting the wheels nearer the corners. Just after the first 4,000 were shipped in mid-1992, a dealer phoned to say that a washer on one car's suspension had snapped during a test drive. Then-chairman Lee Iacocca had a big decision to make. ■ As matters stood, a single car needed fixing, and as far as Iacocca knew, it was the only one with a bad five-cent washer. Fifty cars were already with their new owners, who could discreetly be notified of the problem. Another option seemed the least palatable, recalling all 4,000 cars and going public with the reason. If the LH car introduction failed, Chrysler would be hard-pressed to find the funds to underwrite a new car-development program.[1]

FORECASTING

WHY FORECASTING IS IMPORTANT

All plans are based on assumptions or premises that we make about the future. When you plan your route to school, you implicitly (or explicitly) make some assumptions about traffic patterns, for instance. Similarly, IBM's strategy in the 1990s will reflect the assumptions the company makes regarding the demand for mainframe computers in the foreseeable future. Chrysler's LH car plans were also based on forecasts of consumers' tastes. **Forecast** means to estimate or calculate in advance or to predict.[2] According to one expert it is "a service whose purpose is to offer the best available basis for management expectations of the future, and to help management understand the implications for alternative courses of action."[3] The purpose of this section is to explain the more popular forecasting methods.

TYPES OF FORECASTING METHODS

There are two broad classes of forecasting methods: *quantitative* and *qualitative*. These are illustrated in Figure 7.1.[4] **Quantitative forecasting** uses statistical methods to examine data and find underlying patterns and relationships. **Qualitative forecasting** methods emphasize human judgment. Quantitative methods can be classified as either time series methods or causal models. Qualitative methods include technological and judgmental methods.

QUANTITATIVE FORECASTING METHODS

Quantitative methods like time series methods, trend lines, and causal models forecast the future based on the past.

TIME SERIES   A **time series** is a set of observations taken at specific times, usually at equal intervals. Examples of time series are the yearly or monthly gross national product of the United States over several years, a department store's total monthly sales receipts, the daily closing price of a share of stock, and the hourly temperatures announced by the New York City Weather Bureau.[5]

If you plot time series data for several years, you may note various patterns. For example, if you were to plot monthly sales of Rheem air conditioning units, you would find seasonal increases in late spring and summer and reduced sales in the winter months. For some types of time series, there may also be an irregular pattern, such as a sudden "blip" in the graph that reflects unexplained variations in the data. For example, monthly sales of Perrier water dropped dramatically in the summer of 1992. This irregular pattern was caused by the fact that Benzene was found in several bottles of Perrier. The basic purpose of all time series forecasting methods is to remove irregu-

FORECAST
To estimate or calculate in advance or to predict.

QUANTITATIVE FORECASTING
Statistical methods used to examine data and find underlying patterns and relationships. These methods can be classified as either time series methods or causal models.

QUALITATIVE FORECASTING
These methods emphasize human judgment and include both technological and judgmental methods.

TIME SERIES
A set of observations taken at specific times, usually at equal intervals.

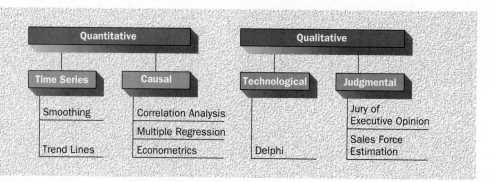

FIGURE 7.1

Forecasting Methods

We can distinguish between two broad classes of forecasting methods, quantitative and qualitative, each with specific techniques.

lar and seasonal patterns so that management can identify the fundamental trend that the data are taking. For example, meteorologists these days are trying to determine if the deterioration of the earth's ozone layer is causing a long-term, fundamental upward trend in global temperatures.

Several methods are used to isolate a time series' underlying trend. **Smoothing methods** average the data in some way to remove seasonal and random variations. One of the simplest smoothing techniques is called simple smoothing average. With a **simple smoothing average** you take an average of, say, the last five months' sales, and forecast that next month's sales will be that average. Then, every month you can drop the first month's sales so that your forecast for the following month is continually an average of the past five months' sales. In that way, you develop a *moving average* as your forecast of the next month's sales. You could, of course, argue that your most recent month's sales should carry more weight, perhaps because they reflect changes in your sales force. With **exponential smoothing** you also average the data, but give more recent data greater weight than their predecessors.

TIME TRENDS   The **trend line method** also involves plotting the data against time, as in Figure 7.2. For example, you plot your monthly sales on a graph, going back five years. But with the trend line method, you then use statistical techniques to fit a "trend line" to the data that best reflect the shape of your data. As in Figure 7.2, the line could be linear or exponential. You can then extrapolate from that line, which means extend it into the future in order to forecast what your sales will be in the following period.

CAUSAL MODELS   Managers often need to understand the causal relationship between two variables such as (1) their company's sales and (2) an indicator of economic activity such as personal income. **Causal methods** develop a projection based on the mathematical relationship between a company factor and those variables management believes influence or explain the company factor.[6] The basic premise of causal models is that a particular factor—such as your company's sales of television sets—is directly influenced by some other, more predictable, factor or factors—such as the number of people unemployed in your state, or the level of disposable income in the United States. The basic assumption is that if you know the historical relationship between, say, TV sales and the level of unemployment, you will be able to project what your TV sales will be if you know what unemployment is now, and what unemployment is projected to be in the immediate future.[7] In other words, **causal forecasting**

SMOOTHING METHODS
These methods average the data in some way to remove seasonal and random variations.

SIMPLE SMOOTHING AVERAGE
An average forecasted for next period, based on the average sales of the last five (or some set number) of periods.

EXPONENTIAL SMOOTHING
Averaging the data of previous periods to forecast next period's average sales, but giving recent periods' data more weight.

TREND LINE METHOD
Involves plotting data on a graph against a period of time, such as five years, and fitting a line to the plots.

CAUSAL METHODS
These methods develop a projection based on the mathematical relationship between the variable being examined and those variables management believes influence or explain the company's variables.

CAUSAL FORECASTING
Involves estimating the company factor (such as sales) based on other factors (such as advertising expenditures).

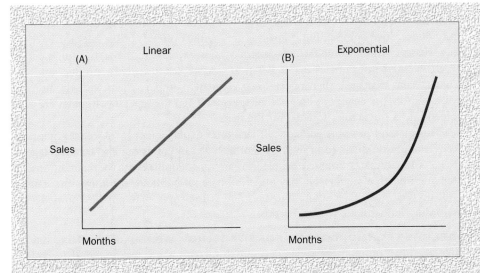

FIGURE 7.2

Monthly Sales Trend Lines

A trend line involves plotting your data against time, such as monthly sales going back five years. The trend line fitted to the points on the graph may be linear or exponential.

involves estimating the company factor (such as sales) based on other factors (such as advertising expenditures, or level of unemployment). Two statistical techniques—*correlation analysis* (How closely are the variables related?) and *regression analysis* (How can we predict one factor if we know the values of related factors?)—are generally used to develop the necessary relationships. With regression analysis, the mathematical techniques involved produce an equation. This presents the magnitude of one variable (say, your company's sales) as a function of the magnitude of the other variables (such as advertising expenditures and unemployment levels). **Econometrics** is a forecasting method in which a series of interrelated regression equations based on economic theory are used to develop forecasts.

QUALITATIVE METHODS

Time series, trend line, and causal forecasting have three big limitations. They are virtually useless when data are scarce, such as for a new product with no sales history. They assume that historical trends will continue into the future.[8] And, they tend to disregard unforeseeable, unexpected occurrences. Yet it is exactly these unexpected occurrences that often have the most profound effects on companies.

Qualitative forecasting techniques emphasize and are based on human judgment. They gather, in as logical, unbiased, and systematic a way as possible, all the information and judgment that can be brought to bear on the factors being forecasted. Techniques here include judgmental techniques such as jury of executive opinion and sales force estimation, and technological methods like the Delphi Technique.[9]

THE JURY OF EXECUTIVE OPINION The **jury of executive opinion** technique involves asking a "jury" of key executives to forecast sales for, say, the next year. Generally, each executive is given data on forecasted economic levels and changes anticipated (in the firm's product or service, for instance). Each jury member then makes an independent sales forecast. Differences can be reconciled by the president or during a meeting of the executives. An enhancement of this approach involves gathering experts from various departments of the company to make the forecast.

This is a simple straightforward way to forecast sales. However, the accuracy of this method is reportedly almost always inferior to the more rigorous quantitative methods.[10] The resulting forecast may also be influenced by a powerful member of the group and the experts' subjective opinions are often influenced in the same direction by general business conditions (all may be overly optimistic in boom times, for instance).

SALES FORCE ESTIMATION The **sales force estimation** method is similar to jury of executive opinion, but it involves getting the opinions of the sales force regarding what they think some factor—generally sales—will be in the forthcoming period. Each salesperson estimates his or her next year's sales, usually by product and customer. Sales managers then review each estimate, compare them with the previous year, and discuss changes with each salesperson. Then the separate estimates are combined into a single sales forecast for the firm.

This method has pros and cons. It facilitates management by objectives by getting each salesperson involved in setting his or her sales quota. It can also be advantageous to get sales estimates from the people who are most familiar with local conditions. On the other hand, a salesperson may underestimate sales if he or she knows the estimate will become his or her quota. Furthermore, salespeople may not be knowledgeable regarding influential economic trends.

DELPHI TECHNOLOGICAL FORECASTING Whereas judgmental techniques like executive opinion are generally used to forecast sales, **technological forecasting** involves predicting future products and innovations.

ECONOMETRICS
A forecasting method in which a series of interrelated regression equations based on economic theory are used to develop forecasts.

THE JURY OF EXECUTIVE OPINION
Involves asking a "jury" of key executives to forecast sales for the next year based on economic levels and anticipated changes.

SALES FORCE ESTIMATION
Involves getting the opinions of the sales force on what they predict sales will be in the forthcoming period.

TECHNOLOGICAL FORECASTING
Involves predicting future products and innovations.

The **Delphi Technique** is the most widely used technological forecasting method. It involves obtaining the opinions of experts on the future technological and economic trends that might affect a company's product or markets. Instead of putting these experts together in one room (where one or two strong personalities might overwhelm the group), their opinions are solicited anonymously and individually through questionnaires. These opinions are then analyzed, distilled, and resubmitted to the experts for a second round of opinions. This process may continue for five, six, or more rounds. In its initial survey, for instance, the company might ask its panel of experts to list the breakthroughs they expect to see in the next 10 years that might prove to be important to the company. These first results are then analyzed, and the ten most frequently mentioned breakthroughs are chosen. Then these ten breakthroughs could be submitted to the panel for an estimate as to the probability that each will occur, and so on.

DELPHI TECHNIQUE
The most widely used technological forecasting method. It involves obtaining the opinions of experts on the future technological and economic trends that might affect a company's product or market.

SCENARIO PLANNING TO BOOST RESPONSIVENESS

Some major companies make projections based on scenario planning. **Scenarios** have been defined as

> hypothetical sequences of events constructed for the purpose of focusing attention on causal processes and decision points. They answer two kinds of questions. (1) Precisely how might some hypothetical situation come about, step by step? And, (2) what alternatives exist, for each situation at each step, for preventing, diverting, or facilitating the process?[11]

SCENARIOS
Hypothetical sequences of events constructed for the purpose of focusing attention on causal processes and decision points.

Shell International Petroleum Company Ltd. is one firm that uses scenario planning. As one of its officers has said, "the Shell approach to strategic planning is, instead of forecast, to use scenarios, which are 'stories' about alternative possible futures. These stories promote a discussion of possibilities other than the 'most likely' one, and encourages the consideration of what if questions."[12]

In developing their current scenarios, Shell looked at "the world as it stood in 1990, in terms of geopolitical change, international economics, and the environment." It saw such things as the cascading collapse of communist regimes in eastern Europe,

Shell International uses scenario planning to project possible futures for the corporation. Such tools may help them make decisions encompassing a complex set of variables, such as whether to expand further into consumer markets in emerging countries.

international economic tensions (as symbolized by some increase in trade tariffs), and increasing pollution concerns. Out of this came two scenarios: global mercantilism and sustainable world.

These two scenarios are summarized in Figure 7.3. In **global mercantilism,** the new post-cold war "international order proves to be too weak to withstand serious political and economic shocks and setbacks." As a result, regional conflicts and frustration with similar international failures leads to a more managed system of trade. For a company like Shell (whose crude oil is a key traded commodity), this could lead to "intermittent over capacity and under capacity and a price 'roller coaster.'" In the **sustainable world** scenario, international economic frictions are resolved, and economic trade flows freely. But here, concern about environmental problems leads to tightened emissions regulation and higher quality standards for energy products. In any case, scenario planning provides Shell managers with a basis for viewing various alternate futures and the consequences these futures might have for Shell and its products.

THE DECISION-MAKING PROCESS

WHY DECISION MAKING IS IMPORTANT

Decision making is the process of choosing between alternative courses of action. It involves four steps: (1) defining the problem, (2) developing alternatives, (3) analyzing the alternatives, (4) making the decision.

Decision making is the essence of what managers do. Planning, organizing, staffing, leading, and controlling are the basic functions of management. However, each of these involves decisions—decisions regarding which plan to implement, what goals to use, and which people to hire.

GLOBAL MERCANTILISM
A scenario that entails looking at the world in terms of geopolitical change and international economic tensions, such that commodities prices, for example, might fluctuate widely.

SUSTAINABLE WORLD
A scenario whereby economic frictions are resolved, economic trade flows freely, and concern about the environment leads to tightened emissions regulation and higher quality standards for energy products.

DECISION MAKING
A four-step process of choosing between alternative courses of action.

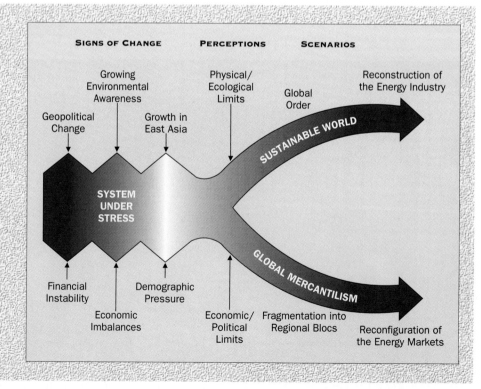

FIGURE 7.3

Scenarios Used by Royal Dutch Shell

Scenario planning involves looking at the events of the world, and creating likely scenarios (such as "sustainable world" and "global mercantilism") along with the implications each of these scenarios would have for the company.

SOURCE: Adam Kahan, "Scenarios for Energy: Sustainable World vs. Global Mercantilism," *Long Range Planning,* vol. 25, no. 4, 41.

Effective decisions are particularly important in the realm of managerial planning. A company like IBM can survive many day-to-day blunders as long as its basic direction—in terms of the market it serves and the product or service it provides—is sound. But where a poor decision is made and a wrong road is chosen, none but the luckiest survive.

It is therefore particularly fitting that we discuss decision making in the context of managerial planning. But remember that decision making actually underlies all five management functions.

STEPS IN DECISION MAKING

Regardless of the type of decision, decision making involves four basic steps. *Identifying the problem* is the first. All decision making is usually driven by the need to improve a situation, and is sparked by some stimulus, like diminishing sales or a machine breakdown. The first decision-making step thus involves determining what that problem is.

You have to be careful not to confuse symptoms and problems. Thus, poor maintenance and particularly inadequate screening of maintenance personnel may be the problems producing symptoms such as machine breakdowns. As another example, IBM spent much of the 1980s and early 1990s watching its market-share erode dramatically. However, declining market share was not the problem, but a *symptom* of the problem, which was an overreliance on selling mainframe computers.

As at IBM, misdefining the problem can lead to poor solutions. In the 1980s, IBM worked hard to boost market share and sales of mainframe computers. Much of that effort might have been better spent reevaluating its strategy, downsizing, and redeploying assets from mainframes to other computer products, such as PCs.

In any case, once the problem is identified, *alternative solutions* can be developed. This is important because it's best to have several alternative solutions from which to choose. In fact, when you don't have a choice, you really don't have any decision to make—except perhaps to take it or leave it.

The next step in decision making is thus to *analyze your alternatives:* Should IBM continue to channel resources into mainframe computers, or concentrate instead on personal computers and work stations? Should the factory manager order machine A or machine B? Then, once the pros and cons of each alternative are compared, the final step is to *make the actual decision.* Techniques for analyzing alternatives and making decisions are discussed below.

PROGRAMMED AND NONPROGRAMMED DECISION MAKING

The decision-making technique used depends on the type of decision to be made. Here we can conveniently distinguish between two types of decisions: programmed and nonprogrammed. Decisions are **programmed** to the extent that they are repetitive and routine and to the extent that definite, systematic procedures exist for making them. Computing weekly payroll taxes is an example. Decisions are **nonprogrammed** to the degree that they are unique and novel, and to the extent that systematic procedures (or "programs") are not available for making them.[13] Reacting to a competitor's new advertising campaign is an example.

Programmed decisions have several characteristics. They generally involve short lead times (say, ordering supplies for the next month or two). They tend to focus on *internal organizational matters* (like computing weekly payroll deductions). Factors that are exogenous or outside the organization (like reactions of competitors) usually do not impact the solution very much. Those making the decisions can thus assume

PROGRAMMED DECISIONS Decisions that are repetitive and routine to the extent that definite, systematic procedures exist for making them.

NONPROGRAMMED DECISIONS Decisions that are unique and novel to the extent that systematic procedures are not available for making them.

they are dealing with a *closed system,* one in which all the factors to be considered, as well as the relationships between these factors, are known and understood. Programmed decisions generally arise from continually recurring problems, like computing weekly production schedules.

NONPROGRAMMED DECISION MAKING Nonprogrammed decisions also have several distinguishing characteristics.[14] Nonprogrammed decisions usually involve long lead times. In making such decisions, managers usually must consider unpredictable factors—factors that are outside the organization (such as the long-term demand for the firm's product and how the firm's rivals are going to react). Managers thus have to deal with more of an open system, one in which unpredictable but interrelated factors must be considered prior to making the decision. The *Digital Equipment* vignette provides an example.

Because so many unpredictable factors must be considered, there are usually no set procedures or decision rules the manager can apply. Instead, he or she must quickly learn as much as possible about the variables involved and then apply experience, intuition, and judgment to get a solution. Nonprogrammed decisions often involve *exceptions,* nonrecurring problems which the organization has never before had to face in exactly the same form. *Crisis decisions*—like Union Carbide's Bhopol, India, chemical plant disaster—are examples. With the rapid changes and displacements of the past few years (as described in Chapters 1 through 3) such nonprogrammed decisions are increasingly prevalent.[15]

Successfully making nonprogrammed decisions involves three things. First, it requires a responsive management system. As we'll see in succeeding chapters, firms for which rapid change and nonprogrammed decisions are the norm establish characteristic management systems or ways of organizing and managing themselves. In other words, the firm is organized and managed so as to facilitate fast, responsive deci-

DIGITAL EQUIPMENT CORPORATION

In early 1992, Digital Equipment Corporation executives made a nonprogrammed decision that they hoped would revolutionize the computer industry. The company unveiled the new Alpha microprocessor chip, a technological breakthrough that could serve as the launching pad for another generation of computers ranging from desktop models to supercomputers. The chip used new technology known as RISC (reduced instruction-set computing), and forecasts showed it could significantly boost sluggish sales.

Still, implementing the decision has not proven easy. Even though the Alpha RISC microprocessor is the fastest yet, rivals like Hewlett-Packard, IBM, and Sun Microsystems have already been using RISC technology for years. Also, DEC's new high-speed chip was designed to run on computers in the $15,000 to $300,000 price range, a tall order in an economically depressed computer industry. The consensus now is that Digital's decision to introduce the new chip may have been too little, too late.

SOURCES: Gary McWilliams, "Did DEC Move Too Late?" *Business Week,* August 3, 1992, 62–64; McWilliams, "Can GQ Give DEC a Winning Makeover?" *Business Week,* August 3, 1992, 64; Esther Dyson, "Recreating DEC," *Forbes,* March 30, 1991, 124; "Dithering," *The Economist,* January 25, 1992; and "Alpha Chips Take Center Stage," *Industry Week,* February 15, 1993, 23.

sion making. Specifically, decision making is decentralized or pushed down to the lower-level employees who are in the best position to make quick, on-the-spot decisions; leaders concentrate on setting a broad direction for the firm and leaving the tactics to subordinates; and upward and interdepartmental not just top-down communications are encouraged, for instance. We'll address these issues starting in Chapter 8.

Successful nonprogrammed decision making requires two other things. First, (since some managers are better at making nonprogrammed than programmed decisions) placing the right manager on the right job becomes doubly important. Finally, different decision-making aids are used for each type of decision. Let us address these last two points in the rest of this chapter.

SYSTEMATIC VERSUS INTUITIVE DECISION MAKERS

One way to improve decision making is to assign managers to tasks based on whether they are better at making programmed or nonprogrammed decisions. For example, researchers McKenney and Keen distinguish between systematic and intuitive decision makers. **Systematic decision makers** "tend to approach a problem by structuring it in terms of some method which, if followed through, leads to a likely solution." At the other extreme, **intuitive decision makers** use more of a trial-and-error decision-making approach. "They are much more willing to jump from one method to another, to disregard information, and to be sensitive to cues that they may not be able to identify verbally." In their study, systematic subjects tended to be preoccupied with defining how to solve the problem. "In contrast, the intuitive subjects tended to jump in,

SYSTEMATIC DECISION MAKERS
People who approach a problem by structuring it in terms of some method which leads to a likely solution.

INTUITIVE DECISION MAKERS
People who use a trial-and-error approach to solve problems.

try something, and see where it led them. They generally showed a pattern of rapid solution testing, abandoning lines of exploration that did not seem profitable."[16] Intuitives therefore tend to excel at making nonprogrammed decisions, while systematics do better at making programmed ones.

Some experts believe such differences are neurologically based.[17] Neurologists and psychologists know that the brain has two hemispheres, and that the left generally controls right-side body movements, while the right controls movements on the left. The two hemispheres also differ in how they solve problems. The left hemisphere tends to specialize in logical, step-by-step decision making. The right hemisphere excels in processing data simultaneously—in other words, "gathering in" a multitude of information and then relating these bits and pieces into a meaningful whole. Whereas accountants and mathematicians might have better developed left hemispheric thinking processes, people like artists and sculptors (and managers) may have to have better developed right hemispheric processes.[18]

This is consistent with some findings by Professor Henry Mintzberg. He discovered that strategic planning (which relies heavily on nonprogrammed decision making) depends heavily on intuition. In his study of 25 strategic decision makers, only in 18 out of 83 decisions did managers mention using explicit step-by-step analyses in arriving at a choice. Sometimes the choice was arrived at after considerable bargaining among managers. More often judgment was used. As Mintzberg says, "typically, the options and all kinds of data associated with them were pumped into the mind of the manager, and somehow a choice later came out. How was never explained."[19]

AIDS FOR PROGRAMMED DECISION MAKING

Programmed decisions are those for which clear decision rules, (like "minimize inventory costs") are available and for which programs (set procedures) can be used to arrive at an optimal choice. Breakeven analysis and decision science are two widely used programmed decision-making aids.

BREAKEVEN ANALYSIS

In financial analysis the breakeven point is that volume of sales at which revenues just equal expenses. Here you have neither a profit nor a loss. **Breakeven analysis** is a financial analysis decision-making aid that enables a manager to determine whether a particular volume of sales will result in losses or profits.[20]

BREAKEVEN CHARTS   Breakeven analysis makes use of four basic concepts: fixed costs, variable costs, revenues, and profits. *Fixed costs* (such as for plant and machinery) are costs that basically do not change with changes in volume. In other words, you might use the same machine to produce 10 units, 50 units, or 200 units of a product. *Variable costs* (such as for raw material) do rise in proportion to volume. *Revenue* is the total income received from sales of the product. For example, if you sell 50 dolls at $8 each, then your revenue is $8 × 50 or $400. *Profit* is the money you have left after subtracting fixed and variable costs from revenues.

A **breakeven chart**, like that in Figure 7.4 is a graph that shows whether a particular volume of sales will result in profits or losses. The fixed cost line is horizontal, since fixed costs remain the same regardless of level of output. Variable costs, however, increase in proportion to output and are shown as an upward sloping line. The total cost line is then equal to variable costs plus fixed costs at each level of output.

The **breakeven point** is the point where the total revenue line crosses the total cost line. Beyond this point (note the shaded area in Figure 7.4), total revenue exceeds total

BREAKEVEN ANALYSIS
A financial analysis decision-making aid that enables a manager to determine whether a particular volume of sales will result in losses or profits.

BREAKEVEN CHART
A graph that shows whether a particular volume of sales will result in profits or losses.

BREAKEVEN POINT
The volume where the total revenue line crosses the total cost line, in other words, where revenue equals expenses.

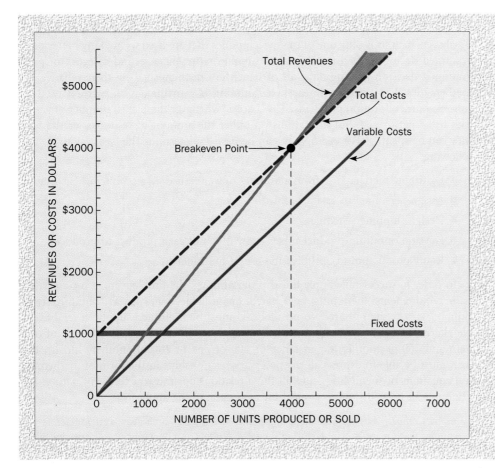

FIGURE 7.4

Breakeven Chart

In this breakeven chart, to-tal costs equal fixed costs plus variable costs, and the breakeven point is at 4000 units, where total revenues just equal total costs.

costs. So in this example, an output of about 4,000 units is the breakeven point. Above this, the company can expect to earn a profit. But if sales are fewer than 4,000 units, the company can expect a loss.

BREAKEVEN FORMULA The breakeven chart provides a picture of the relationship between sales volume and profits. However, a chart is not required for determining breakeven points. Instead, you can use the breakeven formula:

$$P(X) = F + V(X)$$

where

F = fixed costs
V = variable costs per unit
X = volume of output (in units)
P = price per unit

Rearranging this formula, the breakeven *point* is X = F/(P−V). In other words the breakeven point is the volume of sales where total costs just equal total revenues. If, for example, you have a product in which:

F = fixed costs = $1,000.00
V = variable costs per unit = $.75
P = price per unit = $1.00 per unit

Then the breakeven point is $1,000/$1.00 − $.75 = 4,000 units.

LINEAR PROGRAMMING

Breakeven analysis is only one of many techniques that are used for making better programmed decisions. *Decision Science* techniques represent a second category of programmed decision-making aids, all of which are distinguished by their reliance on mathematics. For example, **linear programming** is a mathematical method used to solve resource allocation problems. These arise "whenever there are a number of activities to be performed, but limitations on either the amount of resources or the way they can be spent."[21] For example, it can be used to determine the best way to do the following:

- Distribute merchandise from a number of warehouses to a number of customers.
- Assign personnel to various jobs.
- Design shipping schedules.
- Develop optimum product mixes (how much of each product to produce).
- Route production to optimize the use of machinery.

In order to successfully apply linear programming, the problem must meet certain basic requirements: there must be a stated, quantifiable goal, such as "minimize total shipping costs"; the resources to be allocated must be in limited supply; several feasible alternative courses of action must be available (a firm could produce 200 of one item and 300 of another, for instance or 400 of one or 100 of another); finally, the firm must be able to express all the necessary relationships in the form of mathematical equations or inequalities, and all these relationships must be linear in nature. An example can help illustrate a typical linear programming application:

> Alpha Company has six manufacturing plants and fifteen warehouses scattered across the country. Each plant is manufacturing the same product and operating at full capacity. Since plant capacity and location do not permit the closest plant to fully support each warehouse, Alpha Company would like to determine the factory which should supply each warehouse in order to minimize total shipping costs. Applying linear programming techniques to this problem will provide an optimum shipping schedule for the company.[22]

WAITING LINE/QUEUING TECHNIQUES

Waiting line/queuing techniques are used to solve waiting line problems. For example, bank managers need to know how many tellers they should have. If they have too many, they are wasting money on salaries; if they have too few, they may end up with many disgruntled customers. Similar problems arise when deciding the optimum number of airline reservation clerks, warehouse loading docks, highway toll booths, supermarket checkout counters, and so forth.

STATISTICAL DECISION THEORY TECHNIQUES

Statistical decision theory techniques are used to solve problems for which information is incomplete or uncertain. Suppose a shopkeeper can stock either brand A or brand B, but not both. She knows how much it will cost to stock her shelves with each brand, and she also knows how much money she would earn (or lose) if each brand turned out to be a success (or failure) with her customers. What she does not know is which of the two brands—A or B—will be a success. Her information, in other words, is incomplete. Using statistical decision theory, the shopkeeper would assign probabilities (estimates of the likelihood that the brand will be a success or failure) to each alternative. Then, she could determine which alternative—stocking brand A or brand B—would most likely result in the greatest profits.

THREE DEGREES OF UNCERTAINTY Statistical decision theory is based on the idea that a manager may face three degrees of uncertainty in making a decision. Some decisions are made under conditions of *certainty*. Here, the manager knows in advance the outcome of the decision. From a practical point of view, for example, you know that if you buy a $50 U.S. savings bond, the interest you will earn to maturity on the bond is, say, 4 percent. Managers rarely make decisions under conditions of certainty.

At the opposite extreme some decisions are made under conditions of *uncertainty*. Here, the manager cannot even assign probabilities to the likelihood of the various outcomes. For example, a shopkeeper may have several new products that could be stocked. But because they involve entirely new products, the manager has no idea of the likelihood that one brand will be successful or that another will fail. Conditions of complete uncertainty are also relatively infrequent occurrences.

Most management decisions are made under conditions of *risk*. Under conditions of risk, the manager can at least assign probabilities to each outcome. In other words, the manager knows (either from past experience or by making an educated guess) the chance that each possible outcome (like product A being successful, or product B being successful) will occur.

DECISION TREE A decision tree provides one technique for making a decision under conditions of risk. With a decision tree like the one in Figure 7.5 an *expected value* can be calculated for each alternative. **Expected value** equals (1) the probability of the outcome multiplied by (2) the benefit or cost of that outcome.

For example, in the figure, it pays our shopkeeper to stock brand B rather than brand A. Stocking brand A allows a 70 percent chance of success, so the shopkeeper has to balance the $560 profit she could make against the possibility of the $90 loss. The expected value of stocking brand A is thus $470. By stocking brand B, though, the potential loss—$12—is relatively minuscule. So, the expected value of stocking brand B is a relatively high $588.

DECISION TREE
A technique for making decisions under conditions of risk.

EXPECTED VALUE
A calculated value that equals the probability of the outcome multiplied by the benefit or cost of that outcome.

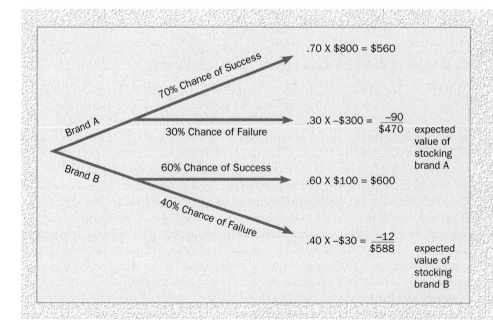

FIGURE 7.5

Decision Tree

A decision tree like this one shows the chance of success and the chance of failure for each alternative (in this case Brand A and Brand B) along with the expected income or loss of each alternative. For 'A' the expected value of introducing that brand is $560 if it succeeds, minus $90 if it fails, or $470.

AIDS FOR NONPROGRAMMED DECISION MAKING

The task of making *nonprogrammed* decisions is often compounded by three basic decision-making mistakes. First, most managers fail to consider, in a systematic and explicit way, strongly different policy alternatives to their current ways of doing things. For example, a company that has consistently followed a policy that opposed vertical integration (producing its own raw materials as well as the finished item) may not systematically explore the alternative of doing so. Instead, the company tends to take the policy as a "given" and make the rest of its decisions on the assumption that the company is locked into its "no vertical integration" policy. This may help to explain why for many years IBM stuck tenaciously to its policy of emphasizing the mainframe computer market.[23]

A second, related mistake is what Professor Chris Argyris calls "the self sealing character" of many organizations. In other words, some organizations make it difficult to mount effective challenges to their traditional ways of doing things. In one company, for instance, Argyris found that although lower-lever managers knew that product X was in serious trouble, they were reluctant to inform their supervisors of this fact. Their reluctance was based on the fact that their supervisors had done the production and marketing studies that led to the decision to produce the product.

The managers knew their supervisors would resist any advice that explicitly or implicitly criticized their decision. As a result, the product was carried for six years beyond the time that it should have been dropped, resulting in a loss of over $100 million to the company.[24]

A third mistake in making nonprogrammed decisions is that criticisms and challenges tend to be directed toward symptoms rather than toward the problem itself. In his study, for instance, Argyris found that when managers saw sales of the product dwindling, they did not react by questioning the validity of the original decision to produce product X. Instead, they reacted by assuming that working harder to advertise and sell the product would solve the problem.[25]

Decision-making aids aimed at minimizing such mistakes include creativity, double-loop learning, and intuitive decision-making processes.

CREATIVITY-STIMULATING TECHNIQUES

CREATIVITY
An organization's ability to invent new ways of doing things, or new ways of interpreting old problems.

Experts have developed a number of techniques aimed at stimulating creative problem solving in organizations. (**Creativity** may be defined as an organization's ability to invent new ways of doing things, or new ways of interpreting old problems.) Perhaps the simplest technique is just to tell people to be creative. Creativity stimulation can be illustrated with Figure 7.6. How many squares are in the box? Your first reaction might be 16. However, if you are told to be creative, you might count again and find that you can find 30 squares in the box. The point is that people tend to accept obvious solutions. This tendency can be avoided by providing specific directions to "be creative."[26]

BRAINSTORMING
A creativity-stimulating technique in which prior judgments and criticisms are specifically forbidden from inhibiting the free flow of ideas.

Brainstorming is a creativity-stimulating technique in which prior judgments and criticism are specifically forbidden from inhibiting the free flow of ideas. A group is assembled, presented with a problem, and encouraged to produce as many ideas and solutions as they can. The important thing is that absolutely no evaluation of any suggestion be permitted until the group has run out of new suggestions. Even impractical suggestions for solving the problem should be welcomed and recorded. Participants often find that even these impractical ideas lead to other, feasible solutions. Then the potential solutions can be evaluated.

FIGURE 7.6

Creativity Test

Creativity can sometimes be stimulated just by telling someone to be creative.

How many squares are in the box?

Now, count again.

Only sixteen?

Take away your *pre*conception of how many squares there are.

Now, how many do you find? You should find thirty!

DOUBLE-LOOP LEARNING

Chris Argyris recommends double-loop learning to improve nonprogrammed decision making. He points out that most organizational decision making tends to reflect "single-loop" learning: managers detect deviations from present policies and then correct these deviations, much as a thermostat detects when the room temperature is too high or too low and then closes the appropriate switch. Single-loop learning enables an organization to carry on its present policies in much the same way that the thermostat permits the house to remain at the temperature set. But what it cannot accomplish, says Argyris, is getting managers to check their assumptions and question their goals any more than a thermostat can question if it should, in fact, be set, say, at 68 degrees.

This can be a real problem. In one study, Argyris and Schon found that almost all of the 1,000 managers they studied were programmed to use only single-loop learning. Ironically, this made it almost impossible for them to admit to themselves that they were single-loop learning (not questioning their assumptions).[27] Compounding the problem was the fact that most of these managers tended to use characteristic tactics in making decisions, such as advocating a position and simultaneously controlling others to win that position. As a result, a sort of "herd mentality" tended to develop, even for the most important, strategic decisions. Everyone just sort of went along with the prevailing way of thinking.

Argyris instead advocates a **double-loop learning** approach. Double-loop decision makers continually question their basic theories and assumptions. The problem, says Argyris, is that most managers think they *are* open-minded, and open to learning new ways of doing things, and having their policies challenged, although they are not. Therefore the only lasting way to make managers double-loop learn, says Argyris, is to get them to see how *closed* their thinking has been in the past. The firm must then get them to develop the habit of checking their assumptions.

Several techniques are used to encourage such double-loop decision making, particularly with respect to strategic planning. One technique is the **advocate approach.**

DOUBLE-LOOP LEARNING
Learning that advocates decision making based on the continual questioning of basic theories and assumptions.

ADVOCATE APPROACH
A technique that involves assigning an alternative plan to an advocate whose job is to see that all the pros and cons of the plan (and any other alternative plans) are covered fully.

Each alternative plan is assigned to an advocate, whose job is to see that all the pros and cons of his or her own and the other alternatives are covered fully. Other experts suggest what they call a *dialectical approach* to strategic planning. This involves a formal four-step process in which (1) all the assumptions underlying each alternative are systematically surfaced and questioned; (2) new alternatives based on a set of counter assumptions are generated; (3) a set of acceptable assumptions (blending the original and counter assumptions) are negotiated; and (4) final strategic alternatives are chosen based on the new, acceptable set of assumptions.[28]

THE RESPONSIVE ORGANIZATION: INTUITIVE DECISION-MAKING PROCESSES

Corporate survival today requires making fast decisions. Whether it's Apple introducing its new computer or the fall of the Soviet Union, organizations that survive are the ones that absorb and process unexpected data the fastest—and then draw the right conclusions faster than their competitors.

As mentioned earlier, there are several ways to foster faster decision making in the firm. The first (as we have seen) is *organizational* and involves designing the management system in such a way as to facilitate fast decisions. We will explain this approach starting in Chapters 8 and 9. In brief, the organizational method involves, for instance, eliminating layers of middle managers and pushing decision making down to those employees who are in the best position to make fast, on-the-spot decisions.[29] A second tactic is to fit the manager to the job—for instance, intuitive managers seem more adept at making nonprogrammed decisions than do systematic ones.

The third option seeks to improve the decision-making process itself. For example, two experts studied managers in 12 computer firms to see how they made fast decisions.[30] Professor Kathleen Eisenhardt, with colleague Jay Bourgeois,[31] found that slow decision makers took 12 to 18 months to do what the quick decision makers did in two to four months. The researchers also noted five major distinctions between the two types of managers. (1) Fast decision-makers immersed themselves in a sea of real-time information, with reams of data on performance and market trends flooding the managers everyday. On the other hand, slow ones relied on "planning and futuristic information." (2) The speeders tended to concentrate on monitoring lots of data on a few key operating measures such as cash, engineering milestones, and sales backlogs, and they often updated their data every day. (3) The speeders also typically scheduled as many as three weekly top-team meetings so they could continually review the implications of the latest trends. (4) Also, the constant computer messages and face-to-face meetings relied on by speeders almost completely replaced the lengthy reports and ponderous group meetings that marked the slow-poke firms. You might expect that flooding managers with so much information would make them drown in a sea of data, but that was not the case. Instead, the flood of information seemed to help the managers get a better intuitive feel for how their firms were doing and what trends were emerging.

Finally, (5) the managers built on all this information by reviewing lots of alternatives at once, not one at a time in sequence. That, in turn, helped them size up the pros and cons of each alternative quickly.

There were several other differences between slow and fast decision makers. The slow decision makers ended up reviewing far fewer alternatives than their speedy colleagues in other firms, and they dissected each possibility in anguishing detail. On the other hand, the speeders critically reviewed a batch of options all at once, which had the very desirable effect of enabling managers to make quick comparative analyses and thus sharpen their preferences for various options. If the slow decision makers' favorite option died, they were often left with nothing, since they spent so much time analyz-

MY OWN MEALS, INC.

When My Own Meals, Inc., was launched, Mary Ann Jackson wasn't concerned about consumer acceptance—she knew they would like her new company's product. Jackson just wondered how close actual sales would come to her projections.

Jackson's confidence wasn't entirely misplaced. She spent a year and a half analyzing her target market, designing and developing her product, and laying out strategies for marketing and distribution. The actual introduction of the packaged children's meals seemed like a movie she'd already seen several times before.

The 35-year old CPA and MBA had spent eight years doing financial and strategic planning at Beatrice Companies. There, and at two big accounting firms before, she oversaw many corporate projects. She said getting MOM off the ground, often a terrifying moment for entrepreneurs, was just another "big project."

Her inspiration was partly due to the guilt some working mothers experience after having to resort to fast food for their children. At Beatrice, she learned the process—retort packaging—by which wholesome foods are vacuum-sealed and pressure-cooked, remaining shelf-stable for a year. A questionnaire, delivered by her diaper service, canvassed interest by other mothers, and she and a group of investors spent $365,000 on market research and product development. They determined there was plenty of consumer interest in children's meals that could be heated in the microwave or in boiling water. With her corporate savvy, Jackson priced her products to make a profit. Sales for 1989 exceeded $1 million, near breakeven. There was no stopping Jackson; she had planned for every contingency.

Or so she thought. Even though Jackson had a plan to counter entry by

FOCUS ON SMALL BUSINESS

large competitors into MOM's original-market, deep down she felt that the inertia of large competitors would give her enough time to establish MOM as the name in its niche of the children's food market. She also had counted on the value of being a mother herself, not a faceless corporation, who was as concerned about the nutritional needs of her customers' children as she was about her own. It was a good plan. But during one week at around 100 Dominick's grocery stores, MOM products found their way into the unusable food bin. Tyson Foods, ConAgra, and George A. Hormel & Company had all launched their own children's dinners. A store manager names a competing sales representative as the perpetrator. "We got annihilated," says Jackson, who had to pay back grocers while saboteurs removed her products from store shelves.

It might have been the end, but something Jackson didn't plan for occurred. Operation Desert Storm was getting underway. No less than the U.S. Army phoned wondering if Jackson could cook up kosher rations with extended shelf lives like MOM. Jackson was interested, but the war didn't last long enough. Trying to fill the order led Jackson to her next market.

There are 6.5 million kosher-food consumers in the United States, and many were having at least some difficulty finding meals, especially when traveling. Jackson consulted with Rabbi Aaron Soloveichik, in charge of kosher production for the large New York matzo manufacturer Aaron Streit. Soloveichik agreed to bless the venture and include his name on the packaging as well. Shortly thereafter, seven adult and three children's kosher meals hit grocery shelves across the United States.

SOURCES: Suzanne Oliver, "The Shiksa Chef," *Forbes,* May 24, 1991, 66–68; Tom Richman, "The New American Start-Up," *Inc.,* September 1988, 54–65.

---

ing just a few options. The speeders also seemed to thrive on the give and take and conflict of reviewing the alternatives; the slow deciders seemed to be hobbled by the need to wait for a painful consensus to evolve.

Differences between the fast and slow decision makers, says Eisenhardt, can be summed up in the word *immersion*. The fast decision makers thrived on immersing themselves in floods of data and alternatives all at once; the slow ones carefully conducted their industry analyses and broad strategic plans in a painfully slow process. However, as Eisenhardt concludes, "the carefully conducted industry analysis or broad ranging strategic plan is no longer a guarantee of success . . . the premium now is on moving fast and keeping pace."[32] The *My Own Meals* Small Business box illustrates how enormously applicable this is to small businesses, too.

SUMMARY

Forecasting is estimating or calculating in advance. It offers management the best available basis for expectations of the future and helps in understanding the implications of alternative courses of action. Broadly speaking, forecasting methods come in two classes: quantitative and qualitative.

Quantitative techniques consist of time series and causal methods. A time series is a set of observations taken at specific, usually equal, intervals. Causal methods develop a projection based on the mathematical relationship between the variable being examined and those factors that management thinks affect a company's variables. Correlation and regression analysis are generally used to develop the necessary relationships.

Qualitative forecasting techniques rely on human judgment, and they include the jury of executive opinion, sales force estimation, and the Delphi Technique. Many companies make projections based on scenarios or hypothetical sequences of events.

Decision making is the process of selecting among alternative courses, and it involves four steps: defining the problem, developing alternatives, analyzing the alternatives, and making the decision. Decisions can be programmed or nonprogrammed, and decision makers can take a systematic or intuitive approach.

Aids in programmed decision making include breakeven analysis and decision science. Linear programming is a mathematical method used to solve resource allocation problems when a number of activities are to be performed. Statistical decision theory techniques are used to solve problems for which information is incomplete or uncertain. A decision tree is a technique for making a decision under conditions of risk.

Aids in nonprogrammed decision making include creativity-stimulating techniques, double-loop learning, and intuitive techniques. Organizations and management systems can be designed to facilitate fast decision making. Immersing oneself in greater amounts of relevant information can lead to quicker, better decisions.

QUESTIONS

■ FOR REVIEW

1. Why is forecasting important, and what are the various methods used in quantitative and qualitative forecasting?

2. List the steps in the decision-making process, and describe the two main types of decision makers.

3. How can organizations be designed to facilitate faster decision making?

■ FOR DISCUSSION

4. Discuss the differences between programmed and nonprogrammed decision making. Give examples of each.

5. Is effective nonprogrammed decision making an art or a science? Do you think managers can dictate specific criteria for evaluating nonprogrammed decisions?

6. Which types of organizations are best suited for quick response, nonprogrammed decision making by employees and which are not? Why?

7. How effective do you think scenario planning is in helping a company prepare for the future?

■ FOR ACTION

8. Develop a scenario describing the changes that are likely to impact college education by the year 2005. How could your university best prepare for these changes?

9. Assume you lost your current job, or if you aren't employed imagine that you were forced to drop out of school. Use some of the creativity stimulating tech-

niques described in this chapter to decide what you would do next. Explain your reasoning.

■ **FOR FOCUS ON SMALL BUSINESS**

10. Critique the situation analysis Jackson conducted for her new company. Do you think she should have been able to anticipate the ultimate outcome?

11. Do you think Jackson was at a disadvantage making her decisions because her firm was so small? Why or why not?

12. Given the small size of MOM, what type of forecasting method would you suggest Jackson use?

CLOSING SOLUTION

CHRYSLER CORPORATION

Iacocca decided to call all the cars back to fix the faulty washers. The 50 owners had their cars picked up, received a free loaner in the meantime, and had their cars redelivered to their homes after being repaired. The service took only a day. The message apparently got through. Production in 1992 was held to 50,000; with a little less emphasis on quality, 100,000 could have been sold. Sales for the following year were projected at 300,000 and *Automobile Magazine* named the LH threesome 1993 Automobile of the Year. Iacocca's crisis decision, an incalculable gamble at the time, turned out to be a watershed moment for Chrysler.[33]

■ **QUESTIONS FOR CLOSING SOLUTION**

1. Describe how Iacocca avoided the three basic mistakes commonly associated with nonprogrammed decision making.

2. What were the possible consequences if Iacocca had decided not to recall all 4,000 cars?

3. Based on the facts presented in this example, would you characterize Iacocca as a fast or slow decision maker? Why?

Forecast	Sales Force Estimation	**KEY TERMS**
Quantitative Forecasting	Technological Forecasting	
Qualitative Forecasting	Delphi Technique	
Time Series	Scenarios	
Smoothing Methods	Global Mercantilism	
Simple Smoothing Methods	Sustainable World	
Exponential Smoothing	Decision Making	
Trend Line Method	Programmed Decisions	
Causal Methods	Nonprogrammed Decisions	
Causal Forecasting	Systematic Decision Makers	
Econometrics	Intuitive Decision Makers	
The Jury of Exective Opinion	Breakeven Analysis	

Breakeven Chart

Breakeven Point

Linear Programming

Waiting Line/Queuing Techniques

Statistical Decision Theory Techniques

Decision Tree

Expected Value

Creativity

Brainstorming

Double-loop Learning

Advocate Approach

CASE FOR ANALYSIS

AN EMPLOYEE WITH AIDS

Nonprogrammed decision making often means moving into the realm of unpredictability. Such was the case when one of Gary Banas's subordinates said he had AIDS. The repercussions were like a large rock landing in a small pond. No one was unaffected. Banas and his other subordinates witnessed the man go through denial, impaired performance, and declining productivity. High morale vanished. Banas thought he'd done his homework and was prepared to deal with the situation. He wasn't altogether wrong, but then again, he wasn't altogether right either.

"Don't let anyone kid you, when you confront AIDS in the workplace, you will face untenable choices that seem to pit your obligation to humanity against your obligation to your organization. Contrary to popular opinion, you will almost certainly fall short in both areas," he said.

Banas is no neophyte. Much of his education regarding how managers should cope with AIDs dates back to the early 1980s. While a personnel officer for the southwestern district of the comptroller of the currency, he regularly attended and even personally organized instructional seminars on the virus. He considered himself one of the more enlightened personnel directors on the subject. When he was transferred to New York in 1987 he had to turn theory into practice.

A mid-level manager began showing signs of illness. His temperament and physical appearance changed, and his performance declined. After being hospitalized, he told Banas he was suffering from tuberculosis, but expected to recover. When the employee returned to work he related to Banas in confidence that he was HIV-positive.

Without realizing it, Banas had undermined his own position and entered into a no-win bargain. The manager was openly homosexual. The office was already rife with speculation. But because of his pledge, Banas had to sidestep countless inquiries with professed ignorance. No one believed him, and the atmosphere deteriorated.

Banas also had another problem. Absenteeism by the affected manager led to deteriorating productivity within his division. But still bound by his pledge, Banas couldn't tell his own supervisor about the problem. He tried shouldering the additional workload himself, but found he didn't have the time. Having only recently transferred into the new office, he feared his well-intentioned oath of silence might ultimately cost him dearly. Banas finally requested, and received, permission to tell his own supervisor about the manager's illness. His boss was understanding and said he would support whatever decision Banas thought best. Banas departed with a sense of relief. It was short-lived.

The manager's periodic hospitalizations continued and obviously did not go unnoticed. After his announced return from one such stay, workers from his division confronted Banas. Confirmed or not, they believed the manager had AIDS, and they wanted an assurance from Banas that they couldn't catch it at the lavatory or the drinking fountain. Banas allayed their fears about contracting the disease through casual contact without confirming anyone's suspicions. The manager was in the office only a couple of hours before becoming ill and departing again.

Banas felt at times that the complexities of the decisions he faced with his subordinates were insurmountable. The organization has an official policy of making special arrangements for employees. It offers flexible schedules, working at home, and leave sharing, among others. To complicate matters further for Banas, his subordinate was inordinately devoted to his career, to the exclusion of both family and friends. Banas knew terminating him would be arduous and difficult. He also feared it would speed the manager's decline. After the manager returned briefly for the final time, Banas was finally forced to take steps to replace him. To his relief, the manager agreed to a reassignment. He died about three months later. To Banas's knowledge, he never admitted to anyone that he was actually suffering from AIDS.

SOURCE: Gary E. Banas, "Nothing Prepared Me to Manage AIDS," *Harvard Business Review,* July–August 1992, 26–33; Jonathan A. Segal, "HIV: How High the Risk?" *HR Magazine,* February 1993, 93.

■ QUESTIONS

1. Do you think Banas made the right decisions in dealing with the subordinate who was suffering from AIDS? What, if anything, could he have done differently?

2. Which decision-making aids described in this chapter could Banas have used to more effectively handle the situation?

3. Based on the information presented in this case, would you describe Banas as a systematic or intuitive decision maker? Why?

A CASE IN DIVERSITY

WOMEN AND DECISION-MAKING

Not surprisingly, when women first started making their mark on the corporate world, the vast majority emulated the autocratic leadership and decision-making styles of their male counterparts. Doing otherwise would have been viewed as upsetting to the status quo. Perhaps ironically, it is the upheaval in the status quo brought on by global competition that may spell the end of authoritarian management. Many now feel that the typical female executive's strengths lend themselves better to leading today's flatter organizations, encouraging teamwork, and opening up communication channels. "Gone are the days of women succeeding by learning to play men's games," says management guru Tom Peters. "Instead the time has come for men on the move to learn to play women's games."

One of the trendier stereotypes ascribed to women executives and how they manage is that they have a tendency to be consensus builders and mold centrarchies—organizations that put the leader in the center rather than on top. But affixing labels usually starts more fights than it settles. A woman may be characterized as strident, while a man with the same management style is considered decisive. "We ought to concentrate on trying to get different races and sexes to work together without adding to the stereotypes," says Jeffrey Sonnenfeld of the Center for Leadership and Career Studies at Emory business school.

Many women admit to soliciting the opinions of subordinates before making a decision. For example, Frieda Caplan, founder of a California-based marketer of unusual fruits and vegetables, says that when facing a hard decision, she always asks employees what they would do if they were in her shoes. Susan S. Elliott, chief of the computer consultant company Systems Service Enterprises, also believes that this approach makes the most business sense. "I can't come up with a plan and then ask those who manage the accounts to give me their reactions," she says. "They have informa-tion I don't have. Without their input, I'd be operating in an ivory tower." But James Autry, author of *Love & Profit: Art of Caring Leadership,* cautions that a disadvantage to this participatory management style is that women sometimes don't know when to stop gathering information and make a decision. It also opens the door to loss of control. "Decisiveness is an area that I think women could probably learn something from men about," he says.

Determing definitively whether women differ all that radically from men in leadership and decision-making methods will require a lot more research and analysis. It has been pointed out that all managers actually have a lot in common no matter what gender they happen to be. Ultimately, the final arbiter will remain the same: whatever style translates the biggest number to the bottom line. Approximately equal numbers of both genders would probably be a safe bet.

SOURCES: Judy B. Rosener, "Ways Women Lead," *Harvard Business Review,* November–December 1990, 119–25; Sharon Nelton, "Men, Women & Leadership," *Nation's Business,* May 1991, 16–22; Jaclyn Fierman, "Do Women Manage Differently?" *Fortune,* December 17, 1990, 115–18.

■ QUESTIONS

1. What do you consider the pros and cons of the participatory decision making style that often is associated with female executives?
2. If there is a difference in decision-making style between men and women, what do you think is its source?
3. Considering the fast changing pace of the business environment, how can managers best determine which decisions warrant consensus building and which are best made unilaterally?

ENDNOTES

1. "Lee Iacocca's Legacy," *Industry Week,* February 15, 1993, 22.
2. *Webster's Collegiate Dictionary of American English* (New York: Simon & Schuster, Inc., 1988).
3. Thomas E. Milne, *Business Forecasting: A Managerial Approach* (London: Longman, 1975), 2.
4. Thomas W. Moore, *Handbook of Business Forecasting* (New York: Harper & Row, 1989), 5.
5. Murray R. Spiegel, *Statistics* (New York: Schaum Publishing, 1961), 283.
6. See, for example, Thomas W. More, op. cit.
7. George Kress, *Practical Techniques of Business Forecasting,* op. cit., 13.
8. A. Chairncross, quoted in Thomas Milne, *Business Forecasting,* 42.
9. John Chambers, Santinder Mullick, and Donald Smith, "How To Choose the Right Forecasting Technique," *Harvard Business Review,* July–August 1971, 45–74; and Moore, *Handbook of Business Forecasting,* 265–90.
10. Moore, *Handbook of Business Forecasting,* 271.
11. Herman Kahn and Anthony Weiner, *The Year 2000: A Framework for Speculation on the Next Thirty-Three Years* (New York: Macmillan, 1967), 6; quoted in George A. Steiner, *Strategic Planning: What Every Manager Must Know* (New York: The Free Press, 1979), 237.
12. Adam Kahane, "Scenarios for Energy: Sustainable World vs. Global Mercantilism," *Long Range Planning,* vol. 25, no. 4 (1992), 38–46.

13. See Herbert Simon, *The New Science of Management Decision* (Englewood Cliffs, NJ: Prentice-Hall, 1971), 45–47; Hillel Einhorn and Robin Hogarth, "Decision Making: Going Forward in Reverse," *Harvard Business Review,* January–February 1987, 66–70; and Richard Kates, "The Gordian Knot: A Parable for Decision Makers," *Management Review,* vol. 79, December 1990, 47–48. For an overview on the decision-making process, see Henry Mintzberg, James Waters, Andrew Pettigrew, and Richard Butler, "Studying Deciding: An Exchange of Views," *Organizational Studies,* vol. 11, no. 1 (1990), 1–16.

14. Henry Mintzberg, Duru Raisinghani, and Andrea Theoret, "The Structure of Unstructured Decision Processes," *Administrative Science Quarterly,* vol. 21, June 1976, 246–75. As one study suggests, at least in small business the top manager may be inclined to use the same decision-making approach for both programmed and nonprogrammed decisions. See Necmi Karagozoglu and Joel Knowles, "Impact of Behavioral Inertia on Strategic Decision Making in Small Business," *International Journal of Management,* vol. 8, no. 2, September 1991, 623–30.

15. See, for example, Gary Dessler, *Winning Commitment: How Top Companies Get and Keep a Competitive Workforce* (New York: McGraw-Hill, 1993), 1–18.

16. James McKenney and Peter Keen, "How Managers Minds Work," *Harvard Business Review,* May–June 1979, 74–90; and Herbert A. Simon, "Making Management Decisions: The Role of Intuition and Emotion," *Academy of Management Executive,* February 1987, 59–60.

17. Henry Mintzberg, "Planning on the Left Side and Managing on the Right Side," *Harvard Business Review,* July–August 1976), 49–58; and W.H. Agor, "The Logic of Intuition: How Top Executives Make Important Decisions," *Organizational Dynamics,* Winter 1986, 5. To make risky decisions, a manager must also have a high level of self-confidence. See, for example, R. Dwayne Ireland, Michael Hitt, and Jay Clifton Williams, "Self-Confidence and Decisiveness: Prerequisites for Effective Management in the 1990s," *Business Horizons,* vol. 35, no. 1, January–February 1992, 36–43.

18. William Taggart and Dan Robey, "Minds and Managers: On the Dual Nature of Human Information Processing and Management," *The Academy of Management Review,* vol. 6, (1981), 187–95; and Orlando Behling and N.L. Eckel, "Making Sense Out of Intuition," *Academy of Management Executive,* February 1991, 46–47.

19. Mintzberg, "Planning on the Left Side." For a recent discussion of the use of intuition in management, see Jagdish Parikh, *Intuition: The New Frontier of Management* (Cambridge, MA.: Blackwell, 1994).

20. For a discussion, see James Van Horne, *Fundamentals of Financial Management* (Englewood Cliffs, NJ: Prentice-Hall, 1977), 161.

21. Maurice Sasieni, Arthur Yaspan, and Lawrence Friedman, *Operations Research* (New York: John Wiley, 1959), 183; and David Cowan, "The Effect of Decision Making Styles and Conceptual Experience on Executives Description of Organizational Problem Formulation," *Journal of Management Studies,* vol. 28, no. 5, September 1991, 463–83.

22. From *Prentice-Hall Encyclopedic Dictionary of Systems and Procedures* (Englewood Cliffs, NJ: Prentice-Hall, 1966), 364: and Donald Mosley, Fabius O'Brien, and Paul Pietri, "Problem Solving Styles Determine Managers' Approach to Making Decisions," *Industrial Management,* vol. 33, no. 5, September–October 1991.

23. Ian Mitroff and James Emshoff, "On Strategic Assumption Making: A Dialectical Approach to Policy and Planning," *Academy of Management Review,* vol. 4 (1979), 2–3.

24. Chris Argyris, "Theories of Actions That Inhibit Individual Learning," *American Psychologists,* September 1976, 638–54; Chris Argyris, "Double Loop Learning in Organizations," *Harvard Business Review,* vol. 15, September–October 1977, 115–25; Ann Langley, "Patterns in the Use of Formal Analysis in Strategic Decisions," *Organization Studies,* vol. 11, no. 1 (1990), 17–45; and William Silver and Terence Mitchell, "The Status Quo Tendency and Decision Making," *Organizational Dynamics,* vol. 18, no. 4, Spring 1990, 34–46.

25. Argyris, "Double Loop Learning," 115.

26. Larry Cummings, Bernard Hinton, and Bruce Gobdel, "Creative Behavior As a Function of Past Environment: Impact of Objectives, Procedures, and Controls," *Academy of Management Journal,* vol. 18, September 1975, 489–99; and Charlene Solomon, "What an Idea: Creativity Training," *Personnel Journal,* May 1990.

27. Chris Argyris and Donald Schon, *Organizational Learning* (Reading, MA: Addison-Wesley).

28. Ian Mitroff and James Emshoff, "On Strategic Assumption Making: A Dialectical Approach to Policy and Planning," *Academy of Msanagement Review,* vol. 4, no. 1, January 1979, 5; for a discussion of a strongly opposing view, see J. Scott Armstrong, "Advocacy as a Scientific Strategy: The Mitroff Myth," *The Academy of Management Review,* vol. 5, no. 4, October 1980, 513–16. For an interesting comparison of systematic vs. intuitive decision makers, see Russ Holloman, "The Light and Dark Sides of Decision Making," *Supervisory Management,* vol. 34, no. 12, December 1989, 33–34.

29. For a discussion on this, see Tom Peters, *Liberation Management* (New York: Random House, 1992) 90–91.

30. "Corporate Decision Making," *Economist,* September 8, 1990, 87–88.

31. Kathleen Eisenhardt, "Speed and Strategic Choice: How Managers Accelerate Decision Making," *California Management Review,* Spring 1990; 39–52; discussed in Peters, *Liberation Management,* 42–43.

32. Eisenhardt, "Speed and Strategic Choice," op cit.

33. "Lee Iacocca's Legacy," op cit.

CHAPTER 8

FUNDAMENTALS OF ORGANIZING

LEARNING OBJECTIVES

After studying this chapter, you should be able to:

- Give examples of how departments are created around functions, product divisions, customers, marketing channels, and geographical areas.

- Describe a matrix organization and the various benefits and drawbacks of this form of departmentalization.

- Give practical examples of hybrid departmentalization in organizations.

- Explain the process of coordination among interdependent company functions, the purpose of coordination in achieving company goals, and the various types of intracompany coordination.

- Identify the sources of organizational authority.

- Describe the process of delegation.

- Compare and contrast tall and flat organizational structures.

Johnson & Johnson is a huge and complex organization. It is made up of nearly 83,000 employees in 166 divisions; its products range from birth control pills to contact lenses, and from microsurgical gear to athlete's foot medicine. Its division presidents are known for their creative abilities and maverick tendencies; some meet with bosses at headquarters as seldom as four times a year. ■ How can the activities of such a disparate organization be effectively coordinated? How can the inevitable redundancies in operating so many separate businesses be avoided, or at least minimized? These are two of the organizational issues now facing chief executive officer Ralph S. Larsen.

SOME BASIC TERMS

There are possibly as many different types of organizations as there are companies in the world. Johnson & Johnson is an example of a huge, highly decentralized organization that produces a wide array of products, and does so successfully. Division presidents are given operational latitude to make key decisions on everything from budgeting to marketing. But the entire operation is tightly coordinated from the top.

Organizing means arranging the activities of the enterprise in such a way that they systematically contribute to the enterprise's goals. An **organization** consists of people who carry out differentiated tasks, which are coordinated to contribute to the organization's goals.

The usual way of depicting an organization is with an **organization chart** as shown in Figure 8.1. The organization chart depicts the structure of the organization, in particular the title of each manager's position and, by means of connecting lines, who is accountable to whom and who is in charge of what department.

The organization chart also shows the chain of command (sometimes called the scalar chain or the line of authority) between the top of the organization and the lowest positions in the organization chart. The chain of command represents the path a directive should take in traveling from the president to employees at the bottom of organization chart or from employees at the bottom to the top of the organization chart.

THE INFORMAL ORGANIZATION

One thing the organization chart does not show is the informal organization that has evolved in the enterprise.

The **informal organization** means the informal, habitual contacts, communications, and ways of doing things that employees always develop. Thus a salesperson might develop the habit of calling a production supervisor in the plant to check on the status of an order. The salesperson might find this route quicker than taking the time to go through the chain of command (by having the sales manager check with the plant manager who in turn checks with the supervisor).

CREATING DEPARTMENTS

Every enterprise must carry out various activities in order to accomplish its goals. In a company, these activities might include manufacturing, selling, and accounting. In a city, they might include the activities of public service agencies like the fire, police, and health protection departments. In a hospital, they including nursing, medical services, and radiology. **Departmentalization** is the process through which an enterprise's activities are grouped together and assigned to managers. It is the organization-wide division of work. It results in *departments*—logical groupings of activities—which also often go by the name *divisions, branches, units,* or *sections.*

The basic question in departmentalization is, around what activities should we organize departments? For example, should departments be established for sales and manufacturing? Or should there be separate departments for industrial and retail customers, each of which then has its own sales and manufacturing units? As we'll see next, many options are available.

ORGANIZING
To arrange the activities of the enterprise in such a way that they systematically contribute to the enterprise's goals.

ORGANIZATION
People who carry out differentiated tasks, which are coordinated to contribute to the organization's goals.

ORGANIZATION CHART
Depicts the structure of the organization, in particular the title of each manager's position and, by means of connecting lines, who is accountable to whom and who is in charge of what department.

INFORMAL ORGANIZATION
Informal contacts, communications, and ways of doing things that employees develop.

DEPARTMENTALIZATION
The process through which an enterprise's activities are grouped together and assigned to managers.

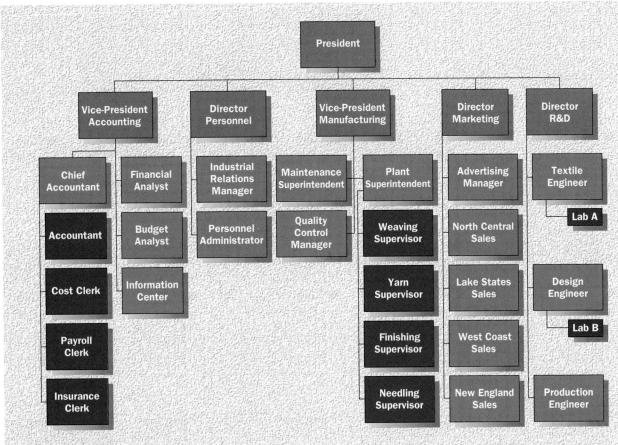

FIGURE 8.1

Organization Chart for a Textile Company

An organization chart like this one shows the title of each manager's position and the departments they manage, as well as who reports to whom.

SOURCE: Richard Daft, *Management*, 3rd ed. (Fort Worth: The Dryden Press, 1994), 292.

CREATING DEPARTMENTS AROUND FUNCTIONS

Functional departmentalization means grouping activities around essential functions such as manufacturing, sales, and finance. This is illustrated in Figure 8.2, which shows the organization structure for the BMW car company. This figure illustrates functional departmentalization by showing how each department is organized around a different business function, in this case sales, finance, and production. At BMW, the production director reports to the chairman and other members of the managing board. He or she manages BMW's domestic production plants and its one foreign-based assembly plant. On the other hand, note that the sales function is divided into domestic sales and overseas sales. One manager is responsible for the domestic market sales. The second is in charge of sales of overseas subsidiaries, including the considerable sales of the firm's U.S. sales company.[1]

FUNCTIONAL DEPARTMENTALIZATION
Grouping activities around essential functions such as manufacturing, sales, and finance.

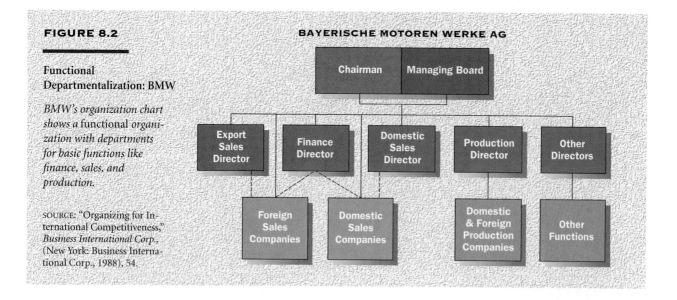

FIGURE 8.2

Functional
Departmentalization: BMW

*BMW's organization chart
shows a functional organization with departments
for basic functions like
finance, sales, and
production.*

SOURCE: "Organizing for International Competitiveness,"
Business International Corp.,
(New York: Business International Corp., 1988), 54.

Service businesses can be built around business functions, too. For example, the
basic business functions around which banks are often departmentalized include operations, control, and loans. Similarly, in a hospital, the "business functions" might
include nursing, medical services, and radiology.

Some firms organize around managerial functions or technological functions.
Building departments around managerial functions means putting supervisors in
charge of departments for management functions like planning, control, and administration. As illustrated in Figure 8.3, departmentalization based on technological functions means the grouping together of activities such as plating, welding, or assembling.
Again, the basic idea of any functional departmentalization is to group activities
around the elemental functions that the enterprise must carry out.

ADVANTAGES AND DISADVANTAGES   Organizing departments around functions has several advantages. It is a simple, straightforward, and logical way to organize. This is because it makes sense to build departments around the basic functions
the enterprise must engage in. Functional organizations also usually have single large
departments for activities like sales, production, and finance that serve all the company's products. As a result, the volume of business done in each department is relatively
high. With this volume typically comes increasing returns to scale—in other words,
employees become more proficient (from doing the same job over and over again),
and the company can afford larger plants and more efficient equipment, for instance.
There also tends to be less duplication of effort in functional organizations. This is
because the same production, sales, and personnel departments typically serve all the
firm's products; a firm does not create separate production, sales, and personnel
departments for each of its products. As a result of advantages like these, functional
organizations are often associated with greater efficiency.

Functional organization has several other advantages. The managers' duties in each
of the functional departments tend to be more specialized (a manager may specialize
in finance or production, for instance); the enterprise therefore need not recruit or
train many general managers—those with the breadth of experience to administer several functions at once. This specialization can simplify both recruiting and training.
Department managers in functional organizations also tend to get information on only

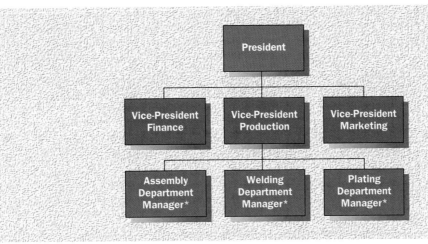

FIGURE 8.3

Departmentalization Based on Technology

This chart shows a special type of functional organization called a technological functional organization, with separate departments for technological functions such as assembly and welding.

part of the "big picture" of the company, that which concerns each manager's own specialized function. This can make it easier for top management to exercise tight control over the activities of department managers.

Functional organizations also have disadvantages. Responsibility for the overall performance of the enterprise lies on the shoulders of one person, usually the president. After all, he or she may be the only one in a position to coordinate the work of the functional departments, each of which is only one element in producing and supplying the company's product or service. This may not be a serious problem when the firm is small or does not work with a lot of products. But as size and diversity of products increase, the job of coordinating, say, production, sales, and finance for many different products may prove too great for one person. At this point, the enterprise could lose its responsiveness. Also, while the tendency for functional departments to result in specialized managers (finance experts, production experts, and so forth) may increase their proficiency, it also makes it more difficult to develop managers with the breadth of experience needed to promote them to general management jobs like that of president. These advantages and disadvantages are summarized in Table 8.1.

CREATING PRODUCT DIVISIONS

With product departmentalization, departments are organized for each of the company's products or for each family of products. Therefore, department heads in this type

ADVANTAGES	DISADVANTAGES	**TABLE 8.1**
1. Managers are functionally specialized and therefore more efficient.	1. Responsibility for overall performance lies with chief executive only.	Advantages and Disadvantages of Functional Departmentalization
2. Less duplication of effort than in other types.	2. Can overburden chief executive.	
3. Increased returns to scale.	3. Reduces the attention paid to specific products, customers, markets, or areas.	
4. Training is simplified.	4. Results in functionally specialized managers rather than "general" managers.	
5. Simple and proven over time.		
6. Facilitates tight control by chief executive.		

DIVISIONALIZATION (PRODUCT DEPARTMENTALIZATION)
A form of organization in which the firm's major departments are organized so that each can manage all the activities needed to develop, manufacture, and sell a particular product or product line.

of organization are responsible for both producing and marketing a product or family of products. Figure 8.4 shows the organization chart of the Gillette Company. As you can see, a vice-chairman heads Gillette North Atlantic. Three product divisions report to this person, one for blades and razors, one for personal care products, and one for stationery products. Each of these three product divisions then has it's own staff for activities such as production and sales.

Arranging departments around products in this way is often called **divisionalization**. Divisionalization is when the firm's major departments are organized so that each can manage all the activities needed to develop, manufacture, and sell a particular product or product line. The head of such a division usually has functional departments—say, for production, sales, and personnel—reporting to him or her. To that extent, each of these product divisions is thus *self-contained*. Each has control of all or most of the resources needed to create, produce, and supply its product or products.

ADVANTAGES AND DISADVANTAGES Divisionalization can be advantageous. A single manager and department are charged with overseeing all the functions required to produce and market each product. As a result, each product division tends to be more sensitive and responsive to the needs of its particular product or product line. Thus the manager in charge of Gillette's blade and razor group has his or her own blade and razor research, manufacturing, and sales departments. As a result, his or her division could usually respond quickly when, for instance, a competitor brings out a new and innovative razor. This is because the manager would not have to rely on (or seek the approval of) research, manufacturing, or sales managers who are not within his or her own division. This type of organization is therefore appropriate where quick, responsive decisions and flexibility (rather than efficiency) are paramount. The *Xerox* vignette (on page 212) provides an example.

Divisionalization also has other advantages. First, performance is more easily judged. If a division is doing well (or is not doing well), it is clear who is responsible, since one person is managing the whole division. Related to this, being put in charge of the "whole ballgame" can help motivate the manager to perform better. These self-contained divisions can also be good training grounds for an enterprise's future executives because they are exposed to a wider range of problems, from production and sales to personnel and finance. Finally, divisionalization can help shift some of the management burden from the top management to division executives. For example, imagine if Gillette's president had to coordinate the tasks of designing, producing, and marketing each of Gillette's many products, which range from Gillette razors to Papermate pens. The diversity of problems he or she would face would be enormous. Therefore, virtually all very large companies with diverse products and customers have divisionalized.[2]

Organizing around divisions also creates disadvantages. For one thing, divisions breed duplication of effort. The fact that each product division is self-contained implies that there are several production plants instead of one, several sales forces instead of one, and so on, since each product division often has its own. Such duplication is very expensive. Furthermore, the company's customers (such as a drugstore) may become annoyed at being visited by salespeople representing different divisions.

Divisionalization can also diminish top management's control. The division heads often have great autonomy, since they are in charge of all phases of producing and marketing their products. Top management therefore tends to have less control over each division's day-to-day activities. For example, a division might run up huge expenses before top management discovers there is a problem. In fact, striking a balance

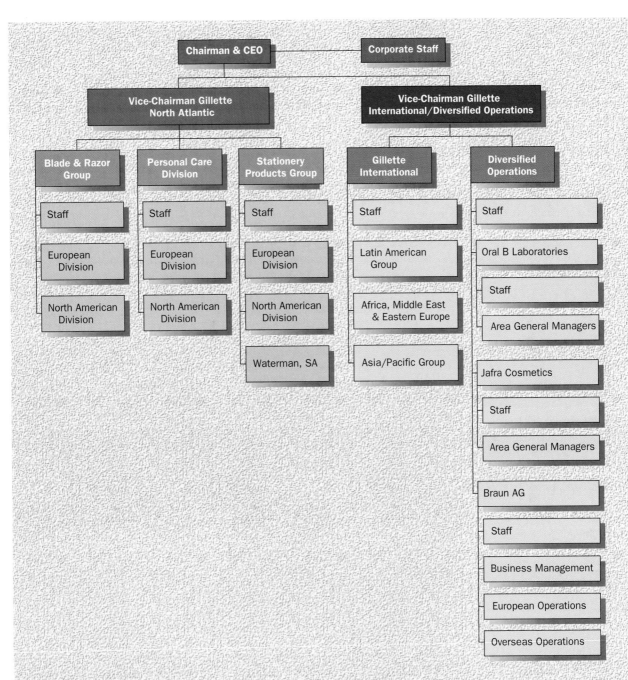

FIGURE 8.4

Product Departmentalization: Gillette Company

In a product departmentalization like this one, separate departments or divisions are set up for products—in this case, blades and razors, personal care, and stationery.

SOURCE: "Organizing for International Competitiveness," *Business International Corp.* (New York: Business Corp., 1988), 77.

XEROX

Up until the early 1990s, Xerox was organized around functions such as sales, manufacturing, and R&D. But in 1992, the company decided to set up operations in a way that would place heavier emphasis on what Xerox considered its primary target: the customer. These customers consist of individuals, small businesses, office document systems, and engineering systems, among others. The new organizational structure is built around product divisions, and established nine businesses (such as duplicating) to go after the various customers. Manufacturing plants were altered so that different factories could produce especially for specific business and customers.

Chief executive officer Paul Allaire calls the building blocks of these team-led businesses "microenterprise units." "We've given everyone in the company a direct line of sight to the customer," he says.

SOURCE: Thomas A. Stewart, "Are You Flat, Lean, and Ready for a Bold New Look? Try High-Performance Teams, Redesigned Work, and Unbridled Information," *Fortune,* May 18, 1992, 42–44.

Xerox facilities, like this copier cartridge plant in Rochester, NY, were reorganized in 1992 to produce for specific customers and businesses. Employees are encouraged to think of the customer first.

between providing each division head with enough autonomy to run the division and still maintaining top management control is crucial.

Divisionalization also requires managers with general management abilities. Because each product division is, in a sense, a miniature company, each has its own production plant, sales force, personnel department, and so forth. Therefore, divisional managers cannot just be sales, production, or personnel specialists.

Advantages and disadvantages of product (divisionalization) departmentalization are summarized in Table 8.2.

CREATING CUSTOMER DEPARTMENTS

Customer departmentalization is similar to organizing around product divisions except that departments are organized to serve the needs of specific groups of customers. Figure 8.5, for instance, shows the organization chart for the Alcoa Aluminum Company. Notice how the company's main divisions are organized to serve the needs of particular customers, such as metals and chemicals customers, packaging systems customers, aerospace and industrial customers, and the international group.

CUSTOMER DEPARTMENTALIZATION
Similar to organizing around product divisions except that departments are organized to serve the needs of specific groups of customers.

ADVANTAGES AND DISADVANTAGES This method has several advantages. As with product divisionalization, a manager is charged with giving his or her continuous, undivided attention to a customer or group of customers. This can result in faster, more satisfactory service to each of the company's customers, particularly when their needs are substantially different. However, as with product departmentalization, the main disadvantage is duplication of effort. The company may have several production plants instead of one and several sales managers instead of one, each serving the needs of its own customers. This can reduce overall corporate efficiency.

CREATING MARKETING CHANNEL DEPARTMENTS

With **marketing-channel departmentalization,** top-level departments are organized around each of the firm's marketing channels. A marketing channel is the conduit (wholesaler, drugstore, grocery, or the like) through which a manufacturer distributes its products to its ultimate customers. This is a third type of divisional departmentalization (the others are product and customer departmentalization).

MARKETING-CHANNEL DEPARTMENTALIZATION
Top-level departments are organized around each of the firm's marketing channels—conduits through which a manufacturer distributes its products to its ultimate customers.

ADVANTAGES	DISADVANTAGES	TABLE 8.2
1. One unit responsible for giving continuous, undivided attention to the product, so unit is more sensitive and responsive to unique needs of the product.	1. Duplication of effort, perhaps reduced efficiency. In some situations, customers may also be bothered by representatives of more than one division.	Advantages/Disadvantages of Product Departmentalization
2. Lifts part of the burden from shoulders of top manager.	2. Finding and training people to head each division is a more difficult job.	
3. Performance more easily identified and judged; this in turn may motivate performance.	3. Since division heads now do their own coordinating without checking with top manager, the latter could begin to lose control. He or she no longer coordinates and oversees the day-to-day *activities* by which managers do their jobs, just the *ends*—like whether or not division makes a profit at the end of the year.	
4. Provide good training ground for future top executives.		

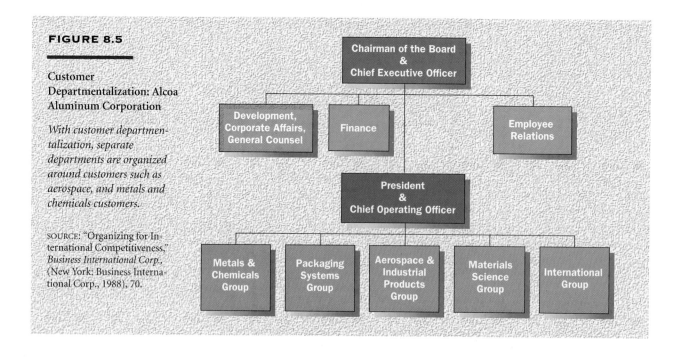

FIGURE 8.5

Customer
Departmentalization: Alcoa
Aluminum Corporation

*With customer departmen-
talization, separate
departments are organized
around customers such as
aerospace, and metals and
chemicals customers.*

SOURCE: "Organizing for International Competitiveness,"
Business International Corp.,
(New York: Business International Corp., 1988), 70.

Marketing-channel departmentalization is illustrated in Figure 8.6. As you can see, it is similar to customer departmentalization, but there are several differences. In customer departmentalization, each customer-oriented department is usually responsible for both manufacturing and selling its own product to its own customers. In marketing-channel departmentalization, the same product (such as Ivory Soap) is typically marketed through two or more channels. Then, a decision is usually made as to

The brand-name products you see on this drugstore shelf may also appear on the shelf in your supermarket or your local cost-cutting warehouse.

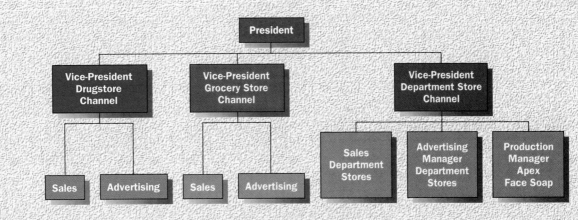

FIGURE 8.6

Marketing Channel Departmentalization

With marketing channels, the main departments are organized to focus on particular marketing channels such as drugstores and grocery stores.

NOTE: Only the department-store channel produces the soap, and each channel may sell to the same ultimate consumers.

which department will manufacture the product for all the other marketing-channel departments.

Organizing around marketing channels assumes that it is the marketing channel's unique needs (rather than the ultimate customer's needs) that must be catered to. For example, Revlon may sell through both department stores and discount drugstores. Yet the demands of these two channels are quite different: the department store may want Revlon to supply specially trained sales people to run concessions in its stores, for instance. The discount druggist may just want quick delivery and minimum inventories. Putting a manager and department in charge of each channel can help ensure that such diverse needs are met quickly and satisfactorily. As with product and customer departmentalization, the resulting duplication—in this case, of sales forces—is a main disadvantage.

CREATING DEPARTMENTS BASED ON GEOGRAPHIC AREAS

With geographic or territorial departmentalization, separate departments are organized for each of the territories in which the enterprise does business. As with product, customer, and marketing-channel organizations, territorial departments are examples of divisional departmentalization: each geographic area often has its own production, sales, and personnel activities. Territorial departmentalization is illustrated in Figure 8.7, which shows the organization chart of Alcoa Aluminum's international group. Notice that the group vice-president, international, has separate managing directors reporting to him or her, each for a different geographic area including Australia, Mexico, and Europe.

FIGURE 8.7

Geographic Organization: Alcoa Aluminum Co.

This is one possibility for a geographic organization with separate departments for geographic areas, such as Europe and Asia.

SOURCE: "Organizing for International Competitiveness," *Business International Corp.* (New York: Business International Corp., 1988), 70.

ADVANTAGES AND DISADVANTAGES   As with other types of divisional organizations, the main advantage of territorial departmentalization is that one self-contained department is charged with focusing on the needs of its particular buyers—in this case, those in its geographic area. This can lead to speedier, more responsive and satisfactory service. Thus, a department store chain such as J.C. Penney's might organize territorially so as to best cater to the tastes and needs of customers in each geographic area. Like product, customer, and marketing-channel departmentalization, territorial departmentalization is advantageous insofar as it ensures quick, responsive reaction to the needs of the company's clients. Also like these forms, however, territorial departmentalization may suffer in duplication of effort. And, again, these types of divisions need to hire and train general managers capable of managing several functions (like production, sales, and personnel).

CREATING MATRIX ORGANIZATIONS

MATRIX ORGANIZATION (MATRIX MANAGEMENT)
Superimposing one or more forms of departmentalization on top of an existing one.

A **matrix organization** (also known as matrix management) is defined as superimposing one or more forms of departmentalization on top of an existing one.[3] In one familiar form, illustrated in Figure 8.8, product departments are superimposed over a functional departmentalization. This company's automotive products division is functionally organized, with departments for functions like production, engineering, and personnel. But superimposed over this functional departmentalization are three product groups—for the Ford project, Chrysler project, and GM project. Each of these product groups has its own product manager (or project leader). One or more employees from each functional department (like production and engineering) are temporarily assigned to each project.

Dual reporting along product and geographic lines is another common matrix approach.[4] For example, one bank is organized geographically with separate officers

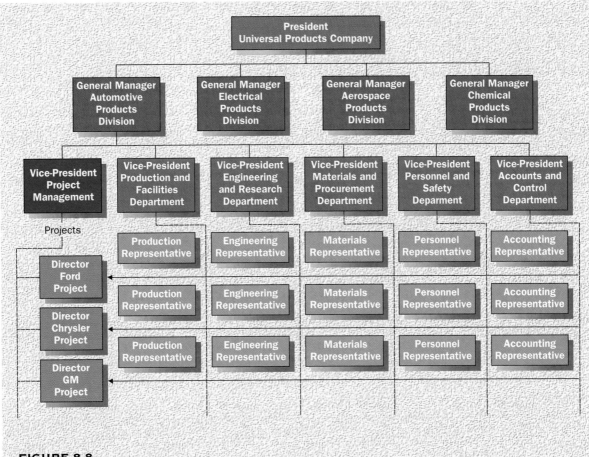

FIGURE 8.8

Matrix Departmentalization

With a matrix organization, a project structure is often superimposed over a functional organization.

in charge of the bank's operations in each of several countries. At the same time, the bank has a product or customer structure superimposed over this geographic organization. For example, project heads at headquarters for, say, major bank customers such as IBM lead teams comprised of bank employees from each country who concentrate on the local and worldwide financial interests of IBM.

Some matrix organizations are more formal than others. Sometimes informal liaisons or temporary project managers are assigned to provide coordination across functional departments with regard to some product or project or customer. Other firms formalize their matrix organizations, sometimes by adding a matrix director to assist each of the project managers and a semi-permanent administrative structure (including, for instance, project employee appraisal forms) to help build the project teams' authority.[5]

Matrix organizations have proved successful. They have been used successfully by a wide range of companies, including Citicorp Bank, TRW Systems, NASA and many of its subcontractors, UNICEF, and various accounting, law, and security firms, to name a few.[6]

ADVANTAGES AND DISADVANTAGES Matrix departmentalization has several advantages. A self-contained department can devote its undivided attention to the needs of its own project, product, or customer; yet the entire organization need not be permanently organized around what may turn out to be temporary projects. Another advantage is that management avoids having to establish duplicate functional departments for each of the several projects.

However, matrix organizations are also subject to problems that, while avoidable, are potentially serious. These problems can be summarized as follows:

- **Power struggles and conflicts.** The potential exists for power struggles and conflicts between managers who head the functional and project groups. Since authority tends to be more ambiguous and up for grabs in a matrix organization, such struggles may be more commonplace in matrix than in traditional organization structures.

- **Time consuming.** Matrix organizations tend to result in more intragroup meetings and therefore often seem to be indecisive and time consuming.

- **Excessive overhead.** Research indicates that matrix organizations may tend to raise costs as the overhead caused by hiring more managers and secretaries rises.

DEPARTMENTALIZATION IN PRACTICE: A HYBRID

Most enterprises actually use several forms of departmentalization: in other words, they are hybrids. For example, top management might decide to establish functional departments for production, sales, and finance. They then break the sales department into geographic areas, with separate sales managers for the north, east, south, and west.

An example of this type of hybrid is presented in Figure 8.9, which shows the IBM corporate organization. This is basically a divisional structure, with separate departments organized around personal systems, business systems, programming systems, and so forth. However, IBM also uses territorial departmentalization, for instance, with separate officers in charge of Asia, Japan, and the Middle East. As is usually the case with divisional structures, headquarters departments are also organized around managerial functions (general counsel, finance and planning, and law, for instance).

ACHIEVING COORDINATION

THE NATURE AND PURPOSE OF COORDINATION

COORDINATION

The process of achieving unity of action among interdependent activities.

Coordination is the process of achieving unity of action among interdependent activities. Coordination is required whenever two or more interdependent individuals, groups, or departments must work together to achieve a common goal.

In organizations, some departments are more interdependent than others, and so the difficulty of achieving coordination varies from situation to situation.[7] Some departments are highly interdependent. For example, review the BMW organization chart in Figure 8.2. Notice that there are separate directors for the sales, finance, and production functions. To produce a shiny new BMW 750, each department's activities must be closely coordinated by the chairman and managing board. For example, if the sales director projects sales of 50,000 units next year, then the production director must take steps to produce that many cars, and the finance director must be sure that the

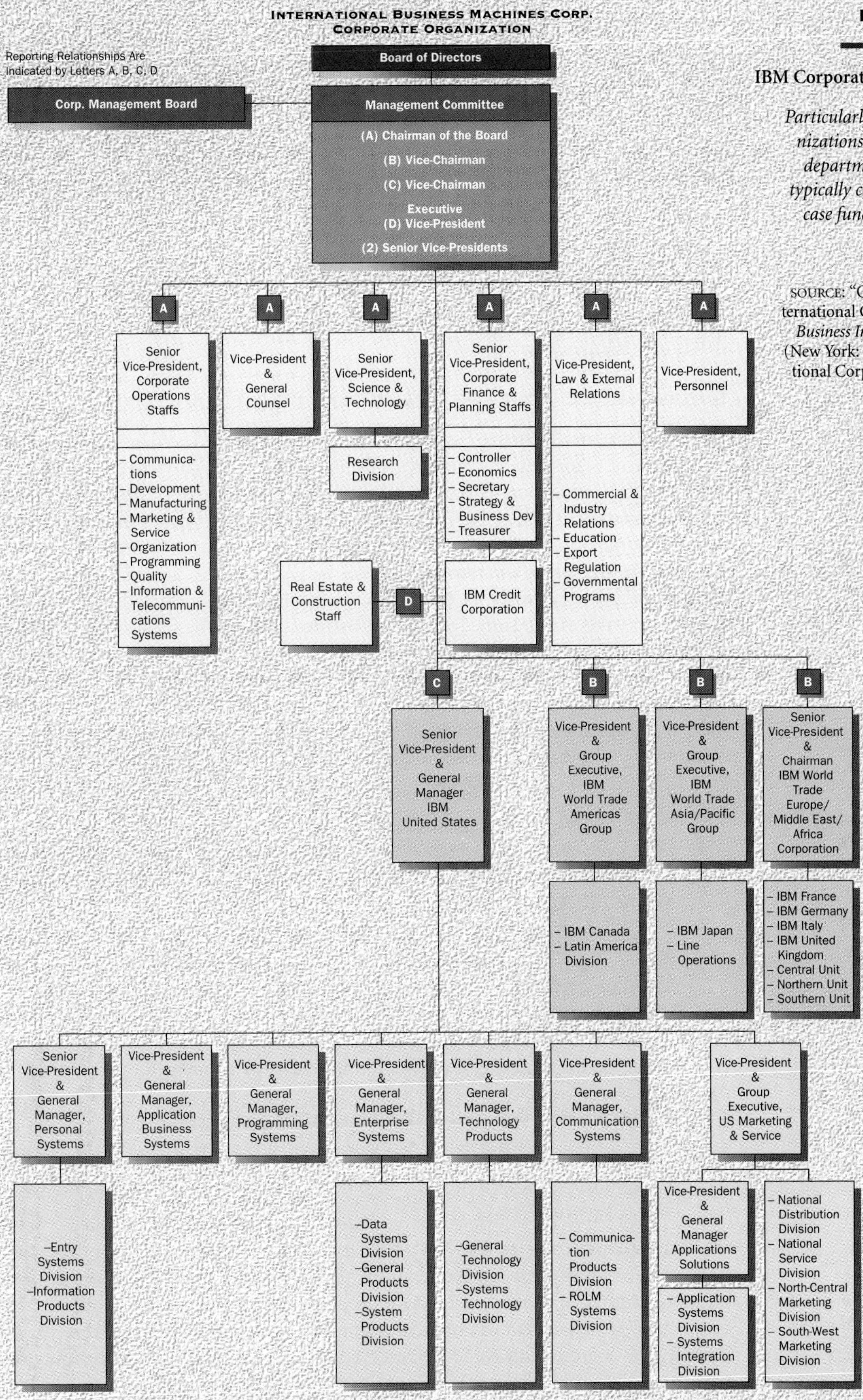

INTERNATIONAL BUSINESS MACHINES CORP. CORPORATE ORGANIZATION

FIGURE 8.9

Reporting Relationships Are indicated by Letters A, B, C, D

Corp. Management Board

Board of Directors

Management Committee

(A) Chairman of the Board

(B) Vice-Chairman

(C) Vice-Chairman

Executive (D) Vice-President

(2) Senior Vice-Presidents

IBM Corporate Organization

Particularly in larger organizations, several types of departmentalization are typically combined, in this case functional, product, and geographic.

SOURCE: "Organizing for International Competitiveness," *Business International Corp.* (New York: Business International Corp., 1988), 108–09.

(A) Senior Vice-President, Corporate Operations Staffs

(A) Vice-President & General Counsel

(A) Senior Vice-President, Science & Technology

(A) Senior Vice-President, Corporate Finance & Planning Staffs

(A) Vice-President, Law & External Relations

(A) Vice-President, Personnel

- Communications
- Development
- Manufacturing
- Marketing & Service
- Organization
- Programming
- Quality
- Information & Telecommunications Systems

Research Division

- Controller
- Economics
- Secretary
- Strategy & Business Dev
- Treasurer

- Commercial & Industry Relations
- Education
- Export Regulation
- Governmental Programs

Real Estate & Construction Staff **(D)** IBM Credit Corporation

(C) Senior Vice-President & General Manager IBM United States

(B) Vice-President & Group Executive, IBM World Trade Americas Group

(B) Vice-President & Group Executive, IBM World Trade Asia/Pacific Group

(B) Senior Vice-President & Chairman IBM World Trade Europe/Middle East/Africa Corporation

- IBM Canada
- Latin America Division

- IBM Japan
- Line Operations

- IBM France
- IBM Germany
- IBM Italy
- IBM United Kingdom
- Central Unit
- Northern Unit
- Southern Unit

Senior Vice-President & General Manager, Personal Systems

Vice-President & General Manager, Application Business Systems

Vice-President & General Manager, Programming Systems

Vice-President & General Manager, Enterprise Systems

Vice-President & General Manager, Technology Products

Vice-President & General Manager, Communication Systems

Vice-President & Group Executive, US Marketing & Service

-Entry Systems Division
-Information Products Division

-Data Systems Division
-General Products Division
-System Products Division

-General Technology Division
-Systems Technology Division

-Communication Products Division
- ROLM Systems Division

Vice-President & General Manager Applications Solutions

- National Distribution Division
- National Service Division
- North-Central Marketing Division
- South-West Marketing Division

- Application Systems Division
- Systems Integration Division

funds are available to produce and sell that many cars. Therefore, the chairman and his or her managing board must coordinate closely with each of these functional departments.

At the other extreme, the work of some departments in some organizations involves almost no interdependence. For example, the separate customer divisions established by Alcoa (see Figure 8.5) are each pretty much self-contained. In other words, each division—such as those for metals and chemicals, packaging systems, and aerospace—has its own research, production, and sales units. In such a divisionalized organization, each division can be managed more or less as an independent, autonomous business. Here, the job of achieving coordination between the autonomous divisions would be relatively simple, since it is not essential for the divisions to work in unison on most day-to-day matters.

HISTORICAL PERSPECTIVE ON COORDINATION

Early management theorists recognized the importance of coordination and considered it one of management's main responsibilities. Henri Fayol viewed it as the binding together of individual efforts to accomplish a common objective, and he identified coordination as one of the five major management functions. Mooney and Reilly defined coordination as "the orderly arrangement of group effort, to provide unity of action in the pursuit of a common purpose" and called it the "first principle of management in that it expresses the principles of organization in toto: nothing less."[8] Most of these early theorists assumed that coordination could best be achieved by just adhering to the chain of command.[9] In other words, the proper way to achieve coordination between the production and sales departments was to refer problems and requests for information up the chain of command to the president to whom both these department managers reported. Although these early theorists saw that other forms of coordination might sometimes be required, these were viewed as exceptions to the rule and as indications of a poorly designed organization. As Gulick pointed out in "Notes on the Theory of Organization":

> In discussions thus far, it has been assumed that the normal method of interdepartmental coordination is hierarchical in its operation . . . in actual practice, there are also other means of interdepartmental coordination which must be regarded as part of the organization as such. . . . [But] whenever an organization needs continual resort to [such] special coordinating devices in the discharge of its regular work, this is proof that the organization is bad . . .[10]

Prescriptions such as these worked fairly well as long as abnormal situations were not the rule. The problem today is that unforeseen events and surprises have indeed become the rule. Depending on the chain of command can thus take too much time. New techniques for achieving coordination have therefore emerged.

TECHNIQUES FOR ACHIEVING COORDINATION

Theorists Jay Galbraith[11] and Henry Mintzberg,[12] working independently, have developed descriptions of the techniques managers use to achieve coordination. These techniques are summarized next.

MUTUAL ADJUSTMENT
Achieving coordination through interpersonal communication.

COORDINATION THROUGH MUTUAL ADJUSTMENT   According to Mintzberg, **mutual adjustment** achieves coordination by relying on interpersonal communication. Mutual adjustment is used for coordination in both the simplest and most complex of situations. For example, in a simple situation such as two people moving a heavy log, coordination could be achieved by just having one person count "one, two, three, lift," at which time both people lift the log in unison.

But mutual adjustment is also used in the most complex of situations. In these cases the situation changes so quickly and the work to be done is so unpredictable that standard procedures and following the chain of command will not suffice. A platoon of marines planning its attack, for instance, may follow formal procedures and stick to the chain of command. But when the marines hit the beach, most coordination will likely take place through an ongoing process of mutual adjustment as the group attempts to respond to problems as they arise.

COORDINATION BY RULES OR PROCEDURES: STANDARDIZATION OF WORK PROCESSES If the work to be done is predictable and can be planned for in advance, a supervisor can specify ahead of time what actions his or her subordinates should take. *Rules and procedures* are thus useful for coordinating routine, recurring activities. They specify in detail, ahead of time, what course of action each subordinate should take if a particular situation should arise. Thus, a restaurant manager could have a rule that "bussers will bus tables as soon as customers finish eating." This ensures that the table is clear before the next course is served and that the work of the waiters and bussers is coordinated.

COORDINATION THROUGH DIRECT SUPERVISION: USING THE HIERARCHY *Direct supervision* achieves coordination by having one person coordinate the work of others, issuing instructions to them and monitoring their results.[13] Thus, when problems arise that are not covered by rules or procedures, subordinates are trained to bring the problem to their manager. In addition to using rules and mutual adjustment, all managers use the chain of command to achieve coordination. Doing so—having two or more subordinates come to their supervisor for a decision—works well when the number of exceptions or problems to be brought to the boss is not too great. If too many problems or disagreements are brought to the boss, he or she will become overloaded and unable to function effectively. Then other coordination techniques like those discussed next are required.

COORDINATION THROUGH DIVISIONALIZATION Divisionalization facilitates coordination. For example, in a divisional organization, the president does not have to work as hard coordinating the efforts of his or her product divisions because they are not as interdependent as are the production, finance, and sales departments in a functional organization. As a rule, functional departmentalization creates additional demands for presidential coordination, since the functional departments are interdependent. Product (or customer, market channel, or area) departmentalization reduces such interdependence and makes it easier for the president to achieve coordination.

COORDINATION THROUGH STAFF ASSISTANTS Some managers hire a staff assistant to make the job of coordinating subordinates easier. When subordinates bring a problem to the manager, the assistant can compile information on the problem, research the problem, and offer advice on what alternatives are available. This effectively boosts the manager's ability to handle problems and coordinate the work of his or her subordinates.

COORDINATION THROUGH LIAISONS When the volume of contacts between two departments (like production and sales) grows, some firms use special liaisons to facilitate coordination. For example, the sales department manager might appoint a salesperson to be his or her liaison with the production department. This liaison is based in the sales department but travels frequently to the factory to learn as much as possible about the plant's production schedule. Then, when an order came in to the sales department, the sales manager could quickly determine from this liaison what the production schedules were and would then know whether a new order could be accepted and delivered when promised.

COORDINATION THROUGH COMMITTEES Many firms achieve coordination by appointing interdepartmental committees, task forces, or teams. These are usually composed of representatives of five or six interdependent departments. They meet periodically to discuss common problems and ensure interdepartmental coordination.

INDEPENDENT INTEGRATOR
Coordinates the activities of several interdependent departments, but is independent of them.

COORDINATION THROUGH INDEPENDENT INTEGRATORS[14] An independent integrator coordinates the activities of several interdependent departments. Integrators differ from liaison personnel since integrators are *independent of* (not attached to) the departments they coordinate. Instead, they report to the manager who oversees the departments they coordinate.

This technique has proved useful in high-tech firms where the work of several interdependent departments must be coordinated under rapidly changing conditions. In the plastics industry, for instance, developing new products requires close coordination between the research, engineering, sales, and production departments in a situation where competitors are always introducing new and innovative products. Some successful plastics firms have thus established new-product development departments. Their role is to coordinate (or *integrate*) the research, marketing analysis, sales, and production activities needed for developing and introducing a new product.

ACHIEVING COORDINATION BY STANDARDIZING TARGETS, SKILLS, OR SHARED VALUES Firms also achieve coordination by standardizing the efforts of their employees. This can be accomplished in three ways. First, you can standardize the *goals* or targets that the employees are to reach. For example, as long as the sales, finance, and production managers reach their assigned goals, the president can be reasonably sure that their work will be coordinated, since adequate financing and production will be provided to meet the sales target.

Standardizing *skills* also facilitates coordination. That's one reason why firms like Saturn spend millions of dollars training their workers. Whether a work team is installing door panels or solving a problem, training ensures that each team member knows how his or her efforts fit with the others; and how to proceed. Standardized skills thus reduce the need for outside coordination.[15]

Finally, many firms facilitate coordination by creating *shared values* among their employees. They do this by carefully screening and socializing their employees and by establishing a set of values and a philosophy that permeates the organization and guides what employees do. For example, every year Unilever brings 300 to 400 of its managers to its executive development center and also gives 100 to 150 of its most promising overseas managers temporary assignments at corporate headquarters.[16] This policy gives the visiting managers a strong sense of Unilever's strategic vision and values. Such knowledge helps to ensure that, wherever they are around the world, Unilever managers will contribute in a coordinated way to that vision, while adhering to the values of the firm. As one of its managers put it, "The experience initiates you into the Unilever club and the clear norms, values, and behaviors that distinguish our people—so much so that we really believe we can spot another Unilever manager anywhere in the world."[17]

RESEARCH FINDINGS Several studies shed light on when to use the various coordination techniques. For example, Lawrence and Lorsch studied companies in the plastics, foods, and containers industries. They found that in the most unpredictable environment—in the relatively high-tech plastics industry—coordination was best achieved with special integrating "new product development" departments.[18] At the other extreme, in the relatively predictable and unchanging container industry, interdepartmental coordination was best achieved via the chain of command.

A second study underscores why it is important to fit the coordinating technique to the task. This study focused on employees in offices of the administrative headquarters of a large state employment agency. The findings, presented in Figure 8.10, illustrate how coordination and the task are intertwined. As the uncertainty of the tasks undertaken by a work unit increases, the use of impersonal coordination techniques like rules and plans decreases significantly. As the same time, the use of interpersonal and group coordination techniques increases significantly. According to the researchers, the departments with the most unpredictable tasks relied very little on rules and very heavily on personal, mutual adjustment-based coordination techniques such as scheduled and unscheduled group meetings.[19]

AUTHORITY IN ORGANIZATIONS

SOURCES OF AUTHORITY

Authority is the right to take action, to make decisions, and to direct the work of others. It is an essential feature of organizing, since managers and employees must be *authorized* to carry out the jobs assigned to them.

Authority derives from several sources, one of which is the person's position or rank. For example, the president of IBM has more authority based on rank than does one of his senior vice-presidents.

AUTHORITY
The right to take action, to make decisions, and to direct the work of others.

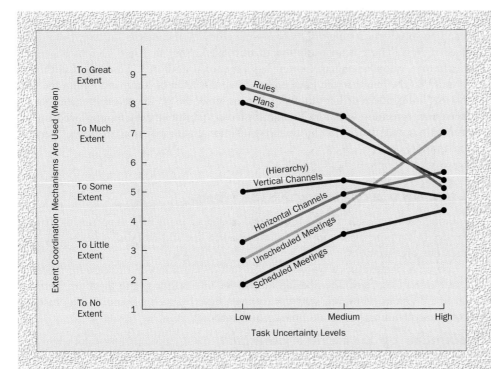

FIGURE 8.10

Coordination Mechanisms Used at Different Levels of Task Uncertainty

This study concluded that personal coordination techniques like meetings were used more for unpredictable, fast-changing tasks, while rules, plans, and the chain of command were useful as long as the task was fairly routine.

SOURCE: Andrew Van de Ven, Andre Delbecq, and Richard Koenig, Jr., "Determinants of Coordination Modes within Organizations," *American Sociological Review*, vol. 41 (April 1976), 330.

But authority can stem from other sources, too. Some people are able to command authority because of their personal traits, such as intelligence or charisma. Others are acknowledged experts in some area or have some knowledge that requires others to depend on them. Thus even the president of IBM might have to defer on some highly technical matter to the head of R&D.

Some management writers argue that authority must come from the bottom up and be based on the subordinate's acceptance of the supervisor's orders. Theorist Chester Barnard was an early proponent of this view. Barnard argued that for orders to be carried out they must lie within the subordinate's "zone of acceptance" (in other words, they must be viewed as acceptable). From a practical point of view, there is a great element of truth in this. A president might have considerable authority based on rank, but not be able to get anyone to follow his or her orders unless subordinates view those orders as acceptable. Experts such as Rosabeth Moss Kanter and Tom Peters argue that acceptance-based authority is increasingly important today, given the growing emphasis on empowered workers and team-based organizations.

LINE AND STAFF AUTHORITY

LINE MANAGER
A managerial position authorized to issue orders to subordinates down the chain of command.

STAFF MANAGER
A managerial position, such as Personnel Manager, which generally cannot issue orders down the chain of command; can only assist and advise line managers.

FUNCTIONAL AUTHORITY
Authority to issue orders down the chain of command within the very narrow limits of his or her authority.

Managers distinguish between line and staff authority. The way the terms are generally used, two basic differences exist between the two. First, line managers, like the president, production manager, and sales manager, are always in charge of essential activities such as sales. Second, they are always authorized to issue orders to their subordinates. **Line managers,** in other words, can always issue orders to subordinates down the chain of command. **Staff managers,** on the other hand, generally cannot issue orders down the chain of command (except in their own department); staff managers can only assist and advise line managers. For example, a personnel manager—even a senior vice-president—can advise a production supervisor regarding the types of selection tests to use. However, it would be unusual for the personnel/human resource manager to order the supervisor to hire a particular employee. On the other hand, the production supervisor's boss—the production manager—usually could issue such orders. (There is an exception to this rule: a staff manager such as a personnel/human resource manager often has functional authority. **Functional authority** means that the manager can issue orders down the chain of command within the very narrow limits of his or her authority. For example, the president might state that no personnel screening tests can be administered without first being approved by the human resource manager, who thus has functional authority over the use of personnel tests.)

LINE AND STAFF ORGANIZATIONS

Although some organizations use only line managers, many have departments that are headed by staff managers too. The latter are called line and staff organizations; the former, line organizations.

Figure 8.11 illustrates a typical line and staff organization, in this case for the General Electric Company. The division heads have line authority and these are therefore all line divisions. However, staff departments have been established, in this case for corporate planning, corporate finance, and corporate legal.

SOURCES OF LINE-STAFF CONFLICT   Line-staff conflict results when disagreements occur between a line manager and the staff manager who is giving him or her advice. For example, a production manager may want to use a particular personnel

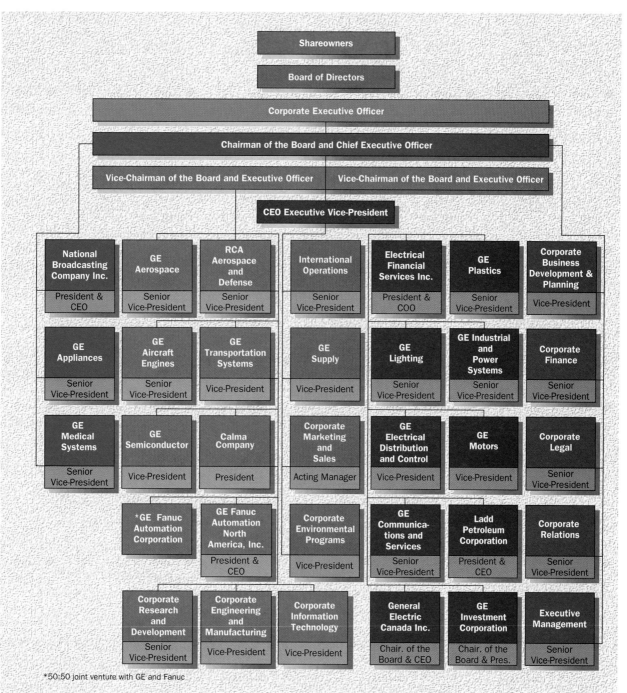

FIGURE 8.11

Typical Line and Staff Organization: General Electric Corporation

Most organizations, especially in larger firms, contain both line and staff managers. At GE the CEO and GE aerospace managers are line officers, while the heads of corporate development and planning and finance are staff managers.

SOURCE: "Organizing for International Competitiveness," *Business International Corp.* (New York: Business International Corp., 1988), 16.

test but the human resource manager insists that the test not be used. Conflict usually results when line managers feel that staff managers are encroaching on their duties and prerogatives. For their part, staff managers may feel that line managers are unnecessarily resisting their good advice. One way to reduce such conflict is to make it clear who is responsible for what, in this case with respect to personnel testing.

THE PROCESS OF DELEGATION

DELEGATION
The pushing down of authority from supervisor to subordinate.

Organizing departments would be impossible without **delegation,** which we can define as the pushing down of authority from supervisor to subordinate. The assignment of responsibility for some department or job traditionally goes hand-in-hand with the delegation of authority to get the job done. It would be inappropriate, for example, to assign a subordinate the responsibility for designing a new product and then deny him or her the authority to hire designers or choose the best design.

But although authority can be delegated, responsibility cannot. A manager can assign responsibility to a subordinate. However, the manager is still ultimately responsible for ensuring that the job gets done properly. Since the supervisor retains the ultimate responsibility for the job's performance, delegation of authority always entails the creation of *accountability*. Thus, subordinates become accountable to the supervisor for the performance of the tasks assigned to them.

Today, the terms *delegation* and *empowerment* are closely intertwined. They differ in that the term *empowerment* is the broader of the two. Specifically, **empowerment,** as the term is increasingly used, means authorizing *and enabling* workers to do their jobs. Thus the assembly workers at Toyota do not just have the authority to solve problems on the line. In addition, they are given the training, tools, and management support required to enable them to solve these problems. In this way, Toyota workers are empowered to analyze and solve problems on the line and continuously improve production quality.

EMPOWERMENT
Authorizing and enabling workers to do their jobs.

The *Westhaven Services* Small Business box illustrates some of the problems managers encounter when trying to delegate.

THE DECENTRALIZED ORGANIZATION

DECENTRALIZED ORGANIZATION
An organization in which authority for most decisions is delegated to the department heads, while control over essential company-wide matters is maintained at the headquarters office.

A **decentralized organization** is one in which authority for most decisions is delegated to the department heads (usually the heads of product divisions), while control over essential company-wide matters is maintained at the headquarters office.

Decentralization at the best decentralized organizations such as GE always represents a shrewd balance between delegated authority and centralized control. On the one hand, division managers have considerable autonomy and the means for designing, producing, and marketing their own products. On the other hand, GE headquarters maintains control of its far-flung company by centralizing (retaining control over) major decisions regarding activities such as capital appropriations, managing incoming cash receipts, and division profitability. Thus, decentralization always involves both selective delegation of authority *and* centralized control over essential matters.

Some firms are referred to as "decentralized" while others are "centralized." To appreciate the difference between these two, it is useful to understand that there is both a communication aspect and a delegation aspect to decentralizing.[20] First, the communication aspect of decentralization refers to the extent to which employees must channel all their communications directly through the head or *hub* of the organization. For example, must the finance, production, and sales managers communicate with each other *only* through the president, or are they permitted to communicate directly when arriving at a joint decision? The more that all communications must

WESTHAVEN SERVICES COMPANY

Mary Lou Fox is an enigma. Her greatest gifts—an entrepreneur's spirit and an innate sense for both marketing and problem solving—are also her greatest handicaps. The problem: no one to whom she delegates ever seems to react the way she would have, and the way she would have reacted is always the best way. Just ask her!

"I've spent years saying, 'How hard would it be to clone me?' I keep thinking, if I can do this, a high school graduate from an idiot town, why can't you?" she asks.

Under Fox's near sole stewardship, Westhaven Services Company, an institutional pharmacy, which sells to such clients as hospitals, has risen from nothing to an $18 million company in 15 years. She took over Westhaven from her husband on one condition: she wanted absolute control. Admittedly not a businessperson, Fox got a rough baptism the first year. She was sued once, had to sue a computer company herself, and came to work one day to find state licensing board investigators, working on an anonymous tip, perusing her in-house files. "It was all harassment and politics," she says. "I was not a pharmacist, and the pharmacists hated me for it."

Those institutional pharmacies, her nameless competitors, generally emphasized price when trying to attract business. Occasionally they sent fruit baskets. Fox intuitively sensed the dearth of marketing zip and did what she knew how to do best—she entertained. Fox sent out poinsettia arrangements, and pens that nurses could wear around their necks. "It says we are thinking of you," she says. "The best way for us to deliver quality care is to be in good communication with the nursing staff." She also threw bashes that became part of the Perrysburg, Ohio lore. Fox knew what she wanted customers to feel, and she drew on her own life experiences to design ways to make them feel it. Westhaven didn't break even for three years, and through that period the line that separated Mary

FOCUS ON SMALL BUSINESS

Lou Fox and Westhaven first blurred and then finally disappeared.

Fox decided to get her employees to manage themselves. She would grow executives and instill in them what she already knew: that Westhaven sold service, not drugs. Once indoctrinated, they would carry out departmental objectives in support of Westhaven's corporate goals. But something went wrong. Fox said they couldn't delegate; the executives said she wouldn't. Nearly all of them burned out and left. Todd Herzog, one of the original appointees, said, "You get so much piled on you that you cannot survive. It pulls you to the bottom of the pond and you can't get back to the top."

Next Fox tried hiring experienced managers. She tapped Garth Tebay, an accountant. He discovered managing for Fox meant dealing with an endless stream of problems but never having the authority to keep them from recurring. He lost 35 pounds and even Fox said he looked like a gray ghost. He left.

Fox's next tact was an effort to continue Westhaven's customer closeness tradition. Four teams of the company's key people, led by a marketing representative, would concentrate on about 35 nursing homes each. Fox had selected four team captains. All left within a year, grousing that they were given plenty of responsibility, but little authority. Fox in turn said none of them tackled problems like she would have.

Fox is alone again. She refuses to hire anyone, saying she's no good at it. A remaining subordinate says Fox is starting to let certain authority trickle down. Another says she has even started to delegate real authority. Someone suggested that Fox is nearing the conclusion that there might even be another, maybe better, way to run Westhaven.

"This business is a reflection of me, and I personally care about what our customers think," Fox says. "What I know isn't hard to identify. But it takes time to mold it into something I can [delegate]. Maybe it's just too tough."

SOURCE: Hyatt, "No Way Out," *Inc.*, November 1991, 78–92.

be channeled through the president, the more centralized the firm is. The more that the managers can communicate directly with each other, the more decentralized the firm is.

Second, there is a delegation aspect of decentralization. In particular, the more decisions and the more areas in which authority is delegated from the president to his or her subordinates, the more decentralized the organization is.

Companies organized around product divisions are usually referred to as "decentralized." Managers of product divisions are often in charge of the amount of time to give to their own miniature companies. All or most of the decisions that have anything to do with their product are within their own domains and can be made by the divisional managers with little or no interaction with the other divisions or the firm's CEO.

The *NASA* vignette illustrates some of the issues involved in balancing decentralized decision-making and centralized control.

SITUATIONAL DETERMINANTS: HOW MUCH SHOULD AN ORGANIZATION DECENTRALIZE?

Practicing managers and management consultants are usually in agreement about the advantages of decentralization. Peter Drucker, in an early analysis of decentralization at the General Motors Corporation, found that decentralization led to speedier, more responsive decisions, improved management development, and increased motivation on the part of the managers to do a good job and be rewarded for it.[21] Another expert argues that the advantages of decentralization include quicker and better decisions, better manager development, fewer organizational levels, and the freeing of supervisors to concentrate on their broader responsibilities.[22]

Yet we know that decentralized, divisionalized structures are not always "best." Remember that one of the drawbacks of the product division structure is duplication of effort: there may be several production plants (one for each product) instead of one, for instance, and several different sales forces. The question, then, is this: Under what conditions do decentralized, divisionalized structures seem to work best? Here are some pertinent research findings:

1. *The greater the diversity of products, the greater the decentralization.* Alfred Chandler, in a study of firms in a wide range of industries, found that divisionalized structures were most often found in companies that market a wide range of products. Here, product divisions are typically set up, and decision making is decentralized. The reason, says Chandler, is that the problems of doing business in many diverse markets are so varied that a single manager cannot handle them all. Thus, companies like Westinghouse and General Electric opted very early for a divisionalized, decentralized structure.[23]

2. *In general, the larger the enterprise, the more likely it will use the decentralized, divisionalized structure.* Studies of both American and British firms indicate that larger enterprises are usually more decentralized than smaller ones.[24] However, there are some big exceptions to this rule. For example, the largest companies in the steel and paper industries still have structures built around business functions and most important decisions remained centralized. For companies like these, efficient management is of overriding importance and responsiveness is not the key concern. They have thus retained the more efficient functional, centralized organization structures, those in which duplication of effort is held to a minimum.[25]

3. *The more rapidly changing the environment, the more decentralized the decision making.* Where companies depend on a single, predictable customer (as does, say, a WalMart supplier), most decisions remain centralized and the firms remain functionally structured. Where environments are less predictable, decision making is usually more decentralized and the firms tend to be divisionally structured. Here, intense competition, new product developments, and similar unexpected changes require a more responsive organization. This means one where lower-level managers are authorized to make quick, on-the-spot decisions. Decentralization, here, is the rule.[26]

NASA

From its inception, NASA administrators have tried to create a cooperative coalition out of the ten field centers that make up NASA. All manner of reporting schemes have been tried. Nothing worked. The centers became stronger and more autonomous, while headquarters weakened, particularly in important areas such as systems analysis, cost estimating, and contract monitoring.

The roots of the problem stretched back to the founding of the space agency in 1958. NASA was the amalgamation of three entities: the National Advisory Committee for Aeronautics, the Army Ballistic Missile Agency, and elements of the Naval Research Laboratory. The agency was never properly centralized in the beginning, and, hence, could never be properly decentralized either. Funding cuts in the 1980s exacerbated the problem. Instead of cooperation, shrinking budgets led to competition among centers for new projects.

But now, with budget cutbacks, NASA will have to provide firm centralized direction of the programs carried out by its field centers. In the areas of basic research and project development, some operational latitude will still be permitted, but under much greater supervision than in the past. Strong central direction will also be mandatory for major projects in their advanced development, implementation, and operations phases.

TALL AND FLAT ORGANIZATIONS
AND THE SPAN OF CONTROL

FLAT VERSUS TALL ORGANIZATIONS

When he took over as CEO of a sprawling GE in the late 1980s, Jack Welch knew he had to make some dramatic organizational changes—and fast. Welch had climbed the ranks and saw how GE's chain of command was draining the firm of its creativity and responsiveness. For instance, business heads had to get approval from the headquarters staff for almost every big decision they made, so that in one case the light bulb business managers spent $30,000 producing a fancy film to demonstrate the need for some production equipment they wanted to buy. The old GE, Welch knew, was wasting hundreds of million of dollars and missing countless opportunities because managers at so many levels were busily checking and rechecking each others' work.

Therefore, the first thing he did as CEO was strip away unneeded organizational levels and flatten GE's structure. For example, before he took over, "GE's business heads reported to a group head, who reported to a sector head, who reported to the CEO. Each level had its own staff in finance, marketing, and planning, checking and double checking each business."[27] Welch disbanded the group and sector levels, thus dramatically flattening the organizational chain of command. No one stands between the business heads and the CEO's own office now. In disbanding those two levels Welch got rid of the organizational bottlenecks they caused and the salaries of the almost 700

The Jet Propulsion Laboratory in Pasadena is one of NASA's 10 field centers. The last row of computers in Mission Control, shown here, monitor the Deep Space Network planetary probe. The centers, which have operated fairly autonomously in the past, will be subject to more centralized control now that NASA's budget has been cut.

corporate staff that comprised them. Now that it is flatter and leaner, GE is a much more responsive company, and its corporate results reflect its new effectiveness.

The restructuring at GE has been repeated tens of thousands of times in the past few years at tens of thousands of companies. Everywhere you look, from GM to IBM to Levi Strauss to Pratt and Whitney, CEOs are hammering down their chains of command and shoving authority down to lower levels.[28]

Actually, management experts have long known about the advantages of flat organizations. One of the first and most extensive empirical studies on the effect of flat and tall organizations was carried out by James Worthy many years ago in the Sears, Roebuck Company.[29] He found that in many Sears units the merchandising vice-president and store managers each had more than 40 managers reporting directly to them. As we'll see, this was an extraordinarily high number of subordinates: early management writers had suggested keeping the number of subordinates reporting to a manager down to a more manageable seven or eight.

Worthy found that because each vice-president and store manager had so many managers reporting to them (had such a "wide span of control") subordinates all ended up with more autonomy and therefore with higher morale. What happened was that each store manager had so many people reporting to him or her that the manager couldn't demand that their subordinates keep coming to them for approval of their actions. If they did, the store managers and their merchandising vice-presidents would have been swamped. So at Sears (and, increasingly today, at thousands of other firms) the organization chart was kept flat. There were relatively few levels and each manager had a relatively high number of subordinates reporting to him or her. The result was an organization in which employees tended to have high autonomy, and this autonomy seemed to lead to higher morale and better and faster decisions.[30]

THE SPAN OF CONTROL

The **span of control** is the number of subordinates reporting directly to a supervisor. In the typical country organization of Eastman Kodak shown in Figure 8.12, the span of control of the country general manager is 13: six business managers, six directors, and one innovation manager report to the general manager.

SPAN OF CONTROL
The number of subordinates reporting directly to a supervisor.

A correlation exists between the number of people reporting to a manager and the number of management *levels* in an organization. For example, if an organization with 64 workers to be supervised contains a span of control of eight, then there will be eight supervisors directing the workers and one manager directing the supervisors (a flat organization). If, on the other hand, the span of control were four, the same number of workers would require 16 supervisors. They would in turn be directed by four

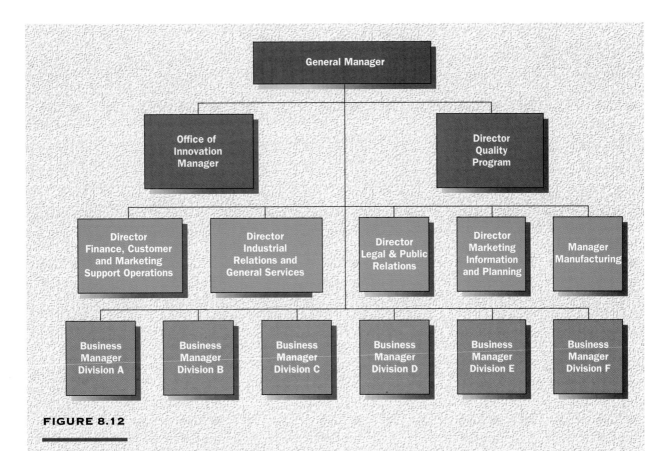

FIGURE 8.12

Typical Country Organization: Eastman Kodak Corporation

In this chart the span of control of the general manager is 13—six business managers, six directors, and one manager.

SOURCE: "Organizing for International Competitiveness," *Business International Corp.* (New York: Business International Corp., 1988), 43.

managers. These four managers would in turn be directed by one manager (a tall organization). There would be an extra management level.

Classical management theorists such as Henri Fayol believed that tall organizational structures (with narrow spans of control) improved performance by requiring close supervision.[31] However, as recent experience at firms like GE has shown, tall organizations and narrow spans are not panaceas; in fact, they can and do backfire by slowing the decision-making process. Therefore, as the rate of technological change and new-product introductions has increased, the number of firms opting for flatter structures and wider spans has escalated.[32] We will pursue this point in the following chapter.

Organizing is the arranging of an enterprise's activities in such a way that they systematically contribute to the enterprise's goals. An organization consists of people accomplishing differentiated tasks, which are coordinated to contribute to the organization's goals.

Departmentalization is the process through which an enterprise's activities are grouped together and assigned to managers. Departments can be grouped around functions, either technological or managerial; products; customer groups or marketing channels; or geographic areas.

A matrix organization, or matrix management, is defined as superimposing one or more forms of departmentalization on top of an existing one. In practice, most enterprises use several forms of departmentalization, called hybrids.

Coordination is the process of achieving unity of action among interdependent activities. It is required when two or more interdependent entities must work together to achieve a common goal. The techniques for achieving coordination include mutual adjustment; the use of rules or procedures; the use of direct supervision; the use of departmentalization, a staff assistant, a liaison, a committee, or independent integrators; and standardizing targets, skills, or shared values.

Authority is the right to take action, to make decisions, and to direct the work of others. Managers usually distinguish between line and staff authority. Departments could not be organized without delegation, which is defined as the pushing down of authority from superior to subordinate. But barriers exist to the process of delegation. In a decentralized organization, authority for most decisions is delegated to the department heads.

Organizations typically either have a tall or flat structure. Many companies are adopting flatter structures in an effort to eliminate duplication of effort, inspire creativity, and increase the responsiveness of the company. The span of control in a company is the number of subordinates reporting directly to a supervisor.

SUMMARY

QUESTIONS

■ FOR REVIEW

1. What are some of the essential functions around which activities can be grouped in an organization?

2. What form of departmentalization do most companies use in practice?

3. What are some of the advantages of decentralization?

■ FOR DISCUSSION

4. Compare the advantages and disadvantages of creating departments around functions as opposed to product divisions.

5. Explain the difference between delegating authority and delegating responsibility. Discuss why one can occur, and the other cannot.

6. In light of the current trend toward decentralization, do you think the traditional bureaucratic structure will soon become a thing of the past?

■ FOR ACTION

7. Contact a publicly held company's personnel department and ask if you can obtain a copy of their organizational chart. Is it an example of a tall or flat structure? Is it centralized or decentralized? Why do you think it's organized the way it is?

8. Divide the class into two groups. Assign each the task of organizing the structure of Hallmark Greeting Cards, a company that produces some 40,000 different cards

with a creative staff made up of some 700 writers, artists, and designers. Would you divide the departments by function, product, customer group, or geographic area? Compare your results.

9. Find out how your university or college is organized. What concepts described in this chapter apply to the structure in place at your school?

■ FOR FOCUS ON SMALL BUSINESS

10. Discuss the reasons why a manager like Fox would assign subordinates responsibility for jobs but not give them the authority to carry them out.

11. What barriers to delegating do you think this case illustrates?

12. Do you think Fox's reluctance to delegate is characteristic of entrepreneurs? Why or why not? If so, how would you explain this?

CLOSING SOLUTION

JOHNSON & JOHNSON

Corporate America may only recently have awakened to concepts like decentralization, employee empowerment, and the higher effectiveness of small, self-governing work units. But it has been standard practice at Johnson & Johnson for better than 50 years.

The company has long been a model of how a decentralized organization should work, but the company isn't resting on any laurels. The holy grail is still finding the optimum balance between encouraging entrepreneurial spirit while maintaining corporate structure and control. Coordinating all of it into a cohesive, functional organization is no easy task.

"We will never give up the principle of decentralization, which is to give our operating executives ownership of a business," CEO Larsen says. "They are ultimately responsible."

What might be a recipe for chaos in most companies is the lifeblood of one like Johnson & Johnson. Creative thinking is critical at Johnson & Johnson because innovation plays such a key role in its viability and growth. That reality is graphically illustrated when the following is considered: new products introduced within the past five to six years now account for 25 percent of total sales.

Larsen isn't inclined to diverge off the path of decentralization, and based upon the numbers Johnson & Johnson has generated throughout his tenure, he shouldn't. Since 1980 the company's annual profit gains have averaged 19 percent, and sales have increased 10 percent in five of those years. He once likened his role at Johnson & Johnson to a maestro leading a talented symphony orchestra.

■ QUESTION FOR CLOSING SOLUTION

1. Describe J&J's organizational structure, as best as you can. In what ways could coordination among the 166 divisions be improved?

2. Do you think the benefits of decentralization at J&J outweigh the drawbacks? Why or why not?

3. If you were to succeed Ralph Larsen, what changes, if any, would you make in the company's organizational structure? Why?

CASE FOR ANALYSIS

Organizing

Organization

Organization Chart

Informal Organization

Departmentalization

Functional Departmentalization

Divisionalization

Customer Departmentalization

Marketing-channel
  Departmentalization

Matrix Organization
  (Matrix Management)

Coordination

Mutual Adjustment

Independent Integrator

Authority

Line Manager

Staff Manager

Functional Authority

Delegation

Empowerment

Decentralized Organization

Span of Control

CASE FOR ANALYSIS

CYPRESS SEMICONDUCTOR CORPORATION

T. J. Rodgers has proved a few things during his tenure as chief executive officer of San Jose, California–based Cypress Semiconductor Corporation. Namely, that calling competitors unkind names garners many press clippings and that accusing semiconductor executives of backward management practices makes them angry. But, he has learned something else as well. Those that live by the sword die by it, and in the Silicon Valley, you're often only as good as your last success.

Rodgers' "in-your-face" management style is extremely aggressive. For a long time, he refused to delegate, trying instead to directly control every project in the works at Cypress. When growth made that impossible, he resorted to a system where he could review a synopsis of every technical document and select the ones he wanted to read in detail. At weekly meetings, employees outlined projects, goals, and deadlines. Rodgers designed software to track progress and sound the alarm when completion was overdue. "I can't be involved in everything anymore," he says. "But if I'm in it, I'm running it, because I'm the boss. If I'm out of it, I review it once every quarter, and I'll fire the guy if he's not doing a good job or give him a raise if he's doing well. It's hard for me to be involved halfway."

Among other things, Rodgers has referred to large American chip makers as dinosaurs. And he guaranteed that even through the expansion process, the $300 million Cypress would not fall victim to the bureaucracy of titans like Intel or Texas Instruments. When branching into a new business, Rodgers creates a company around the new product division, complete with board members and president. The product line or manufacturing processes are funded venture-capital style from the parent entity. The original projections had better be on the mark. Subsidiaries that fail to produce cash flow have to sell equity back to Cypress, a reality that tends to make them lean producers.

This style of operation extends to Cypress as well, and once again, the process is taken to the extreme. Nearly all internal departments are set up as profit centers within the company. That means product managers who need quality testing are charged by that department for the service. As a result, they tend not to request testing that isn't really necessary. "We've gotten rid of socialism in the organization," Rodgers says.

A large reason for the success at Cypress is flexible manufacturing processes, which enable the company to respond to customer demand and quickly create a massive variety of specialized chips. Still, with its fast memory chips known as SRAM, or static random-access memory, Cypress has largely been a niche player. But its 37 percent annual growth rates and profit margins of 15 percent in an industry where 5 percent is the norm were eventually noticed.

When Motorola and Micron Technology entered the SRAM fray, a price war ensued. Rodgers discovered barbed rhetoric was no match for deep pockets. Cypress, which derived nearly a third of its total revenues from SRAM sales saw the price of some fall more than a half.

One of Rodgers' staunchest critics, and his former boss, had maintained that when the market areas Cypress was exploiting grew large enough, Rodgers wouldn't like what followed. "He was mugged by reality," said Advanced Micro Devices CEO W. J. Sanders, III. After years of relentlessly lambasting fellow chip manufacturers, Rodgers was forced to emulate them. He shifted assembly work to Thailand and issued pink slips to 21 percent of his 2,000-plus work force. He had to abandon his micro-management tendencies as well. "It's a defeat," Rodgers admitted. "I've had to change my mind-set."

Revenue erosion wasn't the only problem. Cypress engineers were discovering they had too many balls in the air. They were trying to stay out front with innovations while still upgrading the company's 2,500 existing products. Nothing was coming in on schedule. Cypress fell months behind Motorola and Micron on the next generation SRAM 1-megabit chip. A Cypress subsidiary was a year late delivering a new chip to Sun Microsystems. Texas Instruments took that business away. Rodgers turned to outside consultants to reduce design time. He also decided to prune the product line by a quarter and cancel a number of development projects.

Rodgers will have to identify another niche, and he had better do it sooner rather than later. The move offshore is expected to save $17 million when completed. Cutting product lines and focusing on those that are most profitable should also help. But perhaps the biggest changes may have to come from Rodgers himself. Fred B. Bialek, a former executive from National Semiconductor and now a Cypress director had an observation. After commending Rodgers' efforts at keeping his fingers out of every pie, he said, "In the area of technology, the guy's fantastic. But I want him out of the things that he doesn't have . . . insight into."

SOURCES: David R. Altany, "Bull in a Chip Shop," *Industry Week,* July 6, 1992, 15–18; Richard Brandt, "The Bad Boy of Silicon Valley," *Business Week,* Dec. 9, 1991, 64–70; Richard Brandt, "Humble Pie for T. J. Rodgers," *Business Week,* Nov. 23, 1992, 81–82.

■ QUESTIONS

1. Using some of the concepts explained in the chapter, describe as best you can how Rodgers has organized Cypress Semiconductor to accomplish his goals. What are the advantages and disadvantages associated with organizing the company in this fashion?

2. Based on the information contained in this case, would you say that Rodgers has been effective in coordinating the activities of the various groups within the company? Why or why not?

3. How effective has Rodgers been in delegating authority? Would you consider Cypress a decentralized organization? Discuss.

A CASE IN DIVERSITY

MONSANTO CHEMICAL GROUP

In the late 1980s, Monsanto Chemical Group of St. Louis, MO awakened to the discovery that a lot of talented women and minorities were leaving because they had the sense that management neither appreciated nor really understood them. The company had a three-year-old diversity-management program underway, but it was obvious that something else was needed. After some statistical analysis and a lot of deliberation, management settled on the use of consulting pairs. The hope was that cross-cultural communication channels could be enhanced by the employees themselves, and that the effort itself would signal Monsanto's commitment to its entire workforce.

In a given company setting, problems between employees of differing ethnic backgrounds are often grounded in erroneous, and perhaps more importantly, unarticulated perceptions. When ethnic, gender, racial, or similar conflicts arise at Monsanto, consulting pairs of trained volunteers are assigned to mediate. Ideally, the consulting pair selected will very closely reflect the backgrounds of both of the workers who are unable to come to agreement. That means a young Hispanic female who can't come to an accord with a 57-year-old white male can expect to see, as nearly as is possible, a consulting pair of the same age, gender, and ethnicity. Matters are kept confidential when the quartet made up of two combatants and two mediators get together. The focus of these meetings is to get at the heart of the matter, whatever it may be.

Most of the resources are focused on an aspect of the program called "join-up." Designed to smooth the supervisor-subordinate relationship, join-ups occur whenever an employee begins reporting to a new boss. Although it takes time for any employee to fully understand what a new boss expects of him or her, research has shown that the process is three to four times more difficult when the worker is a woman or minority. Consulting pairs moderate a two-hour get-together where expectations are outlined and the foundations of effective communication laid. Even if such meetings don't result in an outstanding level of rapport, they do allow both sides to put their cards on the table and avoid unexpected surprises later on.

Consulting pairs and the join-up program provides Monsanto employees with an avenue for airing grievances and learning both what they can expect, and what is expected of them. And one of the primary reasons it has been effective is because employees know it's available. The company's turnover rate for the target group of women and minorities has flattened. Another benefit that might be even more important is every employee now realizes there is a forum where they can be heard.

SOURCE: Jennifer J. Laabs, "Employees Manage Conflict and Diversity," *Personnel Journal,* December 1993, 30–36.

■ QUESTIONS

1. List some possible reasons why the relationship between a new boss and a subordinate is even more difficult when the employee is a woman or a minority.

2. What do you consider the primary benefits of a program such as consulting pairs?

3. How could the consulting pairs program be used to facilitate coordination?

ENDNOTES

1. *Organizing for International Competitiveness: How Successful Corporations Structure Their Worldwide Operations* (New York: Business International Corp., 1988) 52–57.

2. Ernest Dale, *Organization* (New York: AMA, 1967), 109.

3. See, for example, Lawton Burns and Douglas Wholey, "Adoption and Abandonment of Matrix Management Programs: Effects of Organizational Characteristics and Interorganizational Networks," *The Academy of Management Journal,* vol. 36, no. 1, February 1993, 106–38.

4. *Organizing for International Competitiveness,* 117.

5. Burns and Wholey, "Adoption and Abandonment," 106.

6. For a discussion of this type of organization and its problems, see Stanley Davis and Paul Lawrence, *Matrix* (Reading, MA: Addison-Wesley, 1967); and Davis and Lawrence, "Problems of Matrix Organizations," *Harvard Business Review,* May–June 1978, 131–42.

7. For a discussion, see James Thompson, *Organizations in Action* (New York: McGraw-Hill, 1967).

8. James D. Mooney and Alan C. Reilly, *The Principles of Organization* (New York: Harper & Row, 1939), 5.

9. Mary Parker Follett, *Dynamic Administration,* eds. Henry C. Metcalf and L. Urwick (New York: Harper, 1942); and Sherman Krupp, *Pattern in Organization Analysis* (New York: Holt, Rinehart & Winston, 1961).

10. Luther Gulick, "Notes on the Theory of Organization," in *Papers of the Science of Administration* by L. Gulick and L. Urwick (The Institute of Public Administration, 1972), 31–37.

11. Jay Galbraith, "Organizational Design: An Information Processing View," *Interfaces,* vol. 4, no. 3 (1974), 28–36; and *Organizational Design* (Reading, MA: Addison-Wesley, 1977).

12. Henry Mintzberg, *Structure in Fives: Designing Effective Organizations* (Englewood Cliffs, NJ: Prentice-Hall, 1983) 4–9.

13. Mintzberg, *Structure in Fives,* 4.

14. Paul Lawrence and Jay Lorsch, *Organization and Environment* (Cambridge, MA: Harvard University Press, 1967).

15. Ibid., 6.

16. Christopher A. Bartlett and Sumantra Ghoshal, "Matrix Management: Not a Structure, a Frame of Mind," *Harvard Business Review,* July–August 1990, 138–45.

17. Bartlett and Ghoshal, "*Matrix Management,*" 143–44.

18. Lawrence and Lorsch, *Organization and Environment,* 95; and Andrew H. Van de Ven, Andre L. Delbecq, and Richard Koenig, Jr., "Determinants of Coordination Modes within Organizations," *American Sociological Review,* vol. 41, April 1976, 330.

19. Lawrence and Lorsch, *Organization and Environment.*

20. Kenneth MacKenzie, *Organizational Structure* (Arlington Heights, OH: AHM, 1978), 198–230.

21. Peter Drucker, *Concept of the Corporation* (New York: John Day, 1946), 47–48.

22. Harold Stieglitz, *Organizational Planning* (New York: The National Industrial Conference Board, Inc., 1962).

23. Alfred Chandler, *Strategy and Structures* (Cambridge, MA: MIT Press, 1962).

24. Dale, *Organization,* 110; John Child, "Predicting and Understanding Organization Structure," *Administrative Science Quarterly,* June 1973, 168–85; see also Daniel Robey, M. Baker, and Thomas Miller, "Organizational Size and Management Autonomy: Some Structure Discontinuities," *Academy of Management Journal,* vol. 20, no. 3 (1977), 378–97.

25. Dale, *Organization,* 10; Chandler, *Strategy and Structure,* 325.

26. Sergio Mindlin and Howard Albrich present a good review of this concept in "Interorganizational Dependence: A Review of the Concept and a Reexamination of the Findings of the Aston Group," *Administrative Science Quarterly,* vol. 20 (September 1975), 382–91.

27. Judith H. Dobrzynski, "Jack Welch: How Good a Manager?" *Business Week,* December 14, 1987, 94.

28. See, for example, Brian Dumaine, "The Bureaucracy Busters," *Fortune,* June 17, 1991, 36–40; and Todd Vogel, "Where 1990s Style Management Is Already Hard at Work," *Business Week,* October 23, 1989, 92–97.

29. James Worthy, "Organization Structures and Employee Morale," *American Sociological Review,* vol. 15 (1950), 169–79.

30. For findings that cast some doubt on the generalizability of this conclusion, see Lyman Porter and Edward Lawler, III, "The Effects of Tall Versus Flat Organization Structures on Managerial Job Satisfaction," *Personnel Psychology,* vol. 17 (1964), 135–48.

31. See, for example, Henri Fayol, *General and Industrial Management,* trans. by Constance Storrs (London: Sir Isaac Pittman, 1949).

32. For a discussion of the contingencies affecting span of control (task uncertainty, professionalism, and interdependence), see, for example, Daniel Robey, *Designing Organizations,* 3rd ed. (Homewood, IL: Irwin, 1991), 258–59.

THE RESPONSIVE ORGANIZATION

LEARNING OBJECTIVES

After studying this chapter, you should be able to:

- Differentiate between mechanistic and organic management systems.

- Outline organizational structures that are appropriate for different technologies, such as unit and small batch.

- Give examples of the major ways a manager might improve the responsiveness of an organization.

- List some typical duties of self-managing work teams.

- Discuss the characteristics of formal, informal, and electronic networks and the functional aspects of each.

- Define boundaryless organization, and give examples of authority, task, political, and identity boundaries.

OPENING PROBLEM
HEWLETT-PACKARD

Hewlett-Packard was the Silicon Valley trendsetter for progressive management and technological breakthroughs for over 45 years. It was a fixture atop the list of best-run U.S. firms. But by the early 1990s, "the HP way," designed to encourage communication and break down the chain of command, had solidified into an unresponsive giant. It once took seven months and 100 people on nine separate committees just to name a new computing package. "There was a lot of decision overhead," is how HP CEO John A. Young put it. ∎

HP thus found itself in an organizational straight-jacket that was diminishing its responsiveness. Regaining its former dominance in the industry would clearly require organizational changes.

A wave of reorganizations—actually, de-organizations—is sweeping companies as firms like Hewlett-Packard grapple with the challenges of rapid change.[1] In the early 1990s Zurich-based ABB Asea Brown Boveri cut its headquarters staff by 95 percent and "de-organized" 215,000 people into 5,000 largely independent profit centers that average only 50 people each.[2] At IBM, CEO Richard Gerstner is stripping away the vestiges of the ponderous central staff and bureaucratic procedures that helped to slow IBM's responsiveness, substituting instead decentralized decision making and small organizational units. At GM's Saturn Corporation plant in Spring Hill, Tennessee, the "organization" is hardly an organization at all: instead, virtually all activities are carried out by self-managing work teams within the framework of the values of quality and teamwork that drive this new firm.

Around the globe the traditional and neat organization chart, with its rigid chain of command and specialized division of labor, is undergoing massive change. The organizational structures that worked so well in the past are being replaced by structures that are allowing firms to respond to fast technological change.

THE DETERMINANTS OF ORGANIZATION

Traditional organization charts are being transformed into more responsive ones because the determinants of organization are themselves changing. Several major studies illustrate the link between these determinants and how the organization should be structured. Let us look at these studies next.

THE IMPACT OF ENVIRONMENT: THE BURNS AND STALKER STUDIES

Tom Burns and G. M. Stalker are two British business experts who were among the first to study the determinants of organization structure. After studying some 20 industrial firms in the United Kingdom, they concluded that the firms' environment was one such major determinant. In particular, they concluded that:

> when novelty and unfamiliarity in both market situations and technical information become the accepted order of things, a fundamentally different kind of management system becomes appropriate from that which applies to a relatively stable commercial and technical environment.[3]

The companies they studied came from a variety of industries, including a rayon manufacturer and several firms in the electronics industry.

The rayon mill was at one extreme organizationally. To be successful in this highly price-sensitive industry, the firm had to keep costs to a minimum and be as efficient as possible. Therefore, its existence depended on keeping unexpected occurrences to a minimum and maintaining steady, high volume production runs. Responsiveness was not a big requirement. Burns and Stalker described this organization as a "pyramid of knowledge." It was highly centralized and run on the basis of all-encompassing policies, procedures, and rules. Job descriptions were highly detailed, and everyone from the top of the firm to the bottom had a very specialized job to do.

The electronics firms were at the other extreme. The survival of these firms depended on their ability to introduce new and innovative electronic products continuously. They therefore had to be very alert to new innovations by their competitors, which came frequently and often unexpectedly. And, they had to be able to respond fast when such new products were introduced. The organizations here were thus organized to be responsive. Employees' tasks "were defined almost exclusively as the consequence of interaction with superiors, colleagues, and subordinates; there was no specification by the head of the concern."[4] Everyone recognized the need for common beliefs and goals, and these common goals helped ensure that all could work together with little or no guidance. Some of these firms had no organization charts at all, since jobs changed so fast. Employees' jobs changed from day-to-day and week-to-week and when a problem arose an employee simply took it to the person he or she felt was in the best position to solve it—even if this meant bypassing the "formal" chain of command. Decision-making authority was pushed down to the lowest levels.

Burns and Stalker were ultimately led to distinguish between two different management systems, which they called mechanistic and organic, each appropriate to a specific environment. Each system is summarized in Figure 9.1. The rayon mill reflected the typical mechanistic organization: jobs were specialized; employees were told to adhere to their job descriptions; everyone was expected to stick to the chain of command for achieving coordination; communication was vertical—between superior and subordinate—rather than horizontal; and decision-making authority was centralized. On the other hand, organic systems of management exhibited continual redefinition of individual tasks through interaction with others; avoidance of defining one's responsibilities just as a limited set of rights, obligations, and methods; a network structure of control, authority, and communication; lateral rather than vertical

CHARACTERISTICS OF ORGANIC SYSTEMS OF MANAGEMENT

- The encouragement of employees to contribute their special knowledge and experience to the common task of the concern

- The "realistic" nature of the individual task, which is seen as set by the total situation of the concern

- The adjustment and continual redefinition of individual tasks through interaction with others

- The shedding of "responsibility" as a limited field of rights, obligations, and methods

- The growth of commitment to the concern beyond any technical definition

- A network structure of control, authority, and communication

- Omniscience no longer imputed to the head of the concern; location of knowledge about the technical or commercial nature of the present task located anywhere in the network

- A lateral rather than a vertical direction of communication through the organization; also, a communication between people of different rank, resembling consultation rather than command

- Content of communication consisting of information and advice rather than instructions and decisions

- Commitment to the concern's task and to the "technological ethos" of material progress and expansion more highly valued than loyalty and obedience

- Importance and prestige attached to affiliations and expertise valid in the industrial, technical, and commercial environments outside the firm

FIGURE 9.1

The Organic and Mechanistic Management Systems

SOURCE: Tom Burns and G. M. Stalker, *The Management of Innovation* (London: Tavistock Publications, 1961), 120–22.

FIGURE 9.1

continued

CHARACTERISTICS OF MECHANISTIC SYSTEMS OF MANAGEMENT

- The specialized division of functions, to which the problems and tasks facing the concern as a whole are broken down
- The abstract nature of each worker's task, which is pursued with techniques and purposes more or less distinct from those of the concern as a whole
- The use of the formal hierarchy for coordination
- The precise definition of rights, obligations, and technical methods attached to each functional role
- The translation of rights, obligations, and methods into the responsibilities of a functional position
- Hierarchic structure of control, authority, and communication
- A reinforcement of the hierarchic structure by the location of knowledge about activities exclusively at the top of the hierarchy
- A tendency for interaction between members of the concern to be vertical; i.e., between superior and subordinate
- A tendency for operations and working behavior to be governed by the instructions and decisions issued by superiors
- Insistence on loyalty to the concern and obedience to superiors as a condition of membership
- A greater importance and prestige attaching to internal (local) than to general (professional) knowledge, experience, and skill

communication; more decentralized decision making; and an emphasis on commitment to the company's task.

TECHNOLOGY AS A DETERMINANT OF ORGANIZATION STRUCTURE: THE WOODWARD STUDIES

British researcher Joan Woodward's contribution lies in her discovery that a firm's production technology (the processes it uses to produce its products or services) also determine how the firm should be organized.[5] Studying firms in the area of South Essex, England, Woodward and her team were surprised to find that there seemed to be no relation between how a firm was organized and whether or not it was effective. On the face of it, the firms she studied were organized in a multitude of ways, and no rhyme or reason could explain which type of organization structure produced the best profits.

However, it soon became apparent that different organization structures were appropriate for different technologies. As Figure 9.2 shows, the researchers stumbled across this discovery after classifying their firms into three main groups, according to production technology:

1. Unit and small-batch production, such as custom-built cars.

2. Large-batch and mass production, such as mass-produced cars.

3. Long-run process production of the same product, such as chemicals.

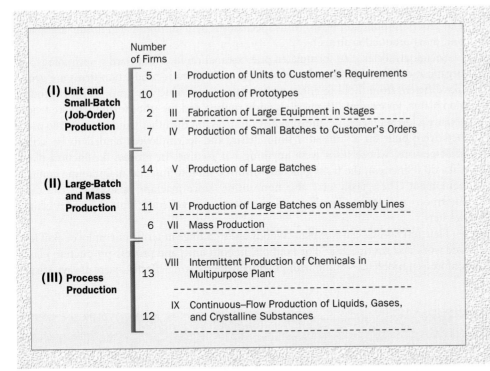

FIGURE 9.2

Organizations Classified by
Production Technology

*Woodward classified the
firms she studied according
to the production technology they used, with three
main categories—unit and
small batch, large batch,
and process.*

SOURCE: Joan Woodward, *Industrial Organization: Theory
and Practice* (London: Oxford
University Press, 1965), 39.

How the best firms were organized was determined partly by the production process
that the individual firms used. Woodward's results are summarized in Table 9.1. For
example, firms with unit and process technologies relied mostly on verbal communications, whereas mass-production firms relied more on formal, written communications. Jobs tended to be more specialized in mass-production firms than in either unit

CHARACTERISTICS	UNIT AND SMALL-BATCH PRODUCTION	LARGE-BATCH AND MASS PRODUCTION	PROCESS PRODUCTION	TABLE 9.1
Lower levels	Informally organized narrow spans of control	Organized by formal process; wide spans	Organized by techno-logical task demands; narrow spans of control	Summary of Woodward's Research Findings on the Or-ganizational Structures of Successful Firms
Higher levels	Informally organized; no distinction between line and staff	Organized by administrative processes with line-staff separation	Informally organized; no distinction between line and staff	*In general, unit and production firms were less formally struc-tured and more organic; mass production firms were more mechanistic.*
General characteristics	Few levels; narrow spans of control; low "organizational consciousness"; no clear chain of command; low ratio of ad-ministrative to nonadministra-tive personnel	More "organiza-tional conscious-ness"; more clearly defined positions; clear chain of command	Many levels; less "organizational consciousness"; high ratio of ad-ministrative to nonadministrative personnel	SOURCE: Gary Dessler, *Orga-nizational Theory* (Englewood Cliffs, NJ: Prentice-Hall, 1980), 72.

or process firms. Organic management systems also tended to predominate in the unit- and process-production firms, while mechanistic systems dominated in the large-batch and mass-production firms.[6]

Sociologist Peter Blau formulated one explanation for Woodward's "technology and organization" findings. Blau found that the tasks in mass-production firms are generally different from those in either unit- or process-production firms. In mass-production plants, for example, the work is fairly routine and the labor force therefore tended to have a low skill level. In unit-production firms, on the other hand, customized products were built on a "one at a time" basis, and so employees tended to be skilled craftspersons, whose tasks were anything but routine. In process-production plants (like oil refineries), the tasks generally involved monitoring and maintaining complex equipment. These tasks were also nonroutine (since machine breakdowns can cause enormous problems). These plants therefore were generally staffed by very skilled workers.

When he took over, Compaq chairman Eckard Pfeiffer moved quickly to reposition the company by changing marketing strategies, speeding up production, and dropping prices.

Blau and his associates explain Woodward's findings in terms of employee skill level and work task routineness.[7] For example, in both unit- and process-production plants, unforeseen problems—some with potentially devastating effects—were always arising.

Therefore, these plants had to be organized to be more responsive, so they could react quickly to unforeseen problems. Also, since unit and process employees were highly skilled, they did not have to be closely supervised. In unit and process plants, therefore, structures were organic, and more emphasis was placed on self-management than on close supervision.[8] The *COMPAQ* vignette illustrates how technology can determine an organization's structure.

HOW ORGANIZATIONS PROCESS INFORMATION

Findings like these suggest that the rate of change and predictableness of the information with which the organization must cope influences how the firm should be structured. In other words, some organizations are better able to cope with unpredictable events than are others because they are structured to be more responsive. For

COMPAQ

It was clear where Eckhard Pfeiffer was placing his bets after he took over as Compaq Corporation's CEO in late 1991. Pfeiffer increased the advertising budget 60 percent while cutting the number of engineers by 200 and implementing other cost-cutting measures. The future of the personal computer business, according to Pfeiffer, would require getting the next generation of machines to stores quickly and marketing them effectively, while keeping costs down.

In its heyday, Compaq had matched IBM prices while delivering more innovative products. But charging high prices left Compaq vulnerable, and clone makers promptly moved in. Compaq needed to lower costs, and to do so Pfeiffer made price a priority second only to product quality. To speed production, he oversaw the reorganization of Compaq's engineering team. The four engineering organizations were cut in half, and one of the remaining groups focused on product development while the other focused on production. Processor boards that in the past were redesigned an average of 14 times before going into production were now reworked no more than 3 times.

In the future, Compaq computers will not only be produced faster and more cheaply, they'll be easier to find. Twice as many outlets now sell Compaq computers, including discount sellers such as Office Depot. Mail and phone sales are a possibility. Pfeiffer thinks Compaq can be the market leader in the industry by 1995. He's already experienced how suddenly things can change in the industry, and he knows how important it is to keep on the pressure to move in the right direction. "But we have to move faster," he says. At Compaq as at other firms, responsiveness will be the key to success, and this will impact how the firm is organized.

SOURCES: David Kirkpatrick, "The Revolution at Compaq Computer," *Fortune,* December 14, 1992, 80–88; Julie Pitta, "Identity Crisis," *Forbes,* May 25, 1992, 82; and Mark Ivey et al., "Compaq's New Boss Doesn't Even Have Time to Wince," *Business Week,* November 11, 1991, 41.

example, in explaining that "extrinsic factors determine which management system is best," Burns and Stalker conclude that

> these extrinsic factors are all, in our view, identifiable as different rates of technical or market change. By change we mean the appearance of novelties; i.e., new scientific discoveries or technical inventions, and requirements for products of a kind not previously available or demanded.[9]

In a similar vein, Henry Mintzberg points out, "It is not the environment per se that counts but the organization's ability to cope with it—to predict it, comprehend it, deal with its diversity, and respond quickly to it—that is important."[10] Another expert on this subject, Jay Galbraith, defines uncertainty as "the difference between the amount of information required to perform the task and the amount of information already possessed by the organization." He argues that

> the basic proposition is that the greater the uncertainty of the task, the greater the amount of information that has to be processed between decision makers during the execution of the task [and so the more organic the structure must be].[11]

We can now summarize the discussion to this point as follows: How you design an organization—its organization structure—is strongly influenced by the organization's task and specifically by the rate of change and predictableness of the information with which the organization will have to cope. At one extreme are organizations for performing predictable, routine efficiency-oriented tasks such as running a rayon mill. In such firms, efficiency is emphasized, and successful organizations tend to be mechanistic. They stress adherence to the rules and to the chain of command, are highly centralized, and have a more specialized, functional departmentalization as well as a preplanned set of policies and rules for making decisions. At the other extreme, enterprises such as high-tech electronics firms have more unpredictable tasks and are continually confronted by the need to create new products and to respond to new competitors' innovations. Responsiveness, creativity, and entrepreneurial activities are paramount if the firm is to survive; organization structures here therefore tend to be organic. Employees are not urged to stick to the rules or to abide closely to the chain of command. Jobs are enlarged and self-contained, employees are self-managing, and communications take place via a constantly shifting network of often informal interactions and mutual adjustments. It is this latter increasingly unpredictable environment that firms must face today, and so for the remainder of this chapter we will focus on organizational methods for fostering innovation and responsiveness.[12]

THE RESPONSIVE ORGANIZATION

Early management theorists were not oblivious to the fact that organizations had to be responsive—at least, occasionally. Most of these experts, such as Henri Fayol, Frederick Taylor, and Luther Gulick, were managers or consultants. They were therefore experienced enough to know that there are times when "sticking to the chain of command" simply resulted in too ponderous a response. Henri Fayol, for instance, said that orders and inquiries should generally follow the chain of command but that in very special circumstances a "bridge" communication could take place, say between a salesperson and a production supervisor, if a decision was needed immediately.

Prescriptions like these worked fairly well as long as abnormal situations were not the rule. As long as a company was operating in an environment in which novel, unexpected occurrences were at a minimum, then giving every employee a specialized job and then achieving coordination by making most everyone stick to the chain of command was an effective way of doing things. But as the number of unexpected problems and issues to be dealt with—new competitors, new product or technological innovations, customers suddenly going out of business, and so on—becomes unmanageable, such a mechanistic organization becomes overloaded and errors begin to mount. Today, says management expert Tom Peters, success in the marketplace "is directly proportional to the knowledge that an organization can bring to bear, how fast it can bring that knowledge to bear, and the rate at which it accumulates knowledge."[13] In other words, companies must be organized to respond—and to respond fast. Divisionalized structures and special "integrating" mechanisms (discussed in Chapter 8) are two ways to accomplish this responsiveness. New organizational techniques have emerged as well, as we will explore next.

SIMPLIFY/REDUCE STRUCTURE

As mentioned in Chapter 8, one thing most firms are doing today to boost responsiveness is simplifying and reducing their structures. In practical terms this means (1) several layers are squeezed out of the chain of command; (2) the remaining managers have wider spans of control; (3) managers must then reduce the amount of attention given to each of their subordinates, who therefore end up with much more decision-making authority than they originally had.[14] Some specific tactics here follow.

REDUCE LAYERS OF MANAGEMENT   Reducing management layers is perhaps the most widespread tactic used. When he took over the troubled Union Pacific Railroad (UPRR) in the mid-1980s, CEO Mike Walsh found an extremely bureaucratic and sluggish organization. Consider this typical example from Mr. Walsh:

> Suppose a customer was having difficulty [finding] a railroad car—it was either not the right one, or wasn't where the customer needed it for loading or unloading. The customer would go to his UPRR sales representative—who "went up" to the district traffic manager, who in turn "went up" to the regional traffic manager. The regional boss passed the problem from

The late Michael Walsh, former CEO of Union Pacific, drastically cut levels of management to provide better, faster responses to customer complaints and to streamline the company's decision-making process.

his sales and marketing organization, across a chasm psychologically wider than the Grand Canyon, to the operations department's general manager. The general manager then "went down" to the superintendent, who "went down" to the train master to find out what had gone wrong.[15]

After that, of course, the whole cumbersome approval process was repeated, but in reverse. The information went up the operations hierarchy, then down the sales and marketing hierarchy until—often several days later—the annoyed customer finally got his or her answer. Multiplied hundreds or thousands of times a week, that sort of unresponsiveness helped to explain, Walsh knew, why Union Pacific was losing customers, revenues, and profits.

The first thing he did was flatten the railroad's 30,000-person operations department, squeezing out five layers of middle management. The results are shown in Figure 9.3. When Walsh arrived, there were nine layers of managers between the executive VP of operations and the railroaders themselves. After the reorganization only four levels remained. In about three months, Walsh stripped out five layers and 800 middle managers from the operations chain of command.[16]

REASSIGN SUPPORT STAFF As part of their simplify/reduce structure campaigns, many firms are also moving headquarters staff people like industrial engineers out of headquarters, and assigning them to the divisional officers who are actually running the business teams. For example, candy maker Mars, Inc., is a $7 billion company with only a 30-person headquarters staff. Mars does have staff employees. But, as in more and more firms, these staff employees are assigned directly to the individual business units. Here they can help their business units be successful in the marketplace rather than act as gate keepers who check and recheck divisional managers'

FIGURE 9.3

Union Pacific Railroad Hierarchy: 1987 and 1990

SOURCE: Tom Peters, *Liberation Management* (New York: Knopf, 1992), 91.

FIGURE A	FIGURE B
PRIOR TO 1987 REORGANIZATION	1990
Executive VP Operations	*Executive VP Operations*
VP Operations	VP Field Operations
General Manager	Superintendent Transportation Services
Assistant General Manager	Manager Train Operations
Regional Transportation Superintendent	Yardmaster
Division Superintendent	*Railroaders*
Division Superintendent Transportation	
Trainmaster/Terminal Superintendent	
Assistant Trainmaster/ Terminal Trainmaster	
Yardmaster	
Railroaders	

plans for the firm's top executives. When Percy Barnevik took over as CEO of Sweden's ASEA, it had a central staff of 2,000, which he quickly reduced to 200. When his firm then acquired Finland's Stromberg company, its headquarters staff of 880 was reduced within a few years to 25.[17]

WIDEN SPANS OF CONTROL One consequence of squeezing out management layers is that it results in wider spans of control. Not too long ago, one researcher found that the average span of control in the United States was one supervisor to ten nonsupervisors. The Japanese ratio was one to 100 (and often one to 200).[18] Today, flattening the hierarchy has widened U.S. spans, by eliminating managers.

EMPOWER If the supervisors are not there to supervise, then who makes all their decisions? The answer, increasingly, is "the employees themselves." Thus, at firms like ABB, GE, and Scandinavian Air Systems, employees who previously had to consult their supervisors before taking some action like approving a refund are now making the decisions themselves.

The Pratt and Whitney engine division of United Technologies Corporation provides one example. When CEO Bob Daniell took over, one of the first problems he had to address was Pratt and Whitney's deteriorating reputation with its customers. Firms like American Airlines and United Airlines threatened they would never buy another Pratt engine unless they started getting faster answers to their complaints. Pratt soon saw its engine orders slip by over 25 percent. Part of Daniell's solution was to boost the number of service representatives in the field by nearly 70 percent. Then these field reps were given authority to approve multimillion dollar warranty replacements on the spot, instead of waiting weeks for headquarter's approvals. Customers found the improvements startling, and the Pratt and Whitney division quickly turned around.[19]

TEAM-BASED STRUCTURES

Many firms today are also organizing more activities around self-managing teams to achieve "enhanced focus, task orientation, innovativeness, and individual commitment."[20] We explain this fully in Chapter 17, and just provide some relevant examples here.

SELF-CONTAINED/SELF-MANAGING WORK TEAMS Many firms boost responsiveness by organizing their activities around self-contained and self-managing work teams. At Johnsonville Foods in Sheboygan, Wisconsin, CEO Ralph Stayer has organized much of the firm's activities around 12-person work teams. Teams like these do have their primary responsibilities, as do any work groups. At Johnsonville, specific work teams might be responsible for maintaining the firm's packaging equipment, for instance. But under traditional management practices, if something went wrong, or if the work group wanted to change one of its practices, the issue would have to go for approval up the chain of command.

Not in self-contained/self-managing work teams. At many firms around the world such teams are empowered to literally manage themselves and thus make fast, on-the-spot decisions. For example, some of the duties of a typical 12-person Johnsonville work group include:

- Recruit, hire, evaluate, and fire (if necessary) on their own.
- Formulate, then track and amend, their own budget.
- Make capital investment proposals as needed.
- Handle quality control, inspections, subsequent trouble shooting, and problem solving.

- Develop quantitative standards for productivity and quality, and then monitor them.
- Suggest and develop prototypes of possible new products and packaging.
- Routinely work on teams with counterparts from sales, marketing, and product development.[21]

The *Chesebrough-Ponds* vignette illustrates how another firm moved to a team-based organization.

NETWORK-BASED ORGANIZATIONS

Many firms use organizational networks to boost organizational responsiveness. In general, we can define a network as "a group, system, etc. of interconnected or cooperating individuals."[22] By networks, some managers mean ". . . a global web of alliances and joint ventures [between companies]."[23] We discussed such strategic networks in Chapter 6. In this section we will describe three other organizational networks used for boosting responsiveness: formal organizational networks, informal organizational

CHESEBROUGH-POND'S USA

Back in 1989, employees at Chesebrough-Pond's USA, a subsidiary of Unilever United States, Inc., were comfortable with the way their plant operated, and they didn't want it to change. But after their Quest to be the Best program was implemented, changes were required.

Under the program, a functional organization was replaced with multiskilled, cross-functional, and self-directed teams which now run the plant's four product areas. Hourly employees make employee assignments, schedule overtime, establish production times and changeovers, and even handle cost control, requisitions, and work orders. They are also solely responsible for quality control under the plant's Continuous Quality Improvement Challenge, a program in which anyone can post a *challenge* to improve quality. Sherry Emerson summed up employee sentiments: "The empowerment is exciting. If we see something that will affect the quality to customers, we have the freedom to stop a process. They [management] trust us."

The results have been extraordinary. Quality acceptance is 99.25 percent. Annual manufacturing costs are down $10.6 million, work-in-process inventory was reduced 86 percent, and total inventory was down 65 percent. Chesebrough-Pond's was named one of America's best plants. The enthusiasm still amazes plant manager Joseph M. Roy, but he's ever-vigilant. "We have to continue to instill the realization that no matter how good we are, the competition is still there—and getting better too."

SOURCE: William H. Miller, "Chesebrough-Pond's at a Glance," *Industry Week,* October 19, 1992, 14–15.

networks, and electronic information networks. We then describe two network and team-based organizational forms, *boundaryless structures,* and *horizontal structures.*

FORMAL NETWORKS

A **formal organizational network** has been defined as "a recognized group of managers assembled by the CEO and the senior executive team . . . The members are drawn from across the company's functions, business units, and geography, and from different levels of the hierarchy. The number of managers involved almost never exceeds 100 and can be fewer than 25—even in global companies with tens of thousands of employees."[24]

The cross-functional nature of formal networks is apparent in Figure 9.4. Notice that network members are typically drawn from several organizational levels and departments.

Formal networks differ from teams, cross-functional task forces, or ad hoc groups in three main ways.[25] First, unlike most task forces, networks are not temporary. On the contrary, it is the managers' ongoing experience in the network that helps to build the shared understanding among the network members that boosts the network's effectiveness.

Second, unlike most teams and task forces, networks take the initiative in finding and solving problems. In other words, they do not just solve the specific problems they are given.

Third, the existence of the formal network changes—or should change—the nature of top management's job. With the networks in place, CEOs "no longer define their jobs as making all substantive operating decisions on their own."[26] Instead, (while they still make many decisions), their main role involves creating the setting—in terms of the company's management practices and the personal relationships of the managers in the networks—that will improve the network's ability to make good decisions.

FORMAL ORGANIZATIONAL NETWORK
A recognized group of managers assembled by the CEO and the senior executive team. The members are drawn from across the company's functions, business units, geography, and from different levels of the hierarchy.

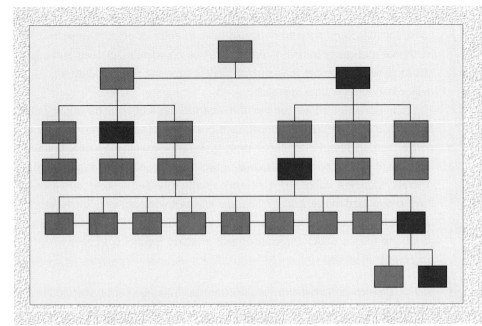

FIGURE 9.4

How Networks Reshape Organizations—For Results

The members of a formal network may be selected from various departments and organizational levels.

SOURCE: Ram Charan, "How Networks Reshape Organizations—For Results," *Harvard Business Review,* September–October, 1991.

Consider one such formal network, at the railroad firm Conrail. Here, 19 middle managers constitute the firm's operating committee. The managers influence most of the firm's key operating decisions through this committee. They meet for several hours on Monday mornings to review and decide on various tactical issues (delivery schedules and prices, for instance) and work on longer-term issues such as five-year business plans as well.[27] The *Electrolux* vignette illustrates another firm's use of formal networks.

INFORMAL NETWORKS

Many firms, particularly multinationals, also use informal organizational networks. As one expert puts it, "[Informal] networking is one method of beating international competition in the long-term . . . Creating confidence in the work of colleagues around the world and building up personal relationships are the key factors."[28] But unlike the formal network with its defined membership and purpose, **informal organizational networks** consist of cooperating individuals who are interconnected only informally. They share information and help solve each other's problems based on their personal knowledge of each other's expertise.

There are several ways to develop the personal relationships on which informal networks depend. For example, multinationals like Phillips and Shell build relationships through international executive development programs, bringing managers from around the world to work together in training centers in New York and London. Oth-

INFORMAL ORGANIZATIONAL NETWORK
Consists of cooperating individuals who are informally interconnected.

ELECTROLUX

When Leif Johansson took over an Electrolux division that stretched from Norway to Italy, he inherited a daunting task that went beyond the widespread geography. Electrolux's line included 20 products, numerous companies that had been acquired, and more than 200 plants. Each presented unique market positions, capabilities, plant capacity, and competitive situations. Johansson recognized he would have to seize opportunities across functional and geographic borders, as well as coordinate activities and capabilities, if he were to derive maximum benefit from the multi-product, multi-plant, multinational operation.

Local managers convinced him that abandoning local brands would jeopardize existing distribution channels and customer loyalty. But how could he derive the benefits of Electrolux's large scale while maintaining local brands' autonomy? His solution was a formal network comprised of managers from different countries. Johansson's network structure helped to keep operations flexible and responsive. Local managers still had wide authority to deliver local brands. But Johansson's formal network helped provide overall multinational and multi-product coordination that enabled Electrolux to obtain economies of scale.

SOURCE: Christopher Bartlett and Sumantra Ghoshal, "What Is a Global Manager?" *Harvard Business Review,* September–October 1992, 62–74.

Electronic conferences, expert networks, E-mail, and other new forms of communication via computer disseminate information to more users more quickly than do traditional means. As noted on page 254, such electronic networks can boost organizational responsiveness.

ers like Olivetti have international management development centers in their home cities, to which they bring their managers.

Development programs like these help build networks in several ways. They help to steep the managers in the firm's "corporate culture," its shared values and expectations. Furthermore, the socializing that takes place builds personal relationships among managers from the firm's facilities around the world. Such personal relationships then facilitate global networking and communications as the needs arise. So, if a new Shell Latin America sales manager needs to get in to see a new client, she might call a Shell Zurich manager she knows who has a contact at the client firm.

Moving managers from facility to facility around the world is another way to build informal networks. Transferring employees enables managers to build relationships that then can be tapped all around the globe, and some firms, such as Shell, transfer employees around the world in great numbers. At one firm, for instance:

> [International mobility] has created what one might call a "nervous system" that facilitated both corporate strategic control and the flow of information throughout the firm. Widespread transfers have created an informal information network, a superior degree of communication and mutual understanding between headquarters and subsidiaries and between subsidiaries themselves, as well as a stronger identification with the corporate culture, without compromising the local subsidiary cultures.[29]

ELECTRONIC NETWORKING

Interconnecting employees' computers throughout the firm (and indeed among firms) is another way to use networks to boost a firm's responsiveness. In this case the network is electronic. Here's how one expert describes one such application:

> An example of [such] networks was developed in the late 1970s when science advisors to state legislators joined together with technical professional societies, federal labs and public interest research groups to form Legitec Network. . . . [Using the network], for example, one frost-belt state posed the question: "What are alternatives to road salt for dealing with icy highways without polluting water supplies?" Another state, having recently dealt with the problem, responded, as did associations and labs that knew of relevant research on the topic. Other frost-belt states joined the topic to get the benefit of inquiry responses that might help their states as well as the inquiring state . . .
>
> Electronic organization and [networks] are more powerful than familiar [computer aided communication] forms, such as electronic mail and computer conferencing . . . [networking] is less formal than most other writing and in fact seems more like talking . . . the medium is more interrogative than declarative. Interacting more than expounding becomes the norm. Questions are often asked. The best answers frequently come from surprising sources. An unknown peer with irrelevant experience can sometimes provide better help than the more famous expert, who may be less accessible or less articulate.[30]

We will discuss electronic networking in greater detail in later chapters.

THE BOUNDARYLESS ORGANIZATION

"Old-style" organizations are often described as having "boundaries." Vertically, the chain of command implies clearly defined authority boundaries: the president gives orders to the vice-president, who gives orders to the managers, and so on down the line. There are also clearly delineated horizontal or departmental boundaries: the production department has its responsibilities, the sales department has its own, and so on. If the company happens to be divisionalized, then the work of each division is self-contained and each division often proceeds on the assumption that it is a sealed vessel, one that can (and should) do its job with little or no interaction with the other product divisions.[31]

We've seen that such hierarchical organizations served a very useful purpose given the tasks that most companies faced until quite recently. Jobs were specialized, lines of communication were well defined, and the slow-arriving problems could be solved in a relatively mechanical, step-by-step manner, by an organization in which everyone knew exactly where they stood.

Things are different today. Rapid change demands a more responsive organization, as we've seen. As a result, yesterday's neat organizational boundaries are disappearing. As two experts summarized it, "Companies are replacing vertical hierarchies with horizontal networks; linking together traditional functions through interfunctional teams; and forming strategic alliances with suppliers, customers, and even competitors."[32] In so doing, they are creating boundaryless organizations.

A **boundaryless organization** is one in which widespread use of teams, networks, and similar structural mechanisms means that the boundaries that typically separate organizational functions and hierarchical levels are reduced and made more permeable.[33] In fact, taken to the extreme, the boundaryless company is one in which not only internal organizational boundaries are stripped away but those between the company and its suppliers and customers are removed as well. (Recall our discussion of the virtual corporation in Chapter 6.) The *Atmospheric Processing* Small Business box illustrates how even a small business can benefit from a boundaryless organization.

BOUNDARYLESS ORGANIZATION
An organization in which widespread use of teams, networks, and similar structural mechanisms means that the boundaries that typically separate organizational functions and hierarchical levels are reduced and made more permeable.

ATMOSPHERIC PROCESSING, INC.

When the 1990 recession hit, Atmospheric Processing, Inc. CEO Gail Hering took a look at her organizational chart and decided that she had to downsize. At the time her company, which heat-treats automobile parts, had 170 employees; when she was finished 56 were left.

Hering was never big on hierarchical organizational structures. She believed that employees in such organizations focus too much on pleasing managers, who are either peering over shoulders or building alliances and protecting their turfs. "That mentality dooms a company," she says.

Hering had other problems with the standard organizational chart. An employee's first concern tended to be pleasing the person he or she was reporting to. Her solution is a boundaryless organization. She says her newly flattened organization is now full of unclassifiable, cross-trained workers because she got everyone, herself included, to focus on what makes a company really work: good products and happy customers. The problem is,

says Ms. Hering, pleasing superiors may be good for longevity, but it doesn't do much to improve output or creativity. In fact, making the immediate boss happy often supplanted company goals.

The old organizational chart had another flaw in Hering's view. Increasing profits and satisfying customers often become secondary to Machiavellian exercises that aimed at helping

FOCUS ON SMALL BUSINESS

one's career. Managers wanted bigger departments to boost their egos. Customers often complained about the layers they had to penetrate to get a decision.

In place of the traditional hierarchical chart, Hering adopted a sometimes confusing hub-and-spoke chart. At its center is customer satisfaction. Positioned around the hub in slices are functions like engineering, scheduling, staffing, shipping, billing, and paying. Encircling that comes customer service,

followed by CEO and COO, and finally the company board of directors. Generally, new employees are totally confused, but during a two-week orientation, they discover that they will learn and be responsible for a lot more than they might have under the traditional setup. "We require that new employees understand how the entire company earns a profit. We teach that if [they] don't understand something, instead of referring it to a supervisor, go directly to the person from whom it came and solve the confusion," Hering says.

Customer satisfaction displaces the CEO at the center of the circular chart. Surrounding this with company functions illustrates the need to bring about customer satisfaction *through* employees, says Hering. Putting all the functions side-by-side promotes cross department boundaryless communication channels.

Hering seems satisfied. "Now," she says, "API is a flattened organization. No one's productivity is constrained by the structure." Customers are happier, and she has control of her organization again.

SOURCE: Teri Lammers, "The New, Improved Organization Chart," *Inc.*, October 1992, 29–37.

In practice, four specific boundaries must be overcome. These are the authority boundary, the task boundary, the political boundary, and the identity boundary.[34] A summary of these four boundaries and the tensions and feelings that must be addressed in order to bridge them is presented in Figure 9.5.

THE AUTHORITY BOUNDARY Even a relatively boundaryless company still has an authority boundary, since some people still lead, while others follow. In other words, superiors and subordinates—even those found in self-managing teams or formal networks—always meet at an **authority boundary.**

Therein lies the problem: to achieve the responsiveness we want from our flat, team-based, network structure, just issuing and following orders "is no longer good enough."[35] For example, a manager in a formal network who happened to be a vice-president would inhibit the network's effectiveness if she demanded the right to give orders based solely on the fact that she was the highest ranking person in the network. Achieving boundarylessness across the authority boundary thus requires several things. Bosses must learn how to lead while remaining open to criticism. They must be willing to accept "orders" from lower ranking employees who happen to be experts on the

AUTHORITY BOUNDARY
Superiors and subordinates, even those found in self-managing teams or formal networks, always meet at an authority boundary, where some people still lead, and others follow.

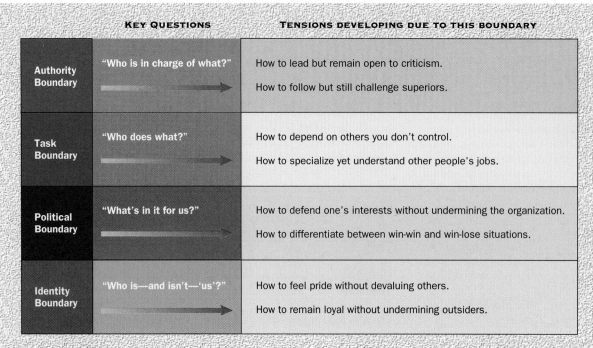

FIGURE 9.5

The Four Organizational Boundaries That Matter

In setting up a boundaryless organization, four boundaries must be overcome, but doing so means dealing with the resulting tensions.

SOURCE: Larry Hirschorn and Thomas Gilmore, "The New Boundaries of the Boundaryless Company," *Harvard Business Review,* May–June 1992, 92, 107.

problems at hand. And "subordinates" must be trained and encouraged to follow but still challenge superiors if an issue must be raised.

THE TASK BOUNDARY   Creating a boundaryless organization also requires managing the **task boundary**, which means determining who does what when employees from different departments must divide up their work. Managing the task boundary and thus achieving effective networks and teams therefore means that employees must be trained to rid themselves of the "it's not my job" attitudes that typically compartmentalize one employee's area from another's:

> Indeed, their own performance may depend directly on what their colleagues do. So, while focusing primarily on their own task, they must also take a lively interest in the challenges and problems facing others who contribute in different ways to the final product or service.[36]

THE POLITICAL BOUNDARY   Differences in political agendas often separate employees as well. For example, manufacturing typically has a strong (political) interest in smoothing out the demand for its products and in making the firm's products as producible as possible. Sales, on the other hand, has an equally legitimate (political) interest in maximizing sales (even if it means taking in a lot of last-minute rush orders). The result of such conflicting agendas is often a conflict at the department's **political boundary.**

TASK BOUNDARY
Determining who does what when employees from different departments must divide up their work.

POLITICAL BOUNDARY
The differences in political agendas that often separate employees and cause conflict.

Creating a boundaryless organization thus means managing this political boundary, too. Members of each special interest group in a boundaryless firm may still ask, "What's in it for us?" when a decision must be made. But the employees will know how to defend their interests without undermining the best interests of the team, the network, or the organization.

THE IDENTITY BOUNDARY Everyone identifies with several groups. For example, a General Motors accountant might identify with her colleagues in the accounting profession, with her coworkers in the GM accounting department, and perhaps with the General Motors Corporation itself, to name a few. In any case, the distinctive feature of such identification is that it tends to foster an "us" versus "them" mentality. The **identity boundary** means that we tend to identify with those groups with which we have shared experiences and with which we believe we share fundamental values.

The problem at the identity boundary arises because people tend to trust insiders (those who they identify with) but distrust outsiders. Attitudes like these can undermine the free-flowing cooperation that responsive, networking, team-based organizations require.

Achieving boundarylessness thus means managing the identity boundary, and there are several ways to do this. One is to train and socialize all the firm's employees so that they all come to identify with the company and become committed to its goals. Another is to emphasize that while the team spirit employees may have developed within their own groups may be laudable, they must avoid "devaluing the potential contribution of other groups."[37]

> **IDENTITY BOUNDARY**
> The tendency employees have to identify with those groups with which they have shared experiences and with which they believe they share fundamental values.

THE HORIZONTAL CORPORATION

In many firms today, *boundaryless* translates into what management gurus call a horizontal corporation. As illustrated in Figure 9.6, the horizontal corporation is organized around *basic processes* such as new product development, sales and fulfillment, and customer support. Virtually everyone works together in multidisciplinary teams, with each team performing one or more of the firm's core customer-oriented processes such as product development. In its purest form, a horizontal corporation structure is one that virtually eliminates functional departments and instead sprinkles functional specialists throughout the key process teams. Where they work together with other functional specialists to accomplish the process-oriented team's mission, be it product development, sales and fulfillment, customer support, or some other. The horizontal structure usually has a small team of senior executives to insure strategic direction and to provide essential staff support functions like human resource management.[38]

Companies are organizing horizontally for several reasons. Many firms (including AT&T and Dupont) found that just downsizing did not change the fundamental way that their departments accomplished their work. The work of the organization—from getting the sales order to processing an invoice—was still handed from department to department like batons in a relay race. At truck rental firm Ryder Systems, for instance, purchasing a vehicle for subsequent leasing required as many as 17 "handoffs," as the documents made their way from one department to another. Since such handoffs went both horizontally and vertically, the amount of time and energy wasted was enormous, and could be reduced by establishing a purchase process group.

Horizontal structures also help to obliterate the sorts of organizational boundaries we mentioned earlier. Even in divisionalized firms, functional areas tend to grow into fiefdoms in which protecting one's own turf takes priority over satisfying customer needs. Such territorial thinking is less likely to occur where the "departments" are not

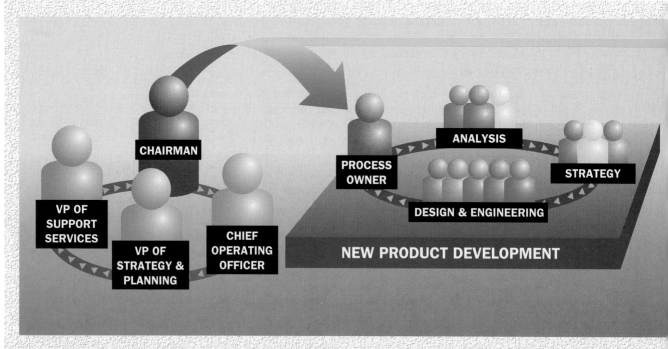

FIGURE 9.6

The Horizontal Corporation

In the horizontal corporation the work is organized around cross-functional processes with multi-function teams carrying out the tasks needed to service the customer.

SOURCE: John A. Byrne, "The Horizontal Corporation," *Business Week*, Dec. 20, 1993, 80.

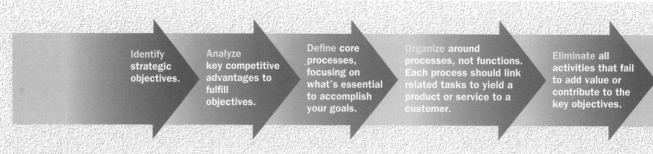

FIGURE 9.7

How to Create a Horizontal Corporation

Creating a horizontal organization involves several steps, starting with determining the firm's strategic objectives, and including such steps as flattening the hierarchy, and using teams to accomplish the work.

SOURCE: John A. Byrne, "The Horizontal Corporation," *Business Week*, Dec. 20, 1993, 80.

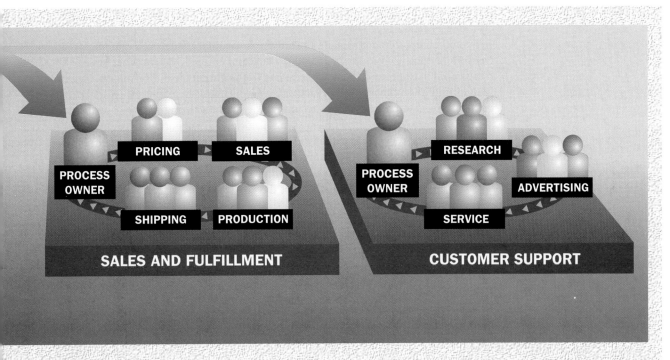

FIGURE 9.6

continued

FIGURE 9.7

continued

departments at all, but are essentially multifunctional teams organized around basic customer-oriented processes.

Several companies are moving toward the horizontal model. For example, AT&T's Network Services division with 16,000 employees identified 13 core processes and then reorganized itself around them. General Electric's lighting business similarly organized around multidisciplinary teams, each carrying out more than 100 processes and programs, from new-product design to improving manufacturing machinery efficiency.

As in Figure 9.7, the heart of creating a horizontal corporation involves defining the firm's core processes and then organizing your teams around these, linking each process team's task to specific customer-related performance objectives. Once the horizontal heart of the organization is thus in place, the firm can cut away the functions, levels, and staff departments that do not directly add value or contribute to the work of the process-oriented teams.

The traditional corporate structure, with its formal chain of command and division of labor, is undergoing massive changes in companies throughout the world. Contingency factors, such as changing markets and technological breakthroughs, now dictate the organizational structure most appropriate for a company. Manufacturers of products in relatively unchanging environments often employ a mechanistic approach in which employees strictly adhere to job descriptions. Firms that rely on the ability to introduce innovations continuously usually take an organic approach, giving employees more latitude for decision making and communication outside the formal chain of command.

SUMMARY

Team-based, or self-contained/self-managing work groups, can enhance responsiveness by conducting activities virtually autonomously. Team responsibilities range from hiring to budgeting to participation in corporate-level strategic planning.

Three types of organizational networks exist. Formal networks are often comprised of the chief executive officer, a senior executive team, and perhaps 50 or so managers. Informal networks consist of cooperating individuals informally connected by personal relationships and sharing of information. These personal relationships facilitate networking. Electronic networking is built on the interconnecting of computers throughout a firm and is another way of boosting responsiveness.

The new boundaryless organization relies on self-managing work teams and the use of networking. It reduces or eliminates internal boundaries that separate functions and hierarchical levels. The four main boundaries to be managed include the authority boundary, the task boundary, the political boundary, and the identity boundary.

The horizontal corporation structure is organized around core customer-oriented processes, with each process team comprised of various functional specialists.

QUESTIONS

■ **FOR REVIEW**

1. Explain the difference between mechanistic and organic management systems. Which one do you think is more prevalent? Why?

2. Name some of the ways an organization can become more responsive. What are the pros and cons of each?

3. Describe the inherent boundaries within an organization. Why do each of them exist?

■ **FOR DISCUSSION**

4. Discuss how technology influences organization structure.

5. List, in order of importance, the techniques you consider most effective for improving a company's responsiveness. Explain your reasoning.

6. Do you think that in the future, boundaryless organizations will become more the rule than the exception? What are the difficulties that can arise in this type of organization?

■ **FOR ACTION**

7. Go to the library and look through the last few issues of a weekly business magazine. How many examples can you find of companies that have reorganized in order to become more responsive to changing market forces?

8. Order an annual report from a Fortune 500 company. What insight does it give into how the company is organized? List all the examples of the concepts described in this chapter.

9. Think back to a job you have held. Describe the various boundaries you encountered in your line of work.

▪ FOR FOCUS ON SMALL BUSINESS

10. Is Atmospheric Processing an example of a mechanistic organization or an organic system of management? Explain.

11. Which of the organizational techniques described in the chapter has Atmospheric Processing adopted?

12. Hering successfully eliminated boundaries among her 56 employees. Would the same approach be more difficult at a large corporation? Why or why not?

CLOSING SOLUTION

HEWLETT-PACKARD

To speed up product development, CEO Young abandoned the company's linear product development method in favor of what he called a concurrent engineering approach. Cross-functional product development teams were formed, and every department thus had input from day one. Young also flattened HP's organization and divided the company's computer business into two main groups: one to oversee personal computers, printers, and products sold through dealers, and the other in charge of sales of workstations and minicomputers to large clients. Bob Frankenberg, who had been forced to try and extract a product development consensus from 38 committees, was ecstatic. "The results are incredible," he said. "We are doing more business and getting products out quicker with fewer people."

▪ QUESTIONS FOR CLOSING SOLUTION

1. Discuss some of the possible reasons why HP's organizational structure had become so unresponsive.

2. Which of the strategies described in this chapter were implemented by John Young?

3. What can Young do to ensure that the company does not revert to its unresponsive structure?

KEY TERMS

Formal Organizational Network	Task Boundary
Informal Organizational Network	Political Boundary
Boundaryless Organization	Identity Boundary
Authority Boundary	

CASE FOR ANALYSIS

PHILADELPHIA ELECTRIC COMPANY

Philadelphia Electric Company (PE) used to be the kind of company everyone loved to hate. The company was an environmentalist's punching bag. Philadelphians dubbed the downtown headquarters the Darth Vadar building. Ridicule by comedians always earned a big laugh.

The slide began in 1987. Inspectors from the Nuclear Regulatory Commission (NRC) caught a couple of plant operators at PE's Peach Bottom facility playing video games or fast asleep. Because of previous warnings, NRC lowered the boom, shutting down the plant for more than two years. The cost was more than $250 million in lost revenues and fines, and the effects rippled throughout the company.

At the same time, PE was in the process of getting its Limerick No. 2 generating station on line. The addition of No. 2 to an existing plant 35 miles northwest of Philadelphia had faced a host of problems since 1982. Initially, the need for the extra capacity was questioned. By the time the go-ahead was given, Pennsylvania's Public Utility Commission (PUC) had laid down onerous conditions. Costs couldn't exceed $3.197 billion and Unit 2 had to be on line by the fourth quarter of 1990. Nettlesome groups like Limerick Ecology Action took exception with the utility's accident and evacuation plans. Another environmental watchdog in Delaware raised issues that delayed completion of a pumping station at Point Pleasant on the Delaware River.

Joseph F. Paquette, Jr., had been PE's CEO through 1986 before leaving to become president and chief operating officer at Consumers Power Company in Michigan. He returned to PE in 1988, just in time to jump into the rate increase fight that involved bringing Limerick No. 2 on line. Miraculously, PE had completed the plant $400 million under projections and nine months early. But the PUC only approved a 7.7 percent rate increase. Construction costs, overcapacity, and the rate of return on equity were cited as excessive. The PUC lopped $307 million off the company's original request of $549 million.

Paquette, who had spent 30 years at PE, faced a daunting task in turning things around. He brought in Corbin McNeill, an ex-commander of nuclear-powered naval vessels, to run the Peach Bottom plant. McNeill had turned around New York Power Authority's Fitzpatrick unit in 1983. He didn't mince words when getting across the message that Peach Bottom was in crisis. Podiums were pounded, and at one meeting furniture flew. Said plant manager Kenneth Powers, "He shared our frustrations and passions."

Upon taking over, McNeill immediately noted a lack of leadership and management skills in the plan for getting the plant started up again. Employees were promoted based on seniority, not on their skills, and the company has had as many as 10 to 12 management levels.

With its monopoly in a highly regulated industry, PE had also become complacent. The company did not even have a customer service department. Beth Rubino, manager of management development, acknowledged that the utility focused principally on procedures. That was useful in ensuring that PE operated a safe plant and acted as a reliable source of energy for customers, but it had its drawbacks. "Everything became focused on the technical end. Anything that was technical got lots of attention and money thrown at it. When something broke, we would write a new procedure to fix it, instead of looking at why it was broken and what we could do differently," Rubino says.

Not everything at PE needed changing. Many of the employees were second and third generation members of the same family to work for the company. Turnover was less than 2 percent a year. And PE had achieved world-class status in the nuclear business, with its original Peach Bottom I plant serving as a prototype for others in the industry. But as it shifted its focus to the new Limerick plant, Peach Bottom had started to lag. "We became complacent about how we managed Peach Bottom. Finally, the NRC came in and shut it down. This was after lots of people at the station were crying for help but really weren't being heard by the corporation. We threw contractors at all of our problems instead of managing our problems," Rubino says. "I believe it was the first time in the industry that a plant was shut down for human resources reasons."

Immediately after the shutdown, the company reacted first by making cosmetic changes to spruce up the plant. But when criticism began flooding in from other regulatory agencies, company officials knew they had to do more.

SOURCES: "The Luck of the Irish," *Financial World,* May 29, 1990, 28–29; Manjeet Kriplani, "Transformation," *Forbes,* April 27, 1992, 132; and Jennifer J. Laabs, "Plant Shutdown Forces Changes in Operations," *Personnel Journal,* March 1993, 112–22.

■ QUESTIONS

1. Using some of the concepts described in the chapter, detail how you think PE could be reorganized in order to be more effective.
2. By 1992, PE management had turned things around. The company not only was profitable again, but it also had improved its public image. Find some articles in the university library that detail how the company changed and compare the actual events with the plan you outlined in the first question.
3. Do you think PE's problems stemmed largely from the fact that it was a monopoly in a highly regulated industry? Please discuss.

A CASE IN DIVERSITY

DISABILITY HIRING INITIATIVE BY CEOS

Even before the Americans with Disabilities Act pushed the recruitment and hiring of disabled persons to the forefront of public consciousness, a group of top corporate executives had already undertaken their own initiative. Called the Disability 2000–CEO Council, the group ambitiously set as its goal the doubling of the number of employed disabled persons by the year 2000. But the group isn't simply focusing on filling slots and presenting statistics. The aim is to enhance communication between disabled workers and their colleagues, upgrade their skill levels, and bring about changes in perception that in the past have effectively been boundaries to their development and growth. So far, progress has been an admirable cooperative effort between government and corporate America.

U.S. West Corporation founded its FRIENDS program in 1990. Designed to attract applicants with disabilities, this support group now has almost 100 members company-wide. The effort begins with human resource personnel visiting campuses to focus recruitment efforts on qualified graduates with disabilities. To get the most from these new-hires, career assistance and developmental counseling is available on an on-going basis. Disabled employees also actively deal with customers who have similar impairments, creating what the company considers a competitive advantage.

Westinghouse received the Opportunity 2000 Award in 1992 from the U.S. Department of Labor. The award is presented to the company that best exemplifies in-place affirmative action programs such as skills training, upward mobility, 'glass ceiling' issues, and work and family life programs. Among other achievements, the company created specialized medical equipment specifically designed to assist disabled workers. Westinghouse designed a stand-up wheel chair, a blink switch with voice synthe-

sizer enabling communication strictly by eye movement, and a Computer Aided Design workstation for quadriplegic employees.

The Target Corporation actively recruits disabled workers, and some stores establish a mentor for new employees. Called the buddy system, a department supervisor pairs the disabled employee with a current staffer. The set-up affords the new-hires the benefit of their mentor's experience when problems or unfamiliar tasks arise. Target believes the program is not only beneficial to customers, but also to the employees who serve as buddies to disabled workers.

Besides coming into compliance with the law of the land, the Disability 2000–CEO Council believes promoting higher employment among qualified persons with disabilities makes good business sense. They also think eliminating the kind of tunnel-vision in which employees only communicate and relate to their own narrow peer group will create all sorts of ideas and opportunities.

SOURCE: "The Disability 2000–CEO Council," *Business Week*, Oct. 28, 1991, 32–33; *Willing and Able*, National Organization on Disibilities.

■ **QUESTIONS**

1. What effect will the efforts of the Disability 2000–CEO Council have on the identity boundary in the workplace?
2. Is it possible to completely eliminate an "us" versus "them" mentality among diverse workers? Why or why not?
3. US WEST, Westinghouse and Target have developed programs aimed at integrating disabled employees into the work force. Can you think of any other approaches companies could take?

ENDNOTES

1. George Stalk, Phillip Evans, and Lawrence E. Shulman, "Competing on Capabilities: The New Rules of Corporate Strategy," *Harvard Business Review*, March–April 1992, 87–94.
2. Tom Peters, *Liberation Management* (New York: Alfred Knopf, 1992), 9.
3. Tom Burns and G. M. Stalker, *The Management of Innovation* (London: Tavistock Publications, 1961), vii.
4. Ibid., 94.
5. Joan Woodward, *Industrial Organization: Theory and Practice* (London: Oxford University Press, 1965).
6. Woodward, *Industrial Organization*, 64. Some more recent findings provide support for this assertion. See Robert Keller, et al., "Management Systems, Uncertainty, and Continuous Process Technology," *Proceedings of the Academy of Management*, 33rd Annual Meeting, August 1973, 507–508.
7. Peter Blau, et al., "Technology and Organization in Manufacturing," *Administrative Science Quarterly*, March 1976, 110–16.
8. Other contingency factors including organizational size, operating variability, and life cycle have also been found to influence organization structure. See, for example, Derek Pugh, et al., "The Context of Organization Structures," *Administrative Science Quarterly*, vol. 14 (1969), 15–16; John Kimberly, "Organizational Size and the Structuralist Perspective: A Review, Critique, and Proposal," *Administrative Science Quarterly*, vol. 21 (December 1976), 380–84; Guy Geerarts, "The Effect of Ownership on the Organization Structure in Small

Firms," *Administrative Science Quarterly,* vol. 29, no. 2, June 1984, 172–76; and Robert Marsh and Hiroshi Mannari, "Technology and Size as Determinants of the Organizational Structure of Japanese Factories," *Administrative Science Quarterly,* vol. 26, no. 1 (March 1981), 33–57.

9. Burns and Stalker, *Management in Innovation,* 96.

10. Henry Mintzberg, *Structure in Fives: Designing Effective Organizations* (Englewood Cliffs, NJ: Prentice-Hall, 1983), 136–37.

11. Jay Galbraith, *Organization Design* (Reading, MA: Addison-Wesley, 1977), 36–37.

12. For an additional perspective on how firms structurally respond to increased innovation see, for example, John Child, "Information Technology, Organization, and a Response to Strategic Challenges," *California Management Review,* Fall 1987, 81–84; Alfred Marcus, "Responses to Externally Induced Innovation: Their Effects on Organizational Performance," *Strategic Management Journal,* vol. 9 (1988), 387–402; and Danny Miller, "Relating Porter's Business Strategies to Environment and Structure: Analysis and Performance Implications," *Academy of Management Journal,* vol. 31, no. 2 (1988), 280–308.

13. Peters, *Liberation Management,* 310.

14. Except as noted, this section is based on Tom Peters, *Thriving on Chaos* (New York: Harper & Row, 1987), 425–38; and Peters, *Liberation Management,* 90–95.

15. Peters, *Liberation Management,* 88.

16. Based on Peters, *Liberation Management,* 90.

17. Peters, *Liberation Management,* 49–50.

18. James O'Toole, *Work and the Quality of Life: Resource Papers for Work in America* (Boston, MA: MIT Press, 1974), 18–29.

19. Todd Vogel, "Where 1990s-Style Management Is Already Hard at Work," *Business Week,* October 23, 1989, 92–100.

20. Tom Peters, *Thriving on Chaos,* 256.

21. Tom Peters, *Liberation Management,* 238.

22. *Webster's New World Dictionary,* 3rd college ed. (New York: Simon and Schuster, Inc., 1988), 911.

23. Ram Charan, "How Networks Reshape Organizations—For Results," *Harvard Business Review,* September–October 1991, 104–15.

24. Ibid., 105.

25. Based on Charan, "How Networks Reshape Organizations," 106–107.

26. Charan, "How Networks Reshape Organizations," 106.

27. Ibid., 108.

28. Tom Lester, "The Rise of the Network," *International Management,* June 1992, 72.

29. Paul Evans, Yves Doz, and Andre Laurent, *Human Resource Management in International Firms* (London: Macmillan, 1989), 123.

30. Chandler Harrison Stevens, "Electronic Organization and Expert Networks: Beyond Electronic Mail and Computer Conferencing," Sloan School of Management Working Paper No. 1794–86, Massachusetts Institute of Technology, Management in the 1990s Research Program, May 1986. Reprinted in Peters, *Liberation Management,* 123–24.

31. Mary Anne Devanna and Noel Tichy, "Creating the Competitive Organization of the 21st Century: The Boundaryless Corporation," *Human Resource Management,* vol. 29, no. 4, Winter 1990, 455–71.

32. Larry Hirschhorn and Thomas Gilmore, "The New Boundaries of the 'Boundaryless' Company," *Harvard Business Review,* May–June 1992, 104.

33. This is based on Hirschhorn and Gilmore, "The New Boundaries," 104–108.

34. Except as noted, the remainder of this section is based on Hirschhorn and Gilmore, "The New Boundaries," 107–109.

35. Hirschhorn and Gilmore, "The New Boundaries," 107.

36. Ibid., 108.

37. Ibid., 109.

38. Except as noted, this section is based on John A. Byrne, "The Horizontal Corporation," *Business Week,* December 20, 1993, 76–81.

CHAPTER 10

THE STAFFING FUNCTION AND HUMAN RESOURCE MANAGEMENT

LEARNING OBJECTIVES

After studying this chapter, you should be able to:

- Define human resource management.

- Describe the legal framework of the personnel function, including equal employment laws.

- Discuss the six steps in staffing an organization: job analysis, personnel planning, recruiting, interviewing, testing and selection, and training and development.

- Explain five employee selection techniques.

- Discuss the processes of orienting, training, and developing new employees.

- Compare and contrast the four main forms of direct and indirect compensation and employee benefits.

- Describe why performing employee appraisals is important.

OPENING PROBLEM

BECKER CPA REVIEW COURSE LTD.

Small-business owner Newton D. Becker achieved a nationwide first in late 1992. As founder of the Encino, California–based Becker CPA Review Course, Ltd. (a company that helps accountants to prepare for competency exams), Becker knew he had to make accommodations for deaf students under the Americans with Disabilities Act. After reading the law, which lists "written notes" as an acceptable accommodation, he dutifully furnished them. ■ Apparently unsatisfied, the U.S. Department of Justice told Becker it would take action against his firm unless he hired sign-language interpreters for the hearing impaired by December 24, 1992. Becker says he complied on the deadline date. Four days later the department went ahead and sued him anyway, giving Becker the dubious distinction of being the first person ever sued under the ADA. No one at the Justice Department would comment. "They won't take yes for an answer," said Becker.[1]

THE CENTRAL ROLE OF HUMAN RESOURCE MANAGEMENT

WHAT IS HUMAN RESOURCE MANAGEMENT?

HUMAN RESOURCE MANAGEMENT
The management function devoted to acquiring, training, appraising, and compensating employees.

Human resource management (also sometimes called *staffing* or *personnel management*) is the management function devoted to acquiring, training, appraising, and compensating employees. All managers are, in a sense, personnel managers, since like Newton Becker they all get involved in activities like recruiting, interviewing, selecting, and training. But most firms also have a human resource department with its own human resource manager. As shown in Figure 10.1, this department is responsible for the firm's personnel-related activities.

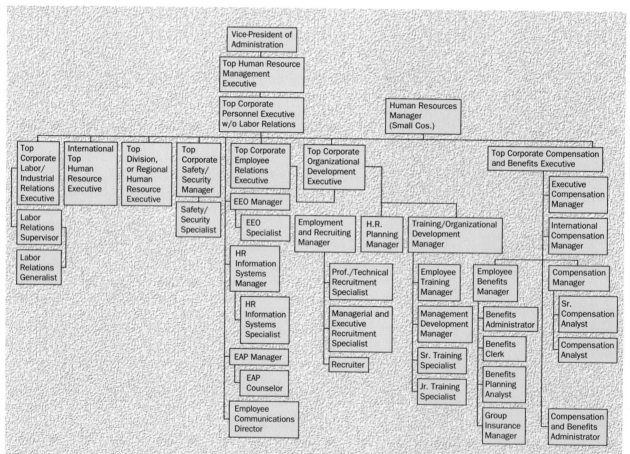

FIGURE 10.1

Human Resource Department in a Large Organization

This shows the organization chart of the human resource department in a very large firm. Even in a small firm, however, the same personnel functions, such as labor relations, safety, equal employment, and training must be addressed.

SOURCE: Gary Dessler, *Human Resource Management,* 6th ed. (Englewood Cliffs, NJ: Prentice-Hall, 1994), 7.

THE EVOLVING IMPORTANCE OF HUMAN RESOURCE MANAGEMENT

The human resource function is increasingly important in today's fast-changing world. That helps to explain why some former personnel officers are today top CEOs. For example, Ronald W. Allen, chairman, president, and CEO of Delta Airlines, was formerly the company's top personnel officer and spent almost ten years overseeing Delta's personnel department. Janet Colson moved from vice-president of human resources for the Restaurant Enterprises Group to senior VP of financial and administrative services. Dave Pringle parlayed jobs as head of human resources for United Airlines and White Motor Corporation into the president of Louisville Ladder Corp., an Emerson Electric Company subsidiary.[2]

Personnel's growing importance derives in part from competitive changes taking place today. As seen in previous chapters, several trends—such as global competition, an increased rate of technological change, increasingly sophisticated customers, more service and "knowledge-based" jobs, and a more sophisticated work force—are forcing companies to organize more responsively. Companies are now flattening their pyramids, relying more on self-managing work teams, empowering workers, and getting "closer to their customers," in part by giving employees more authority to handle customer complaints and requests.

Changes like these require a more high-powered and motivated work force. In particular, promoting teamwork, trust, and in general creating a highly committed work force are increasingly crucial as companies battle each other for dominance. And as the management function charged with the tasks of hiring, training, and compensating the firm's employees, human resource management plays a central role in molding a company's work force into a motivated and committed team.

THE LEGAL FRAMEWORK OF HUMAN RESOURCE MANAGEMENT

In Minnesota, an apartment manager with a passkey entered a woman's apartment and assaulted her; the apartment building's owner was found to be the cause of personal injury to the tenant because the owner had failed to exercise reasonable care in hiring the apartment manager.[3] Time Warner's Home Box Office unit recently was sued by a 58-year-old former employee who charged he was turned down for an HBO job because he was too old.[4] Cases like these emphasize an important fact of life regarding human resource management: more than any other management function, the personnel function is subject to a myriad of federal, state, and local laws.

EQUAL EMPLOYMENT LAWS

The equal employment laws that prohibit employment discrimination are among the most important of these personnel laws (see Table 10.1). For example, **Title VII of the 1964 Civil Rights Act** bars discrimination because of race, color, religion, sex, or national origin. Its requirements are enforced by the federal Equal Employment Opportunity Commission. This is a five-member commission, appointed by the president with the advice and consent of the Senate. It receives, investigates, and may file charges regarding job discrimination complaints on behalf of aggrieved individuals. Other important antidiscrimination laws include the Equal Pay Act of 1963 (which requires equal pay for men and women performing similar work), the Pregnancy Discrimination Act of 1978 (which prohibits discrimination in employment against

TITLE VII
From the Civil Rights Act of 1964, this bars discrimination because of race, color, religion, sex, or national origin.

TABLE 10.1

Summary of Important
Equal Employment
Opportunity Legislation

SOURCE: Gary Dessler,
*Human Resource Manage-
ment*, 6th ed. (Englewood
Cliffs, NJ: Prentice-Hall,
1994), 47.

ACTION	WHAT IT DOES
Title VII of 1964 Civil Rights Act, as amended	Bars discrimination because of race, color, religion, sex, or national origin; instituted EEOC
Executive orders	Prohibit employment discrimination by employers with federal contracts of more than $10,000 (and their subcontractors); establish office of federal compliance; require affirmative action programs
Federal agency guidelines	Guidelines used by federal agencies covering enforcement of laws barring discrimination based on sex, national origin, and religion, as well as employee selection procedures; for example, they require validation of tests
Supreme court decisions: *Griggs v. Duke Power Co., Albemarle v. Moody*	Ruled that job requirements must be related to job success; that discrimination need not be overt to be proved; that the burden of proof is on the employer to prove the qualification is valid
Equal Pay Act of 1963	Requires equal pay for men and women for performing similar work
Age Discrimination in Employment Act of 1967	Prohibits discriminating against a person 40 or over in any area of employment because of age
State and local laws	Often cover organizations too small to be covered by federal laws
Vocational Rehabilitation Act of 1973	Requires affirmative action to employ and promote qualified handicapped persons and prohibits discrimination against handicapped persons
Pregnancy Discrimination Act of 1978	Prohibits discrimination in employment against pregnant women, or related conditions
Vietnam Era Veterans' Readjustment Assistance Act of 1974	Requires affirmative action in employment for veterans of the Vietnam war era
Wards Cove v. Atonio; Patterson v. McLean Credit Union	These Supreme Court decisions made it more difficult to prove a case of unlawful discrimination against an employer
Morton v. Wilks	This case allowed consent decrees to be attacked and could have had a chilling effect on certain affirmative action programs
Americans with Disabilities Act of 1990	Strengthens the need for most employers to make reasonable accommodations for disabled employees at work; prohibits discrimination
Civil Rights Act of 1991	Reverses *Wards Cove, Patterson,* and *Martin* decisions; places burden of proof back on employer and permits compensatory and punitive money damages for discrimination

pregnant women), and the Americans with Disabilities Act of 1990 (which requires employers to make reasonable accommodations for disabled employees at work).

At work, antidiscrimination laws mean employers should adhere to certain procedures. For example, employers should confirm that selection tests they use do not unfairly screen out minorities, and should avoid inquiring about an applicant's ethnic, racial, or marital status.

AFFIRMATIVE ACTION PROGRAMS

AFFIRMATIVE ACTION
Requires the employer to make
an extra effort to hire and promote those in the protected
(women or minority) group.

Whereas equal employment opportunity aims to ensure equal treatment at work, **affirmative action** requires the employer to make an extra effort to hire and promote those in the protected (women or minority) group. Affirmative action thus includes specific actions (in recruitment, hiring, promotions, and compensation) that are designed to eliminate the present effects of past discrimination. An example would be setting a goal of promoting more minorities to middle management jobs.

SEXUAL HARASSMENT

Sexual harassment is illegal in the United States. **Sexual harassment** may be defined as unwelcome sexual advances, requests for sexual favors, and other verbal or physical conduct of a sexual nature that takes place under conditions including the following: where such conduct is made, either explicitly or implicitly, a term or condition of an individual's employment; submission to or rejection of such conduct by an individual is used as the basis for employment decisions affecting the individual; or such conduct has the purpose or effect of unreasonably interfering with an individual's work performance or creating an intimidating, hostile, or offensive work environment.

Any manager should keep two facts in mind with respect to sexual harassment. First, in addition to being unfair and detestable, it is also illegal. In fact, in one famous case, *Meritor Savings Bank, FSB v. Vinson,* the U.S. Supreme Court indicated that employers should establish meaningful complaint procedures and head off charges of sexual harassment before they occur.

Second, sexual harassment is a widely occurring problem. Upwards of 60 percent of female employees (as well as a large percentage of male employees) report having experienced sexual harassment.[5] At Stanford University, Dr. Frances Conley, one of the first female neurosurgeons in the country, recently resigned from the School of Medicine saying she had endured years of subtle sexual harassment at the school, most of which, she said, took the form of demeaning remarks from coworkers. However, Conley said she also had to fend off physical contacts and sexual comments by other doctors.[6] The *Corning, Inc.* vignette shows how one firm deals with and prevents sexual harassment.

OCCUPATIONAL SAFETY AND HEALTH

The **Occupational Safety and Health Act** was passed by Congress "to assure so far as possible every working man and woman in the nation safe and healthful working conditions and to preserve our human resources." The Act sets safety and health standards, standards that apply to almost all workers in the United States. The standards themselves are contained in five volumes and cover just about any hazard one could think of at work including, for instance, what sorts of ladders to use, fire protection, and how to guard against accidents when using machines and portable power tools.

LABOR-MANAGEMENT RELATIONS

Various labor laws govern union-management relations. For example, the Norris-LaGuardia Act guarantees each employee the right to bargain with employers for union benefits. The Wagner Act outlaws unfair labor practices such as employers interfering with, restraining, or coercing employees who are exercising their legally sanctioned rights of organizing themselves into a union. The Taft-Hartley Act prohibits unfair labor practices by unions against employers (like refusing to bargain with the employer). The Landrum-Griffin Act protects union members from unfair practices against them perpetrated by their unions.

OTHER EMPLOYMENT LAW ISSUES

Other employment-related laws impact virtually every personnel-related decision that you will make at work. The **Fair Labor Standards Act,** for instance, specifies a

SEXUAL HARASSMENT
Unwelcome sexual advances, requests for sexual favors, other verbal or physical conduct of a sexual nature, and actions creating a hostile work environment.

OCCUPATIONAL SAFETY AND HEALTH ACT
An act passed by Congress to set safety and health standards that apply to almost all workers in the United States.

FAIR LABOR STANDARDS ACT
Specifies a minimum wage ($4.25 per hour as of 1995), as well as child-labor and overtime pay rules.

CORNING, INC.

A year after the Senate confirmation hearings on the nomination of Clarence Thomas to the Supreme Court, the Equal Employment Opportunity Commission reported a 50 percent increase in charges of harassment. Anita Hill's charge of harassment affected almost every company in the nation. Labor lawyers, consultants, and advocacy groups reported that companies were scrambling for information, with calls coming in at three times the previous rate.

Corning, Inc., tackled the issue of women's treatment in the workplace well before the hearings. It developed a policy for those suffering harassment: confront the harasser and let him or her know your feelings. If that fails, bring the problem to the attention of management. And if the first two steps aren't successful, go forward and take part in the investigation and the process of rectifying the behavior. The New York advocacy group, Catalyst, selected Corning as one of only four companies to receive its award for commitment to women.

Future managers will have to come to grips with the fact that the workplace is the most probable arena for sexual harassment to occur. Most would also agree that preventing the problem is preferable to lawsuits or a public airing like the Thomas hearings.

SOURCES: Michele Galen, Joseph Weber, and Alice Luneo, "Sexual Harassment Out of the Shadows," Business Week, October 28, 1991, 30–31; and Geoffrey Smith, "Consciousness-Raising among 'Plain Old White Boys,' " Business Week, October 28, 1991, 32.

When exit interviews with women and blacks in the mid-1980s consistently revealed that they felt their chances for advancement at Corning were limited, the company created an internal affirmative-action plan, part of which deals with issues of sexual harassment. Dawn Cross, Corning's director of diversity, sees artificial barriers to advancement slowly being removed.

minimum wage ($4.25 per hour as of 1995), as well as child-labor and overtime pay rules. The Employee Polygraph Protection Act of 1988 outlaws almost all uses of the polygraph or "lie-detector" machine for employment purposes. Under certain legislation such as the Federal Privacy Act of 1974 and the New York Personal Privacy Protection Act of 1985, employees may have legal rights regarding who has access to information about their work history and job performance. Under the Whistle-Blower Protection Act of 1989, some employees who "blow the whistle" on their employers for the purpose of publicizing dangerous employer practices are subject to legal protection.

STAFFING THE ORGANIZATION

The term **staffing** is often used to refer to actually filling a firm's open positions, and it includes six steps (as summarized in Figure 10.2): job analysis, personnel planning, recruiting, interviewing, testing and selection, and training and development.

JOB ANALYSIS

Developing an organization chart (discussed in Chapters 8 and 9) results in jobs to be filled. **Job analysis** is the procedure used to determine the duties of the jobs and the kinds of people (in terms of skills and experience) who should be hired for them.[7] It provides data on job requirements, which are then used to develop a job description (a list of duties showing what the job entails) and job specifications (a list of the skills and aptitudes showing what kind of people to hire for the job).

A **job description** like the one in Figure 10.3 identifies the job, provides a brief job summary, and then lists specific responsibilities and duties of the job. The **job specification** specifies the human qualifications in terms of traits, skills, and experiences required to accomplish the job.

PERSONNEL PLANNING

Personnel planning involves forecasting personnel requirements and the supply of outside candidates and internal candidates, and then producing plans that describe how candidates will be trained and prepared for the jobs that will be opening up.

Thanks to computers, personnel planning today is becoming increasingly sophisticated. Many firms maintain computerized information systems containing employee

STAFFING
Refers to actually filling a firm's open positions, and it includes six steps: job analysis, personnel planning, recruiting, interviewing, testing and selection, and training and development.

JOB ANALYSIS
The procedure used to determine the duties of the jobs and the kinds of people (in terms of skills and experience) who should be hired for them.

JOB DESCRIPTION
Identifies the job, provides a brief job summary, and then lists specific responsibilities and duties of the job.

JOB SPECIFICATION
Specifies human qualifications in terms of traits, skills, and experiences required to accomplish the job.

PERSONNEL PLANNING
Involves forecasting personnel requirements and the supply of outside candidates and internal candidates, and then producing plans that describe how candidates will be trained and prepared for the jobs that will be opening up.

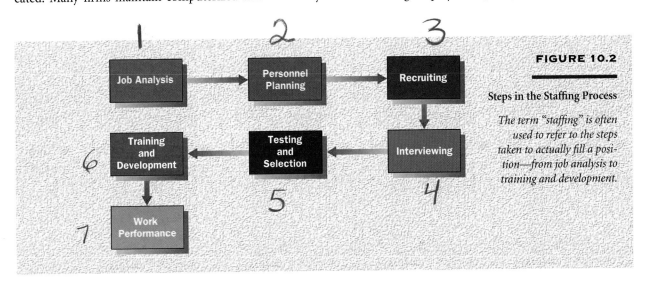

FIGURE 10.2

Steps in the Staffing Process

The term "staffing" is often used to refer to the steps taken to actually fill a position—from job analysis to training and development.

FIGURE 10.3

Sample Job Description

SOURCE: Richard Daft, *Management*, 3rd ed. (Fort Worth, TX: The Dryden Press, 1994), 412.

AmericanAirlines

JOB DESCRIPTION

Title: Associate - Corporate Development

Department: Corporate Development

Location: Corporate Headquarters
              Dallas/Fort Worth Airport, Texas

Reports To: Managing Director - Corporate Development

American Airlines is seeking an Associate for its Corporate Development Department. This position supports the growing diversification activities of AMR Corporation, American Airlines and other subsidiaries.

Functional Description:

Responsibilities include identifying, analyzing and negotiating merger and acquisition transactions in a diverse group of industries. Position involves interaction with senior management as well as the Legal, Tax and operating departments.

Qualifications:

MBA degree required. The successful applicant will have excellent communication and analytical skills. Prior experience in mergers and acquisition and knowledge of PC financial modeling techniques are preferred.

P.O. BOX 61616, DALLAS/FORT WORTH AIRPORT, TEXAS 75261-9616, CABLE ADDRESS AMAIR

information on hundreds of employee traits (like special skills, product knowledge, work experience, training courses, relocation limitations, and career interests).[8] The availability of so much employee data facilitates planning for and filling positions in big companies. It also has intensified the need to create better ways to protect the privacy of the personal data that are stored in the firm's data banks.

EMPLOYEE RECRUITING

RECRUITING
Attracting a pool of viable job applicants.

Recruiting—attracting a pool of viable job applicants—is a crucial personnel function. If only two candidates appear for two openings, the manager may have little choice but to hire them. But if 20 or 30 applicants appear, then you can use techniques like interviews and tests to screen out all but the best. The main sources of applicants are discussed next.

INTERNAL SOURCES OF CANDIDATES   While recruiting often brings to mind employment agencies and classified ads, *current employees* are often your largest source of recruits.

Filling open positions with inside candidates has both benefits and drawbacks. On the plus side, employees see that competence is rewarded and morale and performance may thus be enhanced. Inside candidates are also known quantities in terms of their performance and skills and may already be committed to your organization and its goals. On the other hand, current employees who apply for jobs and do not get them may become discontented. Furthermore, promotion from within can lead to inbreeding: when an entire management team has been brought up through the ranks, there may be a tendency to maintain the status quo, when an innovative and new direction is called for.

ADVERTISING AS A SOURCE OF CANDIDATES As you know from the many help-wanted ads that appear in your local newspaper, advertising is a major source of attracting applicants. The main issue here is selecting the best advertising medium, be it the local paper, *The Wall Street Journal,* or a technical journal. The medium chosen depends on the type of job. The local newspaper is usually the best source for blue-collar help, clerical employees, and lower-level administrative employees. For specialized positions, employers can advertise in trade and professional journals like *American Psychologist, Sales Management,* and *Chemical Engineering.* Executive jobs are often advertised in *The Wall Street Journal.*

EMPLOYMENT AGENCIES AS A SOURCE OF CANDIDATES An employment agency is basically an intermediary whose business is to match applicants with open positions. There are basically three types of agencies: (1) those operated by federal, state, or local governments; (2) those associated with nonprofit organizations; and (3) those that are privately owned.

Public state employment agencies exist in every state and are often referred to as job service or unemployment service agencies. Agencies like these are a major free source of hourly blue-collar and clerical workers and are increasingly establishing themselves as agents for professional and managerial-level applicants as well.

Other employment agencies are associated with nonprofit organizations. For example, most professional and technical societies such as the Academy of Management have units that help their members find jobs.

Private agencies charge fees for each applicant they place. Their fees are usually set by state law and are posted in their offices. Whether the employer or the candidate pays the fee is mostly determined by market conditions. However, the trend in the last few years has been toward fee-paid jobs in which the employer and not the candidate pays the fees. Such agencies are important sources of clerical, white-collar, and managerial personnel.

EXECUTIVE RECRUITERS AS A SOURCE OF CANDIDATES Executive recruiters (also known ominously as head hunters) are agencies retained by employers to seek out top management talent for their clients. They fill jobs in the $40,000 and up category, although $50,000 is often the lower limit.

These firms can be very useful. They have many business contacts and are especially adept at contacting qualified candidates who are employed and not actively looking to change jobs. They can also keep a firm's name confidential until late in the search process. The recruiter can also save management time by doing the preliminary work of advertising for the position and screening what could turn out to be hundreds of applicants. The recruiting process will typically begin with the executive recruiter meeting with the client company's executives to formulate a clear written description of the position to be filled and the sort of person needed to fill it. The recruiter will then use various sources and contacts to identify viable candidates, interview these people, and present a short list of three or four candidates to the client's executives for final screening.

EXECUTIVE RECRUITERS
Agencies retained by employers to seek out top management talent for their clients.

REFERRALS OR WALK-INS AS A SOURCE OF CANDIDATES Particularly for hourly workers, "walk-ins"—people who apply directly at the office—are a major source of applicants. Encouraging walk-in applicants may be as simple as posting a hand-written Help Wanted sign in your office or plant window. On the other hand, some organizations encourage walk-in applicants by mounting employee referral campaigns. Here, announcements of openings and requests for referrals are made in the company's bulletin or posted on bulletin boards.

OLDER WORKERS AS A SOURCE OF JOB CANDIDATES   As of the early 1990s, 44 percent fewer eighteen- to twenty-five-year-olds have been entering the work force than there were in 1979. This reduction has caused many employers to begin looking to alternative sources to help meet their employment needs.[9] For many employers this means harnessing America's "gray power," by encouraging current retirement-age employees to stay with the company, or actively recruiting applicants who are at or near (or beyond) retirement age.[10]

EMPLOYEE SELECTION AND PLACEMENT

With a pool of applicants, the firm can turn to screening and selecting. This involves using one or more techniques including application blanks, interviews, tests, and reference checks to assess and investigate an applicant's aptitudes, interests, and background. The company then chooses the best candidate, given the job's requirements.

Employee selection is important for several reasons. First, as a manager, your own performance will always hinge on the performance of your subordinates. A poor performer will drag a manager down, and a good one will enhance your own performance. Therefore, the time to screen out undesirables is before they have their foot in the door—not after.

Screening applicants is also expensive, so it is best to do it right the first time around. Hiring a manager who earns $60,000 a year may cost as much as $40,000 or $50,000 once search fees, interviewing time, and travel and moving expenses are added up. In fact, the cost of hiring even nonexecutive employees can be $3,000 to $5,000 apiece or more.

Employee selection is also important because it is the first chance the company has to instill in the employee the values and culture the company cherishes. We will return to this point but should first review some popular employee selection techniques.

APPLICATION BLANKS

APPLICATION BLANK
A form that requests information like education, work history, and hobbies, and is a good means of quickly collecting verifiable and fairly accurate historical data from the candidate.

The selection process usually begins with an application blank, although some firms first require a brief, prescreening interview. The **application blank** is a form that requests information like education, work history, and hobbies.[11] It is a good means of quickly collecting verifiable and therefore fairly accurate historical data from the candidate.

TESTING FOR EMPLOYEE SELECTION

TEST
A sample of a person's behavior, used in personnel management for predicting a person's success on the job.

A **test** is basically a sample of a person's behavior. It is used in personnel management for predicting a person's success on the job.

The use of tests for hiring, promotion, or both has increased in recent years after two decades of decline.[12] It appears that about half of all employers use tests of some sort for employee screening: about two-thirds use skill tests (like typing tests) while only about 17 percent use so-called personality tests.

Actually, many different types of tests are available to be used at work. For example, intelligence (IQ) tests are designed to measure general intellectual abilities. Intelligence is often measured with the Standord-Binet test or with the Wechsler or Wonderlic tests.

For some jobs, managers will also be interested in testing an applicant's other abilities. For example, the Bennett Test of Mechanical Comprehension (shown in Figure 10.4) helps to assess an applicant's understanding of basic mechanical principles and might be useful for predicting success on a job like machinist or engineer. A test like the Stromberg Dexterity Test is used to measure the applicant's speed of finger, hand, and arm movements. This would be useful if the job in question involves manipulating small items (for instance, assembling computer circuit boards).

It is also sometimes useful to measure the applicant's personality and interests. For example, you probably would not want to hire someone into an entry-level job as accounting clerk if he or she had no measurable interest in working with figures.[13] With the burgeoning number of service workers these days, service management expert Karl Albrecht says that jobs that involve high levels of *emotional labor* will increase. Emotional labor is any kind of work in which the employee's feelings are the tools of his or her trade (for instance, an airline reservation clerk would be expected to deal courteously with each and every caller). Most of us have already had some experience dealing with service people who are obviously not well suited psychologically for such jobs. A personality test might have screened them out.

A **management assessment center** is another approach to selection. In such centers, about a dozen management candidates spend two or three days performing realistic management tasks (like making presentations) under the observation of expert appraisers. Each candidate's potential for management is thereby assessed or appraised.[14] The center's activities might include individual presentations, objective tests, interviews, and participation in *management games*. Here participants would

MANAGEMENT ASSESSMENT CENTER
A center in which management candidates spend two or three days performing realistic management tasks under the observation of expert appraisers.

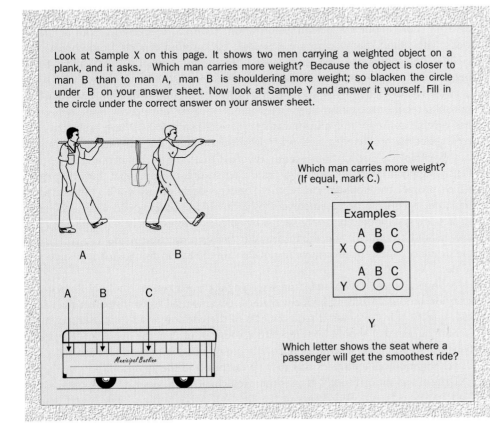

FIGURE 10.4

Bennet Test of Mechanical Comprehension Example

Human resource managers often use personnel tests, like this one, to measure a candidate's skills and aptitudes.

SOURCE: Gary Dessler, *Human Resource Management*, 6th ed. (Englewood Cliffs, NJ: Prentice-Hall, 1994), 164.

Look at Sample X on this page. It shows two men carrying a weighted object on a plank, and it asks. Which man carries more weight? Because the object is closer to man B than to man A, man B is shouldering more weight; so blacken the circle under B on your answer sheet. Now look at Sample Y and answer it yourself. Fill in the circle under the correct answer on your answer sheet.

X

Which man carries more weight?
(If equal, mark C.)

Examples

A B C
X ○ ● ○

A B C
Y ○ ○ ○

Y

Which letter shows the seat where a passenger will get the smoothest ride?

engage in realistic problem solving, usually as members of two or three simulated companies that are competing in a mock marketplace.

INTERVIEWS

Both before and after any testing occurs, several interviews will usually be in order.

Although an interview is probably the single most widely used selection device, the usefulness of interviews is often questionable. One question concerns their *reliability:* Will different people interviewing the same candidate come to similar conclusions about the applicant's acceptability for the job? A second interviewing and testing question concerns validity: Do the results of the interview (or test) accurately predict success on the job?

A manager can boost the reliability and validity of selection interviews in several ways.[15] One way is to decide ahead of time what the characteristics of a good employee for the job are and then formulate questions that are aimed at identifying these specific characteristics. Thus, if a hotel is interested in hiring a front-desk clerk, the candidate's ability to get along with people and be empathetic might be two very important traits. In this case, the interviewer might ask questions like "Could you tell me about an instance at college when someone brought you a problem to solve; how did you handle that situation?"[16] An interview questionnaire is shown in Figure 10.5 on pages 280–81.

OTHER SELECTION TECHNIQUES

Various other selection techniques are used to screen applicants. Most employers (estimates range up to 93 percent) do at least some reference checking on final candidates. These background checks can take many forms. However, most companies at least try to verify an applicant's current position (or previous position) and salary with his or her current employer by telephone. Others call current and previous supervisors to discover more about the person's motivation, technical competence, and ability to work with others. Some employers also get background reports from commercial credit-rating companies; this can provide information on an applicant's credit standing, indebtedness, reputation, character, and lifestyle.

With so many employees working in jobs in which honesty is important—such as in banks, retail stores, and managing restaurants—paper-and-pencil "honesty testing" has become an important mini-industry.[17] Several psychologists have expressed concern about the proliferation and potential misuse of such tests. However, the American Psychological Association recently reported that "the preponderance of the evidence" supports the notion that some of the tests work, meaning that they can predict which prospective employees may prove undependable or dishonest.[18] At the same time, the association urged employers to be careful in choosing and using such tests. In fact, any tests should be administered by qualified professionals, the applicant's privacy should be assured, and the relationship between test results and subsequent job performance should be ascertained to make sure the test is doing what it is supposed to do.

A physical examination and drug screening are often two of the final steps in the selection process. A preemployment medical exam is used to confirm that the applicant qualifies for the physical requirements of the position and to discover any medical limitations that should be taken into account in placing the applicant. By identifying health problems, a physical exam can also reduce absenteeism and accidents and detect communicable diseases that may be unknown to the applicant.

Drug abuse, unfortunately, is a serious problem at work. Counselors at the Cocaine National Help Line polled callers of the 800-COCAINE hotline. They found that 75

HATTERAS HAMMOCKS

Hatteras Hammocks of Greenville, North Carolina, needed a new controller. Executive vice-president Jay Branch picked a standout from a big field of applicants: his choice had received his undergraduate degree in accounting, earned an MBA from Indiana University, and had worked as a CPA. The applicant was recommended by a personal friend, so after a brief chat with his former employer, Branch brought him aboard.

Six months later the man was gone. Soon after that, Branch discovered that the firm was missing about $60,000. The impressive résumé and credentials were fabricated. Apparently, the new controller had omitted his areas of greatest expertise: fraud, forgery, and embezzlement.

"The whole episode taught me the necessity of checking thoroughly," says Branch, "no matter how good a recommendation is."

The nightmare at Hatteras Hammocks underscores the importance of screening and background checks when selecting new employees. However the potential for lawsuits can make reference checking perilous and costly. So how does a human resource manager determine how far is far enough? By applying sound judgment, common sense,

FOCUS ON SMALL BUSINESS

and sticking to queries that have a factual relevancy to the particular job being filled.

For example, Voca Corporation of Columbus, Ohio, provides care to mentally retarded and developmentally disabled persons. Patient safety is naturally one of the paramount concerns, so applicants who will be in direct contact

with residents are carefully screened for any history of abuse, neglect, or mistreatment. As the process begins, staffers give applicants the opportunity to explain or clarify anything that might come to light later. Fingerprinting follows. "It's our way of . . . demonstrating we're serious," says Hilary Franklin, director of human resources. "And it's pretty darn effective."

The company protects itself by adhering to strict guidelines throughout the process. Checks are only run on people to whom a job offer has been extended. Adverse discoveries, such as felony convictions, are kept strictly confidential. A prospective employee who would be in charge of transporting clients could expect his or her driving record to be scrutinized; a receptionist applicant would not. Everyone signs a release giving the company permission to verify the information the applicant has provided.

SOURCE: Michael Cronin, "This Is a Test," *Inc.*, August 1993, 65–66.

percent admitted to occasional cocaine use at work, 69 percent said they regularly worked under the influence of a drug, and 25 percent reported daily use at work.[19] As a result, more employers are including drug screening as part of their prehiring program. In one survey, testing rose from 21 percent of surveyed firms in 1986 to 48 percent in December 1988.[20]

The *Hatteras* Small Business box describes the screening steps two small businesses take, and why they now take them.

SELECTING EMPLOYEES FOR RESPONSIVE ORGANIZATIONS

Management expert Tom Peters says that in today's fast-changing world "the task of transforming raw recruits into committed stars . . . begins with the recruiting (and selection) process per se." Peters says that when it comes to recruiting and selecting employees, the most responsive companies follow three rules, "unfortunately ignored by most: (1) spend time, and lots of it; (2) insist that line people dominate the process; and (3) don't waffle about the qualities you are looking for in candidates."[21]

The selection process at Mazda's Flatrock, Michigan, plant illustrates the time these firms devote to staffing.[22] Almost from the day in 1984 that Mazda announced it was building a plant in Michigan, the company's managers emphasized that they would be

FIGURE 10.5

Structured Applicant Interview Guide

SOURCE: Gary Dessler, *Human Resource Management*, 6th ed. (Englewood Cliffs, NJ: Prentice-Hall, 1994), 202–04.

Applicant Interview Guide

To the interviewer: This Applicant Interview Guide is intended to assist in employee selection and placement. If it is used for all applicants for a position, it will help you to compare them, and it will provide more objective information than you will obtain from unstructured interviews.

Because this is a general guide, all of the items may not apply in every instance. Skip those which are not applicable and add questions appropriate to the specific position. Space for additional questions will be found at the end of the form.

Federal law prohibits discrimination in employment on the basis of sex, race, color, national origin, religion, disability, and, in most instances, age. The laws of most states also ban some or all of the above types of discrimination in employment as well as discrimination based on marital status or ancestry. Interviewers should take care to avoid any questions which suggest that an employment decision will be made on the basis of any such factors.

Job Interest

Name _____ Position applied for _____

What do you think the job (position) invloves? _____

Why do you want the job (position)? _____

Why are you qualified for it? _____

What would your salary requirements be? _____

What do you know about our company? _____

Why do you want to work for us? _____

Current Work Status

Are you now employed? _____Yes _____ No. If not, how long

have you been unemployed? _____

Why are you unemployed? _____

If you are working, why are you applying for this position? _____

When would you be available to start work with us? _____

Work Experience

(Start with the applicant's current or last position and work back. All periods of time should be accounted for. Go back at least 12 years, depending upon the applicant's age. Military service should be treated as a job.)

Current
or last employer _____ Address _____

Dates of employment: from _____to _____

Current or last job title _____

What are (were) your duties? _____

Have you held the same job throughout your employment with this company?

_____Yes._____No. If not, describe the various jobs you

have had with that employer, how long you held each of them, and the main

duties of each. _____

_____

What was your starting salary? _____What are you earning now? _____

Comments _____

Name of your last or current supervisor _____

What did you like most about that job? _____

What did you like least about it? _____

Why are you thinking of leaving? _____

    Why are you leaving right now? _____

    Interviewer's comments or observations _____

_____

What did you do before you took your last job? _____

Where were you employed? _____

Location _____ Job title _____

Duties _____

Did you hold the same job throughout your employment with that company?

_____Yes _____No. If not, describe the

jobs you held, when you held them and the duties of each. _____

_____

What was your starting salary? _____ What was your final salary? _____

Name of your last supervisor _____

May we contact that company? _____Yes _____No.

What did you like most about that job? _____

What did you like least about that job? _____

Why did you leave that job? _____

Would you consider working there again? _____

Interviewer: If there is any gap between the various periods of employment,

the applicant should be asked about them. _____

Interviewer's comments or observations _____

What did you do prior to the job with that company? _____

What other jobs or experience have you had? Describe them briefly and explain

the general duties of each. _____

Have you been unemployed at any time in the last five years? _____Yes

_____No. What efforts did you make to find work? _____

What other experience or training do you have which would help qualify you for

the job you applied for? Explain how and where you obtained this experience

or training. _____

Educational Background

What education or training do you have that would help you in the job for which

you have applied? _____

Describe any formal education you have had. (Interviewer may substitute techni-

cal training, if relevant.) _____

Off-Job Activities

What do you do in your off-hours? _____Part-time job

_____ Athletics _____ Spectator sports _____ Clubs _____ Other

Please explain. _____

Interviewer's Specific Questions

Interviewer: Add any questions to the particular job for which you are interview-

ing, leaving space for brief answers. (Be careful to avoid questions which may be

viewed as discriminatory.) _____

_____

_____

Personal

Would you be willing to relocate? _____Yes _____No

Are you willing to travel? _____Yes _____No

What is the maximum amount of time you would consider traveling? _____

_____

Are you able to work overtime? _____

What about working on weekends? _____

Self-Assessment

What do you feel are your strong points? _____

_____

What do you feel are your weak points? _____

_____

Interviewer: Compare the applicant's responses with the information furnished

on the application for employment. Clear up any discrepancies. _____

Before the applicant leaves, the interviewer should provide basic information
about the organization and the job opening, if this has not already been done.
The applicant should be given information on the work location, work hours, the
wage or salary, type of remuneration (salary or salary plus bonuses, etc.), and
other factors that may affect the applicant's interest in the job.

Interviewer's Impressions

Rate each characteristic from 1 to 4, with 1 being the highest rating and 4 being
the lowest.

Personal Characteristics

Personal appearance _____

Poise, manner _____

Speech _____

Cooperation with interviewer _____

Job-related Characteristics

Experience for this job _____

Knowledge of job _____

Interpersonal relationships _____

Effectiveness _____

Overall rating for job

1	2	3	4	5
_Superior	_Above Average	_Average	_Marginal	_Unsatisfactory
	(well qualified)	(qualified)	(barely qualified)	

Comments or remarks _____

_____

_____

Interviewer _____Date _____

Copyright 1992 The Dartnell Corporation, Chicago, IL. Adopted with permission.

Potential employees who make it through Mazda's lengthy screening process may end up working on a state-of-the-art auto assembly line like this one at the Flatrock, Michigan plant.

very selective in choosing employees. Forget the standard application blanks and background checks. Instead, Mazda would evaluate applicants in a way that no American automaker had ever evaluated hourly employees before.[23]

Consider the case of applicant Wayne Dodd. Two years after mailing in a Mazda job application that had appeared in the local newspaper, Dodd was working at a Burger King restaurant. He received a letter from Mazda inviting him to come to an abandoned school just outside Flatrock for a series of written aptitude tests. These tests were the second step in Mazda's five-step recruiting and selecting process (the first was the application that had appeared in the newspaper).

Dodd breezed through the two-hour battery of tests (which dealt mostly with basic math and reading comprehension) but did not do quite as well on a test that evaluated his ability to detect quality defects. In this test, applicants were given a series of illustrations (such as six light bulbs) and had to pick out the quality defect (such as the one with the small crack in its base).

However, Dodd did well enough to be invited back for the third step in the screening process, a personal interview. The interview lasted 30 minutes, during which a man and woman inquired about Dodd's enthusiasm and asked questions about how he liked working as part of a team at Burger King. He was asked if he would have trouble at the auto plant if his supervisor asked him to pitch in to help out another team member who was having trouble completing a job on time. The interviewers, both Americans, wore the same blue and khaki Mazda uniform and both introduced themselves by their first names. There were still two steps to go in Mazda's screening process.

In the fourth step of the screening process, Dodd was asked to come to the auto plant itself at Flatrock for a group problem-solving assessment. Dodd and several other employees were organized into teams of varying sizes and put through a six-hour series of problem-solving exercises aimed at evaluating traits like the applicant's ability to contribute to a consensus decision. They were therefore asked to solve problems such as creating a rewards program that ranked perfect attendance, a flawless safety record, and other achievements in their order of importance. Mazda's assessors then ranked each team's (and individual's) efforts. They were looking for things like how well the members expressed their ideas, how well they listened to one another, and how well each applicant participated in the group's discussions.

In a second problem-solving exercise, Dodd was asked to join a new team in what Mazda called "*kaizan* projects." Group members were issued toy blocks and told to work together as a team to assemble "air boats." The group was then instructed to use the *kaizan* process of constant improvement to find ways of more efficiently assembling the boats. For example, could the piles of toy blocks be arranged more efficiently so blocks could be found more quickly? The group problem-solving sessions went on for six hours.

In the fifth and final series of tests, Dodd and the final group had to pass a simulated work exercise. Applicants (who already showed they had the intelligence and interpersonal skills required of Mazda team members) now had to exhibit the physical coordination and endurance needed to build cars.

Why such an enormous investment of time in hiring employees? According to David Merchant, the personnel vice-president at Flatrock, it was because Mazda would be investing so heavily in developing each employee. Mazda viewed the employee-employer relationship as a marriage, said Merchant, not a casual date, and it was therefore important for each party to know each other very well. Merchant and Mazda were looking for very bright, flexible, and motivated team members—not the rigid and often alienated worker more often associated with the auto industry of previous years.[24]

The experiences at other responsive firms including Hewlett-Packard and Saturn help to underscore two other aspects of staffing at responsive firms. First, an emphasis is placed on getting line managers (rather than just the personnel department) involved in the actual screening. After all, no one knows what they are looking for in a colleague like the people who will actually be working with the new employee. The best companies, therefore (as Tom Peters points out), deemphasize the role of the personnel department and emphasize the importance of getting line managers involved in the interviewing and screening.

Such companies also emphasize the sorts of "soft skills" and values that the company really cherishes. At Mazda, for instance, testing for technical skills like the mechanical ability to use tools was the last step in the screening process. First, evaluators looked for skills in problem solving, identifying quality defects, and cooperating in team efforts.

TRAINING AND DEVELOPMENT

Once employees are recruited, screened, and selected, they must be prepared to do their jobs, and this is the role of employee orientation and training.

Employee **orientation** traditionally means providing new employees with basic information about the employer, information that they need to perform their jobs satisfactorily. This basic information includes how to get on the payroll, how to obtain identification cards, what the working hours are, and who the new employee will be working with. In many companies, employees receive an orientation handbook containing information like that summarized in Figure 10.6. As you can see, the orientation process is aimed at familiarizing the new employee with the company and his or her coworkers, providing information about working conditions (coffee breaks, overtime policy, and so on), and generally reducing the sorts of first-day jitters that commonly are associated with starting a new job.

This initial orientation is usually followed by a training program, one aimed at ensuring that the new employee has the basic knowledge required to perform the job

ORIENTATION
Providing new employees with basic information about the employer, information that they need to perform their job satisfactorily.

FIGURE 10.6

Contents of Orientation Program

In many organizations, new employees receive a package of orientation materials or a handbook, containing information on matters like the ones shown in this checklist.

SOURCE: Gary Dessler, *Human Resource Management,* 6th ed. (Englewood Cliffs, NJ: Prentice-Hall, 1994), 236.

Orientation Checklist
(Small southern manufacturing company)

HOURLY & SALARIED EMPLOYEE ORIENTATION GUIDE CHECKLIST
NOTE: ALL APPROPRIATE INFORMATION MUST BE DISCUSSED WITH EACH NEW EMPLOYEE

SUPERVISOR: This form is to be used as a guide for the orientation of new employees in your department.

In order to avoid duplication of instruction the information indicated below has been given to the employee by the Personnel Department.

PERSONNEL DEPARTMENT

EEO BOOKLET	ABSENCES, TARDINESS	
INSURANCE PROGRAM BOOKLET	VETERANS RE-EMPLOYMENT RIGHTS & RESERVE STATUS	
SALARY CONTINUANCE INSURANCE BOOKLET	UNITED FUND	
SAFETY BOOKLET	VACATIONS	
PENSION PLAN BOOKLET	JURY DUTY	
EMPLOYEE HANDBOOK/LABOR AGREEMENT/RULES BOOKLET	SICK BENEFITS A & S LIMITATIONS, ETC.	
MATCHING GIFTS	LEAVE OF ABSENCE, MATERNITY, MEDICAL, ETC.	
EDUCATIONAL ASSISTANCE PROGRAM	SERVICE AWARDS	
PATENT AGREEMENT	VISITORS	
I.D. CARD	HOLIDAYS	
CREDIT UNION	FOOD SERVICES	
STOCK PURCHASE PLAN	FIRST AID & REQUIREMENTS OF REPORTING INJURY	
SAVINGS BOND PLAN	DIFFICULTIES, COMPLAINTS, DISCRIMINATION & GRIEVANCE PROCED	
PROBATIONARY PERIOD	MILL TOUR	
PAY, SALARY, PROMOTIONS, AND TRANSFERS	TERMINATION NOTICE AND PAY ESP. VACATION ALLOWANCE (VOLUNTARY RESIGNATION)	
TRANSPORTATION		
TIME SHEET	INTRODUCTION TO GUARDS	
PERSONAL RECORDS	(OTHERS)	
BULLETIN BOARDS		
PERSONAL MAIL		
PARKING FACILITIES		

SIGNATURE OF EMPLOYEE:	WITNESS:	DATE

SUPERVISOR: The following is a checklist of information necessary to orient the new employee to the job in your department. Please check off each point as you discuss it with the employee and return to the Personnel Department within three days following employee placement on the job:

INTRODUCTION TO FELLOW EMPLOYEES	HOURS OF WORK, OVERTIME, CALL IN PROCEDURES	
TOUR OF DEPARTMENT	REST, LUNCH PERIODS	
EXPLANATION OF NEW EMPLOYEE S JOB. RESPONSIBILITIES AND PERFORMANCE EVALUATIONS	SUPPLY PROCEDURES	
	LINE OF AUTHORITY	
LAVATORY		
PHONE CALLS PERSONAL/COMPANY		

SIGNATURE OF SUPERVISOR:		DATE

I have received a copy of the appropriate materials listed above and have had explained to me the information outlined. I understand this information concerning my employment with (Company name). Also, in case of voluntary separation (resignation) I understand the Company s policy, that in order to be eligible for any due vacation allowance, I must give my supervisor at least two weeks notice in writing prior to my last day of work.

SIGNATURE OF EMPLOYEE:	WITNESS:	DATE

satisfactorily. Techniques traditionally used here (and discussed more fully in Chapter 18) include on-the-job training, lectures, and perhaps other techniques using, for example, audiovisual tools and computers.

ORIENTATION AND RESPONSIVENESS Orientation plays a central role in building the employee commitment that is essential in today's decentralized, empowered, and responsive firms.

Consider once again the experience of Wayne Dodd and other workers hired at Mazda's Flatrock facility.[25] At Mazda, the aim of orientation and training is not just to familiarize workers with their new jobs. Instead, it is to foster a level of commitment to and identification with Mazda and its goals that far exceed anything usually attained in U.S. companies. This is why Mazda interviewers typically asked the job applicants questions like, "What would you do if your neighbor was having trouble with a Mazda automobile?"[26] Initially, candidates were taken aback by this question and were unsure of how to answer it. However, by the end of the applicants' ten- to twelve-week orientation and training program it was clear what the answer should be:

> Those Americans who had been hired by Mazda would, it was expected, answer this question without hesitation: "I would try to solve the problem, and I would apologize to my neighbor on behalf of Mazda." By then they would understand that standing behind a company and its products was the only correct thing for a worker to do. They would have grown to identify with their company, Mazda, in a way that was less American and more Japanese.[27]

The orientation and training program at responsive firms like Mazda and Saturn are therefore extensive. At Mazda, the first few days of orientation involve paperwork and administrative details, and employees are fitted for safety shoes and measured for the blue-and-khaki Mazda uniforms worn by everyone at the plant. Implicit and explicit throughout the orientation and training program, however, is a recurring theme: a Mazda employee is expected to "take the initiative." Thus, when the top personnel officers spoke to the new employees, they reiterated that message:

> It may have been okay to just follow orders where you worked before, they would tell all hirees, but at Mazda things would be different. Here, everyone will be expected to take the initiative and participate in the management of the plant. This participation will take many forms: not only will workers be contributing ideas to the design and constant improvement of their own jobs, they will be expected to help maintain quality control standards throughout the shop floor.[28]

There is a similar emphasis on getting new employees to identify with the firm and its cherished values at other responsive companies. At the new Saturn plant, new arrivals face five days of "awareness training." The purpose of this training is to teach workers how to work in teams and build a consensus. This is followed by from 100 to 750 hours of training, including time spent learning to read balance sheets (the company expects employees to know how their operations are doing profit-wise).[29] Similarly, when Nissan moved to its new Smyrna, Tennessee, plant, it spent almost $63 million, about $30,000 per person, training 2,000 workers before the plant even started operation. Such extensive training not only ensures a highly knowledgeable and flexible work force, it also sends the strongest message possible to workers that "you're important to us."[30] Orientation and training thus play a central role in producing the sort of committed and flexible work force that companies increasingly need to stay competitive. The *Motorola* vignette describes another example of this.

COMPENSATING AND APPRAISING EMPLOYEES

BASIC FORMS OF COMPENSATION

Employee compensation refers to all forms of pay or rewards that go to employees and arise from their employment.[31] It includes direct financial payments in the form

MOTOROLA

According to the American Society of Training and Development, 15,000 employers—less than one percent of the total— spend 90 percent of the $30 billion annually allocated to company-funded training programs. Motorola is one of the big training spenders. Integrated within its Schaumburg, IL, corporate headquarters are a collection of computer-equipped classrooms and laboratories known as Motorola University. Here an effort is made to customize the training to the particular production process at hand. Factory employees learn robotics, customized manufacturing techniques, and computer-aided design. Motorola U employs a faculty made up of consultants, engineers, scientists, and former managers instead of professional educators. In 1992, the company spent $120 million on education, or about 3.6 percent of total payroll. That is more than double the 1.5 percent Bill Clinton urged companies to reinvest in employees during his presidential campaign.

Motorola U president William Wiggenhorn says, "When you buy a piece of equipment, you set aside a percentage for maintenance. Shouldn't you do the same for people?"

Analyzing the results makes it difficult to argue with him. Over five years, profits have increased 47 percent and sales per employee have doubled. The company estimates that every $1,000 spent on continuing education returns $30,000 in increased productivity over a three-year period. Such production upgrades and the elimination of waste resulting from training has resulted in savings of $3.3 billion, and a more motivated and committed workforce.

SOURCE: Ronald Henkoff, "Companies That Train Best," *Fortune,* March 23, 1993, 62–68.

FIXED SALARY (HOURLY WAGES)
The main component of most employees' pay.

FINANCIAL INCENTIVE
Any financial reward that is contingent on a worker's performance.

of wages, salaries, incentives, commissions, and bonuses, and indirect payments in the form of financial fringe benefits like employer-paid insurance and vacations.

A **fixed salary** or **hourly wages** are the main component of most employees' pay. For example, blue-collar workers and clerical workers are often paid hourly or daily wages; this is often called day work. Some employees—managerial, professional, and often secretarial—are salaried. They are compensated on the basis of a set period of time (like a week, month, or year), rather than hourly or daily.

Financial incentives are increasingly important and today are often referred to as "pay for performance." A **financial incentive** is any financial reward that is contingent on a worker's performance. Thus salespeople are often paid financial incentives called commissions, which represent a portion of the items or services they actually sell. Production workers are often paid a financial incentive called piecework: piecework means that an employee is paid a standard sum for each item he or she produces. Many employees periodically receive merit pay or a merit raise, which is any salary increase that is awarded to an employee based on his or her individual performance. Merit pay differs from a bonus, which represents a one-time financial payment.

Managers have sought to formulate effective incentive plans for many years. One such plan was developed many years ago by Joseph Scanlon, a union official for the United Steel Workers. In his plan workers participate in making cost-savings sugges-

Training at Motorola University helped this purchasing team cut a requisition-handling process from 30 hours to 3 hours, winning them top prize in the company's annual quality contest. They came in first out of 4,000 entrants.

tions and then share whatever benefits result from these suggestions. The Scanlon plan is an early version of what today is known as a **gainsharing plan,** an incentive plan that engages many or all employees in a common effort to achieve a company's productivity objectives; the resulting cost-savings gains are shared among employees and the company.[32] As with the Scanlon plan, virtually all gainsharing plans involve two components: the participation and cooperation of employees in making cost-cutting suggestions and a formula by which employees then share in any resulting cost-savings gains.

EMPLOYEE BENEFITS

Employee benefits are any supplements to wages or pay that employees get based on their membership in the organization. They typically include health and life insurance, vacation, pension, and education plans. Many of these benefits are legally mandated. For example, under federal and state law, **unemployment insurance** is available to most employees and is paid by state agencies to workers who are terminated through no fault of their own (the funds come from a tax on the employer's payroll). **Worker's compensation,** another legally mandated benefit, is a payment aimed at providing sure, prompt income and medical benefits to work-related accident victims or their dependents, regardless of fault. Most employers today also offer hospitalization, medical, and disability insurance because of the expense employees would have to absorb if they

GAINSHARING PLAN
An incentive plan that engages many or all employees in a common effort to achieve a company's productivity objectives and in which they share in the gains.

EMPLOYEE BENEFITS
Any supplements to wages or pay that employees get based on their membership in the organization.

UNEMPLOYMENT INSURANCE
Insurance available to most employees that is paid by state agencies to workers who are terminated through no fault of their own (the funds come from a tax on the employer's payroll).

WORKER'S COMPENSATION
A payment aimed at providing sure, prompt income and medical benefits to work-related accident victims or their dependents, regardless of fault.

had to obtain such insurance themselves, as individuals. Many companies also offer their employees membership in a health maintenance organization (HMO). This is a medical organization consisting of several specialists (surgeons, psychiatrists, and so on) that provides routine, round-the-clock medical services at a specific site. Social Security is another federally mandated benefit paid for by a tax (of a total of 15.02 percent of pay as of 1994) on the employee's wages; employees and their employers share equally in this tax, up to a set limit. Among other things, Social Security provides beneficiaries with retirement benefits after they leave the company. Sick leave, vacations, and severance pay (a one-time payment when an employee is terminated) are other frequently used benefits. The *Starbucks* vignette illustrates how one firm uses benefits to boost employee loyalty and commitment.

EMPLOYEE APPRAISAL

Appraising performance serves several purposes. People want and need feedback regarding how they are doing, and appraisal provides an opportunity for management to give employees that feedback. And, if performance is not up to par, the appraisal conference provides an opportunity to review a subordinate's progress and map out a plan for rectifying any performance deficiencies.

Managers use several techniques to appraise their employees' performance. Probably the most familiar is a performance appraisal form like the one shown in Figure 10.7. This form lists several job characteristics and provides a rating scale from out-

STARBUCKS

Starbucks of Seattle, WA, has almost 160 specialty coffee stores, most concentrated in the northwest. But the firm bucks a prevailing industry trend: most retailers like to avoid paying benefits because of high turnover. Starbucks, on the other hand, wants loyalty. "Our only sustainable competitive advantage is the quality of our work force. We're building a national retail company by creating pride—and a stake in the outcome of our labor," says Howard Schultz, the firm's CEO. To get it Schultz places a big emphasis on a benefits package that features deductible-exempt physicals, dental coverage, eye care, and company-paid disability and life insurance. Also included are stock options, training programs, career counseling, and product discounts for *all* employees, full-time and part-time.

If that sounds like a potential financial hemorrhage, it hasn't been so far. Even though the benefits are generous, they make up only a quarter of Starbucks labor costs and have stabilized there. Schultz sees stock options and benefits as the intercompany bond that ties workers to the company and inspires loyalty. Perhaps more importantly, he thinks employees that are treated right treat customers with the same kind of care. "The future of Starbucks," says Schultz, "lies in increasing shareholder value—and increasing employee value will [do that]." Some might argue his theory, but it's hard to argue with his results.

SOURCE: Matt Rothman, "Into the Black," *Inc.,* January 1993, 59–65.

standing to unsatisfactory along with short definitions of each of these possible ratings. This particular appraisal form is relatively objective, calling as it does for specific ratings. However, also notice (as is often the case) that the form provides space for more subjective examples of particularly good or particularly bad incidents of the employee's performance.

Experts including Tom Peters emphasize the importance of continuous (rather than annual) appraisals. In Japan, for instance, specific feedback to an average employee is meted out daily. Peters recommends spending a lot of time in the appraisal, both on a day-to-day basis and in preparing and providing useful feedback for the more formal semiannual and annual appraisal meetings. The trend is also to move away from using formal forms like that in Figure 10.7 and to instead focus more on specific job-related outcomes and behaviors. For example, in their book *Workplace 2000,* Joseph Boyett and Henry Conn say that many companies are already totally revising their approach to performance appraisal and that we may even soon see that:

> Instead of a rating form, most companies will use nothing more than a blank sheet of paper on which employees and their bosses list specific objectives to be accomplished during the appraisal period. These objectives will encompass areas including learning and development goals (such as training the employee will participate in, skills to be developed and used); teamwork goals (such as personal contributions the employee agrees to make to help his or her team improve feedback); communication or problem-solving such as participating on a

Howard Schultz, CEO and president of Starbucks (center), gives the same attention to the quality of his employees as he does to the flavor of the coffee he sells. Each employee receives 25 hours of training before starting behind the counter—a cost to Starbucks of roughly $1,000, an unheard-of investment in the retail world, where low wages and high turnover are the norm.

FIGURE 10.7
Performance Appraisal Chart

This is a page from a typical performance appraisal form. Supervisors use it to rate the employee's performance on factors like quality and productivity.

SOURCE: Gary Dessler, *Human Resource Management*, 6th ed. (Englewood Cliffs, NJ: Prentice-Hall, 1994) 335.

Performance Appraisal for:

Employee Name _____   Title _____

Department _____   Employee Payroll Number _____

Reason for Review: ☐ Annual   ☐ Promotion   ☐ Unsatisfactory Performance

☐ Merit   ☐ End Probation Period   ☐ Other _____

Date employee began present position _____ / _____ / _____

Date of last appraisal _____ / _____ / _____   Scheduled appraisal date _____ / _____ / _____

Instructions: Carefully evaluate employee's work performance in relation to current job requirements. Check rating box to indicate the employee's performance. Indicate N/A if not applicable. Assign points for each rating withnin the scale in the corresponding points box. Points will be totaled and averaged for an overall performance score.

RATING IDENTIFICATIION

O – Outstanding – Performance is exceptional in all areas and is recognizable as being far superior to others.

V – Very Good – Results clearly exceed most position requirements. Performance is of high quality and is achieved on a consistent basis.

G – Good – Competent and dependable level of performance. Meets performance standards of the job.

I – Improvement Needed – Performance is deficient in certain areas. Improvement is necessary.

U – Unsatisfactory – Results are generally unacceptable and require immediate improvement. No merit increase should be granted to individuals with this rating.

N – Not Rated – Not applicable or too soon to rate.

GENERAL FACTORS	RATING	SCALE	SUPPORTIVE DETAILS OR COMMENTS
1. **Quality** – The accuracy, thoroughness, and acceptability of work performed.	O ☐ V ☐ G ☐ I ☐ U ☐	100–90 90–80 80–70 70–60 below 60	Points
2. **Productivity** – The quantity and efficiency of work produced in a specified period of time.	O ☐ V ☐ G ☐ I ☐ U ☐	100–90 90–80 80–70 70–60 below 60	Points
3. **Job Knowledge** – The practical/technical skills and information used on the job.	O ☐ V ☐ G ☐ I ☐ U ☐	100–90 90–80 80–70 70–60 below 60	Points
4. **Reliability** – The extent to which an employee can be relied upon regarding task completion and follow up.	O ☐ V ☐ G ☐ I ☐ U ☐	100–90 90–80 80–70 70–60 below 60	Points
5. **Availability** – The extent to which an employee is punctual, observes prescribed work break/meal periods, and the overall attendance record.	O ☐ V ☐ G ☐ I ☐ U ☐	100–90 90–80 80–70 70–60 below 60	Points
6. **Independence** – The extent of work performed with little or no supervision.	O ☐ V ☐ G ☐ I ☐ U ☐	100–90 90–80 80–70 70–60 below 60	Points

problem-solving task force; taking on leadership responsibility in meetings; and plans for personal contribution to team goals such as quality improvement, cost reduction, or improvements in customer service.[33]

PROMOTIONS, TERMINATIONS, AND DISCIPLINE

PROMOTION
Rewarding the employee's efforts by moving that person to a job with increased authority and responsibility.

Performance appraisal often leads to personnel actions such as promotion, termination, and discipline. A **promotion** generally means rewarding the employee's efforts by moving that person to a job with increased authority and responsibility. Ideally, promotions (like rewards in general) should be awarded based on proven competence.

Unfortunately, that is often not the case today, for two reasons. First, with the wave of downsizings and consolidations that have taken place over the past few years there are often not enough middle management (and higher) positions available into which to promote worthy employees. As a result, companies today are relying more on lateral "promotions" to broaden employees' experiences and to help them gain additional skills. Being transferred from a post such as sales manager to one as personnel manager may not have the same impact as a traditional promotion. However, it can at least reignite the initial interest and excitement that the employee felt in his or her first job, and it gives the person additional skills that may be useful later.

Unfortunately, for most women, promotions into management are particularly hard to come by. According to one study, only 2 percent of top executives in Fortune 500 companies are women.[34] Similarly, female vice-presidents earn 42 percent less than men in the same jobs.[35] What accounts for this? The answer, to many experts, is that there is a glass ceiling, one that effectively holds down the promotion possibilities for women and minorities. The term *glass ceiling* refers to the fact that the barriers to promotion are invisible ones, a product of things like the relative inability for women and minorities to take advantage of male-dominated "old-boy" networks, as well as implicit discrimination.

Breaking through these kinds of invisible barriers will be increasingly important over the next few years. With almost all the growth in the labor force comprised of minorities or women, promotion ladders for everyone—not just men—will have to be strengthened and assured.

DISCIPLINE AND GRIEVANCES A grievance is a complaint that an employee lodges against an employer, usually one regarding wages, hours, or some condition of employment like unfair supervisory behavior. Most union contracts contain a *grievance procedure* which provides an orderly system of steps whereby employer and union determine whether or not some clause of the contract has been violated. Steps typically include discussing the problem with one's supervisor, then referring the matter to the department head, personnel department, and finally the employer's facility head. Thus a supervisor may fire an employee for excessive absences. The employee might then file a grievance stating that the supervisor had issued no previous warnings or discipline related to excessive absences as called for in the union agreement, and that the firing was thus unwarranted. Many nonunionized companies also offer grievance procedures.

A supervisor often has to discipline a subordinate, usually because a rule or procedure was violated. A company should have clear rules (such as "no smoking allowed when dealing with customers") as well as a series of progressive penalties that all employees know will be enforced if the rule is broken.

One way to set up a discipline system is to follow the so-called FRACT model: get the *facts,* obtain the *reason* for the infraction, *audit* the records, pinpoint the *consequences,* and identify the *type* of infraction before taking remedial steps.

A recent innovation in this area is called discipline without punishment. With this disciplinary technique, for example, an employee first gets an oral reminder for breaking the rule and then a written reminder if the rule is broken again. Then a paid one-day "decision making leave" is mandated if another incident occurs in the next few weeks. If the rule is broken again, then the employee may be dismissed.

DISMISSALS Employees have always been dismissed for unsatisfactory performance, for insubordination, or if the company suffers a downturn. Over the past few years, however, a multitude of mergers, consolidations, and downsizings have also triggered wholesale dismissals at companies like Wang Computer and IBM.

GRIEVANCE
A complaint that an employee lodges against an employer, usually one regarding wages, hours, or some condition of employment, such as unfair supervisory behavior.

SUMMARY

Human resource management is the management function devoted to acquiring, training, appraising, and compensating employees. All managers are, in a sense, personnel managers.

Human resource management has evolved in importance because of the increasing employee commitment and sophistication required by companies.

The failure of employers to exercise due diligence in hiring practices can result in litigation. Human resource managers are required to be familiar with all aspects of equal employment laws, affirmative action programs and their applicability, the varying degrees of sexual harassment, and the Occupational Safety and Health Act, among others. Knowledge of the rights guaranteed under such labor laws as the Norris-LaGuardia Act and its guarantees to employees also are important.

When staffing an organization, a manager should follow six steps: job analysis, personnel planning, recruiting, interviewing, testing and selection, and training and development.

Job analysis entails determining job duties and the kinds of people who should carry them out, and it results in job descriptions and job specifications.

Personnel planning and recruiting involve forecasting personnel requirements and the supply of candidates, and planning how candidates will be prepared for available jobs.

Employee recruiting is a crucial function and includes screening internal candidates, advertising for applicants, consulting with agencies or executive recruiters, and relying on referrals.

The interviewing/employee selection and placement process involves screening and selecting the most qualified candidate through the use of applications, interviews, tests, and reference checks.

The selection process has become more challenging in today's fast-changing world and should include three key ingredients: spending considerable time with the prospect under consideration, insistence that line people dominate the process, and strict adherence to the qualities desired in the employee.

Employee orientation means providing new employees with information both about the employer and the procedures for performing their jobs.

Compensating workers includes all direct forms of compensation such as wages, salaries, incentives, commissions, and bonuses, as well as indirect forms of compensation like financial fringe benefits, company-paid insurance, and vacations.

The appraisal of an employee can be pivotal in improving performance through feedback and, if problems exist, for rectifying deficiencies. Methods include quantitatively rating an employee's performance or outlining objectives and evaluating performance at the end of a specified period. Employee appraisals should be conducted on a frequent, recurring basis.

Personnel actions stemming from employee appraisals can include promotion, termination, or disciplinary action. The recent wave of downsizing has complicated this process considerably, often resulting in lateral promotions designed to broaden an employee's exposure.

QUESTIONS

■ FOR REVIEW

1. Describe some of the abuses employment laws are designed to prevent.

2. Name the six steps employers must follow when staffing an organization.

3. Explain the difference between direct and indirect forms of compensation.

■ FOR DISCUSSION

4. Which of the many federal laws outlined in this chapter do you think have had the greatest impact on the workplace? Why?

5. Discuss the advantages and disadvantages of various employee recruiting methods.

6. Do you agree that human resource management has become more difficult in recent years? Why or why not?

■ FOR ACTION

7. Do additional research on one of the employment laws mentioned in this chapter, for example, the Occupational Safety and Health Act or Americans with Disabilities Act. Summarize the key points of the law and their implications.

8. Contact the investor relations department of a publicly traded company. Ask for a 10K or other document that outlines how top executives of the company are compensated. Describe the direct and indirect forms of compensation.

9. Find a classified ad for a job you might like to have after graduating. Describe the requirements for the job. What kind of training would the position require?

■ FOR FOCUS ON SMALL BUSINESS

10. Given the expense involved in screening applicants, are small businesses with limited resources at a disadvantage when selecting employees? Discuss your answer.

11. Compare and constrast honesty testing with background checks. What are the strengths and weaknesses of each approach?

12. Do you think that selecting employees is more difficult today than in the past? Why or why not?

CLOSING SOLUTION

BECKER CPA REVIEW COURSE, LTD.

With the best of intentions, Congress passed the ADA in 1990. It is designed to ensure fair treatment for 43 million Americans deemed disabled, and went into effect in July of 1992. Since the law applies to any company with 25 or more workers, it impacts virtually every employer in the country, including Becker CPA Review Course, Ltd. Persons protected under the act include people in wheelchairs, hearing or visually impaired persons, people who suffer from AIDs and other contagious diseases that do not represent a threat to coworkers, as well as rehabilitated drug users and alcoholics, persons at high risk of sustaining on-the-job injury, obese persons, and cosmetically disfigured persons.

But the purpose of the act goes further than barring discrimination. Under ADA, employers like Becker must make whatever "reasonable accommodations" are required for disabled (but otherwise qualified) workers to perform the "essential functions" of a job. That kind of phrasing in legislation, along with the absence of any sort of precedents, can trip up even the best of attorneys. "The real difficulty that every lawyer in the land has is, what in the world should that advice and counsel be?" said Phillip McCrury, a Texas attorney. "We don't know what the statutes mean, and it will take years of lawsuits before we do."

■ QUESTIONS FOR CLOSING SOLUTION

1. How could a company's personnel recruiting and selection activities be tailored to account for ADA requirements for handicapped or disabled applicants?

2. What do you think would be reasonable accommodations for a disabled person, say, for the job of engineer? What do you think would constitute undue hardship if you were the owner of a company?

3. What do you consider the benefits and drawbacks of the ADA, both from a theoretical and a practical standpoint?

KEY TERMS

Human Resource Management	Application Blank
Title VII	Test
Affirmative Action	Management Appraisal Center
Sexual Harassment	Orientation
Occupational Safety and Health Act	Employee Compensation
Fair Labor Standards Act	Fixed Salary (hourly wages)
Staffing	Financial Incentive
Job Analysis	Gainsharing Plan
Job Description	Employee Benefits
Job Specification	Unemployment Insurance
Personnel Planning	Worker's Compensation
Recruiting	Promotion
Executive Recruiters	Grievance

CASE FOR ANALYSIS

MANAGING DIVERSITY

A diverse work force and diversity training brings advantages but human resource managers who are not vigilant in dealing with multiethnic employees risk paying a price in both lawsuits and lost customers. Consider the following examples.

Problems at Lucky Stores, Inc. began after the Dublin, California-based grocery store chain initiated a diversity training program aimed at controlling prejudice in the work place. During one exercise, managers were asked to list common stereotypes for minorities and women. The idea was to elevate awareness of potential bias and enhance effectiveness with employees. But one female worker was incensed after reading notes from the seminar that contained such statements as "black women are more aggressive," and "women cry more." In a $155 million lawsuit against the company, she claimed such prejudices were the reason she and others hadn't advanced at Lucky. In August 1992, a judge found Lucky Stores guilty of discrimination, but maintained the seminar notes weren't the only reason for ruling against the chain. Still, legal experts said the case put all human resource managers in a quandary. "On the one hand, if employers don't conduct the training, they run the risk of breaking affirmative action and equal employment opportunity statutes," says Kirby Wilcox, Lucky's lead counsel in the case. "The catch-22 is that if the training is conducted, statements made by managers during the course of the training may be used against the company as evidence that its managers hold gender- or racial-stereotypical attitudes."

In the case of Flagstar Company, the firm's diversity awareness program proved to be too little, too late. The company employs 120,000 people in a restaurant empire that includes Hardee's, Denny's, and other eateries. Signs of trouble surfaced in early 1992, when customers in California charged a prepayment policy was applied disproportionately to blacks. The problem gained momentum as other black customers surfaced charging they were ignored altogether by waitpersons. While the Justice Department began investigating, Flagstar CEO Jerry Richardson fired or transferred a number of employees and began meeting with civil rights groups. He also assembled a cultural diversity team to heighten awareness about racism. Two months after reaching a deal with the Justice Department, six black members of the Secret Service who went to a Denny's in Annapolis, Maryland, complained that they were denied service while their white coworkers were served promptly. The six agents also filed suit against Flagstar.

Unfortunately, Richardson's best efforts at mending fences with customers didn't speak as loudly as some of the company's human resources actions. Flagstar had no blacks among the ranks of its senior managers, officers, or directors, and only one of the 163 Denny's franchise owners was African American. Richardson began working with the NAACP to increase minorities in the company, but many believed his efforts were merely a token effort brought on by adverse circumstances.

U.S. conglomerates haven't been immune from discrimination charges either. A New Jersey court ruled an AT&T Technologies manager was guilty of defamation based upon the performance evaluation and eventual termination of Margaret Cary, an African American woman who had worked at the company for 23 years. From the time she was hired in1964, Cary's evaluations had been above average to outstanding. In 1985 she was transferred to a construction accounting group, and shortly thereafter she was moved again, this time to a temporary post. The transfer prompted her to file a complaint against her supervisor alleging racial and sexual discrimination. Cary's evaluation was poor the following year, and because of a new company policy, the performance appraisal put her job at risk. Under an AT&T downsizing plan, the lowest performers were targeted for layoffs if the company could not get enough employees to leave voluntarily. When Cary's position was eliminated, she was offered a lower-level job. She refused and was fired. Her supervisor also happened to be black, and Cary believed he was jealous of her for winning a company black achievement award. She filed suit against the company for both defamation and discrimination.

The New Jersey court denied Cary's discrimination charge, but ruled the company defamed her through her performance evaluation. The potential for companies to be held liable for performance appraisals raises questions about how such appraisals should be formulated in the future. Evaluations by committee and basing terminations and promotions on more than a single year's evaluation are possibilities.

As these examples illustrate, the challenges of human resource management have taken on added complexity since the advent of equal employment opportunity, a culturally diverse work force, and affirmative action laws. Diversity awareness and sensitivity is an essential ingredient in everything from staffing to employee selection and training. Sometimes even the best intentions don't lead to favorable outcomes, but animosities left unaddressed can turn into problems that are costly in both dollars and shattered morale.

SOURCES: Andrew E. Serwer, "What to Do When Race Charges Fly," *Fortune*, July 12, 1993, 95–96; Chuck Hawkins, "Denny's: The Stain That Isn't Coming Out," *Business Week*, June 28, 1993, 98–99; S.C "Employees Use Diversity-training Exercise Against Lucky Stores in Intentional-Discrimination Suit," *Personnel Journal*, April 1993, 52; "Diversity Training Goes to Court," *Training & Development*, November 1991, 11–12; and Betty Southard Murphy et al., "Jury Finds Employee Defamed in Performance Evaluations," *Personnel Journal*, June 1992, 26.

■ QUESTIONS

1. How have equal employment laws and affirmative action programs impacted hiring and training decisions?
2. Based on your answer to the first question, how could managers at Lucky Stores, Flagstar, and AT&T Technologies have avoided some of the problems described in this case?
3. What could these companies do to go beyond the letter of the law and increase their effectiveness in dealing with a diverse work force?

A CASE IN DIVERSITY

WHITE MALES IN THE WORKPLACE

Increasingly, white males feel that they are the most aggrieved victims of job discrimination. Without question, they are in a crossfire. Companies are eliminating management layers in an effort to cut costs and become more responsive and competitive. Human resource executives are redoubling efforts to make sure that their staffs are reflective of the society as a whole. That means women and ethnic minorities are usually given the nod in hiring decisions that are otherwise too close to call. But that leads to other questions. Is it fair? Are white males being punished for inequities they had nothing to do with? Finally, is all the brouhaha detracting from what should be everyone's most important concern, that being what is best for the company as a whole?

Before too many crocodile tears are shed, it's important to remember that white males still far and away comprise the dominant segment of the job market. But since the original intent of civil rights legislation was that everyone be judged strictly on the basis of qualifications, white males have a right to expect at least an even break in the hiring process, or so many people believe.

In many cases, personnel managers have set out to diversify their companies' work forces. That fair-minded intention notwithstanding, subjectivity invariably enters into the equation. For whatever reason, women often get priority. In one 12-month period, for instance, the Torrance, California-based search firm Corporate Directions was asked by five companies to fill middle-manager slots with women. Four of the five firms said they would conduct interviews with men, but made it clear they would hire only a woman. The fifth company said not to bother sending any men at all. Korn/Ferry International, the country's largest search firm, says around 4 percent of its business specifically calls for women to be hired. That sort of predetermined focus can lead to equally unfair discrimination against groups like ethnic minorities, disabled persons, older workers, and a host of others.

The solution to the problem of diversifying a company's work force may be years away. It's hard to find anyone who'll quibble with the benefits, but how best to put the right staff in place without fracturing overall company morale remains elusive. Most company managers want a work force that reflects their customer base or the society in general. Accomplishing that, and putting the right people in the jobs they are most qualified to perform, will be a challenge for managers of the future.

SOURCES: Charlene Marmer Solomon, "Are White Males Being Left Out?" *Personnel Journal*, November 1991, 88–94; and Joann S. Lublin, "Firms Designate Some Openings for Women Only," *The Wall Street Journal*, February 7, 1994, B-1, B-6.

■ QUESTIONS

1. What do you think about the contention of some white males that affirmative action programs have resulted in reverse discrimination?
2. How can human resource managers best manage the tensions of white males who feel discriminated against due to affirmative action?
3. Do you think today's work force continues to reflect the effects of past discrimination. Why or why not?

ENDNOTES

1. This problem was researched from Bradford McKee, "The Disabilities Labyrinth," *Nations Business*, April 1993, 18–25.
2. Diane Filipowski, "Life After HR," *Personnel Journal*, June 1991, 64–71.
3. *Ponticas v. K.M.S. Investments*, 331n.w. 2d 907 Minn. (1983).
4. See Wade Lambert and Arthur Hayes, "Overqualified Ruling May Presage Suits," *The Wall Street Journal*, January 29, 1991, B6.
5. David Terpstra and Susan Cook, "Complaint Characteristics and Reported Behaviors as Consequences Associated with Formal Sexual Harassment Charges," *Personnel Psychology*, vol. 38, no. 2 (Autumn 1985), 559–74.
6. "Stanford Doctor to Face Charges," *The New York Times*, June 28, 1991, A9.
7. Wayne Cascio, *Applied Psychology in Personnel Management* (Reston, VA: Reston, 1978), 132.
8. Donald Harris, "A Matter of Privacy: Managing Personnel Data in Company Computers," *Personnel*, February 1987, 37.
9. Harold E. Johnson, "Older Workers Help Meet Employment Needs," *Personnel Journal*, May 1988, 100–05.
10. Based on Robert W. Goddard, "How to Harness America's Gray Power," *Personnel Journal*, May 1987, 33–40.
11. Stephen J. Vodanovich and Rosemary H. Lowe, "They Ought to Know Better: The Incidence and Correlates of Inappropriate Application Blank Inquiries," *Public Personnel Management*, vol. 21, no. 3, Fall 1992, 363.
12. See Paul Blocklyn, "Pre-Employment Testing," *Personnel*, February 1988, 66–68.

13. Mel Kleiman, "Employee Testing Essential to Hiring Effectively in the '90s," *Houston Business Journal,* vol. 22, no. 38, February 8, 1993, 31; and Gerald L. Borofsky, "Pre-Employment Psychological Screening," *Risk Management,* vol. 40, no. 1, January 1993, 47.

14. Louis Olivas, "Using Assessment Centers for Individual and Organizational Development," *Personnel,* vol. 57, May–June 1980, 63–67; Tim Payne, Neil Anderson, and Tom Smith, "Assessment Centres, Selection Systems and Cost-Effectiveness: An Evaluative Case Study," *Personnel Review,* vol. 21, no. 4, Fall 1992, 48; and Roger Mottram, "Assessment Centres Are Not Only for Selection: The Assessment Centre as a Development Workshop," *Journal of Managerial Psychology,* vol. 7, no. 1, January 1992, A1.

15. For a full discussion of this, see Gary Dessler, *Human Resource Management* (Englewood Cliffs, NJ: Prentice-Hall, 1994), Chapter 6.

16. "Personal Bias Can Threaten Interview Process," *HR Magazine,* vol. 37, no. 9, September 1992, 504.

17. John Jones and William Terris, "Post-Polygraph Selection Techniques," *Recruitment Today,* May–June 1989, 25–31.

18. Gilbert Fuchsberg, "Prominent Psychologists Group Gives Qualified Support to Integrity Tests," *The Wall Street Journal,* March 7, 1991, B2, B7.

19. Ian Miners, Nick Nykodym, and Diane Samerdyke-Traband, "Put Drug Detection to the Test," *Personnel Journal,* vol. 66, no. 8, August 1987, 191–97.

20. Eric Rolfe Greenberg, "Workplace Testing: Who's Testing Whom," *Personnel,* May 1989, 39–45.

21. Tom Peters, *Thriving on Chaos: Handbook for a Management Revolution* (New York: Harper & Row, 1987), 379.

22. This is based on Joseph J. Fucini and Suzy Fucini, *Working for the Japanese* (New York: The Free Press, 1990), 1–2, 49–52.

23. Ibid.

24. For a complete discussion of these matters, see Fucini and Fucini, *Working for the Japanese,* 58–59.

25. Based on Fucini and Fucini, *Working for the Japanese,* 67–87.

26. Fucini and Fucini, *Working for the Japanese,* 67.

27. Ibid., 67.

28. Ibid., 68–69.

29. See Gary Dessler, *Winning Commitment* (New York: McGraw-Hill, 1993), 84–85.

30. Tom Peters, *Thriving on Chaos,* 390.

31. This is based on Dessler, *Human Resource Management,* 341–415.

32. Barry W. Thomas and Madelyn Hess Olson, "Gainsharing: The Design Guarantees Success," *Personnel Journal,* May 1988, 73–79.

33. Joseph Boyett and Henry Conn, *Workplace 2000* (New York: Dutton, 1991), 56–57.

34. *Time,* December 4, 1989, 82–85.

35. Charlene Marmer Solomon, "Careers Under Glass," *Personnel Journal,* April 1990, 97.

CHAPTER 11

ACHIEVING CONTROL

LEARNING OBJECTIVES

After studying this chapter, you should be able to:

- Explain the reasons managers need controls.
- List the three steps in the control process.
- Give examples of the basic types of control, including steering, yes-no, and post-action controls.
- Discuss budgetary control techniques such as sales forecasts, production budgets, income statements, and budgeted balance sheets.
- Contrast zero-based budgeting with traditional budgeting methods.
- Illustrate the use of ratio analysis in the budget control process.
- Define strategic control and the various types of strategic control methods.
- List several responses and consequences, both intended and unintended, of implementing controls.
- Determine what type of control is most appropriate for a situation and how to move from imposed control to self-control and commitment.

The Control Process
Steps in the Control Process
Basic Types of Control
Controlling Actions, Results, and Personnel

Budgetary Control Techniques
Budgets and Performance Reports
Basic Steps in the Budgeting Process
Zero-Based Budgeting
Ratio Analysis and Return on Investment

Strategic Control and Responsiveness
The Need for Strategic Control
Strategic Control Methods

Human Responses to Control
Control—A Central Issue in Managing
Some Unintended Human Consequences of Controls

Control, Commitment, and Organizational Responsiveness
Imposed Versus Self-Control
Moving from Imposed Control to Self-Control and Commitment

OPENING PROBLEM
SATURN CORPORATION

The 1980s was a bleak period for domestic auto makers. Foreign competition was eroding market share as more Americans found that the lowest cost, highest quality automobiles were manufactured in Japan. General Motors set a goal of recapturing the small-car market by creating "a different kind of company." ■ Classifying the Saturn Corporation as different is an understatement. The company philosophy called for exceeding customer expectations and providing an unparalleled buying and ownership experience that resulted in customer enthusiasm. To achieve that end, Saturn had to reinvent the way cars were made and marketed. The company expected a commitment from workers; trust and respect for the individual from management; and a dedication to customer enthusiasm, continuous improvement, and self-control from both. Workers, suppliers, and managers would become partners in team decision making. The collegial corporate culture would extend from the assembly line to the dealership floor. It would also mean a whole new way of keeping operations under control. At inception it all sounded progressive. But at an estimated $3 billion investment, no one was really certain it would work.[1]

THE CONTROL PROCESS

After plans are set and the organization is designed and staffed, the manager takes steps to ensure that the firm's plans are carried out or, if conditions warrant, to ensure that the firm's strategies, plans, and goals are modified.[2] As William Newman has said, managerial control is "the series of steps a manager takes to assure that actual performance conforms as nearly as practical to plan."[3] In the most general terms, therefore, **controlling** means setting a target, measuring performance, and taking corrective action.

CONTROLLING
Setting a target, measuring performance, and taking corrective action.

All control methods collect and transmit information on profits, sales, or some other factor, and all control methods are aimed at influencing employee behavior. *Control* may just mean establishing and monitoring a monthly budget, like the one you may use to make sure your expenditures don't "get out of control." Or, as at Saturn, it could mean fostering employees' self-control. But in the broadest sense, control refers to *all* the manager's efforts to influence behavior. As one expert put it:

> In their desire to gain control over the behavior of people, business organizations use a variety of mechanisms, including personal supervision, job descriptions, rules, standard operating procedures, performance appraisal, budgets, standard costing, accounting-information, and incentive compensation systems. Taken together, these mechanisms comprise the "organizational control system."[4]

Managers need controls for basically two reasons. The traditional explanation for control is that employees do not always do what they are supposed to do:

> If all personnel always did what was best for the organization, control—and even management—would not be needed. But, obviously, individuals are sometimes unable or unwilling to act in the organization's best interest, and the set of controls must be implemented to guard against undesirable behavior and to encourage desirable actions.[5]

Today's fast-changing world, however, presents a second need for control. Plans today can quickly become outdated; when that happens, an effective control system is needed to inform management that some change in the plan is required.

The word *planning* is always used along with the word *control,* for two reasons. First, all control systems monitor planned targets, standards, or goals.[6] Second, in a more general sense, control expert Kenneth Merchant says that one of the most important characteristics of any control system is that it be future oriented. "The goal is to have no unpleasant surprises in the future."[7]

STEPS IN THE CONTROL PROCESS

Whether the person doing the controlling is the assembly line supervisor or the mayor of New York, the control process generally involves three steps:

1. Establishing a standard, goal, or target.
2. Measuring actual performance against this standard.
3. Identifying deviations and taking corrective action.

Budgeting expert Glen Welsch points out that, in practice, control is more complicated than this. Controlling also involves analyzing the reasons for the deviations, reviewing alternative courses of action, and, finally, choosing and implementing the most promising solutions.[8]

ESTABLISH STANDARDS   Control begins by setting standards. These standards are typically expressed in terms of money, time, quantity, or quality (and perhaps a combination of these). Often these standards are expressed in monetary terms. Thus, a salesperson might be told that his or her quota is to sell $8,000 worth of products per month; or a production supervisor may be told to cut costs by $2,000 per week. Standards of performance are also expressed in terms of time—such as having to meet a certain sales quota in a week or complete a report by May 1.

Other standards are quantitative. Thus, production supervisors are usually responsible for producing a specified number of units of product per week. The number of labor hours used per unit of time is another example of a quantity standard. Still other standards are expressed in terms of quality, such as the reject rates in quality control, the grades of products sold (such as "grade A"), or the quality of a requested report or forecast. For each area (quantity, quality, and so on), the normal procedure is to choose a yardstick and then set a standard, as summarized in Figure 11.1. In terms of quantity, for instance, yardsticks include units produced per shift and grievances filed per month.[9] The *Benchmarking* vignette illustrates another approach to setting standards.

MEASURE ACTUAL PERFORMANCE AGAINST STANDARDS The second control step is to measure actual performance against the standards and determine whether or not any deviations exist.

In organizations, monitoring performance is accomplished through both personal and impersonal means.[10] Personal observation is the simplest and probably most common way of measuring actual performance against standards. For example, while a new employee is getting on-the-job training, her performance might be personally observed by a supervisor.

While nothing substitutes for the immediate feedback provided by personal supervision, as the manager assumes more responsibilities, it becomes increasingly impossible to personally monitor everyone. As we saw in Chapters 8 and 9 (Organizing), one way to handle this problem is by adding supervisors; for example, a hospital director might hire two assistant directors to observe employees on different floors. But from a practical point of view, personal control must be supplemented by formal, impersonal (and usually written) control reports. Budgetary control reports, quality control reports, and inventory control reports are three examples of impersonal techniques used for monitoring actual performance and comparing it to standards.

IDENTIFY DEVIATIONS FROM STANDARDS AND TAKE CORRECTIVE ACTION This final step requires applying all of the management functions. In terms of decision making, for instance, the manager will have to distinguish between symptoms and problems and determine why performance is not up to par. The deviation might mean, for instance, that the plans themselves should be revised, or that poor staffing has put an employee in place who is just not up to the task.

AREA TO CONTROL	POSSIBLE YARDSTICK	STANDARD/GOAL TO ACHIEVE
Quantity	Number of products produced	Produce 14 units per month
Quality	Number of rejects	No more than 10 rejects per day
Timeliness	Percent sales reports in on time	Return 90% of sales reports on time
Dollars	Percent deviation from budget	Do not exceed budgeted expenses by more than 5% during year

FIGURE 11.1

Examples of Control Standards

BENCHMARKING

General Motors Europe formalized its benchmarking program in the late 1980s. Why? Because, says John F. Smith, chairman and CEO, "We need to compare our plants with similar plants around the world and understand what we are spending our money for and how it compares with how the best competition spends their money." Such comparisons are known as **benchmarking**. They provide standards a firm can then use to better manage its own operations.

Smith acknowledges that getting into every plant is impossible, but says access to enough companies is available. GM doesn't usually exchange information. "We exchange plant visits," says Smith, and adds that you have to pick up what's needed on your own.

GM's special relationships with other car companies place it in a more advantageous position than most competitors. Besides joint ventures with both Toyota and Suzuki, GM is also a big stockholder in Isuzu Motors. That alliance came in handy when GM decided to benchmark Isuzu's V-6 engine plant in Ellsmere Port, England.

GM had been through an Isuzu plant that was producing a similar engine with a lower investment and much lower per-piece cost. The highly automated plant used machinery GM Europe hadn't heard of and required fewer employees per engine.

Plant director Nick Reilly says GM Europe now produces a V-6, benchmarked against the BMW and the Japanese, that he thinks can capture a large segment of the market. But don't think the information was easily available. If you ask just how much GM/Isuzu is saving per engine at Ellsmere Port, the answer will be a polite, no comment.

SOURCE: Sharon Reier, "Does Macy's Tell Gimbel's?" *Financial World,* September 17, 1991, 32.

BENCHMARKING
Intercompany comparisons that provide standards which a firm can use to better manage its own operations.

BASIC TYPES OF CONTROL

Professor William Newman distinguishes between three types of controls: steering controls, yes-no controls, and post-action controls.

STEERING CONTROLS With **steering controls**, results are predicted and corrective action is taken *before* the operation or project is completed.[11] For example, the flight control of a spacecraft aimed for the moon is tracked continuously. Its trajectory is modified so that flight-path corrections are made days before the spacecraft is due to reach the moon. Steering controls play an important role in today's organizations because they provide a mechanism for correcting deviations while the actual results are still being shaped.

YES-NO CONTROLS A **yes-no control** means that work may not proceed to the next step until it passes an intermediate control step. For example, most large companies have a rule forbidding any employee from entering into a contract with a sup-

STEERING CONTROLS
Results are predicted and corrective action is taken before the operation or project is completed.

YES-NO CONTROL
Work may not proceed to the next step until it passes an intermediate control step.

GM's success in international markets (profits ran $2.7 billion on foreign operations in 1989), probably can be partly attributed to its benchmarking program.

plier or customer unless the agreement has been approved ahead of time by the firm's legal staff.

POST-ACTION CONTROLS With **post-action controls**, the particular action being controlled is completed first, and then results are measured and compared to the standard. Budgets are examples of post-action controls, as are your end-of-term college grades. As with grades, the problem with post-action controls is that it is usually difficult to do much about the situation once the final exam is over and the grades are in. Just as most students prefer to find out how they are doing during the semester, organizational post-action controls are less useful for taking corrective action than are steering controls. Responsiveness, in particular, requires steering controls.

POST-ACTION CONTROLS
The particular action being controlled is completed first, and then results are measured and compared to the standard.

CONTROLLING ACTIONS, RESULTS, AND PERSONNEL

We can also classify controls according to the object of the control system. For example, the owner of a small retail store will want to control who uses the cash register, how the customers are treated, and whether a particular item is accepted as a return. However, regardless of what you are controlling, you have a choice of controlling either specific *actions, results,* or *personnel.* Figure 11.2 summarizes various specific control tools, according to whether the object of the control is specific actions, results, or personnel.

CONTROL OF SPECIFIC ACTIONS[12] First, you can control specific actions. Specific action controls such as physical locks, security guards, work rules, policies and procedures, and direct supervision aim to ensure that employees perform (or do not perform) specific actions that are known to be desirable (or undesirable). For example, a manager can install physical locks to prevent unauthorized employees from using the cash register. Managers also use work rules and codes of conduct to define the limits of acceptable actions and to punish deviants: disciplinary procedures are used to punish employees who violate work rules, for instance. Preaction reviews—observing

FIGURE 11.2

Possible Control Tools based on Object of Control

Locks and work rules can help control specific actions; budgets help maintain control based on employee results; selection and training can help employees better control themselves.

SOURCE: Kenneth Merchant, "The Control Function of Management," *Sloan Management Review*, Summer 1992.

OBJECT OF CONTROL

TO CONTROL SPECIFIC ACTIONS

Behavioral Constraint:
—physical (e.g., locks, security guards)
—administrative (e.g., separation of duties)
—work rules
—policies and procedures
—codes of conduct

Preaction Review:
—direct supervision
—approval limits
—budget reviews

TO CONTROL EMPLOYEES' RESULTS

Results Accountability:
—standards
—budgets
—management by objective (MBO)

TO CONTROL PERSONNEL THEMSELVES

Upgrade Capabilities:
—selection
—training
—assignment

Improve Communication:
—clarify expectations
—provide information for coordination

Encourage Peer Self-Control:
—work groups
—shared goals

the work of others before the activity is complete—is another way to control specific actions, for instance, through direct supervision or with a yes-no control that limits signing agreements without prior approval.

CONTROL OF RESULTS Managers can also maintain control by focusing not on employees' specific actions, but on their *results*. This is usually referred to as **results accountability**. This means that while the supervisor is still responsible for the work of his or her subordinates, the subordinates are accountable for their results. These results are typically itemized in specific standards, budgets, or perhaps management-by-objectives–set goals.

RESULTS ACCOUNTABILITY
When managers control activities by focusing not on employees' specific actions, but on their results.

CONTROL OF PERSONNEL Finally, control can be achieved by relying on the employees to do what is best for the organization. An approach like this is the ultimate in steering controls: the employees themselves are responsible for continually monitoring their behavior and keeping it in line with what is best for the organization.

Firms like Toyota and Saturn rely very heavily on personnel types of controls. For example, they upgrade employees' capabilities through selection and training, which ensures that the employees are capable of building high-quality cars and are motivated to do so; they institute extensive two-way communication systems to help individual employees know and understand their jobs better and how they can best coordinate their efforts with those of the other groups in the organization; and they encourage the work teams themselves to monitor and control their own work. Personnel control essentially means fostering self-control. It is achieved by winning the employees' commitment to the goals and the aims of the firm. We will discuss some popular control tools before returning to the topic of self-control.

BUDGETARY CONTROL TECHNIQUES

BUDGETS AND PERFORMANCE REPORTS

BUDGETS
Financial expressions of a manager's plans and one of the most widely used control techniques.

Budgets are among the most widely used control tools, and are formal, financial expressions of a manager's plans. They show targets for yardsticks such as revenues, cost of materials, expenditures, and profits, usually expressed in dollars. These planned targets are the standards against which actual results are compared and controlled. Budgets are widely used. Each manager, from the first-line supervisor to top management, usually has his or her own budget to use as a standard of comparison.[13] However, budgets (as shown in Figure 11.3) only represent the standard-setting step in the control process. Actual performance still has to be measured and compared to the budgeted standards. Then, corrective action must be taken.

The organization's accountants are responsible for collecting data on actual performance. They then compile the financial data and feed them back to the appropriate managers. The most common form of feedback is a performance report like that shown in Figure 11.4. Typically, the manager receives a report like this for his or her unit at the end of some time period (say, each month). As in Figure 11.4, the performance report shows budgeted or planned targets. Next to these figures, the budget shows the department's actual performance. The report also lists the differences between budgeted and actual amounts (these are usually called **variances**). A space on the report for the manager to explain any such variances is also sometimes provided. After reviewing the performance report, the manager and supervisor can then take any corrective action that seems warranted.

BASIC STEPS IN THE BUDGETING PROCESS

As suggested in Figure 11.5, the first step in budgeting is usually to develop a sales forecast and sales budget. For this step, a variety of factors—including economic conditions, the availability of credit, competitors' actions, and seasonal fluctuations—are taken into account to ensure as accurate a forecast as possible. The **sales budget** itself shows the number of units to be shipped in each period (usually per month) as well as the sales revenue expected, based on some assumed sales price per unit.

Next, you may want a production budget. The **production budget** outlines the number of units that must be manufactured to meet monthly sales requirements and

VARIANCES
The difference between budgeted and actual amounts.

SALES BUDGET
Shows the number of units to be shipped in each period (usually per month) as well as the sales revenue expected, based on some assumed sales price per unit.

PRODUCTION BUDGET
Outlines the number of units that must be manufactured to meet monthly sales requirements and maintain proposed inventory levels.

BUDGET FOR MACHINERY DEPARTMENT, JUNE 1994

Budgeted Expenses:	Budget
Direct Labor	$2,107
Supplies	$3,826
Repairs	$ 402
Overhead (electricity, etc.)	$ 500
TOTAL EXPENSES:	$6,835

FIGURE 11.3

Example of a Budget

PERFORMANCE REPORT FOR MACHINERY DEPARTMENT, JUNE 1994

	BUDGET	ACTUAL	VARIANCE	EXPLANATION
Direct Labor	$2,107	$2,480	$373 over	Had to put workers on overtime.
Supplies	$3,826	$4,200	$374 over	Wasted two crates of material.
Repairs	$ 402	$ 150	$252 under	—
Overhead (electricity, etc.)	$ 500	$ 500	0	—
TOTAL	$6,835	$7,330	$495 over	

FIGURE 11.4

Example of a Performance Report

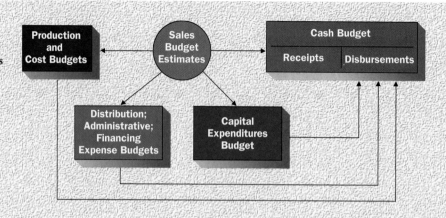

FIGURE 11.5

The Sales Budget Is the Basis for Other Budgets

The first step in budgeting is usually to develop a sales forecast and budget.

maintain proposed inventory levels. Then based on this, a materials-used and materials-purchased budget can be compiled. This budget shows the amount and cost of the raw materials needed to produce the units of goods specified in the production budget. In addition, expense budgets covering other items such as direct labor (the actual cost of the worker input utilized in producing the goods), indirect labor (including electricity to run the plant and plant maintenance), as well as administrative expenses (advertising and sales expenses, insurance, depreciation, taxes, and so forth) are created at this point.

On the basis of these budgets, a budgeted profit and loss or income statement can be prepared. The **income statement** summarizes the expected sales revenue, expenses, and income for the budgeted year (or other planning period). Cash does not usually flow into the firm from sales in such a way as to coincide precisely with the amount and frequency of cash disbursements. Therefore, a cash budget is usually prepared at this point. The **cash budget** estimates the firm's month-to-month cash needs based on the monthly levels of operations as outlined in the sales, production, and expense budgets.

Finally, based on these budgets, a budgeted balance sheet is developed. The **budgeted balance sheet** provides information to management, owners, and creditors about the company's probable financial picture in terms of assets, liabilities, and net worth (or owners' equity—equal to the excess of assets over liabilities) at the end of the budget period.

In most firms the appropriate budgets are then distributed to managers throughout the organization. These budgets describe managers' plans in financial terms. They also provide measurable targets as well as the vehicles through which actual performance can be fed back to management and deviations identified. However, even the most elaborate budgeting system can produce misleading results, as the *U.S. Army* vignette illustrates.

ZERO-BASED BUDGETING

Traditional budgeting methods have serious drawbacks. In particular, new budget requests are often based on current, ongoing projects, although these projects may no longer be useful. For example, many federal government programs are routinely continued from year to year simply because "they've always been in the budget," in spite of the fact that they may no longer be needed.

INCOME STATEMENT
Summarizes the expected sales revenues, expenses, and income for the budgeted year (or other planning period).

CASH BUDGET
Estimates the firm's month-to-month cash needs based on the monthly levels of operations as outlined in the sales, production, and expense budgets.

BUDGETED BALANCE SHEET
Provides information to management, owners, and creditors about the company's probable financial picture in terms of assets, liabilities, and net worth at the end of the budget period.

U.S. ARMY

In an effort to hold agencies more accountable for resources, Congress passed the Chief Financial Officers Act in 1990. It mandated audits of many agencies, including the U.S. Army and its $350 billion in gross assets. What General Accounting Office auditors found would earn failing marks for even a first-year accounting student.

Munitions shipped from a central depot to a base are expensed immediately and dropped from the balance sheet, even though they might languish in a warehouse for months. Durables like truck parts are fully expensed upon assignment to a unit. GAO turned up $400 million in cash in the hands of disbursement officers. The money was nowhere to be found on army financial statements. Records accounted for two trucks on one base; auditors found 27. One set of books showed 559 engines in inventory; there were only 77, or a shortfall of $222 million. Even more shocking, very little in the way of potential liability record keeping was done. Ticking financial timebombs, like chemical weapons destruction, hazardous waste clean-up, and other environmental pollution claims amounting to upwards of $18 billion, weren't recorded as future expenses.

An army spokesperson contended that ledger entries aren't the issue, it's military preparedness. U.S. Comptroller General Charles Bowsher had a different view. "It's long overdue that we have the same kind of reporting requirements for the federal government as for the private sector."

SOURCE: Todd Gunter, "Cheese It! The Auditors," *Forbes,* December 21, 1992, 270.

Lax accounting procedures make it difficult to determine exactly how much it costs to keep the U.S. Army running. Recent government-mandated audits have turned up shocking inaccuracies and billions in unaccounted-for surplus munitions and supplies.

To deal with problems like this, some companies and many government agencies have adopted special budgeting methods, one of which is fairly widely used: zero-based budgeting.

Zero-based budgeting is a technique that forces managers to defend all their programs every year and to rank them in order of priority based on the ratio of their benefits and costs. With zero-based budgeting, both an organization's ongoing and proposed programs and agencies are identified, and alternative funding levels for these programs or agencies are specified and compared. Basically, each manager has to rank all his or her different programs or agencies every year and defend that ranking. This gives top management an opportunity to reevaluate the need for ongoing programs, compare ongoing to proposed programs, and consider reducing or eliminating the funding for ongoing programs so that new programs with higher priorities can be implemented.[14]

RATIO ANALYSIS AND RETURN ON INVESTMENT

Many organizations (particularly those in which interdivisional profitability comparisons must be made) control overall performance through a network of interlocking financial ratios. A **financial ratio** compares one financial indicator to another. The **rate of return on investment** (or ROI) is an important measure of overall company performance and represents net income divided by total investment. It is a useful standard against which the performance of the individual divisions can be measured. Control of ROI does not view profit as an absolute figure, but rather in relation to the investment in the business; thus, a $1 million profit would be much more impressive in a business with a $10 million investment than one with a $100 million investment.

THE INTERLOCKING RATIOS   Some commonly used financial ratios are summarized in Figure 11.6. Figure 11.7 shows how combining these ratios can help to keep actual performance under control. For example, the absolute level of sales by itself is less informative than the ratio of sales to total investment (or *capital turnover*). Similarly, sales divided by earnings (the *profit margin*) reflects management's success or failure in maintaining satisfactory cost controls. As another example, the ratios show that the ROI can be influenced by such factors as excessive investment. In turn, excessive investment might reflect inadequate control of inventory levels, accounts receivable, or cash.

STRATEGIC CONTROL AND RESPONSIVENESS

THE NEED FOR STRATEGIC CONTROL

Strategic control basically means monitoring not just actual performance relative to that planned, but the basic premises of the plan itself. When it comes to monitoring progress in carrying out strategic plans, the traditional three-step control process can be ineffective and misleading. The three-step process—set standards, compare actual performance to standards, and take corrective action—basically detects problems and deviations after they occur. However, relying on these three steps to control strategic issues can be dangerous for several reasons.[15]

First, the post-action nature of most control systems (such as budgets) is a problem when the plan's basic assumptions are changing quickly and unpredictably. In a world in which technological change, strategic alliances, and nations' borders change

---

ZERO-BASED BUDGETING
A technique that forces managers to defend all their programs every year and to rank them in order of priority based on the ratio of their benefits and costs.

FINANCIAL RATIO
Compares one financial indicator to another.

RATE OF RETURN ON INVESTMENT (ROI)
Represents net income divided by total investment and is an important measure of overall company performance.

T. Boone-Pickens, head of Mesa Inc., hopes to take advantage of a growing demand for natural-gas vehicles, a demand that he has helped create to keep his company alive. His forward-thinking approach is a good example of strategic control.

almost overnight, a company can hardly afford the luxury of setting a strategy in motion on the assumption that the strategy's premises won't shift—and shift dramatically. In one study, 60 percent of the 93 company presidents responding identified "uncontrollable factors" in their firm's external environments as adversely impacting their abilities to implement their strategic decisions.[16] In a rapidly changing world, managers need a *real-time* method of monitoring both their strategy's effectiveness, *as well as the underlying assumptions on which that strategy was built.*

A related problem is that traditional controls usually assume that performance standards are correct and that deviations from standards are therefore bad.[17] This may be true enough for short-term standards (such as what a manager's 12-month sales levels should be). However, when dealing with long-term strategic issues, the fact that the strategy is not working may mean that the plan itself needs changing. Double-loop learning of the sort discussed in Chapter 7 can help overcome this particular problem by forcing managers to examine both the deviations *and* the plans, as well as the assumptions on which those plans are built. But, in general, managers today are recognizing that a special control technique is required to monitor and control the company's strategy.

FIGURE 11.6

Widely Used Financial Ratios

NAME OF RATIO	FORMULA	INDUSTRY NORM (ASSUMED MERELY AS ILLUSTRATION)
1. Liquidity Ratios (measuring the ability of the firm to meet its short term obligations)		
Current ratio	$\dfrac{\text{Current assets}}{\text{Current liabilities}}$	2.6
Acid-test ratio	$\dfrac{\text{Cash and equivalent}}{\text{Current liability}}$	1.0
Cash velocity	$\dfrac{\text{Sales}}{\text{Cash and equivalent}}$	12 times
Inventory to net working capital	$\dfrac{\text{Inventory}}{\text{Current assets–Current liabilities}}$	85%
2. Leverage Ratios (measure the contributions of financing by owners compared with financing provided by creditors)		
Debt to equity	$\dfrac{\text{Total debt}}{\text{Net worth}}$	56%
Coverage of fixed charges	$\dfrac{\text{Net profit before fixed charges}}{\text{Fixed charges}}$	6 times
Current liability to net worth	$\dfrac{\text{Current liability}}{\text{Net worth}}$	32%
Fixed assets to net worth	$\dfrac{\text{Fixed assets}}{\text{Net worth}}$	60%

continued on next page

FIGURE 11.6

continued

NAME OF RATIO	FORMULA	INDUSTRY NORM (ASSUMED MERELY AS ILLUSTRATION)
3. Activities Ratios (measuring the effectiveness of the employment of resources)		
Inventory turnover	$\dfrac{\text{Sales}}{\text{Inventory}}$	7 times
Net working capital turnover	$\dfrac{\text{Sales}}{\text{Networking capital}}$	5 times
Fixed-assets turnover	$\dfrac{\text{Sales}}{\text{Fixed assets}}$	6 times
Average collection period	$\dfrac{\text{Receivables}}{\text{Average sales per day}}$	20 days
Equity capital turnover	$\dfrac{\text{Sales}}{\text{Net worth}}$	3 times
Total capital turnover	$\dfrac{\text{Sales}}{\text{Total assets}}$	2 times
4. Profitability Ratios (indicating degree of success of achieving desired profit levels)		
Gross operating margin	$\dfrac{\text{Gross operating profit}}{\text{Sales}}$	30%
Net operating margin	$\dfrac{\text{Net operating profit}}{\text{Sales}}$	6.5%
Sales margin	$\dfrac{\text{Net profit after taxes}}{\text{Sales}}$	3.2%
Productivity of assets	$\dfrac{\text{Gross income less taxes}}{\text{Total assets}}$	10%
Return on capital	$\dfrac{\text{Net profit after taxes}}{\text{Net worth}}$	7.5%
Net profit on working capital	$\dfrac{\text{Net operating profit}}{\text{Net working capital}}$	14.5%

STRATEGIC CONTROL
This technique is the critical evaluation of plans, activities, and results, [as well as the basic premises underlying them].

Strategic control is that technique. It has been defined as "the critical evaluation of plans, activities, and results, [as well as the basic premises underlying them]."[18] In general, *strategic control standards* tend to be nonfinancial, qualitative performance measures, or "strategic milestones" that are essential for achieving long-term competitive advantage in the industry.[19] Examples of such standards include market share relative

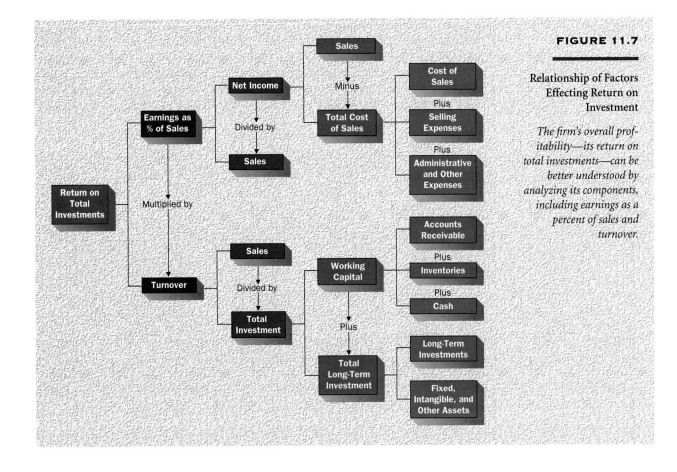

FIGURE 11.7

Relationship of Factors
Effecting Return on
Investment

*The firm's overall prof-
itability—its return on
total investments—can be
better understood by
analyzing its components,
including earnings as a
percent of sales and
turnover.*

to other leading competitors or (in a research-intensive business such as Merck Pharmaceuticals) some measure of the quality of the new drugs in the firm's R&D
pipeline.[20]

Strategic control is similar to the steering controls discussed earlier in this chapter.[21] It is future-directed and anticipatory, and it employs what management experts
call a feed-forward approach to control. In essence, strategic control monitors changes
inside and outside the firm on a continuous basis, predicts their effects on the company's strategy, and evaluates the firm's strategic objectives in the light of those changing conditions.

STRATEGIC CONTROL METHODS

Three unique strategic control methods are available. **Premise control methods**
"involve the systematic and continuous checking of environmental conditions to see
if previously established planning premises are still valid."[22] **Strategic surveillance
methods** represent a broad search activity aimed at early detection of events that may
threaten or demand modification of existing strategies. Finally, special alert control
methods aim to deal with crises, "low probability, high impact threatening events."[23]
All three methods are aimed at monitoring whether the strategies themselves should
be modified due to changing situations. We will look more closely at these three methods next.[24]

PREMISE CONTROL Strategic plans (like any plans) are formulated based on
assumptions or premises regarding what the future holds. Premise control means

PREMISE CONTROL METHODS
A strategic control method that
involves the systematic and
continuous checking of environmental conditions to see if
previously established planning
premises are still valid.

**STRATEGIC SURVEILLANCE
METHODS**
Represent a broad search activity aimed at early detection of
events that may threaten or demand modification of existing
strategies.

ENVIRONMENTAL MONITORING
Involves tracking previously identified events, trends, and other premises that were uncovered when the strategy was first formulated and are thus deemed of particular importance to the firm.

ENVIRONMENTAL SCANNING
Aimed at identifying previously unidentified or undetected critical events that could influence the company's strategy.

engaging in environmental monitoring to track previously identified events, trends, and other premises that were (1) uncovered when the strategy was first formulated and are thus (2) deemed of particular importance to the firm. In practice, **environmental monitoring** means systematically and continuously checking the previously identified premises to see if any of the strategic plan's basic assumptions have changed, a fact that might call for modifying the strategy. For instance, qualified individuals and departments can be assigned to monitor environmental information related to matters such as competitors' actions, inflation, and new product developments. For example, the introduction of videotape should have signaled to Polaroid in the 1980s that its instant moving film process was probably doomed.

STRATEGIC SURVEILLANCE   By definition, monitoring premises focuses on the previously identified assumptions on which the strategic plan was built. Strategic surveillance control relies on **environmental scanning,** which is defined as identifying previously *un*identified or undetected critical events that could influence the compa-

FIGURE 11.8

Worksheet For Environmental Scanning

SOURCE: Rowe et. al., *Strategic Management: A Methodological Approach,* 3rd ed. (Reading, MA: Addison-Wesley, 1989).

Economic Factors
(e.g., business cycle, inflationary trends, consumption, employment, investment, monetary and fiscal policies)

_____

_____

_____

_____

Political Factors
(e.g., political power, different ideologies; interest groups, social stability, legislation, and regulation)

_____

_____

_____

Social Factors
(e.g., age distribution, geographic distribution, income distribution, mobility, education, family values, work and business attitudes)

_____

_____

_____

ny's strategy. Environmental scanning for strategic surveillance is necessarily a more open, less focused activity since the firm is scanning its environment to detect events for which it is not specifically looking.

Environmental scanning begins by dividing the firm's environment into manageable sectors (economic, political, social, and so on), perhaps using a worksheet such as that in Figure 11.8. These individual sectors (such as the economic sector) are then further subdivided into dimensions that may have particular relevance for the company (such as interest rates and employment trends within the economic sector).

The sectors and individual measures are then continuously scanned to detect events and trends that could be significant for the organization and its strategy.

Such scanning can be accomplished in several ways. Company employees can be chosen and assigned the responsibility of tracking particular events and trends, perhaps by monitoring publications such as *The New York Times, Business Week,* and *The Wall Street Journal,* as well as consultants' reports, information services, and industry

FIGURE 11.8

continued

Technological Factors
(e.g., rate of technological change, future raw material availability, raw material cost, technological developments in related areas, product life cycles)

_____

_____

_____

_____

Competitive Factors
(e.g., entry and exit of major competitors, major strategic changes by competitors, competition size, number, capacity, location, methods, production/market segments)

_____

_____

_____

Geographic Factors
(e.g., plant/warehouse location, relocation of facilities, headquarters, foreign markets)

_____

_____

_____

newsletters. Increasingly, outside experts called *environmental scanners* (individuals who read and abstract a wide variety of publications) are retained to search for environmental changes that could impact the firm. Forecasting techniques including trend analysis, Delphi, and the use of scenarios can be used to fine-tune and focus the results of the information coming in. In any event, environmental scanning's purpose is to scan a very wide range of information sources on a continuous basis and in an organized way in order to identify previously unidentified events or trends that could impact the company and its strategy.

SPECIAL ALERT CONTROLS
A subset of strategic surveillance that are aimed at identifying crises or other events that may have very low probabilities of occurring, but which may threaten the very viability of the firm.

SPECIAL ALERT CONTROLS Special alert controls are a subset of strategic surveillance and are aimed at identifying crises or other events that may have very low probabilities of occurring, but which may threaten the very viability of the firm.

There are several ways to perform such crisis audits. For example, Heinz, Inc., uses brainstorming sessions to develop a better picture of the crisis that might develop and impact its business, as well as alternatives for how those crises will be dealt with.[25] Other firms develop worst-case scenarios to better clarify the sorts of crises that might leave them vulnerable.

HUMAN RESPONSES TO CONTROL

CONTROL—A CENTRAL ISSUE IN MANAGING

Every organization has to ensure that its employees are performing as expected. Because of this fact, how to maintain control lies at the core of a manager's job. Every day managers are faced with questions such as, "How can I make sure that Marie files her sales reports on time?" and "How can I make sure John doesn't close the store before 10:00 P.M.?" To a large extent, the answer to both questions is "By imposing controls."

But if tightly controlling employees was the only (or best) way to ensure effective performance, we could disregard more than half of this book. For example, we would not need to know very much about what motivates people, what leadership style is best, or how to win your employees' commitment.

But the fact is that managers can't rely exclusively on controls for keeping employees' performance in line. For one thing, it is virtually impossible to produce a system of rules and controls so complete that you can keep track of everything your employees say or do. For this (as we will see later in this chapter, and in the following chapters as well) you will have to rely more on self-control, which can be fostered with various motivational practices. The *Whole Foods* small business box provides an example.

Furthermore, a manager cannot rely exclusively on controls because employees can and will *retaliate* against controls, using what will often seem to be extraordinarily ingenious techniques. In terms of ingenuity, for instance, consider this true story. The owner of a chain of dry cleaning stores tried to control stealing by requiring store managers to give a cash register receipt to each and every customer. To reinforce this policy, the owner placed a large sign by the register that said, "If you don't get a cash register receipt, your order is free. Please call us at 348-6283." Sure that he could now track all the cash coming into the store, the owner happily went home every night, handing over the store at 5:00 P.M. to his store manager. However, every evening at 5:15 sharp, the store manager pulled out his own cash register, which he had secreted away during the day, and then spent about an hour happily taking in the owner's cash, and giving each satisfied customer a cash register receipt. Then he would replace the owner's cash register, and pocket his loot.[26]

WHOLE FOODS MARKET, INC.

Ask an employee of a firm that has a policy handbook what it's used for, and the answer will often range from doorstop to paperweight. Small businesses often don't even bother to prepare written policies. Many companies could learn from Whole Foods natural foods supermarket of Austin, Texas. Instead of a list of rules, Whole Foods' manual explains where the company came from and why it exists. Perhaps more importantly for a small, aggressive business, it lets employees know where they stand within the organization, and why the company does things the way it does. The company even offers advice on how to go about initiating changes employees believe are needed.

Whole Foods' founder and CEO John Mackey thinks spelling out how a business works is the best way to instill the idea that everyone is a part of it. "When people come into a business," he says, "they don't know what to expect." Growth means new employees, and they are often as inquisitive about why things need to be done a certain way as what needs to be done. Mackey's manual lists the rules, but the reasons behind them follow. For example, workers can't park in the store lot *because* it's not very big and if the

employees take up all the space, the customers won't have anyplace to park. The idea behind the dress code is much the same. It's made clear that employees are expected to serve the customers and not shock them.

Another practical (and in most companies, unheard of) element of the Whole Foods manual is the alteration it undergoes whenever the need arises. When accidents became a problem, Mackey instituted a safety program. Eventually, a couple of pages on job safety tips were incorporated into the manual. The number of mishaps de-

FOCUS ON SMALL BUSINESS

creased. Managers also gradually sensed curiosity on the part of workers about salary information. The next updated manual included a chart listing what employees could expect to earn at the various levels of the company.

Employees have had a hand in shaping policy, and their suggestions have gone into the manual. After a rousing debate about amending the dress code to include shorts, it was finally agreed that khakis with pockets would be acceptable. Employees also managed to

get their food discount extended to meats and produce. It had been thought that low margins on those two items made reductions unfeasible, but after double-checking it was discovered that was no longer the case. The 20 percent price break was extended across the board.

Mackey thinks the key to Whole Foods' success is based on communication, and the manual is a big part of it. "It helps us give people a sense of the past, the present, and the future," he says. "It's how we tell them about the game we're playing." He admits that this form of policy making may not work for every company because rapport between managers and employees has to be high. Employees have rules reasonably presented and logically explained. Managers must have justification for their actions and can be challenged if their instructions run contrary to the manual. "We try to build consensus," says Mackey. "If people don't have input, it isn't alive for them. But if you invest time and energy explaining things, employees take the whole program more seriously." And that helps ensure that employees keep their own actions "under control."

SOURCES: Betsy Spethmann, "Nature's Bounty," *Brandweek*, September 6, 1993, 18; and Bruce G. Posner, "The Best Little Handbook in Texas," *Inc.*, February 1989, 84–88.

SOME UNINTENDED HUMAN CONSEQUENCES OF CONTROLS

As you can see, one of the main problems with overrelying on controls is that they frequently result in unintended, undesirable, and often harmful employee reactions. Professor Kenneth Merchant classifies these potentially harmful reactions as behavioral displacement, gamesmanship, operating delays, and negative attitudes.[27]

BEHAVIORAL DISPLACEMENT Behavioral displacement occurs when the behaviors encouraged by the controls are inconsistent with the company's objectives. This often manifests itself in a tendency for employees to try to look good in terms of the control standards. In other words, they concentrate their efforts where results are measured, often disregarding the organization's more important goals.

BEHAVIORAL DISPLACEMENT
Occurs when the behaviors encouraged by the controls are inconsistent with the company's objectives.

This problem stems mostly from incomplete standards. In one classic example, employees in a state employment agency found that they were measured on the number of job seekers they *interviewed,* rather than on the number they placed on jobs. The number of interviews soared, but little attention was focused on adequately counseling applicants. When what was happening became apparent, several new standards (such as the ratio of placements to interviews) were devised.[28] In a similar example, a plant manager refused to modify production schedules to accommodate rush orders, although those orders could be large and very profitable for the company. His reasoning was that he was evaluated in terms of his costs, not in terms of his plant's profits, and last-minute rush orders drove up his costs.[29]

GAMESMANSHIP
Refers to management actions that are aimed at improving the manager's performance in terms of the control system without producing any positive economic effects.

GAMESMANSHIP Gamesmanship refers to management actions that are aimed at improving the manager's performance in terms of the control system without producing any positive economic effects. For example, Professor Merchant describes a manager who depleted his stocks of spare parts and heating oil at year's end although he knew these stocks had to be bought back shortly thereafter at higher prices. By reducing his stocks, though, the manager reduced his expenses for the year and made his end-of-year results look better, although in the long run the company lost out.[30] In another example, a division of a large company overshipped products to its distributors at year-end. The aim, apparently, was to ensure that management could meet its budgeted sales targets even though the managers knew the products would be returned.[31]

OPERATING DELAYS Operating delays—such as those that occur when a manager has to wait for approval from his supervisor before accepting a sales order—are another unfortunate and frequently unintended consequence of many control systems. They are particularly dangerous when quick, responsive decisions are needed. At some major corporations, for instance, managers often describe how the approvals needed to move from a new product's concept to detailed engineering and finally to sales can take so long that competitors introduce similar new products years ahead.[32]

NEGATIVE ATTITUDES In addition to the problems of displacement, gamesmanship, and operating delays, controls can have a more insidious effect by undermining employees' attitudes. In one study (which focused on the reactions of first-line supervisors to budgets), Professor Chris Argyris found that budgets were viewed as pressure devices. The supervisors came to view the budgets as "prods" by top management; in turn, they used their budgets to prod their own subordinates. As a result of this pressure, employees formed antimanagement work groups and the supervisors reacted by making narrow, shortsighted decisions.[33] Consider, for example, how the control tags in the *Employee IDs* vignette may well affect employee morale.

CONTROL, COMMITMENT, AND ORGANIZATIONAL RESPONSIVENESS

A number of years ago, Tom Burns and G. M. Stalker carried out a study of how British firms managed innovation, that is, organized and managed themselves in order to respond effectively under conditions of fast technological and market change. As we saw in Chapter 9 (The Responsive Organization), they found that a textile mill had established what they called a "mechanistic" management system. It was organized bureaucratically with clearly defined and specialized individual tasks, centralized decision making, and the traditional, "hierarchic structure of control, authority and com-

EMPLOYEE IDs

Italy's Olivetti holds the basic patent on the active-badge system and began marketing it commercially around the beginning of 1993. When asked how many people will be wearing active badges in five to ten years, one Olivetti lab director responded, "Everybody."

The active badge looks like a clip-on ID. But it's actually a small computer that emits infrared signals to strategically located sensors, which can then effectively track the wearer anywhere within an equipped facility. The system can even keep tabs on most visitors, revealing who they are and when they stopped by.

What may sound like a dream come true for companies trying to safeguard technological secrets could become an Orwellian nightmare for employees. The inventor, Roy Want, agrees. "It's great technology in the right hands. But if you've got a bad manager, he's going to make your life hell."

Besides Olivetti, Digital Equipment Corp., Xerox, and the Media Laboratory of MIT also currently use some variation of the system, and they find there are advantages. Knowing where people are avoids interruptions, wasted phone calls, and useless trips to empty offices.

But the questions loom: How much privacy in the name of control can managers expect employees to surrender? How much is too much control? Proponents say effective safeguards can be implemented. Critics fear that once such a system is in place, there will be no defense against capricious abuse, and no turning back.

SOURCE: Peter Coy, "Big Brother, Pinned to Your Chest," *Business Week,* August 17, 1992, 38.

As ID badge's become more sophisticated, generating a trail of an employee's whereabouts during the day, privacy issues become of great importance.

munication."[34] Here the employees' work behavior was governed by the rules, regulations, and close supervision of the firm's managers.

On the other hand, recall that for the electronics firms operating in the most rapidly changing conditions, "organic" management systems were the norm for the best-run companies. In this high-tech industry, jobs were continually adjusted and redefined, and decision making was pushed down so that first-line employees could make quick, on-the-spot decisions. Control was achieved not by preplanned rules and continually observant supervisors, but by employee commitment, and the realization of all employees that they had to be responsible for doing what was best for their firms.[35]

Fast-forward to the 1990s, when management expert Tom Peters found much the same in the firms that most effectively dealt with rapid external change. In fact, says Peters, when organizational responsiveness is the key to the firm's success, an extraordinary paradox emerges: "You are out of control when you are 'in control.' You are in control when you are 'out of control.' " The executive, says Peters,

who knows everything and who is surrounded by layers of staffers and inundated with thousands of pages of analyses from below may be 'in control' in the classical sense but in fact really only has the illusion of control. The manager has tons of after-the-fact reports, on everything, but (almost) invariably a control system and organization that's so ponderous that it's virtually impossible to respond fast enough even if a deviation is finally detected.[36]

That kind of imposed control is not the best, says Peters, in an era when rapid technical and market changes often demand quick, on-the-spot, innovative decisions, *now*. As he says:

> In fact, you really *are* in control when thousands upon thousands of people, unbeknownst to you, are taking initiatives, going beyond job descriptions and the constraints of their box on the organization chart, to serve the customer better, improve the process, work quickly with a supplier to nullify a defect . . .[37]

In other words, under rapidly changing conditions, companies must rely more on the self-control of their employees than on keeping the firm on track by enforcing rules, monitoring budgets, and closely supervising what everyone does. Self-control, many experts agree, is an essential ingredient of the responsive organization.

IMPOSED VERSUS SELF-CONTROL

The idea that control can range from self-control to imposed control has a long and distinguished history in management theory. Professor Herbert Simon (who went on to win a Nobel prize in economics for his work on decision making) has compared the two control approaches:

> Decisions reached in the higher ranks of the organization hierarchy will have no effect upon the activities of operative employees unless they are communicated downward. Consideration of the process requires an examination of the ways in which the behavior of the operative employee can be influenced. These influences fall roughly into two categories: (1) *establishing in the operative employee himself* attitudes, habits, and a state of mind which leave him to reach that decision which is advantageous to the organization, and (2) *imposing on the operative employee* decisions reached elsewhere in the organization. The first type of influence operates by inculcating in the employee organizational loyalties and the concern with efficiency, and more generally by training him. The second type of influence depends primarily upon authority and upon advisory and informational services. It is not insisted that these categories are either exhaustive or mutually exclusive . . .[38]

The social psychologists Daniel Katz and Robert Kahn make a very similar point. At one extreme, they say, organizations can get the behaviors they need from their employees through **legal compliance.** Legal compliance basically means the rule-enforcement approach to control. It means encouraging employees to do their jobs according to the rules by convincing them that those rules derive from a legitimate authority, much as sergeants are trained to jump when the general tells them to move. Katz and Kahn contend that legal compliance can bring about acceptable levels of individual performance, particularly when the employees' tasks are very routine.

However, for evoking *innovative* behavior, they say, managers must depend more on the employees' self-control. At the other extreme of the control spectrum is a form of self-control that Katz and Kahn call "internalized values and the self-concept." This basically means gaining employees' self-control by winning their personal commitment to the firm and its goals. In this situation, employees do their jobs right because they want to and because the company's goals and theirs have merged into one.[39]

RESEARCH FINDINGS Is a high reliance on self-control really the way to go under conditions of rapid change? The preponderance of evidence suggests that the answer is yes. For one thing, the anecdotal evidence based on case studies of firms from Burns and Stalker to Tom Peters supports that contention.

LEGAL COMPLIANCE
Encouraging employees to do their jobs according to the rules by convincing them that those rules derive from a legitimate authority.

Furthermore, several well thought out behavioral science studies also suggest that the answer is yes. In one study, for instance, the researcher found that the extent to which an employee was allowed to exercise self-control (as measured by questions like "To what extent do you control your job and the general pace of your work?") was a function of how predictable the task was: the more unpredictable the work demands confronting the employee, the greater the likelihood that he or she would exert a high degree of self-control.[40] Another study by Professors Paul Lawrence and Jay Lorsch focused on managers in three industries: foods, plastics, and containers. In the plastics and food firms, managers at all levels—first-line supervisors, department managers, and plant managers—were encouraged to exercise a good degree of self-control. But in the container firms, only top-level managers exerted much influence; lower-level managers had very little control or influence over how they did their jobs and to that extent were just following top management's dictates.

In interpreting their findings, Lawrence and Lorsch concluded that control has to fit the predictableness of the situation. In the plastics and food firms, responsiveness, innovation, and creativity were paramount. Quick decisions had to be made. It was therefore relatively important that all managers have a good deal of influence so they could make quick, on-the-spot decisions. In the container firms, on the other hand, efficiency (not responsiveness) was paramount. Here it was consequently more important for everyone to "stick to the rules" and be highly efficient. Control therefore was more hierarchical, with top managers exercising a great deal of control or influence, and lower-level managers basically following orders and sticking to the rules.[41]

MOVING FROM IMPOSED CONTROL TO SELF-CONTROL AND COMMITMENT

Harvard Professor Richard Walton writes that a transformation is taking place in organizations today, a transformation from what he calls "control to commitment."[42] As it becomes more important that firms respond to change and to customer demands for quality products and services, firms around the world—from the Saturn car company to Penney's department stores—are finding they must rely more on, and thus cultivate, their employees' self-control. This certainly does not eliminate the need for traditional control tools like enforcing rules, monitoring budgets, or exercising some degree of personal supervision. It simply means that in a world in which organizations must increasingly rely on their employees to make the right fast, on-the-spot decisions, the relative importance of self-control has grown.

The question, then, is "How do companies win such self-control?" Developing employees' self-control is essentially a behavioral matter, one linked inextricably to topics like motivating employees, creating shared values, and winning employees' commitment. To answer this question, we must therefore leave the topic of traditional control per se and move on to Part III: Behavior and Management.

SUMMARY

With plans set and the organizations designed and staffed, managers have to take the necessary actions to ensure that performance conforms to the plan—that *control* takes place.

Steps in the control process include establishing a standard, goal, or target; measuring performance against this standard; and identifying deviations and taking corrective action. The three basic types of control are steering controls, yes-no controls, and post-action controls. Organizations have many activities that must be controlled. These include specific actions, results, and personnel.

Budgets are formal, financial expressions of a manager's plans. Accountants' reports reflect actual performance versus planned targets, allowing managers to take corrective actions where needed.

The budgeting process begins with a sales forecast or budget. Then a production budget is created, reflecting the number of units to be produced and what the cost will be. From this budget an income statement is derived, along with a cash budget showing month-to-month cash needs. Finally, from all of this information, a budgeted balance sheet is developed.

Zero-based budgeting eliminates some shortcomings of traditional budgeting. This technique forces managers to defend and rank programs based on a ratio of benefits and costs.

Many organizations control and compare interdivisional performances through interlocking financial ratios. Financial ratios compare one financial variable to another; multiplying these ratios together eventually results in the rate of return on investment.

Traditional control processes are often ineffective and misleading in monitoring strategic plans because they detect problems after they have occurred. In a fast-changing environment, managers are forced to examine not only deviations from the set plan, but also the plan itself. This process, called strategic control, includes premise control, strategic surveillance, and special alert control.

Overreliance on control techniques can result in adverse effects such as behavioral displacement, gamesmanship, operating delays, and poor work attitude.

Establishing an effective control system is difficult, complicated, and can often be self-defeating. In most contemporary organizations, where fast response is paramount, relying on employee self-control is more important than imposing rigid top-to-bottom controls. Employees who exercise self-control and react to customer demand within acceptable parameters are usually those who have greater commitment to the organization and its goals.

QUESTIONS

■ FOR REVIEW

1. List and detail each step in the control process.

2. Outline the basic steps in the budgeting process and the budgetary control techniques used in each.

3. Name the content and purpose of the three strategic control methods.

4. Describe some of the most common problems associated with human control.

5. What is the difference between mechanistic and organic management control systems, and in which types of firms are each most appropriately employed?

■ FOR DISCUSSION

6. Contrast traditional budgeting with the requirements of zero-based budgeting. What are the advantages and disadvantages of the two methods?

7. Describe the types of control measures your professor uses in the classroom. What is your response to them?

8. How do you think employees are likely to respond to an active badge system that allows the company to track their every move? Why?

9. Discuss the pros and cons of fostering employees' self-control, instead of imposing rigid controls over their activities.

■ FOR ACTION

10. Devise a budget for your personal spending in the upcoming week and do your best to stick with it. At the end of seven days, review how successful you were in controlling your expenditures. Discuss your observations during the next class period.

11. Assume you are a top executive at Exxon Corporation the day after the *Valdez* oil spill. Devise a basic plan for controlling the negative repercussions that are sure to follow. What decisions would you make?

12. Write a short description of the managerial control techniques at your current place of employment or a business you know of. Which ones do you think are the most effective?

■ FOR FOCUS ON SMALL BUSINESS

13. What steps have Whole Foods managers taken to help ensure that employees do not retaliate against the control measures outlined in the company handbook?

14. Is the handbook an example of imposed control or self-control? Explain.

15. Do you think that small companies find it easier to maintain control than do large ones? Why or why not?

CLOSING SOLUTION

SATURN CORPORATION

Today, the Saturn plant in Spring Hill, Tennessee, is made up of small, autonomous, and self-directed work teams. Workers have control over everything from their own budgets to hiring new help. Saturn does not have a personnel department. Teams take part in day-to-day strategic decision making and each runs its operation like a small business.

The main problem the company must still overcome is low productivity. Despite absenteeism of only 2.5 percent (other GM plants average 10 to 14 percent) and between 300 and 700 hours of instruction per worker, it still takes 35 hours to build a car. The goal of producing a car in 20 hours remains well in the distance.

Saturn can certainly be pleased with sales. Cars are moving faster than they can be built, and they are winning high marks for quality and the company's stated goal—customer satisfaction. From all appearances, Saturn has achieved another goal as well. Using an innovative approach, it is producing a car that is meeting and beating the Japanese, while relying on the self-control of its employees.

■ QUESTIONS FOR CLOSING SOLUTION

1. Will the team approach at Saturn help management avoid the unintended human consequences of controls described in the chapter? Why or why not?

2. Using GM and Saturn plants as examples, discuss the merits of imposed versus self-control.

3. Describe some of the traditional means of control that are necessary even in a self-managed work environment like Saturn.

KEY TERMS

Controlling

Steering Controls

Yes-no Controls

Benchmarking

Post-action Controls

Results Accountability

Budgets

Variances

Sales Budget

Production Budget

Income Statement

Cash Budget

Budgeted Balance Sheet

Zero-based Budgeting

Financial Ratio

Rate of Return on Investment (ROI)

Strategic Control

Premise Control Methods

Strategic Surveillance Methods

Special Alert Control Methods

Environmental Monitoring

Environmental Scanning

Behavioral Displacement

Gamesmanship

Legal Compliance

CASE FOR ANALYSIS

OVERLY MANUFACTURING COMPANY

As the saying goes, even the best laid plans often go astray. In 1991, Terry and David Reese bought Overly Manufacturing Company of Greensburg, Pennsylvania. They had their sights set on growing the $12 million a year specialty door and roofing manufacturer into a $50 million company. And with the changes they saw titans like AT&T, General Electric, and Hewlett-Packard embracing, they thought they knew exactly how to do it.

The giant firms were abandoning their hierarchical structures in favor of flexibility, higher product quality, customer satisfaction, and quicker response. The brothers Reese, along with company president John Harts, therefore thought it was time to jettison the authoritarian culture at the 105-year-old Overly plant. Worker empowerment was the ticket for the future.

Harts, who had spent the last 41 years in the door industry, began by naming 12-member teams of designers, salespeople, welders, press operators, and plant supervisors. Following a few days instruction on how teams are supposed to work, they were given the assignment of getting the company's new, low-cost method for manufacturing sound-retardant doors under way.

The team was enthusiastic, but progress often seemed to take two steps forward, followed by three steps back.

First of all, the assignment was far more complicated than anyone expected. One team figured out a way to save space by eliminating scrap metal piles, but no one could decide where to put the production line. A consultant suggested putting it in a segregated area so workers doing different jobs could move about freely, but then some employees said they didn't think the Steelworkers' Union would appreciate press operators putting in door insulation.

The team established plans to build doors four feet wide, which was perfect until salespeople began coming around with orders for wider ones. There was a lot of doubt and dissension about business school theories and how things happen in the real world. After things finally got under way, the new line was a creaky operation indeed. Cost projections turned out to be wildly optimistic.

Things were worse elsewhere in the shop. Slowdowns in the manufacture of heavy bank-vault and blast doors had long been a problem at Overly. The team tackling this problem decided an overhead crane was needed so welders could move these 4,000-pound behemoths without waiting around for lift trucks. A chorus of objections ensued, from management to coworkers. Management told the stunned team members to rethink the problem. Welder Ken Guidas summed up the general sentiment on worker empowerment. "It's going to take a lot longer than anyone thought to get it accomplished," he said.

Terry Reese thinks things will come around. "It takes a while, especially when you've been in an environment where it's 'Sit down, shut up and do what I tell you,' " he says. And the changes have not been without benefit. Workers on the floor opened a free-flowing line of communication with engineers. Because of direct worker input at regular meetings, the engineers have learned to smooth off the more difficult elements of their design specifications. Other such ideas have lowered costs through inventory reduction, better storage, and realigning equipment. And a new-product team's first production run, which rolled off the line in June 1993, may be a winner. An exuberant Harts said of the sound-retardent door line, "It's going to knock the market dead."

Perhaps so, but Overly isn't out of the woods, and plenty of finger pointing is going on. Managers complain that they don't know what they can promise customers because they no longer have any idea what they can deliver. Subordinates now beat a path to their manager's door with their latest, greatest idea, and simply telling them to get back to work is viewed as counter-culture. Not surprisingly, workers who see their ideas ignored doubt management's commitment to the new way of doing things. Gene James, who runs the company's computer systems, offered a particularly insightful viewpoint. "There's some vague idea that Overly wants to become a new democratic organization, empowering people," he says. "But we've lost the old structure before the new structure is in place, and the chaos [really] scares me."

Pinpointing exactly why the corporate makeover at Overly hasn't been successful is difficult. Workers who feel their suggestions are ignored or delayed resist when called upon to learn new job skills. Managers who tried to embrace the new system now see no end in sight to the confusion and misdirected energies. More than a few wouldn't mind turning back the clock.

Terry Reese remains optimistic. Emphasizing people resources is the wave of the future, and he won't be deterred. "In 10 years," he predicts, "anybody who runs a business on the hierarchical model isn't going to be in business."

Before it's all over, Terry Reese may become familiar with another old saying: Success has a thousand fathers, but failure is an orphan.

SOURCE: Marc Levinson, "Playing with Fire," *Newsweek*, June 21, 1993, 46–48.

■ QUESTIONS

1. Have Overly managers lost control of their employees, or is this simply an example of maintaining control by allowing workers to exercise self-control? Discuss.
2. Why is the company having so many problems with its empowerment program? How could the system be improved?
3. Do you agree with Terry Reese's prediction that hierarchical businesses will not survive?

A CASE IN DIVERSITY

NEW YORK NATIONAL BANK

When Serafin Mariel was managing a Bankers Trust branch in the South Bronx, New York, he thought he spotted an opportunity. His own bank and other big institutions were shuttering most of their inner city branches and exiting in droves. Conventional wisdom held that the market offered too much in the way of risk and too little in the way of profits. The city's biggest minority institution, the $100 million Freedom Bank, folded in 1990. The question was, had Mariel identified a lucrative niche to be exploited, or was he walking into a trap?

Mariel and a group of investors bought one of the Bankers Trust branches and created New York National Bank (NYNB) in 1982, now the city's largest minority owned commercial bank. But Mariel's familiarity with his market didn't insulate the institution from recessionary forces near the end of that decade. Pressure from regulators to clean up bad loans resulted in a $1.5 million loss in 1987. More red ink recurred in 1990. Mariel was faced with the necessity of implementing controls that satisfied the regulators, and put NYNB back on a path to continued profitability.

The initial priority was to wring out the loan book, concentrate on workouts, and bite the bullet where write-offs were the only alternative. Regulators were also insisting reserves be increased, hurting the banks liquidity position. Mariel put the bank's portfolio in order, and later completed a stock offering that netted nearly $1 million in working capital. He also acquired additional branches designed to serve local businesses and generate healthy new loan business. The goal was to double NYNB's assets and facilitate economies through growth and expansion.

Because of the market NYNB served, capital was a principle concern. Mariel's approach was innovative, and perhaps a bit ironic. He sought out some of the institutions that formerly served his customer base. "I've been working with the major banks trying to formulate what I call a 'CRA alliance' so they will invest some Tier 1 capital into New York National Bank. Those funds would enable us to make the acquisitions and go forward." Mariel has tapped two other sources of capital, the minority bank funding source Minbanc, and the Business Consortium Fund, which directs funds to minority-owned businesses.

Serafin Mariel says that despite the problems he has encountered, he likes being a banker, and he thinks his role is critical. In his opinion, big banks' community reinvestment efforts, which were channeled through state or municipally sponsored pro-grams, fell short of the mark. Mariel says what's needed are more local institutions, familiar with the market and customer base, operating under the right fiscal controls. Those types of institutions can book profitable local loan customers and remain flexible enough to operate efficiently. In Mariel's view, a renaissance in the South Bronx or any other inner city borough with businesses that have limited access to capital sources, won't come from government or big banking Manhattan-based institutions. It will come from responsive home-grown fast-movers like NYNB.

SOURCES: Franklin Smith, "Minority Bank Toughs It Out in New York," *American Banker,* November 18, 1992, 1 and 8.

■ QUESTIONS

1. Which of the following types of controls did Mariel use to guide NYNB to profitability: steering controls, yes-no controls, post-action controls?
2. Describe some uncontrollable factors that the bank likely has encountered in its external environment.
3. Do you think regulators should apply different control standards to NYNB because it is a minority bank?

ENDNOTES

1. This problem was researched from Dorothy Cottrell et al., "Sales Training and the Saturn Difference," *Training & Development,* December 1992, 38–43; "On Another Planet," The *Economist,* October 17, 1992, 9–11; and David Woodruff, "Where Employees Are Management," *Business Week,* Reinventing America Issue, 1992, 66.

2. Kenneth Merchant, "The Control Function of Management," *Sloan Management Review,* Summer 1982, 43.

3. William H. Newman, *Constructive Control* (Englewood Cliffs, NJ: Prentice-Hall, 1975), 5.

4. Kenneth Merchant, *Control in Business Organizations* (Boston: Pitman, 1985), ix.

5. Kenneth Merchant, "The Control Function of Management," *Sloan Management Review,* Summer 1982, 43.

6. See, for example, T. K. Das, "Organizational Control: An Evolutionary Perspective," *Journal of Management Studies,* September 1989, 459–75.

7. Merchant, "The Control Function of Management," 44.

8. Glenn A. Welsch, *Budgeting: Profit Planning and Control* (Englewood Cliffs, NJ: Prentice-Hall, 1988), 16.

9. Thomas Connellan, *How to Improve Human Performance: Behaviorism in Business and Industry* (New York: Harper & Row, 1978), 68–73.

10. For a discussion, see Joan Woodward, *Industrial Organization: Behavior and Control* (London: Oxford, 1970), 37–56.

11. This section is based on William Newman, *Constructive Control* (Englewood Cliffs, NJ: Prentice-Hall, 1975), 6–9.

12. This is based on Merchant, "The Control Function of Management," 45–47; and Merchant, *Control in Business Organizations,* 18.

13. Charles Horngren, *Accounting for Management Control* (Englewood Cliffs, NJ: Prentice-Hall, 1970), 188.

14. Mark Dirsmith and Stephen Jablonski, "Zero Base Budgeting as a Management Technique and Political Strategy," *The Academy of Management Review,* vol. 4, no. 4, October 1979, 555–65.

15. See John Preble, "Towards a Comprehensive System of Strategic Control," *Journal of Management Studies,* vol. 29, no. 4, July 1992, 391–408; and David Asch, "Strategic Control: A Problem Looking for a Solution," *Long-Range Planning,* vol. 25, no. 2 (1992), 105–10.

16. L. Alexander, "Successfully Implementing Strategic Decisions," *Long-Range Planning,* vol. 18, no. 3 (1985), 91–97.

17. G. Schreyogg and H. Steinman, "Strategic Control: A New Perspective," *Academy of Management Review,* vol. 12, no. 1 (1987), 91–103.

18. Ibid., 91; and Arye Globerson, Shlomo Globerson, and Judith Frampton, *You Can't Manage What You Don't Measure: Control and Evaluation in Organizations* (Brookfield, VT: Gower Publishing, 1991), 71–72.

19. Stephen Bungay and Michael Goold, "Creating a Strategic Control System," *Long-Range Planning,* vol. 24, no. 3 (1991), 32; and Charles Bonini, Robert Jaedicke, and Harvey Wagner, eds., *Management Controls: New Directions in Basic Research* (New York: Garland Publishing, 1986), 63.

20. Ibid., 32; and David Asch, "Strategic Control: A Problem Looking for a Solution," *Long-Range Planning,* vol. 25, no. 2, April 1992, 105–10.

21. Preble, "Towards a Comprehensive System," 393; and Alfred D. Chandler, Jr., "The Functions of the HQ Unit in the Multi Business Firm," *Strategic Management Journal,* vol. 12, Winter 1991, 31–50.

22. "Towards a Comprehensive System," 394; and Stephen Bungay and Michael Gold, "Creating a Strategic Control System," *Long-Range Planning,* vol. 24, no. 3, June 1991, 32–39.

23. "Towards a Comprehensive System," 402. For discussion of the emphasis on self-control in various countries, see Paul Boreham, "The Myth of Post-Fordist Management: Work Organization and Employee Discretion in Seven Countries," *Management Decisions,* vol. 30, no. 6, November 1990, 100–09.

24. Except as noted, the remainder of this section is based on Preble, "Towards a Comprehensive System," 397–405. See also Patricia Galagan and Michael Donovan, "Beyond Hierarchy: The Search for High Performance," *Training & Development,* vol. 46, no. 8, August 1992, 20–26.

25. "How Companies Are Learning to Prepare for the Worst," *Business Week,* December 1985, 74–76; and Michael Rigg, "Increased Personal Control Equals Increased Individual Satisfaction," *Industrial Engineering,* vol. 24, no. 2, February 1992, 12–14.

26. As described by the owner of a chain of dry cleaning stores to the author. For a discussion of how to evaluate standards, see Dennis Arter, "Evaluate Standards and Improve Performance with a Quality Audit," *Quality Progress,* vol. 22, no. 9, September 1989, 41–43.

27. The following, except as noted, is based on Merchant, *Control in Business Organizations,* 71–120. See also Robert Kaplan, "New Systems for Measurement and Control," *The Engineering Economist,* vol. 36, no. 3, Spring 1991, 201–18.

28. Peter Blau, *The Dynamics of Bureaucracy* (Chicago: University of Chicago Press, 1955), 4–6. As we will see in Chapter 15 (Motivation and Innovation), at least one motivation theory today emphasizes individuals' propensity to control their efforts in light of the goals they have accepted. See, for example, Howard Klein, "An Integrated Control Theory Model of Work Motivation," *Academy of Management Review,* vol. 14, no. 2 (1989), 150–72.

29. Eric Flamholtz, "Organizational Control Systems as a Managerial Tool," *California Management Review,* vol. 22, Winter 1979, 50–59; and Michael Gould, "Strategic Control in the Decentralized Firm," *Sloan Management Review,* vol. 77, Winter 1991, 69–81.

30. Merchant, *Control in Business Organizations,* 98.

31. "Did Warner-Lambert Make a $468 Million Mistake?" *Business Week,* November 21, 1983, 123; quoted in Merchant, *Control in Business Organizations,* 98–99.

32. See, for example, "The Shrinking of Middle Management," *Business Week,* April 25, 1983, 55.

33. Chris Argyris, "Human Problems with Budgets," *Harvard Business Review,* vol. 31, no. 1, January–February 1953, 97–110.

34. See, for example, Tom Burns and G. M. Stalker, *The Management of Innovation* (London: Tavistock Publications, 1961), 120–21.

35. Ibid., 121.

36. Tom Peters, *Liberation Management* (New York: Alfred A. Knopf, 1992), 465–66.

37. Ibid., 466.

38. Herbert A. Simon, *Administrative Behavior* (New York: The Free Press, 1976), 11.

39. See Daniel Katz and Robert Kahn, *The Social Psychology of Organizations* (New York: John Wiley, 1966), 238–45. For a recent discussion of similar ideas see Richard E. Walton, "From Control to Commitment in the Workplace," *Harvard Business Review,* March–April 1985, 77–83.

40. Gerald Bell, "The Influence of Technological Components of Work Upon Management Control," *Journal of the Academy of Management,* vol. 8, no. 2 (1965), 127–32.

41. Paul Lawrence and Jay Lorsch, *Organization and Environment* (Boston: Harvard University, 1967), 140–45; for an additional view on some of these ideas see T. K. Das, "Organizational Control: An Evolutionary Perspective," *Journal of Management Studies,* vol. 26, no. 5, September 1989, 459–75; and R. Goffee and R. Scase, "Proprietorial Control in Family Firms: Some Functions of 'Quasi-Organic' Management Systems," *Journal of Management Studies,* vol. 22, 1985, 53–68.

42. See Walton, "From Control to Commitment in the Workplace."

FLORIDA POWER CORPORATION

VIDEO CASE

The business environment today is constantly shifting and reinventing itself. Companies that adapt to this evolution will be the companies that succeed through the next decade and beyond.

There are many innovative strategies that allow organizations to manage change. Some involve very flexible decentralized structures with employees empowered to make decisions as needs arise. Other organizations rely on long-term planning and carefully developed centralized systems to predict and respond to change from a centralized location.

Still, other organizations change their systems of operations to adapt to customer needs. The ability to simultaneously manage change and maintain a high level of customer service has become vital to the success of some companies in this era of constant flux.

One organization using a combination of these strategies is Florida Power Corporation. Based in St. Petersburg, Florida Power provides electrical service to over 1.2 million residential, commercial, and industrial customers in 32 counties across Florida. Florida Power currently operates in a highly regulated environment with many customers having no real alternative source for electric power. Even so, Florida Power realizes the value and need of providing quality customer service. Recognizing that "those who provide the service are the service," they recently invested $50 million to develop a new customer service system. This system provides their employees with the information and flexibility needed to provide the best service possible and allows Florida Power to remain ahead in the increasingly competitive utilities business.

Like other industries that have seen increasing competition (telecommunications and express package delivery), technology will play a key role for companies like Florida Power who are trying to stay competitive in the utility industry. Don Higgins, Director of Information Services, said, "We see the company moving into a much more competitive environment and we need a system that allows us to compete in that environment." Florida Power and Andersen Consulting have developed high-tech information systems to provide state-of-the-art customer service for their customers and their employees.

The new system also required significant change in the training of both new and current customer service representatives. Adjustments had to be made when moving from a mainframe-based system to a PC system. Current customer service representatives had to be trained not only on a new system, but platform differences as well (such as using a mouse). They also had to be educated on the benefits of the new system so that they would be mo-

tivated to want to use it. Trainers, however, quickly recognized the efficiencies of the new system—nearly all new hires will enter Florida Power with some base of PC knowledge from which to build.

Carefully planned development of this system provides Florida Power employees with the information they need to provide better service. Customers who call the utility company will be speaking with service representatives who have instant access to current customer records, energy usage patterns, payment history, all past correspondence with that customer and other information to better answer customer questions. The new system will also help representatives respond more efficiently to unusual conditions that affect or interrupt the delivery of electricity. These innovations answer the needs of the customer at the same time they are responding to the changing needs of the business environment. The utility is also counting on the system to help its representatives sell customers on new services, such as energy conservation devices, said company spokesperson Karen Ralhill. This same system should provide managers with data to plan for changes that will affect Florida Power both today and in the ever-changing competitive years ahead.

SOURCE: Robert Trigaux, "Utility Looks for High-Tech Future," *St. Petersburg Times,* March 22, 1994.

■ QUESTIONS

1. Why should Florida Power expect a more competitive environment in the future? What might occur to make this a more competitive business environment? Can you name another service industry which experienced a major change in its competitive environment?
2. Describe the structure of authority and control at Florida Power from a customer service standpoint. Is authority and control centralized or decentralized? Explain.
3. How will the system changes described in the case affect the work of the human resource department at Florida Power? Staffing? Selection and Placement? Compensation and Appraisal?

CHAPTER 12

EMPOWERING EMPLOYEES AND BUILDING COMMITMENT

LEARNING OBJECTIVES

After studying this chapter, you should be able to:

- Define employee commitment and explain its implications for achieving company goals.
- Outline the commitment building process found in modern-day high-commitment organizations.
- List the practices and organizational experiences that trigger commitment in the workplace.
- Identify the processes and three basic tenets of value-based hiring.
- Illustrate the relationship between job security and employee commitment.
- Explain the role of financial rewards and profit sharing in winning employee commitment.
- Discuss several practices that help individual employees self-actualize.

OPENING PROBLEM
APPLE COMPUTER

Employees at Apple Computer were long known for their steadfast commitment to the company. Many hired on for the opportunity to change the world. But when former chairman and CEO John Sculley, responding to dwindling profit margins and changes in the industry, made the alarming announcement that employee layoffs were planned, the reaction of some disillusioned workers was equally alarming. ■ A 500-member protest group, Employees for One Apple, called for collective bargaining. Just mentioning the possibility of forming a union among Apple's maverick work force had previously been unthinkable. Many employees were ambivalent or afraid of the so-called *U* word, but they acknowledged it would afford them some protection. ■ Sculley's greatest challenge was to rally his work force, convince them of the severity of the crisis, and emphasize that the only way out was for everyone to pull together. In essence, he asked them to rediscover the soul of Apple Computer and to recommit to it.[1]

THE QUESTION OF HOW TO GET EMPLOYEES TO COMPLY

We said in Chapter 11 that it is not enough for a manager to simply assign tasks to subordinates; in addition, he or she has *to ensure that those tasks are carried out*—that *compliance* takes place. For an organization to function with any degree of effectiveness, each person must be confident that the people he or she directs will comply with orders. When orders are not obeyed and when employees do not (in the absence of orders) unilaterally take steps to help the company succeed, there is no way to ensure that the organization will function effectively. As a result, the question of compliance—of how to get employees to carry out their tasks—has long been a holy grail of management theorists.

IN SEARCH OF COMPLIANCE

SCIENTIFIC MANAGEMENT   The question of compliance was a main concern of early twentieth-century management theorists like Frederick Winslow Taylor. Taylor knew that putting the right worker on the right job would not by itself guarantee high productivity; instead, some plan for motivating workers to do their best and to comply with their supervisor's instructions was required. Taylor, a Puritan by background, proposed a system of financial incentives in which each worker was paid in direct proportion to how much he or she produced rather than according to a basic hourly wage. Today Taylor is often criticized as the man who almost single-handedly operationalized the degrading, demoralizing, machine-like existence for many of the workers of his age. However, despite our vision of armies of workers silently carrying out highly simplified jobs and blindly following orders in return for the financial incentives they are owed, Taylor's original objectives may have been just the opposite. He said that scientific management was "not just an efficiency device, or a new scheme of paying men, or a bonus system," but instead

> involves a complete mental revolution on the part of the working man engaged in any particular establishment or industry—a complete mental revolution on the part of these men as to their duties toward their work, toward their fellow men, and toward their employees. And it involves the equally complete mental revolution on the part of those on the management side—the foremen, the superintendent, . . .
>
> The greater revolution that takes place in the mental attitude of the two parties under scientific management is that both sides take their eyes off the division of the surplus as the all-important matter, and together turn their attention toward increasing the size of the surplus until the surplus becomes so large that it is unnecessary to quarrel over how it shall be divided. They come to see that when they stop pulling against one another and instead both turn and push shoulder to shoulder in the same direction, the size of the surplus created by their joint effort is truly astonishing.[2]

Taylor's ideas thus seemed to be firmly founded upon a desire for worker-management harmony and increased worker benefits. The problem lay not in Taylor's motives but in his assumptions, which were the prevailing utilitarian-rational assumptions of his day. Taylor lived in an era of efficiency, in which worker tasks were relatively routine and repetitive as factories pressed forth to satisfy the burgeoning demand for goods. Under conditions like these, close supervision and financial incentives were indeed useful techniques for ensuring compliance.

THE CHANGING ENVIRONMENT   Extraordinary changes took place during the early decades of the 1900s. Although World War II required industry to convert to military production, the technological and managerial advancements of the war years resulted in a postwar boom as firms used their expanded capacities to add more diversified product lines. This period was therefore characterized by product diversification and by increasingly differentiated, complex, and rapidly changing industrial environments.[3]

The Depression (in which about 30 percent of Americans were put out of work and in which many began to question the blind pursuit of efficiency) plus the product diversification and innovation of the postwar years, coincided with dramatic changes in how management experts suggested obtaining employee compliance.

The work of Rensis Likert is representative of the trends taking place in management theory at this time. Likert's thesis was that effective organizations differ markedly from ineffective ones in several ways. The effective organization encourages its supervisors to "focus their primary attention on endeavoring to build effective work groups with high performance goals." In contrast, the less effective organization follows the prescriptions of classical writers like Frederick Winslow Taylor. These less effective, "job-centered" organizations break the total operation into simple component parts and then use close supervision and financial incentives to ensure that these tasks are carried out.[4] For Likert,

> The leadership and other processes of the organization must be such as to ensure a maximum probability that in all interactions and all relationships with the organization each member will, in the light of his background, values, and expectations, view the experience as supportive and one which builds and maintains his sense of personal worth and importance.[5]

Social psychologists Daniel Katz and Robert Kahn synthesized the approaches of experts like Taylor and Likert.[6] As we saw in Chapter 11, Katz and Kahn argued that control techniques could be envisioned as ranging from imposed control to self-control:

IMPOSED CONTROL   Type I is legal or **imposed control**.[7] Employees comply with rules or orders because they either consider them legitimate job demands or because they fear sanctions. Under imposed control, employees assume that any rule or directive from the proper authority should be obeyed because it is the law of the organization, and they accept these orders as part of the "contract" they agreed to when joining the organization.[8] The problem with such control, say Katz and Kahn, is its inability to motivate employees for anything but routine compliance with the demands of their jobs.[9]

IMPOSED (OR LEGAL) CONTROL
Employees comply with rules or orders because they either consider them legitimate job demands or because they fear sanctions.

FINANCIAL INCENTIVES   Frederick Taylor's solution to this problem was the use of **financial incentives**, which represent the second of Katz and Kahn's four compliance techniques. Here, rewards are linked to desired behaviors. Doing one's job becomes instrumental in obtaining the desired financial rewards.

FINANCIAL INCENTIVES
Rewards that are contingent on performance.

JOB IDENTIFICATION   Legal compliance (Type I) and the use of rewards (Type II) both depend on external reminders to get employees to do their jobs. Katz and Kahn's next two types of techniques are both aimed at encouraging *self-control*. Type III, say Katz and Kahn, involves **job identification**. A job that is sufficiently challenging and interesting provides the employee with an opportunity for self-expression and achievement. The employee complies—carries out the job assigned—not because rules, supervision, or incentives are imposed but because he or she identifies with the job and gets satisfaction from carrying it out.

JOB IDENTIFICATION
The person views the job as his or her "own," usually because the job is challenging and interesting and provides an opportunity for self expression and achievement.

INTERNALIZATION   The fourth technique offered by Katz and Kahn involves getting the employee to **internalize** the organization's goals. Here the company's goals become identical with those of the employee. The person complies or is motivated to

INTERNALIZATION
When the person accepts the organization's goals as his or her own.

accomplish the task because by achieving the organization's goals, he or she is also achieving his or her own. This employee becomes committed to the firm and its goals.

Katz and Kahn argue that each of these four techniques is appropriate for encouraging a different type of organizational behavior. Legal compliance (Type I) is usually not too effective for attracting people into a system or holding them there, except in such instances as military service. But it can bring about acceptable levels of individual performance, particularly if the job is very routine. To ensure compliance above minimum standards, rewards (Type II) must be used. But while rewards can be useful for attracting people to the organization and ensuring dependable behavior, they do not guarantee innovation and spontaneous behavior, say Katz and Kahn.

For this, managers must depend more on the employee's self-control, say Katz and Kahn. Building opportunities for deriving satisfaction from the job itself into the job and managing the organization so that its goals and those of its employees become synchronized are the ways to evoke innovative and spontaneous behaviors, they say. In other words, the most powerful technique for ensuring compliance—where **compliance** means being innovative, doing one's best, and going that extra mile—is to get each employee to adopt the organization's goals as his or her own; in other words, to win the employee's commitment.

COMPLIANCE

Carrying out the job's duties, including following orders and instructions. We distinguished between imposed control and self control as two ways to obtain compliance.

CREATING COMMITMENT: THE RESEARCH EVIDENCE

Few would disagree that the most powerful way for a firm to get things done right is to synchronize its goals with those of its employees until the two sets of goals are essentially the same. Creating commitment means forging just such a synthesis.[10]

THE MEANING OF COMMITMENT

Researcher Richard Steers says that commitment can be defined as the relative strength of an individual's identification with and involvement in an organization. He says commitment is characterized by three things: (1) a strong belief in and acceptance of the organization's goals and values, (2) a willingness to exert considerable effort on behalf of the organization, and (3) a strong desire to maintain membership in the organization.[11] Similarly, researcher Bruce Buchanan says that commitment embodies three separate but closely related attitudes: (1) a sense of identification with the organizational mission, (2) a feeling of involvement or psychological immersion in organizational duties, and (3) a feeling of loyalty and affection for the organization as a place to live and work, quite apart from the merits of its mission or its purely instrumental value to the individual. Furthermore, he says, identification implies the alignment of individual and organizational goals. **Employee commitment** therefore exists when an employee comes to think of the organization's goals in personal terms and to incorporate them into his or her own goal system.[12] Creating commitment means synchronizing employee and company goals and thus creating self-motivated employees.

EMPLOYEE COMMITMENT

When an employee comes to internalize the organization's goals as his or her own and to incorporate them into his or her own goal system.

RESEARCH EVIDENCE

How can companies create such commitment? This question has been studied by many researchers.

BUCHANAN STUDY   Bruce Buchanan studied 279 managers in eight large U.S. organizations to identify the factors that these managers thought encouraged the growth of commitment.[13] Of the factors he studied, five had the most significant impact on commitment for the total group of managers: personal importance, work group experiences, realization of expectations, valuing high commitment, and first-year job challenges.

Personal importance was "the experience of being considered a productive and valuable member of the organization." It measured the extent to which a manager sensed that the work he or she did was viewed as a genuine contribution to the success of the company. As Buchanan puts it, "Managers who felt they were indispensable or important were much more likely to report strong commitment than those who lacked this feeling."

Work group experiences represented a second commitment-enhancing factor. In particular, the more cohesive, friendly, and close-knit the manager's work group, the more positive the group's overall feeling toward the organization and the more likely was the manager to report strong commitment.

High commitment among these managers also depended on their ability to *realize their expectations*. Managers were asked to evaluate their organizations in terms of questions like "Has my organization fulfilled its promises to me and met my expectations in areas I care about?" Those that answered yes also reported greater commitment, in part because employees seem to bring to their positions hopes and expectations developed over years of preparation that they expect to see satisfied.

Organizations that obviously *valued high commitment* had managers who were more highly committed, too. In other words, managers who sense that their organizations expected them to be more committed were more committed.

Finally, managers who were given greater levels of *first-year job challenge* remained more committed to their organizations, even after that first challenging year.

Overall, the best route to employee commitment, says Buchanan, is "for the organization to take the time and the trouble to provide each manager with the experience he or she needs—even craves—at each stage of his or her career." The most important implication is that employee commitment and employee career development are intertwined. When recruiting employees companies should avoid career-related practices that can have an adverse effect on commitment, such as allowing candidates to develop unrealistic or inaccurate expectations regarding what working for the company will entail. In selection, prospective employees should be evaluated not just based on skills and competencies but on the basis of the person's destiny, values, and sense of him or herself. Individual jobs should be designed to be both valuable to the organization and relevant to the personal needs of the individual, and the employee's progress should be monitored to ensure that his or her career expectations are being met.

STEERS STUDY   In another study, Richard Steers surveyed almost 400 employees in several midwestern organizations. He found that factors like *organizational dependability* (how dependably the organization was seen to carry out its commitments to employees), the person's *perceived personal importance to the organization,* and the degree to which he or she was assigned to *challenging tasks* influenced the employee's commitment:

> Individuals come to organizations with certain needs, desires, skills, and so forth and expect to find a work environment where they can utilize their abilities and satisfy many of their basic needs. When the organization provides such a vehicle (for example, where it makes effective use of its employees, is dependable, and so forth), the likelihood of increasing commitment is apparently enhanced. When the organization is not dependable, however, or where it fails to provide employees with challenging and meaningful tasks, commitment levels tend to diminish.[14]

OTHER STUDIES Another representative study involved almost 500 employees of a manufacturing plant.[15] This study found a clear connection between the company's employment practices and the commitment of its employees. In this plant, internal mobility, company-sponsored training and development, and employment security all correlated with higher levels of employee commitment. For example, employees who had been promoted and who believed the company was pursuing a promotion from within policy were more committed to the company; so were those who received company-provided training and development and who believed the company was working hard to provide employment security for its employees. The researchers' conclusions underscore the importance of providing opportunities for career development and self-actualizing when it comes to boosting employee commitment:

> These results suggest that psychological commitment is higher among employees who believe they are being treated as resources to be developed rather than commodities to buy and sell. Even controlling for other known antecedents, employees are committed to the extent that they believe the company is providing a long-term, developmental employment opportunity.[16]

Another study focused on 264 bank tellers, a job notorious for high turnover and lack of commitment.[17] Many of the tellers that were studied were career tellers who viewed the job as a starting point on a career path and planned to eventually move into supervisory positions. For these people, commitment was enhanced by allowing them to participate more in decision making, by providing them with more challenging job assignments, by giving them promotion opportunities, and by offering a more people-oriented supervisory style.

Several studies have sought to determine if some people are more predisposed to high levels of commitment than are others as a result of certain personality or demographic traits. Employee commitment and employee age do tend to be directly related and, in at least one study, women were more highly committed, too. (The researchers' explanation was that women had to fight harder for jobs and promotions so that advancements meant more to them and they were more committed to their companies as a result. This would be similar to the implicit rationale behind the sort of hazing and initiation rights that certain private clubs put their members through as the price of admission.)[18] Similarly, people with strong work ethics and for whom work is more important—a *central life issue* to use the psychological term—do seem predisposed to being more highly committed.

Yet it would be a mistake to assume that a manager can elicit high commitment by simply screening out potential low-commitment employees. For example, in a study of 367 management employees, two researchers concluded that generally there is no "commitment-type" of individual. Instead, as they put it, employees come to the organization with certain needs, desires, skills, and so forth and expect to find a work environment where they can utilize their abilities and satisfy many of their basic needs.[19] The researchers found that this high-commitment environment was characterized by employee participation in decision making, clear communications about the organization's intentions, activities, and performance, autonomy (rather than close supervision), and a sense of cohesion among employees. In their study, for instance, it was "standard practice for the top management of the company to meet monthly with all lower level managerial employees in order to keep them informed about corporate performance and plans, and to gather their reactions to these plans."[20] As they concluded, "when the organization commits to the individual, the individual commits to it."

The *State Farm* vignette shows how one firm wins commitment by applying career-enhancing ideas like these.

STATE FARM

State Farm agents operate strictly as independent contractors. The company's compensation package isn't as attractive as the competition's. State Farm doesn't pick up any of its agents' expenses either. But if you think this leads to a revolving door, with agents moving in then quickly moving on, think again.

Despite the lower average commission rate, State Farm agents typically make more money than their counterparts at other companies. Most of them stick around longer, too. On average, 80 percent of State Farm agents are still on the job after 4 years; most agents have at least 13 years experience. The rest of the industry doesn't approach that level of tenure. How does State Farm do it? Through the use of a system designed to engender loyalty from employees and customers alike.

To begin with, State Farm agents set up offices—their own businesses—in the neighborhoods of the clients they serve. The system lets the agents do as well as they are capable of doing, since the sky, so to speak, is the limit. Through personal service to customers they construct lasting relationships, after expanding coverage from auto to home to life. The company encourages this long-term approach by offering the same commission rates for renewals as for new policies. As an added benefit, one agent servicing the entire range of products saves the company money, resulting in a 10 percent sales and distribution advantage over competitors.

It all pays off. More than 90 percent of State Farm clients renew, tops among national insurers that work through agents. The company has learned that fundamentally altering business practices and adopting a loyalty-based system is the best way to sustain profitability over the long haul.

SOURCE: "Loyalty-Based Management," *Harvard Business Review,* March–April 1993, 71–73.

COMMITMENT IN UTOPIA

One of the most comprehensive investigations of commitment focused not on businesses, but on utopian communities such as the Shakers and the Oneida. Most of those communities were formed in the United States in the 1800s, usually with the aim of having their people live together cooperatively, create their own government, and operate according to a "higher order" of natural and spiritual laws.

Communities like these, as Rosabeth Moss Kanter notes from her research, are held together not by coercion but by commitment: in utopia, what people *want* to do is the same as what they *have* to do. The interests of the individuals are congruent with those of the group, and personal growth and freedom also entail responsibility for others.[21] Group life in the successful communities was organized to support what Kanter calls "commitment building processes." These included sacrifice, investment, communion, and transcendence. All of these processes, as we will see, are used by modern-day high-commitment organizations.

SACRIFICE   Community members had to give up something as a price of membership. Once the new members made their sacrifices or paid their dues, "membership [became] more valuable and meaningful."[22] Sacrifice, says Kanter, operates on the basis of a simple psychological principle: the more it costs someone to do something, the more valuable he or she will consider it, in order to justify the psychic expense. Signing over one's worldly goods, taking a vow of poverty, and pledging abstinence in one form or another constituted sacrifice in these nineteenth-century communes. We will see later that extensive applicant testing and screening processes that border on initiation rites often constitute such sacrifice today.

INVESTMENT   All successful communes also demanded investment from their members, to ensure that they had a stake in the fate of the community. If one commits his or her profit to the group, then leaving the group becomes more costly. To that extent commitment tends to be a function of the irreversibility of the person's investment: if you cannot get it back, you are more committed to stay. Nineteenth-century communes thus demanded that members commit their profits to the group; modern-day high-commitment firms are more likely to create golden handcuffs with their pension plans.

COMMUNION   The dictionary defines communion as a sharing or possession in common; as Kanter says, "Connectedness, belonging, participation in a whole, mingling of the self and the group, equal opportunity to contribute and to benefit—all are part of communion."[23] Communion, in turn, helps to create commitment.

Kanter found that utopian communities used several practices to foster feelings of communion. For example, "a certain amount of homogeneity of background facilitated communion in successful 19th century communities, for members shared a fund of common experiences to ease mutual role taking and identification with one another and the collectivity." Members often had a common religious background, similar social or educational status, or a common national or ethnic origin. In addition, "members of every successful community had some prior acquaintance with one another before coming together to form the community."[24]

This sense of communion was further heightened by communal sharing: joint ownership of property helped to create a "we" feeling, for example.[25] Furthermore, there was communal work, "with all members, as far as possible, performing all tasks for equal rewards."[26] As Kanter found,

> [Job] rotation can be extremely effective as a commune mechanism, for it increases the area of the individual's responsibility to the group rather than limiting it to one task, and it emphasizes that the member is ready to perform any service the community may require of him, regardless of personal preference.[27]

TRANSCENDENCE   Commitment in utopian communes was also fostered by what Kanter calls transcendence, the feeling among members that they were part of something bigger than themselves, something all-embracing. These communities, after all, were more than merely social clubs whose members banned together to enjoy each other's company. All the successful communities had a mission—often a spiritual one—as well as shared values, beliefs, and a comprehensive ideology that all members could commit to. Orientation and socialization activities aided in the ideological conversion of new recruits; an elaborate system of legends and ceremonial meetings served to remind members of the community's ideological traditions. High commitment firms today similarly formulate visions, missions, ideologies, and hard work to win their employees' commitment to them.

THE CONSEQUENCES OF COMMITMENT

What are the consequences of high employee commitment? Several conclusions are warranted, based on the research evidence.

COMMITMENT AND ATTENDANCE

First, committed employees tend to have better attendance records, longer job tenure, and less early job withdrawal than do less committed employees.[28] In one representative study of 367 managers, employee commitment was found to be strongly associated with both the desire to leave and turnover; in another study of 315 clerical employees, uncommitted employees were much more likely to quit during the earliest stages of their employment.[29]

COMMITMENT AND PERFORMANCE

The results regarding the relationship between employee performance and commitment, though, are fairly mixed. In several studies, committed employees had higher job performance, while in others they did not; in still others, committed employees had higher performance as measured by objective indices like output, but not when measured by subjective supervisory ratings.[30]

Mixed performance results like these are not surprising, since employee commitment should not necessarily lead to high performance for every job. In many jobs, employees could not perform well even if they wanted to, due to lack of training or extraneous problems like a lack of tools. And many routinized jobs are so closely paced that employee commitment should have little or no effect.

COMMITMENT AND RESPONSIVENESS

However more and more jobs today do rely on employees' spontaneity and self-control, and so require initiative and "going that extra mile." It is here that employee commitment does have a positive effect.

For example, in one study the researchers found that "having a membership that shares the organization's goals and values can ensure that your individuals act instinctively to benefit the organization."[31] They found that in this study, "critical voluntary behaviors that are not specified by job descriptions are largely a function of identification and internalization [with the organization and its goals, rather than financial rewards]."[32] Similarly, in another study, organizational commitment was associated with organizational responsiveness, and specifically with the employees' and the organization's ability to respond to unforeseeable occurrences.[33]

The study by British researchers Tom Burns and G. M. Stalker illustrates this link between commitment and company responsiveness. Recall that their work focused on how management practices in companies were related to their external environments and in particular to the rates of change in the scientific techniques and markets of the selected industries. They drew the following conclusion:

> When novelty and unfamiliarity in both market situation and technical information become the accepted order of things, a fundamentally different kind of management system becomes appropriate from that which applies to a relatively stable commercial and technical environment.[34]

Some companies, recall, had become particularly adept at responding to rapid change exemplified by the appearance of novelties, new scientific discoveries, or technical innovations and "requirements for products of a kind not previously available or demanded." Burns and Stalker called these *organic* organizations. They were characterized by lateral rather than vertical communications, a strong sense of shared values, and, perhaps most importantly for us at this point, "the growth of commitment to the concern." As with more and more firms today, the distinctive feature of these organic systems was the

> pervasiveness of the working organization as an institution. In concrete terms this makes itself felt in preparedness to combine with others in serving the general aims of the concern. . . . The individual's job ceases to be self-contained; the only way in which "his" job can be done is by participating continually with others in the solution of problems which are real to the firm, and put in a language of requirements and activities meaningful to them all. Such methods of working put much heavier demands on the individual.[35]

In Burns and Stalker's responsive, organic organizations, jobs were continually being redefined. Responsibilities, therefore, could not be defined in terms of a limited obligation in which if conditions changed employees could just opt out by saying, "No, that's not my job." Under rapidly changing conditions like these, it was the employee's commitment to the firm that ensured that each employee would go the extra mile to carry out his or her changing job. Of course, it is precisely this type of organization and job that increasingly prevails today.

HOW COMPANIES BUILD COMMITMENT

MANAGEMENT PRACTICES

Several commitment-building practices surface repeatedly in studies like those summarized earlier; these include fostering a sense of community, building cohesive work teams, providing jobs that challenge employees' minds, maintaining open communications, hiring people with some similarity of values, and enabling employees to self-actualize and to be all they can be. Studies and conclusions like these help to explain how managers win employee commitment.

In this section, we will look more closely at some of the actual techniques companies use to build employee commitment, based on the results of one recent study. Two things will be apparent from this discussion. First, companies do not win employee commitment with any one technique such as quality circles or management by objectives. Instead, building commitment requires a comprehensive management program that consists of concrete management practices and personnel policies. Second, these practices are not exclusively behavioral; instead, we will see that building employee commitment draws on all the management functions and on many of the practices that we have already touched on in our discussions of managerial planning, organizing, staffing, leading, and controlling. In other words, building employee commitment requires a multifaceted, multifunctional set of management practices, all focused on boosting commitment. In this sense, building commitment thus bridges the management functions discussed in Chapters 5 through 11 and the behavioral topics—many of which aim to build commitment—that follow this chapter. Let's look at some of these specific commitment-building practices.

PEOPLE-FIRST VALUES

The practices that foster employee commitment are usually built on a strong foundation of what may be called people-first values. These firms literally put their people first: they trust them; they assume that their employees are their most important assets; they believe strongly in respecting their employees as individuals and treating them fairly; and they are relentlessly committed to each employee's welfare. Research indicates that firms do at least four things to institutionalize such values: firms should know what they want, put it in writing, hire and indoctrinate, and "walk the talk."

KNOW WHAT YOU WANT *Knowing what you want* (in terms of people-first values) is first. Here is how one UAW officer at Saturn Corporation's Spring Hill, Tennessee, plant put it:

> Our philosophy is, we care about people—and it shows. We involve people in decisions that affect them. I came from the Mesina, New York GM foundry and managers there, like a lot of the other managers you'll come across, take the position that "I'll tell you what to do, and that's what you'll do." In fact, some of those managers from the foundry are here now. But on the whole those who are here now are different, and the basic difference is wrapped up in the question, "Do you really believe in people?" Saturn's commitment really comes down to how you feel about people—your attitudes—more than anything, because all the other Saturn programs—the work teams, the extensive training, the way people are paid—all stem from these people attitudes.[36]

CODIFY Second, these firms *codify* their people-first values by frequently mentioning them in company brochures, handbooks, and handouts. For example, Saturn employees carry a card that lists the firm's values, one of which is expressed in these words:

> *Trust and respect for the individual:* We have nothing of greater value than our people. We believe that demonstrating respect for the uniqueness of every individual builds a team of confident, creative members possessing a high degree of initiative, self-respect, and self-discipline.[37]

HIRE AND INDOCTRINATE The UAW officer's comment that "commitment really comes down to what you feel about people" underscores a third way in which people-first values are institutionalized throughout many firms: they *hire managers* who have people-first values from the start. In fact, it is almost impossible for antisocial "Theory X" people to move into management—or to stay. For example, at Federal Express all supervisory candidates must enroll in the firm's multistage leadership selection program. This is where they prove they have the values and skills to be Federal Express managers. About 20 percent drop out after the first "Is Management for Me?" phase of the program. This one-day session familiarizes candidates with the manager's job. This session is followed by about three months of self-evaluations and supervisory assessments of the candidate's values and leadership skills. Next come peer assessments and panel interviews with senior managers; this phase takes several days. Management training sessions then reinforce and indoctrinate the new managers in the firm's principles and people-first values.

WALK THE TALK Finally, managers in these firms *walk the talk;* in other words, people-first values permeate everything these firms' managers say and do. The idea that the firm's people-first values should be applied to every one of its decisions was summed up by one officer at retailer J. C. Penney this way:

> Our people's high commitment stems from our commitment to them, and that commitment boils down to the fundamental "respect for the individual" that we all share. That respect goes back to the Penney idea—"To test every act in this wise: Does it square with what is right and just?" As a result, the value of respect for the individual is brought into our management process on a regular basis and is a standard against which we measure each and every decision that we make.[38]

EXTENSIVE TWO-WAY COMMUNICATIONS

Many managers also recognize that commitment is built on trust, and that trust requires a flood of two-way communication. Managers in firms like Saturn, Federal Express, and GE thus do more than express a willingness to hear and be heard. They also establish programs that guarantee two-way communications. We will discuss these much more fully in Chapter 16. However, at least four types of communications programs are typically employed here: *guaranteed fair treatment* programs for filing grievances and complaints, *speak up* programs for voicing concerns and making inquiries, *periodic survey* programs for expressing opinions, and various *top-down* programs for keeping employees informed.

Federal Express has the *guaranteed fair treatment* procedure (GFTP), which is a good example of an effective grievance process. Readily available forms make filing the grievance easy; employees are encouraged to use the system; and the highest levels of Federal Express's management are routinely involved in reviewing complaints.

In many firms *speak up* programs also encourage and facilitate upward communications and thus foster commitment. At IBM, for instance, speak up forms let employees air anonymous inquiries and complaints to special speak up administrators. They, in turn, get the answers while protecting the inquirer's anonymity. Similar programs—ranging from informal open-door programs at Delta Airlines and J. C. Penney to formal written programs at Federal Express and an anonymous phone hotline at Toyota Motor Manufacturing, USA—help ensure that employees always have a channel through which to air all their concerns, thereby fostering commitment.

Other firms today enhance upward communication through periodic *opinion surveys*. The Survey-Feedback-Action (SFA) program at Federal Express includes an anonymous survey. This lets employees express feelings about the company and their managers and to some extent about service, benefits, and pay. Each work group's manager then uses the SFA results to help design a plan for boosting work group commitment.

Many firms also give their employees *extensive top-down data* on the performance of, and prospects for, their operations. For example, Toyota offers twice-a-day five-minute team information meetings at job sites, where employees get the latest news on the plant. A television set in each work site break area runs continuously, presenting plantwide information from the in-house Toyota Broadcasting Center. The company also supports quarterly roundtable discussions between top management and selected nonsupervisory staff and an in-house newsletter. Such information helps to cultivate a feeling of partnership and thus commitment to the firm and its goals.

BUILDING A SENSE OF SHARED FATE AND COMMUNION

Many firms today also work hard to encourage a sense of communion and shared fate. As in the utopian communities in Kanter's study (summarized earlier), the firms do so by pursuing what Kanter called commonality, communal sharing, communal work, and regularized work contact and ritual. Together these factors create a sense of shared fate and communion and contribute to employee commitment.

COMMONALITY These firms pursue commonality in several ways. They do so not in the sense of discriminatory employment practices, of course, but by seeking employees whose values and interests are compatible with those of the firm. For example, Ben & Jerry's Homemade has a policy of paying executives no more than seven times the firm's lowest entry-level wage. This helps ensure that the firm attracts only those managers whose values and social philosophies fit the firm's. As one Ben & Jerry's man-

Creating a company which values employee feedback and acts on it is difficult, but can pay off in the long run, as at Bell Atlantic, where the pictured team cut customer service hookup lead time from 16 days to a matter of hours.

ager put it, "If you're motivated by money, this is not the place for you. You come here for the firm's social side, and because you believe in the values of the firm."[39] In many firms, *commonality* means, in part, trying hard to hire only team players (although firms must guard against inhibiting dissent and creativity by doing so). Here is one example that Tom Peters presents:

> When I taught in Stanford University's MBA Program, I observed students returning from a long day of interviewing at [Hewlett-Packard], baffled that the interviewer seemed to take little interest in their ability to manipulate a balance sheet or understand which direction electrons flow in. Instead, HP interviewers were determined to figure out whether or not they'd be good team players. A typical "question" might go like this: "Describe in detail an experience you had working in an intense, long-lasting small group." It makes sense, of course, given that so much of HP's work is carried out by small teams engaged in high pressure projects.[40]

SENSE OF SHARING Communion is also fostered by building a sense of sharing, a sense that "we're all in this together." Firms do this in several ways. One is to avoid the status differences that often set top management apart from employees. For example, the entire office staff of Toyota Motor Manufacturing in Tennessee works in one huge open room, without offices, walls, or partitions. President Fujio Cho is there, along with secretaries, public relations people, vice-presidents, and data entry clerks. Executives at Ben & Jerry's have private offices, but they are spartan compared with those that you will find in most firms; the company's founders worked in a trailer at the foot of a hill on which the plant is situated until a few years ago. Similarly, you may find that few firms that take commitment seriously have executive parking spots.

COMMUNAL WORK The sense of community nurtured by homogeneity and communal sharing is often further enhanced by encouraging joint effort and communal work. In early communes (and in some communities today), all the citizens would gather for a "house raising," in which everyone in the community worked together to build a new community member's house. In companies, this sense of joint effort and communal work can be accomplished in several ways. At Toyota, new employees are quickly steeped in the terminology and techniques of teamwork: there are no employees in the plant, only team members. Toyota has no employee handbook; instead it provides a team member handbook. Teamwork training begins during the employee's initial orientation as new members meet their teams and are trained in the interpersonal techniques that make for good teamwork. The closeness is enhanced by letting work teams recruit and select their own new members. Periodic job rotation then further fosters the sense that everyone is sharing all the work.

REGULAR CONTACT Kanter found that the feeling that "we're all in this together" is further enhanced by activities that bring individual employees into regular contact with the group as a whole.[41] Ben & Jerry's hosts monthly staff meetings in the receiving bay of its Waterbury, Vermont, plant. Similarly, Ben & Jerry's has a "joy gang." Its function is to organize regular "joy events," including Cajun parties, ping-pong contests, and "manufacturing appreciation day," all aimed at getting everyone together and fostering a sense of sharing and communion.

PROVIDING A VISION

Rosabeth Moss Kanter says that "leaders need new and more effective incentives to encourage high performance and build commitment" and that one of these incentives is giving employees a sense of mission.[42] She adds that "good leaders can inspire others with the power and excitement of their vision and give people a sense of purpose and pride in their work. Pride is often a better source of motivation than the traditional corporate career ladder and the promotion-based reward system."[43]

In fact, committed employees need missions and values to be committed to. With such missions, the workers at firms like Saturn and Ben & Jerry's become not just workers but almost soldiers in a crusade, one that allows them to redefine themselves in terms of an ideology and a mission. In that way, says Kanter, the employee can "find himself anew in something larger and greater."[44] The commitment in high-commitment firms thus derives in part from the power of the firm's mission and from the willingness of the employees not just to accept the company's aims as their own, but to acquiesce to the needs of the firm for the good of achieving its mission.

CREATING IDEOLOGY Companies take several steps to achieve the feeling among employees that they are part of something "larger and greater" than themselves. Some firms create an ideology that lays out a basic way of thinking and doing things, which all employees are expected to share. This idea is illustrated by the 14 business principles of Goldman Sachs, shown in Figure 12.1. A comprehensive set of principles like these help to make it clear to all employees what the firm is (in terms of its values) and what its basic mission is, too.

CHARISMA Second, firms create what we might call "institutional charisma" by linking their firm's missions and values to a higher calling or to ultimate moral values. Ben & Jerry's is a good example. The company's mission symbolizes the founders'

FIGURE 12.1

The 14 Business Principles
of Goldman Sachs

*Companies such as
Goldman Sachs put their
basic principles and values
—their ideologies—in
writing to help ensure
that their employees
understand and are
committed to them.*

SOURCE: Gary Dessler, *Winning Commitment* (New York: McGraw-Hill, 1993), 72–73.

1. Our clients' interests always come first. Our experience shows that if we serve our clients well, our own success will follow.

2. Our assets are people, capital and reputation. If any of these are ever lost, the last is the most difficult to regain.

3. We take great pride in the professional quality of our work. We have an uncompromising determination to achieve excellence in everything we undertake. Though we may be involved in a wide variety and heavy volume of activity, we would, if it came to a choice, rather be best than biggest.

4. We stress creativity and imagination in everything we do. While recognizing that the old way may still be the best way, we strive always to find a better solution to a client's problems and pride ourselves in having pioneered many of the practices and techniques which have become standard in the industry.

5. We make an unusual effort to identify and recruit the very best person for every job. Although our activities are measured in billions of dollars, we select our people one by one. In a service business, we know that without the best people, we cannot be the best firm.

6. We offer our people the opportunity to move ahead more rapidly than is possible at most other places. We have yet to find the limits of responsibility which our best people are able to assume. Advancement depends solely on ability, performance, and contribution to the firm's success, without regard to race, color, age, creed, sex, or national origin.

7. We stress teamwork in everything we do. While individual creativity is always encouraged, we have found that the results of a team effort are often better than the sum of the parts. We have no room for those who put their personal interests ahead of the interests of the firm and its clients.

8. Our profits are a key to our success. They replenish our capital and attract and keep our best people. It is our practice to share our profits generously with all who helped create them. Profitability is critical to our future.

9. The dedication of our people to the firm and the intensity of their effort to their jobs are greater than one finds in most other organizations. We think it is an important part of our success.

10. We consider our size an asset which we try hard to preserve. We want to be big enough to undertake the largest project that any of our clients could contemplate, yet small enough to maintain the loyalty, the intimacy, and the esprit de corps which we all treasure and which is an important part of our success.

11. We strive constantly to anticipate the rapidly changing needs of our clients and to develop new services to meet those needs. We know that the world of finance will not stand still and that complacency can lead to extinction.

12. We regularly receive confidential information as part of our normal client relationships. To breach a confidence or to use confidential information improperly or carelessly would be unthinkable.

13. Our business is highly competitive, and we aggressively seek to expand our client relationships. However, we are always fair competitors and must never denigrate other firms.

14. Integrity and honesty are at the heart of our business. We expect our people to maintain high ethical standards in everything they do, both in their work for the firm and in their personal lives.

unique idea of what a business should be. It also provides the firm and its employees with an ideology that represents a higher calling to which employees can commit. Ben & Jerry's mission (including its unique social mission to recognize "the central role that business plays in the structure of a society") is presented in Figure 12.2.

IDEOLOGICAL CONVERSION Finally, companies promote the ideological conversion of their employees to the missions and values of their firms. Social psychologists Daniel Katz and Robert Kahn refer to this as socialization and point out that "the

FIGURE 12.2

Ben & Jerry's Mission

Ben & Jerry's mission is "charismatic" in that it links employees' actions with the transcendent goal of helping humankind.

SOURCE: Ben & Jerry's Homemade, Inc.; *Employee Handbook*

Ben & Jerry's is dedicated to the creation and demonstration of a new corporate concept of linked prosperity. Our mission consists of three interrelated parts:

Product Mission: To make, distribute, and sell the finest quality all natural ice cream and related products in a wide variety of innovative flavors made from Vermont dairy products.

Social Mission: To operate the company in a way that actively recognizes the central role that business plays in the structure of a society by initiating innovative ways to improve the quality of life of a broad community—local, national, and international.

Economic Mission: To operate the company on a sound financial basis of profitable growth, increasing value for our shareholders and creating career opportunities and financial rewards for our employees.

Underlying the mission of Ben & Jerry's is the determination to seek new and creative ways of addressing all three parts, while holding a deep respect for individuals, inside and outside the company and for the communities of which they are part.

adult socialization process in the organization can build upon the personal values of its members. . . . People can thus identify with the organizational mission."[45]

In many companies today, this process begins by carefully hiring new employees whose values are consistent with the firm's and then carefully orienting and training them. This is one reason why Toyota Motor Manufacturing calls its orientation an *assimilation* program: Its aim is to steep new recruits in the ideology of the firm. While covering usual topics such as company benefits, the assimilation program is mostly intended to convert Toyota team members to the firm's ideology of quality, teamwork, personal development, open communication, and mutual respect and teamwork.

Consider the schedule for Toyota's four-day orientation program. Day 1 begins at 6:30 A.M. with an overview of the program and a welcome to the company. About an hour and a half is devoted to discussing Toyota's history and culture, and about two hours are spent discussing employee benefits. The rest of the day is then devoted to a discussion of Toyota Motor Manufacturing policies, including the emphasis on product quality and employee teamwork. Much of day 2 is devoted to communication training, which the firm refers to as "The TMM Way of Listening." In day 3, the first two and a half or three hours is devoted to communication training and then the discussion turns to the techniques of problem solving and quality assurance. Day 4 is then devoted mostly to teamwork-related topics such as teamwork training. The main point is this: just having an ideology and set of values will not do. Many firms also work hard to socialize their employees into their firms' values by using hiring practices, orientation, and training programs that help to merge the employees' values with the company's own. The small business box shows how one small organization fosters commitment.

VALUE-BASED HIRING

In *Thriving on Chaos,* Tom Peters makes this observation:

The task of transforming raw recruits into committed stars, able to cope with the pace of change that is becoming normal, begins with the recruiting process per se. The best three tenets, unfortunately ignored by most: (1) spend time, and lots of it; (2) insist that line people dominate the process; and (3) don't waffle about the qualities you are looking for in candidates.[46]

CHILDREN'S MEDICAL CENTER OF DALLAS

Joan McGuigan's job usually isn't pleasant. As a registered nurse at the Small Children's Medical Center of Dallas, she spends her days caring for children in some of the worst conditions imaginable. Sometimes their parents are in even worse shape. It's a high-stress, often sad job, yet she says she loves it.

McGuigan could easily work someplace else. But she's been at Children's Medical Center for more than eight years, working 24-hour shifts, because she likes being on the cutting edge of children's health care. She might be an anachronism, but McGuigan says she's committed to her employer because the hospital enables her to be the best at what she does.

An employee like McGuigan sounds like a dream come true, but unfortunately, they don't come around that often. In a business environment where most companies are reducing human resources budgets, prospective employees are increasingly looking out for themselves. Factors contributing to this attitude include company downsizings, low compensation, even policies relating to child care and family leave issues.

"It's earned loyalty—in both directions," says Suzanne Kenney, manager of Employee Listening Practice for the Hewitt Associates consulting firm. "Employees are now asking, Is my company loyal to me?"

Children's Medical Center seems to have overcome the sorts of loyalty-based problems that plague most hospitals. For example, the rate of turnover for registered nurses is notoriously high. The reasons range from stress and burnout to the need to be

FOCUS ON SMALL BUSINESS

home with a family. But the Dallas hospital took steps to encourage nurses to stay on board. They were given the opportunity to participate and grow—in a sense, to become partners—in the hospital's achievements.

The hospital established a "clinical ladder," which offers the potential for career enhancement for nurses. Research, in-service work or other projects all can result in increased salary levels. If a nurse spots a case where a

new diagnosis was possible, he or she can put together the data and present it.

Offering employees greater involvement in decision making also helps engender loyalty to the institution. Teams formed by the nursing department coordinate care methods at the patient level. Under a program called "independent practice," standout nurses are urged to exercise their own judgment regarding the most appropriate types of treatment. The result is better care, better nurses, and a feeling on the part of the staff that their abilities are being utilized for maximum benefit. They also have an enhanced sense of recognition and purpose.

The medical center, in conjunction with a consulting firm, also spelled out the organization's mission and communicated it to the nurses. Letting employees know where the hospital was headed and what their individual roles were in that mission provided an inspirational bond for employees. Shirley Lopez, a vice-president of human resources summed it up: "If I work for a company that knows where it's going and can share that with me, then I'm going to be more committed to that as a direction."

SOURCE: "The Loyalty Factor," *Personnel Journal*, September 1992, 52.

Indeed, as we saw in Chapter 10 (Staffing), an increasing number of firms today use value-based hiring practices. Instead of just looking at an applicant's job-related skills, they try to get a sense of the person and his or her personal qualities and values; they identify common experiences and values that may flag the applicant's fit with the firm; they give their applicants realistic previews of what to expect; and they usually end up rejecting large numbers of applicants. In short, they put enormous effort into interviewing and screening to find the best people. As one Toyota, USA vice-president put it:

> You might be surprised, but our selection or hiring process is an exhaustive, painstaking system designed not to fill positions quickly, but to find the right people for these positions. What are we looking for? First, these people must be able to think for themselves . . . be problem solvers . . . and, second, work in a team atmosphere. Simply put, we need strong minds, not strong backs. . . . We consider the selection of a team member as a long-term investment decision. Why go to the trouble of hiring a questionable employee only to have to fire him later?[47]

Toyota's hiring process involves about 20 hours and six phases, spread over five or six days. The Kentucky Department of Employment Services conducts phase 1. Here applicants fill out application blanks summarizing their work experience and skills and view a one-hour video describing Toyota's work environment and selection system. Phase 2 is aimed at assessing the applicant's technical knowledge and potential and is also conducted by the Kentucky Department of Employment Services. In phase 3, Toyota itself takes over the screening to assess the applicant's interpersonal and decision-making skills, and all applicants participate in four hours of group and individual problem-solving and discussion activities in the firm's assessment center. (This is a separate location where applicants engage in exercises under the observation of Toyota screening experts.) Also in phase 3 is a production line assembly simulation. Candidates play the roles of the management and work force of a firm that makes electrical circuits. The team decides which circuits to manufacture and how to effectively assign people, materials, and money to produce them.

In phase 4 groups of candidates discuss their accomplishments with Toyota interviewers. This phase helps give Toyota a more complete picture of each candidate, in terms of what each is proudest of and most interested in. Phase 4 also gives Toyota another chance to watch their candidates interact with each other. Those who successfully complete phase 4 then undergo two and a half hours of physical and drug-alcohol tests at area hospitals (phase 5). Finally, phase 6 involves closely monitoring, observing, and coaching the new employees on the job to assess their performance and to develop their skills during their first six months at work.

Value-based hiring like this does much more than ensure that only those with the best skills are brought on-line. Value-based hiring is also a prerequisite for building employee commitment. Fostering a sense of communion and shared values is facilitated by the sacrifice of the extensive screening process. Commonality is then fostered by a process that filters out applicants who do not have the organizationally desired values—such as a belief in putting people first and a love of teamwork and quality.

THE ROLE OF JOB SECURITY

JOB SECURITY
The firm is committed to not dismissing employees for nondisciplinary reasons, except in event of the most serious economic problems.

Job security and employee commitment go hand in hand. For one thing, the costs involved in value-based hiring and in extensively training, empowering, and building employee capabilities presumes the firm is committed to keeping them around. That is why Toyota's president has been quoted as saying, "At Toyota we hire people who will stick around for 30 or 40 years or the remainder of their working years. So we always try to remember that hiring a 30-year employee who will earn $30,000 or $40,000 a year is really a million dollar plus decision for us."[48] Commitment is also a two-way street: Employees become committed to companies that are committed to them, and few things express an employer's commitment like job security. That's why both Kanter and Peters recommend that firms build in all the job security that they can.

A high-commitment firm like Federal Express is thus dedicated to "providing the maximum job security for all of our employees."[49] However, at Federal Express (as at other firms that try to do this), *job security is usually a commitment, not an ironclad policy.* Although it offers no guarantees, the firm is on record as having a strong commitment to make every effort not to lay off personnel except in the most extreme economic circumstances as determined by the chief executive officer.[50] In fact, Federal Express has avoided layoffs since its incorporation on June 24, 1971. The most notable example occurred when the firm discontinued its facsimile products (Zap mail) in the early 1980s. More than 1,000 employees assigned to that area were retained and reassigned without a loss in pay. The *job security* vignette presents some insight into job security in Japan.

JOB SECURITY IN JAPAN

Even though Japan is famous for offering job security, only about 25 percent of workers in Japan are protected with a guarantee of lifetime employment. Despite its seeming attractiveness, lifetime job security is not without risk or cost for both the employer and the employee.

Japanese firms that hire workers for life usually make a hefty investment in the individual. Education and training are costly, and shaping an employee's thinking to coincide with the company's way of doing things takes time. From that perspective, it's understandable that companies would loath to see that kind of investment walking out the door.

The Japanese system does have its advantages. Turnover is almost zero. The expertise of individual employees is enhanced. Commitment to the company is bolstered. And upper-managers, technical personnel, and supervisors, unburdened by the fear of termination, feel much freer to impart knowledge to subordinates.

But the security of lifetime employment is not for everyone. The long hours, reduction of leisure time, and particularly the separation from family members is too much for some. "Life involves almost all working," Sam Okamaoto said of his time in Japan. "I couldn't accept that kind of environment." He now works in Southern California.

SOURCE: "The Loyalty Factor," *Personnel Journal,* September 1992, 52.

It remains to be seen what the long-term effects of risutora, re-structuring, will be on Japan's industry. An oversupply of both manufacturing capacity and employees has led companies to cut costs where they can. Companies are still trying to avoid lay-offs, but these have become more common in the land of lifetime employment.

FINANCIAL REWARDS AND PROFIT SHARING

In Chapter 15 we will see that in his classic explanation of why money cannot buy commitment, Frederick Herzberg says that "hygiene" factors like pay only result in short-term motivation. With pay, he says, the motivation disappears as soon as the incentive is removed. Furthermore, firms that rely on pay become caught in a vicious cycle. They must continually ratchet up pay rates as employees become accustomed to their current salaries. Yet pay rates rarely fall when times get bad. Pay should be satisfactory to get and keep good people, Herzberg contends. However, to win employee commitment you must appeal to other employee needs, such as the needs to achieve, to affiliate, and to become all that we can be.[51]

But, while firms may not be able to buy commitment, most firms don't try to get commitment without healthy financial rewards. Intrinsic motivations like work involvement, a sense of achievement, and the feelings of oneness that communion bring are not enough. To paraphrase psychologist Abraham Maslow, you can't appeal to someone's need to achieve until you've filled his or her belly and made the person secure. That is why Rosabeth Moss Kanter says that "entrepreneurial incentives that give teams a piece of the action are highly appropriate in collaborative companies."[52]

When it comes to pay, for instance, the J. C. Penney Company may be one of the best kept secrets in retailing, a situation that goes back to 1902. On April 14 of that year, James Cash Penney, age 26, opened The Golden Rule, a dry goods and clothing store in Kemmerer, Wyoming, in partnership with his former employers, merchants Thomas Callahan and William Johnson. In 1903, Penney's partners offered him a one-third partnership in their new Rock Springs, Wyoming, Golden Rule store and asked him to supervise it. At the same time, Penney recommended a new Golden Rule store in nearby Cumberland, Wyoming, and also became its one-third partner. By 1907 Johnson and Callahan had sold Penney their interests in the Kemmerer, Cumberland, and Rock Springs stores and Penney and his new partners (all former sales clerks) began building their own chain of Golden Rule stores. As the chain spread across the country, Penney followed the same practice of giving hard-working clerks the opportunity to manage the stores, also with a one-third partnership—the same opportunity Johnson and Callahan had given him back in 1902. When the J. C. Penney Company was incorporated in 1913, the partnership incentive was retained by offering one-third stock interests in new stores to managers. If the purpose of commitment is to synchronize the employees' goals with those of the firm, the Penney's partnership concept helped fill that bill.

While the structure of the plan has changed, the heavy incentive value of the partnership concept remains intact today at J. C. Penney. Entry-level merchandise manager trainees straight out of college start off at perhaps $20,000 to $25,000 per year. But after three years or so they usually find themselves making more than other middle managers in the industry and the gap continues to widen as they move up the chain of command.[53]

The portion of salary that is based on bonus depends on the person's job and the size of the store. For store managers in the smallest J. C. Penney's stores, for instance, 90 percent of their annual pay would typically come from salary and only 10 percent from bonus, with a total annual pay of perhaps $110,000 per year. For some of the biggest stores, however, only about $80,000 per year of the manager's pay would come from an annual salary. About $110,000 would come from an at-risk incentive bonus, one tied to the store's sales and gross profits.

At Federal Express, quarterly pay reviews and periodic national and local salary surveys are used to maintain salary ranges and pay schedules that are very competitive. For virtually all Federal Express positions, base salary alone would probably make pay competitive with market rates. However, Federal Express also places a big emphasis on pay-for-performance. As we explained in more detail in Chapter 10, some of the company's pay-for-performance or variable pay programs include the following:

- *Merit programs.* All salaried employees (and many hourly employees) receive merit increases based on their individual performance.
- *Pro pay.* Many hourly Federal Express employees can receive pro pay, which are lump-sum merit bonuses offered to employees who have reached the top of their pay range.
- *Star/superstar program.* Salaried employees with a specified performance rating may be nominated for a bonus through the star/superstar program.

SELF-ACTUALIZATION

As a manager, you will come to a point when you'll ask if you've achieved all you could have achieved, given your skills, gifts, and dreams, and woe to the firm that prevented you from doing so. Few needs are as strong as the need to fulfill our dreams, to become all we are capable of being. In Chapter 15 we will see that psychologist Abraham Maslow said the ultimate need is "the desire to become more and more what one is, to become everything that one is capable of becoming." Self-actualization, to Maslow, meant that "what man *can* be, he *must* be . . . it refers to the desire for self-fulfillment, namely, to this tendency for him to become actualized in what he is potentially."[54] Building on the motivation theories of psychologists such as Maslow and Herzberg, many firms today implement practices to help their employees to actualize, in other words to become all that they can be. This in turn helps build employee commitment, as the studies presented earlier in this chapter showed.

Firms use at least three sets of practices to actualize employees: *committing to the goal of actualizing* all employees, aggressively *promoting employees from within,* and *empowering employees* at work. Note that actualizing does not have to be reflected in just promotions. Certainly, these are important. But the real question is whether employees get the opportunity to develop and use all their skills and become, as Maslow would say, all they can be. Training employees to expand their skills and to solve problems at work, enriching their jobs and empowering them to plan and inspect their own work, and helping them to continue their education and grow are some other ways to accomplish employee self-actualization.

COMMITTING TO SELF-ACTUALIZATION   The process often begins by having the firm explicitly commit to the idea of helping its workers to self-actualize. Here's how one Saturn assembler put it as he walked on the plant floor:

I'm committed to Saturn in part for what they did for me: for the 300 hours of training in problem solving and leadership that help me expand my personal horizons; for the firm's Excel program that helps me push myself to the limit; and because I know that at Saturn I can go as far as I can go—this company wants its people to be all that they can be. But I'm also committed to Saturn for what I saw where I came from: the burned out workers, the people who were so pressed down by the system that even if they saw their machines were about to break from poor maintenance, they'd say, "Leave it alone. Let management handle it." This is like a different world.[55]

Similarly, one Federal Express manager described his firm's commitment to actualizing employees as follows:

At Federal Express, the best I can be is what I can be here. I have been allowed to grow with Federal Express. For the people at Federal Express, it's not the money that draws us to the firm. The biggest benefit is that Federal Express made me a man. It gave me the confidence and self-esteem to become the person I had the potential to become.[56]

PROMOTING FROM WITHIN   For many employees becoming all you can be does boil down to career progress. Many firms recognize this and so institute comprehensive promotion-from-within programs.

The distinction between promotion-from-within *programs* and *policies* is important. Many firms have promotion-from-within policies. At J. C. Penney, "We believe in promotion-from-within whenever a unit's requirements and an associate's qualifications provide a suitable match. Promotions are based primarily on such factors as performance (including productivity), dependability, initiative, and availability."[57] At Federal Express, "Open positions are filled, whenever possible, by qualified candidates from within the existing work force."[58] At Delta Airlines, "Delta hires at entry-level, then trains and develops personnel to promote them to higher levels of responsibility."[59]

But there is more to a successful promotion-from-within program than just a policy statement. Promotion from within at high-commitment firms generally means a five-part program, of which a promotion-from-within policy is only part 1.

Next, promotion-from-within also involves *value-based hiring.* Firms like Delta and Federal Express hire applicants who have the potential for promotion. The reason for this is that it is unwise to commit to promotion from within when a firm hires people who do not have the potential to be promoted eventually. Hiring people with promotion potential and values that are in synch with the firm's is thus a requisite step in promotion-from-within programs.

Many firms also provide the *career assessment and development* assistance needed to help employees identify and develop their promotion potential. At Ben & Jerry's, career development is encouraged through programs of career planning, company internships, and tuition assistance. Employees are encouraged to attend a sequence of eight four-hour career planning seminars, the aim of which is to help employees think about and plan their careers. Employees who have completed the seminars and want to learn about other jobs within the firm can then spend two or three days interning at another company job, on paid time. At Saturn Corporation, a career-growth workshop uses vocational guidance tools (including a skills-assessment disk) to help employees identify the career-related skills they need to develop.

Next, promotion from within is facilitated by *career-oriented performance appraisals.* These firms do not just assess past performance. Instead, the supervisor and the appraisee are charged with linking the latter's performance, career preferences, and developmental needs in a formal career plan.

J. C. Penney provides an example. As Figure 12.3 illustrates, its management appraisal form requires both a promotability recommendation and projections for associate development. Every year the employee and supervisor meet and review all the jobs at Penney's that the employee might aspire to. They then have a frank discussion regarding the employee's potential fit for those jobs and the developmental effort that will be needed to attain them.

A *career records and job posting system* is often the final element in the promotion-from-within program. Its purpose is to ensure that an inside candidate's career goals and skills are matched openly and fairly with promotional opportunities. For example, the Internal Placement Center (IPC) at Goldman, Sachs and Company, aims to give employees interested in pursuing jobs in different areas of the firm the information to locate and apply for job openings. Employees interested in applying for an open position with the firm submit an IPC application and current resume. The IPC then investigates the possibility of a match.

Date & Initials Midyear Follow Up
9/10/90 GPT/LS

Management Characteristics and Strategic Directions: Fill in letter for each using ratings below. See reverse for definitions.
Ratings: **O** = Outstanding **G** = Good **S** = Satisfactory **ND** = Needs Development **TN** = Too New to Rate or Not Applicable

I. **Leadership** G II. **Awareness** ND III. **Sense of Urgency** ND IV. **Judgement** G V. **Planning & Organizing** G VI. Team **Process Participation** G VII. **Fashion Credibility** G VIII. **EEO Management** G

Additioanl Comments, Strengths and Opportunities Lee achieved very solid results in Men's -- nice sales, good team development and depth of lines. Shoes is a real opportunity for Lee. Many decisions must be made more quickly by Lee, using merchandise systems better.

OVERALL PERFORMANCE RATING 3
(See reverse for instructions)

Manager Signature	Date of Appaisal	Reviewer Signature	Date of Review	Associate Signature	Date of Appaisal	Is this associate willing to move residence? (Check One)
Gary P. Turner	4-15-91	Phil Adams	4-1-91	Lee Smith	4/15/91	[X] Yes [ ] Not Now

See Associate Career Grid for Instructions

Promotability Recommendation: Enter letter here → B

A This Year **B** Second or third year **C** Fourth or fifth year
D Can grow with job **E** Recommend lateral transfer **F** Is at responsibility level
G Recommend less responsibility **H** Promotable this store **I** Too New To Rate

High Potential: Check if this associate has exceptional growth potential, top 5% in drive and ability [ ]

Projections for Associate Development	Year 19 92		Year 19___	
	Position Title	Position Code/Volume	Position Title	Position Code/Volume
First Choice Projection	Sr. Merch. Mgr.	4300		
Alternate Projecton				

DP. 2036 (Rev. 2/90) T.O.C. # 008-7427-1000

FIGURE 12.3

Portion of J. C. Penney's Management Appraisal Form

When the performance appraisal is career-oriented the information can be used to further the employee's self-development by identifying realistic career paths and development needs.

SOURCE: Gary Dessler, *Winning Commitment* (New York: McGraw-Hill, 1993), 139. Reprinted with permission from J. C. Penney.

Federal Express has its own career records/job posting system called JCATS (Jobs Change Applicant Tracking System). Announcements of new job openings via this electronic system usually take place every Friday. All employees posting for the position receive numerical scores based on job performance and length of service and are told whether they have been chosen as candidates.

Empowering employees—discussed next—is another method that helps employees self-actualize, and which thus helps build commitment.

EMPOWERING EMPLOYEES
Authorizing and enabling employees to do their jobs with greater autonomy.

EMPOWERING EMPLOYEES

EMPOWERING DEFINED

Empowering employees is an increasingly popular phrase today and means authorizing (giving power to) and enabling employees to do their jobs with greater autonomy. As such, empowerment is inherently a motivational concept since boosting employees' feelings of **self-efficacy**—of being able to influence important aspects of their world—is fundamentally a motivating experience.[60]

SELF-EFFICACY
Being able to influence important aspects of your world.

Empowering employees is also motivational because it appeals to an employee's need to self-actualize. As we will explain in more detail in Chapter 15 (Motivation) and as we touched on earlier, most people are strongly motivated by this need to self-actualize. To the extent that empowering workers broadens their influence and thus helps satisfy this need, empowerment can and will motivate employees and boost their commitment to the firm.

ENRICHMENT
Building challenge and achievement into a worker's job by changing the job's content.

Firms like Delta, Saturn, and Federal Express therefore help their people to self-actualize by enriching their jobs and empowering their activities. **Enrichment** means building challenge and achievement into a worker's job by changing the job's content—letting workers order and inspect their own goods, schedule their own day, and so forth. Empowerment, again, means authorizing *and enabling* workers to do their jobs with greater autonomy. To enrich and empower their employees, firms do three things: (1) expand the employees' job descriptions to allow them to plan their own work, control their own scrap, and obtain their own supplies, for instance; (2) provide the training, tools, and support employees need to enable them to do their new jobs; and (3) insist all managers follow through by actually letting the workers use their new, broader authority.

EMPOWERING IN PRACTICE

Saturn Corporation provides a good example of worker empowerment in action. At Saturn, self-managing work teams accomplish all the work, and all work team assignments are highly enriched. As you can see in Figure 12.4, each team is responsible for a broad range of duties. These include resolving its own conflicts, planning its own work schedule, determining its own job assignments, making selection decisions of new members, performing within its own budget, and obtaining its own supplies.

But assigning broad responsibilities is not enough. The teams also get the training, skills, and tools to empower them to do their jobs. For example, they receive training and decision-making tools needed to improve consensus decision making. Firms like Saturn also make sure their managers actually let their people do their jobs as assigned. Here's a sampling of how Saturn team members describe this sort of empowerment:

> If an issue comes up the work team handles it—all on our team must be agreeable or we don't leave the room until we're 100 percent committed, 70 percent comfortable.

> Here you know there's no one else to do it. If something is wrong you must fix it yourself. We bring in suppliers if there is a problem and work with them to rectify it.

> The old world treats you like a kid. Here, for example, we're trusted with a lot of confidential information like the financials of the company.[61]

Not all examples of empowerment involve such comprehensive programs. At Scandinavian Air Systems (SAS), for instance, empowering the work force meant letting employees make more decisions themselves; thus the ticket agents now have the authority to reticket passengers or even move the passenger up a class, if the agent feels the situation warrants it. At one Marriott chain subsidiary each and every hotel employee from management to maintenance is empowered to offer guests a free night's stay if the hotel has, in the employee's opinion, been lax in serving the guest. And at engine maker Pratt & Whitney, salespeople can now authorize multimillion dollar repairs on the spot, instead of having to wait for approvals from up the line. In virtually all such cases, employees find empowerment to be exciting, while employers find it helps workers to self-actualize and to that extent boosts motivation and employee commitment.

FIGURE 12.4

Sampling of Saturn Work
Team Functions

*As you can see from this
sampling of the duties,
Saturn work teams are em-
powered. Each unit is
responsible for and trained
to make many of the deci-
sions formerly made by
managers.*

SOURCE: Gary Dessler, *Winning Commitment* (New York:
McGraw-Hill, 1993), 139.
Reprinted with permission
from *Saturn Work-Team
Functions*, a company training document.

Each Saturn team will:

1. Use consensus decision-making: No formal leader [will be] apparent in the process. . . . All members of the work unit who reach consensus must be at least 70% comfortable with the decision, and 100% committed to its implementation.

3. Make their own job assignments: A work unit . . . ensures safe, effective, efficient, and equal distribution of the work unit tasks to all its members.

5. Plan their own work: The work unit assigns timely resources for the accomplishment of its purpose to its customers while meeting the needs of the people within the work unit.

6. Design their own jobs: This should provide the optimum balance between people and technology and include the effective use of manpower, ergonomics, machine utilization, quality, cost, job task analysis, and continuous improvement.

8. Control their own material and inventory: Work directly in a coordinated manner with suppliers, partners, customers, and indirect/product material resource team members to develop and maintain necessary work unit inventory.

9. Perform their own equipment maintenance: Perform those tasks that can be defined as safe, and those they have the expertise, ability, and knowledge to perform effectively.

13. Make selection decisions of new members into the work unit: A work unit operating in a steady state has responsibility for determining total manpower requirements, and selection and movement of qualified new members from a candidate pool will be in accordance with the established Saturn selection process.

14. Constantly seek improvement in quality, cost, and the work environment: The work unit is responsible for involving all work unit members in improving quality, cost, and the work environment in concert with Saturn's quality system.

18. Determine their own methods: The work unit is responsible for designing the jobs of its team members consistent with the requirements of the Saturn production system and comprehending the necessary resources and work breakdown required.

21. Provide their own absentee replacements: The work unit is responsible for the attendance of its members. . . . The work unit will be required to plan for and provide its own absentee coverage.

22. Perform their own repairs: The work unit will have the ultimate responsibility for producing a world-class product that meets the needs and requirements of the customer. In the event a job leaves the work unit with a known or unknown non-conformance to specification, the originating work unit will be accountable for corrective action and repair.

SUMMARY

Perhaps the most powerful method of ensuring that the work of a firm is done right is to synchronize company goals with those of its employees.

Commitment exists when employees come to think of the aims of the organization in personal terms and to incorporate them into their own goal system. It is characterized by factors such as a strong belief in and acceptance of the organization's goals and values, a willingness to exert considerable effort on behalf of the organization, and a strong desire to maintain membership in the organization.

A study of utopian communities formed in the 1800s found that commitment building processes include sacrifice, investment, communion, and transcendence. All of these processes continue to be used today by high-commitment organizations.

Studies indicate that organizational experiences that play a role in creating employee commitment include personal importance, work-group experiences, open communications, realization of expectations, and first-year job challenges.

Many companies have found that the best way to foster employee commitment is through comprehensive management programs, packages that combine management practices and personnel policies, all focused on the aim of boosting commitment.

Some of the management practices that build employee commitment include people-first values, trust and respect for individuals, extensive two-way communications, building a sense of shared fate and communion, and outlining a clear company mission.

Companies can help ensure that employees share a common vision by implementing hiring and training practices that help merge workers' values with those of the firm. For example, in value-based hiring, an applicant's personal qualities and values are considered in addition to the applicant's job-related skills.

Employee commitment and job security also go hand in hand; employees become committed to companies that are committed to them.

Firms cannot rely solely on financial rewards and profit sharing as a means of building commitment, but most managers also know that employee commitment is difficult to achieve without financial rewards.

Few needs are as strong as the need to fulfill life aspirations, so many firms commit to the goals of actualizing all employees, enriching and empowering employees at work, and aggressively promoting employees from within. In essence, the firms must provide employees the wherewithal to achieve maximum potential.

QUESTIONS

■ FOR REVIEW

1. List the factors in the commitment building process that are found in both utopian communities and modern-day high-commitment organizations.

2. Describe some of the management practices that can lead to a higher level of employee commitment.

3. What are the basic tenets of value-based hiring?

4. How can companies help employees self-actualize or become all that they can be?

■ FOR DISCUSSION

5. Discuss the validity of the following statement: "Companies can increase the level of commitment among the work force by changing managers' behavior."

6. Are the management methods that foster employee commitment any different from practices that foster commitment in relationships outside of the workplace? Why or why not?

7. Describe some of the ways a manager can spot a potentially committed employee during the hiring process.

8. Why are generous financial rewards and profit sharing not enough to keep employees committed to their jobs? Discuss.

▉ FOR ACTION

9. Formulate a list of actions that a company could take to keep employees committed during a major downsizing.

10. Go to the university library and look through some recent business periodicals. Find an example of a company that has been able to foster employee commitment. Describe the methods it has used.

11. Interview your parents or any happily married couple that you know and ask them to describe some of the methods they use to keep the commitment alive in their relationship. Could any of the same practices be applied in the workplace?

▉ FOR FOCUS ON SMALL BUSINESS

12. Which of the commitment-building methods discussed in the chapter helped foster commitment among the nurses at Children's Medical Center?

13. How can a mission statement, such as the one drafted by the hospital, help encourage employee commitment?

14. Do you think it's really feasible for a small business to foster commitment—for instance, there are few jobs to be promoted to? Explain a commitment-building program you would install in a small business.

CLOSING SOLUTION

APPLE COMPUTER

Sculley decided that the way to move the company forward and reinspire employee commitment was by utilizing the talents of individuals in a concentrated, coordinated manner, instead of allowing people to pursue their own agendas. "Large organizations cannot run without a very high degree of process and teamwork," he said.

Aware of the symbolic impact of examples, Sculley took a 15 percent pay cut, and rolled back salaries at the director level and above between 5 and 15 percent. Equally important, Sculley ensured that a dialogue between upper-management and the work force was maintained through companywide meetings. Often these group sessions were broadcast. Additionally, he established an employee executive group in which 12 employees, randomly chosen, traveled to the corporate headquarters for a give-and-take session with upper managers. Videotapes of these dialogues were distributed throughout the company to demonstrate that candid exchanges with the top brass were not only possible, but useful as well.

To a large degree, Sculley did feel it was useful for employees to remember certain things that had, in a sense, become mythological under Apple-founder Steve Jobs such as the company's loose, informal working environment and the idea that individual employees can make a difference. But he was also adamant in his thinking that changes in the external environment could only be coped with by internal organizational changes. Given the company's past, it seemed the only alternative for long-term survival. With that vision in mind, Sculley resigned in 1993, leaving the company in the hands of his right-hand man and now chief executive officer Michael Spindler. It would be up to Sculley's successor to guide Apple and its employees into the future, in part by recultivating the commitment they were once known for.[62]

■ QUESTIONS FOR CLOSING SOLUTION

1. Is it possible that Apple ended up with workers who pursued their own agendas because the company put too much emphasis on employee self-actualization? Discuss your answer.

2. Do you think Sculley did enough to regain the commitment of disgruntled employees? Why or why not?

3. Based on the concepts described in this chapter, what other steps could Apple executives have taken to ensure the commitment of the workforce?

KEY TERMS

Imposed Control	Employee Commitment
Financial Incentives	Job Security
Job Identification	Empowering Employees
Internalization	Self Efficacy
Compliance	Enrichment

CASE FOR ANALYSIS

CATERPILLAR, INC.

"We never thought he'd actually go that far," United Auto Workers Local 145 President John Paul Yarbrough said. He was talking about Caterpillar chairman Donald V. Fites's threat to replace 12,600 striking workers during the 1992 strike. Fites had moved into the top spot at Cat two years earlier, intent on completing the remake of the $10 billion company. He shook up marketing and broke Cat into pieces. Former chairman Lee L. Morgan called him one of the most determined men he'd ever met. But change at Caterpillar, Fites was to find, wouldn't come without cost.

The showdown, according to Fites, concerned the production efficiency required to compete on a global scale. The UAW's Detroit leaders saw it another way. Its members stubbornly clung to the notion that industry contracts should apply across the board, regardless of individual company situations. Fites was adamant that these so-called pattern contracts denied him the right to manage the company.

How Fites wanted to manage Caterpillar was based on practical experience acquired in his years overseas with the company. In Japan, he saw unions committed to the success of their employer. Workers first worried about the welfare of the company, then their own. He also admired the way the Japanese groomed managers by exposing them to engineering, production, and sales. In South Africa, Fites had to contend with pricing structures handed down from on high that ignored realities of the market. The experiences instilled in him a desire to make Caterpillar a more responsive organization.

Fites got his chance in 1985. Using then unheard of cross-functional teams, he integrated marketing, design, and manufacturing personnel and cut new product development time in half. People in the far reaches of the globe received the authority to make decisions. Salaried personnel were eventually reduced by 2,000; 5,500 hourly workers also received pink slips. Caterpillar was sectioned into 14 profit centers expected to produce a robust return of 15 percent on assets. Some that didn't were summarily sold. But through it all, Fites nurtured a company value system of empowered employees, work teams, and cooperation. Since 1986, Cat's productivity increased 30 percent. "He has completely changed the culture," says industry consultant Frank Manfredi.

But on the issue of wages the company and the union ran into irreconcilable differences. Fites estimated the wage-scale disadvantage against Komatsu of Japan at 25 percent. The union said it was nearer to 6 percent and said that didn't even take into account the higher productivity of Caterpillar's workforce. Fites countered with the reminder that the company had laid out $1.9 billion in capital expenditures over the past ten years. He further contended that average pay of $44,000 annually, 3 to 4 percent yearly pay increases, job guarantees for six years, and free health care was a fat enough compensation package. Neither side would budge.

In April 1992, Fites's threat to replace workers effectively busted the union, as employees began to return to work. Just months after that, union members and their families gathered to stage a mock trial outside company headquarters in Peoria, Illinois. The outcome had Fites dangling by the neck in effigy. The remains were buried with the chairman's final pay offer. The leadership hadn't made it available for a vote, but members were working under the exact terms being buried. Despite a total of 12 strikes since 1948, Cat employees had never worked without a contract before. But they had little choice; the strikers had effectively lost.

In the aftermath of the labor rift at Caterpillar it was difficult to determine who the winners were, if in fact there were any. The slogan No Contract, No Peace could be spotted around Cat plants everywhere. Many workers donned T-shirts that read Permanently Replace Fites. The union began a campaign to slow production. Fites was the object of personal attacks by union officials. The UAW insisted that company labor policies caused a decline in product quality. Meanwhile, Caterpillar moved to transfer production stateside from Japan and Great Britain, but most of it was to be shifted to nonunion plants in North Carolina. Reportedly, many workers were mulling over the idea of dumping the UAW altogether and starting a company union unfettered by problems in Detroit.

Putting things back the way they were at Caterpillar may be a lot like the story of Humpty Dumpty. But Fites, who insists he did not set out to replace his workers, is as stubborn in his optimism as he was in negotiations. "I'm sure of one thing," he says. "Caterpillar is going to survive one way or another as a global leader. We hope we can do that from a U.S. manufacturing base. That's the best thing for the company, the union, and the country."

sources: Gary Slutsker, "What's Good for Caterpillar... ," Forbes, December 7, 1992, 108–10; Kevin Kelley et al., "Caterpillar's Don Fites: Why He Didn't Blink," Business Week, August 10, 1992, 56–57; "Bulldozing Labor Peace at Caterpillar," Industry Week, February 15, 1993; and Allison Rogers, "Now Playing in Peoria," Fortune, July 12, 1993, 11–12.

■ QUESTIONS

1. Do you agree with Fites's decision to force an end to the strike by threatening to permanently replace union workers, or do you think his hard-line stance will have a negative impact on the company in the long run? Discuss your answer.
2. If you were Fites, how would you now go about rebuilding a sense of commitment among alienated union workers?
3. Will Caterpillar ever be able to recapture the old sense of teamwork and camaraderie among employees? Why or why not?
4. Do you think these problems would have occurred if the company had worked to make Caterpillar a high commitment company in the first place? Why or why not?

A CASE IN DIVERSITY

JAPANESE AND EMPLOYEE COMMITMENT

Creating a workplace environment that engenders maximum commitment on the part of employees is never easy. When foreign companies establish plants on U.S. soil the challenge is exponentially greater. Japanese manufacturers and industrialists are probably in a class by themselves when it comes to the number of difficulties they must surmount in turning American workers into dedicated company-persons. So far they have been successful, principally by devising strategies that make employee and company interests coincide.

Japanese managers, particularly car makers, are nothing if not pragmatic about really visceral issues like layoffs. And sometimes they can have their cake and eat it too. Having already made substantial plant investments from Ohio to Michigan to Indiana, auto makers like Mazda, Subaru-Isuzu, and Honda have cut production back home rather than furlough U.S. workers. And although the strategy is no doubt welcome news to the rank-and-file, it's also purely a business decision. Even during the recessionary period of the early 90s, foreign car companies opted to cancel overtime or reduce work week hours in lieu of letting people go. The reasons are simple. Factories in Japan were operating with big overhead costs. Scaling back there was more cost-effective. Labor economist Harley Shaiken succinctly summed up another critical factor. "Laying somebody off is like signing them up for the UAW," he says.

The biggest Japanese companies are holding fast to the lifetime-employment policy as a means of earning employee commitment. Firms such as steel manufacturer NKK Corp. and heavy-equipment builder Hitachi Zosen have gone so far as to ex-

pand outside their principle business sphere in order to create positions for employees that would otherwise get pink slips. This approach is in keeping with another Japanese philosophy, and despite appearances, it has the company interest at its core. Resisting layoffs during cyclical down-times may foster loyalty on the part of U.S. workers to their Japan-based company. Japanese managers also think it keeps the company poised to capitalize when conditions do improve. "If the economy does not come back quickly," says Mark Mori, managing partner of Andersen Consulting, "then their management will have a challenge."

Although Japanese companies operating in the United States have enjoyed good success in gaining employee commitment from American workers, there are still areas where substantial improvement is needed. United States-based executives complain that their bosses across the Pacific operate in ivory towers and ignore cultural differences. They welcome input but don't provide much in the way of feedback. They also are often secretive, and tend to treat other Japanese better than Americans. As for workers on the factory floor, Japanese managers fail to recognize, let alone offer encouragement for, work well done. And perhaps ironically, Japanese managers who have experienced plenty of prejudice themselves, have racked up a dismal record when it comes to hiring minorities in the United States.

In all likelihood, the level of investment Japanese companies have made in U.S. plants and equipment will eventually bring about increased efforts at garnering commitment from employees.

SOURCES: Matthew D. Levy et al, "Foreign Ownership: Japanese in U.S. Overcome Barriers," *Management Review,* December 1992, 10–15; James B. Treece et al, "Japanese Carmakers Are Coddling Their U.S. Kids," *Business Week,* March 4, 1991, 21; John Teresko, "Japan Rethinks Manufacturing," *Industry Week,* September 6, 1993, 50–57.

QUESTIONS

1. Life-time employment undoubtedly helps foster loyalty among workers. But is it enough to offset such negatives as lack of recognition?

2. Is it feasible for U.S. companies to adopt the Japanese policy on life-time employment?

3. How could U.S. executives help encourage their Japanese counterparts to be more sensitive to cutural differences?

4. What do you think accounts for this alleged cultural insensitivity?

ENDNOTES

1. Laurie Kretchmar, "Biting Apple," *Fortune,* July 29, 1991, 43.
2. Frederick W. Taylor, "What Is Scientific Management?" Reprinted in Michael Matteson and John Ivancevich, *Management Classics* (Santa Monica: Goodyear, 1977), 5–8.
3. Alfred Chandler, *Strategy and Structure* (Cambridge, MA: MIT Press, 1962), 19–51.
4. Rensis Likert, *New Patterns of Management* (New York: McGraw-Hill, 1961), 6.
5. Ibid., 103.
6. For a similar perspective, see Herbert A. Simon, *Administrative Behavior* (New York: Free Press, 1976), 11.
7. Simon refers to this as imposed authority. Ibid., 116–17.
8. See also Chester Barnard, *The Functions of the Executive* (Cambridge: Harvard University Press, 1968).
9. Daniel Katz and Robert L. Kahn, *The Social Psychology of Organizations* (New York: John Wiley, 1966), 336.
10. Except as noted, this chapter is based on Gary Dessler, *Winning Commitment: How to Build and Keep a Competitive Workforce* (New York: McGraw-Hill, 1993).
11. Richard Steers, "Antecedents and Outcomes of Organizational Commitment," *Administrative Science Quarterly,* vol. 22, March 1977. For an additional view, see Rick Hackett et al, "Further assessments of Meyer and Allen's (1991) Three Component Model of Organizational Commitment," *Journal of Applied Psychology,* February 1994, 15–24.
12. Bruce Buchanan, "To Walk an Extra Mile: The What's, When's, and Why's of Organizational Commitment," *Organizational Dynamics,* Spring 1975, 67–80; reprinted in Jerome Schnee, E. Kirby Warren, and Harold Lazarus, *The Progress of Management* (Englewood Cliffs, NJ: Prentice-Hall, 1977), 452–69.
13. Ibid. See also Randall Dunham et al, "Organizational Commitment: The Utility of an Integrative Definition," *Journal of Applied Psychology,* June 1994, 370–381.
14. Richard M. Steers, "Antecedents and Outcomes," 53.
15. Karen Gaertner and Stanley Nollen, "Career Experiences, Perceptions of Employment Practices, and Psychological Commitment in the Organization," *Human Relations,* vol. 42, no. 11, 1989, 975–91.
16. Ibid., 87.
17. Penny Wright, "Teller Job Satisfaction and Organization Commitment as They Relate to Career Orientations," *Human Relations,* vol. 43, no. 4, 1990, 369–81.
18. For a discussion of personal traits that influence commitment see Richard Mowday, Lyman Porter, and Richard Steers, *Employee-Organization Linkages: The Psychology of Commitment, Absenteeism, and Turnover* (New York: Academic Press, 1982), 30–31.
19. Thomas DeCotiis and Timothy Summers, "A Path Analysis Model of the Antecedents and Consequences of Organizational Commitment," *Human Relations,* vol. 40, no. 7, 1987, 445–70.
20. Ibid., 466. For discussion of other factors influencing commitment see, for example, Hal Gregersen, "Commitments to a Parent Company and a Local Work Unit During Repatriation," *Personnel Psychology,* Spring, 1992, 29–55.
21. Reprinted by permission of the publisher from Rosabeth Moss Kanter, *Commitment and Community: Communes and Utopias in Sociological Perspective* (Cambridge: Harvard University Press, 1972), 1. Copyright 1972 by the Presidents and Fellows of Harvard College.
22. Ibid., 76.
23. Ibid., 93.
24. Ibid., 94.

25. Ibid.

26. Ibid., 95.

27. Ibid., 96.

28. See, for example, Mowday et al., *Employee-Organization Linkages,* 36–37. See also Robert Tett and John Meyer, "Job Satisfaction, Organizational Commitment, Turnover Intention, and Turnover: Path Analysis Based on Meta Analytic Findings," *Personnel Psychology,* Summer 1993, 259–294.

29. See Thomas DeCotiis and Timothy Summers, "A Path Analysis," 463; and Cathy Kline and Lawrence Peters, "Behavioral Commitment and Tenure of New Employees: A Replication and Extension," *The Academy of Management Journal,* vol. 34, no. 1, March 1991, 194–204.

30. For discussions see Mowday et al., *Employee-Organization Linkages;* and DeCotiis and Summers, "A Path Analysis."

31. Charles O'Reilly III and Jennifer Chatman, "Organizational Commitment and Psychological Attachment: The Effect of Compliance, Identification, and Internalization on Pro-Social Behavior," *Journal of Applied Psychology,* 1986, vol. 71, 493.

32. Ibid., 497.

33. Harold Angle and James Perry, "An Empirical Assessment of Organizational Commitment and Organizational Effectiveness," *Administrative Science Quarterly,* March 1981, vol. 26, 1–13.

34. Tom Burns and G. M. Stalker, *The Management of Innovation* (London: Tavistock Publications, 1961), vii.

35. Ibid., 125.

36. Personal interview. See Gary Dessler, *Winning Commitment,* 27–28.

37. Ibid., 28.

38. Ibid., 30.

39. Ibid., 56.

40. Tom Peters, *Thriving on Chaos* (New York: Harper & Row, 1988), 380.

41. Dessler, op. cit.; 64.

42. Rosabeth Moss Kanter, "The New Managerial Work," *Harvard Business Review,* November–December 1989, 91.

43. Ibid.

44. Dessler, op. cit., 69.

45. Daniel Katz and Robert Kahn, *The Social Psychology of Organizations* (New York: John Wiley, 1966), 366.

46. Peters, *Thriving on Chaos,* 379.

47. Dessler, op. cit., 89.

48. Fujio Cho speech.

49. *Federal Express Employee Handbook,* 103.

50. Ibid., 21.

51. Discussed in Dessler, op. cit., 118.

52. Kanter, "The New Managerial Work," 91.

53. Personal interview with Penney's compensation manager, December 1991.

54. Abraham Maslow, 336.

55. Interview with assembler Dan Dise, March 1992.

56. Personal interview, March 1992.

57. *J. C. Penney Associate Handbook,* 3.

58. *Federal Express Employee Handbook,* 28.

59. *Delta Policies and Procedures Manual.*

60. Kenneth Thomas and Betty Velthouse, "Cognitive Elements of Empowerment: An Interpretative Model of Intrinsic Task Motivation," *Academy of Management Review,* 1990, vol. 15, no. 4, 666–81.

61. Personal interviews at Saturn Corporation, March 1992.

62. This discussion is based on Michael Meyer, "From Champ to Chump," *Newsweek,* July 26, 1993, 36–37; Charlene Marmer Solomon, "The Loyalty Factor," *Personnel Journal,* September 1992, 52; "Apple's Plan to Survive and Grow," *Fortune,* May 4, 1992, 68–70; Richard Brandt et al., "The Toughest Job in the Computer Business," *Business Week,* March 19, 1990, 118–22; and "Corporate Antihero John Sculley," *Inc.,* October 1987, 49–59.

CHAPTER 13

LEADERSHIP

LEARNING OBJECTIVES

After studying this chapter, you should be able to:

- Define leadership and its importance in management.
- Describe at least five types of power that serve as sources of a leader's influence.
- Discuss trait theories of leadership.
- Give examples of behavioral leadership theories.
- Explain situational theories of leadership.
- Compare and contrast the situational leadership theories developed by Fiedler, House, and Vroom.
- List characteristics that enable transformational leaders to inspire subordinates to perform beyond expectations.

OPENING PROBLEM
ROBERTO GOIZUETA

When Roberto C. Goizueta took over the Coca-Cola Company in 1981, all seemed well. Operations were so tranquil that no one seemed interested in trying any new ideas or methods of operation. Still, Goizueta had a problem. The world's most valuable trademark was affixed to but one product. And annual growth levels weren't robust enough to suit him. So he decided to make some changes. ■ Word went out that Coke wasn't going to be a nice company, but a growth company. The Cuban-born Goizueta was atypical for the somewhat staid corporate hierarchy; he was a visionary leader and a risk taker. Aiming at the sweet-tooth of the next generation of soft-drinkers, he decided to launch New Coke. He also extended the brand name to Diet Coke, a large gamble at the time. And he exploded tradition by laying out $692 million to buy Columbia Pictures. Coca-Cola in Hollywood? Goizueta edged himself out onto a risky venture in pursuit of his leadership vision.[1]

INTRODUCTION TO LEADERSHIP

In May 1991, General Norman Schwarzkopf gave a televised explanation of the strategy and tactics that won Operation Desert Storm, and few who watched him could have come away unimpressed with his enormous leadership skills. The operation was brilliantly conceived and flawlessly executed, and, while any loss is tragic, fewer than 150 Americans lost their lives. In a few months, the general had not only planned, organized, and staffed an astonishingly complex and potentially risky operation, in addition, he had somehow ignited his troops, so that by and large they felt driven to accomplish Desert Storm's mission.

LEADERSHIP

Occurs whenever one person influences another to work toward some predetermined objective.

Leadership occurs whenever one person influences another to work toward some predetermined objective, so most would agree that General Schwarzkopf is a great leader.[2] Yet there would be no unanimity about what makes General Schwarzkopf (or any other great leader) so effective. Are the Norman Schwarzkopfs, Margaret Thatchers, and Roberto Goizuetas of the world born with traits like intelligence that make them great leaders? Does their greatness come from their leadership style, the way they behave? Or is it something else? As we will see in this chapter, four types of leadership theories have been advanced: trait theory, behavioral style theory, contingency theory, and transformational leadership theory. Each theory has its proponents. Each also contributes to what we know about what makes a leader great.

The question of what makes a leader great came up again recently. A new book about General Schwarzkopf and Desert Storm (while not diminishing his military accomplishments) describes the General's rages. His anger against his subordinates at one point became so intense that Defense Secretary Cheyney had to send a three-star general to Schwarzkopf's command post to act as a buffer between Schwarzkopf and his subordinates. At various times, for instance, General Schwarzkopf threatened to fire and court marshal his air, land, and navel commanders. The image of an undeniably brilliant leader raging at his troops this way underscores what is probably the impossibility of finding a final answer to the question, "What makes a leader great?"

What makes a leader great? Were General Norman Schwartzkopf's accomplishments in Operation Desert Storm a result of his character traits, the way he behaved, or the situation in which he found himself?

LEADERSHIP AND THE RESPONSIVE ORGANIZATION

Leadership—the ability to influence one's team to move in a chosen direction—has always been an important management element. However, in today's fast-changing environment, good leadership is more important than it has ever been before, because it is the leader who must initiate change, and provide a unifying vision.

INITIATE CHANGE First, leaders initiate change. As two experts say:

> In a world characterized by global competition, deregulation, sharp technological change and political turmoil, discontinuous [sudden] organization change seems to be a determinant of organization adaption. Those firms that can initiate and implement discontinuous organization change more rapidly and/or prior to the competition have a competitive advantage. While not all change will be successful, inertia or [evolutionary] incremental change in the face of altered competitive arenas, is a recipe for failure. [Therefore] executive leadership is the critical factor in the initiation and implementation of large-system organization change.[3]

PROVIDE VISION In addition to triggering change, the leader's vision becomes the glue that assures a coordinated sense of direction for the firm.

This is very important. In many firms today the coordination provided by a tight chain of command is gone. Instead, employees in responsive organizations often work in boundaryless teams, largely directing themselves. This can be problematical without a shared sense of purpose that channels employees toward a coordinated effort. The authors Tom Peters and Robert Waterman say the answer is a "loose-tight phenomena," which means "co-existence of firm central direction and maximum individual autonomy."[4] Thus a firm like 3M is loose in that small groups of employees often meet to develop projects with little supervision. Yet such looseness must be matched with a tight commitment to a vision and shared values, which means in this case that the teams must adhere to 3M's belief in customer-oriented service and engineering excellence.

The leadership tasks of initiating change and providing a vision are increasingly important today. And so we will see in this chapter that the study of leadership effectiveness has evolved from a preoccupation with leadership traits to a focus on the *transformational* (vision-setting) aspects of leadership. Raymond Gillmartin, CEO of medical equipment maker Beckton Dickinson, is a good example of a visionary leader. With competition rising, Gillmartin knew that his firm needed a way to encourage his employees to take the initiative and form teams to innovate and go after new business in new ways.[5] To keep employees and teams working in unison, he laid out a broad vision to "develop innovative new products and beat the competition to the market with them." He then let his 15 divisions develop their own business strategies to meet their individual needs. "We set the strategy and the team carries it out," is the way one division head puts it.[6]

POWER AND LEADERSHIP INFLUENCE

Leaders must influence others to achieve the organization's goals. Therefore, before proceeding, we should briefly review the sources of influence.

One description was formulated by the sociologists French and Raven. They define **power** as the ability of one person to influence another to do something the latter would not otherwise do.[7] They propose five types of power: reward power, coercive power, legitimate power, referent power, and expert power.[8]

REWARD POWER Reward power is power whose basis is the ability to reward. According to French and Raven, the strength of the reward power one person holds over another rises with the magnitude of the rewards the leader can provide. Therefore,

POWER
The ability of one person to influence another to do something the latter would not otherwise do.

REWARD POWER
Power whose basis is the ability to reward.

leaders have influence to the extent that they can decide the positive rewards (such as money) accruing to the other person. The leader also has power to the extent that he or she can reduce the negative rewards (such as poor working conditions) the other person might otherwise have to endure.

COERCIVE POWER Coercive power stems from a person's real or imagined expectation that he or she will be punished for failing to conform to his or her leader's demands.

LEGITIMATE POWER Legitimate power, says French and Raven, "is characterized by the feeling of 'oughtness' on the part of a subordinate." The actual source of this legitimate power might be *tradition* (as in the case of a monarch), or it might derive from the leader's *office*. For example, upon agreeing to join General Motors, its salespeople accept the right of the sales manager to assign them work, this being a legitimate right of the office of sales manager.

REFERENT POWER Referent power is based on the fact that one person identifies with and is highly attracted to a leader, perhaps due to the leader's charismatic personality.

EXPERT POWER Finally, expert power stems from the fact that one person is viewed as an expert in some area; others must therefore depend on him or her for advice and counsel. For example, even a company's president may find herself or himself deferring to one of her firm's research scientists in those areas in which the scientist has the knowledge and expertise to solve some critical product problem.

A leader can build and supplement influence over subordinates in other ways. Thus, researchers have identified other leadership influence tactics, including *rational persuasion, pressure tactics, ingratiation, consultation,* and *inspirational appeals.*[9] Similarly, Professor Gary Yukl points out that in addition to attempts at overt influence, a leader's indirect efforts to exercise power might include political tactics such as forming coalitions, coopting opponents, and gaining control for key decisions.[10]

Such sources of influence notwithstanding, it seems apparent that there must be more to effective leadership than just the use of power. And, in fact, several theories have been proposed to explain what makes some leaders effective and others ineffective. We turn to these next.

TRAIT THEORIES OF LEADERSHIP

BACKGROUND

Trait theories of leadership assume that effective leaders have a number of identifiable traits or characteristics that distinguish them from ineffective leaders. These theories grew out of work done by the American Psychological Association at the beginning of World War I.[11] A committee of psychologists had been appointed to assist the U.S. Army in screening and selecting military personnel, and the early, *traitist* leadership research grew out of this personnel testing movement.

Most of the early research on leadership traits was inconclusive. Specific traits were related to leadership effectiveness in specific situations, but none were found to be so related in a variety of different studies and situations.[12] However, subsequent studies over the past 40 or 50 years suggest that effective leaders *do* differ from ineffective ones in some measurable ways. For example, after an extensive literature review, leadership expert Dr. Bernard Bass had this to say:

Margin glossary

COERCIVE POWER
Stems from a person's real or imagined expectation that he or she will be punished for failing to conform to his or her leader's influence attempts.

LEGITIMATE POWER
Characterized by the feeling of oughtness on the part of a subordinate; the actual source of this legitimate power might be tradition or the supervisor's office.

REFERENT POWER
Based on the fact that one person identifies with and is highly attracted to a leader, perhaps due to the leader's charismatic personality.

EXPERT POWER
Stems from the fact that one person is viewed as an expert in some area; others must therefore depend on him or her for advice and counsel.

TRAIT THEORIES OF LEADERSHIP
Assume that effective leaders have a number of identifiable traits or characteristics that distinguish them from ineffective leaders.

The leader is characterized by a strong drive for responsibility and task completion, vigor and persistence in pursuit of goals, venturesomeness and originality in problem-solving, drive to exercise initiative in social situations, self-confidence and sense of personal identity, willingness to accept consequences of decision and action, readiness to absorb interpersonal stress, willingness to tolerate frustration and delay, ability to influence other persons' behavior, and capacity to structure social interaction systems to the purpose at hand.[13]

LEADERSHIP TRAITS TODAY

Recent studies corroborate Bernard Bass's assertion that such leadership personality traits do exist.[14] For example, effective leaders must want to exert influence, as well as experience *self-efficacy,* which means the feeling that they are competent in exerting influence and assuming a leadership role.[15] Similarly, Professor Robert J. House argues that effective leaders are predisposed to be influential.[16] Henry Mintzberg notes that a leader needs the "will" while also being confident about his or her leadership "skills."[17] Professor James G. Hunt says there is a "predisposition to use power" in effective leaders, and that the leader also must possess a self-confidence, competency, and self-efficacy that combine to make the person believe that "he or she can be a leader and exert influence."[18] Similarly, Professor Gary Yukl concludes that

> traits that relate most consistently to managerial effectiveness or advancement include high self-confidence, energy, initiative, emotional maturity, stress tolerance and belief in internal locus of control. With respect to interest and values, successful managers tend to be pragmatic and results-oriented, and they enjoy persuasive activities requiring initiative and challenge.[19]

J.B. Miner and his colleagues found that "motivation to be a manager" is another important leadership trait and that its elements include a desire for power, a positive attitude toward authority figures, and a desire to compete with peers.[20] In summary, effective leaders do seem to be characterized by a number of personality traits.

BEHAVIORAL THEORIES OF LEADERSHIP

Trait theorists generally focus on what the leader *is,* in terms of measurable, characteristic personality traits such as intelligence. Behavioral leadership theories focus on what the leader *does* and how he or she behaves, particularly in relation to subordinates. So behavioral leadership theorists focus on the leader's *observed behavior,* on the way that he or she acts. The *Goodyear* vignette illustrates leadership style.

WORK-CENTERED AND EMPLOYEE-CENTERED LEADERS

As you might imagine, many different terms have been used to describe how leaders behave toward their subordinates. However, most of the early work in this field (up to about the 1980s) focused on either work-centered behavior or employee-centered behavior.[21] **Work-centered leaders** are variously described as authoritarian, autocratic, production-oriented, or as a type that needs to initiate structure. **Employee-centered leaders** are variously described as democratic, employee-oriented, or considerate. As a rule, says Bass, the same leaders who are described as autocratic or authoritarian will also be described as directive, concerned with production, initiator of structure, production centered, and task oriented. Similarly, employee- or follower-centered leaders may also be described as considerate, democratic, consultative, and participative. The *Scitor* small business box describes an employee-centered entrepreneur.

WORK-CENTERED LEADERS
Leaders who are authoritarian, autocratic, production-oriented, or a type that needs to initiate structure.

EMPLOYEE-CENTERED LEADERS
Leaders who are democratic, employee-oriented, or considerate.

GOODYEAR TIRE & RUBBER COMPANY

Before Stanley Gault took over as CEO at Goodyear Tire & Rubber Company, the company was undergoing a near-death experience coping with a $3.7 billion debt load and a dearth of new-products. His reputation as a tough cost cutter and innovative marketer were legendary from his days as head of Rubbermaid. In 11 years, that company grew four-fold and earnings increased by a factor of six. But few expected the disarmingly down-to-earth style of leadership Gault exhibited at Goodyear. His first day on the job in June 1991, he was given the keys to the ornate cabinets in his office. Lots of people come and go in the evenings, it was explained, some of them union people. He handed the keys back. "I don't give a damn," he said, "this company should be run on the basis of trust."

Since then Gault has made many small changes that carry big impact. Like his friend, the late Sam Walton, he insisted employees be referred to as associates. He likes the leveling effect it has among employees of different ranks. "We don't work for each other," he says, "we work with each other." Gault announces Goodyear's quarterly performance to 800 invitees and then fields questions from the group. Tapes of the proceedings go out to company plants around the globe. Gault also personally presides over twice-monthly meetings where associates recount improvements they have made and are then rewarded.

Lifting $11 billion Goodyear out of the doldrums involved more than egalitarian gestures. Gault redesigned the company's marketing organization and opened channels of distribution with Sears, Kmart, Wal-Mart, and other chains where people increasingly shopped for tires. He also moved decisively in divesting the company of noncore businesses and tripled the rate of new product introductions.

Gault has a well-earned reputation as a considerate leader who grasps the importance of issues large and small. On the one hand, he reduced Goodyear's debt by $1 billion in seven months. On the other, he's also managed to get the janitors that work around his office to call him Stan.

SOURCES: "No One Excluded," *Fortune*, December 14, 1992, 104–105; Zachary Schiller, "Goodyear's Miracle Man?" *Business Week*, June 17, 1991, 35; and Peter Nulty, "The Bounce Is Back at Goodyear," *Fortune*, September 7, 1992, 70–72.

Each type of leader—work centered or employee centered—exhibits characteristic behaviors. Bass describes these as follows:

A task-focused leader initiates structure, provides the information, determines what is to be done, issues the rules, promises rewards for compliance, and threatens punishment for disobedience. The follower-focused leader solicits advice, opinions and information from followers and checks decisions or shares decision-making with the followers. The . . . task-focused leader uses his or her power to obtain compliance with what the leader has decided.

SCITOR CORPORATION

CEO Roger E. Meade, cofounder of Sunnyvale, California-based Scitor Corporation, believes everything his company does should be geared toward enhancing competitiveness and productivity. How does the company do this? "To increase productivity you start by first understanding the human heart," Meade says. "Only [then] will you know how to stir the passion that fuels productivity." Impractical sounding? Maybe, but Scitor has marked 13 years of uninterrupted profits and growth, which Meade regards as by-products of doing the job right and making customers happy. The company, which provides products and services for program management, systems engineering, and customized computer information systems, doesn't even establish goals for earnings or revenues. Instead, Scitor's theory is that satisfying customers can't help but lead to increases in both.

Meade's most central policy calls on employees to make their own decisions. But before doing so, he asks them to employ their best judgment and to make sure it's fair, honest, and within the context of company objectives. If all the answers are yes, employees are given the green light to go ahead, with a reminder that everyone will be held accountable. Meade expects employees to challenge management if, in their own best judgment, they decide that in-

structions are out of sync with what needs to be done. Meade is particularly intolerant of employees saying they are "just following orders," an excuse that he calls inexcusable.

Meade's approach to doing things is a result of his experience at larger organizations that inhibited their employees' capabilities. "I always used to feel frustrated with how organizations operate," he says. "People at the lowest level always [know] what [has] to be done. Management should always remember that we are ignorant of what is really happening because we simply aren't involved in the day-to-day work."

FOCUS ON SMALL BUSINESS

He thinks policy manuals should be eliminated. Great leaps always ensue, he says, when managers really listen to employees. His own policy is to take part in employee discussions on strategy, but he won't participate in the final decision making.

In the area of work-family policy, Meade thinks an analytical—not emotional—approach makes the most sense. The company pays for sick days but doesn't keep track of them, funds a generous health care plan, picks up $1,400 a year for dental expenses, and

allows even new hires three weeks a year vacation. The company provides a care center for slightly sick kids and offers in-home care in emergency situations. Paid maternity leave extends to 12 weeks, and when the mother returns to work she is given a flexible schedule. Anyone who works more than 17.5 hours weekly is eligible for flextime, job-sharing, and benefits. The company also throws in 49er football tickets, as well as ski, picnic, wine, and road rally trips. It's all capped off by Scitor's fiscal year kickoff meeting hosted at sumptuous resorts throughout the state. All 200 employees and their guests are invited at company expense.

How do employees respond to a company leader who puts people first and is almost wholly reliant on trust and allowing workers to do what they consider to be the right thing? On average, Scitor workers are out five days a year. The company's turnover rate for engineers is just over 2 percent; the rate for the rest of California is eight times that high. Nine out of ten new mothers stay on after giving birth. To Meade, being people focused is pretty basic and makes the most sense. "I believe in the worth of the individual," he says. "Individual initiative is the fuel on which our company and our nation run."

SOURCE: Michael A. Verespej, "Roger Meade: Running on People Power," *Industry Week*, October 18, 1993, 13–18.

The follower-focused leader uses his or her power to set the constraints within which followers are encouraged to join in deciding what is to be done.[22]

The following research evidence suggests that employee-centered leaders' styles are usually associated with higher employee satisfaction; however, the effects of a work-centered style are inconsistent in that it seems to vary with the type of situation.

STRUCTURING AND CONSIDERATE STYLES

Initiating structure and *consideration* are two specific work-centered/employee-centered descriptions of leader behavior. They were developed from a research project that was launched in 1945 at The Ohio State University.[23] A survey called the Leader Behavior

Description Questionnaire (LBDQ) was produced and was further refined by subsequent researchers.[24] The two leadership factors it measured that survive to this day—*consideration* and *initiating structure*—have become synonymous with what experts in the field call The Ohio State Dimensions of Leadership:

> **Consideration:** Leader behavior indicative of mutual trust, friendship, support, respect, and warmth.

> **Initiating Structure:** Leader behavior by which the person organizes the work to be done, and defines relationships or roles, the channels of communication, and the ways of getting jobs done.

RESEARCH RESULTS　Considerate leaders generally have the most satisfied employees, but their effects on employee performance are inconsistent. One of the original studies on this subject was carried out in a truck manufacturing plant. Leader consideration was generally positively related to the employees' satisfaction. However, no consistent relationship was found between leader consideration and employee performance. Findings like these led researcher Gary Yukl to conclude that "the research literature indicates that in most situations, considerate leaders will have more satisfied subordinates."[25]

However, the effects of leader initiating structure on both subordinate satisfaction and performance are inconsistent. In one study that is representative of those in this area, leader structure and employee grievance rates were directly related; the more structuring the leader was, the more grievances were filed. However where the leader was also very considerate, leader structure and grievances were *not* related. In general, we can conclude that: (1) leader consideration is positively related to employee satisfaction, but its effects on employee performance are inconsistent; and (2) we cannot generalize about the effect of initiating structure, except to say that its relation to both employee satisfaction and performance may be positive, negative, or nonexistent, depending on the situation.[26]

PRODUCTION-CENTERED AND EMPLOYEE-CENTERED LEADERSHIP STYLES

At about the same time that researchers at Ohio State were developing their LBDQ, a similar program was underway at the University of Michigan Survey Research Center.[27] This line of research led to the identification of two leadership styles: employee orientation and production (job) orientation. Employee-oriented leaders, according to researcher Rensis Likert, focus on the individuality and personal needs of their employees and emphasize building good interpersonal relations. Production or job-centered leaders focus on production and the job's technical aspects. Based on his own review of the research results, Likert concluded the following:

> Supervisors with the best record of performance focus their primary attention on the human aspects of their subordinates' problems and on endeavoring to build effective work groups with high performance goals.[28]

CLOSE AND GENERAL STYLES OF LEADERSHIP

Other experts distinguish between close and general styles of leadership; this line of research also evolved out of work begun at the University of Michigan.[29] *Close supervision* was conceptualized as "one end of a continuum that describes the degree to which a supervisor specifies the roles of subordinates and checks up to see that they comply with the specifications."[30] The laissez faire leader who takes a completely

Stanley Gault, CEO of Goodyear Tire, visits tire stores, both his own and rivals, with regularity on Saturdays. His disarmingly low-key style and open-door policies, both characteristics of employee-centered leadership, have won the loyalty of Goodyear's 96,000 employees, enabling them to work together to reduce Goodyear's debt.

hands-off policy with subordinates is at the other extreme, with a general leader somewhere in the middle of the continuum.

The research findings here are much clearer with respect to employee morale than they are with employee performance. Generally speaking, they indicate that most people do not like being closely supervised or having, in effect, someone frequently watching them and telling them what to do. Close supervision is therefore usually associated with lower employee morale.[31] Yet no consistent relationship seems to exist between close (or general) styles of leadership and employee performance. Here again, other factors apparently determine whether performance is high or low.

Vernon Jordan's skills as a leader were honed in the civil-rights movement of the 1960s. His stints as director of the United Negro College Fund and as head of the National Urban League have earned him a place on the boards of many corporations.

SITUATIONAL THEORIES OF LEADERSHIP

The preceding research results seem to underscore the importance of situational factors in explaining leader effectiveness.[32] As we have seen, no one style of leadership has been found to be universally effective, a fact that led Tannenbaum and Schmidt to conclude that "effective leadership depends on the leader, his followers, the situation, and the interrelationships between them."[33] Research in succeeding years therefore focused on identifying the conditions under which some leadership traits or styles were or were not effective. The work of Fred Fiedler, Robert House, and Victor Vroom are illustrative of this situational approach to leader effectiveness.

FIEDLER'S LEADERSHIP THEORY

Fred Fiedler's contingency model of leader effectiveness grew out of a program of research he began at the University of Illinois in 1951.[34]

THE THEORY Fiedler originally sought to determine whether a leader who was lenient in evaluating associates was more or less likely to have a high-producing group than the leader who was demanding and discriminating. At the core of this research is the "least preferred coworker" (or LPC) scale. The person who fills it out is asked to think of all the people with whom he or she has ever worked and to focus on the one person with whom he or she had experienced the most difficulty in getting a job completed, that is, his or her least preferred coworker. The rater is then asked to describe this person via a series of descriptive scales, the extremes of which are labeled in the following fashion:

Pleasant <------------> Unpleasant
Smart <--------------> Stupid

Fiedler originally argued that the LPC was measuring a personality trait. However his more recent work suggests that the LPC is actually measuring a style of leadership, ranging from considerate leadership (high LPC) to structuring leadership (low LPC).

According to Fiedler's theory, three situational factors combine to determine whether considerate or structuring leader styles are appropriate:

1. **Position power:** The degree to which the position itself enables the leader to get his or her group members to comply with and accept his or her direction and leadership.

2. **Task structure:** How routine and predictable the work group's task is.

3. **Leader-member relations:** The extent to which the leader "gets along" with workers and the extent to which they have confidence in and are loyal to him or her.

Based on his studies, Fiedler concluded that "the appropriateness of the leadership style . . . is contingent upon the favorableness of the group-task situation."[35] As shown in Figure 13.1, Fiedler argued that where the situation is either favorable or unfavorable to the leader (where leader-member relations, task structure, and leader position power are either very high or very low), a more task-oriented, structuring leader is appropriate. On the other hand, in the middle range, where these factors are more mixed and the task is not as clear-cut, a more considerate, relationship-oriented leader is appropriate. To explain these findings, Fiedler says:

> In the very favorable conditions in which the leader has power, informal backing, and a relatively well structured task, the group is ready to be directed and the group members expect to be told what to do. . . . In the relatively unfavorable situation, we would again expect that the task oriented leader will be more effective than will be the considerate leader who is concerned with interpersonal relations [since the group will fall apart without the leader's active intervention and control]. . . . In situations which are only moderately favorable [or moderately unfavorable] for the leader, a considerate relationship-oriented attitude seems most effective. . . . Here the leader must provide a nonthreatening, permissive environment if members are to feel free to make suggestions and to contribute to discussions.[36]

THE THEORY TODAY   On the assumption that it is easier to change a situation than one's basic leadership tendencies, Fiedler and his associates next developed a leadership training program. The basic idea of his **leader match program** is that by manipulating the three situational variables—leader member relations, task structure, and position power—a leader who knows his or her LPC style can change the situation to best suit that style. Thus a task-oriented leader who assesses the situation as moderately favorable could increase its favorability by demanding of the boss the right to allocate all rewards. Fiedler and Mahar report the results of 12 studies that they say support the usefulness of leader-match training."[37] But several writers, including Fiedler, have recently described deficiencies in the contingency model and in leader match.[38]

POSITION POWER
The degree to which the position itself enables the leader to get his or her group members to comply with and accept his or her direction and leadership.

TASK STRUCTURE
How routine and predictable the work group's task is.

LEADER-MEMBER RELATIONS
The extent to which the leader "gets along" with workers and the extent to which they have confidence in and are loyal to him or her.

LEADER MATCH PROGRAM
The basic idea of this program is that by manipulating the three situational variables—leader-member relations, task structure, and power position—a leader who knows his or her LPC style can change the situation to best suit that style.

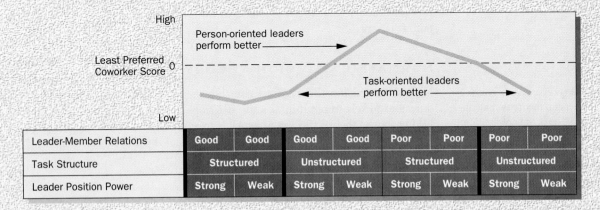

FIEDLER'S CLASSIFICATION OF SITUATION FAVORABLENESS

	Very Favorable		Intermediate				Very Unfavorable	
Leader-Member Relations	Good	Good	Good	Good	Poor	Poor	Poor	Poor
Task Structure	High		Low		High		Low	
Leader Position Power	Strong	Weak	Strong	Weak	Strong	Weak	Strong	Weak
Situations	I	II	III	IV	V	VI	VII	VIII

HOW LEADER STYLE FITS THE SITUATION

High

Least Preferred Coworker Score   0

Low

Person-oriented leaders perform better ⟶

Task-oriented leaders perform better ⟶

Leader-Member Relations	Good	Good	Good	Good	Poor	Poor	Poor	Poor
Task Structure	Structured		Unstructured		Structured		Unstructured	
Leader Position Power	Strong	Weak	Strong	Weak	Strong	Weak	Strong	Weak

FIGURE 13.1

Fiedler's Contingency Theory of Leadership

Fiedler concluded that structuring leaders were most effective under very favorable and very unfavorable conditions; relationship-oriented leaders were best in intermediate situations where the task was not so clear cut.

SOURCE: Fred. E. Fiedler, "The Effects of Leadership Training and Experience: A Contingency Model Interpretation," *Administrative Science Quarterly* 17 (1972), 455. As presented in Richard Daft, *Management*, 3rd ed. (Fort Worth, TX: The Dryden Press, 1994), 489, Exhibits 14.4 and 14.5. Reprinted by permission of *Administrative Science Quarterly*.

Fiedler's contingency theory has therefore continued to evolve. In its most recent version, Fiedler and Garcia stress the importance of what they call **cognitive resources** in explaining leader effectiveness.[39] They argue that some leaders have better cognitive resources, such as in terms of intelligence and job-related knowledge. Fiedler's new Cognitive Resource Theory predicts, for example, that directive (low LPC) behavior only results in good performance when the leader has high cognitive resources.

HOUSE'S PATH-GOAL THEORY OF LEADERSHIP

According to the **path-goal theory of leadership** as formulated by Robert J. House, the functions of a leader consist largely of increasing the personal rewards that subordinates receive for attaining goals and making the path to these rewards easier to follow

COGNITIVE RESOURCES
Resources, such as intelligence and job-related knowledge, that enhance leadership effectiveness.

PATH-GOAL THEORY OF LEADERSHIP
A leader should increase the personal rewards that subordinates receive for attaining their goals, and smooth the path to these rewards by clarifying it, reducing road blocks, and increasing the opportunities for personal satisfaction en route.

by clarifying it, reducing road blocks and pitfalls, and increasing the opportunities for personal satisfaction en route. The path-goal theory is based on the expectancy theory of motivation, which states that motivation is a function of a person's ability to accomplish the task and his or her desire to do so. House says that a leader can increase an employee's motivation by ensuring that the person has the ability to accomplish the task. To do this, the leader provides structure (in terms of instructions, and so forth) when needed.[40]

House's basic thesis is that ambiguous, uncertain situations are potentially frustrating. In such situations, the structure provided by the leader will be viewed as legitimate by subordinates. On the other hand, in routine situations (such as might be encountered on assembly-line tasks), the leader's additional structure might be viewed as redundant by the subordinates, who might therefore become dissatisfied. Reviews of this research suggest that specific leader behaviors such as clarifying roles, planning the work, and setting specific objectives can boost motivation in ambiguous, uncertain situations.[41]

NORMATIVE DECISION THEORY

NORMATIVE DECISION THEORY A leadership theory that identifies the degree of participation most likely to result in effective decisions in a particular situation.

Normative decision theory is a leadership theory that identifies the decision procedures most likely to result in effective decisions in a particular situation.[42] Vroom and Jago propose a theory, the aim of which is to guide leaders in choosing the right degree of participative leadership. Their theory consists of three basic components:

1. A set of management decision styles.
2. A set of diagnostics questions.
3. A decision tree for identifying how much participation the situation calls for.

THE FIVE MANAGEMENT DECISION STYLES   First, Vroom and Jago say that participation is not an either/or leadership style and that there are actually different degrees of participation. As summarized in Figure 13.2, the degree to which leaders allow their subordinates to participate in decision-making can range from no participation (or highly autocratic), in which "the leader solves the problem or makes the decision him or herself," to consensus management (or highly democratic), in which "you share a problem with your subordinates as a group and together you generate and evaluate alternatives and reach agreement."

DIAGNOSTIC QUESTIONS   Next, Vroom and Jago say that the appropriate degree of participation depends on eight attributes of a situation, including the importance of the quality of the decision, the extent to which the leader possesses sufficient information to make a high-quality decision by him or herself, and the extent to which the problem is routine and structured or ambiguous and complicated. These eight attributes are summarized in Figure 13.3. The corresponding questions in that figure allow the leader to diagnose the presence or absence of each of these eight attributes for the situation at hand.

THE DECISION TREE   Finally Vroom and Jago provide a chart in the form of a decision tree, also presented in Figure 13.3. To use this figure, you work from left to right. First determine whether the quality of the decision is important, then determine if you have sufficient information to make a high-quality decision, and so forth. By starting on the left of the figure and answering each question, you can work your way across the decision tree. You can therefore identify (1) the nature of the situation that you as a leader find yourself in and (2) the degree of participation that is best.[43]

	Decision Style	Description
Highly Autocratic ↑	**AI**	You solve the problem or make the decision yourself using information available to you at that time.
	AII	You obtain the necessary information from your subordinates and then decide on the solution to the problem yourself.
	CI	You share the problem with relevant subordinates individually, getting their ideas and suggestions without bringing them together as a group. Then you make the decision.
	CII	You share the problem with your subordinates as a group, colectively obtaining their ideas and suggestions. Then you make the decision.
↓ **Highly Democratic**	**G**	You share a problem with your subordinates as a group. Your role is much like that of chairman. You do not try to influence the group to adopt "your" solution, and you are willing to accept and implement any solution that has the support of the entire group.

FIGURE 13.2

Normative Leader Decision Styles

Vroom and Jago said that there are five degrees of participation that leaders can engage in.

SOURCE: Reprinted from *The New Leadership: Managing Participation in Organizations* by Victor H. Vroom and Arthur G. Jago, Englewood Cliffs, NJ: Prentice-Hall, 1988. Copyright 1987 by V. H. Vroom and A. G. Jago. As presented in Richard Daft, *Management,* 3rd ed. (Fort Worth, TX: The Dryden Press, 1994), 267. Used with permission of the authors.

HERSEY AND BLANCHARD'S SITUATIONAL THEORY

Paul Hersey and Kenneth Blanchard have developed a Situational Leadership Model to describe the manner in which the leader's style must be adjusted to the task. Like the Ohio State researchers, Hersey and Blanchard propose that there are two basic styles of leadership: relationship-oriented and task-oriented. These combine in a matrix to produce four types of leader behavior, namely delegating (low task, low relationship), participating (low task, high relationship), selling (high task, high relationship), and telling (high task, low relationship). The type of style that is best depends, say Hersey and Blanchard, on the followers' ability and willingness to be led. Thus, followers with the ability and willingness may get more delegation and participation. Those without the willingness or ability require more of a selling or telling approach.

IN SUMMARY: YUKL'S CONCEPTUAL FRAMEWORK

Professor Gary Yukl is optimistic that these lines of leadership research—trait, styles, and situational—are gradually converging.[44] His conceptual framework for integrating the various leadership theories is summarized in Figure 13.4. Yukl basically argues that the leader's traits influence both his or her behaviors and personal power. In turn, the leader's behavior and power, and particularly the extent to which they are appropriate to the situation, influence outcomes such as performance and morale.

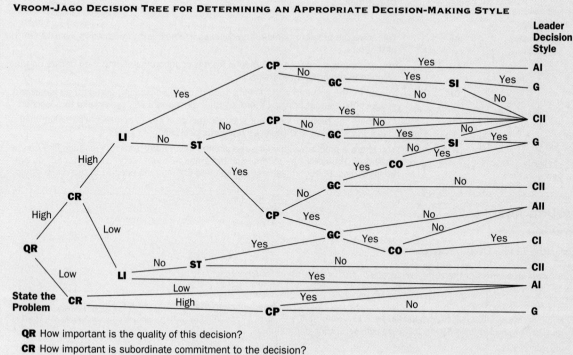

VROOM-JAGO DECISION TREE FOR DETERMINING AN APPROPRIATE DECISION-MAKING STYLE

QR How important is the quality of this decision?
CR How important is subordinate commitment to the decision?
LI Do you have sufficient information to make a high-quality decision?
ST Is the problem well structured?
CP If you were to make the decision by yourself, is it reasonably certain that your subordinates would be committed to it?
GC Do subordinates share the organization goals to be attained in solving this problem?
CO Is conflict among subordinates over preferred solutions likely?
SI Do subordinates have sufficient information to make a high-quality decision?

FIGURE 13.3

Vroom-Jago Decision Tree for Determining an Appropriate Decision-Making Method—Group Problems

Vroom and Jago contend that leaders can choose how participative he or she should be in a specific situation by asking the question posed in a series.

SOURCE: Reprinted from *The New Leadership: Managing Participation in Organizations* by Victor H. Vroom and Arthur G. Jago, Englewood Cliffs, NJ: Prentice-Hall, 1988. Copyright 1987 by V. H. Vroom and A. G. Jago. As presented in Richard Daft, *Management*, 3rd ed. (Fort Worth, TX: The Dryden Press, 1994), 268. Used with permission of the authors.

TRANSFORMATIONAL LEADERSHIP AND THE RESPONSIVE ORGANIZATION

As with many other human endeavors, leadership research and theorizing tend to reflect the environment in which they evolve. For most of the early 1900s, firms stressed efficiency, and managers generally focused their efforts not on responsiveness but on economies of scale and the efficiency that bigger organizations could provide. In this context, the researchers' preoccupation with identifying the measurable per-

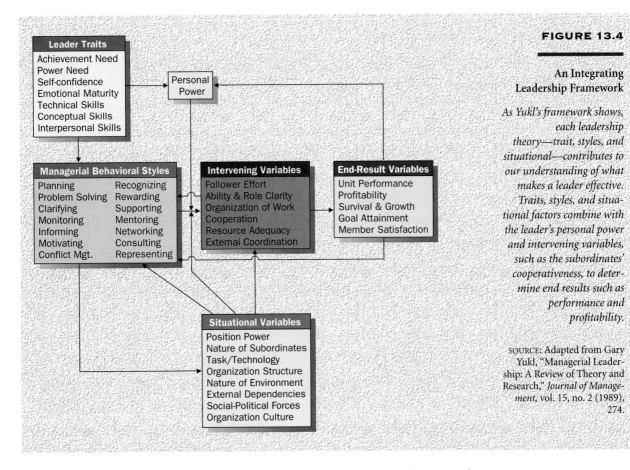

FIGURE 13.4

An Integrating Leadership Framework

As Yukl's framework shows, each leadership theory—trait, styles, and situational—contributes to our understanding of what makes a leader effective. Traits, styles, and situational factors combine with the leader's personal power and intervening variables, such as the subordinates' cooperativeness, to determine end results such as performance and profitability.

SOURCE: Adapted from Gary Yukl, "Managerial Leadership: A Review of Theory and Research," *Journal of Management*, vol. 15, no. 2 (1989), 274.

sonality traits that distinguish between effective and ineffective leaders made sense and allowed for easier testing. Similarly, the postwar preoccupation with human relations and employee morale was consistent with the emerging interest in employee or job-centered leadership styles. The situational leadership approach then grew, in part, out of the realization that different organizations had to cope with different rates of change as the pace of change in some industries like electronics began to curve up in the 1960s.

TRANSFORMATIONAL AND TRANSACTIONAL LEADERSHIP

In the late 1970s, James McGregor Burns wrote a book called *Leadership*, which had a major impact on the course of leadership theory.[45] Basically, Burns argued that leadership could be viewed as either a **transactional** or a transformational process.[46] He said that some leadership resulted from an exchange (or *transaction*), which was based on promises of rewards by the leader. In politics, for instance, transactional political leaders are those who "approach followers with an eye to exchanging one thing for another: jobs for votes, or subsidies for campaign contributions."[47] Leader behaviors like initiating structure and consideration are essentially based on such quid pro quo transactions. Specifically, such transactional behaviors are "largely oriented toward accomplishing the tasks at hand and at maintaining good relations with those working with a leader [by exchanging promises of rewards for performance]."[48]

In his book Burns describes the central role of what he calls transformational leadership in organizations today. He says "**transformational leadership** refers to the process of influencing major changes in the attitudes and assumptions of organization

TRANSACTIONAL LEADERSHIP
Leadership resulting from an exchange or transaction which was based on promises of rewards by the leader.

TRANSFORMATIONAL LEADERSHIP
Leadership that involves influencing major changes in the attitudes and assumptions of organization members and building commitment for the organization's mission, objectives and strategies and for the leader's vision for the firm.

members and building commitment for the organization's mission, objectives and strategies."[49]

Like other leadership theories, transformational leader theory is partly a product of its time, a time when "many companies in the United States had finally acknowledged the need to make major changes in the way things are done in order to survive in the face of increasing economic competition from foreign companies."[50] Transformational leaders are leaders that bring about "change, innovation and entrepreneurship."[51] They are responsible for a process of corporate transformation that "recognizes the need for revitalization, creates a new vision, and institutionalizes change."[52]

WHAT DO TRANSFORMATIONAL LEADERS DO?

Transformational leaders engage in several specific activities. They encourage and obtain performance beyond expectations by formulating visions and then inspiring their subordinates to pursue them. In so doing, transformational leaders cultivate employee acceptance of and commitment to their visions.[53] Transformational leaders "attempt to raise the needs of followers and promote dramatic changes of individuals, groups and organizations."[54] Transformational leaders do this by articulating a realistic vision of the future that can be shared, stimulating subordinates intellectually, and paying attention to the differences among these subordinates.[55]

Transformational leaders are characterized by four factors: charisma, inspiration, individual consideration, and intellectual stimulation.[56]

Transformational leader Herb Kelleher, head of Southwest Airlines, says he looks first for a sense of humor in his employees, who are encouraged to throw themselves into their jobs.

Transformational leaders are first *charismatic.* They have what Bass refers to as the ability to generate great symbolic power with which the employees want to identify. Employees often idolize and develop strong emotional attachments to the charismatic leader. Transformational leaders are also *inspirational,* in that "the leader passionately communicates a future idealistic organization that can be shared. The leader uses visionary explanations to depict what the employee work group can accomplish."[57] The inspired employees are then motivated to achieve these organizational aims.

Third, Bass says that for transformational leaders *individual consideration* goes beyond just being considerate. Such leaders treat employees as individuals and use a developmental orientation that encourages employees to self-actualize and become all they can be. Finally, transformational leaders use *intellectual stimulation* to "encourage employees to approach old and familiar problems in new ways."[58] This enables employees to question their own beliefs and use creative ways to solve problems by themselves. Southwest Airlines' Herb Kelleher, as described in the accompanying vignette, is one such transformational leader.

STUDIES OF TRANSFORMATIONAL LEADERS IN ACTION

Transformational leadership has been studied in many settings.[59] In one study, researchers found that high-performing managers in an express delivery firm used significantly more transformational leader behaviors than did less successful managers in the firm.[60] Another study found that successful champions of technological innovations—the men and women charged with carrying a technological change through an organization to its completion—used more transformational leader behaviors than did less successful champions.[61]

Several studies were conducted by Bass and his associates using a survey called the Multifactor Leadership Questionnaire (MLQ).[62] Examples of the transformational leadership questions are as follows:

1. *Charisma.* "I am ready to trust him or her to overcome any obstacle."
2. *Individualized consideration.* "Treats me as an individual rather than just a member of the group."
3. *Intellectual stimulation.* "Shows me how to think about problems in new ways."
4. *Inspirational leadership.* "Provides vision of what lies ahead."[63]

Studies using the MLQ have found that transformational leadership was related more strongly to subordinates' extra effort than were transactional or laissez-faire leadership.[64] Transformational leadership was also more closely associated with leader effectiveness and employee satisfaction with the leader than were transactional types of leadership.[65]

CREATING THE VISION

Being a transformational leader requires a vision. Transformational leaders achieve their ends through committed employees, and committed employees need visions and missions and values to be committed to. That is why Warren Bennis and Bert Nanus identify *vision* as a basic component of good in leadership:

> To choose a direction, a leader must first have developed a mental image of a possible and desirable state of the organization. This image, which we call a vision, may be as vague as a dream or as precise as a goal or mission statement. . . . The critical point is that a vision articulates a view of a realistic, credible, attractive future for the organization, a condition that is better in some important ways than what now exists.[66]

HERB KELLEHER

Herb Kelleher constantly tells his employees at Southwest Airlines Company that they must be ready for change. "Sometimes only in change is there security," he says. When facing the titans of his industry, he has consistently made them all look like a cavalry on horseback going up against his modern war machine.

Almost without question, the 9,500 employees at the $1.2 billion airline regard Kelleher as a battler, winner, and their chief inspiration. Besides being one of the smartest lawyers around, colleagues say he combines a keen judgment of people with real sincerity and approachability. Four times a year Kelleher loads baggage, takes tickets, or works as a flight attendant on regularly scheduled trips.

In the early days, Kelleher shepherded tiny Southwest through the minefield of the airline giants. He combines charm and cunning with unshakable vision to create a transformational style of leadership that has garnered the commitment of employees and the respect of competitors.

SOURCE: Edward O. Welles, "Captain Marvel," *Inc.,* January 1992, 44–47.

Not all managers or management experts agree. Several months after taking over as CEO of IBM in 1993, Louis Gerstner, Jr., astonished many reporters at his first press conference by saying that "the last thing IBM needs right now is a vision." Instead, *The Wall Street Journal* reported, he said that "IBM needs textbook blocking and tackling: Lower costs and better market focus in every division."[67]

His statement raised a good question: Can a good corporate mechanic—one who knows how to reorganize, cut costs, and restaff organizations—fix a company without a strategic vision for its future? "[That's] an accountant's answer, not a leader's," said one management consultant. "If he [Gerstner] is trying to get his people to turn the company around and be innovative and fast he has to give them another reason."[68] That reason (this consultant implies) is an inspiring corporate vision. On the other hand, Microsoft Corporation's Bill Gates disagreed. "Being a visionary is trivial," Gates said, "being a CEO is hard. All you have to do to be a visionary is give the usual speech, 'everything will be everywhere, everything will be converged.' Everybody knows that. That's different from being the CEO of a company and seeing where the profits are."[69]

Others argue that vision certainly is important in today's fast-changing environment. It is especially important says one expert where environments are "volatile and carry in them the seeds of rapid and potentially hostile change."[70] Here, "the faster a chief executive officer can conceive a future vision where new products are positioned within emerging product markets the greater is the ability of the firm to control its destiny and affirm a sense of direction."[71] Says another, "One of the first requirements of recovery is the development of that sense of direction and the visualization of the kind of organization people aspire to and markets accommodate, in the longer term."[72] And to that extent visionary, transformational leaders are at the heart of responsive organizations.

SUMMARY

Leadership occurs when one person influences another to work toward some predetermined objective. Good leaders are more important than ever in today's fast-changing environment because they are required to initiate change and provide vision for the organization. The ability of one person to influence another to do something can stem from five types of power: reward, coercive, legitimate, referent, and expert.

Various leadership theories have been proposed to explain what makes some leaders more effective than others. Trait theories of leadership assume that effective leaders have a number of identifiable traits or characteristics that distinguish them from ineffective leaders. Traits that relate most consistently to managerial effectiveness include high self-confidence, energy, initiative, emotional maturity, stress tolerance, and belief in internal locus of control—that leaders must control their own actions.

Behavioral leadership theories focus on what leaders do and how they act, especially when dealing with subordinates. Researchers have distinguished between employee-centered leaders, who focus on the individuality and personal needs of their employees and emphasize good interpersonal relations, and work-centered leaders, who stress production and the technical aspects of the job. Other experts differentiate between close supervision and laissez-faire styles, with general leaders falling somewhere in the middle.

Situational theories of leadership hold that the traits required to be a leader are largely determined by the situation in which the leadership is to be exercised. Fiedler argued that which leadership style is best is influenced by position power, or the degree to which the position enables the leader to get group members to comply; task structure, or the routineness and predictability of the work; and leader-member relations, or the extent to which the leader gets along with workers. According to House's path-goal theory of leadership, the functions of leaders consist largely of increasing personal rewards for subordinates for goal attainment and of making the path to these rewards easier to follow. Normative decision theory, developed by Vroom and Jago, identifies the degree of participation most likely to result in effective decisions in a particular situation. A review of the various leadership theories concludes that the different lines of research are gradually converging.

Leadership also can be viewed as either a transactional or a transformational process. Transactional leadership results from an exchange based on promises of rewards by the leader. Transformational leaders obtain performance beyond expectations by formulating visions and then inspiring their subordinates to pursue them. Transformational leaders are characterized by charisma, inspiration, individual consideration, and intellectual stimulation. They also formulate a vision in order to guide the organization in a changing environment and provide a sense of direction and purpose for employees.

QUESTIONS

■ **FOR REVIEW**

1. Describe the various types of power that can serve as sources of a leader's influence.

2. Explain the reasoning behind trait theories of leadership.

3. Name some typical leader behaviors or styles.

4. Why is a leader's effectiveness influenced by situational factors?

5. How have leadership traits and behavior theories evolved over the last century?

■ FOR DISCUSSION

6. Opinions differ as to what makes a leader great. Which characteristics described in this chapter do you consider most important in the making of a great leader?

7. What type of leadership behavior do you think would be most appropriate when dealing with employees in the following situations: (a) line workers at a computer assembly plant; (b) auditors at the Internal Revenue Service; (c) sales representatives at a toy company? Explain your reasoning.

8. To what degree should leaders allow their subordinates to participate in decision making? Does the answer depend on the situation? Discuss.

9. Do you think transformational leaders are born or made? Discuss your response.

■ FOR ACTION

10. Describe someone whom you consider to be a transformational leader and his or her effect on your life.

11. Think of a person in public life whom you consider to be a great leader. Using sources of information researched at the library, write a leadership profile including traits, styles, vision, and so forth of the person you selected.

12. Assume that a local Fortune 500 company has given your professor the opportunity to select three students to participate in a special management training program that could lead to a lucrative position after graduation. Use the Vroom and Jago decision tree to help the professor determine whether students should be involved in deciding who is selected to participate.

■ FOR FOCUS ON SMALL BUSINESS

13. Describe Meade's style of leadership using the terms defined in the chapter.

14. Based on Fiedler's theory, is Meade's leadership style appropriate for the situation. Explain.

15. Do you think the top executive's leadership style is more important in a small firm than a large firm? Explain your answer.

KEY TERMS

Leadership	Initiating Structure
Power	Position Power
Reward Power	Task Structure
Coercive Power	Leader-member Relations
Legitimate Power	Leader Match Program
Referent Power	Cognitive Resources
Expert Power	Path-goal Theory of Leadership
Trait Theories of Leadership	Normative Decision Theory
Work-centered Leaders	Transactional Leadership
Employee-centered Leaders	Transformational Leadership
Consideration	

CLOSING SOLUTION

ROBERTO GOIZUETA

Goizueta eventually affixed the Coca-Cola name to seven soft drinks. He borrowed money, another taboo, and invested $2 billion to enter the bottling business. He imparted his personal sense of entrepreneurship to managers, encouraging sensible risks, and in the process transformed the company culture from the top down. Goizueta made operations managers cognizant of the cost of money by insisting they adopt his "economic profit" computation, defined as after-tax profits from operations less the cost of funds used to create those earnings. Other easily discernible Goizueta accomplishments at Coke include a market capitalization of $56 billion in 1993, up from $4 billion in 1980, and a ten-year total return to investors that averaged nearly 30 percent, up from less than 1 percent previously. Launched in 1982, Diet Coke is the third biggest soft drink in the world and considered perhaps the most successful consumer product introduction of that decade. Goizueta stumbled somewhat with Columbia Pictures, if you can call it that. He never quite got a handle on moviemaking and had to settle for a $1.1 billion dollar gain after selling in 1989. All told, a good example of successful, visionary leadership on Goizueta's part.

■ QUESTIONS FOR CLOSING SOLUTION

1. How would you describe Goizueta's vision for the company and the sources of his power?

2. In your opinion, is Goizueta a transformational leader? Why or why not?

3. Goizueta has been at the helm at Coca-Cola for more than a decade. Can a case be made for bringing in new leadership, even if the company continues to enjoy success? Discuss your response.

CASE FOR ANALYSIS

MRS. FIELDS, INC.

Debbi Fields was the quintessential hands-on CEO and founder of the cookie company that bears her name. Impromptu visits to stores, where she gave the operation a thorough once over and the manager an interrogation, were commonplace. But she was far from the unreasonable taskmaster type; she simply wanted things done exactly as she envisioned. If they weren't, she usually rolled up her sleeves and did it herself. "Debbi can go into a store after visiting [once]," says husband Randy, "and remember not only a staff person's name but the names of members of her family, or what the telephone bill was at that store two months ago."

Fields emerged as something of a business icon, invoking comparisons ranging from Col. Sanders to Margaret Thatcher. She penned an autobiography—*One Smart Cookie*—gave lectures, and did guest spots on *Hollywood Squares*. Having herself been a homecoming queen and bathing beauty, she became the embodi-

ment of the self-made woman, and an inspiration to anyone who aspired to do it all in their own business.

Just over a decade after its inception in Palo Alto, California, in 1977, Mrs. Fields Cookies totaled 543 stores in six countries. The debt load multiplied, but earnings in 1987 were $18 million on revenues of $104 million, or a very attractive 17.5 percent of sales. The company stock, issued in London on an unlisted exchange, was soaring. But things were not as rosy as they seemed. The break-neck pace had placed too many stores in expensive locations. The onset of the recession made consumers think twice about paying a dollar for a cookie. Most importantly, Fields discovered that trying to singlehandedly stay on top of it all wasn't good for her, or the company.

Her bankers agreed. Closing 97 stores resulted in a $19 million loss in 1988 while Mrs. Fields started learning to delegate. With some help, she came to the realization that her business niche was as that of a specialty retailer. To exploit this position, her existing stores would have to keep the product pipeline flowing with introductions that took advantage of her name. A licensing arrangement with a Marriott Corporation division opened Mrs. Fields stores along freeway interchanges and in airports. Fifty locations are planned through 1995. Mrs. Fields also entered a licensing deal with Ambrosia Chocolate to sell semisweet chocolate chips in supermarkets. The company is also currently opening bakery-café shops featuring soups and sandwiches along with the signature cookies and brownie treats.

Fields's efforts did not prove to be enough to satisfy lenders who forced her out as president and CEO in the first quarter of 1993. The deal forgave $94 million in debt in exchange for 80 percent ownership stake in the company. Although she no longer has a hand in operations, she remains the largest shareholder and retains the position of chairwoman.

SOURCES: Alan Prendergast, "Learning to Let Go," *Working Woman,* January 1992, 42–45; Robin Pogribin, "What Went Wrong with Mrs. Fields?" *Working Woman,* July 1993, 9–11; Harris Collingwood, "Kitchen Too Hot for Mrs. Fields?" *Business Week,* March 1, 1993, 46; Stephen Madden, "Tough Cookies?" *Fortune,* February 13, 1989, 112; and Katherine Weisman, "Succeeding by Failing," *Forbes,* June 25, 1990, 160.

■ QUESTIONS

1. Was Debbi Fields's hands-on management style essential to the company's success or did it contribute to the later problems? Discuss your answer.
2. Using the theories outlined in the chapter, describe Fields's leadership traits and behavior.
3. How could Fields have been more effective in initiating change and providing vision for the company?
4. Would you describe Debbi Fields as a transformational leader?

A CASE IN DIVERSITY

J. BRUCE LLEWELLYN

J. Bruce Llewellyn isn't known for his patience. Although he might personally like some of the Hollywood and sports luminaries who invest with him, he quickly becomes annoyed when their lack of business acumen leads them to ask time-wasting questions. What drives the 62-year-old entrepreneur/businessperson is achievement. And that's something he's amassed plenty of already, earning him the distinction of being the nation's most powerful African-American businessman.

The Philadelphia Coca-Cola Bottling Company was the nation's 15th-largest when Llewellyn took it over in 1983. After identifying and exploiting new routes and with the help of added equipment, sales increased 50 percent over a two-year period and the bottler is now ranked eighth in the country.

Llewellyn regards television as a vast wasteland, but it didn't stop him from snapping up ABC's Buffalo affiliate. He couldn't resist the profit margins that can reach 30 percent. His strategy is to acquire around five or six more stations, in disparate locations, to smooth out profit and loss gyrations as various regions of the country experience economic fluctuations.

Llewellyn's portfolio also includes South Jersey Cable, for which he paid $420 million with a group of partners. He is the CEO for the technically sophisticated operation, which is a leader in pay-per-view programming and serves 170,000 subscribers.

All his business holdings combined have given Llewellyn economic power that is unmatched by other African-American business owners. He has come a long way from his roots as the son of Jamaican immigrants, but Llewellyn never forgot the lessons his father taught him. "You're going to have to work twice as hard to get half as much," his father used to say. But Llewellyn also learned that prejudice could be overcome by education and hard work.

Working harder than everyone else has always been one of Llewellyn's habits. "In Bruce's mind," says attorney J. Burton

Rubin, "the biggest sin is being unprepared." Llewellyn has some other basic rules he strictly adheres to. The job at hand gets all his energy, with no thought given to what comes next. He thinks everyone must be confident enough to believe they can perform as well as anyone else. Like preparation, he's certain that education is vital to becoming successful. "You've got to have the skills," he says.

Llewellyn isn't shy about proffering other opinions. He admits racism still exists and African Americans still face obstacles like glass ceilings and old-boy networks. But he thinks things have improved, and that actions speak volumes. He and his partners borrowed $300 million for the cable company. "We paid it back," he says, "we didn't take the money and run. That establishes a track record and helps all minorities."

As for the long term, Llewellyn thinks African-American businesspeople must stop making distinctions about the customers they serve. "If you don't do that," he says, "you're walking away from 90 percent of the population."

SOURCE: Glen Macnow, "Business Is the Emancipator," *Nation's Business,* September 1990, 41–43.

■ QUESTIONS

1. Based on the facts presented in this case, would you characterize Llewellyn as a transactional or transformational leader?
2. How would you describe Llewellyn's vision for aspiring African-American entrepreneurs?
3. What personality traits do you think have made Llewellyn a good leader?

1. This problem was researched from John Huey, "The World's Best Brand," *Fortune,* May 31, 1993, 44–54; Thomas Moore, "He Put the Kick Back into Coke," *Fortune,* October 26, 1987, 46–52; and Patricia Sellers, "Leaders of the Most Admired Companies," *Fortune,* January 29, 1990, 46–50.

2. Defining leadership is not as simple as it might appear. As Bass points out, for instance, "a definition that identifies a thing for the factory manager or agency head is not necessarily the most useful for the development of broad theory." For some other aspects of the definition of Leadership, see Bernard M. Bass, *Stogdill's Handbook of Leadership* (New York: The Free Press, 1981), 14–16. For another view, see William Paganis, "The Work of the Leader," *Harvard Business Review,* November–December 1992, 118–127.

3. David Nadler and Michael Tushman, "Beyond the Charismatic Leader: Leadership and Organizational Change," *California Management Review,* Winter 1990, 94.

4. Thomas Peters and Robert Waterman, Jr., *In Search of Excellence* (New York: Harper and Row, 1982), 318.

5. Based on Bryan Dumaine, "The Bureaucracy Busters," *Fortune,* June 17, 1991, 42.

6. Dumaine, "The Bureaucracy Busters," 42.

7. For several definitions of power and a discussion of the sources of power as it applies to leadership, see, for example, Bass, *Stogdill's Handbook,* 169–91; and Jeffrey Pfeffer, "Understanding Power in Organizations," *California Management Review,* Winter 1992, 29–49.

8. John French, Jr., and Bertram Raven, "Studies in Social Power" (Ann Arbor, MI: Institute for Social Research, 1959). Reprinted in Henry Tosi and W. Clay Hamner, *Organization Behavior and Management* (Chicago: St. Claire Press, 1977), 442–56.

9. Gary Yukl and C. Falbe, "Influence Tactics in Upward, Downward and Lateral Relations." Unpublished manuscript, State University of New York, Albany; and Gary Yukl, "Managerial Leadership: A Review of Theory and Research," *Journal of Management,* vol. 15, no. 2 (1989), 256.

10. Gary Yukl, *Leadership in Organizations,* 2nd ed. (Englewood Cliffs, NJ: Prentice-Hall, 1989); and Yukl, "Managerial Leadership." See also Antoinette Phillips and Arthur Bedeian, "Leader-Follower Exchange Quality: The Role of Personal and Interpersonal Attributes," *Academy of Management Journal,* August, 1994, 990–1002.

11. Ralph Stogdill, "Historical Trends in Leadership Theory and Research," *Journal of Contemporary Business,* vol. 3, no. 4, Autumn 1974, 1–17.

12. See, for example, Ralph Stogdill, "Personal Factors Associated with Leadership: A Survey of the Leadership of the Literature," *Journal of Psychology,* vol. 25 (1948), 35–71.

13. Bernard Bass, *Stogdill's Handbook of Leadership,* 81.

14. Except as noted, this discussion is based on James Hunt, *Leadership: A New Synthesis* (Newbury Park, CA: Sage Publications, 1991), 106–43.

15. Douglas McClelland, *Human Motivation* (Glenview, IL: Scott Foresman, 1985); and R. Wood and A. Bandura, "Social Cognitive Theory of Organization Management," *Academy of Management Review,* vol. 14 (1989), 361–84.

16. Robert J. House, "Power and Personality in Complex Organizations," L.L. Cummings and B.M. Staw, ed. *Research in Organizational Behavior,* vol. 10 (Greenwich, CT: J.A.I. Press, 1988), 305–57.

17. Henry Mintzberg, *Power in and Around Organizations* (Englewood Cliffs, NJ: Prentice-Hall, 1983).

18. Hunt, *Leadership,* 107.

19. Yukl, "Managerial Leadership," 260.

20. F.E. Berman and J.B. Miner, "Motivation to Manage at the Top Executive Level: A Test of the Hierarchic Role-Motivation Theory," *Personnel Psychology,* vol. 38 (1985), 377–91.

21. For a discussion, see Bass, *Stogdill's Handbook of Leadership,* 289–91.

22. Ibid., 292.

23. Ralph Stogdill and A.E. Coons, "Leader Behavior: Its Description and Measurement" (Columbus: Bureau of Business Research, Ohio State University, 1957).

24. Ralph Stogdill, *Managers, Employees, Organizations* (Columbus: Bureau of Business Research, Ohio State University, 1965).

25. Gary Yukl, "Towards a Behavioral Theory of Leadership," *Organizational Behavior and Human Performance,* vol. 6, no. 4, July 1971, 414–40.

26. Chester Schriesheim, Robert J. House, and Steven Kerr, "Leader Initiating Structure: A Reconciliation of Discrepant Research Results and Some Empirical Tests," *Organizational Behavior and Human Performance,* vol. 15, no. 2, April 1976.

27. Rensis Likert, *New Patterns of Management* (New York: McGraw-Hill, 1961).

28. Ibid.

29. Daniel Katz and Robert Kahn, "Leadership Practices in Relation to Productivity and Morale," in *Group Dynamics,* D. Cartwright and A. Zander, eds. (Evanston, IL: Rowe Peterson, 1960), 550–70.

30. Robert Day and Robert Hamblin, "Some Effects of Close and Punitive Styles of Leadership," *American Journal of Psychology,* vol. 69 (1964), 499–510.

31. See, for example, Nancy Morse, *Satisfactions in the White Collar Job* (Ann Arbor, MI: Survey Research Center, University of Michigan, 1953).

32. Ralph Stogdill, "Personal Factors Associated with Leadership: A Survey of the Literature," *Journal of Psychology,* vol. 25 (1948), 35–71.

33. Robert Tannenbaum and Warren Schmidt, "How to Choose a Leadership Pattern," *Harvard Business Review,* vol. 36, March–April 1958, 95–101.

34. Frederick E. Fiedler, *A Theory of Leadership Effectiveness* (New York: McGraw-Hill, 1967), 147.

35. Ibid.

36. Ibid.

37. Fred Fiedler and Linda Mahar, "The Effectiveness of Contingency Model Training: A Review of the Validation of Leader-Match," *Personnel Psychology,* vol. 32, Spring 1979, 45–62.

38. See, for example, G. Graen, K. Alvares, J.B. Orris, and J.A. Martella, "Contingency Model of Leadership Effectiveness: Antecedent and Evidential Results," *Psychological Bulletin,* vol. 74 (1970), 285–96; and Terrence Mitchell, Anthony Biglan, Gerald Onken, and Frederick Fiedler, "The Contingency Model: Criticisms and Suggestions," *Academy of Management Journal,* vol. 13, no. 3 (September 1970), 253–67.

39. F.E. Fiedler and J.E. Garcia, *New Approaches to Effective Leadership: Cognitive Resources and Organizational Performance* (New York: John Wiley & Sons, 1987); and R.T. Vecchio, "Theoretical and Empirical Examination of Cognitive Resource Theory," *Journal of Applied Psychology,* April 1990, 141–47.

40. Robert J. House and Terrence Mitchell, "Path Goal Theory of Leadership," *Contemporary Business,* vol. 3 (1974), 81–98. See also Abraham Sagie and Meni Koslowsky, "Organizational Attitudes and Behaviors as a Function of Participation in Strategic and Tactical Change Decisions: An Application of Path Goal Theory," *Journal of Organizational Behavior,* January, 1994, 37–48.

41. Gary Yukl, "Managerial Leadership," 263–65.

42. Ibid.

43. For a discussion, see Victor H. Vroom and Arthur Jago, *The New Leadership: Managing Participation in Organizations* (Englewood Cliffs, NJ: Prentice-Hall, 1988) 54–69.

44. Gary Yukl, "Managerial Leadership," 274. For a discussion of the Hersey Blanchard Theory in particular, see John Weitzel and Stephen Green, "A Test of the Situational Leadership Theory," *Personnel Psychology,* Autumn 1990, 579–595.

45. J.M. Burns, *Leadership* (New York: Harper, 1978).

46. For a discussion, see Ronald Deluga, "Relationship of Transformational and Transactional Leadership with Employee Influencing Strategies," *Group and Organization Studies,* vol. 13, no. 4, December 1988, 457–58.

47. Bass, *Stogdill's Handbook,* 20.

48. Joseph Seltzer and Bernard M. Bass, "Transformational Leadership: Beyond Initiation and Consideration," *Journal of Management,* vol. 16, no. 4 (1990), 694.

49. Gary Yukl, "Managerial Leadership," 269.

50. Ibid. See also Jane Howell and Bruce Avolio, "Transformational Leadership, Transactional Leadership, Locus of Control and Support for Innovation: Key Predictors of Consolidated-Business–Unit Performance," *Journal of Applied Psychology,* December 1993, 89–101.

51. N.M. Tichy and M.A. Devanna, *The Transformational Leader* (New York: John Wiley and Sons, 1986).

52. Seltzer and Bass, "Transformational Leadership," 694.

53. Deluga, "Employee Influencing Strategies," 457.

54. Frances Yamarino and Bernard Bass, "Transformational Leadership and Multiple Levels of Analysis," *Human Relations*, vol. 43, no. 10 (1990), 976.

55. Ibid.

56. Bernard M. Bass, *Leadership and Performance Beyond Expectations* (New York: The Free Press, 1985); and Deluga, "Employee Influencing Strategies," 457–58.

57. Deluga, "Employee Influencing Strategies," 457.

58. Ibid.

59. For a review, see Robert Keller, "Transformational Leadership and the Performance of Research and Development Project Groups," *Journal of Management*, vol. 18, no. 3 (1992), 489–501.

60. J.J. Hater and Bernard M. Bass, "Superiors' Evaluations and Subordinates' Perceptions of Transformational and Transactional Leadership," *Journal of Applied Psychology*, vol. 73 (1988), 695–702.

61. J.M. Howell and C.A. Higgins, "Champions of Technological Innovations," *Administrator Science Quarterly*, vol. 35 (1990), 317–41.

62. Bass, *Leadership and Performance Beyond Expectations*.

63. Yamarino and Bass, *Human Relations*, 981.

64. Ibid., 975.

65. Deluga, "Employee Influencing Strategies," 456. For another view, of how leaders impact innovation, see, for example, Susanne Scott and Reginald Bruce, "Determinants of Innovative Behavior: As Path Model of Individual Innovation in the Workplace," *Academy of Management Journal*, June 1994, 580–608.

66. Warren Bennis and Bert Nanus, *Leaders: The Strategies for Taking Charge* (New York: Harper and Row, 1985). Quoted in Andrew Campbell and Sally Yeung, "Case: Mission and Strategic Intent," *Long Range Planning*, vol. 24, no. 4 (1991), 145–47.

67. Michael Miller and Laurie Hays, "Gerstner's Non-Vision for IBM Raises a Management Issue," *The Wall Street Journal*, July 29, 1993, B-1, B-12.

68. Ibid., B-1.

69. Ibid.

70. M.S.S. Lel-Namaki, "Creating a Corporate Vision," *Long Range Planning*, vol. 25, no. 6, 25.

71. Ibid.

72. Ibid.

O R G A N I Z A T I O N A L
C U L T U R E   A N D
S H A R E D   V A L U E S

LEARNING OBJECTIVES

After studying this chapter, you should be able to:

■ Define culture and its importance for an organization.

■ Describe the building blocks of organizational culture, including shared values and group norms.

■ Give examples of how a company's culture can be a force for either good or ill.

■ Explain why shared values are the nucleus of any firm's culture and are often codified in formal statements.

■ Identify ways in which the value systems of high-performing firms focus on supporting customers, employees, and shareholders.

■ Discuss how a firm's leaders create and sustain the corporate culture.

■ Detail how signs, stories, rites, and ceremonials can be used to symbolize a firm's values.

■ Compare and contrast ways in which some cultures support adaptiveness, while others impede it.

■ Review reasons why cultures that help organizations adapt to environmental change are associated with superior performance.

■ Explain why cultures sometimes must be changed.

As the chief executive of Taligent, Joe Guglielmi, a 30-year IBM veteran, has his work cut out for him. Taligent is the software joint venture between IBM and Apple, which the two firms created to develop a new computer operating system to compete with Microsoft/DOS. But as Guglielmi is finding out, the technical challenges are not as tough as the social challenges, given the vastly different cultures that exist between Taligent and its parent firms. ■ While it's changing, IBM historically was known as a relatively stiff and formal company. As Guglielmi puts it, "IBM is a very hierarchical company. Plans go up, are consolidated, and come back down as one worldwide strategy."[1] On the other hand, says Guglielmi, "Apple is a group of empowered individuals doing great things with great technology. Decisions are made at very low levels all the time."[2] ■ The differences don't end there. Apple was known for its laid-back style, a style that manifested itself in the most informal of dress codes. IBM, on the other hand, was known for gray suits and white button-down shirts. Similarly, his Apple employees tended to resist Guglielmi's attempts to measure performance or to monitor their progress. "You can't do this, you can keep track of this or that process," they would tell him. ■ IBM valued formality and hierarchy and a precise procedural way of doing everything (including making decisions). Apple, on the other hand, valued informality and empowerment and letting whoever was best qualified jump in and make the decision. ■ Of course the cultures of IBM and Apple do have much in common: employees in both companies share values like hard work, quality, and going the extra mile for the customer. Both firms also shared a commitment to respecting and supporting their employees. But in total, creating a culture in a firm with employees from two such different cultures was still quite a challenge.[3]

CULTURE DEFINED

WHAT IS ORGANIZATIONAL CULTURE?

ORGANIZATIONAL CULTURE
The interdependent set of values and ways of behaving that are common to the organization and that tend to perpetuate themselves, sometimes over long periods of time.

VALUE
A value is a basic belief about what you should and should not do, and what is important and what is not.

In organizations, **culture** represents the values and ways of behaving that are common to the organization and that tend to perpetuate themselves, sometimes over long periods of time.[4] A **value** is a basic belief about what you should and should not do, and what is important and what is not.

While most experts focus on the central role of shared values in culture, others view culture in broader terms. They include in culture not just values but the underlying beliefs and principles that organizational members share, as well as the employee behaviors that exemplify and reinforce those basic values, beliefs, and principles.[5] Others include "the shared meanings, assumptions, norms and values that govern work-related behavior."[6] Although experts may disagree about precisely how culture is defined, most definitions have this in common: culture reflects the shared values, norms, and behaviors that are characteristic of the society (or the employees of the firm). These shared values and behaviors must be learned. Firms that put mechanisms in place to help employees become acquainted with the company's preferred values and behaviors can thus preserve their organizational cultures even as employees come and go.

WHY CULTURE IS IMPORTANT

Organizational culture is important because a firm's culture reflects its shared values, and it is values which help guide and channel people's behavior. People's values lay out "what ought to be, as distinct from what is."[7] At the United States Military Academy at West Point, the values of "duty, honor, country" are drilled into cadets so as to provide the nation's future military leaders with the moral compasses they will need to carry out their duties in the years ahead. Walmart founder Sam Walton adhered to the values of hard work, honesty, neighborliness, and thrift, and these values became the touchstones of behavior for Walmart's employees as well, and the core of Walmart's culture.

The corollary is also true: to change employees' actions, you usually have to change the organization's culture—its underlying values—too. If Taligent's Joe Guglielmi wants his IBM employees to be more responsive and to make more decisions themselves, he will have to do more than just change the organization chart. He will have to change the shared values that the employees have adopted as their own. The *Chaix & Johnson* vignette provides another example.

BUILDING BLOCKS OF ORGANIZATIONAL CULTURE

Values and norms are two building blocks of organizational culture. Figure 14.1 illustrates this. As you can see, shared values are "important concerns and goals that are shared by most of the people in a group (and) that tend to shape group behavior." Examples might include the fact that the firm's managers "care about customers" and are risk-prone and therefore "like long-term debt." The values themselves are invisible—

CHAIX & JOHNSON

When sales and personnel at the L.A. design firm Chaix & Johnson declined a potentially lethal 25 percent, the remaining 30 employees were understandably distracted. Instead of pulling together to set the firm back on the road to profitability, they were looking over their shoulders and wondering how long they would be around.

Managing director Scott Kohno tried a lot of things to redirect focus. But the most effective change also turned out to be one of the simplest. He abandoned the enclosure of his private office and resituated his desk right in the midst of his subordinates. "It shocked everybody," Kohno says. It made a big difference, too, in Chaix & Johnson's culture.

Interactions on decisions big and small rose exponentially. Everyone's input increased, Kohno's included, and the company was again on the move at a pace not seen in some time. He notes that the energy that used to be wasted concealing or passing problems along now goes into getting them resolved. Private meetings suddenly seem silly. Kohno transformed a no-cost symbolic gesture into just the kind of substance his firm needed and sent an unmistakable signal that openness and teamwork are what Chaix & Johnson are all about.

Scott Kohno, a managing director at Chaix & Johnson, broke down traditional boss-employee barriers by moving his desk into the middle of the work floor. Open office architecture is being experimented with by many large and small companies.

FIGURE 14.1

Culture in an Organization

Shared values and the more-visible group behavior norms are two main building blocks that together represent what we call organizational culture.

SOURCE: John Kotter and James Heskett, *Corporate Culture and Performance* (New York: The Free Press, 1992), 5.

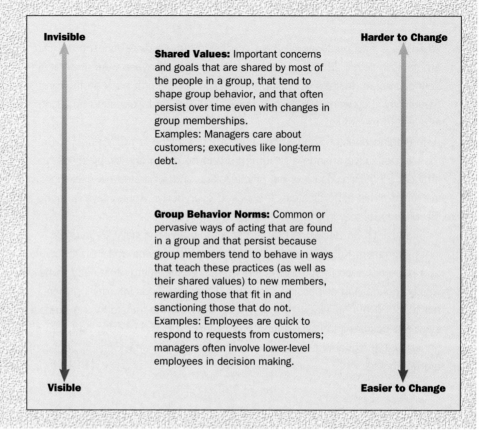

Invisible   Harder to Change

Shared Values: Important concerns and goals that are shared by most of the people in a group, that tend to shape group behavior, and that often persist over time even with changes in group memberships.
Examples: Managers care about customers; executives like long-term debt.

Group Behavior Norms: Common or pervasive ways of acting that are found in a group and that persist because group members tend to behave in ways that teach these practices (as well as their shared values) to new members, rewarding those that fit in and sanctioning those that do not.
Examples: Employees are quick to respond to requests from customers; managers often involve lower-level employees in decision making.

Visible   Easier to Change

people don't wear name tags that state their shared values. Group norms manifest themselves in obvious behaviors and thus are relatively visible says management theorist John Kotter. Group norms are "common or pervasive ways of acting that are found in a group."[8] Examples might include the fact that employees are quick to respond to customers' requests and that managers often involve lower-level employees in decision making.

James G. Hunt says we should delve deeper to understand the origins of a firm's culture. His idea (based on the work of Edgar Schein) is summarized in Figure 14.2. Hunt says studying organizational culture requires one to sift through several layers of culture's building blocks. In layer 1 are cultural artifacts, the obvious signs and symbols that an organization leaves behind such as written rules, office layouts, organizational structure, and dress codes.[9]

Beneath this layer of these obvious manifestations of a company's culture lie *patterns of behavior.* These include the company's ceremonial events, written and spoken comments, and the actual behaviors that the firm's managers and other employees engage in (such as hiding information, politicking, or expressing honest concern when a colleague needs assistance).

In turn these obvious artifacts of culture are a product of the values and beliefs that lie beneath the culture's surface in layer 3. Values and beliefs (such as "the customer is always right," or "duty, honor, and country") are guiding standards that lay out "what ought to be, as distinct from what is."[10]

Management's stated values and beliefs sometimes differ from what the managers really value and believe. If so, this will show up in their actual behaviors. In other

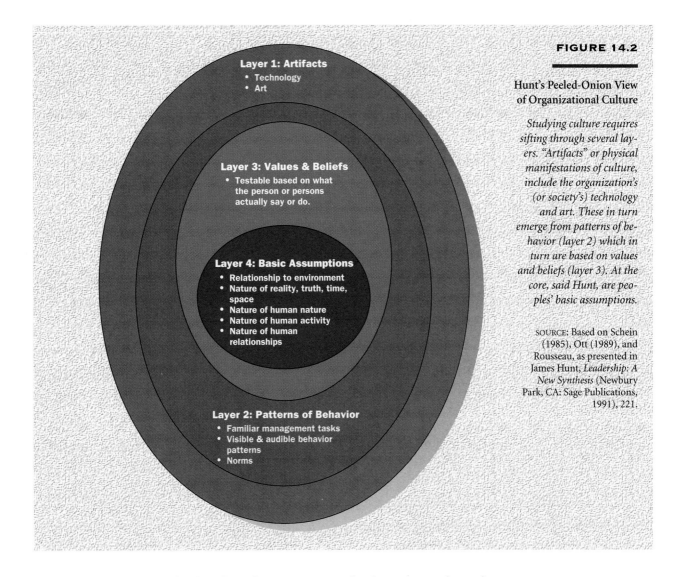

FIGURE 14.2

Hunt's Peeled-Onion View of Organizational Culture

Studying culture requires sifting through several layers. "Artifacts" or physical manifestations of culture, include the organization's (or society's) technology and art. These in turn emerge from patterns of behavior (layer 2) which in turn are based on values and beliefs (layer 3). At the core, said Hunt, are peoples' basic assumptions.

SOURCE: Based on Schein (1985), Ott (1989), and Rousseau, as presented in James Hunt, *Leadership: A New Synthesis* (Newbury Park, CA: Sage Publications, 1991), 221.

words, you can infer a firm's values from the actions its people take. For example, Fred Smith, the founder and chairman of Federal Express, has said that many firms say they believe in respecting their employees and putting their people first.[11] However, in many firms it is not what managers say they believe but how they actually behave—insisting on time clocks, routinely downsizing at the first indications of an economic down turn, and so on—that make it clear where their values really lie.

Therefore, management's basic assumptions are really at the core of a firm's culture, says Hunt. A selection of illustrative assumptions is presented in Figure 14.3. For example, is top management's assumption about human nature that people are inherently good or bad? Such assumptions, in turn, influence the emergent values about, for instance, what top management should do about giving employees more control over their own day to day activities.

EXAMPLE OF ORGANIZATIONAL CULTURE

The corporate culture of Procter & Gamble provides a good example. It reflects what management theorist Daniel Denison calls the firm's legendary emphasis on "thoroughness, market-testing, and ethical behavior," values that are transmitted to new

FIGURE 14.3

Five Basic Types of Assumptions

Assumptions mold values, which in turn mold behavior and the physical manifestations of a person's behavior, like policies and rules.

SOURCE: Based on Schein (1983), 16. As presented in James Hunt, *Leadership: A New Synthesis* (Newbury Park, CA: Sage Publications, 1991), 223.

---

1. Organization's Relationship to Environment. Extent to which key organizational members see this relationship as one of dominance, submission, harmonizing, finding an appropriate niche, and the like.

2. Nature of Reality, Truth, Time, Space. The linguistic and behavioral rules that define what is real, and what is not, what is "fact," how truth ultimately is to be determined, and whether truth is "revealed" or "discovered"; basic concepts of time as linear or cyclical, monochronic (one kind only) or polychronic (several different kinds); basic concepts such as space as limited or indefinite and property as communal or individual; etc.

3. Nature of Human Nature. What does it mean to be "human," and what attributes are assumed to be intrinsic or ultimate? Is human nature evil, good or neutral? Are human beings perfectible? Is theory X or Y more appropriate?

4. Nature of Human Activity. What is the "right" thing for humans to do, on the basis of the above assumptions; should they be active, passive, self-developmental, fatalistic, or what? What is work and what is play?

5. Nature of Human Relationships. What is assumed to be the "right" way for individuals to relate to each other, to distribute power and love? Is life cooperative or competitive; individualistic, group, collaborative, or communal; based on traditional lineal authority, law, or what?

---

employees through the firm's recruitment, socialization, and internal promotion processes.[12] To foster its values P&G also reportedly combines internal competition and promotion from within in a process that results in a sort of tournament that determines the victors or leaders of the firm.[13]

Procter & Gamble has a strong corporate culture in that its underlying values exert a powerful influence on all P&G employees. Basic elements of its culture can be traced back to the firm's founders, William Procter and James Gamble. They founded P&G in Cincinnati in 1837 with the mission of producing relatively inexpensive household products that were technically superior to the competition, quickly consumed, and an integral part of their customer's lifestyle.[14] The founders' intention was to "foster growth in an orderly manner, to reflect the standards set by the founders, and to plan and prepare for the future."[15]

In addition to an emphasis on thoroughness, market testing, and ethical behavior, several other underlying values constitute the P&G culture. One is a system in which, according to one expert, "individual identity is always minimized and sometimes lost." A new recruit soon learns to say "we" instead of "I."[16] One P&G manager was quoted as saying, "Everyone at P&G is like a hand in a bucket of water—when the hand is removed, the water closes in and there is no trace."[17]

The founders' emphasis on orderly growth also manifests itself in "tremendous conformity."[18] As one manager described it, "conform and you succeed; question and you are gone." In turn, this conformity results in precisely the thoroughness and methodical approach desired by the company's founders. Its result, according to one past chairman, is a "consistency of principles and policy that gives us direction, thoroughness, and self-discipline."[19]

An emphasis on research is also part and parcel of P&G's culture. Research is an integral part of P&G's thoroughness, as well as a product of its aim of "removing personal judgment from the equation" by testing and continually retesting all of its products. P&G's aim is to produce products that consistently win in consumer blind tests.

The emphasis on written rather than oral communication is another manifestation of the firm's stress on the value of thoroughness. All significant events are preserved in writing and all records can be re-created at any point. Managers are taught to condense their comments to fit a one-page format. New P&G recruits reportedly "tell horror stories" about their first memos being ripped to shreds by the boss.[20]

Secrecy is a final element of P&G's culture. As far back as the late 1800s, the firm had tried to stop giving detailed financial reports to its stockholders; as recently as the late 1980s, reports confirm that financial information was still very closely held and that P&G "maintains a mistrust of outsiders who are overly curious about P&G."[21] New employees are instructed not to talk about the company to outsiders.

As is usually the case, Procter & Gamble's culture reflects and is sustained by concrete management practices. Graduates are recruited and placed in highly competitive situations, and those who cannot learn the system are quickly weeded out, with the remainder enjoying the benefits of promotion from within. As a result, no one reaches middle management without five to ten years of very close scrutiny and training. This in turn creates what one researcher called "a homogeneous leadership group with an enormous amount of common experience and strong set of shared assumptions."[22]

Other management practices contribute to creating and sustaining P&G's culture. New recruits may assume major responsibility for projects almost immediately, but the authority for most big decisions is made far-up the chain of command, usually by committees of managers. Nearly everything must be approved through the memo process. Stories abound that reinforce this system; one regards the decision on the color of the Folger's coffee lid, supposedly made by the CEO after four years of extensive market testing.[23] The internal competitive system is fostered by the brand management system at P&G. Brands compete for internal resources, have their own advertising and marketing, and act as independent cost centers. The extensive use of memos, the continual rechecking of each other's work, and the rigid time line for promotions also contribute to (and reflect) P&G's strong corporate culture.

In summary, corporate culture represents a firm's shared values and characteristic behaviors. These shared values often have their roots with the firm's founders and subsequent top executives, whose behaviors and policies then help to mold and sustain the firm's culture. The firm's shared values then manifest themselves in characteristic behaviors—such as thorough research and development at P&G.

UNHEALTHY ORGANIZATIONAL CULTURE

A company's culture can be a force for good or for ill. Procter & Gamble's strong and largely healthy culture has contributed to making P&G a highly competitive firm, one that dominates its industry. Yet, in other firms, unhealthy corporate cultures have led to much less satisfactory results. Xerox is reportedly a case in point. According to several reports, Xerox was long known for its social responsibility and innovation, and for its founders' principles of ". . . faith in people, concern for customers, and economic power through innovation, marketing, patents and world-wide presence."[24]

By the 1970s, however, and into the early 1980s when a turnaround began, Xerox's culture became unhealthy in terms of its effects on the company. The firm reportedly became increasingly insular and "most of the decisions (were) made around issues of turf, career advancement and those kinds of things."[25] Gradually, "the culture of Xerox also became somewhat intolerant of initiatives and leadership from the ranks . . . experimentation was often discouraged, and error was not tolerated well."[26]

Xerox is reportedly recovering, but still damage was done. Clearly, unhealthy corporate cultures can undermine a firm's effectiveness. During the decades in which the firm's culture was insular and anti-innovative, Xerox's market share lead in duplicating machines dropped dramatically.

CAUSES OF UNHEALTHY CULTURES   It is therefore useful to review the origins of unhealthy organizational cultures. In Figure 14.4, Professors John Kotter and James Heskett summarize these origins. As illustrated, a firm's initial success creates pressure to manage the growing firm and misplaced self-confidence on the part of the managers that they are unbeatable. The need to manage success drives the firm to permit an administrative bureaucracy to develop in which shuffling papers and getting the work done becomes more important than providing visionary direction for the firm. As a result, a strong but arrogant corporate culture develops as these managers

FIGURE 14.4

The Origins of Unhealthy Corporate Cultures

Success can lead to unhealthy, unresponsive organizational cultures if the pressure causes management to focus on building the internal bureaucracy rather than on serving the customer.

SOURCE: John Kotter and James Heskett, *Corporate Culture and Performance* (New York: The Free Press, 1992), 73.

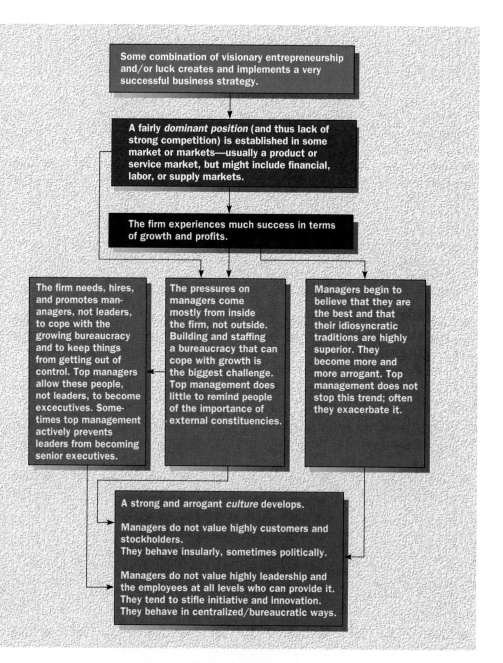

concentrate on the internal mechanisms of the firm rather than on the company's customers or stockholders. Gradually, the company's forward motion falters.

THE CENTRAL ROLE OF SHARED VALUES

CREATING THE CORE VALUE STATEMENT

Shared values are the nucleus of any firm's culture. In many firms, the core values are codified in formal statements. Figure 14.5 (as reproduced from Figure 3.4) summarizes the core values or credo of the Johnson & Johnson Company. These values include "we believe our first responsibility is to the doctors, nurses, and patients, to mothers and all others who use our products and services. In meeting their needs, everything we do must be of high quality."[27]

As you probably recall, Johnson & Johnson faced a crisis several years ago when someone tampered with its Tylenol capsules, and the firm used its values to guide it out of the crisis. According to one manager, "crisis planning did not see us through the tragedy nearly so much as the sound business management philosophy that is embodied in our credo. It was the credo that prompted the decisions that enabled us to make the right early decisions."[28] In five months, the firm had produced a new tamper-resistant Tylenol product and regained 70 percent of its recent market share; within several years, its market share was fully restored.

CREATING VALUES FOR THREE CONSTITUENCIES

Professors John Kotter and James Heskett found that high-performing firms actually had shared values that supported three key constituencies: customers, employees, and shareholders. They found that the firms that have been the most successful at adapting to change did not just concentrate on or develop shared values for customers, or for employees, or stockholders alone. Instead, the most successful firms adhere to values regarding the firm's basic posture with respect to all three constituencies. Albertson's Markets, for instance, had a "corporate creed" stating the firm's responsibility to customers, employees, community, shareholders and society. American Airlines' commitment to all of its constituencies—stockholders, passengers, and employees alike—is part of its statement of "corporate vision." Kotter and Heskett conclude:

> When managers do not care about all three key constituencies and about leadership initiatives throughout the management hierarchy, the net results always seem to be less effective adaptation. This is perhaps most obvious when a high concern for customers and/or leadership is lacking. But this is also true in a firm with a strong customer orientation but without much concern for employees or stockholders.[29]

CREATING AND SUSTAINING CORPORATE CULTURE

Let us now examine how firms create and sustain their corporate culture.

THE ROLE OF LEADERSHIP

The firm's leaders generally play a major role in creating and sustaining any firms culture, through the actions they take, the comments they make, and the visions they espouse.

FIGURE 14.5

The Johnson & Johnson Credo

Core values like these are at the heart of Johnson & Johnson's culture.

SOURCE: "Corporate Ethics: A Prime Business Asset," *The Business Roundtable*, February 1988.

OUR CREDO

- We believe our first responsibility is to the doctors, nurses and patients, to mothers and all others who use our products and services.
- In meeting their needs everything we do must be of high quality.
- We must constantly strive to reduce our costs in order to maintain reasonable prices.
- Customers' orders must be serviced promptly and accurately.
- Our suppliers and distributors must have an opportunity to make a fair profit.
- We are responsible to our employees, the men and women who work with us throughout the world.
- Everyone must be considered as an individual.
- We must respect their dignity and recognize their merit.
- They must have a sense of security in their jobs.
- Compensation must be fair and adequate, and working conditions clean, orderly and safe.
- Employees must feel free to make suggestions and complaints.
- There must be equal opportunity for employment, development and advancement for those qualified.
- We must provide competent management, and their actions must be just and ethical.
- We are responsible to the communities in which we live and work and to the world community as well.
- We must be good citizens—support good works and charities and bear our fair share of taxes.
- We must encourage civic improvements and better health and education.
- We must maintain in good order the property we are privileged to use, protecting the environment and natural resources.
- Our final responsibility is to our stockholders.
- Business must make a sound profit.
- We must experiment with new ideas.
- Research must be carried on, innovative programs developed and mistakes paid for.
- New equipment must be purchased, new facilities provided and new products launched.
- Reserves must be created to provide for adverse times.
- When we operate according to these principles the stockholders should realize a fair return.

The process of molding shared values (and thus culture) usually begins with the company's founders. As theorist Edgar Schein has said:

> By far the most important for cultural beginnings is the impact of founders. Founders not only choose the basic mission and the environmental context in which the new group will operate, but they choose the group members and bias the original responses that the group makes in its efforts to succeed in its environment and to integrate itself.[30]

The Walmart discount chain is a good example. As Harry Cunningham (who founded competitor Kmart stores while CEO of SS Kresge Company) put it:

> Sam's establishment of a Wal-Mart culture throughout the company was the key to the whole thing. It's just incomparable. He is the greatest businessman of this century.[31]

The foundations of Walmart's values can be traced to Sam Walton's personal guiding values of "hard work, honesty, neighborliness, and thrift."[32] Under Walton's leadership, for example, the firm developed an almost religious zeal for doing things efficiently, and working hard became a requirement for getting ahead. Walmart stressed honesty (for instance in identifying the sources of its merchandise), and its neighborliness was epitomized by the greeters at its doors. The entire thrust of its strategy—from low prices and locations away from the center of town to satellite-aided distribution—was aimed at making "Walmart" synonymous with "thrift." Walton also worked hard to underscore his company's emphasis on thrift by downplaying his own billionaire's status: until the day he died he drove an old pickup truck, a fact which he explained with the rhetorical question "If I drove a Rolls Royce, what would I do with my dog?" He also worked hard to make sure other Walmart employees (many of whom had become millionaires on company stock) did not flaunt their wealth. As he said, "maybe it's none of my business, but I have done everything I can to discourage our folks from getting too extravagant with their homes, their meals and their lifestyles."[33]

But there was more to Walmart culture than just hard work, honesty, neighborliness, and thrift. Sam Walton wanted to create a culture of enthusiasm, fun, and unpredictability and how he did it says a lot about how cultures are formed. Walton would fly from store to store in his own plane leading Walmart's employees in their morning cheer ("Give me a W! Give me an A! Give me an L!" and so on). In 1984, Walton lost a bet to President David Glass and had to pay up by donning a grass skirt and doing the hula on Wall Street. Store managers became known for what Walton called "crazy kinds of things." For example, the Nairbury, Nebraska, store, had a "precision shopping cart drill team" that marched in local parades. The members all wore Walmart's smocks and pushed their carts through a routine of whirls, twists, and circles.[34]

THE ROLE OF MANAGEMENT PRACTICES

James G. Hunt has described the process through which founders like Sam Walton create and sustain their companies' cultures. The founders' values, beliefs, and basic ideas on how to succeed merge into a vision of what the firm should be and is then translated into specific management practices. One crucial practice is the founder's tendency to *hire* people whose values, ideas, and beliefs are similar to his or her own. These "right-type" people then move into management positions and attract new generations of right-type people, who in turn become socialized into the firm's way of doing things.

The *socialization process* itself, says Hunt, consists of numerous signs, symbols, and rituals through which the firm's leaders express the firm's cherished values. Walton's displeasure with outward signs of affluence, and his encouragement of slightly "crazy" activities like the precision shopping carts drill team are examples of such outward signs, symbols, and rituals.

Notice that *transformational leadership* (discussed in Chapter 13) also plays a role in creating and sustaining a company's culture. For example, when he took over GE in 1981, Jack E. Welch saw the need to make GE more adaptive by creating a leaner and more responsive organization. He knew he had to change GE's culture. Welch's strategic vision of GE emphasized such values as leanness, agility, creativity, leadership, candor/openness, and simplicity. These characteristics spawned the values that would eventually form the foundation of the new GE.[35]

USE SIGNS, SYMBOLS, STORIES, RITES, AND CEREMONIALS At Saturn Corporation—a firm known for its strong culture of quality, teamwork, and

Founders Ben Cohen (left) and Jerry Greenfield (right) of Ben and Jerry's have gone out of their way to create a corporate culture that emphasizes doing good while doing well financially. Having fun and giving back to the community are tenets of the corporate mission.

SIGNS AND SYMBOLS
Used throughout strong culture firms to create and sustain the company's culture.

STORIES
Used widely in organizations to illustrate important company values.

RITES AND CEREMONIALS
Used to symbolize the firm's values and to help convert employees to these values.

respect for the individual—one of the firm's top managers had this to say about company culture:

> Creating a value system that encourages the kind of behavior you want is not enough. The challenge is then to engage in those practices that symbolize those values [which] tell people what is really O.K. to do and what not [to do]. Actions, in other words, speak much more loudly than words.[36]

Signs, symbols, stories, rites, and ceremonials are examples of such actions.

Signs and **symbols** are used throughout strong-culture firms to create and sustain the companies' cultures. At Ben and Jerry's, for instance, the firm has a "joy gang" as a concrete symbol of the firm's values (values that emphasize charity, fun, and goodwill toward fellow workers). The joy gang is a voluntary group that meets once or twice a week to create new ways to inject fun into what the Ben and Jerry's people do, often by giving out "joy grams," which are "five hundred quick, easy, no-strings attached dollars for long term improvements to your work area."[37] Sam Walton's hula dance on Wall Street is another example of a culture-building symbol.

Stories illustrating important company values are also widely used in all of these firms. Thus at Procter & Gamble

> There are many stories about relatively trivial decisions going all the way to the top of the company. One example is the decision regarding the color of the lid on Folger's coffee, a decision supposedly made by the CEO.[38]

At IBM, stories also abound that support the company culture, such as stories about IBM salespeople who took dramatic steps (such as driving all night through snow storms) to get needed parts to the company's customers.

Rites and **ceremonials** are also used to symbolize the firm's values and to help convert employees to these values. At J.C. Penney (where loyalty and tradition are core values) new management employees are inducted at ritualistic conferences into the "Penney Partnership." Here, they vow to commit to the firm's ideology as embodied in its statement of core values. Each inductee solemnly swears allegiance to these values and then receives his or her "H.C.S.C. lapel pin." These letters symbolize Penney's basic values of honor, confidence, service, and cooperation.

Tom Peters and Robert Waterman, in their book *In Search of Excellence,* emphasize that it is the leader's responsibility to create strong cultures by shaping norms, instilling beliefs, inculcating values, and generating emotions.[39] Leaders do this by establishing management practices that embody and symbolize the firm's core values and specifically by using symbols, stories, rites, and ceremonials. The *Rosenbluth Travel* vignette provides an example.

ADAPTIVE CULTURES

COMPANY CULTURE AND THE RESPONSIVE ORGANIZATION

In his book *Corporate Culture and Organizational Effectiveness,* Daniel Denison writes that three aspects of responsiveness are likely to impact an organization's effectiveness: its ability to perceive and respond to the firm's external environment in general and its customers and competitors in particular; the firm's ability to respond to internal customers (and in particular cordial and free-flowing communications between departments and divisions); and the ability to restructure and change behaviors and processes to better allow the organization to adapt. Each of these three aspects of

ROSENBLUTH TRAVEL

Rosenbluth Travel thinks first-impressions can be lasting. That's why the company spends a lot of time from day one getting a few basic core values across to new hires. An innovative, two-day orientation starts employees on the right track.

What Rosenbluth's is about and what differentiates the travel agency—elegant customer service—is stressed first. Sincerity is the linchpin of the company slogan, "Live the Spirit." Even though it may sound empty, employees learn that this core value is strictly upheld by ensuring all company messages are both consistent and true. Finally, company president and CEO Hal Rosenbluth feels strongly that time and energy invested in his staff reaps enhanced service output. He makes new employees the focal point of a formal tea party at the conclusion of the familiarization process, and he keeps a handle on the sentiments of his staff through his twice-yearly Happiness Barometer survey. Information gleaned from this survey has led to a number of useful improvements.

All of this has resulted in Rosenbluth Travel gaining an excellent reputation. For one thing, in one recent year the company received 21,000 job applications for 800 openings.

SOURCE: Nancy K. Austin, "Wacky Management Ideas That Work," *Working Women,* November 1991, 42–44; and Ellyn E. Spraging, "First Impressions," *Inc.,* December 1991, 157.

A formal tea at Rosenbluth Travel is a ritual which follows orientation for new employees. Though seemingly off-beat, Rosenbluth's creative ways of dealing with both customers and employees have paid off for the company.

responsiveness are in turn supported (or not supported) by the firm's underlying culture and shared values. In other words, some cultures support responsiveness while others may impede it.[40] Corporate culture—the values and beliefs a firm's employees share—affects all aspects of organizational responsiveness in two main ways.

SOME VALUES SUPPORT RESPONSIVENESS   First, some values support responsiveness better than do others. For example, the apparent emphasis on the values of politicking and on hampering internal communications at Xerox hampered the firm's ability to make a coordinated and rapid response to its competitors' moves. At the other extreme, GE's emphasis on the values of agility and candor/openness help keep interdepartmental lines of communication open and emphasize the value of fast decision making in a rapidly changing world. Thus, some shared values encourage and facilitate responsiveness, while others may hamper it.

VALUES AS GUIDES   The firm's shared values can also boost responsiveness by providing a common set of standards that all employees can use as guides. Consider an example described by Tom Burns and G.M. Stalker, in their book *The Management of Innovation*. They found several "organic" organizations that were structured to respond to rapidly changing technical, market, and competitive conditions. These electronics firms were organized to react to unpredictable, unexpected events and make fast, on-the-spot decisions. Such shared values were particularly important here, say Burns and Stalker, since they helped guide empowered employees who had to make their own fast on-the-spot decisions:

> Such concerns have to rely on the development of a "common culture" of a dependably constant set of shared beliefs about the common interest of the working community and about the standards and criteria used in it to judge achievement, individual contributions, expertise, and other matters by which a person or a combination of people are evaluated. A system of shared beliefs of this kind is expressed and visible in a code of conduct, a way of dealing with other people. This code of conduct is, in fact, the first sign to the outsider of the presence of a management system appropriate to changing conditions.[41]

Peters and Waterman discovered how a set of shared values can provide the guidelines employees use to keep themselves on track. Excellent firms' basic beliefs and values, say Peters and Waterman, provided the glue these firms needed to stay "tight but loose": they were loose in terms of letting everyone have a great deal of authority for decisions and not relying on a rigid, hierarchical decision-making process, so that decisions could be spontaneous and the firms responsive. Yet such looseness required a "tightness" on the part of employees: top management could delegate considerable authority, *as long as it knew the employees' decisions would be consistent with the firm's basic values* (such as P&G's emphasis on quality, integrity, and thoroughness). As a result, the best employees in such responsive firms "are those who have internalized the organization's goals and values—its culture—into their cognitive and effective make-up and therefore no longer require strict and rigid external control."[42]

A strong culture, in other words, makes responsiveness possible by enabling the firm to depend on employees' self-control. Sociologist Amitai Etzioni has said that while mechanistic organizations rely on traditional control systems like rules and procedures, responsive organizations depend more on "normative control." To Etzioni, normative control meant eliciting and directing the required efforts of an organization's members by controlling the underlying values, thoughts, beliefs, and feelings that guide their actions. As one expert put it:

> Under normative controls, members act in the best interest of a company not because they are physically coerced, nor purely from an instrumental concern with economic rewards and sanctions. It is not just their behaviors and activities that are specified, evaluated and

rewarded or punished. Rather, they are driven by internal commitment, strong identification with company goals, [and] intrinsic satisfaction from work.[43]

In other words, employee behavior is guided by a strong set of shared values, beliefs, and traditions—a strong culture.

THE NATURE OF RESPONSIVE CULTURES

Based on their study of corporate culture, John Kotter and James Heskett conclude that "only cultures that can help organizations anticipate and adapt to environmental change will be associated with superior performance over long periods of time."[44]

They found that the values and traditions of adaptive cultures emphasize a risk-taking, trusting, and proactive approach to life, as well as an emphasis on having employees actively support one another's efforts to identify all problems and implement workable solutions.[45] On the other hand, nonadaptive cultures are usually bureaucratic: employees are reactive and quick to blame, and they are risk averse and not very creative. Similarly, communications do not flow quickly and easily throughout the organization, in part because negative values such as "guard your turf" are emphasized over "get the job done."

Kotter and Heskett therefore say the message from their data is clear:

> In the firms with more adaptive cultures, the cultural ideal is that managers, throughout the hierarchy, should provide leadership to initiate change in strategies and tactics whenever necessary to satisfy the legitimate interest of not just stockholders, or customers, or employees but all three. In less adaptive cultures, the norm is that managers behave cautiously and politically to protect or advance themselves, their product, or their immediate work groups.[46]

The differences between adaptive and unadaptive corporate cultures are summarized in Figure 14.6. As you can see, core values in adaptive, responsive cultures emphasize caring deeply about customers, stockholders, and employees and also highly

	Adaptive Corporate Cultures	Unadaptive Corporate Cultures
Core Values	Most managers care deeply about customers, stockholders, and employees. They also strongly value people and processes that can create useful change (e.g., leadership up and down the management hierarchy)	Most managers care mainly about themselves, their immediate work group, or some product (or technology) associated with that work group. They value the orderly and risk-reducing management process much more highly than leadership initiatives.
Common Behavior	Managers pay close attention to all their constituencies, especially customers, and initiate change when needed to serve their legitimate interests, even if that entails taking some risks.	Managers tend to behave somewhat insularly, politically, and bureaucratically. As a result, they do not change their strategies quickly to adjust to or take advantage of changes in their business environments

FIGURE 14.6

Characteristics of Adaptive Versus Unadaptive Corporate Cultures

SOURCE: John Kotter and James Heskett, *Corporate Culture and Performance* (New York: The Free Press, 1992), 51.

valuing people and the processes that can create useful change. As a result, common behaviors almost always exemplify adaptive cultures: managers make it clear by their actions that they pay close attention to all three constituencies (employees, stockholders, and customers), and they willingly initiate change when needed, even if doing so entails taking some risks. Thus, under the (transformational) leadership of Chairman Bob Crandall, American Airlines, faced with a drastic change in its industry, made hundreds of changes in the early 1980s.[47] For example, "the firm cut costs, created hubs, altered routes, re-wrote labor contracts, grounded a whole fleet of 707s, invented frequent flyer programs, automated processes, and consolidated functions and facilities.[48] In other words, openness and change are encouraged.

Of course, adaptive cultures do not create changes like these, they just allow and encourage them to occur. The shared values inspire the employees to be open to change, to support each other, and to focus on the other values (like quality, teamwork, or thoroughness) that can make the company great. The firm is then positioned to implement the changes required for it to survive and thrive. The *Ryder International* vignette shows how one small firm applies these ideas.

CHANGING ORGANIZATIONAL CULTURES

WHEN CULTURES MUST BE CHANGED

At the giant Dutch firm Phillips Electronics, CEO Jan Timmer thought he had done most of what was needed to make his company more responsive. Taking over in 1990, Timmer reportedly eliminated 45,000 jobs, consolidated and sold off businesses, and put his firm on the offensive with innovative new consumer electronic products. Yet, a recent drop in earnings and delays in launching new products had made it clear that Europe's last big integrated electronics group wasn't changing fast enough. With all his cuts, the firm was reportedly slow moving and bureaucratic. The digital compact cas-

Frank Ryder, founder of Ryder International, wanted his company to be a reflection of his personal values and interests. His main hobby—building and flying airplanes—has turned into another business for him.

RYDER INTERNATIONAL

There's not much that could be called conventional about Frank Ryder or his product-development company Ryder International of Arab, Alabama. Ryder and his 300 employees generate $25 million a year in revenues by moving fast and largely ignoring all the rules. But even though almost every aspect of the operation is out of the ordinary, everything has an underlying purpose, from the layout of the company headquarters to the way employees are expected to tackle their jobs.

Ryder International designs and develops all kinds of products but specializes in medical and health-care products. It targets company managers in need who don't have a year or more to wait on an in-house design. Ryder International can usually deliver a prototype in a couple of weeks. That kind of speed comes from a structure devoid of hierarchical layers. "The people here have the authority to act without going through a lot of red tape and paperwork," says CEO and president Dick Rabenau. Lunchtime napkin designs often get rushed straight to the model builder.

Frank Ryder made his company a reflection of his own value system. "Everyone should enjoy what they do," he says. The atmosphere at the 190-acre headquarters is family-like. Picnic areas dot grounds connected by 1.5 miles of bike paths. An exercise room is available for workouts. The more leisurely inclined can fish in one of seven stocked lakes, but they have to throw the catch back. Ryder says the fish are for the kids, and he doesn't want any disappointments. "Every time the little tykes go fishing here, I want them to be able to catch a big one."

By eliminating the typical confines of a restrictive corporate culture, Ryder has succeeded in maximizing the creative energies of every employee. In turn, he has made the strength of his company greater than the sum of its parts, and created a highly responsive organization.

SOURCE: David R. Altany, "Frank Ryder: Inventor, Entrepreneur, Dreamer," *Industry Week*, May 3, 1993, 31–33.

sette that should have been introduced in mid-1992 was months behind schedule and getting mixed reviews; others were talking about abandoning Phillips' satellite-based television system in favor of another one (developed in the United States), which can send signals by cable as well as by satellite.

The bottom line seems to be that CEO Timmer may not have made his company nimble enough, fast enough. "You just can't change a deep-rooted corporate culture in one or two years," he says. "It takes at least five years or longer." Whether he's got the five years, only time will tell.[49]

Leaders like Timmer have probably always had to grapple with the need for cultural change, but such change is particularly prevalent during today's chaotic times. In the United States, for instance, deregulation means that airlines had to become lean and adaptive almost overnight; one of the distinguishing differences between successful firms like American and those that failed was probably the latter's inability to change their cultures fast enough. Thus the highly politicized, antiunion, bureaucratic culture at Eastern was probably one of the factors that hampered the firm's success.

Various events can force a firm to change its culture.[50] A dramatic crisis, such as deregulation or the introduction of an entirely new technology by a competitor, can force the firm's leaders to confront the need for cultural change. Turnover in top management and other levels provides the firm with an opportunity for new values and beliefs to be introduced. The firm's stage in its organizational life cycle—from rapid growth to maturity to decline, for instance—can also create the need for cultural change. Thus, the laid-back, loose, and somewhat crazy culture that defined Apple Computers during its formative years gradually gave way to a more formal, restricted, and hierarchical way of doing things as the computer business matured. Management needs to be cognizant of such events and of the need to watch for them.

EXAMPLES OF CULTURAL CHANGE

In our rapidly changing world, many companies have had to implement major cultural changes. These firms range from General Electric to Nissan, American Express, Bankers Trust, and British Airways.[51]

Two experts conclude that regardless of the industry, "the single most visible factor that distinguishes major cultural changes that succeed from those that failed was competent leadership at the top."[52] Here leaders "knew how to produce change and were willing to do just that.[53] In each instance the leader

> created a team that established a new vision and set of strategies for achieving that vision. Each new leader succeeded in persuading important groups and individuals in the firm to commit themselves to that new direction and to energize the personnel sufficiently to make it happen, despite all obstacles. Ultimately, hundreds (or even thousands) of people helped to make all the changes in strategies, product, structures, policies, personnel and (eventually) culture. But often, just one or two people seemed to have been essential in getting the process started.[54]

GENERAL ELECTRIC   The transformation of General Electric in the 1980s from "a sluggish, diverse set of businesses into a lean, cohesive market leader" is a good example of cultural change, one driven by the need to change the company's strategy.[55] The chief strategist and transformational leader in this case was Chairman John Welch, Jr.. Welch spent the early 1980s downsizing the firm, a process that, for better or worse, left him with the nickname "Neutron Jack" (after the neutron bomb, which destroys the people but leaves the equipment and hardware standing). Next, according to Welch, one of his first steps in establishing a new GE culture was to create a GE value statement. Welch then turned to the task of living each of these values by instituting management practices that epitomized them. He pushed authority down while fostering teamwork by promoting values like candor and trust. He instituted a training center in Crotonville, New York, that helps turn GE's managers into people who thrive on turmoil. He pushes hard to make GE managers "win-aholics," strong competitors who are driven to make their divisions number 1 or 2 in their industries.[56] He also instituted hundreds of "work-out" sessions aimed at encouraging candor and openness throughout the firm.

DIGITAL EQUIPMENT CORPORATION   Vice-President Willow Shire had to change her division's culture after the computer maker ousted its CEO Ken Olsen. Bob Pommer, his replacement, quickly restructured the firm around nine new businesses (including Shire's) and began demanding improved performance.[57]

As a result, Shire reportedly spends much of her time purging her division's old corporate culture:

We are in the process of a cultural revolution. . . . First we have to get rid of that old engineering idea: build a good box, and they will come. And we have to focus on accountability. In the past, if you were terribly charming and quite influential, you could pretend that you were successful. But we didn't focus on the customer, and we paid no attention to the underlying profitability of what we were doing.[58]

Those old values were purged thanks to Shire's actions. For example, she learned that one of her salespeople had been selling disk drives to a hospital but had not met the hospital's head in three years. She insisted that the sales rep take her on a sales call, and she soon learned that the hospital director had just invested millions of dollars in Hewlett-Packard computer equipment. As Shire says, "yet here we were patting ourselves on the back because we had a multimillion dollar contract to sell disk drives."[59]

Shire has also taken other steps. For one thing, she is now carefully choosing the right people for the right jobs, and letting those who cannot change go. As she says, "there is a lot of nervousness around here, and there should be." Shire is thus working hard to transform her division's culture from a relatively insular, unresponsive, easy-going, and non–customer-oriented one to one with a new sense of urgency, drive, and customer orientation—just the sort of culture Digital will need to survive in the competitive and turbulent 1990s.

SUMMARY

Culture represents the values and ways of behaving that are common to an organization and tend to perpetuate themselves over time. Since people's behavior is always a product of their values and beliefs, changing employees' actions involves changing the company's culture. Shared values and group norms are two building blocks of organizational culture, but several other layers may exist as well. A company's culture can be a force for good or ill.

Shared values are the nucleus of any firm's culture and often are codified in formal statements. High-performing firms typically have a value system that supports customers, employees, and shareholders. Firms create and sustain their corporate culture through the actions of the firm's leaders. Visionary leaders create an ideology that summarizes the firm's most important values and then promote the conversion of their employees to these values. Signs, stories, rites, and ceremonials can be used to symbolize a firm's values.

Some cultures support adaptiveness, while others impede it. A firm's shared values can boost adaptiveness by providing a common set of standards that all employees can use as guides. Cultures that can help organizations respond to environmental change will more likely be associated with superior performance over a long period of time.

QUESTIONS

■ FOR REVIEW

1. What characteristics do most definitions of culture have in common?
2. List some of the building blocks that make up an organization's culture.
3. Describe the role a firm's leaders play in creating and sustaining the firm's culture.
4. Give several examples that illustrate the statement: When it comes to changing culture, actions speak louder than words.
5. Explain how a company's underlying culture can either support or impede adaptiveness.

■ FOR DISCUSSION

6. How can a company ensure that its employees abide by the values codified in its formal statements.
7. If a firm's leaders are dishonest, will that inevitably be reflected in the company's culture? Discuss your response.
8. What steps can a company take to ensure that it can quickly respond in today's rapidly changing world?
9. More companies are making the transition from hierarchical, bureaucratic structures to flatter, looser organizations. What implications does this have for corporate cultures?

■ FOR ACTION

10. In 1993, Procter & Gamble announced a major restructuring. Research the changes that took place and how they have affected the company's culture to date.
11. How would you describe the culture at your university?
12. Develop a core value statement to help guide your professional career aspirations.

CLOSING SOLUTION

TALIGENT

Guglielmi decided that adopting a workable culture at Taligent should begin in his own office. Even though he had long enjoyed extensive staff support, he dispensed with personnel both at the Cupertino headquarters and on the road. The change yielded instant benefits. The support strata had always served as a de facto buffer between Guglielmi and Taligent's employees. Now, instead of learning about problems in reports, he was in position to react from his own impressions. Guglielmi didn't miss the old IBM chain of command, but he found it more difficult to shed the desire to keep tabs on departmental performance levels. He therefore insisted on data and keeping track of processes. Gradually, the Apple free spirits and the IBM white shirts met him somewhere in the middle. The consensus was that rigid hierarchy leads to creaky execution, but empowered renegades without structure leads to anarchy. As for the company dress code, Guglielmi's decree was clear as a bell: Don't say anything about my outfit, and I won't say anything about yours.[60]

■ **QUESTIONS FOR CLOSING SOLUTION**

1. What factors lead to organizational cultures that are as vastly different as those at IBM or Apple?

2. What else could Guglielmi do to create a sense of shared values at Taligent?

3. Based on the facts presented in this chapter, would you say that Taligent has developed an adaptive culture? Discuss your answer.

Organizational Culture

Value

Signs and Symbols

Stories

Rites and Ceremonials

KEY TERMS

CASE FOR ANALYSIS

WANG LABORATORIES

The history of Wang Laboratories has all the elements of great theater. It rose to almost $3 billion in sales through the leadership of a charismatic CEO whose ideas were the single overriding factor in shaping the company culture. But it crashed back to earth, and bankruptcy, in just four years, leaving many unresolved questions about publicly held companies run as family operations and what obligations that family has to shareholders and employees.

After emigrating from Shanghai and earning a doctorate at Harvard, company founder An Wang invented a magnetic storage device that became a mainstay in computers until the advent of the memory chip. The best was still ahead. In 1964, he scored big with the first version of the desktop calculator. Wang's market sense was unerring. Quick to grasp the low-margin, commodity-type aspects of calculators, he next introduced the Wang Word Processing System. Wang Laboratory revenues shot up astronomically. In the five years between 1977 and 1982, the company grew by a factor of ten and the number of employees rose from 4,000 to 24,800.

Wang privately charted the growth of his company and IBM, predicting he would catch up by the mid-1990s. But he ignored those who urged him to emulate Big Blue with a Wang all-purpose computer. Wang's word-processors and midsize models were soon blindsided by the PC onslaught, and Wang market share plunged. Matters were made worse by customers wanting systems that were compatible with other computer makers. Wang cultivated a culture that inhibited development of open compatible computer systems. The company's proprietary equipment—which only worked with Wang programs—returned big margins, until customers stopped buying.

An Wang's most critical mistake may be traced to Chinese tradition and his desire for a corporate culture that reflected his family-centered ideology. "As the founder, I would like to maintain sufficient control so that my children might have a chance to demonstrate whether they can run the company," he wrote in his autobiography. In a move that symbolized his traditional values, Wang installed his son Fred as president of the company in 1986, despite muted objections by board directors that Fred Wang lacked the experience and know-how to do the job. "He is my son," Wang responded. "He can do it."

The magnitude of that miscalculation quickly became clear. In Fred Wang's less than three-year tenure, the company failed to introduce anything significant in the way of product upgrades, and it added around $1 billion in debt. With cash reserves low and a unanimous thumbs-down from the company's bankers, An Wang made what must have been the most heart-rending decision of his life. He fired his son. The elder Wang died the following year.

"What happened at Wang was a cultural thing," says one analyst. "Chinese businesses are run very differently than American businesses. The Chinese tradition (no matter how large the firm) is to keep the business in the family."

Richard Miller, who had been something of a miracle worker at GE, took the helm, and he immediately began taking steps to transform the Wang culture and make it more adaptive. He sold noncore businesses, instituted layoffs, and finally directed Wang Labs into compatible systems manufacturing. A deal was struck under which Wang agreed to resell IBM machines in exchange for cash, but after a $25 million outlay, further investment was withheld. With few options remaining, Miller took Wang Labs into bankruptcy.

Miller's next miracles will be worked someplace other than Wang Labs. He was replaced in early 1993 by Joe Tucci, recruited from Unisys. By then the computer maker had lost just under $2 billion over four years and product demand had reached an all-time low. Recognizing that the company's history as a hardware maker was over, Tucci hoped Wang could emerge as a smaller company specializing in producing and servicing imaging software capable of storing computerized documents. But he knew that changing the company's deep-rooted anti-change culture would take time.

An Wang exhibited sound and often ingenious judgment in the nearly forty years he presided over Wang Labs, creating a company culture that revolved around him and his ideas. But it is arguable that the same elements that made Wang Labs soar are also what caused its downfall.

SOURCES: Donna Brown, "The Dilemma of Family Succession," *Management Review,* November 1989, 26–27; Andrew E. Serwer, "Wang Laboratories—Can This Company Be Saved?" *Fortune,* April 19, 1993, 86–90; "An American Tragedy," *The Economist,* August 22, 1992, 56–58; and Charles C. Kennedy, "Fall of the House of Wang," *Computerworld,* February 17, 1992, 67–68.

■ QUESTIONS

1. Explain some of the reasons Wang's culture could be described as unhealthy.
2. What factors have made it essential for Wang's new leadership to change the corporate culture?
3. How can Tucci make Wang's corporate culture more adaptive?

A CASE IN DIVERSITY

ORGANIZATIONAL CULTURE AND THE BABY BUSTERS

In the future, both top executives and human resources managers will face new challenges in shaping their firm's organizational culture. Just as careful selection of basic raw materials plays one of the biggest roles in the overall quality of the final product, the values and beliefs of a company's work force also must be addressed when managers go about creating the company culture. Those values and beliefs are undergoing some changes, at least among the so-called baby buster generation born between 1965 and 1975. Their idea of what constitutes success can be radically different from the thinking of their predecessors.

Objectives used to be easily identifiable on the organizational chart. Careerists could set their sights as high as they wished and do whatever was required to get there. While advancement remains a priority, large numbers of recent graduates place the quality of their work environment on an equal footing. Sometimes even a fat paycheck isn't enough to compensate for a work environment that they think stifles personal growth and life experiences. "I didn't find the banking industry very satisfying," says Kirk Odegard, who spent two years with Bank of America. "I didn't anticipate being happy for a long period of time." Though he scored well on both the GRE and LSAT exams, Odegard opted to pursue a masters in education and teaches high school social studies.

Managers and supervisors will face a number of complex challenges in getting the most out of the younger members of their work force. Many have already begun likening the oversight role to that of a parent. Respecting individualism is a high priority, but recognizing the right moment to offer input is equally important. "Not having the flexibility to manage each worker as an individual won't work with the baby bust generation because their needs are so diverse and varied," says author Claire Raines. "If we leave our managers no flexibility, they're going to fail with this generation."

One company that appears to have mastered the skills necessary for dealing with the younger generation is California-based Patagonia, which manufactures products for outdoor enthusiasts. In order to keep baby busters happy, the company encourages flexible work schedules. It also allows employees to take unpaid personal leaves of absences of up to four months a year. Patagonia tries to make the work environment as stimulating as possible by allowing twentysomething employees to make their own decisions and take calculated risks. The tactics seem to be working. Nearly 40 percent of the company's work force is made up of employees in their twenties.

SOURCE: Charlene Marmer Solomon, "Managing the Baby Busters," *Personnel Journal,* March 1992, 52–59.

■ QUESTIONS

1. How can a firm identify shared values and achieve ideological conversion when its work force is made up of baby boomers and baby busters with radically different views?
2. Do you think companies should change their organizational cultures in order to adapt to the values of the twentysomething generation, or take the opposite approach and try to change these younger employees' values and beliefs?
3. As baby busters achieve top managerial ranks, are we likely to see changes in corporate cultures? Discuss.

ENDNOTES

1. This opening discussion is based on John Huey, "Managing in the Midst of Chaos," *Fortune,* April 5, 1993, 44.
2. Ibid., 44.
3. Ibid.
4. John Kotter and James Heskett, *Corporate Culture and Performance* (New York: The Free Press, 1992), 141.
5. Daniel Denison, *Corporate Culture and Organizational Effectiveness* (New York: John Wiley and Sons, 1990), 2.
6. Gideon Kunda, *Engineering Culture* (Philadelphia: Temple University Press, 1992), 8.
7. James G. Hunt, *Leadership* (Newbury Park, CA: Sage Publications, 1991), 221.
8. Based on Kotter and Heskett, *Corporate Culture,* 5. See also Mary Jo Hatch, "The Dynamics of Organizational Culture," *Academy of Management Review,* October 1993, vol. 18, N4, 657–80.
9. Based on Hunt, *Leadership,* 220–24.
10. Ibid., 221.

11. *Blueprints for Service Quality: The Federal Express Approach* (New York: AMA Membership Publications, 1991), 13.

12. These two examples are based on Daniel Denison, *Corporate Culture,* 147–74.

13. Denison, *Corporate Culture,* 147.

14. Ibid., 148.

15. Ibid.

16. Ibid., 151.

17. Ibid.

18. Ibid.

19. Ibid.

20. Ibid., 152.

21. Ibid., 153.

22. Ibid., 154.

23. Ibid., 155.

24. John Dessauer, *My Years with Xerox* (Garden City, NY: Doubleday, 1971). Quoted in Kotter and Heskett, *Corporate Culture,* 76.

25. Kotter and Heskett, *Corporate Culture,* 76.

26. Ibid., 76–77. For a discussion of how culture also impacts employee retention rates see John Sheridan, "Organizational Culture and Employee Retention," *Academy of Management Journal,* December 1992, 1036–57.

27. Richard Osborne, "Core Value Statements: The Corporate Compass," *Business Horizons,* September–October 1991, 29.

28. Ibid., 29.

29. Kotter and Heskett, *Corporate Culture,* 54.

30. Edgar Schein, *Organizational Culture and Leadership,* Second Edition, (San Francisco: Jossey-Bass Publications, 1992), 211–212.

31. Sam Walton and John Huey, *Sam Walton: Made in America, My Story,* (New York: Doubleday, 1992), 14.

32. Ibid., 14. For a discussion of culture's role in ethics, see, for example, Ishmael Akaah, "Organizational Culture and Ethical Research Behavior," *Journal of the Academy of Marketing Science,* Winter 1993, 59–64.

33. Ibid., 171.

34. Ibid., 161.

35. Richard Osborne, "Core Values Statements," 30.

36. Gary Dessler, *Winning Commitment: How to Build and Keep a Competitive Work Force* (New York: McGraw-Hill, 1993), 85.

37. Ibid., 85.

38. Denison, *Corporate Culture,* 155.

39. Thomas J. Peters and Robert Waterman, *In Search of Excellence* (New York: Harper & Row, 1982), 81.

40. Denison, *Corporate Culture,* 12.

41. Tom Burns and G.M. Stalker, *The Management of Innovation* (London: Tavistock Publications, 1961), 118–19.

42. Gideon Kunda, *Engineering Culture: Control and Commitment in a High-Tech Corporation* (Philadelphia: Temple University Press, 1992), 10.

43. Ibid., 11.

44. Kotter and Heskett, *Corporate Culture,* 44.

45. Ibid.

46. Ibid., 50.

47. Ibid., 53–54.

48. Ibid., 53. For another view of culture's impact, see Raymond Zammuto and Edward O'Connor, "Gaining Advanced Manufacturing Technologies' Benefits: The Roles of Organization Design and Culture," *Academy of Management Review,* October 1992, 701–29.

49. William Echikson, "Phillips Electronics: How Hard It Is to Change Culture," *Fortune*.

50. Hunt, *Leadership*, 234–36.

51. Kotter and Heskett, *Corporate Culture*, 85.

52. Ibid., 84.

53. Ibid.

54. Ibid.

55. Richard Osborne, "Core Value Statements: The Corporate Compass," *Business Horizons*, September–October 1991, 29.

56. Judith Dobrzynski, "Jack Welch: How Good a Manager?" *Business Week*, December 14, 1987, 92–98.

57. John Huey, "Managing in the Midst of Chaos," *Fortune*, April 5, 1993, 47–50.

58. Ibid., 48

59 Ibid. Ironically, Willow Shire was asked to leave Digital in 1994. For an additional view on the need to change culture, see Jennifer Chatman and Karen Jehn, "Assessing the Relationship Between Industry Characteristics and Organizational Culture: How Different Can They Be?," *Academy of Management Journal*, June, 1994, 522–54.

60. "Corporate Culture School: An IBM-Apple Computer Joint Venture," *Fortune*, April 5, 1993, 44.

MOTIVATION AND BEHAVIOR

OPENING PROBLEM
THE EQUITABLE COMPANIES

If the 1980s were a parable, The Equitable Companies might qualify as a corporate prodigal son. It wandered far from core insurance operations. Ventures into real estate and junk bonds proved profligate. A money market account deal that promised customers big returns ended up costing the company millions when interest rates headed down. In 1990 Equitable's insurance business lost $300 million; the year after that the red ink reached a half-billion. The company's looming insolvency got plenty of press. People who didn't read the newspaper heard even more sinister versions gleefully recounted by competitors. Equitable agents increasingly hit a wall of skepticism from leery customers. The company turned to Richard Jenrette and Joe Melone, two highly regarded executives from the brokerage and insurance industries. Together they had to come up with a strategy that cut costs and raised capital. Perhaps more importantly, they had to find a way to motivate a badly dispirited sales force.[1]

INDIVIDUAL DETERMINANTS OF BEHAVIOR

Part of Equitable's dilemma was that what motivates one person might not motivate any other. Any stimulus—an order from the boss, an offer of a raise, or a kick in the pants—will have different effects on different people. One person might leap at the chance for a $100 raise, while another might shun it. One person might emerge from training with excellent skills, while another will learn nothing. One might jump whenever the boss gives orders, while another will laughingly ignore them.

To a large extent, these anomalies occur because people differ in their perceptions, personalities, abilities, and needs. As illustrated in Figure 15.1, these factors act much like filters, adding to, detracting from, and often distorting the stimulus's effects. Let us therefore start our discussion of behavior and motivation by examining personality, perception, and abilities.

PERSONALITY

Personality is probably the first thing that comes to mind when most people think of what determines behavior. We tend to classify people as introverted, dominant, mature, or paranoid, for instance, and by and large these labels conjure up visions of particular kinds of behavior.

For our purpose, we can define **personality** as "the characteristic and distinctive traits of an individual, and the way the traits interact to help or hinder the adjustment of the person to other people and situations." Psychologist Raymond Cattell used observations and questionnaires to identify sixteen illustrative primary personality traits.[2] These were then expressed in pairs of polar words, such as reserved/outgoing, submissive/dominant, and trusting/suspicious. Based on his work, Cattell and his colleagues developed a questionnaire that produced a personality profile for individuals. Figure 15.2 shows the average personality profiles for people in three occupational groups: writers, airline pilots, and business executives.

Such traits do not just represent characteristics that people possess. People do not possess "submissiveness" or "sensitivity." Instead, they act and feel submissive (or sensitive) under most circumstances (although they may act in a dominant way in others). Thus, we can define someone's personality in terms of his or her traits and these traits will generally reflect how he or she will act in a given situation.

PERSONALITY
The characteristic and distinctive traits of an individual, and the way the traits interact to help or hinder the adjustment of the person to other people and situations.

FIGURE 15.1

Individual Determinants of Behavior

A particular stimulus may evoke different behaviors among individuals, since each person's perceptions, personality, abilities, and needs will influence how he or she reacts to the stimulus.

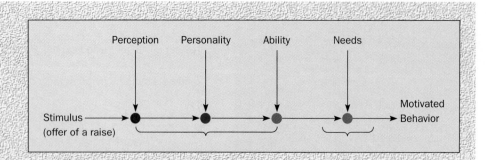

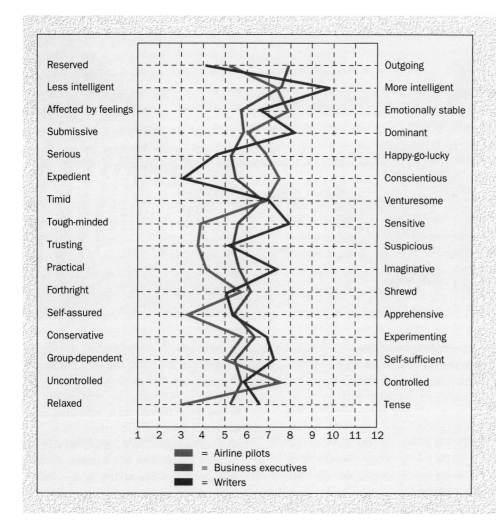

FIGURE 15.2

Cattell's 16 Personality Factors

The personalities of various people and even various groups of people are characterized by particular packages of traits, such as intelligent, dominant, sensitive, and shrewd.

SOURCE: Gregory Northcraft and Margaret Neale, *Organizational Behavior* (Fort Worth, TX: The Dryden Press, 1994), 87.

Recent studies of personality traits have tended to focus on the so-called Big Five traits: extraversion/intraversion, emotional stability, agreeableness, conscientiousness, and openness to experience.[3]

Extraverts of course tend to be outgoing and gregarious while introverts are shy. Emotional stability (the second of the primary traits) reflects such things as anxiousness and insecurity. Agreeable people tend to be cooperative and flexible. Conscientiousness reflects behaviors such as thoroughness and dependability. Individuals high on the fifth, "openness to experience" dimension tend to be imaginative and curious.[4]

PERCEPTION

WHAT IS PERCEPTION? We all react to, and behave on the basis of stimuli that reach us via our sense organs, but how we define or perceive these stimuli depends on what we bring along with us from past experiences, and what our present needs and personalities are.[5] In other words, our behavior is not motivated just by the actual stimuli out there, but by our **perceptions** of those stimuli, and our perceptions are distorted by our experience, situation, and needs.

This kind of perceptual distortion is probably most familiar when it involves inanimate objects. For example, consider what happens when we try to match the sizes of

PERCEPTION
How we define or perceive stimuli, depending on what we bring along with us from past experiences, and what our present needs and personalities are.

Measure on this page the height (perspective size) of the nearest arch and compare it with the height of the distant arches. You will find that the near arch is more than four times as high (in perspective size) as the distant arch, although it only looks about twice as large because your expectations mold your perceptions.

near objects with those of far ones. When we look down a row of arches, the farthest one usually looks smaller than the closest one, and its perspective size is in fact smaller (because it is farthest away). Based on our experience, however, we know that the arches are actually equal in size, so what we perceive is a compromise between the perspective size of the arch and its actual size. In the above photo, the nearest arch seems about twice the size of the farthest arch. But if you measure the arches you will see that the size of the nearest arch is actually more than four times that of the farthest arch. What happens is that our desire to see objects as we expect them to be causes us to perceive the difference in the height of the arches as less than it actually is.

PERCEPTION AND PEOPLE   Just as we read stable, permanent characteristics into objects, we also read them into people. This is called stereotyping. For example, we tend to associate characteristics like industriousness and honesty with certain socioeconomic classes, but not with others. We tend to assume (or once tended to assume) that women were fit only for certain jobs, but not for others. Similarly, we tend to stereotype people according to age, sex, race, or national origin and to attribute the characteristics of this stereotype to everyone we meet who is of that age, sex, race, or national origin. In other words, we all learn to associate certain meanings with certain groups of people. This process helps us to deduce more quickly (with varying degrees of accuracy) the important characteristics of the people we meet and to avoid having to make fresh guesses every time.[6] Thus managers often tend to (incorrectly) assume that older workers are not as flexible or effective as younger workers,[7] and that managers are more honest than union representatives, for instance.[8]

FACTORS THAT AFFECT PERCEPTION   How we "see" or perceive the world results from a multitude of influences. Some important influences are listed here:

- *Needs.* A person's needs affect his or her perceptions. For example, when shown fuzzy and ambiguous pictures of objects, hungry people tend to "see" them as food while others do not. Similarly, tell an insecure employee that you want to see him in your office later in the day, and he might spend the day worrying about being fired, although you only wanted to discuss some small matter.

■ *Stress.* People who are under stress tend to perceive things less objectively than those who are not. In one experiment, a group of employment interviewers were put under pressure to hire more employees. They subsequently perceived candidates' qualifications as being much higher than did a group of interviewers who were not under pressure.

■ *Experience.* Our perceptions are also influenced by our experiences. Based on our experiences, for example, we learn to associate certain groups with certain behaviors (in other words, stereotype them). We then tend to expect everyone from that group to behave in the same fashion.

■ *Position.* A person's position in the organization is another important factor. Production managers tend to see problems as production problems, while sales managers see them as sales problems, for instance.

■ *Attribution.* What people perceive is also strongly influenced by their *attributions.* **Attributions** may be defined as the meanings people give to the causes of actions and outcomes. For example, suppose another driver cuts you off as you drive to work. How you perceive his or her actions and how you react to them will depend in part on your attributions. Thus if you attribute the other driver's actions to temporarily losing control of his car, you may drive on without further thought. If you attribute his actions to intentionally cutting you off out of anger, you may decide to take evasive action to avoid further encounters with someone you now perceive as a hothead.

ATTRIBUTIONS
The meanings people give to the causes of actions and outcomes.

We can summarize our discussion with the following three principles.[9]

1. Although two people may share the same event, each one's perception of the experience will be different.

2. We experience the world subjectively; that is, we interpret it.

3. Human behavior is actually responses to perceptions; we respond or react to our mental image of the outside world.

ABILITIES AND PERFORMANCE[10]

A person's performance is also always a function of abilities and motivation; one without the other won't suffice. In other words even the most highly motivated person will not perform well—as a golfer, a company president, or a machinist—unless he or she also has the ability to do the job. Conversely, even the most able employee will not perform satisfactorily if not motivated. Some experts summarize this interaction this way: Performance = Ability × Motivation.

TYPES OF ABILITIES Abilities come in many types. Mental abilities include intelligence and its building blocks like memory, inductive reasoning, and verbal comprehension. Mechanical ability would be important for mechanical engineers or machinists, who must be able to visualize how a particular piece of machinery works. Psychomotor abilities include dexterity, manipulative ability, eye-hand coordination, and motor ability. Such abilities might be important for employees who have to put together delicate electronic components, or who work as card dealers in Las Vegas. People also differ in their visual skills, for example, in their ability to discriminate between colors and between black and white detail (visual acuity).

In addition to these general abilities that we all have, there are also job specific abilities learned through training, experience, or education. We test for these abilities when we are interested in determining the candidate's proficiency on a job, such as computer programmer, typist, or chemical engineer.

INTRODUCTION TO MOTIVATION

MOTIVATION
The intensity of a person's desire to engage in some activity.

NEED-BASED THEORIES
These emphasize the role of the person's personality and needs in motivation.

EXPECTANCY-BASED THEORIES
These hold that motivation is a function of whether or not the person expects his or her effort to result in performance and therefore rewards.

REINFORCEMENT THEORIES
These hold that people are motivated by the consequences of their behavior and that they tend to continue behaviors that are rewarded and to cease those that are unrewarded or punished.

NEEDS-HIERARCHY THEORY OF MOTIVATION
Maslow's theory of motivation, based on the proposal that people have five increasingly higher-level needs: physiological, safety, social, self-esteem, and self-actualization.

PREPOTENCY PROCESS PRINCIPLE
Maslow's theory that people become motivated as they move up through the hierarchy, satisfying the lower-order needs and then, in order, each of the higher-order needs.

PHYSIOLOGICAL NEEDS
The most basic needs that include the need for food, drink, and shelter.

SAFETY NEEDS
When physiological needs are reasonably satisfied, your personal safety, security, and protection needs become potent forces in your behavior.

SELF-ESTEEM NEEDS
These needs relate to one's self-esteem, needs for self-confidence, independence, achievement, competence, and knowledge, and needs that relate to one's reputation, needs for status, recognition, appreciation, and the deserved respect of others.

Motivation can be defined as the intensity of a person's desire to engage in some activity. Along with personality, perception, and ability it is a major determinant of behavior and performance at work. Motivation theories that explain the cause of motivation can be classified as need-based theories, cognitive process theories, expectancy theories, and reinforcement theory. **Need-based theories** emphasize the role of the person's personality and needs in motivation. Cognitive process theories assume that motivation is essentially a process of self-regulation, and focus on the decision process through which motivation comes about. **Expectancy-based theories** hold that motivation is a function of whether or not the person expects his or her effort to result in performance and therefore rewards. **Reinforcement theory** basically holds that people are motivated by the consequences of their behavior and that they tend to continue behaviors that are rewarded and to cease those that are unrewarded or punished.

NEED-BASED THEORIES OF MOTIVATION

MASLOW'S NEEDS-HIERARCHY THEORY

Maslow's **needs-hierarchy theory of motivation** is typical of need-based theories, and is the basis for the other need-based theories discussed in this section.

Maslow proposed that people have five increasingly higher-level needs: physiological, safety, social, self-esteem, and self-actualization. According to Maslow's **prepotency process principle,** people become motivated as they move up through the hierarchy, satisfying the lower-order needs and then, in order, each of the higher-order needs.[11]

Maslow's hierarchy can be envisioned as a pyramid as in Figure 15.3. According to Maslow, lower-level needs (once satisfied) become the foundations that trigger the potency of higher-order needs. Let us look at each of Maslow's five categories of needs before discussing this point further.[12]

PHYSIOLOGICAL NEEDS   Anyone who has heard a baby crying at four o'clock in the morning knows that people are born with certain **physiological needs.** These are the most basic needs, including the needs for food, drink, and shelter.

SAFETY NEEDS   Maslow says that when these physiological needs are reasonably satisfied—when one is no longer thirsty and has enough to eat, for instance—then the **safety needs** become potent or activated. In other words, if you are starving or in the middle of a desert with nothing to drink, the lower-level need for food or water will drive your behavior, and you might even risk your life and safety by pursuing it. But once you have enough to eat or to drink, your personal safety, security, and protection become potent forces in your behavior.

SOCIAL NEEDS   Once you feel reasonably secure and have had enough to eat and drink, **social needs** begin to drive your behavior, says Maslow. These are the needs people have for affiliation, for giving and receiving affection, and for friendship.

SELF-ESTEEM   At level four are the **self-esteem needs.** Psychologist Douglas McGregor says these include "ego needs":

1. Those needs that relate to one's self-esteem—needs for self-confidence, independence, achievement, competence, and knowledge.
2. Those needs that relate to one's reputation—needs for status, recognition, appreciation, and the deserved respect of others.[13]

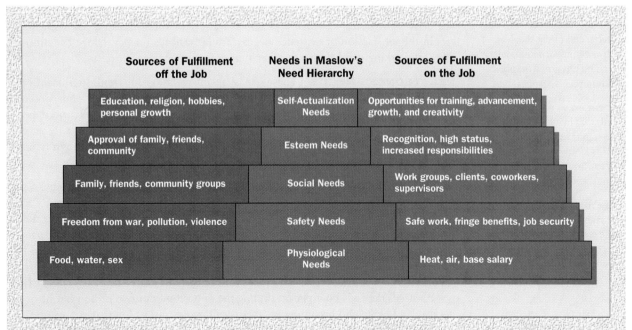

FIGURE 15.3

Maslow's Hierarchy of Needs

Maslow argued that people have a hierarchy of needs, each of which may be satisfied by various on-the-job and off-the-job sources of fulfillment. Each lower need must be reasonably well satisfied before higher-level needs can motivate behavior.

SOURCE: Richard Daft, *Management*, 3rd ed. (Fort Worth, TX: The Dryden Press, 1994), 516.

Like the social and safety needs, self-esteem needs do not begin to drive behavior (says Maslow) until the lower-level needs are fairly well satisfied. But McGregor and other psychologists argue there is a big difference between ego needs (and the top-level self-actualization needs) and lower-level physiological, safety, and social needs: higher-level needs for things like self-respect and recognition are insatiable—we never get enough of them. Lower level needs are relatively easily satisfied.

SELF-ACTUALIZATION NEEDS Finally, there is an ultimate need that only begins to dominate a person's behavior once all lower-level needs are reasonably satisfied. This is the need for self-actualization or fulfillment, the need we all have to become the person we feel we have the potential for becoming. **Self-actualization needs,** as McGregor says, drive us to realize our own potentialities, continue self-development, and to be creative in the broadest sense of that term.

ALDERFER'S EXISTENCE-RELATEDNESS-GROWTH THEORY

Clayton Alderfer's **existence-relatedness-growth (ERG) theory** was designed to improve on Maslow's theory in two ways. First, Alderfer classifies needs into three groups (existence, relatedness, and growth needs) rather than into five as Maslow proposes. Second, he says these three needs are all active at the same time, and that it is not necessary to satisfy lower-level needs before higher-level needs become activated.

SELF-ACTUALIZATION NEEDS
Needs that only begin to dominate a person's behavior once all lower-level needs are reasonably satisfied; the need for self-actualization or fulfillment is the need we all have to become the person we feel we have the potential for becoming.

EXISTENCE-RELATEDNESS GROWTH (ERG) THEORY
Designed by Clayton Alderfer to improve on Maslow's theory in two ways: first, needs are classified into three groups (existence, relatedness, and growth needs) rather than into five groups as Maslow proposes; second, these three needs are all active at the same time, and it is not necessary to satisfy lower-level needs before higher-level needs become activated.

EXISTENCE NEEDS
Needs that include all the various material and physical drives, such as eating, drinking, salary level, and physical working conditions.

RELATEDNESS NEEDS
Needs that involve relationships with significant other people, such as family members, superiors, coworkers, subordinates, friends, and enemies.

GROWTH NEEDS
Needs that impel a person to make creative or productive effects on himself or herself and the environment.

EXISTENCE NEEDS[14]   Existence needs include all the various material and physical drives. For example, when a person is hungry or thirsty this represents deficiencies in the satisfaction of existence needs. Similarly, needs for pay, fringe benefits, and physical working conditions are other types of existence needs.

RELATEDNESS NEEDS   These needs "involve relationships with significant other people" such as family members, superiors, coworkers, subordinates, friends, and enemies.[15] One basic characteristic of **relatedness needs** is that their satisfaction depends on sharing or mutuality. People satisfy their relatedness needs by mutually sharing their thoughts and feelings, by interacting with other individuals, or through families, work groups, friendship groups, or professional groups.

GROWTH NEEDS   Alderfer says people also have **growth needs** that "impel a person to make creative or productive effects on himself and the environment."[16] Existence needs might be satisfied by, for instance, eating food or drinking water. Relatedness needs are satisfied by developing mutual relationships with other people. Growth needs are satisfied when a person engages in problems "which call upon him or her to utilize his or her capacities fully."[17] Satisfying growth needs lets a person experience "a greater sense of wholeness and fullness as a human being."[18] Satisfying growth needs depends on a person finding the opportunities to do or be what he or she is capable of being and becoming (as the recruiting ads put it) "all that you can be."

In addition to using three, rather than five, categories of needs, Alderfer is not as strict as Maslow in insisting that lower-level needs must be satisfied before higher-level needs become important. Thus, ERG theory would argue that even a very hungry person still has a need for affiliation and for growth. The difference is one of degree: Maslow argued that lower-level needs should be "fairly well" satisfied before higher-level needs become potent; Alderfer says that even at the same point in time all three classes of needs are usually fairly important in driving a person's performance.[19]

NEEDS FOR POWER, ACHIEVEMENT, AND AFFILIATION

Researchers David McClelland and John Atkinson say there are three needs that are particularly important for managers to understand: the need for achievement, the need for power, and the need for affiliation.[20]

NEED FOR ACHIEVEMENT
Represents the need people have to accomplish challenging tasks.

NEED FOR ACHIEVEMENT   The **need for achievement** represents the need people have to accomplish challenging tasks. A person with a relatively high need for achievement concentrates a lot of energy on doing his or her job better, accomplishing unusual and important things, or advancing his or her career. People with high achievement needs like situations in which they can take personal responsibility for finding solutions to problems, have a strong desire for concrete feedback as to how well they are doing, and tend to set moderate achievement goals and to take calculated (but not crazy) risks.

NEED FOR POWER
Represents a need some people have to gain influence and control others.

NEED FOR POWER   People with a high **need for power** tend to spend their time thinking about how to gain influence and control over others, such as how to win arguments, change other people's behavior, or gain positions of authority and status. People with a strong need for power usually attempt to influence other people directly, for instance by making suggestions, giving their opinions and evaluations, and by trying to talk others into things. They are also usually seen by others as forceful and outspoken, but also as somewhat hard-headed and demanding. Some studies suggest that successful top executives not only have strong needs for achievement, but are strongly motivated by the need for power as well.[21]

NEED FOR AFFILIATION   Other people focus more on thinking about and developing warm, friendly, compassionate relationships; these people have a relatively high **need for affiliation.** They are likely to pay close attention to the feelings of others and to concentrate on establishing friendly relationships, often by agreeing or giving emotional support. They derive a majority of their satisfaction from being liked and accepted in the group.

HERZBERG'S MOTIVATOR-HYGIENE THEORY

Psychologist Frederick Herzberg and his colleagues basically argue that people have a lower- and higher-level set of needs, and that the best way to motivate someone is to offer to satisfy the higher-level needs. Satisfying physiological or safety needs by offering a person a raise or better working conditions is no way to motivate someone, says Herzberg, because lower-level needs like these are quickly satisfied, and when satisfied the only way to motivate the person is to offer even more money or better working conditions in an endlessly escalating process. Therefore, says Herzberg, the best approach is to arrange the job in such a way that the person derives a sense of achievement, accomplishment, and fulfillment out of doing it, because people have an infinite craving to satisfy such higher-level needs.

EXTRINSIC AND INTRINSIC MOTIVATION FACTORS   The idea central to Herzberg's **two-factor theory** is that there are two classes of work motivators: extrinsic and intrinsic factors. They are listed here:[22]

EXTRINSIC FACTORS	INTRINSIC FACTORS
1. Company policy and administration	1. Achievement, or completing a challenging task successfully
2. Supervision	2. Recognition (for instance, being singled out for praise)
3. Relationship with supervisor	3. The work itself, and particularly whether it provides a challenge to employees and utilizes their skills and thinking abilities
4. Work conditions	4. Responsibility for one's own or others' work
5. Salary	5. Advancement, or the opportunity to be promoted
6. Relationship with peers	6. Growth, or the opportunity to expand one's knowledge or skills
7. Job security	

In Herzberg's theory, two important differences exist between extrinsic factors and intrinsic factors. First, intrinsic factors are derived from the job itself. In fact, **intrinsic factors** are often called **job content** or motivator factors, since opportunities for achievement, responsibility, advancement, growth (and of course the nature of the work itself) are intrinsic to the work. On the other hand, **extrinsic** (or *"hygiene"*) **factors** are generally external to the work itself. They include pay, company rules, and the nature of the employee's relationship with his or her supervisor and peers at work.

The second difference between intrinsic and extrinsic factors is that they satisfy different sets of needs. Extrinsic factors like pay and job security are important at work because (says Herzberg) they can satisfy employees' lower-level needs, such as their physiological desires, safety needs, and affiliation with one's peers. Intrinsic factors, on the other hand, appeal to employees' higher-level needs, such as the need for self-esteem or the opportunity to self-actualize and be fulfilled.

Herzberg and his colleagues conducted interviews with professionals like engineers and accountants and arrived at several important conclusions about how extrinsic and intrinsic factors affect motivation and satisfaction. He says that if extrinsic hygiene factors like salary are missing or inadequate, employees will become dissatisfied.

NEED FOR AFFILIATION
Represents the need some people have to think about and develop warm, friendly, compassionate relationships.

TWO-FACTOR THEORY
Herzberg's theory that there are two classes of work motivators—extrinsic and intrinsic factors.

INTRINSIC FACTORS
Derived from the job itself, where opportunities for achievement, responsibility, advancement, growth, and the nature of the work itself are intrinsic to the work. Also called *motivator* or *job content* factors.

EXTRINSIC FACTORS
Factors that are external to the work itself, such as pay, company rules, and the nature of the employee's relationship with his or her supervisor and peers at work. Also called *hygienes.*

However, adding more of these hygienes to the job is not the best way to motivate employees. This is because, as stated earlier, lower-level needs are quickly satisfied, and when they are satisfied, employers will have to escalate their offers to further motivate employees. Extrinsic hygiene factors like salary and working conditions are, says Herzberg, really only good for preventing dissatisfaction. This is important, because if an employee's lower-level needs are dissatisfied, the manager cannot appeal to the employee's relatively unlimited higher-level needs.

However, according to Herzberg, intrinsic, job content, motivator factors (like opportunities for achievement) accomplish the task of motivating employees by appealing to higher-level needs, needs which are never completely satisfied. Herzberg argues that the best way to motivate employees is to build challenge and opportunities for achievement and fulfillment into their jobs, so that merely doing the job provides intrinsic motivation. The *OurTown* vignette shows how one firm applies some of these ideas.

JOB ENRICHMENT   Job enrichment is the method Herzberg recommends for applying his theory. **Job enrichment** means building motivators like opportunities for achievement into the job by making it more interesting and challenging. This is often accomplished by *vertically loading* the job, which means giving the worker more autonomy and allowing the person to do much of the planning and inspection normally done by the person's supervisor.

Job enrichment can be accomplished in several ways:[23]

1. *Form natural work groups.* Change the job in such a way that each person is responsible for or "owns" an identifiable body of work. For example, instead of having the typist in a typing pool do work for all departments, make the work of one or two departments the continuing responsibility of each typist.

2. *Combine tasks.* Let one person assemble a product from start to finish, instead of having it go through several separate operations that are performed by different people. Combining tasks in this way is also often called *job enlargement.*

3. *Establish client relationships.* Let the worker have contact as often as possible with the client of that person's work. For example, let an assistant research and respond to customers' requests, instead of automatically referring all problems to his or her boss.

4. *Vertical loading.* Let the worker plan and control his or her job, rather than having it controlled by others. For example, let the worker set a schedule, do his or her own troubleshooting, and decide when to start and stop working.

5. *Open feedback channels.* Finally, find more and better ways for the worker to get quick feedback on his or her performance.

JOB ENRICHMENT
Building motivators like opportunities for achievement into the job by making it more interesting and challenging.

COGNITIVE-PROCESS MOTIVATION THEORIES
These assume that motivation is essentially a process of self-regulation, and focus on the decision process through which motivation comes about.

EQUITY THEORY
Adams' theory that assumes that people have a need for, and therefore value and seek, fairness in employer-employee relationships.

COGNITIVE PROCESS THEORIES OF MOTIVATION

Cognitive-process motivation theories focus on the decision-making process through which a person's motivation develops.

ADAMS' EQUITY THEORY

Adam's **equity theory** basically assumes that people have a need for, and therefore value and seek, *fairness* in employee-employer relationships.[24] People are therefore strongly motivated to maintain a balance between what they perceive as their inputs, or con-

OURTOWN PRODUCTIONS

Steven Rosenbaum says his television production company, OurTown Productions, produces programming with one-half to two-thirds the staff that other companies require. He claims his 18 employees are more productive as well, even though they could make more money working elsewhere. So, how does he elicit the necessary motivation?

When Rosenbaum and his partner started OurTown in Saratoga Springs, New York, right out of college, they couldn't compete with the salaries other local stations were paying. They had to find something to make OurTown attractive enough to attract the talent they wanted. Their solution was to accommodate employees' needs for accomplishment and fulfillment by customizing their jobs to fit their tastes. For example, OurTown's story coordinator, Steve Mendes, also likes to weld. Rosenbaum needed a story coordinator, didn't have a welder, and got both when he hired Mendes. "Letting me weld makes me a happier person here," says Mendes.

Rosenbaum takes such expansion of his employees' job descriptions in stride. In fact, he spends a lot of time trying to find out what his workers love and hate about their jobs. Of course, creating the perfect job is still out of reach. However, Rosenbaum can usually find someone interested in a job that another finds distasteful. He says that figuring out ways to keep his employees motivated by letting them satisfy their needs is well worth the effort.

SOURCE: "Managing People," *Inc.*, September 1991, 125–26.

Job enrichment involves building motivators into jobs by making them more challenging in a number of ways. Steven Rosenbaum of OurTown Television Productions has attracted and kept a talented staff who could be making more money elsewhere by custom-fitting task to employee and allowing them to expand beyond standard job descriptions.

tributions, and their rewards. Basically, equity theory states that if a person perceives an inequity, a tension or drive will develop in the person's mind, and the person will be motivated to reduce or eliminate the tension and perceived inequity.

According to equity theory, exactly how the person goes about reducing what he or she perceives as an inequity depends on how the person is paid:

1. If a person is paid on a piece-rate basis and thinks he or she is *overpaid,* the quantity the person produces should stay the same or may decrease, because producing more would simply increase the financial inequity from the point of view of the employee. However, quality should increase since this should allow an increase in the inputs a person is providing, thus reducing the perceived inequity. However, if the piece-rate person is *underpaid,* work quality should go down and quantity might increase.

2. If a person is paid a salary (regardless of output) and believes he or she is *overpaid,* then quantity, quality, or both should increase since this will reduce the perceived inequity. If a person believes he or she is *underpaid,* then quantity and quality should both decrease. The effects of perceived inequity are summarized in Figure 15.4.

Adams' theory is one of several organizational justice theories that try to explain how employees' drives for justice and fairness influence their motivation and behavior. On the whole, empirical findings regarding *underpayment,* at least, are consistent with Adams' theory. For example, people paid on a piece-rate reduce quality and boost quantity when they believe they are underpaid. Those paid a straight hourly rate or salary tend to reduce both quantity and quality. Interestingly, though, overpayment inequity does not seem to have the positive effects on either quantity or quality that Adams' theory would predict for it.[25]

LOCKE'S GOAL THEORY OF MOTIVATION

Goal-based theories of motivation, like Locke's, assume that once someone chooses to pursue a goal, that person regulates his or her behavior to try to ensure that the goals are reached.[26] In this case the cognitive process giving rise to motivation focuses on the person's goals, rather then on equity. Locke and his associates argue that the goal a person has consciously decided to pursue is a main motivator of that person's behav-

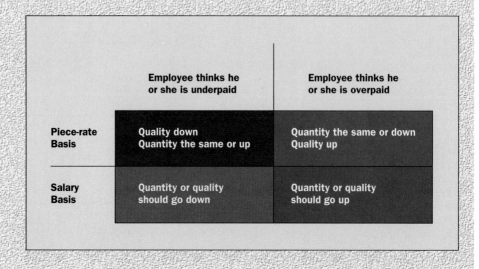

FIGURE 15.4

How a Perceived Inequity Effects Performance

According to equity theory, how a person reacts to under- or over-payment depends on whether he or she is paid on a piece-rate or salary basis.

	Employee thinks he or she is underpaid	Employee thinks he or she is overpaid
Piece-rate Basis	Quality down Quantity the same or up	Quantity the same or down Quality up
Salary Basis	Quantity or quality should go down	Quantity or quality should go up

ior.[27] Rather than focusing on the employee's needs, Locke and his colleagues thus view a person's goals as the most potent determinants of action. They contend that a person's goals provide the mechanism by which unsatisfied needs are translated into action.[28] In other words, a person's unsatisfied needs prompt the person to seek ways of satisfying those needs, and goals are then formulated that become the precursors to action.[29]

Most of the research in this area has been conducted in laboratory settings, with undergraduates as subjects. While findings like these do not necessarily generalize to industrial settings, the findings do tend to support Locke's basic theory. The most consistent finding here is that people who are assigned *and who adopt* difficult and specific goals outperform people who are simply told to do their best.[30] These findings have recently been extended to field settings. Here the evidence suggests rather strongly that people assigned (and who adopt) specific and difficult goals tend to outperform people without such performance goals.[31] The *Da Vinci* vignette shows how one manager applied this idea.

EXPECTANCY THEORIES OF MOTIVATION

Expectancy theories of motivation assume that before working on a task, individuals size up both their expectations for success and the value (to them) of the outcome and then choose their tasks and levels of effort so as to maximize their benefits and minimize any negative effects.[32] A theory formulated by psychologist Victor Vroom, called valence-instrumentality-expectancy theory, is a good example.

According to Vroom the force on a person to choose to exert a certain level of effort is a function of three components, expressed as follows: Force = E × I × V. In the

EXPECTANCY THEORIES OF MOTIVATION
A theory that assumes that before embarking on a task, individuals size up both their expectations for success and the value of the outcome and then choose their tasks and levels of effort so as to maximize their benefits and minimize any negative effects.

DA VINCI SYSTEMS

Dan Vena, director of sales at Da Vinci electronic mail systems based in Raleigh, North Carolina, was facing a crisis. His 12-person sales force had badly missed its sales goals for four months in a row. The ultimatum from above was clear: the following month was do or die.

Vena felt certain he'd communicated to his salespeople what each needed to do to meet targets. But when a consultant asked them to write down major job responsibilities, Vena saw that they weren't at all sure what they were supposed to be doing. They had largely become passive rather than proactive with customers.

Vena also realized that in the past he'd done little more than tell his people to increase sales and do as many "test-drive" installations as possible. The consultant pointed out that the most important step for Vena was to set specific goals that could be monitored and measured. The salespeople now started planning how many calls they would make, who they would talk to, and when it would get done. The result was an almost immediate and sustained boost in sales as employees adjusted their behaviors to their new goals.

SOURCE: "Managing Employees' Accountability," *Inc.,* March 1993, 34.

EXPECTANCY
The probability that a person's efforts will lead to performance.

INSTRUMENTALITY
The perceived correlation between successful performance and obtaining the reward.

VALENCE
Represents the perceived value a person ascribes to the reward.

equation, E represents the person's **expectancy** (in terms of probabilities) that her or his effort will lead to performance; I represents **"instrumentality"** or the perceived correlation between successful performance and obtaining the reward; and V represents **valence,** which represents the perceived value the person ascribes to the reward.[33]

Thus, to be motivated to perform, the person must expect that effort will lead to performance, that performance will result in obtaining the reward, and that the reward that results from the performance will be of value.

Notice that Vroom makes no mention of needs or motives. In his theory, the level of aroused motivation is simply a product of expectancy (that effort will lead to performance), instrumentality (the perceived correlation between performance and rewards), and valence (or the extent to which the outcomes of performance have any value to the person).

Research results generally provide support for Vroom's theory, particularly in studies investigating job choice. The results suggest that expectations, instrumentalities, and valence combine to influence a person's motivation to choose specific jobs.[34]

REINFORCEMENT THEORY

You may be familiar with the work of Russian physiologist Ivan Pavlov, who conducted a series of studies in the early 1900s. In his most famous experiments he put a dog in a harness to see how it responded to various stimuli. By hooking a special tube to the dog's mouth, Pavlov was able to determine when the dog salivated. In one experiment, a light was turned on in front of the dog and then after a few seconds some meat powder was delivered to the dog's feeding tray. Since the dog was hungry it salivated, and ate. Pavlov found that the dog soon learned to associate the light with the following meat powder so that after several trials the dog salivated even without the meat, simply in response to the light. In other words, the dog's response (salivation) had become **conditioned** on the appearance of the light. These trials were therefore called experiments in classical conditioning. They focused on **respondent behavior,** behavior (like salivating) that simply responds to a stimulus (like Pavlov's light bulb).

Psychologist B. F. Skinner knew that a great many behaviors occurred that could not be explained by this so-called stimulus-response theory. For example, if you wanted to train your dog to roll over, you probably would not do it by ringing a bell and then hoping it would eventually learn to roll over: that could obviously take years. In all likelihood, you would encourage the dog to roll over (perhaps by gently nudging it down and around yourself) and then would reward it with some treat. Fairly quickly, no doubt, your dog would learn that if it wanted a treat it would have to roll over. Before you knew it, Fido would probably be rolling throughout your house. In Skinner's theory, the dog's rolling would be called **operant behavior.** This is because it operates on its environment, specifically by *causing* its owner to give it a treat. In other words, classical conditioning means the stimulus (like a light) causes the respondent behavior (salivation); in operant conditioning the operant behavior (dog rolling over) seems to cause the reinforcing stimulus (dog getting the treat). In operant conditioning the main emphasis is on strengthening the association between the stimulus (treat) and the operant behavior response (dog rolling over).[35]

CONDITIONED RESPONSE
An act or response previously associated with one stimulus becomes associated with another.

RESPONDENT BEHAVIOR
Behavior that simply responds to a stimulus.

OPERANT BEHAVIOR
Behavior that results from a reward that appears to be a consequence of the subject operating on its environment—such that its behavior "leads to" the stimulus. See operant conditioning.

OPERANT CONDITIONING
Conditioning in which the operant behavior seems to cause the reinforcing stimulus and the operant behavior response.

BEHAVIOR MODIFICATION
Changing or modifying behavior through the use of contingent rewards or punishment.

BEHAVIOR MODIFICATION

The principles of **operant conditioning** are often applied through behavior modification. **Behavior modification** means changing or *modifying* behavior through the use of contingent rewards or punishment, and it is built on two principles: (1) that behavior which appears to lead to a positive consequence (reward) tends to be repeated, while behavior that appears to lead to a negative consequence (punishment) tends not to be repeated; and (2) therefore, by providing the properly scheduled rewards, it is possible to change a person's motivation and behavior.[36] There are two central factors in behavior modification. They are the types of reinforcement and the schedules of reinforcement.

TYPES OF REINFORCEMENT Assume you are a manager whose employees are chronically late for work. You want to use behavior modification to train them to come in on time. You could choose from four types of reinforcement: positive reinforcement, negative reinforcement, extinction, and punishment.

First, you could focus on reinforcing the *desired* behavior (which in this case is coming to work on time). To do this, you could use either positive or negative reinforcement. **Positive reinforcement** involves giving rewards like praise or raises each time the desired behavior—in this case coming to work on time—occurs. **Negative reinforcement** also focuses on reinforcing the desired behavior (coming to work on time). But instead of providing a positive reward, the "reward" is that the employee avoids some negative consequence. For example, the employee avoids being harassed or reprimanded for coming in late. The *reward* is thus a negative one—employees who come in on time will avoid some negative consequence like harassment or a reprimand.

Alternatively, you might focus on reducing the *un*desired behavior (coming in late) rather than on rewarding the desired behavior. With behavior modification, you can use two types of reinforcement to reduce undesired behavior: extinction and punishment. People tend to repeat behavior that they have learned leads to positive consequences; with **extinction,** reinforcement is withheld so that over time the undesired behavior disappears. For example, suppose your employee learns from experience that coming to work late invariably leads to a scolding by you, which in turn leads to much laughter and attention on the part of the worker's peers. That laughter represents a positive reinforcement to the worker for coming in late. Extinction would involve ignoring the employee or disciplining that person in the privacy of your office, thus removing the attention and laughter—the reinforcement the worker receives from his or her friends.

Punishment is a second way to reduced undesired behavior. Here, for instance, you might reprimand or harass late employees. Punishment is the most controversial method of modifying behavior. Skinner recommends extinction rather than punishment for decreasing the undesired behavior's frequency. Positive reinforcement is preferred.

SCHEDULES OF POSITIVE REINFORCEMENT The schedule through which you apply the positive reinforcement is the second most important aspect of behavior modification. There are basically four schedules you can use to apply positive reinforcement.

With a **fixed interval schedule** the person gets a reward only when the desired response occurs and only after the passage of a specified fixed period of time since the previous reinforcement. For example, at the end of each week you might go around and praise each employee who came to work on time every day that week.

Variable interval schedules also are based on time. However, your worker is reinforced at some variable interval around some average. For example, suppose you want to provide reinforcement on the average of once a day for all employees who come to work on time. You might then visit them once on Tuesday, skip Wednesday, three times on Thursday, and so forth, in such a way that the praise averages out to once a day.

POSITIVE REINFORCEMENT
Involves giving rewards like praise or raises each time the desired behavior occurs.

NEGATIVE REINFORCEMENT
Involves achieving the desired behavior by avoiding some negative consequence.

EXTINCTION
Reinforcement is withheld so that over time the undesired behavior disappears.

PUNISHMENT
A way to reduce undesired behavior by punishing the person, for example, reprimanding or harassing late employees.

FIXED INTERVAL SCHEDULE
A person receives a reward only when the desired response occurs and only after the passage of a specified fixed period of time since the previous reinforcement.

VARIABLE INTERVAL SCHEDULE
Based on time, the worker is reinforced at some variable interval around some average.

Many garment industry workers are paid on a fixed rate schedule, that is, by the number of pieces they produce, regardless of how long it takes to produce them.

FIXED RATIO SCHEDULE
Based on units of output, rather than on time. Rewards are delivered only when a fixed number of desired responses occur.

VARIABLE RATIO SCHEDULES
Based on units of output, the number of desired outcomes necessary to elicit a reward changes around some average.

A **fixed ratio schedule** is based on units of output, rather than on time. With a fixed ratio schedule, rewards are delivered only when a fixed number of desired responses occur. Most piece-rate incentive pay plans are on a fixed ratio schedule. The worker is rewarded every time he or she produces a fixed number of pieces.

Variable ratio schedules are also based on units of output, but the number of desired outcomes necessary to elicit a reward changes around some average. Las Vegas slot machines are examples of rewards administered according to variable ratio schedules. The number of times you can expect to hit a jackpot with such machines, *on the average* over the long term, is predictable. But because the jackpots come randomly on a variable interval schedule, you might get no jackpots for five times and then hit two jackpots in a row; or, you might go fifty times without a jackpot and then get one. The *Electronics Company* vignette provides an example.

Some schedules are more effective than others in maintaining the desired behavior:

1. In general, the fastest way to get someone to learn is *not to put them on a schedule at all.* Instead, reinforce the desired behavior continuously, each and every time it occurs. The drawback is that the desired behavior also diminishes very quickly once you stop reinforcing it.

2. Las Vegas-type variable ratio reinforcement is the most powerful at sustaining behavior. With this schedule people will continue producing the desired response for a long time even without reinforcement, since they are always expecting to hit the jackpot on the next try.

3. Fixed and variable ratio schedules are both better at sustaining behavior than are either of the interval schedules.

EVOLVING VIEWS OF MOTIVATION

THE CHANGING NATURE OF WORK

In a way, motivation was not a major issue in the early factories of Henry Ford. This was not because his workers were particularly satisfied or particularly well treated, since they were not. As you can see from the photos on the next page, the work on Ford's early assembly lines was dirty, hot, and demeaning. As one historian described it, "Men faced a seemingly endless line, moving at a pace they could not control and which did not allow for any variations in speed among individuals. As the assembly line became increasingly standardized, a deep sense of frustration became the rule in the shops."[37] To many Americans, Ford's assembly lines meant they could finally have their own cars, and this gave them a new freedom. But, ironically, to the Americans who were building those cars, "the line" meant some of the most restrictive jobs the world had ever known.

Yet they generally worked, and worked hard, and the fact that they were not particularly motivated did not really seem to matter for several reasons. In 1913, Henry

THE ELECTRONICS COMPANY

Behavior modification has been used in many companies, for instance to improve worker safety and reduce absenteeism. In one application, an electronics manufacturer found that it had an absenteeism and tardiness problem and concluded that behavior modification could reduce the problem. Under the program, employees could qualify for a monthly drawing of a prize only if they had perfect attendance and punctuality records for the month. Thus, eligibility for the monthly drawings was contingent upon work attendance. The reward itself—winning the monthly lottery—is an example of variable ratio reinforcement. While an employee probably would not win it every month, over the period of a year employees could at least informally assess the odds that their number would come up.

In this program, all absences of any kind precluded employee eligibility. A drawing was held on the last work day of each month in which the winner was selected at random from a bowl containing the names of all employees who had maintained perfect attendance and punctuality records for that month. A small cash prize was awarded to the winner of each monthly lottery. In addition, the names of all employees who qualified were listed on the plant bulletin board. The program apparently improved attendance and decreased sick leave expenditures about 30 percent during its first year of operation.

SOURCE: Jerry Wallin and Ronald Johnson, "The Positive Reinforcement Approach to Controlling Employee Absenteeism," *Personnel Journal*, August 1976, 390–92.

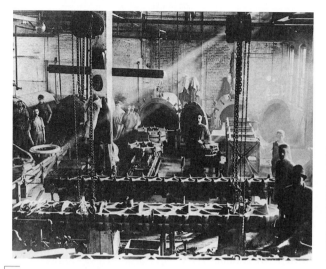 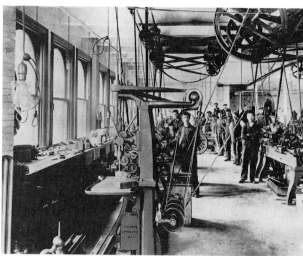

*Although jobs on early auto pro-
duction lines were narrowly
defined and filled with repetition,
workers were never in short supply
because the pay was better than
average.*

Ford paid his workers the then unheard of sum of almost $1.00 per hour, and there
was never any lack of qualified labor. Second, as you can see from the photos above,
the genius of the assembly line was that it reduced each worker's job to one very narrow task which he or she then carried out time after time, repetitiously. The entire
idea of the line was to minimize variability—in the parts that were used, in the efforts
of the workers, and in the final product that was produced. The effect was to create a
situation in which *motivation* as most of us use the term today was unimportant. Jobs
were so specialized that they required very little thought and certainly no creativity or
improvisation; foremen could patrol the line, insuring compliance; and workers that
would not toe the line could easily be replaced from the crowds of applicants waiting
to get in.

We face a very different world today. In the book *Made in America,* for instance
researchers analyzed the factors that made some firms highly successful in manufacturing today.[38] Here's what they say about how the role of workers is changing:

> In the most successful firms today the role of production workers is shifting from one of
> passive performance of narrow, repetitive tasks to one of active collaboration in the organi-
> zation and fine-tuning of production.[39]

TWO WAYS TO OBTAIN COMPLIANCE

Earlier we said that there are two basic methods available to obtain compliance. You
can, first, *force* someone to comply, perhaps by holding a gun to their head or by giving them narrow, standardized jobs that can be closely supervised. At the other
extreme, you can tap that person's internal *desire* to perform—to get them to genuinely *want* to do the job. The thing to remember is that close supervision and enforcing the rules does not work very well in most of today's service, knowledge, and high-
tech production jobs. An employer can force a worker to tighten a bolt correctly, over
and over again. But when it comes to tapping the worker's initiative—getting her to
create a new computer circuit board or getting him to be extra nice to a client when
no boss is around—holding a gun to the employee's head will not do. Winning commitment and getting employees to genuinely *want* to do their jobs and "go the extra
mile" is thus the goal of motivation theory today.

MODERN MOTIVATION PRACTICES

Comprehensive programs aimed at winning employee commitment are a primary way some firms obtain such self-motivated behavior today, as explained earlier in Chapter 12. In addition, managers use three specific motivation techniques to encourage self-motivation: pay for performance and profit sharing, appealing to workers' higher-level needs, and self-management programs and job enrichment.

PAY FOR PERFORMANCE AND PROFIT SHARING

Companies today increasingly deemphasize across-the-board salary increases and instead emphasize **pay for performance.** As Rosabeth Moss Kanter says:

> Entrepreneurial incentives that give teams a piece of the action are highly appropriate in collaborative companies. Because extra rewards are based only on measurable results, this approach also conserves resources.[40]

As a result, variable pay, pay for performance, and nontraditional incentive plans are flourishing today. For example, variable pay plans for nonexecutive employees (pay plans that included such things as companywide bonuses based on company performance, as well as individual and group/team bonuses) were used by 51 percent of companies responding to one recent survey.[41] The *DuPont* vignette provides an example. Another survey found that 54 percent of the responding organizations used nontraditional incentives to motivate their employees. For example, spot bonuses—spontaneous cash awards for extraordinary individual performance—were found to be awarded by 26 percent of the surveyed organizations. Many other firms have also implemented individual or group incentive plans and cash profit-sharing plans or so-called gainsharing plans. A **gainsharing plan** is an incentive plan that engages many or all employees in a common effort to achieve a company's productivity objectives; resulting incremental cost savings gains are shared among employees and the company.[42]

APPEALING TO EMPLOYEES' HIGHER-LEVEL NEEDS

Managers today also use various practices that are aimed at motivating employees by appealing to their higher-level needs. These practices—which are all ultimately aimed at increasing the responsiveness and flexibility of organizations and their employees—include quality improvement programs, worker empowerment, and continuous learning programs. We will discuss each of these in subsequent chapters; here we will just illustrate the higher-level needs motivational aspect of each of these types of programs.

QUALITY IMPROVEMENT PROGRAMS As we will see in Chapter 19, **quality improvement programs** are often built around **quality circles.** These are groups of 5 to 10 specially trained employees who meet for an hour once a week for the purpose of spotting and solving problems in their work area. Often working with a specially trained *facilitator*, these groups are usually expected to identify work-related problems in their work areas, and apply statistical and other problem analysis techniques to solve these problems. They then present the proposed solution to management for implementation. At the heart of most quality circle programs is the extensive training that group members receive. This typically takes four days or more and emphasizes techniques such as statistics, histograms, and basic problem-solving techniques. The thrust of programs like these is to get employees involved in a concrete way in analyzing and solving problems at work on the assumption that the people actually doing the work

PAY FOR PERFORMANCE
Salary increase based on merit or performance rather than the standard across-the-board salary increase.

GAINSHARING PLAN
An incentive plan that engages many or all employees in a common effort to achieve a company's productivity objectives; resulting incremental cost savings gains are shared among employees and the company.

QUALITY IMPROVEMENT PROGRAMS
Programs built around quality circles for the purpose of spotting and solving problems in their work area.

QUALITY CIRCLES
Groups of 5 to 10 specially trained employees who meet for an hour once a week for the purpose of spotting and solving problems in their work area.

DUPONT CHEMICAL COMPANY

The DuPont Chemical Company's new achievement sharing program illustrates how one firm instituted a variable pay plan for virtually all its employees.

The Achievement Sharing Program, implemented in the company's huge fibers department, is based on a simple concept: the better the department does in achieving its earnings objective, the more its employees will benefit. It is a variable pay system, which means that employees' earnings will rise and fall according to the department's yearly earnings. That way, all participating employees share in both the rewards as well as some of the risks involved in meeting (or not meeting) their earnings projections.

Basically, with Achievement Sharing an employee's monthly compensation has two components: a fixed component and a variable at-risk component. The fixed component is based on what the employee has historically earned and what employees in equivalent positions in other DuPont departments are earning. The employee earns this base component every month, regardless of department performance. However (and this is where the variable-pay component comes in), at the beginning of the year employees can put part of their base component "at risk." If they decide to put, say, 6 percent of their base component at risk and the department doesn't meet its earnings projection, then their subsequent monthly earnings are reduced by 6 percent. However, if the department's earnings projections are met, then they get that 6 percent back each month, plus an additional 2 percent. Of course, the more the department exceeds its earnings projections, the higher the monthly bonus each at-risk employee would earn.

For a company like DuPont (or any other, for that matter), this kind of plan offers three big advantages. First, if for some reason earnings projections are disappointing, the company gets to conserve a lot of cash, since the employees' at-risk pay will not be paid to them. Second, the plan's incentive feature focuses all employees' attention on their department's earnings and hopefully boosts motivation, so that higher performance and earnings should thereby result. Finally, a program like this provides a very equitable and solid financial foundation that employers can build on in their attempts to appeal to employees' higher-level needs via programs like job enrichment.

SOURCE: Robert McNutt, "Sharing Across-the-Board: DuPont's Achievement Sharing Program," *Compensation and Benefits Review*, July–August 1990, 17–24. Decreased earnings during the 1990–1991 recession and employee pressure for more control over the amount of their pay they put at risk caused DuPont to discontinue its variable pay program in 1991. See Joyce Santora, "DuPont Returns to the Drawing Board," *Personnel Journal*, February 1991, 34–36.

When you shop at Home Depot, the boss waits on you every time. Home Depot building supply stores are owned by their employees. Programs like this are powerful motivators; if the store does well, the workers do well.

are often in the best position to understand how to solve the problems in their workplace.

To the extent that programs like these are successful, it is because workers can satisfy higher-level needs, such as for affiliation and achievement, by participating in the programs. Working together in a relatively small, cohesive group with the goal of solving concrete problems together appeals to most workers' affiliation needs and is therefore a motivating experience. Perhaps more important, though, the opportunity to use one's analytical skills to solve problems at work appeals to most workers' needs for achievement and provides the sort of challenging opportunity that McGregor would suggest most employees want. And the recognition and feedback that comes from having management approve and implement a suggested solution further contributes to most employees' sense of achievement.

EMPOWERING WORKERS According to management expert Tom Peters, **empowering** really boils down to taking someone seriously. As Peters says, "No one denies where the answers are: on the firing line. How do we get people to come forth and give the answers, to take risks by trying new things bound to fail at times?"[43] According to Peters, "empower them."

As explained in Chapter 12, many companies are therefore taking steps to empower their employees. At Sweden's Scandinavian Airlines System, for instance, Chief Executive Jan Carlzon accomplished this by granting broad responsibility to workers on all levels. For example, an SAS ticket clerk can switch a ticket or give vouchers to disgruntled passengers without a lot of red tape. Similarly (as we will discuss further in Chapter 21, Service Management), flight attendants can serve free alcoholic beverages after a delay without getting prior approval and without fear of bureaucratic wrangling.[44]

Worker empowerment succeeds in part because it motivates employees—"turns them on"—by appealing to their higher-level needs. Worker empowerment literally gives employees greater power and more authority over their jobs and to that extent boosts the challenge and sense of achievement that can be derived from them.

CONTINUOUS LEARNING Continuous learning at work is often the foundation upon which worker motivation is built. Managers, faced with the need to provide improved services and higher quality products and to manage high-tech flexible manufacturing plants require, as we have seen, highly trained and self–motivated employees. As a result, more companies recognize today what many foreign firms have known for years: motivating workers to do a better job and to use their heads goes hand in

EMPOWERING
Giving someone the responsibility for a significant task, and the tools and authority required to do it.

CONTINUOUS LEARNING
Providing resources for employees to continue building on their store of knowledge.

hand with training. As one recent report put it, "It is a powerful combination: workers who equip themselves [through training] to be competitive and employers who provide them with challenging jobs."[45]

In fact, the report *Made in America* concludes that one of the big differences between highly competitive countries like Japan and West Germany and less competitive countries is that Japan and West Germany "use on the job training to develop general, transferable skills as well as specialized capabilities."[46] In West Germany, for instance, 16 year olds enter apprenticeships on leaving school and then receive extensive broad-based training after going to work. In Japan training has such high priority that a manager's skill as a teacher carries great weight in the person's promotions. Most Japanese firms make extensive use of rotation through various departments (a form of training), off-the-job training in special company institutes, specific job-related skills training, and broader training (for instance, to build problem-solving skills).

Such on-the-job training pays off in several ways. The employer, of course, gets a highly skilled and relatively flexible work force comprised of employees able to move easily from job to job and communicate more easily with colleagues in other departments. Furthermore, this skills training also results in a more highly motivated work force. "Knowledge is power," a philosopher once said, and workers who know they have the knowledge and skills to accomplish challenging tasks are usually more motivated to do so. The process of learning and developing new skills also contributes to the workers' sense of achievement and to their sense that the company is helping them to self-actualize and to become all they are able to become.

SELF-MANAGEMENT/JOB ENRICHMENT PROGRAMS

Other firms use self-managed teams (fully discussed in Chapter 17) and other types of job enrichment programs to motivate employees today. At Corning's Blacksburg, Virginia, plant, for instance, highly trained employee teams carry out most of the tasks previously assigned to supervisors. They make many of their own managerial decisions, such as inspecting their own quality, disciplining fellow workers, and choosing vendors.

Many firms have instituted job enrichment programs. Thus in one AT&T department the enrichment program involved reorganizing clerks' jobs. Previously, customers' complaints were handled sequentially: one unit got the complaints, a second researched the problem, a third corresponded with the customer, and so forth. Jobs were reorganized so that each clerk was responsible for receiving, researching, and responding to customers' complaints, and motivation and productivity increased dramatically.

MOTIVATION TECHNIQUES FOR INNOVATING AND THRIVING ON CHAOS: EXAMPLES

In his books *Thriving on Chaos* and *Liberation Management,* management expert Tom Peters argues that the way for companies to achieve flexibility and responsiveness is by motivating their people, by empowering them and by giving them more influence over their jobs. Here, says Peter, is how world-class companies motivate their workers[47]:

INVOLVE EVERYONE IN EVERYTHING   Peters says that "the chief reason for our failure in world-class competition is our failure to tap our workforce's potential."[48] The root of the problem, he says, is the attitude of management, an attitude that seems to assume (as McGregor would say) that employees do not like to work and must be closely supervised and restricted in relatively narrow jobs to make sure that they get their jobs done. Instead, says Peters, managers have to ask themselves if they "genuinely believe that there are no limits to what the average person can accomplish, if well trained, well supported, and well paid."[49] And, he says, employers must put their money where their mouths are, by involving "everyone in everything." A General Motors Delco-Remy plant in Fitzgerald, Georgia, shows how far involvement can go. Here, most individual workers

- handle all quality control (experts are on tap only if needed in specific cases);
- do all maintenance and make minor repairs on machines;
- keep track of their own time (there are no time cards and no time clocks);
- handle the "housekeeping" (there are no janitors);
- participate in a pay-for-performance program (for learning almost every job in the plant);
- are organized into teams that engage in regular problem-solving activities;
- are responsible for safety;
- have full-time access to the lock-free tool room;
- do budget preparation and review (capital and operating budgets);
- help determine staffing levels;
- advise management on equipment layout and generate requirements for new equipment;
- are in charge of all recruiting and run the assessment center for new recruits;
- decide on layoff patterns (whether to lay people off or have everybody work shorter hours, for example); and
- rotate as leaders of work teams.[50]

MAKE EVERY EMPLOYEE A BUSINESS PERSON Many firms, says Peters, do not just involve workers in decision-making: they turn employees into business people who are individually in charge of their own self-contained businesses. For example, at Indianapolis's 1,041-bed St. Vincent Hospital, says Peters, there were 598 separate job classifications, most with just a single job incumbent.[51] Such specialization caused at least two problems, he says. First, employees were not particularly motivated by such narrow and highly specialized jobs. Second, customer service suffered, since the job of attending to a single customer or patient was split among several employees. As an alternative, here is what was suggested for this hospital:

- Care givers are cross-trained to provide 80 to 90 percent of the services their patients need—including traditional bedside nursing, basic X-ray films, routine lab work, respiratory care, and EKGs. Appropriate X-ray and lab equipment is redeployed to the unit. As a result, patients seldom leave the unit and almost never requiring scheduling . . . [or] major transportation . . .
- Care givers truly "own" their patients. Continuity is maintained across shifts and across days of stay. Care givers admit their own patients and perform medical record coding and abstraction. They perform even the mundane tasks of linen changing, tray passing . . . three day stay patients no longer interact with 55 employees; they interact with fewer than 15 . . .
- Routine ancillary services are performed for the convenience of patients and doctors, not as dictated by central departments. Turnaround times outperform current levels . . .
- Documentation now consumes less than 30 minutes per care giver per day. Medical records can now be measured in millimeters, not inches. Quality is more transparent. We no longer need to be satisfied with merely auditing the process of care.

MATHSOFT

MathSoft cofounders David Blohm and Allen Razdow are firm believers that you can create a successful family business even if no one in the office is related. According to them, the secret is in people's attitudes, not their bloodlines.

Blohm and Razdow run their $10 million Cambridge, Massachusetts, software business without much in the way of corporate structure. They deal with one another in a relatively personal way, and this same type of communication extends to employees. In fact, Blohm believes that the nearer they can come to making employees feel like partners in the company, the better employee work performance will be. If that sounds like an attempt to build the same sort of vested interest in success that a family business member would feel, it is.

Blohm and Razdow hold quarterly employee meetings and are candid about the company's financial condition, as well as where they are headed in the future and how they plan to get there. They also try to be energetic about recognizing standout employees

or announcing promotions. The company is managed through a committee of ten people, all of whom own stock options.

Blohm and Razdow also like to delegate what they call ownership responsibility as well. For example, MathSoft's director of product development, Mariann Ivey, has also assumed ownership responsibility for handling customer phone calls. Blohm and Razdow have always insisted on

**FOCUS ON
SMALL BUSINESS**

emphasizing personal service, and Ivey picked up on that. Although Ivey's background was in technical support, her commitment to looking after customer needs really shows; Blohm says he regularly gets letters complimenting her work.

The career ladder at MathSoft also bears strong resemblance to a family business. Even though very little planning goes into the process, employee

responsibility grows and evolves as their time with the company increases. The cofounders have always used an informal management style keyed to employee individuality, and they have extended this approach to issues such as maternity leave, part-time work, and working at home. For example, Blohm and Razdow weren't surprised when members of their R&D department said they no longer would wear shoes. "I don't think we're by any means a zoo of a place that encourages odd behavior," Razdow says, "but we make accommodations for other people's working styles. We're more results-oriented."

Blohm and Razdow are convinced that giving people objectives and then letting them operate as they see fit is itself motivational, since it's tantamount to expressing confidence in their ability to perform. How exactly they do their jobs is then up to them, as long as they continue to produce to the level expected. Both stock ownership and responsibility ownership thus play a role in an employee's sense of belonging with the company.

SOURCE: "Why Every Business Can Be a Family Business," *Inc.,* March 1992, 80.

- Long-term, sustainable reductions in personnel on the order of 15 to 20 percent are possible.[52]

The *MathSoft* small business box shows how one firm applied many of these ideas.

USE SELF-CONTAINED WORK TEAMS   We will discuss this further in Chapter 17, but Peters found that firms are widening their spans of control and shifting the supervisor's duties down to self-managing work teams. For example, recall from Chapter 7 that at Johnsonville Foods, members in a typical 12-person work group

- recruit, hire, evaluate, and fire (if necessary) on their own;
- regularly acquire new skills as they see fit, then train one another as necessary;
- formulate, then track and amend, their own budget; and
- make capital investment proposals as needed.[53]

LISTEN/CELEBRATE/RECOGNIZE   We've seen that people have a need to be recognized, in part because such recognition provides material confirmation of their achievements. Perhaps that is why Peters found that many firms today establish a multitude of opportunities for recognizing their employees' accomplishments. Specific practices here (in addition to annual bonuses or incentive payments or merit raises) include the following:

- Federal Express supervisors are authorized to present Alpha-Bravo awards. These might range from tickets to a show to several hundred dollars and are used spontaneously to recognize the efforts of individual employees.

- Peters says "consider a ritual like that of the top property manager of Marriott's in Albuquerque, New Mexico. He makes it a rigorous habit to send out at least 100 thank you notes a month to his staff for jobs well done.[54]

- Schedule periodic events such as special meals at the company cafeteria to celebrate accomplishments such as "90 days of meeting the promise of 95% fulfillment within 24 hours of receiving an order," suggests Peters. Use "90 days at 95%" hats or t-shirts to emphasize the accomplishment.[55]

- Stop at the bakery on the way to work several times a month and pick up donuts to reward a project team that passed a minor milestone the day before.[56]

SPEND TIME LAVISHLY ON RECRUITING We know from expectancy theory that if people are not right for the job they probably will not be motivated to do it. After all, how motivated would you be to do a job that you believed you could not do, or do well? We discussed employee recruiting and selecting in Chapter 10. Suffice it to say here that Peters argues that motivating employees requires that you spend time "lavishly" on recruiting people who have the capability to do the job and the values to help ensure that they'll fit in with your other employees.[57]

TRAIN AND RETRAIN Training (see Chapter 18) is a multi-faceted motivation booster. It boosts motivation by increasing employees' expectancies regarding success, and by broadening their skills and abilities and thereby helping them to self-actualize.

This helps to explain why Peters found so many firms that invest in human capital by lavishly training and retraining all their employees. At a General Motors assembly plant, Pat Carrigan, the first woman to manage a GM assembly plant, dramatically improved the plant's performance, largely by extensively training employees. For example, she immediately instituted a two-week pre-start-up training program for everyone; this followed a long shut-down that resulted from a recession. Next, she instituted an ongoing training program that gave 3,000 people a total of about 360,000 hours of training over a two-year period.[58] (In fact, it's not unusual for firms to give all their employees—not just their new ones—several weeks of training every year. For example, both Toyota Motor Manufacturing, Inc., and Saturn Corporation give their employees at least two weeks of training each year, and everyone at Federal Express including the CEO is required to take one week of training each year.)

The training these employees receive is not just technical training that helps the person to do his or her current job better. At Saturn and Toyota training involves improving problem-solving skills, developing analytical skills, and learning accounting and planning, for instance. At Ben & Jerry's, employees are encouraged to attend college to broaden their horizons and better prepare them for bigger jobs. The point is that in all of these firms training is not just aimed at boosting the company's performance. Training is also a motivational technique in that it broadens the employees' vistas and helps the employee become the person he or she has the potential to become—to self-actualize.

PROVIDE AN EMPLOYMENT GUARANTEE Finally, Peters suggests providing an employment guarantee. As discussed in Chapter 12, such an employment guarantee does not necessarily have to mean that no one is ever fired. But firms that are successful in fostering the commitment and motivation that breeds responsiveness and innovation know they have too much of an investment in their workers to let them go except under the worst economic conditions. They also know that it is difficult or impossible for employees to develop a sense of partnership or ownership with the firm—to treat the firm and its customers like their own—unless they see that the firm is also committed to their security. Most of these sorts of firms therefore work very hard to avoid layoffs. At Ben & Jerry's, for instance, the firm did not lay off employees when production at one of its plants had to be slowed down. Instead, it redeployed all of the employees to projects like painting fire hydrants in the town. The town viewed the effort as socially responsible (which it was), and the employees appreciated being kept on the payroll. Then, when demand picked up, the employees returned to the plant.

S U M M A R Y

Motivation can be defined as the intensity of an individual's desire to engage in some activity. Motivation theories can be classified as need-based, cognitive-process-based, expectancy-based, and reinforcement.

Maslow's needs-hierarchy theory is a typical need-based theory of motivation. It states that people have five categories of needs—physiological, safety, social, self-esteem, and self-actualization—and that individuals move upward through the hierarchy, satisfying lower-order needs and progressing to higher needs.

Alderfer's existence-relatedness-growth theory of motivation was designed to improve on Maslow's theory by classifying needs into three groups—existence, relatedness, and growth needs—and by saying the three groups are all active at the same time.

David McClelland and John Atkinson say there are three needs of particular importance for managers to understand: the needs for achievement, power, and affiliation.

Herzberg's motivator-hygiene theory agrees that people have a lower and higher set of needs, but argues that the best way to motivate someone is to offer to satisfy the higher-level needs. Herzberg says the best approach is to design a job so that a person derives a sense of achievement, accomplishment, and fulfillment from doing it. Central to Herzberg's theory is the idea that there are two classes of work motivators: extrinsic and intrinsic factors.

Of the cognitive process theories of motivation, Adam's equity theory basically assumes that people need, value, and seek fairness in employee-employer relationships. Locke's goal theory of motivation argues that a goal an individual has consciously decided to pursue becomes a main motivator of that person's behavior.

Expectancy theories of motivation assume that persons try to maximize their benefits and minimize any negative effects and in the process size up both the potential rewards of doing the task, as well as the likelihood that efforts will indeed lead to the reward.

Reinforcement theories can be applied in organizations through the process of behavior modification. This is based upon the principles that behavior that leads to a positive consequence tends to be repeated, while behavior that leads to punishment is not repeated. The four types of reinforcement are positive, negative, extinction, and punishment.

Contemporary views on how to motivate workers have led to a broadening of tasks for workers. This challenges and taps workers' intrinsic motivation to do a job, as opposed to trying to force them to perform. Three practices that characterize modern motivational practices today are pay for performance and profit sharing, appealing to workers' higher-level needs, and an emphasis on self-management and job enrichment.

Q U E S T I O N S

■ FOR REVIEW

1. List Maslow's five categories of needs from the lowest to the highest. How does his theory differ from the need-based theories of motivation developed by Aldefer, McClelland and Atkinson, and Herzberg?

2. Name some examples of positive and negative reinforcement and the various behaviors to which they can be applied.

3. Explain why Theory X prescriptions are usually not effective in today's business environment.

■ FOR DISCUSSION

4. Describe some of the ways a manufacturer could meet the higher-level needs of employees. How important would pay be in determining their level of on-the-job satisfaction?

5. Do you believe that work behavior can be modified over the long term, or do you think employees will inevitably fall back into bad habits?

6. What are some of the pitfalls that can be associated with motivating employees through empowerment?

7. Which do you think is more effective: pay for individual performance or company profit sharing? Why?

■ FOR ACTION

8. Go to the library and look through recent business periodicals. Find one or two examples of companies that are using job enrichment to satisfy their employees' needs for accomplishment and fulfillment.

9. Using the modern motivation practices outlined in this chapter as your guide, interview your boss or a local business executive to find out how many of these strategies are being implemented at the company.

10. Your instructor will divide the class into two teams. One half of the class must formulate ideas for motivating engineers employed at a high-tech software company. The other half of the class must devise ideas for motivating migrant farm workers. Compare the strategies.

■ FOR FOCUS ON SMALL BUSINESS

11. How do MathSoft's founders meet employee needs for achievement, power, and affiliation as described in the chapter?

12. Which of the motivational practices advocated by management expert Tom Peters have been implemented at MathSoft?

13. As the company grows, will some of its motivational practices become impractical? Why or why not?

CLOSING SOLUTION

THE EQUITABLE COMPANIES

CEO Jenrette and COO Melone initially concentrated on selling Wall Street investment analysts on the sweeping changes at Equitable. It was an impressive pitch; Equitable's public offering eventually raised $2.5 billion. They also tapped Jim Benson as senior executive vice-president. His job was to reconvert the formerly faithful sales force. He decided to take the direct approach, visiting 70 of the company's 90 agencies and inviting Jenrette and Melone along on about half of the visits. Collectively the trio tried to hit all of the agents' hot-buttons. Melone provided reassurance. Jenrette stressed that the 134-year-old company would be around a while longer, and that it wouldn't be run from an ivory tower in New York. Benson told them what they really needed to hear—Equitable still offered the best products in the business. The company would make selling them easier through automated work stations. Computerization would make timely client and policy information available to all offices. Revamped commission schedules would mean higher income for top producers. And new agents as well as seasoned veterans would receive ongoing training. "If there is any group of people within the company that doesn't get much support, it's the established agents," Benson says. He pledged that agents would have the necessary product and expertise to exploit opportunities in the marketplace.

Benson's aim was to put Equitable agents back on the offensive in selling the company's products, and give them greater confidence and direction. To do that he had to convince them the overall workings of the company had really changed. A big part of that was achieved through incentive pay increases, and a real commitment to agent development through training and education. Benson talked to a total of 8,300 agents. The result was an increase in sales of 24 percent.

■ QUESTIONS FOR CLOSING SOLUTION

1. Which of the techniques outlined in the chapter did Equitable use to motivate its agents?

2. Why is ongoing training an important part of motivating the veteran agents?

3. Beyond the increase in revenue, how else would the company benefit from a motivated sales force?

KEY TERMS

Personality	Motivator Factors
Perception	Job Enrichment
Attributions	Cognitive-process Motivation Theories
Motivation	Equity Theory
Need-based Theories	Expectancy Theory
Expectancy-based Theories	Theories of Motivation
Reinforcement Theories	Expectancy
Needs-hierarchy Theory of Motivation	Instrumentality
Prepotency Process Principle	Valence
Physiological Needs	Conditioned Response
Safety Needs	Operant Behavior
Social Needs	Operant Conditioning
Self-esteem Needs	Behavior Modification
Self-actualization Needs	Positive Reinforcement
Existence-relatedness Growth (ERG) Theory	Negative Reinforcement
Existence Needs	Extinction
Relatedness Needs	Punishment
Growth Needs	Fixed Interval Schedule
Need for Achievement	Variable Interval Schedule
Need for Power	Fixed Ratio Schedule
Need for Affiliation	Pay for Performance
Two-factor Theory	Gainsharing Plan
Intrinsic Factors	Quality Improvement Programs
Job Content	Quality Circles
Extrinsic Factors	Empowering
Hygienes	Continuous Learning

CASE FOR ANALYSIS

PEOPLE EXPRESS AIRLINES, INC.

Donald Burr founded People Express Airlines with two things in mind. He wanted to make flying affordable to everyone, and he wanted to create the perfect place to work. He began with 250 employees and three used Boeing 727s in 1981. Four years later, People Express was the ninth largest airline in the United States, with $1 billion in revenues, 4,000 employees, and 71 jets, four of which were 747s. A million passengers a month were flying the no-frills discount airline. People's Newark, N.J. terminal, formerly inhabited mostly by rodents, was refurbished to elegance and glowed with every color of the rainbow. But despite his unerring entrepreneurial instincts, Burr never quite made it to the real rainbow's end.

The goals of People Express were based on six precepts Burr expected everyone to live by. The first was three-fold: top service, growth, and development of employees. People Express would also be the best provider of transportation; it would develop top leaders; it would be a role model; it would employ a simple approach; and it would make as much money as possible.

Burr's revolutionary approach at People Express emphasized motivating his people. Its cornerstones were self-management and voluntary cooperation. He was an early pioneer of eliminating organizational hierarchy and specialization. Cross-utilization is the description Burr selected for employee responsibilities at People. The term somehow seemed inadequate. Everyone rotated through jobs. Pilots not only flew planes, they checked baggage and took reservations. Every employee was required to become a stockholder. Those that couldn't afford to were given interest-free loans. And education never stopped. "Everybody is a teacher and a learner," said team manager Jim Miller. "Training is a very, very big part of People Express. We're in the business of training leaders, so we have no training budget—whatever it takes is what we'll spend."

Another of Burr's chief concerns was that employees be happy. The airline lived by the axiom that everyone is basically honest and trustworthy, and given an open environment, would do the right thing for the company. During the nearly four-year rise of People, maintaining that culture was easy. The momentum seemed unstoppable, growth was spectacular, and no one doubted People was on the way to conquering the airline world. Of those heady days, Burr said, "People Express had a mystique; we couldn't do anything wrong. We just bought planes, hired people, and put them in the air. Grow, grow, grow."

But that growth led to a loss of the sense of family among employees. Burr's solution was to splinter the airline into 10 mini-airlines. Since its founding, the airline had operated with every employee serving as either a customer service manager, flight manager, or maintenance manager. Rotating assignments could lead an employee into recruitment, training, marketing, or accounting. Groups of a few hundred managers representing all three job classifications were led by team managers, general managers, and a managing officer just below the CEO. These groups ran all aspects of assigned flight schedules, including hiring and training. "When people are needed in my group," Jim Miller said, "my group hires them and trains them and makes them feel like part of our family right from the start."

The mystique and the family atmosphere began to unravel in late 1984 and continued into the following year. The airline began losing money after competitors began price cutting. Suddenly, it seemed problems were cropping up everywhere. Morale sank. The seven-day-a-week grind started getting to people. New ways of doing things had to be implemented, and anxiety and uncertainty were rampant. The potential of unionization also loomed. Workers wondered whether People was doing enough for them. Burr had to resell the company vision hard on the heels of the company's first ever suspension of profit-sharing checks.

Plenty of critics inside and outside the industry had views on why dissension now ran so deeply through People. Burr himself wondered if it were possible for employees to put his six precepts in practice given the fact that the company had been adding new employees at a rate of three or four every day. Others pointed to the reliance on self-direction and lack of structure, which left the airline vulnerable to a vocal minority bent on fomenting discord. Burr thought his more human method of operation was communicated directly to customers via better service; critics charged he had forgotten he was running a business that had to turn a profit.

The ultimate undoing of People Express didn't come from within. A combination of factors, the principle of which was their acquisition of Frontier Airlines in late 1985 for $300 million, sealed the discount airliner's fate. Labor troubles and more fare wars ensued, and Frontier was bankrupt less than a year later. People's own service and load factors also began declining. Burr's effort to create a place where employees wouldn't have to "check their freedom, their humanity, at the door when they went to work," did not survive. In 1986, Burr announced the sale of People Express to Texas Air Corp. "I will grieve about People Express all of my life," he said.

SOURCES: George Newman, "The Morning After," *Across the Board,* September 1992, 11–12; Amy Barrett, "The Last Romantic," *Financial World,* May 14, 1991, 50–51; James Norman et al., "Nice Going Frank, But Will It Fly?" *Business Week,* September 29, 1986, 34–35; Geraldine Spruell, "Will Competition Knock the People out of People Express?" *Training and Development Journal,* May 1986, 50—54; Kenneth Labich, "How Long Can Quilting-Bee Management Work," *Fortune,* November 25, 1985, 132; and "Bitter Victories," *Inc.,* August 1985, 25–35.

■ QUESTIONS

1. Do you think Burr took his theories for motivating and empowering employees too far? Why or why not?
2. Which theories of motivation explained in the chapter best describe the management philosophy at People Express?
3. Based on the information outlined in this case, which of the following do you think played the greatest role in People's demise: unconventional management practices, rapid growth, industry factors beyond the airline's control?

A CASE IN DIVERSITY

MOTIVATED ENTREPRENEURS

There was a time when a corporate position meant a measure of security, a challenging career, and ongoing training. Motivated employees who did their jobs well could look forward to ascending the company ladder. But when security became a thing of the past, and disillusionment took its place in many cases, a lot of those same self-motivated managers began opting out of the corporate arena in favor of heading up their own operations. Few find the work any easier, especially those who face the added challenge of being at the helm of a minority-owned business. But the right kind of entrepreneurial risk-takers have found the economic and personal rewards are worth going it alone.

The lack of a regular paycheck wasn't the only drawback Anna Garcia discovered when she launched ANKO Metals Services, Inc., of Denver, Colorado. Operational hassles, employee tax filings, and workers who didn't show up caused plenty of headaches. She also had to fight the prejudices she encountered by virtue of the fact that she was both a woman and Hispanic. "Hispanics do not own corporations, they work for corporations. Women aren't the frontrunners. Women are the administrative support. That was the mindset," she says.

Garcia had been motivated to launch her own business more by circumstance than personal aspiration. She had ten years in the steel industry and planned to stay with Reynolds Aluminum forever when the company closed the Denver office and laid her off. Garcia perceived a glass ceiling at her old company. She wishes she'd paid more attention before she went on to head up her own steel company. But she must have picked up a few pointers; sales figures have grown steadily, topping $2 million annually.

Often, lack of financing is another obstacle minority business owners face. Rey G. Salinas, president of Horizon Telephone Systems, Inc., which serves the Texas cities of San Antonio, Houston, and McAllen, funded his company by tapping into his personal savings. While that may have left him feeling vulnerable, he says he never felt any great sense of security, even when he was with Southwestern Bell. This despite the fact that he received eight promotions. But the allure of running his own operation even overcame this kind of recognition. Salinas is quick to attribute a lot of his current success to the experience he gained in the corporate ranks. "The training and development I got was worth a million dollars," he says. Everything from administration to policy skills to the way he put together his infrastructure and operations were the result of things learned at Bell.

To some it may seem that abandoning a corporate ship to launch a start-up operation, by choice or otherwise, amounts to jumping from the frying pan into the fire. They may be right, but it all boils down to perspective. Lifetime job security is no longer a reasonable expectation, and often the ax can fall without warning. Entrepreneurs like Salinas and Garcia discovered that in a world without job guarantees, the best place to be is in the driver's seat calling the shots.

Source: Irene Middleman Thomas, "Me, Inc." *Hispanic,* October 1992, 57–60.

■ QUESTIONS

1. Which of Maslow's hierarchy of needs have the entrepreneurs profiled in this case satisfied by launching their own business?
2. Do you think the fact that they are minority business owners meant Garcia and Salinas had to be exceptionally motivated to start their businesses? Why or why not?
3. Now that they are business owners, what can these entrepreneurs do to ensure that their own employees are motivated?

ENDNOTES

1. Charles Butler, "Man on a Mission," *Sales & Marketing Management,* March 1994, 58–65.
2. R. Lattel, *The Scientific Analysis of Personality* (Baltimore: Penguin Books, 1965). See also G. Northcraft and M. Neale, *Organizational Behavior* (Hinsdale, IL, Dryden 1994) 64–240.
3. J. M. Digman, "Personality Structure: Emergence of the Five Factor Model," *Annual Review of Psychology,* vol. 41 (1990), 417–40.
4. Digman, "Personality Structure," 417–40.
5. Ernest R. Hilgard, *Introduction to Psychology* (New York: Harcourt, Brace and World, 1962), 186.
6. Timothy Costello and Sheldon Zalkind, *Psychology in Administration* (Englewood Cliffs, NJ: Prentice-Hall, 1963), 315–16.
7. Benson Rosen and Thomas Jerdee, "The Influence of Age Stereotypes on Managerial Decisions," *Journal of Applied Psychology,* vol. 61, no. 4 (August 1976), 428–32.
8. Maison Haire, "Role Perception in Labor Management Relations: An Experimental Approach," *Industrial and Labor Relations Review,* vol. 8, no. 2 (March 1955), 204–16.
9. Hilgard, *Introduction to Psychology,* 476. See also R. Heneman, et al, "Attributions and Exchanges: The Effects of Interpersonal Factors on the Diagnosis of Employee Performance," *Academy of Management Journal,* June 1989, 466–478: and Mary Ann Glynn, "Effects of Work Task Cues and Play Task Cues on Information Processing, Judgment, and Motivation," *Journal of Applied Psychology,* February 1994, 34–46.

10. Based on Ernest J. McCormick and Joseph Tiffin, *Industrial Psychology* (Englewood Cliffs, NJ: Prentice-Hall, 1974), 136–74. See also Marilyn Gist and Terence Mitchell, "Self-Efficacy: A Theoretical Analysis of Its Determinants and Malleability," *Academy of Management Review*, April 1992, 183–202.

11. See, for instance, Kanfer, "Motivation Theory," *Handbook of Industrial and Organizational Psychology*, 1990. See also Robert Hersey, "A Practitioner's View of Motivation," *Journal of Managerial Psychology*, May 1993, 110–15.

12. See Douglas M. McGregor, "The Human Side of Enterprise," in Michael Matteson and John M. Ivancevich, *Management Classics* (Santa Monica, CA: Goodyear, 1977), 43–49.

13. McGregor, "The Human Side of Enterprise," 45.

14. Based on Clayton P. Alderfer, *Existence, Relatedness, and Growth: Human Needs in Organizational Settings* (New York: The Free Press, 1972), 9–26.

15. Ibid., 10.

16. Ibid., 11.

17. Ibid.

18. Ibid., 12.

19. For a discussion see Alderfer, *Existence, Relatedness, and Growth,* 27.

20. Based on George H. Litwin and Robert A. Stringer, Jr., *Motivation and Organizational Climate* (Boston: Division of Research, Graduate School of Business Administration, Harvard University, 1968), 14–24.

21. Ibid., 19.

22. For a discussion see, for example, Frederick Herzberg, "One More Time: How Do You Motivate Employees?" *Harvard Business Review,* January–February 1968, reprinted in *Motivation Series,* reprints from *Harvard Business Review,* #21137, 54–63; and John P. Campbell and Robert Pritchard, *Motivation Theory in Industrial and Organizational Psychology,* Marvin D. Dunnette, *Handbook of Industrial and Organizational Psychology* (Chicago: Rand McNally College Publishing, 1976), 100–101; and John Hudy, "The Motivation Trap," *HR Magazine,* December 1992, 63–68.

23. See, for example, J. Richard Hackman, et al., "A New Strategy for Job Enrichment," *California Management Review,* vol. 17, no. 4 (1973), 57–71.

24. Kanfer, "Motivation Theory, 102. See also Robert Bretz and Steven Thomas, "Perceived Equity, Motivation, and Final-Offer Arbitration in Major League Baseball," *Journal of Applied Psychology,* June 1992, 280–89.

25. See, for example, J. Greenberg, "A Taxonomy of Organizational Justice Theories," *Academy of Management Review,* vol. 12 (1987), 9–22.

26. For a discussion, see Kanfer, "Motivation Theory," 124.

27. Campbell and Pritchard, *Motivation Theory,* 110.

28. Edwin A. Locke and D. Henne, "Work Motivation Theories," in C. L. Cooper and I. Robertson, eds., *International Review of Industrial and Organizational Psychology* (Chichester, England: Wiley, 1986), 1–35.

29. Kanfer, "Motivation Theory," 125.

30. A. J. Mento, R. P. Steel, and R. J. Karren, "A Meta-analytic Study of the Effects of Goal Setting on Task Performance: 1966–1984," *Organizational Behavior and Human Decision Processes,* vol. 39 (1987), 52–83.

31. Gary Latham and T. W. Lee, "Goal Setting," in Edwin A. Locke, ed., *Generalizing from Laboratory to Field Settings* (Lexington, MA: Lexington Books, 1986), 101–19.

32. Kanfer, "Motivation Theory," 113.

33. For a discussion, see John P. Campbell and Robert Pritchard, "Motivation Theory in Industrial and Organizational Psychology," in Marvin Dunnette, *Industrial and Organizational Psychology,* 74–75; and Kanfer, "Motivation Theory," 115–16.

34. See, for example, Terrence Mitchell, "Expectancy-Value Models in Organizational Psychology," in N. P. Feather, ed., *Expectations and Actions: Expectancy-Value Models in Psychology* (Hillsdale, NJ: Erlbaum, 1982), 293–312. See also Mark Tubbs, et al, "Expectancy, Valence, and Motivational Force Functions in Goal Setting Research: An Empirical Test," *Journal of Applied Psychology,* June 1993, 36–49.

35. For a recent review of operant conditioning, see Fred Luthans and R. Kreitner, *Organizational Behavior Modification and Beyond: An Operant and Social Learning Approach* (Glenview, IL: Scott Foresman, 1985).

36. W. Clay Hamner, "Reinforcement Theory in Management and Organizational Settings," in Henry Tosi and W. Clay Hamner, *Organizational Behavior and Management: A Contingency Approach* (Chicago: Saint Claire, 1974), 86–112. See also Donald J. Campbell, "The Effects of Goal-Contingent Payment on the Performance of a Complex Task," *Personnel Psychology*, vol. 37, no. 1, Spring 1984, 23–40.

37. Warner Phlug, *The UAW in Pictures* (Detroit: Wayne State University Press, 1971), 11.

38. Michael L. Dertouzos, Richard K. Lester, and Robert M. Solow, *Made in America* (Cambridge, MA: The MIT Press, 1989), 137.

39. Ibid., 137.

40. Rosabeth Moss Kanter, "The New Managerial Work," *Harvard Business Review*, November–December 1989, 91. See also J. Brudney and S. Condrey, "Pay for Performance: Explaining the Differences in Managerial Motivation," *Public Productivity and Management Review*, Winter 1993, 129–34; D. Marsden and R. Richardson, "Performing for Pay? The Effects of 'Merit Pay' on Motivation in a Public Service," *British Journal of Industrial Relations*, June 1994, 243–62.

41. See Bureau of National Affairs, *Bulletin to Management*, February 21, 1991, 55.

42. Barry Thomas and Madeline Hess Olson, "Gainsharing: The Design Guarantees Success," *Personnel Journal*, May 1988, 73–79. See also K. Sigler and T. Santone, "Linking Pay to Company Performance," *Journal of Compensation and Benefits*, September–October 1993, 49–53.

43. Tom Peters, *Thriving on Chaos* (New York: Harper & Row, 1988), 525.

44. Kenneth Labich, "An Airline That Soars on Service," *Fortune*, December 31, 1990, 96.

45. John Hoerr, "Sharpening Minds for a Competitive Edge," *Business Week*, December 17, 1990, 72.

46. Dertouzos, Lester, and Solow, *Made in America*, 87.

47. Peters, *Thriving on Chaos*, 328. For empirical evidence regarding Peter's suggestions, see, for example, "Performance, Productivity and Motivation. (A special selection of abstracts of articles covering the latest research and developments in Personnel Management)." *Personnel Review*, July 1993, 39–49.

48. Ibid., 345.

49. Ibid., 342.

50. Ibid., 350–51.

51. Tom Peters, *Liberation Management* (New York: Alfred A. Knopf, 1992), 229.

52. Ibid., 230.

53. Ibid., 238.

54. Peters, *Thriving on Chaos*, 372.

55. Ibid.

56. Ibid., 385.

57. Ibid., 388.

58. Ibid., 390.

ORGANIZATIONAL COMMUNICATION

LEARNING OBJECTIVES

After studying this chapter, you should be able to:

- Define communication and its importance in management.

- Describe the five basic elements of a communications model.

- Name interpersonal and organizational factors that can be barriers to effective communication.

- Explain how managers can reduce communication barriers.

- Distinguish between upward, horizontal, and downward organizational communication, and give examples of each.

- Discuss methods managers can use to encourage horizontal communication among employees.

- Rank communication media based on the speed of feedback, variety of communication channels employed, personalness of the source, and richness of language.

OPENING PROBLEM
COLGATE-PALMOLIVE CO.

Colgate-Palmolive Company initiated an employee communication program in its domestic division to discover why profits weren't up to par. The program was aimed at rallying middle management support for needed changes. But a cross section of the division's top 300 managers—queried on such topics as growth, common vision, teamwork, trust, communication, and understanding consumers—unearthed hidden hostilities. The survey of managers revealed a lack of leadership and direction in the domestic division. Even top-producing teams had little sense of continuity or cooperation. Most importantly, few of the respondents had a feel for what their primary objective really should have been: the customers. The behavioral issues revealed by the survey showed that sagging profits may have stemmed from other concerns.[1]

THE COMMUNICATION PROCESS

COMMUNICATION DEFINED

COMMUNICATION
The exchange of information and the transmission of meaning.

Psychologists Daniel Katz and Robert Kahn define **communication** as "the exchange of information and the transmission of meaning."[2] In fact, to most experts, communication does not even occur unless a listener can perceive "and re-create in his own mind the meaning contained in the mind of the communicator."[3] Managers—indeed, all employees—operate on the basis of what they know about things, like competitors' tactics, the supply of raw materials, or assembly line delays. It is not the actions themselves (of competitors, of supplies decreasing, or of delays) that prompt managerial action, but rather the information about these things. At Colgate-Palmolive's domestic division, for instance, the survey provided a clear picture of weaknesses that were keeping profits down. Armed with that information, management was able to take steps to improve the division's financial performance. Getting information from one place to another, clearly, quickly, and without distortion is always a critical part of managing any organization.

THE MANAGER AS A COMMUNICATOR

Much of what managers do has always revolved around the process of communicating, of getting information from one place or person to another place or person.[4] In fact, most studies of what managers do always conclude that they spend the lion's share of their time communicating. For example, one study of supervisors in a DuPont lab found that 53 percent of their time was occupied by meetings, 15 percent in writing and reading, and 9 percent on the telephone. In fact, when you count meetings, interacting with customers and colleagues, and the vast array of other ways in which managerial communication takes place it's estimated that managers typically spend from 60 to 80 percent of their time communicating, with the majority of communication occurring face-to-face.[5]

A COMMUNICATION MODEL[6]

Stripped to its essentials any communication process has five basic elements. These elements are depicted in the basic communication model shown in Figure 16.1.

SENDER   First someone or something must actually send the information.[7] In organizations, *people*—employees, customers, vendors, and the like—often send information. But *things*—fire alarms, machine breakdowns, and so on—send messages, too.

COMMUNICATIONS CHANNEL
A vehicle or vehicles that carry the message.

CHANNEL   Whether a person or a thing sends the message, the message and the information it contains must travel along a communication channel. A **communication channel** is a vehicle or vehicles that carry the message. Direct, face-to-face communication is the most familiar and widely used communication channel in organizations. However, many other channels are used as well. Memos, reports, policies and procedures manuals, videotaped reports, computerized information, and (in the navy) even flashing-light semaphores are some other possible channels.

NOISE SOURCE   Notice that the information sent is not necessarily the same as the information received. This is because all information channels (including face-to-face conversations, television, and semaphores) are subject to *noise,* specifically, distortions of various kinds. Thus, a face-to-face conversation in a noisy restaurant may lead to misunderstandings when the message is overwhelmed by the conversation from surrounding tables.

RECEIVER   The receiver is the person or persons to whom the information is sent. However, your experiences will confirm that the person to whom the information is

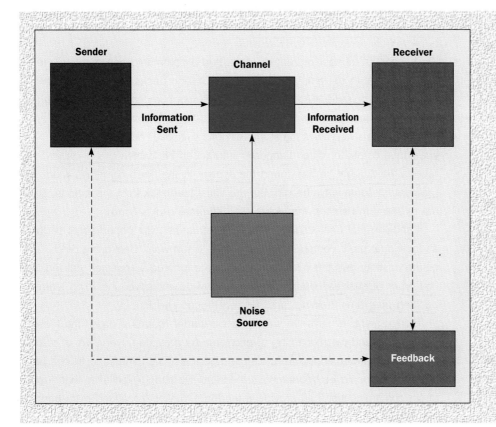

FIGURE 16.1

Basic Communication
Process Model

*Whether or not the message
is accurately received depends on the existence of
noise and the nature and
quality of the channel,
among other things.*

sent does not always "get the message." Various *communication barriers* exist. Noise in the channel may have so distorted the message that the message received is indecipherable or just wrong. Also, if the communication channel is not well-designed to suit the purpose, it is possible that the message will never arrive or will arrive too late. People's perceptions can also distort what a message is intended to mean. For example, if as a manager you innocently mention to a subordinate that you would like to speak to him in your office, you may create a nervous wreck. You may just have planned to discuss vacation schedules, but the insecure employee misperceived your tone and assumed you were about to fire him. We'll discuss communication barriers shortly.

FEEDBACK Finally, the communication process usually includes some type of feedback from receiver to sender. **Feedback** represents the receiver's response to the message that was actually received. For example, air-traffic controllers (and good managers) continually confirm and expect confirmation of the messages they send.

SUMMARY Our communication model summarizes important aspects of the communication process. Notice that a communication system is no stronger than its weakest link. If too much noise passes between sender and receiver, if the receiver misperceives the message, or the sender accidentally telegraphs the wrong message, then, strictly speaking, communication will not take place. The model also emphasizes how important both the channel and the feedback can be. For example, if your company's communication channel requires copious and highly detailed reports and approvals before a customer's request can be addressed, then the customer may be long gone before she finally gets an answer. The *Lantech* vignette shows how one firm rearranged its communication channels and feedback mechanisms to boost its effectiveness.

FEEDBACK
The receiver's response to the
message that was actually received.

LANTECH, INC.

Pat Lancaster, founder of Lantech, Inc., had a communication problem. He couldn't seem to get employees at his $50 million packaging-machinery manufacturer in Louisville, Kentucky to level with him completely. By wandering around the plant conducting impromptu question and answer sessions, Lancaster did get everyone's latest impressions. However he learned little of substance or depth. When Lancaster introduced his written group-leader reports, he thought he had found the answer to the firm's communication problem. In some ways he did, but the initial feedback from the reports, filled out by the firm's six top managers, was something of a horror.

It showed that Lantech's decentralized structure, with departments set up as individual profit centers, was vulnerable to turf wars, backbiting, and blame casting, and the customer needs were ignored. Lancaster realized the first order of business would be a companywide makeover, including team-building programs, training, and customer-focus checks.

Today Lancaster says the weekly group-leader reports sharpen the focus of meetings and the monitoring of problems by providing overviews of possible problem areas, and it takes his managers just five minutes to fill one out. Responses should be spontaneous, he says. He strongly believes that such direct communication can provide a feedback device for valued managers and employees, as well as a warning signal of trouble before it grows unmanageable. A group-leader report is shown on page 453.

SOURCE: Elizabeth Conlin, "The Vital-Signs Assessment," *Inc.*, April 1993, 127–29.

COMMUNICATION PATTERNS

The role played by communication channels and feedback in organizational performance was first illustrated by a series of studies carried out a number of years ago; these are now known as the **communication patterns studies**.[8] In brief, the studies showed that how the organization channels information (in particular, who can talk to whom and to what extent feedback is permitted) effects the accuracy and speed of decision-making.

These early studies experimented with several communication patterns, two of which are shown in Figure 16.2 on page 454. In most of these studies, each subject was placed in a compartment at a table in such a way that his communication was restricted (most of these early studies involved male subjects only). In the circle network shown in the figure, the subject could communicate only with the subjects to his left and to his right. Subjects in the wheel network could communicate only with the subject in the central position in the network but this central person could communicate with the four other subjects in the network. All the lines in the networks show two-way linkages. The overall structure of the network for any group was unknown to the subjects. All a person knew was to whom he could send messages and from whom he could receive them.

As summarized in Table 16.1 on page 455, the wheel and circle patterns produced very different results.[9] The circle pattern (which most experts associate with more free-

COMMUNICATION PATTERNS STUDIES
A series of studies carried out several years ago showing the role played by communication channels and feedback in organizational performance.

Group Leader: *John Doe*   Date: *March 25, 1994*

GROUP LEADER REPORT
(To be submitted every Thursday.)

MORALE AND CLIMATE IN YOUR GROUP

-- Personal energy level is: ✓ High ___ Medium ___ Low

Factors contributing to this level: *Just returned from vacation -- feeling energetic*

-- Morale in my group this week is: ___ High ___ Medium ✓ Low

Based upon the following events/issues: *Confused & have lost self-confidence -- it's not one event, just a general feeling*

-- Overall, the climate in the group feels: *Hopeful, but not yet committed*

INTERGROUP RELATIONSHIP AND COMMUNICATIONS

-- Group Leaders with whom I am carrying issues (large or small) this week (place an * next to those issues to be addressed this week):

Name: *Joe*

Issue: *Joe is late on deliveries again. When is he going to get his act together? I thought you spoke to him.*

-- Apparent deadlock issues which will probably require PRL's attention in the near future: _____

GROUP ISSUES

-- Customer contact or feedback issues of the week: *Heard thru' the grapevine that XYZ customer is unionizing. Sounds like trouble for us -- already seeing signs that their shop is less flexible.*

-- Quality Objectives status (attach metrics, if available): *Start-up defects shot up this month because the vendor missed specifications*

-- Important associate interactions this week:

Name: *Jean*   Action: *Awarded employee of the month*

-- Group issues on which I would like to consult with PRL

Issue: *Compensation strategy. I'm still not clear how it works.*

Scope of requested assistance: *Consultation with Pat*

-- Current/upcoming events that I find myself ruminating on this week:

Issue: *Large order due at end of month -- worried might not come through*

Intervention requested? ___ Yes ✓ No

OTHER IMPORTANT INFORMATION

-- Particular difficulties I'm experiencing with PRL this week:

Issue: *Don't understand your position* Plan to confront? ✓ Yes ___ No When? *Thursday lunch meeting*

-- Items of interest to Lantech overall or information which helps PRL to grasp the big picture more fully: *Did you know ZYX competitor just got order for 10 machines? Did you see article in Wall Street Journal on tax investment credits?*

-- Potential areas where I'm gaining awareness of inability to meet strategic goals: *December vacations coming up. Might make it hard to make deadlines.*

-- Self-inventory on expectations this week (place an * next to areas where you would like some dialogue on the topic): *Having a difficult time scheduling enough time with customers!*

This is an example of a Lantech, Inc. group leader report, as described in the vignette on page 452. It is one of several channels Lantech's president uses to communicate with his department managers.

flowing, decentralized types of organization structures) has multiple message channels. It tends to be better than the more restrictive wheel pattern, in terms of accessibility of members to one another, morale, number of messages sent, and adaptability to changes in assigned tasks. For routine sorts of tasks, though, the centralized wheel network produced the fastest and best solutions. The moral of these studies seemed to be that centralized structures were fine for routine tasks, but that adaptability required a more decentralized communication structure.

Like the researchers who designed these communication pattern studies, managers also have options for how they structure organizational message flows, a point we will return to later. First, however, we should look more closely at how managers deal with communication barriers such as misperceptions and channel noise.

DEALING WITH COMMUNICATION BARRIERS

INTERPERSONAL COMMUNICATION BARRIERS[10]

We can conveniently distinguish between interpersonal communication barriers and organizational communication barriers. Let us look first at some interpersonal factors that can distort messages, and thereby inhibit effective communication.

PERCEPTION We all view the world through a window tainted by our own experiences, personality, and point of view. Perception is the meaning or interpretation that a communication receiver applies to the message he or she receives.

PERCEPTION
The meaning or interpretation that a communication receiver applies to the message he or she receives.

FIGURE 16.2

Two Basic Communication Patterns

In the centralized wheel pattern each person (A–E) could communicate only with the central, "A" person; in the more decentralized circle, messages could flow more freely from person to person.

NOTE: Letters refer to people in communication networks.

SOURCE: Wayne Pace and Don Foules, *Organizational Communication* (Englewood Cliffs, NJ: Prentice-Hall, 1989), 136.

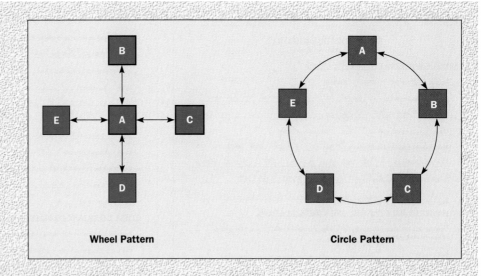

Wheel Pattern   Circle Pattern

As explained in chapter 15, we all perceive the world through our senses, through our eyes, ears, noses, and senses of touch. Therefore, we are continually getting sensory inputs—hot, cold, up, down, words, pictures, and so forth—literally through our nerve endings, a process called **sensation**.[11] As far as psychologists are concerned, these sensations themselves have no meaning in and of themselves; they are, quite literally, just electrical impulses that whisk through our nervous systems back to our brains. Perception is the process of interpreting or assigning meaning to these sensations. Our perceptions are therefore influenced by a variety of factors, and it is probably safe to say that no two people will perceive the same stimulus or message in exactly the same way.

For one thing, people tend to perceive things in a manner that is consistent with what they believe. If you believe that people are inherently good, trustworthy, and honest, then you may tend to perceive people's actions and their comments in a supportive way. People also perceive *selectively*. At the moment, for instance, you are probably concentrating on this book (we hope!) and may therefore be virtually unaware of the radio blasting in the background. Similarly, people tend to select out messages that they do not want to hear or simply tune out low-priority or unwelcome information.

SENSATION
Sensory inputs such as hot, cold, up, down, words, pictures, etc., that are channeled through nerve endings.

SEMANTICS
The meaning of words.

SEMANTICS Semantics, the meaning of words, is another barrier, since words mean different things to different people. For example, you might tell an employee to "clean-up that oil spill as soon as you can" only to find that ten minutes later it has not been cleaned up and that someone has slipped on it. Ask why she did not clean the spill, and the employee may say "but you said to do it as soon as you can and I was busy." In other words, what you meant by "as soon as you can," was not the same thing as what she thought you meant by "as soon as you can."

NONVERBAL COMMUNICATION According to one expert, "it has been estimated that in a conversation involving two people, verbal aspects of a message account for less than 35 percent of the social meaning, whereas nonverbal aspects of a message

ORGANIZATIONAL COMMUNICATION VARIABLE	WHEEL PATTERN	CIRCLE PATTERN
Accessibility of members to one another	Low	High
Control of message flow	High	Low
Morale or satisfaction	Very low	High
Emergence of leader	High	Very low
Accuracy of solutions	Good	Poor
Speed of performance	Fast	Slow
Number of messages sent	Low	High
Emergence of stable organization	Fast	Very slow
Adaptability to job changes	Slow	Fast
Propensity to overload	High	Low

TABLE 16.1

Effects of Two Communication Patterns on Ten Organizational Communication Outcomes

By restricting communication through the "hub," the centralized wheel pattern resulted in fast, good, decisions for simple tasks, but slow adaptability to task changes. Decentralized circle patterns were much more responsive.

SOURCE: Wayne Pace and Don Foules, *Organizational Communication* (Englewood Cliffs, NJ: Prentice-Hall, 1989), 137.

account for 65 percent of the social meaning.[12] In other words, people pick up cues regarding what you mean not just from your words but from your **nonverbal communication,** your manner of speaking, facial expressions, bodily posture, and so on. Thus, coming in to work looking perturbed because you were caught in a traffic jam may "communicate" to employees that you are dissatisfied with their work, although that message was not what you intended.

NONVERBAL COMMUNICATION
A person's manner of speaking, facial expressions, body posture, etc.

AMBIGUITY If a statement seems ambiguous, it means that the person on the receiving end is somewhat uncertain of how to interpret it. Three types of ambiguities can distort messages. Ambiguity of *meaning* occurs when the person receiving the message simply is not sure of what was meant by the person who said or wrote the message. (For example, does "see me in my office as soon as you can" mean immediately or next week after you've finished your project?) Ambiguity of *intent* means that, while the words may be clear, the sender's intentions are not. (For example, your subordinate might ask, "Why does he want to see me in his office *now*?") Finally, ambiguity of *effect* represents the receiver's uncertainty about predicting what the consequences of responding to the message might be. Thus, you might understand your boss's note as well as her intentions but still not be able to accurately gauge how noncompliance will affect you.

ORGANIZATIONAL COMMUNICATION BARRIERS

In addition to interpersonal barriers to effective communication, the organization itself and the way it restricts information flow can distort messages and create communication barriers.

ORGANIZATIONAL POSITION   The organizational positions of the sender and receiver can influence the accuracy with which the message is received. This is a familiar aspect of organizational life, and probably one with which you are already familiar. For example, subordinates tend to be somewhat deferential toward their bosses, and often tell them what they want to hear or withhold unwelcome information. Employees also tend to be myopic when it comes to interpreting information and understanding organizational problems. Thus, the president's message that "costs are too high" might prompt the sales manager to claim that "production should get their costs under control" while the production manager argues that "we are selling too wide a range of products."[13]

COMMUNICATION RESTRICTIONS   As we saw in Chapters 8 and 9 (in our discussions of organizing), some firms are more restrictive regarding communication flows than are others. For example, functional organizations often tend to operate like the wheel patterns shown in Figure 16–2. Each functional vice-president (sales, manufacturing, personnel, finance) might, at the extreme, be restricted from communicating with each other; instead, virtually all messages must go through the president. In this case, the restriction itself is a barrier to communication, one that can lead to a variety of message distortions, particularly when the president gets overloaded with work. (We will discuss information overload later in the chapter.)

ORGANIZATIONAL CULTURE   In Chapter 14 (Organizational Culture and Shared Values), we saw that the organization's culture—its shared values and traditional ways of doing things—can influence how messages flow throughout the organization. Thus, when Jack Welch took over as GE's CEO, he inherited an organization that he felt did not adequately encourage lower-level employees to speak their minds. One of Welch's first tasks was therefore to re-create GE's culture so as to encourage all employees to communicate openly, quickly, and with candor.[14] He did this by emphasizing the value of open communication and by instituting organizational changes to encourage employees to speak their minds.

OVERCOMING COMMUNICATION BARRIERS

Like Welch, managers need not be helpless victims of communication barriers. Instead, they can take steps to reduce communication barriers and distortion, including:

ESTABLISH MORE THAN ONE CHANNEL OF COMMUNICATION   For example, we've seen that top management at firms like Federal Express have instituted special channels such as Survey Feedback Action through which employees throughout the organization can make their attitudes and ideas known to top management. Other firms, like Toyota, also set up special communication channels that encourage employees to express attitudes and complaints and make inquiries by sending their requests directly to upper-level managers. For example, if a Toyota employee has a complaint, a gripe, or an important question that he or she thinks cannot be expressed to the immediate supervisor, the anonymous message can be sent on the Hotline for top management review. Similarly, more firms are moving away from wheel types of communication networks (functional organizations) and instead are encouraging more free flowing communication amongst all employees.

ELIMINATE THE INTERMEDIARY BETWEEN THE SENDERS AND THE DECISION MAKERS   For example, many firms today are flattening their organizational hierarchies and delegating more authority to lower-level employees. Since messages do not have to thread their way up and down a long hierarchy, distortions are minimized and decisions get made faster.

CREATE A NEW CULTURE   Managers like GE's Jack Welch know that you first must change the shared values in the firm—in GE's case toward more openness and candor. Once employees truly share those values, the organizational modifications needed to reduce communication barriers and distortions can be put into place. The *Datatec* vignette describes how another firm solved its communication problem.

Now let's look more closely at how firms overcome communication barriers.

ORGANIZATIONAL COMMUNICATION

We've seen that organizational communication is subject to barriers and distortion caused by organizational factors such as restricted communication flows and different organizational positions of senders and receivers. In this section, we will look more closely at how firms overcome communication barriers.

DIRECTIONS OF INFORMATION FLOW

Organizational communication can flow downward, laterally, and upward. Downward communication is transmitted from superior to subordinate and consists of messages

DATATEC

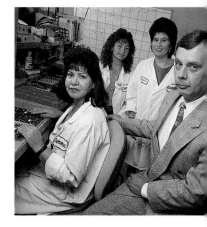

Some communication barriers are a little more obvious than others. Larry Tourjee, Datatec's vice-president of manufacturing, really had to go back to basics to get his message across to his diverse work force. Misunderstandings weren't a problem; understanding at all was. The communication barriers came to light when the Fairfield, New Jersey, computer installation company decided to bring manufacturing in house, using a work force that previously had done only light assembly. Bringing the largely Hispanic group up to speed on the more technical work meant overcoming the language barrier. First, special care had to be taken in choosing an instructor to provide English lessons, since a good deal of technical jargon went with the job. Tourjee screened the instructor candidates, then asked his own employees to make the final choice.

Total cost of the program has been $55,000 over three years, but according to Tourjee, that's 40 percent less than the cost of training brand new workers. Tourjee also used innovative methods to get his workers serious about the program. One worker became an English-only speaker every Friday. Another decided to sponsor a less advanced colleague. English-speaking volunteers attended weekly lunches with the Hispanic employees, yielding a double benefit. The employees learned the new language, and the volunteers gained insight into problems and concerns of their fellow workers. Tourjee says turnover is now practically nonexistent at Datatec, production line failures are way down, and the communication barriers have all but disappeared.

SOURCE: Phaedra Hise, "When English Isn't So Plain," *Inc.*, November 1993, 127.

regarding things like what the job entails, procedures and practices to be followed, and evaluations of job performance. Lateral (or horizontal) communication involves messages between departments or between people within the same department. Organizational communication can also flow upward. Upward communication (from subordinates to superiors) can provide management with valuable information concerning how the organization and its employees are functioning.

FORMAL AND INFORMAL COMMUNICATION

We can also distinguish between formal and informal organizational communication. **Formal communication** refers to messages that are recognized as official by the organization; they include orders (from superiors to subordinates) and various formal, written reports on sales levels, status of projects in progress, and so on. **Informal communication** is communication that is not officially sanctioned by the organization; the grapevine (or rumors) is the most familiar example.

BUILDING UPWARD COMMUNICATION

In an organization, **upward communication** generally represents the messages that flow from subordinates to supervisors. Experts have long praised the benefits of upward communication. Such messages provide supervisors with valuable information on which to base decisions,[15] encourage gripes and grievances to surface,[16] and cultivate commitment by giving employees an opportunity to express their ideas and suggestions.[17] Upward communication also provides feedback through which supervisors can ascertain whether subordinates understand their goals and instructions, and it can help employees "cope with their work problems and strengthen their involvement in their jobs and with the organization."[18]

This being the case, numerous upward communication methods have been devised. For example, R. Wayne Pace and Don Faules list the following as a checklist of upward communication methods:[19]

- suggestion systems
- grievance procedures
- attitude and information surveys
- counseling interviews
- rumor clinics
- question boxes
- employee roundtables
- manager's luncheons
- performance appraisals
- dial-the-boss telephone systems
- employee letters
- organizational development activities
- human resource development and training
- reports and memos
- union publications
- the grapevine

Here is a sampling of upward communication methods used by firms today.

FORMAL COMMUNICATION Messages that are recognized as official by the organization, i.e., orders from superiors to subordinates, sales reports, and status reports.

INFORMAL COMMUNICATIONS Communication not officially sanctioned by the organization, i.e., rumors heard through "the grapevine."

UPWARD COMMUNICATION Represents the messages that flow from subordinates to supervisors.

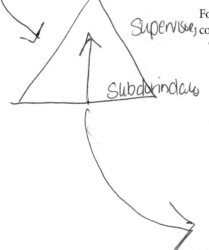

FEDERAL EXPRESS'S GUARANTEED FAIR TREATMENT PROCEDURE (GFTP)   GFTP is available to all permanent Federal Express employees and provides them with a vehicle through which grievances and discontent can be expressed to upward management. As noted earlier, in Chapter 12, it covers concerns regarding matters such as promotions, compensation policies, and discipline affecting the individual complainant. Basically, as the firm's handbook points out "if for any reason you are a recipient of discipline, you will have access to GFTP."[20]

In brief, the Federal Express guaranteed fair treatment procedure contains three steps. In step 1, *management review,* the complainant submits a written complaint to a member of management. Then, that manager reviews all relevant information, holds a conference with the complainant, and makes a decision to either uphold, modify, or overturn the original supervisor's actions.

In step 2, *officer review,* the complainant can submit a written complaint to a vice-president or senior vice-president of his or her division. That person then reviews all relevant information, conducts an additional investigation, and makes a decision to uphold, overturn, or modify management's action.

Finally, in step 3, *executive appeals review,* the complainant can submit a written complaint that goes to an appeals board consisting of Federal Express's CEO, president, and chief personnel officer as well as two other senior vice-presidents. They then review all relevant information and make a decision to uphold, overturn, or initiate an investigative board of review. (The latter is used when there is a question of fact.)

IBM'S SPEAK UP!   IBM's Speak Up! program aims to solicit employee opinions, and uses special Speak-Up! forms to protect the employee's identity. The form itself is a combination letter-envelope, which is easily available to all employees and is self-addressed to the Speak-Up! administrator. On the top is a detachable stub where employees print their names, home addresses, and IBM locations and indicate if they prefer to discuss the matter with a qualified person (usually by phone). The form also has a space for handwritten concerns, along with a note to the effect that the Speak-Up! entry will be typed so that the "handwriting cannot be identified." The form is then completed, folded, and mailed.

When the form is received, a Speak-Up! administrator removes the name stub and assigns the form a file number. The stub itself is secured in a locked box and no one, except the Speak-Up! administrator, ever sees the writer's name. The Speak-Up! opinion or complaint is then typed and assigned to an investigator for an answer. The latter then sends the response to the Speak-Up! administrator who returns the answer to the employee.

TOYOTA'S HOTLINE   Toyota Motor Manufacturing tells its employees, "don't spend time worrying about something . . . speak up!" At Toyota, the primary upward communication channel is called "Hotline." Its purpose is to give team members an additional channel for bringing questions or problems to the company's attention.

The hotline is available 24 hours a day. Employees are instructed to pick up any phone, dial the hotline extension (the number is posted on the plant bulletin board), and deliver their messages to the recorder. All inquiries received on the hotline are guaranteed to be reviewed by the human resources manager and to be thoroughly investigated. If it is decided that a particular question would be of interest to other Toyota team members, then the question, along with the firm's response, is typed up and posted on plant bulletin boards. If a personal response is desired, employees must leave their names when they call. However, employees know that no other attempt will be made to identify a particular hotline caller.[21]

GENERAL ELECTRIC'S "WORK-OUT"[22]   As part of his attempt to build openness and candor at GE, CEO Jack Welch initiated a series of classroom sessions with his executives in what, for better or worse, became known as the "pit." In these sessions, GE executives were encouraged to put aside decorum and engage Welch in the "rough and tumble debate he relishes."[23] By 1988, however, Welch was concerned that the same candor he was experiencing with his executives in the pit meetings was not being carried over to lower-level GE employees, and the work-out was born.

Like the pit, **work-out** is basically a place. One observer described it as a forum in which participating employees get a mental work-out while engaging in enthusiastic discussions aimed at taking unnecessary work out of their jobs and working out problems together.[24] Welch himself compares his work-outs to New England town meetings. A group of 40 to 100 employees, "picked by management from all ranks and several functions, goes to a conference center or hotel."[25] The three-day sessions are usually kicked off by a talk by the group's boss, who soon leaves. An outside consultant/facilitator then breaks the group into five or six teams, each of which addresses problems, list complaints, and debates solutions. Later the boss returns and the team spokesperson makes the team's proposals. Under work-out's rules, the boss can make only three responses: he or she can agree on the spot, say no, or ask for more information, "in which case he must charter a team to get it by an agreed upon date."[26]

The work-out sessions are useful for solving problems and for getting information up the line. For example, as one GE electrician responded when told his comments had made his boss really sweat, "When you've been told to shut up for 20 years and someone tells you to speak up—you're going to let them have it."[27] The work-out sessions do not just produce profitable solutions to GE's unit problems. They also enable employees to express their ideas upwards with openness and candor.

WORK-OUT
A forum in which participating employees get a mental work-out while engaging in enthusiastic discussions aimed at taking unnecessary work out of their jobs and working out problems together.

BUILDING DOWNWARD COMMUNICATION

Downward communication represents the messages that flow from positions of higher authority to those of lower authority. This includes a variety of essential types of information regarding, for instance, job instructions, rationales for jobs (including how jobs are related to other tasks and positions in the organization), organizational policies and practices, employee performance, and the organization's mission.[28] In many firms today, the scope of downward communication has been dramatically expanded: the aim is to provide newly empowered employees with information about their companies and tasks so they can do their jobs better.

In addition to the usual channels like job descriptions, policies and procedures manuals, and face-to-face and written messages, firms today use several means to get data "down to the troops." At Saturn Corporation assemblers describe communications as excellent and say "we get information continuously via the internal television network and from financial documents."[29] The firm also has monthly townhall-like meetings, usually with 500 to 700 people attending. The net effect is that all employees are quite familiar with Saturn's activities and performance.

Toyota Motor Manufacturing has five-minute team information meetings at job sites twice a day, where employees get the latest plant news. Toyota also puts a television set in each worksite break area, which runs continuously and presents plantwide information from the in-house Toyota Broadcasting Center. The company also sponsors quarterly roundtable discussions between top management and selected nonsupervisory staff, and an in-house newsletter. The hotline described earlier is another channel of top-down information, insofar as it gives management a chance to publicly answer questions team members might have. The plant's top management is also often on the shop floor, fielding questions, providing performance information, and ensur-

KROY, INC.

Deducing what was wrong at Kroy, Inc., did not require a high-priced consultant. A leveraged buyout in the mid-1980s had loaded the company with debt. Sales headed down to the point where net operating income at this labeling equipment maker was insufficient to cover interest payments. The cash shortage led to neglect of new product development, making dealers unhappy. The dearth of capital also led to unannounced, seemingly random layoffs. Skittish employees walked on eggs wondering when the other shoe would drop. Esprit de corps was lower than profits. Rumors were rampant, largely owing to top management's halt to any form of communication.

The future, if there was to be one, hinged on reducing debt. The firm filed for Chapter 11 bankruptcy to give it a chance to work out its problems. New CEO Howard Klemmer came on board in late 1990. Next to reducing debt, his assessment of Kroy's next most critical shortcoming was symbolized by his first move on the job: communication, he said, would be central to Kroy returning to financial health. Managers would never again wall themselves off from

the rest of the company, even if they wanted to. The day he arrived, Klemmer ordered all doors removed from executive offices.

The ensuing days found Klemmer actively participating in companywide meetings at the Scottsdale, Arizona, headquarters. His message made clear that sweat, toil, and trouble lay ahead, but he made it equally clear that with a commitment from every employee, the company would survive. Workers were

FOCUS ON SMALL BUSINESS

invited to ask job-related questions. No, was the answer to their most pressing concern—no one's job was guaranteed. Many left, but putting it all on the table relieved a good deal of the anxiety that had plagued the company. Turnover afterward was minimal.

To ingrain the new channels of communication effectively, managers met regularly with various employees. Klemmer became ubiquitous throughout the office, keeping employees

abreast of the latest developments and helping quash further rumors by his presence. Meetings between the CEO, top brass, and employees became a monthly occurrence. Everything from planned cost-cutting measures to proposed staffing reductions was aired. Honesty was the main theme. Employees were also given the most up-to-the-minute status reports of the company's position. Workers too shy to broach topics in the open got the option of dropping their queries into boxes throughout the offices. A manager would then research the answer for announcement the following month without ever identifying the employee.

Howard Klemmer made companywide communications his number one priority and the centerpiece of his management strategy at Kroy. His active and on-going participation in the process, along with the rest of his management staff, made it clear that his commitment to open, honest exchanges between members of the company was more than rhetoric. By the time Kroy emerged from Chapter 11 bankruptcy, employee morale was up, and so were profits.

SOURCE: Suellyn McMillan, "Squelching the Rumor Mill," *Personnel Journal,* October 1991, 95–101.

ing that all general managers, managers, and team members are "aware of Toyota's goal and where we are heading."[30] The *Kroy, Inc.* small business box shows how one small business improved its communications processes.

BUILDING HORIZONTAL ORGANIZATIONAL COMMUNICATION

THE PROBLEM OF INFORMATION OVERLOAD

Reducing communication barriers is necessary in part because firms today are overloaded with information. As one expert has said, "in many ways, people resemble a computer. They can process so much information and store that information in their brains—but only so much. Both people and machines have what is called a channel capacity. When that channel capacity is reached, the same thing happens to the person and the machine—they break down."[31] Researcher James Miller and his associates found seven means by which people adjust to such "information overload":

- *Omission*—not processing some of the information
- *Errors*—incorrectly identifying some of the information
- *Queuing*—delaying a response during heavy loads and catching up during slack periods
- *Filtering*—systematically omitting certain types of information, usually by some priority system
- *Approximation*—giving a less precise response
- *Multiple channels*—using parallel sub-systems for processing information (for example, using both audio and visual cues, if available)
- *Escape*—leaving the situation or cutting off the input of information

These kinds of adjustments happen in organizations, too. Managers, say Daniel Katz and Robert Kahn, are decision makers and coordinators and thus occupy roles in the organization that require them to assimilate information from sources like subordinates, peers, superiors, and outside vendors and competitors. They must then interpret this information and make decisions that result in a coordinated effort, while meeting deadlines.[32] If a firm can't process information fast enough, errors will occur.

Managers and their organizations get overloaded in part because the industrial environment is becoming so unpredictable. Potential sources of supply may diminish and require additional search for new ones. Markets for products grow and decline. Competitors introduce new products, initiate advertising campaigns, change pricing strategies, and buy new, more efficient equipment. As a result, managers are continually faced with the dilemma of (1) having to make decisions and coordinate activities within a given time period, while at the same time (2) having to deal with unpredictable, rapidly changing environments and floods of information.[33] One way to deal with this dilemma is to institute better, faster ways of sharing information horizontally, across the organization. (Chapter 9 discusses reorganizing using network structures.)

BUILDING BETTER HORIZONTAL COMMUNICATION

Horizontal communication refers to the sharing of information among peers within the same work unit or among employees across functional boundaries or departments.

Managers work hard today to boost horizontal communication, for several reasons.[34] Doing so facilitates interdepartmental coordination, since coordinating almost always requires communicating. Doing so also enhances organizational responsiveness, by helping employees pierce departmental or geographic barriers and get right to the source when quick decisions must be made. Methods for building horizontal communication include the following.

BOOST OPPORTUNITIES FOR HORIZONTAL INTERACTION   First, managers build horizontal communication by establishing more opportunities for employees in different departments or on different teams to interact. For example, in their study of excellent companies, Tom Peters and Robert Waterman found that the "intensity and sheer volume of communications are unmistakable." Here are some examples of what Peters and Waterman found:[35]

1. Communications systems are informal. At Walt Disney Productions, for instance, everyone from the president down wears a name tag with just his or her first name on it. At 3M there are endless meetings, few of which are sched-

Open, informative interdepartmental meetings like this one are a good way to boost horizontal, interdepartmental communication.

uled; most, instead, are characterized by the casual getting together of people from different disciplines to talk about problems in a campus-like, shirt sleeves atmosphere.

2. Communication intensity is extraordinary. At the more successful companies, meetings and presentations are held in which "the questions are unabashed; the flow is free, everyone is involved. Nobody hesitates to cut off the chairman, the president or board members."[36] What is encouraged, in other words, is an open confrontation of ideas in which people go after issues bluntly and straightforwardly. Meetings in these excellent companies are thus not highly formal and politicized affairs. Instead, they are open, informative discussions in which all points of view can safely be aired.

3. Communication is given physical support. In these companies, physical supports, like blackboards and open offices, facilitate and encourage frequent informal interaction. In one high-tech firm, for instance, all employees from president down work not in offices, but in six-foot high doorless cubicles that encourage openness and interaction among employees. Corning Glass installed escalators (rather than elevators) in its new engineering building to increase the chance of face-to-face contact.[37] Similarly, another company got rid of its small, four-person dining room tables, substituting instead, long rectangular ones that encourage strangers to come in contact, often across departmental lines. Similarly, managers are encouraged to get out of their offices, walk around, and strike up conversations with those both in and outside their own departments.

What this all adds up to, says Peters and Waterman, is "lots of communication." In most of these firms, they say, you cannot wander around long without "seeing lots of people sitting together in a room with blackboards working casually on problems."[38]

ENCOURAGE SOCIAL ACTIVITIES Many companies encourage horizontal communication by organizing social activities such as bowling teams at which employees from different departments can get together and at which much horizontal communication occurs. For example, Toyota Motor Manufacturing has an annual picnic.

USE QUALITY CIRCLES   A quality circle is a group of employees, usually at the same level, who meet once a week on company time to analyze and share work-related problems. The employees are generally specially trained in the use of problem-solving tools such as graphs. Perhaps the most obvious benefit of such circles is that they can create employee enthusiasm by giving workers the relatively challenging task of analyzing and solving work-related problems. They can also, of course, produce financial savings for the firm. In addition, though, quality circles build horizontal communication. They do this both among employees in the same department, and among the representatives of different departments who may be serving on interdepartmental quality circles.

COMMUNICATION AND THE RESPONSIVE ORGANIZATION

THE IMPORTANCE OF OPEN COMMUNICATION

Peters and Waterman's finding that in responsive firms communication systems are informal, communication intensity is extraordinary, and communication is given physical support illustrates how important intense and open communication is to responsive organizations today. As they have observed:

> Excellent [and responsive] companies are a vast network of informal, open communications. The patterns and intensity cultivate the right people getting into contact with each other, regularly, and the chaotic-anarchic properties of the system are kept well under control simply because of the regularity of contact and its nature.[39]

They go on to note that

> the astonishing by-product is the ability to have your cake and eat it too: that is, rich informal communication leads to more action, more experiments, more learning, and simultaneously to the ability to stay better in touch and on top of things.[40]

The fact that open, intense (and frequently informal) communication is a distinguishing characteristic of responsive organizations has been re-affirmed by other experts. For example, Rosabeth Moss Kanter writes:

> More challenging, more innovative, more partnership-oriented positions carry with them the requirements for more communication and interaction. One needs more time for meetings in a post-entrepreneurial workplace, where divisions interact in the search for synergies, job territories overlap, people might report to more than one manager, and projects require the coordination of a number of people, each with specialized responsibility.[41]

Hundreds, probably thousands of other firms thus use various techniques to boost their communication effectiveness. The work-out forum at General Electric (as described earlier) is one example. Several other examples follow.

UNION PACIFIC RAILWAY, OPENING UP COMMUNICATIONS   When Mike Walsh took over as CEO of Union Pacific Railway, employees routinely addressed each other with the formal Mr. or Mrs., and teamwork between departments was almost nonexistent.[42] Walsh viewed the firm as bureaucratic and militaristic.

One of the first things Walsh did to boost communication was to institute so-called townhall meetings throughout the 19 state rail system. In each meeting, Walsh met with between 300 and 1,000 employees, explaining the firm's new strategy and his vision for it, and how that new vision would affect Union Pacific and its employees. Employees were asked to contribute their ideas.

"FRESH AIR" AT MATTEL TOYS You do not always need townhall-type meetings to open up communication. For example, when John Amerman became CEO of Mattel Toys, he told employees he wanted to let in some fresh air to the firm and enable employees to have some fun. In a company that was described as "an out-of-control money-loser" that had "spent big to introduce a series of toys that bombed," and in which morale was low, Amerman's ideas triggered a big change in culture.[43]

To put his "fresh air" ideas in place, he began wandering around the firm, eating in the cafeteria, and meeting regularly with employees. Suggestions were soon forthcoming; to his surprise, "many employees recommended that their departments be pruned or totally scrapped."[44]

GETTING PERSONAL AT BROOKS FURNITURE Bob Crawford, founder and CEO of Brooks Furniture Rental similarly emphasizes two-way communication. As he says, "people will put every effort into advancing the businesses in which they can communicate their ideas freely."[45] Crawford takes a more personal approach to communication. He walks through his company's huge warehouses, greeting every worker by name and chatting about work and personal matters. Crawford emphasizes the importance of listening and says "the secret of good human dynamics is a balance between talking and listening."[46]

PLANNED NOSINESS AT CHIAT/DAY/MOJO At advertising agency Chiat/Day/Mojo (CDM), creativity is the hallmark, and "everything and everyone serves that idea."[47] The agency has no organization chart, business cards have no titles, everyone works out of open, low-partition offices, and the whole personnel system from selection through compensation and appraisal is aimed at encouraging a love for work and hypercreativity.

Not surprisingly, employees at CDM emphasize open communication to foster the firm's famous creativity.

"Nosiness feeds creative energy" is how one staffer put it. "You can pop in and out of offices and exchange ideas, look at story boards or ads. By being close together, creatives can bounce more ideas off each other. Our physical structure encourages communications. And our philosophy demands not hiding things."[48]

THE MEDIA RICHNESS MODEL

Several academic researchers have contributed what is at least a partial explanation for responsive firms' reliance on floods of open, face-to-face communication. Robert Taft and R. Lingel have proposed that communication media can be viewed along a continuum of media "richness."[49] They say that the richness of a media reflects its capacity to resolve ambiguity. Four characteristics of the media define that media's richness: speed of feedback, variety of communication channels employed, personalness of source, and richness of the language used.

On their continuum, face-to-face is the richest communication medium, followed by telephone, and (at the other end of the continuum) written documents. An important point, they say, is that the media's richness (in terms of communication) needs to match the ambiguity level of the task. Thus, the sort of ambiguity prompted by the rapidly changing and unpredictable situations that responsive organizations must deal with lend themselves particularly well to rich communication media like face-to-face. (Here, after all, there is plenty of opportunity for immediate feedback and the use of multiple channels, including both verbal and nonverbal communications.) At the other extreme, in relatively unambiguous and unchanging highly routine situations, a reliance on memos and documentation may be quite adequate.

SUMMARY

Managers spend most of their time communicating, or trying to get information from one place to another quickly and without distortion. A basic communications model has five elements: sender, channel, noise source, receiver, and feedback. Communication patterns studies have shown that how information is channeled will influence the accuracy and speed with which decisions are made.

A number of communication barriers exist that can make a manager's job more difficult. Interpersonal factors, such as individual perception, semantics, nonverbal messages, and ambiguity, can lead to distorted messages. Organization factors also can hinder effective communication, with the positions of the sender and receiver, the freedom of communication flow, and the organizational culture all playing a role. Managers can reduce communication barriers and distortion by establishing more than one channel of communication, eliminating intermediaries between the senders and the decision makers, and creating a new culture.

Organizational communication can flow downward, horizontally, or upward, and can be either formal or informal. Upward communication flows from subordinates to supervisors and includes such methods as suggestion systems, grievance procedures, and surveys. Downward communication includes everything from job instructions to employee performance appraisals. In building horizontal communication in an organization, excellent companies seek to establish more opportunities for employees to interact with one another and install communication systems that are informal, intense, and supported by physical structures within the organization. Researchers have determined that the richness of communication media depends on the speed of feedback, the variety of communication channels employed, the personalness of the source, and the richness of the language used. Therefore, face-to-face communication is richer than a written document and is more appropriate under fast-changing conditions.

QUESTIONS

▪ FOR REVIEW

1. Using the five basic elements of the model described in this chapter, outline the communication process based on a situation in which you have recently taken part.

2. List the two types of factors that can serve as barriers to effective communication, and give several examples of each.

3. What steps can managers take to minimize barriers in the communication process?

4. Grievance procedures, rumor clinics, and performance appraisals are examples of what types of communication methods?

5. How do people adjust to information overload?

▪ FOR DISCUSSION

6. Discuss the pros and cons of using memos, reports, and electronic mail to communicate with large numbers of employees. How can inherent weaknesses in each type of communication system be strengthened?

7. In what ways do circle patterns of communication tend to be better than the more restrictive wheel patterns?

8. Do you believe it is possible to eliminate all communication barriers in an organization? Why or why not?

9. Which of the upward, downward, and horizontal communication methods used by firms described in this chapter do you think are most effective? Explain.

■ **FOR ACTION**

10. Your professor will divide the class into two groups and pass out a copy of the crossword puzzle from a daily newspaper to each student. One group will work on the puzzle individually, while the other group will discuss possible solutions among themselves. Compare your group's results with those of the other group. What does this exercise reveal about the importance of horizontal communication in organizations?

11. What methods does your professor use to promote upward and horizontal communication in class? Since students go to class to be taught by the professor (downward communication) why are upward and horizontal communication important?

12. How would you interpret the following commonly used financial terms? Compare your answers with other students': *balloon, crash, hedge, dumping, estate, net, bear, float, par, street,* and *takeover.*

■ **FOR FOCUS ON SMALL BUSINESS**

13. Which of Klemmer's actions do you think were most effective in overcoming communication barriers within the company?

14. How do you think small firms differ from large ones when it comes to reducing communication barriers? How are they similar?

13. What else could Klemmer have done to improve communication at the company?

CLOSING SOLUTION

COLGATE-PALMOLIVE CO.

The top managers at Colgate-Palmolive decided to let the trickle of information from the domestic division's survey become a flood. After reviewing the findings at the yearly management meeting, the company conducted a day-long, no-holds-barred discussion. A nationwide tour of each of the company's plants was used to establish better lines of communication. Every employee got an overview of the profit picture and upcoming changes. The company launched two publications that detailed both the current financial numbers and the future strategy. A task force was created to revamp the customer-service department with greater emphasis on flexibility and streamlining business operations. Three-fourths of the squabbling top management team was replaced, unmistakably signaling sincerity in the company's dedication to teamwork. The company made employee input a part of doing business through ongoing townhall-type get-togethers at individual plants. And, profitability increased by a factor of four.

■ **QUESTIONS FOR CLOSING SOLUTION**

1. Using the terms defined in the chapter, describe how Colgate-Palmolive management overcame obstacles to communication?

2. What are some other ways the company could build upward communication?

3. Do you think the improved communication will make the company more responsive? Why or why not?

KEY TERMS

Communication

Communications Channel

Feedback

Communication Patterns Studies

Perception

Sensation

Semantics

Nonverbal Communication

Formal Communication

Informal Communication

Upward Communication

Work-out

Information Overload

CASE FOR ANALYSIS

EURO DISNEY

In the final analysis, the French and the Walt Disney Company probably have a lot more in common than either would like to admit. Disney's close-to-the-vest methods of operation and rigid standards often smacked of effrontery to many French. The French, on the other hand, exhibited a level of snobbery uncommon even for a country known for its nationalist sentiments. Disney officials faced a litany of challenges in building and operating Euro Disney, and if it will begin turning a profit is still not certain.

Communication between Disney and the French public was not good from the very beginning. A chorus of criticism erupted with the March 1987 announcement that the Euro Disneyland theme park would be built outside Paris. Local tradespeople claimed they were shut out. A large trade union complained of poor working conditions, leading to an investigation by French union leaders. Not to be outdone, the intellectual community weighed in with its own blistering attacks, decrying everything from government subsidies to the supposed loss of French cultural identity the park surely would bring on. One critic labeled Euro Disney a cultural Chernobyl. When chairman Michael Eisner visited Paris to announce the company stock offering, his welcome was marred by a pelting of eggs and ketchup.

Disney officials believed they had responded to the complaints by making changes where possible. Various attractions and policies were altered while maintaining the integrity of the Disney formula. English and French became the two official languages at the park. "In planning, there was a great deal of discussion on various philosophies of how we should handle the language and cultural variances. It has been an interesting challenge," said Ron Logan, vice-president of creative show development and executive producer of all live performances. "The most important thing was to be true to our Disney philosophy and not do anything just for the sake of making it European. If it worked, we did it, if we felt it wouldn't, we weren't about to force it."

From Euro Disney's inception, it was Eisner's conviction that in order for the park to succeed it would have to attract visitors from all over Europe. He believed the key would be the ability of park personnel to greet and communicate with visitors in their own language. Because of extensive recruitment in 28 cities in the European Community, almost 40 percent of Euro Disney's 16,000-person work force is from countries other than France. Even officials at EC headquarters in Brussels concede that Euro Disney is probably Europe's most multinational work place.

Company specialists have been quick to make marketing and merchandising changes at Euro Disney. Despite the sentiments of the French intelligentsia regarding American pop culture, visitors clamored for authentic American entertainment. Frivolity won out over genuine substance in product offerings. Mickey Mouse hats, mugs, and other knickknacks pushed more expensive items off the shelves. Cheaper meals, especially for children, and ready access to take-out food resulted in the elimination of formal restaurants in favor of cafeterias and fast-food carts. Popcorn was changed from salted to sugared, and then back to salted again.

French visitors were originally expected to make up around 50 percent of Euro Disney's clientele. To date, they have constituted only a small percentage of the gate, but the difficulties at Euro Disney cannot all be attributed to French snobbery. On average, a family of four spends $280 at Euro Disney. Combine that with long lines, parking problems, and bad weather, and the recipe for losses is complete. The company lost just over $200 million in the first half of 1993, and many analysts are predicting Euro Disney may not get into the black for years, if then.

The Disney company's characteristic penchant for secrecy was again in evidence when officials denied concern over the park's performance while simultaneously slashing admission rates 25 percent and launching a huge promotional effort directed at neighboring Parisians. But even here, the knife cuts both ways. Attendance figures improved dramatically as a result of the advertising campaign, but the discounts meant that the revenues remained anemic. The French finally came out, but it took an admissions cut to move them, and commuter business from nearby Paris did little to improve the occupancy rates of surrounding hotels, stuck at around 37 percent.

Disney gathered information from the first six million visitors to the park. Even though Euro Disney has been beset with more than its share of start-up and operational problems, officials believe they now understand what customers want. They have already experienced the difficulty in absorbing and communicating the information necessary to run a theme park that aims to attract visitors of varied cultures from an entire continent to its gates.

SOURCES: Stewart Toy et al., "The Mouse Isn't Roaring," *Business Week,* August 24, 1992, 38; "Ducking Doom," *The Economist,* July 10, 1993, 73–74; "Waiting for Dumbo," *The Economist,* May 1, 1993, 74; Keith H. Hammonds, "Storm Clouds over Disney Land," November 1, 1993, 43; Barbara Rudolph, "Monsieur Mickey," *Time,* March 25, 1991, 48–49; and Steven Bergsman, "The Ground Floor," *Barron's,* October 14, 1991, 50.

■ **QUESTIONS**

1. What barriers to communication did managers of Euro Disney face, both with employees and the French public?
2. How could some of those barriers be overcome? How would you rate Euro Disney's efforts so far?
3. Should management's primary focus now be on building upward communication, downward communication, or horizontal communication? Explain your answer.
4. How do you think Disney's "penchant for secrecy" backfired at Euro Disney?

A CASE IN DIVERSITY

ASIAN AMERICANS AND ORGANIZATIONAL COMMUNICATIONS

Asian culture tends to inculcate workers with a sense of deference to superiors, an emphasis on maintaining harmony, loyalty, and control of emotions, and staying the work course without complaint. But those virtues, on the U.S. side of the Pacific, can lead to misunderstanding and acrimony for Asian-American workers. Things often get worse when some of those same Asian Americans aspire to managerial positions.

J.D. Hokoyama decided to do something about the problem. He operates the Los Angeles-based Leadership Education for Asian Pacifics, Inc., a nonprofit workshop group designed to identify messages Asian-American managers may be conveying to employees. He admits it is a double-edged sword.

Although Asian Americans are usually recognized as hard workers, some employers don't think they can fill the bill as managers because they are perceived as too indecisive and unassertive. Those who do put their foot down are branded as aggressive and dictatorial. "All of a sudden, you can't win either way," says Hokoyama.

The problem comes down to cultural mores. Where confrontation and competition are the norm in the U.S. workplace, consensus and continuity are the objective in the same Far Eastern settings. One of Hokoyama's typical training sessions includes role-playing. Participants are urged to strive for eye contact, begin sentences with *I,* emphasize key themes through repetition, and exhibit correct body language. Real-world work situations are often re-enacted, with trainers and fellow participants offering criticism and suggestions. Managers who have difficulty issuing

direct orders, but who aren't having success with mere suggestions, are steered to some agreeable median point.

It's not always easy. After attending training sessions, some Asian-American workers wonder if altering long-standing codes of conduct is worth the price of success. Perhaps with good reason, they question whether office shouting matches or publicly dressing down employees are really the best motivational methods. In the final analysis this may get to the heart of the benefits that can be derived from diversity in the workplace. Managers who can select and employ the best elements of management from both continents will probably enjoy the edge on those who don't.

SOURCE: Vivian Louie, "For Asian Americans, a Way to Fight a Maddening Stereotype," *The New York Times,* August 8, 1993, 9.

■ **QUESTIONS**

1. Do you agree with the theory that Asian-American workers need to alter their communication skills in order to get ahead in the U.S. business world. Why or why not?
2. Which of the communication barriers described in the chapter are Asian-Americans most likely to encounter in the work place, and how can these best be overcome?
3. Can you think of other ethnic cultures with communication traditions that differ from those that predominate in the United States.

ENDNOTES

1. Isadore Barmash, "More Substance Than Show," *Across the Board,* May 1993, 43–45.
2. Daniel Katz and Robert Kahn, *The Social Psychology of Organizations* (New York: John Wiley, 1966).
3. Raymond Ross, *Speech Communication,* 6th ed. (Englewood Cliffs, NJ: Prentice-Hall, 1983), 8. For an added view, see Chris Argyris, "Good Communication that Blocks Learning," *Harvard Business Review,* July–August 1994, 77–89.
4. George Miller, *Language and Communication* (New York: McGraw-Hill, 1951), 10. Discussed in Gary Hunt, *Communication Skills in the Organization,* 2nd ed. (Englewood Cliffs, NJ: Prentice-Hall, 1989), 29.

5. This is discussed in and based on Fred Luthans and Janet Larsen, "How Managers Really Communicate," *Human Relations,* vol. 39, no. 2 (1986), 162.

6. This model is based on the classic and best-known communication model by Claude E. Shannon and Warren Weaver and is adapted by using several improvements suggested by Sanford, Hunt, and Bracey. Both models are presented in Hunt, *Communication Skills,* 34–36.

7. This section is based on Hunt, *Communication Skills,* 34–36.

8. For a recent discussion of these studies, see R. Wayne Pace and Don Faules, *Organizational Communication* (Englewood Cliffs, NJ: Prentice-Hall, 1989), 136–38.

9. Ibid., 137.

10. This section on "Dealing with Communication Barriers" is based on Pace and Faules *Organizational Communication,* 150–62, unless otherwise noted. See also Tom Geddie, "Leap Over Communication Barriers," *Communication World,* April 1994, 12–17.

11. Gregory Northcreft and Margaret Neale, *Organizational Behavior* (Chicago: The Dryden Press, 1990), 88–92.

12. Pace and Faules, *Organizational Communication,* 153.

13. For further discussion, see Pace and Faules, *Organizational Communication,* 157–60.

14. Thomas Stewart, "How G.E. Keeps Those Ideas Coming," *Fortune,* August 12, 1991, 41–49.

15. Jitendra Sharma, "Organizational Communications: A Linking Process," *The Personnel Administrator,* vol. 24, July 1979, 35–43. See also Victor Callan, "Subordinate-Manager Communication in Different Sex Dyads: Consequences for Job Satisfaction," *Journal of Occupational and Organizational Psychology,* March 1993, 13–28.

16. William Convoy, "Working Together . . . Communication in a Healthy Organization," (Columbus, OH: Charles Merrill, 1976). See also David Johnson, et al, "Differences Between Formal and Informal Communication Channels," *The Journal of Business Communication,* April 1994, 111–24.

17. Dessler, *Winning Commitment: How to Build and Keep a Competitive Workforce* (New York: McGraw-Hill, 1993).

18. Pace and Faules, *Organizational Communication,* 105–106. See also Joanne Yates and Wanda Orlinkowski, "Genres of Organizational Communication: A Structurational Approach to Studying Communication and Media," *Academy of Management Review,* April 1992, 299–327.

19. Ibid., 110–11.

20. *Federal Express Employee Handbook,* 89.

21. *Team-Member Handbook,* Toyota Motor Manufacturing, USA, February 1988, 52–53.

22. Based on Thomas Stewart, "G.E. Keeps Those Ideas Coming," *Fortune,* August 12, 1991, 41–49.

23. Ibid., 42.

24. Ibid.

25. Ibid.

26. Ibid., 43.

27. Ibid.

28. Pace and Faules, *Organizational Communication,* 99–100.

29. Personal interview, March 1992.

30. Personal interview, March 1992.

31. Hunt, *Communications Skills,* 216. See also Rick Tetzeli, "Surviving Information Overload," *Fortune,* July 11, 1994, 60–67.

32. Based on James G. Miller, "Adjusting to Overloads of Information," in *Organizations: Structure and Behavior,* Joseph L. Litterer, ed. (New York: John Wiley and Sons, 1969), 313–22.

33. Katz and Kahn, *The Social Psychology of Organizations,* 230–34.

34. See, for example, "How GE Keeps Those Ideas Coming," op. cit.

35. Tom Peters and Robert Waterman, *In Search of Excellence* (New York: Harper & Row, 1982), 219.

36. Ibid.

37. Ibid., 22.

38. Ibid., 122–23.

39. Ibid., 122.

40. Ibid., 124.

41. R. Moss Kanter, *When Giants Learn to Dance* (New York: Touchstone, 1989), 275.

42. Faye Rice, "Champions of Communication," *Fortune,* June 3, 1991, 111–20.

43. Ibid., 43.

44. Ibid.

45. Ibid., 112.

46. Ibid., 116.

47. Tom Peters, *Liberation Management* (New York: Alfred A. Knopf, 1992), 172–75.

48. Ibid., 174.

49. R. L. Taft and R. H. Lingel, "Information Richness: A New Approach in Managerial Behavior and Organization Design," in *Research in Organizational Behavior,* Larry Cummings and Barry Staw, eds. (Greenwich, CT: JAI Press, 1984), 190–233. Discussed in Janet Faulk and Bryan Boyd, "Emerging Theories of Communication in Organizations," *Journal of Management,* vol. 17, no. 2 (1991), 409–11. See also Susan Strauss and Joseph McGrath, "Does the Medium Matter? The Intersection of Task Type and Technology on Group Performance and Member Reactions," *Journal of Applied Psychology,* February 1994, 87–99.

MANAGING TEAMS

LEARNING OBJECTIVES

After studying this chapter, you should be able to:

- Define employee involvement programs and explain their role in boosting productivity.

- Rank eight possible levels of employee involvement.

- Explain how group norms regulate and regularize the behavior of group members.

- List several factors that determine a group's cohesiveness or the attraction of the group for its members.

- Describe the main types of work teams.

- Name the five stages an organization must undergo to move to the point where work is carried out by self-directed teams.

- Compare and contrast characteristics of productive and unproductive teams.

- Identify approaches companies use to build effective teams.

- Discuss the role work teams play in total quality management programs.

OPENING PROBLEM
JOHNSONVILLE FOODS

In 1986, a big food company asked Johnsonville Foods CEO Ralph Stayer whether Johnsonville's Sheboygan, Wisconsin, plant was up to the task of manufacturing sausage under a private label. Stayer knew that the additional workload would push plant capacity to the limit, and the required hours would likely push his 200-person work force beyond theirs. He decided against taking on the project, but almost as an afterthought, he called his people together. Ever since his work force had been organized into teams of 5 to 20 members, Stayer had been pleasantly surprised at the increased efficiency and product quality. He felt he owed it to his staff to at least ask their opinion on the offer. Bonuses were based on profits, and the economies that would come with a bigger operation could mean more money to them. It would also mean a brutal work schedule and might even result in a decline in the quality of Johnsonville's product. The work force took ten days to mull it over.[1]

EMPLOYEE INVOLVEMENT PROGRAMS

At the General Mills cereal plant at Lodi, California, work teams run the plant and productivity has never been higher.[2] In one team, Carmen Gomez, Ruby Liptack, and Bill Gerstner operate the cereal-manufacturing machinery, while Donald Owen, William Walker, and Irma Hills help maintain the machinery. The manager, Denny Perak, is not a manager in the traditional sense at all: instead, he "coaches the team on management techniques and serves as the team's link with headquarters."[3] At Johnsonville Foods, similar self-managing teams now recruit, hire, evaluate, and fire (if necessary) on their own. Although many of the factory workers have little or no college background, they also train one another, formulate and track their own budgets, make capital investment proposals as needed, handle quality control and inspection, improve every process and product, develop their own quantitative standards, and create prototypes of possible new products.[4]

A work team like the one at General Mills or Johnsonville Foods can be defined as "a small number of people with complementary skills who are committed to a common purpose, set of performance goals, and approach, for which they hold themselves mutually accountable."[5] There are, as we will see in this chapter, several types of teams. But, regardless of type, the use of work teams is now widespread throughout the United States. For example, one study of team usage concluded that 82 percent of all U.S. firms have organized at least some of their employees as members of a working group that is identified as a team. Thirty-five percent of all U.S. organizations also have at least one team classified as self-directed or semi-autonomous (which generally means that the team supervises itself).[6]

Self-managed teams are examples of *employee involvement programs* and managers increasingly rank such programs as their biggest productivity boosters. For example, the editors of *National Productivity Review* mailed a survey several years ago to subscribers. They found that "increased employee involvement in the generation and implementation of ideas was ranked the highest priority productivity improvement action by the respondents." Employee involvement "was similarly ranked number one as the top cause of improvement over the past two years at these firms." (The other eight causes of improvement in descending order were quality programs, improved process methods, top management, equipment, technology, training, computers, and automation.)

EMPLOYEE INVOLVEMENT DEFINED

EMPLOYEE INVOLVEMENT PROGRAM
Any formal program that encourages and permits employees to participate in formulating important work decisions or in supervising all or part of their own work activities.

An **employee involvement program** is any formal program that encourages and permits employees to participate in formulating important work decisions or in supervising all or part of their own work activities.[7] In practice, many degrees of employee involvement are possible. After a comprehensive study of employee involvement programs and self-directed work teams in the United States, five researchers presented what they described as "an informal, non-scientific" list of employee involvement levels, as summarized in Figure 17.1.[8] Based on this, levels of employee involvement (ranked from level 1, low, to level 8, high) were as follows:[9]

- *Level 1: Information sharing.* Managers make all important operational decisions, inform employees, and then respond to employee questions.
- *Level 2: Dialogue.* Managers make the final decisions, but only after an open discussion between managers and employees. Typically, for instance, a group that

**Employee Involvement in Your Company:
An Informal Checklist**

☐ 1. Managers make decisions on their own, announce them, then respond to any questions employees may have.

☐ 2. Managers usually make the decisions, but only after seeking the views of employees.

☐ 3. Managers often form temporary employee groups to recommend solutions for specified problems.

☐ 4. Managers meet with employee groups regularly—once a week or so—to help them identify problems and recommend solutions.

☐ 5. Managers establish and participate in cross-functional employee problem-solving teams.

☐ 6. Ongoing work groups assume expanded responsibility for a particular issue, like cost reduction.

☐ 7. Employees within an area function full-time with minimal direct supervision.

☐ 8. Traditional supervisory roles do not exist; all or most employees participate in self-managing teams.

FIGURE 17.1

Eight Levels of Employee Involvement

SOURCE: Jack Osburn, et al., "Self-Directed Work Teams," (Homewood, IL: Business One Irwin, 1990), 30.

works together regularly might meet for an hour once a month, with their boss or other managers, in order to discuss important issues.

■ *Level 3: Special problem solving.* Managers assign selected employees to explore a limited issue or problem and recommend a course of action. This temporary task force might then meet weekly or monthly to formulate a solution to this pre-defined problem.

■ *Level 4: Intragroup problem solving.* Managers solicit employees' suggestions for solving operational problems within a given area. This involvement level often involves the formation of a *quality circle,* a group of from six to ten employees who meet for an hour or so each week to analyze or solve work-related problems.

■ *Level 5: Intergroup problem solving.* Experienced, trained, cross-functional teams of employees meet regularly with a manager to work on problems across several organizational units.

■ *Level 6: Focused problem solving.* The big difference here is that managers "empower the group to make decisions and take action affecting an important organizational issue (such as service quality, just-in-time delivery, or cost reduction)."[10] This level involves substantially more autonomy than levels 1 through 5, because the employees here do not just gather data and analyze problems. Instead, they identify opportunities for improvements and implement changes as well, all without direct supervision.

■ *Level 7: Limited self-direction.* Self-directed teams are limited to selected sites within the company, but at those sites the multiskilled members (such as those at the General Mills Lodi plant) "turn out a well-defined segment of work, and themselves manage their own efforts."[11]

■ *Level 8: Total self-direction.* At level 8, "every employee belongs to a self-directed team, starting with a highly interactive executive group."[12] Level 8 often involves establishing what is sometimes called a *team concept organization,* in which the company rearranges its entire organization structure and all its systems to support the teams. The managers themselves (also usually members of self-directed teams) devote their major effort toward helping their subordinates manage themselves and develop a sense of commitment.[13]

A BRIEF HISTORY OF EMPLOYEE INVOLVEMENT PROGRAMS

Employee involvement programs have been around for many years (although the self-directed teams popular today are of relatively recent origin). Even in the late nineteenth century, formal schemes for eliciting employee involvement existed in the United States. For example, Straiton & Storm, the largest cigar manufacturing firm in the nation in the early 1880s, used a labor-management board of arbitration to resolve disputes, and Boston's Filenes Department Store had a similar plan in 1898.[14] In the early 1900s, the Lincoln Electric Company instituted a famous incentive plan that included a suggestion system; the Lincoln plan is still in effect at the Lincoln Electric Company today. In 1937, Joseph Scanlon, a United Steel Workers Union official, developed an incentive plan based on a philosophy of cooperation between workers and management. In what subsequently became known as the Scanlon Plan, departmental-level and executive-level employee committees formulated productivity improving suggestions and then shared in any savings. In the late 1950s, Rensis Likert and his associates formulated what they called an employee-centered or *System IV* approach to managing. This plan consisted of decentralized, disbursed decision making, upward communications, and letting employees exert considerable self-control over their daily activities.

The 1970s saw the implementation of more sophisticated employee-involvement programs. For example, at Sweden's Saab Automobile Company, employee turnover had become so bad in the late 1960s that the firm decided to experiment with team assembly of cars.[15] One Saab plant organized to facilitate small-group assembly of auto engines. The work was laid out in such a way that all the basic components for an engine—cylinder heads, engine block, spark plugs, and so on—were supplied to one of seven production teams. Each team then planned its own work, made its own assignments, and assembled its own engines. The engines were then sent to the testing and shipping departments.[16]

Closer to home, General Motors joined with Toyota to jointly manage one of GM's plants in Fremont, California. The joint venture—known as New United Motor Manufacturing, Inc., or NUMMI, for short—involved re-opening what had become one of GM's worst plants in terms of absenteeism, grievances, and productivity. Within 18 months this plant used Toyota management methods and self-directed work teams to become one of the most productive auto plants in the United States. Partly because of this success, the growth of self-directed teams has increased enormously over the past few years.

GROUP

Two or more persons who are interacting with one another in such a manner that each person influences and is influenced by each other.

SMALL GROUP

A group of twenty or fewer members, usually fewer than five or six.

FUNDAMENTALS OF GROUP DYNAMICS

GROUPS AND TEAMS

A **group** is defined as two or more persons who are interacting with one another in such a manner that each person influences and is influenced by each other person. In psychological literature, a **small group** is generally defined as a group of twenty or fewer members, and usually fewer than five or six members.[17] As a result, all **teams** are groups, but a group is not always a team. Whether referring to a football team, a commando team, or a self-managing work team, a team is always distinguished by the fact that its members are "committed to a common purpose, set of performance goals, and approach for which they hold themselves mutually accountable."[18] Groups in general need not have such unanimity of purpose, but since all teams are groups, we should briefly review some small-group concepts before moving on.

DEVELOPMENT AND ENFORCEMENT OF GROUP NORMS

Group norms are defined as "the informal rules that groups adopt to regulate and regularize group members' behavior."[19] They are "rules of behavior, proper ways of acting, which have been accepted as legitimate by members of a group [and which] specify the kind of behaviors that are expected of group members."[20]

Work groups, enforcing their norms, can have an enormous influence over the behavior of their members.[21] In fact, studies reveal that "group norms may have a greater influence on the individual's performance than the knowledge, skills and abilities the individual brings to the work setting."[22] This fact was first popularized by the Hawthorne researchers. They described, for instance, how production that exceeded the group's norms triggered what the workers called *binging,* in which the producer's hand was slapped by other workers.

GROUP COHESIVENESS

In turn, the extent to which a group can influence its members' behavior depends largely on the attraction of the group for its members, on its **group cohesiveness.**[23]

Group cohesiveness depends on several factors. First, *proximity and contact* are prerequisites for both group formation and group cohesiveness; not only do they provide an opportunity for individuals to interact, but without them individuals would have no opportunity to become attracted to one another. On the other hand, proximity is no guarantee that people will discover they have something in common; if the individuals should find they have little in common, the effects could be just the opposite.[24]

Cohesiveness is also a function of the presence or absence of an *interpersonal attraction* between the people involved. In turn, individuals are usually attracted to a group because they find its activities or goals attractive, rewarding, or valuable or because they believe that through the group they can accomplish something they could not accomplish on their own. Such attractiveness, in turn, fosters cohesiveness.

Several other factors influence group and team cohesiveness. For one thing, group cohesiveness tends to decline as *group size* increases; beyond about 20 members, cohesiveness tends to diminish.[25] Also, *intergroup competition* can foster cohesiveness (particularly for the winning group), while *intragroup competition* (competition between the group's members) tends to undermine cohesiveness.[26] People join groups in part because they believe the group can help them accomplish their goals; *agreement over goals,* therefore, boosts cohesiveness, while differences reduce it.[27]

TYPES OF TEAMS

Most firms have several types of teams functioning at the same time. The main types of work teams are discussed next.

TEAMS THAT RECOMMEND THINGS: THE QUALITY CIRCLE

Companies have long used decision-making committees at the management level for analysis, advice, and recommendations. Often called task forces, project groups, or audit or safety groups, their role is to identify problems or opportunities and to recommend courses of action.[28]

After being widely used at the management level for many years, such analysis and recommendation teams have become common in nonmanagerial ranks as well. The quality circle is the most familiar example here. A **quality circle** is a team of 6 to 12 employees that meets once a week at work to solve problems affecting its work area.[29] Such teams are first trained in problem analysis techniques (including pareto analysis and basic statistics). Then the quality circle usually meets on company time to engage in problem solving and analysis.[30] In practice, this process involves five steps: problem identification, problem selection, problem analysis, solution recommendations, and solution review by top management. One study estimates that "perhaps several hundred thousand U.S. employees belong to QC circles," and that most of these are front-line manufacturing employees.[31]

The original wave of employer enthusiasm and support for quality circle programs began to fade several years ago. Perhaps the biggest reason for this decline in popularity was that many circles failed to produce measurable cost savings for the employer. Some circles' bottom line aims were too vague. In other firms, the participative quality circles proved incompatible with the autocratic management styles and cultures already in existence.[32]

Many firms today are taking steps to make their quality circles more effective. At Northrop, for instance, the groups are no longer voluntary and now involve all workers on the shop floor. The groups are responsible for setting improvement targets, keeping progress reports, and competing with other groups to achieve goals. At Honeywell Corporation the firm has replaced about 700 of their original quality circles with about 1,000 new work groups. These new groups are generally not voluntary;

QUALITY CIRCLE
A team of 6 to 12 employees that meets once a week at work to solve problems affecting its work area.

Work teams, like this crew assembling a Boeing 757, progress through several distinct stages in the course of their life.

they involve, instead, most shop floor employees and, in contrast to the bottom-up approach of quality circles, problems are usually assigned to work groups by management.[33]

TEAMS THAT MAKE OR DO THINGS: THE SELF-DIRECTED WORK TEAM

These teams usually consist of first-line employees who work together (making or doing things) full time. Increasingly, these types of teams include front-line employees who are responsible for the basic activities of the business, including assembling the product, customer sales, and product service.[34]

Self-directed teams are examples of teams that make or do things. A **self-directed work team** "is a highly trained group of employees, from 6 to 18 [people], on average, fully responsible for turning out a well-defined segment of finished work."[35] We will look more closely at self-directed work teams later in this chapter, but the *Rolls Royce* vignette provides one example.

SELF-DIRECTED WORK TEAM
A highly trained group of employees, from 6 to 18 people on average, fully responsible for turning out a well-defined segment of finished work.

ROLLS-ROYCE MOTOR CARS

Rolls-Royce, a name that has become synonymous with the highest possible quality, has altered production methods. The company has eliminated layers of management, trimmed its work force, and through it all dramatically improved operations. The driving force for its success has been the adoption of self-managed teams.

In the nearly 90-year history of Rolls-Royce, the 24 months beginning in 1991 represent the company's bottom. The automaker lost $150 million, and sales dropped by half. Michael J. Donovan, the company's commercial, managing director, moved quickly to implement team concepts across the company spectrum, from new product development to the factory floor, from blue-collar to white-collar workers.

The factory now consists of 16 zones each operating as profit centers under a manager. Costs, quality, and delivery to the next zone are the responsibility of a team that includes engineers, material-control, and maintenance specialists. Most zones consist of 10 teams with 6 to 10 members. Leaders are elected. Specific work requirements are not necessarily based on specialities, and each team member considers him- or herself responsible for pushing product on to the next zone. As a result, the teams are highly flexible, motivated units.

Donovan says the process isn't magic, but rather involves encouraging everyone to apply initiative, creativity, and take risks. He points out that since the team concept was implemented, defects that need to be corrected before shipping have been reduced from 150 to 47 per automobile. Now, says Donovan, "We aren't driven by dogma or senior-management dictates but by customer needs and the work place decisions of employees."

SOURCE: Brian S. Moskal, "The Rescue of the Gilded Lady," *Industry Week,* January 17, 1994, 15–18.

Workers on the line at Rolls-Royce have shifted to a team approach which blurs distinctions between blue- and white-collar jobs. Members of each zone's team are equally responsible for moving the product to the next stage of production.

VENTURE TEAM

A small group of people who operate as a semi-autonomous unit to create and develop a new idea.

PROJECT AND DEVELOPMENT TEAMS: THE VENTURE TEAM

Project and development teams are generally composed of white-collar professionals (marketing experts or engineers, for example) who collaborate on specific projects such as designing new processes (process design teams) or new product development (new product development teams or venture teams).

A **venture team** "is a small group of people who operate as a semi-autonomous unit to create and develop a new idea."[36] Venture teams are growing in popularity. The classic example is the IBM team organized in Boca Raton, Florida, in the 1980s to develop and introduce the firm's first personal computer. As is usually the case with venture teams, the unit was semi-autonomous in that it had its own budget and leader and the freedom to make decisions within broad guidelines.

As it turned out, IBM's PC venture team illustrates both the pros and cons of the venture team approach. Working semi-autonomously, it was able to create and bring to market in less than two years a new computer system. This might otherwise have taken IBM many years to develop and introduce if it had followed its usual hierarchical approach to product development.

On the other hand, many believe that the PC venture team's autonomy eventually backfired against IBM. Not bound by IBM's traditional policy of using only IBM parts, the team went outside IBM, both to Microsoft (for its DOS or disk operating system) and to Intel (for the computer processor). This certainly facilitated an early introduction of the IBM PC. Unfortunately, it also allowed Intel and Microsoft to sell the same PC parts to any PC manufacturer, and led to the proliferation of IBM clones.[37]

MAKING TASK FORCES WORK In *Liberation Management,* Tom Peters says that "project structures aren't new," and that task forces "were the rage for a while."[38] The problem, he says, is that "committee-itis" tends to set in, and as a result, many task forces become inward-looking and reflective rather than responsive. He suggests taking the following steps to keep project teams on track:

- *Set goals or deadlines for key subsystem tasks.* Successful project teams are characterized by a clear goal and by concrete milestones. Remember that committees *deliberate* while project teams *do.*

- *Let the project leader do the appraising.* The project boss, not the functional boss (if there is one) should have the main responsibility for evaluating a team member's performance.

- *Aim for full-time assignments to the team.* The project team's members should be highly committed, and such commitment usually requires full-time appointments. Key members should thus be given full-time assignments for the duration of most routine projects.

- *Allot space so that team members can "live" together.* If possible, set the team up in a separate space away from headquarters. At the very least team members should be able to work within the same facility.

- *Construct a self-contained system.* The team, says Peters, should have its own work stations, local area network, data base, and so on. This may lead to some duplication of equipment or support, but it is necessary to create a committed, integrated team.

- *Let teams pick their own leaders.* A self-designated champion, approved by management, may get the project underway. However, the most successful project teams usually select their own leaders.[39]

TEAMS THAT RUN THINGS

In September 1993, IBM's new chairman, Louis Gerstner, Jr., announced the appointment of a new IBM executive-level panel to help him run IBM. The eleven-person panel is to include (in addition to Gerstner) a number of senior vice-presidents and a vice-chairperson: John Thompson, with overall responsibility for mainframes and minicomputers; Ellen Hancock, who oversees networking and high-end software; Patrick O'Toole, responsible for chips, disk drives, printers, and specialized industry software; the head of the firm's personal computer business; the head of human resources; the head of North American marketing operations; the head of overseas marketing; the head of corporate strategy; the chief financial officer, and IBM's vice-chairperson.

Most large firms have numerous senior officers, of course. The difference in this case is Gerstner's desire to turn these individual executives into a smoothly functioning team.

Gerstner plans to transform these eleven strong individuals into a cohesive team by identifying them as members of his top-level executive committee, and by requiring them to focus on overall corporate results (not individual unit performance). The executives will thus be compensated, not based on the performance of their individual units, but on companywide results. They will all report to Gerstner, and together they will run IBM. The aim is to overcome what the *Wall Street Journal* refers to as "the formidable problem of coordinating IBM's divisions."[40]

SELF-MANAGING TEAMS

In many firms today, self-directed (also called self-managing) work teams are the ultimate manifestation of employee involvement programs. As mentioned earlier, a "self-directed work team is a highly trained group of from six to eight employees, on average, fully responsible for turning out a well-defined segment of finished work."[41] The "well-defined segment" might be an entire refrigerator, or an engine, or a fully processed insurance claim. In any case, the distinguishing features of self-directed work teams are that the teams are empowered to direct their own work and the work itself is a well-defined item. The *Globe Metallurgical* vignette illustrates what happened when a union strike forced one small firm to organize around self-managing teams.

STEPS IN MOVING TO SELF-DIRECTED TEAMS

Based on their practical experience in establishing and working with self-directed teams, one consulting group suggests that five stages are involved in moving the organization to the point where all or much of its work is carried out by self-directed teams. These five stages are as follows:

STAGE 1: START-UP Prior to start-up, an executive steering committee establishes the feasibility of a team structure, develops a mission statement, selects the initial team sites, designs a multilevel network of teams, and organizes the teams. Then, at start-up, the teams and supervisors begin figuring out their specific roles in the new team organization. These experts contend that "the dominant feature of start-up is intensive training for all involved." Team members must learn how to communicate and how to listen, how to use administrative procedures and budgets, and other similar skills. Supervisors must learn how to become facilitators and supporters rather than top-down supervisors.[42]

STAGE 2: STATE OF CONFUSION Once the initial enthusiasm wears off, the organization and its teams may enter a period of some confusion. Team members may become concerned regarding whether their new (probably self-imposed) higher work

Globe Metallurgical's turnaround was a direct result of its commitment to total quality concepts, earning it a Malcolm Baldrige Award.

GLOBE METALLURGICAL

Globe Metallurgical is the first small-company winner of the Malcolm Baldrige Award, and it didn't come by the honor easily. Back in 1984, the company appeared to be waiting its turn to join the list of defunct commodity metal suppliers dotting the rust belt. At the urging of customers, and after cost-cutting measures had failed, Chairman Arden C. Sims attended a seminar on total quality. More intensive training was to come later, but it's safe to say nothing was ever the same again at Globe.

Sims made several observations when he took over Globe, none of them good. R & D was virtually nonexistent, productivity and quality were low, and the company was bureaucratic and unresponsive. Though he had no experience with total quality management, work teams, or empowerment, Sims was certain of one thing. He had to get a handle on the production processes. To do so, he initiated the quality, efficiency, and cost program, or the QEC. In a two-year period between 1986 and 1988, Globe eliminated $11.3 million of costs. The company became the most efficient producer in the industry.

Sims's next objective was to make plant workers more conscious of product quality. But the flexibility he needed from employees put him at odds with the United Steelworkers Union, which had strict rules about job functions. A strike ensued, during which Sims ended up working maintenance, the dirtiest job in the plant. "I still don't know who made the assignment," he says. He and his managers got some practical experience in cross-functional teams and the most efficient methods of operations. Managers formed into eight-member teams because it seemed to be the most efficient division of labor. Several weeks after they took over, output increased 20 percent. Before the strike, it took 350 workers to run the plant. It's now run with 120 workers using the ideas Sims scribbled in a notebook every day on the job.

Globe is now an industry leader in cost, productivity, quality, sales—and profit increases. The company operates between 90 and 100 percent of its capacity utilization rate; the average rate for the rest of the industry is around 40 percent. Sims insists the company's quality program and use of teamwork wasn't some trendy attempt to alter the company culture. "It was about digging our way out of a real crisis," he says. It was also the right idea, just in time.

SOURCE: Bruce Rayner, "Trial-by-Fire Transformation: An Interview with Globe Metallurgical's Arden C. Sims," *Harvard Business Review*, May–June 1992, 117–29; Warren Stugaith, *World Trade,* March 1993; and "Does the Baldrige Award Really Work?" *Harvard Business Review*, January–February 1992, 126–47.

standards are liable to backfire at compensation time; supervisors may become increasingly concerned about their apparently shrinking role in day-to-day operations.

STAGE 3: LEADER-CENTERED TEAMS   Ideally, the team's confidence should grow at this point as the team members master new skills and find better ways to apply their new authority and accomplish their work. The chief danger in this stage, according to these experts, is that the teams become too reliant "on their internal leaders." Rather than remaining self-directed, some teams may slip into the habit of letting an informally elected team member carry out the former supervisor's supervisory role. A way to avoid this is "to make sure everyone continues to learn and eventually exercise leadership skills, . . . or allow anyone to exercise leadership functions as needed."[43]

STAGE 4: TIGHTLY FORMED TEAMS   The self-directed teams, somewhat blinded by their newfound authority and ability to manage their own affairs, may allow loyalty to their coworkers to mask problems within the team. For example, the other team members might hide a poorly performing member to protect the person from outside discipline in a misguided fit of loyalty. Management's job here is to reemphasize the need for both interteam cooperation and the team's responsibility for adequately supervising its own members.

STAGE 5: SELF-DIRECTED TEAMS   Once the new teams rid themselves of the intense team-oriented loyalties that often accompany building self-directed teams, the organization can move to what researcher Jack Orsburn calls "the period of true self-direction."[44] Gradually, the teams develop a powerful commitment, not just to their own members and missions but to achieving corporate goals as well.

The empowerment of self-directed teams can reportedly be a heady experience for all concerned. As one vice-president of a midwestern consumer goods company said of organizing his firm around teams, "people on the floor were talking about world markets, customer needs, competitors' products, making process improvements—all the things managers are supposed to think about."[45] The *Published Image* small business box describes how one small business successfully implemented self-directed teams.

BUILDING EFFECTIVE TEAMS

COMMON WORK TEAM PROBLEMS

Requiring several people to work together does not make the group a team, certainly not an effective team. An underperforming team might simply lack the initiative and sense of urgency that coaches traditionally try to ignite during half-time breaks. But a lack of initiative is often the least of the problems with which a team has to cope. The purpose of a team is to harness divergent skills and talents toward specific objectives; members' divergent points of view may lead instead to tension and conflict.[46] Power struggles—some subtle, some not—can similarly undermine the group's effectiveness; for instance, individual members may make subtle attempts to undermine potentially productive ideas with the implicit goal of "winning the day rather than doing what's best for the team." In addition, some team members may be ignored, thus eliminating a potentially valuable resource.[47]

Irving Janis also described another team problem, a phenomena he called "group think," "the tendency for a highly cohesive group, especially one working on special projects, to develop a sense of detachment and elitism."[48] This sense of detachment, Janis found, leads to a tendency for the group to press for unanimity and a reluctance to examine different points of view. The opinions of group members thus tend to be

PUBLISHED IMAGE, INC.

Aside from one key difference, Eric Gershman's aspirations were pretty similar to those of most entrepreneurs: Grow his business. Make some money. But lose his job?

Strange but true. Almost from the day he founded Published Image, Inc., and organized the newsletter into self-managed teams, Gershman had in mind the day his own position would become superfluous. His viewpoint is that employees capable of preparing their own work schedules, budgets, and bonuses certainly shouldn't have much use for a boss.

Gershman's team approach is nothing new in larger corporations, but it is rare for operations like Published Image, which has a total work force of only 26. For firms that size, the chasm between theory and practice can be wide indeed. For one thing, it's costly, in both time and tangible resources, to implement successful self-managed work teams. "You have to seriously re-design the organization to make them most effective," says Edward Lawler III, director of the University of Southern California's Center for Effective Organizations.

Gershman has always been something of a contrarian, dating back to his first job at a Boston ad agency. Luckily,

he's also resilient. Getting sacked didn't change his viewpoint in the least. "I always felt I had better ways of doing things than my boss," he says.

With the growth of mutual funds, Gershman correctly predicted the need for shareholder newsletters, and he spent his entire savings getting Published Image off the ground. Eleven clients and $600,000 in revenue later things looked rosy, except for several problems. Turnover was high, morale low, factual errors commonplace, and a third of the clients were opting out an-

FOCUS ON SMALL BUSINESS

nually. The company was also about to go bust. Gershman's characteristic certitude led him to the inescapable conclusion that changes had to be made. He came up with a 250-page plan of action.

"We blew up the whole company and totally changed people's thinking about what their job is," Gershman says. Published Image was divided into four virtually independent teams responsible for clients, sales staff, editorial content, and production workers.

Everyone performed a specialty, but everyone shared responsibility for daily deadlines as well. "We work like a unit and pitch in to get out on time whatever has to get done," says Shelley Danse. Her day as an account executive can stretch from research to proofreading to laying out artwork.

Not surprisingly, the team approach at Published Image engenders a sense of ownership of the collective output, as well as an enhanced appreciation of the work of fellow members. Planning is easier and efficiency has improved. Turnover has been reduced to zero. Clients are also impressed. "We have one group of people who know all facets of our job, and we can contact any of them during the process," says Peter Herlihy, vice-president of mutual-fund marketing at Fleet Financial Group.

Gershman may soon get his wish of working himself out of a job. Revenue doubled in 1993 to $4 million, and more than a third of the 20 percent profit margin occurred in the fourth quarter. Perhaps not coincidentally, that was just after the teams were put in place.

SOURCE: Michael Selz, "Testing Self-Managed Teams, Entrepreneur Hopes to Lose Job," *The Wall Street Journal*, January 11, 1994, B-1.

---

self-centered and **groupthink** sets in, in which one powerful point of view prevails—even though powerful and cogent arguments against it may exist in the group.

SYMPTOMS OF UNPRODUCTIVE TEAMS

Researcher Glenn Varney says that various symptoms make it fairly easy to recognize unproductive teams. Typical symptoms include the following:[49]

- *Cautious or guarded communication.* When people fear some form of punishment, ridicule, or negative reaction, they may either say nothing or be guarded in what they do say.

- *Lack of disagreement.* Lack of disagreement among team members may reflect an unwillingness to share their true feelings and ideas.

GROUPTHINK
When one powerful point of view prevails in a group, even though powerful and cogent arguments against it may exist in the group.

- *Use of personal criticism.* Personal criticism, such as "If you can't come up with a better idea than that, you better just keep quiet," is a sign of unhealthy team member relations.

- *Malfunctioning meetings.* Unproductive teams often have malfunctioning meetings characterized by boredom, lack of enthusiastic participation, a failure to reach decisions, and one or two people dominating all discussions.

- *Unclear goals.* Productive teams have a clear sense of mission, while members of unproductive teams are often unable to recite their own team's objectives.

- *Low commitment.* Without a clear sense of purpose, unproductive teams tend to have low commitment, because no sense of purpose has been established for members to commit to.

- *Conflict within the team.* Unproductive teams are also often characterized by a suspicious, combative environment within the team and conflict among team members.

CHARACTERISTICS OF PRODUCTIVE TEAMS

Of course, it is not unproductive teams you want to foster but productive, highly effective ones. A team, remember, can be defined as "a small number of people with complimentary skills who are committed to a common purpose, set of performance goals, and approach for which they hold themselves mutually accountable."[50] The core characteristics of productive teams are implicit in this definition. In particular, based on their extensive study of teams at work, Katzenbach and Smith found that productive teams have the following characteristics.

A COMMON COMMITMENT   Katzenbach and Smith found that "the essence of a team is common commitment. Without it, groups perform as individuals; with it, they become a powerful unit of collective performance."[51] In turn, productive teams must have a crystal clear purpose to be committed to, whether it is expressed as "Let's beat the Japanese by producing a world-class quality car" or "Let's prove that all children can learn." In any case, it is the team's clarity of mission and purpose that first sets it apart from unproductive teams.[52]

Katzenbach and Smith found that productive teams usually developed this sense of purpose and commitment by themselves, over time, often "in response to a demand or opportunity put in their path, usually by higher management."[53] This is not to say that productive teams do not often get their initial direction from outside the team, such as from top management. In fact, top management may provide the basic charter, rationale, or challenge. However, Katzenbach and Smith found that the most productive teams developed commitment around their own definitions of management's assigned aims: "the best teams invest a tremendous amount of time and effort exploring, shaping, and agreeing on a purpose that belongs to them both collectively and individually."[54]

SPECIFIC PERFORMANCE GOALS   Productive teams also translate their common purposes (such as "build world-class quality cars") into specific performance goals (such as "reduce new-car defects to no more than four per vehicle"). In fact, "transforming broad directives into specific and measurable performance goals is the surest first step for a team trying to shape a purpose meaningful to its members."[55]

RIGHT SIZE, RIGHT MIX   Best-performing teams generally have fewer than 25 people, and usually have from 7 to 14 people. Team members also have to complement each other in terms of their skills. For example, accomplishing the team's mission often calls for technical or functional expertise, problem-solving and decision-making skills, and interpersonal skills. The best teams have the right mix.

COMMON APPROACH   Productive teams also develop a strong commitment to a common approach, which outlines how they will work together to accomplish their purpose. In practice, a common approach leads team members to agree about who will do particular jobs, how schedules will be set and adhered to, what skills would need to be developed, what team members will have to do to earn continuing membership in the team, and how decisions will be made and modified.

MUTUAL ACCOUNTABILITY   In addition to a common purpose and a common approach, the most highly productive teams also develop a sense of mutual accountability. Productive team members develop a sense that "we are all in this together" and that "we all have to hold ourselves accountable for doing whatever is needed to help the team achieve its mission." Katzenbach and Smith found that such mutual accountability cannot be coerced. Instead, it emerges from the commitment and trust that come from working together toward a common purpose.

BUILDING TEAM PERFORMANCE

Good coaches know that productive teams do not emerge spontaneously; instead, they are a product of careful selection, training, and management. Researchers have identified many of the approaches companies use to build effective teams, and several of those approaches are listed here.

CAREFUL SELECTION   The time to begin building team effectiveness is before, not after the team is organized. Good football coaches do not choose players at random and then hope they will be effective athletes. As Katzenbach and Smith point out, "no team succeeds without all of the skills needed to meet its purpose and performance goals."[56] Members of productive teams therefore tend to be chosen both for their existing skills and their potential to improve existing skills and learn new ones. Remember that for teams, this includes technical or functional expertise, problem-solving and decision-making skills, and interpersonal skills.[57] Note that, in many situations, technical and even problem-solving skills are not enough. Instead, interpersonal skills and "a willingness to see the world from the other's point of view" are important characteristics, and indeed the team's effectiveness may depend on them.[58]

Firms like Toyota Motor Manufacturing also aim to select people not just on the basis of technical skills or work history, but on the sorts of values (such as cooperativeness and quality orientation) that fit best with the company's basic ideology. In fact, Toyota provides a good example of the team selection process. Toyota management looks first for interpersonal skills because of the firm's emphasis on team interaction.[59] Similarly, because the entire thrust of Toyota's quality improvement process is to improve work processes through worker commitment, recruits are carefully screened for their reasoning and problem-solving skills. Also, because quality is one of Toyota's central values, the firm also seeks a history of quality commitment in the people it hires. This is one reason for the firm's group interview, during which each applicant discusses his or her accomplishments. The net result, as at Toyota, is that teams are built around high-potential team members from the start.

TRAINING   Productive teams are usually highly trained teams. As one expert put it, "when moving toward team-oriented environments, companies tend to underestimate the need for new types of training."[60] Firms with productive teams therefore devote one or more weeks per year toward upgrading team members' skills (in addition to the initial training all team members receive). At a minimum, team training emphasizes three categories: (1) job skills (the technical skills required for job performance), (2) team interaction skills (the interpersonal and communication skills needed by team members, such as giving and receiving feedback), and (3) quality/action skills (including identifying problems and implementing improvements).[61]

One interesting development in training is the use by many firms of so-called wilderness programs for team building. These programs, such as one run by the Santa Monica, California-based Pacific Crest Outward Bound School, moves the firm's employees into outdoor wilderness settings in order to build trust and teamwork through a series of outdoor activities. For example, team members might be required to participate in a "trust fall," where participants stand on a ledge, perhaps 15 feet high, with their backs to the ground. A group of seven to ten of their colleagues await with outstretched palms, and the team member is expected to slowly fall backward into the waiting arms of his or her colleagues. Exercises like the trust fall and traversing a ravine by rope aim to build trust and to illustrate vividly the need for teamwork.[62]

CREATE A SENSE OF PURPOSE As we discussed in Chapter 12 (Empowering Employees and Building Commitment), the teams at firms like Toyota and Saturn work with a clear sense of purpose and mission as laid down by their respective firms. At Saturn, for instance, employees are driven by the mission of building a car to compete with the best of the Japanese and of producing vehicles that are "world leaders in quality, cost, and customer satisfaction through the integration of people, technology and business systems."[63] In other words, team building begins with knowing what the firm wants to achieve and what the role of each team should be in achieving that mission. Each team can then formulate specific goals and approaches for doing so.

OPEN COMMUNICATIONS A work team's effectiveness depends in part on operating under open and unrestricted information conditions. For example, in a study of about 200 companies with effective teams, it was found that "employees believe that greater access to information about corporate operations is critical if they are to improve their effectiveness in decision making."[64] In other words, it is not just the nature of the team and whether or not it has a clear mission—the team's context is important too, and in particular whether it has access to the corporate information and resources it needs to do its job.

OTHER APPROACHES SHARED BY MANY SUCCESSFUL TEAMS Katzenbach and Smith identified a number of other managerial actions that appear to distinguish successful from unsuccessful teams. These are summarized in Figure 17.2. As you can see, they include establish urgency, set demanding performance standards and direction, set clear rules of behavior, and challenge the group regularly with fresh facts and information.

SPECIAL TEAM-BUILDING TECHNIQUES

In some cases, the situation necessitates instituting special team-building activities, either to improve the way the team accomplishes its tasks or to overcome the interpersonal or other problems that are inhibiting the group's effectiveness. A number of special so-called organizational development techniques are available.[65]

FAMILY GROUP DIAGNOSTIC MEETING
A team or "family" group in which all team members report to the same manager.

FAMILY GROUP DIAGNOSTIC MEETING In the case of a **family group diagnostic meeting,** the team is a "family" group in which all team members report to the same manager. The diagnostic meeting's overall aim is to get a general reading on the group's overall performance (and in particular its current problems and how they

Establish urgency, demanding performance standards, and direction. All team members need to believe the team has urgent and worthwhile purposes, and they want to know what the expectations are.

Select members for skill and skill potential, not personality. The wise manager will choose people both for their existing skills and their potential to improve existing skills and learn new ones.

Pay particular attention to first meetings and actions. Initial impressions always mean a great deal. When potential teams first gather, everyone monitors the signals given by others to confirm, suspend, or dispel assumptions and concerns. If a senior executive leaves the team kickoff to take a phone call ten minutes after the session has begun and he never returns, people get the message.

Set some clear rules of behavior. All effective teams develop rules of conduct at the outset to help them achieve their purpose and performance goals. The most critical initial rules pertain to attendance (for example, "no interruptions to take phone calls"), discussion ("no sacred cows"), confidentiality ("the only things to leave this room are what we agree on"), analytic approach ("facts are friendly"), end-product orientation ("everyone gets assignments and does them"), constructive confrontation ("no finger pointing"), and,

often the most important, contributions ("everyone does real work").

Set and seize upon a few immediate performance-oriented tasks and goals. Most effective teams trace their advancement to key performance-oriented events. Such events can be set in motion by immediately establishing a few challenging goals that can be reached early on.

Challenge the group regularly with fresh facts and information. New information causes a team to redefine and enrich its understanding of the performance challenge, thereby helping the team shape a common purpose, set clearer goals, and improve its common approach.

Spend lots of time together. Common sense tells us that team members must spend a lot of time together, scheduled and unscheduled, especially in the beginning. This time need not always be spent together physically; electronic, fax, and phone time can also count as time spent together.

Exploit the power of positive feedback, recognition, and reward. Positive reinforcement works as well in a team context as elsewhere. There are many ways to recognize and reward team performance beyond direct compensation, from having a senior executive speak directly to the team about the urgency of its mission to using awards to recognize contributions.

FIGUR

Managerial Actions for Building Successful Teams

SOURCE: Adapted from Jon Katzenbach and Douglas Smith, "The Discipline of Teams," *Harvard Business Review,* March–April 1993, 118–19.

should be worked on in the future), by getting away from the work itself and analyzing data about the group and its current problems.

The consultant may conduct interviews or collect data from team members before the diagnostic meeting. However, most of the data generation usually takes place at the meeting itself. One approach is to engage the entire team into a discussion in which everyone presents ideas to the group. Another is to break the team into smaller groups, which then have intensive discussions and develop a list of prioritized issues to be addressed. The consultant may also feed back to the group his or her diagnostic findings based on preliminary discussions with team members.

Once the problems have been made public, the team and consultant will next prioritize and categorize them into, for instance, "communications" or "tight resources." The next step is to develop action plans, steps the team will take to manage the problems that were identified.

THIRD PARTY INTERVENTION FOR CONFLICT RESOLUTION Practitioners occasionally use **third party intervention** to resolve interpersonal conflicts between team members. These interventions involve what researcher Richard Walton refers to as dialogue.[66] The third-party consultant in this type of intervention tries to help the parties to interact with each other directly and to thereby "facilitate their diagnosis of the conflict and how to resolve it."[67]

THIRD PARTY INTERVENTION
The third party consultant in this type of intervention tries to help the parties to interact with each other directly and to thereby facilitate their diagnosis of the conflict and how to resolve it.

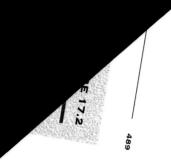

TOTAL QUALITY MANAGEMENT PROGRAMS

WHAT IS TOTAL QUALITY MANAGEMENT?

Work teams are often elements in **total quality management (TQM) programs.** TQM programs may be defined as organization-wide programs that integrate all functions of the business and related processes such that all aspects of the business including design, planning, production, distribution, and field service are aimed at maximizing customer satisfaction through continuous improvements.[68] W. Edwards Deming, who is credited with bringing quality control to Japan in the early 1950s, is generally regarded as the intellectual father of total quality management. His concept of total quality is based on the following 14–point system, which he says must be implemented at all organizational levels:

1. Create consistency of purpose toward improvement of product and service and translate that into a plan.
2. Adopt the new philosophy of quality.
3. Cease dependence on inspection to achieve quality. In particular, eliminate the need for inspection on a mass basis by building quality into the product from the beginning.
4. End the practice of choosing suppliers based solely on price. Move toward a single supplier for any one item and toward a long-term relationship of loyalty and trust.
5. Improve constantly and forever the production and service system in order to improve quality and productivity and thus constantly decrease cost. In other words, aim for continuous improvement.
6. Institute extensive training on the job.
7. Shift your focus from production numbers to quality.
8. Drive out fear, so that everyone may work effectively for the company.
9. Break down barriers between departments. People in research, design, sales, and production must work as a team to foresee problems of production as well as problems that may occur after sale when the product or service is actually used.
10. Eliminate slogans and targets for the work force for zero defects and new levels of productivity, particularly where new methods for achieving these targets are not put in place.
11. Eliminate work standards (quotas) on the factory floor.
12. Remove barriers that rob employees of their right to pride of workmanship. Among other things, this means abolishing the annual merit rating and all forms of management by objectives or management by numbers.
13. Institute a vigorous program of education and self-improvement.
14. Create a structure within top management that will push every day on the above 13 points. Make sure to put everybody in the company to work to accomplish the transformation.[69]

In Japan, (and since 1986 outside of Japan) the Deming prize for quality is awarded by the Union of Japanese Scientists and Engineers. The prize recognizes outstanding achievement in quality control management. In 1987, the U.S. Department of Commerce created the **Malcolm Baldrige Award,** named after President Reagan's Secretary

MALCOLM BALDRIGE AWARD
A prize created in 1987 by the U.S. Department of Commerce to recognize outstanding achievement in quality control management.

of Commerce who died while in office. Most U.S. manufacturing firms, service firms, and small businesses are eligible to apply for the Baldrige. Winners include Motorola, Inc., Federal Express Corporation, Cadillac Motor Car Company, and Xerox Business Products and Systems.

STEPS IN TOTAL QUALITY MANAGEMENT

In deciding on the Baldrige Award winners, several agencies (including the National Institute of Standards and Technology of the U.S. Department of Commerce and a Board of Examiners consisting of quality experts), evaluate and visit the sites of applicants. Overall, the applicants are judged on the extent to which they are continually improving value to customers while maximizing their overall productivity and effectiveness.[70] In evaluating applicants, the judges focus on a number of core issues such as customer-driven quality and continuous improvement, issues which are grouped into seven categories. These seven categories represent the core of the Baldrige application, and they are also illustrative of the elements in any total quality management program.[71] The key relationships among the seven Baldrige categories are summarized in Figure 17.3.

CATEGORY 1: SENIOR EXECUTIVE LEADERSHIP Judges focus on two things here: top management's symbolic commitment to quality and the day-to-day quality leadership by senior staff. Symbolic gestures (including taking the same courses lower-level employees are expected to take in preparation for the TQM programs), talking to customers about quality, and meeting with employees regarding quality are examples.

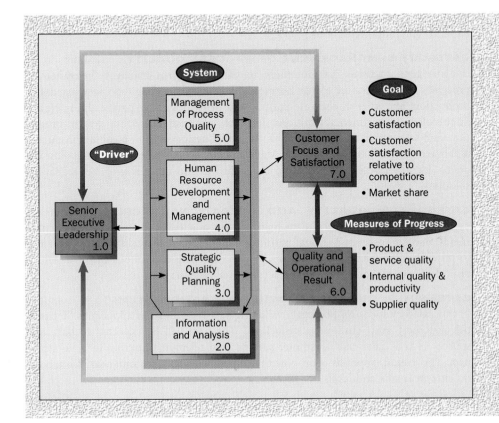

FIGURE 17.3

Baldrige Award Criteria Framework

Senior executive leadership is the "driver" of total quality management, with each of the other six elements, or Baldrige Categories, playing a crucial role.

SOURCE: U.S. Department of Commerce, 1992.

CATEGORY 2: INFORMATION AND ANALYSIS   Company applicants must show that they have gathered and used data that demonstrates both their quality performance and the fact that they are seeking continuous improvement. Applicants are expected to have a very adequate system for collecting statistical data on matters such as product or service quality and customer satisfaction.

Benchmarking refers to the process of comparing one's own firm's statistical results in key areas with those of other firms. The firm is expected to report which companies it benchmarked, what has been learned, and how the information was used.[72]

CATEGORY 3: STRATEGIC QUALITY PLANNING   In a general sense, strategic quality planning refers to the adequacy of the firm's planning process and how all key quality requirements are integrated into the firm's overall business planning process. In practice, examiners also typically review two or three goals the firm has set to determine how well it has met them. For example, goals might include answering all customer telephone calls by the second ring or increasing on-time customer deliveries by 80 percent.

CATEGORY 4: HUMAN RESOURCE DEVELOPMENT AND MANAGEMENT   Judges evaluate the firm's achievements with respect to developing and realizing the full potential of its employees to pursue the firm's quality and performance objectives. They also examine the firm's efforts to build and maintain an environment and culture for quality excellence, one conducive to full participation and personal organizational growth.[73]

In practical terms, examiners in this category tend to focus on the extent to which human resource management and organizational behavior techniques (such as enrichment, empowerment, training, and career development) are used to fully tap each employee's potential. For example, employees should be trained to use problem-solving tools and group decision-making skills. The teams and employees should also have enriched and empowered jobs.

CATEGORY 5: MANAGEMENT OF PROCESS QUALITY   Examiners in this category tend to focus on the extent to which the firm manages the systematic processes that are critical to the business. For example, rather than viewing design, production, and sales as separate entities, top firms usually recognize the integrated nature of the departments' work. For instance, representatives from design, production, and sales might work together on the initial design so as to facilitate production and maximize customer satisfaction. Many Baldrige winners develop process-flow diagrams, identify bottleneck areas, and use statistical and other approaches to develop solutions.[74]

CATEGORY 6: QUALITY AND OPERATIONAL RESULTS   Firms are expected to provide statistical data reporting on quality levels, quality improvement trends, and company operational performance and supplier quality. One aim here is to provide data which shows that the firm is achieving continuous improvement in critical operational areas, such as in service quality levels.

CATEGORY 7: CUSTOMER FOCUS AND SATISFACTION   The examiners in this category focus on objective, validated data regarding the applicant's "focus on the customer" and "customer satisfaction." The firm will be expected to have used sources such as sales calls, customer surveys, and telephone hotlines to generate the data. The overall emphasis is on how the company assesses customer satisfaction and on current trends and levels of satisfaction.

S U M M A R Y

The use of work teams for employee involvement is now widespread throughout the United States. Generally speaking, an employee involvement program is any formal program that encourages and permits employees to participate in formulating important work decisions or supervising all or part of their work activities. Such programs are increasingly ranked by managers as their most important productivity boosters. Eight possible levels of employee involvement, ranked from lowest to highest, include information sharing, dialogue, special problem solving, intragroup problem solving, intergroup problem solving, focused problem solving, limited self-direction, and total self-direction. Although self-directed teams originated recently, employee involvement programs have been around, in one form or another, for more than a century.

A group is defined as two or more people who are interacting with one another in such a manner that each person influences and is influenced by each other person. Group norms are the informal rules adopted to regulate and regularize the behavior of group members. Behavioral scientists have long recognized that work groups, enforcing their norms, can have an enormous influence over the behavior of their members. But the extent to which a group (or a team) can influence behavior depends largely on the attraction of the group for its members, or its cohesiveness.

Most firms will have not one, but several types of teams functioning at the same time. The main types of work teams include those that recommend things, make or do things, design new products or processes, run things, and those that are self-managing. An organization must pass through at least five stages to move itself to the point where work is carried out by self-directed teams. These stages include start-up, state of confusion, leader-centered teams, tightly formed teams, and self-directed teams.

Power struggles, lack of initiative, and group think are common work-team problems. Various symptoms make it fairly easy to recognize unproductive teams. These include cautious or guarded communication, lack of disagreement, use of personalized criticism, malfunctioning meetings, unclear goals, and low commitment. In contrast, productive teams are characterized by a common commitment, specific performance goals, the right size and right mix, a common approach, and mutual accountability. Researchers have identified many of the approaches companies use to build effective teams, such as careful selection, training, creation of a sense of purpose, open communication, and special team-building techniques. Work teams are often elements in total quality management programs, which are aimed at maximizing customer satisfaction through continuous improvements.

Q U E S T I O N S

■ FOR REVIEW

1. List and describe the eight possible levels of employee involvement. How do they relate to the main types of work teams described in this chapter?

2. Describe a self-managing work team. What main characteristic distinguishes it from other work teams?

3. Name some problems that can develop with work teams and the symptoms that accompany them.

4. What are the three most important components of successful team building? Explain the processes underlying each one.

5. Explain the five stages an organization undergoes in moving to the point where self-directed teams accomplish the majority of company work.

6. What is total quality management?

■ FOR DISCUSSION

7. Should a high level of employee involvement be the ultimate goal of all firms? Why or why not?

8. Can a team that is organized with existing employees be as effective as one with members that were hired and trained specifically for the task? Discuss.

9. Do you think total quality management is a passing fad or here to stay? Defend your position.

■ FOR ACTION

10. Recall a time when you were a member of a team. Describe any problems the team experienced and how they were resolved.

11. Saturn Corporation offers one of the best-known examples of the effective use of work teams. Gather information on the company and its parent, General Motors Corporation. Write a report contrasting the two firms' approaches.

12. Obtain a list of Malcolm Baldrige Award recipients. Find out if their quality efforts have translated into improvements in the companies' profitability. What conclusions can you reach from your research?

■ FOR FOCUS ON SMALL BUSINESS

13. Why do you think the team approach is not widely used in small business?

14. Discuss the reasons that Gershman was able to successfully implement self-managed work teams despite the small size of his work force.

15. If the self-managed work teams continue to be effective, will Gershman's job actually become obsolete? Why or why not?

CLOSING SOLUTION

JOHNSONVILLE FOODS

Ralph Stayer's workers came back with three responses. They were certain about one, pretty sure about the other, and just speculating on the third. They felt like they would have to work seven-day weeks for a while. But they didn't think that would last long. What they were positive about was that they could do it; they could handle the extra load and the company wouldn't suffer any loss of product quality. Collectively they offered projections on how much new machinery would be needed, and even roughed out schedules of what the plant would need to produce per day. "If I had tried to implement it from above," says Stayer, "we would have lost the whole business." The move ultimately led to a big expansion of the facility. Since 1986, productivity has increased by 50 percent.

■ QUESTIONS FOR CLOSING SOLUTION

1. Based on the eight levels of employee involvement described in the chapter, how would you describe the team set-up at Johnsonville Foods?

2. What factors do you think influence group cohesiveness at the company?

3. Do you think it was a risky move for Stayer to accept the workers' recommendations? Why or why not?

Employee Involvement Program

Group

Small Group

Teams

Group Norms

Group Cohesiveness

Quality Circle

Self-directed Work Team

Venture Team

Groupthink

Family Group Diagnostic Meeting

Third Party Intervention

Total Quality Management Programs

Malcolm Baldrige Award

CASE FOR ANALYSIS

SUNBEAM-OSTER COMPANY

It's not every day that a CEO turns a multimillion-dollar-losing company into a huge profit maker in just a few years. Even more rare is the CEO who can accomplish this feat, make his senior officers millionaires, and still alienate them to the point that they vote for his dismissal.

In 1990, former Goldman Sachs & Company investment banker Paul B. Kazarian spearheaded a hostile takeover of Sunbeam while the company was still in bankruptcy. His Japonica investment group, along with limited partners Steinhardt Partners and Mutual Shares Corporation, paid $660 million for the Pittsburgh-based consumer products maker. The company had just lost $95.3 million. Kazarian moved the corporate headquarters to Providence, Rhode Island, and instituted what he later called management by "constant humility, of being no better than anybody else." Competition between departments was encouraged, and it became mandatory for top executives to wear beepers all day, every day. Thirty managers were allocated a total of two secretaries. Kazarian's approval was required on any capital expenditure over $5,000, and he was fast gaining a reputation as an extremely control-oriented micromanager.

"He sure made a lot of people nuts," says Foote, Cone & Belding Communications managing director Mitchel Engel. Foote Cone was the Chicago advertising agency that James J. Clegg, Sunbeam's household products division chief, selected for a $3.7 million television and print promotion contract. When Kazarian learned of the deal he faxed a cancellation, terming the expenditure unauthorized. The advertiser promptly sued.

Very soon after moving the company to Rhode Island, one former executive described the atmosphere as that of a military barracks. Bad language was common, and employees described Kazarian as going out of his way to malign and degrade suppliers and other adversaries in negotiations. It was also alleged that he fired a BB gun at empty chairs during a meeting while shouting "die, die," narrowly missed his controller's head with a thrown container of juice, destroyed phones, and publicly issued lascivious comments to women. Senior officers, it was also charged, were routinely dressed down in front of colleagues. Kazarian denies any of it happened.

If any of these events did happen, they should not have come as that big of a shock. Members of the group that worked on Sunbeam's (then known as Allegheny International) bankruptcy recall similar bad-taste antics that occurred during those proceedings. Kazarian's idea of professional attire consisted of blue jeans, a baseball cap, and no sign of a haircut. During a meeting with lawyers, according to Bruce McCollough, counsel for Allegheny, Kazarian bit a portion of a cigar off and promptly spit it back out. Here too, he was alleged to have used profanities, and McCollough says matters nearly came to blows at one point. Kazarian also denies McCollough's recollection of events.

While he may not have earned high marks in charm school, no one can deny Kazarian's effectiveness in turning Sunbeam-Oster around. "It was one of the best analytical jobs I've seen of demonstrating value where [previous] management didn't see it," says Harvard business school professor Steven R. Fenster. When Kazarian took the helm, the company was a smorgasbord of businesses, many of them money-losing black holes. The unprofitable divisions were sold off quickly, and the appliance division was restructured. Kazarian located a number of undetected assets, including the somewhat amazing discovery of $60 million in foreign bank accounts. New products were introduced, and the company began operating at lower costs.

Rebounding from the 1990 loss, Kazarian managed Sunbeam-Oster to a $47 million profit the following year. The company earned $120 million in 1992. An offering of Sunbeam stock raised $236 million, imputing a total worth of the company in the $1 billion-plus range.

"You don't change a company in bankruptcy without making a few waves," Kazarian points out. "I wasn't there to be a polite manager. I was there to create value for shareholders." No one can argue that he didn't do that. Steinhart and Mutual's original investment is now worth around $1 billion. Kazarian sued Sunbeam-Oster over his ouster, and he was awarded a $173 million settlement that he will split with two of his partners. The company will also have to pick up just under $4 million of his salary because his departure was technically without cause. The merits, and shortcomings of how Kazarian went about transforming Sunbeam-Oster will likely be debated for a very long time.

SOURCES: Geoffrey Smith et al., "How to Lose Friends and Influence No One," *Business Week,* January 25, 1993. 42–43; "Corporate Moonbeam at Sunbeam-Oster," *Time,* January 25, 1993, 19–21; Agis Salpukis, "Sunbeam

to Settle Kazarian Suits for $173 Million," *New York Times,* July 23, 1993, C15 (N); and Sabra Chartrand, "Sunbeam-Oster Picks Chief to Replace Ousted Leader," *New York Times,* August 3, 1993, C3 (N).

■ QUESTIONS

1. Contrast Kazarian's success at controlling numbers with his apparent failure in the area of human relations.
2. Could Kazarian have been more successful in running the company if he had relied less on imposed, top-to-bottom control and more on employee involvement? Discuss?
3. Explain how you might have used self-directed teams to accomplish the same financial turnarounds.

A CASE IN DIVERSITY

GE SILICONES

Achieving team cohesiveness can be difficult, even when the majority of members share similar backgrounds and experience. Reaching a consensus when members of the group have varying ethnic and gender makeup can be more challenging. But the payoff can be even greater for the manager who is able to bring such a disparate group together and get them all pulling in the same direction.

GE Silicones (GES) of Waterford, New York launched some critical initiatives in the late 1980s. The company created a total-quality department, expanded its research and development staff, and added technologies to the overall manufacturing infrastructure. GES, which manufactures a wide variety of silicone products, decided to add something else to the company. While the company ranks remained stilted in favor of white males, graduates from the best engineering schools were increasingly female and minorities. The company decided to be a participant in the future instead of waiting for it to roll over them. Before long, almost a third of GES new-hires were drawn from these groups.

Top managers quickly learned that implementing changes in a company's culture is a lot more complicated than just putting a stop to off-color ethnic humor and adding a few ladies' rooms. How this came about may lend credence to the theory that the work force is often the most knowledgeable about company problems, and is best equipped to do something about them. Groups of recently hired women and minorities began meeting spontaneously to talk about work problems. Minority workers vented anger about challenges to their ideas that seemed to occur far more frequently than to those of their white male counterparts. Women lamented reluctance on the part of superiors to extend responsibility. They also expressed frustration at the inability to mention issues relating to their families, fearing they would impact career aspirations adversely. One thing quickly became apparent. Nothing much would change unless management became aware of the problems they were experiencing.

GES top managers came to a quick conclusion: a total quality program, increased R&D or the adding of plant capacity had a far better chance of success if every employee felt free to make his or

her maximum contribution. A combination of managers and a volunteer steering committee used teamwork and diversity training to address a list of cultural-diversity problems first raised by employees. In turn, teams of workers were formed to look into everything from family leave to personal development to mentoring. The results included an employee wellness and fitness program, enhanced minority recruitment, on-site support groups for women and minorities, and periodic surveys where employees could offer feedback relating to career opportunities.

The cultural-diversity program took root quickly at GES, largely because of real commitment and action on the part of management. A woman was selected to fill the top spot in the total quality department; minorities now also hold key managerial posts at R&D and the maintenance sector. Another R&D manager points to a key departure from the past. "There's more talking and listening going on," says Rich Allen.

Most agree that there are two important reasons that the GES cultural-diversity program made such rapid progress. Its makeup, through the use of teams of employees rather than managers, made participation seem natural. It also gave workers a sense of responsibility for the outcome, while allowing them direct input into the program's direction and content.

SOURCE: Vicki Clark, "Employees Drive Diversity Efforts at GE Silicones," *Personnel Journal,* May 1993, 148–153.

■ DIVERSITY QUESTIONS

1. What special challenges is a work team likely to face if its membership is culturally diverse?
2. Why do you think GES' top managers didn't anticipate the problems their minority and women hiring program triggered? Do you think such dissatisfaction and problems are inevitable? Discuss.
3. List the benefits of the added perspectives made possible by a diverse team.

1. Brian Dumaine, "Who Needs a Boss," *Fortune,* May 7, 1990, 52–60.

2. Ibid.

3. Ibid., 52.

4. Tom Peters, *Liberation Management,* (New York: Alfred Knopf, 1992), 238–39.

5. John Katzenbach and Douglas Smith, "The Discipline of Teams," *Harvard Business Review,* March–April 1993, 112.

6. Jack Gordon, "Work Teams: How Far Have They Come?" *Training,* October 1992, 60–65.

7. For employee involvement survey data, see Lee Towe, "Survey Finds Employee Involvement a Priority for Necessary Innovation," *National Productivity Review,* vol. 9, no. 1, Winter 1989–1990, 3–15.

8. Jack Orsburn, Linda Moran, Ed Musselwhite, John Zenger, and Craig Perrin, *Self-directed Work Teams: The New American Challenge* (Homewood, IL: Business One Irwin, 1990), 30–34.

9. These are based on Ibid., 31–34.

10. Ibid., 32.

11. Ibid., 33.

12. Ibid.

13. Ibid., 34. See also Charles Manz, "Self-Leading Work Teams: Moving Beyond Self-Management Myths," *Human Relations,* vol. 45, no. 11 (1992), 1119–41.

14. Raymond Hogler, "Employee Involvement and Electromation, Inc.: An Analysis and a Proposal for Statutory Change," *Labor Law Journal,* May 1993, 261–74.

15. "Job Redesign on the Assembly Line: Farewell to Blue Collar Blues?" Reprinted in Denis Organ, *Applied Psychology of Work Behavior* (Dallas: BPI, 1978), 270.

16. "Job Redesign on the Assembly Line: Farewell to Blue Collar Blues?" *Organizational Dynamics,* vol. 2, no. 2 (1973), 51–67.

17. These definitions are from Marvin E. Shaw, *Group Dynamics: The Psychology of Small Group Behavior* (New York: McGraw-Hill, 1976), 11.

18. See, for example, Katzenbach and Smith, "The Discipline of Teams," 112–13. Note that many researchers do not, however, distinguish between groups and teams. See, for example, Gary Coleman and Eileen M. Van Aken, "Applying Small-Group Behavior Dynamics to Improve Action-Team Performance," *Employment Relations Today,* Autumn 1991, 343–53.

19. Daniel Feldman, "The Development and Enforcement of Group Norms," *Academy of Management Review,* vol. 9, no. 1 (1984), 47–53.

20. A.P. Hare, *Handbook of Small Group Research* (New York: The Free Press, 1962), 24. See also S. Barr and E. Conlon, "Effects of Distribution of Feedback in Work Groups," *Academy of Management Journal,* June 1994, 641–56.

21. See Stephen Worchel, Wendy Wood, and Jeffrey Simpson, *Group Process and Productivity* (Newbury Park, CA: Sage Publications, 1992), 245–50.

22. Ibid., 245.

23. For a discussion of the difficulty of measuring and defining cohesiveness, see Peter Mudrack, "Group Cohesiveness and Productivity: A Closer Look," *Human Relations,* vol. 42, no. 9 (1989), 771–85. See also R. Saavedra, et al, "Complex Interdependence in Task-Performing Groups," *Journal of Applied Psychology,* February 1993, 61–73.

24. Sell Marvin Shaw, *Group Dynamics* (New York: McGraw-Hill, 1976), Chapter 4.

25. Stanley C. Seashore, *Group Cohesiveness in the Industrial Work Group* (Ann Arbor, MI: Survey Research Center, University of Michigan, 1954), 90–95. See also Joseph Litterer, *The Analysis of Organizations* (New York: Wiley, 1965), 91–101. See also J. Haleblian and S. Finkelstein, "Top Management Team Size, CEO Dominance, and Firm Performance: The Moderating Roles of Environmental Turbulence and Discretion," *Academy of Management Journal,* August 1993, 844–64.

26. Robert Blake and Jane Mouton, "Reactions to Inter-Group Competition under Win–Lose Conditions," *Management Science,* vol. 7 (1961), 432.

27. John R. P. French, Jr., "The Disruption and Cohesion of Groups," *The Journal of Abnormal and Social Psychology,* vol. 36 (1941), 361–77.

28. Katzenbach and Smith, "The Discipline of Teams," 116–18.

29. Everett Adams, Jr., "Quality Circle Performance," *Journal of Management,* vol. 17, no. 1 (1991), 25–39.

30. Ibid.

31. Eric Sundstrom, Kenneth DeMeuse, and David Futrell, "Workteams: Applications and Effectiveness," *American Psychologist,* February 1990, 120.

32. See, for example, Adams, "Quality Circle Performance," and Gilbert Fuchsberg, "Quality Programs Shows Shoddy Results," *The Wall Street Journal,* May 14, 1992, B-1, B-4.

33. Gopal Pati, Robert Salitore, and Saundra Brady, "What Went Wrong with Quality Circles?" *Personnel Journal,* (December 1987), 83–89.

34. Katzenbach and Smith, "The Discipline of Teams," 116; and Sundstrom, DeMeuse and Futrell, "Workteams," 121.

35. Orsburn, et al., *Self-Directed Work Teams,* 8.

36. Philip Olson, "Choices for Innovation Minded Corporations," *The Journal of Business Strategy,* January–February 1990, 86–90.

37. In many firms, the concept of a venture team is taken to what may be its natural conclusion in that new venture units and new venture divisions are established. These are separate divisions devoted to new product development. See, for example, Christopher Bart, "New Venture Units: Use Them Wisely to Manage Innovation," *Sloan Management Review,* vol. 35, Summer 1988, 35–43; and Robert Burgelman, "Managing the New Venture Division: Research Findings and Implications for Strategic Management," *Strategic Management Journal,* vol. 6 (1985), 39–54.

38. Peters, *Liberation Management,* 208.

39. Ibid., 208–10.

40. Leslie Scism, "Gerstner Moves to Coordinate IBM Businesses," *The Wall Street Journal,* September 14, 1993, A-4.

41. Jack Orsburn, et al., *Self-Directed Work Teams,* 8.

42. Ibid., 20–27.

43. Ibid., 21.

44. Ibid., 22.

45. Ibid., 22–23.

46. Based on Erin Neurick, "Facilitating Effective Work Teams," *SAM Advanced Management Journal,* Winter 1993, 22–26.

47. Ibid., 23.

48. Ibid.

49. The following, except as noted, is based on Glenn H. Varney, *Building Production Teams: An Action Guide and Resource Book* (San Francisco: Jossey-Bass Publishers, 1989), 11–18. See also P. Bernthal and C. Insko, "Cohesiveness Without Group Think: The Interactive Effects of Social and Task Cohesion," *Group and Organization Management,* March 1993, 66–88.

50. Katzenbach and Smith, "The Discipline of Teams," 112. See also C. Meyer, "How the Right Measures Help Teams Excel," *Harvard Business Review,* May–June 1994, 95–106.

51. Ibid.

52. See G. T. Shea and R. A. Guzzo, "Groups As Human Resources," in *Research in Personnel and Human Resources Management,* vol. 5, K. M. Roland and G. R. Ferris, eds. (Greenwich, CT: JAI Press, 1987), 323–56. See also Sundstrom, DeMeuse, and Futrell, "Workteams," 123.

53. Katzenbach and Smith, "The Discipline of Teams," 112.

54. Ibid., 113.

55. Ibid. The evaluation process is important as well. See R. Saavedra and S. Kwun, "Peer Evaluation in Self-Managing Work Groups," *Journal of Applied Psychology,* June 1993, 450–63.

56. Ibid., 118.

57. Ibid.

58. Erin Nurick, "Facilitating Effective Work Teams," 26.

59. Gary Dessler, *Winning Commitment: How to Build and Keep a Competitive Workforce* (New York, McGraw-Hill, 1993), 94–95.

60. Richard Wellins, "Building a Self-Directed Work Team," *Training & Development,* December 1992, 27.

61. Ibid. See also Paul Brauchle and David Wright, "Training Work Teams," *Training & Development,* March 1993, 65–67.

62. Jennifer Laabs, "Team Training Goes Outdoors," *Personnel Journal,* June 1991, 56–63.

63. Dessler, *Winning Commitment,* 75.

64. Richard Magjuka and Timothy Baldwin, "Team-Based Employee Involvement Programs: Effects of Design and Administration," *Personnel Psychology,* vol. 44 (1991), 806.

65. Except as noted, this is based on Thomas Cummings and Christopher Worley, *Organization Development and Change* (Minneapolis: West Publishing Company, 1993) 214–28.

66. Richard Walton, *Managing Conflict: Interpersonal Dialogue and Third Party Roles,* 2nd ed. (Reading, MA: Addison-Wesley, 1987).

67. Cummings and Worley, *Organization Development,* 212. For a discussion of fitting the team to the task to bolster team performance, see S. Keck and M. Tushman, "Environmental and Organizational Context and Executive Team Structure," *Academy of Management Journal,* December 1993, 314–48.

68. Based in part on Joel E. Ross, *Total Quality Management: Text, Cases and Readings* (Delray Beach, FL: St. Lucie Press, 1993), 1.

69. Ibid., 2–3, 35–36.

70. Richard M. Hodgetts, *Blueprints for Continuous Improvement: Lessons from the Baldrige Winners* (New York: American Management Association, 1993), 13.

71. Except as noted, the following is based on Hodgetts, *Blueprints for Continuous Improvement,* 15–22; and Ross, *Total Quality Management,* 4–5.

72. Hodgetts, *Blueprints for Continuous Improvement,* 19.

73. Ross, *Total Quality Management,* 4.

74. Hodgetts, *Blueprints for Continuous Improvement,* 21.

CHAPTER 18

ORGANIZATIONAL CHANGE AND DEVELOPMENT

LEARNING OBJECTIVES

After studying this chapter, you should be able to:

- Differentiate between incremental and strategic changes and between reactive and anticipatory changes.

- Identify the risks and benefits of implementing organizational changes.

- List the sources of resistance to organizational change.

- Describe the three steps that make up Lewin's change model.

- Name the six main steps involved in making both incremental and strategic changes.

- Compare and contrast the main targets for change, such as strategy, structure, tasks, technologies, culture or attitudes, and skills.

- Discuss the six overlapping steps in the critical path approach to change.

- Give examples of the leadership activities carried out by change advocates.

- Define four categories of interventions in organizational development programs.

- Describe how change is managed by overcoming employees' resistance to change, developing political support for the change, and motivating employees to implement the change.

OPENING PROBLEM
WARNACO, INC.

Back in 1986, Linda Wachner, formerly president and CEO of Max Factor, Inc., set her takeover sights on an apparel maker named Warnaco, Inc. Her timing could not have been worse. The economy was starting to nosedive. Consumers were pinching pennies, and many department store chains were going bankrupt. Wachner soon found herself presiding over Warnaco's portfolio of 15 businesses, many of which were doing poorly financially. The investment required to make them competitive would cost millions. Interest payments would cost millions more. Warnaco costs were also out of line. Wachner had some hard organizational change decisions to make: She had to set a new direction for the firm, improve the firm's finances, and get Warnaco's employees to work with her to implement her new vision.[1]

THE NATURE OF PLANNED CHANGE

TYPES OF CHANGE

INCREMENTAL CHANGES
Changes that only affect selected organizational components, perhaps by changing the organization's structure, introducing a new production technology, or developing employees so as to reduce interdepartmental conflict.

STRATEGIC ORGANIZATIONAL CHANGE
Changes that impact the entire organization and fundamentally redefine what the organization is or change its basic framework, including strategy, structure, people, processes and in some cases, core values.

REACTIVE CHANGE
Changes that are made in direct response to an external event.

ANTICIPATORY CHANGE
Changes that are initiated not because of the need to respond to an immediately pressing event but rather because senior management believes that change in anticipation of events still to come will provide competitive advantage.

Organizational change experts David Nadler and Michael Tushman say that "organizations go through change all the time" but that the nature, scope, and intensity of such changes vary considerably.[2] For example, experts distinguish between *strategic* and *incremental* changes. **Incremental changes,** while significant, only affect selected organizational components, perhaps by changing the organization's structure, introducing a new production technology, or developing employees so as to reduce interdepartmental conflict. Changes like these are intentionally limited in their scope and occur "within the general framework of the strategy, mode of organizing and values that are already in place."[3] At the other extreme, **strategic organizational changes** impact the entire organization and "fundamentally redefine what the organization is or change its basic framework, including strategy, structure, people, processes and (in some cases) core values."[4] It was such strategic changes that Warnaco's CEO Linda Wachner had to define and implement.

Organizational changes also differ in the extent to which they are *anticipatory* and planned or just *reactive*. A **reactive change** is made in direct response to an external event. Thus, when Lee Iacocca assumed Chrysler's presidency, the firm's impending bankruptcy denied him the luxury of implementing a carefully planned change over a period of years. Instead, his organizational changes had to be implemented almost at once in reaction to the firm's desperate financial situation.

At the other extreme, **anticipatory changes** are initiated not because of the need to respond to an immediately pressing event "but rather because senior management believes that change in anticipation of events still to come will provide competitive advantage."[5] Such anticipatory change (particularly anticipatory *strategic* change) is the type instituted by Jack Welch when he became president of General Electric. Compared to Iacocca, Welch had the luxury of creating a vision of a more agile, open, and adaptive General Electric. He also had the years required to remake the firm's business mix, culture, structure, and operating practices. Between 1981 (when Welch took over GE) and 1989

he had squeezed 350 product lines and business units into thirteen big businesses, each first or second in its industry. He had shed $9 billion of assets and spent $18 billion on acquisitions. He collapsed G.E.'s management structure, a wedding cake that had towered up to nine layers high, and scraped its ornate frosting of corporate staff; 29 pay levels became five broad bands.[6]

As we have seen, Welch successfully changed GE's culture by reformulating its values and aims, and he implemented hundreds of organizational practices that opened up communications. He then took steps to encourage employees to live out such new GE values as leanness, agility, and candor or openness.

THE ORGANIZATIONAL CHANGE MATRIX Combining these two change dimensions—strategic versus incremental change and reactive versus anticipatory change—means that four types of changes can be identified (see Figure 18.1). Nadler and Tushman refer to an incremental and anticipatory change as *tuning*. This is the simplest type of change to conceive and implement: It combines relatively limited incremental modifications of specific organizational components with the luxury of making those changes slowly, in anticipation of future events. When incremental change is initiated reactively, it is referred to as *adaptation*. Incremental changes like these are also relatively limited in scope. However they are reactively implemented as

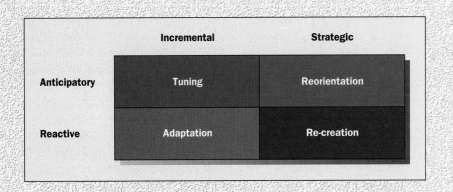

FIGURE 18.1

Types of Organizational Changes

Organizational changes can be classified as either incremental or strategic and either anticipatory or reactive.

SOURCE: David Nadler and Michael Tushman, "Beyond the Charismatic Leader: Leadership and Organizational Change," *California Management Review,* Winter 1990, 80.

a result of the time constraints associated with unexpected, unanticipated fluctuations in the firm's environment. Similarly, strategic changes initiated in anticipation of future events are known as **reorientations,** while strategic changes like Chrysler's that are prompted by immediate crises are called **recreations.**[7]

IMPLEMENTING STRATEGIC CHANGES Whether anticipatory or reactive, strategic changes—redefining as they do the organization's basic direction—are among the riskiest changes managers can implement. We can summarize the research results as follows:

1. *Strategic organizational changes are usually triggered by factors outside the organization.* External threats or challenges including deregulation, intensified global competition, or dramatic technological innovations (such as those occurring now in the computer and telecommunications industries) are usually the ones that drive organizations to make systemwide, strategic changes. These changes may be either anticipatory (as at General Electric) or reactive (as at Chrysler).[8]

2. *Strategic organization changes are often required for survival.* Nadler and Tushman found that while strategic organization change did not guarantee a firm's success, those organizations that failed to change generally failed to survive. In particular, they found that what they called *discontinuous* environmental change—change of an unexpected nature, such as what happened when electronic chips replaced mechanical watches—required quick and effective strategic change for the firm to survive.

3. *Recreations—major, systemwide changes implemented under crisis, reactive conditions—are highly risky.* The study concluded that of the four types of organizational changes, recreations were riskier "if only because they are initiated under crisis conditions and under short time constraints." Further, recreations almost always involve a change in core values.[9] Since core values tend to be resistant to change, recreations tend to trigger the most serious individual resistance to change and heighten political behavior.

REORIENTATIONS
Strategic changes initiated in anticipation of future events.

RECREATIONS
Strategic changes that are prompted by immediate crises.

The recreations that did succeed usually involved changes in the senior leadership of the firms involved and often replacements from outside the firm. This was the case at U.S. Steel, Chrysler, Singer Corporation, and particularly IBM. Here the board of directors was finally prompted to replace CEO John Ackers with outsider Louis Gerstner in the hopes that Gerstner could create and implement the massive strategic changes that were required.

4. *Reorientations are usually more successful.* Reorientations (systemwide, strategic changes implemented in a planned, anticipatory fashion) were usually more successful than were the recreations that occurred under crisis conditions. For example, GE's reorientation has been extraordinarily successful at reshaping GE's core values and operating practices and thus positioning the firm ahead of competition. But reorientations can also be risky: they involve making the right strategic bets, usually well ahead of the competition and so well ahead of concrete knowledge about which way the markets and competitors may actually be heading. Thus, Jack Welch's 1981 bet that the 1990s would place a premium on leanness and responsiveness may not have worked so well if the emphasis today turned out to be on research and development instead of efficiency.

The *Lexmark* vignette demonstrates how correctly assessing a company and implementing changes to avoid a crisis are mandatory for survival.

Employees of Lexmark, formerly IBM's information products arm, had to rethink every process by which they worked when their company was spun off in 1991.

LEXMARK

When IBM spun off its Lexington, Kentucky, Lexmark printer manufacturing plant, rumors were rampant that the plant would be closed, or, at best, big layoffs would occur. New CEO Marvin L. Mann faced the formidable task of first winning the trust and then the hearts and minds of former IBMers who were steeped in Big Blues' company culture.

Mann eliminated four of eight management layers. He also put an end to different department heads bickering over one another's proposals. He granted each more operational latitude and told them to focus on beating the competition. He initiated the use of teams with decision making power on the plant floor.

Production manager and 32-year IBM veteran Roger Hopwood found installing teams was easier said than done. He pointed out that empowerment would take time and training and was meaningless unless workers thought they really would have ownership of what was produced. "We're helping our people realize that it's okay to learn from mistakes," Hopwood says. "We're seeing results by improving employee attitudes toward empowerment."

Mann's strategy has resulted in a work force that now acts instead of reacting. When a newspaper columnist complained of difficulty in obtaining IBM typewriter ribbon, a Lexmark employee saw to it a big supply was shipped that morning. After shipping achieved its 100 percent rate of correctly filled orders, curious employees began checking with customers about delivery time. Not happy with what they learned, they prevailed upon management to change trucking firms. Mann knew before taking over Lexmark that success in the printer business against the likes of Hewlett-Packard, Apple, and Canon wouldn't be easy. But by correctly assessing the company he was taking over and the transformation it needed to make to be competitive, he made all the required changes before a crisis erupted.

SOURCE: Patrick Flanagan, "IBM One Day, Lexmark the Next," *Management Review,* January 1994, 38–44.

SOURCES OF RESISTANCE TO CHANGE

Many years ago, Niccolo Machiavelli, a shrewd observer of Italian politics, pointed out that "there is nothing so difficult to implement as change, since those in favor of the change will often be small in number while those opposing the change will be numerous and enthusiastic in their resistance to change."[10] Indeed, even the most effective change agents would agree that implementing wide scale change is enormously challenging. No less an advocate than GE's Jack Welch has been quoted as saying that even after ten years of almost continual change, he expected it to take at least another ten years to completely rejuvenate GE's culture.[11]

Just because a change may be advisable or even mandatory doesn't mean the organization's employees will accept it. As Machiavelli observed, individuals, groups, even entire organizations may resist a change, and this resistance stems from several sources:[12]

HABIT People become accustomed to the usual way of doing things and may then resist change solely because they assume it is more convenient or less costly to just keep doing things "the usual way." For instance, many executives resist switching from manual to computerized systems in part because the present way of doing things is familiar, comfortable, and (from their point of view) workable.

RESOURCE LIMITATIONS Resource limitations can also stymie change. For many years, Eastern Airlines executives knew that they would not be able to compete effectively with their outdated fleet of planes, but resource limitations made it impossible for them to rejuvenate their fleet. This inability to instill a key renovation helped lead to the airline's demise.

THREATS TO POWER AND INFLUENCE A number of years ago, Harvard Professor Paul Lawrence pointed out that it is usually not the technical aspects of a change that employees resist, but rather the social consequences of the change, "the change in their human relationships that generally accompany the technical change."[13] For example, they may see in the change diminished responsibilities for themselves and therefore lower status in the organization and less job security. Threats to one's power and influence often underlie resistance to change.

FEAR OF THE UNKNOWN Sometimes it is not fear of the probable consequence of a change but of its unknown consequences that produce resistance. For example, several years ago J.C. Penney Company decided to move its headquarters from New York City to Dallas, Texas. The fact that most employees elected to relocate is testimony to the firm's ability to minimize the move's unknown aspects. The company made extensive efforts to prepare its employees by describing housing conditions and prices, school quality, and lifestyles in the Dallas/Fort Worth area.

LEWIN'S CHANGE MODEL

Given such possible resistance, social psychologist Kurt Lewin formulated a model of change to summarize what he believed were the basic steps in a good planned change effort (whether an incremental/strategic change or an anticipatory/reactive change). To Lewin, all behavior in an organization was a product of two forces: those striving to maintain the status quo and those pushing for change. Implementing change thus meant either reducing the forces for the status quo or building up the forces for change. Lewin's planned change process consisted of these three steps:

1. *Unfreezing.* **Unfreezing** means reducing the forces that are striving to maintain the status quo, usually by presenting a provocative problem or event to get people to recognize the need for change and to search for new solutions. Without such unfreezing, said Lewin, change will not occur. Attitude surveys, interview results, or participatory value-molding meetings like those held by Jack Welch and his GE managers are often used to provide such provocative events. With respect to attitude surveys, for instance, survey results may show extremely low morale, and knowing about this problem may galvanize a skeptical manager into action. Similarly, losing a big sale because of a communication breakdown or an intergroup rivalry may convince top management that some change is in order.[14]

2. *Moving.* Lewin's second step aims to shift or alter the behavior of the individuals, departments, or organization in which the changes are to take place. **Moving** usually means developing new behaviors, values, and attitudes, sometimes through organizational structure changes and sometimes through the sorts of

UNFREEZING
Reducing the forces that are striving to maintain the status quo, usually by presenting a provocative problem or event to get people to recognize the need for change and to search for new solutions.

MOVING
Developing new behaviors, values, and attitudes, sometimes through organizational structure changes and development techniques.

organizational change and development techniques we will discuss later in this chapter.

3. *Refreezing.* Lewin assumed that organizations tended to revert to their former ways of doing things unless the changes were reinforced, which could be accomplished by **refreezing** the organization into its new state of equilibrium. Lewin therefore advocated instituting mechanisms that would support and maintain the changes that were made. This is why, for instance, GE's Jack Welch instituted a new executive performance appraisal system to appraise and reward managers based on their adherence to the firm's new values of leanness, adaptability, and openness or candor.

THE ORGANIZATIONAL CHANGE PROCESS

Unfreezing, moving, refreezing underpin the change process itself which can be summarized as consisting of six main stages:

Stage 1: Becoming aware of the pressure for change

Stage 2: Recognizing the need for change

Stage 3: Diagnosing the problem

Stage 4: Planning the change

Stage 5: Implementing the change

Stage 6: Following up on the change

BECOMING AWARE OF THE PRESSURE FOR CHANGE Most organizational changes are carried out in reaction to or in anticipation of pressures from inside or outside the organization. Outside the organization, technological innovations like "cable-less" cable television, microprocessors, and automated factories force managers to confront a constantly changing competitive terrain. Within the firm, conflicts arise, employees retire or resign, and pressures mount as the organization outgrows its old ways of doing things. Pressures like these (or the anticipation of such pressures) demand changes in the structure, technology, tasks, and people in the organization.

Pressures for change are particularly prevalent today because of the rapid increase in the rate at which the world is changing. One expert has noted, for instance, that typesetting was accomplished by hand, letter by letter, for more than 400 years (from the early 1400s, when Johannes Guttenberg invented movable type, to the 1880s, when mechanized typesetting became prevalent). Only 70 years later, in the 1950s, new photo offset methods of creating type became commonplace, and just 20 years later computerized desktop publishing made many forms of typesetting obsolete. The times between these innovations—480 years, 70 years, and 20 years—illustrate the increased speed with which change is taking place.[15]

Another change expert, writing in an article entitled "Managing Change in a Turbulent Business Climate," lists the following pressures for change that face many industries and firms today:

- Divestiture (telecommunications industry)
- Consolidation (pharmaceutical and insurance industries)
- Deregulation (banking and transportation industries)
- Increased regulation (brokerage/investment banking and health care industries)
- Globalization of consumer and producer markets (including electronics and automobiles)
- Unstable currencies

- United European trading market
- The growing need for investment in East European economics
- A rush toward democratization throughout the world and particularly in the former Soviet Union.[16]

RECOGNIZING THE NEED FOR CHANGE   Even within the same industry, some firms have been more adept at recognizing the need for change than others. For example, Bill Gates at Microsoft successfully recognized the pressures driving the computer industry toward greater reliance on personal computers. He created an enormously successful firm as a result. At the same time, top executives at IBM seemed to let their firm drift throughout the 1980s, dramatically underestimating the effects that the personal computer would have on their industry. The *Union Pacific* vignette depicts the positive circumstances that evolve when management recognizes the need for change.

DIAGNOSING THE PROBLEM   Recognizing that change is needed is not enough: the manager then must diagnose the pressure for change—be it an impending bankruptcy or a new technology—to determine how it may affect the firm and what the consequences will be.

Various *diagnostic tools* are available for doing this. The advantages and disadvantages of some diagnostic tools are shown in Figure 18.2. For example, change programs may first involve preliminary *interviews* with at least a cross-section of employees, because such interviews allow management to probe freely into a range of possible subjects and to build rapport and support for the imminent change program. *Questionnaires* are relatively easy to use with large numbers of employees, and the resulting information can be quantified and easily summarized. Survey data can also be a good starting point for gaining employees' commitment to the change and for analyzing alternative solutions.

Other techniques are also popular. *Observing* the employees produces data regarding actual behavior (rather than reports of behavior), and is in real time (rather than retrospective, as are interviews and questionnaires). Finally, *secondary data* (such as

Schwinn, an American institution since 1895, had fallen on hard times before being purchased by Scott Sports Group in 1994. Ignoring global markets helped put them in bankruptcy.

UNION PACIFIC RAILROAD

In the mid-1980s, Union Pacific Railroad had reached a low point. Customers were irate, and trucking companies were happily siphoning off freight business. To turn things around, the company decided to eliminate 800 middle managers and five layers of bureaucracy. But that was only the beginning. When top management solicited employee input as to what other changes were needed, they got a surprisingly direct response: "The problem is you."

"When we asked our front-line managers what was preventing them from being customer-responsive, they said the bureaucracy was standing in the way," explained Richard Davidson, a Union Pacific veteran who was named chief executive in 1991. "It was like we found the enemy, and the enemy was us."

In addition to downsizing the structure, executives took on the unions as well. They trimmed Union Pacific's payroll by almost 32 percent, from 43,000 to around 29,500. Also, the company's authoritarian command structure was scrapped in favor of a more relaxed approach that allowed more latitude for decision making in the lower ranks. "As long as customers are satisfied and [managers] maintain safety standards and their budgets, they never hear from us," says Davidson.

Operations also were centralized, with a new emphasis on computer technology. Through the mid-1980s, customer orders and invoicing were handled by thousands of agents scattered throughout the western United States. Still more railroad yard offices acted as the usually snail-paced conduit between the actual train crews and the corporate hierarchy. In the re-created company structure, all of these operations were centralized in a customer-service center in St. Louis, Missouri.

The makeover at Union Pacific included cost-cutting measures as well. The company concluded that short-haul, low-density runs added little profitability and were better left to small operators with lower overhead and nonunion employees. As a result, Union Pacific abandoned almost 3,000 miles of track. These savings were plowed back into the company.

The massive restructuring has been good for Union Pacific's bottom line. The company earned a record $665 million in 1992 on revenues of $4.9 billion, and it expected to earn $725 million in 1993 on revenues of $5.1 billion. Union Pacific's new structure and culture have made the company more responsive to market realities and customer needs, and there will be no trips to the boneyard anytime soon.

SOURCES: James P. King, "On Track with Customers," Training & Development, August 1993, 31–40; Sandra D. Atchison, "This Train Keeps A-Rollin'," Business Week, January 11, 1993, 59; and Roula Khalaf, "The Enemy Was Us," Forbes, January 6, 1992, 173.

FIGURE 18.2

A Comparison of Four
Diagnosis Methods

*Diagnosing the problem to
better ascertain what sort
of change is needed is a big
step in implementing a
change.*

source: David Nadler, *Feedback and Organization
Development: Using Data-
based Methods* (Reading, MA:
Addison-Wesley, 1977), 119.

METHOD	MAJOR ADVANTAGES	MAJOR POTENTIAL DRAWBACKS
Interviews	1. Adaptive—allows data collection on a range of possible subjects 2. Source of "rich" data 3. Empathic 4. Process of interviewing can build rapport	1. Can be expensive 2. Interviewer can bias responses 3. Coding/interpretation problems 4. Self-report bias
Questionnaires	1. Responses can be quantified and easily summarized 2. Easy to use with large samples 3. Relatively inexpensive 4. Can obtain large volume of data	1. Nonempathic 2. Predetermined questions may miss issues 3. Data may be over-interpreted 4. Response bias
Observations	1. Collects data on behavior rather than reports of behavior 2. Real time, not retrospective 3. Adaptive	1. Interpretation and coding problems 2. Sampling is a problem 3. Observer bias/reliability 4. Costly
Secondary data/ unobtrusive measures	1. Nonreactive—no response bias 2. High face validity 3. Easily quantified	1. Access/retrieval possibly a problem 2. Potential validity problems 3. Coding/interpretation

that regarding employee turnover or productivity) can be used for quantifying the problem.

The breadth of the diagnosis will depend on how widespread the problem itself seems to be. In some cases, **organizational analysis**—in which the organization's goals, plans, environment, practices, and performance are studied—is appropriate. At other times, the problem may involve just one department, group, or individual, and the diagnosis can appropriately focus there.

ORGANIZATIONAL ANALYSIS
An analysis of the organization's goals, plans, environment, practices, and performance.

PLANNING THE CHANGE   The next step is to plan the change. This involves answering the questions: What should we change? When should we change it? and How should we change it?

Regarding what to change, Harold Leavitt contends that all organization changes can be classified as changes in structure, task, technology, or people.[17] Changing the structure might involve reorganizing departments, revising the span of control, or decentralizing. Changing the task might involve enriching jobs or, at the other extreme, further specializing them. Changing the technology might include installing a new production line or inventory control system or instituting new selection procedures. Managers can also change the people in the organization through training or through other development activities explained later in this chapter.

Beyond structure, task, technology, or people, other aspects of the organization often can and may be changed. The firm's strategic control and monitoring processes may identify a need to change the firm's strategy, for instance, thus possibly driving the firm into new markets and areas. As we saw in Chapter 14 (Organizational Culture and Shared Values), cultural changes often demand changing the prevailing values in the firm so as to foster greater openness, creativity, or customer-orientation. Decisions regarding how the change will be made (the specific techniques to be used) and when to schedule each activity will also be made in this planning stage.

IMPLEMENTING THE CHANGE The next step is to implement the change by actually changing the structure, technology, task, people, strategy, or culture in the organization. We will return to implementation in a moment.

FOLLOW UP ON THE CHANGE (REFREEZE) The next step is to evaluate the effects of the change and to institute the procedural modifications that will ensure that the change continues to be implemented. For example, to refreeze GE's new set of values, Welch made the values a key element in the firm's performance and reward processes:

> We've told the business leaders that they must rank each of their officers on a scale of 1–5 against the . . . characteristics in that [value] statement. . . . We have to know if our people are open and self-confident, if they believe in honest communication and quick action, if the people we hired years ago have changed.[18]

ORGANIZATIONAL CHANGE TARGETS

As mentioned earlier, managers can focus on various change targets. They can, in other words, change the *strategy, culture, structure, tasks, technologies,* or *attitudes* and skills of the people in the organization.

STRATEGIC CHANGE Organizational change often starts with **strategic change,** a change in the firm's strategy, mission, and vision. Strategic change may then subsequently require other organizational changes, for instance, in the firm's technology, structure, and culture.

The strategic change initiated at Fuji-Xerox by President Yotaro Kobayashi provides an example.[19] In response to declining market share, a dearth of new products, and increasing customer complaints, Kobayashi and his team formulated a new vision for Fuji-Xerox, what they called the New Xerox Movement, which was based on total quality control. Thus, the firm's new strategy emphasized the core values of quality, problem solving, teamwork, and customer emphasis. To implement the necessary cultural change (and thus support the strategic change) Fuji's executive team instituted what two experts referred to as a "dense infrastructure of objectives, measures, rewards, tools, education and slogans, all in service of total quality control and the 'new Xerox.'"[20]

STRATEGIC CHANGE
Change in a firm's strategy, mission, and vision.

CULTURAL CHANGE As at Fuji, strategic change often necessitates cultural change, in other words a change in the firm's shared values and aims. In order to implement cultural change, Fuji-Xerox created a new set of heroes, as individuals and teams were publicly congratulated whenever their behaviors reflected the best of Fuji's new values. Kobayashi and his team also continually reinforced, celebrated, and communicated their new vision of a Fuji-Xerox based on excellence.

STRUCTURAL (ORGANIZATIONAL) CHANGE Reorganization involves a redesign of the organization's structure, that is, a change in the departmentation, coordination, span of control, reporting relationships, or centralization of decision making in an organization. Reorganization is a relatively direct and quick method for changing an organization, and the technique is widely used and often effective.

Structure is often a change target today, particularly given recent demands for lean and responsive organizations. Before he began the process of building openness, candor, and communications at GE, Jack Welch collapsed GE's management structure from nine layers to as few as four, reduced 29 pay levels to five broad bands, and reorganized 350 product lines and business units into 13 big businesses.[21]

The aim today is often to create organic, or adaptive, organizations. Here committed and empowered teams supervise their own efforts within the framework of top management's vision and communicate with colleagues horizontally and vertically throughout the firm as the need arises.[22]

REDESIGNING TASKS The tasks and authority of individuals and teams within the organization are often changed as well. For example, to gain its employees' commitment to quality, auto work teams at Saturn are empowered to hire their own team members and supervise their own work.

TECHNOLOGICAL CHANGE Technological changes are modifications to the work methods used by the organization to accomplish its tasks. They include introducing new production technologies, new selection and screening procedures, and new performance appraisal methods, for instance. Thus, the new rewards and systems instituted by Yotaro Kobayashi at Fuji-Xerox illustrate technological change, in this case technological change implemented to support cultural and strategic changes.

CHANGING ATTITUDES AND SKILLS Sometimes the employees themselves must change. A variety of techniques are used to change the people in the organization and these techniques vary in the extent to which they involve in-depth emotional involvement on the part of the employee.[23] Surface techniques such as lectures, conferences, and on-the-job training are often used to provide new or present employees with the skills they need to perform their jobs adequately, for instance; such surface techniques involve little emotional involvement on the employee's part. The *Rogers Corporation* vignette shows how one company put such ideas into practice.

ROGERS CORPORATION

Rogers Corporation lowered labor costs by relocating two electronic and automotive materials and components plants south of the border. But the wage savings were wiped out by other cost increases. The scrap rate on flexible printed circuits averaged 25 percent. Only around one-third of output was delivered on time. Keeping people on board was also tough; one in five employees moved on. Establishing the assembly plants just across the border from Douglas, Arizona, looked like an expensive bust. Something had to be done.

Daniel Murillo was put in charge of the largest of the two plants, and he literally used textbook methods to change the plants. He distributed Spanish-language versions of *World-Class Manufacturing: The Lessons of Simplicity Applied* to his engineers and managers. Together they read a chapter a week, putting theory into practice as they went. Quality problems were eliminated by training employees and by shifting the quality control function to the production employees themselves. Three years later, quality is measured in defective parts per million instead of percentage of scrap. On-time deliveries are at 96 percent, and turnover is less than half the former level.

SOURCE: William H. Miller, "Textbook Turnaround," *Industry Week,* April 20, 1992, 11–12.

A multitude of products, including electronic components, four-color books, and even musical instruments, are now being manufactured in Mexican maquiladora (American-owned border) plants.

At the other extreme, adds theorist Roger Harrison, in-depth **organizational development interventions** (such as the sensitivity training discussed below) are aimed at changing the employees' attitudes, values, and behavior. The aim here is often to encourage them to develop more open, supportive, organic types of organizations.

ORGANIZATIONAL DEVELOPMENT INTERVENTIONS In-depth interventions such as sensitivity training aimed at changing the employees' attitudes, values, and behavior through the involvement of the employees.

THE CRITICAL PATH TO CORPORATE RENEWAL

WHY A CRITICAL PATH APPROACH?

One of the interesting aspects of successful change programs like the one at GE is their apparent informality. While such programs are certainly well thought out, much of the change results not from formal programs like management by objectives or total quality management, but by putting the firm's employees into situations that force them to act differently than they might otherwise behave. For example, during GE's "work-out" meetings, workers are brought together, away from the job, and spend time listing complaints, debating solutions, and preparing presentations to their managers. The managers then must come back and field proposals by team spokespersons. "I was ringing wet within half an hour," said one manager after a half an hour of this kind of give and take.[24]

Based on a four-year study of organizational change at six large corporations, three change experts—Michael Beer, Russell Eisenstat, and Bert Spector—found that, as at GE, the firms involved in the most successful organizational transformations usually did not focus on formal programs for changing formal structures or systems. Instead, "they created ad hoc organizational arrangements to solve concrete business problems. By aligning employee roles, responsibilities and relationships to address the organization's most important competitive task [such as boosting responsiveness] . . . they focus energy for change on the work itself, not on abstractions such as 'participation' or 'culture.' "[25]

These experts contend that most change programs fail because "they are guided by a theory of change that is fundamentally flawed."[26] Too many programs, they say, are based on the assumption that the company has to change the knowledge and attitudes of individuals; such attitudinal changes then supposedly lead to changes in individual behavior and then (it is hoped) to organizational change. In fact, says Beer and his associates, this theory gets the change process backwards. Individual behavior is powerfully shaped by the organizational role that people play. These experts contend that the most effective way to change behavior is to put people into a new organizational context that imposes new roles, responsibilities, and relationships on them. Beer emphasizes the need for "task alignment," which means "aligning employee roles, responsibilities and relationships to address the organization's most important competitive task."[27] This is usually easiest in small units, such as plants or departments, where goals and tasks are most clearly defined. Here, refocusing employees' roles, responsibilities, and relationships to solve specific business problems is most easily accomplished.

USING THE CRITICAL PATH APPROACH

Beer and his colleagues found that managers who had the most successful organizational changes used a sequence of six steps, which Beer called the *critical path*. The steps were as follows:

MOBILIZE COMMITMENT TO CHANGE THROUGH JOINT DIAGNOSIS OF BUSINESS PROBLEMS   This is analogous to Lewin's unfreeze stage. Joint diagnosis of business problems should lead to a shared understanding of what can and must be improved, and thereby mobilize the commitment of those who must make the change.

DEVELOP A SHARED VISION OF HOW TO ORGANIZE AND MANAGE FOR COMPETITIVENESS   The next step is to conceptualize the change. At one firm, a 20-person task force produced a vision in which cross-functional teams would take over the tasks involved in new product development. Under this plan, a team composed of the general manager and his staff would set the unit's strategic direction and review the work of lower-level teams. Meanwhile, business area teams would develop plans for specific markets. Product development teams would then manage new products from initial design to production, while production process teams identified and solved quality and cost problems in the plant. Beer and his associates point out that the entire thrust of the proposed change was to organize the employees' efforts around getting the product development done and done right—in other words, task alignment.

FOSTER CONSENSUS FOR THE NEW VISION, COMPETENCE TO ENACT IT, AND COHESION TO MOVE IT ALONG   Not all employees will be involved in the preceding design of the reorganized approach to work. The aims of this next step are thus (1) to encourage (through communication and further involvement) the other employees to support the new effort and (2) to develop the employees' competencies to make the new approach work.

SPREAD REVITALIZATION TO ALL DEPARTMENTS WITHOUT PUSHING IT FROM THE TOP   Beer and his associates point out that "the impulse of many general managers [is] to force the issue—to announce, for example, that now all parts of the organization must manage by teams."[28] Successful top managers usually did not do this, however. Instead, each department was allowed to "find its own way to the new organization."[29] In one case, an engineering department spent nearly a year analyzing how to implement the team concept, conducting surveys, holding off-site meetings, and analyzing various alternatives before deciding on a matrix management approach that the department members felt would work for them.

INSTITUTIONALIZE REVITALIZATION THROUGH FORMAL POLICIES, SYSTEMS, AND STRUCTURES By putting employees into new organizational arrangements that allowed them to focus their efforts on essential tasks like new product development, several firms in this study achieved substantial productivity improvements. They did so with virtually no formal changes in reporting relationships, evaluation procedures, compensation, or in operating practices. However, the researchers found that "when the opportunity eventually arose, general managers in the successful firms did make changes in their firm's formal organization and practices, changes that were aimed at institutionalizing the new ways of doing things."[30] For example, when one vice-president for operations left his firm, the position was left vacant so that the two departments—engineering and manufacturing—which previously reported to him now reported to the general manager. This helped to formalize the cross-functional nature of the new team approach at this firm.

MONITOR AND ADJUST STRATEGIES IN RESPONSE TO PROBLEMS IN THE REVITALIZATION PROCESS Changes do not always go as planned. It is therefore important to create, says Beer, an organization "capable of adapting to a changing competitive environment."[31] In one firm this involved appointing an oversight team composed of managers, a union leader, an engineer, and several others to monitor the cross-functional team process. In another firm, regular surveys were used to monitor employee attitudes.

SUMMARY The advantage of this six-step critical-path approach, conclude these experts, is that it provides "a way to elicit renewal without imposing it."[32] In the successfully transformed firms, the employees became committed to a vision and then became willing to accept a new pattern of management—such as the ad hoc, cross-functional, product-development team structure. In turn, participation in this team structure led to changes in employee behavior. Over time, these behavior changes helped the employees to adapt their attitudes and values to their firms' changing needs. The *Leegin* small business box shows how one small business implemented a similar organizational change process.

THE ROLE OF CHANGE ADVOCATES

Organizational changes almost never take place spontaneously; instead, they are pushed or driven by change advocates. The change advocate may be the chairperson of the board (as at GE), the general manager of the plant (as in several of the critical path changes just described), or simply a **champion** who assumes the role of cajoling, inspiring, and negotiating a new invention or other innovation successfully through the firm until it is produced. In any case, change advocates play a major role in any organizational change.

ROLE OF EXECUTIVE LEADERSHIP IN STRATEGIC ORGANIZATION CHANGE

Nowhere is the role of a change advocate more obvious or more important than in the sorts of organization-wide strategic changes implemented at firms like GE by Jack Welch or at Fuji-Xerox by Yotaro Kobayashi. A careful analysis of the methods of executive leaders like these suggest three sets of executive-change leadership activities.

LEEGIN CREATIVE LEATHER PRODUCTS, INC.

Leegin Creative Leather Products, Inc., isn't what it used to be. A decade ago the belt manufacturer's sales stalled around $10 million. Salespeople had to make big trips to write little orders. Staying abreast of the latest designs kept the factory in perpetual disarray. Interdepartmental warfare was the office norm. Passing the buck and watching your back was everyone's chief priority. Perhaps only to get out of town for a few weeks, company founder Jerry Kohl headed east to the Harvard Business School. He returned with a vision for a revitalized firm.

Kohl's salespeople started carrying computers. On calls, they first would inventory belts and input the data by color and sizes.

Then, when it was time to sell their products, the salespeople did something unusual. They showed the store owner what products were hot, what was not, and where he or she might increase sales with the next order. The numbers didn't lie. Store owners now knew exactly what to restock, and salespeople didn't waste time pushing belts that didn't move. The result was trust, cooperation, and orders. "Thanks to them," says store owner Don Zuidema,

"we make a lot of money in the small space we use for belts." The transition was not without problems; some salespeople quit. But Kohl eased the process with training-and-discussion seminars held several times annually.

As Kohl remade his sales approach, he dissolved his small firm's structure. The order-processing, customer-service, and credit-and-collection departments were fused. Two account specialists per territory were assigned to

FOCUS ON SMALL BUSINESS

perform these functions. More employees left, and Kohl sent the rest to training classes. "You lose some people as they get frustrated," he says, "but we were getting people to feel more a part of the company." The classes and refinements to computer software never stopped. No expenses were spared making the job easier. Customers noted both the expeditiousness and the accuracy. "I can call and place an order, and they ship it right out," says store man-

ager Lottie Shamie. "Another company we deal with, their orders get messed up all the time."

Kohl shook up his factory floor next. In an effort to consolidate the assembly-line-type belt-making process, he selected 20 workers and assigned them the entire manufacturing process on specific belt designs. The piece-rate pay plan was changed to an equivalent hourly wage. Quality increased, but productivity sank, and deliveries fell behind. The assembly group was further divided into four or five smaller teams under an incentive pay scheme. Output climbed back to the former levels and gradually surpassed it. Eventually, 10- to 12-person teams were found to work best. By 1990, every production line had been revamped, with cross-trained workers creating different types of belts throughout.

Leegin now makes more than a thousand different belts, or five times what it used to. The number of accounts the company services has tripled to 6,000. Every other aspect of production, quality, delivery time, and prices have improved. As for those sales that seemed stuck around $10 million—they were projected to be $65 million in 1993.

SOURCE: John Case, "A Business Transformed," *Inc.,* June 1993, 84–91.

These activities help to explain why some executives are more successful than others at implementing systemwide change.[33] The three leadership activities have been called charismatic leadership, instrumental leadership, and "spreading the Gospel of change" through leadership.

CHARISMATIC LEADERSHIP   Nadler and Tushman say that successful leadership for change requires, first, **charismatic leaders,**[34] who possess "a special quality that enables the leader to mobilize and sustain activity within an organization through specific personal actions combined with perceived personal characteristics."[35]

Charismatic leadership for change is composed of three behaviors: envisioning, energizing, and enabling. As summarized in Figure 18.3, the charismatic leader is first an *envisioning leader,* capable of articulating a compelling vision, setting high expectations, and being a model of behaviors which are consistent with that compelling vision. The charismatic leader (like Jack Welch) is also an *energizing leader,* one who is able to demonstrate personal excitement, express personal confidence, and seek, find,

CHARISMATIC LEADERS
Individuals who possess a special quality that enables the leader to mobilize and sustain activity within an organization through specific personal actions combined with perceived personal characteristics.

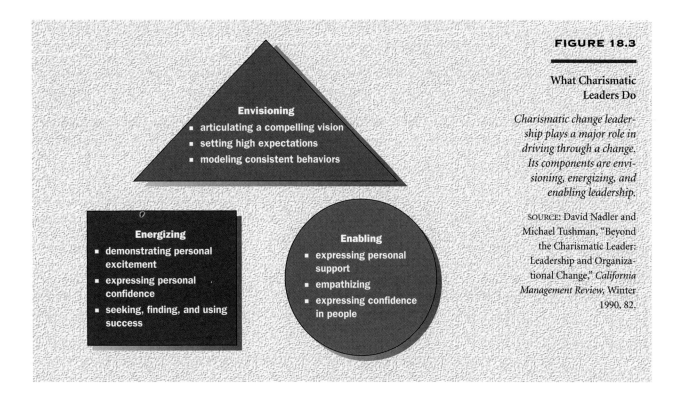

FIGURE 18.3

What Charismatic
Leaders Do

*Charismatic change leader-
ship plays a major role in
driving through a change.
Its components are envi-
sioning, energizing, and
enabling leadership.*

SOURCE: David Nadler and
Michael Tushman, "Beyond
the Charismatic Leader:
Leadership and Organiza-
tional Change," *California
Management Review,* Winter
1990, 82.

and use success among his or her colleagues. Finally, the charismatic leader is an
enabling leader, one who is able to express personal support, empathy, and confidence
in people and thereby inspire them to undertake the required changes.

INSTRUMENTAL LEADERSHIP Charismatic leadership alone does not explain
the sort of success that executives like Welch have had at transforming firms like GE.
As Nadler and Tushman point out, "effective leaders of change need to be more than
just charismatic."[36] The second change leadership role is "to build competent teams,
clarify required behavior, build in measurements, and administer rewards and punishments so that individuals perceive that behavior consistent with the change is essential for them in achieving their own goals." Nadler and Tushman call this second leadership role **instrumental leadership.** It is the aspect of executive leadership that puts
the instruments in place through which the employees can accomplish their new tasks.

This involves three types of instrumental leader behavior. The first is *structuring.*
Leaders like Welch must ensure that the necessary structure is in place to carry out
the change, and so must invest time in building teams, creating new organization
structures, setting goals, establishing standards, and defining roles and responsibilities.[37] Instrumental change leadership also means establishing successful *controlling*
mechanisms, "the creation of systems and processes to measure, monitor and assess
both behavior and results and to administer corrective action."[38] Finally, instrumental
change leadership involves *rewarding.* This means instituting the material (and non-
material) rewards and punishments that are needed to reinforce behaviors that are
consistent (or discourage behaviors that are inconsistent) with the desired organizational change.[39]

SPREADING THE GOSPEL OF CHANGE THROUGH LEADERSHIP Few
leaders—not even Jack Welch—are capable of turning huge organizations around
by themselves; instead, they must enlist the aid of and develop leadership ability

INSTRUMENTAL LEADERSHIP
The aspect of executive leadership that puts the instruments in
place through which the employees can accomplish their new
tasks.

throughout the firm. They must then depend on these new leaders to spread the top manager's gospel of change.

Successful executive leaders thus seek to extend their change leadership to three other groups—their own senior team, senior management, and leadership throughout the organization. They generally look first for opportunities to extend and institutionalize their vision for the firm to the group of individuals who report directly to them. This, in part, is why CEOs seeking to implement major organizational changes often seek out and hire new subordinates whose values and visions are consistent with theirs. For example, Louis Gerstner quickly hired several new senior vice-presidents for finance, human resource management, and several other functions within months of assuming the reigns at IBM.

The CEO must then encourage managers below the top executive team to buy into and become missionaries of his or her vision and plans for change. Unfortunately, those below the senior management level often feel they are not in position to lead such a change. They may even feel more like unwitting participants or observers in the changes occurring around them. Yet, this tier of managers is actually in a unique position in the chain of command, sitting, as they do, between the majority of the firm's employees and the firm's top management team. As a result, "the task is to make this group feel like senior management, to get them signed up for the change and to motivate and enable them to work as an extension of the senior team."[40]

Finally, the "gospel of change" needs to be spread throughout the organization, by creating cadres of employees who are capable and eager to exhibit leadership with respect to implementing the necessary changes. GE does this, in part, by annually training hundreds of employees—not just managers, but engineers, chemists, and others throughout the firm. In this way, GE provides employees with the values and skills they will need to make their units consistent with Welch's vision of a lean, competitive, agile organization.[41]

ENTREPRENEURS, CHAMPIONS, AND INNOVATION

A firm's ability to create and bring to market technological innovations can mean the difference between success and failure for the firm. IBM's introduction in the late 1960s of the system 360 made the firm a great success, while Dell Computers' recent inability to bring several advanced models to market created serious financial problems for that firm.

Many factors, including the availability of resources and the technical competence of the firm's engineers, contribute to the speed with which a firm can introduce technological innovations. However, "highly enthusiastic and committed individuals who are willing to take risks" always play a major role too.[42] In an organization's early years, the firm's entrepreneur plays this role. As the economist J. A. Schumpeter has put it, the entrepreneur

> reforms or revolutionizes the pattern of production by exploiting an invention, or more generally, an untried technological possibility for producing a new commodity or producing an old one in a new way, by opening up a new source of supply of materials or a new outlet for products by reorganizing an industry.[43]

CHAMPION
A change advocate who assumes the role of cajoling, inspiring, and negotiating a new invention or other innovation successfully through the firm until it is produced.

CHAMPIONS   The problem is that as firms grow, they tend to become increasingly resistant to change. The innovation process may then grind to a halt. In one study of major product innovations of the twentieth century, for instance, Schoen found that in virtually all instances the new idea encountered sharp resistance and that overcoming this resistance required vigorous promotion.[44] Overcoming this resistance required someone to champion the idea; in other words, someone had to assume burden that in smaller firms is carried by the entrepreneur.

Other studies have found that successful innovations had several champions, filling a different role. For example, researcher Ed Roberts identified two champi

Product champion: A member of an organization who creates, defines, or adopts an id a new technological innovation and who is willing to risk his or her position and pr to make possible the innovation's successful implementation.

Executive champion: An executive in a technological firm who has direct or indirect ence over the resource allocation process and who uses this power to channel resourc.. new technological innovation, thereby absorbing most, but usually not all, of the risk of the project.[45]

The striking finding of this study was that the executive, not the product champion usually emerged as the main contributor to the product's successful introduction. That executive had to have the power, respectability, and status needed to channel the resources necessary to keep the innovation alive.[46]

ORGANIZATION DEVELOPMENT

WHAT IS ORGANIZATION DEVELOPMENT?

Organization development (OD) is one special set of organizational change methods; it has been defined as "a systemwide application of behavioral science knowledge to the planned development and reinforcement of organizational strategies, structures, and processes for improving an organization's effectiveness."[47] OD's distinguishing feature is its emphasis on improving the organization's ability to solve its own problems. As a result, (1) the typical OD program is aimed at changing the attitudes, values, and beliefs of employees so that the employees themselves can identify and implement the technical, procedural, or structural changes needed to improve the firm's functioning; and (2) OD programs are always "intended to change the organization in a particular direction, toward improved problem-solving, responsiveness, quality of work, and effectiveness."[48]

A FOCUS ON ACTION RESEARCH   While not always the case, action research is usually the common denominator underlying OD programs. **Action research** is "the process of systematically collecting research data about an on-going system relative to some objective, goal, or needs of that system; feeding that data back into the system; taking action by altering selected variables within the system based both on the data and on hypotheses; and evaluating results of action by collecting more data."[49]

WHY USE ORGANIZATION DEVELOPMENT?

OD proponents vigorously argue that today's turbulence and rapid change make OD programs (with their emphasis on fostering organizational learning, responsiveness, and problem solving) more effective than they have ever been before. As Cummings and Worley put it:

Organization development is playing an increasingly key role in helping organizations to change themselves. It is helping organizations to assess themselves and their environments and to revitalize and to rebuild their strategies, structures, and processes. OD is helping organizational members to go beyond surface changes to transform the underlying assumptions and values governing their behaviors.[50]

520

INTERVENTION
A set of planne intended to increase i

tige to make possible the innovation's successful implementation.

EXECUTIVE CHAMPION
An executive in a technological firm who has direct or indirect influence over the resource allocation process and who uses this power to channel resources to a new technological innovation, thereby absorbing most, but usually not all, of the risk of the project.

ORGANIZATION DEVELOPMENT
An application of behavioral science knowledge to the planned development and reinforcement of organizational strategies, structures, and processes for improving an organization's effectiveness, usually using action research.

ACTION RESEARCH
The process of systematically collecting research data about an ongoing system relative to some objective, goal, or needs of that system; feeding that data back to the employees; taking action by altering selected variables within the system based both on the data and on hypotheses; and evaluating results of action by collecting more data. Basically, the employees themselves analyze the data and develop the solutions.

TYPES OF OD INTERVENTIONS

Traditionally, an OD effort is called an **intervention,** "a set of planned change activities intended to help an organization increase its effectiveness."[51] Most successful interventions have three key characteristics: (1) they are based on "valid information about the organization's functioning," usually collected by the employees themselves, or with their assistance; (2) the intervention (under the guidance of the change agent/consultant) provides employees with opportunities to make their own "free and informed choices" regarding the nature of the problems and their preferred solutions; (3) interventions are aimed at gaining the employees' personal commitment to their choices.[52]

The number and variety of OD interventions have increased substantially over the past few years. OD got its start with what were called **human process interventions.** These interventions were generally aimed at enabling employees to develop a better understanding of their own and others' behaviors for the purpose of improving that behavior in such a way that the organization benefited.

Today, as illustrated in Figure 18.4, a much wider range of interventions is available. Indeed, the once-clear lines between OD interventions and other types of orga-

---

change activities
help an organization
effectiveness.

HUMAN PROCESS INTERVENTIONS
Interventions aimed at enabling employees to develop a better understanding of their own and others' behaviors for the purpose of improving that behavior in such a way that the organization benefits.

FIGURE 18.4

Examples of OD Interventions and the Organizational Levels They Impact

OD interventions or change efforts may be classified as human process, techno-structural, human resource, or strategic; however, they generally all rely on action research, in other words, on letting the employees develop solutions based on their review of the data on the organization.

SOURCE: Adapted from Thomas Cummings and Christopher Worley, *Organizational Development and Change,* 5th ed. (Minneapolis: West, 1993), 167.

INTERVENTIONS	PRIMARY ORGANIZATIONAL LEVEL AFFECTED		
	INDIVIDUAL	GROUP	ORGANIZATION
HUMAN PROCESS			
T-Groups	X	X	
Process consultation		X	
Third-party intervention	X	X	
Team building		X	
Organization confrontation meeting		X	X
Intergroup relations		X	X
TECHNOSTRUCTURAL			
Formal structural change			X
Differentiation and integration			X
Cooperative union-management projects	X	X	X
Quality circles	X	X	
Total quality management		X	X
Work design	X	X	
HUMAN RESOURCE MANAGEMENT			
Goal setting	X	X	
Performance appraisal	X	X	
Reward systems	X	X	X
Career planning and development	X		
Managing workforce diversity	X		
Employee wellness	X		
STRATEGIC			
Integrated strategic management			X
Culture change			X
Strategic change			X
Self-designing organizations		X	X

nizational change efforts (such as reorganizing the firm) are beginning to blur. This is because OD practitioners have become increasingly involved in changing not just participants' attitudes, values, and beliefs, but the firm's structure, practices, strategy, and culture directly.

Cummings and Worley distinguish between four categories of interventions: *human process interventions, technostructural interventions, human resource management interventions,* and *strategic interventions.*

HUMAN PROCESS INTERVENTIONS The OD techniques in this category generally aim first at improving employees' human relations skills. The aim is to provide them with the insight and skills needed to more effectively analyze their own and others' behavior so they can more intelligently solve interpersonal and intergroup problems. Perhaps the most widely used technique here is called *sensitivity training.*

Sensitivity, laboratory, or t-group training (the *t* is for training) was one of the earliest OD techniques, and while its use has diminished, it is still used today. Sensitivity training's basic aim is to increase the participant's insight into his or her own behavior and the behavior of others by encouraging an open expression of feelings in the trainer-guided t-group. In a typical t-group, 10 to 15 people meet, usually away from the job, and no activities or discussion topics are planned. The focus is on the here and now (specifically, the feelings and emotions of the members in the group). The participants are encouraged to portray themselves in the group rather than in terms of past experiences or future problems. As a result, the t-group's success depends largely on the feedback process and in particular on participants' willingness to inform one another of how their behavior is being perceived. A climate of "psychological safety" is therefore necessary if participants are to feel safe enough to reveal themselves to the group, to expose their feelings, to drop their defenses, and to try out new ways of interacting.[53]

T-group training is obviously very personal in nature, so it is not surprising that it is a very controversial technique, and its use has diminished markedly since its heyday in the 1970s. Some argue, for instance, that t-group training can be unethical, since when participation in a t-group is "suggested" by one's superior, attendance cannot be considered strictly voluntary.[54] Others argue that it can actually be a dangerous exercise if led by an inadequately prepared trainer.

The characteristic OD stress on action research is perhaps most evident when the OD program is used for **team building,** improving the effectiveness of a team. Data concerning the team's performance are collected and then fed back to the members of the group. The participants then examine, explain, and analyze the data and develops specific action plans or solutions for solving the team's problems.

According to experts French and Bell, the typical team-building meeting begins with the consultant interviewing each of the group members and the leader prior to the meeting. They are asked what their problems are, how they think the group functions, and what obstacles are keeping the group from performing better. The consultant might then categorize the interview data into themes and present the themes to the group at the beginning of the meeting. (Themes might be culled from such statements as "I don't have enough time to get my job done" or "I can't get any cooperation around here.") The themes are then ranked by the group in terms of their importance, and the most important ones become the agenda for the meeting. The group then explores and discusses the issues, examines the underlying causes of the problems, and begins working on some solutions to the problems.

Other human process interventions aim to bring about intergroup or organization-wide change. Organization **confrontation meetings** can help clarify and bring into the open intergroup misperceptions and problems so that these problems can be solved.

SENSITIVITY TRAINING
Also called laboratory or t-group training, the basic aim is to increase the participant's insight into his or her own behavior and the behavior of others by encouraging an open expression of feelings in the trainer-guided t-group.

TEAM BUILDING
Techniques used to improve the effectiveness of a team.

CONFRONTATION MEETINGS
Organizational meetings that can help clarify and bring into the open intergroup misperceptions and problems so that these problems can be solved.

The basic approach here, as we will see below, is one of action research, in that the participants themselves provide the basic data for the meeting (in terms of how they perceive themselves and the other groups) and then confront and thrash out any misperceptions in an effort to reduce tensions. **Survey research** requires that employees throughout the organization fill out attitude surveys. The data are then used as feedback to the work groups and provide a basis for problem analysis and action planning. In general, such surveys are a convenient and widely used method for unfreezing an organization's management and employees by providing a lucid, comparative, graphic illustration of the fact that the organization does have problems that should be solved.

System IV management is a program based on the work of Rensis Likert and his colleagues. Its premise is that the most effective organizations have supportive, trusting leaders, open communication, clear goals, and an emphasis on employee self-control.

TECHNOSTRUCTURAL INTERVENTIONS　OD practitioners are increasingly involved in efforts to change the structures, methods, and job designs of firms. As compared with human process interventions, such technostructural interventions (as well as the human resource management interventions and strategic interventions described in the following section) generally utilize the traditional OD action research approach but focus more directly on productivity improvement and efficiency.

OD practitioners use a variety of technostructural interventions. For example, the *formal structures* change program involves having the employees collect data on and analyze existing formal structures. The purpose is to jointly redesign and implement new organizational structures (including matrix structures and the sorts of network structures described in Chapters 8 and 9). OD experts also use as interventions the employee involvement-type programs described in earlier chapters including *quality circles, total quality management,* and *employee commitment.*

HUMAN RESOURCE MANAGEMENT INTERVENTIONS　Companies recognize that human resource management practices such as performance appraisal and selection and testing can mold employee commitment, motivation, and performance. OD practitioners are therefore increasingly involved in using action research to enable employees to analyze and change their firm's personnel practices. Targets of change include the firm's performance appraisal system and reward system, as well as workforce diversity programs aimed at boosting cooperation among a firm's diverse employees.

STRATEGIC INTERVENTIONS　Among the newest additions to OD are strategic interventions, organization-wide interventions aimed at bringing about a fit between a firm's strategy, structure, culture, and the firm's external environment. *Integrated strategic management* is one example. This program consists of four steps:

1. *Analyzing current strategy and organization design.* Managers and other employees utilize models such as the SWOT matrix to analyze the firm's current strategy, as well as its organization design.

2. *Choosing a desired strategy and organization design.* Based on the OD consultant-assisted analysis, senior management formulates a strategic vision, strategic objectives, a strategic plan, and an organizational structure for implementing them.

3. *Designing a strategic change plan.* The group designs a strategic change plan, which "is an action plan for moving the organization from its current strategy and organization design to the desired future strategy and design."[55] It explains

how the strategic change will be implemented, including the specific activities involved as well as the costs and budgets associated with them.

4. *Implementing a strategic change plan.* The final step involves actually implementing the strategic change plan and measuring and reviewing the results of the change activities to ensure that the process is proceeding as planned.[56]

CONFLICT AND CONFLICT MANAGEMENT TECHNIQUES

Anyone who has ever worked in an organization knows that conflict exists and that it can have extremely dysfunctional effects on the organization and the people that comprise it. Opposing parties tend to put their own aims above those of the organization, and the organization's effectiveness suffers. Time that could have been used productively is wasted as the opposing parties hide valuable information from each other and jockey for position, each thereby preventing the other from carrying out its assigned tasks. Those involved in the conflict can become so personally enwrapped in the tensions it produces that it often undermines their emotional and physical well-being. Perhaps the most insidious effect of organizational conflict is that it doesn't remain organization-bound for long. Its effects are observed by customers and stockholders and are taken home by the opponents whose innocent families are often caught in the fallout.

Despite its adverse effects, most experts today view conflict as a potentially useful aspect of organizations since it can, if properly channeled, be an engine of innovation and change. This view recognizes the necessity of conflict and explicitly encourages a certain amount of controlled conflict in organizations. The basic case for this view is that some conflict is necessary if an organization is to avoid stagnation and myopic decision making. An example often cited is a paper by Janis called "Group-Think." In this paper, Janis describes how potential critics of the abortive Bay of Pigs invasion in Cuba were put under tremendous pressure not to express their opposing viewpoints. For example, then Attorney General Robert Kennedy at one point took aide Arthur Schlesinger aside and asked him why he was opposed to the invasion. According to Janis, Kennedy listened coldly and then said, "You may be right or you may be wrong, but the President has made his mind up. Don't push it any further. Now is the time for everyone to help him all they can."[57]

Janis argues that if Kennedy and his staff had encouraged the expression of more criticism, many of their questionable assumptions would have been challenged and much better decisions would have resulted.

This generally positive picture of conflict appears to be supported by surveys of management practice. In one survey of top and middle managers, for example, managers rated "conflict management" as of equal (or slightly higher) importance than topics like planning, communication, motivation, and decision making. The managers spent about 20 percent of their time on conflicts; yet they did not consider the conflict level in their organization to be excessive. Instead, they rated it as about right—that is, at the midpoint of a scale running from "too low" to "too high."[58]

INDIVIDUAL, INTERPERSONAL, AND ORGANIZATIONAL CONFLICT

At least three kinds of conflict can be identified in organizations. **Role conflict** is a familiar example of conflict *within the individual.* Role conflict occurs when a person is faced with conflicting orders, such that compliance with one would make it

ROLE CONFLICT
Conflict within the individual occurring when a person is faced with conflicting orders.

difficult or impossible to comply with the other. Sometimes role conflict arises out of obviously conflicting orders, as when a corporal receives orders from a captain that would force him to disobey an order from his sergeant. Sometimes, however, the source of the role conflict is not quite so obvious, as when obeying an order might force a person to violate his or her own cherished values and sense of right and wrong. In any case, role conflict is a serious problem in organizations, one that can be stressful to the persons involved, and adversely affect their morale and performance.[59]

INTERPERSONAL CONFLICTS
Conflicts occurring between individuals and/or groups.

Conflicts in organizations can also be **interpersonal** and occur between individuals, or between individuals and groups. Sometimes, of course, such conflicts arise from "legitimate" sources, as when real differences in goals or objectives exist between the parties involved. Often, however interpersonal conflicts arise not from legitimate differences, but as a result of the personalities involved. Some people are more aggressive and conflict prone than others, for example, and others are so hypersensitive that every comment is viewed as an insult.

INTERGROUP ORGANIZATIONAL CONFLICTS
These are conflicts that may occur between organizational units such as production and sales departments or between line and staff units.

Finally, there are **intergroup organizational conflicts,** conflicts, for example, between line and staff units, or between production and sales departments. Effectively managing such conflict is especially crucial today, as firms increasingly try to move towards the kinds of boundaryless organizations envisioned by GE's Jack Welch and discussed in Chapter 9. We will focus on the causes and management of intergroup conflicts in the remainder of this section.

CAUSES OF INTERGROUP CONFLICT

There are many sources of intergroup conflict, but research findings suggest that four factors create most of the problems: interdependencies and shared resources; intergroup differences in goals, values, or perceptions; authority imbalances; and ambiguities.

INTERDEPENDENCIES AND SHARED RESOURCES Groups (or individuals) who work interdependently, or who must compete for scarce resources may eventually come into conflict. Conversely, groups that do not have to depend on each other or compete for scarce resources, will generally not get involved in intergroup conflicts.[60]

Examples of how interdependence or competition for scarce resources lead to conflict abound. For example conflicts are often a way of life for members of quality control and production departments, sales and production departments, and departments which depend on each other and are interdependent. On the other hand, intergroup conflict is less likely to occur between the finance and quality control departments, since the people in these departments are not too interdependent. Similarly, competition for scarce resources, such as when two or more departments must compete for limited funds, or for the services of a typing pool, generally leads to "office politics," hiding of information, and conflict.

Of course interdependence does not have to necessarily lead to intergroup conflicts; just the opposite. If the situation is managed correctly, or if the groups' overall aims are similar, interdependence can provide an incentive for collaboration rather than conflict; this is one reason why the conflict management techniques we discuss later in this chapter are important.[61]

INTERGROUP DIFFERENCES IN GOALS, VALUES, OR PERCEPTIONS
Persons who agree in terms of their goals, values, or perceptions are less likely to find themselves arguing than are those with fundamental differences.

Differences in goals are one familiar source of intergroup conflict. Researchers Richard Walton and John Dutton, for example, have found that the preference of production departments for long, economical runs conflicted with the preference of sales units for quick delivery for good customers, and that these differing goals often led to intergroup conflict.[62] Other fundamental differences in goals that have been found to lead to intergroup conflicts include an emphasis on flexibility versus stability, on short-run versus long-run performance, measurable versus intangible results, and organizational goals versus societal needs.[63] In summary, when the goals of two groups are similar or identical, there is little chance of serious conflict arising; but when there is a fundamental difference in goals, conflicts will likely arise. Similarly, when two groups differ in terms of their values or how they perceive a situation, conflicts are more likely to arise.

Researchers Paul Lawrence and Jay Lorsch said that what they call "organizational differentiation" is another source of intergroup conflict.[64] Basically, they found that as each department in an organization tries to cope with the unique demands of its own environment, it necessarily develops its own types of procedures, cherished values, and point of view. For example, a research department in a chemical firm might be run very democratically, and its personnel might develop a rather long-term time perspective since most of the things they are working on will not reach fruition for years. On the other hand, the production department might be run more autocratically, and its managers might be expected to put a much greater emphasis on immediate results. Lawrence and Lorsch believe that the greater the differentiation between departments, the more potential for conflict there is. However, they found that whether conflict in fact emerges depends on several things, including how departments settle their differences.

AUTHORITY IMBALANCES   We also know that when a group's actual authority is inconsistent with its prestige, intergroup conflicts are more likely to develop. For example researcher John Seiler found that in one company, the production department had to accept instructions from a production engineering department composed of employees with skills no greater than (and in fact quite similar to) those possessed by production employees. As a result, "production managers spent an inordinate amount of time checking for consistency among the various items produced by production engineering."[65]

AMBIGUITY   Finally, difficulty in assigning credit or blame between two departments increases the likelihood of conflict between units. For example, if both the quality control and production departments can claim credit for the cost savings resulting from a change in production procedures, a conflict may well result. Similarly, if it is difficult to place the blame for a problem, conflicts may emerge as departments attempt to shed themselves of the blame, for, say, a cost overrun or machine breakdown. Conflict is also sometimes found in organizations where departmental responsibilities are not clearly delineated, and where "power vacuums" arise and intergroup conflicts ensue as each department fights to fill those vacuums by taking on increased responsibilities.

TECHNIQUES FOR MANAGING ORGANIZATIONAL CONFLICT

There are many techniques for managing or resolving conflicts but they generally fall into one of four categories. The first involves establishing superordinate goals and thus creating an area of commonality between the previously competing groups, for example, by convincing each that they share a common enemy. Second, there are various structural approaches that involve, for example, reducing the interdependencies between the competing groups or referring the disagreement to a common superior.

Third, various conflict resolution "modes," or ways of solving problems, can be tried. Finally, organizational development conflict resolution techniques can be used.

USING COMMON GOALS TO MANAGE CONFLICT　One of the most familiar and sensible ways of short-circuiting conflicts is to find some common ground that the parties can agree on. In labor-management negotiations, for example, arbitrators generally begin their work by finding some point that both sides can agree on, and then build a solution from that one point of agreement. As another example, national leaders, such as Cuba's Fidel Castro, often use the ploy of claiming that their countries are about to be attacked to bring about unification of the opposing factions in their own countries. Creating a shared vision (as at GE) is another option.

STRUCTURAL APPROACHES TO CONFLICT MANAGEMENT　One can also use various structural approaches to managing and resolving intergroup conflicts, for example, by having the groups appeal to a common superior.[66] In fact, the most common way of resolving disagreements between departments is still to refer the disagreements to a common superior. For example, if the vice-presidents for sales and production cannot reach agreement on some point, they would typically refer their disagreement to the president for a final, binding decision.

Another structural way to reduce the potential for conflict is to reduce the interdependencies or the need to compete for scarce resources. Sometimes the changes here are as simple as separating the units physically so that the members of each group no longer have to confront each other each day.[67] Another change is to increase the available resources so that both groups can get basically what they want.

Lawrence and Lorsch, in the study mentioned earlier, found that many companies have reduced interdepartmental conflict by setting up special liaisons between the conflicting departments. In the high-technology plastics industry, for example, successful companies set up special departments whose job it was to coordinate the work of the research, sales and manufacturing departments.

CONFLICT RESOLUTION MODES　There are different ways to settle an argument, and some are better than others. For example, having both parties meet to confront the facts and hammer out a solution is usually more effective than simply smoothing over the conflict by "pushing the problems under a rug."

Lawrence and Lorsch in their study of conflict resolution found that managers used either confrontation, smoothing, or forcing to resolve conflicts. They present the following as actual examples of each:

Confrontation. "In recent meetings we have had a thrashing around about manpower needs. At first we did not have much agreement but we kept thrashing around and finally agreed on what was the best we could do."

Smoothing. "I thought I went to real lengths in our group to confront conflict. I said what I thought in the meeting, but it did not bother anybody. I guess I should have been harsher. I could have said I won't do it unless you do it my way. If I had done this, they couldn't have backed away, but I guess I didn't have the guts to do it. I guess my reaction was—well, I made a fool of myself in the meeting and nothing happened so I will sit back and feel real comfortable. I guess I didn't pound the bushes hard enough."

Forcing. "If I want something very badly and I am confronted by a roadblock, I go to top management to get the decision made. If the research managers are willing to go ahead (my way), there is no problem. If there is a conflict, then I take the decision to somebody higher up."[68]

Of these methods, the confrontation approach usually got the best results, especially when the conflict involved major issues like salaries and promotions.[69]

OD: THE CONFRONTATION MEETING OD techniques including t-groups and the confrontation meeting are sometimes used to manage conflict. For example, firms use the confrontation meeting to "clear the air" and resolve intergroup conflicts.[70] The technique usually requires the use of an outside consultant who is skilled in its use. Confrontation meetings seem to be especially useful when misperceptions are at the root of the intergroup conflict, such as when each group misperceives or misunderstands the opposing group's true position. The typical confrontation meeting lasts from four to eight hours and usually begins with the consultant discussing in general terms such topics as organizational communication, the need for mutual understanding, and the need for members of the management team to share responsibility for accomplishing the organization's goals. In such a meeting, the discussion might turn to an analysis of the organization's operating problems, including how advertising budgets are arrived at, how sales commissions are computed, and how financial controls are imposed. On the other hand, some confrontation meetings focus exclusively on human relations problems like conflict between line and staff personnel. Thus, in one case, the two groups of employees were assigned to separate rooms and were asked to discuss three questions: 1) What qualities best describe our group? 2) What qualities best describe the other group? 3) What qualities do we predict the other group would assign to us?[71]

Each group was asked to develop a list of words or phrases that they felt best described their answers to each question. The two groups of employees then assembled together and proceeded to discuss their own lists as well as those developed by the other group. They questioned each other about the lists, and after several hours "it appeared as if each side moved to a position where they at least understood the other side's point of view."[72]

MANAGING CHANGE

Regardless of the nature of the change, the change itself must be managed. By this change experts mean overcoming employee resistance to the change, developing political support for the change, and motivating employees to implement the change.

OVERCOMING RESISTANCE TO CHANGE

As we explained earlier, overcoming employee resistance to the change is a critical feature of any change program. The resistance may stem from various sources, including a preference for a habitual way of doing things, fear of the unknown, or a feeling that one's personal power or security are at stake. Whatever the source, the resistance must be addressed.

In Figure 18.5, John Kotter and Leonard Schlesinger have summarized some methods for dealing with resistance to change, as well as each method's advantages and drawbacks. For example, *education and communication* is appropriate where a lack of information or inaccurate information is contributing to employee resistance to change. *Facilitation and support* (which might include providing training and new skills, employee time off after a demanding period, or simply listening and providing emotional support) can reduce resistance where fear and anxiety are at the heart of the resistance. *Participation and involvement* (which might involve presenting the problem to a group of employees and letting them collect and analyze data and select the solution) can be particularly useful where management does not have all the information needed to design the change, or where management believes that employee

APPROACH METHOD	COMMONLY USED IN SITUATIONS	ADVANTAGES	DRAWBACKS
Education + communication	Where there is a lack of information or inaccurate information and analysis.	Once persuaded, people will often help with the implementation of the change.	Can be very time-consuming if lots of people are involved.
Participation + involvement	Where the initiators do not have all the information they need to design the change, and where others have considerable power to resist.	People who participate will be committed to implementing change, and any relevant information they have will be integrated into the change plan.	Can be very time-consuming if participators design an inappropriate change.
Facilitation + support	Where people are resisting because of fear and anxiety.	No other approach works as well with adjustment problems.	Can be time-consuming, expensive, and still fail.
Negotiation + agreement	Where someone or some group will clearly lose out in a change, and where that group has considerable power to resist.	Sometimes it is a relatively easy way to avoid major resistance.	Can be too expensive in many cases if it alerts others to negotiate.
Manipulation + co-optation	Where other tactics will not work, or are too expensive.	It can be a relatively quick and inexpensive solution to resistance problems.	Can lead to future problems if people feel manipulated.
Coercion	Where speed is essential, and the change initiators possess considerable power.	It is speedy, and can overcome any kind of resistance.	Can be risky if it leaves people angry at the initiators.

FIGURE 18.5

Six Methods for Dealing with Resistance to Change

To overcome employee's resistance to the change, its usually wise to fit the method for overcoming the resistance to the specifics of the situation.

SOURCE: John Kotter and Leonard Schlesinger, "Choosing Strategies for Change," *Harvard Business Review*, vol. 57, no. 2, March–April 1979, 111.

resistance can be a particular problem. However, in some situations (such as some labor-management disagreements), *negotiation and agreement* may be appropriate, because one group will clearly lose out in the change and that group has considerable power to resist. *Manipulation and co-optation* (for instance giving a key resistor a key role in the change) works well where other tactics will not work or are too expensive. Finally, where speed is essential and the manager responsible for the change possesses considerable power, management can deal with resistance by *coercing* others to go along with the change. Coercion—simply forcing the change—can be a speedy way of pushing through a change and is probably widely used, particularly when speed is essential. But it can be a risky tactic if it leaves influential employees with a residue of ill will against the company. The *Breiner Construction* vignette shows how one business owner applied several of these methods to change her firm.

BREINER CONSTRUCTION, INC.

Rosemary Montoya Breiner knows the saying "it takes two to tango" isn't misplaced in the construction business. Her late husband, Jim, started Breiner Construction, and he knew all about estimating jobs and putting buildings where only grass used to grow. But the firm has survived through some tough recessionary times because Rosemary Breiner recognized that the administrative and bookkeeping ends of the business are equally important.

Rosemary Montoya Breiner took over Breiner Construction after her husband's death, making herself equally at home in the office and on the job site.

From 1972 to 1985, Breiner's Denver base of operations was booming. But by 1990, the drop in profits meant that Breiner had to ram through a change. She first laid off 40 percent of the work force. She scaled back plans to diversify the company, which had always concentrated on federal jobs, because jumping on an unfamiliar horse in the midst of a crisis didn't seem wise. "My feeling was, this was what we did well and were known for in the market," she says. "It wasn't the time to abandon one market and look for another foothold."

Breiner thinks the difficult times were good for one thing at least. She used to manage the company's changes with little outside assistance. Now, she says, input from employees provides a welcome alternative perspective. Weekly meetings allow everyone to vent whatever is on their minds. Rosemary Breiner has a word of advice to construction companies that have to weather hard times in the future; it doesn't matter how skilled you are at your particular trade or occupation; if you don't have someone equally competent at tracking receivables, paying the insurance, and keeping in touch with the customers, your company's history may be woefully short.

SOURCE: Steve Pergsman, "Rosemary Montoya Breiner, Breiner Construction, Inc.," *Hispanic Business,* April 1991, 32.

DEVELOPING POLITICAL SUPPORT

Organizations are often composed of individuals and groups with different preferences and interests. Attempts to change the organization may thus threaten the balance of power, resulting in political conflicts and struggles.[73] Kotter and Schlesinger contend that building political support for the change should therefore begin with assessing the power of the person initiating the change. In this way, the change agent can assess how much support he or she can expect and the most effective manner in which his or her power might be used. Key stakeholders in the change—staff groups, unions, and informal employee leaders, for instance—should then be identified. The change agent (who might be the manager in charge) can then turn to influencing these key stakeholders and building political support for the change (perhaps using education, communication, participation, facilitation, negotiation, manipulation/co-optation, or coercion).

MOTIVATING CHANGE

The best way to get someone to change is first to get them to see the need for change. Whether it is getting someone to study more, or to lose weight, or to change a particularly disruptive habit, few people change just because someone else tells them to; instead, they must be shown the need for change—they must "unfreeze".

The same is true when motivating change in an organization. Effective change leaders like GE's Jack Welch often begin by educating their employees regarding the pressures for change, be they increased competition, new technology, poor product quality, or high production costs. The leader may then go on to reveal gaps between current and desired states, laying out, as they do, a vision of the situation as they would like to see it unfold. They also, according to Cummings and Worley, convey "credible positive expectations" for the change, in terms of specific behavioral outcomes that the manager expects from the employees, along with expressions of his or her confidence that the employees can achieve them.[74]

S U M M A R Y

Organizations go through change all the time, but the nature, scope and intensity of those changes vary considerably. Incremental changes only affect selected parts of the organization, while strategic changes impact the entire organization. Changes made in direct response to an external event are called reactive, while those that are planned are called anticipatory. Combining these two dimensions of change—strategic versus incremental and reactive versus anticipatory—results in an organizational change matrix. Implementing change involves both risks and benefits.

Resistance to change within an organization may stem from a number of sources including habit, resource limitations, threats to power and influence, and fear of the unknown. According to Lewin's change model, the three-step process for change involves unfreezing (or reducing status quo forces), moving (or shifting the behavior of individuals), and refreezing (or reinforcing the new state of equilibrium). The entire change process can be summarized by the following six stages: becoming aware of the pressure for change, recognizing the need for change, diagnosing the problem, planning the change, implementing the change, and following up on the change.

Managers can choose various targets for change including strategy, structure, tasks, technologies, culture, attitudes, and skills of people in the organization. The special critical path approach to change involves six overlapping steps: mobilizing commitment to change through joint diagnosis of business problems; developing a shared vision of how to organize and manage for competitiveness; fostering consensus for the new vision, competence to enact it and cohesion to move it along; spreading revitalization to all departments without pushing it from the top; institutionalizing revitalization through formal policies, systems, and structures; and monitoring and adjusting strategies in response to problems in the revitalization process.

Changes are typically driven by change advocates. The activities required for such a role have been described as charismatic leadership, instrumental leadership, and "spreading the gospel of change" through leadership.

Organization development focuses on improving the organization's ability to solve its own problems. OD interventions include those aimed at improving the human relations skills of individuals; efforts to change firms' structures, methods, and job designs; those targeted at changing personnel practices; and those designed to bring about a fit between a firm's strategy structure, culture, and the external environment.

All change must be managed by overcoming employee resistance to change, developing political support for the change, and motivating employees to implement the change.

Q U E S T I O N S

■ FOR REVIEW

1. Describe the types of changes that make up the organizational change matrix.

2. What are some sources of resistance to change within an organization?

3. Compare Lewin's change model with the critical path approach to change.

4. Name some of the most common targets of change in today's organizations.

5. Explain the essential activities carried out by change advocates.

6. How is organizational development used in helping organizations change themselves?

■ FOR DISCUSSION

7. In terms of change, how would you describe the spate of downsizings sweeping corporate America.

8. Assume you are serving as a consultant to a local bank that plans to shift its focus from major real estate lending to consumer financing and eliminate some employees in the process. What kind of resistance is the bank likely to encounter and how would you suggest overcoming it?

9. Even the most successful companies eventually face the need for change. Discuss some of the reasons why change is inevitable.

10. How might the U.S. government use the critical path approach to reform the nation's health care system?

■ FOR ACTION

11. Think of a strategic change that would benefit your university. Outline the six main steps that would be involved in the change process.

12. Go to the library and find an example of a company that has changed as a result of one of the following pressures: divestitures, consolidation, increased regulation, globalization, or the rush toward democratization. Write a brief report describing the changes.

■ FOR FOCUS ON SMALL BUSINESS

13. Did the fact that Leegin is a small business make the change easier or harder to implement? Why?

14. Outline the changes at Leegin using the six-step organizational change model described in the chapter.

15. Discuss Jerry Kohl's role as the company's change advocate. Which leadership activities did he carry out?

CLOSING SOLUTION

WARNACO, INC.

Wachner decided the money and patience required to resuscitate most Warnaco divisions wasn't a good gamble in the cutthroat apparel trade. Shortly after she took over, all but two Warnaco divisions were gone. Intimate apparel now generates around 60 percent of company revenues, with men's wear making up most of the rest. Warnaco established itself as an innovative company. It has entered licensing agreements with Valentino, Ungaro, Scaasi, and Bob Mackie to produce high-dollar women's undergarments. In two other deals, the company supplies private-label goods for Victoria's Secret and the Fruit of the Loom label. Men's wear is manufactured under the Christian Dior, Hathaway, Ralph Lauren's Chaps, and Jack Nicklaus names. Wachner established herself as a tightfisted cash manager. Debt has been reduced by more than 40 percent. Operating cash flow has nearly doubled. The company was taken public again in October 1991. The stock price has been as high as 75 percent over the initial offering. Wachner, who is the only woman CEO of a Fortune 500 industrial company, can now spend time watching her own cash. Her 10 percent stake is worth somewhere around $72 million.[75]

■ QUESTIONS FOR CLOSING SOLUTION

1. Would you characterize the changes at Warnaco as a reorientation or recreation? Why?
2. What are some of the sources of resistance to change that Wachner most likely encountered?
3. Which of the change leadership activities discussed in the chapter best describes Wachner's actions?

Incremental Changes

Strategic Organizational Change

Reactive Change

Anticipatory Change

Reorientations

Recreations

Unfreezing

Moving

Refreezing

Organizational Analysis

Strategic Change

Organizational Development Interventions

Champion

Charismatic Leaders

Product Champion

Instrumental Leadership

Executive Champion

Organization Development

Action Research

Intervention

Human Process Interventions

Sensitivity Training

Team Building

Confrontation Meetings

Survey Research

System IV Management

Role Conflict

Interpersonal Conflicts

Intergroup Organizational Conflicts

CASE FOR ANALYSIS

UNITED WAY OF AMERICA

For 22 years it was difficult to dispute the effectiveness of William Aramony's leadership of the United Way of America (UWA)—or the results. Annual receipts more than tripled from 1970 to just over $3 billion. A high-profile partnership with the National Football League brought gridiron heroes together with afflicted youngsters in donated Sunday afternoon T.V. spots. Even the most grizzled pro-football fans were moved to make donations to their local United Way chapter.

The UWA does little fund raising; its primary function is providing training and services. It is supported by dues from the 2,100 chapters around the country. This is the grassroots level where the tough money-raising work gets done. United Way personnel collect donations and disburse them to worthy local charities. Since 1946, each year's contributions surpassed the preceding one.

Until 1992. Those same hard-nosed contributors, and a lot of substantial corporations and other people, were shocked upon learning that Aramony's annual salary and benefits package topped $460,000. Other revelations struck decidedly uncharitable

chords as well. The president liked flying first-class on domestic hops and preferred the ultra-expensive Concorde for trans-Atlantic jaunts. Ground transportation was equally cushy. United Way picked up over $92,000 in limousine tabs. Las Vegas turned out to be a frequent stopover; the expense-account bite on 29 trips to that stop for Aramony and his associates was nearly $38,000. There were other allegations of how contributions were spent. Aramony resigned in March 1992.

With a number of local chapters effectively stiff-arming the national headquarters and hanging on to contributions, Elaine L. Chao took the helm at UWA eight months later. "We are going to have a new reverence for donors' dollars," said Chao, who previously headed the Peace Corps. She instituted a new policy of making managers responsible for their own budgets. Senior vice-presidents would oversee outlays on a monthly basis, and senior executives' expenses would be scrutinized by outside auditors. Local United Way chapters would have input at national headquarters. Half the seats on six new steering committees—including budget, ethics, and compensation—would be filled from the field level. Fifteen seats on the board were also created to be filled by local personnel. Future airline travel would be coach-class, with limited stipends for meal expenses. Chao also cut administrative staff levels by a third. On the community level, donors could now direct contributions, which were sometimes matched by a corporate donation, to their own particular worthy charity.

Despite Aramony's expenditures, few agree on what's at the root of the recent decline in contributions. United Way officials point to the recession. People on the ground say Aramony's gilded lifestyle led to widespread cynicism. Whatever the cause, Chao faces a formidable challenge. If a violation of trust is the root cause, it will be a hard road back for the United Way. But one thing is certain. Without restructuring and new controls to restore confidence and credibility, the tightfisted response of former donors could linger a long time.

SOURCES: Nanette Byrnes, "The Nonprofit Business," *Financial World*, August 3, 1993, 68; David Gergen, "Reforming Welfare at the Very Top," *U.S. News & World Report*, April 20, 1992, 43; and Michael Duffy, "Charity Begins at Home," *Time*, March 9, 1992, 48.

■ QUESTIONS

1. Elaine Chao has already made a number of internal changes since taking over the United Way in November 1992. Do you think she has gone far enough or would you suggest further restructuring?
2. What other changes can the United Way make to repair its tattered public image?
3. Describe the changes in core values that will inevitably have to be part of the United Way's recreation. What is likely to be the chief resistance to the changes?

A CASE IN DIVERSITY

ORGANIZATIONAL CHANGE AT AVON AND PRUDENTIAL

More and more companies are discovering that establishing, maintaining, and getting the most out of a diverse work force doesn't happen overnight and takes a lot of sustained effort. But old habits often die hard. Many managers literally find themselves in foreign territory when trying to make the organizational changes necessary to relate to disparate ethnic groups. Two companies that are redoubling efforts are The Prudential of Newark, New Jersey, and New York-based Avon Products, Inc.

Prudential started out by using a survey to determine why its African-American workers were leaving for other jobs in droves. The results revealed that minority employees felt diversity issues warranted little more than lip service from management. The company decided to devise a human-resource strategy that would maximize the input of every employee while increasing productivity and improving customer satisfaction.

Every mid- and upper-level manager underwent training. The managers had to create action plans detailing activities designed to enhance organizational diversity. Recruitment and development of minorities, communication, teamwork, and training were all integral to these plans. The follow-up entailed more than lip service. Senior managers began drawing up business-unit action plans that summarized core diversity problems and suggested solutions. Task forces tracked progress of the company's overall diversity program and different ethnic managers audited sentiments of various affected groups.

Avon encountered little difficulty in attracting women and minorities. But transforming this work force into a cohesive unit proved more difficult. One of the corporate policies called upon employees to set aside differences and assimilate. Nevertheless, personal concerns and career development increasingly took precedence. The company's Managing Diversity Program was designed to make workers aware of negative stereotypes in the workplace.

Like Prudential, Avon workers were in for increased training, but with a different twist. Everyone, from secretaries to upper-management, attended the same seminars. Six networks were established to address the concerns of employee minority groups. Every Avon location was assigned a representative who focused on how diversity issues affected sales and customer service. The company took the additional step of addressing family issues, child care, as well as lifestyle differences. Avon also emphasized empowerment through cross-functional, self-managed work teams.

It hasn't been all smooth sailing at Prudential or Avon. Prudential found that the time required to train employees was a lot greater than originally anticipated. Coping with individual prejudices and bias also proved more difficult than expected. At Avon, women now comprise three-quarters of all managers, but the company has found that its diversity program has had to be slowed at times because it sometimes runs contrary to immediate business needs. Despite the occasional fits and starts, Avon maintains that it is committed to diversity for the long haul.

SOURCE: Vivian Louie, "Successful Companies Realize that Diversity Is a Long-term Process, Not a Program," *Personnel Journal*, April 1993, 54–55.

■ QUESTIONS

1. Do you consider the implementation of diversity programs at Prudential and Avon part of anticipatory or reactive organizational changes? Explain
2. What sources of resistance to change are the companies likely to encounter in pursuing the diversity programs?
3. Based on the facts presented in this case, do you think Avon and Prudential followed the critical path approach in attempting to change attitudes among their diverse work forces? What process and methods would you have used?

1. Susan Caminiti, "America's Most Successful Businesswoman," *Fortune*, June 15, 1992, 102–8; Laura Zinn, "We Had to Be an Owner," *Business Week*, June 8, 1992, 81; and Maggie Mahar, "The Measure of Success," *Working Woman*, May 1992, 70–107.

2. David A. Nadler and Michael Tushman, "Beyond the Charismatic Leader: Leadership and Organizational Change," *California Management Review*, Winter 1990, 79.

3. Ibid., 49.

4. Ibid., 79.

5. Ibid.

6. Stewart Thomas, "G.E. Keeps Those Ideas Coming," *Fortune*, August 12, 1991, 42.

7. See Nadler and Tushman, "Beyond the Charismatic Leader," 79; see also David A. Nadler and Michael Tushman, "Organizational Frame Bending: Principles or Managing Reorientation," *Academy of Management Executive*, vol. 3 (1989), 194–202.

8. Nadler and Tushman, "Beyond the Charismatic Leader," 80; and Alfred Marcus, "Responses to Externally Induced Innovation: Their Effects on Organizational Performance," *Strategic Management Journal*, vol. 9 (1988), 387–402.

9. Nadler and Tushman, "Beyond the Charismatic Leader."

10. Check Niccolo Machiavelli, *The Prince*, translated by W.K. Marriott (London: J.M. Dent & Sons, Ltd., 1958).

11. Richard Osborne, "Core Values Statements: The Corporate Compass," *Business Horizons*, September–October 1991, 28–34.

12. Based on Gregory Northcraft and Margaret Neale, *Organizational Behavior* (Fort Worth: The Dryden Press, 1990), 716–21.

13. Paul Lawrence, "How to Deal with Resistance to Change," *Harvard Business Review*, May–June 1954. See also Andrew E. Schwartz,"Eight Guidelines for Managing Change," *Supervisory Management*, July, 1994, 3–5; Thomas J. Werner and Robert F. Lynch, "Challenges of a Change Agent," *The Journal for Quality and Participation*, June, 1994, 50–54; and Larry Reynolds, "Understand Employees' Resistance to Change," *HR Focus*, June, 1994, 17–18.

14. Kurt Lewin, "Group Decision and Social Change," T. Newcomb and E. Hartley, eds., *Readings in Social Psychology* (New York: Holt, Rinehart & Winston, 1947); see also Thomas Cummings and Christopher Worley, *Organization Development and Change* (Minneapolis: West Publishing Company, 1993), 53.

15. Beverly Goldberg, "Manage Change Not the Chaos Caused by Change," *Management Review*, November 1992, 39–40.

16. Jerome Want, "Managing Change in a Turbulent Business Climate," *Management Review*, November 1990, 38–41.

17. Harold J. Leavitt, *New Perspectives in Organization Research* (New York: John Wiley and Sons, 1964).

18. Noel Tichy and Ram Charan, "Speed, Simplicity, Self-Confidence: An Interview with Jack Welch," *Harvard Business Review*, September–October 1989, 112–20. Reprinted in Richard Osborne, "Core Values Statements: The Corporate Compass," *Business Horizons*, September–October 1991, 32.

19. Based on David Nadler and Michael Tushman, "Beyond the Charismatic Leader: Leadership and Organizational Change," *California Management Review*, Winter 1990, 77–97.

20. Ibid., 78.

21. Stewart Thomas, "G.E. Keeps Those Ideas Coming," *Fortune*, August 12, 1991, 42.

22. See, for example, Bryan Dumaine, "The Bureaucracy Busters," *Fortune*, June 17, 1991, 36–50.

23. Roger Harrison, "Choosing the Depth of Organization Intervention," *Journal of Applied Behavioral Science*, vol. 2, (April–May–June 1970), 181–202.

24. Stewart, "G.E. Keeps Those Ideas Coming," 44, 43.

25. Michael Beer, Russell Eisenstat, and Burt Spector, "Why Change Programs Don't Produce Change," *Harvard Business Review*, November–December 1990, 158–66.

26. Ibid., 159. See also Ritta Smeds, "Managing Change Towards Lean Enterprises," *International Journal of Operations & Production Management*, March 1994, 66–83.

27. Ibid.

28. Ibid., 163.

29. Ibid., 163.

30. Ibid., 164.

31. Ibid., 164.

32. Ibid.

33. The following is based on Nadler and Tushman, "Beyond the Charismatic Leader," 77–97.

34. Ibid., 82.

35. Ibid.

36. Ibid., 85.

37. Ibid.

38. Ibid.

39. The perceptive reader will note that Nadler and Tushman's concept of instrumental leadership is in some respects the same as saying that the successful executive leader of change is really a successful manager in that he or she is able to successfully plan, organize, staff, lead, and control the various elements of the change.

40. Ibid., 92.

41. Ibid., 93–94.

42. Modesto Maidique, "Entrepreneurs, Champions and Technological Innovation," *Sloan Management Review,* Winter 1980, 59–76.

43. J.A. Schumpeter, *Capitalism, Socialism, and Democracy* (New York: Harper & Row, 1975), 132.

44. Discussed in Maidique, "Entrepreneurs, Champions and Technological Innovations," 60.

45. "What Do We Really Know about Managing R & D" (a talk with Ed Roberts), *Research Management,* November 1978; discussed in Maidique, "Entrepreneurs, Champions and Technological Innovations," 63–64.

46. Ibid., 61–62.

47. Thomas Cummings and Christopher Worley, *Organization Development and Change* (Minneapolis: West Publishing Company, 1993), 2.

48. Ibid., 3.

49. Wendell French and Cecil Bell, Jr., *Organizational Development* (Englewood Cliffs, NJ: Prentice-Hall, 1978), 88.

50. Ibid., 4.

51. Cummings and Worley, *Organization Development and Change,* 163. See also Herbert A. Marlowe, William S. Hoffman and Steven Bordelon, "Applying Organizational Development Processes: The Challenge of Downsizing—A Cognitive Approach," *Journal of Managerial Psychology,* November, 1992, 22–33.

52. Ibid.

53. Based on J.T. Campbell and M.D. Dunette, "Effectiveness of T-Group Experiences in Managerial Training and Development," *Psychological Bulletin,* vol. 7 (1968), 73–104. Reprinted in W.E. Scott and L.L. Cummings, *Readings in Organizational Behavior and Human Performance* (Homeward, IL: Irwin, 1973), 571.

54. Robert J. House, *Management Development* (Ann Arbor, MI: Bureau of Industrial Relations, University of Michigan, 1967), 71; Louis White and Kevin Wooten, "Ethical Dilemmas in Various Stages of Organizational Development," *Academy of Management Review,* vol. 8, no. 4 (1983), 690–97; and Louis White and Kevin Wooten, "Ethical Dilemmas in Various Stages of Organizational Development," *Academy of Management Review,* vol. 8, no. 4 (1983), 690–97.

55. Cummings and Worley, *Organization Development and Change,* 501.

56. For a description of how to make OD a part of organizational strategy, see Aubrey Mendelow and S. Jay Liebowitz, "Difficulties in Making OD a Part of Organizational Strategy," *Human Resource Planning,* vol. 12, no. 4, 317–29.

57. I.L. Janis, *Victims of group think* (Boston: Houghton Mifflin, 1972), Steven Robbins, "Managing Organizational Conflict," in Jerome Schnee, E. Kirby Warren and Harold Lazarus, *The Progress of Management* (Englewood Cliffs, NJ: Prentice-Hall, 1977), 163–76. For another

example of conflict's benefits, see Richard T. Pascale, "International Breakdowns and Conflict by Design," *Planning Review,* June, 1994, 12–17.

58. Kenneth Thomas and Warren Schmidt, "A Survey of Managerial Interests with Respect to Conflict," *Academy of Management Journal* (June 1976), 315–18.

59. See, for example, John Rizzo, Robert J. House, and Sydney I. Lirtzman, "Role Conflict and Ambiguity in Complex Organizations," *Administrative Science Quarterly,* 15 (June 1970), 150–63. For additional views on sources of conflict, see Patricia A. Gwartney-Gibbs and Denise H. Lach, "Gender Differences in Clerical Workers' Disputes Over Tasks," *Human Relations,* June 1994, 611–40; and Kevin J. Williams and George Alliger, "Role Stressors, Mood Spillover, and Perceptions of Work-Family Conflict in Employed Parents," *Academy of Management Journal,* August 1994, 837–69.

60. See, for example, Richard Walton and John Dutton, "The Management of Interdepartments Conflict: A Model and Review," *Administrative Science Quarterly,* 14, no. 1 (March 1969), 73–84.

61. Ibid., 73–84.

62. John Dutton and Richard Walton, "Interdepartmental Conflict and Cooperation: Two Contrasting Studies," *Human Organization,* 25 (1966), 207–20.

63. H.A. Lansberger, "The Horizontal Dimensions in a Bureaucracy," *Administrative Science Quarterly,* 6 (1961), 298–333.

64. Paul Lawrence and Jay Lorsch, *Organization and Environment* (Boston: Harvard University, Graduate School of Business Administration, division of research 1967).

65. John A. Seiler, "Diagnosing Interdepartmental Conflict," *Harvard Business Review* (September–October 1963), 121–32.

66. Ross Stagner, "Corporate Decision Making: An Empirical Study," *Journal of Applied Psychology,* 53 (1969), 1–13; Georg Wieland and Robert Ulrich, *Organization: Behavior, Design and Change* (Homewood: Irwin, 1976) 271–73. For another approach, see Al Galves, "The Interface Meeting as a Tool for Addressing Intergroup Conflict," *Supervision,* August 1994, 3–6.

67. Eric Neilson, "Understanding and Managing Intergroup Conflict," in Paul Lawrence, Lewis Barnes, and Jay Lorsch, *Organizational Behavior and Administration* (Homewood: Irwin, 1976), 294. See also Robin L. Pinkley and Gregory B. Northcraft, "Conflict Frames of Reference: Implications for Dispute Processes and Outcomes," *Academy of Management Journal,* February 1994, 193–206.

68. Lawrence and Lorsch, *Organization and Environment,* 74–75.

69. See, for example, Patricia Renwick, "Impact of Topic and Source of Disagreement Conflict Management," *Organizational Behavior and Human Performance,* 14 (December 1975), 416–25.

70. Warren Bennis, *Organization Development: Its Nature, Origins and Prospects* (Reading, MA: Addison-Wesley, 1969), 4–6.

71. Ibid., 4–6.

72. Ibid., 4–6. For a discussion of additional third-party interventions, see Donald E. Conlon, Peter J. Carnevale, and Keith J. Murnighan, "Intravention: Third-Party Intervention with Clout," *Organizational Behavior & Human Decision Processes,* March, 1994, 387–411.

73. David Nadler, "The Effective Management of Change," *Handbook of Organizational Behavior,* J. Lorch, ed. (Englewood Cliffs, NJ: Prentice-Hall, 1987), 358–69; and Cummings and Worley, *Organization Development and Change,* 152–54. See also Paul Strebel, "Choosing the Right Change Path," *California Management Review,* Winter, 1994, 29–52; and Clay Carr, "Seven Keys to Successful Change," *Training,* February 1994, 55–60; and Jeanie Daniel Duck, "Managing Change: The Art of Balancing," *Harvard Business Review,* November–December 1993, 109–19.

74. D. Eden, "OD and Self-Fulfilling Prophecy: Boosting Productivity by Raising Expectations," *Journal of Applied Behavioral Science,* vol. 22 (1986), 1–13.

75. Susan Caminiti, "America's Most Successful Businesswoman," *Fortune,* June 15, 1992, 102–8; Laura Zinn, "We Had to Be an Owner," *Business Week,* June 8, 1992, 81; and Maggie Mahar, "The Measure of Success," *Working Woman,* May 1992, 70–107.

DELL COMPUTER CORPORATION

Entrepreneurs are living examples of the American dream. Resourceful, committed, confident, and focused, entrepreneurs are the mavericks in this era of change. Few people fit that description better than Michael Dell, owner and founder of Dell Computers. In 1984 at the age of 19, Dell began selling computers from his college apartment under the name PCs Limited (changed to Dell Computer Corp. in 1987). Using IBM computers purchased at cost from retailers' surplus stock, Dell would customize them for resale by adding graphics cards and hard disks. By 1993, the company had grown to $2 billion in sales, with growth of 285 percent occurring from 1991 to 1993. This rapid growth has led to some growing pains, but has yet to leave any permanent scars. Both Michael Dell and Dell Computer Corporation are currently experiencing many of those growing pains. Dell, the organization, is making changes in its structure while Dell, the individual, is seeing an evolution in his role as leader and motivator.

For many successful entrepreneurs, the business eventually outgrows their managerial capabilities. Some, like Bill Gates of Microsoft Corp., are able to lead their enterprises from small beginnings to sustained growth as a large corporation. Others, like Steve Jobs of Apple Computer Inc. and Rod Canion of Compaq, find themselves unable to handle this transition and are left behind. Microsoft's Gates said entrepreneurs need to question their skills when the number of products and employees reach a certain breadth. "That's where you say, 'Wow, I have to play a different role,'" Gate's said. Dell is finding himself in that position now.

The low cost, tightfisted management approach of the entrepreneurial days is changing at Dell. The days of renting office space and outsourcing the assembly of PCs no longer addresses the quality and growth needs of a $2 billion, 5,000-plus employee company that sells PCs in 120 countries. Recognizing this overwhelming need for systems and managerial controls, Dell has hired several new managers and doubled the budget for internal information systems to link every operation at Dell. New plans are also in the works to build several new assembly plants around the world. This is in response to Dell competitors, Compaq and IBM, who argue that they have more control over quality than Dell does due to in-house assembly of most of their machines.

Dell will not change the assemble-to-order and the direct response business models, two things which he feels best meet customer needs and the customer-focused corporate culture.

The assemble-to-order system at Dell works in the following way. Orders are taken by telephone representatives, then printed on the manufacturing floor. Dell stocks and builds third-party hardware into the computer per the customer's specifications. They then preload, configure and test the customer's software at the factory. For example, Exxon placed a PC order that required Dell to load proprietary software. The computers were delivered directly to the gas stations and they were ready to run as soon as they were pulled out of the box. Orders are shipped in two to five business days.

Dell's customer-focused corporate culture has grown out of the entrepreneurial days. Employees at Dell are empowered to answer and respond to customer needs. "All of our people know that the customer is God, not just king," said Joel Kocher, president of Dell U.S.A. He added, "Our people don't know any other way of doing business than focusing on customers and doing backflips for them every minute." Having a group of employees who understand this mission and are driven to carry it out is a tremendous competitive advantage. Dell employees are confident they are doing the right thing and they are rewarded for doing so. All this combines to create a positive internal environment in which to work.

Even with the astronomical growth in the last three years, the Dell culture remains strong. The culture does not accept a non-customer attitude, and people who do not accept the standards are quickly turned out. Perhaps this is why Dell achieves a 70 percent repeat purchase rate. Joel Kocher said that in the 90s the customer will define value, not the supplier. "We subscribe to the fact that there's no average customer, one size fits one, and value engineering your business around a customer-directed value model works . . . because the customer has the power, not us."

SOURCES: Mollie Neal, "Dell Takes a Megabyte of the PC Market," *Direct Marketing*, May 1, 1993. Stephanie Anderson Forest, Catherine Arnst, Kathy Rebello, and Peter Burrows, "The Education of Michael Dell," *Business Week*, March 22, 1993. Peter Burrows and Stephanie Anderson Forest, "Dell Computer Goes into the Shop," *Business Week*, July 12, 1993. Neal Boudette, "A Reorganized, Matured Dell to See Q2 Payoffs, *PC Week*, May 23, 1994. "Making the Right Choices for the New Consumer," *Planning Review*—publication of the *Planning Forum*, September 1, 1993.

■ QUESTIONS

1. Why was it important for Dell Computer Corporation to hire several new high-level managers?
2. What other changes might be necessary in the structure of Dell Computer Corporation as the corporation's product lines grow?
3. How important is maintaining the current corporate culture at Dell Computer Corporation both now and in the future?

PART IV

MANAGING OPERATIONS AND SERVICES

CHAPTER 19

OPERATIONS MANAGEMENT

LEARNING OBJECTIVES

After studying this chapter, you should be able to:

- Define operations management.
- Describe the elements that make up any production system: inputs, a conversion subsystem, and outputs.
- Identify four basic production design system decisions.
- Discuss the various elements in the production planning and control process.
- Give examples of popular network planning and control methods.
- Explain the ABC and EOQ systems for managing inventory.
- List the aims of design for manufacturability.
- Name some of the techniques used to monitor and control product quality.
- Describe the production techniques and management systems used by world-class manufacturers.
- Explain the purpose of linear programming and queuing techniques.

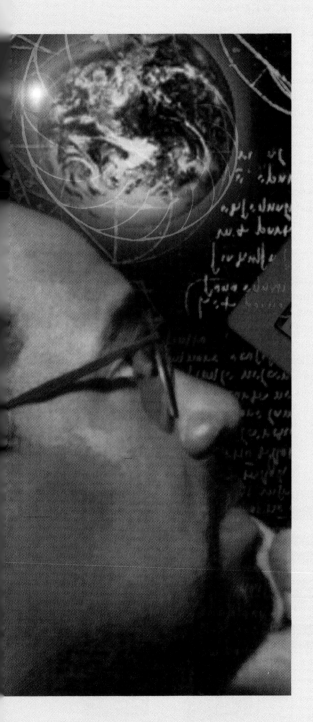

OPENING PROBLEM

FEDERAL SIGNAL
CORPORATION

When Joseph Ross assumed the role of president and COO at Federal Signal Corporation, the prospects for the multiproduct manufacturing company weren't encouraging. Few expected the company's markets to grow, and factory efficiency was below par. The Signal division, which made lights and sirens for emergency vehicles, was producing all 2,500 of its products on one assembly line, a single run at a time. As a result, the company either had to carry a wide inventory at substantial cost or customers had to wait months for products not in stock. Investment in working capital was high, and return on equity and operating margins were unsatisfactory. Ross came to two quick conclusions. Federal would have to become a leaner manufacturer to lower costs, and if its markets continued to shrink, the company would have to develop other products to fill the void.[1]

BASICS OF OPERATIONS MANAGEMENT

OPERATIONS MANAGEMENT DEFINED

OPERATIONS MANAGEMENT
The process of managing the resources required to produce the organization's goods and services.

Operations management is the process of managing the resources required to produce the organization's goods and services.[2] Like any managers, operations managers plan, organize, staff, lead, and control. However, unlike other managers, operations managers focus on the *direct production resources* of a firm, often called the five Ps of operations and production management: people, plants, parts, processes, and planning and control systems. These production resources are outlined in Figure 19.1.[3] The *people* include the direct and indirect work force, such as assembly workers, inventory clerks, and clerical staff. The *plants* are the factories or service branches where production is carried out. The *parts* include the raw materials and other inputs that will be transformed into finished products or services. The *processes* represent the technology, the equipment and the steps necessary to accomplish production. Finally, the *planning* and control systems are the procedures that management uses to operate the system, such as the steps followed to schedule the work, and control quality.[4]

THE PRODUCTION SYSTEM

INPUTS
Resources required for the manufacture of the product or service.

CONVERSION SYSTEM
A production system that takes inputs and converts these into products or services called outputs.

As summarized in Figure 19.2,[5] any system for producing something must have *inputs,* a *conversion subsystem,* and *outputs.* **Inputs** are all the resources required for the manufacture of the product or service. These include materials and supplies, personnel, and capital goods. Inputs also include market inputs; these primarily include data on the competition, the product, and customer desires. Environmental inputs are also informational. They include data on the legal aspects of doing business, social and economic trends, and technological innovations.

Any conversion system takes inputs and converts these into products or services called outputs. The **conversion system** (also sometimes called the production process or technology) has several elements. These include the machinery and their physical

FIGURE 19.1

Components of Operations

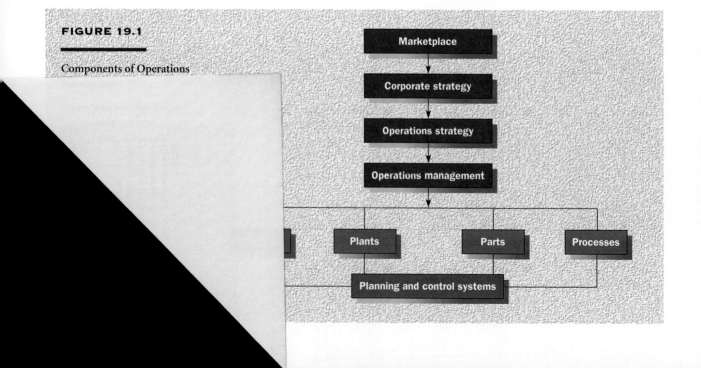

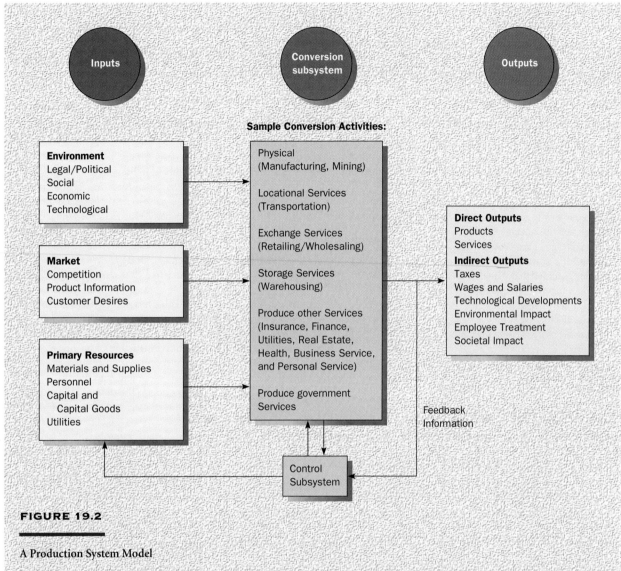

FIGURE 19.2

A Production System Model

Every production system is built around a conversion subsystem that takes various inputs and converts these into outputs such as products or services

SOURCE: Norman Gaither, *Production and Operations Management,* 5th ed. (Fort Worth, TX: The Dryden Press, 1992), 20.

layout, the transport services that bring in the inputs and deliver the final products to customers, storage services for goods awaiting shipment, and similar resources. Finally, the production system's **outputs** may be divided into direct outputs (the firm's products or services) and indirect outputs (such as taxes, wages, and salaries). Production system design can be especially important for a small, fledgling firm, as the *Aladan* small business box shows.

As summarized in Table 19.1, the input-conversion-outputs sequence remains basically the same whether the output is tangible (such as a car) or intangible (such as a

OUTPUTS

Direct or indirect outcomes of a production system, such as the firm's products or services, or taxes, wages, and salaries.

ALADAN CORPORATION

Julian H. Danielly might agree with the saying that timing is everything. The widespread AIDS awareness that occurred in the late 1980s brought with it a shortage of protective gloves. With little in the way of other job options, Danielly combined this growing health concern with his own background as an executive at a latex-glove manufacturing company to find financing for his own start-up, Aladan. An old friend and colleague Larry Povlacs worked up plans for a $3 million glove-manufacturing machine that would outperform competitors in both quantity and quality. Danielly began looking for ways to obtain the money to build a factory where his partner could install the innovative machine.

Danielly sold investors $2 million in stock. He was also convincing enough to obtain $3 million in tax-free, industrial-development bond financing, a rare feat for a fledgling outfit. But he first had to get a bank to back the bond issue. Before South Trust Bank would agree to underwrite, it insisted that Danielly sign customers to long-term contracts. He shortly returned with one $25 million order and several others that extended as long as five years. July 1987 marked the groundbreaking for Aladan's first plant in Dothan, Alabama. That particular site was selected because of tax incentives and a nearby airport. It also was Povlacs's home.

Latex gloves are essential for people in the medical field, but profit margins are notoriously slim and manufacturing and selling the gloves is often risky. Since 1986 the price for one hundred gloves has ranged from $2 to $12. In that same period, the market tripled in size to around $300 million. Danielly had performed miracles getting his factory built. He knew keeping it running would require staying on top of the latest manufacturing technology, good

FOCUS ON SMALL BUSINESS

marketing, and reducing risks through product diversification. Foreign competition posed the greatest immediate threat. Povlacs would have to design factory equipment efficient enough to outproduce the Pacific Rim companies, where labor was cheaper.

"A lot of what we've done here is incorporate improvements we had thought of over the years, but never had the opportunity to build," says Povlacs. "Starting from scratch was a real advantage for us from a manufacturing standpoint." The yearly output for each of Povlacs's machines totalled 200 million gloves. Aladan pioneered triple-dipping, a process that vastly increased the impenetrability of the gloves, exceeding the Food and Drug Administration standard. Competitors had no choice but to match the product quality level or be left behind. Povlacs even designed and built Aladan's drying equipment in house. His machines were twice as expensive as others available, but they also were six times as efficient.

Aladan has spearheaded other quality improvements. After an investment of $1 million, it reduced the labor requirements of the more expensive powder-free gloves, making the product feasible for a vastly expanded market.

Aladan has funneled $30 million into company plant and equipment. Danielly used ingenuity in raising funds for the construction of the first factory. Povlacs applied innovation in the design of equipment, and the quality of the product is the standard the rest of the industry strives to attain. Sales per employee were $126,000 in 1993, and profit margins range between 10 and 20 percent. Aladan took advantage of rising demand for its principal product, but it was obviously more than good timing that turned the company into an industry leader.

SOURCE: Teri Lammers, "What's Luck Got to Do With It?" *Inc.*, December 1993, 90–98.

service). For example, the primary inputs for an automobile factory include purchased parts, raw materials, supplies, paints, and personnel.[6] Such a factory's conversion system would include the lines of machines and tools that transform steel and other raw materials into finished cars. The outputs, of course, would be cars.

The same sequence applies to a service business like a university, where inputs would include students, books, supplies, professors, and buildings. The conversion subsystem would consist of the technology (lectures, computerized instruction and so forth) used to transmit information to the students. The output would be (it is hoped) educated persons.

PRODUCTION SYSTEM	PRIMARY INPUTS	CONVERSION SUBSYSTEM	OUTPUTS
1. Pet food factory	Grain, water, fish meal, personnel, tools, machines, paper bags, cans, buildings, utilities	Converts raw materials into finished goods	Pet food products
2. Hamburger stand	Meat, bread, vegetables, spices, supplies, personnel, utilities, machines, cartons, napkins, buildings, hungry customers	Transforms raw materials into fast-food products and packages	Satisfied customers and fast-food products
3. Automobile factory	Purchased parts, raw materials, supplies, paints, tools, equipment, personnel, buildings, utilities	Transforms raw materials into finished automobiles through fabrication and assembly operations	Automobiles
4. Trucking firm	Trucks, personnel, buildings, fuel, goods to be shipped, packaging supplies, truck parts, utilities	Packages and transports goods from sources to destinations	Delivered goods
5. Department store	Buildings, displays, shopping carts, machines, stock goods, personnel, supplies, utilities, customers	Attracts customers, stores goods, sells products	Marketed goods
6. Public accounting firm	Supplies, personnel, information, computers, buildings, office furniture, machines, utilities	Attracts customers, compiles data, supplies management information, computes taxes	Management information, tax services, and audited financial statements
7. Automobile body shop	Damaged autos, paints, supplies, machines, tools, buildings, personnel, utilities	Transforms damaged auto bodies into facsimiles of the originals	Repaired automobile bodies
8. College or university	Students, books, supplies, personnel, buildings, utilities	Transmits information and develops skills and knowledge	Educated persons
9. County sheriff's department	Supplies, personnel, equipment, automobiles, office furniture, buildings, utilities	Detects crimes, brings criminals to justice, keeps the peace	Acceptable crime rates and peaceful communities
10. National Marine Fisheries Service	Supplies, personnel, ships, computers, aircraft, utilities, office furniture, equipment	Detects offenders of federal fishery laws, brings them to justice, preserves fishery resources	Optimal stock of fish resources

TABLE 19.1

Some Typical Production Systems

All production systems consist of inputs, a conversion subsystem, and outputs.

SOURCE: Norman Gaither, *Production and Operations Management*, 5th ed. (Fort Worth, TX: The Dryden Press, 1992), 22–23.

PRODUCTION SYSTEMS DESIGN

Four basic production system design decisions must be made: Where will the facility be located? What type of production process will be used? What will be the layout of the plant or facility? And what will be the layout of the production system itself?

MAKING THE FACILITY LOCATION DECISION

Deciding where to locate the facility is usually a crucial question for management. For a service firm like a retail store or fast-food restaurant, even placing the facility on the wrong side of the road can spell disaster if the spot is inaccessible. For a manufacturer, plant location will influence factors such as transportation costs and labor availability.

Locating a factory involves applying both subjective and objective criteria. On the subjective side are things like the owner's personal preference. If Mr. Suarez loves to sail, and his whole family is in Miami, then the plant may be located in Hialeah, even if transportation costs are somewhat higher.

But, as a rule, selecting a site primarily rests on objective criteria such as labor costs, and outbound and inbound distribution costs.[7] Some facility site location variables are summarized in Table 19.2.[8] The objective variables in Table 19.2 include labor availability, waste disposal costs, the power supply, communications, the tax structure, and property costs. Inbound distribution costs are influenced by factors like the closeness of the site to its supply sources. Outbound distribution costs depend on the nature of the product and the site's closeness to the firm's markets.

BASIC TYPES OF PRODUCTION SYSTEMS

We can distinguish between two broad types of production processes: *intermittent production* systems and *continuous production* systems.

INTERMITTENT PRODUCTION Production is performed on a start-and-stop basis.

INTERMITTENT PRODUCTION In **intermittent production** systems, production is performed on the product on a start-and-stop basis.[9] Manufacturing operations like automobile repair shops, custom cabinet shops, and building contractors are examples. They are generally characterized by made-to-order products and relatively low product volumes, as well as frequent schedule changes and the use of general purpose equipment that can be used to produce a variety of models or products.

LABOR FACTORS	TRANSPORTATION FACTORS	UTILITIES FACTORS	CLIMATE, COMMUNITY ENVIRONMENT, AND QUALITY OF LIFE FACTORS	STATE AND LOCAL POLITICAL FACTORS
Labor supply	Closeness to sources of supply	Water supply	Climate and living conditions	Taxation policies
Labor-management relations	Closeness to markets	Waste disposal	Schools (elementary and high schools)	Tax structure
Ability to retain labor force	Adequacy of transportation models	Power supply	Universities and research facilities	Opportunity for highway advertising
Availability of technical and executive personnel	Costs of transportation	Fuel availability and cost	Community attitude	
Labor rates		Communications	Religious factors Property costs	

TABLE 19.2

Factors Influencing Facility Site Location

SOURCE: James Evans, David Anderson, Dennis Sweeney, and Thomas Williams, *Applied Production and Operations Management* (St. Paul, MN: West Publishing, 1990), 261.

A **mass production** process is a special type of intermittent production process in which standardized methods and single-use machines are used to produce long runs of standardized items. Most mass production processes use assembly lines. An assembly line is a fixed sequence of specialized (single-use) machines. In a typical assembly line, the product moves from station to station where one or more employees and/or specialized machines perform tasks such as inserting bumpers or screwing on doors. Mass production systems are intermittent production processes. However they may in fact run more or less continuously and may stop and start very few times over the course of a year.

CONTINUOUS PRODUCTION Continuous production processes run for very long periods without the start-and-stop behavior associated with intermittent production. Chemical plants, paper plants, and petroleum refineries are examples of continuous production process plants. Enormous capital investments are involved with building continuous process facilities such as these. They are therefore always built for high product volume and use special purpose equipment.

As we will see later in this chapter, the traditional dividing line between intermittent and continuous processes is beginning to blur. For example, computer-assisted manufacturing processes are being used to merge the flexibility of intermittent production with the efficiency of continuous production.

FACILITY LAYOUT

Facility layout refers to the configuration of all the machines, employee work stations, storage areas, internal walls, and so forth that constitute the facility used to create the firm's product or service. Facility layout objectives include reducing materials-handling costs, providing sufficient capacity, and allowing for safe equipment operation and ease of maintenance.

Facility layout is also important for service firms. Retailers lay out their stores to improve sales, customer satisfaction, and convenience, for instance, and office managers seek to promote communication between departments, and provide adequate privacy.

PRODUCTION SYSTEM LAYOUT

Four options are available for laying out the production system itself. In a **product layout**, *every item* to be produced follows the same sequence of operations from beginning to end, moving from one specialized tool and operation to another. An assembly, or production, line is one example. However, product layouts are not restricted to manufacturing. For example, automatic car washes use product layouts, as Figure 19.3 illustrates.[10]

In a **process layout**, similar machines or functions are grouped together; for example, all drill presses may be positioned in one area and all lathes in another. As Figure 19.4 illustrates,[11] universities and hospitals are usually organized around process layouts; separate locations exist for classrooms, libraries, offices, and computer centers, for instance. In a **fixed-position layout**, the product stays at one location and the manufacturing machines and tools required to build the product are brought to that location as needed. Bulky or heavy products such as ships are built in this way.

In **cellular manufacturing**, machines are grouped into *cells,* each of which contains all the tools and operations required to produce a particular product or family of products. As Figure 19.5 shows,[12] cellular manufacturing layouts combine aspects of both

MASS PRODUCTION
A special type of intermittent production process in which standardized methods and single-use machines are used to produce long runs of standardized items.

CONTINUOUS PRODUCTION
Processes that run for very long periods without the start-and-stop behavior associated with intermittent production.

FACILITY LAYOUT
Refers to the configuration of all the machines, employee work stations, storage areas, internal walls, and so forth that constitute the facility used to create the firm's product or service.

PRODUCT LAYOUT
Every item to be produced follows the same sequence of operations from beginning to end, moving from one specialized tool and operation to another.

PROCESS LAYOUT
Similar machines or functions are grouped together.

FIXED-POSITION LAYOUT
The product stays at one location and the manufacturing machines and tools required to build the product are brought to that location as needed.

CELLULAR MANUFACTURING
Machines are grouped into cells, each of which contains all the tools and operations required to produce a particular product or family of products.

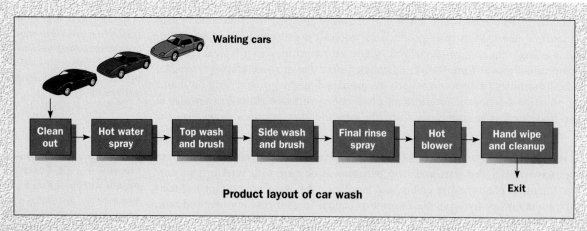

Product layout of car wash

FIGURE 19.3

Product Layout

A car wash is an example of an assembly-line-type product layout, where each special-purpose machine performs its function as the product moves from station to station.

SOURCE: Everett Adam, Jr., and Ronald Ebert, *Production & Operations Management* (Englewood Cliffs, NJ: Prentice-Hall, 1992), 254.

FIGURE 19.4

Process Layout

In a process layout like this, each process has its own area, and the "product" (in this case the patient) is directed to the processes (such as X-ray and pediatrics) that are appropriate.

SOURCE: Everett Adam, Jr., and Ronald Ebert, *Production & Operations Management* (Englewood Cliffs, NJ: Prentice-Hall, 1992), 254.

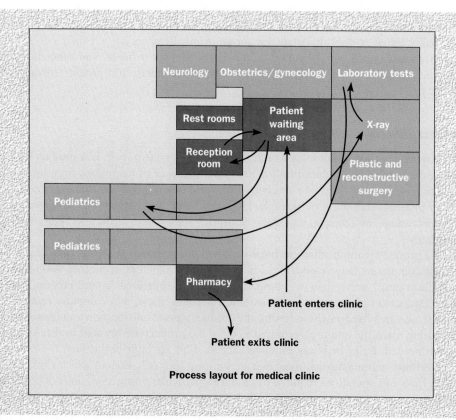

Process layout for medical clinic

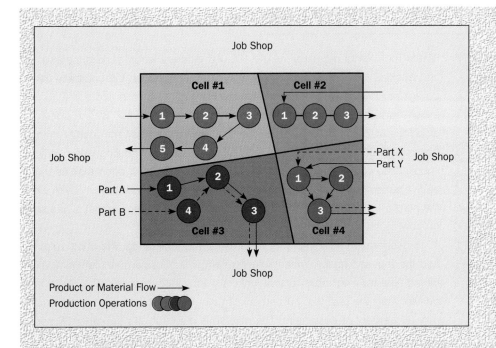

FIGURE 19.5

Cellular Manufacturing

When production is organized around cells, each cell contains the processes or production tools to manufacture a specific part or group of parts. Within each cell, all the production operations (such as sanding, filing, and drilling) required to complete one part or subassembly are placed together.

SOURCE: Norman Gaither, *Production & Operations Management*, 5th ed. (Fort Worth, TX: The Dryden Press, 1992), 135.

process and product layouts. As in product layouts, each cell is dedicated to producing particular parts or products; but like process layouts, each cell is designed to perform a specific set of manufacturing operations (such as all of the grinding and buffing needed to produce one of the valves that goes into the company's car engines). The *Illinois Tool* vignette shows how cellular manufacturing helps one firm to compete.

PRODUCTION AND OPERATIONS PLANNING AND CONTROL

THE PRODUCTION PLANNING AND CONTROL PROCESS

Whether producing cars or a Broadway show, you must have a system for planning and controlling production. **Production planning** is the process of deciding what products to produce and where, when, and how to produce them. **Production control** is the process of ensuring that the specified production plans and schedules are being met.

Figure 19.6 on page 554 provides a bird's-eye view of the production planning and control process.[13] The process includes several elements:

AGGREGATE OUTPUT PLANNING The **aggregate output planning** shows the aggregate (overall) volume in units of products (or services) that need to be produced to achieve each product's (or service's) dollar sales forecast.

MASTER PRODUCTION SCHEDULING (MPS) The amounts of all products to be produced and the date when individual products are to be produced can be

PRODUCTION PLANNING
The process of deciding what products to produce and where, when, and how to produce them.

PRODUCTION CONTROL
The process of ensuring that the specified production plans and schedules are being met.

AGGREGATE OUTPUT PLANNING
Shows the aggregate (overall) volume of products (or services) that need to be produced to achieve each product's (or services) sales forecast.

ILLINOIS TOOL WORKS

Illinois Tool Works produces nearly 100,000 different kinds of nails, screws, and buckles for everything from cars to pet collars. When the company came up against low-cost competitors from the Far East, it had to find a way to cut expenses without sacrificing innovation or quality. Its solution was to boost efficiency at its factories, such as the one in Elgin, Illinois. The factory manufactured 2,500 different kinds of self-drilling screws. Scheduling was nearly impossible, work-in-process covered the plant floor, and it often took as many as five weeks for products to progress from one stage to the next. Even with the help of a mainframe computer, managers couldn't track or get a handle on how much it all was costing.

In desperation, ITW implemented cellular manufacturing, the 80/20 rule, and the focused factory manufacturing concepts. Cellular manufacturing eliminated time-wasting cross-factory junkets with work-in-process. The *80/20 rule* derives from the fact that 80 percent of plant business typically comes from only 20 percent of customers. The reverse is also true. It's the other 80 percent of customers that force the company to frequently retool for low-volume runs, slowing overall production considerably. ITW overcame this problem by moving the small orders to a designated section of the factory. The third concept—*focused factories*—meant the spinoff of nine high-volume production lines into single-line plants throughout Wisconsin. The plants required only about 25 workers who in effect became entrepreneurs. "It's like we own our own little factory," says Thelma Douglas, a worker in one Illinois plant. "It makes you feel like you belong to something."

The low-tech approach of reconfiguring production, segregating low-volume runs, and spinning off some lines into focused factories has lowered costs and added market share. Productivity has tripled in the eight years since the manufacturing changes were implemented, and ITW weathered the recession of 1991 with only a 1 percent drop in profits.

SOURCE: "Cash In on U.S. Companies That Are Hammering the Japanese," *Money,* April 1992, 69–70; and Ronald Henkoff, "The Ultimate Nuts & Bolts Co.," *Fortune,* July 16, 1990, 70–73.

MASTER PRODUCTION SCHEDULE
The amounts of all products to be produced and the date when individual products are to be produced.

MATERIALS REQUIREMENTS PLAN
A computer-based system that reviews the master production schedule and specifies the required raw materials, parts, subassemblies, and assemblies needed each week to meet the master production schedule.

found on the **master production schedule.** It shows, on a yearly or monthly basis, when incoming sales orders can be scheduled into production, given current backlogs and delivery schedules.

MATERIAL REQUIREMENTS PLANNING (MRP) Also known as the MRP, the **materials requirements plan** is a computer-based system that reviews the master production schedule and specifies the required raw materials, parts, subassemblies, and assemblies needed each week to meet the master production schedule. This is sometimes also called *manufacturing resource planning.*

The MRP computer program is tied in with several other computerized manufacturing data bases. For example, most manufacturing firms maintain bills of materials.

A few of the thousands of types of screws manufactured by Illinois Tool Works, which has successfully retooled for the future, tripling productivity in the last eight years.

BILL OF MATERIALS
Lists the required parts and materials for each product manufactured.

INVENTORY FILE
Shows the specifications for each required part, as well as where it can be purchased or produced.

SHOP FLOOR CONTROL
The process of overseeing the weekly and daily production schedules to most effectively implement the master production schedules on a week by week basis.

LOADING AND SEQUENCING
Assigning individual jobs to machines and work centers.

LOAD SCHEDULE
Compares the labor and machine hours needed to carry out the master production schedule with the labor and machine hours actually available each week.

DETAILED SCHEDULING
Specifying the actual start times and finishing times for all jobs at each machine or work center, as well as each job's labor assignments.

GANTT CHART
A chart showing the production schedule where the time is presented on the horizontal scale and for each order, the start and stop times of each operation are shown.

The **bill (or list) of materials** lists the required parts and materials for each product manufactured. If an organization does not have such a list, it might need to hire a specialist to analyze each customer's order and develop a list of required parts. Most firms also maintain an **inventory file,** which shows the specifications for each required part, as well as where it can be purchased or produced. The MRP program dips into the computerized bills of materials and inventory files to identify the component parts and other materials required to fill the company's orders in the foreseeable future. It also calculates how much time the firm will need to purchase or produce these components.

SHOP FLOOR CONTROL   The process of overseeing the weekly and daily production schedules to most effectively implement the master production schedule on a week by week basis is referred to as **shop floor control.** It consists of four elements. **Loading and sequencing** means assigning individual jobs to machines and work centers. It is based on a **load schedule,** which compares the labor and machine hours *needed* to carry out the master production schedule with the labor and machine hours actually *available* each week.[14] **Detailed scheduling** means specifying the actual start times and finishing times for all jobs at each machine or work center, as well as each job's labor assignments. Finally, the movement of products and materials from operation to operation must be monitored and adjusted, a process known as *expediting*.

SCHEDULING AND GANTT CHARTS

Production schedules are often presented on charts that show specifically what operations are to be carried out, and when. The **Gantt chart** shown in Figure 19.7 is one example.

Henry Gantt, a scientific management pioneer, actually devised several versions of his chart. In the example shown in Figure 19.7, time is presented on the horizontal scale, and for each order, the start and stop times for each operation are shown sequentially. In another type of Gantt chart, each operation is listed vertically, while time is

FIGURE 19.6

The Operations Planning
and Control System

SOURCE: Adapted from
Everett Adam, Jr., and
Ronald Ebert, *Production &
Operations Management*
(Englewood Cliffs, NJ:
Prentice-Hall, 1992), 374.

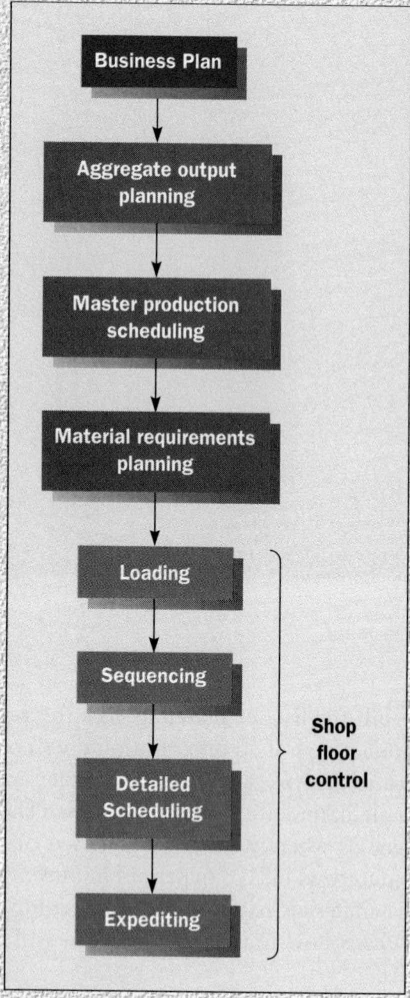

Business Plan

↓

Aggregate output
planning

↓

Master production
scheduling

↓

Material requirements
planning

↓

Loading

↓

Sequencing

↓

Detailed
Scheduling

↓

Expediting

Shop
floor
control

again shown horizontally. That way, the start and stop times for all operations in a
complex project can be scheduled and visually tracked.

In practice, schedulers work from the required delivery date backward. They determine how long each assembly will take, how long it will take to obtain raw materials,
and so forth. Based on the results, schedulers can determine whether the required
delivery date can be met and what bottlenecks they must prepare to unclog.

NETWORK PLANNING AND CONTROL METHODS

**NETWORK PLANNING AND
CONTROL METHODS**
Methods for planning and controlling projects by graphically
representing the projects' steps
and the timing and linkages between these steps.

Network planning and control methods are methods for planning and controlling
projects by graphically representing the project's steps and the timing and linkages
between these steps. A *project* is a series of interrelated activities aimed at producing
a major, coordinated product or service. Examples of a project include introducing a
new Mustang automobile or planning a wedding reception.

A relatively simple project (with not too many subassemblies or activities) may be
managed with versions of the Gantt chart. However, more complex projects usually

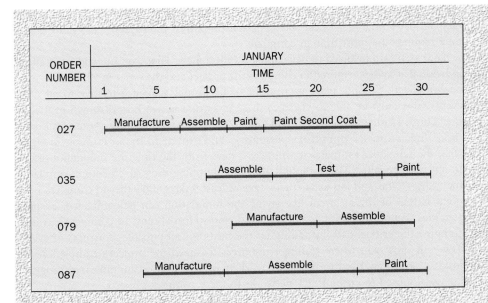

FIGURE 19.7

A Gantt Chart

This particular Gantt Chart shows the steps and timing of each step for each order.

require computerized network charting methods to show how one activity impacts the others.

PERT and CPM are the two most popular network planning and control methods. PERT (program evaluation review technique) and CPM (critical path method) were invented at about the same time and are similar, although several details set PERT apart from CPM.

Events and *activities* are the two major components of PERT networks. As Figure 19.8 shows, **events,** depicted by circles, represent specific accomplishments such as foundation laid. **Activities** are the time-consuming aspect of the project (like laying

EVENTS
A major component of a PERT network, events represent specific accomplishments.

ACTIVITIES
The time-consuming aspect of the project, represented by arrows in the PERT method.

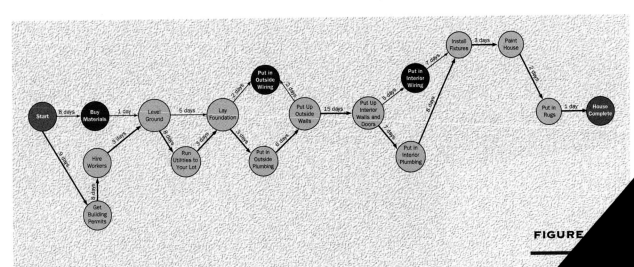

FIGURE

PERT Chart for Buil

In a PERT Chart like this one, each event is shown in its proper relationship to the other events. The darke
critical—or most

CRITICAL PATH

The sequence of events that in total requires the most time to complete.

the foundation) and are represented by arrows. By studying the PERT chart, the scheduler can determine the *critical path*. The **critical path** is the sequence of events that in total requires the most time to complete.

Four steps are involved in developing a PERT chart. First, you must identify all the individual activities required to complete the project and the order in which they must be completed. Second, place each event in its proper sequence relative to all other events. You must be able to visualize these tasks in a network as is shown in the figure. Third, estimate how long it will take to complete each activity. (Some estimators make three estimates: optimistic, pessimistic, and expected.) In our example in Figure 19.8, the scheduler estimates it will take 4 days from the time the foundation is laid to put up the walls. (Notice though, that the plumbing must go in before completing the walls, so the wall job will actually take at least 9 days altogether to complete.) The point is that before an event like laying the foundation can be completed, *all* prior activities (running utilities, leveling ground, and so forth) must be completed. Fourth, compute the critical path by adding up the times for all possible sequences of events. This will show you where to direct resources to speed the project's completion (for instance, you may need to put more workers on overtime). Computerized programs are usually used to create PERT networks for very complex projects.

PURCHASING

Most firms must purchase some or all of the materials required to create their firm's final products or services. All firms therefore do purchasing. Purchasing departments buy all the materials and parts the firm needs to conduct its business. These materials and parts include the raw materials that go into the firm's products, as well as machinery, tools, purchased components, and even paper clips and computer paper.

Purchasing is a more important function than many managers realize. Some experts estimate that 60 percent of a manufacturer's sales dollars are paid to suppliers for purchased materials.[15] Furthermore, manufacturers who are striving to maintain world-class levels of quality quickly learn that the quality of their finished products can be no better than the quality of the subassemblies that were used to make them. This point was illustrated a few years ago when Saturn had to recall tens of thousands of cars because of faulty alternators. Purchasing departments can therefore impact a firm's cost-effectiveness, as well as its quality reputation.

Purchasing managers engage in several activities.[16] They maintain a data base of available suppliers to facilitate supplies and materials purchases. They are also generally responsible for selecting suppliers and negotiating supply contracts with them.

Purchasing managers also try to minimize the costs of materials and supplies, but it would be an oversimplification to say that this is their only (or even main) concern. For many firms high quality or reliable, on-time deliveries outweigh costs. The purchasing manager working in these industries might well choose a somewhat more expensive (but much more reliable) supplier.

Today, in fact, many firms work closely with suppliers to foster better quality parts. ny firms, such as Ford, send out engineers to help their suppliers boost their qual- management systems.

INVENTORY MANAGEMENT

HE ROLE OF INVENTORY MANAGEMENT

irms keep inventories of five types of items.[17] *Raw materials and purchased parts* are tems obtained from outside suppliers and used in the production of the firm's finished products. *Components* are subassemblies that are awaiting final assembly. *Work*

19.8
...ding a House
...ed circles show the
...me-consuming path.

in process refers to all materials or components on the production floor in various stages of production. *Finished goods* are final products waiting to be purchased or about to be sent to customers. Finally, *supplies* are all items the firm needs but that are not part of the finished product, such as paper clips, duplicating machine toners, and tools.

Inventory management may be defined as the process of ensuring that the firm has adequate inventories of all parts and supplies needed, within the constraint of minimizing total inventory costs. In practice, the inventory manager must address four specific sets of costs. **Ordering costs** are the costs involved with placing the order or setting up machines for the production run. For purchased items, ordering costs might include clerical order-processing costs and the cost of inspecting goods when they arrive. Similarly, set-up costs are usually incurred when manufacturing a product, and might include the labor involved with setting up the machine and the cost of preparing the paperwork for scheduling and controlling the production run.

Ordering costs are usually fixed, meaning that they are independent of the size of the order. On the other hand, acquisition costs are not fixed. **Acquisition costs** are the total costs of all units bought to fill an order. Acquisition costs do vary with the size of the order. For example, ordering required parts in larger quantities may reduce each unit's cost due to quantity discounts. This will in turn lower the total acquisition costs of the order. On the other hand, ordering smaller quantities may raise the unit cost.

Inventory managers focus on two other inventory costs. **Inventory-holding** or **inventory-carrying** costs refer to all of the costs associated with carrying parts or materials in inventory. The biggest specific cost here is usually the firm's cost of capital, which in this case is the value of a unit of the inventory times the length of time it is held times the interest rate at which the firm borrows money.[18] Finally, **stockout costs** refer to the costs associated with running out of raw materials or finished-goods inventory. For example, if a company cannot fill a customer's order, it might lose both the customer and any profits or future sales the customer may have delivered.

Inventory managers want to avoid three basic problems. The first is *over investment* in inventories, which ties up money, crowds available space, and hikes losses due to product deterioration and obsolescence. At the other extreme, inventory managers want to avoid *underinvestment*, which makes the firm unable to fill production orders and discourages customers. The third problem is *unbalanced inventory,* which results when some items are understocked while others are overstocked.

BASIC INVENTORY MANAGEMENT SYSTEMS

Many quantitative and nonquantitative systems are available for managing inventory. Two of the most popular systems are the ABC and EOQ systems.

ABC INVENTORY MANAGEMENT The basic idea of an **ABC inventory management** system is to divide the inventory into three value categories (A, B, and C). Most firms find that a small proportion (25 or 30 percent) of the parts in their inventory account for a large proportion (70 or 80 percent) of their annual dollar volume of inventory usage. A part's annual dollar volume is computed by multiplying its cost per part by the number of parts used in a year. When using the ABC system, the manager divides the inventory into three dollar-volume categories—A, B, and C—with the A parts the most active. The inventory manager then concentrates most of his or her checking and surveillance on the A parts. For example, the A parts are ordered most often so that their total in inventory is minimized and so that they are not in the inventory bins too long.

At the other extreme, the inventory manager might find that perhaps 50 percent of the parts in inventory account for perhaps only 15 percent of annual dollar volume.

INVENTORY MANAGEMENT
The process of ensuring that the firm has adequate inventories of all parts and supplies needed, within the constraint of minimizing total inventory costs.

ORDERING COSTS
The costs involved with placing the order or setting up machines for the production run.

ACQUISITION COSTS
The total costs of all units bought to fill an order.

INVENTORY-HOLDING OR INVENTORY-CARRYING COSTS
Refer to all of the costs associated with carrying parts or materials in inventory.

STOCKOUT COSTS
Refers to the costs associated with running out of raw materials or finished-goods inventory.

ABC INVENTORY MANAGEMENT
An inventory system that divides the inventory into three value categories (A, B, C).

ECONOMIC ORDER QUANTITY (EOQ)

An inventory management system used to determine the most economic quantity to order in order to minimize total inventory costs.

Why spend as much time closely monitoring all those parts when in total they account for only 15 percent of the firm's annual dollar volume of inventory usage? The idea, instead, is to focus on the high annual dollar volume A inventory items, while focusing to a lesser extent on the B items and even less on the C items.

THE ECONOMIC ORDER QUANTITY INVENTORY MANAGEMENT SYSTEM   The idea behind the **economic order quantity** (EOQ) system or model is to determine the most economic quantity to order, in other words the quantity that will minimize total inventory costs. Developed in the early 1900s, EOQ is the best-known and probably oldest inventory system. Figure 19.9 illustrates the relationships involved. As shown, the two major costs, *inventory carrying costs* and *ordering costs*, vary inversely with each other. For example, ordering in large quantities usually allows the firm to do so more economically, but means higher storage costs (because the firm would have, on average, more inventory in stock).

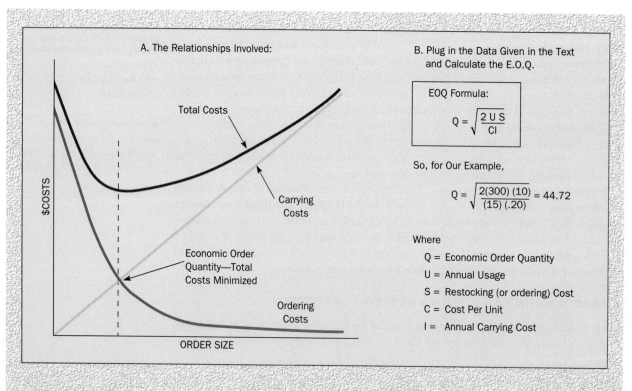

FIGURE 19.9

The Economic Order Quantity Model

As in this example, when order size goes up, ordering costs per order go down, but carrying costs go up because more items are left longer in inventory. The Economic Order Quantity (E.O.Q.) is that order size at which total costs are minimized.

NOTE: As the order size goes up, costs per order go down —due to reduced ordering costs and other factors. But as order size goes up, the inventory manager will order less often and carry more inventory, which means that carrying costs will go up.

In its simplest form the economic order quantity is

$$Q = \sqrt{2US/CI}$$

where Q is the economic order quantity (the most economical quantity to order), U is the annual usage of that item, S is the restocking or ordering costs, C is the cost per unit, and I is the annual carrying costs.

This EOQ equation is widely used, but it is based on some simplified assumptions. For example, it assumes that the same number of units are taken from inventory periodically, such as ten units per day. It also assumes that the supplier does not offer quantity discounts for ordering in larger batches. More sophisticated EOQ versions are available for handling these and other complications.[19]

CONTROLLING FOR QUALITY AND PRODUCTIVITY

QUALITY DEFINED

Quality may be defined as the totality of features and characteristics of a product or service that bears on its ability to satisfy given needs. To put this another way, "quality measures how well a product or service meets customer needs.[20] This definition highlights several important characteristics of quality. First, the customer's needs are the basic criteria for assessing something's quality: thus an airplane seat in coach can be as high quality as one in first class, in terms of the coach passenger's expectations and the competitor's services. Second, high quality does not necessarily mean high price. Again, the basic consideration should be the extent to which the product or services meets the customer's expectations.

QUALITY
The totality of features and characteristics of a product or service that bears on its ability to satisfy given needs.

TOTAL QUALITY MANAGEMENT

Quality control in many firms today means a total, companywide effort. This is exemplified by the Baldrige Award for quality. The firm's total quality commitment (not just the extent to which defects are caught by inspectors at the end of the line) is what is important. The Baldrige National Quality Award raters therefore assign points for a range of company quality activities, including *senior executive leadership,* quality *values, competitive comparisons* and benchmarks, *employee involvement, quality education* and training, design and *introduction of quality products* and services, *supplier quality* results, and *determining customer requirements* and expectations.[21] Quality standards are increasingly international. For example, doing business in Europe often means that a firm must show that it complies with **ISO 9000,** the quality standards of the European Community (EC). If required to do so by a customer, the vendor would have to prove that its quality manuals, procedures, and job instructions all comply with the ISO 9000 standards.

ISO 9000
The quality standards of the European Community (EC); establish standards for quality manuals, procedures, and job instructions.

Several things characterize quality control at total quality organizations like Toyota Motor Manufacturing in Lexington, Kentucky (which produces the Camry). The *assemblers themselves* complete a 100 percent inspection of all the items they produce, and those responsible for making bad items are also responsible for reworking them. Workers also have *line-stop authority;* this means they may stop the production line (usually by pushing a button or pulling an overhead cord) when a defect is found that requires time to repair. In fact, a single employee might cause the whole plant to shut down for a serious quality problem. Under such circumstances, an observer might see

WILSON SPORTING GOODS COMPANY

At Wilson Sporting Goods Company's Humboldt, Tennessee, plant, total quality control is essential. The facility produces almost 100 million golf balls a year, and it considers them the world's best.

One of the plant's shining success stories is its reduction of manufacturing costs. With employees participating and through the use of Wilson's new Demos Control Chart System (which integrates plant quality data), waste was cut by 67 percent and quality cost savings reached almost $10 million over a seven-year period. Under Demos, employees log and compare quality data against projections for various operations. Areas where improvements are needed are identified. Standards are continually upgraded, and teams formulate ways to achieve them.

Plant manager Al Scott believes in breaking down barriers between management and line workers and emphasizing a team approach. These concepts are primarily responsible for the plant moving from one of Wilson's worst to near first in productivity and efficiency. Since concentrating golf ball manufacturing at Humbolt, market share has shot from 2 to 17 percent. Total inventory dropped by two-thirds while production has shot up by a factor of eight. Factory productivity is up 121 percent.

Scott admits the plant's transformation exceeded all his expectations. But he'll continue to seek more and better methods of operation. He has to; poor quality at the Humboldt plant might mean the product doesn't perform.

SOURCE: John H. Sheridan, "Wilson Sporting Goods," *Industry Week,* October 19, 1992, 59–61.

---

assembly employees from throughout the plant walking toward the source of the line stop to provide assistance. The *Wilson* vignette shows how one manufacturer applies some of these ideas. (For more on total quality, review pages 490–492.)

QUALITY CONTROL METHODS

ACCEPTANCE SAMPLING
When only a portion of the produced items are inspected, perhaps only 2 percent or 5 percent of the items.

QUALITY CONTROL CHARTS
Used to control product quality, quality control charts identify the range within which some measurable characteristic of the product is to remain. The chosen characteristic is then inspected and measured.

Various quality control tools and techniques are used to monitor and control product quality. First, most firms have a formal *inspection procedure,* in which inspectors test and measure the merchandise against the quality standards. In some manufacturing processes (such as the production of heart pacemakers), a 100 percent inspection is typical, and every unit is inspected. More often *acceptance sampling* is used. With **acceptance sampling,** only a portion of the items are inspected, perhaps only 2 or 5 percent.

Many firms also use **quality control charts** like the one in Figure 19.10 to control product quality. Quality control charts come in many types, but the basic idea is always the same. First, upper and lower control limits are drawn on the chart to identify the range within which some measurable characteristic of the product is to remain. Then the chosen characteristic, such as its length or weight, is inspected and measured. (Thus, Kellogg's might want to make sure each box of corn flakes contains no more

Although inspectors make a last check on golf balls produced at Wilson Sporting Goods' Humboldt plant before they are shipped, quality control is built into the production process from the beginning.

than 20 ounces and no less than 19.5 ounces.) If the measures begin to move toward the upper or lower control limits, then quality may be going out of control, and the reason for the trend must be ascertained.

When employees themselves monitor quality problems, they typically use several tools. Some of these are summarized in Figure 19.11.[22] For example, a *scatter diagram* is a graph that shows the magnitude of one trait (such as the number of defects) versus a second trait (such as time). A *cause and effect* (or *fishbone*) diagram outlines the

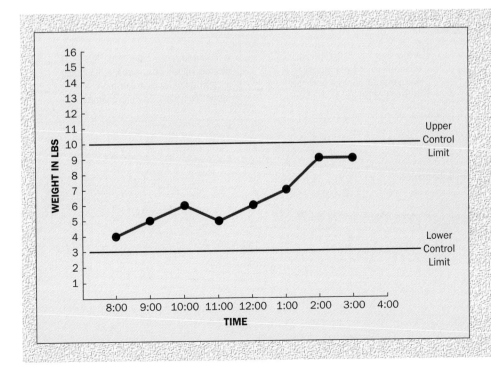

FIGURE 19.10

Example of Quality Control Chart

The idea behind any quality control chart is to track quality trends to ensure they don't go out of control.

These tools do not substitute for judgment and process knowledge. They help deal with complexity and turn raw data into information that can be used to take action.

Process Flow Chart

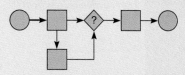

A picture which describes the main steps, branches and eventual outputs of a process.

Pareto Analysis

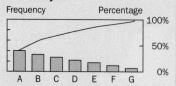

A coordinated approach for identifying, ranking, and working to permanently eliminate defects. Focuses on important error sources. 80/20 rule: 80 percent of problems are due to 20 percent of causes. (A, B, etc., are error sources).

Run Chart

A time sequence chart showing plotted values of a characteristic.

Data Collection

Always have an agreed upon and clear reason for any data you collect. Prepare in advance your strategy for both collecting and analyzing the data. Questions that might be asked of data collection: Why? What? Where? How much? When? How? Who? How long?

Histogram

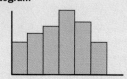

A distribution showing the frequency of occurrences between the high and low range of data.

Scatter Diagram

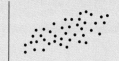

Also known as a correlation chart. A graph of the value of one characteristic versus another characteristic.

Checksheet

An organized method for recording data.

Causes and Effect Diagram

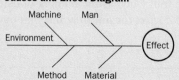

A tool that uses a graphical description of the process elements to analyze potential sources of process variation.

Control Charts

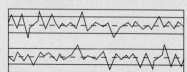

A time sequence chart showing plotted values of a statistic, including a central line and one or more statistically derived control limits.

FIGURE 19.11

Tools Commonly Used for Problem Solving and Continuous Improvement

A selection of tools employee teams can use to monitor and analyze quality.

SOURCE: Richard Chase and Nicholas Aquilero, *Production & Operations Management,* 6th ed. (Homewood, IL: Irwin, 1992), 197.

four main categories of problems—machine, man (personnel), method, and material—and helps to analyze the problem and devise solutions.

DESIGN FOR MANUFACTURABILITY

Many firms today rely on a process called **design for manufacturability.** This may be defined as designing products with ease of manufacturing in mind. The aims of designing for manufacturability are to develop a product that can

- Have the desired level of quality and reliability.
- Be designed in the least time with the least development cost.
- Make the quickest and smoothest transition into production.
- Be assembled and tested with the minimum cost in the minimum amount of time.
- Satisfy customer's needs and compete well in the marketplace.[23]

One reason why designing for manufacturability is so important is because, as one expert points out, "by the time a product has been designed, only about 8 percent of the total product budget has been spent. But by that point, the design has determined 80 percent of the cost of the product!"[24] For example, Hewlett-Packard's Laser Jet III printer has dozens of parts more than does the IBM laser printer. Because IBM's printers have fewer points where assembly errors can take place, they can be manufactured more quickly, less expensively, and with fewer initial defects. In summary, as one expert said,

> "The *design* determines the manufacturability. It is not determined by the factory, no matter how sophisticated it may be. In fact, the more advanced the factory is, the *more* it depends on good designs. Automation places many constraints on the design, which design for manufacturing accounts for."[25]

Designing for manufacturability often means designing products in multidisciplinary teams with representatives from sales, product design, and manufacturing, for instance. This team approach is also called *simultaneous design* or **concurrent engineering.** It helps to ensure that all the departments involved in the product's success make contributions to its design.

WORLD-CLASS MANUFACTURING AND THE RESPONSIVE ORGANIZATION

THE WORLD-CLASS MANUFACTURER

Today, no firm—even one in the heartland of America—can assume it will be immune from global competitors.[26] Virtually every firm today finds its industry globalized, which means that competitors face not only local firms but foreign firms as well. This globalization has intensified competition as firms around the world strive to improve quality, lead time, customer service, and costs in the hope of gaining a stronger competitive advantage.

World-class companies are those that can compete based on quality and productivity in an intensely competitive global environment. Firms such as Coca-Cola, Sony, Motorola, to name a few, set the performance standards for their industries and are able to respond swiftly and effectively to changing conditions. As two experts put it,

DESIGN FOR MANUFACTURABILITY
Designing products with ease of manufacturing in mind.

CONCURRENT ENGINEERING
Designing products in multidisciplinary teams with representatives from sales, product design, and manufacturing, for instance.

WORLD-CLASS COMPANIES
Organizations that can compete based on quality and productivity in an intensely competitive global environment.

WORLD-CLASS MANUFACTURERS
Organizations that use modern production techniques and management systems to boost manufacturing productivity, quality, and flexibility.

JUST-IN-TIME (JIT) SYSTEM
Refers to the production control methods used to attain minimum inventories by ensuring delivery of materials and assemblies just-in-time, in other words, just when they are to be used. Also refers to a philosophy of manufacturing that aims to optimize production processes by continuously reducing waste.

"being world-class in manufacturing means that the company can compete successfully and make a profit in an environment of international competition, not only now, but also in the future."[27]

World-class manufacturers use modern production techniques and management systems to boost manufacturing productivity, quality, and flexibility. These production techniques and management systems include *total quality management* (already described) and *just-in-time manufacturing, computer-aided design and manufacturing, automation and robotics, flexible manufacturing systems,* and *computer-integrated manufacturing.* These and other components of world-class manufacturing are summarized in Figure 19.12 and discussed next.

JUST-IN-TIME SYSTEMS (JIT)

The **just-in-time (JIT)** concept has two related meanings. In the narrowest sense, JIT refers to the production control methods used to attain minimum inventories by ensuring delivery of materials and assemblies "just in time," in other words, just when they are to be used. But JIT also refers to a philosophy of manufacturing that aims to

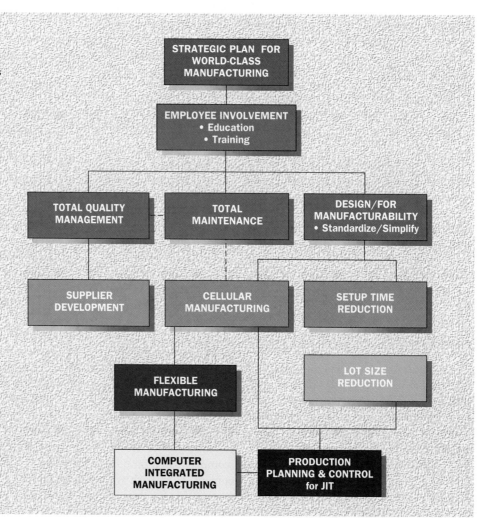

FIGURE 19.12

Components of World-class Manufacturing

Shown here are components of world-class manufacturing and how they interact. A basic aim is to reduce the lot sizes needed for economic production, while reducing set up time, so that the firm gains the advantages of mass production costs, but small-lot-size flexibility.

SOURCE: Adapted from Harold Stradel and Paul Desruelle, Manufacturing in the 90s (New York: Van Nostrand Reinhold, 1992), 11.

optimize production processes by continuously reducing waste. One expert explains the benefits of JIT this way:

> JIT streamlines production, based on demand-driven, just-in-time arrival of components at each assembly's stage. JIT strives to simplify manufacturing and reduce material burden by operating with minimum lot sizes, no queues, and minimum inventory levels . . . JIT means producing each day only that day's demand, so material "flows" through production. [But] JIT also can serve as a focal point for other approaches to world-class manufacturing . . . JIT demands zero defects and other total quality management efforts to eliminate waste. It calls for individual responsibility and empowerment. The ideal of continuous improvements—making products ever better, cheaper and faster—is likewise the mission of JIT.[28]

The idea of reducing seven main wastes lies at the heart of JIT. As summarized in Figure 19.13,[29] they include waste of *overproduction,* waste of *waiting, waste of transportation,* waste of *processing,* waste of *stock,* waste of *motion,* and waste of making *defective products.* As you can see from this comprehensive list of wastes, JIT is a thorough management approach. It is sometimes called **lean manufacturing** or **value-added manufacturing** (meaning that any manufacturing process that does not add value to the product for the customer is wasteful.)[30]

As a management philosophy, JIT consists of eight basic elements, starting with focused factory networks:[31]

LEAN MANUFACTURING OR VALUE-ADDED MANUFACTURING The idea that any manufacturing process that does not add value to the product for the customer is wasteful.

---

1. *Waste of overproduction.* Eliminate by reducing setup times, synchronizing quantities and timing between processes, compacting layout, visibility, and so forth. Make only what is needed now.

2. *Waste of waiting.* Eliminate through synchronizing work flow as much as possible, and balance uneven loads by flexible workers and equipment.

3. *Waste of transportation.* Establish layouts and locations to make transport and handling unnecessary if possible. Then rationalize transport and material handling that cannot be eliminated.

4. *Waste of processing itself.* First question why this part or product should be made at all, then why each process is necessary. Extend thinking beyond economy of scale or speed.

5. *Waste of stocks.* Reduce by shortening setup times and reducing lead times, by synchronizing work flows and improving work skills, and even by smoothing fluctuations in demand for the product. Reducing all the other wastes reduces the waste of stocks.

6. *Waste of motion.* Study motion for economy and consistency. Economy improves productivity, and consistency improves quality. First improve the motions, then mechanize or automate. Otherwise there is danger of automating waste.

7. *Waste of making defective products.* Develop the production process to prevent defects from being made so as to eliminate inspection. At each process, accept no defects and make no defects. Make processes failsafe to do this. From a quality process comes a quality product—automatically.

FIGURE 19.13

The Seven Wastes

Just-in-time is aimed at eliminating the seven wastes: overproduction, waiting, transportation, processing, stocks, motion, and defective products.

SOURCE: R. Hall, *Attaining Manufacturing Excellence* (Homewood, IL: Dow-Jones-Irwin, 1987), 26. As reprinted in Everett Adam, Jr., and Ronald Ebert, *Production & Operations Management,* 5th ed. (Englewood Cliffs, NJ: Prentice-Hall, 1992), 259, 5th Edition.

FOCUSED FACTORY NETWORKS   The Japanese business community (where JIT was invented) tends to build small specialized plants rather than large ones. This is because it is easier to manage smaller plants and because it is easier to organize the work flow and to staff plants that are highly specialized. Few Japanese plants have as many as 1,000 employees; most have fewer than 30 employees, and the rest have between 30 and 1,000 employees.[32]

GROUP TECHNOLOGY   Inside their plants, the Japanese tend to lay out the facilities around the cell or group technology discussed earlier. The process production departments that form the core of many U.S. firms—such as those specializing in grinding, drilling, pressing, and so forth—are not used in JIT firms. Instead, cells are formed in which the processes required to complete a major part of the product are grouped together. One employee may then perform all the activities needed. The worker will have to be more highly trained and flexible, but the moving and waiting time between processes is reduced.

***JIDOKA*—QUALITY AT THE SOURCE**   JIT-based firms function on the idea that every worker is personally responsible for the quality of the item he or she produces. Thus, quality goes in at the source, when the product is actually made. These firms do not rely on end-of-the-line quality inspectors to catch defects. **Jidoka** means "stop everything when something goes wrong." In such firms, defects do not just travel down the line. If a defect is found, the entire line is stopped (usually by the employees, who have push-buttons or cords to signal the need for a line stop).

JUST-IN-TIME PLANNING AND CONTROL   Just-in-time planning and control systems aim to reduce the waiting time for all parts and materials to zero. The firm thus hopes to minimize inventory investment and shorten production lead times. That way, finished products can be produced relatively quickly, instead of being delayed for weeks or months waiting for components before finally being assembled.

***KANBAN* PRODUCTION CONTROL SYSTEM**   Just-in-time production is a *pull* system. This means that whenever an item—such as a car—is sold, it pulls the need for another item—such as an engine—which in turn pulls the need for engine components, and so forth. At Toyota, the control system is called **Kanban,** from the Japanese word "card." When a part is used, a *Kanban* card goes back to the parts depot. Containers for the parts travel with the *Kanbans* (cards) requisitioning the parts and are returned with the parts.

UNIFORM PLANT LOADING   Just-in-time systems depend on scheduling production so that it is as predictable and smooth as possible. Many Japanese plants therefore use **uniform plant loading.** This usually means that monthly production plans are established for the plant and are then adhered to. For example, the monthly production quantities of each model of the items to be produced are set and then daily quantities are computed. From this data the plant manager determines the cycle time, or the amount of time that elapses between identical units coming off the production line. The plant management uses this information to compute the hourly amounts of parts and the materials and labor required.

MINIMIZE SETUP TIMES   Uniform plant loading allows concentrating on small production lots. However, it can also require that in one day a plant is going to produce several models—say sedans, coupes, and convertibles—requiring additional machinery setups and changes. Many JIT-based Japanese firms therefore use industrial engineering and behavioral science methods to dramatically reduce machinery changeover times. For example, a well-trained team might be able to change the tooling on an 800 ton press in ten minutes in Japan, a job that is estimated to take six hours in the United States and four hours in West Germany.[33]

JIDOKA
A Japanese term that means "stop everything when something goes wrong."

KANBAN
From the Japanese word "card," this production control system operates on the theory that whenever an item is used, it pulls the need for another item, which in turn pulls the need for another, and so on.

UNIFORM PLANT LOADING
Monthly production plans are established for the plant and are then adhered to in order to ensure a scheduling of production that is as predictable and smooth as possible.

Dana Corporation's lessons in just-in-time manufacturing were applied at several of its plants, including the award-winning Minneapolis Valve plant and its Spicer Systems assembly facility in Lugoff, South Carolina.

RESPECT FOR INDIVIDUALS The productivity and quality improvements obtained by JIT firms would be impossible without employee commitment. This commitment depends in part on the "respect for people" philosophy instilled in most of these firms. The *Dana* vignette on page 570 shows how important this can be.

COMPUTER-AIDED DESIGN AND COMPUTER-AIDED MANUFACTURING

Computer-aided design (CAD) is a computerized process for designing new products or modifying existing ones. Designers are able to sketch and modify their designs on a computer screen, usually with an electronic pencil. In addition to facilitating the actual design of the item, CAD makes it easier to modify existing products and lets designers expose their designs to simulated stress factors such as wind resistance.

Computer-assisted manufacturing (CAM) refers to using computers to plan and program production equipment to produce manufactured items. For instance, CAM allows for computerized control of tool movement and cutting speed so that a machine can carry out several sequential operations on a part, all under the guidance of the computer-assisted system.

For many applications, CAD and CAM are used together. For example, with the design already in place within the CAD system, the computer "knows" a component's specifications and can thereby "tell" the production equipment how to cut and machine it.

AUTOMATION AND ROBOTICS

Automation may be defined as the automatic operation of a system, process, or machine. A *robot* is a programmable machine capable of manipulating items and designed to move materials, parts, tools, or specialized devices through programmed motions.

The photos on the next two pages suggest the range of applications for automated machinery today.[34] The first photograph shows automated quality control testing at Hewlett-Packard in Grenoble, France. The next photograph shows automated process control at Warren Papers in Michigan, where a worker monitors an automated process

COMPUTER-AIDED DESIGN (CAD)
A computerized process for designing new products or modifying existing ones.

COMPUTER-ASSISTED MANUFACTURING (CAM)
Refers to using computers to plan and program production equipment to produce manufactured items.

AUTOMATION
The automatic operation of a system, process, or machine.

Automated machinery handles many tasks today, from quality control testing, shown here at Hewlett-Packard's Grenoble microcomputer plant to running complete production systems, as at Warren Paper's Muskegon paper-making facility.

FLEXIBLE MANUFACTURING SYSTEM (FMS)
A system in which groups of production machines are connected by automated materials-handling and transfer machines, and integrated into a computer system.

control system, which controls a system that produces paper from wet pulp to the finished product.

FLEXIBLE MANUFACTURING SYSTEMS

A **flexible manufacturing system (FMS)** is "a system in which groups of production machines are connected by automated materials-handling and transfer machines, and integrated into a computer system."[35] Computers route parts and components to the appropriate machines, select and load the proper machine tools, and then direct the machines to perform the required operations. The items are then moved from machine to machine by computerized automated guided vehicles (AGV). These basically form a computer-guided cart system that picks up and delivers tools and parts to and from multiple-work stations.

Several elements work together to give a flexible manufacturing system its flexibility: machine set-up times are reduced by computerized instructions; each machine can be quickly retooled to produce a variety of parts; reduced set-up times cut required manufacturing lead times; automated guide vehicles move parts with relative speed and efficiency; and the firm can respond more quickly to new competing products or changing consumer tastes by using CAD to redesign products and CAM to reprogram its machines. In fact, says Toshiba President Fumio Sato, the aim of flexible manufacturing at his firm "is to push Toshiba's two dozen factories to adapt faster to markets . . ."[36] customers wanted choices. They wanted a washing machine or TV set that was precisely right for their needs. We needed variety, not mass production."[37]

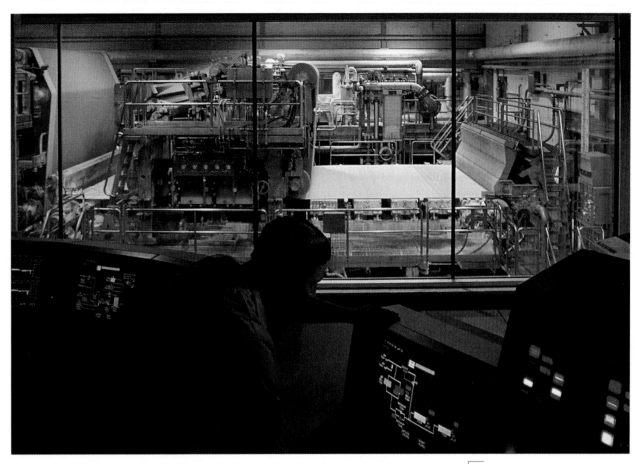

Automated process control at Warren Papers in Michigan.

Flexible manufacturing has allowed Toshiba and other firms to merge the advantages of customized, one-at-a-time production with mass production's efficiency. At the Toshiba plant in Ome, Japan, for instance, workers efficiently assemble nine word processor models on one line and 20 laptop computer models on another.[38] Such flexibility lets Toshiba be very responsive to customer requirements.

The National Bicycle Industrial Company, a subsidiary of electronics giant Matsushita, is another example.[39] With only 20 employees National Bicycle's factory can produce more than a million variations of 18 bicycle models, each custom-made to a customer's unique requirements. At the retail store, the customer sits on a special frame, and the shopkeeper measures him or her and faxes the person's measurements to the factory. There the information goes into a computer-assisted design system, which creates a computerized blueprint for the custom-made bike. A bar code is printed for the bike and each part, and from there on every part that goes into the bicycle moves from work station to work station on computerized automated-guided vehicles. As this example shows, the goal of flexible manufacturing is not just to instill adaptable production processes, but to maximize the responsiveness of the whole company, including its sales effort, to customer demand.

Firms like General Motors are taking further advantage of their increasingly flexible facilities by running them on round-the-clock schedules. For example, instead of closing GM's unprofitable Lordstown, Ohio, assembly plant, managers there boosted output from 260,000 to 400,000 cars a year by running the plant all night; the goal was recently raised to 450,000 cars a year.[40]

DANA CORPORATION

When Dana Corporation division managers traveled to Japan to see just-in-time (JIT) manufacturing processes in action, they learned much that was useful. Some of the Japanese businesspeople were forthright enough to tell them exactly why they didn't think most American workers would ever excel at it. Americans, they were told, were terrific innovators but made poor team members. JIT methods ran contrary to the typical individualistic company culture in the United States, and changing culture is difficult.

Upon their return, the managers indeed discovered that implementing the various components of JIT was easier said than done. Management leadership and employee education, eliminating waste, cellularization, *Kanban* pull systems, and quick changeover to processes all sound good and work well. But, as Dana managers discovered, they must also work together, and coordinating the processes isn't an overnight undertaking. Dana managers first had to win the hearts and minds of both supervisors and employees by getting the staff just as committed to JIT processes as the managers were themselves.

Dana began at its Minneapolis valve plant. A vision of what the manufacturing system could be was explained to every employee. The reasons behind the changes were spelled out. Plant leaders made their commitment clear. Everyone would participate in continuing education and would actively support his or her respective team. Contrary to (and perhaps because of) their Japanese hosts' warnings, Dana managers made work teams the driving force of the entire JIT implementation.

The transformation was neither painless nor easy. But despite earlier predictions to the contrary, Dana's Minneapolis valve plant was awarded the 1991 Shingo Prize for excellence in manufacturing, thanks in large part to its successful implementation of JIT.

SOURCE: Hank Rogers, "What Dana Learned from Japan," *Industry Week,* July 15, 1991, 36–40.

COMPUTER-INTEGRATED MANUFACTURING (CIM)

COMPUTER-INTEGRATED MANUFACTURING (CIM)
The total integration of all production-related business activities through the use of computer systems.

The aim of many firms is to integrate components including automation, JIT, flexible manufacturing, and CAD/CAM into one self-regulating production system. **Computer-integrated manufacturing (CIM)** is defined as the total integration of all production-related business activities through the use of computer systems.[41] By combining the strengths of CAD/CAM, JIT, automation, total quality control, and flexible manufacturing, the basic aim of CIM is to give the firm a manufacturing competitive advantage based on speed, flexibility, quality, and low cost. The components of CIM are summarized in Figure 19.14 on pages 572–73.[42] For example, the objectives for computer-aided design include improving design productivity and reducing design lead-time. The objectives of automated-guided vehicles include reducing material handling costs and improving inventory control. CIM integrates these world-class manufacturing system components, thus combining their benefits.

CIM's advantages usually exceed the sum of its component parts. In other words, CIM can yield synergistic results. For example, computer-aided design facilitates computer-aided manufacturing by feeding design changes directly to the machinery tools. Automated-guided vehicles can facilitate just-in-time systems by eliminating human variabilities from the system.[43]

Eventually, some firms link CIM with their other systems. For example, Caterpillar, Inc., is working on a computer system that will link its plants, suppliers, and dealers with a worldwide electronic information network that will help make the firm one of the most efficient producers of earth-moving equipment. As part of its plan, the firm is junking its antiquated production methods in favor of a flexible manufacturing system aimed at cutting Caterpillar's manufacturing costs by 20 percent, which amounts to about $1.5 billion a year.[44]

Why is such an approach important? As one Japanese executive put it, "in the past, manufacturing was characterized by large (production run) quantities, with few varieties. Today's customers are asking for small quantities in very many varieties. CIM adds flexibility to help make those ever shorter production runs economical."[45] As such, CIM can be a cornerstone of organizational responsiveness. The *Allen-Bradley* vignette shows how one firm uses its version of computer-integrated manufacturing.

ALLEN-BRADLEY COMPANY

Product variety at the Allen-Bradley Company is high, but volume is low. The company, which produces printed circuit board assemblies (PCBs), uses what it calls electronic manufacturing strategy, or EMS1, to stay flexible and economical.

With their sophisticated EMS1 system, ten varieties of circuit boards can be on the same continuous conveyor. An overhead loop detours products past unneeded processes, even though the boards can contain a half-million integrated circuits and other electronic components. Allen-Bradley produces more than 110 products and anticipates adding as many as 100 more. Product quality has also been exceptional. "This is not just another computer-integrated-manufacturing (CIM) facility," says Glenn Eggert, vice-president of operations for Allen-Bradley Operations Group. "EMS1 is a solution to a complete business approach."

A number of factors gave rise to EMS1. It was necessary to bring more products to market faster and with fewer defects and to increase manufacturing capacity. The capacity to handle new products, increase customer satisfaction, and attain the lowest total life-cycle cost of the product were also key requirements. Benchmarking visits to firms such as Digital Equipment and Northern Telecom, as well as Japanese plants, made it clear Allen-Bradley was on track with its EMS1 processes. The firm was able to obtain a competitive advantage through the low volume production of a wide variety of circuit boards.

SOURCE: Joseph F. McKenna, "Allen-Bradley," *Industry Week,* October 19, 1992, 41–42.

COMPONENTS	SUMMARY	STAND-ALONE OBJECTIVES
Computer aided design (CAD)	The application of computer technology to automate the design process including geometric modeling, stress and strain analysis, drafting, storing specifications, and allowing simulation of a mechanism's parts.	• Improve design productivity • Reduce design lead-time • Better design quality • Improve access to and storage of product designs • Increase capability to design a variety of products
Flexible manufacturing (FMS)	Flexible manufacturing systems can react quickly to product and design changes. An FMS includes a number of work stations, an automated material handling system, and system supervisory computer control. Central computer control provides real-time routing, load balancing and production scheduling logic. An FMS can incorporate AGV, AS/RS and robotics to decrease time to change tools and fixtures, load and unload machines, and move materials to and from manufacturing cells.	• Increase capability to produce a variety of products while at the same time reducing delivery lead times and inventory requirements • Enable manufacturing to build volume across products to achieve economies of scope • Enable firms to produce specialized designs for more finely tuned market segments • More rapid response to frequent changes in product design, production requirements and market demands • More consistent product quality
Cellular manufacturing	Cellular manufacturing is the physical layout of the factory into product oriented work centers. Each center or cell includes the machines and tools necessary to efficiently produce a family of parts.	• Reduce material handling • Simplify tool control • Reduce expediting and in-process inventory • Improve operator expertise

Group technology (GT)	Group technology is a process of coding and classifying families of parts according to similarities in their geometric characteristics, material or manufacturing requirements.	• Enable scheduling within families of parts to:
		  • Reduce set-up time
		  • Reduce lead time
		  • Improve productivity
		  • Simplify process planning (reduce complexity of sequencing operations, simplify routings, eliminate unnecessary routings)

Computer numerical control (CNC)	The application of computer technology to numerical controlled (NC) machines by utilizing computer hardware and software to control machine operations.	• Reduce direct labor costs • Improve product quality/precision • Reduce time to load NC software

FIGURE 19.14
━━━━

World-Class Manufacturing Components Integrated by CIM

Computer integrated manufacturing uses computers to combine the components listed in this figure. By doing so, the combined effect is greater than the sum of the stand-alone objectives of the individual components. CIM ties together the elements that make up world-class manufacturing.

SOURCE: Adapted from Mark Vonderemble and Gregory White, *Operations Management* (St. Paul, MN: West, 1988), 44–45.

COMPONENTS	SUMMARY	STAND-ALONE OBJECTIVES
Computer aided manufacturing (CAM)	The application of computer and communications technology to enhance manufacturing by linking CNC machines, monitoring the production process, and providing automatic feedback to control operations.	• Improve manufacturing control and reporting • Enhance coordination of material flow between machines • Enhance rerouting capabilities
Computer aided process planning (CAPP)	Computer aided process planning is a decision support system which generates instructions for the production of parts. Based upon information concerning machining requirements and machine capabilities, CAPP plans machining operations and determines routings between machines.	• Enable manufacturing to cope with the complexity of process planning in a multiple product environment • Reduce the cost and effort required to create and revise process plans
Automated materials handling Automated guided vehicles (AGV) Automated storage and retrieval (AS/RS)	Material handling systems may include AGV and AS/RS components. An AGV is a computerized cart system capable of delivering parts and tools to and from multiple work centers. AGV may be used with an AS/RS which is a computerized system for storing and retrieving parts and tools.	• Reduce material handling costs • Improve inventory control • Reduce land and building costs • Improve safety and control of material movement • Reduce work-in-process inventory on the shop floor
Robotics	An industrial robot is a general-purpose, programmable machine possessing certain human-like capabilities (e.g., grasping, sensing and vision).	• Reduce direct labor costs • Improve quality/precision in repetitive tasks • Avoid risk to humans in hazardous working conditions • Increase throughput
Just-In-Time (JIT)	Just-In-Time is a business strategy for designing manufacturing systems which are more responsive to precisely timed customer delivery requirements. This strategy focuses on reducing lead times, reducing set-up times, and improving product quality.	• Improve customer service • Reduce delivery lead time • Reduce set-up time • Improve product quality • Reduce work-in-process, raw material, and finished goods inventory • Improve factory design (i.e., distance between work centers and factory floor space requirements) • Uncover work flow problems hidden by work-in-process inventory

FIGURE 19.14 (CONTINUED)

SUMMARY

Operations management is the process of managing the resources required to produce an organization's goods and services. The direct production resources of a firm are often called the five P's of operations/production management—people, plants, parts, processes, and planning and control systems. Any production system consists of inputs, a conversion subsystem, and outputs. Inputs are the primary resources used in the direct manufacture of the product or service. The conversion system converts those inputs into useful products or services called outputs. The production system is the heart of the operation. Four production design system decisions include the facility or plant location, the type of production processes that will be used, the layout of the plant or facility, and the layout of the production system itself.

Production planning is the process of deciding what products to produce, and where, when, and how to produce them. Production control is the process of ensuring that the specified production plans or schedules are being met. Several elements make up the production planning and control process: aggregate output planning, master production scheduling, material requirements planning, and shop floor control. The production schedule is often presented on a chart, which shows specifically what operations are to be carried out and when. Network planning and control methods are used to plan and control projects, usually by graphically representing the project steps and the timing and interrelationships between these steps. Purchasing departments buy the materials and parts the firm needs to conduct its business.

Inventory management ensures that the firm has adequate inventories of all parts and supplies needed, within the constraint of minimizing total inventory costs. Many quantitative and nonquantitative systems are available for managing inventory. ABC and EOQ systems are two of the most popular.

Quality reflects how well a product or service meets customer needs. Many firms use a process called design for manufacturability to improve quality. Quality control in many firms today involves a total, companywide effort. A number of quality control techniques are used to monitor and control product quality, including inspection procedures and acceptance sampling.

World-class companies can compete based on quality, productivity, and responsiveness in an intensely competitive global environment. World-class manufacturers use modern production techniques and progressive management systems to boost manufacturing productivity, quality, and flexibility. These production techniques and management systems include total quality management, just-in-time manufacturing, computer-aided design and manufacturing, automation and robotics, flexible manufacturing systems, and computer integrated manufacturing. In the chapter appendix, linear programming is described as a mathematical method used to solve resource allocation problems. Queuing techniques are used to solve waiting line problems.

QUESTIONS

■ FOR REVIEW

1. Describe the five direct production resources on which operations managers focus.

2. What are the four principal questions that must be addressed in production system design?

3. Explain the differences between production layouts, such as product layout, process layout, fixed position layout, and cellular manufacturing.

4. What are the objectives of the design for manufacturability process?

5. List the steps that make up the production planning and control process.

6. Compare and contrast the ABC and economic order quantity (EOQ) inventory management systems.

■ **FOR DISCUSSION**

7. Describe some of the ways operations management has changed over the years. What do you consider the biggest advantages to modern production techniques?

8. Discuss the processes, control methods, and guiding philosophy that makes up just-in-time manufacturing. Why do you think it has been so effective?

9. Do you think computer-assisted manufacturing will eventually make the traditional factory worker obsolete? Why or why not?

■ **FOR ACTION**

10. Arrange to take a tour of a local factory. Which of the methods described in this chapter are in place there?

11. Go to the library and research the production methods of a major U.S. auto manufacturer and a Japanese counterpart. How do they differ, if at all?

12. Identify a world-class company and research its manufacturing techniques. Discuss what makes them outstanding.

■ **FOR FOCUS ON SMALL BUSINESS**

13. Would you consider Aladan a world-class manufacturer as defined in the chapter?

14. Aladan made huge investments in its company's plant and equipment. Discuss the risks and potential payoffs of funneling large sums of money into the manufacturing process when the firm is relatively small, like Aladan.

15. Like many U.S. companies, one of Povlac's goals was to outperform foreign manufacturers. Do you think doing so is easier or harder for a small business like Aladan? Why?

CLOSING SOLUTION

FEDERAL SIGNAL CORPORATION

Ross dispensed with the batch assembly system, replacing it with work cells where workers could oversee product manufacturing from start to finish. The improvements in quality were dramatic. In addition, a new manufacturing-to-order policy lowered Signal's inventory costs from $24 million to $10 million in four years. The company made capital investments in new product designs, like using aluminum in fire engines and producing street sweepers that had dumping capabilities and could travel at freeway speeds. Ross also bargained hard with suppliers on prices. Many Federal factories began working under what has been called vendor partnering, lowering supplier costs as much as 20 percent. Overhead has also been cut, from headquarters to the factory floors. Federal now has higher sales and more labor hours functioning in about 60 percent of the space used before the changes were installed.

■ **QUESTIONS FOR CLOSING SOLUTION**

1. Why do you think Federal Signal's switch to cellular manufacturing resulted in a dramatic improvement in quality?

2. Federal Signal significantly reduced its inventory levels. Based on the concepts described in this chapter, discuss the importance of that move.

3. What else might the company do to improve its operations?

<table>
<tr><td>

KEY TERMS

</td><td>

Operations Management
Input
Conversion System
Output
Intermittent Production
Mass Production
Continuous Production
Facility Layout
Product Layout
Process Layout
Fixed-position Layout
Cellular Manufacturing
Production Planning
Production Control
Aggregate Output Planning
Master Production Schedule
Materials Requirements Plan
Bill (or list) of Materials
Inventory File
Shop Floor Control
Loading and Sequencing
Load Schedule
Detailed Scheduling
Gantt Chart
Network Planning and Control
  Methods
Events
Activities
Critical Path

</td><td>

Inventory Management
Ordering Costs
Acquisition Costs
Inventory-holding or Inventory-
  carrying Costs
Stockout Costs
ABC Inventory Management
Economic Order Quantity (EOQ)
Quality
ISO 9000
Design for Manufacturability
Concurrent Engineering
Acceptance Sampling
Quality Control Charts
World-class Companies
World-class Manufacturers
Just-in-Time (JIT) System
Lean Manufacturing or Value-added
  Manufacturing
Jidoka
Kanban
Uniform Plant Loading
Computer-aided Design (CAD)
Computer-assisted Manufacturing
  (CAM)
Automation
Flexible Manufacturing System (FMS)
Computer-integrated Manufacturing
  (CIM)

</td></tr>
</table>

CASE FOR ANALYSIS

NABISCO BISCUIT CO.

When Nabisco Biscuit Company launched its SnackWell's Devil's Food Cookie Cakes, it anticipated there might be problems. Convincing people that a fat-free chocolate and marshmallow cookie is not only tasty but good for them is a tall order. But it's what Nabisco didn't anticipate that has customers peeved. The company can't manufacture the cookies fast enough. One lady was reportedly angry enough to chase a delivery truck driver all the way back to a distribution center. Resigned officials have given up trying to furnish explanations and simply urged cookie lovers to try one of Nabisco's other offerings. The company can't make the product fast enough, and no one is happy about it.

Skeptics wonder how an operation that produces 600 million pounds of cookies annually can't just turn up the volume. It turns out that there's more to the process than the average snacker might think. "There is no such thing as a simple cookie," says Brian Beglin, senior director of operations services. "But the Devil's Food Cookie Cake is the hardest one we make." Cookies that aren't coated with chocolate on all sides can be run along a conveyor and deposited into a waiting container. The marshmallow cream center of the Snackwell's cookie gets chocolate all over. It sticks to everything, including conveyor belts.

So Snackwell's cookies are produced through the use of a pin-trolley system, a process that has gone largely unaltered for 70 years. Baked cookies are skewered on a little double-pronged fork. They then make a one-mile trip through the bakery getting doused and dolloped with marshmallow and chocolate and a final glazing. Things don't get any easier after that. The fat-free chocolate covering can't be chilled, which would make the cookies congeal, so the cookies must be air dried. Because of these special requirements, the process takes four hours. By comparison, creating a bag of Chips Ahoy! cookies take 30 minutes from start to finish.

Nabisco acquired the necessary custom-made machinery to make Snackwell's from a Sioux City, South Dakota, bakery owned by Interbake Foods, Inc. That also happens to be the only place the equipment is available. Increasing capacity would be neither easy nor cheap. The company has three production lines running overtime and will soon add another. But that will reportedly do it for the machine-building capacity of the Interbake plant. More cookie production after that will cost the company a lot more money.

Using 1920s-era processes to produce Snackwell's didn't result in a lot of finger-pointing at Nabisco. The company has produced cookies that require the use of the pin-trolley system for many years. The problem, if it can be called that, is that no one expected Snackwell's to be so popular. The key to what made the cookie

such a hit may be in the different process that went into making it. By using cocoa instead of chocolate, reducing the fat content wasn't difficult, and the fat-free cookie tastes authentic. Nabisco's big decision is what to do now.

Customers are still clamoring for more product, and it seems inconceivable that they will simply be left standing in line. On the other hand, adding costly capacity could backfire if the fad fades. None of this has escaped competitors. Keebler has launched its own reduced-fat cookie line. Despite racking up over $100 million in sales in just its first year, there are no guarantees about the sometimes fickle sweet tooths of consumers. But no one need shed tears for Nabisco. After all, the company knew that some kind of problem always arises launching a new product.

SOURCES: Kathleen Deveny, "Man Walked on the Moon but Man Can't Make Enough Devil's Food Cookie Cakes," *The Wall Street Journal,* September 28, 1993, I-1, I-2; Julie Liesse, "Sharon Rothstein-Snackwell's," *Advertising Age,* July 5, 1993; Julie Liesse, "Snackwell's Soars at Nabisco," *Advertising Age,* April 5, 1993; and "Cookies Offer Food for Thought—RJR Nabisco," *Financial Times,* August 24, 1993.

■ **QUESTIONS**

1. Is the Snackwell's product shortage indicative of operations management problems, the marketing department's failure to accurately gauge demand for the cookies, or both? Explain your answer.
2. What steps could the company take to improve the situation?
3. Should Nabisco invest the money required to develop a more sophisticated production process? Would more automation come at the expense of product quality?

A CASE IN DIVERSITY

OLDER WORKERS AT CHRYSLER

At the Chrysler Corporation's Jefferson North plant, the shift is 10 hours a day, six days a week. Jeep Grand Cherokees roll off the line as fast as workers can put them together. The defect level is as good as any factory in the world, from Stuttgart to Tokyo and everywhere in between. What's surprising is the workers putting out a product that is selling as fast, and sometimes faster, than they can make it don't look like they used to. Or more accurately, they look exactly like they used to, a lot older.

Not long ago the average assembly line in almost any manufacturing industry was primarily staffed with personnel who were generally 35 years old. But lean years, layoffs, and restructurings put this less-senior group out of work first. Having been burned once, many weren't interested in ever coming back. Those who remain are the wily veterans. They are smarter, more experienced workers, but even they will admit that they've lost a step or two over the years.

"The traditional way of improving productivity has been to speed up the line," says Harley Shaiken, an industrial relations professor at the University of California, Berkeley, "but you can't do that with older workers." Shaiken is quick to add that only a few adjustments are necessary in order for older workers to pro-

duce just as efficiently as their younger counterparts. The numbers bear this out.

About 20 years ago, the plant that Jefferson North replaced put out a quarter-million vehicles annually using a 5,000-person work force. Today, half that many workers produce the same number of cars at Jefferson North, which opened in 1991. It's no secret that Chrysler, and every other automaker, made big investments in technology. Plants are now roomier, and engineers were careful to make the Cherokee design easier to put together than before. But the fact remains that the workers at Jefferson, whose average age is 52, or six years more than the rest of the industry, can produce as efficiently as anyone.

Besides such strain savers as conveyer systems that actually tilt the entire vehicle for easier access and mechanical devices that take care of heavy lifting, older workers receive intensive training. Courses in problem solving and teamwork have made them more agile and flexible where they need to be: at making decisions on the factory floor. With automation eliminating most of the least palatable back-breaking aspects of the job, they can channel those many years of experience into producing high-quality cars as efficiently as possible.

It's expected that younger workers will eventually return to the manufacturing sector. When they do, they will find factories that are a radical departure from the past. For now, workers at Jefferson North are disproving the myth about teaching old dogs new tricks. They also serve as an example of how operations managers must be prepared to make necessary adjustments in a changing work environment.

SOURCE: Doron P. Levin, "The Graying Factory," *The New York Times,* February 20, 1994, Section 3, 1.

■ QUESTIONS

1. Describe the production techniques and management approaches Chrysler has used to boost productivity by accommodating the aging of its manufacturing work force.
2. How has the dawn of high-tech manufacturing changed the role of the production worker? Do you think Chrysler would have been able to maintain its older work force even without the technological advances?
3. What lessons can other companies learn from the Chrysler experience?

ENDNOTES

1. This problem was researched from Gary Slutsker, "We Know Them All," *Forbes,* December 20, 1993, 240–41; Jarlan S. Byrne and Pauline Yuelys, "Federal Signal," *Barron's,* April 27, 1992, 31–32; and Ret Autry, "Companies to Watch: Federal Signal," *Fortune,* December 31, 1990, 98.
2. Richard Chase and Nicholas Aquilano, *Production & Operations Management* (Homewood, IL: Irwin, 1992), 5.
3. Id., 6.
4. Id.
5. Norman Gaither, *Production and Operations Management* (Fort Worth, TX: The Dryden Press, 1992), 20.
6. Id., 22.
7. Chase and Aquilano, *Production & Operations Management,* 375–78.
8. James Evans, David Anderson, Dennis Sweeney, and Thomas Williams, *Applied Production and Operations Management* (St. Paul: West Publishing Company, 1990), 261.
9. Gaither, *Production and Operations Management,* 132–33.
10. Everett Adam, Jr., and Ronald Ebert, *Production & Operations Management* (Englewood Cliffs, NJ: Prentice-Hall, 1992), 254.
11. Id., 254.
12. Gaither, *Production and Operations Management,* 135.
13. Adam and Ebert, *Production and Operations Management,* 374.
14. Gaither, *Production and Operations Management, 869.*
15. Id., 551.
16. Id., 551–53.
17. Evans, et al., *Applied Production,* 500–501.
18. Id., 511.
19. See, for example, Steven Replogle, "The Strategic Use of Smaller Lot Sizes Through a New EOQ Model," *Production and Inventory Management Journal,* Third Quarter, 1988, 41–44; T.C.E. Cheng, "An EOQ Model with Learning Effect on Set-Ups," *Production and Inventory Management Journal,* First Quarter, 1991, 83–84.
20. Evans, et al., *Applied Production,* 39.
21. 1991 Application Guidelines, Malcolm Baldridge National Quality Award (Gaithersburg, MD, U.S. Department of Commerce, National Institute of Standards and Technology, 1991), 5. For a description of three recent Baldridge winners, see "Three Electronics Firms Win 1991 Baldridge Award, *Quality Progress,* November 1991, 39–42.
22. Chase and Aquilano, *Production & Operations Management,* 197.
23. These traits quoted from David Anderson, *Design for Manufacturability* (Lafayette, CA: CIM Press, 1990), 9.
24. Id., 16.
25. Anderson, *Design for Manufacturability,* 15. See also F. Robert Jacobs and Vincent Mabert, *Production Planning, Scheduling, and Inventory Control* (Norcross, GA: Industrial Engineering and Management Press, 1986), 96–100; and Otis Port, Zachary Shiller, Gregory Miles, and Amy Schulman, "Smart Factories, America's Turn," *Business Week,* May 8, 1989, 142–48.

26. Valerie Reitman, "Global Money Trends Rattle Shop Windows in Heartland America," *The Wall Street Journal*, November 26, 1993, A-1.

27. Harold Steudel and Paul Desruelle, *Manufacturing in the 90s* (New York: Van Nostrand Reinhold, 1992), 2.

28. David Mandel, "JIT: Strategic Weapon for Aerospace and Defense?," *Industrial Engineering*, February 1993, 48. Just in time can also be used to improve performances of service organizations. See, for example, W. Calvin Waco, Robert Stonehocker, and Larry Feldman, "Success with JIT and MRP II in a Service Organization," *Production & Inventory Management Journal*, Fourth Quarter, 1991, 15–22.

29. Adam and Ebert, *Production & Operations Management*, 568.

30. Id., 568.

31. These elements based on Kenneth Wantuck, "The Japanese Approach to Productivity" (Southfield, MI: Bendix Corporation, 1983); and Chase and Aquilano, *Production & Operations Management*, 261–72.

32. Chase and Aquilano, *Production & Operations Management*, 261.

33. Id., 270.

34. Gaither, *Production & Operations Management*, Plate 3, Plate 5, Plate 7, page 201.

35. Adapted from ibid., 6–8. See also David Woodruff, "A Dozen Motor Factories—Under One Roof," *Business Week*, November 20, 1989, 93–94.

36. Thomas Stewart, "Brace for Japan's Hot New Strategy," *Fortune*, September 21, 1992, 64.

37. Ibid., 64.

38. Ibid.

39. Susan Moffat, "Japan's New Personalized Production," *Fortune*, October 22, 1990, 132–35.

40. James Treece and Patrick Oster, "General Motors: Open All Night," *Business Week*, June 1, 1992, 82–83.

41. Gaither, *Production & Operations Management*, 866.

42. Mark Vonderem and Gregory White, *Operations Management* (St. Paul: West Publishing, 1988), 44–45. For more information on computer integrated manufacturing, see Michael Baudin, *Manufacturing Systems Analysis* (Englewood Cliffs, NJ: Prentice-Hall, 1990), 2–5.

43. For additional information, see, for example, Alan Luber, "Living in the Real World of Computer Interfaced Manufacturing," *Production & Inventory Management*, September 1991, 10–11; and Jeremy Main, "Computers of the World, Unite!" *Fortune*, September 24, 1990, 115–22. See also John Teresko, "Japan's New Idea," *Industry Week*, September 3, 1990, 62–66.

44. Bryan Bremner, "Can Caterpillar Inch Its Way Back to Heftier Profits?" *Business Week*, September 25, 1989, 77–78.

45. John Teresko, "Manufacturing in Japan," *Industry Week*, September 4, 1989, 35–79.

APPENDIX FOR CHAPTER 19

QUANTITATIVE OPERATIONS MANAGEMENT TOOLS

LINEAR PROGRAMMING APPLICATIONS IN OPERATIONS MANAGEMENT

Linear programming is a mathematical method used to solve resource allocation problems. Resource allocation problems often arise in manufacturing management, where a number of activities must be performed but there are limitations on the amount of available resources to carry them out. For example, linear programming can be used to determine how to best

1. Distribute merchandise from a number of warehouses to a number of customers.
2. Assign personnel to various jobs.
3. Design shipping schedules.
4. Develop optimum product mixes (how much of each product to produce).
5. Route production (to optimize the use of machinery).

To apply linear programming successfully, the problem must be reviewed for certain basic requirements as follows:

1. First, as a manager you must state the quantifiable goal you are attempting to achieve. For example, you might want to minimize total shipping costs, maximize profits, or minimize total salaries.
2. Second, the resources to be allocated must be in limited supply. For example, there must be a limited number of warehouses from which you wish to ship your goods, a limited number of machines for producing your goods, or a limited amount of materials out of which to produce your merchandise.
3. You must also identify a series of feasible alternative courses of action. For example, if you have enough leather to produce 600 belts, you could produce 200 of one belt and 400 of another, or 300 of one and 300 of the other, and so forth.
4. Finally, you must be able to express all the necessary relationships in mathematical equations (or inequalities), and all these equations or inequalities must be linear in nature. For example, suppose the profit on belt A is 30¢ and the profit on belt B is 50¢. Then you can present the profit in the form of an equation as follows, where P represents the profit:

$$P = 0.30A + 0.50B$$

This profit relationship is linear since the profit would rise or fall in direct proportion to the rise or fall in sales of belts.[1]

WAITING LINE OR QUEUING TECHNIQUES

Queuing techniques are used to solve waiting line problems. For example, bank managers need to know how many tellers they should have. If they have too many, they are wasting money on salaries; if they have too few, they may end up with disgruntled customers. Similar problems arise when managers must determine the optimum number of airline reservations clerks, warehouse loading docks, highway toll booths, supermarket checkout counters, and so forth.

Waiting line or queuing techniques can be used to analyze alternatives and arrive at solutions to many of these problems. It is necessary to know how often customers arrive, how long it takes to service them, and the order in which arriving customers are served. With these data, a waiting line problem can be solved with queuing techniques. An example of a typical waiting line problem is as follows:

A bank has two tellers working on savings accounts. The first teller handles withdrawals only. The second teller handles deposits only. The service time for both deposits and withdrawals averages three minutes per customer. Depositors arrive in a predictable fashion throughout the day with a mean arrival rate of 16 per hour. Withdrawers also arrive in a predictable fashion with a mean arrival rate of 14 per hour. What would be the effect on the average waiting time for depositors and withdrawers if each teller could handle both withdrawals and deposits? What would be the effect if having tellers handle both transactions could only be accomplished by increasing the mean service time to 3.5 minutes?

[1]See Marvin Agee, Robert Taylor, and Paul Torgerson, *Quantitative Analysis for Management Decisions* (Englewood Cliffs, NJ: Prentice-Hall, 1976), Chapter 12.

CHAPTER 20

INFORMATION TECHNOLOGY AND MANAGEMENT SYSTEMS

LEARNING OBJECTIVES

After studying this chapter, you should be able to:

- Define information technology.
- Differentiate between information and knowledge.
- List the characteristics of good quality information.
- Explain why managers at different levels in the organization require different types of information.
- Name the main elements of a computer system.
- Describe the four basic types of computers: microcomputers, minicomputers, mainframes, and super computers.
- Discuss the basic types of information systems used in management.
- Define telecommunications and its role in managing organizations.
- Identify the information systems applications spawned by telecommunications.
- Explain the effect computerization and information technology have had on organizational structure and responsiveness.

OPENING PROBLEM

BANC ONE CORPORATION

Banc One is a contradiction. While most banks shun technology, Banc One usually finds itself out front embracing innovations that enhance service. It was the first institution to use automatic teller machines and led the way in offering cash management accounts. In another startling deviation from industry standards, Banc One annually allocates 3 percent of its earnings to technology research and development. But what may be the institution's most ambitious, and potentially risky, innovation to date is the implementation of its Strategic Banking System for its member branches. The System is designed to enhance service and product marketing. But with a price tag of over $100 million, the strategy could turn into an expensive mistake if it doesn't translate into increased business. It is unclear whether banking customers will perceive that they have received better service simply because Banc One embraces the latest technological improvements, and skeptics warn that the capital outlay might prove too rich for an industry known for conservative operations.[1]

MANAGEMENT IN THE INFORMATION AGE

In 1988, management expert Peter Drucker made a prediction:

> The typical large business twenty years hence, will have fewer than half the levels of management of its counterpart today, and no more than one third the managers. In its structure, and in its management problems and concerns, it will bear little resemblance to the typical manufacturing company, circa 1950, which our textbooks still consider the norm. Instead, it is far more likely to resemble organizations that neither the practicing manager nor the management scholar pays much attention to today: the hospital, the university, the symphony orchestra. For like them, the typical business will be knowledge-based, an organization composed largely of specialists who direct and discipline their own performance through organized feedback from colleagues, customers, and headquarters. For this reason, it will be what I call an information-based organization.[2]

The rapid deployment of *information technology* in organizations has promoted the transformation of many businesses today into the information-based organizations that Drucker foresaw. Essentially, **information technology** refers to any processes, practices, or systems that facilitate the processing and transportation of information. You are no doubt already very familiar with modern components of information technology. For example, you may use a personal computer and be familiar with management information systems from the work you do. You probably use cellular phones, facsimile machines, and the increasingly ubiquitous voice-mail answering systems. Information technologies like these have dramatically altered the way people do their jobs and how organizations are managed. How information technology at firms like Banc One impacts management is the subject of this chapter.

INFORMATION TECHNOLOGY
Refers to any processes, practices, or systems that facilitate the processing and transportation of data information.

THE NATURE OF INFORMATION

Information is data presented in a form that is meaningful to the recipient.[3] "Information," as Drucker has said, "is data endowed with relevance and purpose."[4] **Knowledge,** on the other hand, has been defined as "information that has been distilled via study or research and augmented by judgement and experience."[5]

To put these definitions into managerial terms, consider this example. PepsiCo, Inc., wants to determine why consumers are not buying its new Pepsi Light clear cola drink. To search for an answer, the company's market researchers conduct a survey containing 25 multiple-choice questions. The answers to the questions are put on computer tapes, and by themselves would appear to the untrained eye as nothing but long streams of unrelated numbers (in this case the *data* resulting from the survey). When market researchers summarize this data for presentations to management, though, the result is *information,* such as graphs showing average responses by age level and other demographic traits for each question. The marketing department can then apply its *knowledge* to draw meaningful conclusions, such as, in PepsiCo's case, why older consumers seem less inclined to purchase Pepsi Light than are younger ones.

INFORMATION
Data presented in a form that is meaningful to the recipient.

KNOWLEDGE
Information that has been distilled via study or research and augmented by judgment and experience.

INFORMATION QUALITY

Good quality information has several characteristics.[6] As with the PepsiCo example, good information must be *pertinent* and related to the problem at hand. Good quality information must also be *timely.* For example, the Pepsi Light survey information would be useless if it came rolling in two years after the product was called off the shelf. Good information must also be *accurate.* Finally, good information reduces *uncertainty.* **Uncertainty** may be defined as the absence of information about a particular area of concern.[7] In the PepsiCo example, the survey should thus have been

UNCERTAINTY
The absence of information about a particular area of concern.

designed so that the information helped the marketing manager answer the question, "Why aren't people buying Pepsi Light the way we thought they would?"

Yet, even good information is relatively useless without the *knowledge* that comes from analysis, interpretation, and explanation.[8] Managers today are, if anything, deluged by information—on competitor practices, consumer buying habits, machinery breakdowns, and an array of other relevant issues. The role of information technology at work is thus not just to generate and transfer more (or even better quality) information. It is to contribute to the manager's knowledge of what is happening through analysis, interpretation, and explanation.

MANAGEMENT'S REQUIREMENT FOR INFORMATION

Managers at different levels in the organization require different types of information, as is summarized in Figure 20.1.[9] First-line managers (like Ford production supervisors or the front-desk manager at a Hilton Hotel) tend to focus on short-term, operational decisions. At this level, information should emphasize operational activities such as accounts receivables information, order entry information, inventory control information, and cash management information.

Middle managers tend to focus more on intermediate-range decisions, like those events that might affect the company in the coming year or so. They therefore require information for use in budget analysis, short-term forecasting, and variance analysis.

Top managers (including the CEO and the firm's top vice-presidents) focus more on long-range, strategic decisions. They therefore require information that will enable them to make, for example, factory location decisions, merger and acquisition decisions, and new product planning decisions. We will see in the next section that these different information requirements translate into different types of information systems at each level in the organization.

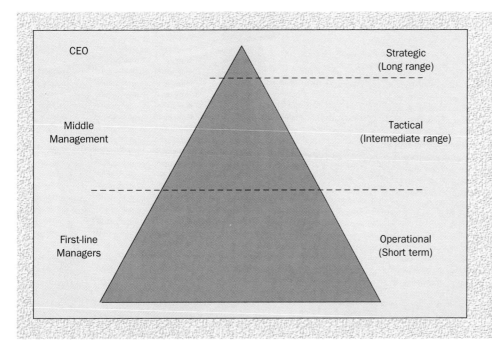

FIGURE 20.1

Management Information Requirements

The information needs of managers at each organizational level differ because their orientations—strategic, tactical, operational—differ.

SOURCE: Carroll Frenzel, *Management of Information Technology* (Boston: Boyd and Frazer, 1992), 11.

COMPUTER INFORMATION SYSTEM COMPONENTS

ELECTRONIC DIGITAL COMPUTERS
Automatic, electronic devices composed of circuitry through which electricity can flow in such a way as to represent data as numbers.

INPUT DEVICES
These devices receive instructions and data, convert them into electrical impulses, and then transfer the impulses to the computer's storage unit.

OUTPUT DEVICES
These devices receive the electrical impulses from the computer and convert them to a form we can read or use.

CENTRAL PROCESSING UNIT (CPU)
The heart of a computer system that contains three main components: a primary storage unit, an arithmetic/logic unit, and the control unit.

When most business people refer to computers today, they mean **electronic digital computers.** These are automatic, electronic devices composed of circuitry through which electricity can flow in such a way as to represent data (including numbers and alphabetical data) as numbers. In practice, a computer by itself is of little use; instead, computer *systems* are used, which consist of several components.

Computer systems have two main elements, hardware (equipment) and software (programs for guiding the equipment's operation). All computer systems contain several types of hardware. **Input devices** receive instructions and data, convert these into electrical impulses, and then transfer these impulses to the computer's storage unit. Typewriter terminals and devices for reading floppy disks are familiar input devices. **Output devices** receive the electrical impulses from the computer and convert these to a form we can read or use. Output information is often presented on typed printouts or on television-like computer screens.

The **central processing unit** (CPU) is the heart of a computer system (the part that is technically "the computer"). It contains three main components. The *primary storage unit,* or memory, is the component that stores the data to be used during processing. The next component is the *arithmetic/logic unit,* which is capable of doing

Technicians at Bell Atlantic work on a highly sophisticated network, but each station is made up of the basic computer system components: input device, output device, central processing unit, and software.

addition, subtraction, multiplication, and division and determining whether a number is positive, negative, or zero. This unit also has a logic ability in that it can compare two numbers and decide if one is greater than, equal to, or less than the other. Finally, the CPU's *control unit* monitors the instructions programmed into the computer. It then commands the input unit to supply information, the arithmetic/logic unit to perform the program instructions, and the output device to produce usable output.

Software is a computer system's second main element. **Software** usually refers to computer programs, which are instructions that tell the computer which steps to take, which data to work on, and what to do with the results. The control unit then takes these program instructions and issues commands to the computer system's input, output, and central processing unit elements regarding what to do next.

Computer systems are available in four basic classes: microcomputers, minicomputers, mainframes, and super computers. **Microcomputers** are relatively small in size but may have considerable computer power and speed. Personal computers, including laptop computers (small enough to fit on one's lap) and home computers are examples. **Work stations** are microcomputers that offer relatively high computer power. They are often used for engineering and manufacturing applications and may cost several times what a personal computer costs. Mid-range or **minicomputers** are designed for multiple users and have much greater speed and storage capacity than microcomputers.[10] **Mainframe computers** are large-scale systems often used for high-volume processing jobs (such as preparing thousands of payroll checks). Finally, **super computers** are the fastest computers available. They are used for applications that require that enormously complex calculations be made quickly; for instance, the weather bureau uses super computers to forecast weather patterns.

TYPES OF INFORMATION SYSTEMS

WHAT IS AN INFORMATION SYSTEM?

An **information system** may be defined as a set of people, data, and procedures that work together to retrieve, process, store, and disseminate information to support decision making and control.[11] In this chapter, we will focus on computerized information systems. These are information systems in which computers play a central role in retrieving, processing, storing, and disseminating the information. Similarly, we focus on *management* information systems, which are systems that support *managerial* decision making and control. The *Bissett* small business box shows how one small business used an information system to dramatically boost its business.

Information systems form a hierarchy corresponding to the fact that the decisions made at each organizational level tend to be unique to that level. This hierarchy is illustrated in Figure 20.2.[12] For example, *executive support systems* provide information for strategic-level decisions regarding matters such as five-year operating plans. *Management information systems* and *decision support systems* provide middle management reports regarding matters such as current versus historical sales levels. *Office automation systems* operate on a more short-term basis and combine components such as word processors and electronic mail to facilitate interpersonal communications. *Transaction processing systems* provide detailed information on the most short-term, daily activities, such as data regarding accounts payables and order status. Let us look at each of these systems (and several others) in more detail.

SOFTWARE
Refers to computer programs, which are instructions that tell the computer which steps to take, which data to work on, and what to do with the results.

MICROCOMPUTERS
Computers that are relatively small in size but may have considerable computer power and speed.

WORK STATIONS
Microcomputers that offer relatively high computer power.

MINICOMPUTERS
Designed for multiple users and have much greater speed and storage capacity than microcomputers.

MAINFRAME COMPUTERS
Large-scale systems often used for high-volume jobs.

SUPER COMPUTERS
The fastest computers available. They are used for applications requiring enormously complex calculations that must be made quickly.

INFORMATION SYSTEM
A set of people, data, and procedures that work together to retrieve, process, store, and disseminate information to support decision making and control.

BISSETT NURSERY CORP.

Back in the early 1980s, Jim Bissett could have been happier, but things could have been a lot worse, too. Long Island, New York, was in the midst of a building boom, and Bissett Nursery couldn't have handled any more business. Bissett's son Jimmy spent his days sprinting around trying to service customers, many of whom then had to wait up to 25 minutes for a hand-written invoice. Bookkeeping was a month behind, receivables sometimes took 90 days to meander back, and inventory control basically didn't exist. Both Bissetts knew booms invariably turned to busts, and the company—a wholesaler of nursery materials, hard goods, and lumber—would have to change to make it through tougher times. The younger Bissett had ideas about expanding through vertical integration without taking on big labor costs. He thought the best way to do so would be with the help of brother-in-law Bob Pospischil, an ex-fighter pilot who knew his way around both sophisticated computer hardware and the financial data it could produce. "My goal was not to change the business," says Pospischil, "but to use technology to meet the business needs." The elder Bissett was skeptical. He'd seen competitors go the same route, only to find it an expensive mistake, but he finally relented.

Pospischil signed on as the company's chief financial officer. He spent 60 days getting a handle on buying, sales, shipping, and accounting, and then spent $135,000 on the company's first IBM System 36. Order-entry employees took turns visiting the software vendor to learn the new system. After the first 30 minutes of operation, the network

crashed. Convinced the curse of computers had finally descended on his house, a frantic Jim Bissett insisted everyone return to the old manual system. The snafu was ironed out in 15 minutes and the elder Bissett gradually became accustomed to the new technology.

What Jim Bissett senior soon gained from the information system was a new perspective on practically every phase of his business operation. Instead of haphazard strategic planning, he could order with precision based upon his customers' historical needs. He was also able to make Bissett Nursery indispensable to them while at the same time providing better service. He could easily show small contractors their annual

FOCUS ON SMALL BUSINESS

needs for nonperishable goods, enabling them to purchase in bulk and save money. When water conservation became an issue in the region, Bissett was out in front steering clients to heartier plants that thrived in drier conditions. Bissett Nursery's customer base shot from 600 to 7,500, and Pospischil was only beginning to hit his stride.

Marketing was costing Bissett $130,000 annually, and better than 60 percent of that budget went to producing the ads and catalogs. Pospischil had an easier time selling the elder Bissett on the idea he could do more timely promotions with an in-house desktop publishing system. The price tag was $40,000, but the company never felt a

ripple. "With the first catalog, we saved enough to pay for the system," says Pospischil.

The next technological innovation was the greatest challenge. It also provided the nursery's customers their biggest competitive advantage. Landscapers face big barriers with homeowners because they have to sell the aesthetics of their products either by driving potential clients by past jobs or through the use of pictures. It's not always easy to get a customer to visualize how a tree or row of shrubbery six blocks away would look in their front yard. That changed when a software company sold Bissett on an imaging system that could produce a rendering of how the planned trees and plants would look in front of the customer's house.

The new technology gave Bissett Nursery a huge edge when the building boom turned into a recession. More than 95 percent of landscape contractors who used Bissett's computer-generated images sold the job and came back to fill orders at the nursery. "We were a very strong company going into the recession," says the younger Bissett, "and I feel we've stayed fairly strong."

Despite the fact that the nursery and landscape businesses are generally not regarded as being in the vanguard of high technologies, the Bissetts have proved otherwise. Using the latest information systems, they have managed the enviable feat of producing more efficiently, providing better service, and making themselves indispensable to customers.

SOURCE: Donna Fenn, "Picture the Image," *Inc.*, February 1994, 66–71.

	SALES	MANUFACTURING	ACCOUNTING	FINANCE	PERSONNEL
EXECUTIVE SUPPORT SYSTEMS (ESS)	**STRATEGIC-LEVEL SYSTEMS**				
	5-year sales trend forecasting	5-year operating plan	5-year budget forecasting	Profit planning	Personnel planning

	SALES	MANUFACTURING	ACCOUNTING	FINANCE	PERSONNEL
MANAGEMENT INFORMATION SYSTEMS (MIS) **DECISION SUPPORT SYSTEMS (DSS)**	**MANAGEMENT CONTROL-LEVEL SYSTEMS**				
	Sales management	Inventory control	Annual budgeting	Capital investment analysis	Relocation analysis
	Sales region analysis	Production scheduling	Cost analysis	Pricing/ profitability analysis	Contract cost analysis

OFFICE AUTOMATION SYSTEMS (OAS)	**KNOWLEDGE-LEVEL SYSTEMS**				
	Engineering workstations		Graphics workstations		Managerial workstations
	Word processing		Image storage		Electronic calendars

	SALES	MANUFACTURING	ACCOUNTING	FINANCE	PERSONNEL
TRANSACTION PROCESSING SYSTEMS (TPS)	**OPERATIONAL-LEVEL SYSTEMS**				
		Machine control	Payroll	Auditing	Compensation
	Order tracking	Plant scheduling	Accounts payable	Tax reporting	Training & development
	Order processing	Material movement control	Accounts receivable	Cash management	Employee recordkeeping

FIGURE 20.2

Information Systems Hierarchy

Managers at each level of the organization have unique information requirements and various types of information systems have thus been developed to serve the needs at each management level.

SOURCE: Kenneth Laudon and Jane Laudon, Management Information Systems (New York: Macmillan, 1991), 7.

TRANSACTION PROCESSING SYSTEMS (TPS)

A **transaction** is an event that affects the business. Hiring an employee, selling merchandise, paying an employee, and ordering supplies are some examples. In essence, transaction processing systems collect and maintain detailed records regarding the business's (or organization's) transactions. Transaction processing is crucial for any business to remain viable. For example, a university must know what students are registered, which have paid fees, which members of the faculty are teaching, and what secretaries are employed in order to conduct its business.

The collection and maintenance of such day-to-day transactions were two of the first procedures to be computerized in organizations. As is the case today, early transaction processing systems automated the collection, maintenance, and processing of

TRANSACTION
An event that affects the business, such as hiring an employee, selling merchandise, and ordering supplies.

basic information for mostly repetitive transactions. Examples include computing withholding taxes and net pay, and processing accounts payable checks.

Transaction processing systems (TPS) can be put to one or more of five uses.[13] The TPS may have to *classify* data based on common characteristics (such as all sales employees or all plant employees, for instance). They are used to do routine *calculations* (such as computing net pay after taxes and deductions for each employee). They can be used for *sorting* (for instance, grouping invoices by zip code to more efficiently distribute them. The TPS can also be used for *summarization* (such as summarizing for each department's manager what his or her average payroll is compared to the other departments). Finally, the TPS can be used for *storage* (for example, storing payroll information for, say, the past five years).

MANAGEMENT INFORMATION SYSTEMS (MIS)

MANAGEMENT INFORMATION SYSTEM (MIS)
An information system that provides decision support for managers by producing standardized, summarized reports on a regular basis.

The term management information system is sometimes used generically to describe any computerized information system, the purpose of which is to facilitate managerial decision making and control. However the traditional definition of management information system is narrower. Specifically, a **management information system (MIS)** provides decision support for managers by producing standardized, summarized reports on a regular basis.[14] An MIS generally produces reports for longer term purposes than typical transaction processing systems. In a university, for instance, a TPS is used to print class rolls and grade rolls. An MIS is used to measure and report class size and enrollment trends by department and by college. The deans and academic vice-presidents can then use the MIS reports to increase or decrease the class sizes or to drop some courses from the next semester's schedule, while adding others. In other words, management information systems condense, summarize, and manipulate information derived from the organization's transaction processing systems. They then present the results in the form of routine summary reports to management, often with exceptions flagged for control purposes.[15]

DECISION SUPPORT SYSTEMS (DSS)

DECISION SUPPORT SYSTEMS
Information systems that help managers make decisions that are relatively unstructured when compared to those addressed by the typical MIS.

Decision support systems help managers make decisions that are relatively unstructured when compared to those addressed by the typical MIS. At the university, for instance, an MIS is used to make course addition and deletion decisions, decisions which are fairly routine. However, suppose the university's faculty threatens to strike. The university could use a decision support system to estimate the impact on university revenues of having to drop various combinations of classes.

An MIS differs from a DSS in several ways.[16] A DSS is more capable of analyzing various alternatives, in part because decision support systems let the user (in this case, the vice-president for academic affairs) include more different sub-programs showing how various components of the university are related. More distinctively, perhaps, a DSS does not just draw on internal information from the transaction processing system the way an MIS typically does. Instead, a DSS is built to absorb new external information into the analysis. Thus, our university's academic vice-president, faced with a strike, may want to include in her or his analysis an estimate of the likelihood that a number of the university's students will move across town to a competing university given that competing university's ability (or inability) to expand its class offerings.

EXECUTIVE SUPPORT SYSTEMS (ESS)

EXECUTIVE SUPPORT SYSTEMS
Information systems designed to help top level executives acquire, manipulate, and use the information they need to maintain the overall company's effectiveness.

Executive Support Systems are information systems designed to help top-level executives acquire, manipulate, and use the information they need to maintain the overall effectiveness of the company. Such systems often focus on providing top management with information for making strategic decisions. They help top management match changes in the firm's environment with the firm's existing and potential strengths and weaknesses.

As summarized in Figure 20.3,[17] managers use executive support systems for several specific tasks. Executives like Cypress Semiconductor's Tom Rogers use their ESS for *keeping informed* of and monitoring the pulse of their organizations. Rogers uses an ESS to monitor the weekly compliance of all 4,000 Cypress employees (for instance, to review how each worker is doing in terms of project progress and sales productivity). Second, executives use ESS to *identify and understand* evolving new situations quickly. You may recall from Chapter 7 on Decision Making that the fastest strategic decision makers "swim" in what Tom Peters calls "a deep turbulent sea of real-time information."[18] A university president could thus use an ESS to keep tabs on and analyze the following situational questions:

- Is the average student taking fewer courses?
- Are costs for labor or maintenance substantially higher than they have been in the past?
- Is there a significant shift in the zip codes from which most of our students come?

Executives use these systems for several other purposes. First, an ESS provides for easy browsing through the data. One executive describes this *browse capability* this way:

I like to take a few minutes to review details about our customers, our manufacturers or our financial activities first hand. Having the details flow across the screen gives me a feel for how things are going. I don't look at each record, but glance at certain elements as they scroll by. If something looks unusual, it will almost jump out at me and I can find out more about it. But if nothing is unusual, I will know that, too.[19]

FIGURE 20.3

How Executives Use an ESS

Top managers use executive support systems for such things as keeping informed and being able to understand a new situation or trend more quickly.

SOURCE: James Senn, *Information Systems in Management* (Belmont, Wadsworth, 1990), 575.

REASON	EXPLANATION
To keep informed	Enables executives to stay abreast of day-to-day activities by viewing firsthand information from representative business activities and transactions without getting bogged down in details
To understand a new situation quickly	Enables rapid access to details describing business activities that provide insight into an unexpected or recently uncovered situation
To browse through data	Provides a firsthand view of activities that often cannot be achieved through the review of reports and business summaries
To maintain surveillance	Allows monitoring of a situation of special interest through specified details
To perform strategic scanning	Enables viewing of information that provides insight into a particular strategy or opportunity or brings to light the opportunity to develop a new strategy having significant potential for the organization
To analyze data	Enables examination of data or alternative scenarios through creation of spreadsheets or other forms of models; supports both "what is" and "what if" forms of analysis
To get at data directly	Enables viewing of data without waiting for staff to retrieve and extract details; also enables viewing of actual details before summarization

The top executive can also use an ESS to *monitor* a situation. Thus the university's president could use an ESS to monitor the new dining facilities management firm running the university's student cafeteria by reviewing information such as student usage, student complaints, and revenues. Executives also use ESS to perform *strategic scanning*. For example, a wealth of information is available in commercial computerized data banks, including financial information on tens of thousands of U.S. companies. Executives can use an ESS to tap into such data banks in order to glean competitive data regarding other firms in their industry. An ESS can also support *analytical needs*. For example, an ESS may allow our university president to create "what if" scenarios that show the probable effects on university revenues of increasing faculty salaries or adding new programs. Finally, an ESS may enable the executive to get at *data directly*. Using his or her terminal and a telephone line, the executive can use an executive support system to tap directly into the company's data files in order to get the specific information that may be of interest without waiting for others to assemble the data.[20]

EXPERT SYSTEMS AND ARTIFICIAL INTELLIGENCE

An **expert system** is an information system in which computer programs store facts and rules *(often called a knowledge base)* to replicate the abilities and decisions of true human experts. For example, one early application involved closely watching an investment advisor's decision making in order to identify the rules the advisor used to determine what investments to recommend to investors who fit into various demographic and risk-propensity categories. Those observations were then used to develop a computer program that replicated most of the investment decisions the investment officer expert would have made.

Expert systems are used in all fields of business, from manufacturing to sales to finance. Increasingly, though, some of the most well-publicized uses have been in the area of finance and investments. For example, Manufacturers Hanover's TARA (Technical Analyses and Reasoning Assistant) aids this bank's foreign currency traders in New York. Basically, TARA is an expert information system that tracks foreign currency prices as well as the prices of options to buy foreign currency in all markets around the world. Continually monitoring enormous quantities of currency data, it then flashes signals to the bank's currency traders, based on TARA's analysis of price movements. In doing so, TARA basically replicates the currency-monitoring and decision-making habits of professional foreign currency trading experts. However, TARA undoubtedly makes those decisions faster and processes considerably more foreign currency data than the average trader could have processed.[21]

The term **artificial intelligence** is often used in association with *expert systems* because they both are related to replicating human thought processes. However, expert systems are relatively straightforward information systems comprised of programs that contain decision rules. These decision rules (when combined with the facts of the situation) allow the expert system to mimic the expert's decision-making style.

Artificial intelligence leaps beyond that sort of logical problem solving. Basically, *artificial intelligence* may be defined as "teaching computers to accomplish tasks in a manner that is considered 'intelligent,' and is characterized by learning and making decisions."[22] Ultimately, says one expert,

> Such systems would be able to learn natural languages; accomplish coordinated physical tasks (robotics); develop and utilize a perceptual apparatus that informs their physical behavior and language, and, finally, exhibit logic, reasoning, intuition, and just plain common sense—qualities that we associate with human beings.[23]

Dramatic as this sounds, many experts today believe that such thinking machines are a long way off. One expert, for instance, contends that "artificial intelligence is the snake oil of the information age."[24] Others simply throw up their hands and conclude that "the truth is, nobody knows what AI means."[25] In any case, it would seem that we are some years away from being able to replace either faculty members or students with such so-called thinking machines. Some modest applications have been implemented, though, as the *Tulare County* vignette shows.

THE COMPUTER-INTEGRATED BUSINESS

Many businesses today are moving toward the point at which their various transaction processing systems, decision support systems, expert systems, executive support systems, and the management information systems within each functional area and for the company as a whole are fully integrated. One writer defines the **computer-integrated business** as "an enterprise whose major functions—for example, sales, finance, distribution, manufacturing—exchange operating information quickly and constantly via computer."[26] Such information exchange will usually then depend on telecommunications, to which we now turn.

COMPUTER-INTEGRATED BUSINESS
An enterprise whose major functions exchange operating information quickly and constantly via computer.

TULARE COUNTY

The cutting edge of technology has surfaced in an unlikely locale. People in need of public assistance in Tulare County, one of California's poorest, file requests with an artificial intelligence program as part of the qualification process. "We knew there had to be a better way of handling point-of-contact client entry," says deputy county executive Gerard Kersten. "And this is it."

Tulare always had more than its share of people in need of assistance, due to the area's low income levels. But California counties—not the state—shoulder the burden of actually administering the aid. Adding additional personnel threatened to break Tulare's budget. The answer turned out to be what are called *eligibility kiosks,* which interview applicants via computer. IBM PCs linked to a mainframe each display an interactive presentation from a video disk player. A bilingual image converses with users while an artificial intelligence program tallies replies. When the answers are all in, the program produces an 11-page form and evaluates whether the applicant qualifies.

The county's demand for human services has climbed steadily for the past several years, but the use of the artificial intelligence interviewer has kept personnel additions to a minimum. The system even carried the load when unemployment jumped 4 percentage points. Human services costs per recipient in Tulare County are now lowest or next to lowest, and that includes the entire state. Officials are now considering installing artificial intelligence kiosks that will enable residents to do everything from paying property taxes to making reservations to visit county campgrounds.

SOURCE: David H. Freedman, "Read This, Al Gore," *Forbes ASAP,* October 25, 1993, 151–54.

Tulare County in California uses a sophisticated set of automation systems to speed up access to services. Child protection worker Prudence Morris, pictured here, uses a laptop when in the field, enabling her to tap into case information back at the office.

ADVANCES IN MANAGERIAL DATA AND TELECOMMUNICATIONS

THE NEW TELECOMMUNICATIONS

TELECOMMUNICATIONS

The electronic transmission of data, text, graphics, voice (audio), or image (video) over literally any distance.

TELECOMMUNICATIONS SYSTEM

A set of compatible telecommunications devices that link geographically separated devices.

TERMINALS

Input-output devices that send or receive data.

LINE ADAPTERS

Modify the signal from the terminal and computer so that it matches the characteristics of the telecommunications line.

Telecommunications refers to the electronic transmission of data, text, graphics, voice (audio), or image (video) over literally any distance. In practice, the transmission may travel from machine to machine within an office, from office to office, between cities, around the globe; or even further, such as between NASA headquarters and the transmitter on the Venus probe.[27]

A **telecommunications system** is a set of compatible telecommunications devices that link geographically separated devices.[28] A telecommunications system's purpose is to connect information processing devices (such as personal computers, telephones, and video displays) for the purpose of exchanging data and information.[29]

As depicted in the simple telecommunications system in Figure 20.4,[30] several elements exist in any telecommunications system. The *telecommunications lines or links* are the medium through which signals are transmitted. These might consist of copper wires, coaxial cables, optical fibers, or microwave transmissions, for instance. **Terminals** are input-output devices that send or receive data. One or more *computers* can be used to process information. **Line adapters** modify the signal from the terminal and computer so that it matches the characteristics of the telecommunications line. (This is important because many popular telecommunications links, such as telephone lines, are not suited for the type of signal produced by computerized input and output devices.) The most familiar line adapter is called a *modem*.[31] Finally, *telecommunica-*

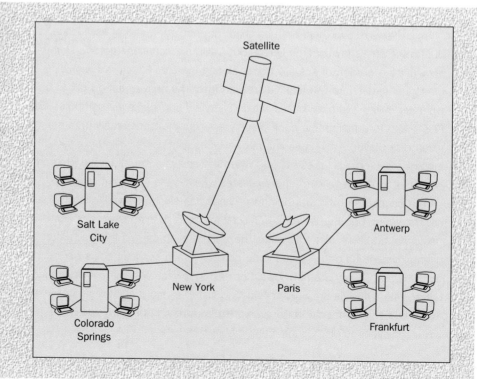

FIGURE 20.4

A Telecommunications System

A telecommunications system like this one is a set of compatible telecommunications devices like lines, adapters, and computers that link geographically separated devices.

SOURCE: Carrol Frenzel, *Management of Information Technology* (Boston: Boyd & Frazer, 1992), 164.

Digitized automobile designs in Dearborn, Michigan, travel via telecommunication to become full-sized mockups in Turin, Italy.

tions software is the computer program that controls input and output activities and other communications network functions.

Telecommunications play an important role in managing organizations today. For example, apparel manufacturer Levi Strauss uses a sophisticated telecommunications system to link its own inventory and manufacturing facilities with point of sale processing devices at retail customers such as Wal-Mart. Detailed sales information can thus be transmitted directly to headquarters, where it is analyzed for trends and buying patterns. Management can then make decisions regarding inventories and production plans. Similarly, one large toy retailer uses telecommunications to manage in-store inventories. Its buyers get instant access to sales information from the stores and can modify their purchasing actions accordingly.

As another example, Ford designers at its Dearborn, Michigan, headquarters use computers to develop designs for new cars such as the Lincoln Continental. As shown in the above photos,[32] digitized designs are then sent via telecommunications, and they are reproduced at Ford's design facility in Turin, Italy, where styrofoam mockups are made automatically to reproduce Dearborn's design, 4,284 miles away.

Another reason telecommunications is important is because more and more computer systems applications rely on it. For example, Levis depends on telecommunications in its computerized inventory control systems; radiologists rely on telecommunications for X-rays taken by their technologists, which can then be read from remote locations; your college or university may rely on telecommunications to allow you to access library information from your office or home; computer-assisted manufacturing systems rely on telecommunications to transmit information from one location in the plant to another; and banks rely on telecommunications to make their remote automatic teller machines operational. At the same time, telecommunications fosters the development of new management computer systems applications, some of which we now discuss.

WORK GROUP SUPPORT SYSTEMS

Work groups play an increasingly important role in managing organizations, as we have seen in previous chapters. A work group usually consists of up to 25 people who work together to achieve a common goal.[33] The work group might be a door-assembly team at Saturn cars, the sales department at a Levi Strauss subsidiary, or a project team set up in a manufacturing plant to solve a quality control problem. A work group might be relatively permanent (as it would be if it were a sales department) or temporary (such as a group formed to solve a one-time quality control problem). The work group's members might all be at a single site, or they might be dispersed around the city or even around the world. For example, the work group might consist of the separate country IBM representatives devoted to advising Ford on its worldwide computerized systems. In any event, work group information systems facilitate communication among a work group's members. These information systems range from electronic mail to video conferencing.

Many of these work group support applications also represent examples of office automation. *Office automation systems* "provide electronic mail, word processing, electronic filing, scheduling, calendaring capability and other support to office workers."[34]

ELECTRONIC MAIL (E-MAIL)
A computerized information system that lets group members electronically create, edit, and disseminate messages to each other, depositing each message in the recipient's electronic mail box.

ELECTRONIC MAIL   Electronic mail (E-mail) is a computerized information system that lets group members electronically create, edit, and disseminate messages to each other, depositing each message in the recipient's electronic mail box. E-mail's aim is to speed and facilitate intra-group communication and thereby bolster intragroup coordination. Some applications are fairly simple. At one law firm, for instance, a manager points out that "we used to have a downstairs and an upstairs receptionist. . . . People had to go upstairs and downstairs to check messages and sometimes there would be a lag time of two hours before someone got a message. Now all the messages are input on [our] E-mail system and there is a lag time of 5 to 10 minutes at the most."[35]

VIDEO CONFERENCING
Meetings among dispersed group members via television links.

GROUP CONFERENCING
A set of telecommunications-based methods that lets group members interact directly with or leave messages for a number of other group members simultaneously.

VIDEO CONFERENCING   Video conferencing is one example of **group conferencing**, a set of telecommunications-based methods that lets group members interact directly with or leave messages for a number of other group members simultaneously. Video conferencing refers to meetings among dispersed group members via television links. Thus, with video conferencing, the top attorneys of Royal Dutch Shell subsidiaries around the world could hold a conference without any of them leaving their offices. One firm—International Open Systems (IOS) of Peabody, Massachusetts—provides video conferencing via desktop personal computers. It lets users send live video and audio messages (with a few seconds delay).[36] An **electronic bulletin board** is another example of video conferencing. It lets one or more group members file messages on various topics to be picked up later by other group members.

ELECTRONIC BULLETIN BOARD
Allows one or more group members to file messages on various topics to be picked up by other group members.

Video conferencing can significantly improve communications and coordination among group members and thereby help a work group achieve its aims more quickly than the group could otherwise. For example, the team developing the Boeing 777 made extensive use of video conferencing for meetings with engine suppliers and key airlines regarding the new aircraft's design.[37]

COLLABORATIVE WRITING SYSTEMS
Allows a work group's members to create long written documents (such as proposals) while working simultaneously at one of a number of interconnected or network computers.

OTHER WORK GROUP SUPPORT SYSTEMS   Other work group support systems are also available. For example, **collaborative writing systems** let a work group's members create long written documents (such as proposals) while working simultaneously at one of a number of interconnected or network computers. As team members work on different sections of the proposal, each member has automatic access to the rest of the sections and can modify his or her section to be compatible with the rest. The *group decision support system* described earlier in this chapter represents

HILL & KNOWLTON

When one of Hill & Knowlton's principal clients filed for Chapter 11 bankruptcy, the big public relations firm found itself in uncharted waters. The company had to make quick decisions about how to release the news. At stake was the company's stock price, not to mention a host of suppliers and distributors who might panic before a workable reorganization was formulated. H & K vice-president Mayer G. Becker remembered an intriguing demonstration of a group decision support system (GDSS) he'd recently seen at a computer trade show. He hurriedly gathered nine members of the account team and herded them to a firm equipped with an electronic brainstorming room.

The team assembled around a conference table with a PC at each station. Everyone began typing in their ideas. "Within 10 minutes, we had 47 excellent ideas," says Becker. "By the end of the hour, we had discussed them, voted on them, ranked them in order of priority and walked out with printed documentation in hand." What the PC-linked team didn't have to worry about were organizational or personal problems. Intimidation of subordinates, long-winded speeches, and other extraneous distractions didn't have the opportunity to detract from the PC-based proceedings.

SOURCE: Alice LaPlante, "'90s Style Brainstorming," *Forbes ASAP,* October 25, 1993, 45–61.

---

another work group information system. (See the *Hill and Knowlton* vignette above for an example.) A **group scheduling system** lets each group member put his or her daily schedule into a shared data base, which enables group members to identify the most suitable times for meetings to be scheduled or to attend currently scheduled meetings. The *work flow automation system* permits the use of a system such as E-mail to automate the flow of paperwork.[38] For example, if a proposal requires four signatures, it can be sent electronically from mailbox to mailbox for the necessary signatures rather than having the actual paperwork be sent.

TELECOMMUTING Today, millions of people around the world do most of their work at home and commute to their employers electronically. **Telecommuting** has been defined as the substitution of telecommunications and computers for the commute to a central office.[39]

The typical telecommutor falls into one of three categories. Some are not employees at all, but are independent entrepreneurs who work out of their homes—perhaps developing new computer applications for consulting clients, for instance. The second (and largest) group of telecommutors includes professionals and highly skilled people who work at jobs that involve a great deal of independent thought and action. These employees—computer programmers, regional salespersons, textbook editors, or research specialists, for instance—typically work at home most of the time, coming into the office only occasionally, perhaps for monthly meetings.[40] The third telecommutor category includes workers who carry out relatively routine and easily monitored jobs such as data entry or word processing.[41] The *Chiat/Day* vignette shows how one firm uses telecommuting, as well as networks, to which we turn next.

GROUP SCHEDULING SYSTEM
Allows each group member to put his or her daily schedule into a shared data base, which enables group members to identify the most suitable times for meetings to be scheduled or to attend currently scheduled meetings.

TELECOMMUTING
The substitution of telecommunications and computers for the commute to a central office.

CHIAT/DAY

Science fiction writer Jules Verne might have eventually dreamed up Jay Chiat if he had lived a little longer. The chairman of Chiat/Day, an advertising agency with billings of $620 million in 1992 and clients that include Apple, Nissan, Reebok, and Energizer, among others, hasn't mastered time travel yet. But he does think he's found the next best thing, and he works without ever departing his East Hampton, Long Island, base of operations.

Chiat expects his company to become the world's first "virtual agency." Chiat/Day will keep the wires and airwaves humming with brainstorming sessions, electronic mail exchanges, and video conferencing. Frequent flier miles will be a thing of the past. So will the standard work day. With all employees interconnected by cellular phone and notebook computers equipped with E-mail, his employees' locations do not really matter.

According to Chiat, besides being an incredibly cool place to hang out, tomorrow's new work place will feature a CD-ROM library and state-of-the-art software that instantly transfers words, pictures, sound, and video to any CD receiver in the world. Stations to plug in laptops will be provided, since they will be the all-purpose communication device at the virtual agency. Chiat says relying on telecommuting will reinvent the way work is done and spell doom to long-held habits of the past that don't necessarily add anything in the way of increased productivity. Chiat maintains he came up with his virtual agency idea whooshing down a ski slope. He says he also sometimes solves company problems in the shower. "And now that the technology exists to work from anywhere," he says, "the real question is, can we use it without being dehumanized in the process?" He apparently thinks so.

SOURCE: Richard Rapaport, "Jay Chiat Tears Down the Walls," *Forbes,* October 25, 1993, 25–28.

NETWORKS

Computerized networks have proliferated in the past few years. At the University of Michigan's Angell Hall, students flock to 320 personal computers that are wired up to networks all over campus and the world. They use the computers to send E-mail to each other, to post notes about Rousseau and Locke on a special bulletin board for members of a political science class, and to communicate with fellow students and researchers all around the globe.[42] At home today, tens of thousands of subscribers use on-line network services such as Prodigy to shop for apparel, airline tickets, or seats to Broadway shows.

Companies and other organizations also make extensive use of networks to better manage their operations. A **network** "is a group of interconnected computers, work stations or computer devices (such as printers and data storage systems)."[43] Four examples of managerial networks include local area networks (LAN), wide-area networks (WAN), value added networks (VAN), and distributed networks.

LOCAL AREA NETWORK (LAN)
A communications network that spans a limited distance such as a building or several adjacent buildings using the company's own telecommunications links.

LOCAL AREA NETWORKS　A local area network (LAN) spans a limited distance such as a building or several adjacent buildings using the company's own telecom-

Advertising agency Chiat/Day's far-out building in Venice, California, may become obsolete if chairman Jay Chiat's "virtual office" idea takes off.

munications links (rather than common-carrier links such as those provided by AT&T's phone lines). In an office, a LAN may be used to support a work group information system such as E-mail, and a factory may use a LAN to link computers with computer-controlled production equipment. More generally, LANs are used for one or more of the following reasons: for the distribution of information and messages (including E-mail) and to drive computer-controlled manufacturing equipment; for distribution of documents (such as engineering drawings from one department to another); to interconnect the LAN's computers with those of a public network such as Prodigy or Internet; and, given the high cost of certain equipment such as laser printers, for equipment sharing (including not just printers but disk storage files servers, for instance).

In part because LANs facilitate communication and allow sharing of expensive devices such as color graphic plotters and large disk files, local area networks are growing in popularity. One survey of 500 U.S. microcomputer installations found that 81 percent either had LANs or intended to add them in the future.[44]

WIDE AREA NETWORKS Wide area networks (WANs) are networks that serve microcomputers over larger geographic areas, spanning distances from a few miles to around the globe. Early WANs utilized common carrier networks, such as the telephone linkages provided by AT&T and MCI. However, many firms today own their

WIDE AREA NETWORK (WAN)
Networks that serve microcomputers over larger geographic areas, spanning distances from a few miles to around the globe.

own wide area networks, which are thus essentially private, computerized telecommunications systems. For example, the Benetton retail store chain can use a wide area network to enable both store managers and the headquarters staff to identify trends and improve inventory and production management. The stores accumulate sales data during the day and keep them on computer disks. At night, another, larger computer at corporate headquarters polls the individual retail stores' computers, thus accessing the data that are then transmitted over telephone lines back to headquarters. Here, the information is processed and a summary of sales trends is forwarded to headquarters and to the individual store managers.[45]

DISTRIBUTED NETWORKS   As in the Benetton example, wide area networks are often used to achieve *distributed processing*. **Distributed processing** generally refers to the use of small local computers (such as point-of-sale systems) to collect, store, and process information, with summary reports and information sent to headquarters as needed.[46] Computer expert James Senn lists the features of distributed processing as follows:

- Placing computing facilities at remote locations.
- Having these systems do the majority of the data processing for that location on the site (rather than transmitting data for processing to a centralized facility).
- Linking these locations to a central facility or other locations in a communication network.[47]

THE INFORMATION SUPERHIGHWAY

We are fast approaching the day when we will be able to sit in our homes and access an enormous number of computerized data bases. We will use them to do everything from browsing through the Louvre Museum, to purchasing a bomber jacket, to ordering a showing of *Gone With the Wind,* to planning a weekend trip to New York. All of these services—from phone calls to televised shop-at-home retailers—will be available to us through the **information superhighway.** This superhighway (as outlined in Figure 20.5) is a high-speed digital communications network that may combine telephone lines, cable lines, microwave transmissions, and fiber optics to let anyone anywhere use interactive television, telephones, PCs, or other devices to interact with data bases around the world. Already, it has been estimated that consumer-oriented interactive services are now used in almost 3.5 million of the 92 million U.S. households, and the number is growing more than 30 percent a year.[48]

On-line, interactive services like these are already dramatically changing how customers buy, how companies do business, and how managers manage. In shopping, for example, the Prodigy Service (jointly owned by IBM and Sears) offers on-line catalogs, not just from Sears but also from other merchants such as J.C. Penney and Spiegel.[49] In Denver, Tele Communications, Inc., and U.S. West have joined AT&T to test one of many video-on-demand cable television services.[50] In Japan, used car dealers meet via computer to take part in weekly electronic auctions, buying and selling cars by the press of a button.[51]

Micro Electronics and Computer Technology Corp. (MCC), an Austin, Texas, consortium of major high-tech firms, has a service that provides a glimpse of the new electronic marketplace. Once plugged into their EINET (Enterprise Integration Network), a buyer looking for, say, office products will find potential sellers by scrolling through a national directory similar to the Yellow Pages. Buyers will also be able to exchange E-mail messages with sellers, enter purchase orders, make payments, and even hook themselves to sellers electronically to facilitate just-in-time delivery and automatic inventory replenishment.[52] Wal-Mart already has such links with suppliers

DISTRIBUTED PROCESSING
The use of small local computers to collect, store, and process information, with summary reports and information sent to headquarters as needed.

INFORMATION SUPERHIGHWAY
A high-speed digital communications network that may combine telephone lines, cable lines, microwave transmissions, and fiber optics to let anyone anywhere use interactive television, telephones, PCs, or other devices to interact with databases around the world.

FIGURE 20.5

The Information Superhighway

Components of the information superhighway include computers, copper cable, fiber optics, and satellite transmissions, all working together to allow users to interact with each other and with numerous databases.

SOURCE: Anthony Failola, "Superhighway: Delivering Data to Your Door," *The Miami Herald*, 1K.

A ROAD MAP TO YOUR TV

Like typical highways — I-95, I-75, I-595 — the fiber-optic information superhighway won't take information all the way to your home. Initially it will take data most of the way, then let smaller, copper wires carry it to your TV.

SATELLITE
1. Program information is transmitted to a satellite in space which forwards the information to a regional Earth station. In the future, scientists expect fiber-optic wires to run through the U.S.

HEADEND STATION
2. This station receives the signals and sends them to nodes, via fiber optics.

NODES
3. In the first systems to go on line, nodes will translate light signals into electrical impulses to be transmitted over wires.

Node	Node	Node	Node
1,800 homes	1,800 homes	1,800 homes	1,800 homes

4. Each node would serve a neighborhood, with a typical configuration handling 1,800 homes. Four main trunk cables, each containing dozens of wires, would be strung from each node. From those trunks, hundreds of branch wires would take signals to homes.

450 450 450 450 450 450 450 450 450 450 450 450

5. Once the signals reach the home, a mini-computer, or cable box, that sits on top of your television, takes over, translating the signal into pictures and sound.

THE 'HIGHWAY'

■ A fiber-optic cable is a bundle of glass strands that carry light pulses. For typical cable TV service, the bundle might include 24 strands.

HOW IT WORKS

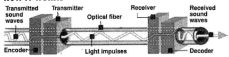

Transmitted sound waves — Transmitter — Optical fiber — Receiver — Received sound waves
Encoder — Light impulses — Decoder

■ Sound and data are converted to electronic digital information. That information is converted to light pulses and sent through the fibers by a laser flashing on and off at very high speeds.

■ At the receiving end, the light is converted back to electronic digital information, then decoded to reproduce sound or data.

Glass strands where light pulses travel through

Metallic casing that protects glass strands

A SMART, NEW BOX

The cable boxes of the future will be more of a computer, with an electric eye that operates an "air mouse" — the television version of computer mouse. You could plug your television, telephone, computer and video camera into the boxes.

Computer
Telephone
Video camera
Television

WHAT YOU WILL GET

The data superhighway will eventually offer countless options, from 500 cable channels, to video telephone calls, to home shopping with the touch of a remote control.

INTERACTIVITY

Interactivity means two-way communication, and interactive TV means sending information through your TV as well as receiving it. Options include home shopping, video games, movies on demand, educational games, and college courses.

MULTIMEDIA

Multi-media services give you the option of using more than one communication device at once. The most popular example is video telephone calls, where you talk through the telephone, look through a video camera and watch your caller through the TV.

FIBER OPTICS VS. COPPER CABLE

The new technology uses light pulses traveling though glass fiber to transmit information. Conventional telephone cable uses electricity traveling through copper wire.

WHY IT'S BETTER
■ Light can travel much farther before a costly amplifier is needed to boost the signal.
■ Optical fibers can carry more information.
■ Optical fibers aren't affected by electrical or radio interference or lightning.

COPPER WIRE
A conventional 3-inch-thick cable contains 1,200 pairs of copper wires. It can carry 14,400 telephone converstions.

FIBER FOR PHONES
A half-inch-thick fiber-optic cable for telephone use can include 72 pairs of fibers that transmit 3.5 million conversations.

like Procter & Gamble. Links like EINET will also give many more buyers and sellers the option of sending their data in code, so that they will be able to do business on public networks without fear of eavesdropping or intrusion.[53]

COMPUTER SECURITY

Security-conscious organizations like banks and the armed forces have long understood the need to protect their computer systems from outside intrusion. However, more and more firms are finding that, with the increased use of interactive networks, additional computer security steps are not just wise, but mandatory. Part of the reason is today's widespread ownership of PCs with modems, which make it relatively easy to sign on to company networks. Another reason is the change in the nature of most firms' computer centers. The old computer center was often a large and highly secure complex of rooms. Today, the "computer centers" are often vast networks of desktop computers, each of which provides a potential doorway into the firm's computer data bases.

A firm's computer system (and its computer networks in particular) are subject to two types of security threats.[54] **Passive threats** come from unauthorized individuals or organizations who monitor the firm's data transmissions in order to obtain unauthorized information. **Active threats** consist of attempts to alter, destroy, or divert data or to act as an authorized network terminal point, thus exchanging information with legitimate sites and obtaining free network services.[55] In either event, firms are taking a number of steps to boost computer security. These steps fall into one of these five categories:[56]

- Physical security and isolation of certain computer equipment and data media.
- Authentication of the identity of authorized users.
- Careful definition of user authorization.
- Inscription of transmitted and sensitive stored information.
- Audit trails, coupled with meaningful accountability.

The *Computer Security* vignette describes a somewhat more controversial method for boosting computer system security.

INFORMATION TECHNOLOGY AND THE RESPONSIVE ORGANIZATION

DECENTRALIZED OPERATIONS AND CENTRALIZED CONTROL

For many years, experts have debated how computerization would change the way in which organizations are structured. Most early predictions suggested that computerized organizations "would become more centralized, and that middle management would tend to disappear over time because computers would give central, high-level managers all of the information they require to operate the organization without middle-management intervention."[57] An early study by Thomas Whisler, for instance, focused on how computers effected an organization's structure. From his analysis of the research evidence, he concluded that the introduction of a computer system in an organization generally tends to cause the following changes in the organization's structure:

1. Departments are consolidated.
2. The number of levels in the hierarchy is reduced.

PASSIVE THREATS
Threats that come from unauthorized individuals or organizations who monitor the firm's data transmissions in order to obtain unauthorized information.

ACTIVE THREATS
Threats that consist of attempts to alter, destroy, or divert data or act as an authorized network terminal point, thus exchanging information with legitimate sites and obtaining free network services.

COMPUTER SECURITY CONSULTANTS

The search for a secure computer system sometimes takes companies down controversial paths. Former computer hacker Scott Chasin, founder of his own security consulting firm, claims people like him are a company's best hope of warding off security breaches by old cohorts. Ex-hackers scoff at the notion that conventional security consultants could ever equal their penetration skills. Prosecutors and other law enforcement officials think voluntarily opening up a company's system to so-called reformed hackers is asking for trouble.

Chasin gained infamy as a member of the Legion of Doom hacker group. Though never convicted of crimes himself, the group wreaked havoc penetrating a number of telephone company systems. Chasin now manages personal computer networks for Amoco in Houston and freelances as a computer security consultant. Mainstream security professionals were apoplectic when they learned he was marketing his questionable expertise to corporate clients. Sour grapes, countered Chasin. "These guys just didn't want the competition," he says. "How would you feel if some young guy who knew all the tricks was entering your line of work?"

Many industry experts wonder why companies would risk hiring a Scott Chasin when they could get the same or better evaluations and services from someone like Peter Goldis, a subcontractor for Coopers & Lybrand and others. He arrives armed with a binder full of programs designed to get around security safeguards on mainframes. Goldis is sometimes able to breach a system in as little as 20 minutes. He points out that hackers excel at cracking PC and Unix-based systems, and that most corporations are moving fast toward just that type of client/server system.

Some believe that a lot of big corporations are putting hackers in security positions and keeping quiet about it. Trumpeting the background of quasi-criminal staffers makes little sense and makes bad publicity a possibility. The irony is that many companies may already have ex-hackers employed and not know it. What remains to be seen is whether the former hackers have truly retired or are merely on sabbatical until an opportunity too tantalizing to resist presents itself.

SOURCE: David H. Freedman, "The Goods on Hacker Hoods," *Forbes ASAP,* September 13, 1993, 32–40.

3. The span of control is reduced.

4. Parallel (product-oriented) departments are replaced by functional departments.

5. Control becomes more centralized.

6. Control is shifted laterally between major executives and departments.

7. The (computer) technology becomes a part of the control structure.[58]

Most of these changes would shift an organization's structure toward the more centralized, mechanistic end of the structural spectrum. For example, this would occur if spans of control were reduced (number 3 on the list), if divisionalized "profit center" structures were replaced by the more traditional functional departmentalization (number 4), and if control becomes more centralized (number 5).

In practice, computerization and information technology has not had quite this effect on organization structure. In fact, in many ways its effect has been just the opposite. On the one hand, the flattening of the hierarchy that Whisler predicted has no doubt come about. In other words, computerization does seem to have reduced the need for so many layers of management. As Peter Drucker has said, "it turns out that whole layers of management neither make decisions nor lead. Instead, their main, if not their only function, is to serve as 'relays,' human boosters for the faint unfocused signals that pass for communications in the traditional pre-information organization."[59] These management layers have been eliminated in many firms.

Yet it does not appear that computerization has led to the sort of centralized decision making that early writers predicted. On the contrary, information technology has actually boosted the depth and range of decisions that lower-level operational employees can make, in part because information technology provides top level managers with the security of real-time monitoring of subordinates' progress. As information technology expert Carroll Frenzel puts it:

> Information technology, especially telecommunications systems, offers executives the potential to have the best of both worlds. Decision-making and operational control can be delegated to operational units; control information can be available to headquarters on a real-time basis.[60]

Such computerization has occurred at a propitious time for the world's business firms. Technological and competitive trends, globalization, and deregulation have made organizational responsiveness a prerequisite for survival. Responsiveness, in turn, demands increased decentralization of decision-making, so that operating units can respond more quickly to customer needs and to competitive threats and opportunities. Whether information technology by itself would have led to more or less decentralization can be debated. However, combined with the pressures for increasingly responsive organizations, groupware, networks, and other forms of information technology have helped to spawn decentralized and responsive organizations by letting managers decentralize more decisions while monitoring overall progress on a real time basis.

INFORMATION TECHNOLOGY'S ROLE IN STRATEGIC ALLIANCES

A recent *Business Week* article pointed out that "in today's world of fast-moving global markets and fierce competition, the windows of opportunity are often frustratingly brief."[61] Most firms wishing to capitalize on these opportunities do not have the time or in-house capabilities to design and launch the required complex products quickly enough to satisfy such fast-changing needs. Therefore, *virtual corporations* are, as we've seen, increasingly important vehicles for boosting a firm's responsiveness. A virtual corporation, in turn, can be defined as "a temporary network of independent companies—suppliers, customers, even erstwhile rivals—linked by information technology to share skills, costs, and access to one another's market."[62]

Such business alliances—and, thus, such responsiveness—would be impossible without information technology, as exemplified by an actual alliance organized to build a new generation of jet engine. The alliance consists of five companies, one each in the United States, Japan, Italy, Great Britain, and Germany. The alliance was organized to build engines for 2,000 new aircraft over the next 20 years. According to one expert, a highly complex and geographically dispersed effort like this relies for its existence on information technology. Specifically, "it is possible only because a 24-hour communications network transfers data on design control, bills of material, parts catalogues, tool design, and many other items among the firms."[63]

MANAGERIAL APPLICATIONS OF INFORMATION TECHNOLOGY

It is one thing to discuss information systems and advances in telecommunications but another thing to see how information technology is actually being applied to assist managers today. The following examples outline some of the managerial applications of information technology.

DELL: GETTING CLOSER TO ITS CUSTOMERS[64]

Dell Computer, the direct-sales computer firm we first met in Chapter 1, relies heavily on information technology to stay close to its customers and their changing needs. At the present time, Dell gets about 35,000 calls or E-mail messages every day. Employees who take these calls work on PCs linked by a network to a large central computer that contains the company's customer data base. As the calls come in, the telephone representatives input the information to the data base and follow up inquiries by triggering the mailing of customized sales letters to inquiring customers.

Dell uses its information systems in other ways, too. For example, it fine-tunes its mailing lists to target specific customer needs. (Why send information on office networking to a customer who is obviously just an at-home user?) The data base also helps Dell boost add-on sales, for instance, by alerting telephone reps to sell extended warranties to all those ordering computers above a particular dollar amount.

AMERICAN EXPRESS: TELECOMMUTING[65]

When you call American Express for travel advice, chances are that the travel counselor you speak with will not be at Amex headquarters, but back home keeping one eye on the kids. For a company that spends over $1 billion annually on information

American Express travel counselor Faye Compton commutes to work via personal computer.

■ Here's how Price Waterhouse put together a proposal in four days and won a multimillion-dollar consulting contract by using Lotus's Notes software for groups. On Thursday a Price Waterhouse executive learned that a major securities firm was about to award a big consulting contract to help develop a complex new trading operation. Price Waterhouse was invited to bid, but there was a hitch: The proposals were due Monday. A Price Waterhouse competitor had been working on its own bid for weeks.

THE FOUR Price Waterhouse executives who were needed to write the proposal were in three different states. But they were able to work together using Notes, which allowed them to conduct a four-way dialogue on-screen. They also extracted key components of the proposal from various databases on Notes. From one, they pulled résumés of the Price Waterhouse experts from around the world who could be assigned to the job. From another, they borrowed passages from similar successful proposals.

FIGURE 20.6

Winning the Job with Groupware

SOURCE: David Kirpatrick, "Groupware Goes Boom" *Fortune*, December 27, 1993, 100–101.

technology, it is probably not surprising that by the end of 1993, more than 100 Amex travel counselors in 15 locations will have shifted to homework, up from just 25 in the late summer of 1993. American Express connects its "homeworkers" to its phone lines and data lines for a small one-time expense of about $1,300 each, including hardware. After that, the travel counselors can easily bounce information from their homes to the nearest reservation center, and thus look up fares and book reservations on their home PCs. Supervisors continue to be able to monitor agents' calls, thus ensuring good control.

This information technology application has been good for both American Express and its travel counselors. The homeworker counselors handle 26 percent more calls at home than in the office, resulting in about $30,000 more in annual bookings each. For travel counselors, working at home means saving three hours a day on commuting, and less wear and tear on both the travel counselor and her or his family.[66]

WINNING THE JOB WITH GROUPWARE[67]

Groupware refers to computer software programs that make it easier for groups to work together. For example, when Price Waterhouse accounting manager Rick Richardson arrives at his office each morning, he checks his computer to review the average 20 to 25 E-mail messages he gets in a typical day. Price Waterhouse also maintains electronic bulletin boards on more than 1,000 different subjects. About 18,000 Price Waterhouse employees in 22 countries can use these electronic bulletin boards to get updates on various matters. For instance, on a board called PW alert, employees can post general information and inquiries. In one recent example, a Price Waterhouse Dublin employee asked if anyone had experience auditing a cheese plant processing 100 million gallons of milk a year.[68]

Figure 20.6 summarizes how a Price Waterhouse team won a consulting job by using groupware.[69] The four Price Waterhouse executives who needed to write the proposal (which was due in three days) were in three different states. But they were able to use their Lotus Notes Groupware to conduct a four-way dialogue on their screens to extract key proposal components from various PriceWaterhouse data bases. For example, they could pull up resumes of the key Price Waterhouse experts from around the world and borrow passages from similar proposals. Then they could use Notes to fine-tune the proposal and put it into final form. The team met the deadline and got the contract.

Groupware has helped make many firms more responsive. For one thing (as one manager at a New York insurance brokerage firm put it), it is helping to dissolve the old corporate hierarchy "because even non-supervisory office workers plugged into groupware networks have information and intelligence previously available only to their bosses." Similarly, "networks . . . can give the rank and file new access: the ability to join in on-line discussions with senior executives. In these interactions, people are judged more by what they say than by their rank on the corporate ladder."[70]

Groupware has flattened corporate hierarchies and abolished the chain of command in many other ways, too. For example, when Mary Joe Dirkes, a young employee at an insurance firm, posted a particularly well done memo on the network about the firm's workers compensation efforts, her good work was immediately noticed by top management in New York; she thereby soon broadened her responsibilities. Her message and the network also altered the chain of command.

> She now gets requests for help from around the firm via the network. When a client in Ohio needed someone with experience in cutting workplace injuries in plastics factories, Ms. Dirkes clicked into a groupware data base to find an expert that could help. "Before, people would have called or sent a memo to my boss, then he'd assign it to me. . . . Now I do it on my own."[71]

Information technology refers to any processes, practices, or systems that facilitate the processing and transportation of data information. The increasingly rapid deployment of information technology in organizations has sped the transformation of many businesses today into information-based organizations.

Information is data presented in a form that is meaningful to the recipient. Knowledge, on the other hand, has been defined as information that has been distilled via study or research and augmented by judgment and experience. Good quality information must be pertinent, timely, accurate, and reduce uncertainty. But even good information is relatively useless without knowledge. The role of information technology at work is to contribute to the manager's knowledge of what is happening through analysis, interpretation, and explanation.

Managers at different levels in the organization require different types of information. First-line managers tend to focus on short-term, operational decisions and therefore need information that focuses on operational activities. Middle managers tend to concentrate on the intermediate range and so require information for use in such tasks as budget analysis, short-term forecasting, and variance analysis. Top managers make long-range plans and therefore require information that will enable them to make better strategic decisions.

The two main elements of a computer system are the hardware, which includes input and output devices and the central processing unit, and the software or computer programs. The four basic classes of computer systems are microcomputers, minicomputers, mainframes, and super computers.

Information systems are people, data, hardware, and procedures that work together to retrieve, process, store, and disseminate information to support decision making and control. The hierarchy of information systems used in management include executive support systems, management information and decision support systems, office automation systems, and transaction processing systems. An expert system uses computer programs to store facts and rules and replicate the abilities and decisions of human experts. Artificial intelligence involves teaching computers to accomplish tasks in a manner that is considered intelligent and is characterized by learning and making decisions. The departments and other components of computer-integrated businesses exchange operating information quickly and constantly via computer.

Telecommunications is playing an increasingly important role in managing organizations today. The term refers to the electronic transmission of data, text, graphics, voice, or image over any distance. Telecommunications systems connect geographically separated devices through the use of lines or links, terminals, computers, line adapters, and software. Telecommunications has fostered the development of numerous new computer systems applications, such as work group support systems, networks, and the information superhighway. The increasing use by businesses of interactive networks underscores the importance of computer security.

Computerization and information technology have reduced the need for management layers. They have also boosted the depth and range of decisions that lower-level operational employees can make while giving top-level managers the security of decentralizing decision-making while monitoring the progress of subordinates. Certain types of strategic alliances, such as the virtual corporation, would be impossible without information technology.

■ FOR REVIEW

1. What are the different types of information needed by front-line, middle, and top managers?

2. Give some examples of information systems, and explain how each of them work.

3. What are the functions and limitations of expert systems and artificial intelligence?

4. Describe the components and necessary technologies that make up a virtual corporation. What market conditions have given rise to them?

5. List some ways that companies use telecommunications to run their businesses. What changes in work habits has the new technology spawned?

6. What steps should companies take to ensure the security of computer systems?

■ FOR DISCUSSION

7. How do you think firms may conduct business in the future using interactive services and the information superhighway?

8. Discuss how the changes brought about by computerized information technology affect lower-level employees and upper managers. How can information technology enhance a firm's competitiveness in today's global economy?

9. Many people today consider themselves computer illiterates. Do you think it will be possible to succeed in business in the future without an extensive knowledge of computers? Discuss your response.

■ FOR ACTION

10. Develop a description of a typical corporation in the year 2050, taking into account the technological innovations that are likely to influence its organizational structure.

11. Contact a computer software store that is willing to give you a demonstration of one of the systems described in this chapter. Describe it.

12. Think of one or more examples of how you use telecommunications in your personal, professional, or academic life. How have you benefited as a result?

■ FOR FOCUS ON SMALL BUSINESS

13. Many managers who, like Bissett, are accustomed to old manual systems, are initially suspicious of information technology. If you were working as an information systems consultant, how would you go about convincing such managers of the value of innovation?

14. Describe what you consider the primary benefit that a small firm like Bissett Nursery derived from using the latest information systems?

15. What obstacles is a small business like Bissett likely to encounter in making the transition to an information-based organization?

CLOSING SOLUTION

BANC ONE CORPORATION

In implementing its Strategic Banking System, Ohio-based Banc One entered a partnership with Electronic Data Systems Corporation. The bank shifted from reliance on big mainframe systems to a local area network of PCs on the desktops of customer service representatives, loan officers, and new account managers. Because of the system's enhanced data-gathering ability (it keeps up with customer facts ranging from marital status to the birth dates of children), Banc One employees have access to a broader range of marketing, sales, and service needs, which are displayed on a customer-by-customer basis. Also, as it turned out, Banc One didn't stray too far afield from its conservative banking roots in handling the cost of SBS. EDS assumed the majority of the cost and risk of developing the system. In exchange, it retained the right to market SBS to other financial institutions. Even though SBS is available to other institutions, Banc One again finds itself two to three years out in front of the competition because it was first in recognizing both the savings and service enhancements of implementing the latest technological innovations.

■ QUESTIONS FOR CLOSING SOLUTION

1. Why is the information that the new technology will provide important to Banc One's success?
2. With technology progressing at such a rapid pace, what criteria should a company like Banc One use to determine if its existing systems have become obsolete?
3. How do you think technology will change banking in the future? Discuss your response.

KEY TERMS

Information Technology
Information
Knowledge
Uncertainty
Electronic Digital Computers
Input Devices
Output Devices
Central-processing Unit (CPU)
Software
Microcomputers
Work Stations
Minicomputers
Mainframe Computers
Super Computers
Information System
Transaction
Management Information System
Decision Support System
Executive Support System
Expert System

Artificial Intelligence
Computer-integrated Business
Telecommunications
Telecommunications System
Terminals
Line Adapters
Electronic Mail (E-mail)
Video Conferencing
Group Conferencing
Electronic Bulletin Board
Collaborative Writing Systems
Group Scheduling System
Telecommuting
Local Area Network (LAN)
Wide Area Network (WAN)
Distributed Processing
Information Superhighway
Passive Threats
Active Threats

Perhaps it is easy to understand how Aetna Life and Casualty had grown a little stodgy. The $90 billion in assets Hartford, Connecticut-based insurer was writing policies while Abraham Lincoln was delivering the Gettysburg Address. The next century and a quarter saw the company evolve into an impenetrable bureaucracy that left customers waiting months to get claims settled. Getting questions answered satisfactorily sometimes took weeks. Chairman and CEO Ronald E. Compton resolved to remake the monolith, and he didn't mince words about what the company's primary objective would be. "Either serve the customer superbly or don't even try," he said.

Aetna, the largest publicly held insurance company in the United States, had three primary divisions. Compton splintered these into 15 more responsive strategic business units (SBUs), eliminating 5,000 employees in the process. Compton let it be known he expected these SBUs to pull their weight. He established performance criteria for each, and he quickly dispelled any notions he would tolerate failure to meet projections. He cancelled one unit for failure to measure up and sold another. He withdrew Aetna from the auto insurance business in Massachusetts in early 1992 at a cost of $88 million.

Better service at lower costs meant changing the most fundamental aspects of the company and, especially, computerizing. Virtually all business operations are being revamped as manual processes are replaced with technology-driven applications. It is no easy undertaking. Personal and commercial lines of property and casualty insurance were formerly serviced by two huge computerized systems that didn't communicate with one another. Putting them together was a Herculean task, but worth the effort. The new mainframe system can be accessed by laptop allowing employees or agents to perform functions ranging from crediting payments to filing loss reports. As a result, the company was able to eliminate 43 claim centers and saved as much as $100 million by 1995. Aetna also now utilizes a computer system linked to its office suppliers. Employees use a desktop terminal system to log purchases that are processed and paid for centrally. By-passing the purchasing department saved the company $20 million in 1992, and the efficiencies are expected to compound further in the future.

Aetna's small business market group in Hartford is now using laptops in the enrollment process. Life and health applications that were manually produced and mailed to small businesses used to take a couple of months in the process. With the laptops and Canon BJ-10 printers, the same job can now be completed in a single morning. Estimates are the company will pare $700,000 in annual costs thanks to this computer application.

Savings from implementing the latest information technolo-

gies are essential for survival, according to Compton. An overview of Aetna reveals that this contention isn't hyperbole. A pall of uncertainty surrounds the Clinton administration's efforts to reform health care. The outcome could have far-reaching repercussions for the company. Health and life operations make up around a third of revenues at Aetna and represent a significant portion of earnings. Earnings have been hard to come by elsewhere in the company. Aetna was at the forefront of aggressive real estate lending, and the collapse in property values in many areas of the country has left it perilously exposed. The insurer has already written down or foreclosed $635 million in real estate loans. A potentially cataclysmic $2.9 billion in mortgage loans remain questionable. Some analysts estimate that as much as $4 billion of Aetna's $21 billion real estate portfolio may be troubled or underperforming.

Some critics don't think Compton's reengineering efforts will lead to anything but high expectations and dashed hopes. Dick Lochridge, president of the management consulting firm Lochridge & Company, doubts the likelihood of any quick fixes at Aetna. "That's what Roger Smith tried to do at General Motors when he automated all the plants," he says. "It's people who make the difference."

Reengineering expert Michael Hammer agrees, to a point. "I've never claimed that reengineering is the only answer or solution to the world's business problems," he says. "Reengineering is about achieving world-class operations. You can have that and still get killed by other things."

Compton's assessment is matter-of-fact. The changes at Aetna will make the company flexible enough to allocate resources where they can earn the biggest return. Costs will go down, and maybe the company can then perform up to its true potential. Once again, he minces no words about the future if it fails to do so. "There are going to be no survivors," he says, "only big winners and the dead."

SOURCE: Linda Grant, "Avoiding the Wreckage," *U.S. News & World Report,* June 21, 1993, 49–52; Glenn Rifkin, "Reengineering Aetna," *Forbes ASAP,* June 7, 1993, 78–86; and Adrienne Hardman, "Reinventing Aetna," *Financial World,* November 24, 1992, 22–23.

■ QUESTIONS

1. Do you think information technology will be the key to Aetna's long-term survival? Why or why not?
2. How has computerization already changed the company?
3. What else could Compton do to improve operations at Aetna?

A CASE IN DIVERSITY

MINORITY IS MANAGERS

Carl Williams' information systems career has been enviable. He moved up the ladder to a senior vice-president and director of a MIS post at the Needham Worldwide Inc. advertising agency before taking over as president of The Intertechnology Group Inc., a New York-based IS consultancy firm. He admits encountering varying degrees of racism, even at the upper levels, along the way. But he says taking charge of his own destiny was the key to maintaining upward momentum. "A lot of talented blacks never got beyond a certain point in their IS careers," he says. "I would sit down with managers at every level in my career and make them understand the contribution I thought I was capable of making to the company."

Wilma Horne can relate to what Williams is talking about, and she used a similarly innovative approach in her career climb. The New York Port Authority IS director says she analyzed the mostly white, mostly male business spectrum to identify opportunities for herself. If she didn't find any, she tried to create them. "I decided what I wanted to do, I prepared myself to do it, and then I did it," she says.

Williams and Horne agree on one thing—persistence is important, and keeping a sharp eye out for opportunities and pouncing on them quickly when they come along. That can mean changing companies. "You've got to talk to people about where you want to be," says Williams, "but if it looks like getting ahead is not going to be possible in that corporate structure, then go to where it will be." Having made six job-related moves in 20 years, Horne is in accord with this view. "I took the risk. I had to go to where the opportunity was," she says.

As a black male and a black female at the top of the IS heap, both Horne and Williams acknowledge they can be positive role models for others just starting out. And they agree that simply being available to seize opportunities won't mean much if future IS professionals aren't educationally qualified to fill the position. Neither presume to be in the advice business, nor do they assume that methods employed in their careers will work for everyone else. Both spend time giving a little something back. Horne speaks to high school students about an IS career. Williams does the same with college and graduate students. What they have to say carries considerable weight because of what they've already accomplished. "It's a credibility factor," says Williams. "It's more credible for me to say to a young black MBA that, hey, here are some of the things you're going to have to go through, and here are some of the options you have for handling those situations."

SOURCE: Lory Zottola, "Striving Against All Odds," *Computerworld*, January 21, 1991, 58.

■ QUESTIONS

1. Given the right educational background, do you think minorities have the same opportunities to succeed in an information-based organization as their non-minority counterparts? Why or why not?

2. How can successful IS managers like Williams and Horne best help other minorities who are considering a computer-related career?

3. What advice would you give to a manager who is encountering discrimination on the job?

ENDNOTES

1. This problem was researched from Alice LaPlante, "Shared Destinies: CEOs and CIOs," *Forbes ASAP*, September 13, 1993, 32–38; and "Mightier than Its Parts," *Economist*, December 19, 1992, 76.

2. Peter F. Drucker, "The Coming of the New Organization," *Harvard Business Review*, January–February 1988, 45.

3. James Senn, *Information Systems in Management* (Belmont, CA: Wadsworth Publishing Company, 1990), 58.

4. Drucker, *Coming of a New Organization*, 46.

5. Carroll Frenzel, *Management of Information Technology* (Boston: Boyd & Fraser, 1992), 10.

6. See, for example, David Kroenke and Richard Hatch, *Management Information Systems* (New York: McGraw-Hill, 1994), 20.

7. Senn, *Information Systems*, 58.

8. Kenneth Laudon and Jane Price Laudon, *Management Information Systems* (New York: Macmillan Publishing, 1991), 25.

9. Frenzel, *Management of Information Technology*, 11.

10. Senn, *Information Systems*, 21.

11. Based on Senn, *Information Systems*, 8; and Laudon and Laudon, *Management Information Systems*, 5.

12. Laudon and Laudon, *Management Information Systems*, 7.

13. Senn, *Information Systems*, 14–15.

14. See, for example, Kroenke and Hatch, *Management Information Systems*, 51.

15. Laudon and Laudon, *Management Information Systems,* 43.

16. See, for example, Laudon and Laudon, *Management Information Systems,* 43.

17. Senn, *Information Systems,* 575.

18. Tom Peters, *Liberation Management* (New York: Alfred Knopf, 1992), 42.

19. Senn, *Information Systems,* 576.

20. This discussion is based on Senn, *Information Systems,* 576–77.

21. This example is from Laudon and Laudon, *Management Information Systems,* 684.

22. Senn, *Information Systems,* A-11.

23. Laudon and Laudon, *Management Information Systems,* 662.

24. Herb Grosch, "The Artificial Intelligence Scam," *Management Technology,* March 1984; reprinted in Laudon and Laudon, *Management Information Systems,* 663.

25. Kroenke and Hatch, *Management Information Systems,* 745.

26. Jeremy Main, "Computers of the World, Unite!!" *Fortune,* September 24, 1990, 115–22.

27. For the definition of telecommunications, see G. Michael Ashmore, "Telecommunications Opens New Strategic Business," *Journal of Business Strategy,* March–April 1990, 58.

28. Laudon and Laudon, *Management Information Systems,* 321.

29. Frenzel, *Management of Information Technology,* 159–60.

30. Ibid., 160.

31. The term *modem* is derived from the functions of modulation and demodulation, basically because its function is to modulate or superimpose on the telephone line's analog signal the digital information from the computer input device. See, for example, Frenzel, *Management of Information Technology,* 161.

32. "How to Bolster the Bottom Line," *Fortune,* Autumn 1993, 14–15.

33. Kroenke and Hatch, *Management Information Systems,* 336.

34. Frenzel, *Management of Information Technology,* 44.

35. Deborah Donston, "E-Mail Finds a Solid Niche in Business World," *Buyers Guide.*

36. Stephen Loudermilk, "Desk Top Video Conferencing Getting for Prime Time," *PC Week,* October 19, 1992, 81.

37. Paul Saffo, "The Future of Travel," *Fortune,* Autumn 1993, 119.

38. Kroenke and Hatch, *Management Information Technology,* 359.

39. Robert Ford and Michael Butts, "Is Your Organization Ready for Telecommuting?" *SAM Advanced Management Journal,* Autumn 1991, 19.

40. Ibid.

41. See also Sandra Atchison, "The Care and Feeding of Loan Eagles," *Business Week,* November 15, 1993, 58.

42. Michael Miller, "Contact High," *The Wall Street Journal,* November 15, 1993, R-4.

43. Senn, *Information Systems,* 415.

44. Laura Cooper McGovern, "Local Area Networks Are Now the Rule, While Multilan Use Continues to Grow," *PC Week,* February 6, 1989, 126; and Frenzel, *Management of Information Technology,* 177.

45. See, for example, Senn, *Information Systems,* 418.

46. Ibid., 427.

47. Ibid.

48. David Kirkpatrick, "Hot New PC Services," *Fortune,* November 2, 1992, 108.

49. Ibid., 110.

50. Ibid., 114.

51. Thomas Stewart, "Boom Time on the New Frontier," *Fortune,* Autumn 1993, 153.

52. Ibid., 158.

53. Ibid., 158–59.

54. Carroll Frenzel, *Management of Information Technology,* 476–79.

55. Ibid., 476.

56. Kenneth Weiss, "Controlling the Threat to Computer Security," *Management Review,* June 1990, 55–56.

57. Laudon and Laudon, *Management Information Systems,* 125.

58. Thomas Whisler, *Information Technology and Organizational Change* (Belmont, CA: Wadsworth, 1970), 68.

59. Peter F. Drucker, "The Coming of the New Organization," *Harvard Business Review,* January–February 1988, 46.

60. Frenzel, *Management of Information Technology,* 498.

61. John A. Byrne, Richard Brandt, and Otis Port, "The Virtual Corporation," *Business Week,* February 8, 1993, 99.

62. Ibid., 99.

63. Wayne Ryerson and John Pitts, "A Five-Nation Network for Aircraft Manufacturing," *Telecommunications,* October 1989, 45; and Frenzel, *Management of Information Technology,* 402.

64. Stratford Sherman, "How to Bolster the Bottom Line," *Fortune,* Autumn 1993, 18.

65. Ibid., 24–25.

66. *Fortune,* Autumn 1993, 28.

67. David Kirkpatrick, "Groupware Goes Boom," *Fortune,* December 27, 1993, 100–101.

68. David Kirkpatrick, *Fortune,* December 27, 1993, 99.

69. Figure from Kirkpatrick, "Groupware Goes Boom," 100–101.

70. John Wilke, "Computer Links Erode Hierarchical Nature of Workplace Culture," *The Wall Street Journal,* December 9, 1993, A-7.

71. Ibid.

CHAPTER 21

MANAGING SERVICES

LEARNING OBJECTIVES

After studying this chapter, you should be able to:

- Understand how a companywide approach to maximizing the quality of service is implemented.
- List reasons why service management is important.
- Distinguish between the different requirements in managing services and managing production processes.
- Define the core concepts in Karl Albrecht's service triangle.
- Discuss a service blueprint and the type of information it provides the service manager.
- List the functions and uses of a service audit.
- Explain the upside-down pyramid and worker empowerment, and their importance in service organizing.
- Name the three essential steps in service control.
- Explain the five steps involved in implementing a service management program.

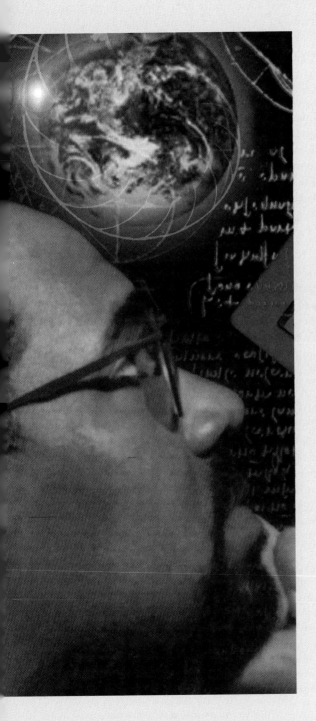

OPENING PROBLEM
KinderCare Learning Centers, Inc.

CEO Tull Gearreald of KinderCare Learning Centers, Inc., was paying for the excesses of his predecessors. Poorly thought out expansion by former parent Enstar Group forced the child care company into bankruptcy. Critics, many of them teachers, were calling Kinder-Care facilities the McDonald's of preschool education, little more than holding pens for latchkey children. Not surprisingly, teacher turnover was high. Low wages, long hours, and watching cranky toddlers for 13 hours a day didn't help. Worse still, most of the company's personnel had to deal with both children and parents on the job, adding to already high stress levels. Child care is an estimated $4 billion a year business, and is expected to grow from 4 percent to 5 percent annually as baby boomers try to juggle work and family priorities. In order to survive and prosper, KinderCare had to learn how to combine high quality service with low cost. In a business so highly charged with emotion, it wouldn't be easy.

THE ROLE OF SERVICES TODAY

It's likely that after college you will go to work for a service firm. As you can see from Figure 21.1, the number of people employed in goods-producing industries (including manufacturing, construction, mining, and agriculture) will stay about the same—at about 27.6 million people—through the year 2000. But the number of people employed in service-producing industries is exploding, from about 51.5 million people in 1972 to about 75 million people in 1990. By the year 2000 there will be almost 96 million people employed in service-producing industries like transportation, communications, wholesale and retail trade, finance and insurance, government, and the legal, educational, and health sectors. In fact, just about every new job added by the U.S. economy over the next few years will be in service-producing industries. Even today, about 75 percent of the people working are employed in the service-producing sector.

As you can see, the role of service firms like KinderCare in our economy today is enormous. As a result, we turn in this chapter to the topic of managing services.[1]

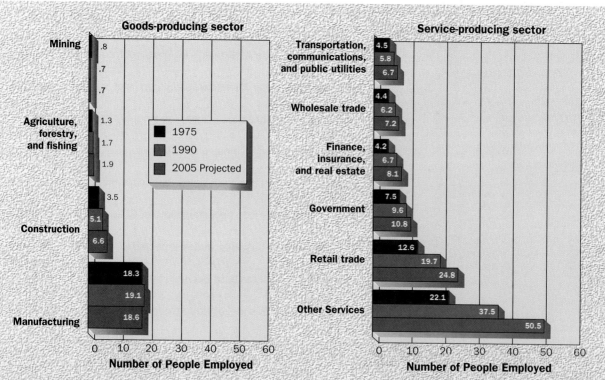

FIGURE 21.1

Goods-Producing Versus Services-Producing Employment by Industry 1975, 1990, and Projected 2005 (in millions)

The number of people employed in goods-producing sectors like manufacturing and construction will stay about the same, but employment in the service sectors will expand rapidly.

SOURCE: "Industrial Growth," *Occupational Outlook Quarterly,* Fall 1991, 18.

THE CHALLENGE
OF SERVICE MANAGEMENT

SAS TAKES OFF

When it comes to managing services, few people equal the exploits of Jan Carlzon, president of Sweden's Scandinavian Airlines System (SAS). Taking over the airline in 1980 (at the relatively young age of 39), he spent the decade building it into a world-class competitor using top-notch service as the airline's competitive edge.[2]

When he took over as president, Carlzon inherited an undistinguished, unprofitable airline during a period in which the world economy was being pummelled by the second oil shock. His airline had already lost money two years running and was pointing nose down toward an imminent crash landing. Due to relatively high wage rates, Carlzon knew he had no chance to compete with other airlines based on low prices.

Carlzon's great insight was recognizing that with his country's reputation for high quality products, he could make high quality service the centerpiece of his airline's turnaround strategy. He decided to reposition SAS as the airline of choice for business travelers and to focus all of his people's efforts on boosting the quality of service that these travelers would get.

Carlzon's service management effort at SAS involved taking a total, companywide approach to maximizing the quality of service for these service-conscious business travelers. He and his staff had first-class cabins removed on most flights; they replaced them with enlarged business-class service so that more businesspeople could afford to travel in plush, leather-lined style. To make sure these business travelers kept coming back, Carlzon and his people had meeting after meeting with employees emphasizing to them the importance of treating the customers right. Carlzon even coined the term "the moments of truth," by which he meant all the key points at which a traveling customer interacts with an SAS employee. Carlzon emphasized to employees that the traveler's overall perception of the quality of service he or she was getting would be molded by all these moments of truth (such as if a hassled passenger got some extra friendly help during check-in or if a problem arose).

Carlzon knew, though, that to get his employees to provide such top-notch service, he had to give them the power to carry out their jobs. For example, what good would it do to encourage an SAS ticket agent to smile and try to be friendly to a traveler who would miss her plane if the agent had no power to reroute the passenger or write a new ticket? Carlzon therefore *empowered* his employees, granting them much broader authority to do things like write new tickets than other airline employees ever had.

To do this he had to make many of the SAS systems more customer oriented. For example, the procedures had to be changed to allow clerks to give vouchers to disgruntled passengers or to let flight attendants distribute free drinks if their planes were delayed. On the ground new systems had to be instituted to speed up check-ins at the airport and to make business facilities (like FAX machines) more widely available for traveling customers.

This example illustrates why Karl Albrecht, a famous service management expert defines service management like this:

> Service management is a total organizational approach that makes quality of service, as perceived by the customer, the number one driving force for the operation of the business.[3]

As this definition shows, service management means much more than just managing a service firm. Certainly, Jan Carlzon was a service manager insofar as he was the president of SAS, which is a service firm. But "service management" also means managing an enterprise (whether it is a service firm like SAS or a manufacturing firm like

Honda) in such a way that quality of service as perceived by the customer becomes the number one driving force for the operation of the business.

WHY SERVICE MANAGEMENT IS IMPORTANT

Service management is important because of the intense global competition that all enterprises face today. As we've explained throughout this book, deregulation and the growth of global competitors have increased the level of competition for virtually all companies and organizations. That means everyone has to fight harder for customers than ever before. Therefore, service management is important today for at least three specific reasons:

SERVICE AS A COMPETITIVE ADVANTAGE   Back in Chapter 6, we explained that one way to compete is for a company to differentiate its product or service by creating something that is perceived as unique.[4] Recall that there are many approaches to doing so: some (like Mercedes) create a high quality image; some (like Caterpillar Tractor) create a strong dealer network, while others use technology, special product features, and other forms of differentiation.

Many firms today differentiate themselves, at least in part, based on customer service. In other words, they use customer service as a competitive weapon. For example, Mercedes-Benz North America offers its customers an 800 number they can call 24 hours a day, seven days a week if they need road assistance. Crown Cork and Seal custom builds a can manufacturing plant near each major customer, thereby providing customized services for each one of them. SAS, as explained earlier, offered top-notch service for its business travelers that set the airline apart from its competitors.

BAD SERVICE LEADS TO LOST CUSTOMERS   Good service is also important because most companies never hear from most of their dissatisfied customers. In other words, bad service leads to lost customers.

This point is illustrated by a series of studies undertaken by the Technical Assistance Research Program, Inc. (TARP), in Washington, D.C.[5] TARP found that the average business never even hears from 96 percent of its unhappy customers. In other words, if a company gets four complaints, there are probably another 96 or so unhappy customers that it never hears from. However, TARP also found that while the company may not hear from these unhappy customers directly, they are out there spreading the word nevertheless. For example, each of those unhappy customers will tell an average of nine or ten people about the problems that they had with the firm. So in addition to reducing its competitive edge, bad service will siphon off many of the firm's current and potential customers. The *T & K Roofing* vignette illustrates how one service business solicited its customer's opinions and thoughts to save profits and customers.

CUSTOMER DEFECTIONS DRAIN PROFITS   Effective service management is also crucial because (in most industries) the longer a firm keeps a customer, the more profit it stands to make from that customer.[6]

There are three reasons for this. First, long-term customers tend to spend more than new customers. Second, they tend to generate profits in other ways like through referrals. Third, as summarized in Figure 21.2 customers generally become more profitable over time. For example, it usually costs a credit card company about $51 to recruit a new customer. If that customer then stays only about a year and uses the card once or twice before leaving in disgust over an error on his bill, the credit card company might not even earn back that $51 acquisition cost. On the other hand, if the company can keep that customer for several years, her value to the company rises because the customer generates a profit in each of those years through credit card fees.

T & K ROOFING

One of the worst things about running a service business that creates customer dissatisfaction is the drop in profits and then the finger-pointing that goes on afterwards. Tom Tjelmeland, T & K Roofing Company CEO, had seen his profit margins slip from 5 percent to 1 percent. More than the usual number of his bids were being rejected, and his 68 percent market share was eroding. He wanted some answers, but he was skeptical about some of the information his salespeople were relaying back. In frustration, he turned to a method that he believed might solve his problem.

Tjelmeland had his son design a questionnaire—the Lost-Job Survey—that was a bit out of the ordinary. He not only wanted to know why his bids were being rejected, but he also wanted to hear anything else customers had to say about his company that they thought didn't measure up. He discovered that such forms can rekindle broken business relationships. Bad questionnaire feedback from a client results in an immediate call from Tjelmeland, and he questions clients about every aspect of the job that didn't measure up. Many clients receive dinner certificates or what Tjelmeland calls a value-added apology.

Although Tjelmeland has 29 years in the business, the surveys taught him to focus on what customers want instead of trying to provide what he thought they needed. Where before he presumed everyone preferred a roof that would last a lifetime, he learned that some people can't afford the expense. As a result, he added cheaper product lines. Because of the surveys, T & K has moved from low-margin contract bidding to the more profitable, negotiated-bid projects it had been missing out on before. Ever since the company began using the Lost-Job survey, its revenues have doubled, and Tjelmeland says perusing them from time to time is good for something else too. "It keeps me humble," he admits.

SOURCE: Teri Lammers, "The Lost-Job Survey," *Inc.*, April 1992, 78–79.

Furthermore, the more a customer uses the credit card the more profitable those fees become: for example, it costs the same 90 cents to generate and mail the monthly bill for someone with $10 worth of credit card purchases as for someone with $100 worth of purchases. Two experts writing in the Harvard Business Review conclude that companies can boost profits by almost 100 percent by retaining just 5 percent more of their customers every year. This alone is an excellent reason for effective service management.

WHY MANAGING SERVICES IS A SPECIAL CHALLENGE

Service management is different from managing the creation of tangible products for two big reasons.[7] First, a service is generally created the instant it is used and cannot be produced and held in stock awaiting demand. Furthermore (and second), services

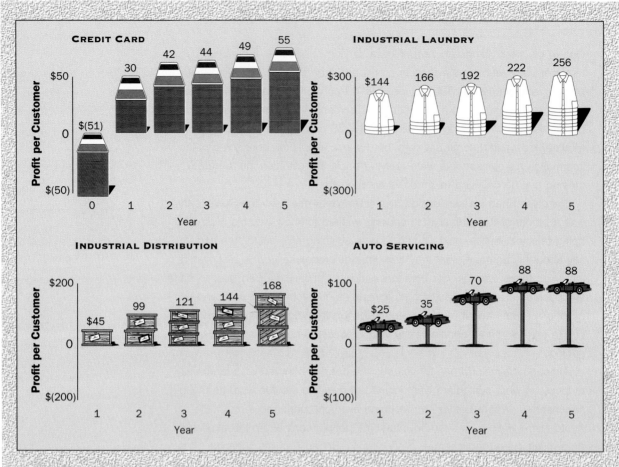

FIGURE 21.2

How Much Profit a Customer Generates Over Time in Four Industries

The longer a customer stays with the company, the more profitable each of his or her transactions becomes for the company. For example, longer-term customers tend to buy more per transaction, so the same monthly cost of mailing a bill is spent on someone with $100 worth of purchases instead of $10.

NOTE: Customers who are with a company longer produce more profits; it therefore pays to keep present customers happy.

SOURCE: Frederick Reichheld and Earl Sasser, Jr., "Zero Defections: Quality Comes to Services," *Harvard Business Review,* September–October 1990, 106–07.

are usually provided with little or no supervision. Goods and products usually get a series of quality checks on their way to the warehouse where they await shipping. Services, though, are usually provided without the checks that are familiar aspects of production processes. Usually no production supervisor or quality control clerk is hovering around the arrogant waiter who ruins a customer's meal, for example. The nature of services thus makes managing services a special challenge.

KARL ALBRECHT'S SERVICE TRIANGLE©

The actual techniques of service management focus on three core concepts: the moment of truth, the triangle of service, and service cycles.[8]

THE MOMENT OF TRUTH

The core concept in service management is the **moment of truth,** which service management expert Karl Albrecht defines as "that precise instant when the customer comes into contact with any aspect of your business and, on the basis of that contact, forms an opinion about the quality of your service and, potentially, the quality of your product."[9]

The moment of truth plays a central role in service management because it is, as Albrecht says, "the basic atom of service, the smallest indivisible unit of value delivered to the customer."[10] When you as a customer call Federal Express or go to a movie or theater or supermarket, you experience moments of truth—precise instants when you come into contact with any aspect of the business. On the basis of those accumulated moments of truth you then form an opinion about the quality of the service you have received and, potentially, about the quality of the product as well.

For example, here are some typical moments of truth in a supermarket shopping experience:

1. You look for a place to park in the supermarket's lot.
2. You walk to the supermarket from your car.
3. You look for a shopping cart.
4. You get your check approved.
5. You ask a clerk for directions to a product.

MOMENT OF TRUTH
A core concept in service management that is the precise instant when the customer comes into contact with any aspect of the business and, on the basis of that contact, forms an opinion about the quality of service and, potentially, the quality of the product.

The friendly efficiency of Federal Express delivery persons plays a large role in the opinions customers form of the company.

6. You pick up your items.

7. You wait in the checkout line.

8. Your order is added up.

9. Your items are placed in the bag.

10. You take your purchases back to your car.

This is a simplified example, of course, but consider how many opportunities the supermarket's management has to create a good (or bad) service quality impression on you. In fact, if your supermarket was really interested in improving quality, they would have to manage the service experience in such a way that *each of those moments of truth proved to be as positive an experience as possible.* How might they do this? By taking actions like reducing waiting time at the checkout lines, expediting the check approval process, and ensuring that stock clerks are ready and eager to answer your questions.

One of the main points service management experts like Albrecht make is that when the moments of truth go unmanaged the quality of service quickly deteriorates. In other words, if the supermarket manager does not actually sit back and consider what his or her customer's typical moments of truth are and then see that they are positive experiences, the moments of truth will likely be unhappy ones. And for the supermarket (or for almost any other business, for that matter) this accumulation of negative experiences embodied by the bad moments of truth will undermine the customer's perceptions of the quality of the service of the firm. In today's highly competitive world, that could be deadly. To take our supermarket example, management may stock the shelves with the finest products and perhaps even offer competitive prices. But if the moments of truth go unmanaged and the customer's experience is sufficiently bad the market will lose out to its competitors down the road.

THE CYCLE OF SERVICE

Albrecht therefore suggests thinking of the organization's moments of truth in terms of a **cycle of service.** Start with the first instance in which a customer comes into contact with any aspect of the organization, and then proceed through every other contact between the customer and the organization.

The manager and his or her team will want to map out a cycle of service for three reasons. First, by carefully thinking through each contact from beginning to end, a complete list of all the moments of truth can be identified. Second, once identified, the most critical moments of truth can then be focused on. Finally, with a list of moments of truth (and particularly the critical ones), management can turn to actually managing the service experience. But such service management also means creating a *service strategy* and attending to the *service people* and the *service system.* We discuss these next. The *Stew Leonard* small business box shows how far one small business will go to keep its service quality top-notch.

THE COMPONENTS OF THE SERVICE TRIANGLE

Along with the moments of truth and service cycles, the service triangle is a basic service concept. Perhaps the best way to introduce the *service triangle* is to review the example of Jan Carlzon and his efforts at SAS. Recall that upon taking over the airline in 1980, Carlzon decided to build its competitive advantage around high quality customer service. He therefore formulated a service *strategy* that involved giving business travelers the top-notch service they were willing to pay top-notch prices for. But

CYCLE OF SERVICE
Starts with the first instance in which a customer comes into contact with any aspect of the organization, and then proceeds through every other contact between the customer and the organization.

STEW LEONARD

Don't look for a lot of frills at Stew Leonard's, just good products at reasonable prices. The sign outside the Danbury, Connecticut, store reads, Our Mission Is to Create Happy Customers! Stew Leonard means it—and does it. Even though the Danbury location—which is actually a tent—carries only about 800 items, less than 5 percent of a typical supermarket, sales are an impressive $500,000 per week. And the original 115,000-square-foot Stew Leonard's store in nearby Norwalk racks up numbers that would make Sam Walton envious. Annual sales there are $115 million, or $3,470 per foot of floor selling space.

Stew Leonard, Sr., opened the first store in 1969. His sons Stew, Jr., and Tom run things now, but they still heed the founding father's input. Slippages in product quality seldom escape their eyes. Like the time the sons and several managers were preparing to meet with a high-priced consultant. Stew, Sr., wasn't able to be there, but one son called to see if any critical company matters were on his mind that he could analyze. "As a matter of fact," Stew, Sr., said, "I bought some corn yesterday—and it wasn't really sweet."

The son reminded his father that this was to be a strictly big-issue meeting dealing with strategy, merchandising, and other such matters of pressing import. He asked again if his father had anything along those lines. "Yeah," he replied, "the corn isn't really, really sweet."

Stew Leonard, Sr., has always had clear-cut ideas of what's important and what's not. The way he puts it, his customers, "come here to save money on

FOCUS ON SMALL BUSINESS

good stuff," and he does whatever it takes to make sure his stuff is good. Stew Leonard Stores therefore quickly redid the scheduling for corn delivery. Instead of receiving it in the evenings for sale the following day, the farmer now brings it in the day it is picked. The corn then goes on sale and when it does, it's really, really sweet.

Tom Leonard runs the Danbury store and claims he likes customer complaints. "When people call up," Tom says, "and they have a problem with an item, I thank them so much for calling, because I can go out and solve the problem right now." The Leonards are inquisitive as well. Twelve times a year, Stew, Jr., rounds up a dozen customers for a 60-minute focus group session. For their trouble, each gets a $20 store certificate, and the Leonards think it's money well spent. "Some of the ideas that have come out of that have been incredible," says Stew, Sr. One such suggestion led to merchandising fresh fish on ice instead of in the standard plastic packages found in most grocers. A new merchandising display had to be constructed, but sales doubled. Stew, Sr., said it might have taken him a hundred years to come up with an idea he got from a customer for a store voucher.

The Leonards know that their limited selection means customers must make a special stop at their stores. They also know the key to long-term success comes from paying attention to that sign out front.

SOURCES: Pheadra Hise, "Pushing the Customer Service Envelope," *Inc.*, July 1993, 24; and Michael Barrier, "A New Sense of Service," *Nation's Business*, June 1991, 16–21.

---

he knew that to implement his strategy, Carlzon had to modify both the *people* and the *system* at SAS. For example, the SAS people had to be trained and retrained and empowered to cut through red tape to help the customers. In terms of the systems, Carlzon had to eliminate first-class service, expand business-class service, institute new check-in systems for business customers, install business equipment like FAX machines that his customers could use, and so forth.

Albrecht says it's useful to think of a successful service management effort in terms of a **service triangle,** as presented in Figure 21.3. As you can see, three key factors form the corners of the service triangle:

1. A vision, or strategy, for the service product.
2. Customer-oriented front-line people.
3. Customer-friendly systems.[11]

SERVICE TRIANGLE
Three key factors form the service triangle: vision for the service product; customer-oriented front-line people, and customer-friendly systems.

FIGURE 21.3

The Service Triangle©

Successful service management means formulating an effective service strategy, creating customer-oriented front-line people, and then building customer-friendly systems.

SOURCE: Karl Albrecht and Ron Zemke, *Service America: Doing Business in the New Economy* (Homewood, IL: Dow Jones-Irwin, 1985), 41. ©1984 Karl Albrecht.

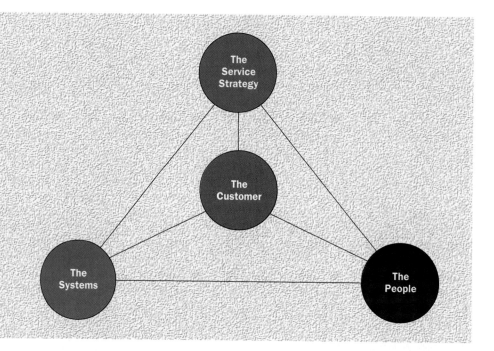

Service management experts know that these three key factors must perform together to maintain a high level of service quality. Here's how Albrecht describes each one of them:

> A well-conceived strategy for service. The outstanding organizations have discovered, invented, or evolved a unifying idea about what they do. This service concept, or service strategy . . . directs the attention of the people in the organization toward the real priorities of the customer. This guiding concept finds its way into all that people do. It becomes a rallying cry, a kind of gospel, and the nucleus of the message to be transmitted to the customer.
>
> Customer-oriented front-line people. By some means the managers of such organizations have encouraged and helped the people who deliver the service to keep their attention fastened on the needs of the customer . . . This leads to a level of responsiveness, attentiveness, and willingness to help that marks the service as superior in the customer's mind and makes him or her want to tell others about it and then come back for more.
>
> Customer-friendly systems. The delivery system that backs up the service people is truly designed for the convenience of the customer rather than the convenience of the organization. The physical facilities, policies, procedures, methods, and communication processes all say to the customer, 'This apparatus is here to meet your needs.'[12]

Later in this chapter, we will look more closely at the methods managers use to formulate service strategies, recruit and train front-line people, and develop customer-friendly systems.

EVERYONE HAS A CUSTOMER   Remember that everyone in the organization has a customer. A company's service management effort necessarily focuses a lot of attention on the company's front-line people—the cabin attendants, cashiers, food servers, and telephone operators, for instance—who actually interact with the company's customers. It is therefore easy for a company's managers to neglect the vast array of employees who are in background jobs—like accounts payable and inventory control—who normally have no direct contact with the company's ultimate customers.

And yet it is a big mistake to neglect these important background, non-front-line employees. In fact, service management experts emphasize that "If you're not serving the customer, you'd better be serving someone who is."[13] The point they make is that "internal" service—services by a company's employees for a company's employees—is as important as the service provided by front-line employees and needs to be managed just as carefully.

MAKING THE BUSINESS CUSTOMER DRIVEN: SERVICE MANAGEMENT TOOLS

A number of tools are available to facilitate the analysis and improvement of service systems. Several are discussed next.

DESIGNING THE SERVICE SYSTEM: THE SERVICE BLUEPRINT

A service blueprint is a detailed graphical presentation of the sequence of steps needed to produce and render the service to a customer. A blueprint (like the simple one for a corner shoeshine in Figure 21.4) provides a picture that helps identify the nature of a company's service system and determine the points at which that system has to be improved.

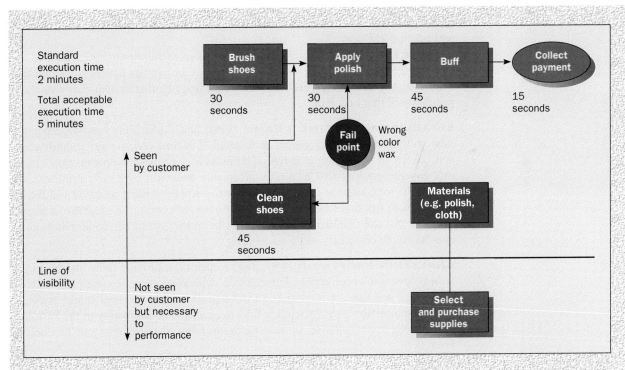

FIGURE 21.4

Blueprint for a Corner Shoeshine

Using a "blueprint" like this to outline the service steps and potential failpoints can help a service firm improve the quality of its service.

SOURCE: Lynn Shostack, "Designing Services That Deliver," *Harvard Business Review*, January–February 1984, 134.

For example, consider the corner shoeshine in the figure. Above the "line of visibility" are all those activities seen by the customer (brush shoes, apply polish, and buff). Below the line of visibility are activities like "select and purchase supplies," which are not seen by the customer but are still vital to successful service performance.

A blueprint like this one provides the service manager with four types of information.[14]

IDENTIFYING PROCESSES   The first step in creating your blueprint is to map out the processes or activities that constitute the service. In this case, these activities include brushing shoes, applying polish, and buffing, for example. While this blueprint was intentionally kept simple, a service manager would normally want to provide more detail. For example, it might be useful for the owner to show how the buffing step will be performed. And of course for more complicated services like tax preparation, the number of activities and decision points will be much, much greater.

The blueprint distinguishes between those activities that are seen and those not seen by the customer, and it's important not to underestimate the role of those activities which are out of the customer's line of visibility. For example, the actual act of buying substandard supplies might not be seen by the customer, but its effects would probably become noticeable rather quickly. Much the same can be said of an airline's purchase of in-flight meals or a bank's decision to change its computer system.

ISOLATING FAIL POINTS   Once the service designer has laid out all the activities or processes involved, it becomes easier to identify those points at which the system might break down.

Having identified possible fail points, it then becomes easier to anticipate and plan to avoid them. For example, if one possible fail point (in the figure) is "wrong color wax" our proprietor might institute a color coding or other system that reduces the possibility of that occurring.

ESTABLISHING A TIME FRAME   Costs and profitability tend to depend on time, so the next thing to consider is the amount of time each activity should take. As you can see in the figure, it is typical to provide a standard execution time (in this case two minutes) as well as a total acceptable execution time (five minutes). This reflects the total amount of time a customer is actually willing to spend waiting and having his or her shoes shined. After five minutes, of course, the proprietor's research indicates that the customer's perception of the quality of the service declines quickly and that some customers will actually leave.

ANALYZING PROFITABILITY   The blueprint can provide some insight into the service operation's profitability. For example, depending upon how the proprietor values his or her time, a standard execution time of two minutes might make the shoeshine profitable, while spending four minutes (while acceptable to the customer) might make it unprofitable, by halving the number of shines that can be done per hour.

THE CUSTOMER REPORT CARD

The customer report card lists the *service attributes* that your customers are looking for, as well as the relative weights or *priorities* of each attribute and how the customers *score* your company on each of these attributes. If the information can be obtained, it's also useful to add your competitors' scores on each attribute for comparison purposes. One way to obtain the information required to compile the report card is to conduct in-depth interviews with a sample of the company's customers.[15]

DESIRABLE SERVICE ATTRIBUTES	CUSTOMER PRIORITY	OUR MOVIE'S SCORE (BASED ON AUDIT)	TABLE 21.1
Convenient parking	High	Medium	
Safe parking	High	Low	Report Card for Downtown Ten-Plex Movie Theater
First-run movies	High	High	
Clean theater	High	Medium	
Unobstructed view	High	High	
Comfortable seats	Medium	Medium	
Courteous clerks	Low	Low	
Short waits for tickets	Medium	Low	

An example of a report card for the Downtown Ten-Plex Movie Theater is presented in Table 21.1. As you can see, the movie theater's customer research lists eight service attributes that typical theatergoers look for in the Ten-Plex Theater. These service attributes include convenient parking, first-run movies, and a clean theater. In the next column, each of these attributes are given a priority ranking, to reflect the fact that some attributes are more important than others. For example, convenient parking, safe parking, and first-run movies are all high-priority services, while courteous clerks (while a significant service attribute) is rated relatively low. Finally, the customer report card includes a space called "Our Score" toward the right. Management can use this space to record how customers rated the Downtown Ten-Plex Movie Theater on each of these service attributes. Finally, while the report card for Ten-Plex does not include one, a final column may be added on the right to list the competitors' scores. This can in turn be important information when formulating a service strategy for our Ten-Plex Theater.

Thomas Raffio, senior vice-president at Delta Dental Plan, meets with member dentists to solicit face-to-face feedback. Constant communication with customers has enabled Delta to retain accounts and improve its internal procedures.

DELTA DENTAL

Delta Dental Plan exploits its customers, and the customers don't seem to mind. The Medford, Massachusetts firm sells and administers dental benefits to 300,000 employees and dependents at 2,000 companies.

Delta's customer service system utilizes the best source available to evaluate client satisfaction—the customers themselves. Under the program, Delta surveys its client companies, their employees, and the dentists. Corporate customers are contacted quarterly by phone or mail. Dentists give feedback once a year, and are also encouraged to attend meetings where suggestions on improving service are discussed. Employees of the various companies are called randomly for their impressions.

Delta's seven-point service guarantee, the foundation of the company's "no-hassle" customer-service program, is another interesting feature. Should Delta fail to fulfill any of its service pledges, the customer gets a check. Customers who haven't received their ID card within 15 days of signing up get $25. Not getting a phone call returned within 24 hours is worth $50. Even more surprisingly, if a corporate customer switches to Delta and the changeover isn't hassle-free, that month's administration fee is waived. Such charges can be as high as $7,500, and it's entirely the customer's decision.

The company paid out almost $25,000 for service glitches in 1992, but senior vice-president Thomas Raffio thinks it's worth it. "We look at this as an opportunity to improve," he says. "We let employees have the authority to do this without being concerned about the cost." It's hard to argue with him. Delta is keeping clients at a rate of between 97 and 99 percent.

SOURCE: Roberta Maynard, "What Do Customers Think of Your Firm?" *Nation's Business,* April 1993, 62–63.

THE SERVICE AUDIT

SERVICE AUDIT
An ongoing periodic audit accomplished most often by questionnaire or survey which is used to take the pulse of how the company is doing with respect to each of the service attributes.

Many companies (see the *Delta Dental* vignette above) also conduct regular examinations or surveys of how they are doing on each of the report card service attributes. Such a **service audit** is an ongoing periodic audit—most often accomplished by questionnaire or survey—which is used to take the pulse of how the company is doing with respect to each of the service attributes. The *Restek* vignette on page 631 shows how one firm runs a more informal but still effective service audit.

THE MANAGEMENT PROCESS IN A SERVICE WORLD

The planning, organizing, staffing, leading, and controlling techniques that managers might use for a manufacturing firm like General Motors are often somewhat different from those used to run service firms. We'll look briefly at the management functions as they apply to services in this section.

RESTEK

Employees of Restek, a $9.2 million manufacturer of lab equipment parts, take customer service seriously. Everyone from secretaries to graphic artists attend the company's product awareness course and know who the big customers and competitors are.

Over 25 employees have completed technical training and take turns working the technical service lines answering routine questions and handling customer complaints.

In addition, volunteer employees contact between 200 and 300 customers each month to "follow-up" on Restek's performance and make sure the customers are completely satisfied. "When customers complain about a product, the follow-up call might be made by the person who manufactured or tested it," says technical marketing director Neil Mosesman, "so they really want to know why something didn't work, and they feel like they have to bend over backward to fix the problem." Other customers may be people that haven't ordered anything for 12 months or first-time buyers who can give valuable feedback about the timeliness of arrival and how a product is working. Ideas about new products are solicited from customers as well.

Still, one might wonder why people don't just shunt service calls over to the customer service department. There's an easy answer to that one. At Restek, everyone is a customer service rep.

SOURCE: *Inc.,* November, 1993, 123, "Every Employee a Service Rep" *Business Ethics,* March/April 1994, Vol.8, No. 2, 30.

Customer service is at the heart of Restek's success. All of its 70 employees are familiar with the company's product line. In addition, roughly one-third of the staff has had further technical training, enabling them to field calls on the tech-support line.

SOME CHARACTERISTICS OF SERVICE PLANNING

Some planning techniques generally are not as useful for service firms as they are for industrial ones. For example, project planning techniques (like Gantt and PERT charts discussed in Chapter 19) are of relatively little use in creating a service that is consumed at the moment it is produced. Similarly, production planning control techniques (such as order control) are of little use.

On the other hand, service firms do engage in strategic and tactical planning. Techniques such as industry analysis, formulating competitive and corporate level strategies, and using the SWOT analysis to analyze the company's strengths, weaknesses, opportunities, and threats are all used by service firms.

Many service firms also use a service planning tool that researcher John Shaw calls the **client/customer service spectrum,** which assumes that some services are more easily standardized than are others. As illustrated in Figure 21.5,[16] the left side of the client/customer service spectrum is for services that require unique solutions to complex problems: a specialized medical diagnosis, a unique legal difficulty, or an international accounting problem are service examples. Clients facing challenging medical or legal problems like these usually have little choice but to use the services of the highly trained specialists that provide them.

CLIENT/CUSTOMER SERVICE SPECTRUM
A service planning tool that assumes that some services are more easily standardized than are others.

FIGURE 21.5

The Service Spectrum: How Customized Is the Service?

A service firm's plans are influenced in part by the degree to which its service is, or can be, standardized. For example, a law firm could spin off a separate division to provide packaged wills while the parent firm continues to concentrate on complex legal problems.

SOURCE: Adapted from John Shaw, *The Service Focus* (Homewood, IL: Dow Jones-Irwin, 1990), 31.

Unique	Mixed	Routine
1	2	3
Client need: Unique solutions to complex problems (Highly customized)	Client/customer need: Experience-based solutions to more routine problems	Client requirement: Generic solutions to common requirements (Not customized at all)
Example: Complex medical or legal problem	Traffic tickets; broken bones	Prepackaged incorporations or wills
Provided by: Highly trained specialists	Less specialization required	Can be provided by Paralegals or nurses

In the middle of the spectrum are service problems that lend themselves to somewhat more routine problem solving. Local law firms handling relatively routine civil matters (such as traffic tickets), individual medical practitioners handling sore throats and broken bones, and accountants handling small business tax returns fit in this category.

To the right of the spectrum are service firms that provide *standardized* solutions to common requirements. Legal service companies that offer prepackaged incorporation documents or divorces, discount brokerages that merely buy and sell securities but offer little research or advice, and fast-food chains like McDonald's would fit in this category.

The client/customer service spectrum planning tool helps the service firm identify what its service strategy is and what it should be. For example, many service firms start out offering a unique and indispensable service, the sort found at the left of the spectrum. As more competitors enter the market, and clients become more sophisticated the services provided often become increasingly standardized, and the service shifts to the center of the spectrum. Then, even later in the service's life, computerization and other advances might actually turn the service into a highly standardized commodity service.

For example, consider the work done by many certified public accounting firms. Many years ago, the auditing practices of these firms aimed at solving relatively unique and complex problems and were thus toward the left of the client/customer service spectrum. Today, the auditing practices of many (or most) accounting firms have become almost a commodity product. In other words, the audit services do not differ very much among the accounting firms and tend to be routine and aimed at providing standardized solutions to what have become common, industrywide requirements.

This is where the service spectrum comes in. In considering what its strategy should be, a company could use the service spectrum to consider whether it has inadvertently slipped "down-scale" by offering more prepackaged solutions (perhaps in order to get more customers and thus keep total billings up), or whether it should do so. Or, it may suggest that a CPA firm might want to diversify away from sole reliance on relatively routine audits, and add a management consulting practice.

SOME CHARACTERISTICS OF SERVICE ORGANIZING

Service organizing has some unique characteristics, in part because of service firms' heavy dependence on front-line customer-contact people. In particular, there are at least two important characteristics of service organizing: the *upside-down pyramid* and *worker empowerment*. First, service management experts recommend turning the traditional authority pyramid upside down so that it looks like the one in Figure 21.6. This emphasizes that the customers are the real bosses of the firm, and that managers and support units exist to ensure that the front-line service employees have what they need to service their customers. Drawing the pyramid in this way (and publicizing it throughout the firm) has several consequences. For example, it draws attention to the fact that job descriptions for customer service people and those of support units and managers should emphasize supporting customers and front-line employees.

Expanding front-line employees' authority, in other words, *empowering* them, is a second characteristic of service organizing. Customers (such as irate airline passengers) usually want service, and they want it *now*. It is deadly to make your front-line

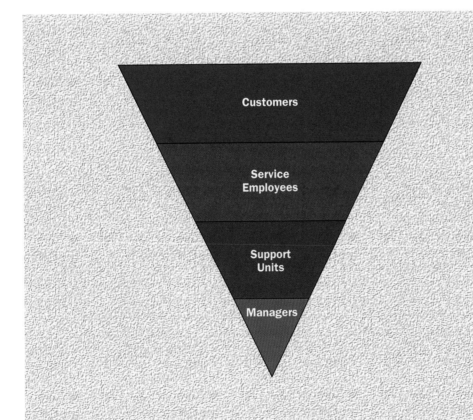

FIGURE 21.6

Turning the Authority Pyramid Upside Down

It is important for a service firm to think of its organization as being an upside-down pyramid. It is the customer on top (not the president) that drives decision making, and the managers and support units exist to help the front-line service employees serve the customer.

NOTE: The upside-down pyramid suggests management must support the front-line employees who serve the customers.

SOURCE: Karl Albrecht, *At America's Service* (Homewood, IL: Dow Jones-Irwin, 1988, 107.

Customers

Service Employees

Support Units

Managers

people simply claim "I've got to check with my boss first." This is why empowering front-line employees was one of Jan Carlzon's service building blocks at SAS.

A program at the Hampton Inn hotel chain illustrates the benefits of worker empowerment.[17] In order to build a competitive advantage, the new, fast-growing Hampton Inn chain decided to institute an unconditional 100 percent satisfaction guarantee for its customers. The guarantee states that if a guest has a problem or complaint at any time during his or her stay and is not satisfied by checkout time, the chain will give the guest one night's stay for free. Guarantees that are invoked are transmitted by computer to the chain's Memphis headquarters so management is kept aware of service weaknesses.

As Ray Schultz, the President and Chief Executive of Hampton Inn hotels puts it, "The secret to making the guarantee work is giving our employees the authority to implement it." For example, the program authorizes all employees—not just the hotel manager or the front desk personnel—to take whatever action is needed to keep the customer satisfied. If a housekeeper notices a guest who is upset because her key won't work in the door, the housekeeper does not have to refer the frustrated guest to the front desk. The housekeeper (indeed, all employees) are empowered to get a new key, change the lock, or arrange for a different room. If the guest still isn't happy, any employee may offer to refund the cost of the room for the night—without contacting the manager.[18] In other words, worker empowerment is the key to Hampton Inn's service strategy.

SOME CHARACTERISTICS OF SERVICE STAFFING

Imagine this: you are scheduled to fly out on Flight 504 but as you wait for your flight to be called the announcer says, "504 has been cancelled, please come to the passenger agent to rebook your flight." You race to the agent, only to find that you're about 40th in line. After what seems like an eternity, you finally make it to the front and tell the agent, "I'd like the next flight to Topeka." Whereupon she glares at you, and screams at the top of her lungs, "You're not the only one with a problem around here, you know, and if you don't think I'm working fast enough you can go to the back of the line for all I care."

Such episodes underscore one of the most challenging characteristics of service staffing—the need to recruit, select and train customer service people who must deal with high levels of *emotional labor*. Emotional labor basically means the degree to which the employee's feelings are important on the job. Of course, even car assembly line workers use their feelings on the job. However, assembly jobs tend to be relatively low in emotional labor. Front-line employees like airline reservations clerks, telephone operators, accountants, front-desk clerks, and (to a greater or lesser extent) all employees whose job it is to interact with customers directly have high emotional labor jobs. It is therefore especially important that employees who deal with the public be carefully recruited and tested and screened, so that antisocial types don't slip through.

Service staffing is also characterized by *wall-to-wall training*. Basically, this involves short bursts of 100 percent participation training: a service management program is kicked off by having every employee in the organization brought together (perhaps divided into large groups). They are all trained at about the same time during a one- or two-day period.

Wall-to-wall training programs first became popular after the approach was used at SAS. There, Carlzon retained a training firm to ensure that every employee from manager to baggage handler went through an intensive two-day workshop devoted to the new SAS.[19] A similar program was recently instituted by the Alamo Rent-A-Car firm, where employees were exposed to a five-day combined orientation and training session.[20] With respect to orientation, the program focused on such basics as Alamo's history, its growth and expansion, benefits, and company expectations and work ethics. The customer service training portion emphasized the importance of outstanding customer service, explained how to define it, and identified the specific skills (like active listening, for instance) needed to deliver it.

SOME CHARACTERISTICS OF SERVICE LEADERSHIP

One of a service management leader's most important tasks is to mold a company culture that fosters high quality service. As several experts put it:

> The individual employee's willingness to do the "extras," to do the little things, to add a touch of grace to the service is influenced directly by the organizational culture in which the employee functions. Culture, after all, defines what is important, what is valued in the organization. How can we expect even the most self-motivated individuals to try extra hard for customers day after day and week after week if the organization does not respond to this behavior, if no one in the organizational hierarchy seems to notice—or care?[21]

Successful service leaders, like Jan Carlzon at SAS, must also formulate and promulgate a customer-oriented *vision* of the business, one that makes *customer satisfaction* the nucleus of the firm's strategy. They effectively *communicate* this vision to all employees through techniques like wall-to-wall training and personal example. Effective service leaders like Hampton Inn's Ray Schultz also create a feeling among the employees that they and the firm share a common fate. Employees then conduct themselves in ways that reflect high-quality service, even if there's no supervisor around to make them do so. Creating that kind of commitment is the essence of effective service management leadership.

SOME CHARACTERISTICS OF SERVICE CONTROL

The basic control process in a service company is essentially the same as in any firm and involves three steps: setting standards, measuring performance, and taking remedial action. The standards in this case are generally *service standards,* like those summarized in Figure 21.7. As you can see, customer-contact employees at MBank are given specific courtesy standards to follow when dealing with the bank's customers. Standards like these "present customer expectations in a language that service providers understand and find meaningful."[22] Wall-to-wall training and communications devices like service newsletters are used to make sure these standards (and the reasons for them) are understood.

Service audits and similar types of ongoing customer-satisfaction surveys form the basis of the second, *measurement* stage of service control. Measurement may take the form of a service audit survey, customer interviews, tracking complaints, or similar means. In any case, employees must see that the firm takes the standards seriously and is measuring performance to see that they are met.

In the third, *remedial action* stage of control, service management experts usually recommend rewards, not punitive measures. Rewards include direct financial rewards, nonfinancial recognition, and career advancement.[23] For example, in its President's Special Quality Award Program, Metropolitan Life Insurance Company issues 1,000 annual awards of $1,000 each to employees who demonstrated "an obsession with quality" in serving their customers.[24] Customers and employees nominate individuals for the awards by writing a letter of recommendation to the president. Winners are selected based on consultations with managers familiar with each nominee.

FIGURE 21.7

Customer Courtesy Standards at MBank

SOURCE: Leonard Berry, David Bennet, and Carter Brown, *Service Quality* (Homewood, IL: Dow Jones-Irwin, 1989), 171. Reprinted by permission of MBank. A separate set of standards has been developed for telephone encounters.

- Smile sincerely and make eye contact when you greet customers. Don't avert your eyes or look down when a customer approaches you. Say "Hello," "How are you," and "May I help you" in a friendly way.

- *Introduce yourself* either when the customer first walks up or immediately when you answer the telephone.

- *Use the customer's name twice.* In many instances, you will have the customer's name right in front of you—on a deposit slip check, or on the CRT—so use it. It makes the customer feel important.

- *Give the customer your undivided attention.* When you're talking to a customer, put aside the papers at your desk, quit adding up a column of numbers or writing a report.

- *Answer questions accurately and completely.* Don't guess. If you're not sure of the answer, check with someone who knows and get back to the customer immediately.

- *Refer the customer to another MBanker by introducing the customer and explaining the situation.* If the customer is in the bank, call ahead to the person who you are referring them to.

- *Give specific directions to other areas of the bank.* Say, "The Personal Banking Center is in the southwest corner of the first floor across from Customer Service"—rather than "on the first floor."

- *Say "Please" and "Thank You."*

Service companies also use recognition to reinforce high-service performers.[25] Northwest Corporation's annual reports often contain full color photos of excellent service employees. It also awards a "highly visible" five foot tall trophy every month to the branch providing the best service in the system. This lets branch employees know they have done a good job, and that their customers are going to know it too.

FIVE STEPS IN IMPLEMENTING A SERVICE MANAGEMENT PROGRAM

It would be useful to conclude this chapter with a quick summary of the process involved in creating a service-oriented, customer-driven organization.[26] Service management experts Karl Albrecht and Ron Zemke say this involves five steps:

STEP 1: THE SERVICE AUDIT

The first step in making a company service oriented is to conduct a service audit and formulate a customer report card. As we have seen, this step involves determining the service attributes that are important, prioritizing them, and then determining how your company rates when it comes to these various factors.

STEP 2: STRATEGY DEVELOPMENT

The second step is to formulate a service strategy, which has been defined as "a distinctive formula for delivering service; such a strategy is keyed to a well-chosen benefit premise that is valuable to the customer and that establishes an effective competitive position."[27] In the simplest terms, the service strategy should answer the question, "Why should the customer choose us?" It should be clear and brief enough to be easily communicated to and grasped by all the company's employees. McDonald Corporation's strategic emphasis on "quality, service, cleanliness, and price" and Carlzon's SAS strategy emphasizing "high-quality service for business travelers" are examples.

STEP 3: EDUCATION

The next step in implementing a service program is to spread the gospel of service throughout the organization. As we've seen, wall-to-wall training is often the method of choice here: it enables all the firm's employees to quickly get up to speed regarding the firm's new service effort.

STEP 4: IMPLEMENTATION

The next phase involves the "implementation of grass-roots improvements in the way the organization produces and delivers its service products."[28]

Several activities are involved here: *service quality task forces* are often created. Each serves as a source of specific recommendations on how to improve service as well as functioning as a conduit of information back to the departments. Another implementation technique is the *application lab.* Here, a trainer (often a member of the firm's human resource department) is invited to meet with a department to discuss the group's service mission with them and to identify aspects of operation that the department would like to improve. Other companies use *service quality circles,* a small group of employees who meet on a regular basis to identify and solve service problems. Useful tools include the service blueprint and an analysis of the moments of truth and the cycle of service.

The most important implementation activity involves redesigning service systems. It often turns out that employees either cannot or will not do their jobs effectively because the firm's systems prevent them from doing so. For example, in one bank, the system requires that you stand in one line to get the check approved and then stand in a second, longer line to pick up your money!

Redesigning service systems can involve many things. Albrecht defines a customer-impact system as "any organizational structure, procedure, method, or rule that causes a result the customer can perceive."[29] Therefore, implementing grass-roots improvements might involve modifying organization structures, data systems (to avoid having to respond to customer concerns with "Sorry, the computer can't do that"), customer rules, and serial procedures (the actual sequence of steps the company uses to handle the customer's problem). The idea is to let the front-line employees do their jobs.

STEP 5: MAINTENANCE—MAKING THE CHANGE PERMANENT

Making the change permanent requires effective service management, in terms of planning, organizing, staffing, leading, and controlling. For example, making high-quality service the norm means the firm must continually audit customers to ensure that the service attributes (such as speed of delivery) do not have to be revised and to continually assess each attribute's relative importance. Employees need to be empowered and reminded that the customer comes first. Employee selection and training must be effective so the high-emotional labor jobs are properly staffed. Top managers have to walk their talk and show by word and deed that they do take service seriously. Service standards must be set, performance measured, and rewards distributed to ensure that customer service remains top-notch. Making the change permanent thus requires a coordinated application of the management functions of planning, organizing, staffing, leading, and controlling.

SUMMARY

The number of people employed in service-producing industries is growing rapidly. The increasing intensity of global competition makes service management even more important. Better service can be a competitive advantage, and poor service can result in lost customers and decreased profits. Managing services is different from managing the creation of a product because services are created and used simultaneously and are often provided without supervision.

The moment of truth is that instant when customers come in contact with any aspect of a business and form an opinion about the quality of its service and potentially the quality of its product. These various moments should be regarded in terms of a cycle of service. The three key corners of the service triangle are a concept, or strategy, for the service product, customer-oriented front-line people, and customer-friendly systems.

A service blueprint is a detailed graphical presentation of the sequence of steps needed to produce and render the service to a customer. It identifies processes, highlights potential fail points, establishes a time frame for activities, and provides insight into profitability. A customer report card lists and prioritizes the service attributes customers want and scores performance on each. Some companies also conduct surveys, or service audits, to discover how customers rate performance in each report card service category.

The planning, organizing, staffing, leading, and controlling techniques used to run service firms are often different from those used in manufacturing firms. Many service firms use a planning tool called the client/customer service spectrum, which assumes some services are more easily standardized than others. Two important characteristics of service organizing are the upside-down pyramid and worker empowerment. Customer service jobs involve high levels of emotional labor, and employees must be properly screened. Staffing is characterized by short, intensive, participative training. Service leadership begins by molding a company's culture and setting standards required for high quality service. Service leaders must also have a customer-based vision that makes customer satisfaction the center of the firm's strategy, and they must communicate this to all employees.

The five steps in implementing a service management program include the service audit, strategy development, education, implementation, and maintenance (making changes permanent).

QUESTIONS

■ FOR REVIEW

1. List at least three reasons why service management is important.

2. Describe the three core concepts that serve as the corners of Karl Albrecht's service triangle.

3. Give several examples of the type of information contained in a typical service blueprint.

4. How do management techniques in a service firm differ from those in a manufacturing firm?

5. What are the essential steps involved in creating a service-oriented and customer-driven organization?

■ FOR DISCUSSION

6. Why do you think service-producing industries are experiencing such explosive growth?

7. Consider the following statement: "A company with a superior product and low

prices will succeed, even if its customer service is deficient." Do you agree or disagree? Discuss.

8. Identify a company that you think has exceptional customer service. What makes it so special?

9. Compare the management training that might be required to manage a service firm with the management background that would be most appropriate for a manufacturing firm.

■ FOR ACTION

10. Visit a local retail store with the aim of evaluating the level of customer service. Describe the moments of truth, and explain how they influenced your opinion of the establishment.

11. Create a basic service blueprint for a service firm of your choice. Identify the processes that constitute the service, isolate fail points, and establish a time frame for each activity.

12. Interview someone who is employed by a high-quality service organization. Ask them to describe the customer-service training they received.

■ FOR FOCUS ON SMALL BUSINESS

13. What steps does Stew Leonard's take to ensure that its customers' moments of truth are as positive an experience as possible?

14. Create a sample report card that Stew Leonard's could use to conduct a service audit.

15. Based on the facts presented in this example, describe what makes Stew Leonard's a service leader. Would a large firm use the same methods? Why or why not?

CLOSING SOLUTION

KINDERCARE LEARNING CENTERS, INC.

After KinderCare emerged from bankruptcy in April 1993, Gearreald implemented a strategy that anyone managing services would do well to emulate: he listened to customers and followed up on what they wanted. To directly attack one of parents' biggest gripes—teacher turnover—Gearreald made it policy that everyone at the company's 1,160 centers take a fully-paid, 12-hour training course. The agenda included teaching techniques and different approaches for dealing with parents. "We hope the training tells them, 'We think you're valuable, so we're making an investment in you,'" Gearreald says. Along with the training, additional programs were introduced to enrich children's daily learning experiences, including computers for homework or games. KinderCare also seized upon offering services to large corporations. The company now operates centers for around 40 megafirms, Citicorp and Walt Disney among them, and is actively seeking others. Gearreald also found a more cost-effective way to pursue the company's expansion goals. Instead of constructing million dollar, free-standing facilities, he discovered it was quicker and cheaper to establish locations in malls or strip shopping centers. He even opened a center just a few steps away from an Illinois train station, enabling harried commuters to drop off their children on their way to work.[30]

1. Discuss the unique challenges of managing services in the child care industry.

2. How could KinderCare benefit from a service blueprint?

3. Does the new KinderCare exhibit any of the characteristics of high quality service? If so, which ones?

Moment of Truth	Service Audit	**KEY TERMS**
Cycle of Service	Client/Customer Service Spectrum	
Service Triangle		

CASE FOR ANALYSIS

FOUR SEASONS HOTEL

Isadore Sharp, CEO and founder of the 32-year-old Four Seasons Resort and Hotel chain, sounds finicky to an extreme when it comes to service. A room at a Four Seasons hostelry will cost 20 percent more on average, yet the hotel consistently maintains 90 percent occupancy levels. A big part of the reason is the hotel's near-zero tolerance for unsatisfied customers. For Sharp, even one disenchanted guest out of a hundred won't do, because compounded over 25 hotels, that becomes a significantly unacceptable figure. "All of a sudden you've got 1 million people a year who won't use us," he says.

But even the best in the business face occasional challenges. One of Sharp's biggest tests came in 1992 with the opening of the Four Seasons Hotel Chinzan-so in Tokyo. Japan is known for its unique customer service, which many believe is superior to any available in the United States. Four Seasons had to find a way to blend its hotel's employees' Eastern traditions with its own exceptional Western service.

Senior vice-president of human resources John Young sums up the strategy this way: "What's really required is to build into employees over time the ability to distinguish between different guests' needs, and to adjust their behavior accordingly." Young continues, "We need to help people understand, and allow them to improvise, the way North Americans typically behave. That is where good service comes from: clarity of role, confidence and competence."

In order to achieve its objectives, however, Four Seasons management first had to find a way to overcome the obstacles it was facing. For starters, it did not have complete control over staffing as part of its hotel management contract. Hotel employees were hired and fired by Fujita Tourist Enterprises Company, Ltd., the firm that owned the Chinzan-so. In keeping with the Japanese way of doing business, Fujita promoted people based on loyalty and length of service, rather than on technical capabilities. Other differences were ingrained in the employees themselves. Japanese

workers tended to move through the hotel quickly, unlike their Western counterparts, who had been taught to take a more measured approach. To Western guests, the Japanese employees looked as if they were constantly dealing with an emergency. To Japanese hotel visitors, the Western employees appeared not to care about their duties.

Other procedural changes also proved difficult. While Four Seasons encouraged employees to solve problems on their own, Japanese staffers were accustomed to being told the right and wrong way of doing things. Japanese customer service "works much more by rote, and it lacks that interpersonal dynamic that someone who really felt the desire to provide good service would demonstrate," Young says.

On the positive side, plenty of similarities could be found between the Four Seasons' way and the Japanese way of doing business. The kind of service a guest at Four Seasons can expect in Japan, or anywhere else, covers a broad spectrum, starting with being greeted by name when checking in. Operators use this same personal approach when answering calls. Fresh flowers, fine china, and silver are also part of the process. Sharp doesn't think such touches can be overemphasized.

Since the typical guest is busy and living out of a suitcase, delivery of high-quality services on time, and time and time again, does not escape notice. It has become common knowledge throughout the travel industry as well. "Four Seasons is probably the premier luxury hotel chain," says Daniel Daniele, director of hospitality consulting for Ernst & Young of Chicago. "They've lived up to that reputation, and other hotel companies try to emulate them."

Many view the Four Seasons' emphasis on service as a direct reflection of Sharp himself. Marketer Bob Bloch notes the corporate culture and sense of purpose in everyone employed at Four Seasons. "I think aspects of the company which contribute to the culture are the commitment to quality, and the effort put into training the staff and orienting them to take pride in their work," he says. "I continually see Izzy's personality showing through in the attitudes and decisions of managers."

Sharp thinks a key to satisfying customers is to hold on to employees who are happy with their jobs. Toward that end, he offers good pay and benefits. And he carries the effort further with a never ending quest to eliminate what are called "potential employee dissatisfiers," which can include everything from uncomfortable uniforms to unpleasant working conditions. An additional motivator Sharp considers one of the most important is the Four Seasons incentive plan. Begun in 1980 and refined since through trial-and-error, Sharp thinks he's finally weeded out the problems most commonly associated with employee incentive programs.

"We decided to take the risk out of the program by funding pensions separately, and by basing most of our incentives on individual hotels and performance," he says. "We now have a bonus arrangement that sustains our strategy and helps set goals."

Sharp doesn't really expect perfection; he knows there will be occasional breakdowns. But he thinks keeping service concerns uppermost in everyone's mind, from the busboys to the hotel managers, engenders an attitude, which can transform the occasional problem into an opportunity when employees step in

quickly and conscientiously to correct it. The future, he's convinced, will not be kind to those who don't adopt this approach to service. "Customer retention will become sacred," he says.

SOURCES: Minda Zetlin, "When 99 Percent Isn't Enough," *Management Review*, March 1993, 49–52; Stephen Madden, "Home, Sweet Hotel," *Fortune*, December 19, 1988, 175–76; and Alicia Johnson, "An Incentive System for All Seasons," *Management Review*, August 1986, 58–60.

■ QUESTIONS

1. Do you think the level of commitment to customer service at Four Seasons will be such that it will overcome cultural differences between Japanese and western employees.

2. How would you suggest that Four Seasons go about training its Japanese employees? Should it try and make them conform to the hotel's North American standards or allow workers to continue with their typically Japanese approach?

3. Can Four Seasons hope to please both its Japanese and U.S. guests equally? What approach would you take?

4. Explain how you think Mr. Sharp may have applied The Service Triangle in creating his high service quality hotel chain.

A CASE IN DIVERSITY

JUGGLING CAREER AND FAMILY

Margaret Johnsson has proven she has both an eye for spotting talent and trends in corporate business practices. Her three-year old, Chicago-based J & A Corporate Financial Solutions provides consulting services to companies carrying out big-ticket projects. So far it's been a big success. How she's managed to pull it all together may also qualify her as a master magician and juggler.

About the same time Johnsson identified a host of available consulting opportunities with corporations that needed help with outside projects, she also took note of a growing number of professional women who wanted sufficient flexibility to both work and care for children. She was able to attract a staff of consultants, all CPAs, the majority with MBAs, with 10 or more years of experience. Except for one, the mothers had children and did the majority of their work out of their homes using a computer and modem. They agreed to be paid only when they worked, lowering overhead and eliminating social security contribution requirements. Even though insurance was available, most were covered under their spouse's company policy. This combination put J & A in an enviable competitive position when it came to pricing its services; Johnsson could often charge half of what other consultants were quoting. She expects revenues for 1994 to reach $750,000, twice the amount of the previous year.

J & A clients believe Johnsson is on to something. "You have a lot more highly qualified women in the work force who are looking for a balance between family and work," says Bryan DeLoatch, a manager with a Philip Morris Companies unit that uses J & A's consulting services. "It would be a mistake not to tap these re-

sources." And J & A's employees couldn't be happier with the arrangement.

But running the business hasn't been easy. Johnsson not only has had to cope with bolts from the blue from clients, but also unpredictable family crises that inevitably have occurred. To avert the potential for disillusioned clients forced to wait out some delay, Johnsson has put primary and back-up consultants in place to handle all accounts. One client was sufficiently dazzled with the contingency plan that he increased the scope of his project.

There are never any shortages of scheduling and operational headaches at J & A. While many companies are now making the necessary concessions to accommodate working mothers, Johnsson has gone the extra mile to provide flexibility for employees and still ensure the highest quality service to clients.

SOURCE: Barbara Marsh, "A Consulting Business Thrives By Hiring Mothers Part-Time," *The Wall Street Journal*, February 23, 1994, B1.

■ DIVERSITY QUESTIONS

1. List some of the trends that have created the opportunity Johnsson was able to fill.

2. What special challenges does Johnsson face in carrying out the tasks of service management?

3. Can you think of any other group of workers who would be attracted to the flexible work schedule Johnsson has implemented?

1. Note that while about 75 percent of overall employment is in service industries, services represent slightly less than 50 percent of the total gross national product. This is partly because productivity in the goods sectors is higher and growing faster than it is in service sector firms. Henry F. Myers, "Some Service Jobs May Get Less Stable," *The Wall Street Journal,* February 25, 1991, A1.

2. Based on Kenneth Labich, "An Airline That Soars on Service," *Fortune,* December 31, 1990, 94–96.

3. Karl Albrecht, *At America's Service: How Corporations Can Revolutionize the Way They Treat Their Customers* (Homewood, IL: Dow Jones-Irwin, 1988), 20.

4. Michael E. Porter, *Competitive Strategy: Techniques for Analyzing Industries and Competitors* (New York: The Free Press, 1980), 37.

5. Based on a discussion in Karl Albrecht and Ron Zemke, *Service America!: Doing Business in the New Economy* (Homewood, IL: Dow Jones-Irwin, 1985), 6.

6. Based on Frederick F. Reichheld and W. Earl Sasser, Jr., "Zero Defections: Quality Comes to Service," *Harvard Business Review,* September–October 1990, 105–11.

7. Based on Philip Sadler, *Managerial Leadership in the Post-Industrial Society* (Gower), as summarized in "When the Product Is Service," *The Economist,* January 7, 1989, 60.

8. Based on Albrecht and Zemke, *Service America!* 31–47; Albrecht 20–42; and Karl Albrecht and Lawrence J. Bradford, *The Service Advantage: How to Identify and Fulfill Customer Needs* (Homewood: Dow Jones-Irwin, 1990), 24–49.

9. Albrecht and Bradford, *The Service Advantage,* 30.

10. Albrecht, *At America's Service,* 26.

11. Based on Albrecht, *At America's Service,* 31–32.

12. Ibid., 32.

13. Albrecht and Zemke, *Service America!* 106.

14. G. Lynn Shostack, "Designing Services That Deliver," *Harvard Business Review,* January–February 1984, 133–39.

15. Albrecht, *At America's Service,* 162–63; Albrecht and Bradford, *The Service Advantage,* 88–91.

16. Based on Shaw, *The Service Focus,* 28–33.

17. Ray Schultz, "Satisfaction Guaranteed for Customers and Crew," *The Wall Street Journal,* January 28, 1990.

18. Ibid.

19. For a discussion see, for example, Albrecht, *At America's Service,* 185.

20. Based on Joyce Santora, "Alamo's Drive for Customer Service," *Personnel Journal,* April 1991, 44.

21. Berry, Bennett, and Brown, *Service Quality,* 168.

22. Ibid., 170.

23. Leonard Berry, Charles M. Futrell, and Michael Bowers, *Bankers Who Sell—Improving Selling Effectiveness in Banking* (Chicago: Bank Marketing Association, and Homewood, IL: Dow Jones-Irwin, 1985) 120.

24. Based on Berry, Bennett, and Brown, *Service Quality,* 182–85.

25. Ibid., 183–84.

26. Based on Albrecht and Zemke, *Service America!* 169–79; and Albrecht, *At America's Service,* 157–223.

27. Albrecht and Zemke, *Service America,* 174.

28. Albrecht, *At America's Service,* 198.

29. Ibid., 209.

30. Susan Caminiti, "New Lessons in Customer Service," *Fortune,* September 20, 1993, 79–80; "Child Care for Profit, Over There," *The Economist,* August 8, 1992, 58–60; and Chuck Hawkins, "Can KinderCare Put This Puzzle Together?" *Business Week,* February 24, 1992, 54–55.

THE SEAGRAM BEVERAGE COMPANY

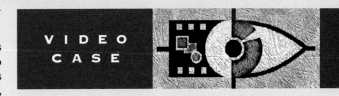

Information systems have a tremendous impact on organizations and the individual managers of today. They allow organizations to perform a variety of tasks more accurately and efficiently, such as processing orders and invoices more quickly, managing inventory, and administering employee benefits more effectively. Individual managers now have instant "on line" access to critical information used in everyday decision making. Information that once took weeks or even months to compile is available immediately. With more information available to us than ever before, the ability to store, process, and access that information is critical. One company that now utilizes the information superhighway is the Seagram Beverage Company.

The Seagram Beverage Company is known for products such as Tropicana, Seagram Wine and Cocktail Coolers, and the new nonalcoholic, fruit-flavored sparkling water, Quest. Seagram must manage in markets that are highly competitive, with both old and new customers constantly looking for new products and services. Because of the competitive nature of these markets, these products require focused promotional and program activities. A more efficient method of tracking the success of these promotions was needed within the Seagram Beverage Company. No vehicle was available to promotion managers and field managers to look at the success of a particular promotion or program activity. Michael Bebel, Director of Finance and Administration, said that promotions tracking was done on a sporadic basis and then only in focused markets. Often the data was there, but a vehicle to store and analyze the data was not available. It might take a month or more before data could be collected and analyzed. "In a highly competitive environment with limited resources, the shotgun approach can't happen. We must focus on those activities that are most effective," Bebel said.

The need for an innovative information system to manage the promotions tracking led to the development of the Marketing Promotion Tracking System at the Seagram Beverage Group. The system captures and analyzes sales volume data and money spent on a particular promotion. Specifically the system measures the volume (number of cases) Seagram sells to its customers (wholesalers/distributors), and the volume they in turn sell to retailers. According to Bebel, "The strategic intent behind the system is to capture customer level activity . . . giving our local field managers a facility from which to implement tactical programs."

Manager of Finance Larry Gandler offers this example: A manager might set up a price discount promotion surrounding a particular event or holiday weekend. The manager puts in the expected increase in sales volume to be achieved and the program's expected cost.

As the actual figures come in, the system will draw a comparison between the expected and actual results. This allows managers to identify the key success drivers of the program, such as which product best responds to this type of promotion and when is the best time period to run promotions of this type. Bebel added, "Eventually, in two to three years, managers will have a historical base of data to draw upon when making decisions on where to spend promotion dollars, data based directly on the levels of success from a specific promotion or program activity." Managers will also be able to identify shifts in consumer tastes as sales increase or decrease for certain products and markets. Responding quickly to the changes in the market will help Seagram stay ahead of the competition.

At the Seagram Beverage Company it is easy to see how field managers will benefit from the data being collected and made available to them through the information system set up for promotions tracking. Decisions on which type of promotion to use and when to implement it can be made for specific products with less guesswork and more substantial data to back it up. Managers, however, still have to utilize this data strategically and take into consideration that the business environment is constantly changing. Those managers and organizations such as Seagram that use the data available through information systems to identify opportunities and anticipate market changes are more likely to remain successful and continue to prosper in this era of change.

SOURCES: Interview with Michael Beber, August 5, 1994. Interview with Larry Gandler, August 8, 1994. "Business as Usual" Ellen R. Marram, President, the Seagram Beverage Company, *Seagram Magazine* (April 1994).

■ QUESTIONS

1. What caused the Seagram Beverage Company to create their new Marketing Promotion Tracking System?
2. How might the Marketing Promotion Tracking System help field managers make everyday, routine decisions? And what about nonroutine, more long term decisions?
3. How might managers at the corporate level benefit from the information available through the Marketing Promotion Tracking System?

MANAGEMENT SKILLS SOFTWARE USER'S GUIDE AND EXERCISES

IMPORTANT NOTE: THIS USER'S GUIDE PROVIDES EXTENSIVE INFORMATION ABOUT MANY FEATURES AVAILABLE ON THE MANAGEMENT SKILLS SOFTWARE. HOWEVER, YOU CAN START QUICKLY BY JUST READING THE FIRST SECTION, "GETTING STARTED."

SUMMARY OF EACH SECTION OF THE USER'S GUIDE

1	Introduction
2	Getting Started
3	Placemarkers
4	Troubleshooting Tips
5	Word Processing
6	Printing
7	Quick Reference For Function Keys (F1–F10)
8	Quick Reference For Word Processing Commands
9	Management Skills Exercises

SUMMARY OF EACH SECTION

SECTION TITLE	Summary
INTRODUCTION	Find out what Management Skills can do for you.
GETTING STARTED	Get the best start in using Management Skills for the first time.
PLACEMARKERS	Leave a "bookmark" at any location in Management Skills so you can easily return.
TROUBLESHOOTING TIPS	Solve any "technical" difficulties you may be experiencing while using Management Skills.
WORD PROCESSING	Learn how to get assistance on the use of the word processor in the exercises where it may be used.
PRINTING	Get printouts of any work you complete and customize Management Skills for your printer.
QUICK REFERENCE FOR FUNCTION KEYS (F1–F10)	Keep this handy by your computer.
QUICK REFERENCE FOR WORD PROCESSING COMMANDS	Keep this handy by your computer.
MANAGEMENT SKILLS EXERCISES	Try your hand at these exercises that accompany the software. There are 12 exercises that tie specifically to chapters in this book as well as 7 more exercises that deal with broader subjects.

SECTION ONE: INTRODUCTION

Your management textbook introduces you to a wide variety of ideas, theories, models and trends in the field of management. The real value of what you learn may be measured by how effectively you apply it. Can you make good decisions? Do you effectively delegate responsibility? What are your capabilities as a leader? How well do you motivate others? Are you open to working with people of a different sex, age, race, or cultural background? How do you land a job which truly interests you and employs your skills and talents? By completing a series of exercises in Management Skills, the software program which accompanies your textbook, you'll be closer to answering these kinds of questions.

Among the subjects you'll cover in the program include:

- Business Ethics
- Decision-Making
- Delegation
- Multicultural Diversity
- Leadership
- Motivation
- Communications
- Budgeting
- Entrepreneurship
- Career Planning

You'll complete one or more questionnaires or activities for each of the management topics listed above. Most of the exercises will help you measure your current levels of awareness and capabilities in addressing a particular management issue. Then, you'll receive personal advice for improving yourself based on your responses. The management skills exercises will also help you to identify your interests, skills and preferred work environment, make decisions about your career direction, and communicate effectively in job interviews. The exercises are located in the last section of this appendix.

SECTION TWO: GETTING STARTED

SYSTEM REQUIREMENTS

- 535,000 bytes of RAM
- Hard Disk with 750,000 bytes of free space OR two 3 1/2″ floppy drives OR two 5 1/4″ high density floppy drives

If you choose to run Management Skills from floppy diskettes, the two floppy disk drives must be of the same size during the initial installation. However, you can later run the program on a computer with one 3 1/2″ drive and one high density 5 1/4″ drive if necessary. For example, you could copy the contents of a 3 1/2″ diskette to a high density 5 1/4″ diskette and then use the 5 1/4″ diskette to run Management Skills.

If you own your computer, you cannot switch between floppy disks and a hard disk when using Management Skills because the software must store your work on ONE disk. That means you cannot use Management Skills on the hard disk of your own computer and then go to the computer lab to run Management Skills on the floppy diskettes. So, before you start on the steps below, choose where you'll be using Management Skills!

1. Decide if you will be using Management Skills on floppy diskettes or a hard disk. If you decide to run the program on floppy diskettes, prepare a blank, formatted diskette and label it as Management Skills Data Disk. Although the program will work with a low density diskette, you are less likely to run out of space later on if you use a high density diskette for your data.

2. Find out if you have enough memory to run Management Skills. Management Skills requires a machine which has a minimum of 640K RAM available. (RAM is different than the amount of space available on the disk.) Here's how to check your memory:

   a. Insert the DOS diskette in Drive A.
   b. Type A: and then press the ENTER key.
   c. At the "A>" prompt, type CHKDSK and then press the ENTER key.

If you are using a computer with a hard disk, skip steps a. and b. above, and just type CHKDSK at the hard disk DOS prompt—such as "C>." When you type this command, you will get some information about your disk first. However, it's the LAST number displayed before returning to the DOS prompt that counts. If the number indicates less than "535,000 bytes free," you will not be able to run all sections of Management Skills.

Many computers in college and university computer labs are connected in "networks." The "CHKDSK" command will not work on networks. If you try this command on a networked computer, you will receive an error message such as "Bad command or file name." Furthermore, computers connected to some networks will not have enough memory to run Management Skills. If you discover that Management Skills is not running properly on a networked computer, consult an assistant in the computer lab who may solve the memory problem or locate computers not connected to the network.

3. Place the Management Skills diskette in Floppy Drive A. (Do NOT write-protect this diskette!)

4. Type A: and then press the ENTER key. The "A>" prompt should now be displayed on the screen. If you prefer, you may use Floppy Drive B in steps 3 and 4 above.

5. Type MS and then press the ENTER key. The Management Skills installation program will give you directions on the screen. Then, return to these directions and continue with the next step.

Once Management Skills has been installed, the program will start immediately the next time you type MS. If you want to install Management Skills again on floppy disks or a hard disk, you must first delete the file MS.INI on the Management Skills diskette.

6. When you see the main menu for Management Skills, select the "Overview" by pressing the ENTER key.

    You will now be looking at the overview for Management Skills. To read ahead, simply press the down arrow key or the Page Down key. To look back at previous text, press the up arrow key or the Page Up key. When you're reading the overview, press the ESC key to return to the main menu.

7. If you are NOT using a color monitor, select "Software Tools," followed by "Screen Configuration," from the main menu for Management Skills.

    Two choices will be displayed: "Color" and "Monochrome." If you are using a portable or notebook computer, the recommended choice is "Monochrome"—unless your computer displays in color or is exceptional at emulating color. If your monitor displays in one color only, such as white, green or amber, select "Monochrome."

8. From the main menu, press the down arrow key once to highlight the "Tutorial" and then press the ENTER key.

    You will now begin the "Tutorial" to learn how to get the most from Management Skills.

9. After completing one or two modules in Management Skills, return again to this guide and read the section, "Placemarkers."

    "Placemarkers" will show you how to mark your place anywhere in Management Skills and return to it later.

IMPORTANT NOTES

1. If you encounter any difficulties installing or running Management Skills, review any class handouts the professor may have given you or the "Troubleshooting Tips" section in this user's guide.

2. If you are running Management Skills on a hard disk, make sure that you first change to the directory where Management Skills is located BEFORE you type "MS." When you turn on your computer, it will usually display a "C>" prompt. Type the following at the "C>" prompt to change to the directory you chose for Management Skills:

    CD C:\[name of directory] and then press the ENTER key.

For example, if you named your Management Skills directory as "MANAGER" you would type:

    CD C:\MANAGER and then press the ENTER key.

Once you're in the right directory, you can type MS to start Management Skills.

SECTION THREE: PLACEMARKERS

PUTTING "BOOKMARKS" AT KEY LOCATIONS

There may be occasions when you want to mark your place in Management Skills and return to it later. You can do it in Management Skills in the same way as you place a bookmark in a book. Let's use the module, "Interests and Fascinations," to learn how to place a mark. It doesn't matter whether you have completed this module already.

1. From the main menu for Management Skills, select "Other Management Topics."

2. From the menu for "Other Management Topics," select "Career Planning."

3. From the menu for "Career Planning," select "Interests and Fascinations."

4. You are now located at the "Overview" for the "Interests and Fascinations" module.

   Notice that "F3–Place Marker" is displayed as an option at the bottom of the screen. Press the F3 key.

5. A "Place Marker" window now pops up with a name already provided for you: "Overview: My Interests and Fascinations."

   Just press the ENTER key to mark your place.

6. Press the ESC key to leave the overview and then press the letter M to return to the "What Do I Want" menu.

7. Return to the main menu for Management Skills by pressing the ESC key, and then select "Place Markers."

8. From the "Place Markers" menu, select "List of Markers."

   Notice that the place you just marked, "Overview: Interests and Fascinations," is displayed and there is room for 16 different placemarkers. It's exactly the same as being able to mark 16 different pages in a book and open to any one of them.

9. With "Overview: Interests and Fascinations" highlighted, press the letter G to "Go to" the location represented by the marker.

   You're now back at the overview for "Interests and Fascinations!"

10. Now move ahead in this module to the "Introduction," and then continue to the exercise where you actually type in your interests.

    Remove any "pop-up" windows, such as "Help," and look at the bottom of the screen, noticing that "F3-Place Marker" is also displayed here. Do not press the F3 key at this time.

You can mark your place at almost any location in Management Skills, just like you could with a book. However, Management Skills will remember to mark your last place, even when you don't use the F3 key. Let's continue to the next section and see how that works.

"LAST PLACE" MARKER

1. Still do not press the F3 key. Just press the ESC key, and then the letter E to exit from Management Skills.

2. We'll pretend that some time has passed by. You're ready to return to Management Skills for another session and continue where you were last. So, load up Management Skills by typing MS—and when you see the main menu, select "Place Markers."

3. This time, select "Last Place."

   Notice that you return immediately to the exercise for listing your interests, even though you didn't mark your place with the F3 key. So, if you just want to pick up where you left off, "Last Place" is the simplest approach.

SECTION FOUR: TROUBLE SHOOTING TIPS

If you cannot get Management Skills to run correctly after trying the troubleshooting tips listed in this section, you may have a defective disk or disk drive. To solve either problem, follow these steps:

1. Use a virus checking program on your DOS disk, the Management Skills disk, and the Management Skills Data Disk.

   A virus can prevent any software program from working correctly. If there's no virus detected, proceed to the next step.

2. Try running Management Skills on a different computer.

   If it works on the next computer, you'll know that the previous computer had a defective disk drive or other problem.

   If it still doesn't work proceed to the next step.

3. Borrow a Management Skills disk from one of your classmates who is successfully running Management Skills. Copy it to a new disk (NOT the disk with the current problem).

4. Prepare a new formatted disk to use as your Data Disk—just in case the current one is causing the problem.

5. Follow the steps in the "Getting Started" section of this user's guide to REINSTALL Management Skills, paying close attention to the "Note" in Step 3 of that section.

The following questions and answers address the most common difficulties students encounter when using Management Skills.

1. When I typed MS to run Management Skills, I received the message, "Bad command or file name".

   ANSWER: If you are running Management Skills from floppy diskettes, make sure that you inserted the Management Skills diskette in the floppy drive. Also, the DOS prompt should be displayed for that floppy drive before typing "MS." For example, if you placed the Management Skills diskette in Drive A, the DOS prompt should be "A>."

If you are running Management Skills from a hard disk, first make sure you are located in the drive and directory you selected for Management Skills when it was first installed. For example, you may have selected Drive "C" and a directory named "CAREER". You would type the following at the "C>" prompt to get into the directory containing Management Skills: CD C:\CAREER and then press the ENTER key. Then you can type MS to start Management Skills.

2. When I inserted the Management Skills Program diskette in the floppy drive and typed "MS," it "crashed" with a "runtime error" message.

ANSWER: Before you run Management Skills, make sure you have ALSO inserted your DATA DISK in the other floppy drive.

Secondly, insert the Management Skills Program disk in the SAME floppy drive (A or B) you selected when you first installed Management Skills. For example, if you placed the Management Skills diskette in DRIVE A when you first installed the program, you must also start Management Skills from now on in DRIVE A.

If you wish to change your choice of floppy drive, you will need to reinstall Management Skills.

3. The program stopped working or "crashed" while I was using it.

ANSWER: If the computer locked up, jumped back to the DOS prompt, displayed a "Runtime Error" message or behaved in some other unexpected way, you may not have enough memory (RAM). Follow the directions under step one of the second section of this user guide, "Getting Started," to find out if you have enough memory.

4. I am unable to get a printout of the work I typed previously. When I press the F8 key, something else gets printed instead, such as the directions for the exercise.

ANSWER: First of all, Management Skills will only print something if the "F8-Print" option is displayed at the bottom of the screen.

Secondly, when you press the F8 key, Management Skills prints whatever is "active" at the present time. So, if a pop-up window for "F1-Help," "F6-Clues" or "F7-Examples" is currently being displayed, the contents of that window will be printed when you press the F8 key.

If you want to print your own work—such as your list of interests or skills—you must first remove the pop-up window by pressing the ESC key. Then, press the F8 key to request a printout of your file.

5. When I requested a printout, the computer "froze" or gave me an error message such as "DOS critical error."

ANSWER: When this happens, you may have to completely reboot the computer by pressing simultaneously the Ctrl, Alt and Del keys. This printing problem usually occurs when the printer is not correctly attached to your computer OR the printer is not ready to print.

Before you try to print again, make sure the power is ON to your printer and that the "On-line" or "Ready" light is ON.

6. I seem to be "stuck" at a certain place and can't move anywhere. None of the keys I've pressed have helped.

ANSWER: Review the options which are currently displayed at the bottom of the screen. One of them will enable you to leave your present location. It is a matter of selecting the right one. The most common keys for leaving the current place are ESC and ENTER keys, but there are times when others are needed, instead. Of course, if only one option is displayed at the bottom of the screen, press that one.

If nothing happens when the keys displayed at the bottom of the screen are pressed, the computer may have "locked up." You will need to reboot your computer or even turn the power off and on to get moving again.

If you are technically inclined: Although there are many reasons why this might happen, the most likely cause is inadequate RAM memory in your computer to run Management Skills. You can find out if this is the case by typing CHKDSK at the DOS prompt. If the last line displayed before returning to the DOS prompt is less than "535,000 bytes free," you may need more memory.

If you have 640K of memory installed on your computer, "free up" more memory, before running Management Skills, by removing TSR's (Terminal Stay Resident), such as DOS shells, pop-up calculators, RAM caches, or unessential device drivers in your "config.sys" or "autoexec.bat" file.

7. I'm not clear about what to do in a particular exercise.

ANSWER: Press the F1 key for help when it is displayed as an option at the bottom of the screen. In some exercises, additional assistance is provided by "F6-Clues" and "F7-Examples."

Note: If you are currently looking at a "pop-up" window such as "Help," first press the ESC key to remove the window. Then, all the options for that exercise will be displayed at the bottom of the screen.

F1-Help" provides basic instructions for completing an exercise, including what keys to press. Look here first.

"F6-Clues" offer extra help by showing you new ways of looking at things or further explaining what needs to be done. For example, in the exercise in which you list your interests, the clues take you through different parts of your life to help you remember what they are.

"F7-Examples" show you how other people responded in the same exercise. Sometimes, the best way to get a clear picture of what you need to do is by looking at an example. For instance, when preparing a letter of introduction, you can see sample letters and an explanation about how they follow each of the guidelines for writing them correctly.

8. The directions for an exercise suggested I press a particular key, but nothing happened when I tried it.

ANSWER: Chances are good that you were reading a "pop-up" window when this happened. For example, you may have been reading some instructions which suggested pressing the F6 key for clues.

You first need to remove the "pop-up" window, by pressing the ESC key, and return to the exercise before pressing the recommended key.

Remember, options such as "F6-Clues" are not available unless they are displayed at the bottom of the screen.

9. I'm having some difficulty getting the word processor to do what I want.

ANSWER: Press the F5 key when it's displayed as an option at the bottom of the screen. Look through each of the options on the word processor menu until you find the command you want. In many cases, you'll also find step-by-step instructions for using that command.

10. I listed more items in an exercise than the computer indicated. For example, I typed in 11 skills and only 9 were counted.

    ANSWER: The reason this happened is you did not press the F10 key after typing in every item. To correct the count, return to the exercise and follow these steps:

    a. Locate the cursor anywhere on the last line of an item which does not display "..." on the line immediately below it.

    b. Press the F10 key.

    The "..." marker will appear below the item, indicating that Management Skills has now counted it. Also, the counter at the top of the screen will show the new total count.

    Repeat steps 1 and 2 for all items which were not originally counted.

11. When I printed my document, instead of getting the appearance I selected, such as underlining, the printer codes I previously entered from the printer appeared.

    ANSWER: This indicates that the printer codes from the printer manual were not correctly entered while using the "Printer Setup Menu." You need to refer again to your printer manual as you repeat the steps in the category, "Setting up your printer for special features," located in "SECTION SIX: PRINTING" of this user's guide.

12. I inserted some words in the middle of a paragraph I previously typed. As a result, the text has shifted past the right margin—or even off the screen. How do I align the paragraph so it fits again within the left and right margins?

    ANSWER: Place the cursor at the beginning of the paragraph and press Ctrl-O-F. This command will realign the paragraph within the current margins.

    For more information about this and other commands for controlling the appearance of your document, select "Formatting" from the Word Processor help menu.

SECTION FIVE: WORD PROCESSING

In the exercises where you can express yourself in your own words, Management Skills provides an easy-to-use word processor. Just begin typing, and your words will wrap automatically to the next line and the window will scroll up to give you more space as you need it.

The word processor also contains many additional features, so you can use it as a practical day-to-day tool for preparing your reports, letters and other documents. All the word processing commands at your disposal are listed and described in the help section in the program. Step-by-step instructions for using the commands are also included, so you won't need to search through this manual to find out how to do something. In fact, the only part of the word processor which is described in this user's guide is how to set up your printer. Here's how to get the word processing help you need:

1. Press the F5 key whenever you see this option displayed at the bottom of the screen: "F5-Word Processor."

   When you press this key, the "Word Processor" menu will appear.

2. Highlight "Tips and Techniques" and then press the ENTER key.

   Read over this section to find out how the help sections are organized, how to press keys correctly to activate commands and how to remember many of these keystroke commands so you won't need to look them up too often.

   Think of "Tips and Techniques" as help on using the other sections of the "Word Processor" menu.

3. After you've read "Tips and Techniques," browse through the other sections.

   Even if you don't use many of the features now, you'll know they are there if you need them. If you find a word processing command particularly intriguing, give it a try. Read the steps for using it and see if you can get it to work.

You can also have the word processor "convert" any of your files into a universal ASCII format—so that you can accurately retrieve them with other word processing programs: refer to the "File" option described in "SECTION SIX: PRINTING" of this user's guide.

CALLING UP WORD PROCESSOR FROM THE "SOFTWARE TOOLS" MENU

Here's how to use the word processor to type letters, reports and other documents:

1. From the main menu for Skills, use the down arrow key to highlight "Software Tools" and then press the ENTER key.

2. Select "Word Processor" from the menu and then press the ENTER key.

   The "Pathname of File" window will appear. It may contain *.* or a phrase, such as B:SKILLS.TXT.

3. Type a name for the file you wish to create. When creating a new file, be sure to use standard DOS naming conventions: no more than eight characters before the period and no more than three characters after it.

   For example, LETTER21.TXT represents the maximum size file name. See your DOS manual for more details about naming or deleting files.

TIPS:

- If you are familiar with DOS commands, the word processor accepts "*.*" and other DOS wildcards, as well as DOS subdirectories in selecting a file.

- If you want to call up a file you already created, but don't remember the name, type: [drive letter]:\[subdirectory name]*.* and then press the ENTER key.

  For example, the command, B:\MYFILES*.* would list all the files on the diskette in drive B in the "MYFILES" subdirectory. If you just type *.* without a drive letter or subdirectory, the files will be listed in the default subdirectory where Management Skills is located.

  Then, highlight the file you want to load into the word processor and press the ENTER key.

4. When you have finished using the word processor, press the ESC key.

Any files currently loaded in the word processor will be saved to disk automatically. So, if you had two files open, both files would be saved.

For more information about opening, closing or saving your files, select "Files" from the Word Processor help menu.

SECTION SIX: PRINTING

QUICK START FOR PRINTING

If you would like to print the file where the cursor is currently located, follow these simple steps:

1. Press the F8 key.

The "Printer Setup" menu will appear with the selection, "Print file now," already highlighted.

2. Press the ENTER key.

Your work will now be printed. Printing operates in the background, so you can continue to work on your document, although the computer will respond more slowly until the print job has been completed.

TIPS:

- To stop a print job at any time, press the F8 key again. An "Abort Printing?" window will pop up. Respond by typing the letter Y for Yes. There may be a few seconds delay before the printer stops.

- If you press the F8 key when a "pop-up" window is displayed, such as "Help" or "Clues," the full contents of the window will be printed instead of your file.

- To print only what is currently displayed on the screen, press the Print Screen (PrtSc) key. On some computers, it is necessary to hold down the SHIFT key while pressing the Print Screen key.

SETTING UP YOUR PRINTER FOR SPECIAL FEATURES

If you want the work you print to display underlining, bolding, italicizing or other special features, you'll first need to set up your printer for the word processor. Here's how:

1. In the manual which came with your printer, look for a section listing "printer control codes" and/or "escape sequences." You'll need it in just a moment.

2. From the main menu for Management Skills, select Word Processor.

A window will appear near the bottom of the screen entitled, "Pathname of File."

3. Type the word, PRINTER, and then press the ENTER key.

4. Press the F8 key.

    The "Printer Setup" menu will now appear.

TIP:

- Notice that the top line of the screen displays the keys you can press. These keys will change as you select different options on the "Printer Setup" menu.

5. Press the down arrow key until the option, "Edit Printer Codes," is highlighted, and then press the ENTER key.

    The "Printer Strings" menu will now be displayed. You'll use this menu for all of the options below.

SETTING UP YOUR PRINTER FOR NEAR LETTER QUALITY AT ALL TIMES

Note: Skip this section if you use a laser printer.

These next few steps will set the default for your dot matrix printer to Near Letter Quality (NLQ). That means your printer will output your documents in NLQ automatically. The printer will be slower using NLQ, but your document will appear much sharper. If your printer does not have an NLQ option, or you prefer not to change the printing default to NLQ, skip this section.

1. Select "Initialization" by pressing the ENTER key.

    The "Initialization" box will now pop up.

2. Press the Scroll Lock key.

    The word, "Literal," will now appear in the lower right hand section of the "Initialization" box.

3. In the printer manual, look up the control code or escape sequence for NLQ. If it is not listed, look for "Double Strike" as an alternative.

    Then, type the code. For example, if the code were ESC G, you would press the ESC key and then the capital letter G.

    The letters and/or numbers you type will appear in the "Initialization" window. If you pressed the ESC key and then G, it would look like this: <Esc>G.

TIPS:

- Be careful about typing upper or lower case letters. They should match exactly what is in your printer manual.

- If you typed the wrong code, press the Scroll Lock key, and the word "command" will appear. Then, press CTRL-BACKSPACE to erase the code. Next, go back to step 2 and continue.

4. Press the Scroll Lock key.

    The word "Command" will appear in the lower right section of the "Initialization" box.

5. Press the ENTER key.

The "Initialization" box will disappear and you will be returned to the "Printer Strings" menu.

SETTING UP YOUR PRINTER FOR BOLD TEXT

1. Select "Bold Text ON" and press the ENTER key.

    The "Bold Text ON" box will now pop up.

2. Press the Scroll Lock key.

    The word "Literal" will appear in the lower right section of the "Initialization" box.

3. In the printer manual, look up the control code or escape sequence for bold text (also called "Emphasized Printing" in some manuals).

    Then, type that code. For example, if the code were ESC E, you would press the ESC key and then the capital letter E. The letters and/or numbers you type will appear in the "Initialization" window. If you pressed the ESC key and then E, it would look like this: <Esc>E.

TIPS:

- Be careful about typing upper or lower case letters. They should match exactly what is in your printer manual.

- If you typed the wrong code, press the Scroll Lock key, and the word "command" will appear. Then, press CTRL-BACKSPACE to erase the code. Next, go back to step 2 to continue.

4. Press the Scroll Lock key.

    The word "Command," will appear in the lower right section of the "Initialization" box.

5. Press the ENTER key.

    The "Initialization" box will disappear and you will be returned to the "Printer Strings" menu.

6. Select "Bold Text OFF" and then press the ENTER key.

    The "Bold Text OFF" box will now pop up.

7. Press the Scroll Lock key.

    The word "Literal" will appear in the lower right section of the "Initialization" box.

8. In the printer manual, look up the control code or escape sequence for cancelling bold text. Then, type that code.

    The letters and/or numbers you type will appear in the "Initialization" window.

9. Press the Scroll Lock key.

    The word "Command" will appear in the lower right section of the "Initialization" box.

10. Press the ENTER key.

    The "Initialization" box will disappear and you'll be returned to the "Printer Strings" menu.

SETTING UP YOUR PRINTER FOR NEAR LETTER QUALITY (NLQ), UNDERLINED, COMPRESSED, OR ITALIC TEXT

Follow the exact same order of steps used to display text in bold, replacing "Bold Text ON" and "Bold Text OFF" with the following printer strings:

For Near Letter Quality: (not needed for laser printers)	Doublestrike ON and Doublestrike OFF
For Underlining:	Underscore ON and Underscore OFF
For Compressed: (also called "Condensed")	Compressed ON and Compressed OFF
For Italics:	Italic ON and Italic OFF

TIPS:

- Before typing in printer codes—such as ESC G—be sure to first press the Scroll Lock key so that the word "Literal" is displayed in the lower right corner. When you want to change or erase what you typed, or press the ENTER key to finish, press the Scroll Lock key again so that the word "Command" is displayed in the lower right corner.

- The options "Superscript" and "Subscript" are not available in this version of the word processor.

SAVING YOUR PRINTER SETUP

After you have entered the correct printer codes for your printer, save them in the "Printer.Pdf" file as follows:

1. If the "Printer Strings" menu is currently displayed, press the ESC key.

   The "Printer Strings" menu is removed, leaving the "Printer Setup" menu in full view.

2. On the "Printer Setup" menu, press the down arrow key until the option, "Save printer setup," is highlighted, and then press the ENTER key.

   The "Printer Definition File" box will now appear.

3. Press the ENTER key.

   The "Printer Definition File" box will disappear and a new box will pop up with the question, "Overwrite File?"

4. Press the letter Y (for Yes).

   The custom setup for your printer will now be saved. Your printer will now output Management Skills documents with such attributes as bolded and underlined text.

5. Press the ESC key.

   The "Printer Setup" menu will disappear, leaving you in the word processor.

6. Press the F5 key.

   The "Word Processor" menu will appear.

7. Press the down arrow key until the option, "Printing," is highlighted and then press the ENTER key.

> The help section on "Printing" will now appear. Use this help section to find out how to prepare text for the special attributes you just set for your printer—such as bolding or underlining.

TIP:

■ If you are using a monochrome monitor, the special attributes will not, of course, be displayed on the screen in color as the "Printing" section would indicate. However, all of these attributes will appear brighter on the screen than the normal text.

8. Press the ESC key twice.

> The "Printing" window and "Word Processor" menu disappear, leaving you back in the word processor itself.

9. Type in some text in one or more of the special display modes—such as underlining.

> For example, to underline your text, you would press Ctrl-U, type in some text, and then press the right arrow key to end underlining.

10. Press the F8 key.

> The "Printer Setup" menu will appear.

11. Press the ENTER key.

> Your printer will now output the text you just typed.

> If the special attributes are not being printed correctly, check the following:

> > Is your printer capable of producing all the special attributes you used? For example, many dot matrix printers will display underlining and bold, but not italics.

> > Did you enter the correct printer codes through the "Printer Strings" menu? Double check your printer manual, and compare these codes with what you actually entered. Be sure any letters you typed match in terms of UPPER or lower case.

> > Did you save your printer setup after entering your codes? Steps 2–4 describe how you do this.

OTHER OPTIONS ON "PRINTER SETUP" MENU

PRINT FILE NOW

Highlight this option and then press the ENTER key to print your file.

NAME OF FILE

Unless you specify otherwise, the file to be printed will be the one where the cursor is currently located. If you want to print a different file, follow these steps:

1. With the "Name Of File" option highlighted, press the ENTER key.

> A "File to print" box will appear.

2. Type in the DOS path for the file.

> For example, if your file were located on Drive C in a subdirectory called MANAGER, you would type: C:\MANAGER\

3. Next, add the file name to the DOS path.

> Continuing with our example, you would add a file named "LETTER1.DOC" in this way: C:\MANAGER\LETTER1.DOC

TIP:

- If you don't remember the name of the file, type the DOS path, followed by *.* in place of the file name. A box will pop up listing all the files in the subdirectory. You can search the subdirectory for the file you want, and then press the ENTER key to add that file to the DOS path.

4. Press the ENTER key to save your selection.

5. Press the up arrow once to highlight the option, "Print file now," and then press the ENTER key.

> The file you just selected will be printed.

AUTO FORMATTING

Under the default setting of "Auto Formatting ON," your document will be printed exactly as you arranged it, including the layout of each page, page breaks and special attributes, such as underlining.

When you set "Auto formatting" to OFF, the word processor will ignore your settings and print the document continuously, with no page breaks or special attributes.

You can toggle between "Auto formatting ON" and "Auto formatting OFF" by pressing the ENTER key when Auto Formatting is highlighted on the "Printer Setup" menu.

FIRST PAGE AND LAST PAGE

Unless you specify otherwise, the word processor will print your entire document when you select "Print file now." "Last Page" shows how many pages your document contains. You can specify exactly which pages you wish to print.

For example, if you had a document 10 pages in length and you wished to print pages 2–4 only, here's how it would be done:

1. With "First Page" highlighted, press the ENTER key.

> The "First Page" box will appear.

2. Type the number 2 and then press the ENTER key.

> "First page" will now show "2" as the new setting.

3. With "Last Page" highlighted, press the ENTER key.

> The "Last page" box will appear.

4. Type the number 4 and then press the ENTER key.

> "Last Page" will now show "4" as the new setting.

That's about all there is to it! Now, when you select "Print file now," pages 2–4 will be the only part of your document printed.

DEVICE

Your printer receives information through a connection (port) on the back of your computer. In most cases that connection will be LPT1. If you get the message, "Printer not responding," and yet the printer is switched on and properly connected to the computer, try the following:

1. With "Device" highlighted, press the ENTER key.

    A "Device" window will pop up.

2. Select LPT2 and then press the ENTER key.

    "Device" will now show "LPT2."

3. Try printing again with "Print file now."

The third option displayed in the "Device" window is "File." By using this option, any file you create in Management Skills can be quickly converted into an ASCII file. As an ASCII file, it can be called up accurately by other word processing programs. For example, you could retrieve, change and print a resume you already created in Management Skills using your favorite word processor.

Here's how to save a Management Skills file in ASCII format:

1. Follow the steps under the earlier PRINTING section, "Name of File," to select a file.

2. With "Device" highlighted, press the ENTER key.

    The "Device" window will pop up.

3. Select "File" and then press the ENTER key.

    The "Print Output File" window will appear.

4. Type in the DOS path and name of the file to which your document will be "printed," and then press the ENTER key.

    "Device" will now display the DOS path and file name.

    For example, if you wanted to "print" your document to a floppy disk, you might type: A:\LETTER1.PRN

TIP:

■ So you don't accidentally overwrite your original file, use a different name for the new file. Consider keeping the first part of the new file name the same, and just changing the extension (the part of the name after the period). For instance, if LETTER1.TXT were the original name, the "printed" file could be called LETTER1.PRN

5. With "Print file now" highlighted, press the ENTER key.

    Your document will be "printed" to the file name you chose in ASCII format. It can now be retrieved accurately by other word processing programs.

USING THE DOS COMMAND, "PRINT"

Once your document has been converted to an ASCII format, you can get a printout of it at any computer without using Management Skills.

1. After making sure you are in the same directory where the DOS program, "Print.com" or "Print.exe" is located, use this format:

    PRINT [DOS path][name of file]

    Continuing with our previous example, you would type:

    PRINT A:\LETTER1.PRN

    . . . and then press the ENTER key.

2. "Name of the list device [PRN]:" will then appear on the screen. You have a

couple of options in responding. If you just press the ENTER key, your file will be sent to your printer through LPT1—the most common location for printer connections.

If your printer uses a different connection, such as LPT2, type in that location and then press the ENTER key. For example, you would type LPT2 and then press the ENTER key.

The printer will now output your document in the same way the word processor would do it! So, you can get accurate printouts of your work at any computer using DOS.

MANUAL PAPER FEED

Set "Manual paper feed" to ON if you wish to have the word processor prompt you to insert a new sheet of paper after each page. When the setting is OFF, the word processor requests the printer to feed paper automatically until the entire document is printed.

USE FORMFEEDS

Set "Use formfeeds" to ON if your printer accepts ASCII character #12 to eject each page. Otherwise, the word processor will fill out the end of each page with blank lines.

SECTION SEVEN: QUICK REFERENCE FOR FUNCTION KEYS (F1–F10)

F1 HELP
Press this key first whenever you want to find out what needs to be done in an exercise. Sometimes, the help is brief, offering simple instructions for what keys to press. At other times, the help is extensive, offering in-depth guidelines and step-by-step instructions.

F3 PLACE MARKER
Places a mark at the current location, in the same way you would place a bookmark. Management Skills will keep track of up to 16 different place marks at the same time. Select "Place Markers" from the main menu to return later to a place you previously marked.

F5 WORD PROCESSOR
Brings up a menu of help sections on how to use the word processor. You can find out what commands are available, what they can do for you and the steps to use them.

F6 CLUES
Provides extra help in completing an exercise. Think of this option as your "personal advisor." It will assist you in thinking differently about the issues so that you can come up with new ideas or better answers.

F7 EXAMPLES
Shows how other people responded in the same exercise. By looking at examples, you will better understand how to complete the exercise and get new ideas to add to your own.

F8 PRINT
Pulls up the "Printer Setup" menu. By pressing the ENTER key when the menu first appears, you can print your current file. Other options on the menu enable you to print any other file on your hard or floppy disks, customize the word processor for your printer, or select the pages you wish to print.

F9 COPY ITEM
Copies an item on a list in one word processing window to another.

F10 COUNT ITEM
"Counts" each item in such exercises as listing interests and skills.

SECTION EIGHT: QUICK REFERENCE FOR WORD PROCESSOR COMMANDS

Note: When pressing a command which involves two or more keys, hold down the first key—such as the CONTROL key—as you press the second key.

CURSOR MOVEMENTS

TO MOVE:	PRESS:
Line above	UP ARROW
Line below	DOWN ARROW
Character left	LEFT ARROW
Character right	RIGHT ARROW
Word left	CONTROL + LEFT ARROW
Word right	CONTROL + RIGHT ARROW
Beginning of line	HOME
End of line	END
Previous page	PAGE UP
Next page	PAGE DOWN
Beginning of document	CONTROL + PAGE UP
End of document	CONTROL + PAGE DOWN

EDITING

TO:	PRESS:
Delete current character	DEL
Delete character left	BACKSPACE
Delete word	CONTROL + W
Delete to end of line	CONTROL + E
Delete line	CONTROL + L
Toggle between insert and overwrite	INS

FORMATTING

TO:	PRESS:
Set left margin	CONTROL + O + L
Set right margin	CONTROL + O + R
Set top margin	CONTROL + O + T
Set bottom margin	CONTROL + O + B
Set tabs	CONTROL + O + S
Set length of page	CONTROL + O + P
Centre line of text	CONTROL + O + C
Format paragraph	CONTROL + O + F
Toggle auto indent	CONTROL + O + I
Toggle tabs and margin display	CONTROL + O + D

BLOCKS OF TEXT

TO:	PRESS:
Mark beginning	ALT + B
Mark end	ALT + E
Copy	ALT + C
Move	ALT + M

| Delete | ALT + D |
| Unmark | ALT + U |

WINDOWS

TO:	PRESS:
Move to next window	ALT + N
Resize active window	ALT + R
Zoom active window to full screen	ALT + Z

SEARCH AND REPLACE

TO:	PRESS:
Search for selected text	CONTROL + S
Replace selected text	CONTROL + R
Go to next occurrence of selected text	CONTROL + N

FILES

TO:	PRESS:
Open	CONTROL + F+ O
Close	CONTROL + F + C
Save	CONTROL + F + S
Get information	CONTROL + F + G

PRINTING

TO PRINT CHARACTERS IN:	PRESS:
Bold	CONTROL + B
Italics	CONTROL + I
Underline	CONTROL + U
Compressed	CONTROL + A
Near letter quality	CONTROL + D

TO:	PRESS:
Display character attributes	CONTROL + O + A

SECTION NINE

BUSINESS ETHICS

Chapter 3, "Management Ethics and Social Responsibility," explained that ethics represents a code of moral principles and values that govern the behaviors of a person or group with respect to what is right or wrong. When all the choices you face may have a potentially harmful effect on one or more parties, including coworkers, the organization, customers, the general public, and you personally, it may not be clear what choice is right. This situation is called an ethical dilemma.

In this exercise, you will be presented with different ethical dilemmas and asked to make choices. Then, the software program will provide some personal feedback about your decisions.

THIS EXERCISE WILL HELP YOU TO

- Clarify your code of business ethics.
- Consider the consequences of your decisions before making them.

HOW TO LOCATE THE EXERCISE

When you see the main menu for Management Skills, select "Other Management Topics." Then select "Business Ethics."

MAKING DECISIONS

Chapter 7, "Planning and Decision-Making Aids," described the classical model for making decisions. One of the key steps in this model is to review the criteria for evaluating the alternatives before making a choice. For example, a retailer is trying to decide where to locate new stores. To help in making this decision, criteria are listed, such as no more than two direct competitors within 3 miles and a neighborhood with an average annual household income of $35,000–$50,000.

The same approach may be used in making job or career decisions. In this exercise, you will explore your decision-making process by listing your criteria for the kind of career or job you want. Later, you can refer to your list in evaluating the alternatives you have listed.

THIS EXERCISE WILL HELP YOU

- Gain a better perspective about the importance of preparation before making important decisions.
- Develop criteria for the kind of work you want upon graduation.

HOW TO LOCATE THE EXERCISE

When you see the main menu for Management Skills, select "Planning." Then select "Making Decisions."

MANAGEMENT SKILLS EXERCISES

CHECK YOUR DECISION-MAKING SKILLS

Chapter 7, "Planning and Decision-Making Aids," explored ways organizations can arrive at the best decisions. Individual versus group decision making was analyzed. Specific methods for bringing out the opinions of participants in the decision-making process were discussed, including brainstorming and interactive groups.

Ultimately, the quality and timeliness of an organization's decisions depend on the capacity and willingness of its employees to make the choices expected of them. If employees are uncomfortable with the responsibilities of decision making, the results will be diminished.

THIS EXERCISE WILL HELP YOU

- Identify how comfortable you feel about making decisions.
- Learn some techniques for improving your decision-making skills.

HOW TO LOCATE THE EXERCISE

When you see the main menu for Management Skills, select "Planning." Then select "Check Your Decision-Making Skills."

HOW WELL DO YOU DELEGATE?

Chapter 8, "Fundamentals of Organizing," emphasized that most organizations today encourage their managers to delegate much of their authority and responsibilities to those below them. That way, employees can respond quickly and flexibly to customers, competitors, changes in technology, and other factors that require an organization to be adaptable.

However, many managers have difficulty depending on others, especially when they still retain the final responsibility. They may not believe that anyone else can do the job besides themselves or they may not want to accept the risk that employees will not complete their assigned tasks correctly or on time.

THIS EXERCISE WILL HELP YOU

- Rate your ability to delegate effectively.
- Learn proven methods for improving your delegation skills.

HOW TO LOCATE THE EXERCISE

When you see the main menu for Management Skills, select "Organizing." Then select "How Well Do You Delegate."

SEXUAL HARASSMENT ISSUES

One of the many subjects covered in Chapter 10, "The Staffing and Human Resource Management Process," was sexual harassment in the workplace. You learned that sexual harassment can take many forms. Even if the perpetrator doesn't direct sexual remarks or actions toward a specific person, sexual harassment may be taking place.

For example, a comment demeaning one gender, such as, "The only way women on the sales force can compete with the men is to use their sex appeal to entice customers to do business with them," would fall into the category of sexual harassment.

Although many offenders know they are sexually harassing someone, others violate a person's rights out of ignorance of what constitutes appropriate behavior with the opposite sex at work. Furthermore, victims of sexual harassment may not know how to handle it.

THIS EXERCISE WILL HELP YOU

- Measure your understanding about what words and actions may be defined as sexual harassment.
- Improve your sensitivity about sexual harassment issues.
- Take appropriate actions if you are subjected to sexual harassment.

HOW TO LOCATE THE EXERCISE

When you see the main menu for Management Skills, select "Organizing." Then select "Sexual Harassment Issues."

MANAGING CULTURAL DIVERSITY

Chapter 10, "The Staffing and Human Resource Management Process," explored how organizations can effectively recruit, train, and utilize the talents and experience of workers from all areas of society. Our ability to manage people depends on how well we understand their perspectives and motivations. All too often, we make assumptions about how people different from ourselves want to be treated. Our ignorance and biases may inadvertently cause offense.

In this exercise, you'll be presented with a series of work situations where the differences between people could lead to conflict or misunderstanding. You'll be asked to choose the best course of action in each scenario.

THIS EXERCISE WILL HELP YOU

- Measure your awareness of how people different from yourself prefer to interact in a work setting.
- Improve your interpersonal effectiveness in motivating and communicating with people in a multicultural workplace.

HOW TO LOCATE THE EXERCISE

When you see the main menu for Management Skills, select "Organizing." Then select "Managing Cultural Diversity."

BEHAVIORAL STYLES

One key theme discussed in Chapter 13, "Leadership," was that leaders cannot expect one approach to work with all people in all situations. The best leaders analyze the personal characteristics of the members of their group and then adopt the best approaches for directing, motivating, and communicating with them. In this section,

**MANAGEMENT
SKILLS
EXERCISES**

you'll have the opportunity to complete a behavioral styles questionnaire about your-self and a different questionnaire for assessing another person's profile of behavior.

THIS EXERCISE WILL HELP YOU

- Become more sensitive to the need to modify your leadership style with different people.
- Develop a specific plan for leading, motivating and communicating with someone based on his or her behavioral style.
- Discover your own behavioral style and its implications for the jobs and careers which may best suit you.

HOW TO LOCATE THE EXERCISE

When you see the main menu for Management Skills, select "Leading," followed by "Behavioral Styles." Then select "Overview" for advice on which options to select on the "Behavioral Styles" menu.

WHAT EMPLOYEES WANT MOST

Although a variety of motivational theories were discussed in Chapter 15, "Motivation and Behavior," all of them emphasized the pivotal role of rewards. Surveys of both managers and employees reveal a gap between what employees actually want most from their jobs and what their managers think they want. In this exercise, you'll have the opportunity to list your own priorities about what you want most from your work and then compare the results with other employees' responses and their superiors'.

THIS EXERCISE WILL HELP YOU

- Motivate others better by first determining what rewards they seek in their work.
- Develop a more flexible approach to motivating others.
- Clarify your own preferences for what you want most from your job.

HOW TO LOCATE THE EXERCISE

When you see the main menu for Management Skills, select "Leading." Then select "What Employees Want Most."

LEADERSHIP POTENTIAL

One section of Chapter 13, "Leadership," explored the concept of autocratic versus democratic styles of leadership. Autocratic leaders tend to centralize authority, using their legitimate, reward, and coercive power to manage subordinates. Democratic leaders delegate authority to others and encourage participation. They rely on their expertise and the respect and admiration of their subordinates to gain cooperation.

The "Leadership Potential" exercise asks you questions that help you learn whether you gravitate toward an autocratic or democratic style.

THIS EXERCISE WILL HELP YOU

- Become more aware of your biases in leading others.
- Explore alternative ways of leading others.

HOW TO LOCATE THE EXERCISE

When you see the main menu for Management Skills, select "Leading." Then select "Leadership Potential."

LEADERSHIP STYLE

In Chapter 13, "Leadership," you learned in the sections on the Ohio State studies and the Leadership Grid that leadership style may be measured according to two factors: concern for people and concern for production. Some studies have shown that the best leaders display both a high concern for people and a high concern for production. Other studies indicate that the best leadership style is more situational. It's helpful to know your leadership tendencies in order to determine whether a given situation already matches your "natural" leadership style or requires you to change it.

THIS EXERCISE WILL HELP YOU

- Identify situations where your favored leadership style works best.
- Improve your versatility as a leader by exploring ways to change your current leadership style in different situations.

HOW TO LOCATE THE EXERCISE

When you see the main menu for Management Skills, select "Leading." Then select "Leadership Style."

SELF-CONTROL

Chapter 17, "Managing Teams," discussed an important method more and more companies are using to improve the quality of their products and services: Total Quality Management (TQM). This approach gives workers rather than managers the responsibility for achieving standards of quality as well as the responsibility of correcting their own errors and exposing any quality problems they discover. Are you prepared to assume this kind of responsibility?

THIS EXERCISE WILL HELP YOU

- Rate your level of diligence in ensuring that tasks are completed correctly and to the best of your ability.
- Learn some ways to improve your self-control on the job.

HOW TO LOCATE THE EXERCISE

When you see the main menu for Management Skills, select "Controlling." Then select "Self-Control."

PERSONAL FINANCES

As you learned in Chapter 19, "Operations Management," companies create operational and financial budgets to determine what they require now and in the future to conduct their business successfully. You experience some of these same responsibilities on a much smaller scale with your own personal finances. It's important to determine your postgraduate expectations and what is required, both financially and professionally, to meet them.

THIS EXERCISE WILL HELP YOU

- Gain firsthand experience in the challenges of preparing and modifying a budget.
- Determine what level of compensation you will need upon graduation to meet your basic expenses for the life-style you want.
- Learn how to determine if a career direction you might pursue will meet those financial expectations.

HOW TO LOCATE THE EXERCISE

When you see the main menu for Management Skills, select "Controlling." Then select "Personal Finances."

ENTREPRENEURIAL QUOTIENT

Did you know that over one million businesses are started each year? In turn, these new enterprises generate over five million jobs annually. However, two out of three businesses fail in the first five years, even though the average entrepreneur works 60 or more hours per week.

Despite the hard work and risks, you may still have the desire at some point to start your own business. It would be helpful to know whether you are personally suited to this kind of venture.

THIS EXERCISE WILL HELP YOU

- Develop a realistic picture of what it takes to become an entrepreneur.
- Gain some personal insights into your inclination toward starting your own business.

HOW TO LOCATE THE EXERCISE

When you see the main menu for Management Skills, select "Other Management Issues." Then select "Entrepreneurship Quotient."

INTERESTS AND FASCINATIONS

The first step in planning your career is self-assessment. An important part of self-assessment is identifying your interests. It is one of the most important exercises in the career planning section of Management Skills, although it may not seem that way

MANAGEMENT SKILLS EXERCISES

now. As you progress through college and into your career, you will discover that anything which interests you is an important clue about your career direction. Most successful people are truly fascinated with their work.

When you are asked to list your interests, take the program's advice and type in as many of your interests as you can, regardless of whether or not you think they are job related.

THIS EXERCISE WILL HELP YOU

- Discover and keep track of your interests.
- Learn that choosing a career which interests you can result in better pay and job satisfaction.

HOW TO LOCATE THE EXERCISE

When you see the main menu for Management Skills, select "Other Management Topics," followed by "Career Planning." Then select "Interests."

LISTING YOUR SKILLS

Another important part of self-assessment is identifying your skills and talents. You'll be surprised at the number of skills you possess. In fact, it's not unusual for students to uncover 50 or more of their skills in this exercise.

By the way, this is not a time to be modest. If you think you have a skill, type it in!

THIS EXERCISE WILL HELP YOU

- Identify many of your skills and talents.
- Discover you possess far more skills than you realized.
- Communicate your value to potential employers.

HOW TO LOCATE THE EXERCISE

When you see the main menu for Management Skills, select "Other Management Topics," followed by "Career Planning." Then select "Listing Your Skills."

PEOPLE PREFERENCES

Here's an exercise about which you'll probably have some strong feelings. Have you ever thought about how you enjoyed a certain job—or hated one—because of the people at work? In this exercise, you will gather all the things you like and dislike about people you have encountered. You will even decide which of those items are so important that the next job you take has to fit that list.

People preferences are yet another part of the self-assessment step of career planning.

THIS EXERCISE WILL HELP YOU

- Develop a clear picture of exactly what kinds of people you prefer to encounter in your work setting.

MANAGEMENT SKILLS EXERCISES

- Learn that the people with whom you work can have a significant impact on job satisfaction.

HOW TO LOCATE THE EXERCISE

When you see the main menu for Management Skills, select "Other Management Topics," followed by "Career Planning." Then select "People Preferences."

WORK PREFERENCES

Have you ever thought about what makes a job appealing or unappealing? Obviously, the actual work you do plays a big part, but there are many other things. In fact, you may have talked to someone who said, "I don't really like what I'm doing, but this is such a great place to work that I don't want to quit." In this next Management Skills Exercise, you'll find out what kind of working conditions you want on the job.

Listing your work preferences completes the group of self-assessment exercises which began with "Interests and Fascinations."

THIS EXERCISE WILL HELP YOU

- Develop a clear picture of exactly what working conditions are important to you.
- Learn that your work environment can be just as important to job satisfaction as the work itself.

HOW TO LOCATE THE EXERCISE

When you see the main menu for Management Skills, select "Other Management Topics," followed by "Career Planning." Then select "Work Preferences."

DATA GATHERING

The second step of career planning involves gathering data on your opportunities and potential choices in the job market. If you're currently employed, it may also mean identifying your options within your own organization.

Before making any decisions about something important—such as choosing a major or deciding on a career or employer—you first need to gather information. That way, you can make an informed decision. It is valuable to not only read about your topic of interest, but to talk with people who are personally involved. For example, you could uncover many facts about a career interest in the *Occupational Outlook Handbook*. However, to get a "sense" for what it's really like on the job, you would need to visit with people who actually do the work.

In gathering your data about an important topic, you'll complete three sections: "Preparing a Plan," "Conducting a Survey," and "Evaluating Results."

THIS SET OF EXERCISES WILL HELP YOU

- Get the exact information you need to make good decisions.
- Learn how to research any topic of interest.
- Discover a method for making valuable contacts, such as potential employers.
- Verify that you have enough information before you make decisions.

HOW TO LOCATE THE EXERCISE

When you see the main menu for Management Skills, select "Other Management Topics," followed by "Career Planning." Then select "Data Gathering."

MANAGEMENT
SKILLS
EXERCISES

INTERVIEW QUESTIONS

The third step of career planning is to make decisions and set goals. What do you want to accomplish in the next few years? What skills and experience do you want to acquire? In fact, many employers are likely to ask these kinds of questions in your job interviews.

The fourth step of career planning is determining how you can pursue your goals, including getting the job you want. Many job opportunities are lost instantly during the job interview, even though the person is qualified for the job, because his or her interview skills are weak. The best way to ensure that your interviews result in a favorable impression is to prepare. That means learning how to best answer the questions you're likely to face.

THIS SET OF EXERCISES WILL HELP YOU

- Understand the reasons why interviewers ask certain questions.
- Prepare effective answers to tough interview questions.
- Convince the interviewer that you are ideally suited for the job.

HOW TO LOCATE THE EXERCISE

When you see the main menu for Management Skills, select "Other Management Topics," followed by "Career Planning." Then select "Interview Questions" followed by "Overview." After reading the overview on the interviewing section, choose from the "Interview Questions" menu the category of questions for which you want to prepare, such as "Goals," "Education" or "Compatibility with Employer."

GLOSSARY

ABC Inventory Management An inventory system that divides the inventory into three value categories (A, B, C).

Acceptance Sampling When only a portion of the produced items are inspected, perhaps only 2 percent or 5 percent of the items.

Acquisition Costs The total costs of all units bought to fill an order.

Action Research The process of systematically collecting research data about an ongoing system relative to some objective, goal, or needs of that system; feeding that data back to the employees; taking action by altering selected variables within the system based both on the data and on hypotheses; and evaluating results of action by collecting more data. Basically, the employees themselves analyze the data and develop the solutions.

Active Threats Threats that consist of attempts to alter, destroy, or divert data or act as an authorized network terminal point, thus exchanging information with legitimate sites and obtaining free network services.

Activities The time-consuming aspect of the project, represented by arrows in the PERT method.

Advocate Approach A technique that involves assigning an alternative plan to an advocate whose job is to see that all the pros and cons of the plan (and any other alternative plans) are covered fully.

Affirmative Action Requires the employer to make an extra effort to hire and promote those in the protected (women or minority) group.

Aggregate Output Planning Shows the aggregate (overall) volume of products (or services) that need to be produced to achieve each product's (or services) sales forecast.

Anticipatory Change Changes that are initiated not because of the need to respond to an immediately pressing event but rather because senior management believes that change in anticipation of events still to come will provide competitive advantage.

Application Blank A form that requests information like education, work history, and hobbies, and is a good means of quickly collecting verifiable and fairly accurate historical data from the candidate.

Artificial Intelligence Teaching computers to accomplish tasks in a manner that is considered intelligent and is characterized by learning and making decisions.

Attributions The meanings people give to the causes of actions and outcomes.

Authority Boundary Superiors and subordinates, even those found in self-managing teams or formal networks, always meet at an authority boundary, where some people still lead, and others follow.

Authority The right to take action, to make decisions, and to direct the work of others.

Automation The automatic operation of a system, process, or machine.

BCG Matrix A widely used portfolio management analysis aid devised by the Boston Consulting Group that helps to identify the relative attractiveness of a firm's businesses.

Behavior Modification Changing or modifying behavior through the use of contingent rewards or punishment.

Behavioral Displacement Occurs when the behaviors encouraged by the controls are inconsistent with the company's objectives.

Bill of Materials Lists the required parts and materials for each product manufactured.

Boundaryless Organization An organization in which widespread use of teams, networks, and similar structural mechanisms means that the boundaries that typically separate organizational functions and hierarchical levels are reduced and made more permeable. These businesses have identifiable functions, levels, and outside limits but these are permeable and do not inhibit the exchange of knowledge, services, and goods in the most efficient way possible.

Brainstorming A creativity-stimulating technique in which prior judgments and criticisms are specifically forbidden from inhibiting the free flow of ideas.

Breakeven Analysis A financial analysis decision-making aid that enables a manager to determine whether a particular volume of sales will result in losses or profits.

Breakeven Chart A graph that shows whether a particular volume of sales will result in profits or losses.

Breakeven Point The volume where the total revenue line crosses the total cost line, in other words, where revenue equals expenses.

Budgeted Balance Sheet Provides information to management, owners, and creditors about the company's probable financial picture in terms of assets, liabilities, and net worth at the end of the budget period.

Budgets Financial expressions of a manager's plans and one of the most widely used control techniques.

Bureaucracy Weber's "ideal" form of organization that involves the following: a well-defined hierarchy of authority; a clear division of work; a system of rules covering the rights and duties of position incumbents; a system of procedures for dealing with the work situation; impersonality of interpersonal relationships; and selection for employment and promotion based on technical competence.

Cash Budget Estimates the firm's month-to-month cash needs based on the monthly levels of operations as outlined in the sales, production, and expense budgets.

Cash Cows Businesses in low-growth industries, but having high relative market shares.

Causal Forecasting Involves estimating the company factor (such as sales) based on other factors (such as advertising expenditures).

Causal Methods These methods develop a projection based on the mathematical relationship between the variable being examined and those variables management believes influence or explain the company's variables.

Cellular Manufacturing Machines are grouped into cells, each of which contains all the tools and operations required to produce a particular product or family of products.

Central Processing Unit (CPU) The heart of a computer system that contains three main components: a primary storage unit, an arithmetic/logic unit, and the control unit.

Champion A change advocate who assumes the role of cajoling, inspiring, and negotiating a new invention or other innovation successfully through the firm until it is produced.

Charismatic Leaders Individuals who possess a special quality that enables the leader to mobilize and sustain activity within an organization through specific personal actions combined with perceived personal characteristics.

Classical School of Management An approach to managing emphasizing concepts and techniques that would cut costs and boost efficiency.

Client/Customer Service Spectrum A service planning tool that assumes that some services are more easily standardized than are others.

Code Law Represents a comprehensive set of written statutes.

Coercive Power Stems from a person's real or imagined expectation that he or she will be punished for failing to conform to his or her leader's influence attempts.

Cognitive Resources Resources, such as intelligence and job-related knowledge, that enhance leadership effectiveness.

Cognitive-Process Motivation Theories These assume that motivation is essentially a process of self-regulation, and focus on the decision process through which motivation comes about.

Collaborative Writing Systems Allows a work group's members to create long written documents (such as proposals) while working simultaneously at one of a number of interconnected or network computers.

Command Economy An economy in which government central planning agencies try to determine how much is produced by which sectors of the economy, and by which plants and for whom these goods are produced.

Common Law Law based on tradition and depending more on precedence and customs than on written statutes.

Common Market No barriers to trade exist among members and a common external trade policy is in force; in addition, though, factors of production, such as labor, capital, and technology, are mobile among member countries.

Communication Patterns Studies A series of studies carried out several years ago showing the role played by communication channels and feedback in organizational performance.

Communication The exchange of information and the transmission of meaning.

Communications Channel A vehicle or vehicles that carry the message.

Company Capability Profile A graphic means of assessing a company's managerial, competitive, financial, and technical strengths and weaknesses.

Competitive Strategy Identifies how to build and strengthen the business's long-term competitive position in the marketplace by analyzing the attractiveness of the business's industry in order to build a relative superiority over competitors.

Compliance Carrying out the job's duties, including following orders and instructions. We distinguished between imposed control and self control as two ways to obtain compliance.

Computer-Aided Design (CAD) A computerized process for designing new products or modifying existing ones.

Computer-Assisted Manufacturing (CAM) Refers to using computers to plan and program production equipment to produce manufactured items.

Computer-Integrated Manufacturing (CIM) The total integration of all production-related business activities through the use of computer systems.

Computer-Integrated Business An enterprise whose major functions exchange operating information quickly and constantly via computer.

Concurrent Engineering Designing products in multidisciplinary teams with repre-

sentatives from sales, product design, and manufacturing, for instance.

Conditioned Response An act or response previously associated with one stimulus becomes associated with another.

Confrontation Meetings Organizational meetings that can help clarify and bring into the open intergroup misperceptions and problems so that these problems can be solved.

Conglomerate Diversification Diversifying into other products or markets that are not related to the firm's present businesses or to one another.

Consideration Leader behavior indicative of mutual trust, friendship, support, respect, and warmth.

Continuous Learning Providing resources for employees to continue building on their store of knowledge.

Continuous Production Processes that run for very long periods without the start-and-stop behavior associated with intermittent production.

Controlling Setting standards (such as sales quotas, or quality standards), comparing actual performance with these standards, and then taking corrective actions as needed.

Conversion System A production system that takes inputs and converts these into products or services called outputs.

Coordination The process of achieving unity of action among interdependent activities.

Corporate Social Audit A rating system used to evaluate the corporation's performance with regard to meeting its social obligations.

Corporate Social Monitoring The process of a firm monitoring how they measure up to the social responsibility aims they have set for themselves.

Corporate Stakeholder Any group which is vital to the survival and success of the corporation.

Corporate-Level Strategy Identifies the portfolio of businesses that, in total, will compose the corporation, and it identifies the ways in which these businesses will relate to each other.

Cost Leadership A strategy that means the business aims to be the low-cost leader in the industry.

Creativity An organization's ability to invent new ways of doing things, or new ways of interpreting old problems.

Critical Path The sequence of events that in total requires the most time to complete.

Custom Union Here trade barriers among members are removed and a common trade policy exists with respect to nonmembers.

Customer Departmentalization Similar to organizing around product divisions except

that departments are organized to serve the needs of specific groups of customers.

Cycle of Service Starts with the first instance in which a customer comes into contact with any aspect of the organization, and then proceeds through every other contact between the customer and the organization.

Decentralization Letting lower level employees make more of their own decisions.

Decentralized Organization An organization in which authority for most decisions is delegated to the department heads, while control over essential company-wide matters is maintained at the headquarters office.

Decision Making A four-step process of choosing between alternative courses of action.

Decision Support Systems (DSS) Information systems that help managers make decisions that are relatively unstructured when compared to those addressed by the typical MIS.

Decision Tree A technique for making decisions under conditions of risk.

Decline That phase in the product's lifecycle when customers' interest in the product diminishes and market saturation occurs.

Delegation The pushing down of authority from supervisor to subordinate.

Delphi Technique The most widely used technological forecasting method. It involves obtaining the opinions of experts on the future technological and economic trends that might affect a company's product or market.

Departmentalization The process through which an enterprise's activities are grouped together and assigned to managers.

Deregulation The act or process of removing restrictions or regulations.

Design for Manufacturability Designing products with ease of manufacturing in mind.

Detailed Scheduling Specifying the actual start times and finishing times for all jobs at each machine or work center, as well as each job's labor assignments.

Development Stage According to the lifecycle theory, products move first through this stage, during which sales are virtually nil.

Differentiation Strategy When a firm seeks to be unique in its industry along some dimensions that are widely valued by buyers. In an increasingly crowded marketplace, businesses may emphasize their unique attributes to capture the consumer's attention. Apple has stressed the user-friendly nature of its line of personal computers from its inception, hoping to differentiate itself from the competition.

Distributed Processing The use of small local computers to collect, store, and process information, with summary reports and information sent to headquarters as needed.

Distributed Computing The ability for every employee with a PC on his or her desk to tap into the firm's computer network and get the information that he or she needs.

Diversification A strategy of expanding into related or unrelated products or market segments. A style of management whereby managers attempt to better utilize their organizational resources by developing new products and new markets.

Divestment Selling or liquidating individual businesses.

Divisionalization (product departmentalization) A form of organization in which the firm's major departments are organized so that each can manage all the activities needed to develop, manufacture, and sell a particular product or product line.

Dogs Businesses that are in low-growth unattractive industries and in which the firm has a low relative market share.

Domestic Organization Division of an organization that focuses on production and sales of domestic markets.

Double-Loop Learning Learning that advocates decision making based on the continual questioning of basic theories and assumptions.

Downsizing Eliminating jobs and the employees that went with them.

Econometrics A forecasting method in which a series of interrelated regression equations based on economic theory are used to develop forecasts.

Economic Integration Refers to attempts by two or more nations to obtain the advantages of free trade by minimizing trade restrictions.

Economic Order Quantity (EOQ) An inventory management system used to determine the most economic quantity to order in order to minimize total inventory costs.

Electronic Bulletin Board Allows one or more group members to file messages on various topics to be picked up by other group members.

Electronic Digital Computers Automatic, electronic devices composed of circuitry through which electricity can flow in such a way as to represent data as numbers.

Electronic Mail (E-mail) A computerized information system that lets group members electronically create, edit, and disseminate messages to each other, depositing each message in the recipient's electronic mail box.

Employee Benefits Any supplements to wages or pay that employees get based on their membership in the organization.

Employee Commitment When an employee comes to internalize the organization's goals as his or her own and to incorporate them into his or her own goal system.

Employee Compensation Refers to all forms of pay or rewards that go to employees and arise from their employment.

Employee Involvement Program Any formal program that encourages and permits employees to participate in formulating important work decisions or in supervising all or part of their own work activities.

Employee-Centered Companies Companies characterized by participation, supportive leadership, and emphasizing the sense of worth of each member of that organization.

Employee-Centered Leaders Leaders who are democratic, employee-oriented, or considerate.

Empower To give authority to employees to make decisions and the training and resources required to make them.

Empowering Employees Authorizing and enabling employees to do their jobs with greater autonomy.

Empowering Giving someone the responsibility for a significant task, and the tools and authority required to do it.

Empowerment Authorizing and enabling workers to do their jobs.

Enrichment Building challenge and achievement into a worker's job by changing the job's content.

Environmental Monitoring Involves tracking previously identified events, trends, and other premises that were uncovered when the strategy was first formulated and are thus deemed of particular importance to the firm.

Environmental Scanning Aimed at identifying previously unidentified or undetected critical events that could influence the company's strategy.

Equity Theory Adams' theory that assumes that people have a need for, and therefore value and seek, fairness in employer-employee relationships.

Ethics The study of standards of conduct and moral judgment; also, standards of right conduct.

Ethnocentric A management philosophy that leads to the creating of ethnocentric or home market-oriented firms.

Events A major component of a PERT network, events represent specific accomplishments.

Exchange Rate Refers to the rate at which one currency can be exchanged for another between two countries.

Executive Champion An executive in a technological firm who has direct or indirect influence over the resource allocation process and who uses this power to channel resources to a new technological innovation, thereby absorbing most, but usually not all, of the risk of the project.

Executive Recruiters Agencies retained by employers to seek out top management talent for their clients.

Executive Support Systems (ESS) Information systems designed to help top level executives acquire, manipulate, and use the information they need to maintain the overall company's effectiveness.

Existence Needs Needs that include all the various material and physical drives, such as eating, drinking, salary level, and physical working conditions.

Existence-Relatedness-Growth (ERG) Theory Designed by Clayton Alderfer to improve on Maslow's theory in two ways: first, needs are classified into three groups (existence, relatedness, and growth needs) rather than into five groups as Maslow proposes; second, these three needs are all active at the same time, and it is not necessary to satisfy lower-level needs before higher-level needs become activated.

Expectancy The probability that a person's efforts will lead to performance.

Expectancy Theories of Motivation A theory that assumes that before embarking on a task, individuals size up both their expectations for success and the value of the outcome and then choose their tasks and levels of effort so as to maximize their benefits and minimize any negative effects.

Expectancy-Based Theories These hold that motivation is a function of whether or not the person expects his or her effort to result in performance and therefore rewards.

Expected Value A calculated value that equals the probability of the outcome multiplied by the benefit or cost of that outcome.

Expert Power Stems from the fact that one person is viewed as an expert in some area; others must therefore depend on him or her for advice and counsel.

Expert System An information system in which computer programs store facts and rules to replicate the abilities and decisions of true human experts.

Exponential Smoothing Averaging the data of previous periods to forecast next period's average sales, but giving recent periods' data more weight.

Export-Oriented An import/export department coordinates all international activities, such as managing foreign sales.

Exporting Selling abroad, either directly to target customers, or indirectly by retaining foreign sales agents and distributors.

Extinction Reinforcement is withheld so that over time the undesired behavior disappears.

Extrinsic Factors Factors that are external to the work itself, such as pay, company rules, and the nature of the employee's relationship with his or her supervisor and peers at work. Also called hygienes.

Facility Layout Refers to the configuration of all the machines, employee work stations, storage areas, internal walls, and so forth that constitute the facility used to create the firm's product or service.

Fair Labor Standards Act Specifies a minimum wage ($4.25 per hour as of 1995), as well as child-labor and overtime pay rules.

Family Group Diagnostic Meeting A team or "family" group in which all team members report to the same manager.

Feedback The receiver's response to the message that was actually received.

Financial Incentive Any financial reward that is contingent on a worker's performance.

Financial Ratio Compares one financial indicator to another.

Fixed Interval Schedule A person receives a reward only when the desired response occurs and only after the passage of a specified fixed period of time since the previous reinforcement.

Fixed Ratio Schedule Based on units of output, rather than on time. Rewards are delivered only when a fixed number of desired responses occur.

Fixed Salary (hourly wages) The main component of most employees' pay.

Fixed-Position Layout The product stays at one location and the manufacturing machines and tools required to build the product are brought to that location as needed.

Flatten the Hierarchy To "slice" out layers of management, letting lower-level employees make their own on-the-spot decisions.

Flexible Manufacturing System (FMS) A system in which groups of production machines are connected by automated materials-handling and transfer machines, and integrated into a computer system.

Focus Strategy When a business selects a market segment and builds its strategy on serving those in its target market better or more cheaply than its generalist competitors.

Forecast To estimate or calculate in advance or to predict.

Foreign Direct Investment Refers to operations in one country that are controlled by entities in a foreign country.

Foreign Exchange Refers to foreign currency.

Formal Communication Messages that are recognized as official by the organization, i.e., orders from superiors to subordinates, sales reports, and status reports.

Formal Organizational Network A recognized group of managers assembled by the CEO and the senior executive team. The members are drawn from across the company's functions, business units, geography, and from different levels of the hierarchy.

Franchising The granting of a right by a parent company to another firm to do business in a prescribed manner.

Free Trade Area A type of economic integration in which all barriers to trade among members are removed.

Functional Authority Authority to issue orders down the chain of command within the very narrow limits of his or her authority.

Functional Departmentalization Grouping activities around essential functions such as manufacturing, sales, and finance.

Functional Strategies Identify the basic courses of action that each of the business's departments will pursue in order to help the business attain its competitive goals.

Gainsharing Plan An incentive plan that engages many or all employees in a common effort to achieve a company's productivity objectives and in which they share in the gains.

Gamesmanship Refers to management actions that are aimed at improving the manager's performance in terms of the control system without producing any positive economic effects.

Gantt Chart A chart showing the production schedule where the time is presented on the horizontal scale and for each order, the start and stop times of each operation are shown.

GE Business Screen A nine-cell matrix originally used by GE to analyze its own diversified portfolio and which plots industry attractiveness and competitive position.

Geographic Expansion A strategic growth alternative that works by aggressively expanding into new geographic markets both domestic and overseas.

Global Corporation Sells essentially a standardized product throughout the world, components of which may be made in or designed in different countries.

Global Manager A manager who views markets and production globally and seeks higher profits for his or her firm on a global basis rather than in terms of what is necessarily optimum for his or her firm's home country.

Global Mercantilism A scenario that entails looking at the world in terms of geopolitical change and international economic tensions, such that commodities prices, for example, might fluctuate widely.

Globalization The tendency of firms to extend their sales or manufacturing to new markets abroad.

Globalizing Production Dispersing part of a firm's production process to various locations around the globe.

Goal Difficulty The level of proficiency or performance sought.

Goal Specificity The degree of precision with which the goal is defined.

Grievance A complaint that an employee lodges against an employer, usually one regarding wages, hours, or some condition of employment, such as unfair supervisory behavior.

Group Cohesiveness The extent to which a group can influence its members' behavior. It depends on proximity and contact, the presence or absence of an interpersonal attraction, group size, intergroup competition, and agreement over goals.

Group Conferencing A set of telecommunications-based methods that lets group members interact directly with or leave messages for a number of other group members simultaneously.

Group Norms The informal rules that groups adopt to regulate and regularize group members' behavior.

Group Scheduling System Allows each group member to put his or her daily schedule into a shared data base, which enables group members to identify the most suitable times for meetings to be scheduled or to attend currently scheduled meetings.

Group Two or more persons who are interacting with one another in such a manner that each person influences and is influenced by each other.

GroupThink When one powerful point of view prevails in a group, even though powerful and cogent arguments against it may exist in the group.

Growth Needs Needs that impel a person to make creative or productive effects on himself or herself and the environment.

Hawthorne Effect The effect which happens when the scientist, in the course of his or her investigation, inadvertently influences the subject's behavior so that it is not the scientist's intended changes that affect the subject's behavior, but how the scientist acts.

Hawthorne Studies A series of studies begun in 1927 at the Chicago Hawthorne Plant of the Western Electric Company, which determined that performance depended on factors other than physical conditions or rate of pay, and that the social situations of the workers (not just working conditions) influenced their behavior and performance at work.

Horizontal Integration Acquiring ownership or control of competitors who are competing in the same or similar markets with the same or similar products.

Human Capital The knowledge, training, skills, and expertise of a firm's workers.

Human Process Interventions Interventions aimed at enabling employees to develop a better understanding of their own and others' behaviors for the purpose of improving that behavior in such a way that the organization benefits.

Human Relations The school of management thought that emphasizes that workers are not just givens in the system—but instead have needs and desires that the organization and task have to accommodate. Laid the foundation for what became known as organizational behavior.

Human Resource Management The management function devoted to acquiring, training, appraising, and compensating employees.

Identity Boundary The tendency employees have to identify with those groups with which they have shared experiences and with which they believe they share fundamental values.

Imposed (or Legal) Control Employees comply with rules or orders because they either consider them legitimate job demands or because they fear sanctions.

Income Statement Summarizes the expected sales revenues, expenses, and income for the budgeted year (or other planning period).

Incremental Changes Changes that only affect selected organizational components, perhaps by changing the organization's structure, introducing a new production technology, or developing employees so as to reduce interdepartmental conflict.

Independent Integrator Coordinates the activities of several interdependent departments, but is independent of them.

Industrial Revolution A period of several decades during which machine power was increasingly substituted for hand labor.

Informal Communications Communication not officially sanctioned by the organization, i.e., rumors heard through "the grapevine."

Informal Organization Informal contacts, communications, and ways of doing things that employees develop.

Informal Organizational Network Consists of cooperating individuals who are informally interconnected.

Information Data presented in a form that is meaningful to the recipient.

Information Superhighway A high-speed digital communications network that may combine telephone lines, cable lines, microwave transmissions, and fiber optics to let anyone anywhere use interactive television, telephones, PCs, or other devices to interact with databases around the world.

Information System A set of people, data, and procedures that work together to retrieve, process, store, and disseminate information to support decision making and control.

Information Technology Refers to any processes, practices, or systems that facilitate the processing and transportation of data information. Merging communications with computers.

Initiating Structure Leader behavior by which the person organizes the work to be done and defines relationships or roles, the channels of communication, and the ways of getting jobs done.

Input Devices These devices receive instructions and data, convert them into electrical impulses, and then transfer the impulses to the computer's storage unit.

Inputs Resources required for the manufacture of the product or service.

Instrumental Leadership The aspect of executive leadership that puts the instruments in place through which the employees can accomplish their new tasks.

Instrumentality The perceived correlation between successful performance and obtaining the reward.

Intergroup Organizational Conflicts These are conflicts that may occur between organizational units such as production and sales departments or between line and staff units.

Intermittent Production Production is performed on a start-and-stop basis.

Internalization When the person accepts the organization's goals as his or her own.

International Business Any firm that engages in international trade or investment, or refers to those business activities that involve the movement of resources, goods, services, and skills across national boundaries.

International Investment The investment of resources in business activities outside a firm's home country.

International Law Agreements embodied in treaties and other types of agreements that countries have agreed to respect, not so much an enforceable body of law.

International Organization Usually coupled with a domestic division, this division focuses on production and sales of foreign markets.

International Trade The export or import of goods or services to consumers in another country.

Interpersonal Conflicts Conflicts occurring between individuals and/or groups.

Intervention A set of planned change activities intended to help an organization increase its effectiveness.

Intrinsic Factors Derived from the job itself, where opportunities for achievement, responsibility, advancement, growth, and the nature of the work itself are intrinsic to the work. Also called motivator or job content factors.

Intuitive Decision Makers People who use a trial-and-error approach to solve problems.

Inventory File Shows the specifications for each required part, as well as where it can be purchased or produced.

Inventory Management The process of ensuring that the firm has adequate inventories of all parts and supplies needed, within the constraint of minimizing total inventory costs.

Inventory-Holding or Inventory-Carrying Costs Refer to all of the costs associated with carrying parts or materials in inventory.

Investment Reduction or Defensive Strategies Corrective actions taken to reduce the company's investments in one or more of its lines of business.

Jidoka A Japanese term that means "stop everything when something goes wrong."

Job Analysis The procedure used to determine the duties of the jobs and the kinds of people (in terms of skills and experience) who should be hired for them.

Job Description Identifies the job, provides a brief job summary, and then lists specific responsibilities and duties of the job.

Job Enrichment Building motivators like opportunities for achievement into the job by making it more interesting and challenging.

Job Identification The person views the job as his or her "own," usually because the job is challenging and interesting and provides an opportunity for self expression and achievement.

Job Security The firm is committed to not dismissing employees for nondisciplinary reasons, except in event of the most serious economic problems.

Job Specification Specifies human qualifications in terms of traits, skills, and experiences required to accomplish the job.

Job-Centered Companies Companies characterized by a focus on specialized jobs, efficiency, and closely supervised workers.

Joint Venture The participation of two or more companies jointly in an enterprise such that each party contributes assets, owns the entity to some degree, and shares risk.

Just-in-Time (JIT) System Refers to the production control methods used to attain minimum inventories by ensuring delivery of materials and assemblies just-in-time, in other words, just when they are to be used. Also refers to a philosophy of manufacturing that aims to optimize production processes by continuously reducing waste.

Kanban From the Japanese word "card," this production control system operates on the theory that whenever an item is used, it pulls the need for another item, which in turn pulls the need for another, and so on.

Knowledge Information that has been distilled via study or research and augmented by judgment and experience.

Leader Match Program The basic idea of this program is that by manipulating the three situational variables—leader-member relations, task structure, and power position—a leader who knows his or her LPC style can change the situation to best suit that style.

Leader–Member Relations The extent to which the leader "gets along" with workers and the extent to which they have confidence in and are loyal to him or her.

Leadership Occurs whenever one person influences another to work toward some predetermined objective.

Leading Getting others to get the job done, maintaining morale, and motivating subordinates.

Lean Manufacturing or Value-Added Manufacturing The idea that any manufacturing process that does not add value to the product for the customer is wasteful.

Legal Compliance Encouraging employees to do their jobs according to the rules by convincing them that those rules derive from a legitimate authority.

Legitimate Power Characterized by the feeling of oughtness on the part of a subordinate; the actual source of this legitimate power might be tradition or the supervisor's office.

Licensing An arrangement whereby a firm (the licensor) grants a foreign firm (the licensee) the right to use intangible ("intellectual") property such as patents, copyrights, manufacturing processes or trade names for a specified period of time, usually in return for a royalty.

Life-Cycle Portfolio Matrix This matrix plots the business unit's competitive position against its industry's life-cycle stage.

Line Adapters Modify the signal from the terminal and computer so that it matches the characteristics of the telecommunications line.

Line Manager A managerial position authorized to issue orders to subordinates down the chain of command.

Linear Programming A mathematical method used to solve resource allocation problems.

Load Schedule Compares the labor and machine hours needed to carry out the master production schedule with the labor and machine hours actually available each week.

Loading Assigning individual jobs to machines and work centers.

Local Area Network (LAN) A communications network that spans a limited distance such as a building or several adjacent buildings using the company's own telecommunications links.

Maastricht Accord In a series of meetings in 1991 held in Maastricht, the Netherlands, the twelve EU countries agreed to submit to their respective legislatures plans for cementing even closer economic ties between them, including plans for a single European currency by 1999 and free movement of labor. The Maastricht Accord was approved by each country by 1993.

Mainframe Computers Large-scale systems often used for high-volume jobs.

Malcolm Baldrige National Quality Award A prize created in 1987 by the U.S. Department of Commerce to recognize outstanding achievement in quality control management.

Management Assessment Center A center in which management candidates spend two or three days performing realistic management tasks under the observation of expert appraisers.

Management Information System (MIS) An information system that provides decision support for managers by producing standardized, summarized reports on a regular basis.

Management By Objectives (MBO) A technique in which supervisor and subordinate jointly set goals for the latter and periodically assess progress toward those goals.

Manager Someone who gets things done through others.

Market Economy The quantities and nature of the goods and services produced are not planned by anyone. Instead, the interaction of supply and demand via market forces decides what is produced, in what quantities, and at what prices.

Market Penetration A growth strategy to boost sales of present products by more aggressively permeating the organization's current markets.

Marketing-Channel Departmentalization Top-level departments are organized around each of the firm's marketing channels—conduits through which a manufacturer distributes its products to its ultimate customers.

Mass Production A special type of intermittent production process in which standardized methods and single-use machines are used to produce long runs of standardized items.

Master Production Schedule The amounts of all products to be produced and the date when individual products are to be produced.

Materials Requirements Plan A computer-based system that reviews the master production schedule and specifies the required raw materials, parts, subassemblies, and assemblies needed each week to meet the master production schedule.

Matrix Organization (Matrix Management) Superimposing one or more forms of departmentalization on top of an existing one.

Maturity Stage During a product's life-cycle it may reach this stage, during which it experiences a long period of flat or modest sales growth.

Mechanistic Management System Management that is appropriate if the company's task was routine and unchanging, and that is characterized by specialized jobs, top-down communications, imposed control, and "sticking to the chain of command" for making decisions.

Microcomputers Computers that are relatively small in size but may have considerable computer power and speed.

Minicomputers Designed for multiple users and have much greater speed and storage capacity than microcomputers.

Mission Statement Broadly outlines the organization's future course and serves to communicate "who we are and where we're heading." Answers the question, "what business are we in?"

Mixed Economy An economy in which some sectors of the economy are left to private ownership and free market mechanisms, while others are largely owned by and managed by the government.

Moment of Truth A core concept in service management that is the precise instant when the customer comes into contact with any aspect of the business and, on the basis of that contact, forms an opinion about the quality of service and, potentially, the quality of the product.

Moral Minimum The standard that corporations should be free to strive for profits so long as they commit no harm.

Moral Standards A set of beliefs regarding right or wrong that address matters of serious consequences to human well-being. These are also characterized by the fact that they cannot be established or changed by decisions of authoritative bodies like legislatures; should override self-interest; and that they are based on universal, impartial considerations.

Motion-Study Principles Tools developed by Frank and Lillian Gilbreth to assist them in their quest for efficiency.

Motivation The intensity of a person's desire to engage in some activity.

Moving Developing new behaviors, values, and attitudes, sometimes through organizational structure changes and development techniques.

Multinational Corporation (MNC) An internationally integrated production system over which equity-based control is exercised by a parent corporation that is owned and managed essentially by the nationals of the country in which it is domiciled.

Multinational Enterprise An enterprise that controls operations in more than one country.

Multinational Firm Each country in which the firm does business may have its own subsidiary

Mutual Adjustment Achieving coordination through interpersonal communication.

Need for Achievement Represents the need people have to accomplish challenging tasks.

Need for Affiliation Represents the need some people have to think about and develop warm, friendly, compassionate relationships.

Need for Power Represents a need some people have to gain influence and control others.

Need-Based Theories These emphasize the role of the person's personality and needs in motivation.

Needs-Hierarchy Theory of Motivation Maslow's theory of motivation, based on the proposal that people have five increasingly higher-level needs: physiological, safety, social, self-esteem, and self-actualization.

Negative Reinforcement Involves achieving the desired behavior by avoiding some negative consequence.

Network Planning and Control Methods Methods for planning and controlling projects by graphically representing the projects' steps and the timing and linkages between these steps.

Non-Normative Judgment Names, defines, or reports a certain state of affairs.

Nonprogrammed Decisions Decisions that are unique and novel to the extent that systematic procedures are not available for making them.

Nonverbal Communication A person's manner of speaking, facial expressions, body posture, etc.

Normative Decision Theory A leadership theory that identifies the degree of participation most likely to result in effective decisions in a particular situation.

Normative Judgment States or implies that something is good or bad, right or wrong, better or worse.

Occupational Safety and Health Act An act passed by Congress to set safety and health standards that apply to almost all workers in the United States.

Operant Behavior Behavior that results from a reward that appears to be a consequence of the subject operating on its environment—such that its behavior "leads to" the stimulus. See operant conditioning.

Operant Conditioning Conditioning in which the operant behavior seems to cause the reinforcing stimulus and the operant behavior response.

Operations Management The process of managing the resources required to produce the organization's goods and services.

Operations Research (management science) The application of scientific methods, techniques, and tools to problems involving the operations of systems so as to provide those in control of the system with optimum solutions to the problems.

Ordering Costs The costs involved with placing the order or setting up machines for the production run.

Organic Management System If innovative, entrepreneurial activities are important, this style of management is more appropriate, and is characterized by enlarged jobs, lateral communications, participative management, and an emphasis on self-control and worker commitment.

Organization People who carry out differentiated tasks, which are coordinated to contribute to the organization's goals.

Organization Chart Depicts the structure of the organization, in particular the title of each manager's position and, by means of connecting lines, who is accountable to whom and who is in charge of what department.

Organization Development An application of behavioral science knowledge to the planned development and reinforcement of organizational strategies, structures, and processes for improving an organization's effectiveness, usually using action research.

Organizational Analysis An analysis of the organization's goals, plans, environment, practices, and performance.

Organizational Culture The interdependent set of values and ways of behaving that are common to the organization and that tend to perpetuate themselves, sometimes over long periods of time.

Organizational Development Interventions In-depth interventions such as sensitivity training aimed at changing the employees' attitudes, values, and behavior through the involvement of the employees.

Organizing To arrange the activities of the enterprise in such a way that they systematically contribute to the enterprise's goals. Includes giving each subordinate a task, setting up departments, delegating or pushing down authority to subordinates, establishing a chain of command, and coordinating the work of the manager's subordinates.

Orientation Providing new employees with basic information about the employer, information that they need to perform their job satisfactorily.

Output Devices These devices receive the electrical impulses from the computer and convert them to a form we can read or use.

Outputs Direct or indirect outcomes of a production system, such as the firm's products or services, or taxes, wages, and salaries.

Passive Threats Threats that come from unauthorized individuals or organizations who monitor the firm's data transmissions in order to obtain unauthorized information.

Path-Goal Theory of Leadership A leader should increase the personal rewards that subordinates receive for attaining their goals, and smooth the path to these rewards by clarifying it, reducing road blocks, and increasing the opportunities for personal satisfaction en route.

Pay for Performance Salary increase based on merit or performance rather than the standard across-the-board salary increase.

Perception How we define or perceive stimuli, depending on what we bring along with us from past experiences, and what our present needs and personalities are.

Perception The meaning or interpretation that a communication receiver applies to the message he or she receives.

Period of Collision A period resulting from environmental conditions which draw people into inescapable proximity and dependency on one another.

Personality The characteristic and distinctive traits of an individual, and the way the traits interact to help or hinder the adjustment of the person to other people and situations.

Personnel Planning Involves forecasting personnel requirements and the supply of outside candidates and internal candidates, and then producing plans that describe how candidates will be trained and prepared for the jobs that will be opening up.

Physiological Needs The most basic needs that include the need for food, drink, and shelter.

Planning Includes setting goals and courses of action, developing rules and procedures, developing plans (both for the organization and for those who work in it), and forecasting—that is, predicting or projecting what the future holds for the firm.

Plans Methods formulated beforehand for doing or making something and consisting of a goal and a course of action.

Policies Set broad guidelines for the enterprise.

Political Boundary The differences in political agendas that often separate employees and cause conflict.

Polycentric A management philosophy oriented toward individual foreign markets.

Portfolio Management Analysis An analytical review or aid that determines, particularly in a multibusiness company, the attractiveness of the firm's various business lines to ascertain whether resources should be shifted from one business to another.

Position Power The degree to which the position itself enables the leader to get his or her group members to comply with and accept his or her direction and leadership.

Positive Reinforcement Involves giving rewards like praise or raises each time the desired behavior occurs.

Post-Action Controls The particular action being controlled is completed first, and then results are measured and compared to the standard.

Power The ability of one person to influence another to do something the latter would not otherwise do.

Power Distance A dimension of cultural differences that refers to the extent to which the less powerful members of institutions accept and expect power to be distributed unequally.

Premise Control Methods A strategic control method that involves the systematic and continuous checking of environmental conditions to see if previously established planning premises are still valid.

Prepotency Process Principle Maslow's theory that people become motivated as they move up through the hierarchy, satisfying the lower-order needs and then, in order, each of the higher-order needs.

Procedures Specify how to proceed if some specific situation arises.

Process Layout Similar machines or functions are grouped together.

Product Champion A member of an organization who creates, defines, or adopts an idea for a new technological innovation and who is willing to risk his or her position and prestige to make possible the innovation's successful implementation.

Product Development Developing improved products for current markets with the goal of maintaining or boosting growth.

Product Layout Every item to be produced follows the same sequence of operations from beginning to end, moving from one specialized tool and operation to another.

Production Budget Outlines the number of units that must be manufactured to meet monthly sales requirements and maintain proposed inventory levels.

Production Control The process of ensuring that the specified production plans and schedules are being met.

Production Planning The process of deciding what products to produce and where, when, and how to produce them.

Programmed Decisions Decisions that are repetitive and routine to the extent that definite, systematic procedures exist for making them.

Promotion Rewarding the employee's efforts by moving that person to a job with increased authority and responsibility.

Punishment A way to reduce undesired behavior by punishing the person, for example, reprimanding or harassing late employees.

Qualitative Forecasting These methods emphasize human judgment and include both technological and judgmental methods.

Quality The totality of features and characteristics of a product or service that bears on its ability to satisfy given needs.

Quality Circle A team of 6 to 12 employees that meets once a week on company time at work to solve problems affecting its work area.

Quality Control Charts Used to control product quality, quality control charts identify the range within which some measurable characteristic of the product is to remain. The chosen characteristic is then inspected and measured.

Quality Improvement Programs Programs built around quality circles for the purpose of spotting and solving problems in their work area.

Quantitative Forecasting Statistical methods used to examine data and find underlying patterns and relationships. These methods can be classified as either time series methods or causal models.

Question Marks Businesses in high-growth industries, but with low relative market shares.

Quotas Legal restrictions on the import of particular goods.

Rapid Growth Stage According to the life-cycle theory, products leave the development stage and enter this stage of introduction as a new and popular product.

Rate of Return on Investment (ROI) Represents net income divided by total investment and is an important measure of overall company performance.

Reactive Change Changes that are made in direct response to an external event.

Recreations Strategic changes that are prompted by immediate crises.

Recruiting Attracting a pool of viable job applicants.

Referent Power Based on the fact that one person identifies with and is highly attracted to a leader, perhaps due to the leader's charismatic personality.

Refreezing The organization may revert to former ways of doing things unless the changes are reinforced through refreezing.

Regiocentric A management philosophy oriented toward larger areas including the global marketplace.

Reinforcement Theories These hold that people are motivated by the consequences of their behavior and that they tend to continue behaviors that are rewarded and to cease those that are unrewarded or punished.

Related Diversification Diversifying into other products or markets in such a way that a firm's lines of business still possess some kind of fit.

Relatedness Needs Needs that involve relationships with significant other people, such as family members, superiors, coworkers, subordinates, friends, and enemies.

Reorientations Strategic changes initiated in anticipation of future events.

Respondent Behavior Behavior that simply responds to a stimulus.

Results Accountability When managers control activities by focusing not on employees' specific actions, but on their results.

Retrenchment The reduction of activities or operations.

Reward Power Power whose basis is the ability to reward.

Rites and Ceremonials Used to symbolize the firm's values and to help convert employees to these values.

Role Conflict Conflict within the individual occurring when a person is faced with conflicting orders.

Safety Needs When physiological needs are reasonably satisfied, your personal safety, security, and protection needs become potent forces in your behavior.

Sales Budget Shows the number of units to be shipped in each period (usually per month) as well as the sales revenue expected, based on some assumed sales price per unit.

Sales Force Estimation Involves getting the opinions of the sales force on what they predict sales will be in the forthcoming period.

Scenarios Hypothetical sequences of events constructed for the purpose of focusing attention on causal processes and decision points.

Scientific Management Developed by Frederick W. Taylor, a set of principles that encouraged managers to study work scientifically in order to identify the "one best way" to get the job done.

Self-Actualization Needs Needs that only begin to dominate a person's behavior once all lower-level needs are reasonably satisfied; the need for self-actualization or fulfillment is the need we all have to become the person we feel we have the potential for becoming.

Self-Directed Work Team A highly trained group of employees, from 6 to 18 people on average, fully responsible for turning out a well-defined segment of finished work.

Self-Efficacy Being able to influence important aspects of your world.

Self-Esteem Needs These needs relate to one's self-esteem, needs for self-confidence, independence, achievement, competence, and knowledge, and needs that relate to one's reputation, needs for status, recognition, appreciation, and the deserved respect of others.

Semantics The meaning of words.

Sensation Sensory inputs such as hot, cold, up, down, words, pictures, etc., that are channeled through nerve endings.

Sensitivity Training Also called laboratory or t-group training, the basic aim is to increase the participant's insight into his or her own behavior and the behavior of others by encouraging an open expression of feelings in the trainer-guided t-group.

Service Audit An ongoing periodic audit accomplished most often by questionnaire or survey which is used to take the pulse of how the company is doing with respect to each of the service attributes.

Service Triangle Three key factors form the service triangle: vision for the service product, customer-oriented front-line people; and customer-friendly systems.

Sexual Harassment Unwelcome sexual advances, requests for sexual favors, other verbal or physical conduct of a sexual nature, and actions creating a hostile work environment.

Shop Floor Control (SFC) The process of overseeing the weekly and daily production schedules to most effectively implement the master production schedules on a week by week basis.

Signs and Symbols Used throughout strong culture firms to create and sustain the company's culture.

Simple Smoothing Average An average forecasted for next period, based on the average sales of the last five (or some set number) of periods.

Single-Issue Monitoring System Intended for use by multiple companies to monitor their performance on a single social responsibility issue.

Situation Analysis An analysis of the features in a company's internal/external environment that will most directly affect its strategic options and opportunities.

Small Group A group of twenty or fewer members, usually fewer than five or six.

Smoothing Methods These methods average the data in some way to remove seasonal and random variations.

Social Responsibility Refers to the extent to which companies should and do channel resources toward improving the quality of life of one or more segments of society other than the firm's own stockholders.

Software Refers to computer programs, which are instructions that tell the computer which steps to take, which data to work on, and what to do with the results.

Span of Control The number of subordinates reporting directly to a supervisor.

Special Alert Controls A subset of strategic surveillance that are aimed at identifying crises or other events that may have very low probabilities of occurring, but which may threaten the very viability of the firm.

Stability or Status Quo Strategy A corporate strategy in which the firm retains its current strategy, focusing on its present products and markets.

Staff Manager A managerial position, such as Personnel Manager, which generally cannot issue orders down the chain of command; can only assist and advise line managers.

Staffing Refers to actually filling a firm's open positions, and it includes six steps: job analysis, personnel planning, recruiting, interviewing, testing and selection, and training and development.

Standing plans Plans established to be used repeatedly, as the need arises.

Stars Businesses in high-growth industries in which the company has a high relative market share.

Statistical Decision Theory Techniques Techniques used to solve problems for which information is incomplete or uncertain.

Steering Controls Results are predicted and corrective action is taken before the operation or project is completed.

Stockout Costs Refers to the costs associated with running out of raw materials or finished-goods inventory.

Stories Used widely in organizations to illustrate important company values.

Strategic Alliance Any close association of corporations to achieve common objectives.

Strategic Change Change in a firm's strategy, mission, and vision.

Strategic Control The process of assessing the firm's progress toward its strategic objectives and taking corrective action as needed. This technique is the critical evaluation of plans, activities, and results, [as well as the basic premises underlying them].

Strategic Management The process of identifying and pursuing the organization's mission by aligning internal capabilities with the external demands of its environment.

Strategic Organizational Change Changes that impact the entire organization and fundamentally redefine what the organization is or change its basic framework, including strategy, structure, people, processes and in some cases, core values.

Strategic Plan Outlines the course of action the firm plans to pursue in becoming the sort of enterprise that it wants to be, given the firm's external opportunities and threats and its internal strengths and weaknesses.

Strategic Surveillance Methods Represent a broad search activity aimed at early detection of events that may threaten or demand modification of existing strategies.

Strategic Alliance Refers to cooperative agreements between potential and actual competitors.

Strategic Planning The process of identifying the business a firm is in today and the business it wants to be in in the future, and the course of action or strategy it will pursue,

given its opportunities, threats, strengths, and weaknesses.

Strategy A course of action which explains how the enterprise will move from the business it is in now to the business it wants to be in.

Strategy Implementation Converting the strategic plan into action and then into results.

Subsidies When a country makes direct payments to help support its producers.

Sullivan Principles A code by Reverend Leon Sullivan that provided for measurable standards by which U.S. companies operating in South Africa could be audited, and contained a number of priciples including non-segregation of the races in all eating, comfort, and work facilities, and equal pay for all employees doing equal or comparable work for the same period of time.

Supercomputers The fastest computers available. They are used for applications requiring enormously complex calculations that must be made quickly.

Survey Research Data collected from attitude surveys filled out by employees of an organization, which is then used as feedback to the work groups and provides a basis for problem analysis and action planning.

Sustainable World A scenario whereby economic frictions are resolved, economic trade flows freely, and concern about the environment leads to tightened emissions regulation and higher quality standards for energy products.

SWOT An acronym for the strengths, weaknesses, opportunities, and threats matrix.

System Any entity that has interdependent parts and a purpose.

System IV Management A program based on the work of Rensis Likert and his colleagues; its premise is that the most effective organizations have supportive, trusting leaders, open communication, clear goals, and an emphasis on employees' self-control.

Systematic Decision Makers People who approach a problem by structuring it in terms of some method which leads to a likely solution.

Systems Approach Viewing an organization as a system means managers remember that a firm's different parts, departments, or subsystems are interrelated and must all contribute to the organization's purpose.

Tariffs Governmental taxes levied on goods shipped internationally.

Task Boundary Determining who does what when employees from different departments must divide up their work.

Task Structure How routine and predictable the work group's task is.

Team Building Techniques used to improve the effectiveness of a team.

Teams A group in which its members are committed to a common purpose, set

of performance goals, and approach for which they hold themselves mutually accountable.

Technological Forecasting Involves predicting future products and innovations.

Technology Transfer The transfer of systematic knowledge for the manufacture of a product, for the application of a process, or for the rendering of a service; does not extend to the mere sale or lease of goods.

Telecommunications The electronic transmission of data, text, graphics, voice (audio), or image (video) over literally any distance.

Telecommunications System A set of compatible telecommunications devices that link geographically separated devices.

Telecommuting The substitution of telecommunications and computers for the commute to a central office.

Terminals Input-output devices that send or receive data.

Test A sample of a person's behavior, used in personnel management for predicting a person's success on the job.

The Jury of Executive Opinion Involves asking a "jury" of key executives to forecast sales for the next year based on economic levels and anticipated changes.

Theory X Assumptions coined by Douglas McGregor; held that most people dislike work and responsibility and prefer to be directed; that people are motivated not by the desire to do a good job, but simply by financial incentives; and that, therefore, most people must be closely supervised, controlled, and coerced into achieving organizational objectives.

Theory Y A set of assumptions which holds that people enjoy work and that an individual will exercise substantial self-control over his or her performance if the conditions are favorable.

Third Party Intervention The third party consultant in this type of intervention tries to help the parties to interact with each other directly and to thereby facilitate their diagnosis of the conflict and how to resolve it.

Time Series A set of observations taken at specific times, usually at equal intervals.

Title VII From the Civil Rights Act of 1964, this bars discrimination because of race, color, religion, sex, or national origin.

Total Quality Management Programs Organization-wide programs that integrate all functions of the business and related processes such that all aspects of the business including design, planning, production, distribution and field service are aimed at maximizing customer satisfaction through continuous improvements.

Trade Control Refers to governmental influences that are usually aimed at reducing the competitiveness of imported products or services.

Trait Theories of Leadership Assume that effective leaders have a number of identifiable traits or characteristics that distinguish them from ineffective leaders.

Transaction   An event that affects the business, such as hiring an employee, selling merchandise, and ordering supplies.

Transactional Leadership   Leadership resulting from an exchange or transaction which was based on promises of rewards by the leader.

Transformational Leadership   Leadership that involves influencing major changes in the attitudes and assumptions of organization members and building commitment for the organization's mission, objectives and strategies and for the leader's vision for the firm.

Treaty of Rome   A treaty signed by France, West Germany, Italy, Belgium, the Netherlands, and Luxembourg, which founded the European Economic Community in 1957.

Trend Line Method   Involves plotting data on a graph against a period of time, such as five years, and fitting a line to the plots.

Two-factor Theory   Herzberg's theory that there are two classes of work motivators—extrinsic and intrinsic factors.

Uncertainty   The absence of information about a particular area of concern.

Unemployment Insurance   Insurance available to most employees that is paid by state agencies to workers who are terminated through no fault of their own (the funds come from a tax on the employer's payroll).

Unfreezing   Reducing the forces that are striving to maintain the status quo, usually by presenting a provocative problem or event to get people to recognize the need for change and to search for new solutions.

Uniform Plant Loading   Monthly production plans are established for the plant and are then adhered to in order to ensure a scheduling of production that is as predictable and smooth as possible.

Upward Communication   Represents the messages that flow from subordinates to supervisors.

Valence   Represents the perceived value a person ascribes to the reward.

Value   A value is a basic belief about what you should and should not do, and what is important and what is not.

Values   Basic beliefs about what is important and unimportant, and what one should and should not do.

Variable Interval Schedule   Based on time, the worker is reinforced at some variable interval around some average.

Variable Ratio Schedules   Based on units of output, the number of desired outcomes necessary to elicit a reward changes around some average.

Variances   The difference between budgeted and actual amounts.

Venture Team   A small group of people who operate as a semi-autonomous unit to create and develop a new idea.

Vertical Integration   Owning or controlling the inputs to the firm's processes or the channels through which the firm's products or services are distributed.

Video Conferencing   Meetings among dispersed group members via television links.

Virtual Corporation   A temporary network of companies, each of which lends the virtual corporation/network its core competence and is committed to the corporation achieving its objectives.

Vision   A general statement of the firm's intended direction that evokes emotional feelings in organization members.

Waiting Line/Queuing Techniques   Techniques used to solve waiting line problems.

Whistle-Blowing   The activities of employees who try to report organizational wrongdoing.

Wholly Owned Subsidiary   A subsidiary that is owned 100 percent by the foreign firm.

Wide Area Network (WAN)   Networks that serve microcomputers over larger geographic areas, spanning distances from a few miles to around the globe.

Work Stations   Microcomputers that offer relatively high computer power.

Work-Centered Leaders   Leaders who are authoritarian, autocratic, production-oriented, or a type that needs to initiate structure.

Work-out   A forum in which participating employees get a mental work-out while engaging in enthusiastic discussions aimed at taking unnecessary work out of their jobs and working out problems together.

Worker's Compensation   A payment aimed at providing sure, prompt income and medical benefits to work-related accident victims or their dependents, regardless of fault.

World-Class Companies   Organizations that can compete based on quality and productivity in an intensely competitive global environment.

World-Class Manufacturers   Organizations that use modern production techniques and management systems to boost manufacturing productivity, quality, and flexibility.

Yes-No Control   Work may not proceed to the next step until it passes an intermediate control step.

Zero-Based Budgeting   A technique that forces managers to defend all their programs every year and to rank them in order of priority based on the ratio of their benefits and costs.

Zone of Indifference   A range within each individual in which he or she would willingly accept orders without consciously questioning the supervisor's authority.

LITERARY CREDITS

p. 13 Figure 1.5 from *In the Era of Human Capital* by Richard D. Crawford. Copyright © 1991 HarperCollins Publishers, Inc. Reprinted by permission of HarperCollins Publishers, Inc. p. 32 Reprinted from October 23, 1992 issue of *Business Week* by special permission. Copyright © 1992 by McGraw-Hill, Inc. p. 34 Reprinted with permission from *World Trade* magazine. p. 36 Reprinted with permission of Guilford Publications, Inc. p. 39 *Fortune* © 1993 Time, Inc. All rights reserved. p. 49 Richard D. Robinson, *Internationalization of Business: An Introduction* (Chicago: Dryden 1984), 270. Reprinted with permission of the author. p. 65 Justin G. Longnecker, McKinney & Carlos Moore, "The Generation Gap in Business," *Business Horizons,* September-October 1989. p. 69 Robert Sweeney and Howard Siers, "Survey: Ethics in Corporate America," *Management Accounting,* Institute of Management Accounting, June 1990. p. 72 Courtesy Johnson & Johnson. p. 92 Used with permission. p. 108 From *Thriving on Chaos* by Tom Peters. Copyright © 1987 by Excel, a California Limited Partnership. Reprinted by permission of Alfred A. Knopf, Inc. p. 155 Reprinted with permission of The Free Press, Macmillan Publishing from *Competitive Strategy: Techniques for Analyzing Industries and Competitors* by Michael E. Porter. Copyright © 1980 by The Free Press. p. 170 Reprinted with the permission of The Free Press, MacMillan Publishing from *Competitive Strategy: Techniques for Analyzing Industries and Competitors* by Michael E. Porter. Copyright © 1980 by The Free Press. p. 173 Reprinted with the permission of The Free Press, Macmillan Publishing from *Competitive Strategy: Techniques for Analyzing Industries and Competitors* by Michael E. Porter. Copyright © 1980 by The Free Press. p. 176 Alan J. Rowe, Richard O. Mason, Karl E. Dickel, and Neil H. Snyder, *Strategic Management: A Methodological Approach,* 3rd Ed. (91–93) © 1989 by Addison-Wesley Publishing Company, Inc. Reprinted by permission of the publisher. p. 186 Reprinted from Adam Kahan, *Scenarios for Energy: Sustainable World vs. Global Mercantilism,* Long Range Planning, vol. 25, no. 4, 41. With kind permission from Elsevier Science Ltd, The Boulevard, Langford Lane, Kidlington OX5, 1GB, UK. p. 248 From *Liberation Management* by Tom Peters. Copyright © 1992 by Excel, a California Limited Partnership. Reprinted by permission of Alfred A. Knopf, Inc. p. 304 Reprinted from "The Control Function of Management" by Kenneth Merchant, *Sloan Management Review* Association. All rights reserved. p. 312 Alan J. Rowe, Richard O. Mason, Karl E. Dickel, and Neil H Snyder, *Strategy Management: A Methodological Approach.* 3rd Ed. (237–238) © 1989 by Addison-Wesley Publishing Company, Inc. Reprinted by permission of the author. p. 346 Reprinted with permission of Ben & Jerry's. p. 392 Reprinted with permission of The Free Press, Macmillan Publishing from *Corporate Culture and Performance* by John P. Kotter and James L. Heskett. Copyright © 1992 by Kotter Associates, Inc. and James L. Heskett. p. 396 Reprinted with permission of The Free Press, Macmillan Publishing from *Corporate Culture and Performance* by John P. Kotter and James L. Heskett. Copyright © 1992 by Kotter Associates, Inc. and James L. Heskett. p. 403 Reprinted with permission of The Free Press, Macmillan Publishing from *Corporate Culture and Performance* by John P. Kotter and James L. Heskett. Copyright © 1992 by Kotter Associates, Inc. and James L. Heskett. p. 453 Courtesy Lantech, Inc. p. 489 Copyright © 1993 by the Presidents and Fellows of Harvard College; all rights reserved. Reprinted by permission of *Harvard Business Review.* Building Team Performance, "The Discipline of Teams," Jon R. Katzenbach and Douglas K. Smith, March-April 1993. p. 503 Copyright © 1990 by The Regents of the University of California. Reprinted from the California Management Review, vol. 32, no. 2. By permission of The Regents. p. 510 David A. Nadler, *Feedback and Organization Development* (119), © 1977 by Addison-Wesley Publishing Company, Inc. Reprinted by permission of the publisher. p. 517 Copyright © 1990 by The Regents of the University of California. Reprinted from the *California Management Review,* vol. 32, no. 2. by permission of The Regents. p. 520 Reprinted by permission from p. 167 of *Organizational Development and Change,* 5th ed. by Thomas Cummings and Christopher Worley; Copyright © 1993 by West Publishing Company. All rights reserved. p. 589 Reprinted with permission of Macmillan Publishing Company from *Management Information Systems: A Contemporary Perspective,* 2nd ed. by Kenneth C. Laudon and Jane Price Lauden. Copyright © 1991 by Macmillan Publishing Company. p. 606 © 1993 Time, Inc. All rights reserved. p. 622 Copyright © 1990 by the President and Fellows of Harvard College; all rights reserved. Reprinted by permission of *Harvard Business Review.* Zero Defections: Quality Comes to Services by Frederick F. Reichheld and W. Earl Sasser, Jr., September-October 1990. p. 627 Copyright © 1984 by the President and Fellows of Harvard College; all rights reserved. Reprinted by permission of Harvard Business Review. *Designing Services That Deliver* by G. Lynne Shostack, January-February 1984.

PHOTO CREDITS

p. 5 Courtesy United Technologies Corporation. Photograph by Fred Gaylor. p. 12 left © Robert Wallis/SABA. p. 12 right © C. Bruce Forster. p. 21 © Steven Pumphrey. p. 31 Courtesy Unilever Corporation. p. 43 © Gerry Gropp. p. 46 © Robert Hampton/Black Star. p. 48 © Stig-Göran Nilsson. p. 52 © Patrick Lim/Black Star. p. 66 © Steve Skoll. p. 71 © Doug Menuez/Reportage. p. 77 © Robin Bowman. p. 80 © Photri/Sygma. p. 90 Culver Pictures, Inc. p. 95 © Dana Fineman/Sygma. p. 97 © 1993 Rich Mays. p. 102 © Dan Pearce. p. 111 © Michael Abramson. p. 122 © Josef Polleross/JB Pictures. p. 125 © 1992 Roger Mastroianni. Photo courtesy Elyria Foundry. p. 128 Photo courtesy Wellington Environmental Consulting & Construction, Inc. p. 132 © Fritz Hoffmann/JB Pictures. p. 137 © Ann States/SABA. p. 146 Courtesy Rocco, Inc. p. 153 © Steve Zavodny. Photo courtesy US West, Inc. p. 159 © David Strick/ONYX. p. 163 © David Young-Wolff/PhotoEdit. p. 172 © 1994 Doug Milner. p. 185 © Jean-Luc Manaud/Matrix. p. 189 Seth Resnick © 1994. All rights reserved. p. 199 © Michael Abramson. p. 212 © John Abbott. p. 214 © Ann States/SABA. p. 230 Roger Ressmeyer-Starlight © 1989. All rights reserved. p. 234 © 1990 Louis Psihoyos/Matrix. p. 244 © Steven Pumphrey. p. 247 © Steven Pumphrey. p. 253 © Katherine Lambert. p. 262 © Brian Smith 1993. p. 272 Mike Greenlar © 1994. p. 282 © Peter Yates/SABA. p. 287 © Michael Abramson. p. 289 © Robert Holmgren. p. 293 © 1993 Chuck Kneysel/Black Star. p. 303 © Heimo Aga. p. 307 © 1990 R.K. Hower/Quadrant. p. 308 © Ben Weaver/SIPA. p. 317 © John Abbott. p. 321 © Ken Kerbs/DOT. p. 337 © Michael Newman/PhotoEdit. p. 343 © John Abbott. p. 349 © Tom Wagner/SABA. p. 357 © 1993 Louis Psihoyos/Matrix. p. 364 © Sygma. p. 371 top JB Pictures © Steven Rubin. p. 371 bottom © J. Markowitz/Sygma. p. 378 © 1994 Louis Psihoyos/Matrix. p. 383 © Mohsen Shandiz/Sygma. p. 391 M. Grecco/Sygma © 1991. p. 400 Seth Resnick © 1994. p. 401 © 1992 Leif Skoogford. Courtesy Rosenbluth Travel. p. 404 © Rich Mays. p. 409 Courtesy Taligent. p. 425 © 1991 John Seakwood. p. 430 © Jeff Greenberg/PhotoEdit. p. 432 left/right Archives of Labor and Urban Affairs, Wayne State University. p. 435 © Andy Freeberg. p. 442 © Mike Malyszko 1993/FPG International. p. 457 © Larry Ford. p. 463 © Patrick Forestier/Sygma. p. 467 © John Abbott. p. 478 © Matthew McVay/SABA. p. 480 © Tom Stoddart/KATZ/SABA. p. 482 © Jim Cunningham/George Hill, Co. Courtesy Globe Metallurgical, Inc. p. 494 © Steve Woit 1994. p. 504 Courtesy Lexmark International, Inc. p. 508 © Michael Newman/PhotoEdit. p. 513 © Richard Perry/Sygma. p. 529 Courtesy Rosemary Breiner. p. 532 © John Abbott. p. 553 © James Schnepf. p. 561 © 1994 Rich Mays. p. 567 Courtesy Dana Corporation. p. 568 Photo courtesy of Hewlett-Packard Company. p. 569 © Arthur Meyerson. Courtesy S.D. Warren Company. p. 575 © Acey Harper/Reportage Stock. All rights reserved. p. 586 © 1994 John Abbott. p. 593 © Ed Caldwell. p. 595 left/right © 1993 Louis Psihoyos/Matrix. p. 599 © Grant Mudford. p. 605 © Louis Psihoyos/Matrix. p. 611 Courtesy Banc One Corporation. p. 623 © David Young-Wolff/PhotoEdit. p. 629 © 1993 Rick Friedman/Black Star. p. 631 Courtesy Restek Corporation. p. 640 © C. Thatcher 1993. All rights reserved.

NAME INDEX

COMPANY INDEX

SUBJECT INDEX